8/9/46
13

OFFERINGS
AT THE
WALL

OFFERINGS AT THE WALL

ARTIFACTS FROM THE

VIETNAM VETERANS MEMORIAL COLLECTION

Turner Publishing, Inc.

ATLANTA

PUBLISHED BY TURNER PUBLISHING, INC.
A SUBSIDIARY OF TURNER BROADCASTING SYSTEM, INC.
1050 TECHWOOD DRIVE, NW
ATLANTA, GEORGIA 30318

LIBRARY OF CONGRESS CATALOGING-IN-PUBLICATION DATA

ALLEN, THOMAS B.
    OFFERINGS AT THE WALL: ARTIFACTS FROM THE VIETNAM VETERANS
MEMORIAL COLLECTION/TEXT BY THOMAS B. ALLEN
        P.   CM.
    ISBN: 1-57036-067-7 (HARDCOVER)
    ISBN: 1-57036-174-6 (PAPERBACK)
    1. VIETNAM VETERANS MEMORIAL (WASHINGTON, D.C.)   2. UNITED STATES—
HISTORY—1961–1969—COLLECTIBLES.   3. VIETNAMESE CONFLICT,
1961–1975—COLLECTIBLES.   I. TITLE.
DS559.83.W18A44   1995
    975.3—DC20   94-46725
                                                                    CIP

DISTRIBUTED BY ANDREWS AND MCMEEL
A UNIVERSAL PRESS SYNDICATE COMPANY
4900 MAIN STREET
KANSAS CITY, MISSOURI 64112

EDITOR—WALTON RAWLS   DESIGNER—MICHAEL J. WALSH
ASSISTANT EDITOR—CRAWFORD BARNETT   PROJECT MANAGER—CHARLES O. HYMAN
COPY EDITOR—LAUREN EMERSON   PICTURE EDITOR— MARTY MOORE

PHOTOGRAPHERS— CLAUDIO VAZQUEZ
AND TAREN Z
PRODUCTION MANAGER—ANNE MURDOCH

FIRST EDITION
10 9 8 7 6 5 4 3 2 1

MANUFACTURED IN THE U.S.A.

PREFACE

AT FIRST, NATIONAL PARK SERVICE rangers did not know what to do with the things they were finding each day at the Vietnam Veterans Memorial, which was dedicated in Washington, D.C., on Memorial Day 1982. The rangers gathered up flags and roses, letters and teddy bears, toy cars and birthday cards, dog tags and service medals, cans of C ration and packets of Army-issue toilet paper. For a time, everyone was puzzled by the status of the objects, many of which were obviously valuable, yet purposely abandoned. But an awareness grew that there was something almost sacred about these objects: They were like tangible bonds between those who fell in Vietnam and those who remembered, a mystic communion with the dead. Everyone who touched these offerings at the Wall knew that they had to be kept—forever. Pamela Beth West, the Park Service's regional curator, suggested that these objects be housed, cataloged, and preserved as what the Park Service calls a museum collection. Her suggestion became the Vietnam Veterans Memorial Collection, which is unlike any other collection because its artifacts were not chosen by a museum curator. "This collection," she says, "is a harvest contributed by living participants, surviving friends, and relatives of those who died on the battlefields of Vietnam. The power of the Memorial and the individual stories behind these objects is really the focus of this collection."

The objects selected for this book were photographed at the Park Service's Museum and Archaeological Regional Storage Facility in Lanham, Maryland, where the collection will be preserved in perpetuity. A section of this huge building was periodically cordoned off to serve as an impromptu studio. Claudio Vazquez, a portrait photographer, and Taren Z., a still life photographer, set up lights and cameras and prepared a pristine white setting for the objects. Each one, labeled and usually sheathed in plastic, was removed from storage, unwrapped, and placed before the camera by the white-gloved hands of curator Duery Felton, Jr., and his assistant, Tony Porco. They patiently moved the objects at the direction of the photographers, who were not allowed to touch them.

Most objects were left at the Wall without any explanation, and those are appropriately presented in this book without captioning. When something pertinent is known about an object, a caption is provided. Excerpts from notes that accompanied an object are italicized in these captions. Full texts or long excerpts used from letters and notes have either been photographed in original form or typeset for clarity.

†

If you know anything about an object left at the Wall, please send your information, including a description of the object and when it was left, to:
Museum and Archaeological Regional Facility (MARS)
P.O. Box 435
Glenn Dale, MD 20769

If you wish to help preserve this collection, please send your tax-deductible contributions to:
National Park Service
Museum and Curatorial Services
1100 Ohio Dr., SW, Room 134
Washington, DC 20242

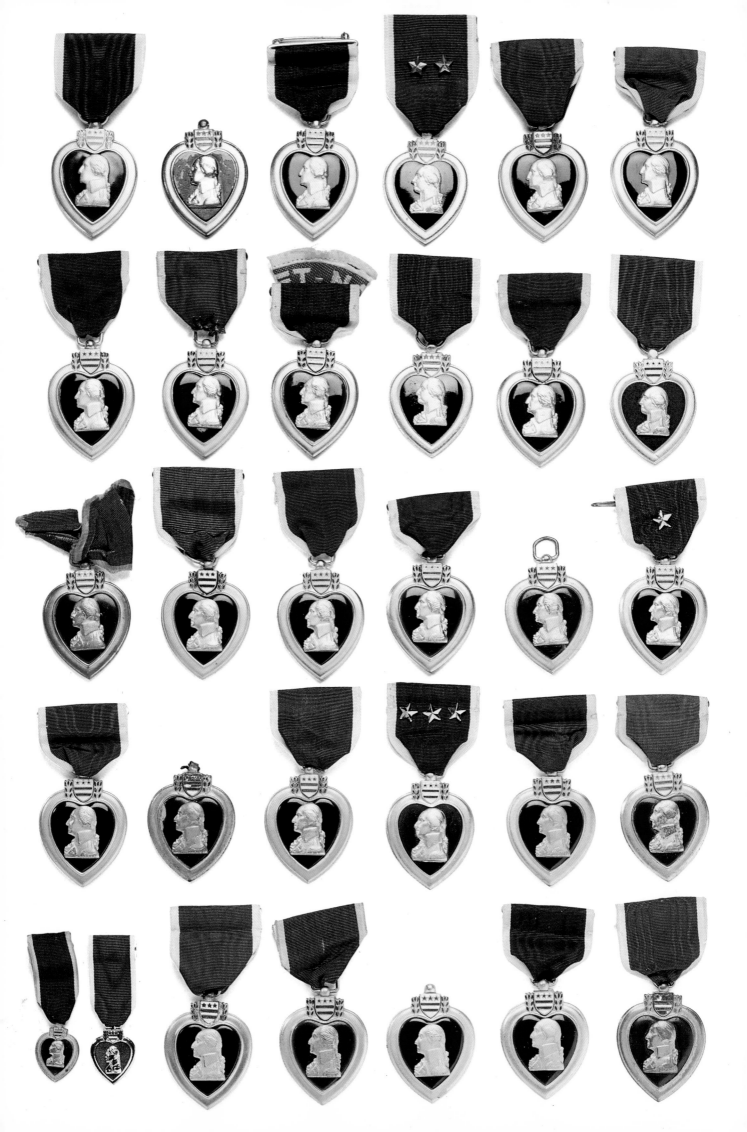

A PLACE FOR MEMORIES

THEY COME TO THE WALL SILENTLY, passing along the walkway where the black stone slabs rise. They walk slowly, seeing their faces mirrored and mingled in the rows of names ... Freddie A. Blackburn ... Daniel Diaz ... Bobby Ray Jones ... Hallie W. Smith—those 58,196 names. Usually they stop and run their fingers along the names, touching a war that this memorial keeps forever unforgotten. For those moments, they are not mere tourists who have arrived at the Vietnam Veterans Memorial while making the rounds of Washington's monuments. They are pilgrims who have journeyed to a place that has become a national shrine and an honored repository for keepsakes of grief.

A FEW STOOP AND LEAVE AN OFFERING—a note hastily written, a flag, a single rose, a burnished plaque, a teddy bear brought from a faraway time. A hat was left with a poem that said, "When we touch the Wall we know that you are there." There are those who prefer the night. They walk past the veterans who are always there and, stepping into the shadow of the Wall, leave a piece of memory to the darkness.

People usually leave ordinary things. The toys of sons and brothers. The badges and the dog tags and the medals of warriors who are parting at last with the past. Birthday cards from mothers. Notes from girlfriends growing old: Linda writes to Gary, Doug, and Billy, high school boyfriends who became names on the Wall—"Well, that time has rolled around and the Class of '65 is having its 20-year reunion. Cheers, cheers for old Orchard Park high school.... After you all died ... I pretty much screwed up for ten years.... Now I'm much better, more responsible. I learned that the pain and loss never goes away. It just changes.... I'm still mad."

A man who had been in the 101st Airborne left a photo of a North Vietnamese man posed with a young girl and wrote a letter:

Dear Sir,

For twenty-two years I have carried your picture in my wallet.

I was only eighteen years old that day that we faced one another on that trail in Chu Lai, Vietnam. Why you did not take my life I'll never know.

You stared at me for so long, armed with your AK-47, and yet you did not fire.

Forgive me for taking your life,

I was reacting just the way I was trained, to kill V.C....

So many times over the years I have stared at your picture and your daughter,

.I suspect. Each time my heart and guts would burn with the pain of guilt.

I have two daughters myself now....

I perceive you as a brave soldier defending his homeland. Above all else, I can now

respect the importance that life held for you. I suppose that is why

I am able to be here today....

It is time for me to continue the life process and release my pain and guilt.

Forgive me, Sir.

A MAN LEFT A COIN AND RING showing membership in Narcotics Anonymous, and with them he spilled these words: "I learned fear. I learned to be ALONE—NEVER let ANYONE in. I learned to be an animal—to take what I wanted, when I wanted. I learned to kill— no—learned it was OK to kill.... I came home and nothing worked—my family did not want me—they were—ARE—afraid of me. I am afraid of me. I pray for your forgiveness for my life/lies...." He ended with the words,

"No more hurt."

They come with burdens and they lay them down at the Wall. They come with words of rage and despair and leave the words at the Wall. But most of the words and the objects come from hearts scarred by loss. There is a watch, stopped at 10:03, and with it a letter to a dead comrade: "When I held you in my arms you felt cold. I would not let them take you from me for as long as I could. And then you were gone." There are two wedding rings that had been placed on a coffin by the widow of a man killed in Vietnam. A friend visiting the grave much later saw the rings, which had somehow worked their way to the surface. He brought his comrade's ring to the Wall—

"where his spirit now resides."

There is a box of cookies from home addressed on its brown paper wrapper to a name that matches a name on the Wall—returned as undeliverable and still unopened.

"Mom & Dad want you to have these cookies & Kool Aid," reads a note.

"It's time they gave these to you...." A man who lost thirteen friends left a dozen cans of beer and a packet of Kool Aid for the kid who never drank.

Men pay off debts, leaving a promised dollar or can of beer or pack of cigarettes. A Special Forces soldier, long ago desperate for a smoke, had broken into a friend's foot locker and snatched a carton, intending to pay for it with two cans of sardines. But before he could do so the friend was killed. After keeping the sardines for twenty years, the borrower sought out his friend's name on the Wall and finally gave him the cans.

On September 23, 1970, a mother wrote a letter to her son in Vietnam: "Dear Al, Everytime we hear the news on the TV or radio, we wonder if you are one of those that are being shot down...." She got the letter back, undelivered. On September 20 her son had been killed when his helicopter was shot down. For years, she held on to those tragically prophetic words. Then one day Al's cousin left the letter at the Wall, with a note, "We thought you should still have it."

Someone else had carried around the stained and creased roster of Alpha Company. Most of the names were typed in capital letters. A few names—newcomers added to the list of "Personnel in Field"—were written in a shaky hand on May 6, 1966, when Alpha Company went into battle. When it was over, name after name was circled. Written after the names was KIA for killed in action, or WIA for wounded in action. The man who held on to the roster for twenty-four years came to the Wall and finally gave it up, writing along the bottom, "Rest in Peace, Gentlemen."

People come to terms with what they have lost. A young woman left two sonograms and a framed note addressed to a name on the Wall: "I don't know if it's a boy or a girl—if the baby is a boy—he'll be named after you. Dad—this child will know you. Just how I have grown to know and love you—even though the last time I saw you I was only 4 mo. old...."

MANY LETTERS BEGIN WITH DAD. "I know you would like Lisa," one says. "You could not ask for a better wife. Dad, you have a granddaughter. Her name is Meghan and when she sees your picture she says, 'That's my pa pa.'" To another Dad: "I've always been told I look like you ... how I wish I could remember you. I was four when you were killed but all I have are visions and childhood dreams of what you were...."

No one expected the Wall to become the country's most visited monument. Nor did anyone expect it to become a pilgrimage site or a shrine of loving words and cherished objects. The Vietnam Veterans Memorial was envisioned to be a place of remembrance and reflection, a way to remember not the Vietnam War but the men and women who died in it. The memorial was the idea of Jan Scruggs, who went to war as a teenage infantryman and came home a wounded man. He wanted his fellow veterans to "have a place to confront and perhaps make peace with the ghosts of their past." The place, he decided, would be a memorial that listed the names of everyone killed in America's longest and most wrenching war.

"We'll accept no money from the government," he vowed. "Dollars will come from the American people." A comedian mocked him later on a television show after he had collected only $144.50 from his fund-raising effort. But Scruggs labored on, working with others to create the nonprofit Vietnam Veterans Memorial Fund. Eventually, more than 650,000 people contributed over $5,000,000 and Congress authorized a site, two acres near the Lincoln Memorial.

The veterans group launched a design competition, setting three requirements: The memorial must contain the names of all the dead and missing, not make any political statement, and be harmonious with the site. Maya Ying Lin, a twenty-year-old senior at Yale, won the competition with her vision of a V of black granite rising out of the earth, its gleaming surface reflecting the images of the living, uniting them with the names of the dead. "I had an impulse to cut open the earth," she later wrote, "an initial violence that in time would heal." Her design was denounced as a "black gash of shame," a tombstone to death and defeat. In a compromise with traditional-minded critics, a flagpole and a representational sculpture group were added to the site. Sculptor Frederick Hart's bronze statue of three young soldiers was placed so that they seem to be looking at the Wall, perhaps searching it for their own names.

IN THE SUMMER OF 1982, a U.S. Navy officer walked up to the trench where the concrete for the foundation of the Wall was being poured. He stood over the trench for a moment, then tossed something into it and saluted. When a workman asked him what he was doing, he said he was giving his dead brother's Purple Heart to the Wall.

That was the first offering.

Since then, more than 30,000 objects and letters have been left at the Wall. As it became a shrine, it also became a place to confront futures that could not be. Tucked into a wreath are the things of an imagined life: new baby shoes for a baby who never would be, pencils and crayons for a first day of kindergarten that never would be, champagne glasses to toast a wedding anniversary that never would be, ornaments for a Christmas tree that never would be. Others have left a birthday card for a fortieth birthday that never would come, a royal flush in spades for a poker game that never would be played.

There are autographed baseballs and marijuana joints and bottles of whiskey. There is a plastic bag with a note that begins: "This is to tell my brothers on the Wall, I know you wanted to grow your beard." The writer of this note had shaved off his own beard and left it as a memento for the dead who "never got your chance."

At first, National Park Service rangers gathered up the objects and the pieces of paper and put them in boxes that were kept at a maintenance yard. The rangers and the volunteers at the Wall knew, instinctively, that everything—the baseballs, the envelope of whiskers, the letters to the dead—had to be saved. Just as instinctively, they knew that sealed letters given to the Wall should never be opened.

Soon the accumulation of unexpected artifacts became the Vietnam Veterans Memorial Collection, an official national heritage with the Park Service as its steward. Twice a day volunteers collect the offerings, but there are a few exceptions to the collect-everything rule. Flowers and floral wreaths are not preserved, but their ribbons and messages are. American flags without messages written on them are given to the Boy Scouts and Girl Scouts and other patriotic organizations. Drugs and drug paraphernalia are routinely confiscated as contraband. However, at least one joint and one roach clip somehow made it into the collection.

Each artifact is tagged with the date it was left and given a reference number. Also recorded is beneath which of the 140 panels of names the object was left, for it probably relates to someone listed on that panel. The day's objects are taken to a storage space in the nearby Lincoln Memorial. Later they are transferred to a huge repository, the Museum and Archaeological Regional Storage Facility (MARS), in Lanham, Maryland, about twelve miles from the Wall. There the artifacts are preserved for posterity, alongside such historic items as weapons from the Battle of Antietam and a life mask of Abraham Lincoln.

FROM A COMPUTERIZED LIST of the collection, a sampler: armband (MP's), berets, Bible, boots, bottles (Jack Daniel's and Budweiser are the leading brands of libation), buttons, can openers, flags in funeral fold, fishing float, foodstuffs (including walnuts, Spam, fruit cocktail, and M&Ms), hats (10-gallon with black band, bush, Australian), insignia, name tapes (Morrison, Murphy, Zepeda, Coveny, Petshke, Despins, Koger), service ribbons, a sock for an amputee's stump, a popsicle stick with writing on it, four mortarboard tassels, a golf trophy, the foil wrapper from a Hershey's kiss.

Many of the objects were not easy to label. They puzzled the white-gloved Park Service employees who handled them, and Vietnam veterans volunteered to help. One of them was Duery Felton, Jr., a black, wounded ex-infantryman. Drafted at nineteen and sent to Vietnam, he was grievously wounded in a battle that he will not describe. He recovered at Walter Reed Army Hospital in Washington, which was and is his hometown. He will not talk about the way he earned his Purple Heart, but he does say, "I was almost a name on the Wall." He still has a look that warns off questions and keeps memories locked, but it was the unlocking and tapping of those memories that gave Duery Felton a new mission in life.

Shown the graffiti on a helmet cover ("Don't shoot, I'm short"), Felton explains that the words were about time, not height. The message indicated that the soldier was a short-timer, having safely reached the last month of his tour in Vietnam. Shown a photo of soldiers facing three rifles hung with helmets and stuck upright in the ground by their bayonets, Felton says, "Memorial service. Lots of times the body hadn't been brought in yet." And, with white-gloved hands, he turns the photo over. On it are written two names and, simply, "new guy." Felton reflects that sometimes a new guy would arrive "and be gone before you knew his name."

LOOKING AT A BAZOOKA BUBBLE GUM WRAPPER left at the Wall, Felton says, "Maybe it was for a guy nicknamed Bazooka. Maybe somebody was remembering how they would take a ditty bag full of trash with them into the field, and how they'd throw the trash around in a wide area when they were being pursued, so the enemy would think there were more men than there actually were." Or he reads words printed on a cigarette—"It ain't broke and it ain't wet"—and explains that a dry, intact cigarette was a prize during monsoon months in Vietnam. Felton might pick up a smooth stone and speculate that it came from the favorite trout stream of someone on the Wall.

His intuition, his lore, his deeply etched memories became so valuable that by 1986 he had been hired as a temporary museum technician.

Now he is curator of the collection, and he treats his job as a sacred trust. The artifacts, he hopes, will help people understand a terrible war and cherish those who died in it. A note, addressed to "Viet Vets," says it well: "Prayerfully we will come to realize your sacrifice. Forgive please our lack of support and understanding. May your healing come soon." Many notes like this one address both the dead and the living. Other objects and notes—many marked "please do not open"—are what Felton calls direct communication between the donor and the dead: a nursing mother's breast pad stained by her milk ... a pacifier ... three ancient Roman coins ... the model airplanes ... the two lollipop trees ...

the two pink washcloths folded in the shape of a rabbit ... the bicycle fender. Trying to fathom them is like staring at rows of votive candles placed before an altar and trying to grasp the prayers flickering within those flames. Was the lollipop tree a family rite at birthday parties? And why two? Felton has examined so many offerings that he often seems able to tug meaning from them. Or, aided by a network of volunteers, he finds ways to reach a donor and gently ask questions. It turns out that the folded washcloths were "Boo-boo Bunnies" that a mother used in treating her dead son's cuts and scratches when he was a little boy. The man who left the bicycle fender explained that a friend of his younger brother, who used to ride a bike without fenders, was killed in Vietnam. "In remembrance of his brother's friend," Felton says, "the donor removed the fenders from his own bicycle and left one at the memorial. Without that information, it was just a fender. Now it has meaning."

The bicycle fender, along with hundreds of other items, became part of a Smithsonian Institution exhibit of the collection. But the overwhelming majority of the artifacts will never be seen in public. They will remain in the chill, windowless repository in Lanham, a hangar-size building that workers call MARS, as much for its location as for its acronym. Objects that are small enough lie in plastic bags in multidrawer cabinets.

Bigger ones—such as the lollipop trees and the painting on a door— stand on platforms in the dimly lit building. Because of the sacred nature of many Native American artifacts in the collection, tribal leaders dispatched a shaman to MARS, instructing him to bless both the objects and the curators. The blessing sanctioned the handling of sacred objects by curators and their viewing by non-Native Americans.

When the Vietnam Women's Memorial was built near the Wall in 1993, the tradition of offering continued. Among the objects left there were eight gold bracelets, each placed on a branch of a tree growing beside a sculptural grouping by Glenna Goodacre that shows three women caring for a wounded soldier. And each bracelet carries the name of one of the eight women who are remembered on the Wall. Flowers and flags, the most frequently found offerings, often appear at the two nearby statuary groups. But it is the Wall that remains the focus of remembrance.

"THE OBJECTS ARE PRIMARY SOURCES, giving validity to a historic event," says David Guynes, site manager of MARS and an authority on the preservation of objects of the past. "People who ordinarily would not be articulate are telling us about an era. They are choosing the things to keep, not a museum curator." Analysts of the collection have discovered, for example, that the higher a unit's casualty count the higher the number of objects associated with that unit. Guynes says that this helps in the understanding of long-term grief.

Through the years, the collection has been changing. At first what was typically left was something personal or a few words spontaneously jotted down on a piece of paper, often the stationery of a Washington hotel. Gradually, as donors became aware of the collection, they carefully prepared their letters or objects, preserving them in advance by enclosing them in plastic or by engraving their words on metal plaques.

Felton sees 1988 as a year of change, following President Reagan's visit to the memorial, where he left a note to "Our young friends.... in our hearts you will always be young, full of the love that is youth, love of life...." After that, Felton says, "There was a validation, as if America was saying, 'It's OK to be a vet.' The letters began saying, 'I've got on with my life.'"

Toys and other objects of the 1950s and early 1960s are now appearing more frequently. Intuitively, Felton senses the effects of a generation passing: The parents of the Vietnam dead are themselves dying. From their attics and closets come the keepsakes of dead children that now pass to brothers and sisters, who bring them to the Wall. They are also bringing their own children, the nieces and nephews who are told of an uncle or an aunt they will never meet. One such brother was a teacher, who brought his fifth graders to see the Wall and show them his older brother's name. He touched the name and began to cry, and then he wrote a letter, which seemed to help. "I'm alright and doing fine," he wrote. "I will love you always."

THE MEMORIAL IS ALSO A RALLYING POINT for demonstrators who come to Washington for a cause. A Medal of Honor became an offering in 1986 when a recipient renounced his medal, the nation's highest award for valor, and left it, with a letter to President Reagan, as "my strongest public expression of opposition to U.S. military policies in Central America."

The Wall has become a permanent site for those who keep alive the prisoners of war issue. When the memorial was built, about 1,150 names were marked with a cross to indicate that the person was missing in action or known to be a prisoner at the end of the war. For the kin of those declared missing in action, the Wall has become a rendezvous of rage and memory. To remind visitors of the unknown fate of these men, MIA-POW organizations keep vigil there.

Long before the Wall, people began wearing bracelets engraved with names of men declared missing in action. They were modeled after the plain brass bracelets given to U.S. servicemen by their Montagnard allies. These bracelets bound their wearers to the hope that the MIAs were still alive somewhere as prisoners of war. Over the years, more than 1,500 people have come to the memorial and relinquished their bracelets, apparently satisfied that the Wall is now custodian of their hopes.

Words and objects supporting or protesting many issues are left at the Wall, which has become a kind of bulletin board for whatever it is visitors need to communicate. Veterans of the Persian Gulf War came and left remembrances of their battles. But it remains, most of all, the place where people leave their thoughts about the Vietnam War. A few come again and again. One mother leaves a decorated Christmas tree every year. Another first brought her son a simple message. Then, year by year, she has brought more and more elaborate collages of words and Xeroxed photos.

She is what the volunteers call a repeater.

The Wall draws many visitors on holidays, and year after year more Christmas cards and Easter baskets are added to the collection. So are Father's Day cards; an estimated four of every ten men on the Wall was a father—or about to become one— when he died. Some offerings are even for people not on the Wall. Gail walked along the Wall and left a letter three days after Jim died. "Although you did not die in Vietnam, a part of you remained there," she wrote. "You were too young to die. This walk was for you."

Others come to mark deaths from causes they attribute to the war, especially to the effects of the herbicide known as Agent Orange. A widow left a model of the Wall and a photograph of her husband, who died in 1985. "My son asked if his Dad's name would be carved on your beautiful face," she wrote. "I had to tell him that it would not, because he did not die *in* Vietnam but from *being* in Vietnam...."

Like so many who come to the Wall, she addresses it directly, as if within its stone lies an understanding that can come from no other source. This is a place where memories weave, where hearts heal. This is a place where people can feel what Lincoln called the mystic chords of memory, "stretching from every battle-field and patriot grave, to every living heart and hearthstone, all over this broad land...."

—THOMAS B. ALLEN

OFFERINGS AT THE WALL

HAPPY FATHER'S DAY - DAD.
HERE ARE THE FIRST
TWO IMAGES OF YOUR
FIRST GRANDCHILD. I
DON'T KNOW IF IT'S A BOY
OR A GIRL - IF THE BABY
IS A BOY - HE'LL BE NAMED
AFTER YOU.
    DAD - THIS CHILD WILL KNOW
YOU - JUST HOW I HAVE GROWN
TO KNOW & LOVE YOU - EVEN
THOUGH THE LAST TIME I
SAW YOU I WAS ONLY 4 MO.
OLD.   I ♡ U DADDY -
            YOUR DAUGHTER,
                JEANETTE
SGT. EDDIE E. CHERVONY (55E 6)
    1ST CAV 1/7, A BTRY

THE VIETNAM VETERANS MEMORIAL COLLECTION

A FRIEND LEFT CASINGS OF THE BLANK CARTRIDGES FIRED IN THE RIFLE SALUTE AT
THE FUNERAL OF A MAN LISTED ON THE WALL.

THIS MARIJUANA CIGARETTE SOMEHOW ESCAPED FEDERAL CONFISCATION—THE FATE OF MOST DRUG
PARAPHERNALIA LEFT AT THE WALL.

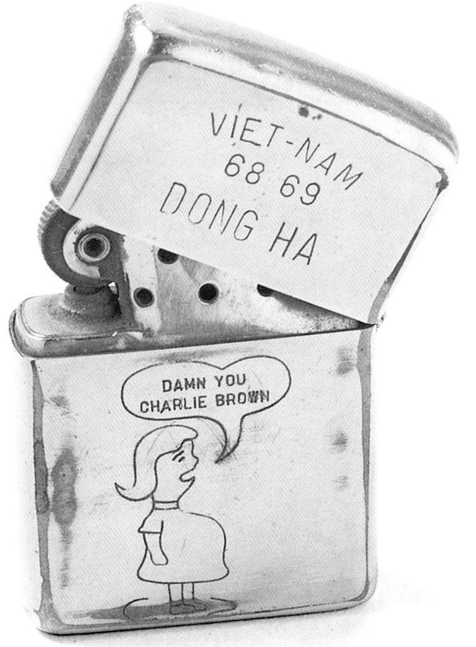
VIET-NAM
68 69
DONG HA
DAMN YOU
CHARLIE BROWN

To all those
commrades who
died for me,
this is all I can
give my Purple
Heart - 1968
Johnny O
USMC-0311 MOS
2   30

LEFT FOR *Our beloved only son*, DEAD AT AGE EIGHTEEN.

We miss you. Mom, Bette, Angela.

Henry L. Bradshaw

On August 11, 1968, I, Corporal _____ remember this as being true facts about this incident concerning Henry L. Bradshaw. On the above date, I and several other soldiers returned to base camp, Charlie Hill. We had been on short patrols north of Qui Nhon, South Vietnam. The Viet Cong had hit Charlie Hill hard in January and February, 1968, during the Tet offensive.

It was known by many that Charlie had been building forces in this area for a takeover of the hill.

The hill was the backbone for communications for all of Southeast Asia.

I had been assigned to the 81mm mortar squad along with Henry and two others. Henry was getting pretty short, so I took most of his patrols. I felt much safer in the bush than in base camp.

In late afternoon our squad returned from patrols.

We had not observed any Viet Cong in the area for several days.

After returning, some of the guys gave me a small birthday party. The next day was to be my 21st birthday.

The guys gave me a pair of boxer underwear

(we hardly had any underwear) and a cold beer, along with a hot shower.

I guess the guys had stolen the water and ice.

After the shower, Henry came to me and advised me that I was on the guard roster that had been posted for the night. I was assigned to the main gate along with a soldier that I did not know very well.

Henry told me that he would take my post and that I could take his some other time.

We agreed on this and at about 0120 hrs. our post was hit and overrun by Viet Cong.

The reports are that Henry, who had taken my post, was the first person to be killed.

Henry was alone when attacked in his bunker. The Viet Cong first threw a grenade in the bunker at him.

He was able to kick it from the bunker before it exploded.

After the grenade was thrown, Henry was shot in the chest area by an AK-47.

He was killed at that point.

I was sleeping at that time. I heard the blast and jumped for cover.

The Viet Cong were all around the camp and had caught us off guard. They were hitting every place they could. We knew we were in deep trouble. The fighting lasted until sunrise. We could not get any support because of our location and the foggy weather. The mortar squad fired over two hundred rounds of mortar shells in and around the camp, trying to keep the Viet Cong out of the camp.

At sunup we had been hit hard and lost a lot of men. The body count was 101 Viet Cong killed.

Henry Bradshaw died for me that night.

If he had not seen the Viet Cong, we all may have been killed.

I dug the bullet that killed Henry out of the bunker wall and have kept it for twenty years.

I think it should be placed to rest along with all the other memories of fallen heroes like Henry.

Henry is always being thought of.

His dedication and memory will live in my life forever. The cause was painful.

Now rest in peace.

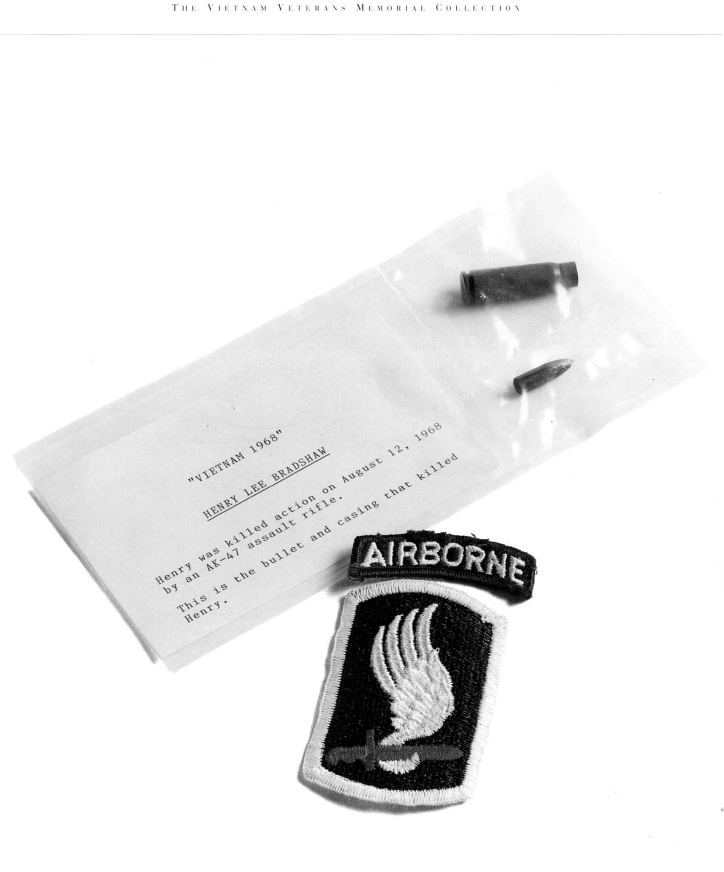

"VIETNAM 1968"

HENRY LEE BRADSHAW

Henry was killed action on August 12, 1968 by an AK-47 assault rifle.

This is the bullet and casing that killed Henry.

We did not fight the enemy. We fought ourselves and the enemy was within us.

THE VIETNAM VETERANS MEMORIAL COLLECTION

1. Sure, Yes drill Sergeant Sure Yes drill Sergeant Sure Yes drill Sergeant
2. Sure Yes drill Sergeant Sure Yes drill Sergeant Sure Yes drill Sergeant
3. Sure Yes drill Sergeant Sure Yes drill Sergeant Sure Yes drill Sergeant
4. Sure Yes drill Sergeant Sure Yes drill Sergeant Sure Yes drill Sergeant
5. Sure Yes drill Sergeant Sure Yes drill Sergeant Sure Yes drill Sergeant
6. Sure Yes drill Sergeant Sure Yes drill Sergeant Sure Yes drill Sergeant
7. Sure Yes drill Sergeant Sure Yes drill Sergeant Sure Yes drill Sergeant
8. Sure Yes drill Sergeant Sure Yes drill Sergeant Sure Yes drill Sergeant
9. Sure Yes drill Sergeant Sure Yes drill Sergeant Sure Yes drill Sergeant
10. Sure Yes drill Sergeant Sure Yes drill Sergeant Sure Yes drill Sergeant
11. Sure Yes drill Sergeant Sure Yes drill Sergeant Sure Yes drill Sergeant
12. Sure Yes drill Sergeant Sure Yes drill Sergeant Sure Yes drill Sergeant
13. Sure Yes drill Sergeant Sure Yes drill Sergeant Sure Yes drill
14. Sure Yes drill Sergeant Sure Yes drill Sergeant Sure Yes
15. Sure Yes drill Sergeant Sure Yes drill Sergeant Sure Yes
16. Sure Yes drill Sergeant Sure Yes drill Sergeant Sure Yes
17. Sure Yes drill Sergeant Sure Yes drill Sergeant Sure Yes
18. Sure Yes drill Sergeant Sure Yes drill Sergeant Sure Yes
19. Sure Yes drill Sergeant Sure Yes drill Sergeant Sure Yes
20. Sure Yes drill Sergeant Sure Yes drill Sergeant Sure Yes
21. Sure Yes drill Sergeant Sure Yes drill Sergeant Sure Yes
22. Sure Yes drill Sergeant Sure Yes drill Sergeant Sure Yes
23. Sure Yes drill Sergeant Sure Yes drill Sergeant Sure Yes
24. Sure Yes drill Sergeant Sure Yes drill Sergeant Sure Yes
25. Sure Yes drill Sergeant Sure Yes drill Sergeant Sure Yes
26. Sure Yes drill Sergeant Sure Yes drill Sergeant Sure Yes
27. Sure Yes drill Sergeant Sure Yes drill Sergeant Sure Yes
28. Sure Yes drill Sergeant Sure Yes drill Sergeant Sure Yes
29. Sure Yes drill Sergeant Sure Yes drill Sergeant Sure Yes
30. Sure Yes drill Sergeant Sure Yes drill Sergeant Sure Yes
31. Sure Yes drill Sergeant Sure Yes drill Sergeant Sure Yes
32. Sure Yes drill Sergeant Sure Yes drill Sergeant Sure Yes
33. Sure Yes drill Sergeant Sure Yes drill Sergeant Sure Yes
34. Sure Yes drill Sergeant Sure Yes drill Sergeant Sure Yes
35. Sure Yes drill Sergeant Sure Yes drill Sergeant Sure Yes
36. Sure Yes drill Sergeant Sure Yes drill Sergeant Sure Yes
37. Sure Yes drill Sergeant Sure Yes drill Sergeant Sure Yes
38. Sure Yes drill Sergeant Sure Yes drill Sergeant Sure Yes
39. Sure Yes drill Sergeant Sure Yes drill Sergeant Sure Yes
40. Sure Yes drill Sergeant Sure Yes drill Sergeant Sure Yes
41. Sure Yes drill Sergeant Sure Yes drill Sergeant Sure Yes
42. Sure Yes drill Sergeant Sure Yes drill Sergeant Sure Yes
44. Sure Yes drill Sergeant Sure Yes drill Sergeant Sure Yes
45. Sure Yes drill Sergeant Sure Yes drill Sergeant Sure Yes
46. Sure Yes drill Sergeant Sure Yes drill Sergeant Sure Yes
47. Sure Yes drill Sergeant Sure Yes drill Sergeant Sure Yes
48. Sure Yes drill Sergeant Sure Yes drill Sergeant Sure Yes
50. Sure Yes drill Sergeant Sure Yes drill Sergeant Sure Yes

THE TOP HAT'S BANDANNA SIGNIFIES MEMBERSHIP IN AN AIR ASSAULT UNIT.

I've missed throwing the baseball to you. You have been on my mind almost daily since 6-9-69.
You wouldn't believe my big three boys and 1 little girl who have taken your place and
now play catch with me....

OFFERINGS AT THE WALL

ONE OF THE MANY NATIVE AMERICAN ARTIFACTS GIVEN TO THE WALL. WHEN THE MEMORIAL WAS DEDICATED,
TRIBAL LEADERS COMMUNICATED WITH THE GREAT SPIRIT AND CHANTED THE NAMES
OF THEIR OWN PEOPLE KILLED IN THE WAR.

A NATIVE AMERICAN, WHO HAD BEEN A PRISONER OF WAR IN VIETNAM, MADE THIS BOX
AND LANCE FROM A CEDAR TREE.

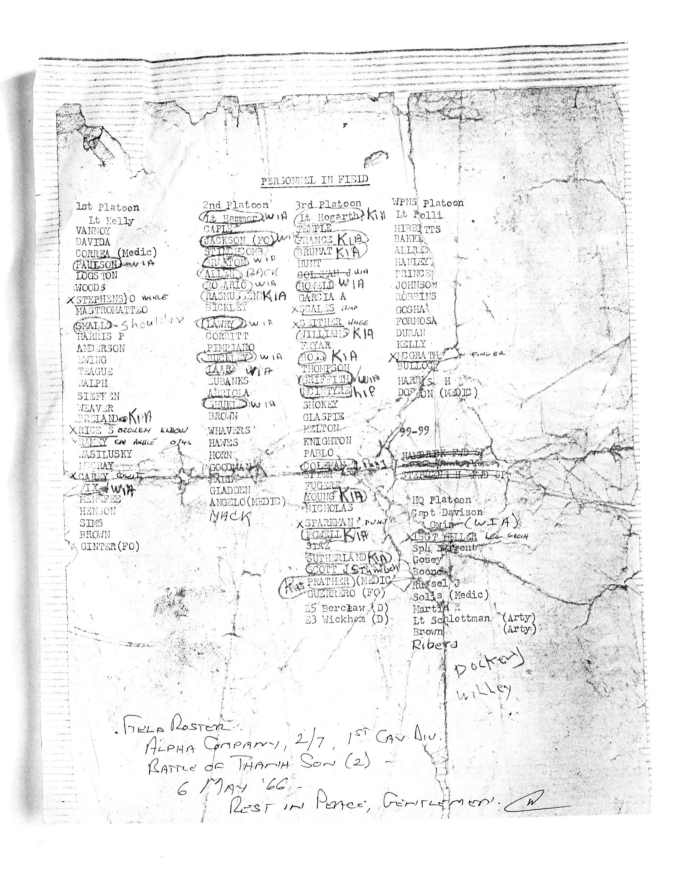

WITH THE COMMUNIST FLAG AND NORTH VIETNAM ARMY SHIRT WAS A NOTE DEDICATING THE OFFERING TO FOUR
MARINES. THEY FOUGHT IN THE BATTLE THAT ENDED WITH THE TAKING OF THESE ENEMY SOUVENIRS.

WEST POINT REMEMBERS THE CLASS OF 1966, WHICH LOST TWENTY-FIVE MEMBERS IN VIETNAM.
THE CLASS OF 1967, WITH TWENTY-SEVEN MEN KILLED IN ACTION OR DEAD OF BATTLE WOUNDS,
HAD THE HIGHEST TOLL IN THE HISTORY OF THE ACADEMY.

Dear Sir,

For twenty-two years I have carried your picture in my wallet.

I was only eighteen years old that day that we faced one another on that trail in Chu Lai, Vietnam.

Why you didn't take my life I'll never know.

You stared at me for so long, armed with your AK–47, and yet you did not fire.

Forgive me for taking your life, I was reacting just the way I was trained, to kill V.C....

So many times over the years I have stared at your picture and your daughter, I suspect.

Each time my heart and guts would burn with the pain of guilt. I have two daughters myself now....

I perceive you as a brave soldier defending his homeland.

Above all else, I can now respect the importance that life held for you.

I suppose that is why I am able to be here today....

It is time for me to continue the life process and release my pain and guilt.

Forgive me, Sir.

GARY, WHO WAS ALWAYS ASKING HIS BUDDY THE TIME, WAS LEFT THIS WATCH.

When I held you in my arms you felt cold. I would not let them take you from me for as long as I could.

And then you were gone.

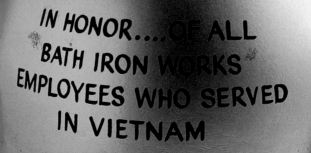

DAVID W. WICKHAM
GUY D. JOHNSON
LEE E. NORDAHL
BILLIE D. CARTWRIGHT
EDWARD F. GOLD
MAX E. LUCKENBACH
ROBERT T. HANSON
JOSEPH V. MURRAY
THOMAS A. GLASSON
LARRY M. JORDAN
KENNETH W. PUGH
REUBEN B. HARRIS
MICHEAL R. ZERBE
DAVID S. UNDERHILL
JOHN ABBOTT
WILLIAM L. TROMP
JACK E. KELLER

BILLY O. HOOPER
CHARLES A. FAHLNOWER
JACOB D. LOGAN
CARL B. AUSTIN
CEDRIK B. BOE
ELLIS E. AUSTIN
ROBERT F. WEIMERTS
WILLIAM B. NICKERSON

COME ON ALL YOU BIG STRONG MEN
UNCLE SAM NEEDS YOUR HELP AGAIN
HE'S GOT HIMSELF IN A HELL OF A JAM
WAY DOWN YONDER IN VIET NAM
SO PUT DOWN YOUR BOOKS
AND PICK UP A GUN
WE'RE ALL GONNA HAVE SOME FUN
SO IT'S
ONE, TWO, THREE, WHAT ARE WE FIGHTING FOR
DON'T ASK ME, I DON'T GIVE A DAMM
NEXT STOP IS VIET NAM
FIVE, SIX, SEVEN, OPEN UP THE PEARLY GATES
WELL IT AINT NO TIME TO WONDER WHY
WERE ALL GONNA DIE

LOSES: U.S.S. KITTY HAWK
APRIL 1965 – MAY 1966

IN HONOR.....OF ALL
BATH IRON WORKS
EMPLOYEES WHO SERVED
IN VIETNAM

It's a beautiful day. We'd be playing golf. I'd be beating you by two strokes, sucker.

The Vietnamese sign says, "Bad Land," probably warning of land mines. With the sign came a memo book, its words blurred by rain and time: *I lived and died a thousand nights.*

MANY VIET CONG USED U.S.-DISTRIBUTED SAFE-CONDUCT PASSES TO GET FOOD AND MEDICAL AID,
BUT THEN RETURNED TO WAR.

THE REPUBLIC OF VIETNAM'S CROSS FOR GALLANTRY, WITH PALM, WAS LEFT AT THE WALL.

U.S.ARMY
STEVE MALMBERG
13th AVIATION BN
64-65.
Ben Benson
Commander
Viet Nam Brother of
Viet Nam Veterans
P.O. Box 1985
Vacaville, Calif.
95688
MONTY FAPP
ROD GEORGE
HELPED Pull Guard
WHEN YOU CUT OUT
Chuck Bowen
DALE Vollbrecht
101st AHC
69-70
ROBERT McSmith
JOHN E. PASELL
101st ABN DIV
CURTISS BROWN
JOHN SMALLEN
ECO. 26TH ENG
BN. AMERICAL DIV
ROGER McGILL
25th INF DIV
3/4 CAV
1965-1966
Cu Chi
TIM SCHAEFER
HELL ON WHEELS
"LEST WE FORGET"
ED HOKERS
VIET NAM
HUNTING CLUB
POW MIA

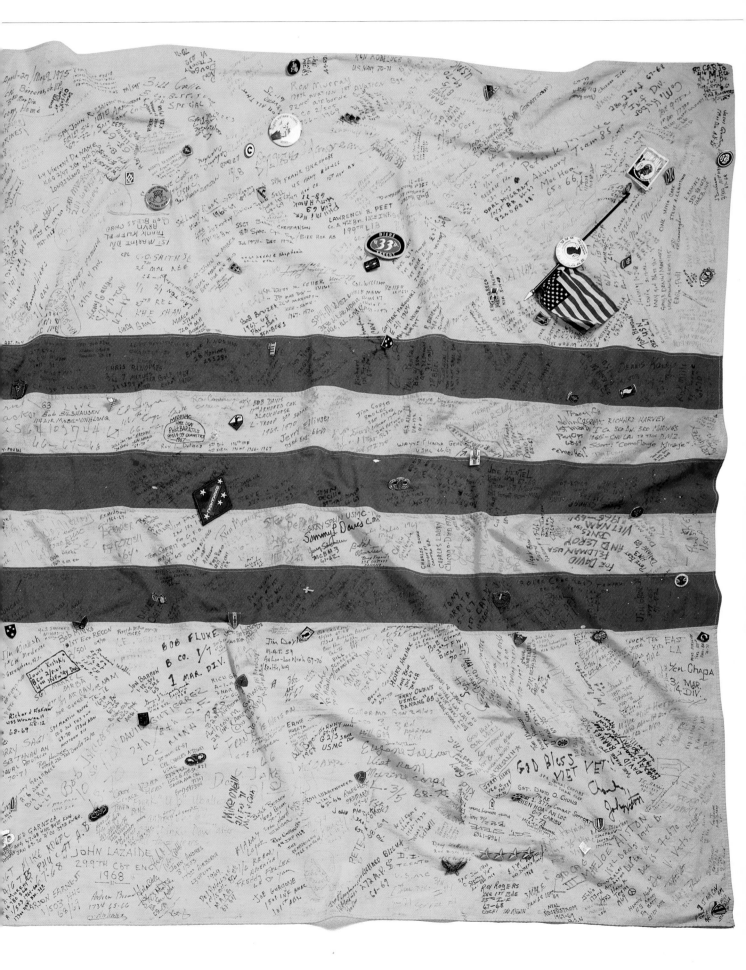

Tìm Thấy Mào Tử Phi Tổn Số Phi Sư Tự do
chôn ở Nhà Mào Tử Đấy
Me Trái đất Sẽ Thừa Kiện (Các) Anh
đất Của Anh Thân Thể đi Xuống

— — — — —

Find The Cost of Freedom
Buried in The ground
Mother Earth will Claim you
Lay Your Body Down

BETWEEN MEMORIAL DAY AND SEPTEMBER 1986 THERE WERE LEFT AT THE WALL FIVE SEPARATE RUBBINGS
OF THE NAME J. C. STORY. WITH THE RUBBINGS WERE SEVERAL MEDALS AND RIBBONS FOR MEDALS OF
COMMENDATION AND SERVICE. J. C. STORY WAS IN THE ARMY, YET ONE RIBBON IS FOR THE
NAVY GOOD CONDUCT MEDAL, AND THE ANCHOR CAP DEVICE SIGNIFIES A NAVY PETTY OFFICER.
NO NOTES ACCOMPANIED THE RUBBINGS.

Army Regulation 670–1 states that "… insignia will be authorized for wear only after
The Institute of Heraldry, U.S. Army, has determined the propriety and granted approval…." These patches, designed
by their wearers and made by Vietnamese seamstresses, were definitely unauthorized.

President Ronald Reagan   July 29, 1986
The White House
Washington, D.C

Dear President Reagan,

    The enclosed statement of my renunciation of the
Congressional Medal of Honor and its associated benefits,
represents my strongest public expression of opposition to U.S.
military policies in Central America. You have been the
champion of these brutal policies. I hold you most responsible
for their origin and implementation.

    You publically stated your identification with some of the
most ruthless cut-throats in Central American history when you
said, "I'm a Contra too." You insulted every American patriot
when you refered to these killers of children, old men and women
as "freedom fighters," comparable to the founding fathers of our
country.

    In the name of freedom, national security, national
interest, and anticommunism you have tried to justify crimes
against humanity of the most heinous sort. You have made a
global bully of the United States. You would not dare do to
countries capable of defending themselves, what you have done
to tiny nations like El Salvador, Nicaragua and Honduras.

    Mr. President, you are clearly set on a course of U.S.
domination of Central America. There are a lot of us Americans
who do not care to be counted among the oppressors of this world
and we intend to let the government you lead know it by way of
a series of non-violent protests that will end when you stop the
killing, the raping, the torturing, and the kidnapping of poor
people in Central America.

    You are not without company, Mr. President. There are
other Americans who justify the murder of innocents in the same
vigorous way that you do. You are polarizing this nation. One
day you may have to repress your fellow Americans with the same
kind of terror tactics you sanction in Central America.

    I pray for your conversion, Mr. President. Some morning I
hope you wake up and hear the cry of the poor riding on a southwest wind from Guatemala, Nicaragua and El Salvador. They are
crying STOP KILLING US.

    I never met a Central American peasant who did not know
your name.
                    Regretfully,

Charles J. Liteky - Former holder of the Congressional Medal of Honor

1

Desperate for cigarettes, a Special Forces soldier broke into a friend's footlocker and took a
carton, intending to replace it with two cans of sardines. But the friend was killed.
After keeping the cans for twenty years, the borrower found his friend's name
on the Wall and finally gave him the sardines.

THE SAND OF CHU LAI, JANUARY 1969: *Jerry—it ain't that bad!!!*

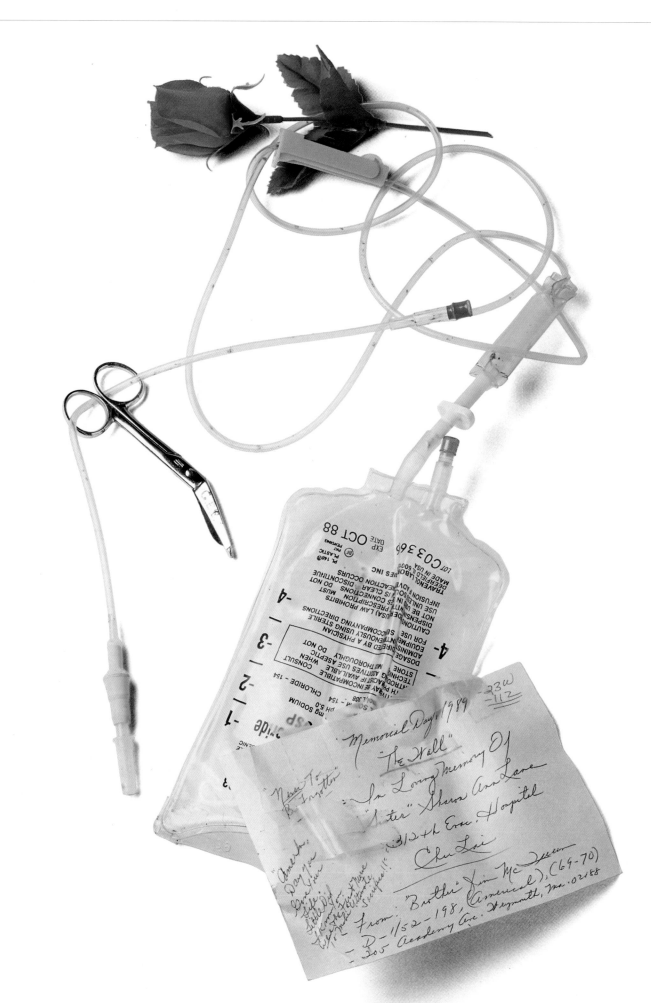

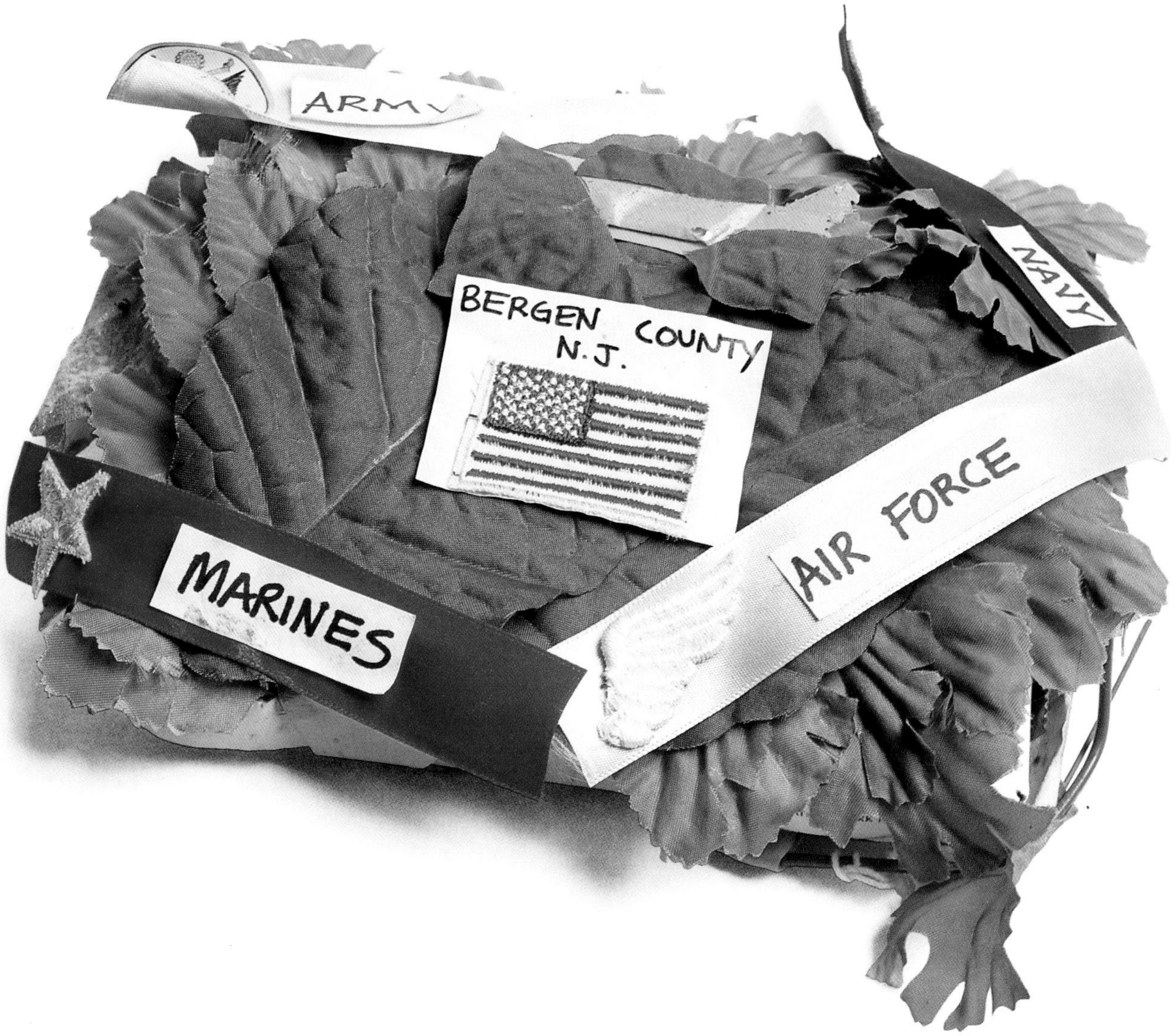
ARMY
BERGEN COUNTY
N.J.
NAVY
AIR FORCE
MARINES

for Tommy + Dave

they said we lost so
they built us a black wall why
expect gratitude

Washington, D.C.
Memorial Day, '92

IN MEMORY OF
DAVID "TEN BEARS" GOMEZ
NAVAJO/ISLETA INDIAN • USMC 3/7 "M" Co.
11/3/46 — 10/25/91
DIED OF AGENT ORANGE
MEMBER OF "THE BROTHERS OF VIET-NAM LA HABRA, CALIF.

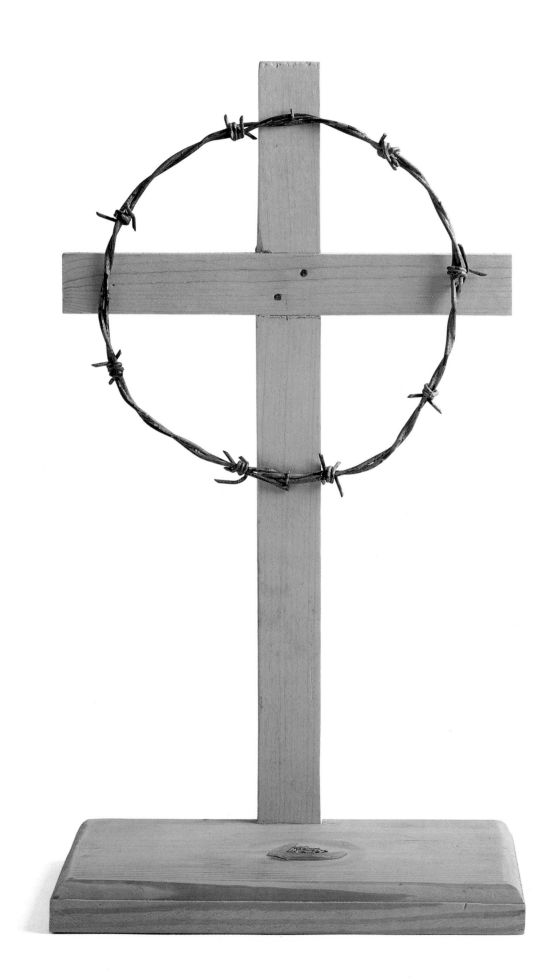

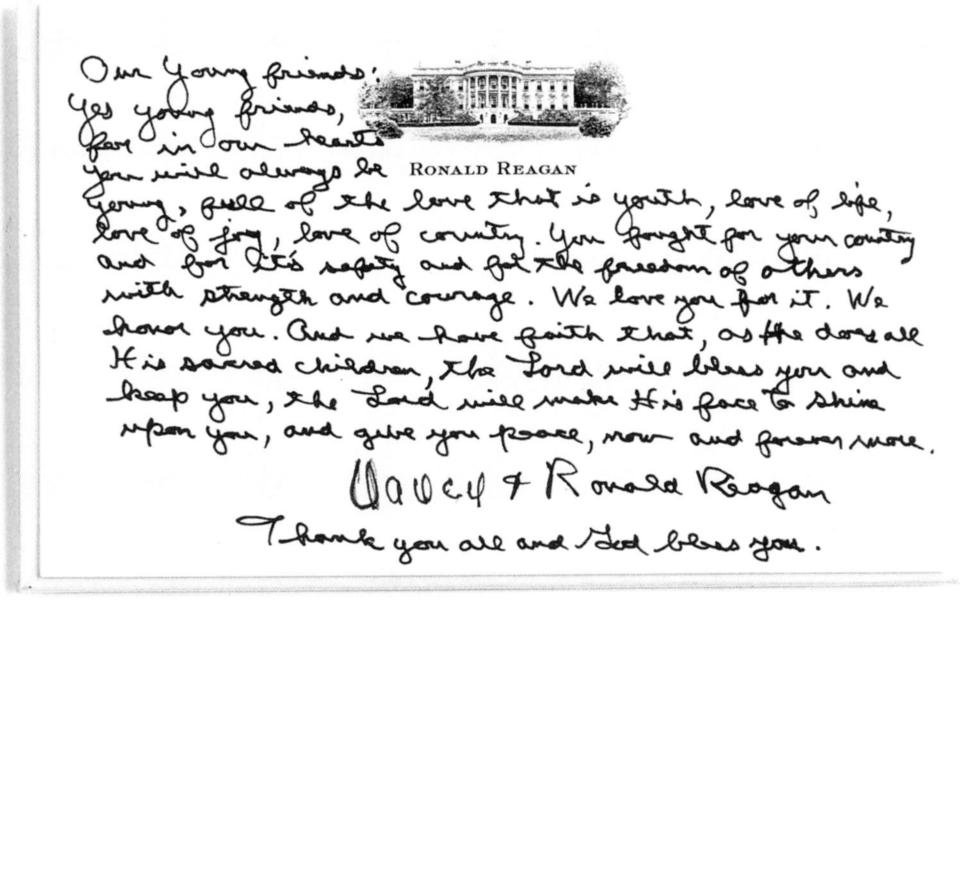

Our young friends:
Yes young friends,
for in our hearts
you will always be
young, full of the love that is youth, love of life,
love of joy, love of country. You fought for your country
and for it's safety and for the freedom of others
with strength and courage. We love you for it. We
honor you. And we have faith that, as He does all
His sacred children, the Lord will bless you and
keep you, the Lord will make His face to shine
upon you, and give you peace, now and forever more.

Nancy & Ronald Reagan

Thank you all and God bless you.

RONALD REAGAN

(OPPOSITE) A NAVY SQUADRON'S PUNCH BOWL AND TWENTY-SIX CUPS, EACH ENGRAVED WITH A FLYER'S NAME.
THE TWO INVERTED CUPS REPRESENT MEN WHO WERE KILLED IN ACTION. THE CUP ON ITS SIDE SIGNIFIES
THE RECOVERY OF ONLY ONE MAN FROM A TWO-MAN CREW.

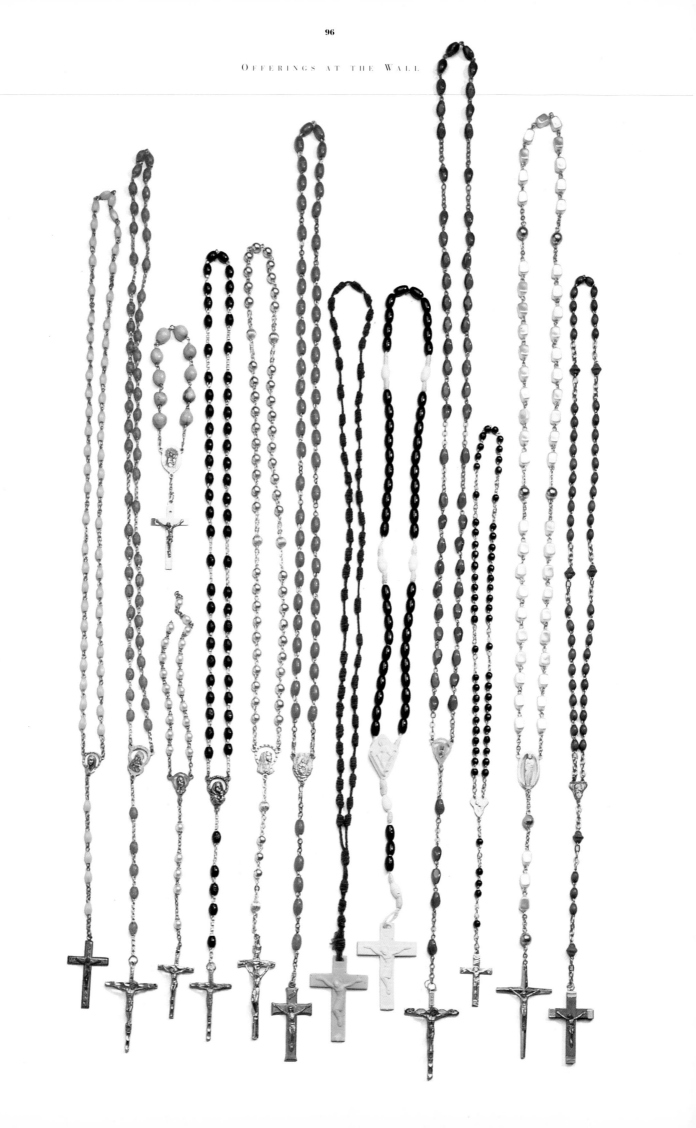

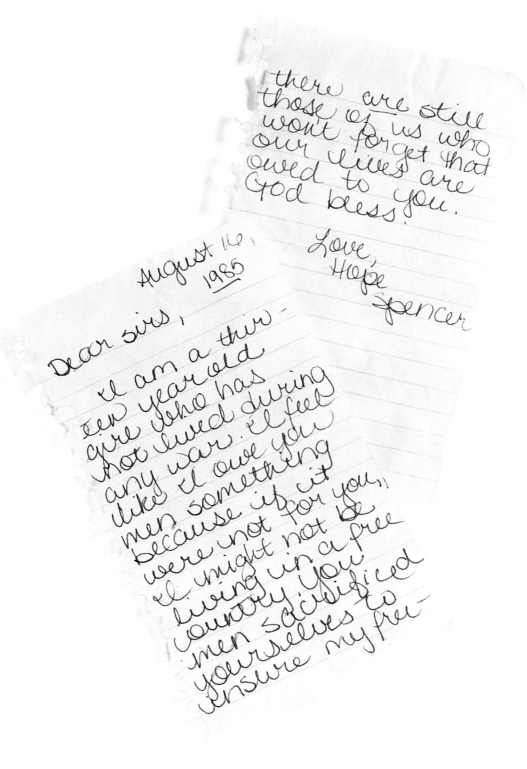

there are still
those of us who
won't forget that
our lives are
owed to you.
God bless you.

Love,
Hope Spencer

August 16,
1985

Dear sirs,

I am a thir-
teen year old
girl who has
not lived during
any war. I feel
like I owe you
men something
because if it
were not for you,
I might not be
living in a free
country. You
men sacrificed
yourselves to
ensure my free-

LEFT AT THE VIETNAM WOMEN'S MEMORIAL, THIS PAINTING OF AN ARMY NURSE IS DEDICATED TO ALL NURSES
WHO SERVED IN THE WAR: *There are those out there who have not forgotten.*

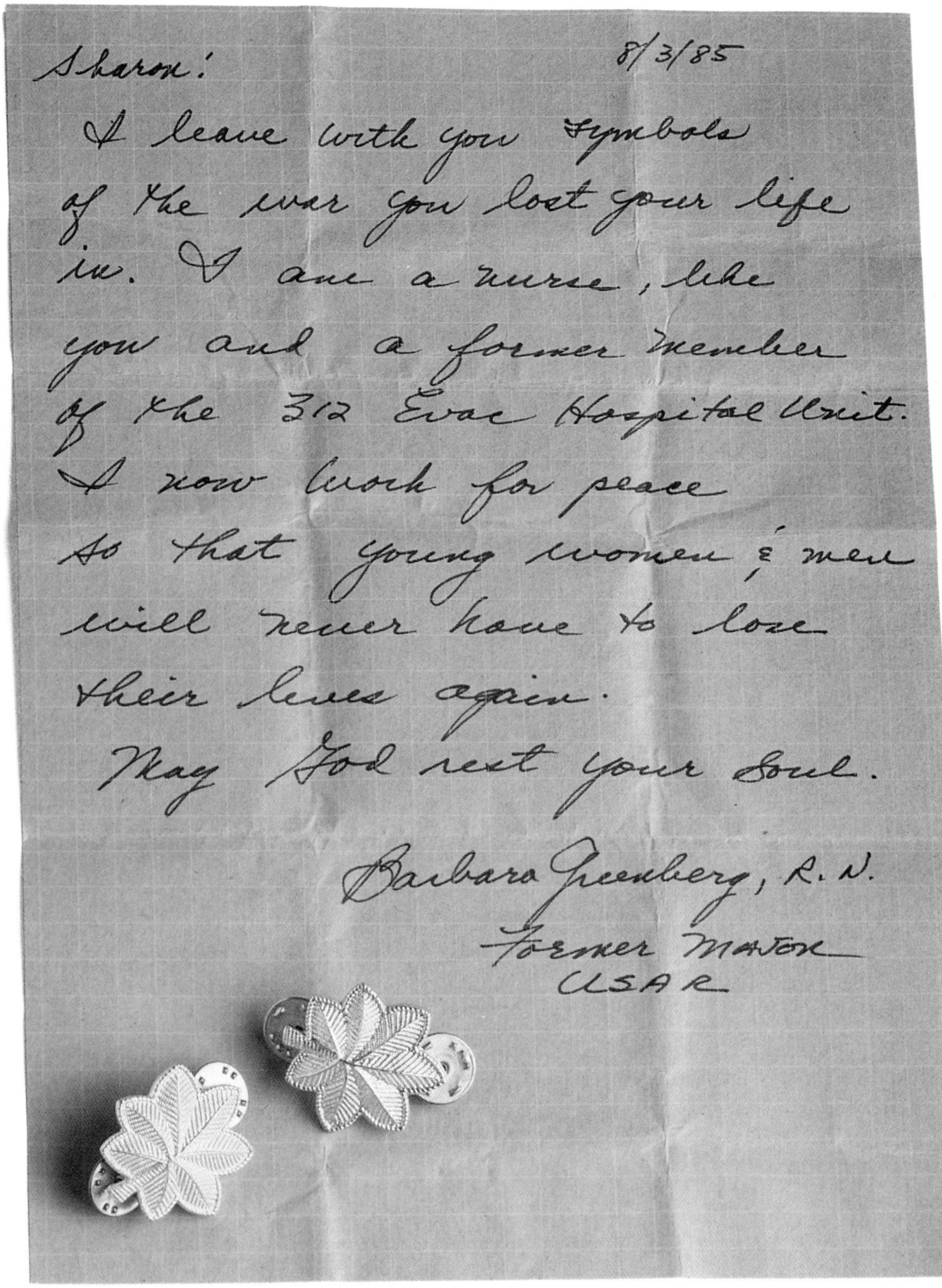

Sharon: 8/3/85

I leave with you Symbols
of the war you lost your life
in. I am a nurse, like
you and a former member
of the 312 Evac Hospital Unit.
I now work for peace
so that young women & men
will never have to lose
their lives again.
    May God rest your Soul.

                    Barbara Greenberg, R.N.
                    Former Major
                    USAR

SSGT
ARLIE || TERRY It Aint BROKE

Someone remembered that a dry, intact cigarette was a rare prize in the monsoon months.
Am I worth dying for? asks a note with it.

GIs called them Ho Chi Min sandals.

ONE HELMET CAME FROM A SON, WHO WROTE ON IT: *Dad—I will never forget you, though
I barely knew you, 1944–1967.* ANOTHER HELMET CAME FROM AN EX-SERGEANT, WITH A RAMBLING NOTE:
*We took good care of our men…. Sorry about Cox being here….
I smoked marijuana…. I hated the 1st Sgt.*

Dear Ed:

Its taken me 22 years to get the courage, but I finally made it.

There hasn't been one day in those 22 years that I haven't thought about you –

talked to you, loved and missed you!

I've seen pictures of the wall and all the things people were leaving,

letters-medals-pictures-etc., just about anything you could think of.

I wanted to bring something so I brought "Worry."

I remember how you laughed when you saw me making that rag-tag doll out of an old sock.

I also remember how you finally helped me finish it and how it became our mascot.

I always put it on my pillow after I made-up my bunk each morning.

I even remember the night I threw it at you as you were leaving one night

after we had had a spat and how you laughed.

"Worry" was baptized with a thousand gallons of tears the day you went down.

When Art came by and told me you had "augered in" I went fucking crazy.

I remember waking up the next morning clutching "Worry"

to my chest like a kid clutching it's security blanket.

Somehow I feel "Worry" will be closer to you here than packed away in my trunk of Viet Nam memories.

So here it is, tear soaked, red Viet Nam dirt and all. I'm keeping your coffee mug

and flight suit (Zips) as we use to call them. It still smells like you.

I have never washed them. Everything turned to shit after you went down. Rainwater and John De Bock

augered in, everyone was spooked. I asked for and got a transfer up north in October,

couldn't stand the memories any longer.

"What the shit – over," you went in the way you wanted "full throttle, guns smoking."

I can just see you up in "Jock" heaven, playing a mean game of poker and knocking back

a few "Pearl" beers. At least your not MIA or a POW.

The country hasn't done well with that issue but we sisters and brothers will never, never give up – never!

God, I miss ya. It's been almost 22 years. I will think of you everyday of my life. Funny, I can still smell Viet

Nam, hear that great music, feel that heat. I can still see your eyes and hear your laugh.

Rest gently darling man. Dream sweet dreams my gallant hero.

Till we meet again, and we will,

Kim

17 September, 1973

John,

The things that I am going to say in this letter are about twenty years and a whole lifetime late, but maybe that won't matter once they've been said.

I've taken the entire responsibility for your death on myself for this whole time. Even now, I intellectually know that there were many mistakes that led to your dying, some of them yours, too. I just have a hard time feeling like it's not my fault.

We trusted each other, implicitly. We depended on each other. We supported each other. We shared a whole lot in the time that we knew each other: pain, hunger, sickness, triumph, laughter, and more than a little excitement. We even shared a lover, Death. Both of us wooed the bitch, but you won her. What a deal for you. You know, I've never forgiven you for leaving me alone. I've been alone and lonely ever since.

Actually, it's probably better that you won. The way things have been back here in the world... you'd have had a hard time. Hell, I've had a hard time and I was always the stable one. You'd have wound up dead or jailed.

I never thanked you for the times that you saved my life. Any more than you thanked me for the times that I saved yours. I kind of thought that it was understood, and didn't matter. I mean, even if one of us had said thanks, the answer would have been "Fuck it. It don't mean nothin'." It does seem to mean something now. It's important. Thanks.

It's just that you've got to know that what happened was done for the best for all of us. We couldn't help you; not without risking us all. We sure as hell weren't going to leave you. It fell to me 'cause I was your partner, I guess. After all, a man shoots his own dog, right? God help me. I can still smell your blood and that damned Wyler's lemonade all over me.

I've been looking for forgiveness for twenty years, now. You can't forgive me, now, even if you thought there was a need to. So, lately, I've been trying to forgive myself. You know, I feel like I got punished for doing what we all knew was the right thing. Nobody would talk about it (not like I would have wanted to); when I got back from R&R they gave me an FNG partner. I felt like it was a death sentence. Even that poor bastard paid for your death by way of my treatment of him.

I want you to know that I avenged your death many times over, that day. The bread that those dinks cast upon the waters was returned to them tenfold. That sounds kind of silly, but I know the vindictive kind of person you were and it would have been important to you. I guess it must have been important to me, but I think that I was trying to die, too. The incompetent bastards just couldn't do me.

A lot of the guys who were there say they feel like they lost something in-country. I know what I lost. I've always said that when you died, it was like killing the other half of myself. Maybe that's not necessarily true. What I did lose was youth... all of the idealism, trust, self-confidence, and personal power that we had, either inside or drilled into us. I'm scared, now, most of the time, and I hurt a lot.

What happened to us has cost me a life as much as it cost you yours. I've never been able to get close to anyone since you died. My wife, my step-daughter, my son. I live in the past, 'cause today hurts too much. I want out of the past. The war is over. I need my war to be over, too.

I never got to say goodbye. So I've come to this monument to have a little memorial service and to say goodbye and to let you go. I'll never forget you, don't worry about that. Hell, I'm a living testimony that you were good at what we did.

Goodbye, John. If there is a caring, Christian God, I hope that he has forgiven both of us and taken you with all of our brother warriors to a peaceful final reward.

Your partner,

Tony C.

A formal set of miniature military medals from the World War II era.

Walker,
I miss you dear friend.
Hope things are peaceful for
you.

315

WALKER SMITH
Fullback

Dedicated to all Vietnam veterans affected by Agent Orange and other herbicides sprayed in S.E. Asia.

In memory of the gay soldiers in Vietnam: Made heroes for fighting other men, shamed for loving other men.

Gay and Lesbian Pride Day · June 14, 1987 · Washington D.C.

Given with love, WROTE THE WOMAN WHO WORE THIS HELMET LINER WHILE WORKING FOR THE RED CROSS
AND ARMY SPECIAL SERVICES IN VINH LONG.

THE VIETNAM VETERANS MEMORIAL COLLECTION

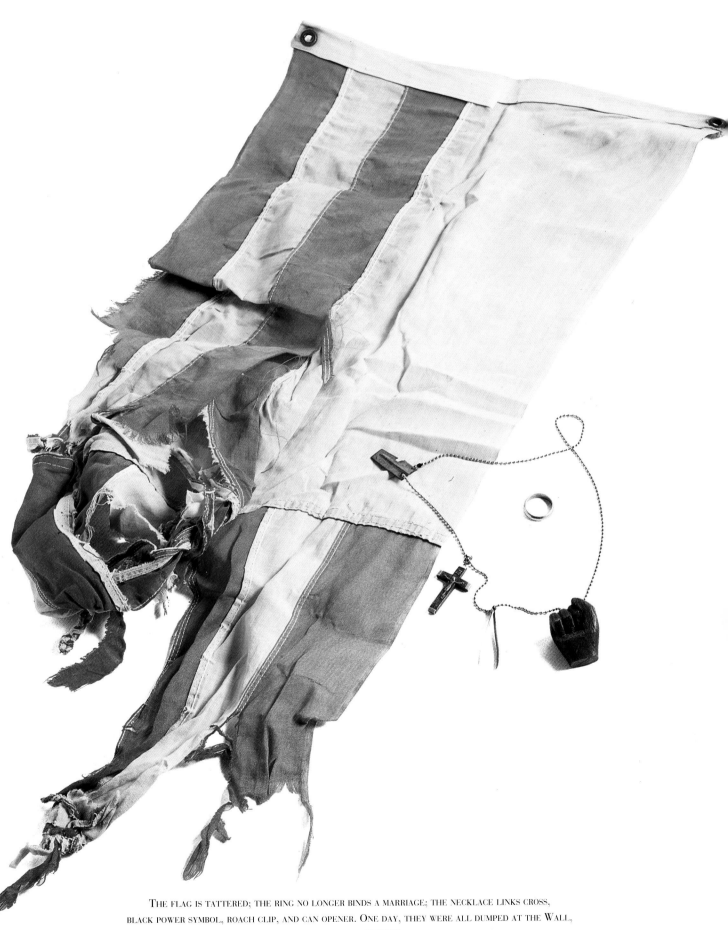

THE FLAG IS TATTERED; THE RING NO LONGER BINDS A MARRIAGE; THE NECKLACE LINKS CROSS,
BLACK POWER SYMBOL, ROACH CLIP, AND CAN OPENER. ONE DAY, THEY WERE ALL DUMPED AT THE WALL,
AS IF IN SELF-EXORCISM.

(OPPOSITE) AT THE END OF A PROTEST DEMONSTRATION AGAINST NUCLEAR WEAPONS,
MARCHERS LEFT THIS SCULPTURE, CALLED *After the Holocaust*.

THESE RINGS BELONGED TO ROBERT F. MELTON, SP4 USA AND JUDY, HIS WIFE.
HE AND JUDY WERE MARRIED IN 1966, SIX MONTHS BEFORE HIS DEATH IN VIET
NAM. HE EXTENDED HIS TOUR THERE TO COME HOME ON LEAVE TO BE MARRIED.
ALTHOUGH HE HAD A RELATIVELY SAFE SUPPLY MOS HE REPEATEDLY
VOLUNTEERED TO RIDE SHOTGUN ON RESUPPLY HELICOPTER MISSIONS TO
FIREBASES AND IN SUPPORT OF FIREFIGHTS. ON ONE OF THESE MISSIONS THE
HELICOPTER HE WAS ON WAS SHOT DOWN SOUTH OF SAIGON.

THESE RINGS WERE PLACED ON HIS CASKET BY HIS MOTHER IN 1966. THEY WERE
WASHED UP FROM THE GRAVE SITE AND FOUND BY ME ON A MEMORIAL DAY VISIT
TO HIS GRAVE IN 1986.

BOBBY, JUDY AND I GREW UP TOGETHER IN LEXINGTON, NC. BOBBY AND I WERE
IN BASIC TRAINING TOGETHER AT FT. JACKSON AND LATER, TOGETHER IN
VIETNAM.

JUDY CHOOSES TO FORGET THIS PART OF HER PAST AND DOES NOT WANT THE
RINGS.

I COULD HAVE PUT THEM BACK ON THE GRAVE BUT I AM FEARFUL THAT A
STRANGER WOULD FIND THEM. I KNOW THAT THESE RINGS MEANT A GREAT DEAL
BOTH TO BOBBY AND JUDY, THEREFORE I FEEL THAT THEY SHOULD BE PLACED AT
THE SITE WHERE HIS SPIRIT RESIDES, WHERE LOVE, FRIENDSHIP AND VALUES
DOMINATE THE DAY.

12-31-87/LAA

Robert F. Melton
Lexington NC
Died VietNam
1966

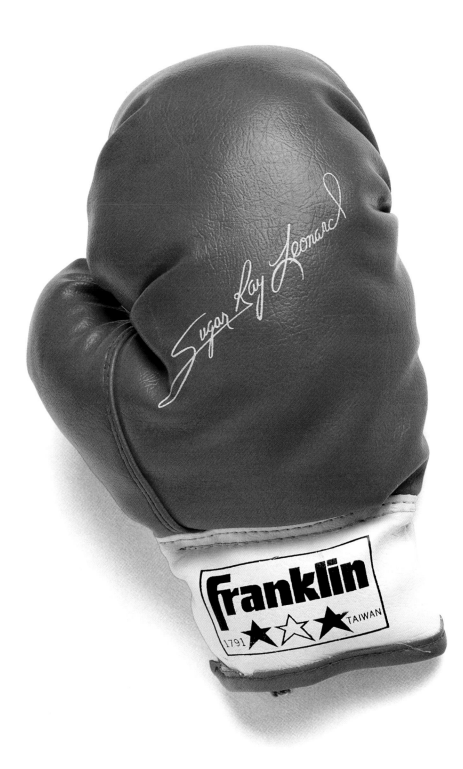

*I sit here and cry…. You know you could never land that left hook…. My little baby Sarah is just
like me (I know that's scary)…. Boy, this is the 1st time I ever wrote a letter to a dead man.
But, Tommy you'll never be gone as far as I'm concerned….*

Cowboy boots were favored by helicopter pilots in Vietnam,
and air assault soldiers wore bandannas like this one.

PFC RAY M. BARKER
KIA 22 AUG 69   AGE 24   19W20
BARKER DIED TRYING TO RECOVER PITTS BODY — HIS FRIEND   WE REME
1/A/3-21ST INFANTRY 196TH LIGHT INFANTRY BRIGADE   1988
picture between hills 407 +378, Que Son Valley
Quang Tin Province, RVN   July 1969

SGT DERWIN B. PITTS
KIA 22 AUG 69   AGE 21   19W97
picture in Vinh Huy hamlet, Que Son Valley
Quang Tin Province, RVN   Jul 1969

PFC CHARLES W. JOHNSON
KIA 22 JUL 69   AGE 20   20W 34
1/A/3-21ST INF, 196TH Lt INF Bde
WE REMEMBER! Memorial Day 88
picture near Chau Lam hamlet, Que Son Valley
Quang Tin Province, RVN   Jul 1969

This bag of soil came from the grave of Lt. Donald P. Candler of Temple, Tx.
May his soul rest in peace and God Bless him. A friend.

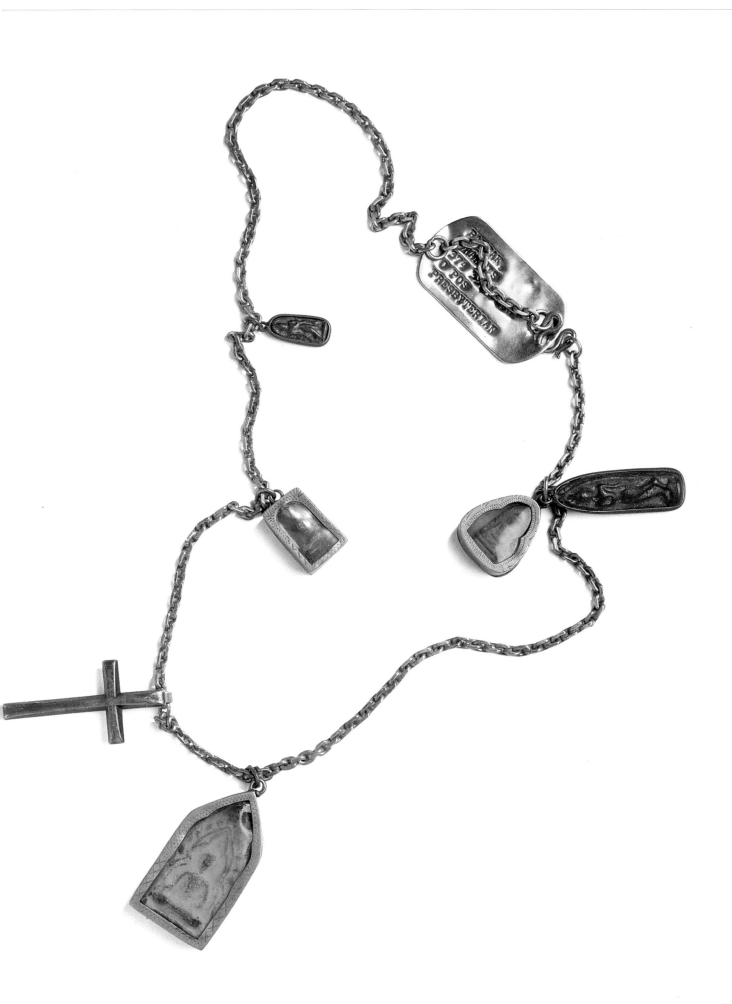

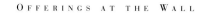

A BROKEN NAVY DRESS SABER, ON WHICH WAS ENGRAVED A STAR OF DAVID AND "NEVER AGAIN,"
WAS LEFT BY A FORMER NAVAL OFFICER AND VIETNAM VET WHO SNAPPED HIS SABER IN TWO
WHEN HE BECAME DISILLUSIONED ABOUT THE WAR.

A FRENCH MAS .36 RIFLE, MOST LIKELY USED BY THE VIET CONG.

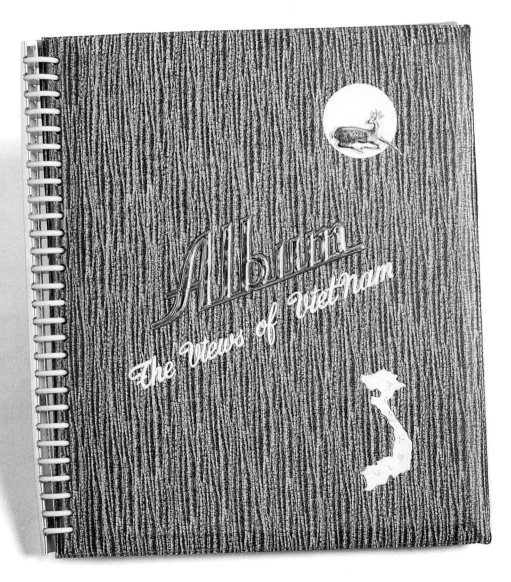

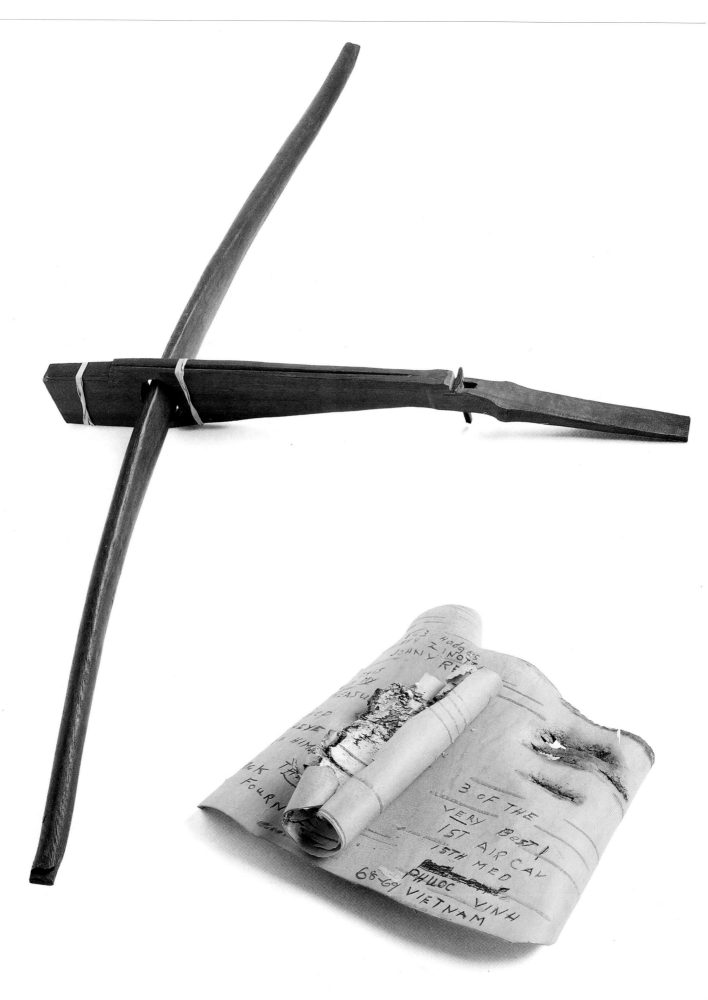

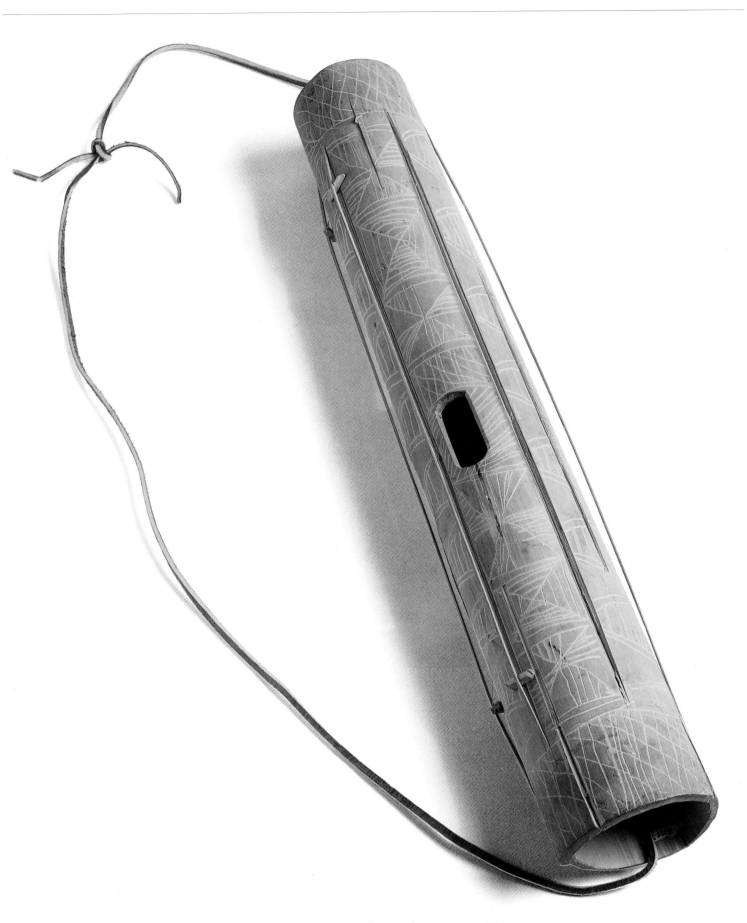

THE MUSICAL INSTRUMENT AND CROSS BOW (OPPOSITE) WERE GIVEN TO U.S. SOLDIERS BY
MONTAGNARD WARRIORS. U.S. SPECIAL FORCES ORGANIZED MONTAGNARD TRIBESMEN INTO
GUERRILLA UNITS TO FIGHT THE NORTH VIETNAMESE.

DURING THE DAY THIS TEDDY BEAR SAT AT THE WALL, CLOTHES AND EQUIPMENT
WERE GRADUALLY ADDED TO ITS OUTFIT.

THE TOY WAS LEFT BY SOVIET VETERANS OF THE AFGHANISTAN WAR,
WHO WERE TAKEN TO THE WALL BY U.S. VIETNAM VETERANS.

FOR A BROTHER, FROM A SISTER: *Dear Jerry: … I remembered that you liked trolls. I miss you.*

A KERCHIEF WORN BY AN AIR FORCE FLYER IN OPERATION RANCH HAND—THE SPRAYING OF THE DEFOLIANT
KNOWN AS AGENT ORANGE. THE CHINESE CHARACTER SIGNIFIES BRAVERY.

VICTORIA CROSS

The Victoria Cross (V.C.) was instituted by Queen Victoria on 29th January 1856 and is the foremost British and Commonwealth gallantry decoration. It is the most prized award that any Australian can earn.

Prior to the Crimean War there was no recognised gallantry medal, but the individual deeds in that war made the creation of such an award, available to Officers and Men alike, necessary.

The Victoria Cross, according to the Instituting Royal Warrant establishing rules and ordinances governing its bestowal, shall only be awarded for the most conspicuous bravery or some daring or pre-eminent act of valour or self-sacrifice or extreme devotion to duty in the presence of the enemy.

Made from Russian cannon captured at Sebastopol during the Crimean War 1854-56, the V.C. can be awarded to men and women of the Navy, Army, Air Force, Reserve Forces, Women's Nursing Services, Merchant Marine or civilians serving under orders.

For further similar acts of bravery bars are awarded. Provisions governing posthumous awards were finalized by a consolidating Royal Warrant in 1920.

The youngest Australian to win the Victoria Cross was Private J. W. A. Jackson, V.C., 17 Battalion who was 18 years 9 months.

The oldest and highest ranking Australian recipient was Lieutenant-Colonel C. G. W. Anderson, V.C., M.C., 2/19 Battalion who was 44 years 11 months.

The highest decorated Australian was Lieutenant-Colonel H. W. Murray, V.C., C.M.G., D.S.O. & Bar, D.C.M., C de G (F).

There have been 96 V.C.'s awarded to Australians covering the period from the South African War to Vietnam by virtue of their birth or service with the armed forces.

AUSTRALIAN VICTORIA CROSS WINNERS

South Africa War (1899–1902)
N. R. Howse
J. H. Bisdee
G. G. E. Wylly
F. W. Bell
J. Rogers
L. C. Maygar

World War I (1914–1918)
A. Jacka
L. M. Keysor
W. J. Symons
*A. S. Burton
W. Dunstan
J. Hamilton
F. H. Tubb
*A. J. Shout
H. V. H. Throssell
*W. T. Dartnell
J. W. A. Jackson
J. Leak
A. S. Blackburn
*T. Cooke
*C. C. Castleton
M. O'Meara
H. W. Murray
F. H. McNamara
*P. H. Cherry
J. C. Jensen
J. E. Newland
T. J. B. Kenny
J. W. Whittle
*C. Pope
G. J. Howell

R. V. Moon
R. C. Grieve
J. Carroll
R. R. Inwood
*F. Birks
J. J. Dwyer
*P. J. Bugden
*L. McGee
W. Peeler
*C. S. Jeffries
S. R. McDougall
P. V. Storkey
C. W. K. Sadlier
W. Ruthven
P. Davey
T. L. Axford
H. Dalziel
W. E. Brown
A. C. Borella
*A. E. Gaby
*R. M. Beatham
P. C. Statton
W. D. Joynt
L. D. McCarthy
B. S. Gordon
G. Cartwright
W. M. Currey
A. D. Lowerson
*R. Mactier
E. T. Towner
*A. H. Buckley
A. C. Hall
L. C. Weathers
M. V. Buckley
J. P. Woods
B. A. Wark

J. Ryan
J. Maxwell
G. M. Ingram

North Russia (1919)
A. P. Sullivan
*S. G. Pearse

World War II (1939–1945)
*J. H. Edmondson
A. R. Cutler
H. I. Edwards
J. H. Gordon
C. G. W. Anderson
*A. S. Gurney
*B. S. Kingsbury
*J. A. French
*W. H. Kibby
*P. E. Gratwick
*R. H. Middleton
*W. E. Newton
R. Kelliher
T. C. Derrick
R. R. Rattey
*A. Chowne
*J. B. Mackey
E. Kenna
L. T. Starcevich
F. J. Partridge

Vietnam War (1964–1973)
*K. A. Wheatley
*P. J. Badcoe
R. S. Simpson
K. Payne

*Indicates a Posthumous Award.

ARMY NURSE ELEANOR ALEXANDER IS ONE OF EIGHT WOMEN WHOSE NAMES ARE ENGRAVED ON THE WALL.

IN LOVING
MEMORY OF OUR
BROTHERS AND
SISTERS WHO DIED
FOR THEIR PEOPLE
IN THE REPUBLIC
OF VIETNAM

———

THE LIVING
MEMORY OF THEM
MOVES US TO BEG
GOD'S HELP TO
ABOLISH WAR, TO
HELP US CREATE A
WORLD OF PEACE
AND JUSTICE. NO
MORE WAR AND
KILLING! NOT IN
SOUTHEAST ASIA,
AND NOT IN
CENTRAL AMERICA

LOVE OUR PEOPLE:
ABOLISH WAR!

LOVE THE CHILDREN:
WAGE PEACE!

LOVE AND HONOR
GOD AND HUMANITY
BY WORKING FOR
PEACE AND JUSTICE.
THEY WILL NOT BE
BROUGHT ABOUT ON
THEIR OWN. WE MUST
CREATE THE WORLD
OF HUMAN BEAUTY
IN WHICH TO LOVE
AND NUTURE OUR
CHILDREN

1ST AIR CAV DIVISION

THE PIN FROM A HAND GRENADE FINALLY IS DROPPED AT THE WALL.

LARRY L. MARSH USN KIA 8 DEC 68

From the innocence of boyhood
filled with springs and summers
playing marbles and baseball
autumns playing football and
winters ice skating — we went to
the reality of manhood and to
the horrors of war I have lost
a very dear friend.
Your Boyhood Friend
USAF 67-68

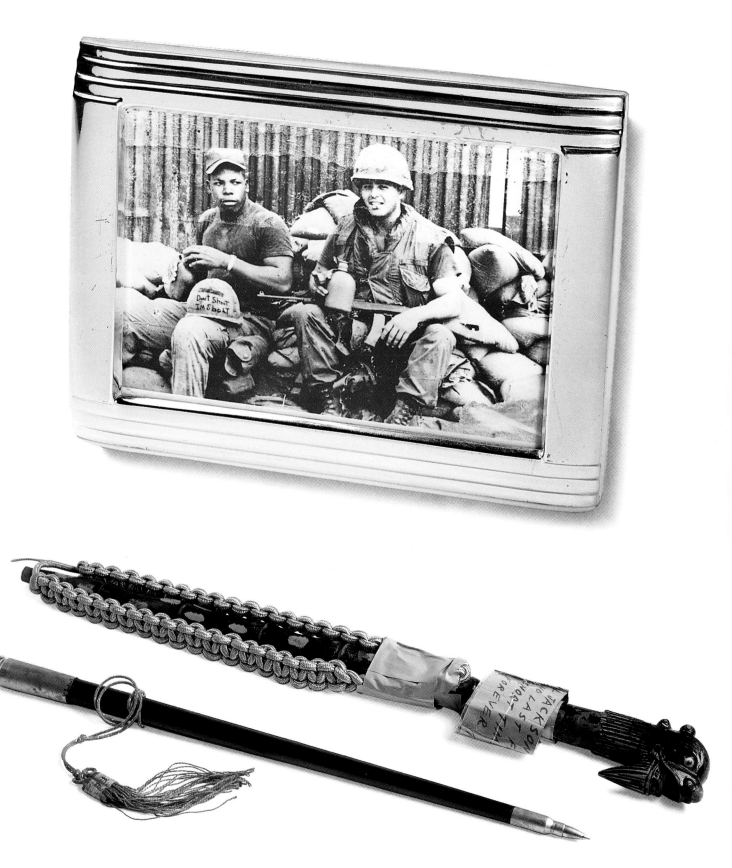

NO NOTE ACCOMPANIED THIS PHOTOGRAPH, BUT GRAFFITI ON THE HELMET AT LEFT READS,
"DON'T SHOOT. I'M SHORT," WHICH INDICATES THAT ITS OWNER HAD LESS THAN A MONTH LEFT TO SERVE OF HIS
ONE-YEAR TOUR IN VIETNAM. "SHORT-TIMER STICKS," LIKE THE SWAGGER STICKS ABOVE,
WERE OFTEN NOTCHED TO RECORD THE PASSAGE OF TIME.

An ammunition pouch worn by a North Vietnamese Army soldier.

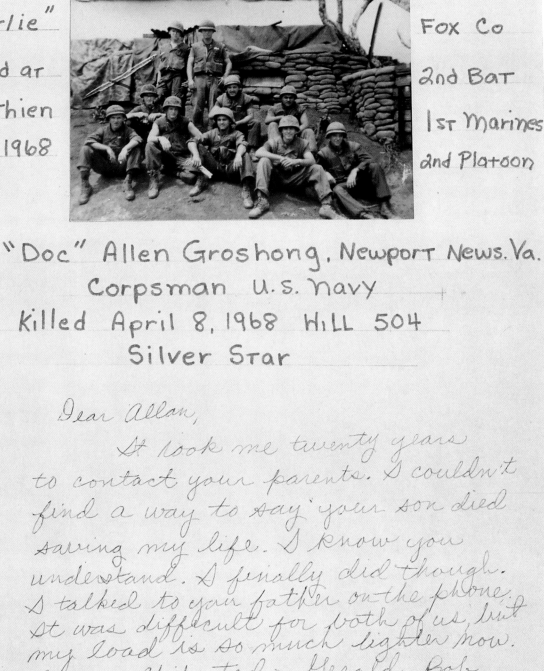

"Charlie"
Squad at
Con Thien
Feb, 1968

Fox Co
2nd Bat
1st Marines
2nd Platoon

"Doc" Allen Groshong, Newport News. Va.
Corpsman U.S. Navy
Killed April 8, 1968 HiLL 504
Silver Star

Dear Allan,
It took me twenty years
to contact your parents. I couldn't
find a way to say your son died
saving my life. I know you
understand. I finally did though.
I talked to your father on the phone.
It was difficult for both of us, but
my load is so much lighter now.
Jonny, chip, ted, Gerald, Bob,
and Sgt Jackson are here with you.
I miss you all   Love Brother
                        Lynn

Lynn Witt 18420 Munlaster Rd. Rockville Md. 20855   48 E-52

AGAIN AND AGAIN THIS SAME PHOTO OF CHARLIE SQUAD HAS BEEN LEFT. EACH TIME A DIFFERENT NAME IS
SINGLED OUT. THE NOTE WITH THE PHOTO FOR DOC GROSHONG TELLS OF A CALL TO THE CORPSMAN'S FAMILY
to say your son died saving my life…. I talked to your father on the phone. It was difficult for both of us,
but my load is so much lighter now. Jonny, Chip, Ted, Gerald,
Bob and Sgt. Jackson are here with you.

To the REMFS who covered my butt & bought it—I made it home. Thanks.
THE INITIALS STAND FOR "REAR-ECHELON MOTHERFUCKERS."

WITH THIS HAT CAME A POEM TO A DEAD BROTHER:
When we touch the wall we know that you are there....

VIETNAM

I learned Fear
I learned to be alone—NEVER let
ANYONE IN
I learned to be AN ANIMAL—to take
what I wanted, when I wanted
I learned to kill—NO—I learned it was OK to kill
I learned to like killing—I needed to kill

I came home and nothing worked—my family
did not WANT me—they were—ARE—afraid of me—
I am afraid of me—

I pray for your forgiveness—for my life/lies
I am doing the best I can....

I can not (or will not?) Remember everything....
I hope to become more at peace with the animal part of me
Please forgive me....

Vietnam (the lie) showed me how different yet alike I am to all mankind.
I try to remember how I felt.
I felt afraid yet excited, for I was one of the chosen.
It all seemed like a big game.
People talking about taking life, destroying life....
I destroyed the enemy better than most.
I liked it, it was the best Rush of my life....

No one close to me!
Good
No more hurt

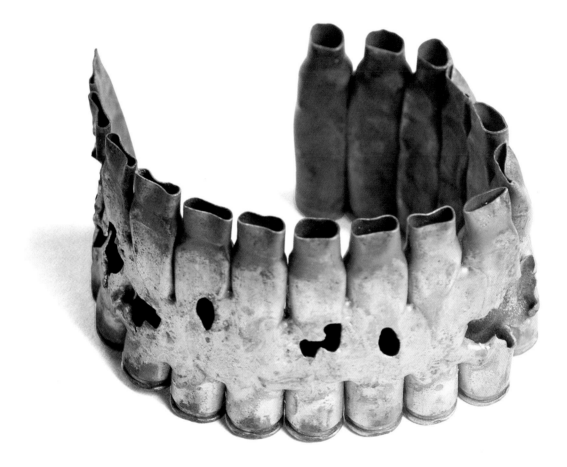

From Native Americans, a blanket representing warmth and safety.

TO BLACK TROOPS THIS WAS KNOWN AS A SLAVE BRACELET.

A RING SAID TO HAVE BEEN MADE OF ALUMINUM TAKEN FROM THE 1,700TH U.S. AIRCRAFT SHOT DOWN
OVER NORTH VIETNAM. *I pray for the pilot and crew of that aircraft.*

FOSTER'S LAGER AND AN AUSTRALIAN FLAG RECALL THE 60,000 AUSTRALIANS WHO SERVED IN VIETNAM;
500 WERE KILLED IN ACTION. THE NOTE, SIGNED *RIP Mate*, TELLS OF A VIETNAM VETERANS'
COMMEMORATION IN AUSTRALIA.

WITH A SLOUCH HAT BEARING A REPUBLIC OF VIETNAM SERVICE MEDAL CAME AN ANTIWAR NEWSPAPER,
PUBLISHED IN CALIFORNIA BUT WIDELY CIRCULATED IN VIETNAM, AND A NOTE ADDRESSED TO DONNY:
I left you in the Intensive Care Unit at Great Lakes Naval Hospital in May of 1968. You had been my
patient for a couple of months. But we never got to know each other. You were unconscious for all but a
brief second. You woke up once…. You looked up at me and asked, "Why?"

ARMY
US
SPECIAL SERVICES

IN MEMORY OF ROZ MUSKAT
WHO WENT TO WAR, TOO...
AS ONE OF 55 CIVILIAN WOMEN
WHO SERVED AND DIED IN VIETNAM

A NOTE ON A FEMALE TEDDY BEAR, LEFT AT THE WOMEN'S VIETNAM MEMORIAL, REMEMBERS THE NAME
OF A WOMAN NOT LISTED ON THE WALL. MORE THAN FIFTY CIVILIAN WOMEN DIED IN VIETNAM
WHILE WORKING IN SUPPORT OF THE ARMED FORCES.

"CHESTY," THE MARINE CORPS MASCOT, GETS ITS NICKNAME FROM THE LEGENDARY
BRIG. GEN. LEWIS B. PULLER, WHOSE SON AND NAMESAKE WAS A MARINE OFFICER IN VIETNAM IN 1968.
WHEN A BOOBY TRAP EXPLODED, HE LOST BOTH LEGS, HIS LEFT HAND, AND TWO FINGERS ON HIS RIGHT HAND.
HIS INSPIRING 1992 AUTOBIOGRAPHY WON THE PULITZER PRIZE. IN 1994 HE KILLED HIMSELF.

David Gaddie Jr.   Brian Dale Upright

David Wayne Larson

IN REMEMBRANCE OF A CEREMONY FOR THREE FALLEN COMRADES, NOW NAMES ON THE WALL.

Offerings at the Wall

After making a great march for peace and nuclear disarmament in 1986,
many marchers left worn sneakers at the Wall.

*Hi Billy, It's been a while since I've been here to see you. Your Mom's gone now but I guess you know
that. I can't really remember your face but I do remember the day we got in "big trouble" with the
fireworks…. Here's a pack of salutes for you…. I'll shoot off another pack for you.*

THE NOTE, ATTACHED TO A GOVERNMENT-ISSUE FORK THAT WAS BEING USED IN A HANOI RESTAURANT,
ENDS WITH A PLEA FOR UNDERSTANDING.

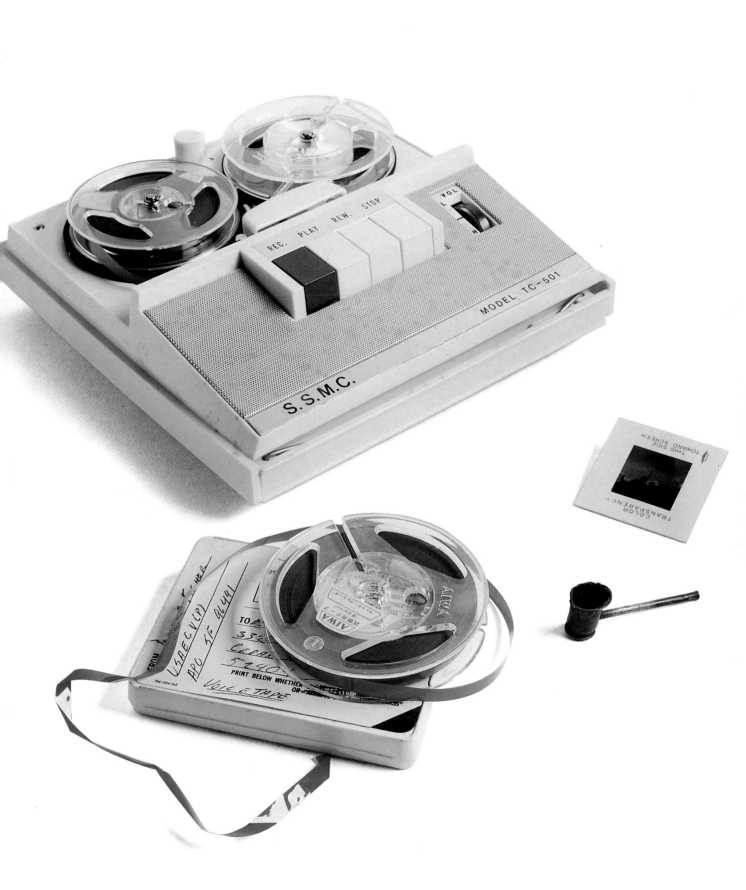

TROOPS OFTEN SENT AUDIO TAPES INSTEAD OF WRITING LETTERS HOME.
LEFT WITH THE RECORDER AND TAPES WAS A SLIDE AND WHAT PROBABLY IS A MARIJUANA PIPE.

Alcoholics Anonymous medallions, tokens of Vietnam service for many veterans,
were left at the Wall at different times.

AN ASHTRAY FROM THE CONTINENTAL PALACE IN SAIGON CAME WITH A WISH:

Dear George: … I'm waiting to have a drink in Saigon. I miss you. I wish it had been me. Michael.

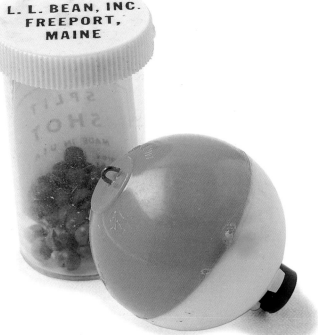

DIRECTOR NORMAN JEWISON, ON BEHALF OF THE CAST AND CREW OF *IN COUNTRY*, LEFT A FILM CANISTER
FROM THE MOVIE, WHICH WAS ABOUT A FAMILY STRUGGLING TO HEAL WOUNDS CAUSED BY THE WAR.
THE GRADUATION PHOTO AND FLOWERS WERE PROPS.

ONE OF THE GENERAL'S REMARKS TO ME BACK IN OCTOBER 1967, "MY HEART GOES OUT TO THE MOTHERS WHO BORE THESE YOUNG FIGHTING MEN AND HAD TO NURSE THEM GROWING UP, FEED THEM, EDUCATE THEM, AND HAD TO SEE THEM COME TO THIS FOOLISH WAR. MY HEART BLEEDS FOR THE MOTHERS. THESE YOUNG MEN ARE THE BRAVEST MEN I HAVE EVER SEEN IN MY LIFE TIME."

MAJ. GEN. BRUNO A. HOCHMUTH WAS THE COMMANDER OF THE THIRD MARINE DIVISION HEADQUARTERS "HUE".

THE GENERAL WAS KILLED IN A HELICOPTER EXPLOSION NOVEMBER 14, 1967

With a box of baseball memories came newspaper clippings that reported
on Chicago-area men killed in action.

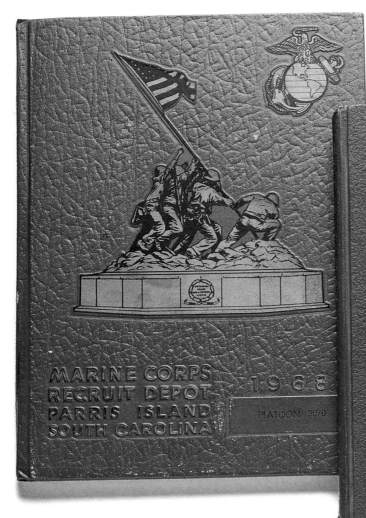

M&Ms MAY HAVE COME FROM SOMEONE WHO REMEMBERED THEIR USE AS PLACEBOS
WHEN NO PAINKILLERS WERE LEFT.

(OPPOSITE) TASSELS FROM COMMENCEMENT MORTARBOARDS SHOW FATHERS LISTED ON THE WALL
THAT THEIR TODDLERS GREW UP AND GRADUATED FROM HIGH SCHOOL AND COLLEGE.
SOME GRADUATES EVEN LEAVE THEIR DIPLOMAS.

WHEN A VIETNAM VETERAN DIED, HIS SON ASKED IF HIS FATHER WOULD BE ON THE WALL. THE BOY'S MOTHER, WHO BLAMED THE DEATH ON AGENT ORANGE, SAID, "HE DID NOT DIE *IN* VIETNAM, BUT FROM *BEING* IN VIETNAM." SHE BROUGHT THIS MODEL AND PHOTO TO THE WALL.

A CIGAR LEFT FOR A MAN ON THE WALL, BECAUSE HIS NAME *is exactly the same as one of my best friends....*
Somehow, I think that you were a lot like my friend.

A GEORGIA HIGH SCHOOL STUDENT TRANSFORMED A DOOR INTO A MEMORIAL LISTING THE NAMES OF
MEN MISSING IN ACTION. THE POW-MIA SYMBOL PERPETUATES THE FAITH OF THOSE WHO, SUSTAINED BY LITTLE
MORE THAN HOPE, BELIEVE THAT MANY MIAS ARE STILL BEING KEPT AS PRISONERS.

13 NOV. 87
Winchester. VA

Sorry about leaving you on the chopper pad, wish
I had stayed and missed my flight to the world,
should have gone to the hospital with you, I didn't
know you was hit that bad, never once did I
think you wouldn't make it. Guess my old knife
didn't help either of us that time. I only live 60
miles on so west of the wall in Winchester,
have tried to go to the wall many times over
last five years but just didn't have the guts,
had to face it, but tomorrow I'm going
and give you this knife for the second
I'll be seeing you before to
I hope I can make myself
think of you and the other
forget. My wife's birthday
never again, will it
go to
old guys have to
guys
is Today,
even happen
at a waste,
do what we
Sorry about that
AF
Henry

Sorry about leaving you on the chopper pad…. I didn't know you wouldn't make it. Guess my old knife
didn't help either of us this time…. I have tried to go to the wall many times …
but didn't have the guts … but tomorrow I'm going to be there and give you this knife for the second
time…. God, I hope I can make myself go to that wall….

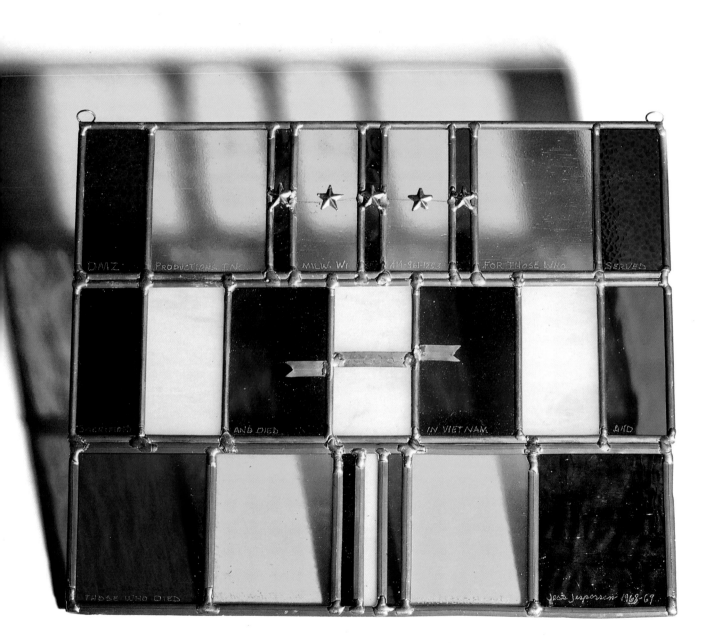

It will be a blue Christmas without you.

SOMEONE LEFT FIVE CANS OF FRUIT COCKTAIL AT FIVE DIFFERENT PLACES ALONG THE WALL.

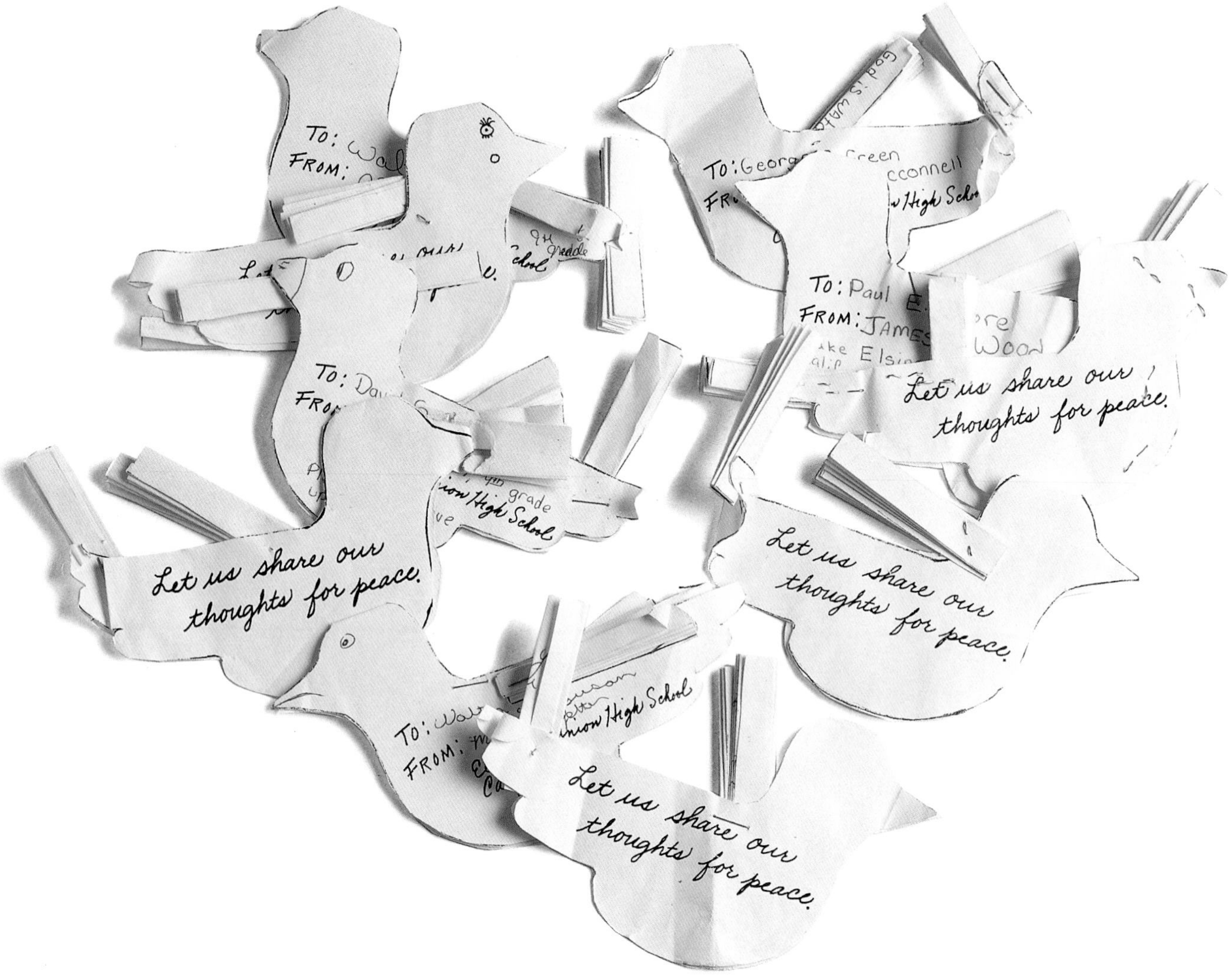

WITH THE MAPLE SYRUP CAME ITS RECEIPT OF PURCHASE AND THE CHANGE.

Bracelets dedicated to each of the eight military women listed on the Wall were left on trees at the Women's Vietnam Memorial.

Wayne, you gave all you had to give to keep me free. I think of you everyday and miss you so much.
I love you, June.

The rifle-and-helmet symbols of death in battle mark a Fallen Comrade Ceremony for the Marines
of C Company. On the back of the photo, two of the fallen are named. The third is simply called
"New guy," killed before his comrades learned his name.

IN THE WEB OF COMBAT STRIKE GEAR IS A NEWSPAPER PHOTO WHOSE CAPTION READS,
"PFC JERRY POFF, CLARA DELAND, FLA., KEEPS LOW AS A SNIPER'S BULLET COMES NEAR HIS POSITION."
SOON AFTER THE ARMY PHOTOGRAPHER TOOK THE PICTURE, POFF WAS KILLED.

ONE VETERAN'S COLLECTION OF WATCHES USED IN VIETNAM—ALL SHORT-LIVED IN THE DAMP AND DIRT OF WAR.

APRIL, 1989

DEAR EDDIE —
IN MEMORY OF THE
GREAT FOOTBALL GAME OF
AUGUST, 1907; EAT *,
DRINK, AND THEN IT'S
"PUFF TIME" (BOUGHT YOUR
FAVORITE BRAND)!
REST IN PEACE
LOVE Jeff
* DON'T WORRY — IT'S NOT
HAM AND "MOTHERS!
P.S. DON'T SCARF IT ALL UP ON
YOUR OWN, SHARE SOME
WITH BERNIE AND
MICHAEL

CPL. EDWARD E. BLUMER U
(CHICAGO ILL.)
D.O.W. SOUTHWEST OF DANANG
B. 9FEB47
D.O.W. 7 NOV. 67
Rest In Peace, MY MAN
From Jeff

BLACK BERET WAS LEFT BY SURVIVING
MEMBER OF 12 MAN TEAM THAT WAS WIPED.
OUT. AGAIN NOV 20 1968 MEMBERS SERVED
IN LONG RANGE PATROL   101ST AIRB DIV.
LOST MEMBERS THAT ARE ON WALL
ALBERT CONTRERAS. 38W LINE 16
TERRY N CLIFTON 38W LINE 15
MICHAEL DEAN REIFF 38W LINE 20
ARTHUR J HERINGHAUSEN JR. 38W LINE 18
THIS BERET WAS LEFT BY
JIM VENABLE WHO WAS WOUNDED.

Dear Daddy
In dedication to our beloved Vietnam Veterans

Mother hurriedly lit my six candles
On the day Saigon fell
She embraced me and your portrait
Whispering: "Dad used to say war is hell"

Mother asked me if I liked to learn English
"'Cause your Dad was a handsome American
He died bravely in a fierce battle
On the hills or down the valleys of Khe Sanh

He came to Vietnam from America
Where the Statue of Liberty stands,
Helping the South stop the North
From stealing the precious piece of lands."

Mother died in the rain at a labor camp
'Cause there was no food or medicine
She was caught for "escape to America"
Where you, Daddy, were growing

I was left a living outcast
Tears dried from missing you, Mom, Dad
Holding onto your spirits each day
That's all your child has had

I secretly heard on the shortwave
Your name is on the Viet Veteran Wall
Proud of you, Dad
You had died for Freedom and Justice for all.

Linh
Veterans Day 1987

IN HONORED REMEMBRANCE

Presented here are the names of Americans who fell in the Vietnam War.
These 58,196 names were on the Vietnam Veterans Memorial when this book
was published. They are arranged much the same as they are on the
memorial's one hundred forty panels.

The memorial consists of two walls that meet at a 125–degree angle, the east wall
pointing toward the Washington Monument, the west wall toward the Lincoln
Memorial. Each wall has seventy granite panels on which the names are inscribed
chronologically by date of casualty. Each name is accompanied by a symbol: a
diamond for death, a cross for anyone missing or imprisoned when the war ended. (A
circle will be inscribed around the cross if a person returns alive.) On the east wall's
first panel are listed the early casualties of the war, beginning in 1959; the east wall
panels continue to list the names chronologically on seventy panels, ending in
May 1968. The list resumes on the seventieth panel of the west wall
and continues back to the first panel, dated 1975.

Here, at the intersection of the walls, the beginning and the end of the war meet.

The names on the following pages are essentially arranged as they
appear on the memorial; the locations of the published names coincide with the panel
and line locations of the names inscribed on the Wall. When a name was etched
incorrectly into the granite, it had to be reinscribed in another location, usually at the
beginning or end of the same line. We have maintained this in publishing the list of
names, printing both the incorrect and correct versions. But the names here are not
accompanied by symbols, and the order in which they appear has been altered
somewhat to reflect the chronology of deaths more accurately. When the memorial
was dedicated, for example, Department of Defense officials listed the war's first death
as 1959. Later, a 1957 death was discovered and that name was inscribed out of
order. Hundreds of names, inscribed after the memorial was completed, could not be
inserted chronologically. The names published here also include five that were added
to the Wall in November 1994. Four were soldiers who died
of combat wounds. The fifth was a naval officer who died in 1966 but
had been inadvertently left off the Wall.

ERIC F. LONG, SMITHSONIAN INSTITUTION

PANEL 1 EAST

ALFONS A BANKOWSKI DALE R BUIS CHESTER A OVNAND CHESTER A OVNARD
FREDERICK T GARSIDE RALPH W MAGEE GLENN MATTESON LESLIE V SAMPSON EDGAR W WEITKAMP JR
OSCAR B WESTON JR THEODORE G FELAND GERALD M BIBER JOHN M BISCHOFF ODIS D ARNOLD
TOM J CRESS HERMAN K DURRWACHTER JR WALTER H MOON BRUCE R JONES FLOYD STUDER JAMES T DAVIS
FRED M STEUER THEODORE J BERLETT MILO B COGHILL FERGUS C GROVES II ROBERT D LARSON
JOSEPH M FAHEY JR FLOYD M FRAZIER STANLEY G HARTSON EDWARD K KISSAM JR JACK D LE TOURNEAU
GLEN F MERRIHEW LEWIS M WALLING JR ROBERT L WESTFALL CHARLES A PULLIAM AL S PADAYHAG
IVAN P WHITLOCK MILTON D BRITTON BARNEY KAATZ JAMES GABRIEL JR WAYNE E MARCHAND
BILLIE L BEARD RONALD E LEWIS HEWETT F COE GEORGE E COLLIER ROBERT L GARDNER
WALTER R MCCARTHY JR WILLIAM F TRAIN III ROBERT L SIMPSON DON J YORK JOSEPH A GOLDBERG
HAROLD L GUTHRIE JAMES E LANE ANTHONY J TENCZA WILLIAM R BUNKER III RICHARD L ELLIS
THOMAS E ANDERSON GERALD C GRIFFIN RICHARD E HAMILTON GERALD O NORTON JERALD W PENDELL
MICHAEL J TUNNEY MIGUEL A VALENTIN JR HERBERT W BOOTH JR TERRY D CORDELL RICHARD L FOXX
JOHNNIE G LEE GARRY C MCFETRIDGE ROBERT D BENNETT WILLIAM B TULLY RICHARD D BENZEL
JACK M LISLE DONALD L BRAMAN WILLIAM L DEAL KENNETH N GOOD CHARLES E HOLLOWAY
CLAYTON A FANNIN CHARLES M FITTS LAWRENCE C HAMMOND BOYCE E LAWSON JAMES D MCANDREW
LEWIS L STONE DONALD B TOTH RAYMOND C WILDE JOHN DUARTE LEON J KRAMER RICHARD E STEPHAN
JOHN P BARTLEY JOHN F SHAUGHNESSY JR JAMES R O'NEILL BERNARD L GRAY ROBERT BURGERT
CRAIG B WOLFORD CHARLES W MCCARY ODES W JEFFERS JAMES H ISHIHARA DAVID WEBSTER
WALTER P GORHAM FLOYD R DAVIS JIMMY R GRIFFIN LAVESTER L WILLIAMS ANDREW C MITCHELL III
JERRY A CAMPAIGNE RAYMOND E DOYLE JR RICHARD L HATLESTAD STANLEY E TRUESDALE RUBE A FREEMAN
PARKER D CRAMER ROBERT J HAIN ROBERT J MAIN JAMES A ELLIS JOHN C MYATT CHARLES E DOERRMAN
JAMES H BRODT NEIL K MACIVER HOWARD M EAKIN JR CHARLES B JOHNSON JR PERCY W HOWELL
G W MAGBEE CONDON H TERRY CURTIS J STECKBAUER RICHARD W GEYER PAUL R SMITH
RAYMOND F PARKS CARL H BALLARD JACK L GOODMAN LAWRENCE E HACKLEY ROBERT K MOSIER
CLARENCE C TESSMAN DONALD V MCGREGOR ARTHUR E BEDAL JOHN H MCCLEAN DONALD G LOGAN
CLAUDE W MCBRIDE EDWARD B CRIBB ARCHIE S BOWEN TIMOTHY M LANG JAMES E WENZEL
WILLIAM G COREY RAPHAEL CRUZ NEIL B MCKINNEY HOWARD P PURCELL JAMES F HILTZ
JAMES H JOHNSON JR FRANKLIN R WHITE DONALD F DAVIDSON MANUEL R DENTON DANIEL K LESSIG
BRUCE C FARRELL WILLIAM T HARRIS LARRY D JAMESON CLAUDE RICE ARTHUR G RICHARDSON
LUTHER E RITCHEY JR RONALD F SKOVIAK CHARLES P TUTHILL CHARLES F WHITEHEAD JR WILBUR T DUNLAP
DEAN A WADSWORTH DONALD C JOHANSEN JOHN C BONZO JAMES W MCNALLY GORDON R BROWN
WOODROW M FITZGERALD CHARLES B LANKFORD WALTER K MORRIS HUMBERT R VERSACE
WILLIAM J EVERHART VERNDEAN A BROCKMAN JAMES D PARKER ATIS K LIELMANIS KENNETH M RORABACK
HOWARD R CODY DUANE E LIMBERG CHESTER D TOWNSEND GARY W BITTON NORMAN R DAVISON
THOMAS F GORTON RICHARD D HILL LOUIS A CARRICARTE WILLIAM E FLOWERS CLARENCE L MOORER
MARSHALL J ANGELL MICHAEL P MARTIN JR NEWMAN R NESMITH TED P NEURA JR RONNY L WOODMANSEE
JAMES H ALLRED JEAN C ESNAULT TERRANCE L LOVENGUTH LLOYD A PAYNE GEORGE W WATSON
SAMUEL E HURD BILLY J COLEY DONALD A MOLLICONE JOHNNY C SANDERS LYNN H ROTHENBUHLER
HUGHIE D ADAMS CLEVELAND W GORDON VINCENT J HICKMAN CARL B MITCHELL CHARLES M HASPER
RAY B BROWNE LOYE T CHRISTMAS RAYMOND P FLYNN WILLIAM H HOUSE GROVER K OLSON
BRYFORD G METOYER JOHN L STRALEY DAVID THOMPSON ROBERT L TAYLOR WILLIAM E JACKSON
ARTHUR W GLOVER DONALD R TAYLOR STANLEY S SHAW PETER M FEIERABEND DONALD E KOELPER
WILLIAM A REID JERRY L TAYLOR BERNARD F LUKASIK WALTER L GLASS PAUL A WILDAUER
MORRIS R MCBRIDE THOMAS W MCCARTHY HERBERT F HARDY JR THOMAS M HERGERT JOHN F SHEA
WYLEY WRIGHT JR THOMAS J BERGIN RICHARD E JAECK ROGER E GAUVIN CARLETON W UPTON
FRANK J HOLGUIN KENNETH A SHANNON THOMAS L LEWIS EDWIN G SHANK JR UWE-THORSTEN SCOBEL
RICHARD L WHITESIDES ROBERT N BRUMET WILLIAM T CAVANAUGH ALBERT L SHIMEK ALAN Y MATSUURA
JOSEPH G GALAMBOS DAVID E MILLER RAYMOND A ADAM JAMES P SPRUILL PETER C MOORE
LOUIS G ONOHAN RONALD D HINES JOHN F SANTOS JR CARMINE A CERVELLINO GEORGE E CHAMBERLIN JR
CLAIR D DOTY GEORGE R GRAHAM CARL W GRIMES COURTNEY P HOLLAR JR WILLIAM J MONTGOMERY
DONALD L NELSON WILLIAM C OSBORN FRANK THORNTON JR BILLY D GOOD IRVING A SELF
JAMES C DYE DEANE A POMEROY DOYD D O'NEAL ARNOLD D KNIFFIN RALPH G REDMOND
ROBERT L GREER FRED T SCHRECKENGOST JESSE A GRAY THOMAS I LEDBETTER HARRY A WALLING
JIMMY CARTWRIGHT MARLIN E MCCAHAN ROBERT L RAGSDALE JAMES P WRIGHT EVERETTE L DONALDSON
WAYNE A ARAKAKI GERALD W DAVIDSON RALPH A DUNN WILLIAM B CAWTHORNE FREDDY D DODSON
CHARLES L KELLY GABRIEL R ALAMO JOHN L HOUSTON LEONARD W LOCKARD THOMAS H MAULTSBY JR
JOSEPH W BURKETT BILLY T HATFIELD RICHARD M SROKA MARTIN STOCKFEDER PAUL R HELTSLEY III
JOHN P DRAKE GEORGE W UNDERWOOD LEO B ABRAMOSKI REED G JENSEN JAMES H MCCLAIN
HOMER C MCINTYRE JR DALE D THOMAS DENNIS C KIDD RICHARD C SATHER FRED C CUTRER JR
LEONARD L KASTER HAROLD L MCNEIL JAMES E CAUGHEY WILLIAM M DEAN WILFRID N BOURGEOIS
ROGER H MULLINS ALAN B HARRIMAN JAMES M COYLE WILLIAM D RAGIN BYRON C STONE TOM WARD
WILLIAM R PATIENCE JR JOHN B MCLAUGHLIN RICHARD D GOSS JAMES E BAILEY RICHARD T LYNCH
JOHN C THOMAS GEORGE E FLYNN III VIRGIL R GREANY JOHN L MCCOY KENNETH E WALKER EDDIE L SMITH
DELBERT L VAUGHN JR THOMAS A BAIN DURWARD D GOSNEY JAMES E HAVEMANN DELBERT C LA FLEMME
GARY R RIGGINS MANFORD L KLEIV GEORGE W MARTIN ROBERT J REILLY JAMES M BECKNER
JAMES A RIAL ROLLIN C SARGENT JR HERMAN TOWERY ROBERT G ARMSTRONG VALMORE W BOURQUE
RALPH MITCHELL ERNEST J HALVORSON THEODORE B PHILLIPS EUGENE RICHARDSON LAWRENCE WOODS
EDWARD S KRUKOWSKI CHARLES P SPARKS GLENN C DYER WILLIAM C TOTH EDWARD A BLAKE
JOHN C KNAGGS RICHARD P BUBAR THOMAS J HANLEY RONALD T O'KEEFE HARRY J SICKLER
THOMAS D WHITLOCK DANIEL G DAWSON HERIBERTO A GARCIA DARL R BLOOM DONALD E SMITH
JOSEPH N HAO EUGENE M PALISKIS WILLIAM R MARTIN EDWIN R EASON OTIS GORDON JR
GEORGE H ALBRECHT LEONARD P HUDSON DAVID NIPPER RICHARD D SLACK JR GORDON L ROBINSON
ROLAND V JAGER JR JAMES G DUNTON GUY T FREELAND WILLIAM R HAMLIN NORMAN W HECK JR
ARTHUR A SHELTON DONALD W BEARD BRIAN J CRONIN BRIAN K SKINNER JOHN F STONEBURNER
DOMINICK SANSONE WOODROW W VADEN WAYNE H KIDD JOHN E KING LEONARD M TADIOS
FRANK D WILLIAMS TOMMIE D EMERT EARL A PATTERSON MEIR ENGEL ROBERT R THRUSTON III
HARRY G CRAMER ROY E CONGLETON JOE PARKS EMMETT H HORN JAMES R HAGEN GERALD R KEENEY
HAROLD G BENNETT ROY G AZBILL REINO A PANULA FRANKLIN D PORTER THEODORE A WINOWITCH
STEPHEN E MORGAN WILLIAM L SIEGRIST DONALD G COOK EDWARD R DODGE KURT C MCDONALD
CHARLES E FULTON GEORGE C BIGLEY JAMES F RAY WILLIAM T REACH ALTON L HORNBUCKLE
LYAL H ERWIN ARTHUR E NORMAN THURSTON A GRIFFITH JR RICHARD S JOHNSON GERALD A BINGER
BENJAMIN B CASTANEDA JAMES T CORDOVA HAROLD E STRONG JR WILLIAM E SWAYKOS ROGER L BUSS
ALFRED A FRYE GEORGE F VLISIDES ROBERT L WHITE JOSEPH K BELANGER DAVID CRAIG III
RALPH W BROUGHMAN EDWARD A DICKSON GERALD D FOUNDS THEODORE LAMB GEORGE MARKOS
ALVIN G PARKER JESSE A PYLE JOHN G WILLIAMS JR EMMETT J BRYANT CARLTON J HOLLAND
DON R LEWIS JOHN W MALAPELLI JAMES H MCLEAN JOHN R URBAN JAMES B ALEXANDER JR
EVERETT L ANDERSON TOMMY J BELCHER ROBERT J BETZ DAVID N CLAYTON HORACE C COLLINS
PAUL E BAYS CLARENCE L COLEMAN DELMER L FERRIS GLENN H KELLEY DALLAS LAWSON
LARRY B MCCLANAHAN ROBERT S MOSIER WALTER L RICKARD HARRY E ROWLEY ERNEST M SCHULTZ III
ROBERT L SIMON JR HARRY L SUMMERS FRANCIS J VALKOS MERLE O VAN ALSTINE MELVIN L WATERS
LAVON S WILSON FLOYD WYNN PETER A SEMMER NORMAN R GARRETT ROBERT W GROVE
RONALD S GAFFNEY ROBERT F RONCA NORMAN ELLIOTT JR LAWRENCE W JORDAN THOMAS C MCEWEN JR
GERALD B ROSE JAMES A STARLEY DWIGHT G FRAKES KURT W GAREISS JAMES I PRATT ELVIS G BARKER
MARK R CHASE DEMPSEY H WILLIAMS III WILLIAM C MATTIS RICHARD D SMITH ROBERT J ACHAS
CHARLES F CLYDESDALE HAROLD D MEYERKORD LOUIE S PARHAM JACK W KLEIN SR WILLIAM H CAMPBELL
JERRY P HAWKINS CHARLES E HUDDLE JR HAROLD R DOLLENS DAVID J WIDDER WILLIAM D REYNOLDS
CHARLES K SIDES KENNETH E HUME MANOLITO W CASTILLO WENDELL T ELIASON JAMES E MAGEL
GERALD W MCKINLEY GERALD C CAPELLE ZLATKO M FAKIN JERRY W OSBORN WAYNE C SIMMONS
JAMES J EVANS GEORGE C SMITH FRANK E BENNETT WALTER F DRAEGER JR JAMES A MAGNUSSON JR
WILLIAM M BARSCHOW JOSEPH R FOSS DAVID W BOWMAN CLARENCE L JONES RAYMOND E RUPCIC
RAFAEL TORRES-RIVERA CHARLES G TUCKER ARTHUR D BAKER JAMES W LEWIS WILLIAM M ROARK
RONALD J FEGAN TERENCE M MURPHY WILLIAM E SWANSON SAMUEL A WOODWORTH JAMES A WHEELER
DANIEL E BISHOP PATRICK P CALHOUN ARTHUR F HENNESSEY JR DOUGLAS D MACK CHARLES F MILLAY
TERRY W MILLS GILBERT OLIVAR GARY L STEELE JOSEF L THORNE ROBERT D WALKER DELOSS W ANDERSON JR
KENNETH L DEAN JR JAMES P SHEA SAYWARD N HALL JR WILLIAM W MCALLISTER WILLIAM R FUHRMAN
ROYAL G ISAACS JR RICHARD H LANGFORD LOWELL H MERRELL ROBERT A BUTTERFIELD PETER R COYMAN
CHARLES M DANSBY JOHN E EHRMENTRAUT JR DONNIE D EZELL JAMES T GRAY THEODORE R LOESCHNER JR
RANDALL K CAMPBELL CARL R WENZEL WILLIAM C SELLERS ROBERT W DOSS EUGENE R FOWLER
GEORGE H KIRBY JR ALVIN K BROYLES JR VICTOR B KELLEY WILLIAM F LE GRAND RONALD E STORZ
CHARLES E SHELTON RAYMOND L HORN ROBERT A STUBBERFIELD WILLIAM T BOWMAN JOHN W IRVING JR
NICKOLAS R KOEHLER JAMES D LA HAYE DAVID A KARDELL ROGER J MCALLISTER JR ROBERT C WISTRAND
DUDLEY W MAYO WILLIAM D BENNING JOHNIE K CULBREATH HENRY A DEUTSCH JHUE F PRICE
AMOS C WATSON HORACE E YOUNG IVAN R SMITH JOSEPH R WYNN JR DONALD E CLOSE
ROBERT GRESKOWIAK JERRY R JONES WAYNE G SCHWARTZ JESSE R ACOSTA JOSE R ARAGON
ROBERT G BELL BRIAN D BROWN CLAUDE M BUNCH JAMES M CALE EDGAR S DONAGHY
SECUNDINO BALDONADO ROBERT L CLARK WILLIAM T CRAWFORD TERENCE D ENGEL AARON G FIDIAM JR
CHARLES N FOX VERNON L HAYNES WILLIAM D HICKS DAVID L HUBBARD JR ARTHUR C JEPSON JR
ANDREW M KEA ERNEST MCFERON CHARLES W RACHAL CLIFFORD H RAULERSON JR DONALD J SEAMAN
BILLY E SHANNON GERALD A SNYDER JAMES E UNDERWOOD LEE C WAGNER JR HAYDEN E WEAVER
CHARLIE G LEWIS DAVID L HRDLICKA LEROY M DONOVAN RICHARD K HARPER RUSSELL W CONDON
ROBERT S FERNANDEZ JIMMY C STINNETT BERNARD J KELLEY RONALD I KRAUSS HARRY R SWIGER
MURREL D THOMAS TROY L WATERS BRICKIE BOWMAN JR EDWARD KENNEY CHARLES R SMITH
ORIEN J WALKER JR MAURICE W MOSHER LYNN W PETERS RAYMOND J VRBA JR FLEMING B BRAINERD III
DOYLE W LYNN PHILLIP D CHILDERS DONALD J FILLERS GEORGE H FRAZEE JR JAMES J MASOTTI
MATTHEW N HARRIS JR RANDOLPH T HICKS RANDOLPH C HOLDER WILLIAM J OAKLEY MYRON M PFOUTZ
EDWARD R PIPER JOHN C SIGG FOSTER F TRIGGS MILLARD R VALERIUS RONALD J WARREN
THOMAS T MCLARNON ROY L MURPHY TYRONE B CARSON CHRISTOPHER J O'SULLIVAN WILLIE D TYRONE
FREDERICK P CROSBY BERNARD W DIBBERT HUGH M ROBBINS DAVID M CHRISTIAN M D MCMICAN
WILLIAM H AMSPACHER JR RICHARD E HEISTER WERNER E LUTZ THOMAS L PLANTS GERALD M ROMANO
CARROLL M BIERMAN JR ROY E STOKES RONALD H MCNEES ROBERT L SHOEMAKER HUGH J SULLIVAN JR
NICOLAUS A DOEDEN CURTIS L FOSTER ALLEN C HERTZ CARL E MCBEE GERALD O MCKAY

PANEL 2E

GARY D TRACY FRANK W WILSON JAMES O CRABTREE HARRY P GAMBLE
HAROLD K STEVENS JR CHARLES A DALE DAVID S DEMMON EDWARD A OWNBY CHARLES D PIZZI
NELSON E VAN GUNDY JOHN W WHITE RONALD E BLAKE WALTER R GRAY FRED M OWENS
JOSEPH J COMPA JR ROBERT L CURLEE JR DONALD C DEDMON CARL L DOUGHTIE RAYMOND C GALBRAITH
CRAIG L HAGEN WALTER L HALL WILLIAM C HOOVER CHARLES O JENKINS JR BRUCE G JOHNSON
WILLIAM R BATCHELDER ZOLTAN A KOVACS EDWARD E KRUKOWSKI BOBBY RUSSELL DONALD R SAEGAERT
MARVIN G SHIELDS JAMES A COY PAUL G DAWSON ALVIN J DIMOND MERLE E ESTES DONALD V HESTER JR
SAMUEL J GANCI JESSE H LAWSON MILO B STIBBINS TERRENCE R TITUS NORMAN C WILLIAMS
DONALD L BAKER FREDERICK N BAKER BILLY G HAMMER LAWRENCE T HOLLAND KENNETH L REED
MICHAEL L WILDES EDGAR C BROWN FRANCISCO X SAENZ ROBERT D GALLUP MICHAEL P MORITZ
JACKIE W SANFORD JOHN R SCHUMANN AARON H WESTERN ANDREW D PARKER JR HAROLD J ROBERTS JR
LEROY A BOURGEOIS JAMES M GEHRIG JR TYRRELL G LOWRY JAMES A MARSHALL WILLIAM E NEVILLE
EDWARD J ANDERS ROBERT L ARMOND ALBERT F ROBERTS JOE C ROBERTSON MELVIN H SUTHONS
FRANK P WATSON HAROLD A ATCHER JOHN R BALL DAVID G LUCAS JAMES L PURSER MICHAEL J ULICSNI
ROBERTO SAMANIEGO JAMES L TALLEY CLAYTON L CRUCE KENNETH W PARKER WILLIAM E CORDERO
ALBERT S KNIGHT III CHARLES K LOVELACE JOHN E MOUGIER JR JESSE JAMES JR FRANK L ADAMSON
EUGENE D FRANKLIN THOMAS C VAN CAMPEN JAMES T BROWN JR ALFRED H COMBS JR CHARLES A JENKINS
GERMAN P ACOSTA DOUGLAS H D'ORSAY MICHAEL J HNAT MICHAEL E WIDENER
ROBERT A EIBER PETER MONGILARDI JR CLARENCE M NEWCOMB ROBERT J SMITH CHARLES A WILLIAMSON
ROBERT A BUTZ ARTHUR B EUSTACE JR JOSEPH P GRUGAN DENNIS L PIERSON FREDERICK J SCHWANGER
GEORGE P ZUPANCIC CARL E JACKSON BILLIE L ROTH MIKE G BUSTOS JERRY R CAMPBELL
EARL G DOWNEY CHARLES G DUDLEY ROBERT L LAIRD MOON W LOCK VINCENT F RISOLDI
THOMAS R AMES RUBIN F BRADLEY SAMUEL P CHAMBERS III ROBERT G LANDRINGHAM CHARLES W STILES
MAURICE R HILL NATHANAEL LEE MARVIN N LINDSEY DENNIS S PITSENBARGER ANTHONY G TATE
DOUGLAS WAUCHOPE WILLIAM F COVEY JR JOHN W FINCH JAMES C HENNEBERRY HARRY W LOVE JR
JOSEPH E PARKER JR BERNARD E TURNER PAUL R WINDLE TERANCE K JENSEN GORDON J DEITZ JR
JAMES C SHERIFF JR ALVIN CHESTER WILLIAM F EISENBRAUN BRYAN E GROGAN WILLIAM A OBERG
ALLEN L HOLT HENRY A MUSA JR ROBERT D STEPANOV JOHN P BURNS RUDOLPH V HERNANDEZ
DAVID L HOWARD ALLEN I JOHNSON MCARTHUR JOHNSON RAYMOND P MEEHAN DURWARD F RAY
JOHNIE E RICE JR THOMAS A SANDERS JOHN D SHAW DON I WILLIAMSON RONALD L ZINN
EDWARD J ALMEIDA RICHARD C BRAM PAUL J BRUNO JOHN F DINGWALL JACK O EITEL DONALD F MARIT
CHARLES D KEARNEY LARRY G MOODY HERBERT SMITH JR STEFAN Z STALINSKI ROBERT J VOSS
IGNACIO ALMANZAR JR WILLIAM L BROWN WILLIAM E FOWLER JAMES A HALL LEON C STEIN
MARSHALL D HOLMAN CLIFFORD A ROBERTS SHERMAN E WILLIAMS GLEN W BRADLEY WILLIAM HORNER
LUIS R JIMENEZ THOMAS E BLUBAUGH BRIAN J GAUTHIER KENNETH A SEISSER DAVID D MCKENZIE
FRANK S REASONER KENNETH L REMMERS ELGIN L STIRLING ELIAS BELL JR HENRY J GALLANT
FRED TAYLOR ROBERT P DIONNE JAMES E PARMELEE DONALD R VINSON RIGOBERTO C CHACON
JAMES M PENNY PATRICK SPIKER JR RICHARD L ZICHEK DARYL L KEEN DANIEL J BENNETT
ROGER PELIKAN DAVID L ROSE MALCOLM A AVORE JOHN J GLASPER SHEPHEN H PHILLIPS
HARRY COHEN LUIS A MIRANDA-CUEVAS VIRGIL L STEPHEN MITCHELL L ANDERSON FAYBERT R BRADSHAW
STANLEY P KIERZEK CLAYTON J MANSFIELD JR ERIE A MARTIN JR JOE M SALINAS JOHNNY R TRIPLETT
JOHN P DAVIS JOHN C HARRIS CLIFFORD D MELTON ROY J BLAKELEY OLIVER C CHASE JR
GARY L DICKEY FRANCIS E GEIGER ROSCOE H FOBAIR ARTHUR F HAMMARSTROM JR LUDWIG P KOHLER
WILLIAM J BARTHELMAS JR JACK G FARR WALTER KOSKO EDWARD D BROWN JR RALPH F GALVIN
JACK W WEATHERBY WILBURN D FELKINS LAWRENCE W JORDAN CURTIS LOCKHART PATRICK P MANNING
LONNIE D SNOW JOHN J DAVENPORT MILTON K MCNULTY VERNARD J SMALL DONALD D WATSON
LESLIE G KING HERMAN W SILVEE RANDALL E FERGUSON WILLIAM W HAIL JOSEPH E BOWER
RICHARD E BROADHURST ALBERT F CALP JAMES R DYER HAROLD E GRAY JR GEORGE T VERDINEK
RICHARD L GOUDY JERRY A JOHNSON WILLIAM E MONTGOMERY HAROLD W SHRADER JAMES C CASTON
PAUL A DEVERS LESLIE I HILDENBRAND LAWRENCE S MAILHES LAVELLE M NOBLES RICHARD J REGAN
DONALD H BROWN JR ROBERT H FUELLHART RONALD C KRAUS GEORGE A DELUCA GENE R COLLAHON
FREDRIC M MELLOR GEORGE H NORTON HARRY E THOMAS JERRY W TOON OVID K WIGGINS
NORMAN E SNODGRASS MICHAEL A LYLES JAMES T CLARK DAVID L FELT ROWLAND J ADAMOLI
ROBERT F BATSON JOHN BELL JR FRANK H BLANK ROBERT G BOUSQUET THOMAS R BRAND
JAMES R BROOKS JR ROBERT F COCHRAN JR OLLIE R COTTEN FRANCIS J DELMARK RYLAND W DRAWDY
JAMES P DE WITT FLOYD E DOADES STEVE G DURAN THOMAS E FIRTH VICTOR FLORES JR
VERLON HADLEY BRUCE J HENRICH CHARLES E IANNUZZI JOHN L JEMISON HENRY C JORDAN
JAMES N KALIL HARRY L KAUS JR EDWARD KOPEC WILLIAM C LAIDLAW EDDIE L LANDRY
ROBERT O LONG MERLIN E MARQUARDT WILLIAM W NICKERSON DONALD G RADCLIFF JON D VANNATTA
ALBERT H RAITT JAMES H SAWYER ROBERT L SCOFIELD DALE K SHAMBAUGH CURLEY SHERELS JR
MITCHELL C SHORT JAMES A SMITH KENNETH D STANKIEWICZ LESSIE K STRICKLAND ROBERT TAGLIONE
ROBERT D BROWN GILBERT R NICKERSON JOHN B TETTE JERRY D THARP DAVID J THOMAS PETER C TOWNE
BRUCE D WEBB WILLIAM N WILSON JAMES L DIERYCK JOE C PAUL WALTER L SMITH WELIE D MEWBORN
JAMES L WHITE NED N LOSCUITO MORRIS O MUSICK JR RONALD P PETRICK VIRGIL W BARTON
ANTONIO D PADILLA FELIZ PERRIS DEPUY R VAN KEUREN RICHARD E CRONK KYLE H HATCHETT
DARRYL MESSER JUSTIN R WHITING IV WALTER J ZIMMER J C CLARK JR GILBERT SMITH JR JAMES J VOTAVA JR
ANTHONY P CHRISTOPHER JEROME ELKINS THOMAS J JOHNSON KENNETH D JOHNSTON GERHARDT JUST
GEORGE G KILBUCK LEVERNE W MCKINLEY CHARLES E NICHOLS EDD D TAYLOR
ROBERT M CARN JR TERRY J NEUMEIER PATRICK F BECK THOMAS C BRONSON DANIEL W DUFFY
JOHN W LAKE JACK D LANELLI JAMES M MITCHELL JR TED W QUALLS ROBERT E RIEDEL DONALD L ARCAND
WILLIAM H EBERHARDT ALVIN C FORNEY GEORGE GUTIERREZ JR MICHAEL G HOYER CARL J MANGOLD
JERRY L ROBERTS LOUIS D ROYSTON JR NELSON E WILSON LESTER O BIEHL JR DOUGLAS L FOLEY
DAVID E GILL MERRILL L LANTRY DALE L TOOLOOSE JOSEPH L TSCHAMBERS GEORGE A ZELINKO
KELLY K HEINZE TONY G ABEYTA GEORGE W BURKHEART FRANCES F NOVELLO THOMAS H BOTTS
JAMES A BRANCH EUGENE M JEWELL WILLIE E HONAKER LAWRENCE E JACKSON WILLIAM J LA GRAND
LEE R JAMES RICHARD C MARSHALL EDWARD B SHAW MICHAEL T BADSING ALLAN R FISCHBACH
LARRY A LINDSEY RICHARD B FITZGIBBON FRANK A HENISS EARL C WILLOUGHBY ORLAND O BEARWALD
CHARLES B GOODWIN GEOFFREY E GREEN ROBERT D RUDOLPH BARNEY E BOYER LEONARD J DADANTE
THOMAS E CZZOWITZ HARRY A HIPKE JAMES W MAHLER PAUL J MARQUEZ ROBERT W REAGAN
ERICH SIMKAITIS LARRY R TAYLOR LEO A BAUER CHARLES M IOPA GLEN E KING HENRY J ZEICHERT
ANDREW J HINDERMAN PAUL W MANSIR JOSEPH E MUIR GEORGE S BALAZY GERALD GREEN
CARROLL E FANKHAUSER WILLIAM A MITCHELL II JOE R MOSSMAN JAMES W STEPHENS DONALD L BENNETT
ROBERT O FRANKLIN JAMES T KEARNS FRANK R SAXON NEIL B TAYLOR BERNARD JAFFE JAMES I BOYER
HAROLD V DAYRINGER JR DAVID D CASE WILLIAM J HENRY KENNETH R IRELAN SAM IVEY DONALD H MEEK
A L PARKS EDUARDO CAMARENA-SALAZAR DEAN A KLENDA GEORGE A WEST ROBERT F BARBER
GARY W GRIMES DAVID E BENSON HAROLD A BIRD FRANK BOYNTON HERBERT J DEXTER LEROY HICKS
GEORGE E BURCHETT JOHNNIE W FAIRCLOTH EDWARD H FOX ERNEST K GERHARDT WALTER N LEVY
BARRY N HAMBLETON JOE L MEEK ERNEST L MILLER EDGAR L PETERSON JR ROBERT E RAWLS PAUL E RYTTER
DUANE C SCHELL ROYNALD E TAYLOR FRED R TICE THOMAS J TOLLIVER WALTER O TRAMEL
LARRY L TRUESDALE JERRY D UNDERWOOD LEONARD F VOGT JOHNNIE P WINFREY LEE E ANDERSON
GRADY K EMBREY EDGAR L HAWKINS DUANE W MARTIN LARRY S PIERCE MARTIN F SCHWICK JR
DONALD R WIEST MANUEL F FERNANDEZ CARL W MANN RICHARD E WINGATE GARY P BLAND
DAVID T GRAHAM JR GEORGE L SHOOK JR DAVID A MORGAN EUGENE L ARANDA GEOFFREY H OSBORN
BENNEL ELLIS WILLIAM E HILL BERNARD P MURRAY FRANK C ALCANTAR JIMMY L CROUCH
PASIA PAIALII GARY L SCHEMEL TROY M THOMPSON JR LUGENE J CLARK EDWIN J FALLOON JAMES P KELLY
HALFORD LOGAN JESUS R MARIANO JAMES E PRUITT DANIEL R ROMANKO THADDEUS ZAJAC
VIRGIL G CRUZ LAURENCE M KING THOMAS E MCMAHAN JR JOHNNIE L SLOAN CARL J WOODS
WALTER J BIENKOWSKI ELLIAS BOULLION GORDON L TAYLOR JAMES WHEATON CHAMBLESS M CHESNUTT
RONALD L DAVIS MICHAEL D CHWAN RAYMOND ELLIS JOHN J FLEMING MELVIN J KILLIAN JAMES D LONG
WILLIAM G MAURONE FRANK L MILLER III CLARENCE E MOORE EMIL R ZISS STEPHEN C BRISUDA
MAUSBY E HYLEMAN MARTIN J MASSUCCI GARY P OFFUTT CHARLES J SCHARF DON R HOOD
JOHN LOWAS DONALD C PATCH THEODORE RICHARDSON ROSCOE AMMERMAN EUGENE L ELLWOOD
ROBERT W ALLEN NELTON R BRYANT LOUIE G FRITTS MICHAEL R FULK PAUL HAMILTON JR
LARRY D HARVEY LEON P LAMPLEY BERNARD J MASNY REGINALD NICHOLAS ADAM E SIMPSON JR
CHARLES W STEVENS JAMES E THOMAS LEROY WILLIAMS JR CHARLES F ALLEN II CHARLES F DE AMARAL JR
JOHN D MUSGROVE WILLIAM W NICHOLS JR DAVID W BLODGETT RICHARD BURGANS KENNETH M HYETT
LON M FLETCHER CLARENCE H GRAY ADHERENE L HAINES JOHN C HAUSCHILDT RUSSELL M HEATH
JERRY L GERRY THOMAS A DVORATCHEK JESSE R HUGHES JR BEN JOHNSON JR JAMES M LONG ABELL MOSES
WILLIAM C MURPHY DEAN A POGREBA THOMAS J SCHINDLER EPHRON WALLACE JR RAYMOND BAILEY
JAMES N HOLBROOK JAMES H KING LARRY V LAKE HECTOR LOPEZ CURTIS R TARKINGTON
ROGER L HUBBARD WILLIAM D PINEGAR BILLIE M CASTLEBERRY RONALD K ASH MICHAEL G BRANCATO
RONALD M DI STEFANO RONALD W GULLEY LEON G HOLTON JACKIE E HUFF RICHARD E LYNCH
BOBBY G MASON GEORGE C RODEN JR GRIJALBA H RON CLAUDE TALBERT JR FRANCIS I TOOPS
CARL E ANDERSON JAMES C BERMINGHAM WAYNE P BREEDING DONALD FREY LAURIANO L LOVATO
DAVID L RIZOR JAMES G BERRY RONNIE M DUNCAN JAMES W FLOYD LAWRENCE A FRANKLIN
HAROLD M HAMBRICK WILLIAM C HARPER HARRY E HIMMELREICH DUANE M NELSON ERNEST PRESIDENT
JAMES J REILLY JR EUGENE M RICK WILFRED R ROBILLARD RONALD K SCHUKAR VAN WILLIAMS
TERRY T WRIGHT JAMES R DISCHERT JAMES T FAULKNER EDWARD A MALEWICZ JR JIMMIE L MINCKS
VICTOR R PARKER JAMES C WARD ROBERT L WOMACK NESTOR L ARGENZIO WILLIAM R ROMANO
ROBERT T EFAW WILBERT C DAVIS CHARLES F KANE JR LEROY F MINNIX SAM M SAVAS JR JOHN M STARKES JR
JACK B LEAF EDWARD L STEWART FRED TOINS GENE W WILLIAMS JERALD L DOZIER WILLIAM J GALLAGHER
DAVID M HALBAUER HAROLD J LANNING MICHAEL LIPTOCK WILLIAM G WHEATLEY DONNY R STEVENS
DUANE C SMITH DAVID G BROWN MICHAEL CAMPBELL LEROY GARRETT JR GARY H JONES
WILLIAM B WOLF ROBERT H SCHULER JR THEODORE R CHAMBLEY JUAN BENITEZ CHARLES R CHEMIS
MICHAEL L CHMURA RODERICK L MAYER STANLEY E OLMSTEAD HARLEY B PYLES WINFIELD W SISSON
JAMES MASSEY PAUL L LE MAY LARRY A THORNE SAMUEL T BAKER MANFRED B MILLER JOHN B WORCESTER
JOSEPH D BAILEY DON G KNOWLTON OWEN T LAVERY RONALD W MACKLIN WESLEY MCDONIAL
FRANKLIN D RACINE NEAL O RICHEY WILLIAM K BARRETT MICHAEL E DAVIS JOSEF S HUWYLER
WILLIAM J JOHNSON HAROLD A PREISENDEFER TIMOTHY J BILKO JAMES L CRAGAR RICHARD K JORDAN
MANUEL GONZALEZ-MALDONA CLIFFORD R HARRY CLAIRE L HAYNER GEORGE G LUIS ROBERT L MANN
JIMMIE L MCBYNUM JAMES A MCEWEN MILTON L OLIVE III THOMAS W PUSSER MIGUEL TREJO
JOHN WEGER JR LEANDER GRIFFIN EDWARD KEMP NORMAN A LEIKAM RICHARD E PETERS

PANEL 2E *(Continued)*

VANN D SHERRILL CHARLES E TANNER DONALD C MCPHEE WILLIAM L MILLER ADOLFO A TABOADA JR
ERNEST HAYWARD WILLIAM L JOHNSON BEN K MCBRIDE WILLIAM R SPATES JR JOSEPH R SWEDA
FRANK A GIVEN DANIEL L CHAPPELL CARL W DEATON GLENN M LANE THOMAS P MILLER JOHN R PETTY JR
WILLIAM R GENDEBIEN JOHN B MCHALE ROBERT E SWANSON WILLIAM J TEBOW RANDELL G TRAIL
DANIEL E ALLUM GARY L DOWELL FRANK O FLOREZ JR CHARLES W ROSE ALMA J STUMPP

PANEL 3E

FRANK D GARRETT WALTER J GELIEN EDWARD E GRABOSKEY WILLIAM A SLAUGHTER JR
THOMAS M CROW ANTHONY R HARDIE JEFFRY L KOCKRITZ JAMES G LEE LARRY P LUSSIER BELTON LYLES JR
ROGER M MANNIE HOMER D NELSON JIMMIE R ORR THOMAS P ROWLAND CARL J SADLER
ROBERT J FAY JOSEPH J SCHUSTER WILLIE J SMITH JR RESTITUTO P ADENIR RONALD V BACCA
RICHARD A CESAR GRANT L CLARK RICHARD A CRAWFORD GARY E ELFORD GERALD L FELTNER
JACKIE J FULGHUM FRANK A GAGLIARDO MARCOS HERNANDEZ ROBERT P JORDAN SEYMOUR P SADBERRY
RAYES C FLORES AARON C MURRELL ROBERT S RUCH HAROLD H SCHOCK PHILIP M SENS
RICHARD D SHARP DENNIS SMITH SAMUEL ADAMS MARVIN E CURRY CHARLES G DUSING
DONALD D HASKINS CHARLES R HEMPEL JR JOHN S MICHALSKI THOMAS MOORE FRANK J NADANY JR
CARRIER PIERRE TRENT R POWERS GEORGE T SAUNDERS JR ALTON E BAKER WAYNE A BALMER
JESUS R BERMUDEZ LUTHER W BURTON CHARLES R DAVIS JR DAVID R DICKENS THOMAS D DUNCAN
GRAT G MYERS NEIL R HANS DANIEL D HARDEN RODNEY C HARRIS JAMES HOOVER JAMES J HOWARD
GORDON S HUGGINS GEORGE C KOSOVICH JR RALPH W ONANA JAMES V POTTKOTTER PETER RUZILA JR
DOMINGO B VINLUAN EVERETT R ANDERSON SAMUEL BESS DWIGHT P BOWLES MARK G HINKLE
KENT D JORDAN WILLIAM B MITCHELL JAMES R PARRETT FLORENDO B PASCUAL GARY W PLATT
KENNETH W SCHMIDT ROBERT A SOLORZANO JAMES H THORNTON ALAN L BARNETT JAMES E CLARK
RICHARD A COFFEY CHARLES C COX CARL S DANIELS ROYAL C FISHER JR WRIGHT B HAMILL
RICARDO MESA EDDIE L HILL JR ROY M HITT JR ROBERT L HURST JAMES H JARZENSKI CHAMP J LAWSON JR
THOMAS A SAGEN RONALD H LUKE WILLIAM J LYONS FRED MOORE JR WALTER B OLIVER RICHARD E STEEL
BENJAMIN R PINKERTON JAMES W SIZEMORE ROBERT A TILLQUIST ROBERT F TOWNSEND JOE T WELBORN
LARIS WHITE JR JERRY D BASDEN WALTER W BROWN CLAYTON COLLINS JOHN P DUCHNOWSKI
RUSSELL E HAMMOND GEORGE C MCCLEARY LARRY A RAYSKI ARLEN C TUTTLE JAMES L ALLEN
CHARLES J ANTONELLY JAMES W BARKSDALE JAMES J CRAFTON CLYDE R HERMAN WILLIAM L HUNT
JOHN T POVEY TIMOTHY H JOHNSON JOHN K KEAO III FELIX D KING JR DENNIS LICHOTA MILES H LOPER JR
JUSTIN M LYNCH THOMAS H MAYNARD JOSEPH P MINNOCK ANTHONY E PENDOLA WILLIAM A SULLIVAN
THOMAS E MURRAY JAMES MOONEY RICHARD A NOELKE EARL G PHILLIPS WILLIE C PICKETT PHILLIP K REA
RUDOLPH RODRIGUEZ DANIEL SANTOS-TRUJILLO VARIS SAVAGE JR LOUIS SHERROD ALVIN C SLIGH
GERALD P METOTT RALPH N SMITH MORRIS E WHEELER RANDLE T WOODS DAVID HOLMES
HENRY J PAWLICK JR JAMES BELTON BRYANT BRAYBOY JR HERMAN BROWN LAWRENCE P HOWARD JR
MAGNO CAMPOS HENRY T CANNON LAVALLE E CARLTON SAMUEL A EIDSON GARY L ELMORE
BYRON J FOSTER EVERETT W GOIAS HAROLD GOLDEN KENNETH E GRAHAM LLOYD V GREENE
JOSEPH T HAMILTON JOHN E HANNIGAN III ROBERT W HARDEN JR CLIFTON W HARRINGTON LEROY HILL
RUDOLPH R AGUILAR REBEL L HOLCOMB JOHN A HUGHLETT WAYNE W HUMPHRIES THEODORE R JONES JR
DAVID L KEEL CLEO LOCKETT VALENTINE MARQUEZ MICHAEL K MATHISON MICHAEL M MEDLEY
JOHN A NATHAN RICHARD L NUZIARD STEVE ORRIS III JERRY L POTTER DANIEL J SOBOTA
CHARLES L MITCHELL JR MICHAEL P RUSSO DENNIS D RUTOWSKI HAROLD M SMITH CORDELL SPENCER
SCIP TATE THOMAS E THAYER JR CLAIR H THURSTON JR SAMUEL S TOLLIVER THOMAS A TURNAGE
JOSEPH A CLANCY DAVID L UGLAND DAVIS UPTAIN GEORGE VINCENT DANNY R WARD KELLY E WHITAKER
NARCISO BERTOMEN JR TROY B WILLIAMS CARL T BAAL DONALD R CLARK GENE T DAVIS DALE L FUGATE
JOHN H VAN WYK LARRY D BELL CLIFTON W HAYS WILLIAM ESPOSITO JR JAMES D HAWES WILLIS W WEBER
ORIN L ALLRED WILBUR W IVANOV GILIVALDO A MARTINEZ JR RICHARD P ROBBLEY THEODORE SHAMBLIN
HAROLD J BATTLE ALLIE W CAMPBELL RAFAEL C CARMONA-MEDINA FRANKLIN L CONN WILLIAM H EADEN
BENJAMIN CASTILLO-LIMA JAMES L DAVIS JOSEPH R DUPERE EDWARD P FERENCE ROGER L FLOYD
THOMAS J FOX JOSEPH C GIORDANO THOMAS G HENSON CHARLES J JANKE HERMAN L JEFFERSON JR
EDWARD JOUJON-ROCHE VIRGIL KIRKLAND JR JAMES W MAYES WILLIAM N MILLER HOOVER MORRIS
JACKIE MCMILLON WARDLOW W PARTEE MARINER PATRICK WAYNE D PROBERTS RAFAEL SANTIAGO-CRUZ
RAYMO SANTILLI EARNEST G SEARS EUGENE TURNER JAMES B WASHINGTON HAROLD E WATKINS
HAROLD E WILKINS DAVE MAYES JR SAMUEL E COKER RALPH A COPELAND LAWRENCE L COVEY
EDDIE BILLUPS JR JACK E GELL BURREL D HUEBNER FLOYD D JOHNSON THOMAS C METSKER LYNN E MINCE
PAUL T MCCLELLAN JR FRANCIS MOODY GILBERT M NICKLAS DONALD R PATRICK RICHARD A WALROD
THOMAS J BARRETT JR RAFAEL A BERLANGA RAMON BERNARD ANTONIO R BERNARD-ROBLES GAIL L DAVIS
BERNARD BIRENBAUM TIMOTHY M BLAKE JOHNNIE L BOSWELL JOHN F BRENNAN THOMAS E BURLILE
NATHANIEL BYRD DAVID J CARNEVALE RALPH W CARTWRIGHT LEO C CHASE JR SIDNEY COHEN
ELIAS ALVAREZ-BUZO CHARLEY H COLLIER WILBUR CURRY JR ROBERT A DAVIS DOMINIC A DE ANGELIS
PAZ H DE LA JR PARIS D DUSCH BILLY R ELLIOTT RONALD D FERGUSON ABRAHAM L FIELDS
DAVID C NEY GEORGE FOXE JOHN L GEOGHEGAN WILLIE F GODBOLDT ROBERT GOMEZ EARL C GRAHAM
BOBBY J HAMES CARL E HARRIS DONALD L HARRISON SCOTT O HENRY HENRY T HERRICK
CHARLES E HERRINGTON JOHN E HIGMAN ROBERT M HILL HERMON R HOSTUTTLER JERRY JIVENS
JOHN S MICHEL NEIL A KROGER DOUGLAS H LEACH ROBERT L LEWIS ROY LOCKHART WILLIAM B MITCHELL
SAMUEL L MCDONALD CHARLES V MCMANUS ROBERT L MOORE CARL L PALMER DONNELL PHILLIPS
PATRICK WILLIAMS TRAVIS O POSS EDDIE L POUCH FLOYD L REED JR DONALD B RODDY JAMES D SMITH
RICHARD A WILLIS ALBERT W SONNIER LEONARD W SRAL ROBERT L STOKES ROBERT E TAFT RICHARD TESTA
THOMAS E TUCKER WILLIAM T VICTORY IVORY WARD JR REGINALD A WATKINS ALEXANDER WILLIAMS
ALBERT WITCHER JOHN R ACKERMAN BENEDICTO P BAYRON CALVIN BOUKNIGHT RICHARD B BRADLEY
DANA E BRANN EDDIE BROWN JR MICHAEL C DE LACY JOHN C ELZY III LUTHER V GILREATH
DONALD G GREEN RONALD R HORNBROOK TOMMIE KEETON BILLY M KNIGHT REAVIS A MONTREY JR
JAMES L RILEY RICHARD W SCHWENDLER BILLY J TALLEY OSVALDO AMODIAS CHARLIE ANDERS
ROBERT H KUNKEL EARL D AULL LAVINE J BANKS OSCAR BARKER JR DONALD A BARNES JIMMIE W BARTON
CHARLES W BASS HARLEY D BECKWORTH SNYDER P BEMBRY CLARENCE V BEVERHOUDT DENNIS W BLACK
ROLLIE L BOLDEN KENNETH C BOLICH JIMMY F BOREN ROY H BOWLING THOMAS G BRANDES
RALPH W BROWN KENNETH E BURCH BARRY T BURNITE WILLIAM R BURTON JR EMMETT L DRESSLER
BRIAN F CARLQUIST DANNY E CARLTON RUBEN G CHAVEZ FRANCISCO CONCEPCION JR MELVIN E COOKS
CHARLES A COLLINS DONALD C CORNETT CHARLES E COX MACK C COX DONALD E CRANE
BERNARD J CREED BUREN R DAVIS ELWOOD W DAVIS JR ROBERT L DAVIS TOMMY A DOAK
MEGDELIO CARABALLO-GARCIA JAMES R DRAGOTI CHARLES L ELLER RALPH H ERNST JAMES W ERVIN
TERRY A CHASE GERALD B EVANS WILLIAM A FERRELL JAMES L FISHER JORDEN D FORRESTER MELVIN F FORT
RUDOLPH J GALARZA JUAN R GARCIA JERELL L GRAYSON MELVIN W GUNTER OTIS J HAMPTON
JIMMY HARRIS FREDERICK C HERIAUD REYNALDO C HERNANDEZ LARRY L HESS JERRY A HIEMER
JERRY J SANDERS JOSEPH R HILLIARD JAMES R HINES ROBERT L HIRST JAMES E HOLDEN SAMUEL L HOLMAN
PHILIP HOWELL DALE F HUDSON PAUL E HURDLE LEROY IRELAND JULIO E MORALES-GONZALEZ
ALPHA R JACKSON DEAN A JACKSON JAMES C JACKSON THOMAS JAMES HARRY F JEDRZEJEWSKI
FRED H JENKINS WILBERT H JOHNSON CECIL W KITTLE JR MARTIN C KNAPP GERALD A KOSAKOWSKI
DUNCAN F KRUEGER RAMON KUILAN-OLIVERAS JOSEPH S LA FASO GARRETT F LEE WILLIAM J LINDSEY
JAMES A GILFORD VINCENT LOCATELLI HENRY T LUNA WAYNE T LUNDELL JACK D LYNN RONALD R MARTIN
RONNIE T MATHIS DAVID L MENDOZA PALMER B MILES MICHAEL J MILLER RONALD A MILLER
ROGER E MERCK MALCOLM E MILLICAN LLOYD J MONSEWICZ ARTHUR R MOODY III CHARLES T MOORE JR
CARL M HUME GLENN E MCCAMMON HAROLD D MCCARN PREZEL MCCULLOUGH ROBERT MORENO
GEORGE S MCHELLON JIMMY D NAKAYAMA ROGER T NELSON THEOPHILOS ORPHANOS ROY L RYSE JR
SHERMAN E OTIS RICHARD D OTT ISMAEL J PAREDES AUGUSTIN C PAREDEZ DONALD C PETERSON
THOMAS C PIZZINO WILLIAM A PLEASANT ROBERT POSIUS LOUIS D RICHARDSON HOWARD G RILEY
FRANK J NOSTADT JR JESSE N RODRIGUEZ CLAYTON G ROGERS JR DARRELL W SANDERS RICHARD P SAWICKI
GUY L SCHAEFFER MURVIN SCHALIPP JR JOHN SCHLECHT III JERROLD J SCHLIESMAN EUGENE C SCOTT
HAROLD SCOTT JOHN A SHAW MATTHEWS SHELTON ROBERT S SHRIVER JR EDWARD L SIMMONS
JOSEPH A FORD III ROGER A SIMRAU GARY D SMITH HENRY F SMITH MICHAEL T SMITH SIDNEY C SMITH
NORMAN W SOLTOW CHARLES T STEINER GEORGE J STEPHENS ROGER A STONE CHARLES W STOREY
FINIS R STUDDARD ERNEST E TAYLOR JESSE J TAYLOR EARTHELL TYLER ROBERT E WALDVOGEL
PAUL E TOLBERT JAMES O VAUGHAN MIGUEL D VERA-DURAN BOBBY C VINSON GEORGE A WILSON
DAVID M VANCELLETTE MACK A WARE NEOPOLIS WIGFALL FRED D WITCHET JOHN H WOODY
JOSEPH M WORKMAN ROBERT G WRIGHT GORDON P YOUNG RICHARD T YOUNG BENJIMAN BROOKS
RONALD H CHITTUM RICHARD C CLARK LINDSEY H CROW LOUIS S GUTIERREZ JOHN F MCDERMOTT
FELIX RODRIQUEZ PAUL H EKLUND ARLIN R JENSEN RAY L NELSON DAVID L REEDER EVERETT B THOMPSON
FRANK D TRYPUS DAVID L VARVELL ROBERT O BALMER RICHARD D BRODA CONNIE L CHANDLER
JOHN P EMERLING ANDRE HAROULAKIS RONALD P JOHNSON JOSEPH P MARA GEORGE MCCUTCHEN
IVAN NOTEBOOM DONALD H PERRICHON KENNETH E SARGENT JOSE W SUAREZ WILLIAM J TAYLOR III
BILLY J WILSON OSCAR E COOPER WILLIE FRANCIS JR WALTER C MILLER KENNETH POLING
DENNIS L TOMS BARRY F ANDERSEN MICHAEL A BERINGER RICHARD R BIGLEY GUST CALLIVAS
JOHN D CAMPBELL RAYMOND CELESTE THOMAS E DOUGLAS DARELL G FREEMAN KENNETH J HAMMOND
ROBERT M LATHROPE BILLY W HEDGE VILIS LISMENTS RICHARD A MILLER VICTOR J PIRKER MOSES C TABOR
FRANCIS E VISCONTI RICHARD G WICK JOHN A WINKLER TERRY WINTERMOYER THEODORE M BEAMON
DAVID G BENAVENTE L C BLAKE ROGER G BRITTEN JOHN V FIORENTIN RICHARD E GEORGE
GUNDER P GUNDERSON GERALD T JENKINS RICHARD JENSEN GLENN D MANN DAVID W MICHAEL
ROBIN A RARIG CLEO SMITH DANIEL F TALLMAN SAMMY L THOMPSON TERRY L BLYTHE
JOHNNY W BOUINGTON NATHANIEL E CARTER III DALE L FUNK ARTHUR M GORDON BENNY G HACK
LESTER KEY RONALD J LOERLEIN WILLIAM M SAVOREN DONALD R BONKO PORTER T DAVIS
DENNIS L LONG DENNIS F AMATO WILLIAM H CRISMAN JOHN M GRASSO JR WEG P VANDER
EDWARD J MONAHAN JR CARL A GRAY LESTER J KERSTEN GUY H MCCAREY JR JAMES W MCNEELY TONY VALE
ROBERT W ANDREASEN MORRIS L BARGY THOMAS O GREEN VIRGIL D GRIFFY MICHAEL G MCMANUS
RALPH G HAMLIN JR GEORGE L STOLTZMAN LESTER E BECKER TYRONE S PANNELL STEPHEN G RICHARDSON
KENNETH M JACKSON JOHN V MCCORMICK THOMAS E REITMANN ROMIRO C RODRIGUEZ CARL B AUSTIN
ARTHUR N MCMELLON MORRIS E JENKINS JACOB D LOGAN GERALD R ROBERTS TOMMY R WILSON
RAFAEL ACEVEDO-RECHANI PETER M BREDBURY STANLEY G JOHNSON THOMAS LEWIS RICHARD W MILLER
WARREN L DEMPSEY WILLIAM R MCPHERSON KIRK I RILEY ROBERT A SINGERHOUSE LAAVALE F TAGATA
ROBERT H WHITE LAWRENCE G BROWN HERMAN ESTRADA-COSTAS GEORGE A OVERWEG RONALD F ROD
JOHN P ROLAND TOM W BROWN STANLEY L SAPP KENNETH L SORENSEN DONALD J TANNER LUZ VIEGRA
JAMES A WATSON DOUGLAS V ANDRE STEVEN H BOYER DAVID L BRODEUR FREDERICK F CADILLE
MORRIS F DIBBLE GEORGE J EISENBERGER RICHARD M FACONDINI HENRY GENTRY JR ROBERT GOINES
JAMES GRAHAM JOHN P GREENE MICHAEL A GRUBER JIMMY D HYDE JORGE M JARAMILLO
NORMAN W JOHNSON JERRY B JOHNSTON GRANDVILLE R JONES JR LEONARD A JONES GEORGE E JOYCE
RAYMOND E KELLEMS RICHARD KILLENS PATRICK W KING CZESLAW KOWALCZYK JOSEPH W LANSKI
O'NEAL LEGETTE MCGEARY LITTLEJOHN JAMES E LOFGREN ROBERT D LOGUE LUIS B LOPEZ
JAMES E LOVE CHARLES E MANZANARES EDWARD K MARSH DONALD W MCCAMMON PHILIP J MCCARTHY
WARREN S OSHIRO JOSEPH D RIGGLE JULIUS ROBERTS JR CARLOS H RUIZ MICHAEL P SCHWEBEL
MILTON SOLOMON NORMAN J SPENARD ROGER W SPRADLIN DON G STALLARD WILLIAM J STEWART
JOHN L THIBEAULT HARRY S THOMPSON DAVID J TUNGATE EDWARD C UPNER WILLIE J WRIGHT
DANIEL A DICKINSON HERBERT A HILFIKER DAYMON D HORN WILLIAM M MEGLIO JR DELMORE B NERVEZA
PAUL A ROBERTSON JOHN T STICHER JOHN W FREDERICK JR THOMAS P LAVIN JAMES D SALA

PANEL 4E

RONALD M CANTER ROBERT K COLLINS JOHN T CORLE ARTHUR E HICKMAN
DONALD W LOVETT DAVID J RICHTSTEIG HARRY C SMITH ODIN E SORENSEN JAMES R BAILEY
LARRY D BORSCHEL JOSE L CABALLERO JOHN B CORDOVA RICHARD L CROXEN RONALD L KOEHLER
BENNY B COE CLANCY G DRAKE ROBERT E EMERY MICHAEL S HARRIS DONALD J REILLY
ROBERT J REILLY JR LARRY D SCARBERRY RICHIE H SCHMITT ANTHONY D SHEFFIELD DONALD W VINCENT
BILLY D HOOPER DENNIS L WEBER ROBERT R BOHLER CHARLES E BOSTON JAMES P BROCK TINSLEY BRYANT
VERNON T CARTER JR RICHARD E CHABOT RONALD E CUMMINGS OMER G DARTY ACIE D HALL
ROBERT L CRAFT WILLIAM E DAVIS JR DONALD E GLICKMAN MICHAEL S GRANNAN ROBERT D HICKMAN
CLAUDE L JOHNSON ROBERT L KECKLER JAMES H LEWIS CHARLES R MCFARLIN JOE MORENO
L C PITCHFORD LESLIE PUZYREWSKI LAWRENCE F RAMAKER RUDY M SAGON RALPH SHANK
BARRY J SITLER LLOYD A VANNATTER JOHN W WILSON JR ROBERT C FELTER DONALD D STEWART
SEAFORD N HEMMINGS ROBERT M HORSKY ROBERTO ITUARTE GORDON J LIPPMAN DENNIS C MANNING
CEPHAS BARNES JR GEORGE P MCKNIGHT MERCEDES P SALINAS ROBERT C BRIX ROBERT M BROWN JR
EUGENE J MARTIN NEIL W POTTER GEORGE R THOMPSON JOSEPH C BRADY JEFF GOUDEAU JR
HARRY R HOSKINSON WILLIAM A JENNINGS III LEO W LE VESQUE NATHANIEL WASHINGTON PAUL J SIMON
RICHARD J BRUNKE JAMES C KINDEL ROBERT J MORONEY PETE A VALASQUEZ JERRY P CLARK
JAMES W GREY RICHARD E MCWILLIAMS JOHNNIE PATTERSON GERARD G SCHNITGER ROBERT E MONTOYA
JOSEPH B BAGGETT JOSE B DUENAS AUBURN W FOREMAN JR RAYMOND S JOY JR WILLIAM R MOORE
JESSE F MORGAN RONALD P SISSON GRAYSON J WEST ROBERT W ABBOTT ROBERT L ABERNATHY
FRANCIS R BUCKLEY JOSEPH A CESTARIC JOHN M CHAPPELL DONALD R HAWLEY THOMAS N SLOAN
RALPH L HINSON CLAUDE W MATHEWS RONALD G MCKINNEY JOHNSON A MEADE DAVID W WICKHAM II
JIMMIE L BROOKS JACK E CLEMMONS DONALD C CRUTCHLEY JAMES E FLAGG MELVIN L FRONTELLA
TOMMIE GARRETT ROBERT A GRAY SAMMIE GRIFFIN DANIEL J GUILMET EDMUND M MASTERSON
PAUL L GORMLEY JR VERNON E HOLLAND GREGORY JEREMICZ DONALD D KARLIN STEPHEN J LUKASIEWSKI
WILLIAM D MCKILLOP JOSEPH E NIMIROSKI RICHARD W PETERSON RONALD W PORTER GEORGE W RICE
FEDERICO SILVA JACK S SWENDER JOSEPH M THIMM JAMES E THOMPSON FRED A TRYON JR
STUART K TWEEDY CLIFFORD L WHIPPLE ROBERT J WILKINS JOSEPH P YATSKO JR LOUIS J CUNNINGHAM
KENNETH L DERHEIM MICHAEL C HALSTEAD KENNETH K HUFFER ERNEST F LOSOYA BENNIE ROMERO
NELS W SWANSON SAMUEL L WOODS CHESTER E WORMAN JR RUSSELL V ALMEIDA LEE E NORDAHL
RONALD M FERO LARY D FOGLE GUY D JOHNSON TERRY F KATTERHENRY GEORGE I MIMS JR
WILLIAM H CRISP WILLIE MITCHELL JR RICHARD F MOODY MARVIN L SHIPMAN DONALD C SMITH
ROBERT D TRIER DAVID J WAX HOWARD L ALLEN ROBERT J CAMPBELL GEORGE S COSTELLO
LEROY E JONES WILLIAM V MOSS RONALD E MULLINAX RONALD W NICKERSON WILLIAM W RICHARD
JIMMIE R ISBELL ALFRED L SPITZFADEN BILLIE J CARTWRIGHT EDWARD F GOLD MAX D LUKENBACH
JOHN D PRUDHOMME JOHN F ASHMAN PAUL D BERTHIAUME JAMES A GRUEZKE JAMES C WISE JR
JOSEPH M BUTLER MARYLAND CHATTEN JOSEPH CHRISTIANO WILLIAM K COLWELL EARL L CROMWELL
JAMES L DOUSE DENNIS L EILERS ARDEN K HASSENGER DERRELL B JEFFORDS GEORGE E JOHNSTON
DENNIS C STANCROFF LARRY C THORNTON PAUL W JANDERSHOVITZ FERNANDO SEDA JR LYNN C RENNER
RICHARD L JOSSENDAL CARL R STEFFEN JOHN O ARNN MARVIN M BELT EDWARD L LOWE LOUIS R RALEIGH
LEONIDAS RAISIS CHARLES A ROBERTS CARL H TORELLO JOHN G TOWNER JOSEPH L DREW
WILLIAM F BROWN JOHN J CARLONE II WILLARD F ELDER JAMES C GUILLORY STEPHEN D JEWETT
OTHAT THOMPSON CHARLES R KIER DAVID A KOVAC WAYNE T LONG PAUL C TAYLOR RICHARD E WILSON
JASPER D CLARDY DONALD C GRELLA GERALD L KUHNLY LUIS A LICIAGA-CONCEPCI EDWARD A LOVELL
JESSE D PHELPS THOMAS RICE JR JOHN S SCHMID KENNETH L STANCIL THOMAS F ELDRIDGE
WILLIAM A BURNETT ARTHUR S HILL JR THOMAS E MURRAY EDGAR A RAWSTHORNE THOMAS P SIMCHOCK
CHARLES E SISSEL DONALD R DUFFY JR JAMES R HICKMAN ROBERT L KRAUS JACK D MCCLURE
CHARLES R ALLEN ROBERT M SWEENEY EMIL J TADEVICH LOUIS B TWINN SR ALVIN R WOODS JR
HAROLD D BARNES ERNEST C KELLY EDWARD S STEFFEK MICHAEL J MCKINSON LARRY J NADEAU
WALLACE E BAKER NOEL M BARTOLF JACK D BIXBY CARL R BROOKS GEORGE E GEOGHAGEN
ROBERT H PRICE HARLOW K HALBOWER JOHNNY H LEAKE GERALD LEVY GARY F LEWIS ELLIOTT L MERKLE
TIMOTHY W AIKEY DONALD C MACLAUGHLIN JR WALTER E MCINTIRE JR JERRY W MORTON
RUBEN C ALSTON VERNON L SHELLMAN ROBERT G SMITH JUVENCIO TORRES-ACEVEDO JOSEPH F COVELLA RALPH A DIDAMO JR
LEO A REMONDINI JR GRANT A RHODES ALLEN R SPINKS FRANCIS W BEAGLE LIONEL J BRYAN JR
CARVER J ENGLISH JR ALTON L GAJAN RONALD L GERRY ROBERT C LANE JOHN J SKALBA HAROLD J BRAZEN
JOSEPH E HETZER JR WALLACE K SINER CLYDE D TAYLOR JUAN B VALTIERRA J R GIPE
DAVID V BILLINGS RICHARD J CALLANAN LEE C DIXON JON A GREENLEY JOHN J HORNYAK
JAMES R LUTE RONALD E NELSON MICHAEL R WEBB LOWELL F WHITE ARVEL D AKERS GERALD V JOHNSON
DONALD R BLAIR NATHAN J COLE JR RONALD E JAHNKE JOHN L ROBINSON MICHAEL V TIMMONS
CHARLES L SCOTT JR JAMES P TYNER GORDON R WITTMAN JAMES R GRIFFEY RICHARD L HOLLINGSWORTH
LOUIS K KANAAR MICHAEL P MORAN DONALD R SANDVE JAMES P SCHIMBERG DANIEL L SHERMAN
RICHARD E TUCKER ROBERT D WARD THOMAS F BRUCK SAM J BURNELL JERRY N HUGHES
MATTHEW J PECHAITIS HUGH F SPAIN CHARLES D SWARTZ LARRY E TENNILL JOHN W THOMAS
EDWARD D AKERS RAYNALD J AMADOR RICHARD C AMATO JAMES V BIGTREE JOSE G BIRCO
DAVID J BYSTEDT ARTHUR CAVANAGH GERALD L DAILEY JOHNNY H GODFREY JOSEPH E HIPP
WILLIAM E JORDAN III NOBLE D MCGEHEE WILLIE J ROBINSON MARVIN B SMITH JR EDWARD J WILLIAMS
RAYMOND E BROWN JOSEPH C CORRELL CARSON E HAIRE RICHARD E HARPER LEON B SMITH II
ROBERT M DOWLING JAIME IRIZARRY-PEREZ ROBERT L KILLABREW RUSSELL W KISTLER LEE E ROSENWASSER
ELIJAH G TOLLETT JR WARREN L ANDERSON BAXTER C CARROLL GEORGE W CRIPPS BYRON H CROTWELL
DANNY M ERWIN THOMAS A FODARO THOMAS F HEFFERNAN EDWARD J HINCEWICZ WAYNE I JONES
MELVIN L HAIRSTON IRWIN L HOFFMAN DORRIS A IVEY ALLEN W JONES ANDERSON H KEY
JOHN W LEWIS JR ROBERT N MIDDLEBROOKS J V PATRICK FLOYD W POHL HERMAN H RITCHIE
RICHARD R RYNKIEWICZ DONALD F WEINMAN GEORGE S EYSTER JR ANDREW L HENRY THEODORE B SILAS
ANDRES GARCIA JOSE R PAGAN-CARTAGENA HEZEKIAH GOSS JR JAMES E HELTON JESSE H HUGHES
LLOYD D LAKE LAURENCE N SOUSA FRANKIE L VARGAS DAVID F WEBER HAL T HOLLINGSWORTH
FRED A NETH CHARLES D SCHOONOVER ROLLAND B SHUBBUCK JAMES E TATE PENI UELI
DONALD WEBB DON C WOOD WILLIAM CUTSHAW SALVADOR R DULAY LARRY FLEMING JR
EARL W FOSTER JR LAWRENCE T HAMMOND DAVID L JACKSON JR JOSEPH R ROBERTS JOSEPH G SERCOVICH
KARL L THOMPSON SELWIN D WISDOM ANTHONY GIANELLI JESSE J MILLER ISRAEL VARGAS-VARGAS
RONNIE J HERRINGTON DENNIS E HIGGINS LARRY NELSON LEANDREW SPENCER JR CLAUDE W THARP
RAYMOND L BOATWRIGHT KENNETH L BAUER JOHN D COFFIELD LEWIS B LONG OLEN W RASNIC
ANTHONY SKODMIN JOHN C STRICKLER JR JAMES V TAURISANO DAVID R BURGESS JAMES T EGAN JR
PETER MARTINEZ WILLIAM S FORMAN GERALD H GAYLOR EDWIN R GRISSETT JR PAUL S PRUSKO
EDMUND H FRENYEA ROBERT R SENNETT ERWIN B TEMPLIN JR DAVID H ELISOVSKY JOHN W ROWLAND JR
ROY S KOBAYASHI DELMAR G BOOZE RAYMOND L BOWEN JR EDWARD J COX LAWRENCE N HELBER
ALBERT PITT JAMES C SPINUZZI DOYLE R SPRICK RICHARD A SULLIVAN WILLIAM H WALLS
CHARLES E ALSTON CHARLES R ASHLEY JR ROBERT C BOWMAN MONTE D BROOKS JAMES P DONNELL JAMES P O'DONNELL
JOHNNIE L BROWN GARY R BRYANT DAVID E BURKES JAMES P COATS HARRY R CRUMLEY
PAUL M BELL JOSEPH DE GENNARO BILLY C DEWEESE EUGENE D DOLLAR DEAN J ELICHKO
CHARLES L ESCHBACH DAVID L GALAN SAMUEL P GIFFARD DONALD R GRIBLER REYNALDO GUZMAN
EDWARD C HANDLY JEROME HERRINGTON JOHN D HETTERLY SR WOODIE L HICKS RADFORD D HOGAN
W D HUBBARD DAVID HUNTER JOSEPH JAMES WALTER B JOHNSON DANIEL G MECHLING
EDWARD Y KIM WOODROW W KING JR ROBERT A KOWALSKI WENCESLEO KUILAN RAY D LEDFORD
JAMES B JONES EDWARD N LEONARD RONALD A MARSH DONALD T MITCHELL JOHN M MYERS
BOBBIE E NOLEN STEVE W PAGE STEPHEN M PASHMAN HENRY PASLEY WILLIAM J PHILLIPS
ERIC SACKETT EDWARD B SMITH EUGENE C SUMMERS ROBERT TILLER WESTOVEL VENABLE
FRANK W WILLIAMS JR LEONARD WILLIAMS HAROLD E WILLIS STUART J ERNHART
GEORGE B FORD WILMER N GRUBB ELVIS G HICKS LESSAINT P HUDSON STEVEN T JEWELL
ARTHUR REGO ALDO ROSSI JR ALENN M TATE JON P TRAVIS RAFAEL A ALGARIN-RIVERA DAVID A LANE
CAREY E BEST BONNIE P CASAS ROBERT L FIELDS III GARY P GAY JIMMY R HARSANYI
HUGHLEN HENDERSON KENNETH R HOLLENBACH JOSEPH E JACKSON JACK E LOCKE HARRY C MCCARTNEY
KENNETH G MCBRIDE JOHN MONKS ROOSEVELT S ROME CHARLES D SENTERS THURMAN B SHOCKLEY JR
WILBUR M WISE EWING C BABBAGE THOMAS R DEVLIN JOHN P FEWELL JR WILLIAM C GEIS
CARLOS FIGUEREDO THOMAS R GRANT JOSE A GUTIERREZ TAYLOR D JOHNSON JOHN E MILENDER
FRED L MCPHERSON HARRY M MORSE THOM T OSBORN JAMES L RICKS NATHANIEL SIMMONS
JAMES R TAYLOR JONATHAN P WORKS CARLOS ZAMORA JR RICHARD E ARNOLD FRANK N BADOLATI
CHARLES J BAIR RICHARD D BEARDEN DENNIS J BROPHY EARL F BROWN MARLIN C COOK
FLOYD A CRIBB EDWARD T DOMIAN JR DONALD L DOTSON JEAN P DOWLING THOMAS S DRAZER
ROY A DUTHU RICHARD B FIELLER CARL J FOX WILLIAM R GLUECKSTEIN WILLIAM H GUYER
JESSE L HANCOCK WILLIAM R HARDIN KENNETH HERSHMAN GEORGE A HOAGLAND III CECIL J HODGSON
HAROLD G HUGHART BOB C HUNT JR DONALD J JACOBSEN CLIFFORD C JOHNSON CLIFFORD T JOHNSON
MICHAEL J KOCHENDORFER ROBERT H LAGRAND GARY R LAMBERT THOMAS A LAWSON JOHN E LAY
PAUL R LEE FORTUNATO LUNA JR FOY M MATHIS RAPHNELL J MERONEY CARL S MILLER JR
EVERETT G MILLER NOE MIRANDA-PEREZ WARREN E PHILLIPS JOSEPH A QUIROZ DAVID L REEVE
ELMER J REIFSCHNEIDER JR JOSE A RIVERA-REYES SAMUEL ROSS HOWARD A SEILHEIMER BERNARD J WAIT
STANLEY K SEMLER ROBERT L SMITH MELVIN J STOCKDALE ROBERT E STPETER ALBERT H TATSUNO
FRANK ROOP RONALD T TERRY CALVIN C TOLLEY JR CLAUDE T TURNER RICHARD WEBSTER
JAMES D WHITE JR ALLAN J WILLIAMS THOMAS D WILLIAMSON TERRANCE D ADAMS SAMMIE L BEDWELL
ROBERT E BEXLEY RICHARD G BILOTTA LARRY O BOOTY DAVID J BUDKA DAVID D GENSEMER III
HOSY CHAPEL RICHARD DAVENPORT RUBEN DELGADO HAROLD T EDMONDSON JR CREIGHTON R GRANT
RAYMOND L HILL ALFRED J HOLDEN WALLACE R JACOBSEN WALLACE K MATAYOSHI BENNIE F PARKER
JOSE NEGRON-RODRIGUEZ JOHN J PALUSCIO RICHARD D PARKER JAMES B ROGOFF GREGORIO VALDEZ JR

245

THE VIETNAM VETERANS MEMORIAL COLLECTION

VICTOR E ANDERSON MELVIN L BENNETT HAROLD E BURKETT ROBERT D DONALDSON GLENN F DRAKE
CHARLES E FREDERICK JOHN E FUQUA KENNETH D GILMORE ROBERT F GUTHRIE EUGENE D HAMILTON
CLARENCE W HOWARD JACK JOHNSON JOHN A JOHNSON MARVIN L LINDLEY EUGENE T MCCOY
RODNEY J OLSON CHARLES L PETEET HOWARD E PHILLIPS JOHN M QUINN JOSEPH A RANDAZZO
DAN R SHEARIN ARMANDO TESILLO JACK THOMAS JR TERRY L WELLER GENRETT WILLIAMS
DAVID B ZIEGLER RICHARD A ALM WALTER P AUGUSTINAS GEORGE A BROWN DILLARD R BURNLEY
JACK W CECIL DONALD L COATES CARL J FORRESTER BILLY G FRY JOHN H GRIFFITH JERRY R RAMBERGER
RUSSELL O HATTON NELSON L HAYES WILLIAM T HAYNES GALEN F HUMPHREY WILLIAM JONES
DODD C KELLER HUBERT B LOHEED RUSSELL B LUKER THOMAS E MCGRAW ALBERT M PREVOST
KALE A SOLBERG HIRAM D STRICKLAND PETER G VLAHAKOS DOUGLAS M WETMORE MICHAEL I SHANER
JESSE T BAILEY JR CRAIG S BLACKNER JOHN I CAMERON JOHN R DUSBABEK SIDNEY J ELYEA RICHARD SMITH
DAVID A FAIRCHILD JAMES L GARDNER GERALD C LYMAN DENNIS M O'NEILL RICHARD G PHILBIN
MICHAEL WILSON WILBUR R BROWN JAMES L CARTER WILLIAM M COOMES RICHARD C YOUNGBEAR
ROBERT T HANSON JR JOSEPH R LANDRY EDWARD M PARSLEY RICHARD C STEWART THERMAN M WALLER
RONALD P ALMARAZ ANTONIO BARBOSA-VILLAFAN WILLIAM A BASON II RONALD L BEUSTER

PANEL 5E
BOBBY L FAVORS RICHARD H MAIN STANLEY J THOMPSON FRANKIE L WALLACE
JIMMY A MARCUM JAMES R NEUBAUER ROBERT R ROY PAUL R SETZER FRANK R STAMPER
JOHN GARCIA ARNOLD E ISON CHARLES E STRADER JOHN H THOMPSON KENNETH A ARVIDSON
JAMES BRADLEY EUGENE N CHESLEY JERRY I HELLAND JOHN E LEER DAN D MCCONNAUGEHAY
GLENN E ASMUSSEN BENARD J SPARENBERG FRANKLIN G TODD WILLIAM L ARMSTRONG SAMUEL L DELLOS
JERRY D ESTES JOSEPH D GUERRERO TIMOTHY L HAYES ROBERT L HOPKINS PHILLIP R LOONEY
STEVEN P MOLLOHAN DENNIS L MORGAN WALTER PIPER JR JAMES W POWERS WILLIAM J STALNECKER
ROY E THOMAS ALEX E VACZI DAVID R VELASQUEZ JAMES B WOODS III BRUCE G BARTH JAMES B O'KANE
CARLOS BETANCOURT-MOJIC DAVID J BROADHEAD WILBERT R BUTLER RALPH BYRD GENE E CHEPELY
RICHARD G CROSSLAND PRINCE C CUNNINGHAM DAVID B GARCIA GUY F SNYDER
JAMES A GARDNER JOHNNIE GRANT WALTER T GUERIN HERMAN L HUEY SYLVESTER JACKSON JR
LEE A JAMES JR FREDERICK P LANGER DERLYN R LEHMANN KONSTANTINS A LUBAVS HAROLD J MARRIETTA
ALFRED L JOHNSON CARL S MAYS DALE R MCINNIS CLIFFORD W MCROBERTS ALEXANDER MONTOYA
JOHN F O'SHAUGHNESSY CHARLES E OSBORNE MORRIS J POWELL THOMAS S RIVERA JIM B ROBISON
DUANE V OLSON KENNETH RUSH JOHN F SANFORD GEORGE J SHUFELT RONALD M SNOW
DA S CORREIA JOHN P VAUGHN ROBERT A WHITE JOHN W COBB CLARENCE GALLOWAY
JERRY M CAIN LESLIE C COUCH LESTER L CROOKS WILLIAM L HINES JR JOHN W OWENS DENNIS R MARTIN
ARTHUR E SANDERS JOHN J SOLLEY GERRALD A STANSELL WENDELL R WHEAT CHARLES R WILLIAMS
DAVID WILLIAMS RICHARD R WOODWARD WILLIAM J AMSTUTZ JR LESLIE H CANTRELL ROBERT K LOVELACE
JOHN D BOWMAN III WILLIAM COOLEY JARMO A KARI JOHN B MECKEL JOHN H MINCEY
ROBERTO PEREZ JOHNNY P PRICE WILLIAM D SETTLEMIRE DON R SHACKELFORD ROBERT S ANDRADE
JOSE ESCAMILLA GARY D HOPPS ALVIN HOSKINS RUSSELL P HUNTER JR GEORGE G WEBB
ERNST P KIEFEL JR M L MCCLELLAN WARREN G PETERSON TEOFILO C PIMENTEL JOHN S VOEGTLI
CHESTER L GABLE KERMIT H YOHO GEORGE K BEERES SEBASTIAN P CANLAS ROBERT O CANTRELL
MOSES M COTTON LEONARD I CRAVEN RAYMOND A DAVIS SAFFORD S PYE DANNY C SCHULTZ
THEODORE F TAYLOR JR JOHN CONNOR JR FREDERIC R DELANGE RONALD W HOBBS KENNETH R HORNE
GAYLORD N KLINEFELTER STEPHEN G LORD DANIEL M MARTZ JR HENRY H MEASLEY JR THOMAS E O'NEILL JR
THOMAS H RHODES RICHARD G THOMAS DENNIS J TULLER ROGER A BISE LEONARD D FORD
HENRY A GRETTEN JOHN M HOAR WALTER KISALA CHARLES T PITTMAN DAVID L SMITH
JOHN W HOUSTON CHARLES L RICHTMYRE DANIEL G ROGERS JAMES E THOMPSON ROBERT K WORLEY
WILLIAM S RIES WALTER N AMMONS ALLEN J AVERY IRA C BOGGS JR DAVID J BOYLE WARREN W PFEFFERLE
BOBBY J BRASWELL GARRY COYLE DONALD E DANIELS LEWIS R DIETZ CORDIE L DIXON
ELOY DURAN FRANKLIN D GAMBRELL HERBERT G GOGGAN JOHN W GROOVER GEORGE E HAYES
TOMMY E HILL JOHN R HILLS WILLIAM A HOOS JR JOSEPH D JARRELL CARLOS D JELKS DENNIS D BACKEN
RICHARD E MARKS AITKEN L MATTHEWS JR WILLIAM R MCKIM GENE C MILLIGAN ELI W NICHOLS
JACK C RODRIGUEZ DAYTON L RUDISILL HENRY M STARKEY ERNEST G TOMPKINS WILLIAM M WOOD JR
TERRY J REED WILLIAM R WALLACE BOBBY R WAYMAN WATSON WILLIS LADD R CONDY
DAVID L FISHER JIMMY GONZALES STEPHEN E LAIER OSCAR MAUTERER ROBERT O NATARTE
RAYMOND R POSTON ANTHONY G SHEPLER JR WAYMOND N STEPHENSON ANTHONY R VALENTINO
ERNEST WATSON WILLIAM H BORDNER FRANK E CRABBE FREDDIE G LLOYD ROSS J PATERSON
JAMES R DINGER RONALD J BENKE III DAVID P BROWN LEN E CARR TORRE L DE LA GARY B GORTON
BOBBY G JOHNSON WILLIAM E LEATHERWOOD JR ROBERT E LEE JUAN A LOPEZ-COLON HUGH A LOVE
JESSE E PETERSON THOMAS E RICE JOHN F SAMPT ROBERT L SMITH SHERDIN J WATKINS
DAVID E WHITTEN MARK H ZELDES GARY R ARTMAN RICHARD F BARNES JOSEPH T BENTON
BOB G BRUMLEY WILLIAM F COLLIER GLENN V CURRY WILLIE E DAVIS DAMION R HILTS
REYNALDO R CAVAZOS CAROL A DRAZBA DANIEL FERNANDEZ ANDREW A GRAZIANO PATRICK J HARRIS
CHARLES M HONOUR JR LEO J HORAN ELIZABETH A JONES LYELL F KING CHRISTOPHER J LANTZ
JAMES W MIZE JR JOSEPH V MURRAY WILLIAM L OAKLEY DOMINIC J PREIRA JR WILLIAM C RIGG
SHEPPARD ROBINSON JR JAMES T RUFFIN THOMAS A SCHROEFFEL DONALD M SHAFER II ALBERT M SMITH
THOMAS W STASKO WALTER A TERLECKI ELZIE J COLLINS JR HURSHEL FRASURE PAUL A GILBERT
FREDDIE W GREEN JOHN M HOELSCHER JACK L JAMES RONALD M KENNY KENNETH W LANTER
ROBERT C LILLY CLARENCE MEDLEY RAYMOND L NAYLOR GEORGE K NEWMAN ROBERT Q ROENTSCH
JERRY D STEWART DOUGLAS J WADE ARFIEN C ALI JAMES O ALLEN THOMAS M DILLARD
EMMITT C ADAMS LEONARD J CHISLOCK WILLIAM A DAVISON JR RICHARD A FILLIATOR PETER T FITZPATRICK
RAYMOND S FORD MARSHALL R FRIZZELL JERRY B HARRIS VICTOR J KOHLBECK MYRON MCCLELLAND
JOHN E KERNS RICHARD P LANCASTER JR JEROME L MCCORMICK JOHN W ROBBINS JAMES R RUTLEDGE
PEDRO SANTOS-PINEDO CHARLIE K SCATES LARRY D STICE RAYMOND D WEIAND CARROLL L WELTY
VERNON G CHASE JOHN A GIROD JR MARSHALL R HIRSCH VERNON A MERRITT CHRISTOPHER E RUBERG
CLINTON R ANDERSON ROBERT L BEATON WILLIAM T CALLERY RICHARD H CASSUBE BILLY B DAY
JAMES L FAIN LYNDSEY F FONGER GARY W GARIS CALVIN R HEBERT JR LEO F KRUMBINE RONALD L POWELL
ROBERT L MACK RALPH A MAXHAM JR MICHAEL W MCDONALD MICHAEL J NEMCHICK VICTOR L NETTLES JR
ADAN M OLVERA WILLIAM B PARNELL RICARDO J PEREZ CHARLES A SOUTHARD III JOE K TAYLOR
DAVID W UTLEY CLARENCE WILLIAMS DONALD B ADAMSON WILLIAM O ALLEN CHARLES E BROOKS
HARMON C BURD WILLIAM H COBURN CHARLES R DALE ARLEN J DUCKETT JR RONALD W DUCKETT
CHARLES E DYSON JR RODGER L EGOLF HONDAH D EL MATTHEW HOUGH JOE N JAMES
DALMER D JUREK GEORGE W MCNEES BURTON C MONTROSS WINSTON MORRIS ISAIAH MULWEE JR
PATRICK C NEVIN TOMMY L NICHOLAS W H NORMAN JACK RABINOVITZ RICHARD RANGEL
KENNETH A REYNOLDS FRANKIE SANCHEZ JIMMY C SEXTON MARSHALL R SMITH TERRENCE L SOUHRADA
WILLIAM J STEPHENSON PAUL J STOCHAJ WILLIAM B WATSON JR MARVIN J WILSON LEE D ANDERSON
JIMMY E BOAN JAMES R BOLAND FELIPE BONILLA-VIERA HARVEY L BOWEN JR ROBERT L CLARK
WILLIE A COOPER JAMES B DETRIXHE JAMES R FOLEY JIMMIE L FOSTER FLEMMON P FREEMAN
GENTRY GRAHAM FLOYD S HARMON THOMAS E HARTUNG RAYMOND H HETRICK RICHARD A MARSHALL
LARRY L KEENER JOE C LILE II ROBERT K LOWE ROBERT D MERRELL GEORGE A MORGAN GEORGE A BELL JR
THOMAS J OGLETHORPE ROBERT D PERDUE ALLEN L PIERCE DONALD C PIPER WILLIE PIPPINS SR
JOSEPH L ROBINSON BENNIE L SIMMONS FREDERICK A SLEMP CECIL Y WARE CHARLES C WHITFIELD
O'DELL ROBINSON ALBERT R WHITE TOMMIE L WILLIAMS JESSE J BOLTON FRANKLIN V BRODNIK
JOHN B CAUSEY PHILLIP A LOTTA NICHOLES SOCHACKI JAMES M TERMINI CLYDE W WITHEE
GEORGE W WOODALL DOUGLAS D ALLEY SIMMIE BELLAMY JR ELMER E BERRY THOMAS C BREWER JR
JAMES T BROWN RONALD C CAVINEE IRVIN CLARKE JR CHARLES E DANIELS CHARLIES E DANIELS JOHNSON F FRANK
LAMAR D FREDERICK JOHN P GILLIAM JACK L HIMES ROBERT L HOSKINS JR DANIEL R JAMES
ERNEST A LAROCHE CLARENCE MITCHELL DONALD S NEWTON FREDERICK E SMITH ROBERT D WILLIAMS JR
BILLIE N PLUM WILLIAM M TARBELL ROBERT L TERRY FRANCIS D WILLS WILLIAM F AYRES RONALD L RUNKEL
DAVID L DANOWSKI EDWARD S GRAVES PAUL E HELSEL JR RICK E KOPKA LAWRENCE B MCCLOUD
JOSEPH J REILLY DONALD W SMITH JAMES M SPENCE ROGER D BULIFANT HENRY C CASEBOLT
WARREN L CHRISTENSEN LESTER H CLEGG PETER W FIELDS WILLIAM FUCHS JR FRANKLIN D GILBERT
JAMES F HUBISZ ARTHUR J JACKSON MARSHALL JESSIE CHARLES JOHNSON PATRICK J KELLY JR
RICHARD R HERCHKORN JAMES B LAIRD RAYMOND E MEYERS KENNETH D MIDDLETON MARK L MORGAN
LARRY E MACDONALD EDWARD J MCCARTHY BRENT A MCCLELLAN GEORGE F MCCOY CURTIS J MCGEE
DANNY J MCGRIFF ANDY MCGUIRE JR JAMES R MCLEMORE JOSE TORRES RICHARD J WOLCHESKI
JAMES G PATZWALL ARTHUR C PEDERSON MICHAEL D PLISKA DARRELL T RAY ALBERT C ROBERTS
MIGUEL E NARANJO JR JOHN H ROBERTS LESTER A ROGERS CHARLES W SIMS CLIFTON L TART
RICHARD F NUGENT CARTER L WILLIAMS JR CLARK N WOODWORTH JR CHARLIE M YOUNG ALBERT F BAIRD
LEONARD J BOCEK WILLIAM M CHRISTENSEN WILLIAM P FORAN WILLIAM D FRAWLEY LONNIE R KING
ROBERT LOPEZ BRUCE L MAROSITES JOHN W WILLIAMS DONALD J WOLOSZYK DONALD ZOBOBLISH
THOMAS J FEARS CARLOS R HATCHER MARSHALL M HOLT JR JACK M HOPKINS BARNETTE G JENKINS
PAUL A MEINERS KARL E WORST CHARLES F COINER ROBERT F FIELDER PAUL H GREENE MAJOR ARNOLD JR
WILLIAM JONES JR LOOMIS OGLESBY III CHARLES W RADER DENNIS L TALKINGTON GARY C ALLEN
RICHARD G ALLEN STEPHEN P ALSTED STUART M ANDREWS HERIBERTO ARMENTA JAMES S COCCHIARA
ALLEN C BAILEY ISIAH BAKER III DANIEL P BIRCH RAYMOND BLANCHETTE WILLIAM W BROWN
LESTER R ATHERDEN NORMAN J BUELL JAMES E BUSH RUPERT S CARVEN III PHILLIP H CLARK
JOHN F CONLON III RICHARD P CORSON BRUCE DAVIS STANLEY T DEMBOSKI SEAN P DODSON
JOHN J EDWARDS REUBEN L GARNETT JR RONALD W GODDARD HARRY M GODWIN ANDREW L HASTINGS
MICHAEL A GILSON WOODROW W HAM JR DAVID M HANN JOHN M HARDEN HARRY P HELT JR
KLAUS J HERMS JOSEPH S HERRON JOHNNY R HOLLOWAY HENRY J HOOPER WILLIAM J HRINKO
LAWRENCE E JOHNSON WILLIAM JOHNSON HARVEY W JONES ARNELL KEYES LEWIS A KIMMEL JR
WILBUR G KIRCHOFF FRANZ J KOLBECK ROBERT B LABBE JACK W LINDSEY FRANK LOPEZ JR DAHL J LAPORTE
ALBERTO A LUCERO DONALD R LUMLEY DIEGO MERCADO VINFORD F MICHAEL PETER G SCAVUZZO
HENRY D ODOM SAMUEL G ORLANDO PAUL G PARSONS JACKIE D REYNOLDS JOSEPH R REYNOLDS
DONNELL D MCMILLIN CRESENCIO P SANCHEZ JAMES R SCOTT MICHAEL A SHANDS ALFRED J SMITH
ROBERT L SMITH JR DWIGHT D TOLLEFSON DELBERT L TRUBE JR ROSCOE L VICK CHARLES D WADSWORTH
THOMAS WARDROP III DAVID B WARREN LESTER A WESIGHAN CHARLES R WETZEL MICHAEL R YOUNG
CHARLES E ANDERSON RAY M BARNWELL DAVID L BAUMGARDNER JOHN H BELL WILLIE J BRAMLET
ANIBAL F AVILES JR KENNETH E BEAUREGARD LEWIS D BELL MICHAEL L BIANCHINI JAMES J BRADLEY
ROBERT BROWN ALBERT CABANAYAN ROBERT M CALIBOSO PHILIP FITCH ROBERT C HESSOM
LELAND F DIXON HENRY J DOSTER JAMES H EDGE CHARLES L EDWARDS THOMAS W EDWARDS
STEVEN A CHURCH GARY W EMMETT THOMAS K EMMONS JOSEPH G EVANS JR RICKEY D GARNER

CHARLES E CRUTCHFIELD RICHARD N GEREAU ROY GONZALES JR ROY F HARBISON LOUIS P HERNANDEZ
ROBERT J HIBBS ROY J HIGGINS JR FRED H HORTON LEONARD A HULTQUIST THOMAS A JENNINGS
ANTONIO JIMENEZ DARRELL L JOHNSON THOMAS P JOHNSTON MARIO C KITTS FREDERICK G LYNCH JR
JOSE E LAGUER HENRY D LANKFORD DENNIS M LYDEN PAUL I MAHER TOMMY R MILLER CECIL W BURTON
WILLIAM D MCCUEN JR CHARLES A MCGEE ALAN C MULFORD DANNY A NETH ROBERT L NUEKU
RICHARD E NUTT CHESTER L O'BRIEN JR DENNIS R ORTWINE JAMES H PAGE JERRY E PARKS
JAMES H ROWDEN DAVID L SABEC JIMMY P SANCHEZ CHARLES S SATCHER CHARLES F SETZENFAND
JOEL RODRIGUEZ ROYCE G SCOGGINS DAVID SHIELDS CONRAD A SIPPLE GARY E SOOTER
MACK D STAINBACK JR JOSEPH G STOUDT CLYDE E TRIEVEL JR RICHARD A WAGNER KERRY L WILLIAMS
LLOYD C WILSON CLIFTON WINNINGHAM WILLIAM R GRAHAM DANNY T HIGGS GREGORY J MONROE
J H ALEXANDER BOBBY J MARSH CYRUS S ROBERTS IV MARIO YBARRA CHARLES L ZOOG PAUL E RUDEEN JR
HARLOW G CLARK JR BARRY A HANSEN EDWARD L HODGE GORDON L PAGE HAROLD V SMITH
BENJAMIN G SPEARS JERDY A WRIGHT JR RICHARD W BOND THOMAS E CONNER PETER S CONNOR
NOLAN F DREWRY HUGH W MERRILL RAYMOND ALLEN FRANCIS T CLARKIN JON I CLIFFORD
WILLARD M COLLINS CHARLES L DAVIDSON WILLIAM D DORFMAN EDWARD F DUNCAN DAVID L FORCE
ROBERT E FOSTER BILLIE A HALL GARY L HENDERSON JAMES M JAROLIMEK PAUL E LA BRECQUE JR
DENIS W MALEWSKI WARREN S MCELHANON CLARENCE E MCKINNIS EDWARD PEREA DELBERT R PETERSON
EUGENE F ROBINSON PHILLIP T STAHL CLARENCE C WILSON CHARLES J FORD WILLIE G HAWKINS JR
ELDON D LONG OWEN F MCCANN FREDERICK PRICE ALAN M TANGUAY JAMES L TAYLOR

PANEL 6E
JOHN R COWAN HARVEY L ENGEL SAMMY L HARTZELL JAMES P MORGAN
KENNETH A BODELL HAROLD E STOELT RICHARD W ARNOLD JAMES W BROWN BRUCE B WARNER
DEAN A DU VALL HOWARD W HENNINGER JOHN H HERLIHY JR JAMES E HUGHES ALBERTO PEREZ-VERGARA
RICHARD K JAMROS EDWIN E MORGAN GERALD E OLSON UDON PARKER ROBERT E PASEKOFF
GENE E DAVIS DAVID J GIER MARSHALL I PAULEY EDWARD D PIERCE ROBERT A STREET
WILEY C BIRKLAND EARLIE J BUTLER JR MARVIN HARPER GERALD W HEUSTON PHIL TABB
ROBERT L HILTON KARL E KLUTE BILLY W MORTON FRANK MULLEN JAMES E PLEIMAN RICHARD F WALLACE
RANDALL S HICKMAN LIONEL RANDOLPH DANIEL F SHARP BILLY R SLADE ROBERT E TAYLOR
STEADMON ADAMS JR DON W CHABOT THOMAS J CHANDLER JR ROBERT L DIAL RAYMOND A RANELLUCCI
DUANE K HEISER ROY J HENDERSON WILLIAM R HOLBROOK DAVID H HOLMES RAYMOND HOOD
GARY E BARTZ IGNACIO HUICOCHEA-REYNA JOHN M NASH HERMAN PENN CARMELO SANCHEZ-BERRIOS
MARTIN R SCOTT GEORGE E SNODGRASS ALLAN STEGALL JR PETER J STEWART DORSEY L TATUM
PEDRO VAZQUEZ-GONZALEZ ROBERT C WILLIAMS GEORGE W ABEY CHARLES A BELL WILLIAM H HUBBARD
JOHN H BEAUCHAMP JR MARION C BROWN ROBERT P GIPSON WILLIAM O GOSSETT JAMES K HUGHES
CHARLES B JEFFRIES JR EDDIE L KNOX KENNETH M KNUDSON JERRY D LEWIS CURTIS C NICKERSON
RONALD L REED JERRY L SEVENBERGEN RICHARD F SMITH WILLIAM N THOMPSON PAUL G UNDERWOOD
CHARLIE C WALKER JERRY G WINSLOW CHARLES A ZIONTS ALBERT K CHRISTY JACK L NEIDRICK
GARLAND C BOBBITT WILLIAM H CRAIG JR MERWIN A DELANO JR BENJAMIN LEE IV VIRGIL A MURRAY
JAMES R REILLY GORDON SHEPHERD JOHNNIE M TENON FRANCIS W CLARK BRENT E DAVIS
THERON S DEMPSEY JAMES W DENNIS JR GASTON D GODFREY DALLAS E HICKMAN THOMAS F HORNBY
JOE D KELLY RAYMOND C MARTIN EVERETT A MCPHERSON ENRICO H PAGNANO JR JIMMIE T SMILEY
DANIEL G STANDS JR RONALD M SUTTON JAMES S WILLIAMS ROBERT H CORLEY MARK FERRELL JR
JAMES E KEELER ALEXANDER D RODARTE JIMMIE L WALLACE JR JAMES P WILLIAMS MARVIN F GOODMAN JR
WILLIAM E CANNON DAVID L DRAKE JR DENNIS D FERGUSON THEODORE L FISCHER DAVID FLORES
ARTHUR J BEACH MARK J GARDELLA RICHARD A GROOVER GEORGE HITZELBERGER TOMMIE L MCFARLAND
CLIFFORD A MCKENNAN JERALD L PINNEKER JOHN H SAVAGEAU GERALD B SCHMIDT HUBERT R SMITH
JOHN R TURNER JOHN A VERGALLITO LOSSY R WANGLER ROY R ALLEN LOUIS A AMBROSE
DENNIS R ANDREW THOMAS A BIRD JR RUSSELL L BISHOP WILLIAM G BLANCHARD JOHN M BOWERS
ROBERT G BROWN DAVID G CALLIS CALVIN K CHOW FRANK R COMPTON WILLARD J FRIESE
RONNIE E CONNACHER ALLAN L ELMORE JOSEPH B FEARNO THOMAS B FLOOD JOHN H FRANKLIN
JAMES H CAVICCHI JR BOBBY G GADIE MARTIN L GILLESPIE JR MARVIN E GLASSBURN GAROLD A HANN
TERRY L HARPER ROGER L HENDERSON MANUEL HERRERA JOHN L HUNTER BENITO IGARTA JR
NOAH M KRAFT RAYMOND E LEIGHTON STEPHAN J MARTIN LESTER G MICHELS JOHN A MITCHELL
MICHAEL G MURRAY JAMES R PACE TERRY L QUINN STANLEY RIFFLE JOHN F SCULL JR WILLIAM K SHOUP
WALTER R SHORTT WALTER G SHULTS WILLIAM A STACY JR RICHARD D SWAYZE JOHN M TIDERMAN
DANIEL TIENDA JULIUS J VALINT JR WILLIAM G WADE BRUCE L WATKINS HAROLD W WILSON
DENNIS R BRUCE WILLIAM E BURKE III JOHNNIE M CURLEE MICHAEL J DELGADO JR PAUL R DRUMMOND
FRANCIS M BOYLE EDWARD J DEVINCENT JR JESSE G EASTMAN FRANK R ESCH ARNOLD J FAULKNER
EDUARDO GONZALEZ-DROZ BILLY HOWARD BRUCE R LANDIS JR JERRY D LEE MARION L LEE JR
JERRY M MCWHORTER ROGER T OKAMOTO JOHN C ROBERTSON RAYMOND W WILSON FRED Y WRIGHT JR
RICHARD A CARUOLO JUAN J CASTRO DONALD E CLARK JR CLYDE D DAWSON SAMUEL E HEWITT
BIENVENIDO G DONA ISIAH FOSTER GEORGE P KING JEROME NIXON RONALD A SAPP
EDMUND L SUDLER JOHN B TAPP ROBERT E BUSH JAMES M CORNETT GENERAL WHITE
JAMES A DOKE ROBERT A DORNER MICHAEL M JACKSON CARL H JOYNER ALBERT M KEEN JR
ROBERT L MACK TOMAS V MARTINEZ JOSEPH A MASON JR LEONARD D MAY JOSEPH G VILLIARD
JESUS A MUNOZ CLYDE E MURR MICHAEL D SCHATZLEY CARL R SMEAD ROBERT E URBANOVSKY
AL J CHATTIN ALLEN G LANE WILLIAM E COPELAND II CHARLES HARMON ANTONIO Q SABLAN
JAMES V DONNELLY RICHARD A ECKVALL HUGH W ELMORE RICHARD M EPPS THOMAS K KING
MICHAEL D LAUX CLYDE D MCDONALD II RONALD M NEUMAN SHIRLEY W O'BOYLE JAMES A WOOD
PATRICK M DOYLE SAMUEL M RAMIREZ PHILIP O ROBINSON CHARLES N RUDD JOHN B SHERMAN
GERALD A LETENDRE CLARENCE A WHITEHEAD CHARLES T COURSON RICHARD K HILL JAMES L HUDSPETH
THEODORE N MISHEIKIS JR DAVID A SIEMANOWSKI JAMES A STCYR JOHN W WILT JR PAUL J BUCK
DAVID COLVIN RICHARD F GRAHAM MERLE E JONES RONALD W JONES ELWIN C WISE
ROBERT B KNUTSON ROGER D REED GEORGE T REYNOLDS HARLAN C RIEHL ROBERT J VAN REYPEN
HORACE A HAMPTON ANTHONY G VELARDO ALDEN B WILLEY STANLEY G YURGAITIS JOHN G BANSAVAGE
MICHAEL R BECK EDMUND F EDDY RONNIE E HALL PAUL E HASSEY WILLIAM F JOYCE RONALD L WAFFORD
RICHARD L MAYES JOHN L MCCARTY THOMAS MCENTEE PEDRO PADILLA RICHARD J PRESKENIS
ALBERT C RISING ANTHONY SILBA LEROY E SIMONS JAMES E TAYLOR WILLIAM R WEST MAARTEN DEGROOT
COLON R RODRIGUEZ GREGORY V ARMSTEAD JOHN L BANKS III THOMAS BINION RICHARD COLEMAN
RAYMOND L FORD FRANCISCO HERRERA RONALD C LOGAN THOMAS E MILES PHILIP C SMITH
THOMAS D VINCENT LEE B TATE JERALD R TOWATER JUAN R TREVINO IVAN ALFEROFF JAMES M ARBUTHNOT
DAVID L ARNOLD PAUL S ASHLINE MARK S BLACK RICHARD A BLANCHFIELD BURTON A BLANTON
LAWRENCE A BRITTEN GEORGE A CANNATA JR CALVIN L CHEIVES MCARTHUR COLEMAN ROBERT J DI REDA
DAVID H ELMAN JAMES W GRADY RICHARD C GROVE LEONARD S HAUSERMAN TYRONE W HISEY
DENNIS E HOLT FLOYD M HORTON JOHNNY HUDSON JOHN G JACKSON ARTHUR L JAMES
DAVID M KNIGHT JAMES N MATTHEWS LEE A MOORE JR CARL L MUNSEY RAYMOND C ROBINSON
CHARLES JOHNSON JR DAVID L MCCONNAUGHEY CLYDE L NORVELLE JR DAVID B POWELL JR DORSE RIGGS
JOHN S SABINE IV RONALD E SHERMAN ELMER J TAYLOR L V THOMAS JR ALFRED L THOMPSON
GIOVANNINO TUMMINIA HENRY L WHALEY CHARLES M WOODS HOWARD O WRIGHT JR LLOYD R TARVER
ROGER L GERTSEN DON C BAKER PATRICK J BREMS HECTOR W BRYAN PAUL R CAPUANO
JESSE J COFFEY WILLIAM R GRAYSON WILLIAM T JOHNSON DAVID J KERN WILLIAM F KOHLRUSCH
CHESTER L LEE DANIEL V MANZARO MICHAEL T MULVANEY RICHARD P RAND RICARDO H SOTO
JAMES L TEWKSBURY MICHAEL D COOK DALE L COURCHANE JULIAN C CUELLAR CURTIS E DORRIS
DONALD R BURTON DAVID M DAVIES GEORGE S FRANKLIN EUGENE E FULLER PAUL A HAINES
WILLIAM D HASTY ALLEN L HIGGINBOTHAN JOHN D HOFFMAN ALEXANDER J MENZIES JAMES MOORE JR
PAUL R HATTABAUGH TERRY R MCLEAN DONALD F MCMILLAN NORMAN N MILLER WELDON D MOSS
THURMAN W OWEN DANIEL J PIOTROWSKI WILLIAM L RICHARDSON JR LARRY E ROSE DAVID G RUSSELL
MICHEAL K MCGUIRE KEITH L SHIPP JIMMY B TAYLOR LESTER J THORNELL FELIBERTO VILLA HENRY M VINSON
RALPH M WILLIAMS RICHARD H WRIGHT DONALD E YOUNG JOHNNY B BOSTON LEO M DONKER
DAVID E HORNBY ROGER D JARRELL MARTIN J LACHER RICHARD L LAWS GARY D NAIL
KENNETH D GOLDEN JR ARTHUR C MORRIS JR LARRY J NICHOLS CASIMIRO PALACIOS JOSEPH W PARENT
DONOVAN J PRUETT TOMMIE L SILLS HAMP J SYKES JR JOHN C WRONSKI CLEVELAND FOSTER
JACK D GILBERT FRANKLIN E HOSLER JOSEPH L KANE JOE F LISERIO STEVEN M SMITH FRANK DE MARCHI JR
JAMES W BROWN GERMAN CHAPARRO-VILLANU MICHAEL R CUNEEN BARNEY M GILES JR
KEITH W KAUFFMAN HAROLD W LOWTHER DANIEL J MACK ISIDRO MARTINEZ NATHANIEL MERRIWEATHER
LAWRENCE MCCREA CHARLIE REED JR PAUL D RODRIGUEZ CARLOS J SANCHEZ JAMES L SLADE JR
EDWARD M STANCHEK FRANKLIN F WEAVER SCOTT T WELBORNE FREDERICK A WENTZ TOMMY L WHITE
ARNOLD WOODSON BERNARD BARRIOS THOMAS A BLEVINS DONALD R BROWN ROBERT BURCIAGA
DENNIS P COOK JAMES W GATES JAMES P HARTEAU DONALD R JOHNSON MELVIN T KRECH
ROBERT A KREUZIGER JOHN W LAFAYETTE JOHN E LITTLE JAMES P MCELHANNON WALTER F ORLEY
THOMAS J RALSTON JACK A SMITH RICHARD C SMITH ROBERT R BARNETT MARIANO R NEGRANZA JR
JOHN M BROWN III MARTIN COX WALTER C FILLMAN SR JOSEPH S GODWIN HARRY G LUTE
ARTHUR J BAYLOR THOMAS T WALKER DAVID O BAILEY CHARLES E PORTER GARY M RADFORD
GEORGE L SAMUELS CHARLES M SHELDON EDWARD H TIMMONS JEFFERSON D HALL THOMAS G WALSTER
LEROY KOLB JR RALPH S KOROLZYK THOMAS W MUIR JIMMY ROLLINGS HARRY D WOODARD
RONALD T SHELTON TOM K TINGLE LOGAN D YOUNG MARION F ACTON CARL D BUCKLEY
CLARENCE E BARNES HOWARD C BLEVINS RICHARD F BUBALA ANDREW J CAMPBELL WILLIAM H CAUSEY
RALPH COLEMAN ZED C CREVELING JOHN A DAVIS DONALD E DERMONT JR DENNIS A DESCO
CHARLES O DIXON JR JOHN H EAGLIN PHILYAW FEE EUGENE GARRETT JR EDWARD L GEORGE BOZY GERALD
DONALD W HALL DAVID A HAMMETT CHARLES E HARVEY NORMAN L HAWKINS ROBERT A JOHNSON
PHILIP A JONES EVERETT E LANGSTON EDWIN H LEVERING RICHARD J MANLEY EMMITT MAYS JR
RICHARD NOYOLA CHARLES H PENN WILLIAM H PITSENBARGER RANDALL B PRINZ
CHARLES D OGLESBY EDWARD W REILLY JAMES W ROBINSON JR RONALD A ROTH RONALD J SEASHOLTZ HENRY A SHIVER
J C SHORT JOSEPH F SMITH THOMAS D STEELE GEORGE C STEINBERG DANIEL E WALDEN
GEORGE H WARD JOHN W WATKINS ERIC WILLIAMS IRVING M WILSON JR JAMES B CONWAY
LAVALL DURR WILLIAM A GLASSON JR REUBEN B HARRIS JOHN M JAMES LARRY M JORDAN
EDMUND H HORNSTEIN RONNIE R LOVETT KENNETH W PUGH WAYNE J SPELLMAN JAMES R TOMAKOSKI
COLEY L WASHINGTON JR FRED A BENNER WILLIAM E BORDER RICHARD D BORIEO JOSEPH W BROWN III
JESSE L CLARK II GREEN CONLEY FRANK A D'AMICO DONALD D DAUGHERTY CLINTON B FACKRELL
LLOYD FIELDS JR PHILLIPS LA MARR RICHARD F MALOY ALEXANDER J MCGLOTHLIN RANDOLPH P VEDROS
JOSE A PACHECO RONALD G SOULE JAMES R TAYLOR MOLIMAU A TELA JOSEPH TIMPA JR
JOHN C MAPE JIMMY R WOLFE DENNIS G HARMON DAVID D HIGDON JR DONALD L SIMMONS

PANEL 6E (*Continued*)

JAMMIE J LANIER BURTON K MCCORD CHARLES J MURPHY JR DENNIS L REEVES HOWARD E ROTHRING JR
LEWIS M THOMAS ROBERT L VADEN CHARLES E COOPER DAVID N EVILSIZER LUSTER C FRIEL
RALPH H LIVESAY JOHN A MCCURDY ROBERT H SANTORELLA GILBERT B SUETOS MICHAEL R ZERBE
WALTER H ANDERSON ANTHONY J BATTISTA VICTOR E CHASE WALTER M COLLINS EMMANUEL D WHITLEY
GALEN D GRETHEN TONY H HUGHES JAMES H KURDELSKI EDGAR B LUEALLEN DANA J MICOLA
MICHAEL J MCGOLDRICK JOHN PARNELLA JAMES E PROMMERSBERGER OKEY L SANDS ERNEST E SIMONS
TOMMIE M CRIPE CLARENCE A TEAS THOMAS N YAGLE WILLIAM H JOHNSON FRANKLIN H QUINTANA
WAYNE H ROWLAND GEORGE E RUTLEDGE LYNN L SMITH WILLIAM L TROMP ROBERT D ARNOLD
DANNY A BOLIN THOMAS H CARUTHERS GERALD W ENGEL FREDERICK HOMEYER RALPH R LIND JR
DAVID J UNDERHILL WILLIAM T MAIN LEE A ADAMS JOSEPH O BROWN HENRY L DEW DANA S FROST
DARRELL Z MAGRUDER A D MOSLEY BENNETT H OWENS JR RICHARD J ROBBINS THELBERT K THOMPSON JR
JOHN ABBOTT FAMOUS L LANE LAWRENCE V PETERS JIMMIE L PLUMLEY RONALD V SILBERSACK
ROBERT C COTHRAN GEORGE J SKAPINSKY GROVER R TAYLOR ROY D WATTS ELLIS E AUSTIN IVAN J BROYLES
CHARLES R GURTLER MICHAEL W HEUER JACK E KELLER CHARLES MILLER FREDRICK W MILLER
CHARLES B NORRIS DANIEL L SAUVE WILLIAM H SCHOLES HENRY C TISDALE
JAMES L EATMON MIGUEL GARCIA JR CLYDE HALL WILLIAM B NICKERSON TERRY A RIPPY
DENIS E ABBOTT ROBERT F WEIMORTS JAMES E COOK FRANCISCO CORREA-MORALES ROBERT R DYCZKOWSKI BERNARD J GOSS
JOHN P ISAACS GERALD B KASPRZYK LARRY F WIRT GEORGE W WOODSON JR ROBERT L ADAMS
WILLIAM E COOPER DONALD L DRYOEL DANIEL B DUFFY JR JOHN A FONTAINE DAVID W TERWILLIGER
ALLEN BRACKINS KENNETH R HALL HENRY P PEREDA RICHARD A RECUPERO TERRENCE D SCOTT
BILLY A THOMPSON KENNETH E TURNER DAVID O BLACKMON FREDERICK C CAIN DALE D DE FORD
KENNETH H DELP AMALIO GONZALEZ RICHARD M LINES ROBERT G MUELLER JAMES D OLSEN EARL STANLEY
WILLIAM L WALTON GEORGE D ADAMS WARREN L ANDERSON BRENT J BAUMERT

PANEL 7E

ROBERT N DAVIS DOYLE E HOLTZLANDER ROBERT J KEENAN KENNETH D MORGAN
EDWARD D REILLY JR JAMES H TUCKER KENNETH W WOLFE JULIAN G CORDERO FRANK D KORNOVICH
GEORGE S EDLEY SAMUEL H GRAHAM II MARTIN R ROBINSON RUBEN L ROCHA
RAMON A PELLOT-RODRIGUEZ FRANCIS W RUCH II JOHNNIE SMITH JR WALTER J TYPE JR HERMAN BROWN JR JOHN A BULPITT
ANDRA CUNEO JR ANTHONY A GENNOCRO CLEMENT B JOHNSTON JR MOSES C LEE MICHAEL A NEWKIRK
JERRY W SANKS STEPHEN C VALLIERE DEANE S VAN DYKE JR JOHN J VICTORY MICHAEL H BALL
TOMMY L BOATWRIGHT LEO S BOSTON LOREN E BRADLEY THOMAS E BROWN DONALD W BRUCH JR
JOSEPH A CRUZ WILLIAM P EGAN VICTOR J FORD ROBERT E FOSTER JR HARRY D HASKINS
JAMES E CUNNINGHAM DAVID D GUMMERE KENNETH E HELEMS DARYL L KADOUS LAWRENCE D KNUTH
JAMES A LEVINGSTON ROBERT B LOWE EDWARD R LUFF JR DENNIS A MAY JAMES R MOLLETTE
WILLIAM F MULLEN LOUIS J PELLIZZARI BOB E POGRE JOSEPH J POLONKO JR WALTER L PUMPELLY
JOSE F RIVERA-BARRETO JASPER STEPHENS JR DAVID STEVENS JR MICHAEL J TRITICO WILBERT E WAXTON
JULIAN B WILLOUGHBY JAMES C WISKUR CARL M GEBHART JR HOWARD R HYSELL ROGER W JENKINS
EDWARD R LETOURNEAU JR HAROLD B MARSHALL MURRAY S MOSELEY JAMES T PRUITT EDWARD T RUSSELL
GEORGE T STRIDIRON PAUL T WHITTINGTON WILLIAM WILKOWSKY JR WILLIAM L BAUER CHARLES B WHITE
JOHN J CARVILLE CARLOS S GONZALEZ DENNIS L KEYER MERLE A KINNEY KARL F SCHRANK
EUGENE G ARMSTRONG SR ALBERT M SINNETT ELMO L DE FORD BILLY DODSON JACOB H FOWNER
KENNETH L FREITAG JAMES J HESSLER GLEN D HINE FERNANDO A HINOJOSA DARRELL W MARTINSON
RONNIE E MATTHEWS WALTER S WOOD EDDIE R DERRITT RICHARD G ENGELMAN DOUGLAS JACKSON
ANTONINE G KOCIPER VIRGIL LINDQUIST ANGELO F MICHELLI JOSEPH A PECORA JR JOHN M PHILLIPS
FRED L RICHARDSON BERNARD J RODZEN JAMES D STOKES CHARLES R TRESCOTT WILLIAM E TUCKER JR
JOSEPH A SCHWERDTFEGER O'NEAL ADDISON AARON B AUMILLER WILLIAM J BARRAGY ROGER L BERG
JOHN A BROWN GEORGE A CLARK ROBERT L CLARK ROGER C COLLETTE JOHN F CONCANNON
CARY CRADDOCK WILLIAM M DENHOFF EDGAR S DOLIBER JOHN A EDDY CHARLES W WOOLIVER
RUSSELL L HAMILTON J D HARRELL MELVIN E HART GENE HAWTHORNE ESTEL HUSKEY JOSEPH E BRUNELLE
MALAKIA JACKSON JR RUDOLPH JACKYMACK CHARLES R KESTERSON JIMMY M MALONE FAIRLEY W MILLS
JERRY R MURPHY JERRY L ONAN MICHAEL SIMPSON JOSEPH J SWAYZE ROBERT E THOMPSON
ROBERT A FENTON EARNEST A TUCKER JR HARDEN B WALKER HOWARD D WEISS REINALDO ZAYAS-CASTRO
WILBERT I ANDREWS CLIFTON L BACON EUGENE CHRISCO JOEL D COLEMAN JOHN J DAWES
THOMAS D EASTMAN DAVID W HARTLEY JAMES R KOVAR JOHN E MCMAHAN MACHUGHLEN MEECE
GEORGE L STOLL BRITT TELL JR KENNETH D THOMAS JR TONY R ARRIAGA BARRIE V BARNES
ROBERT L BOSS CECIL D BRELAND MICHAEL F BRUNAT JOHNNIE E BUTLER DAVID C CARPENTER
JOAQUIN DE JESUS REESE DEVEREAUX DARWIN H ENGMAN MACK L FRANCE JR
ROBERT L ENGBERSON LEONARD I HENRY RICHARD D HOGARTH GLENN A KENNEDY CHARLES R LAWHON WILLIAM C MEEK
JOSEPH C MISSAR JR ELMER F POWELL HARVEY W PRATER NEAL A RASMUSSEN JOHN H REGO
JOSEPH H REID JOSEPH B RUSS RAYMOND P SCHWESINGER DAVID A SCOTT DOUGLAS J WEISS
EARL S SHELTON WILLIAM E SODERSTROM HERBERT L SUTHERLAND STEPHEN E THOMAS JAMES WILLIAMS
OWEN W WORTHEY STEVE G YOUNG JOHN D CHUTER PHILIP P JENKINS JAMES E JOHNSON
HERMANDO S MOYA JOHN VAN DRIESSCHE GILBERT B BUSH MATTHEW J DAVERN
MICHAEL L FAULKNER CARMINE V GENOVESE ARTHUR L JOHNSON ROBERT L MCCAIG TIMOTHY RAY FRANKLIN D WATERS
JESUS L RAMOS JR CHARLES O DAVIS EDWARD L ROARK STEPHEN J STERITI PAUL E SWIM JOHN J TUMINO JOHN BACO
JOHN E CAIL JR AUSTIN M CORBIERE BENNIE L DEXTER ROY E FREEMAN JR DENNIS D KAISER
KEITH R KNOTT FERNANDO O MESQUITA WILLIAM R ROMACK DICKIE D TRINKLER HERBERT N ADAMS
CHARLES K MORAN JR JOHN E BAILEY LARKIN M BEGGS JR JOHN W COATES MARVIN H DAVIS JOEL MELNICK
CSABA F BOROMISSZA TEE W DECKER ROGER DORSEY JOHN J MCCLOSKEY PATRICK C MCCLUSKEY
WILLIE J PEPPERS JR GUY R REED ROBERT N TAMS LEROY W WILLIAMS DAVID C WILLS JR
TOM L AUSTIN ARTHUR J BOWYER GALE V CRAWFORD CHRISTOPHER J DEAN JR JAMES H VILLEPONTEAUX JR
ANDREW C EVANS FRANCIS J FENELEY CLAUDDELL GANDY JAMES R HAUSS DANNY L JONES
HAROLD P KINDLEBERGER GARRY H LINDER ROGER D MANNS ROGER M MATHEWSON WILLIAM F OTTO
BILLY M EDWARDS MARK L ROSENSTOCK BERNARD A TESKE III WAYNE M TRAYLOR ROBERT S VAN DUYNE
EDGARDO CACERES PORTER R CAIN JOHN B CAPEL BERNARD E CLARE BLANCHARD W COCHRANE
GEORGE F DAILEY NEAL A DENNING RALPH G ERDELY JAMES H GRAY GEORGE M HIGHTOWER
JAMES R HOWELL RICHARD W HUNTOON ROBERT E JONES RONALD H JUSTIS JAMES P LA CLEAR
PEDRO MUNOZ WALLACE S PERKINS MICHAEL R POPPAW RONALD F RICE VICENTE Q RODRIGUEZ
MACK R SANDERS ENNIS R SCARBROUGH JOHN J SCHULTZ JR BENJAMIN E SCOLLEY ROBERT J SIMMERMON
ALLEN T WHEATON TOMMY R WHITE DALLAS C YOUNG JR DAVID L BRUNSON MELVIN G CORMIER
LAWRENCE N EDMONDS DAVID A FARROW RONALD J MOOREHEAD RICHARD A SCHMITZ ALBERT DEAN
NORMAND J ASHTON JR REUBEN BUTCHER MICHAEL C DARCY JOHN S DAVIS BOBBY J JACOBS
DONALD L KING STANLEY J KOPCINSKI JOSEPH E LILLEY GEORGE J MACK PAUL W MALEC
WILLIAM W PIERCE FRANK D RALSTON III JAMES F SMALLWOOD DARYL K STANNARD CURTIS L WATSON JR
RALPH C BALCOM JACK R BRADNER GEORGE CANADA JR JAMES D HAKES JR GEORGE W JENSEN
WILLIAM L MADISON KENNETH D MCKENNEY JAMES A PRESTON LAVERN G REILLY ROBERT E SMITH JR
ALBERT E SOMBELON MARSHALL L TAPP GEORGE W THOMPSON JAMES E WILLIAMS EDWARD C WOOD
JOHN C ALBERTS LEO V BEAULIEU JOHN R BOOTH MICHAEL E GEARHART RODGER L TRAMMELL
SKYLER L HASUIKE WILBUR D JACKSON MARTIN F KILLILEA MALVIN L NASWORTHY JR SHERWIN C SCHOPPE
PEKKA TRUNKHAHN LOUIS G TURNER THOMAS H WELSH WILLIAM F WILBER ARTIS W ANDERSON
ALBIN A BARANCZYK SAMMY A BARGA RALPH BASILIERE FREDDIE I BRANCH WILLMATT BROWN
RICHARD W BULLOCK WALTER L BURROUGHS SAMUEL D CARPENTER TERRY W CARPENTER GARY T FUTRELL
LORING W CARPER JR EARL G CLARK TONY DEDMAN DONALD T DEERE KENNETH E DUNCAN
DANNY D DYE RONALD L ECKERT FELIX ESPARZA JR WALTER FELTON BENNY S FLORES
RANDALL J CADENHEAD ROBERT L FOSTER ALLEN M GARRETT EDWARD HAMILTON JOHNNY HARRISON
JIMMY D JORDAN ARTHUR E LEWIS JOHN J MAGYAROSI FREDRICK C MANGAT MICHAEL B MAULDIN
PICARDO R MAYS ROCHESTER MITCHELL GILBERT G MULLEN EDWARD G MYERS HAROLD B NADEAU
VICTOR H O'NEAL ROBERT L PADILLA RICHARD M PATRICK LARRY PAULLEY KENNETH W PICKETT
ROBERT A POTTER JOHN P RANDLES MARTIN D REILLY CLIFFORD G RHODES BILLY E SNIPES
LAWRENCE L RINGGOLD JR RICHARD H SCHMIDT JAMES R STEPHENS BOBBY D SWINDELL JOHN W TEAGUE
RANDY G TOTTEN DALE E UMBENHAUER JESSE F WAGES JAMES E WALKER WILLIAM WALTERS MARVIN L DOOLEY
COSMO L BARONE LEWIS N WELSH ARLOS C WILDER JIMMY L WILLIAMS ARTHUR P WRIGHT JOSE YBANEZ
HOSEA D ADAM DONALD ALLAWAY AQUILA BAKER CHARLES W BAUMAN JERRY W BELL
DAVID L CHAPMAN JAMES L CHERRY STANLEY G COX JOHN E DIECKMANN FELIDELPHIO B GOMEZ
ANDRE R GUILLET CLARENCE E HAGEY LEE D HARLEY BURNIE HARRIS RONALD E HARRISON
RAYMOND C JAJTNER JAMES KENNEDY JR ERNEST E LANE JR ISMAEL LEBRON-LOPEZ MICHAEL G MERRIMAN
WILLIAM J MOORE ANTONIO PARADA-BARRERA ONSBY R ROSE RANDOLPH C SCOTT ALBERT R WILSON
FRANK T SHELTON PRESTON J SNYDER JIMMY G STEWART JERRY M WALL ASTER WATTS
JOSEPH D PELLEGRINO KENNY W BULLARD HARRY E CRISSEY JR MICHAEL D EULER EMMET L JOHNSON
KENNETH ALSTON ROGER E JOZWIAK GARY S KADETZ JASPER L KEEN MICHAEL R KIEHL MICHAEL W KILROY
IRVIN D KNIPPELBERG ANGELO A LONZO GREGORY B NORTON LEON R SCRIBER MARK F UDELL
FRANK MUSCYNSKI WILLIAM R SUTHERLIN RICHARD A UNGERECHT LLOYD G WIEGEL CLINTON R BROWN AUSTIN L DRUMMOND
WILFORD P COLLER DAVID L CROW JACK E GARDNER MICHAEL O GATWOOD DANIEL KNARIAN JAMES F BROOKS JR
GENE M LUTZ GILLIAM MOORE DENNIS L NELSON CARTER REDMOND JAMES H REESE
LAWRENCE S ROBBINS STANLEY I SAGON PHILIP J SERNA OBIE C SIMMONS GEORGE H STAHL JR
RICHARD L WILDMAN WILLIAM F WINTERS RONALD E ANGE ROBERT L BENJAMIN HENRY BENTON
ROSTEN W BISHOP THEODORE J BRADSHAW CLARENCE R BRAME JAMES J BROPHY
LOUIS BUCKLEY JR ROBERT L CLOUTIER DAVID S CROCKER JAMES P DE BRULER
GLEN E WALLACE BARRY W DUFF JAMES W ELENBURG JAMES H FURR CHARLES A GAINES JOHN R GODERRE
BRUCE F GRIFFIN ROBERT L GUERIN PAUL J HARRISON MICHAEL L KING MARSHAL J O'NEAL
ANTONIO P MACIMINIO HAROLD MACK JR DAVID P MANNERS PETER F MEAD PETER R NIEMCZUK
MARVIN K PENLAND WALTER W PHELPS DANIEL G POST DON J RICHARDS CHESTER SCHAPANICK
EDWARD SHEPHERD A V SPIKES JOEL TAMAYO WADE TASTE WALTER A THACKERSON JR
CLEVELAND VINES PAUL D WALKOWSKI LONNIE C WILLIAMS DAVID J CANALES ROBERT H CRUM JR
MICHAEL G CRYAR MICHAEL E DE VOE CHARLES R DEAN JR JOSEPH W DURKIN JR LAWRENCE E FOSTER
THOMAS C GARRETT III GERALD D HOOVER DAVID M JOLLEY JR JOHN E KOCHENSPARGER ALLAN J KOROM
RALEIGH L GODLEY RICHARD F LEASE GERALD E METCALF GARY E PERKINS ALLEN J RITTER
ANGEL RODRIGUEZ-ESTREM CARL C SPANGLER MICHAEL VINASSA DUANE A WAKLEE JOSEPH WILSON
CLYDE A CROW GARY L CALDWELL WILLIAM D GILL FLOYD W HAMILTON DEWEY W KELLEY LOUIS RIDINGS
WILLARD R RYAN FERMIN SALDANA JR STANLEY W SALYER WILLIAM C WRIGHT JR JOHN M BATISTE
THOMAS R ANNIS JIMMY C BETHEA MAURICE A CASEY PAUL L CONRAD JOHN GREEN JR WILLARD D KEERAN
JOSEPH A MACHOWSKI NELSON R MOORE LARRY E CRANFORD TOMPKINS G FOSTER RONALD L GUYER
ROBERT G HUNTER JOHN D KRAMER ARVIN D PENNELL RICHARD H ROYER BOBBY J BAREFIELD
CECIL A BROOME JR JAMES FERRO BENNY E FOSTER GARY A GLANDON TERRENCE H GRIFFEY
GORDON E GULLETT JOHN H MORGAN WILLIAM R REILLY ROBERT SMITH JR THOMAS J WINKELVOSS
GREG WEAVER EUGENE W CASWELL LARRY L GOAR BILLY R MOFFETT JOSEPH L RAPP
CHARLES E STUART JIMMY R BALL MICHAEL T GLYNNE JAMES A HARKLESS ROY M JONES THOMAS M KOCH
JACK R KOONE PHILIP N MADDOX MICHAEL W MULICK LEROY ROBINSON ALDON M ASHERMAN JR
JOHN F BARRY VICTOR D BERMEA DAVID B BRANDON JR GORDON M BRIGGS JAMES W BRILES
THOMAS W BRITTON JR THOMAS D CAMPBELL CHARLIE A CARDEN JAMES E CASALE CLEMENT S CASTALDO
SHELDON R COHEN ROBERT A CORKILL RICHARD E CROWE TERRENCE J DALEY DARREL G DORMAN
DONALD J EVANS ARAMIS GONZALEZ-PEREZ JAMES R HEATH LYLE D HOLLOWAY BILLY J HOLT
DAVID W JOHNSTON R B MARCHBANKS JR NOEL D MARR RICARDO L MORENO RICHARD R ROUNDTREE
JAMES J MACKENNA DONALD MCCONNICO JERRY L NOLAND BILLY R PATRICK ERNEST G PAUL
LEONARD E PEACOCK WALLACE E PILSON ROLAND A PROVENCAL RONALD RALICH ROY J RICHARD
WILBUR R LUCAS ROGER E RODRIGUEZ WALTER J SALLEY EDWARD C SEXTON WALTER B STEVENS
JAMES H STEWART JR SYLVESTER SWINFORD JR JEFFREY G TYNE EARL K TYNES CHARLES E WALKER
WALTER J WETZEL KENNETH W WICKEL DANIEL S BRITTAIN FRANCOIS J BUILAERT GARY A HADNOTT
ROSS A BROWN FREDERICK C BULLINGTON DELNO B COLLINGSWORTH KEVIN M FLAHERTY CARL D VIOLA
THOMAS E COLLINS DARROL O NELSON CHARLES E NICASTRO JOHN R RIDDLE BOBBY J ALBERTON
DARL D BENNETT THOMAS F CASE WILLIAM R EDMONDSON JAMES GRAY DONALD C GREEN
EDWARD R HANSEN ELROY E HARWORTH NED R HERROLD RONALD C KINSKY LEONARD J KROSHUS
DAYTON W RAGLAND LEWIS C ROLLINS ARMON D SHINGLEDECKER MARTIN W STEEN PHILLIP J STICKNEY
EMMETT R MCDONALD HAROLD J ZOOK GERALD W BAYLES MICHAEL D BURT EDWARD S KOPIK
CHESTER A LUTGEN GARY A MILLER FRANK A RAZO PETER F SCHRAMM JOSEPH W SCHUSTER
JIMMIE L SCOTT KENNETH B SYKES ARTHUR BROXTON JR MIGUEL CASTRO-CARRASQUI DELBERT L RYAN
JERRY L FIELDS ROBERT E GAREY THOMAS O GILBERT GERALD C HUNSBARGER III JIMMIE C HUTCHERSON
DOUGLAS M BURNETT HOWARD A MESOYEDZ HAROLD B NELSON LE R PRAIRIE JOSEPH F ROSATO

PANEL 8E

GEORGE D WEEKS RALPH W CASPOLE RUSSELL T CHRISTIAN RICHARD E DABNEY JR
DEBROW DOZIER JOHN O FINNICUM HEZEKIAH GEORGE JERRY W HARMON LUTHER L ROSE
JORGE L ISALES-BENITEZ DONALD L JOHNSON GARTH W KECK JR RUSSELL E KRAUSE THEODORE E KRYSZAK
RICHARD MADDEN JR RUSSELL D MARTIN HAROLD E MULLINS MELVIN T NISHIYAMA CARL S PARKER
STEPHEN H GAYMON HARDING E SMITH SR ERVIN WARREN WILLIAM J WILSON EDGAR B BURCHELL III
DENTON W CROCKER JR PHILIP K DORN GARY J FOSTER CHARLES W GOBER JR WAYNE HYDE
JAMES N SPANGLER EVERETT E LIGHT JEROME W LITKE JAMES LYONS JR RUSSELL E METZGER GARY N NELSON
GEORGE PENDLETON JR CLIFFORD L ROBINSON JACK A SCHNEIDER MILTON J SEU JOHN D SMITH
BENNY T STOWERS GERALD STEED HERSCHEL R WARD MARTIN L WATKINS GARRY WRIGHT FRED E BAILEY
THOMETT D CAMPBELL MICHAEL P DONLON BILLY E GIPSON JOHN P GUERIN DOUGLAS W HOGGE
ELBERT R HUBSCHMITT JR RUFUS L JAMES DONALD F LEUTHOLD BRUCE E MANSFIELD ANTONE P MARKS
HUGH R NELSON JR JERRY D OLDS LESTER L ROBERTS ARTHUR J RUSSELL ALLEN F SCRANTON JR
ELDON C VAN BEBER EPHRAIM VASQUEZ WILLIAM W WEBB CHARLES J WISNIEWSKI JR FRANKLIN W SMITH
THOMAS J FALLON JR MAXIMO P FERNANDEZ VARL E FULFORD MICHAEL J GALBRAITH EDDIE GREEN
ERNESTO DOMINGUEZ WILLIAM D HOPSON RICK L KNIGHT PAUL P PENNINGTON DAVID BASHAW
JERRY D CARTER MARK L CORRIE DAVID L DODSON ROBERT L EMERSON CHARLES S FRANCO
DAVID Z GARCIA RICHARD GARCIA ROBERT B HEMNES TERRY F HUSTON JOHN C JACOBS
JOHN B LASKEY WILLIAM G NORBERG IRA H PERKINS JR MIGUEL A RIVERA ROBERT L SANDNER
RICHARD T TRUJILLO WENDELL O CHATFIELD EDWARD E CHRISTIE REUBEN L CLARK JR ROGER L CONNER
DONALD E COOK JAMES I COURTNEY ARTHUR W DRYNAN DEWEY L FERGUSON AVERY G SMITH
JORGE L FERNANDEZ ROCKFORD W GODDARD PHILLIP H HOLMES JR DAVID B KISER ANTON L MUHM
ROBERT A HILL KENNETH N MACBETH LESTER E MACDONALD ELADIO R MARROQUIN JR DELANEY E MILLER JR
MICHAEL E O'GUINN JOHN R OAKEY DAVID M OLAND GEORGE R PENDYGRAFT TERRILL G PETERSON
FRANCIS E DAILEY FRANCIS C RUMMEL MICHAEL A SHARP PHILLIP R SMITH JOSEPH TORZOK
CHRIS C VURLUMIS THOMAS L YOHN JAMES H BAKER JR WILL P BARTON II ROBERT I BUSH
ALLAN E COMBS DONALD W CONN JR LAWRENCE J DEISHER JOHN T DIXON JOSEPH R ELLMAN
JAMES E FARRAR JR EDWARD T FRODSHAM EDWARD GARCIA ROBERT HANNA ROGER D JACKMAN
EARL W GOODALL GEORGE A MORNINGSTAR ROBERT J PHILLIPS MELVIN REEDER THEODORE J SHORACK JR
JAMES E SHUYLER CHARLES V TURLEY RALPH G WILLIAMS WALTER WILLIAMS JR TOM E BOREN
GREGORY T BUCZYNSKI PETER D GEOGHEGAN EDWARD A IYNDELLIN WARD W MILLS JR MICHAEL T MURPHY GEROLD SCHAEFFER
DAN B PACKARD CHARLES W ROOTH JOHNNIE P SAWYER PAUL F SHOGAN
TERENCE R TANGEN MAX V VASQUEZ III KENNETH G WEIGHTMAN JR LARRY M WIGINTON TERRY L WILES
DERWOOD D STEIGLEMAN JR DONALD C WYLES KENNETH A BABB KENNETH J BOSSIE DANNIE G BRASWELL
RONALD J BRISSETTE DENNIS E BROWN DAVID G BRYAN HENRY BURCH WILLIAM J CALDWELL
THOMAS S CAMERON THOMAS W CHATBURN III WILLIE COLE JR HAROLD T COOKE ERNEST L DURAN
GRADY L ELDER CHARLES E FORD MICHAEL A GARRIS JAMES E HILL LOUIS A JEFFERSON
DONEL R JOHNSON OLIVER JOHNSON GLEN D LOFTON JERRY W LOONEY HERMAN R MENEELY
JOHN E MILLER RICHARD A MITCHELL STANLEY L MOORE TIM A NOE CLAE T NORMAN
JAMES W PHAIR ROY S PITT JACK R PRICE HARVEY J PROFITT RONALD RICHARDS GORDON H BLEXRUDE
JESSIE E SHANNON CHARLES H SHELTON RALPH SIMON DAVID W STEWART MICHAEL T SUKARA
DENNIS R TABOR JOHN R THOMPSON FRANZ X WALLNER J C WILLIAMS RICHARD T ARMSTRONG
DOUGLAS A CLESTER GREGORY J HARRIS THOMAS J KENNEDY JR JAMES T LOCKRIDGE RENE C LOPEZ
RONALD C LOVETT CHARLES W PARSONS ROBERT A POWELL KENNETH E SOMERO BILLY WILLIAMS
CHARLES W BURKART JR JOHN D COOK WILLIAM DELY DONALD A DI SAPIO WILLIAM H GAMBLE
RICHARD L HOGLE EVERETT O KERR GEORGE F LAZAR RUDOLPH A NUNEZ JONATHAN C ROKER
RALPH R SMITH JOHN D YOUNG JACK A BAKER PETER J BRANCATO JR WILLIAM G DUTCHES
JOSEPH H FOREE GEORGE G GIERAK JR JOHN T GLANVILLE JR PAUL M HASLINGER BENNIE R LAMBTON
RONALD M PADILLA GEORGE E PERRY JOSEPH E SHEARIN THOMAS E CARNEY ROBERT H CARR JR
BILLY R FOSTER NATHANIEL HUBBARD RAYMOND H HUDSON LAWRENCE W SHAY JR THOMAS W SHAY
NORBERT G SIMMONS JAMES C WALLACE NORMAN R WILSON CHARLES G WOODS JOHN T ADAMS
GEORGE D BIRDSELL DONALD I BOWERS LEO B BUCKHOLDT GEORGE W COTTRILL JR WILLIAM J GOODSELL
IGNATIUS CARLISI EDWARD S DANIELS GEORGE R DARLING THOMAS D GLAWE TERRY W LORENZ
FRANK E LYONS ALCADIO N MASCARENAS JAMES O MCKINNEY RONALD W MEYER JOSEPH E PACKER JR
TERRY P REDIC RUSSELL J SISLEY NORMAN SPENCER JERRALD R THOMPSON PHILIP VILONE JR
MICHAEL WATERS OLEY N ADAMS ROBERT A CAIRNS RALPH B COBBS CURTIS D COLLETTE
JACK I DEMPSEY THOMAS J EVANS LEON D FLANDERS STANLEY J FRENG CONNIE M GRAVITTE
GENE K HESS CLAIBORNE P MCCALL EDWIN T O'CONNOR JR EDWARD L ROMIG GERALD W WARZECHA
MARCELINO SANTOS-VEGA M J SAVOY DONALD E SIEGWARTH JOSE S SIMBOLA CLEMENT O STEVENSON JR
GEORGE E PERRY III MICHAEL VANCIL BARRY R WALKER LARRY E WASHBURN TERRY W BUCKLER
LOUIS X CABRERA JR SAM CANADA JR CLARENCE G FORMAN ELTON O HARRIS JAMES D HONEYCUTT
WILLIAM JONES JR MICHAEL A NAJARIAN FRANK B PARISH ROBERTO ROCHA JR WILLIAM K STOLL JR
EDWIN R TRAVNICEK RICHARD A BRADLEY GARRY L BURGESS ROBERT W GOLDEN VINCENT G MOELLER
ROY C MCEWEN CHARLES E MCRAE KENNETH R TEMPLES JOSEPH S VESELY JR ERNEST ALSTON JR
REINER W BIEROWSKI HAROLD E BOETCHER CURTIS H BULLARD LONNIE E CLEMENTS ROBERT M COOKE
LELAND R COTTIN FLOYD C DENSON FRED T EARLES MARTIN P EASTHAM JAMES L EMMART
WAYNE L EVITT GABRIEL GALLEGOS LARRY F HERRIN RICHARD HINTON DAVID G HUTCHINGS
ROBERT C JOHNSON RONNIE L JONES JOHN R MCDONOUGH PATRICK T MOONEY ALTON B MUNN
JAMES R MCILWEE GARY E OOTHOUDT FREDERICK A PHOEBUS RICHARD F ROACH EDWIN C ROLLINS
GARY L SANGSTER DONALD F SCHMIDT BOBBY SENTERS MARC A SIVATTA DONALD R SMITH
EDWIN H SORNSON JOHN W TUNNELL EDDIE VASQUEZ RICHARD E WHITING GEORGE A WILLIAMS
MILLARD L WILLIAMSON JAMES G CONDON III JOSEPH H COOPER JR WILLIE FRANCIS JR MICHAEL R HALL
BRUCE M JOHNSON BENJAMIN F LIDDELL III JOHN R MARKILLIE WAYNE H NELSON FREDERICK L RYAN
MANUEL A PEREZ-RIVERA MICHAEL J SOTH JOHN B SULLIVAN III FREDRICK H VESTER CHARLES K WRIGHT
ROBERT C BOICOURT EDMUND D BRENT JR WILFRED A DOIRON JAMES R DUFAULT JAMES E FULLER
ERVELL M GUEVARA THOMAS N HARRISON CHARLES H HILL CECIL HUYLER GARY A ISAACSON
WILLIAM M KELLY WILLIAM LUTZ LARRY L PAGE ROBERT A PEACH ROBERT L REYNOLDS JR
GARY H ROGERS SYLVESTER A SCHAEFER RUDOLPH C SELENKA JR WARREN P SMITH JR BILLY E STEVENSON
THOMAS E SULLIVAN PRISHARDO J TORRES NATHANIEL WILSON JAMES F BALBIRNIE HARRY J BELKNAP
JOHN W CABRERA SHERMAN CHAPMAN JR JAMES R CUMBERPATCH JR FRANCISCO LUNA FREDDY L SAPP
WILLIAM DOWDY ANTHONY GILMORE DELL G HAMPTON JOHN E HAMPTON RICHARD L IANNICELLI
BENTFORD BENNETT JERRY J JOHNSON JAMES T LESTER RALPH E MANNING ANTONIO MORADO
RAYMOND M CARLEY ERNEST E MCALUM GEORGE L MCWILLIAMS HONORIO RAMIREZ JR GENE B SPENCER
RUDOLPH WHITAKER CHARLES C WILLIAMS LARRY D WILLIAMS ADELL A ALSTON ALLAN J ALTIERI
LLOYD H BRAYE WILLIE L COLLIER WILLIAM ELLIS JR DONALD C ESTES OCTAVIO FEBUS VALENTIN G MATULA
ALLAN A GANZY BILLY M GREEN JOHNNY HICKEY GARY R HOLT AARON M HOPKINS DONALD D HANSEN
BOBBY J JAMES RONNIE C JONES KENNETH R KAAIHUE JOHN H KENNY WARREN O KNEPPER JR
RICHARD F LA BARBERA CARL J LATOUR LAWRENCE P LE BRUN LAWRENCE F NYMAN ROBERT D OWEN JR
MELVIN MCCRAY JURIS PUDULS ROBERT W REID HORACE P ROGERS JR LUIS S SANTIAGO
WILLIAM R SAVAGE GORDON R SKYLES WILLIAM E STEIER DELMAS S TOWNSEND CARROLL L TUTHILL
HOLLIS A WALKER JERRY H WILLIAMS LAWRENCE D WOODS HENRY H ALLMAN RONALD L HERBSTRITT LARKIN O VALLERAND
MILLER J BOURG EDWARD G CREED DENNIS J CULLEN ROBERT H DANNEELS CECIL E DAW MELVIN E TAYLOR
CHARLES M EDWARDS THOMAS C EDWARDS ROBERT R EGGLESTON RONALD K GRAY
ISAAC JONES LAWRENCE D KESLER CHARLES W MARIK BRUNO L MARTIN WILLIAM MORRIS
RONALD G MCBETH WILLIAM R REESE JR DAVID E REYNER GARRY L REYNOLDS SANTOS SANCHEZ
ANDREW T BEST RICHARD L STRANGE ERNEST W STREHLE ROBERT D WUERTZ EDWARD C ZIMMERMAN JR
FRANKLIN ALSTON JR ALBERTO A AVALOS HAROLD G AYERS WILBURN H BOYD CHARLES C BROWN
IVOR E BUNCH JAMES COLEMAN JR THOMAS E EDDY RONALD C FORSBACH DONALD E GORE
HACHIRO IMAE LEWIS J JACKSON JACK D JOHNSON ALLAN H MACDONALD JAMES L NORTHROP
HARRY T RICHARDSON JR JOHN M RISNER DOUGLAS ROYSTER LEDELL WILLIS FREDRICK M BINDER
DONALD R BRYANT JACKIE L GOFORTH FRANK L GONDERMAN MARVIN HARRIS JERRY W MCNABB
ARTHUR KEEN BILLY J NAVE EDWARD K PARESA RICHARD T PERRIN GALEN D PETERSEN JOHN S SEELEY
GENE A SMITH DONALD E STAHL ROBERT T VERGANO LOUIS E WALTON ARTHUR M WOOD
MANUEL ALICEA JR MICHAEL F BINGHAM DONALD E BYRUM JAMES W CAPUTO ANTHONY F CAVALLI
GERALD L CROSBY HARRY G DYER CARL E FELL CARL R HUTSON ADRIEN M JORDAN-MOLERO
PEDRO L LAMOURT-TOSADO ARTHUR G MITCHELL RUSSELL L PRICE GERALD R ROLF LAWRENCE F RUNEY

WILLIAM H SCHEIDT JAMES A TAZELAAR THOMAS H WOLFE LELAND W ALBURY JR MALCOLM C BERRY
JOHN J BERTHEL ROBERT M BOWMAN RICKEY D CASTLEMAN CARLOS W CONRAD JESSE C FELDER
HARRY B FORBES FREDERIC W FRITTS DENNIS H GINTER FRANK GRAVES RICHARD L HIDO
TOMMY R JONES ALBERT R POTTER WALDEMAR D SHOWALTER LESLIE R SMITH MOSE SMITH JR
FRANCIS G STEVENS PAUL J SURETTE ROY D BAILEY RICHARD R BANKS DAVID E BAUN
ARNOLDO J CARDENAS DAVID A FERRARO JERALD D FRITZ DAVID K HIGHT PETER E ODENWELLER
RICHARD P HOLIEN DONALD R LONG CHARLES H MILLS BOBBY L MORDEN JOHN D MORGAN
WILLIAM R BUCKLEY RONALD O PATTERSON ERNEST E PEREZ FRANZ G PREDIGER DANNY L SMITH
EARL SMITH EDDIE K WILLIAMS HARRY J YOST RICHARD D ABOLTIN PETER W BAXTER ABRAHAM SCHWARTZ
RONALD W RINGWALL LARRY K DEAL PETER P DOMIANO HAROLD D GIBBS PAUL M LONG GARY N MIYAKE
RICHARD W MCGEE BENJAMIN ORNELAS CHARLES H PETERS JOHN H RABER ROY R ROGERS
ROBERT C WILLIAMS JOHNNY WOODSON JAMES B BARTLETT GERALD L BERG JAMES D BOWERS
HANSEL BROWN DENNIS L BURTON ANTHONY CAPRIGLIONE CHARLES L CHATMON LANCE J CLEVELAND
LAWRENCE J FRAHMAN ELIAZAR E GARZA DAVID E HERBERT NARCISO F HERRERA MICHAEL F JACK
BERNARD E CURTIS JOHN E HOPKINS CHARLES V HOWARD LINWOOD B KRUG LESLIE I MORALES-LUCAS
GARY L NEWPORT FRANK OGBURN JR RUSSELL J PEEK JAY W REYNOLDS RAYMOND L RICHARDSON
JAMES E VAUSE JAROLD A VEACH JAMES E WILSON FRED B BECKERMANN JR CHRISTOPHER E BROOKS
CURTIS BROCKINGTON TOMMIE J CAMPBELL ROBERT P CATLING JULIUS COLLINS JR DONALD J FAWCETT
DANIEL L FIELDS ROBERT H GAGE EUREY L HATCHETT HAZE HOWARD III JOE E JOHNSON ERIC RIBITSCH
HERBERT LAPP WILLIAM E LEWIS RAYMOND L MCGARVEY ROBERT J MORRIS GILBERTO SOTO-GARCIA
DAVID J PHILLIPS JR RALPH J RENO WILLIAM D TAMMEN BERNARD G WALINSKI TERRY K WILKINS
EDWIN J MACNAMARA KENNETH L SCHAEFER HARRY J STATECZNY JR DAVID R STONE JASPER D STURDIVANT
JAMES T NOSS HAROLD B REED ESTEBAN M ALVAREZ LARASETT E AVINGTON JR CHARLES L MOORE
JOHNIE L BLOUNT JR NORRIS J DENTON STEPHEN C FORREST JAMES O GREGORY JR MICHAEL E HOPKINS
GUILLERMO T BONILLAS RAYMOND C GRIFFITHS ROBERT D RICHARDSON ELMER W SCARBOROUGH
GLENN E SPRATLEY DANIEL W STUTLER DAVID W TERRELL HOMERO E TIJERINA RAYMOND WIDMANN
THEODORE WILLIAMS JR CURTIS E BINION MICHAEL M BLANTON JAMES G BROWN DOUGLAS FLORES
WILLIAM F FREESTONE PAUL H PHILLIPS NEIL G REUTER JERRY A ROBERTS WILLIAM C FRALEY
WILLIAM H MAYHAIR WILLIAM A WILL ROBERT R BODE CHARLES W DAVIS ROOSEVELT HESTLE JR

PANEL 9E

PHILIP B HINES GILBERT V KEMPLE JR JOHN F LEE KENNETH C BOUDREAUX
ROGER L LESLIE GARY A MACHADO WILLIAM R MINDACH CHARLES E MORGAN MICHAEL PIASCIK
RILEY JERMANY JAMES A RICHARDSON CONRAD W SHAINA FREDDY L TORRANCE HOWARD J ANDUHA
MARSHALL BURKE JR JOHN B DAVIS III ANTHONY J GUSTIN A T HOWELL WARREN W COBLEY
JOHN L KUKTELIONIS BOOKER T MCCOY JR HORACE G MITCHELL JR HEYWARD W NEDD VICTOR L PAINE
WILLIAM V PHARRIS DENNIS L PHILLIPS CURTIS H RANSDELL ROBERT J RUGGIERO DANNY R SIMPSON
JOHN W HAMM G W WHITAKER LAWRENCE C HARRIGAN MILLARD W LEHMAN RONALD L LONGANECKER
CHARLES C ROBERTS CHARLES E SCHAFER JIM L SMITH ULYSSES ALFORD FREDERICK G ATKINSON
STANLEY W BAKER ROBERT L BARNES JAMES D BENWAY HANS K BRETSCHNEIDER BILLY R CABY
CHARLES E CLARK CHARLES O DE JEAN III EMMETT A DOUGANS ROBERT F FERGUSON CHARLIE FRAZIER JR
JAMES L GRAVES JERRY L HANDLON WILLIE HARPER JR EDWARD L HARRIS JESSE E HERRERA
WALLACE HYMAN BOBBY KING DONALD H MOSES ELVIN PRICE JOHN Q QUESENBERRY
JOHN V RAAUM ROBERT N TETREAULT HOMER E TISCHLER KENNETH L VAN LEW THOMAS J VONTOR
DANIEL L WILSON SHERRILL V BROWN MICHAEL T FITZPATRICK DANNY C KEATON ROBERT W KING
ALBERT F KLESTINEC JR KENNETH C KRAUS JERRY L LEONARDI FRED A LIND HANS P LUTZ
ROBERT W PECK ROBERT P SOUSA JOHNNY R TAGMAN JAMES Q AYDLETT EUGENE JOLLY
JACKIE D JONES ROBERT B MANN RAMIRO MANRIQUE JR DAVID E NANCE ANGELO J SFERRAZZA
GEORGE H WILKINS WILLIAM LEON BRAD W MORAND WILLIAM L ROBERTSON CHARLES R WILLIAMS
GARY L SUNDET GEORGE S YOHNNSON MICHAEL G BARTON RICHARD J JANKOWSKI FELIPE VILLANUEVA
FREDERICK A WATHEN DAVID L COX JR MARSHALL F KIPINA ROBERT G NOPP RICHARD G SCHROEDER
JOHN W SCOTT DONALD E WOOLBRIGHT ORSON H CASE NARCISO R CERNA JR PAUL G HENDRIX
ANDREW P CHAMAJ PAUL R CHAMBERS JAMES W CHERRICK JAMES J CONNELL ROBERT J CROCE
RONALD K CULLERS MICHAEL A CUNNION RICHARD W DEMERS MARK V DENNIS WILLIAM L DOUGLAS JR
ANTHONY G CALVERLEY MICHAEL A GOODEN RICHARD S HOWIE JAMES L LEDIN WILLIAM J LILLY
THOMAS A MCCONAHY JOHN N MORRIS SAMUEL L REED JAMES M REID RALPH V RENAULD JR
CARL W SCHLOEMER HEROLIN T SIMMONS LYNN SPANN STEPHEN S STRYCHARZ JR GERALD E STUBSTAD
ROBERT R TELFER ISAIAH H WILSON JOHN D CAREY CHARLES D CROWE NORMAN E DAWSON JR
JAMES M GODSEY ROY D HEASTER WILLIAM F LA BRECQUE JR RICHARD A MAUL RICHARD S MOHN
GENE S MCMULLEN LARRY E POTTER JESSE B STRIBLING LLOYD B HASKELL JR JAMES L HOGGARD
DANIEL L MORT JAMES D NEWCOMB CHARLES E SMITH STANLEY R SMITH ANTHONY TREVISANO
RICHARD J ANASIEWICZ MICHAEL J BANOVEZ JR LEWIS C BARNARD GARY W BARTLOW RAFAEL E BEECHE
ROBERT H BUTLER JR ULYSSES C COOPER RAMON DESCHAMPS JOSEPH W DUNN PATRICK P DWYER
JAMES W EDWARDS RONALD L EUNICE RONALD E HOEL JOHN T KYSER RUDOLPH H LEFEBVRE JR
CARL R MARRS PETE M MARTINEZ DAVID E PORTERFIELD DONALD J PRIEST MICHAEL R SMITH
JOHN C THOMAS THOMAS M WILLIAMS HEARNE W BEAVER JAMES BESCHEN CHARLES R MALBROUGH
JOHN R BOTTESCH KENNETH M BRANAMAN DANNIE J BREWINGTON THOMAS J BUTLER JR JOHN T DOIKE
RODGER D CLAWSON CHARLES H CRANE JAMES R CROLEY ROSA J DE LA JR TERRY A DENNISON
JACK M BROWN JR STEPHEN W DIAMOND BERNARD DILLARD CHARLES R FLEMING CHARLES L GETMAN
DALLAS E GREEN BOBBY R HOLLEY DAVID W HOLMES EUGENIO ROSADO-RODRIGUEZ ROBERT W RUHL
MEREDITH G HUBBARD LAMOND J JACKSON ALLEN L JELINEK RAYMOND E JOHNSON THOMAS B KEMERER
LEROY BARNES DOUGLAS H KNOTT JOHNNY F LONG CHARLES A MCGUIRK MICHAEL J MUMMEL
YOSHIWA NAGATO JOSEPH E NEWMAN LEROY E PETERSON PATRICK T QUINN JAMES M RADZELOVAGE
JOSE C GOSSE BERNARD A GREEN PHILIP H RATHE SIM H RIGGINS JR TURNER L THOMPSON JR
LAWRENCE H WILSON JR DARRYL G WINTERS STEPHEN A ZUKOV JAMES F ASKIN CLIFFORD S BRATCHER
JOSEPH L BYRNE JR STEPHEN M CAMPBELL TIMOTHY S DAVIES DAVID A DILLON S W GEORGE
CLIFFORD L CARPENTER DENNIS B EASLEY RONALD M FILKINS BRENT I GRIGGS EDWARD F HAP
CASCO D HOWELL LESTER JONES ROLF W JORGENSEN DOUGLAS M KYSER BILLY D NELSON
RONALD J KINKEADE DANIEL A LAMBDIN MERRILL R LEWIS JR ERNEST D MITCHELL WILLIAM H NELSON
COLIN K NICHOLS CRAIG R NOBERT BRADLEY A PEARSON DAVID E PETERS CHARLES S RIDOUT
DANNY L RUTHERFORD CHARLES W SMITH KENT A SMITH WALTER R TATE JR DONALD C WOODRUFF
DAVID L BERRY RICHARD BRIGHT WILLIE B CARY STEPHEN K DIBB DOUGLAS R FRENCH
JAMES X GILCH RICHARD D GILL JR THEODORE GRONOWSKI JR DENNIS L HARMON SAMUEL G HARRIS
LEO E HINTERLONG PEDRO MARTINEZ ROBERT E PULLIAM JR WILBERTO C SANCHEZ JOHN D TYLER
RICHARD F MCNICHOLS MARK E STOLTENBURG RAINFORD TIFFIN LARRY VAN CLIEF OSCAR C BELL JR
LARRY M BERRY JAMES W BETHEL ROY M BROOKS WALTER S BROWN EDWARD W BUTLER
HENRY H DELANO JOHN L DODSON MAXWELL S FRANTZ WESTON D MACLEAN ROY F MENO
DAVID L GAMBLE RICHARD A GILBREATH JOHN C HOLOKA RODNEY A JAMES PAUL W JOHNSON
MITCHELL E COX JOHN J FLEMING DENNIS A LA NORE DORRIS E PATTON JOHN W PERICH
RUSSELL E PESEWONIT PHILLIP M PIERCE JR JOHN W REAGAN JUAN D SANCHEZ CHESTER J SIMMONS
JOHNNIE E SMITH ROBERT E STALLINGS ROBERT J WELLS RODNEY W WESTCOTT GARLAND F WRIGHT
FREDERICK J YOUMANS FRED O BAUGH JR JAMES R BROWN DONALD G DAVENPORT MELVIN FORD
ROBERT F GEARY JR DANIEL M GUNN DAVID W HILL RICHARD D KALER JARVIS C LOWDER
THOMAS V MADISON SAMUEL T MORROW BENJAMIN B NEWSOM STEVEN O SCHULTZ ROBERT L WENGER
GENE T PEMBERTON WILLIAM W SMITH WILLIAM F VOHS ORVILLE D WELLS WILLIE W WILKERSON
ROBIN L ARNOLD BRUCE A BAKER RANDY D BROSNAN PRUITT H CHEANEY RONALD P COATES
GEORGE E COREY OSCAR CRUZ RICHARD J CURRIER JR LAWRENCE E DANIELS LAWRENCE E DENNY
GEORGE G DUKE FRANKLIN C EUCKER RONALD L FENSTERMACHER HUGH C GALBRAITH CHARLIE GRAY
JERRY L HAILEY DANIEL W HARMON WILLIAM H HAWKINS ROBERT M HULSE ROBERT M JOHNSON
JOE M KEMP STEPHEN R KITTLE DENNIS C KNUTSON NORMAN L KOOS JOSEPH S KOPFLER III
SIDNEY J MALONE JR CHARLES G MCINTOSH JAMES K O'LEARY RICHARD N PAYNE RONDA L RAGLIN
JAMES R NASH THOMAS F PRESBY DAVID P SPEARS PAUL J STRAUSSER ROBERT L STUDARDS
RONALD E TINSLEY RAYMOND L TRUDEAU CLIFTON B ANDREWS DAN W BEARGEON WILLIS S BOWMAN JR
GARY N BASS ROBERT J BOKINA DAVID CLEELAND EVERETT A CURRENCE ARTHUR H DYVIG JR
CHRIS F FABRIS JOSE D FLORES MICKEY R GRABLE CHARLES D HATFIELD SAMUEL L HUFFMAN
GERARD M KIESWETTER LEO C LAWSON ROBERT J LYSAGHT ROBERT C MOORE ROBERT R MYLES
JACK PITTMAN DONALD E SCHUMACHER BENNY SENA MILES T TANIMOTO PAUL P VANOVER
JEROME C WINTERS PELLUM BRYANT JR JOHN E CHRISTIANSEN JR JOHN P HICKEY MARVIN C KILLIAN
STEVEN W MARTIN LORENZO C MAULDEN DALE W SCHMIDT JR STEVEN R SHERMAN JOSEPH M THOMAS
JOSEPH L VALLEE THOMAS WALKER DANNY W WANAMAKER JAMES W COLLINS SHELTON L EAKIN
ROBERT J HENNEBERG JOSEPH F HUNT JOE D KEGLEY AGAPITO MOLINA JR GEORGE E THREATS
JAMES L MCCRYSTAL MELVIN W MCDOWELL CARLOS D MOORE BARRY L MOTT HAROLD W REINBOTT JR
JACK J HIEBER JOSEPH C SAMPSON JR JERRY L SCHEMEL ECKWOOD H SOLOMON JR RUTHERFORD J WELSH
ERSKINE B WILDE JIMMY D BACCUS WILLIAM G MAIN JR ROBERT G MALONE JOHN H MCREE
REO OWENS RICHARD D POWER MICHAEL R SAMSON BENNY L SMITH PHILLIP N TROUGHTON
GALILEO F BOSSIO VIRGIL K CAMERON JUAN D CEPEDA VINCENT A CHIARELLO CLAYTON J LUTHER
MICHAEL F COOK DOMINIC A CORONA ROBERT J DI TOMMASO GALE H FELVER ROBERT O GARANT
WILLIAM R GOWER JAMES S HALL ROBERT E HOSKINSON DELMER L LAWS ROBERT V LEECH
BERNARD CONKLIN RAY S LONG JOHN M MAMIYA JAMES A MAXAM DON R SAIN LONNIE D HARTSOCK
HERBERT E SMITH RODNEY C UPCHURCH AKIRA YAMASHITA LEE G JOHNSON EDWARD MALINOWSKI
CHARLES E MCGARVEY LARRY T NELSON CLARENCE L SEXTON JOSEPH C BROWN RICHARD M HARTNELL
LEONARD J BIBBS KENNETH R CARTER GREGORIO M GARCIA RONALD F HOCK ALVIN HOPKINS JR
DANIEL Z POST JR JAMES STEWART JR LESTER A WRIGHT WILLIAM E ANDERSON WENDELL E CHURCHILL
ALLAN L COX GEORGE D CURRY ARTHUR T FINNEY FRANK J GUNDAKER RONALD H KAISER
RICHARD G KITNER JOHN C KWORTNIK JEFFERY L LEDFORD VICTOR MORALES BYRON D ORR
RONALD J RUSSELL ERNEST M SHUMAN JR BILLIE H SMITH DONALD D WALLACE TERRY D CRAIGHEAD
JOSE A RIVERA KENT L AMERINE LARRY K BARNER ROBERT G BURRELL LEONARD D DAVIS
DONALD T ERICKSON GLASCO J FRYAR WILLIAM H GARDNER JR DALE H GIBSON HARLIN HARRIS JR
WILLIAM J HENRY WILLIAM J HOBERT ISAAC E HUNT JR HARRY M KITCHENS HIRAM J KNIGHTON JR
MICHAEL T LEDEBUR HOWARD C MCCARTHY JR JAMES M MCDONOUGH JR EARL MELTON JR JUAN MUNOZ
JOHNIE W MCLAIN BENITO PEREZ DENZIL D PETTIT WILEY L PHILLIPS ALTON D PRICE ROBERT J KUZMANKO
DANNY D PRINCE FRED R SAIZ EDWARD M SIEBEN FRED H STILL GERALD F TRITTSCHUH
JOHN D ROECKL GEORGE G TRUELUCK LARRY E CLINTON HENRY L CRAMER EDWARD T CROOKS

GARY S FERGUSON ROBBIN A GOODWIN HERSCHEL C HOLT ROBERT M HOWELL JR CHARLES E HURD
ALVIN D HUTCHINGS SAMUEL R MOSER ERNEST E ORENDORFF JR FRANK W SELDEN RAYMOND A SHEPARD
JOHN R BURNS RODNEY W CASSELMAN RAYMOND J CHURCHILL JOE L HILL RAY E JOHNSON
DAVID L MANNING TIMOTHY A VELTMAN GEORGE L ELLIS JOHNNY W LLEWELLYN ANDREW M DUNCAN
TYRONE G BURSE RICHARD J WILLETT GERALD V EPPLEY DOUGLAS A JOHNSON CARL F MEIER
DOUGLAS T PATRICK LAWRENCE J PEAK AARON W COCHRAN BOBBY L EATON RAUL FLORES
CHARLES W FRYER ROBERT E GARRETT CLIFFORD D LA CHANCE RICHARD A MORAN ELLIOTT SIMMONS JR
GARY L WILLIAMS TONY L BAKKE RONALD L BELKNAP CLIFTON E BENNETT FRANK L BLEVINS
JUDGE BURROUGHS JR ORRIE J BUSKEY RICHARD J CALLEN BRIAN J CLUNE NORMAN E DECAREAUX JR
DONALD L CORBIN JAMES H FIFE JR MELVIN F FLOYD ERNEST GIBSON LAWRENCE H GOLBERG
CHARLES R GREENE DAVID C HAMPTON BENJAMIN N HAMRICK MARTIS L HAYNES RICHARD V IVES
ANDY JOHNSON JR DOUGLAS W JONES JOHN A KEMP JOHN J KOLZ AADO KOMMENDANT
VERNAL G MARTIN GEORGE E MATUSCSAK RICHARD W MEEHAN LESLIE D NICKELS ERIC R NORDMAN
JOHN P OLT ALFREDO OSTOLAZO-MALDONA MARK E PARKER DEREK B POPE ANDREW M SHERMAN
RICHARD W POWER CHARLES R POWERS RICHARD W ROY RICHARD A SCHAAF DENNIS R SCHMIDT
DONALD A SHERROD JOHN H SHETTERS GERALD S SIMONS FREDERICK STAFFORD BRADLEY H TATE
DAVID L THORPE CHARLES M WALLING CLAUDE F WEIDERMAN JACK A WELCH PATRICK E WYNNE
GLENN M FRIDDLE ALLEN J KAKUK RICHARD T KARGER DENNIS G TAYLOR JIMMY G BRAIS
EDDIE ACHICA ERNEST B AMADOR RICHARD P DONATHAN JAMES T ELROD DAVID L FAUGHT
ALBERT L FRENCH GARY F FUNN ERNEST P GULLEDGE JR DOUGLAS B HADDIX JOHN A HEIKA
ROBERT D HIGBEE WALTER P JACKSON LAWRENCE J KINDRED FREDDIE L KLECKLEY CHEVO G LARA
GREGORY M HOWARD RICHARD J MCSWEENY PHILLIP J MOOG ROBERT W OATES MELVIN ROLLE
RICHARD A SKINNER LAWRENCE T STEINER PAUL E SUDSBURY KENNETH E TASKER EVERETTE A THOMPSON
ROBERT T WALSH RICHARD W WILLIAMSON DAVID C BROSTROM JOHN A CARDOT AUBREY CAULEY
LARRY R DRISKELL JIMMY L HOCKADAY ROMEY E HUGHART JR WILLIAM E IRWIN TOMAS MARROQUIN JR
JERRY PHILLIPS DONALD L RICHARDSON JOHN D SMITH STEPHEN L WEISS THEODORE G WHITE JR
JAMES WRIGHT DAVID J ALLINSON DONALD CONSTANDE JOSEPH B CROWDER ROBERT O DAVIS
GORDON H DUNAWAY JOHN W EDGERLY ROBERT D FINDLEY RONALD E FRIZZELL LEONARD G GOROSPE
KENNETH B HAWLEY CLARENCE E JONES JR WALTER MULLER JR BLAIR C WRYE JOHN I JONES JR
JOHN D WYSZOMIRSKI WILLIAM F COAKLEY DAVID R DEVERS SR GILBERT FERRANTE KENT E GANDY
ERMAN M NEWMAN JR HARVEY W GILBERT PERCY W MCCLATCHY GERALD L MENTZER JOHN J O'NEILL JR

PANEL 10E

JOHN C PETTY II HARRY V PHILLIPS JR JAMES R RICE ROSARIO ROSA-SEIN
GARY L SARGENT BOBBY J SHOCKLEY JOHN C SMITH GARY L VINAS MICHAEL D WALLACE
RONALD L WOODS LAURIE L ALEXANDER WILLIAM M BALDWIN MICHAEL J BILLERO JR WAYLAND DUNN JR
DAVID B BRYANT DARYL R CORFMAN EDWARD J DALTON JR CURTIS A EATON CHARLES E FRANKLIN
FREDDIE B GLOVER ROBERT B HADDEN THOMAS W HANEY JAMES L MORRIS HARRY E OXFORD JR
JEFFREY B WAGMAN HECTOR S ACEVEDO JOHN F BOYCE HARRY G BRANNON FRED BROWN JR
HENRY BUTLER BOBBY J COFFELT WILLIAM M CROY MICHAEL C DUNDAS MANUEL L FONT
ALLEN G FRENCH CANEY GREEN STEVE W HARRIS JOHN L HAWKINS JR KENNETH HAWSEY
SANFORD L JACKSON JR JAMES T LANGLOIS BYRON N LUDWIG JAMES R MORLEY JAMES E PHILLIPS
JAMES R SECHREST DERRELL K SHARP JAMES E SHOWALTER JAMES A SKINNER FRED D SMITH JR
RAYMOND STEPTOE DONALD L SUMMERS WILLIAM E TAYLOR FRED L THOMAS RICHARD J VASCONCELLOS
RICHARD A WALTMAN CHARLES WHITE JOHN J BECKER JR ROBERT L DORSEY RAY FORDYCE
CARL T FUNKHOUSER DAVID E HALL CHARLIE D HOLLY ROBERT A SCHMID JEFFERY W SMITH
JOSEPH W BRAND BASIL P BRASS OSCAR R CARRIERE RONALD L CARTER JAMES A CHRISTY
WELLS E CUNNINGHAM WALTER J DECOTA JIMMIE B DENNEY GEORGE T KRUEGER DONALD M SINGER
FREDDIE KEMP FRANCIS W MACK JOHN R PEARSON ALLEN G WELLS JAMES E BOWERS
DON T ELLEDGE EUGENE J MAJURE JUERGEN A MAYER LYMAN A MCMULLEN EDWARD J RYKOSKEY
HERMAN L TROUPE DENNIS K BAHR MELVIN BARBER ERIC B BARROW JR DAVID E BRACKER
DALE L CLARK PETER DUGNESS ARTHUR H FIKE RONALD E HUMPHRIES BILLY W MACHEN
CHARLES L MAXIE CLIFFORD MCCALL LAWRENCE D WATKINS JR FRANK J AUGUST MICHAEL J COMPTON
LA M FISHER FRANK R GALLAGHER JOHN L HYMES PAUL J KAPPMEYER THOMAS T KASAI
THOMAS R KYLE JR SILBANO MORIN DANIEL E MORRIS ALLEN C ROCK WILLIE J TUCKER
RICHARD M MILIKIN III WILLIAM J SCHULTZ CARL W TUCKER JOSEPH H WALTON LARRY E WHITINGTON
DAN S ALLEN THOMAS A BLANEY WILLIAM R DAVIS JAMES R JOHNSON MATTHEW J KRIST
WILTON P LE BOUEF FELIX R RAMOS JR WILFORD L SPRINKLES HERMAN R ARMSTRONG PETER W BOORAS
BOBBY G CORSI HENRY V DEMPS CHARLES E HEATH MICHAEL LEWIS BILLY R OWENS
NORMAN G POITRAS JAMES L STONE ODIS THOMPSON WALKER N WEEKS LEROY F BARNES
PETER R BINGMAN RONALD L BOWMAN RONNIE L BRAY JAMES R BURDETTE FREDERICK K DEAVER
ANDRE L DUBE R V EDWARDS WILLIE J FRYER KENNETH L GLAZE PHILLIP H GRECO DOUGLAS T PALMER
WILLIAM L HARTLEY DONALD L HEASTON PAUL L HEATER NORMAN A HEFT CHARLES V PICCOLELLA
WILLIAM B HEPBURN RAYFON LOFTON WILLIAM B NORTHCUTT PETER QUILICI JR PAUL M REED
KENNETH P TIERNEY CLIFTON M WALTER DENNIS W WELLMANN CHARLES F AZARA JR JOHN D SANDERSON
WAYNE R BAKER DOUGLAS S DUBOSE BILLY J HARRISON JERRY W NYE ROBERT L PERRY
ANTHONY J ABRUZESE STEPHEN F SNYDER WILLIAM J TARSI PETER H ALBRIGHT TERRY L ALEXANDER
ALFRED J AMBURGEY ADRIAN J ANGLIM HERBERT S BECHTEL JOEL BERNSTEIN GYORGY J BESZE
RICHARD W BILLINGSLEY RAYMOND A BROOKS MAX L BRUBAKER WILLIAM H BULLARD DAVID E CARRAPY
JOSEPH E CANDEAS RICHARD D CLARK THOMAS E CLARK LEO C DIXON JOHN F DOYLE
JAMES E DOZIER OLIVER D DUMAS LAURENCE J DUNN JAMES W EMERSON RUSSELL A ENGREN
STANLEY C CAMPBELL CARL L GLASSCOCK DUANE T GREENLEE CARL R HARBIN JR VERNON G HOLLIFIELD
FRANK P HUDAK ELIAS M KAUHANE LARRY R KELM ARTHUR G KLIPPEN PETER S KNIGHT
SAMUEL J LARKIN DANIEL C LYKINS VERNON A MANHEIM JR RALPH L MASSEY HAROLD E MATSON
EDDIE O MCBROOM JR MATTHEW G MIEDEMA ROBERT F MONTEITH II RONALD P O'ROURKE J C WALKER JR
FELIX PACHECO MAXIE PATTERSON JOHN A RICH BENJAMIN C ROLLER JR JULIUS M SANDERS
WALTER W SHIPLEY JR FREDERICK B SKAGGS FORTUNE SMITH ROBERT L SMITH WILLIAM M SMITH JR
CHRISTOPHER C OAKES RAYMOND M THOMPSON RONALD L WATSON JAMES T BEASLEY JOHN J BLANTON
DANIEL L EARLENBAUGH JERRY W EDDY RICHARD A FRYE DONALD F GIBSON JULES T GIRTANNER
PEDRO R GUERRERO CHARLES E HUTCHINS JR CARY M KISH MARVIN D KOSTROSKI CLIFTON F VAUGHN
DONALD L LEHEW DONALD A LEWIS JAMES E REID ARTHUR B SCARBROUGH DONALD V STEIN
JOHN W JOYS CHARLES F WHITFIELD JR ARTHUR P WILLIAMS ELDRIDGE C AIGELDINGER FRANCIS J ALBERTS
ROBERT L BANKS RANDALL D HOWELL EUGENE R MOREAU KENNETH PARTLOW WILLIAM D PERKINS JR
RAYMOND J PONCURAK EVERETT P RUNNELLS STEPHEN J STEMAC ALEXANDER THARP LEO K THORNTON
MILTON L VAUGHAN JOHN E WATSON ROBERT L BABULA JOHN E BODENSCHATZ JR WILLIAM R TAYLOR
ROBERT C BORTON JR SAMUEL W BREWER DENNIS R CARTER THOMAS R COWLEY WILLIAM A FINKEL
WILLIAM R KELLEY PAUL B MADDEN JOSEPH A MAMMOLITTI JOSE L MORENO ARBAL ROLLINS JR
FRANK L BARBEE DONALD B SMITH VICTOR M TOSADO-HERNANDEZ JOHN R BALLARD MARTIN J CONRAD
VERNON E BRACKINS CHARLES T MCCORKLE RICHARD A OSTEEN JR BRUCE M SMITH WALTER L SMITH
WILLIAM R BUFF PATRICK J CONNORS JOHN T DEMALINE SAMMIE D HOFF KENNETH D ROBINSON
LARRY D TAYLOR ARTHUR E COMSTOCK JR JAMES B HEFFRON ROBERT H LERNER JAMES E METOYER
JAMES A TOOTHAKER ALTON WILKINS III MICHAEL CARROLL LOWELL G EINARSON GEORGE R REYNOLDS JR
COLINNA FEEMSTER JAY A HURD HUBERT C NICHOLS JR BRADFORD S NICKERSON NORMAN SCHMIDT
DAVID W ROBUSTELLINI WILSON C BICKLEY TERRENCE J CATHER JOSEPH Q CONWAY DANIEL J JANHUNEN
HAROLD J KOLLER EVEANS J STULTS STANLEY G TOLER ROBERT P ANDREWS ROY J BULTMAN
CHARLES T DAY DAVID C DE WITT THOMAS E DORAN DANIEL S FERRY THOMAS J MAULDIN
LORENZA GAYLES THOMAS D GRINNELL III CALVIN D HALFORD MAX G HARRIS ROBERT A MASTERSON
CLIFFORD S HEATHCOTE JR EDGAR P HEINEN GUY M HODGKINS MICHAEL H KESSEL CLYDE A LEEDS
ALBERT COLLINS ARTHUR A FREDA JR ELWOOD F NEAD JR JOHN F O'CONNOR DOUGLAS E RAUSCHENBERG
DONALD R ROBINSON WILLIAM P SIMMONS JOSEPH F TRUJILLO RODNEY J WILSON PATRICK J HANNON
DENNIS R HEIHN RALPH L KEELER FLOYD D KING SR ROBERT J LAWLOR PAUL E NADEAU
HARVEY L ROWLAND RAYMOND P SALZARULO JR EDWARD A SHELTON DON E ALLEY ROBERT BEDKER
BRUCE R BENNETT WILLIE E BUNTE WILLIAM B HILL JR MELVIN T HUFFINE WILFRED C JOHNSON JR
MACK A KNIGHT MANUEL LOPEZ LEONARD L MCQUINN JR WALTER S MOONEY RUSSELL B WALKER
NORMAN L BUNDY GARY D JEFFERIS GREGORY A LEIGHTON BILLY R MOORE STANLEY D PFROMMER MICHAEL G HAMILTON
RONALD G PIERCE TOMMY TRAXLER JR JAMES D BASHAM ANTHONY R BOSH
ALEXANDER V HERNANDEZ SAMUEL L KEMP JOSE A LOPEZ JOSEPH A PERRON JOHN H WALKER
WILLIAM B WILSON HAROLD ARNOLD WILLARD F BEVERLY GARY G BLOUNT JAMES W BRYANT
ANTHONY DE RIGGI MICHAEL T DEFIBAUGH CHARLES L HARTLAND WILLIAM O JUERGENS MYLES C SAVELL
WILSON J MAIZE CARL D METROS TOMMY MORALES FRANCIS X NAVA ROBERT L PERRY
PHILLIP A HERRERA JR WILLIAM E REEL MICHAEL G TANDY JAMES E WALLACE EMMITT J WILKEY JR
GERALD B BAGAASON RALPH D CARTER ALBERT C DOODY DAVID B EPHRIAM WOLFGANG W KARASCH
JAMES A BROWN JR JOHN R FISCHER WILLIAM R GILL JR WILLIAM J GILLETTE JOSEPH W MATT
EARL MATTHEWS JR JAMES POSTON KENNETH L SCOTT JAMES W SIMS LEROY WILLIAMS
DENNIS R BALFOUR ALEXANDER L BARNEY DANNY J DOLIN MICHAEL J DOMINGUEZ JOHN M SCOTT JR
LANDER R FRALEY JOHN F GREILING ALLAN H JORDAN THOMAS W KNIGHT THOMAS C NEWKIRK
JAMES A BRANSON HAROLD M PATENAUDE THOMAS G RICHMOND JEFFREY T ROE ALFRED L STONEHOUSE
LAWRENCE B TATUM EDMUND F THORNELL THOMAS C WALSH PAUL G WEIGAND JAMES E WEST
CHARLES A BAKER EARNEST L BEAM CHARLES W DEPP TIMOTHY L HONSINGER EARL E IRVING JR
IVARS LAMA LARRY R LAMBERT MICHAEL R MCLENDON JOHN E PADDOCK GLENN R PHILLIPS JR
JERRY R BLOOMER CHARLES R CROSLEY DAVID R FAULCONER DAVID P KUHNS DANNY L NAILLON
BENJAMIN P NORTON ROLANDO L SOLIZ STANLEY G SPRAGUE M L WILLIS CHARLES S ABEL
KENNETH R BERTSCH LAWRENCE T BORDEN ROBERT E BRYANT ROGER D CHILDERS CHARLES P ELLIS
ALONZA EVANS BENJAMIN B FINZER EDWIN R HIGGINS BRUCE E JASON HOWARD W KAISER
CHARLES LENARTOWICZ HARVEY L LEWIS MILTON B LUSTER RALPH G MAHONEY DONALD G DINGELDEIN
CHARLES M MARTIN JAMES L PALMER NEIL E RILEY JOHN P SKORO JR JOHN E STACKHOUSE
CORNELIUS P KENEALLY WILLIAM E TEER JERRY E COFFEY JESUS C DEL THOMAS C DELL
FELIX HERNANDEZ JULIUS F JONES HAROLD E KNUDSEN JR RICHARD R MILES CLARENCE W STODDARD JR
WILBUR E SWINDELL LARRY G THRASHER PHILLIP A BRANNON ROBERT D BUTLER WILLIAM E CATE
PAUL W FIELDER JOHN M GLASSER JOSEPH L MILLER DOUGLAS R MOWBRAY THOMAS J SCHOUVILLER
JEFFREY R SMALLIDGE LLEWELLYN A SMITH WALTER J SPAINHOUR JR JOSEPH H SULLIVAN JERRY T SUTER
LEONARD WITCHER III JAMES J ANGELIDES JOE M BALLIN JR BERNARD L BLITCH JERRY W MCCULLOUGH
EVERETT L BRACKETT BENJAMIN A CHITKO ALAN DANCE GERALD W EVENHUS HOWARD GARRETT

PANEL 10E (*Continued*)

CHARLIE GAUSE JAMES R GRIFFIN THOMAS H HAWKING BENJAMIN A KENISON JOSEPH M LIGHT
LARRY J BAKER ROBERT W MOODY DAVID L O'CONNOR JOHN O OQUENDO JR DOUGLAS F QUINN
WILBUR D RAINWATER EDWARD G RANKIN JOHN L ROBERTSON WILLIAM J ROHAN JOHN ROSETO
RONALD G STJOHN RICHARD S BATES NICHOLSON BROWN DENNIS L BUNTING LEONARD BURROW
ROBERT G CUMMINGS JR JOHN R CUMMINS JR FRANK F DOUGLAS DENNIS K EAKER ERVIN J EMERSON
MARK A FERGUSON GEORGE R FITZGERALD WILLIAM G FLEMING JR GLENN E INSPRUCKER SHERMAN L IVEY
JAMES A KIGER BILLIE D LANDERS HAROLD P LEAPHART JOHN R LEE DAREL D LEETUN
JAMES A LOCKWOOD JOSEPH B MACK JR CHARLES E MACMICHAEL EDWARD D MCCANN GARY E MCCASLIN
RONALD MCCRACKEN ALFRED MCPHERSON MICHAEL C NATIONS ALAN J O'BRIEN GEORGE B PEARSON III
EDWARD RAMOS MICHAEL C REED ROBERT E ROCKY CLAIBORNE L SHAW WILLIAM F SIEGERT
ATLAS J SMAY CHARLES E STOKES MICHAEL E SURWALD ARTHUR WATSON JR DONALD L ANDERSON JR
JAMES T BAYNE DAVID R BEATTIE JOHN A BRYAN WILLIAM R HINERMAN ELMO ROSARIO-SALABERR
ELMER L BOATMAN GERALD D GEOGHEGAN HERSCHEL P HELM JR THOMAS C JONOZZO STEPHEN P MILLER
JAMES H DUFFETT JR TIMOTHY J MCMAHON VINCENT F MURPHY JAMES P NARD III MCARTHUR NICHOLS
JIMMIE H ROWLETT DANNY R RUNDLE FLORENTINO J SANTANA PHILLIP E TAYLOR LARRY E WASHINGTON
BRUCE B BACKEBERG EARL J BAUCHMANN JERRY L BRANSON FRANK M BROWN JR MANUEL L CARROLL
WILLIAM S DAVIS III MICHAEL D DEROSIER RONALD C DEXTER JERRY W DOWNS LAWRENCE V MCMAHON
MANZIE GLOVER JR WARREN L GOULD GOLLIE L GRANT JOHN M HARRINGTON JAMES J HEETHER II
DAVID A HENRY LINWOOD M HOLMES CHESTER S HUGHES ALBERT S HURTADO CHARLES W JACKSON
LEONARD F LANE JOSE MARTINEZ-SOTO JEROME D MCARTHUR GARY L MILLER GEORGE W MILLER
RONALD L ENGLAND JOSEPH D MCNULTY DON B PARSONS JR RICHARD W PERRY THOMAS H PILKINGTON
ROBERT A POWELL MATIAS T RODRIGUEZ JR RONALD L TAYLOR JIMMY R WALDREP JOHNNY E WILLIAMS
ANDREW W YOUNGKIN JR CHARLES J BLANCO RICHARD M BLOOM JAMES R BRANNEN JAMES M CLARK
HARRY H EGGLESTON LARRY GLOVER WALTER HARRIS MICKY J JOHNS CLARENCE E JOHNSON
JOHN P KAMINSKY JAMES F PANZARELLA HERBERT C PHIPPS ELIAS R RODRIGUEZ MICHAEL D ROSEMAN
GARY E ROSSER BRYAN B STOCKWELL EUGENE UNDERWOOD GLENDON L AMMON JAMES R BAUDER
ARTHUR C ALTERWISHER FRANK ARREY JR JOHN O FREEMAN JOSEPH A FRIEL CARLTON GRIFFIN
LOUIS C HINES NORMAN L HOYT ROBERT L HYDE ROBERT B JACKSON VERNELL JENKINS
JOHN W JOLLEY JR THOMAS J KANE THOMAS P KINDT BILLY L LAUFFER EDWARD A WELLINGS
JAMES B MILLS JAMES L PETTIFORD ANTHONY B PHILLIPS JOHN F SEWELL JR RONALD F VAN RAEMDONCK
RICHARD P BARTLE DENNIS D BRADLEY HUGH C CLAUSEN BILLY J DAILEY JOSEPH N DAVI
WILLIAM J FISHER RONALD A HEINTZ JOE T JOHNSON CHARLES A KNOCHEL SAMUEL E MURPH
BILLY B KING LARRY L LAKEY FRANCISCO H MORENO NORMAN J NAPIERATA JAMES D SMITH

PANEL 11E

JOHN D WILLIAMS GEORGE WYCINSKY JR GERALD W BRASCHE RAYMOND E FLEMING JR
DAVID R AIKEN EMANUEL F DRUMMOND JR ROBERT W GARTH JR LLOYD L GOODING SALVATORE GUARINO
PAUL G HAZEN RAY W HOLEMAN FRANK C HUBICSAK JIMMY A JOHNSON NOE MAGALLAN
ANTONIO R OSUNA WILLIAM P PRESSON JR LARRY L REYNOLDS WILLIAM M SHETRON DAVID R WARGO
CARMELO ROMAN-AGUILAR OLIN R THRUSH JOSEPH T WILLIAMS JOHN T KLUMP
STEPHEN E BURTON ALFREDO CASTANON ESTILL L CHILDERS JACK E CROUCH JR GARRY D DAVIS
CECIL E DORSEY WILLIAM E EBEL WAYNE E ELLISON JOHN H FULCHER JAMES E GRAHAM JR
GERALD J BANNACH ELMER L BUCHANAN ROBERT C HAUSER BURNS W KNOWLTON JR REXFORD A LA ROCK EDWIN J LUCKSTEAD
JOHN C LYNCH GERALD C MCKEEN ROBERT P MINOR HOWARD G MORRISON JEAN USZAKOW
VERNON L RAMEY WILBURN ROBERSON DAVID J ROSE DANIEL J RUSNELL ROBERT P SANTOR
CLYDE MINIX DWIGHT K SATTERWHITE LARRY G SHEFFIELD WAYNE T STRICKLAND JUNIOR L WHITTLE
STEPHEN A ANDERSON GARY A BARNARD JOHN J BARZAN WILLIAM R BEASLEY PETER R BOSSMAN
LARRY J CALLOWAY RONALD M CRAWN CLIFTON E CUSHMAN GARY R DOPP PHILLIP A DUCAT
ROBERT D FELLOWS CHARLES L FORD HERMON E FULLER JR ARTHUR W GREEN DONALD M HENRICKS JR
JAMES E HOLDER ROY D HUTTING HOWARD W JACKSON BRUCE L KENNEDY ERNEST R MARTIE
JAMES E MILLER JERRY L NEWBRAND RONNIE L NOSEFF VERNON H PARKER JR JERRY D PILLSBURY
DAVID W POLICH TERRY L PUNDSACK LOUIS R RANDALL DEAN W REITER KARL A SCHMIDT JR
JAMES D STALLINGS PAUL D TICE JEFFREY P VAUGHN ROBERT M WATERS LARRY W WHITCOME
LAWRENCE WILLIAMS JR WALTER WILLIAMS JR REGINALD L CONE NORMAN L DUPRE ROBERT F GRUNDMAN
JAMES W HOLLIDAY RICHARD C JOHNSON HENRY L MOSBURG GARY R PARSONS MARVIN F PHILLIPS
JERRY W ROSS CHARLES W TURNER CHARLES M CENTENO FRANK E DZIWISZ JR ARVEL H HALL
RONALD G JORDET LAWRENCE F KINNEAR BILLY W LAWS THOMAS A LOWDEN WILLIAM R MASTERS
GROVER C MATHEWS JR GARY P MEYER CARROLL W POWELL ROBERT E ROBINSON JAMES W ROWLETT
DYKE A SPILMAN VICKEY E STANLEY JOSEPH M STINE GARRETT G SUTTON JR ISTVAN SZABO
CHARLES S BURNS III JOHN W GEARY JAMES R HANSON DENNIS T HAYWORTH DANIEL C JONES
KENNETH A KEITH JULIO I MARTIR-TORRES GEORGE G MOLINA MIGUEL F NAJAR GEORGE E O'NEILL
THOMAS J ONTIVEROS GREGG E REED RANDELL F SHANNON LONNIE D SPROUSE DANNY G TAYLOR
RALPH G TILL BENNY E WIMBERLY JACKIE R BROWN JACK CAMPBELL JAMES M HARGROVE
WALTER MARCUM CRISTOBAL MELENDEZ BOOKER SMITH JR SAUL WAXMAN THOMAS L WESTPOINT
LANHAM O BROYLES ELMER E COTNEY WILLIAM T DEUEL LOUIS P GAGNE JR IRVIN J HOPKINS
JOHN T LOGAN RICHARD T MALASPINA HENRY O MARTIN III DAVID I MUSCH RICHARD A SMITH
ROGER L BONNER JR TERRY L SNYDER RICHARD L BISHOP MICHAEL J DE MARSICO CURTIS L FITZPATRICK JR
LEROY FRAZIER WENDELL R GRIZZLE JOE C KELLEY JOE H MOOREHEAD TRAVIS E NUNNERY
WILLIAM L STUBBE EDWARD A URIBE RODRICK P WHALEN JOHN D ANDRADE LARRY W BAILEY
THOMAS E BEGLINGER BOBBY R BRYANT PEPITO CAGUIMBAL JIMMIE D GRAY RICHARD F WALTERS
LOUIS E HADDOCK JR TERRY E HEMMITT VICTOR E KUHNS DOUGLAS R LUECK RONALD H MIS
DUNCAN A MACFETTERS WALTER A MURZIN FLORENTINO R ROQUE FRANCIS P ROYAL ROY SALAZAR
MICHAEL L BYAM BELMIRO TAVARES JR DALE A WAID KENNETH O ALFSTAD BILLY J CLAYTON
JAMES A DANIELS RAYMOND L ECHEVARRIA RANDAL C ENGRAM JAMES H GRAFF WILLIE GREEN JR
JOHN M HENS JOHNNIE L LAWRENCE KENNETH A MALLONEE GEORGE A WALDRON EDDIE L WILLIAMS
JOHN W MARTIN GREGORY D MCKEAGUE RICHARD A ROSBECK JEROME J SMITH DAVID A THORPE
JAMES E JONES HOWARD D ULMER JR BENJAMIN I WARREN RAYMOND L WHEELER DENNIS L WILLIAMS
HAROLD H HIRTLE GEORGE W ALEXANDER JR JOHN T BIRD FRANCIS H BISSAILLON CHARLES M BRADFORD
THOMAS H TREBATOSKI PHILIP M CALLAN HENRY L CREEK SAM W DAILY JOHNNIE L DANIEL JOHN P EYNON
ROBERT O KORNS JOHN H JONES RONALD E LEWIS JAMES G LITTS PINK M LYNCH JR DANIEL P MARLOWE
PHILLIP MILLER RAYFORD J MOSLEY HOMER L PICKETT RICHARD M PROCIV ARMANDO RAMOS
AUGUSTINE D RUSSO DONALD A SMITH JR RONALD K STANEART ROBERT J STEEL DAVID O WEBSTER
KENNETH W WEST WILLIAM R ANDREWS JAMES A BEENE DAVID J BOHN JAMES J CARROLL
ROBERT G DAVIDSON JOHN G DICKERSON III ALBERT E HUFFER MERLIN P LEGAUX PAUL H MITCHELL JR
DAVID L OWENS JOSH PALM JR WALTER F PAYNE JOHN R SMITH RODNEY G THORNTON
JULIO C VARGAS ALBERT L VICICH GARY H BRUX THOMAS DEAN MELVIN L STONE JR
ULYSSES V FRAZIER RICHARD M HECK ROBERT H HOLMES ALFRED J KIBLER RICHARD E RICHARDSON
WILLIAM E JOHNSON RONALD W LEE JOSEPH A MOEN DAVID L MOSER RONALD E PFEIFER
JAMES E BIGGS HOWARD D STROUSE JAMES E WINDHAM JR JAMES W ADKISSON ROBERT F CHAMBERLAIN
GARY W BRAASCH DAVID W BRANCH ROBERT J BROCKMANN RICHARD J CANOVA ORMAN L CROSSLEY JR
JOHN F DALOLA III GARY D DOCTOR VINCENT F GARVEY ROBERT M GILCHRIST JOSEPH T GILE JR
ROBERT W GILLIAM JOHN L HALL JOHN T HENSLEY HARTLEY M JOSEPHSON LARRY D KNIGHT
MICHAEL D MITCHELL JOHNNY L NEAL EUGENE M PABST FRANKLIN M RENSHAW WILLIE J ROUNDTREE
ALVERN W SCHLOTTMAN FRANK M SOKOLOWSKI JAMES A TREECE HARRY T WHETZEL PATRICK F CAMPBELL
FRANCISCO P CHAIRA THOMAS D CONGIARDO HERMAN L COOPER JOHN A FELDHAUS
DENNIS GARLAND KYLE T HARRINGTON KEITH E HIX GERALD E ISAACSON WILLIAM F KERN
KENNETH C FRIDDLE EDWARD D LARSON BILLY LEE ALAN F LUCAS JOHN W MILLER BILLY F MOONEYHAM
WILLIAM L SCHULTZ ROSEVELT SIMMONS JR HALLEY D WHITLOCK PAUL F WIDTFELDT JR ARTURO BARRIGA
JAMES L HATTON JOHN R PIERCE PIERCE I ROBERTSON CHARLES G BOROWSKY PETER H BROWN
GLEN F BULLOCK BRIAN D CLARK LAWRENCE E CLARK MICHAEL S CONFER GLENN W APPLE
LARRY R BILLIE LELAND E HAMMOND RICHARD D HENSLEY ALFRED A KASPAUL RONALD D MILLER
DAVID D PERKINS BRYANT R POWELL JAMES A BARRETT ROBERT E BERRY REGIS P DEBOLD
FRANK C ELKINS LAWRENCE C FREE DAVID H FREEMAN JOHN D GOOD DOUGLAS L JONES
GENE A MENEFEE ALVIN G MORRIS DONALD W ROHLEDER DENNIS E SPRINGSTEEN MURRAY L BORDEN
CARL E GRONQUIST JR DARIUS E BROWN ANDREW CHMIEL LARRY J COX PHILLIP C FOX ANTHONY J NIGRO
JAMES E GARDNER DENNIS D HARRIS JOHN W JARRELL EUGENE T MEADOWS EMERY G MIKULA
WILLIAM J COX ERNEST G PIPKIN JOE L RONJE DAREL L SILLS GEORGE M SMYRYCHYNSKI
DENNIS W WATERMAN HUGH W WELLONS JAMES C DOBSON PAUL E FLOYD JR F G GIPSON JR
WOODWARD S HATFIELD JR DARRELL A JACKSON DAVID H MUELLER ROGER A PETERSEN ROBERT L PRUHS
JACK D SPAULDING JOSEPH N STEVENS DARWIN J THOMAS LOUIS TURCHI ROBERT J BLACK
GERALD L CARMICHAEL GERALD J COLLIER MARVIN DOWDELL MELVIN R ELLIS LAWRENCE H HARRIS
JAMES E JOSLYN WILLIAM T LONDON ROBERT J MARCAVAGE ROBERT D MARLIN DENNIS E PIKE
CARLOS PIREZ-BERGES JAMES S PITTMAN KENNETH E SHRUM WILLIAM J STONE RODGER E TERWILLIGER
DANNY C WHITE CHARLES L BOLING ROY B CANADY ALBERT G HALLOWELL ROBERT C KELLER
PERRY L POOLE GEORGE E SWINNEY JOHN C WILSON EDWARD E ANDERSON HORTON S COKER JR
EDWARD J CORCORAN JOHN T DE BARBER GARETH J DEAL WILLIAM W ENGLISH JR MICHAEL J MCGONAGLE
DAVID A GILBERT WILLIAM M HUBERTY KENNETH J IVORY DALTON E JACKSON EDWARD JACKSON JR
ARTHUR M DOWNS ROBERT W KRALL JAMES C LAMBERT JR FREDERICK W LENNON IRVIN G MILLER
ARTHUR G MCNALLY RAYMOND J ROSS WILLIAM R ROUSSOS EDWARD G SALONISH DAVID L SKINNER
ALLAN E SMITH DAVID P STATES MICHAEL C THOMAS STEVEN H ADAMS RALPH H ANGSTADT
LEONARD W BURNS LAWRENCE CLARK BOBBIE J DENNIS VICTOR O FOWLER JR CHARLES R VESSELS
WILLIAM F HALPIN JAMES W HARGROVE GALE J HAYS ROBERT L HILL FREDERICK H LEWIS
JOHN H LONG EDWARD M MCILVAIN III INZAR W RACKLEY JR EUGENE L SELF JOHN R SHONECK
DAVID L DENNY BRUCE L SIMPSON CHARLES A SLAGER GEORGE E STEWART HUBERT TUCK JR
MICHAEL J BURKE JOSE M CRUZ RAY L GONCE LEONARD J LEWANDOWSKI JR RICHARD E MISHUK
KENNETT K SCOTT THOMAS R TEMPLE JOHN F BURNS JAMES D DANIELS HARRY S EDWARDS JR
JERRY W HAUF CHRISTOPHER J MILLER ROBERT D SISK CHARLES E TOFFERI DAVID R WAGENER
PHILLIP M WILSON RONALD G WOLFE GEORGE H CHACE ROBERT F EHLERS JOSEPH R SIMONE
WILLIAM T GRUDZINSKI HAROLD L HARRIS STANLEY L HORWITZ DANNY E HYDE WILLIAM G MCCANN
DAVID J EARLL DOUGLAS W O'DONNELL ERNEST P PRYOR DAVID C RILEY JUAN A SANTIAGO-MALDONA
ROBERT SMITH SR JOHN O SUNDQUIST BOYD W ANDERSON ROBERT A BATES WILLIAM L CRAWFORD
ELIJAH DANIEL JR DON E DARNALL WILLIAM R DAVIS JAMES L HIGHTOWER THOMAS J HOLDEN
JOHN O JONES JR TEDDY R JORDAN THOMAS C KOLSTAD EARL P MCBRIDE LOUIS J REED
WILLIAM B KLENERT MICHAEL R NEWBERN CHARLES J RILEY ALAN I SMITH ALONZO A TEAGUE
WILLIAM H MEANS JR JOHN C ARDIS SAMUEL J BAKER WILLIAM E BRAND CHARLES F BUSBY GARY B FLABBI
THOMAS F FLAHIVE TULLIO P IODICE JR WILLIAM J NEWTON JIMMY D PHIPPS FRANCIS P ROSEBRUGH
GEORGE BELANGER JOHN F COCHRANE LAWRENCE C DOBRENZ DENIS W GALLOWAY CHESTER W KNIGHT
HUBERT L LEE JR KENNETH D MCCOIN DENNIS A MCKELLAR KIRK A MCLAUGHLIN LEON B TRIEST
ROBERT D WEAVER JOHNNY W WRIGHT ROBERT B GREEN MICHAEL C MILLER COLEMAN L WARREN
RICHARD A NANCE RONALD G PERRYMAN ROBERT L PITT JAKE A SIMMONS LARRY F SMITH
ALVIN L LEVAN JIMMIE E TAYLOR JIMMIE WILLIAMS DEWEY L ALEXANDER WILLIAM R CLEMENTS
CODY A BALISTERI JOSSLYN F BLAKELY JR CHARLES W BOGGS JAMES L BREWER RODNEY B CARTER
NOAH C COLLIER JR RAMON A COPPLE RICHARD E DONAHUE ROBERT L DYKE GEORGE K FARRIS
WILLIAM N FEASTER JOHN F FRANCIS TERRENCE J FREUND FRANK M GARDNER WILLIAM G MCWILLIAMS III
WILLIAM J GARRITY JR JOHN B GEISEN JR JAMES K GRAY JULIAN D HAMMOND JR JOHN E HARDIN
CHARLES T HAFENDORFER JACK H HARRIS GREG E HART JAMES B HUDIS LLOYD P HYDE CLYDE R WELCH
THOMAS M JOYCE JAMES A KELLY JR DANIEL O KERN JAMES A LEE NORMAN S LEVY CHARLES A PHILHOWER
DAVID A LISTE WALTER F MERRICK CLARENCE D MILLER MICHAEL J MONAHAN CLEMENT J MORISETTE
OMAR R FORD GLENN R MORRISON JR JOHN J NUSSBAUMER MICHAEL G PETERSON DONALD W SHANKS
ALVIN M SHIFFLETT JR GERALD W SIEBE JAMES A SMITH THOMAS E SPITZER HOWARD D STRAUSS
WILLIAM A JOHNSON DANIEL L STRONG RONALD E TARDIO FRANKLIN M TUNICK WILLIAM WALLING
JAMES R WELSH HOWARD J YOUNGER JR DAVID A BARUTH MARLIN E BEMBENEK JOHN T BRADFORD
STANLEY S COPE JR RAY E DAVIS EMMANUEL L EATON FRANK A GLOWIAK TERRY L GRUBE
JAMES HAYES JR DALE A JOHNSON HENRY LUCIW KERMITT C PARNELL MICHAEL RAND
ORLANDO S ROACH HOWARD C ROBINSON GARY G RUSHING WALTER J ACKWOOD MICHAEL J BOSKO JR
ALLEN BROOKS SIDNEY L BRYANT JR WALTER J CARROLL AARON D COWAN JESSIE L CRUMP
DANIEL T FLOWERS OSCAR GARCIA PAUL D GUIMOND RICHARD R HENLING WILLIS A KARICKHOFF
THOMAS LEEK JR J C LOVE KENNETH L MADDY ROBERT L MARTINEZ RONALD E MCCLELLAND
GERARD R MCCONNELL LOUIS J RENTERIA FRANCIS D RICE TERRY L SMITH STANLEY R TOMASOVIC
WENDELL L WILSON RONALD WYATT GLEN H YOUNG CARROLL D ABBOTT ROBERT D BENTON
KEMPER S BILLINGS PHILLIP R COLEMAN RAYMOND DOSS CREIGHTON R DUNN WILLIAM G MANSFIELD
TIMOTHY J MEEKER RICHARD F MUSTO DANIEL B NOLFF DENNIS G OLSON ULISES ORTIZ-COLON
RAYMOND PEARL JR DAVID B PEGG ROBERT E POLKINGHORNE THOMAS RESPRESS ROBERT H STEWART
JOHN B TALIANA MILAN E WHITTEN FRANCIS J CASEY DONALD A CHRIST ROGER D CLARK
MICHAEL N CORYELL DAVID A HAAKENSEN DWIGHT W LAWS ADELBERT F MIHALEK IV JOHN W WOODS JR
LINZA NORRIS CHARLES W SMITH EUGENE R TACTAY JR JAMES L WALKER WILMER J WILLINGHAM
DANNY L MCDONALD HENRY ARD JOHN R BOWLING SR NATHANIEL BROWN HOWARD CLANTON

PANEL 12E

WALTER J JANKOWSKI PHILLIP D JOSLEN HARRY W JUNTILLA MICHAEL W KOLEMAINEN
TED T LOCKLAR ELEFTHERIOS P PAPPAS RONALD A VAN SESSEN LEROY BURKS JR DANIEL J ILLI
CHARLES N CARSON JR CHARLES C CLARK LAWRENCE R COSTELLO MARION L DRAPER RICHARD J EDRIS
RONALD A FROMM WILLIAM GARCIA DAVID L HALL DAYTON L HARE JR ANDREW H HODGE
EDWARD P AUSTIN JAMES L HOLCOMB TIMOTHY HOLSTER JOHN E JOHNSON ROBERT I JOHNSON
JOSHUA T JONES JUDD W KENNEDY JOHN F KNOPF DONALD K LAKEY JOSEPH P MACHALICA
DANIEL T MARTINEZ WILLIAM G MENDENHALL ALLAN A MILK THOMAS M MOORE MICHAEL L PUGH
ROBERT L SHUCK MICHAEL H STOFLET GARY L SUBLETTE JOSE A VAZQUEZ KLAUS WARRELMANN
GEORGE R WEAVER JR JERRY P WITT RANDY B WRIGHT BILLIE A ALLEN CHARLES E BROWN JR
THOMAS A DUCKETT LARRY L FULLER CARL F GARRISON ROBERT E KLINE SAMUEL LIGHTMAN
AUGUSTINE LOPEZ JR GILMAN W MCKAY ANDREW J ROBERTSON JESSE SAMARIPA BARRY R WOOD
UPTON F ASHLEY EDGAR H BEASLEY WILLIAM CARPENTER JR RANDOLPH DAVIS KENNETH E SANDERS
RICCARDO B DICKERSON JAMES W EISNER ROBERT L FOWBLE JR JOEL FULLER JAMES J HEALEY
FREDERICK H HENDERSON RONALD E HESSON JOHN R JOHNSON JAMES M KLINK THOMAS A LAWLESS
LARRY L LIBBEE WILLIAM D MONFORE CLYDE J PERKINS DALE A PERKINS GARY L REAM
DONALD T CASSIDY SAMUEL K SOLOMON JR MILBURN H STARNES WALLACE A ABBOTT ROBERT L ADAMS JR
RODNEY E ALTHOFF HOWARD C BARKER WILLIAM C BAROTT JOHN D BELTZ LAWRENCE E BESSON
THOMAS L BLACKMAN ROBERT E BRINCKMANN DENNY L BRUCE DONALD R BRUNNER AARON L THOMAS
BYRON H BUSHAY WILLIAM S BUTLER JR CESARIO CALDERON RICHARD B CARLSON BARRY B MYHR
VINCENT J CONNOLLY GERALD F CURRIER JAMES N FINN JOSE L FONTANEZ-VELEZ JOHN P FRANKEL
FRED A GADDIS DONALD GAGNE EUGENE F GOECKNER THEODORE L HUNDLEY DONALD R JOHNSTON
SEBERN E GRAHAM JR WILLIAM B HUNT DAVID J IGNASIAK BRUCE E KERNDL EDWARD J MERRITT
CARMEN P CARTONIA TITUS MCKINNON JR CHARLES E MITCHAM LESLIE D MOSES ROBERT B NASSER
JAMES R PEARSON LUIS A PEREZ-CRUZ CARL D PRUITT LARRY A RICE ALLAN A SCHWARZKOPF
VINCENT C BOURDEAU VINCENT A SCUNGIO GARY D TACKETT HOWARD L WALKER GARY P WRATTEN
ROBERT L WRIGHT BOBBY YOUNG JAMES R BLEVINS ROY R BLEWETT GERALD L BOURDEAU
JOHN R CANIFF DAVID L CARLSON RICHARD G COLLINS WILLIAM L DENMAN LEX ELSWICK LYNN J RUSSELL
DALLAS G GRUNDY EARL D HUTTON HARRY D LUND JOHN E MILES FREDERICK W MULLEN
DOUGLAS E MURRAY WALTER H MYERS JR ALAN J PERRAULT ALFRED SEVENSKI
RICHARD A SPANGLER GEORGE G STOLL CLAUDE C SUPINGER JERRY D TABER ROBERT E TAYLOR
FERNANDO L TORRES JR ROBERT L VEST ARTIE D WALKER TERRY L WALLS GENE T WINTERS
JAMES L WRIGHT JAMES F BARNES PERCY L CAMPBELL WILLIAM S COCHRAN BILLY M CRAWFORD
WELLINGTON M DONAHUE MELVIN D DUTY ANTHONY J GADDA JR PAUL C HAMBY JR EDWARD P STEFANIK
WILLIAM A HENDON THOMAS J KLEMP NORMAN L LINGLEY ROGER T MACNUTT THOMAS R MURPHY
LAWRENCE E FOWLER CHARLES E PETERS JAMES H SHANNON JR ROBERT G WILSON WILLIAM S MORGAN II
PAUL M BAYLISS ERNEST L CARTER DAVID F DEVOE JIMMIE L DOBBS MICHAEL C DOYLE
LARRY L FONTAINE BENJAMIN H HARRIS CLINNIS H JACKSON DONALD L JACOBSEN JOHN A MEANS
JOSEPH R BACHUS WAYNE A MCCOLLUM MICHAEL E MCCULLOUGH JOHN W MEDLIN ROBERT F PACKARD
JACK D RENFRO EDWARD R STANTON II DAVID E THREADGILL TED N TOLZMANN JAMES R WILSON
BRUCE E YATES EDWARD G BLACKMON LEWIS E BONNIE HOWARD L BOWEN GERALD R BURNS
JOHN D COX II WILLIAM L CYR DAVID B DANN ARTHUR R ERSCHOEN CHARLES M TODD
DONALD E KRAMER JACKIE B HALL JERRY L HAPPEL CLABE HERALD JR VERTIS J HILL JR CALVERT J JOHNSON
JAMES M KELLY BERNARD F KISTLER RANDALL W MOORE RONALD V PUTNAM MICHAEL J QUEALY
HENRY A GARZA MATHEREW D RENFROE EURIPIDES RUBIO JR WALTER J SCHMIDT RAFAEL VEGA-MAYSONET
CASPAR M WALSH III JAMES W WASHKUHN FRED J WILLIAMS JR LESLIE E WRIGHT NATHANIEL WYLEY
RONNIE H BINTLIFF GEORGE E BRYANT DAVID K DEEN WILLIAM A DERKSEMA ROBERT J DONOVAN
ARTHUR GLIDDEN ROBERT E HARRIS CARL D HOFFMAN RANDLE KINNEY CHARLES L ROBERTS
HARLAN N LOCKHART DONALD W MCCANN PATRICK T MCDERMOTT TERRY P SLOAN HARDY W STEBBINS JR
CHARLES F SWOPE JOSEPH BACZALSKI SYLVAN K BRADLEY THOMAS J BROOKS ALFRED CARMICHAEL JR
WILLIAM T CARTER DENNIS L DOOLEY OTIS E JACKSON LEN M JENKINS LLOYD S SMITH
TERRANCE R LYLE THOMAS J MCATEER DAIN W MILLIMAN JOHN E MITCHELL JOHN L O'BRIEN
THOMAS COTTON III JOHN M RIORDAN ERIC J SCHODERER LOWELL E SCHULTZ ROBERT G WILLIAMSON
LYNN BACHMANN JR DONALD L BROWN MARVIN BURNEY RICHARD L BUTT WILLIAM F CALLINAN
GROVER L DICKSON ROGER L EPLEY PAUL J HESS JR MAYNARD J HUMES WALTER R SPEARE III
MARION L KEMPNER HENRY T LEONARD JOHN J LIVINGSTON ARNOLD A LUND ARTHUR S MEARNS
RODOLFO G GONZALEZ LOREN S REEVES TERRENCE M ROONEY EDMOND D SCHOENIG MILTON F SMITH
DEE W STONE JR CARROLL U THOMPSON VERNON B TODD CHARLES E WHITEFIELD DANIEL ACOSTA
ROY G ALVIS CHARLES T ANDERSON JR MANUEL AVILA JR EDUARDO AYALA THOMAS E BIRDSALL
KENNETH H BLACKWELL RONALD E BOCOOK TED D BROOMFIELD JAMES P BROWN CHARLES M GOUDE
ROGER J BRYANT LARRY D DE FILIPPIS HEROLD T DEARDORFF LESLIE P DEDMAN JERRY W DUNIGAN
OTIS S FISHER THOMAS G FITZGIBBON GEORGE A FOGARTY ROBERT C FROSIO NICHOLAS J FULMER
GEORGE H BONNELL III KENT P FURPHY JOHN H GALLAGHER EDUARDO GUZMAN-LUGO LARRY W HOLTZ
JAMES O HUGHES JAMES G JONES JOHN A MCGRATH CHARLES E MEEK DAVID H PAULSEN
RAYMOND L POWELL LLOYD J SADOWSKY ALAN H SHIELDS ROBERT W SMITH DANIEL D YARNELL
JERRY L RUITER CECIL WALKER AARON BLANDING JOHN D BULGER EDWARD CARROLA
CLARENCE L CASTO MOZIE L COLE SAMUEL D DANNA CARL L FALCK JR MICHAEL J MACARELL
JOSEPH X GRANT ROBERT W HATTON ERNEST E LAYAOU JR FRED R LIDER JAMES R NORTHERN
TERENCE D O'BRIEN TERRENCE D O'BRIEN EDWARD J PIANTKOWSKI LOUIS W POTEMPA JOHN R SCHULTZ WILLIAM F SPERRY
TRACY S TENHOFF JUAN TORRES JAMES D TYNER DONALD C VAUGHAN RALPH O WATTS
TERRY L WEBER DANIEL M BENNETT DAVID S BOYD LEON G CHADWICK III RODOLFO M GONZALEZ
RICHARD W HASTINGS JOHN MAYO GLEN A MUSGUIRE NELSON F PULSIFER JR ROBERT T REED JIMMIE TUCH
REXIE L ARMES WILLY S BAKER HARRY G BROCK JAMES W BRUHN HARRY M RAVENNA III
JAMES W CANTRELL JOSEPH R CRAFT JOSEPH A CROSS JIMMY S DAFFRON WALTER E DANIELS
BILLY R HUSSEY THOMAS C JACKSON GERALD JOHNSON JOHN C KEIPER THOMAS C MITCHELL
EDWARD A MCWRIGHT CHARLES G OBERLE FRED M PENNINGTON EDDIE D PEOPLES JIMMIE L PLATO
TED W ADAMS CLYDE M RIDGWAY TEOFILO C RIOS WILLIAM J SEAWRIGHT JR THOMAS SHAW
WESLEY SHIMODA BUDDY A STANLEY EDDIE D STARCHER KENNETH E THORNTON BRUCE A TIMMONS
JAY K BOOKS FRANK DE BERNARDO JR ROBERT R GOMEZ LA M GROW BERNARD J O'DONNELL
DONALD A JACKSON JAMES R JOHNSON SAMMY JONES JR WILLIAM E JOYCE JR DOUGLAS D KERN
OCTAVIANO M HARVEY JOHN B LEAL PETER LITTLE JAMES H MCDONALD ALAN D PITTMANN
EUGENE B RHOADES JESSIE RICHARDSON ROGER D RUOFF HILBERT M SINGLETARY JR WILLIAM J WILDERS
RICHARD L THOMPSON JOE CALDWELL EDWARD C CAYEY JR JOSEPH P FRY NORMAN E GUILLAUME JR
NICHOLAS M HARTMAN CHARLIE LYLES JR ERNEST E ROSS ROBERT E STRAHM MATTHEW WARE
WILLIAM T ARNOLD DUNCAN E BASS JR CARL BROWN JAMES S GILBERT MICHAEL G ISELY
JAMES W LEACH WILLIAM A PALENSKE DONALD P SMITH RAYMOND E SMOOT FREDERICK P VICTORIA
BILLY J WAYMIRE DWIGHT L BASEY TED BELCHER GREGORY C BIELICKI JAMES M JOHNSTONE
MILES D COOPER JOSEPH COUSETTE WILLARD D CRAIG MERL L CRIPE EDMUND V DLUGOKINSKI
RANDALL M CAMPBELL III AUDLEY M FEDERLINE JR JOHN D FITZPATRICK JESSE L HARRIS ALVIN E JACKSON
JAMES H KENNARD LOUIS D KIMES LEWIS R KIRBY DARRELL E LAUSCH ROBERTS MACHADO
JAMES OHLINGER CHARLES T OWEN HOMER L PEASE CARL W PHILLIPS FRANKIE L PRIEST
ROBERT D MCCOWN CHARLES E PHILLIPS ROBERT G RUDOLPH RICHARD D RUSSELL THOMAS R SERRANO
HERBERT C SHUPE MICHAEL D SWANGIN A W TRIPPLETT MARION WATKINS ALAN N WEISMAN
DAVID R WEST COLEY P WHITE JAMES L WHITED ELVIN J WIDEMAN SAMMY R WISWELL
EDWARD W WOODRUFF PAUL O BROWN JOHN W CLAYTON TRAVIS G CRAIN WILLIAM B DORSEY
CHARLES J GAINES PATRICK J GILBERT JIMMIE C HONLEY CHARLES L ISLEY III GLENDELL E YATES
MILTON H LEGRAND RICHARD P MASSINE JAMES A MCCALVY DAVID MENDEZ ARNOLD C PEARSON
PRESTON W POLK HARRY J SHEPHERD JR WILLIAM R SILVER DARYL E SMOCK HARRY K VARNER

ANTHONY F KORPICS WELDON H YOUNG THEODORE A ALKIRE JR GARY D BYFORD LOUIS CASTILLO
EDUARDO CHAVEZ JASPER R CONWAY JOHN M DALTON CARLITO L DORSEY GEORGE EPPINGER
NORMAN C FARRIS LLOYD E GARRETT JOHN L GODFREY RUSSELL L HALLEY RALLS HAWKINS
CHARLES L HICKS HARVEY JOHNSON III MARION E JOHNSON RAY E JOHNSON CARROLL H JONES
WILLIAM E KENNEDY ARNOLD R KRASNOFF ROGER W LAWSON DENNIS R LEHMAN BOBBY W LETBETTER
CHARLES K MALONE GAMALIEL MARCANO-DIAZ LEO G MICHAEL EUGENE E MITCHELL CLIFFORD R STOUT
LARRY D NAASZ HERBERT PEARSALL JR MICHAEL H PENNELL HARRY L POWERS JOSEPH L RABON
JIMMY L RHODES JERRY D SABENS EDWARD J SCAHILL JOSEPH SCICUTELLA SAMUEL W SMITH
WALLACE J MALONE JAMES E SMYTHE JIMMY E STAMEY ANDREW L STEPHENS WILBERT STEWART JR
ALVIN B TUCKER GEORGE A TURNER LESTER E UNGER JR DONALD G VERNON JOHN F WADEN
LEE O WHITE JR MAX M WOODSMALL ROBERT L BORGER GERALD E CHASTAIN EMMETT R DAVIS
RICHARD K FINSTERWALDER ANTHONY T MARTIN THOMAS J MAYER JOHN F MCCABE DOCK J PINION
ROY R ROARK ALOYSIUS J STUHL JAY C TIPTON DENNIS N WILLIAMS GORDON S WILSON
JOSEPH A ARIMENTO JOSEPH D BURNETT JAMES N CAGLEY DAVID A CRABTREE MICHAEL P MCCONAHAY
GEORGE B BELL ALTON O FLAGG JOHNNY M HAIRSTON JIMMY D HUDSON JEAN B INCASHOLA
BERNARD S PLAZA EDWARD J BOIVIN MALCOLM K BROUHARD ARTHUR BRUMAGEN JOHN K THOMPSON
ROBERT CAIN JR JOHN E CANTLON JR DONALD R DUNCAN THOMAS G ERICKSON RUSSELL E FERREBEE
WILLIAM H HARDWICK EDDIE C LOPEZ JAMES W MCCOY GRADY E MCELROY DONALD I RANKIN
RONNIE C ANDERSON JOHN N RODRIGUES DENNIS E WEINBERG GLENN V GARDNER JESSE GUERRERO
RICHARD D MATTSON DAVID T HAKE GEORGE A MYERS ELLIS ORTON JR PHILIP A PURVIS PATRICK O QUINN
CLAUDE N WILLIAMS ARTHUR E WRIGHT III LAWRENCE A BARCKLOW TROY BEALIN HARDY L BELL
JAMES T BOWENS EARL K BURNS JR JERRY W CORKERN DIETER W DIETZ CHARLES L FAULKNER
HAROLD L GRAVES JOSEPH W HARRISON CARROLL G HOGEMAN JOHN R HUMPHREY JAMES E WEBB
EDWARD L KERR RONALD L LA TELLE MARCHELLA R LANZONE BALTAZAR A MALDONADO JESSE L WALTMAN
NORMAN W MCROBIE RONALD D MILES JAMES E OXLEY EVANGELIS PAGAN-RODRIGUEZ JERRY POTTS
ADRIAN F PURNELL ALDEN L RILEY HOLLIE B RUSSELL KARL D SOBOLIK ALAN R STEFFEN
STANLEY R GLEISINGER WILLIAM A LYNCH JR WALTER SUHAR JOE H TRICKEY JR RICHARD E WELCH
PAUL R WEST BOBBY L WILLIAMS DENNIS P WRIGHT ALVIN ECHOLS HENRY W RUST JR
JOHN J STEWART DAVID WISNIEWSKI ROBERT C BOELZNER LARRY F CASTLE WILLIAM R DEVORE
MERCED H GONZALES JOHN H HOEFFS DONAIL MARTIN CARROLL L RODGERS DAVID L SIVERLY
GERALD O TOY JAMES R WILLEFORD WILBERT WILLIAMS JR MICHAEL A BARONOWSKI LINUS G CHOCK
CARROLL J HEBERT HOWARD L JONES DAVID C LOUTHAN DONALD J MILLER TERRY P PIERCE
JOHN M ROPER STEPHEN C SHARP RAYMOND BERNAL JR FRANK W CHADWICK JR HERBERT J NECE
LLOYD H ROHDE LEWIS ALBANESE MELVIN W ANDERSON DENNIS E BENEDETTI WILLIAM R BENNETT
ROBERT E BUTLER STEPHEN W DAY FORREST P DICKEY XAVIER FERNANDEZ JAMES P GALVIN

PANEL 13E

WALTER D LEACH GARY LUMPKIN ALLAN J NELSON JR LUIS A RAMIREZ
WILLIAM J SCHNEIDER CLIFFORD SMITH WILLIAM L WARD WILLIAM J BODZICK JOHNNIE W CARDWELL
RUSSELL P BOTT LEE J BOUDREAUX JR HARVE E BROWN TITUS L BURGESS WILLIAM L CHERRY
BRUCE C DUCAT IRBY DYER III MARK N ENARI KENDALL E GEORGE MEHMET A GILL-BEY
ROBERT R GREGORY DONALD HARRISON TOMMY JONES HENRY I KLEIN JR MONTE L MOORBERG
J C KELSEY DAVID E MCRAE BRUCE A NYSTROM TIMOTHY M O'LEARY LUIZ PINA JR
PATRICK F SCUDIERO WILLIE E STARK DANIEL A SULANDER BILLY B WOODSON PAUL L WORRELL
JACK WEAVER LARRY P CAMPOS MARVIN R FOSTER LOWELL E HARMS EPHRIAM HENRY JR
LELAND R MORGAN WILLIAM F STEIGER ANDREW R YASENOSKY GEORGE M BEVICH JR WALTER G KNIGHT
CHESTER L FREEMAN RICHARD H GRUNBERG GERALD M HUBBARD SAMUEL A JAMES JR DANIEL M JAVA
JOHN M COLE HOWARD V MATSON JR LAWRENCE D MUNGIN III RONALD C OSBORNE JAMES M WILSON
CRAWFORD B PARIS ALVIS O REEVES OLIVER J RIDDLE WILLIAM D ROBBINS WILLIAM V SHORTS
CLIFFORD NICKLEBERRY GREGORIO TRUJILLO JR CURTIS J WILLIAMS LARRY M BARNHILL BURRISS N BEGLEY
THOMAS J GRAGNANI ROYAL T KRELL PAUL MCGAUGHEY JR PAT W MCGEE JERREL C MORTON
DANIEL P TUELL ARTHUR L WARREN RICHARD F CAMPOS RICHARD CORTEZ LEE A GRECO
AUTRY GREEN THEODORE R MCELROY JR SANFORD L NELSON LAWRENCE E PAYNE JAMES E PITTS
GERALD H STEWART FRANCISCO M TAMAYO JR JOHN M TROYER DONALD A WISE RICHARD C BRANDT
JOHN W CARLSON ROGER H COYE CARLOS A FARTO FREDDIE L JOHNSON PATRICK C KOZEL
WILLIAM D LAMBERT JOSE MUNOZ FRANK M MURPHY HARRY W MURRAY DERALD D SWIFT
TILDEN B ZANE DONALD H ASIRE DAVID J BRANSTROM SHELTON L BREAUX SALVATORE P CEMELLI
CHARLES D DAMSGARD MICHAEL T FOUST WALTER L HAMMERSCHLAG GARY L HARBIN FRED D HARDY
MICHAEL L HYDE DANIEL M KELLETT ROGER E LABONTE FRANKLIN J LUMMUS GARY W SMITH
DONALD E JACKSON RONALD J MAHONEY JOHN C MERCIER ERNEST PALMIERI GEORGE C BEDDINGFIELD
ELLSWORTH I DAVIS JR LUCIOUS L EVERETT JOSE B GONZALES ADRIAN J IBROM RICHARD W MCVAY
DOUGLAS THOMAS JR JOHN H OLDS JIMMIE L PATRICK PATRICK J SALYARDS CHARLES E SIVITS J T SMITH
WILLIAM YOUNG WILLIAM H BATOR FRANKLIN E BROOKS JOSEPH CLEMONS MICHAEL L CROUSON
CHARLES J ESBENSEN JOHN D GAYMAN JOHN N GRACHTRUP RANDALL D JARRELL CLIFFORD R SINGLETON
JOHN H KNUDSEN JACK W LOGAN JR DOYLE A MCSHAN DOUGLAS J MILLER JOSEPH G MIXSON
OWEN F NEUMYER JERRY K PATRICK DONALD J RION MARTIN RUIZ JR ROBERT D SAGE
BOBBY HUDSON GEORGE A SANDERS JOHN S SAYER MONTE T SLOAN ROBERT A TWING
PHILLIP T WILEY GERALD O ALFRED JR DENNIS W ANDERSON EDWARD R BASHAM WILLIAM J HOURIGAN
VITO V BRUNO PAUL R BYRNE THOMAS G DE TAMBLE ELMER W DICKENS ROBERT T DOUGHTY
LUDIN BERMUDEZ-QUINONE JOHN W EARNESTY DENNIS HARPER JR WILLIAM O HILL ROBERT E JONES
MICHAEL C KIRBY JOHN E LAWLER JR DONALD L LEE CHARLES H LEWIS JR TOMMIE L MOONEY
ALVIN E KURTZ HENRY MCDONALD CHARLES A MCMASTERS GEORGE MERCADO JIMMIE C POE
MICHAEL R MCCOMMONS EUGENE P RICHARDSON JR ERNIE W ROSSER JAMES H SMITH ANTONIO A SOLIS
BENNY A STARR JOSHUA WELCH JR HOWARD C WEST JOHN E WIDENER HENRY H FORD JR
ROY A GEBHARD PHILLIP B HAYWARD JOHNNY R HOLLAND BERNARD P HOOPII JR LLOYD B JENSEN
DONALD F LEKOVISH RICHARD C MARSH BILLY R MARTINEZ LARRY A MOSS MICHAEL L NOTTAGE
KENNETH RHODES ANTHONY C SCIVOLINO JAMES R VAN CEDARFIELD ERIC W EVANS ERNEST GREEN
JOHNNY L GORDON LARRY D HATFIELD WILLIAM F PRIDDY MELVIN L SHERRELL GEORGE W SMITH III
GEORGE D THEISEN SAMUEL E WATERS JR KIM S BIRD EUGENE E BONNETT ALBERT BRIGHAM
JAMES R BRINK ROBERT COPELAND JAMES H DAULTON ROLAND P GUERETTE CHARLES E HENDERSON
KEITH O ELLEDGE RICHARD J HASTREITER WALTER E HERRMANN III GERALD A HOLMAN WALTER H JONES II
EDWIN L KOENIG LEAMON R LADD RICHARD L MOWREY MICHAEL T NEWELL KENNY R SUZUKI
RANDALL A VANATTA CHARLES E WATKINS KENNETH W WAWERSIK CLAUDE D WILSON JR JERRY B WILSON
ROBERT DI ROBERTO HARRY FISHER KENNETH E GROVE STEPHEN F JALLOWAY DAVID M MILLS
ROBERT H HOLLOWAY RICHARD L OTTE ROBERT E PUGH ROY RATCLIFF JAMES N WYMER LORENZO CLARK
CURTIS L JETER BILLY LEONARD AARON L BRAM CEASAR BRYANT RICHARD L CAROTHERS
HOWARD CHISHOLM WILLIAM D COOK JR CHESTER G COX JACK J DEATON EDDIE D HOLLANDSWORTH
MICHAEL E DENT WILLIE L EARNEST DENNIS K ERDOS ELLIS C ESPINOSA TIMOTHY D EWING
ROBERT G DAVISON ANTONIO GARCIA JESSIE Y GOMEZ JULIUS GREATHOUSE JR JOHN E HORN
ARNOLD M HULL THOMAS F JACKSON RONALD J JOHNSON ALTON R KENNEDY ROGNER A LARSON
DONALD J LEEMHUIS JOE L LEMON ANGEL R LUNA CHARLES H MCCLENNAHAN HENRY J NELSON
RAYMOND D OLZAK ROQUE PERPETUA JR HARRY T POLAND ROBERT L RINGLER JR KENNETH E SCHULTZ
WILLIAM L SEASTROM GEORGE W STINSON JR STEPHEN J SZIJJARTO RAYMOND D TORREY JIMMY VASQUEZ
REGINALD M THOMAS JACK L WILBUR DARRELL W WILSON THURMAN ADAIR WILLIE L BROOKS
MIGUEL R BURRI JOSEPH F CARROLL MARK L ENGLISH LEON V FOX ROBERT P GANDIL
WILLIAM J MADSEN ALBERT J MCAULIFFE JOEL W MCDONNELL JAMES H MURPHY DONALD R PRYOR
SCOTT S WEBBER COLEY L ANDREWS RAYMOND C CLARK DAVID B CONN EDDIE B COOKE JR
ROBERT B COWELL WAYNE E DAWSON RAYMOND N HERRINGTON MACK A JORDAN ALLEN P MILLER
JOSEPH T MCCREIGHT RICHARD E POWELL MARCOS E SAN JAMES E TOOLEY ALEXANDER J VIGH
EUGENE W BURKHART JIMMY D GOLMON JAMES F HARRIS JAMES T HARRIS DAVID A LUM
PEDRO HERNANDEZ JR RICHARD A KOSKY WILLIAM A KUPREVICH DALTON B LOWERY LARRY F LUCAS
AUGUST G MANNION JR TIMOTHY J MCCARTHY GREGORY L MILLER JAY PAUL BRIAN F SMITH
JAMES C THOMAS BOBBY L WADDELL CHARLES H BALL JACK E BEAM EDWARD L BROCK
TIMOTHY E CLARK SPOTSWOOD DE WITT RAY B DEBUSK JR GEORGE R DURHAM MARVIN T HUGHES
JOHN H JOYCE RICHARD V LINDE BRUCE E MILES WILLIAM D MULLINS ROBERT E MURPHY JR
JAMES C MCINTOSH LUIS OLMOS ERNEST ORTEGA BERNARD E STJEAN NORMAN G TOENNIES
JAMES F WENDOLOWSKI ROBERT G WILKIE RICHARD G WORMDAHL VICENTE ZUNIGA GENE L BETTGER
ROBERT C BOYD DARIUS L BROWN FOREST E DUDLEY PAUL O EVANS GERALD L GOODEN
PHILLIP H HESS JAMES S HOLLIS GEORGE W JONES BILLY W LAMB RENOLD W PETERSON
JOHN L SCHMECKER MAX E SLOAN VICTOR TARASUK RALPH W VALT LUIS F ALVAREZ-DELGADO
STEPHEN E DUKEHART BROWNIE HALL JOHN S HALL ARTHUR W KERNS ANTONE PERRY JR
MARVIN G MANTERNACH ROBERT R MARTINEZ BARRY M MOUNCE BERNIS J NOVISKI DONALD R OSWALD
JOHN H REEVES TERRY W SHALHOOB FARLEY D THOMPSON THOMAS L TIGLAS DUANE A VOGEL
ULYSSES WHITE ALBERTO I JARA-VERANO GARY T MCCLAIN MICHAEL E SMITH CARL L YOUNG
WILLIAM D CARSON GIACOMO J CINTINEO CARL M EGOLF GEORGE L FRAGUA MARSHAL L HORTON
ROBERT M KLEVENOWSKI EARL W KNUTSON JR RAYMOND J METTY LARRY REED HERBERT D SURBER
RONNIE H BISHOP DANIEL L BROWN VERNELL D CARLSON RONALD D EVANS GEORGE F FREELAND
DANIEL L GARRISON MICHAEL G ROMANCHUK HARLEY E SHERMAN LARRY A STROM PLUMMER WILLIAMS
LARRY T WOOD SAMUEL Q ASHER ANTHONY C COFFARO RONALD R CONN HUBERT A ERWIN
FREDDIE L BURNETTE ALFRED L DAVIS GREGORY J FISCHER HOWARD S GOLDBERG ARMAND R GRAHAM
ROBERT J HARDESTY RANDALL L HIXSON VICTOR R HOYT PAUL G JACKSON RICHARD A KNAUS
ROBERT D LAJKO DONALD H LEDERHAUS DANIEL L MIRACLE JAMES MOSES JR RONNIE E NORRIS
JAMES E NUNLEY GARY W PEASLEY JERRY E SCHMELTZ RONALD J SHEEHY HUGH G SKIPPER
RODNEY D STATON JERALD D WALLACE BOOKER T WASHINGTON ROGER D WHITE ROSCOE WRIGHT JR
RAY F WILLIAMS LARRY J WILLIS RONALD J ZITIELLO JAMES A ASHECRAFT LONNIE BARBER
OTTO W BAUMANN JR ERIC A BRANNFORS EDWARD D DAVIS JERRY W DAVIS DENNIS F DELASANDRO
DOUGLAS W DOIG LAMONT W FINCH STEPHEN FINNEY CORNEL GIL RONALD GIROUX
GUY L GORDON DENNIS J HAMET DANIEL A HENNESSY BRUCE E HOLDERMAN DOUGLAS D HOUG
RICHARD C JACOBS ERINEO M MENDEZ CARL S MERCER DANIEL M MOBLEY JOSEPH M MOORE
WILLIAM L MCLAUGHLIN CARY NEAL JAMES W PAWLAK RONALD D RICH RONALD K SCHMID
JAMES L SIMS DENNIS M SPAHN EUGENE E STOUT MICHAEL VASQUEZ WALTER L WONNACOTT
JAMES R AARDE LUECO ALLEN JR LEE V BEARDEN MICHAEL R BROWN HERBERT J GABRIEL
THOMAS N CARDIFF JR ELWOOD D COVEY JR BLAINE A DE BOARD JR JAMES B ELDER JR CLARENCE E EVERETT

ALEJANDRO GARCIA JR DAVID R GATTON TERRY D GEMAS JAMES D GREEN TERRY S GUNN
BILLY N HARPER RALPH L HENDERSON JOHN L HOLSTEIN ERNEST KELLY JR RICHARD N LILLIS
ROBERT G PETRIMOULX GARY W PRATHER ROBERT F RATHBUN JOSEPH A RAYNO JOHN F REILLY
JAMES T RENZ CLAUDE B RUSH JR DENNIS G SCHLOTT JACK L SHAFFER RICHARD E SIPES
BOBBY R WILLIAMS CHARLES WILLIAMS HUGH F WINTERHALTER GUY W HUEY ALFREDO J SAENZ
CARL E BOLDEN RANDOLPH S HUTCHINSON JOHN G LARSON RICHARD H LOWERY ERIC C MAGNUSON JR
EDWARD I STARR WILLIE WALKER JAREL W AYERS ZACKRIE BROOKINS JR MARCELI CABRERA-RODRIGUE
DONALD CAMPBELL TERRY A CARLS SAMUEL G CROWELL ROBERT E CURRY DONALD W DRAKE
ROBERT B GLOVER HOWARD M KRAMER DAVID C ORFIELD DANA G ROSE GARY G SCHNEIDER
JAMES H BARKER LARRY A BULLOCK JACK E HOLT ROBERT NADOLSKI ALLAN H SCHULZ
MICHAEL D CANNADAY GEORGE S PHENNEY CHARLES L RAIFORD JR LARRY D ALLEN MAJOR R DALTON JR
ROBERT DAUPHINE JR LARRY D EARLS GARLAND G FUGATE JAMES E GORDON WALTER L GOSHORN
EDWARD E GREENE FRED D HART JOE HERNANDEZ JR JOE D JOHNSON JR ELMER L JUCKETT III
JAMES C KENDRICK JOHN L KINTON ROBERT L KIRKSEY WILBUR L KOHR GEORGE B MENGES
DENNIS G NICOLA JOHN H O'BRIEN GEORGE J SCANLAN ELMER F SPINA THOMAS L TROELSTRUP
NORMAN W VINCENT SAMMY WILLIAMS HAROLD T WILSON TIMOTHY C ABRAMS JR CURTIS T ANDO
RONALD L ARRIGONI DOUGLAS J FENNEY FREDERICO PEREZ JOSEPH R REICHERT ERVIND C STRANDBERG
GARY C RUHLOFF EVERETT L TABOR JOHN S BAGO JOE H KEIFER DONALD G REICH
VINCENT TORRES NORMAN B WENSEL RAY BELTON WILLIAM D BOYD REINALDO L DELGADO
TERRY G FEGELY JOHN HARGETT JR WILLIAM F JOHNSON CLEO L LEVANG JIMMY A MILLER
ROGER C MITCHELL MARTIN W MORENO HARVEY R PARKER DAVID L PEARSON ROBERT L SIMPKINS JR
THOMAS E TOWNSLEY WILLIAM J DUGGAN TONY EVERETT CHARLES D GABRIEL JOHN C GRESENS
RALPH R JUSTICE RONALD W PARKER HAL J ROWLETT CHARLES T SHELTON DANNY C BARNES
PAUL A BENKERT EDWIN S BRAGUE JR EDWARDO E CAZANAS-DIAZ WILLIAM L COVINGTON WILLY V QUAST
JAMES I DANFORD WILLIAM F DITORO RICHARD E FINK SAMUEL D FREEMAN III CONLEY R GARLAND
WILLIAM D GRAVES GEORGE M HANLON JOSEPH F HAYES ROBERT A HECIMOVICH HAROLD J KING JR
PEDRO O CANCEL JOHN M MIZELLE JOHN H MOONEY JR JOHN J MURPHY DONALD F RHODES
ALAN F SCHAEFER JERRY WOODALL DAVID YOUNG LARRY E BURKE JOHNNY A CHAMBERS
RICHARD G CLARK JOHN W DAHR LARRY L DEAN ROBERT W GREEN LYNN A HARRIS
GEORGE E HONSE ROBERT J MANN TIMMY G MATTINGLY JAMES A MESSICK JAMES E PAYTON
WILLIAM R LAWLESS JR ARNEZ F MILLER JR RICHARD A PIERCE HUBERT J PURIFOY CARLOS M RODRIGUEZ
PHILLIP W ROEPKE KENNETH R SCHROM DAVID L SHEEHY NED A SOWLE DOUGLAS J SULLIVAN
FENNELL TATE NATHAN C WILLIAMS JOHN A ABRAMS JAMES R ARTHUR ROBERT W BARTON JR
DAVID L BLUNN MICHAEL J CLEMENS CHESTER D FEWELL TOM FLANAGAN DANA R KELLEY
NATHAN E CHATMON JAMES D GOODMAN CARLYLE L GOULD MICHAEL A KRAFT CLARENCE LOCKHART

PANEL 14E

JOHN J LYNN JR RAYMOND MEDINA ANTHONY P MEOLA DAVID B MERRILL LONNY L MITZEL BRIAN R O'CONNOR
LARRY J NEHRING BOBBY J QUINN DONALD R ROBERSON CHARLES W ROBERTSON CECIL T THOMPSON
VERN L PRAY RICKFORD R SCHMIDT JOHN A SCHOLLARD VENNIE L SMITH JACKIE L WAYMIRE
JOSEPH E WILKINSON III JOHN J BAILEY JUAN J CERVANTEZ WILLIE J COOPER BLAINE M FERGUSON
ROGER E COOPER JAMES P GAULEY LEWIS D GROTHE HARVEY C HARRIS RAYMOND D HOERNER
WILLIE D JONES GLENN D MUSS TIMM C PETERSON LLOYD D PINKERTON DARREL L PRICE
THOMAS R SIEBEN MERRITT STOVES III HENRY J STUCKEY MORRIS C WHEELER THADDEUS E WILLIAMS JR FUIFUITAUA AMISONE
CURTIS M VOSS ROBERT W WHITE ALAN D WHITLOCK TIMOTHY D BERRY WILLIAM R BURNETT
JOHN D BURNS JR LARRY D BUTGEREIT EUGENE CABBAGESTALK DONALD J CALLISON WILLIAM F COYNE
RICHARD E FUCHS CHARLES G HAAS LARRY C HAYLETT ANTONIO HERNANDEZ-SOTO FRANCIS L LANGLEY
FELIX M LOPEZ-AGOSTO ALAN R MOORE ROGER D POLLEY SANDY L ROSS PATRICK L WOOD
ROBERT P SCHENA GARY D SHIELDS G L STETTEN JOHN L STRICKLAND JOHN O WELSH JR
LARRY D MYERS ERNEST H WILSON ALVIE C WYATT JACK L ALLEN MANUEL BARRERA ALLAN D TIMMERMAN
ROBERT E BETHUNE JOHNNY L BRUTON JOHN E BUSCH FREDERICK T CARTER RODNEY G DRAKE
CAREY W ELLENBERGER GARRY D FREEMAN THOMAS A GERG MICHAEL R ISHMAN ANGUS N JACKSON
CHARLES W JOHNSON LLOYD C LAUGERMAN DAVID B MATTHEWS THOMAS E MATUSH DENNIS P NEELEY
CLAYTON C KEMP JR CHARLES D MAXWELL BILLY W MCKEEL WAYNE C REINECKE RENE REYNOSO
SANDER C SANDERSON GUST J SHARLOW THOMAS C SHEA KENNETH L SHUFFITT CHARLES J THOMA
RONALD R VAN REGENMORTER BOBBY J WILSON HECTOR M ALCOCER-MARTINEZ RAYMOND A BIZZELL
MICHAEL R BROTZMAN FRANCISCO D DACANAY JEFFERY T DINES JAMES O DOUBERLY LOUIS E PIZZUTO
JERRY J DUSSEAU JOHN P EADS ROBERT T EDWARDS ROBERT D ERICKSON FORDHAM E FINCH JR
BOBBY G GOLDHAGEN GEORGE H HADDOX EDWIN C HILL BOBBY G JACKSON AARON B JONES JR
ROBERT S KEENER MICHAEL J KEHOE NORMAN L MOORE BRUCE D PATTERSON LE R PIERSON
RICHARD M CUMMINGS WILLIAM L RANDOLPH WESTON H REECE RICHARD A ROBB GERALD STEVENS
HENRY E TEASLEY MORVAN D TURLEY HENRY W WEBSTER LARRY C WEST ROBERT V WOOD
ARLO F BROWN JAMES B CANNINGTON JR FRANKLIN H CANUP JR JOE H EPPS ROBERT C FERRIS
LONNIE A FLOYD ROGER P GALLANT JOHN F GRIEGO JEROME A HAGEN FERRELL HUMMINGBIRD
ARTHUR R LE GROW HARRY L MARION DAVID M MCPHERSON ROBERT D MOORE JUNIOR R MORGAN
ROBERT J MEYER PAUL R NICHOLAS JR JOSEPH D NOEL ARTHUR A O'BRIEN ROBERT L PAINTER
RONALD L PARSLEY JOHN M SULLIVAN JACK R SUTTON FRANK C SUVARA JR ARTHUR K TYSZKIEWICZ
EUGENE WHITE FRANCIS J ZINDA DALE E BENSON A J BOTTOM GARY R BOYETT
NATHANIEL BULLOCK ERNEST W CADELL JR JAMES W CAHALL JAMES G CALLEN HAROLD L MONTANA
TERREL E CARTER ROGER J COOK RALPH D CORDELL TOMMY L CRAFT RICHARD O DE MARIS
ALFRED J DYMERSKI RAYMOND L ELLIOTT FLOYD T FLOWERS RICHARD A FUNELLI JR HERMAN L GURR
THOMAS J HARTY ROGER A HITES ROBERT C HOUGHTION RAYMOND C JACKSON EDWARD B JOHNSON
JAMES S CAMP FRANK H LASKIN ROBERT F MELTON JR DAVID L MILES DANIEL H MORAN JR
DONALD W NEWTON DENIS NICHOLAS RAYMOND S ORR GEORGE I PADILLA JOHN R PRINCE
HOMER L REAVES JOHN J RODGERS CHARLES E SMITH JERRY W SPROUSE ROBERT G STRANGE
KENNETH W TEETER DOUGLAS M THOMAS ARTHUR D WASHINGTON GARY L LININGER ALBERT H SMITH
ANDREW L MOODY JR KENNETH M OTTE MARIO RAMIREZ JESSE RICE CHARLES L ROGERS
FRANK T KRESESKIE JR FRANK L SMITH ROBERT J WELCH ARTHUR W WILKIE LOWELL A WOLFRIES
JEROME V ZERFASS BILLY D BRIGMAN RICHARD B BROCKMAN WILLIAM K COGDELL DAVID A COOPER
HERBERT H CROWDER DANIEL T CUMMINGS HERSCHEL L EPPS JR JAMES ESSARY EDWARD R GLENN JR
LARRY G GRAY JAMES A HARDEN YVON A HEBERT CHARLES W KELLY KENTON D KNAPP
FRANK J KREBS ALVA R KROGMAN ANTHONY P MAGISTRO STEVEN K ODIER JOSEPH R ORTIS
CEFERINO A ORTIZ-PRTIZ EDGAR J SAFFLE JR DALE C SCHUMMER VICTOR L TORRES FREDERICK J WOZNIAK
GARY G WRIGHT JESUS M ARCHULETA GARY O BRENNAN ROGER S BRYANT JOHN W FERRELL
RICKEY L GILLUM LEONARD C GRAY JR DONALD L HELTON JERRY D HUMPHREY GEORGE A JONES JR
THOMAS R KEAVENEY JERRY J KOLAR JR MARLOW E MADSEN JOHN D MCCARTY RONALD J MCCULLOUGH
THOMAS L NARUM DENNIS R O'NEAL CARROLL W PERRY ROBERT L PROVENZANO MICHAEL J SCANLON
PATTERSON SCOTT JR WILLIAM SHOVER LEO V SILBERT CALVIN R WILSON TIMOTHY E WORKMAN
DONALD R ASHBY SR ROSS M BEE STEPHEN A CHILDERS CHARLES E CLARK JOSEPH EDWARDS
DENNIS M EHRLICH CHARLES M EVANS ROGER L PARKER EMMETT F POPE JR DAVID M QUEY
JAMES V RALSTON CLEMMIE J TOMLINSON WILLIAM P YARBROUGH JR EFRAIN ZUNIGA JR GARY S EDWARDS
JULIAN M ALVAREZ MURLIN E BOON JAMES N BYERS FRANCIS E CAMDEN JR JACK L COLLINS
ARTHUR J ABRAMOFF PABLO G CONTRERAS BILLY S DAVIS WILLIAM L DAVIS ARTHUR W GREENE
JOHN L HAYDEN FRED L JOHNSON CHARLES W KAELIN RONALD L KENT REGINALD W LYNCH
WILLIAM J MACK MICHAEL J MARSHMAN GEORGE W MCGHEE ROY M MCWILLIAMS JAMES J NORCIA
CLYDE H O'BRIEN HARRY D RASH HENRY E ROBBINS MORGAN E SAVAGE JAMES B SIMMONS
HIRAM E WIGGINS GARY P WORRELL EUGENE O CONLEY GEORGE G COOPER ALBERT B DOYLE
BOBBY W CORZINE JAMES H DAVENPORT MELVIN G DAVIS MARVIN M DICKS
STEPHEN M DYDYNSKI STEVEN D FRANCIS HERBERT E FRENZELL LARRY W GARDNER EUGENE T GLOWACKI
JIMMY D HESSON JERRY F HOGAN BILLY C JONES WILLIAM A JONES JR GEORGE LOW
HARRY C MAHONEY JR ROBERT E MATSON HARRY J MILLER EDGAR E NUSCHKE HARDY W PEEPLES
MANUEL V TREVINO LOUIS J WANDLER JOHN L WILHELM CHARLES M YATES RAYMOND P ALBIETZ
LEWIS C ANDERSON DANIEL S CASTILLO WILLIE COLEMAN JR CLIFTON FREDERICK JR D C GEORGE
ROWLAND E GIBSON MELVIN T HUNTER DAVID F KIES RONALD L PENDERGIST HAROLD W REYNOLDS
DONALD E SHOEMAKER ROY V WELLS ANTONIO G YESCAS ERIC W ZOLLER TERRY L BRADEN
MARK A CHMIEL ALEXANDER COLES JR WILLIAM E COLLINS JR JULIAN A FINCHER JR JONATHON E THOMAS JR
BILLY W FLYNN THOMAS E HOUSTON KENNETH W KROUS PETER MACIEL JR DANNY D MCGEE
ARTHUR L DANCY DONALD G PEDDICORD GUINN J ROGERS JOHN W VAN CLAKE MICHAEL VITACCO
JOHN C WEBORG DAVID N WOLFE RICHARD T WUCINSKI THOMAS J BARBEE RICHARD A ERICKSON
ANTONIO A ESQUEDA CECIL F FINCHER JR DAVID C GREGORY JIMMIE A HERRERA ROBERT H SMITH
WILLIAM E HINGSTON JR ROBERT W KENNY JOHN A LAMBIE JR RODERICK C PORTELLO MAX C SIMPSON
OWEN D GOODSELL JAMES P SPENCER FRANCIS J THOMPSON THOMAS E VAN HOUTEN CLARK L WALKER
BRIAN D CONLAN JR JEROME CONNER ARTHUR E DONOVAN JOSHUA W EASON ARCHIE M ELLYSON
GEORGE E JONES JR CRAIG S SHELTON FREDERICK A SIMS FRANK J SOMERS WILBUR T STAIR
WILLIAM E GUSEMAN III ARNOLD B WALLACE ARTHUR C AGUIRRE JAMES P BAUER DENNIS W BAXTER
KIRBY W BRADFORD ROBERT L BROWN JERRY H BRYANT THOMAS J CAREY HOWARD H DEAN
CHARLES C CURTIS JR GARY T FRALEY DELL C GEISE ALLAN GUINN CLIFTON O HAIRSTON DAVID JAMISON
JAMES H JONES WILLIAM F KRANZ JR CALVIN L MILLER THOMAS R MORGAN MANSFIELD M TOOGOOD JR
NELSON K RIVERS MARK E ROBINSON LLOYD T RUGGE EARL F SMITH MALCOLM C SMITH
JAMES E MYERS THOMAS R SNAITH RICHARD N STANSELL DOUGLAS L TRACY JOSEPH R WALLEN
EDWIN L YOUNGMAN RUSSELL M ZGRABIK JOSEPH P ARRINGTON ARMAND J AUFIERE JOHN F BANKOWSKI
MARVIN D BENNETT JOSE J BOYLESS MICHAEL S BRYANT LARRY D CLAYBROOK DONALD W EVANS JR
JOHN C FAIDLEY SIDNEY W FLEMING SAMMIE HOWELL OTIS C JONES JR JEROME J RINGENBERG
STEVE W KINGHAMMER ROBERT W MOORE RICHARD J MOSLEY J C NABORS NICHOLAS L NAVARRO
LAVLE J HALL LEROY W PEAGLER FRANK M RHODES ROBERT G ROBERTSON THOMAS Q SABLAN
STEVE A SRSEN ROBERT V THOMAS RICHARD V THOMPSON LAWRENCE S VOGEL JOHN S WOOLHEATER
SAMUEL R BIRD MICHAEL E BRADY WILLIAM R BROAD GARY A DIEU GERALD A DORR JACKYA K GRANT
CLARENCE I HENRY HARVEY G HOWE JR PETER J KELLER JR TERRY L MANZ
JOE F KELLEY FRED L PEDERSEN PAUL B SEVERLOH JAMES L STEINEKE PEDRO A SWENSON JAMES E THOMAS JR
FRANCIS P JELINEK WILLIAM D THORNTON JR CHARLES M TITUS RUSSELL M WAGNER JAMES L WATKINS VINCENT J WEEDO JR
DONALD F YATES JOHN F BERGERSON LARRY W BIEDIGER JOHN I COOK JOHN J SHAW
WILLIAM R DUMAS CHARLES E FAGGETT PERRY L HARRIS ALFRED B MAY LYNN L MILES
FREDERICK M BONANNO RONNIE E REEDER STANLEY A ROBINSON JR CLAUDE A SILVA DONALD S SULLIVAN

PANEL 14E (*Continued*)

PHIL I VALDEZ   GARY E WARD   CHARLES ESTERS JR   RICHARD GARCIA   PAUL D HOLLOWAY
GERALD J MAGUIRE   DANIEL J MYERS   RICHARD L PARHAM   ROBERT L POSEY JR   RUDOLPH REMULAR
JAMES R RHODES   ROBERT E STEIRO   HOWARD L BARDEN   DAVID D BERKHOLZ   GARY E BULLOCK
JOHN T FILPI   EDWARD P HANSHAW   MICHAEL T JONES   ROY R KUBLEY
ERNEST T DUPONT   RONALD K MIYAZAKI   HAROLD H MORRIS   HARVEY MULHAUSER   WILLIAM H STRAUGHN
NICHOLAS E TERRAZAS   LLOYD F WALKER   MERRILL V BEASLEY   WILLIAM A BEYER   JOHN C BOHANNON
JERRY E BROOKS   AUGUST CHIASERA JR   WALTER R DALEY   DAVID J FRISCHMANN   JAMES D HENDERSON
ROBERT C KERI   ERVIN L LAIRD   ROBERT W MARTIN   JAMES P MCGRATH   RICHARD P MCSTRAVICK JR
DAVID W NORTHUP   RAUL ORTA   WILLARD A PHILSON   ROBERT J PRAZINKO   JERRY D WORTHY
LEONARD ROBINSON JR   CARL E RUSSELL   GORDON W RUSSELL   WILLIAM D SCHADDELEE   JOHN H WELCH III
ROBERT V BAIR   JOHN J BENTFELD   JOHN A DABONKA   JOE R FULCHUM JR   ROGER D HERRANDO
ANDREW J HILDEN   PHILIP H JOHNSON   EDWARD E MANNS   THOMAS M MARTINEZ   LUIS G MORA
EDWARD C MCCARTHY   JOHN E MYERS   MARION G RUNION   LARRY E SMITH   LARRY E SMITH
GEORGE C STEWART   JAMES B STEWART   MARCO J BARUZZI   HAROLD E BERG JR
TIMOTHY DALY   RAYMOND C DAVIS   RAYMOND F DEMORY   ADAM FISCHER   JAMES E FORSMAN
JOHN F ANTHONY   EARL W JENNINGS   AUGUST D JOHNSON   PAUL R KARAS   FERNANDO LEAL   HAROLD E LEE
CASIMIR NIESPODZIANY   WILLIAM R PHILLIPS   STEPHEN C SANGER   PAUL T SHORT JR   PHILIP J SMITH
WENDELL SPENCER   JERRY L SPICER   ALVIN G TENNISON   JACKSON THOMAS   ROGER B TJERNBERG
MORTON E TOWNES JR   ROBERT D WARE   DAN T WASHINGTON   DAVID W WEHRS   ROBERT L ARMITAGE
SALVATORE CAMMARATA   ALLAN P COLLAMORE JR   HERB DOBY   ROBERT F HELVESTON   RONALD C KISSINGER
WILLIAM D DAUGHERTY   CHARLES S HYMERS   KENT L JOHNSTONE   GARY L JONES   LARRY E LEE
WILLIAM L LOWMAN   THOMAS R MARK   JOSEPH R MARTINEZ   SAMUEL D MCCLARY   ROBERT W MOYER
FRANK M PIPKIN   RUSSELL A POOR   ROBERT L SHAFER   CHARLES M SHELTON   EDWARD F SMITH
JOHN STORELLI   DONALD E THOMPSON   JOE F WALKER   DENNIS WILBUR   FRANKLIN B WILLIAMS
ROBERT F STARBUCK   WOODROW H WILBURN   JAMES C WINSTON   RICHARD A WOOD   CLIFFORD D BEELER
JAMES E BOSTOCK   JOSEPH M BRADY   ULYSSES G BURROUGHS   DAVID D DAVENPORT JR   LEON N DOUCET
ROBERT R ECKER   ROBERT J ELGAARD   HENRY R LOPEZ   MICHAEL A LOWERY   JAMES R PAUL
GERALD L LARSON   JAMES F MCELYEA   MELVIN G MOFFETT   JIMMY E MUMFORD   ROBERT R PORTEOUS
DAVID E PRICE JR   KENNETH D ROBERTS   JAMES H SCOTT   IRA J SPITTLER III   JAMES A ANGERMILLER
EVERETT ARMSTRONG   SAMUEL W ARRINGTON JR   DONALD R BAIR   MAX E BROWN JR   SAMUEL J BROWN
ROGER V BURKE   JIMMY L BUSSEY   GEORGE J CARRILLO JR   GILMORE W CHRISTY   LARRY E CROSS
RAYMOND M DARRIGAN   PATRICK J FORAN   WILLIAM E FRANKLIN JR   SYDNEY U GOODIN   WILLIAM ROBERTS
WILLIAM E GRAY   DONALD J HALL   LUCIUS L HEISKELL   FRED A JOHNSON   RICHARD A KIBBEY
JAMES A LASCHE   RONALD W MCNEILLY   JAMES O MILLER   MERRHAGE M MOYER   CARLOS N MUNIZ
KENNETH J FLETCHER   MICHAEL C NEWMAN   THOMAS M NOWACK   WILLIAM J ROBBINS   KENNETH H RUD

PANEL 15E

RICHARD D SHEPHERD   CHRISTOPHER S SIGMAN   VICTOR G SPRAY   PATRICK H WOOD
GORDON W STARK   EDDIE L SULLIVAN   ROGER L TANNER   SAMUEL D THOMPSON   CARLOS UGARTE
CHESTER P SIMPSON   RUSSEL L WATSON   HARVEY BREWINGTON JR   BRADLEY T DAIGLE   BOBBY L HAYES
KENNETH L DEAVERS JR   ISAIAH A DOBBINS   JAMES H DUNCAN   BARRY E EVERT   WILLARD A GODFREY
BILLY CHARLES   WILLIAM E HANCOCK   BOBBY J JENNINGS   DWIGHT D JONES   THOMAS E LITHERLAND
JOHN L LOCKWOOD   WILLIAM S MASTER   DANIEL J MCGILVARY JR   WALTER MILLE   RICHARD M MOYERS
TIMOTHY A OLSON   GEORGE K SISLER   RODGER C SNYDER   HAROLD E STIGER   CLARENCE J SWEENEY
JOE E BELL   FLOYD J BERRY JR   KEITH A CAMPBELL   JAMES A DICKENS   GERALD T FETTKETHER
CARL FOSTER   STEVEN M GOLDSBORO   HARRY L JAMES JR   GERRY W LAWSON   MILLARD F MEADOWS
JOSEPH S MEISBURGER   FREDERIC W MILLER   JACK M SECREST JR   PETER M SULLIVAN   RICHARD J WRIGHT
ARMANDO AGUILAR   CHARLES C HARDING   LEROY HENSLEY   WILFREDO PAGAN-LOZADA   MICHAEL F SCOTT
JOHN C HOWLAND   EARL Q QUARTERMAN   ANTHONY THOMAS   OLLIE TUCKER   CHARLES J VITANZA
STEVEN WALDRON   EDWIN E WILSON   ISRAEL ALICEA   PETER BARBERA   WILLIAM J BRYANT JR
PETER F DELANO   MARK D HOLTE   LARRY D JUDKINS   OTIS LEWIS   THOMAS R MANNING
MERRIL A MCKILLIP   PAUL J PERECKO   CHARLES P POHLMAN   FRED C RUSSELL   CHARLES M SWAIM
GEORGE J WIDGER   WILLARD D ARNOLD   RONALD E BERRISFORD   WILLIAM C FORE   DANIEL E HORTON
MILES H NELSON   CLAUDE A ONLEY   ABRAHAM B REESE   RODERICK J RODENBECK   OLIVER G ROWE JR
MARCUS D WHITE   MORRIS E BURNS   ALLEN L BUTLER   STEVE L CAMBY   PAUL V CARLSON
KEVIN J CARROLL   ALLEN DE NICOLA   THOMAS P DEITEMEYER   CLAY E DOWNEY
ROGER W EDWARDS   DONALD J EGAN JR   HAROLD J GILBERT   REX W HIGHFILL   RONALD W HUTSON
TRACY L JONES   ROBERT L KING   ROGER L NIEMI   RICHARD D NOVOTNY   PATRICK H PETTWAY II
HARMON J PIGATT   GERALD RICCI   BERNARDINO SANTIAGO-VAZQUEZ   EDDIE J SCOTT   JERRY P SETZER
JOSEPH D CRAIN JR   RICHARD N SLAVIN   MARTIN J SULLIVAN   CASIMIR S SYLWANOWICZ   COURTNEY E WEISSMUELLER   PETER J YEINGST
WOLFRAM W BISCHOF   RUDOLPH F DUNGEE   JOHN T EVANS   RICHARD C GLIDDEN   BARRY J GOODMAN
JOHN A HAMNER   JOHN R MCKAY JR   CARL W MUELLER   CHARLES L MYERS   LEONARD S PELULLO
R C PERRY JR   CARL G SMITH   JAMES C ULRICH   DONNIE L WARD   JOHNNY WILLIAMS
GALEN L WILSON   HAROLD W WINGET   NAPOLEN K COOPER   EDWARD F RUSHING   MARCUS S TURNER JR
JACOB H CUNNINGHAM III   RAYMOND L HART   ALBERT J HAYES   STEVEN R KING   ROBERT C MARVIN
JAMES E BERARD   OSCAR E RATLIFF   NORMAN R REAGAN   RAYMOND W RICHARDSON   ARTURO RODRIGUEZ
JOHN P BURKE   FLOYD G SAVELL   MICHAEL T SCROGGIN   RUBEN A VAZQUEZ-BERRIOS   LEROY J BORST JR
MERVYN M CARSON   JOSEPH M CASSERLY   ALLEN B CHAMBERLAIN   ROBERT W LINSON
JAMES S CHILDERS   JOHNIE N DANIELS   JOSEPH A FALATO   RONALD C GEHLER   DAVIE J MARTIN
HARVEY M CARKIN   RICHARD A CARVER   KENNETH L HARGRAVE   PHILLIP R JARRETT   JAMES L KRAMER   DONALD S LOWERY
LAWRENCE C CLAUSEN   VAN D MANNERS   DANNY L MCMINN   ROBBIE R MILLS   EDGAR W ODIOT
GARY C PADDOCK   JOHN J RAYMOND   MICHAEL P REILLY   RODNEY H RICKLI   CHARLES L ROBBINS
JAMES L RUSH   CHARLES L SLACK JR   PEDRO A SMITH   LOUIS R SOWARD   ERIC B SPEAK
ROBERT C STEWART   THOMAS TAMILIO   CHARLES M WAYT   LOUIS E WILLETT   EDWARD E FORTENBERRY
CHANNING ALLEN JR   CARLTON AMERSON   WILLIAM L ANDREWS   MICHAEL O BATSON   LEE R BAYS
JEFFREY L BEATY   WILLIAM M BERENWICK   LANNY R BOLDING   STEPHEN Z BORCZYK   RICHARD A LAWRENCE
RAY E BRADLEY   WAYNE N CARD   MICHEAL G CARTWRIGHT   ROBERT W COFFEY   DOUGLAS R COLBERT
AGOSTINO W DASARO   GEORGE E DICKERSON   DONALD R DORMAN   CURTIS L DUCK   JAMES L ELLIOTT
GARY A CURTIS   CHESTER W EDEN   DOMINGO ESCALANTE JR   LARRY S FETHEROLF   MANUEL S FLORES
RICHARD L ADAMS   JOSEPH P FORAN   THOMAS V FORD JR   FRANK F GAGLIANO   GIUSEPPE GIANNELLI
JERRY B GOLDING   WALTER W HARING   CLEMENTE D HERNANDEZ   WILLIAM D HOLDEN
JESSE W IVY JR   EDWARD H JACKSON JR   RODNEY D JOHNSON   LEMEN E JONES   JEFFREY G KAZIKOWSKI
ROBERT E HOLCOMB   ELMER F KEPSEL   TROY L KNIGHT   RICHARD L KOLLMANN   KENNETH L KOSTER   LAWRENCE R KUSILEK
ANASTACIO H BELTRAN   CHARLES R LEWIS   LEE LEWIS   ROY C LITTLEHALES   MARLOW M LOECKER
J L LYLES   MAURICE J MARIER   JAMES H MONROE   NORMAN J MOORE   RONALD G MOTTISHAW
COLIN D MACMANUS   DOUGLAS M MCCRARY   KENNETH W OGLES   JOHN E OOCUMMA   LIONELL POWELL
ANGELO PULLARA   JOHN E QUAM   HOWARD W REECE   JERRY A ROBINSON   UINIFARETI SALEAUMUA
GARY C RICHARDS   KENNETH T RUSSELL   DONALD L SCHNEE   ELMELINDO R SMITH   RICHARD TARKINGTON JR
TOMMY J TERRY   WILLIAM A THOMAS   KENNETH C TITSWORTH   MICHAEL S UHLIG   ROBERT F VERNES   ALTON J ZERANGUE JR
LUIS VIGO-NEGRIN   WILLIAM D WESSELLS   JOSEPH WIGGINS   LARRY P BLACKMAN
GEORGE W CARPENTER   LE R DELGADO JR   ROBERT C DONALD   DONALD A GREEN   RONALD D HART
ERNEST V HENSEL JR   DOUGLAS C REYES   EDMUND R VEDRO   JOHN D VOLNER   BILLY G CONLEY
CHARLES E ANDERSON JR   HERBERT J ARCENEAUX JR   LESTER BRIDGES   JOHNNY E BURTON   JAMES CLEVELAND
DELMAR L CROCKETT JR   DANIEL P DONNELLAN   PATRICK M DORAN   EDWARD J ERNST   WILLIAM I GOULD
THOMAS A GRAY   JOHN R GRIMES   JERRY W HIGGINS   HILARIO B LEANIO JR   MAURO R LO
STEPHEN A MCCORKLE   WILLIAM F MCDONALD   MARK M MCLAUGHLIN   JERRY R MILLER   JOHN T ODOM
PABLO PATINO   LARRY D ROSS   CHARLES SHAFFER   JAMES M SHAPPEE   TONY P BLANKS
WILLIAM M BRANOCK   BRIAN C BROWN   LEONARD C BURRIS   RONALD W HARRILL   SALVATORE V PORCARO
RALPH E HINES   ROGER L HOGSTON   RICHARD KNIGHT   PETER J LIBERATI   VANNY C MAHANA
JOHNNIE MASON   DALE W MOORE   WILLIAM L MYERS JR   CHARLES D NOWLIN   DONALD B POPE
GERALD W GANNON   LESTER W ROBBINS   HAROLD S WILSON   JOHNIE J WRIGHT JR   LARRY B WYNNE
THOMAS E BROMLEY   ELMO BURNEY JR   ERNEST W GAJDOSIK   JOHN L GAMBRELL   RUSSELL C GOODMAN
CHARLES R GUTTILLA   ENOCH JOHNSON   BRUCE S LA PORTE   JOHN E MCCARTHY   GARY L WOOTON
THOMAS H ZEHNER   CHARLES P ALEXANDER   THOMAS E BADAVAS   THOMAS H BAKER   DOMINGO R BORJA
JAMES E ADAMS   I V BOURRAGE   MARVIN R COLE   ROBERT E GELONEK JR   WILLIAM A GILMORE
HAROLD GOMEZ   RAY M HARMON   GLENN A HARRIS   BYRON G HIGHLAND   WALTER L HOWARD
JAMES D HUNTER   JOSEPH L JACOBS   JAMES J LA BARBER   WILBERT G PENNELL   DENNIS M THOMPSON
JOHN D OSSMEN   TERRY J PERKO   JOHN J RUDINEC   JAMES T SEYMOUR   JOHNNIE SPENCER JR
TROY F TOMBLIN   JAMES R WALKER   WALTER WEISS   WAYNE T WOODRUFF   ARTHUR WRIGHT
SOLOMAN D ARLINE JR   CLARENCE A BROWN   DWIGHT S CAMPBELL   OWEN R EMERY   LARRY E FOWLER
EZEKEIL T EXUM   FRANCISCO GARCIA   ALLAN G GRIFFIN   ROBERT M JONES   TIMOTHY M KRANSHAN
JOHN R MCCORD   DANIEL E MOORE JR   WILLIAM J MOORE   PATRICK E O'BRIEN   GEORGE W OVSAK
WILLIAM M POWERS   THOMAS G SHEPHERD   PAUL L STEWART   HOMER URRABAZO   ALEXANDER VIDALES
ROBERT L SHOLL   MICHAEL L UTLEY   CRAIG S VAUGHT   SALVADOR ZABALA JR   LARRY W BRENDEL
JOHN L BYLON   MICHAEL B CARTER   GREGORY C CLEMENT   GEORGE E COLES JR   JULIAN W COUCH
HOWARD D GERSHEN   DELACY GRAY   ROY C GREEN   LEON G HOWARD   JAMES A MASTEN
GEORGE E MCCROBIE   JOHN R MICKNA   MARTIN M MUGAVIN   WILLIAM R SANDERS   FRANKLIN R WATKINS
EARLEY J MESSER   LANDON C RAY   FRANK R SILLS   RANDALL E WALKER   ALBERT B AYRES
WILSON E BIBLER JR   ROGER A CASTLE   DONALD A CHAFFIN   EDWIN E COOPER   RONALD C CRAPO
TERRY L DAVIS   GEORGE H DORSEY JR   JOBIE C DOZIER   JOHNNIE L EVANS   DONALD C GRANEY
PAUL H GRAY   CARL A HUMPHREY   EMORY F JOHNSON   GARY S JORDAN   STEVEN KIRBY
THOMAS E GRAY JR   RAYMON D KESLING   JOSEPH B LUCIDO   HAROLD W MADDOX   CHARLES G MASON
THOMAS MONK   ALBERT C MYERS   VICTOR R PASTRANA   THOMAS F PHILLIPS   RODNEY L RIEGER
LARRY R SCOTT   PHILLIP R SHOOPMAN   WILLIAM L STRUNK   VICTOR V ULLBERG   PAUL E VAN HOOSE
PAUL L VERNON   HILLIARD A WILBANKS   WILLIAM A COGGESHALL   PETER COGILL   LEON D ECKHART
JOE W BARNES   KENDELL D CUTBIRTH   WILLIAM C DAYTON   LAWRENCE A DIRNBERGER   DONOVAN K ELWELL
WILLIAM C FENCEROY   ROBERT H GRANOFF   JOSEPH E GRIFFIS   JOSEPH L HART   ARTHUR A JOHNSON
WILLIAM J FRANKS   CHARLES E HASSLER JR   ROBERT E KARR   GLOVER A PEELER III   HERIBERTO ROMERO-OYOLA
KENNETH F UNDERWOOD   DAVID F VANDERCOOK   ROBERT J WADE   JAMES E WATSON   JOHN M ZELENICK
DAVID T BELL   OVIE E BLANKENSHIP   HARRY P BRIGHTMAN   JOHNNY E BRUMLEY   LARRY R BUTCHER
GEORGE E BYRD   ROBERT T CARNOSKE   BRADLEY CHAVIS   JOHN K DAVIS   JUAN GARCIA
VINCENT J CANNIZZARO   THEODORE H DAVIS   EDWARD J GINTER   ROBERT J GOLD   ROBERT L HARVEY
FELICISIMO A HUGO   LYNN E HUNTER   ALLAN H KATZ   PATRICK B KEANE   RODGER D LEWIS
MICHAEL J LUTZKE   DONALD E MADDEN   HARRY MATHIS JR   CARLOS MEDINA   ROBERT A MILLER
HUGH J MCCORMACK   CALVIN C MORGAN   WARREN F MUHR   RAY NIXON
ARTHUR A NIEDERMEIER   MATTHEW T ORTON   DONALD L PENDER   STEVEN O PERLEWITZ   BRADLEY L POWERS   DANNY R REIGSTAD
CLARENCE H RICKARDS   CESAR E SANCHEZ   GERD F SEELIG   WAYNE K SIPPEY   THOMAS E SMITH
LEONARD R STCLAIR   RICHARD J STERLING   RICHARD E TOMASINI JR   MANUEL A TORREZ   JACK R TRIM
GEORGE T VOLLMAR   GEORGE S WALTON   GARY A WEBB   MAXIMO YABES   JAMES E ABSTON JR
ROBERT C ALLEN   HAROLD J ALWAN   BOBBY J BARCENA   JOHN R CACIOPPO   MICHAEL J CARLEY
WILSON L COOK   JESUS R CRUZ   JAMES L CUNNINGHAM   DONALD G DETMER   DAVID O FJERSTAD
GARY L FULLER   SANTIAGO R GONZALES   ROBERT J HALL   J H HOUSTON   JAMES R HUBBARD
LITCHFIELD P HUIE   JOHN W JACKSON   ROBERT H JONES   EDWARD N LETCHWORTH   TEDDY W STEELMAN
JOSE R LOZANO   SAMMY F MONROE   DOUGLAS E NICHOLS   CHARLES S NORRIS   TIMOTHY E PERRY
ROLAND W RAY   GEORGE ROWLAND JR   BERNARD J SAUSE JR   JOHN P SCOGGINS   MICHAEL E SIMS
DONACIANO F KAUFMAN   OTIS B SINK   ARTHUR C SISCO JR   GARY K SMITH   VIRGIL STANLEY JR
CONRAD F STRAUB   GORDON R TEFTELLER   WALTER R THOMAS   ARTHUR J TURNER   DONALD T VAN HORN
CLARENCE VARNADO   TRAVIS G WALDEN   BRIAN C WEHNER   NEIL S WILLIAMS   RONALD L ZEMPEL
JOHN C AGEE   JAMES ANDERSON JR   DAVID M ANTHONY   JOHNNIE F BARCHAK JR   RICHARD I BERMEJO
CARL E BOCKEWITZ   RICHARD L BOLTZ   DON G BOYD   JAMES T BYRD   ROBERT J CALVILLO
JUAN CASIANO   BRIAN L COLBY   CHARLES COMBS   GARRY K COOK   STEVEN W COUCH
CURTIS E CRAWFORD   RICHARD A DEWANE   RUSSELL W DICKENS   KENNETH M EDWARDS   WILLIAM P FAHEY
DONATUS J GEILEN   MICHAEL J GLYNN   JAMES S GOSS   JOHN H GRAHAM   TOMMY MEZZLES
RONALD G GRUMLING   GILBERTO L GUILLEN JR   CLIFFORD E HAKES   LARRY C HARRIS   WAYNE N HAYES
MICHAEL J HEAL   DAVID C HOLDEN   VICTOR J HOMSLEY   BUDD E HOOD   WILLIAM W HOOD
LA V FOLKERS   JAMES F LAMN   JIMMY L LANGSTON   MATTHEW LEONARD   PATRICK N LYONS
STEPHEN L MILES   STANLEY G MILLER   MICHAEL J MOLINA   JAMES R MOORE   MICHAEL L MYERS
PATRICK M MCKENNEY   RALPH D MCNEW   DANNY R PARKULO   LEE E REUKAUF   DOUGLAS A RIX
JAMES L ROSS   LARRY E ROSS   HARRY T SATTERFIELD   JOHN A SERAVALLI   KENNETH L STEEL
DOUGLAS G STREET   HUBERT O TH-UOT   WILLIAM H THOMPSON   DONALD S VAUGHAN   HAROLD T VAUGHT
JOHN T WETZEL   ROBERT D YORKER   GEORGE D ARNOLD   FRANK D BAZELL   DE W BLACK
DONALD W BOLLMAN   JESSE L BRANDON   DALE V BREMERMAN JR   GARY L BRUSKE   WILLIAM BURTON JR
GREGORY W BUTLER   JERRY D BYERS   REGINALD F CARTER JR   EARL L CRISSELL JR   DAVID R DANIELS
FRANCIS C DONOHUE   THOMAS B DOWD   THOMAS J EVANS JR   JOSEPH J GRANDE JR   GARY A HENDRICKSON
TOMMY D HIGGERSON   ALVESTER HILL   JOSE HOLGUIN JR   ROLAND R JOHN   ROBERT E JOHNSON
KENNETH MITCHELL   VICTOR OHANESIAN   DAVID T RAMIREZ   EDWARD R REID JR   JIMMIE C ROSS
KENNETH P SARGENT   JAY C SHELBY   WILLIE TYLER   JAMES WHEELER   STEPHEN R BANGERT

PANEL 16E

RICHARD B BLINDER   PAUL L CARTER   THOMAS G DENNING   GUADALUPE B GARIBAY
FORREST GOODWIN   RICHARD S GRAHAM   JOHN W HANSCOM   TERRY G HEEKIN   THOMAS W MOORE JR
JACKIE L HARRIS   ROBERT E MARTIN   WALTER P MILLER JR   LAWRENCE T NERECK   GERALD F NOVAK
JOHN P O'DONNELL   TERRY A PATTERSON   WILLIAM SHORTT   GEORGE M SLOAN   HAROLD K SOUTHWICK
LLOYD I STEPHENS   RICHARD W STRAHL   RICHARD H TISSIER   JOSEPH VIERRA   JAMES A WEBB
ADAM E WERSCHING   STEVEN J ADAMS   RONNIE D ADCOX   CHARLES B ALANDT   GALEN L ARSENEAU
CHARLES H BENNETT   ANDREW R BROUSSARD   AUBREY S BROWN   WELBORN A CALLAHAN JR   JESSE J DIXON
CLYDE J CAIRES   WILLIAM L CAMPBELL   DONALD R COLDEBERG   PAUL W CURRAN   EDWARD D DISON
MICHEAL J DRAKE   MICHAEL L EBALD   WALTER J FITZPATRICK   JOHN D FORSHEY   ROBERT T FREED
MARTIN L FREEMAN   MELVIN C GAINES   EARL S GARRISON   RAYMOND R GOODWIN   MOSES GREEN
LARRY D HESSON   JOHN H JOHNSON JR   EDWIN JONES   EUGENE L LAVOY JR   DAVID C PAPESH
THOMAS J MALLON   RONALD L MIKESELL   MICHAEL R PADILLA   NORMAN A RENFRO   FLOYD W RICHARDSON
PAUL W RILEY   CHARLES D ROBY   ANGEL P SAEZ-RAMIREZ   PETER J SCHUTZ   JAMES A SKILES
ROBERT B SMITH   RONALD C SMITH   JOHN R STALTER   LAWRENCE STRACK   JOHN P TAILLON
SELVESTER J VASQUES   ROGER R WILLIAMS   HERBERT WILSON JR   GEORGE K YOCUM   LIONEL S ANTHONY
ERNEST M BEAUCHAMP   ROBERT E BUCKLEY   RALPH L CARLOCK   ROBERT N CLARK JR   ROBERT J GRITTE
DWIGHT L HACKWORTH   WALTER V HULINGS   CHARLIE B INGRAM JR   RUSSELL C JOHNSON   ROY R LA PISH
CHARLES E MURRAY   FRANK E REYNOLDS   ALAN C SHROYER   FRANK D WILEY   WILLIAM A BERRY
GERALD J BREEN   JOSEPH L BRIDGE   DEWEY H BROWN JR   REFUGIO J CANTU   PEDRO LEON JR
JOSEPH M DONOVAN   MAURICE FAULKNER   CHARLES J FEDDEMA   VICTOR C HILL   WILLIAM R JANKA
FREDERICK BURRIS   DENNIS R JENSEN   HAMPDEN C JUDSON JR   LARRY L KNUTSON   KENNETH W LAMPMAN
TIMOTHY J LYNAH   RICHARD C MCKEE JR   JOSEPH L MILOS   REGINALD G MORSE   CARL F MOWERY
ANTHONY M ORLANDO   ORMAN D PHILLIPS   EDWARD G RAY   ROY A SCHAEFER JR   DENNIS W SMITH
CLIFFORD E SPARKS   ROBERT L SPIRES   PHILIPPE B STEPHEN   MAGDALENO TARANGO   DAVID A TAYLOR
GERALD R THOMPSON   RICHARD H TOMA   KENNETH W WELLS   JOE A WHITBY   DONALD E WHITE
RONALD A WILLIAMS   ROBERT E WISE   WALTER R BLALOCK   CHARLES E BOGGS   HOWARD B CARPENTER
JOHN K CLARKE   SAMUEL R DROWN   RUBY E FELTON III   LYNN M FERGUSON   DAVID C FRYC
JESUS GONZALEZ   LAMONT D HILL   RAYMOND HODOROWSKI   EDWARD N KANESHIRO   GLENN A SHEPPARD
HARRY W KLEBER   DOUGLAS L KRAMER   LARRY A LAND   BURGESS A LOVE   RONALD W LYERLY
JIMMIE C MARTIN   DAVID G OUELLET   STEPHEN G PECK   WILLIAM C POOLE   VIRGUS F RAMSEY JR
CLYDE L KEITH   THOMAS J SANCHEZ   THOMAS M SANDS   BURT C SMALL JR   PAUL R SMITH JR
ROBERT N STAUD   HARRY E TAYLOR   LYNWOOD A TIPTON   THOMAS C TUCKER   WAYNE D WAGNER
CAROLD R WAITE   RICHARD WESSEL   BARRY A ZAVISLAN   FREDRICO ARNADO   KENNETH H ARNOLD
RICHARD A BAGLIO   STEPHEN P BLANCHETT   RUDY G BOWMAN   OSCAR E CHAMBERS   BENNIE L CROSS
DEAN F FOX   JOHN C HAINES JR   ROBERT E KASPER   JAMES K KEITH III   CHARLES F KENNEDY
NELSON S LEHMAN JR   DWIGHT B MAYER   CECIL D MCCANN   WAYNE E MEES   ROBERT L MILLER
DANIEL J ORLIKOWSKI   LARRY R RIDDLE   THOMAS L SCOTT   JOHN H SHALLAH   LARRY D WATTS
CHARLES D RIKARD   JOHN A SICKEL III   RALPH L STILLWAGONER   LOUIS F TORRES   LANNY G WRIGHT
STEVEN G BLOOM   JAMES P BYRNE   JOSEPH M CAGNACCI   MANUEL CARDENAS II   CARROLL O CRAIN JR
RONALD E GALVIN   WILBERT J GRESHAM   BUD A GUILLORY   GEORGE E HULSE III   MAX A LOPEZ
JAMES W MAROON   CHARLES R MOUDRY   HARLAN C NELSON   GEORGE F PAWLISH   ROBERT W SKARPHOL
ROBERT L SMITH   JOHN F STIRLING   RICHARD TREMBLAY   ROOSEVELT AMISON JR   GERALD E BARTRAM
LEROY P BOHRER   GEORGE J BOJARSKI   PRENTICE F BRENTON   JOHN M BRONKEMA   CHARLES P BROWN
JESSE R CASTRO   MCKINLEY CAUGHMAN JR   IVEL D FREEMAN   FREDDIE L FRIAR   WILLIS L FURNEY
EDWARD J HABUREY   FRANK C HUFF   CLEVELAND D JONES   AMBROSIOS S JURADO   RICHARD A JURCAK
HAROLD K KETNER JR   LLOYD M KUEHN   WILLIAM G LACEY   CHARLES D LAND   RAYMOND F LEFTWICH
NORMAN G LOZEAU   JOHN M MANSFIELD   ANGEL ORTIZ-RODRIGUEZ   OSCAR W PIERCE   RALPH R SPRINGS JR
RONNIE R PITTMAN   CHARLES L PUTNAM   DANIEL C REESE   ROGER P RICHARDSON   JOHN H ROTH
WOODROW J MUELLER   ROBERT J SOMMERER   MICHAEL F STEARNS   GUS STOVALL JR   LARRY J WADDELL
ROSS J WALKER   JAMES M ALBRIGHT   DAVID BARTOCK   LESTER BELL   DONALD G BROWN
JOEL A BROWN   CECIL L CHAPMAN   JOHN C CRAWFORD   WILLIAM C ECKES   FRANCIS R FERRON JR
JOHN H FLYNN   BERNARD A FREYNE   EDWARD S HALL   BYRON D HAMLETT   LEO C HESTER
JAMES J JOHNSON   WARREN E KECK   ROBERT G KERR   JAMES F LYTAL   LAWRENCE MARTIN
LOUIS P MERINO   CHESTER A MYERS JR   DENNIS O NELSON   ROGER W RABEY   WILLIAM E RAGER
JACOB F STEPAN   HARRY R STEWART   CALVIN P WHITE   MICHAEL E ALDERSON   HARVEY R CHAMBERS
LOREN A ARMLIN   WILLIE J BAKER   EDWARD H BALLARD   MELVIN BALLARD   DONALD L BENNETT
MIKE ARMENDAREZ   DENNIS J DE MICHAEL   WILLIE DOWLING JR   DAVID A DOWNING   FORREST D HOEME
FRANK C ESPOSITO   GARY W FRIEDMANN   ROY E GARDNER   JOSE GARZA JR   DANA L GERALD
CALVIN K GRAESER JR   GUY P GUADAGNO   RICHARD B HEYDT   FREDERICK A HITSON   LARRY L HOBBS
FRANCIS B CONCANNON   JAMES M HOLSWORTH   JAMES E HUTTON   JAMES T KAJIWARA   JOSEPH J KARINS JR
DAVID G KEARNEY   JAMES M KENDRICK   PHILIP J KIMPEL   JOHN R KREIDLER   RAYMOND LOPEZ
RONALD L MANLEY   NORMAN R MAYER   DOUGLAS O MUNDHENKE   JOHN D NOKES
FREDDIE MARSHALL JR   ALLAN B MCCUTCHEON   THOMAS L MCGEE   RICHARD N MCINERNEY   ROBERT C MCKENNA   JERRY M MOODY
CHESTER K NUESSE   FRED W PACK   BRADLEY E PETERSON   GARY A PLUMB   DOYLE W REEVES
RICHARD A ROWELL   RICHARD B SAMS   ROBERT E SCHOPPAUL   ROLAND J SHAW   HAYWARD C SPENCER
LOUIS W TERRELL   ANDREW TRAPANI   GALE K VOGLER   ROBERT C VOLTZ   RICHARD S WOOD
JOSEPH D ADRIAN   STEPHEN F BURLINGAME   HARLAND G CLAUSEN JR   NILS A DRENNEN   CHARLES D SAYLOR
CHARLES W BARRETT   BOYD G GARNER   EDWIN R GOODRICH JR   LAMAR HORNE   RICHARD HUTCHINSON JR
ROBERT E JOHNSON   RONALD L JOHNSTON   STEPHEN E KAROPCZYC   LA M MAJOR   ELMO MARINELLI
DANNY D RHOADS   GORDON R RIGHTLER   VICTOR J RUGGERO JR   ROOSEVELT SCOTT   DOUGLAS W STEGALL
ANDREW T CASTELDA   FILIBERTO G MIRANDA   JAMES P PERRONE JR   ROBERT L VAN GIESON   JACK H SMITH
JERRY L BORGENS   WALTER L CLEMENTS   TIMOTHY R COX   PAUL W HARRIS   FRANKLIN D HITE
JOSEPH W JENKS   DONALD P JOHNSON   CLARENCE A KIMM   LONNIE E PARKER   THOMAS E SAUBLE
THOMAS R BARRY   JAMES A SEARIGHT   MARCO A SERRANO JR   VIRGIL B TERWILLIGER   ANTONIO VEGA
RAY L WILLIAMS   MERLIN E BALL   FRED BEILE   LESLIE P BERNSTEIN   ANGEL L FRAGOSA-GARCIA
HUGH V BEST   MARSHALL E CLEMENTS   HARRY F CONRAD   GEORGE K COOK   JAMES A CRAN
RONALD W BASS   JAMES R CRONIN   JAMES B CUMMINGS JR   SANCHEZ A DE JESUS   CARL M EUBANKS
LEROY J GUILD JR   FRED N HANSHEW JR   MATTHEW HIGGINS   ROBERT W HILL   WILLIAM F HOGAN JR
THOMAS E GARSIDE   EDWIN N HOLLOWAY III   BURLON T HONEYCUTT   ORVILLE N JONES   WILLIAM H KOHO
ROGER S KOHUT   WILLIAM KUHNE   MELVIN LIPSCOMB   LARRY R LUMPKINS   ANGEL M SANCHEZ
EDWARD L MOORE JR   JOSEPH W MORRISON   PATRICK R MURPHY   WILLIAM C PEARCE IV   DENNIS C WILLIAMS
CLARENCE E ROLLEN   CHARLES P TERHUNE   RICHARD L THORNELL   RANDOLPH B WARD   DAVID E WELCH
STEVEN R WITHERS   DONNIE R BEASLEY   ROBERT V CRAIN   KENNETH E DOUGHERTY   DAVID L PARISH
SAMUEL FERGUSON   PETER J FREDERICK   STEVIE R GIBSON   MICHAEL J HUNTER   ALLEN T MAKIN II
DOUGLAS L DISPENSIERO   THOMAS C NICKERSON   THOMAS M OLIN   GARY W OLSON   ALLEN D PAPENFUS
IVORY P PARRISH   RICHARD F RITTER   HERMAN R ROBINSON   HUGH T SANDSTROM   RUPPERT L SARGENT
CLINTON A SMITH   DEAN SMITH JR   JOHN H SNITCH   VICTOR H THOMPSON III   VINCENT M TOMALKA
JAMES P VADBUNKER   ROBERT R ANDERSON   FRANCIS A BENOIT   ELBERT F BLACKBURN   PHILIP BROWNFELD
NORMAN R CATLIN   KENNETH R CHADWICK   MICHAEL J DALEY   MICHAEL C DOMINGUEZ   KEITH D GRIFFIN
ANDREW FEDOR   MICHAEL A GIANNINI   JAMES G GOETZ   JAMES B GORE   JOHN A GRABER JR
FREDERIC R CHESEBROUGH   CHARLEY E GUNN   DONALD E HARPER JR   LARRY E HART   ROGER K HOOSIER
RONALD J IMPERIALE   GEORGE D JOHNSON   CHARLES M KING JR   JAMES E KIRN   LLOYD N KURTZ
WILLIAM C LAMON JR   SYLVESTER LAND   RUSSELL O LEDEGAR   ROBERT S LISZCZ   PEARL W MYERS
NELSON A MATLOCK   ANGEL MENDEZ   CLARK A MILLER   MILLS C MILLER   MICHAEL J MONAHAN
JAMES C LA LONE   GLENN D MCELROY   JULIAN A MCKEE   CLARANCE A MOONEY   DANNY E NICKLOW
JAMES G PATTERSON   DANIEL F PEREZ JR   JAMES E PERRY   ALFRED PINO   FRANK M POKEY JR
RONALD B PRICE   JOHN W RAPEY   DAVID RHOADES   ANTHONY J ROMANIELLO   GARY S ROWLETT

JAMES E SANTOS   JOE L SCHROEDER   ROY N SHOUP   TRAVIS A SIMMONS JR   TED WILLIAMS
GEORGE AGUIRRE   ANDREW A ALDERMAN   LAWRENCE W BARISIC   ROBERT B BEALE   JAMES M BRANDON JR
JAMES H BRAXTON   WAVERIE H BUCHANAN   JERRY M CHUNGES   JOHN J CONWAY   JEFF CURRETHERS
GENE W GOEDEN   DONALD O GRIFFIN   PAUL C HUNTER   WAYNE L JORDAN   JULIO KANEKO
LAWRENCE L LA SALLE   CHARLES W LANTZ   JAMES D LAW   ROBERT G NALLY   STEPHEN B NEAL
WILLIAM T NORRIS   OTTO D TUCKER   RICHARD J VEDDER   RICHARD WOLFINGTON JR   CLAYTON MIDDLETON
DONALD H BROWER   LAWRENCE J CELMER   CHRISTOPHER W DAVIS   WILLIAM R DENNIS III   ALTON SMITH
MYRON T GODDARD   MICHAEL N JOHNSON   KENNETH W JURGENS   JOSEPH T MELENDRES   JOHN H WILLIS
MICHAEL E MCNEAL   JUAN V MINA JR   GEORGE MORGAN   DAVID W MORRILL   ROBERT E PAIGE
HARRY W BRANHAM   MAXIM C PARKER   CHARLES W SANDERS   MICHAEL F SMITH   CHARLIE E THOMPSON
JAMES T BRADSHAW   ROBERT L WESTFALL JR   THOMAS M WHITMAN   RALPH T WOODALL JR   ROBERT W WULFF
BENITO ALANIZ   JOSEPH C AUSTIN   VIRIL L AUSTIN   DAVID BAKER   JAMES P BARTON
JAMES J BATES   DENNIS J BREDA   BRUCE A CORCORAN   THOMAS E COULSON   MARLIN C EVERSGERD
JAMES A BLANCHARD   JAMES R CURRAN   THOMAS J DANDO   JACK M GOSNELL   WINSTON G HOLLENSHEAD
DONALD E JONES   BARNEY J KELLY   ROBERT L LINN JR   DEAN C LOEGERING   PEDRO MARROQUIN JR
THOMAS F MASTROIANNI   PAUL J MCGOWAN   JACK B MEACHAM   WAYNE T MILLER   ALFRED J MOODY
JAMES P NAILEN   FRED H PATTERSON   RUSSELL L ROOT   JAMES J RUFFIN   FRAÑKLIN D RUIS
PETER N SAMARAS   JOSEPH A SANTONE   LOUIS SAS   DONALD L SCHROEDER   JOHN N SHEFFIELD
GILBERT N SMITH   JAMES C TARKENTON III   FRANK TUNSTILL JR   FRANK VALDEZ   MARK A VASQUEZ
DONALD W WALTERS   JOHNNY L WASHBURN   RODNEY R WEED   JOHN C ARNOLD   CHARLES W BROWN JR
JOSEPH BAILEY JR   FRANTZ M BARON   FRANK BARRERAS III   MICHAEL D BIRD   ROBERT E BROWN
EDWARD L BUSH   GORDON L CABLES   RICHARD J CARSON   CARL R CROSIER   RICHARD P CRUZ
JOHN R CUSHMAN   THOMAS D DARLING   RAYMUNDO F DEHERRERA   BARRY R DELPHIN   JOHN W DEVINE
RONALD R FILLMORE   GREG F GOODMAN   NICK J GRCICH   ERWIN J HAARWALDT   THOMAS E HAGGARD
EARL N HAMMOND   GARY C HATFIELD   CLIFFORD R HERRIN   GARY L HOBBS   GREGORY B JOHNSON
MICHAEL H JULIAN   ROBERT L KESSEL   FREDERICK C KUNNA   CORNELIUS A LAU   BENNIE J PAOLANTONIO
MICHAEL L LAWSON   JACK R LICHTE JR   STEVE LOPEZ   DENNIS R MORRELL   DONALD L NEELY
JAMES W LOHREY   CHARLES A MCDANIELS   FRANCIS M MCGUIRE   OSCAR F NICEWANDER   JAMES R NOVOTNY
FREDDIE D JONES SR   DAVID W ROBERTS   JOSE A ROBLES-MIRANDA   GEORGE B ROSS JR   OSWALD C SOUTH JR
ODELL J WERNER   EDWARD M AMATO   HERMAN E ANDERS JR   CARL T ANTHONY   JAMES D BREWER
JUAN P AVILES-AVILES   NORMAN L BALLANCE III   MICHAEL A BALZER   LARRY D BARTON   THO-AS L BELL
RICHARD D BENADUM   GUYE R BENSON   KENNETH G BLANTON   SCOTT C BOWCUTT   ROBERT N BRADLEY
MATTHEW D ATKINS III   ROBERT A BRIED   WILLIAM A BROWN   ROBERT M CARTWRIGHT   JOSEPH CHAMPION

PANEL 17E

JOHN P CRANDALL   JOSEPH J DI LANDRO   TIMOTHY EASLEY   JACK EATON
THOMAS M ELLIOTT   WALTER G ELLIS   CHARLES R EMORY   TONIE L ENGLAND JR   CHARLES R GOODWIN
TENNIS C FERRELL   WALTER H FORBES III   BRIAN F GIBBONS   JAN J GRABOWSKI JR   WILLIE GRANT JR
CHARLES R GREER   JACK D HANGER   EVERETTE E HARDING   JOHN O HARRIS   ROBERT L HENDERSON
JAMES R HINTZ   DANIEL J HOLCOMB   WILLIAM H HOLTHOFF   JAMES H HOPSON   CHARLES E HOSKING JR
KENNETH L JOHNER   JOE R JORDAN   DENNIS KLINE   PETER S LARSON
VIRGIL M LEDFORD   HENRY C LEE   WILLIAM E LUND   WILLIAM E MALLORY JR   MICHAEL G SUDBOROUGH
FLOR MARRERO-BAEZ   HENRY R MATTHEWS   JOHNNIE M MAYO   LEWIS E MILAM   THOMAS F MINOGUE
DAVID E MCLEMORE   JOEL W MOCK   TERRY P MORROW   EDWARD J MULLER   THOMAS J MURPHY
ROBERT L KASTER   MILES J MCLOUGHLIN   PHILIP A MCNINCH   GARLAND A NEWHOUSE   DANIEL J NEWMAN JR   GERMAN L NICHOLSON
ROBERT E OCAMPO   JOHN W ODIERNO   PERCIE E OWENS   THOMAS D PETERKIN   JOHN F PEZZULO
ROBERT M PINNELL JR   STEPHEN D PLEASANT   LAWRENCE E POLLOCK   ROBERT H REINKE   RAY A RHODES
DAVID C ROGERS   JESSE B ROSE   ROGER D ROSEBERRY   THOMAS M SEKLECKI   FREDERICK W SEPUT
JERRY R LONG   ROBERT J SMITH   KEITH P STEPHENSON   DENNIS B STOCKWELL   THOMAS R TALMADGE
ALGERNON P THOMAS   MONTE V THOMAS   HAYZELL C TURNER   LARRY L WARNOCK   VINCENT R WILLIAMS
THEODORE R WOODS JR   CHARLES C ANDERSON JR   ALAN W ANDREWS   ALLEN H ARCHER   FLOYD BARKER JR
JERRY L BELL   KENNETH W BRENWALL   JAMES A CUNNINGHAM   BLAIR E DENNIS   CHARLES M DOUGLAS
JAMES L EVANS   CHARLES E FLETCHER   JOSEPH D FRANCOLINI   FRANK GRANATO   RALPH GRAY
MICHAEL B GRIMES   CHARLES H HABER JR   EARLIE C HAMILTON JR   CHARLES F HARRISON   JACOB A HORN
ANDREW HORVATH   JOSEPH D HURTA   ROBERT D JENKINS   RICHARD D KAMINSKI   WILLIAM T KAUFFER
GARY M LADD   CALVIN D MABERRY   ROBERT L MATTHEWS   RAUL MONTES   GALEN L MOORE
JOHN A MOTT   TIMOTHY X MURPHY   WILLIAM J O'BRIEN   RICHARD PATTERSON   STEVEN C PATTERSON
JOSEPH R PIAMBINO   JERRY L PICKWORTH   DENNIS A PRENTICE   PAUL E REAM   BILLY E REGISTER
GEORGE B RUSNAK   WILLIAM D SANDS III   CALVIN E SCHWARTZ   RICHARD S SEDIES   THOMAS E SHANNON
DANIEL M TAYLOR   JOSE B TIJERINA   THOMAS N TOLESON   DAVID VASQUEZ   RALPH M WENTZEL
FREDERICK G WHEELER   JUNIOR WILKERSON   BILLY J WITZKOSKI   JOHN ZUPAN   FRED S LEA
RONALD E BOHON   JOHN J BRYAR   ALANSON G BYNUM   ROY W CHAMBERLAIN JR   PAUL A CONROY JR
KEVIN M DAILEY   RICHARD F DUNHAM   PAUL L DURAND   JOHN A EWART   JOHN L FULLER JR
ALFRED FUNCK   WAYNE O GAY   JERRY H GEORGES   HAROLD L HALE   JERRY A PHILLIPS
STEVEN R ANDERSON   JOHN T KING   LEROY E LEONARD   ROBERT L PATE III   RANDALL L PERRY
CHARLES W GREENE   JAMES T REDDINGTON   RAYMOND A RYCKO   ISAIAH SAMUELS   JOE A SAUCEDA
MICHAEL D SCHULTZ   ELIJAH H SMITH   MAX P STARKEL   JOHN S SZYMANSKI   THOMAS D UTTER
RICHARD D ADAY   WALTER L ALBRIGHT   ROBERT ALVAREZ   JOHN H ARMSTRONG   FREDERICK H BRODHAGEN
PETER G CODY   EDWARD J CONWAY   CARL COX   DAVID C CUNNINGHAM   CHRISTIAN J ECKERDT JR
JOHN C ELLISON   SAMUEL GALLMAN III   ROGER C HALLBERG   FRANK R HOLLAND   WILLIAM B HOLLOWELL
RICHARD H HOUSH   SAMUEL B HUBBARD   LEIGH W HUNT   PERRY D JAMES   JAMES R KELLY III
LOUIS A LEATHERBURY   HARRY F MCGINNIS JR   JIMMY D MOODY   JOSEPH P MURPHY   WILLIAM I NELSON II
MARVIN T NOAH   JOHN PENA   LOUIS E PERRY   ROBERT B PHILLIPS   REID W STOLTENBERG
LOUIS A PICHON JR   JAMES E PLOWMAN   GARY L PREKKER   FREDERICK J SHUH   WALTER K SINGLETON
HAROLD E NULL   JACK T STEWART   ANTONIO VELASQUEZ   JODIE V WELCH JR   LARRY J WILLIAMS
ERIC M BARNES   FREDERICK W BERGESS   ELMORE BRITTINGHAM JR   CLARENCE H BURSAW   JACKSON E COX
ROBERT CAROVILLANO   DOUGLAS J CARPENTER   CHARLES B CLANTON   DAVID H COOPER II   GEORGE T COX
ROBERT L BURDETTE   RAYMOND R DE MOE   JAMES W EVANS   ALBERT C FILES JR   PEDRO I GARCIA
ROCKWELL S HERRON   JAMES H HISE   KENNETH JOHNSON   CURTIS C JOOSTEN   RAYMOND H KNIGHT
ANTHONY J KORPISZ JR   RICHARD E LEGATE   RAYMOND L MACKLIN   GLENN A MENOWSKY   DONALD MILLS
LOYD L MCBROOM   DOUGLAS E MOORE   JOHN W MOWER   GARY K NEWMAN   FRANKIE D WADE
DUDLEY R PATTY   CHESTER R PAVEY   DONALD R SANDERS   MICHAEL W TWIGG   WARREN D VOUGHT JR
CLARENCE W MONTGOMERY   JOHN K ADAMS   IVY T ANDERSON   JAMES C BATSON   GODFRED BLANKENSHIP
ROBERT T BRINKLEY   ROBERT E BRYSON   CLARENCE J BURLEY   ESIQUIO A CANTU   ROLAND A CUTCHINS
LEROY W CWIKLA   RONALD C DAVIS   JOSEPH C DE JESSA   JACK T DEMPSEY   DOUGLAS E DICKEY
DAVID ESTRADA   RAYMOND B GUARINO   EDWARDO L GUTLOFF   JAMES E HENRY   GOMER D HOSKINS JR
JOHN R HUBBARD   JOHN H JAMES JR   RICHARD S JOHNSON JR   MICHAEL P KELLEY   RANCE A KIRBY
FLOYD M LARRABEE   DOUGLAS W LEE   JAMES A MALECKE   VICTOR H VAN VACTOR   CHARLES H WHITE
THOMAS P MITCHELL   LEON L POLAND JR   BARRY F PRICE   JAMES A SETTER   TERRY D SHAUVER
LARRY J LARSON   STEPHEN M MINICK   RALPH J SMITH   JAMES L VER HELST   CYRIL J WESTLY
GARY L WILCOX   ROGER A BUCHANAN   JOE W CHANDLER   DAVID A DROWN   FREDERICK I FRENIER
KENNETH G GELLERMAN   WORLEY W HALL   DENNIS L HERSHNER   CURTIS W HURLOCK   KENNETH B JORDAN
CHARLES L KELLER   JERRY B KRAFT   THOMAS W MEEK   CHARLES A MORSE   WALTER E MUNNS
AMALIO PAGAN-PAGAN   ALEXANDER J PALENSCAR III   KEVIN M ROHRING   JOHN M TALLION   PAUL E ALBANO
CURTIS R BAKER   BOBBY J BARBER   THO-AS C BEKIEMPIS   DENNIS L BERTSCHINGER   WESLEY C BRENNO
STANLEY DAVIDHEISER JR   LARRY C DYE   CHARLES E DYKE   OTIS R ELLIS JR   STEVE S GALLIS JR
ANTHONY HAWKINS   ARTHUR E JONES   DANIEL R LAIRD   WILLIAM J LENOVER   EDWARD E MORTON
GLENN M MCCARTY   WILLIAM J O'BRIEN   JACK C OWENS   EUGENE J PAYNE III   LAWRENCE J PELLETIER
RONALD W PORTER   JOSEPH R ROBINSON   GLENN W SHAFER   DON L SHOCKLEY   HOWARD S STEVENS
GEORGE M STEVENSON   VERRELL D STILES   WILLIAM F STORCH JR   GERALD J WAHLEN   RICHARD D WEIDNER
PERCY L WILFORD   JOHN L BRIM   KARL A BROWN   GUY J BRUNGARD   JOHN B CABANA JR
JOHN W CLARY   JOHN COYLE   JAMES L FIELDS   DAVID L GLASSCOCK   WILLIAM H HOSEA
STEVEN S CHING   JAMES E HARRELL   MICHAEL P KNIGHT   JIM E OESTRIECH   DENNIS R PUCKETT
HERBERT C RICE   ROBERT E RUONAVAARA   RONALD E AMES   ALBERT G ANTER   RUBEN M ARMENTA
JAMES E BLEVINS   JOHN P BOBO   EDWARD E CANNON   LARRY H CRUMBAKER   ALBERT A CURLEY
JERRY W CURRIN   ROBERT L CURRY   MARTIN M DI ANTONIO JR   HENSLEY M DILWORTH   PATRICK GALLAGHER
EDILBERTO GARCIA   MICHAEL P GETLIN   JAMES E GREEN   STEVEN D GUNDOLF   EDWARD J KEGLOVITS
DONALD W KRICK JR   BRUCE V LE NOUE   RONALD E LIBERTY   JOHN L LOWERANITIS   CLYDE MATHEWS JR
WILLIAM J MCDOWELL   ROBERT L MCGEE   ROBERT W MITCHELL   WALTER J NERAD JR   WILLIAM W PATTERSON
GARY D MILLER   JAMES S OLDFIELD JR   RALPH B PAPPAS   KENNETH PETTUS   JAMES E PRICE
DAVID A SIEMON   ROCKY R SNYDER   DENNIS C STROUD   FRANK H THOMAS JR   ROBERT J WALTRICH
WALLACE WILLIAMS   DANIEL L ALBERTS   ROBERT L BALDWIN   KENNETH L BRESHEARS   ROGER S BRISKIN
JAMES H BRITTAIN   BARRY A CULLISON   CHARLES C DICKEY JR   EDWIN S GARBER   ROMAN R VILLAMOR JR
A G HENSLEY   MANUEL A HICKS JR   RICHARD A HILL   GORDON L HOGAN   MICHAEL J LAURIE
RICHARD A MENEES   PATRICK T MERCIER   JAMES R MORGAN   WILLIAM R PETERSEN   CHARLES R PUTNAM
WILLIAM C RELF   JAMES M RINGLE   GARY F SCHULER   RONALD H SOUTHWORTH   JOE D STOWERS
THOMAS M HANNIGAN JR   THOMAS M SULLIVAN   CHARLES G SUMMERS   JOHN A TODI   DELBERT C TOTTY
JOHN M WEST   FREDDY L AMICK   JAMES M ARRIES   ALLEN M BEALS   CHARLES F BIVETTO
EARNEST C BROWN   ROGER L BRUNO   KENNETH J DANTZLER   GARY L FAUCETT   RENE FERNANDEZ
RAYMUNDO GOMEZ   ROBERT A GOVAN   PHILLIP GRANT   JOHN K HARGRAVE   RAY W RHODUS
GEORGE H JOURDENAIS   LLOYD B MAGBY   ALLEN S MICAN   WILLIAM S MORTIBOY   VICTOR E PRESS
ROLAND H HOWELL   JAMES E PRESSLEY   RAYMOND F QUINN   JOHN O RHODES   CONFESOR RIVERA-MARTES
ROBERT P RUMINSKI   ALTON SMITH   ROBERT W STANLEY   RICHARD J STEWART   BENNIE H STRAIT
DAVID F TAYLOR III   ANGELO TORRES   MANUEL B VALLE   RICHARD M WATERBURY   SAMMIE L WATT
JAMES L WEHR   DAVID R WILLIAMS   JOHN B WOBLE   RAYMOND A AUSTERMANN JR   BARRY W BRICKEY
STEPHEN M CARNAHAN   LIAM S CASEY   ALFRED K EVANS   EARL FAISON JR   ROBERT A MONTGOMERY
THURMAN E FILLINGIM   MASAICHI FUJIMOTO   JOHN R GREGOIRE   JOSEPH L HOCKENBERRY   RALPH C HUTH
JOHN F DANIELS JR   PETER A LAMONT   FRANCIS M LAWRENCE JR   WILLIAM P MARTIN   ALEXANDER L MAYER
ALVIN C MCMANN JR   KENNETH M THIBAULT   VANCE G WILLIAMS   JOHNNY M WOOD   DANIEL L WENTE
CORNELIUS J CHAMBERS   JOHN R CHAPMAN   MICHAEL FERZACCA   CLARENCE F GIPSON   JIMMY H GUINN
DONALD T HELTON   JAMES L PARKER   THOMAS J POTEET   WILLIAM J RICKMAN   ROBERT J SHERWOOD JR
MILFORD D CARTER   LINDELL R STEGALL   VERNON R BAKER   ANDREW C BRUCHER   KENNETH E BYERS
JAMES W COLLIER   HARRY L DAVIS   JAMES E DEWEY   GEORGE R GALBAVY   PAUL V HARRINGTON

CHARLEY C KIBEL   SIDNEY G KREISHER   RONALD F LAKE   JAMES K LINDSEY   DAVID E MARTIN
MICHAEL W MARTINEAU   WILLIS A MATTHEWS   RONALD B SCHRADER   ROBERT T SICKELS   JIMMY J SMITH
EDWARD P SZEYLLER   DONALD F THULIN   LEWIS E AVERY   GLENN T BRISTOW   WILLARD BROOKENS JR
GUY A BYRD   HAROLD L CARVER   THOMAS E COMBS   ROBERT F COTE   REX L CRAIG
ERNEST B CUPP   LEONARD W ELIE   JIMMIE L ELLERBE   RONALD J FITCH   JERRY W MANNING
JAMES H FOWLER   BERT GUERRA III   PAUL L HARRISON   MARION R HUTCHINS   KENNETH R JAMERSON
ALAN J DEAN   WILLIAM P KELLY   KENNETH M KESSINGER   ALFRED G LIRA   EDDIE L MARSHALL
PHILIP R MATTRACION   LEONARD I MOORE   THOMAS A PARKER   DANIEL G PATRICK   ROBERT H PETTIT
CHESTER E ROWE JR   CHARLES L SALTER   RONALD R SCHNAIDT   JOSEPH A SCRUGGS   JOSEPH P WILLIAMS
BROOKE M SHADBURNE   JAMES A SLAGEL   WALTER M SNEAD   GEORGE T SUBERT   HAROLD L TALLEY
ROBERT W REED   RICHARD TOEPRITZ   HARRY E WAGNER   LELAND D ZAHN   ERNEST L GUTIERREZ
ALGER E DURELL JR   RICHARD M DYKES   ROGER E FLAHERTY   CHARLES W FORD   BERNARDINO GONZALEZ JR
JAMES L DARCY   CELISTER HARRISON JR   MICHAEL D HIMMERICK   LEROY C HOTCHKISS III   WILLIAM G SIPOS
JOHNNY E LEWIS   EUGENE MCCRAY   KENNETH E MCFARLAND   VINCENTE MEDINA-TORRES   JOHN R MINUTOLI
RICHARD E NEWTON   ALFONSO ORTIZ-LOPEZ   HENRY E PATENAUDE   EDWARD J PAUL   TED B PETERSON
GEORGE M HARRINGTON   CONRAD E POOLE   ABELARDO ARAUJO   DONALD E BOSTON   HENRY H GAMBLE
JAMES P BOYD   BRUCE W CADE   EDWARD G COURTEAU   KENNETH M CROUT   JACK C DUFF JR
RONALD D ANDERSON   MICHAEL F FLYNN   ROSS A GASTON   DAVID E GORRELL   MICHAEL M KAUFFMAN II
THOMAS J LESTON   DANIEL M MANN   DONALD G MILLER   JERRY R MILLER   LEROY G MITCHELL
ROBERT A O'NEIL   CIPRIANO J PANTOJA JR   ROBERT V PEARSON   JOHN R RHODEHAMEL II   GERALD W WILSON
THOMAS PATTERSON   BERNARD M THOMAS   PATRICK J TRODDEN   TERRY L ANTON   IRVIN S BANKS
JAMES R BANKS   DON C BENFIELD   KENNETH W BOAZ   GARY A CARSTENS   BILLY K CARVER
ROGER D COOPER   TERRENCE G DIXON   TERRY L ELLENDER   JAY F GEYER   DAVID P GIBSON   FRANCISCO A MONTANO
LAWRENCE R HAGEDORN   MANCE K HARGRAVES   JIMMY C HARPER   LARRY G HATCH
JERRY D HATCHER   CHARLES W HEAPS   DAVID E HEVLE   BENNIE L HOUSTON   HOWARD L LE ROY JR
LEONARD F JANTZEN   JAMES N KATRENICS   BOHDAN KOWAL   MICHAEL E KRAFT   DAVID W LAURITSEN
ROBERT R HUSTER   FELIX F LEYVA-PARRA-FRIA   HENRY J MARKOWSKI JR   DON L MICHAEL   EDDIE J MICKENS
ALBERT M GUYER   PETER R MCCARTHY   CHARLES M MCKINNEY   JERRY L MCKINNEY   WILLIAM P NEUTZLING
HIGINIO O OVIEDO   NATHAN E PEACOCK JR   JAMES W PELTIER   JOHN H PERDUE   JAMES A POPP
MICHAEL L PRIEST   ROGER L PUGH   DORSIE E REGISTER   WILLIAM S ROBERTSON III   VICENTE D SANDOVAL
ROGELIO SAUCEDO   JEFFREY A SCHWEIKL   HARRY J SIMMONS JR   LLOYD P STEARNS   JOHN E TARANTOWICZ

PANEL 18E

ROBERT THOMPSON JR   EVARISTO VILANO   MICHAEL A WELCH   GARY E WHIPPLE
JOHN W CHARLTON   THOMAS P CIBOROWSKI   KENNETH A CULLEN   JOHN C DUNLAP   RODNEY C EDWARDS
JOSEPH W FRANCIS JR   ALAN D FREDRICKSON   GEORGE W FROE   CARIO FULLER   FRANK J GARCIA
ARTHUR A GLEASON   KEITH L HARDY   GLENN J HLAVACEK   DOUGLAS C HOLLAND   JAMES L HOLROYD
LOUIS H JILEK   HAROLD B KING   JAMES F MADDEN   WILLIAM C MADISON   RONALD M THOMAS II
DALE E MILAM   ROCKNEY D MONROE   MICHAEL R NELSON   GARY F PAARZ   DALE E PLOTE
ALLEN W PORTER   FRANCIS M RINKER   THOMAS A SMITH   CHARLES A STOKEN   GEORGE TALLMAN
CLIFFORD W JAMES   HAROLD D VAN BUSKIRK   TERRY J WHITTAKER   HOWARD E BEAGLE   LEONARD A CARTER
CHRISTOPHER CRONKHITE   JAMES H EDWARDS   DAVID R FISHER   JAMES W FOSTER   EARL R GROVE
MICHAEL W HERRERA   JAMES W HINTZ   CHARLES J HOFFMANN III   RONALD L JOHNSON   JOSEPH P KRAMER
MICHAEL H LAMB   JODY M LANGLEY   DONALD E LONG   HARRY W MARTIN   SALVADOR M NAVA
JOHN F O'GRADY   ROBERT W RAETZ   MARVIN G SMITH   ISUM M WALKER   LEROY B WEBB
RICHARD A WILLIAMS   BARRY B BROERMAN   KENNETH M BURNETT   BOBBY W COLEMAN   EDWIN E ELLIOTT
JOSE M FLORES   GRANT M GILBREATH   JOHN H HAWLEY   AUDELIZ HERNANDEZ-PENA   KENNETH E JAMES
KENNETH G KONOFF   EUGENE R KRITZ   WILLIAM D LARAWAY   CHARLES LATTIMORE JR   CHARLES RAY
WILFREDO MERCADO-SANTOS   MICHAEL J MIGUEL   OLIVER W MYERS   JAMES D PIPER   JOHN J RABIDEAU
MEDARD A RUEHLE   GARY H SILER   WILLIS W WILLIAMS   DANIEL G ZEGARAC   JACK H ANDERSON
COLBURN BROWN   WILLIAM C CLAY III   RUDI H DUSCHEK   RONALD C HURST   CLYDE REED JR
THOMAS L BARLEEN   MICHAEL J KOTULLA   NICHOLAS KRIMONT   DONALD V LAWSON JR   FRANK A MADISON
MICHAEL J SMITH   CHARLES A SULLIVAN JR   JOHN H TYNDALL JR   VICTORIANO VELEZ   TERRY WELCH
DALE A BISHOP   CHARLES D BLACK   RICHARD E BOYLE   HARRY M BRENN   MARSHALL E BROWN
NEIL R ELLSWORTH   WILLIAM D GARNER   WALTER L GIBSON   CHARLES H HORN   WILLIAM F HORVATH
ROBERT K HICE   NORMAN T KERR   PAUL J LIFRIERI   HAROLD E MAHY   HERMAN E MILLER
VINCENT A RAMIREZ   MICHAEL L SCISNEY   ROY E SHULTS JR   ROBERT A TAYLOR   THOMAS R WALKER
MORRIS B WITT   ROBERT A CHAPP   JAMES R CLIFCORN   JOSEPH W DE ROSA   STEFFAN M FREDSTI
ROY D GALLANT   DAVID A GRAY   JACK M HARRIS   DALE M MCCAULEY   DANIEL F MONAHAN
ROBERT E MCKEE   ROBERT SCHERLAG   JAMES F TINDELL   HOWARD D VANDENACRE   RALPH A WICKHAM
JAMES R BIHLMEYER   GEORGE L CAMPBELL   DAVID A CARRICO   GERALD B DORR   ANTONIO FLORES JR
ROBERT L FLORY JR   RICHARD H GOHEEN   WILLIAM C HURT   LARRY S JENSEN   RAYMOND L KATZENBERGER
DARRYL J KOCH   ROBERT L LAZEAR   JIMMY C MCCARTER   ROBERT A MCCARTNEY   WAYNE L MIDDLETON
RONALD E MCKINNEY   BALDOMERO A NADAL   WALTER J PTASNICK   LAWRENCE J REICHERT   STEVEN J SURMA
ROBERT AGUILAR   FRANK A THOMPSON   JAMES R UTTER   FRANCISCO M VALENCIA   RICHARD A VINAL
BENJAMIN L BARRICK   CHRISTOPHER D BRINE   MARVIN Z BROCK JR   JOHN H BUTCHER JR   DAVID M CHANEY
WALTER A CHATOS JR   VANDIVER L CHILDS   DAVID C GLOVER   JAMES W GODFREY   ARTHUR J GRANT JR
DAVID HELRIEGEL   WILLIAM R HILL   GEORGE A INGALLS   DONALD L KANNEL   RUSSELL A LEFFLER
BILLY B LOUT   DAVID K MONEACHI   RICHARD W PIATT   KARL E SHENEP   JOHNNY W SMITH
LA V WALKER   GORDON O WALSH   RICHARD D WATSON   DAVID E WILLIAMS   WILLIE C WILLIS
DEAN R ZIMMERMAN   ROSARIO R ABBATE   VINCENT J AGIUS   GARY A BILLHIMER   WILLIAM A DISHMAN
BRUCE E BOWERS   RICHARD H BRIDGES   JAMES E CARLTON JR   ALBERT F CLEVELAND   MICHAEL A DE PROFIO
JOHN F BENSE JR   FRANCISCO GARZA   JOHNNY W GOULD   JAMES C HELTON   FITZ-RANDOLPH B MCBRIDE
GRAHAM R HICKLEN   EDWARD M HOWELL   ROYD S KERLEY JR   DONALD L MARTINEZ   JULIO MASSO-PEREZ
EARL L DERBY   JAMES M MCGARVEY   CHARLES MILLER   JOSE H QUINTERO   DAVID A RICHARDSON
JOSEPH R SMITH   EMORY L TAYLOR   RICHARD L TAYLOR   OTHEL THOMAS   JAMES R TREMAYNE
THOMAS WESTON JR   JOSEPH M ARAGON   RONALD D BRUCE   LEROY BUFORD   CHARLES C CLENDENEN
ROBERT J CRABBE   ROBERT B EMRO   PATRICK L HALEY   VERNICE HOLLINGSWORTH   ROY M JONES JR
ROGER E MATHIS   THOMAS D MENDENHALL   CALVIN E NEWELL   RICHARD A RHINE   WILLIE F AMOS
HAROLD J ANABLE   WILLIAM W BISHOP   DENNIS O BOLTON   ROBERT E BROOKS   SAMMY B BRUCE
JOSEPH L COLOTTI   ROBERT J COPE   HARRY L ECCARD   GILBERT EDWARDS   JOHN S HAMILTON
CHARLES E HAWK   STERLING C HENDRICKS   KENNETH E KASA   GREGORY L MARTIN   DAVID E MATTHEWS
BILLY J PATTERSON   JAMES C PEARSON   LARRY R REEVES   JAMES R SCALF   JOHN H SHERMAN
ALFONSO D SIERCHIO   JOSEPH J SYGNATUR   GARY L WESSELMAN   LE R YOUNG JR   JAMES W BARNES JR
GEORGE T BEAN   JAVIER BECERRA   EDUARDO P BRANES   RUFUS R CROOM   DAVID L DE LAUGHDER
GARY R FOX   JAMES A GALUTZ   JOHN H LA DUKE   WILLIAM E LAWSON JR   CECIL E LITTLE
WILLIAM R LUNDBERG   PHILIP G OVERTURF   ERNEST M SKINNER   RODIS J WARREN   LARRY W WILKERSON
GARREL L TEATSWORTH   THOMAS A ARREDONDO   EDDIE P AUSTIN   JOSEPH F BASCO JR   VINCENT J BENEGAS
RONALD M BOLEY   BYRON D BONDS   JEFFERY D BOUTON   RODNEY A BREEDLOVE   DONALD G BROWN
MARC A BROWN   JAMES E CAREY   RONALD R CORMIER   JOHN L DAVIS   RUDOLPH S GALIANA
BENJAMIN BUNN JR   GREGORIO M DEOCAMPO   EDWARD T EGAN JR   SAMMY G EVANS   LOUIS L GOERS
EDWARD D GOULD   LARRY W GREER   ROGER D HAMILTON   GARY R HARTMAN   TAMADGE C STEVENS JR
PAUL A HASENBECK   THOMAS J HOLTZCLAW III   WILLIAM D HUNT   RICHARD L KING   GLENN D KNEPP JR
LANNY R KRAGE   GERALD M KRYSTOSZEK   THOMAS A MANGINO   GARY W MARTINI   JIMMY M MULLINS
RONALD K NEAL   DANIEL R NIDDS   MAURICE J O'CALLAGHAN   JAMES J OWENS   BRUCE C PARMELEE
GARY D GRIMES   JOHN P PAROPACIC   EUGENE A PASTROVICH   DENNIS W PAWLOWICZ   LARRY C PETTAWAY
UVALDO SANCHEZ   RALPH E SCHEIB   GARY A SCOVILL   IVAN J SHACKELFORD JR   JAMES H SHELTON
CHRISTOPHER PODMANICZKY   CHARLES M SMITH   EDWARD J TICE III   GEORGE F VOLK   JOHN W WALL
FREDERICK T WEST   FREDERICK R WILLARD JR   DAVID M WINTERS   JOSEPH D WYLIE II   JIMMIE D CINTRON
JAMES R ADAMS   EDWARD J BELL   KIT BLACKWELDER   ARNOLD L BROCK   LOUIS F CERRANO JR
PETER E COOK   JOSEPH CROSSLEY   EARL K EASTERLING   JAMES P ENGLISH   OTTO R ENSSLIN
DONALD R FIELDER II   ALLAN P FIRMNECK   ALEN L GARDNER   ANDREW L HAMILTON   MARSHALL H ISBELL
DUTLEY JAMES   J L KERR JR   EWELL LEE JR   DOUGLAS H MCCALL   PHILLIP A MOORE
TIMOTHY C PATTERSON   RAUL B PEREZ   WESLEY I PIZER   WILLIAM A PROCTOR   GORDON A ROUSE JR
JAMES E OXLEY   IRA A RICE   KENNETH R RORICK   PAUL L STIMPSON   RAYMOND R TURNER
ROGER L VERWERS   CLARENCE L WAY   HENRY L WEAVER   EUGENE E WEST   ADAM D BALLARD
WAYLAND J BATSON   RAYMOND E BENSON   HOWARD BULLARD   STEPHEN L COLOPY   JOSEPH F DALY
GEORGE R HARRISON   JOSE G HERNANDEZ   JIMMIE HOWARD   DAVID A IVES   LAWRENCE F LEWELLIN
CHARLES R NUNN   RANDALL B RAINVILLE   JAMES L RUSSELL   FREDERICK C SCHMIDT   ROBERT C STEPHENSON
CHARLES J TIGHE   JOHN W VANDEVENTER   GARY M WELCH   EDWARD W WELLS   DOUGLAS B HAMILTON
WAYNE R BARTH   RALPH W CARTER   RAUL CASAREZ   RAYMOND S CASSIDY   JUSTINO E CASTRO-RAMOS
RONALD L BARBER   GARY T COWLES   HOWARD S DOMINIAK   ARMANDO GALLARDO   RICHARD L HADNOT
DANIEL J HEFFERNAN   HERMAN L KNAPP   KENT A LEONARD   CLIVE V MOSIER   BRADLEY A NELSON
GEORGE R OBERMEIER   DANIEL T PEREZ   JAMES G POMERLEAU   GEORGE T POWELL   PHILIP H SAUER
PAUL F RUSZKIEWICZ   WILLIAM W STEWART   JACK L SUTTON   EDWIN B TUCKER   RAYMOND L TWOMEY
ROBERT M WAINZ   JAMES L BELL   LARRY G BONNELL   JERRY CAPE   DALE E CARMICHAEL
EARNEST L COX   DICK D CULVER   GARY L DOOSE   TERRANCE D FRYE   ROBERT L WESKAMP
PATRICK J GAGNON   WAYNE J GAUTZ   MICHAEL G GIBBS   MELVIN L GREEN   JAMES W HAMILTON JR
WILLIAM C JOY   WILLIAM R LATIMER   JAMES V LAWLOR   JOSEPH M LINGLE JR   RONALD L LYVERE
DONALD H MONAT JR   CHARLES S MOORE   CHARLES M NEAL JR   STEPHEN C NELSON   RICHARD C PRATT
JOSEPH E ROYSTER   THOMAS B SHARP   EDWARD G SHARPE   LEONARD H SMITH   ROBERT J STERLING
JOHN G CURTIN   JOHN D STRIPLING III   LEONARD D THOMPSON   JOSHUA A ATKINS III   CHARLES D AUSTIN
JERRY BAGLEY   CLIFFORD C BARNETT JR   FRED E BARNETTE   THOMAS M BARROW JR   DONALD L BERNARD
LYNN S BIERMA   JOHN G BROADBECK   RICHARD T BROWN   LARRY W BUTLER   DANA C DARNELL
ROBERT W DAVIS   JOHN F DUDASH   SHELLY EGLY   MICHAEL J ESTOCIN   EMMANUEL S FENECH
JERRY B FORMEY   PATRICK P FRANCISCO   LARRY F GEIGER   GUY C GETTINGS   LINDY R HALL
WILLIAM T HEDGPATH   ROBERT J HENRY   TILLMON P HITCHCOCK   ISAAC JONES   LEONARD O LA PORT   WALTER L SWAIN
EVERT R MAHARG   JEFFERY R MALONEY   WILLIAM M MEYER   WALTER F MORRIS   JAMES F MURRAY
WILLIAM MCCASKILL   BURNETT NEAL JR   KENNETH W ORTON JR   DAVID R PAGE   HERMAN H PAYNE
TROY D PAYNE JR   PERRY L PEOPLES   THOMAS A PREAUX   KERMIT A RAY   FRANK J RIPORTELLA JR
DAVID E SCHELVAN   RICKEY D SOUTHERN   MICHAEL J STEPHENS   NATHANIEL H STEPHENS JR   RONALD J HENRY
EDWARD S TOWE   BRUCE R WILLIAMS   JOE WILLIAMS JR   STANLEY F BARRETT   RONALD L BECKETT
JAMES A BENTON   JAMES E BOORMAN   JAMES D BRONAKOSKI   WILFRIED BURCK   REINALDO A CASTRO

PANEL 18E (*Continued*)

WILLIAM B CRONIN RICHARD H DALLAS ARTHUR DAVIES JR JAMES C DIXON MANUEL E MESA JR
DAVID C GRIJALVA MICHAEL G HARTNETT RANDY L HEERDT LARRY K LEACH
BLENN C DYER BELVIN LIGHTFOOT THOMAS J MCGEEVER CHARLES W MCKINNIE JR SAMUEL W OSBORNE JR
RONALD K PENNINGTON ANTON PROSZEK JR AUGUSTINE RESENDEZ LONNIE G SKAGGS ROM WORLEY
TERRY L YAWN DONALD R YOUNG JOSEPH J BORICK PAUL J BRAUN FRANKLIN A CARAS
DOMINIC J CIFELLI JAMES D CIRUTI RITSON L CLARKE MORRISON A COTNER KENNETH B MORRIS
TEODORO DAVILA JERRY DELPH ROBERT W EDWARDS DANIEL C FOWLER DANIEL C GILLESPIE
DWIGHT O GILSTRAP ROGER E GOFF JAMES E GREENLEE WILLIAM L HARRIS LINDY E HENRY JAMES E SNOCK
JOHN H HOLLAND BOB JEWITT RONALD H JOHNSON JOHN F LEONE JULIAN MARIN
JOHN H CHEEKS JOSE L MARTINEZ-FELICIA ROBERT H MILLER CARMEN MUSCARA NORMAND A PLANTE
ALBERT J ROSE RICHARD B SEDGWICK EDWARD J SKEBECK JR GEORGE F SMITH JAMES C STEPHENS
JERRY L WAGNER PAUL H WOLOS JAMES A BODA GARY A BURKS LEWIS E CANTRELL
ROGER D CAUDILL JOHN CHLEWA WILLIAM G DAILEY JR DONNIE R DEHART PAUL J LANDRY
CHARLES P DETOMASO FRANCIS T DILLON JOHN F FLEMING JOSEPH GRADEL JACK KURI
PAUL L CYR SIDNEY D LANE JR DONACIANO G LOPEZ GEORGE W MCDANIEL MICHAEL J O'KEEFE
CHARLES R PETCHNICK GEORGE J POLLIN ANTHONY SANSEVERINO FELIX F SOTO MARK L STEPHENSEN
DOUGLAS D WALLACE MARVIN R WHITE EDWIN APONTE KENNETH C APPLEGATE JOHN B APPLETON
BOBBY J ARD DAVID H BASS KAROL R BAUER WILLIAM R BELLER JR FREDERICK W BIVENS JR
DANNY R BROTZ GEORGE B BYRD JR GEORGE A CERVANTES ROBIN L CHILVERE JOHN V CHUTIS
MICHAEL I COLLEY ROBERT L CORNELL CLIFFORD G DAVIS THOMAS E DOUGHER CHARLES H DUTY
BENNIE H HOLBROOK WILLIAM D EARLY GARY W FOX JOE C GARCIA THOMAS G GRAFF GEORGE M SEALL
DAVID S HACKETT DOUGLAS P HALLOCK JEROME M HANRAHAN JR RICHARD HERNANDEZ JERRY W HOOD
TIMOTHY J IVES JULIUS A KESSLER III RICHARD L KINNEY ROBERT J KOTIK DONALD P LINDSLEY
LEONARD MARTIN JR PETER MAZZILLO JR ANTONIO MENDOZA JOSEPH MIECZKOWSKI JOHN T MIKRUT
RANDY N MCPHEE JAMES MINES JR JOSEPH R MITCHELL JR MICHAEL R MORGAN ALEXANDRO NEVAREZ
PETER R OMMEN FRANCIS M PALMA MARVIN PAULSON JR FREDDIE R PITTS HAROLD L POOL
MILTON E PRESCOTT JR JAMES E PRIEBE JAMES A RANDALL SCOTT D RICHARDSON WALTER R ROBINSON JR
WILLIAM J ROLDAN FRANK T ROTH MARVIN A SCHAFER ROBERT J SCHLEY RICHARD T SCHMITZ
JOSE I GARCIA-MALDONADO BRUCE H SCRAGG CHARLES SHIVER JR BARRY J SHORT GENE D SMITH

PANEL 19E

RICKY G SMITH GORDON E STOUDT JOHN F TINO JR JAMES H WHISENHUNT WILLIAM H MYERS PHILLIP A STRIZZI
DORSEY B WILLIAMS JOHN B WOODALL WAYNE H WOODARD EWELL E ACORD JAMES V CHRONISTER
JOHN H BAILEY JAMES B BELL JR LEYBURN W BROCKWELL JR EDWARD W BROWN JR DONALD L BUTE
JOHN M ANDREWS STAN L CORFIELD RICHARD J DESSELLE EARL DILLWORTH JR HERBERT L FARRINGTON III
LEWIS J FOGLER ROGER C GAUGHAN HILARIO H GUAJARDO MICHAEL J HILBURGER BOBBY E HUNT
LAURENCE A INSEL CHARLES C JONES JOHN D LEGG JOSEPH P LIPTON CHARLES E MILLER
WILLIE J MYRICK PEDRO ORTIZ ROBERT F QUINN SAMUEL T SCRIVEN CARL A SMITH
ROBERT L MCCAMBLE DUWAYNE SOULIER LARRY R STEPHAN KENNETH A VARNEY BRADLEY A WALKER
ALFONZA WATSON RICHARD L WOLFE TERRY J ALLEN MICHAEL P BARTELME DANIEL E BIDDLE
JAMES A BOONE EUGENE BREEDING JR CHARLES W BRICKER MARVIN W BUSSEY ANDERSON CARTER JR
GARY L CHASE ANTONIO G CHAVEZ FRANCIS E CLARK CARL J CUE ABE R DE YOUNG
LARRY D DRAVES RALPH V DYE JR THAROLD W ELLIOTT EDWARD A ESCOBAR GERALD M FARRELL
WILLIAM FESKEN GEORGE R FICKLIN JOHN A FRICK SAMMY R HARRISON DANNY M HAYES
WILLIAM T HAYES LLOYD L HEATH JOHN M HENDERSON STEPHEN T HEPNER JAMES E HILL
LAWRENCE J KEENAN THOMAS W MALLON JON L MESSER FRANK D MONTEMAYOR MICHEL L PUGH
JAMES M MCCLURE WILLIE L MOSES PHILLIP D MUNDAY HAROLD E MUNDY DOUGLAS E PARTRIDGE
OTTO P MEYER III MARION E PATRICK JAMES C PHILLIPS JAMES PHILLIPS JR ROBERT P PITTS
RUSSELL L ROBBINS ROY A ROBERTSON JR CLARENCE J SIMMONS DOUGLAS W TALLON WLADMIR W ZUBAR
GENE VAUGHN LAWRENCE G VISCONTI WILLIAM J VLASAK JR KENNETH L WALTERS ALONZO D WOODS
LEOPOLDO P SERNA KENNETH H WRIGHT LARRY E YODER RICHARD H ALMEIDA JOHN S ALMONEY
JAMES ANDERSON JAMES I BALCH DAVID W BARNABY DENNIS P BERGENSTEIN GARY L BIEHL
JAMES D BORAWSKI MONTY D BUTTON TROY M CARNLINE ROBERT H CARR JOSEPH CAUDILLO
CHESTER A CUMMINGS CHARLES C DAVIS TOMMY E DICKERSON CHARLES L DOOM JAMES R DOWDY
WILLIAM K DOWNING KURT C EDIE DONALD W FALWELL JON M FARNER ROBERT E FLANNERY JR
JAMES H FLICKINGER ROBERT W FORBUSH JR RICKY M GILBERTSON AMADOR L GONZALEZ WILLIS R HEAVIN
DAVID K HOLDWAY CHARLES F JOHNSON DARYL L JOHNSON CLIFFORD A JONES EARLIE RAND
CHESTER G JORDAN JOEL C KERVIN DAVID B KOENIG ROBERT H KRUGER JR ROY N MANNS
GARY N KAWAMURA JOSEPH R LA ROSE ROBERT Y LOUIS JR TOMMIE R LUNN NORMAND R MARTEL
JOHN R MEUSE LLOYD A MILLER RALPH E MOORE WILLIAM R MOORE GLENDELL MORGAN
EUGENE MURRY LEONARD PICANSO JR LUCIANO P PLESAKOV ROBERT C POWELL JUAN J RAMIREZ
MICHAEL F HUWEL WINSTON G RAYMO JOHN C RICE BEN ROBERTS ROBERT J ROSE
LEE H RUSS JAVIER A SANCHEZ CLEON L SCHREFFLER PHILLIP C SKINNER EUGENE D SPICER
JOHN E SWEESY JULIO A TORRES-RODRIGUEZ DAVID VERBILLA JAMES G WILLIAMS
JOHN W URICK WILLIAM T WOMBLE JR ROBERT G YAGUES MELVIN L ALLEN EMMETT E BALLREE
ROBERT B BEESON CLARENCE BLANKS THOMAS A BRYNELSEN JOHN S CARTWRIGHT RICHARD A CASSIN
ALLEN F CHAVES WILLIAM A CRENSHAW RALPH W CRYTZER JR PAUL J DENNIS ALEXANDER FORE
JOSE M GOMEZ DAVID A HICKMAN DON R HOLLINGSWORTH THOMAS M JAGGERS
JAMES S GRAHAM PAUL T KOHR ANTHONY E KUNZ JAMES N LAW JACK R LENNER WILLIAM E MCGINNIS II
JESSIE L JOHNSON SCOTT S MCCLOSKEY FREDERICK A MCMAHON DON W MINTON MARSHALL K MORRIS
LEWIS R NICKERSON OSCAR R PARROTT WILLIAM H RIVERS CHARLES E ROGERS ELWOOD C SOVEY JR
FRANKLIN D STALLINGS GEORGE R STAMP HENRY L TURN RICHARD B VAGNONE RICHARD K WHITFIELD
DONALD L WINCKLER JOAQUIN ARZUAGA LAWRENCE P BERECH JOHNNY BLACKMON MARTIN CAVAZOS
KENNETH H HEISSER PAUL J HICKS HARRY L HISSONG MICHAEL G LANGSTON DENNIS J MANNION
HERMAN A MOORE ROCKNE M NOGUCHI MELVIN O'NEAL JR CARL F PEPPLE JR EDWARD J WEIDENBACH
WOODROW WILLIAMS JAMES A PLUMMER JOSEPH P RANDO RICKEY D REVLAND GARY W RODRIGUES PHILLIP L ROUSE
JOE H SAMANIEGO DONALD J SHEEHY JAMES W SMITH ARISTON R TALAN JR JOHN J THOMAS
PIKE P MAYO FRANK C TORRES JR WILLIAM E WHITE JR ARTHUR J WHITNEY JR GREGORY W WOODS
JAMES A BULLINGTON BOBBY W CAMERON CURTIS E CHASE MARVIN C ELLERBROCK GEORGE E HATTEN
VERLIN R BRANDENBURG THOMAS G FANNING RICHARD C GUPTON RONALD L HILDERBRAND
DOUGLAS R HODGSON TIMOTHY W KEARNEY LARRY A LINDELL WILLIAM G RAINEY ROBERT C REYNOLDS
GARY W PRICE CLIFFORD M RHODES JR DONALD R SORENSEN ROBERT J VAN LEEUWEN THOMAS C EVANS
JAY T HENSLEY JOHN J HERMANOWICZ MICHAEL W HOWELL RICHARD A JOHNSON DANIEL M KASTEN
MILTON L HALL FRANKLIN C LEWIS DAVID W LINN RICHARD C MALONE ROBERT A METTERT LOUIS D VIGIL
JOHN W MCCOY TALMADGE RHODEN GEORGE P ROGERS CHARLES L SEEFELDT JR BARRY D THOMAS
EDWARD V ASIP KENNETH V AVERY JON D BAKER WILLIAM C BLADES III JOHN H BOUDREAU
WILLIAM M CAIN MICHAEL CHEROFF JEFFERSON C CHESNUTT DAVID L CLEVELAND LEON L CORNWELL JR
JAMES W CRIBBS CHARLES W DAUT JOSEPH J DODD LEROY ELLIOTT CLINTON A FIELDS
MICHAEL P FINLEY ABEL D GARCIA JR ROBERT J GREEN MICHAEL M GUKICH DONALD L GUSTAFSON
JAMES E HARMON WALTER D HORNER JAMES R HUCKLEBERRY JAMES F HUNDLEY CHARLES JACKSON THOMAS A JOHNSON
LARRY F JANKOWSKI CECIL R JENKINS DENNY L JOHNSON JULIUS J KEARSE
DANIEL L KIRSTEIN JOHN C KOPACSKA GARY H KREH JAMES E LAKEY LARRY M LANGAN
JOHN E LANING JAMES L LESTER JR DURAND G LIGGETT JESUS M LIMONES ROBERT LUDECKER
ROBERT L MARGOLIS ROBERT G MAYES JAMES MAYS JR GARY F MCCUE JIMMY E PAGE
CLYDE E NEWMAN CALVIN A PARKS ARTHUR C PEREZ WILLIAM E PERRY EMMETT J PETERS
JOSE A ROSAS DAVID L ROWELL THOMAS V RUFF JR RONALD W SANDERS GERARD J SCHNEIDER
ROBERT D SELLS JR WILLIAM M SHAW JR JOHN D SLESH JR BOBBY L SLOAN RICHARD A SNYDER
KURT C STAAB THOMAS J STEIMER LEO J SULLIVAN JR JAMES R VALENTINE PHILIP R VANASSE
MELVIN A WADE RALPH H WATINGTON JR HENRY R WICKER DONALD WILLIAMS VOMER O WILSON JR
JOHN E YOUNG RICHARD R BEAN DANIEL S BETTENCOURT GARY R BUTTENBAUM THOMAS J CASE
LAYNE F CLIFTON MORRIS F DIXON JR MERL T DUNN JR MICHAEL L ELMY LAWRENCE L FANT
WILLIAM E CZARNY DAVID F FRALEY FREDERICK W FROMME JR DANNY M GREENE MELVIN W GUNDERSON
RICHARD A HEIN CARMAN K HICKS KENNETH L HOLDER DEL R JACOBS JOSEPH G KLEMENCIC
RONNIE R LANDERS KENNETH J LE CASTRE EDDIE M MANN GREGORY M MCCOOK RONALD E NILES
JAMES M QUIGLEY FRANKLIN S RUTBERG FRANK A RYBICKI JR BOBBY A SEMORE HENRY E SMITH
RONALD M STEIN LYLE S TATE GARDNER TILLSON JR ROBERT J TODD RALPH J TURCOTTE
RAUL VILLA CHARLES R WALLER DENNIS M WARGO TOMMIE J WHITTEN ROBERT E WILLIAMS
HEINZ AHLMEYER JR ELPIDIO A ARQUERO MICHAEL J BEIRNE ALLAN F BERWEGER JAMES M BISHOP
HUGH F BLACKBURN NEIL J CACCIOTTOLO STEVEN L CANNON STEVEN D CHAMBERS LINWOOD E EBRON
LUTHER CHAMBLISS ROGER W CHASTEEN JAMES R COOPER FRANK X CUOZZO ALBERT J DARLING III
ALFRED L BROWN RICHARD J DAVIS STEPHEN D DIXON WILLIAM R FOWLER THOMAS L FOY
JOHN D GILGENBERG HAROLD T GILLIS AARON G GLYNN RANDALL R GRUEBER DAVID M HART
BRIAN C HEWITT LOUIS A HOLTON JR DORIAN J HOUSER AILEY B HURLEY DANNIE D JACOBS
JOHN T KLOC ELDON E KRIEGER BILLY J LAWTON JOHNNY A LEE RICHARD J LOISELLE
PAUL T LOONEY KENNETH W MCGEE MALCOLM T MILLER RUSSELL P MILLER ROGER M NETHERLAND
LEONARD E NISKI PHILLIP A O'BRIEN RAYMOND L PRINCE JOHN M REID DELANCY D TOLBERT
JAMES C RILEY MARCELINO RIVERA-CRUZ ROBERT G ROSS THOMAS SANDERS SAMUEL A SHARP JR
ROBERT L SNYDER DAVID K SUAPAIA NICHOLAS A TAGUE FRED E TATE JOHN C TATE
DONALD A PITTENGER JAMES N TYCZ MICHAEL D WALKER CLARENCE E WASHINGTON RONALD E YOUNG
PERCY E WATSON STERLING S WOODS ROY L BRANHAM PETER J CARLSON RONALD L CHISHOLM
FRANCIS J DUFFY WADDEL EVANS BRADFORD B GREENE TERRANCE E KLARIC FRANK L LUC
JOSEPH T MARTIN CHRISTOPHER J OLEKSA NEELY J SINGLETARY JAMES M AKSTIN CARLOS ASHLOCK
RICHARD L BASINGER JERRY D BASNETT LEONARD A BOHNER JOHN E CARMACK DAVID A DYE
ROBERT BERNTSEN WILLIAM F CLOVER JR CHARLES E COLLENE GARY W COSGRAVE MICHAEL J DAVIDSON
PAUL R EDINGTON JAMES H ESTERGREN GARY A FARLOW RUSSELL T FORD DAVID L GALE
JOHN M GEARY RAYMOND A GIBBS WILLIAM H GOTTSCHALK EARL W GRENZEBACH JR TERRY S HEARON
HORACE A HOLBROOK CHESTER L HOPKINS CLARENCE R HUSK JOHN W JACKSON JAMES M JEFFERSON
GREGORY D JENKINS ROBERT A JOHNSON LEROY H KELLER MARIANO LEIJA JR LAWRENCE E LEWIS
ERNEST G MADDEN EDDIE MANIS JAY A MITCHELL VICTOR H MONTOYA JR WILLIAM P ROGERS JR
ABRAHAM PANGANORAN WILLIE C PENDERGRASS CLOYDE C PINSON JR PETER P PITMAN GERALD A REITER
WILLIAM L SANDERS LOREN M SCHMITZ ANGEL M SOTO-RODRIGUEZ
HARVEY R SANDERS BOBBY G STANFORD ROBERT A STEWART JOHN STRAUDOVSKIS WILLIAM H TRAVIS
DENNIS A TRIMBLE THEODORE R VANCE JAMES E WASHINGTON MICHAEL J WILSON MICHAEL J AMATO
DEAN E ARMSTRONG JOHN M AVILA JAMES D BEDGOOD PETER Q BOETS JR DAVID C BOREY
MICHAEL F BUCKLEY ROBERT E BURNS JOSEPH CAVAROCCHI JOHN W COGHILL JERRY E CORNEY
ANDREW J COOPER DAVID L COOPER DAN M DENNIS JAIME ESQUIVEL MICHAEL D ESTOK
GLEN G BURT RUSSELL I EVANS CABALLERO F FIGUEROA WILLIAM L GARRISON TOMMY W HALEY
LARRY K HEAVNER KENNETH L HIRST JR FRED L HOTTINGER LEROY C HOWE DENNIS L HUBBARD
JIMMY E JOHNSON ANTHONY W KEY BYRON A KIELLEY CARL R KONOPA ALAN LANE
STEPHEN M LEE CARL F LOUVRING JOHN W LOVE PAUL E MANSKE KENNETH C MARLEY
BILLY J MEADOR CHARLES J MILBRANDT JULIO V MORALES RONNIE L PHELPS JOAQUIM V REBELO
MELECIO ORTIZ CHARLES K PURCELL II LARRY L REISSIG JAMES D REYNOLDS ROBERT E ROBINSON
BRUCE L ROTHHAAR WILLIAM A RUSH VIDAL SANCHEZ JR RICHARD T SARAKAS DAVID J SCHARIBONE
JOHN H SIMPSON MICHAEL R SMITH GARY L STEVENS MICHAEL E STEWART ROBERT R SUMMERS
JOSEPH T TIEFENTHALER JAMES H WALLER HULSA D WOLFE GARY R ZYWICA THOMAS ALLEN
DANIEL W BEARY BEN D BONO MICHAEL J BOST STEVEN A BROQUIST JAMES M BRYAN
CHARLES C BURNETT JR JOHN E CRONIN DAVID J DALTON JOSEPH L DUCKETT JR BENITO R GONZALEZ
DAVID N CUMMINGS WINFIELD S FLINT JOSEPH H GOINGS JR FRANK L GUTHRIE JOSEPH C HAILEY
CHARLES E HALFORD DONALD K HALVORSEN HENRY G HAMPTON KENNETH L HEARN JOHN M HICKS
JOSEPH A JIMENEZ DANIEL T JOYCE RONALD W KNOSKY ELDON E LAMBERT ELTON LE BOUEF JR
ERVIN LOVELL AUBURN D MCCOMB JOHNNIE L MCDANIEL GEORGE W MONTGOMERY DALE L OTTO
DENNIS P MOLESE JAMES A NICHOLSON JERRY A NORRIS JOHN M O'BRIEN MICHAEL E PETERSON
PAT E PHILLIPS GARY E SMITH CRAWFORD SNOW FORREST M STAFFORD RAFAEL VALENTIN
DALE A PULLIAM JENNINGS M THOMPSON WILLIAM A ULLMER JR GREGORY J VANDEWALLE JOHN R VRABEL
JAMES T WILLIAMS MILLIGAN R WILLIAMS REIMUNDO AGUILAR JULIAN ALONZO JOE ARREGUIN
NEIL E BATEMAN LONNIE R BUTTS PAUL W CASEY ALLAN R CHAFFIN BRUCE A ILES
RAYMOND M CHASSER DAVID A DIXON PHILIP B EMERSON ROBERT G FULLER ROGER L GARRETT
EARL G GRUBB JACK M HARRIS CHARLES D HILL NORMAN R HOCKER LEE C JAMES JR
JAMES E CHADWICK WOLFGANG A HAEGELE STEPHEN T JARRAS JASPER L JENNINGS JOSEPH T KEESEE

PANEL 20E

WOLFGANG E KRESSE JAMES T MANDLER EDWARD K MEYER ROBERT L SALINAS
JOHN E MCVAY THOMAS E MIDCALF CHARLES R MILTON JR ARTHUR C MOURTGIS JR HOMER J MYERS
DAVID L KRIG REINALDO S ORTIZ GEORGE F PERRY III DONALD M PETERSON ROLAND R RAMOS
MARVIN J SINKLER FRANK TAFOYA JAMES D WEST SAMUEL R ALLEN FLOYD L AMOS
GEORGE R ANNOS ROBERT B BAILEY ROBERT O BARRY WILLIAM W BEDNARZ LEONARD T BISH
LOUIS E BRIZZOLI GERALD A BROWN GEORGE R BUTLER THOMAS W CHAFFIN SIDNEY D CHAPMAN
CLYDE CLARK JR DELMAR F COOK STEPHEN J EICHELBERGER ROSS F FIKE DAVID A FISCH
THOMAS J GUARALDI ARCHIE L GUTHRIE BENJAMIN H INGALLS CHESTER J JOY
DENNIS R HOOKS RICHARD H KRUMM GEORGE R LINDER REUBEN J NEAL PETER J NICOLINI
GERALD V PARMENTIER JOHN C PFEIFFER JAMES L RAY FREDDIE L ROBINSON GERALD A ROBINSON
RALPH D SALERNO JOHN C SILVER DWIGHT R STOCKHOLM DANIEL E TOGNERI BICKETT O WADE JR
HARRY M WADSWORTH GEORGE H WILLIAMS RALPH M WIXSON ROBERT R BOYD
MICHAEL L BRAEUTIGAN BENNY L BUTLER EDWARD O CLAEYS LARRY A CRISCI MARVIN E CUTRER
WHILTON A MCCARTHY WINFRED ALDERMAN EUGENE DAWSON ROBERT M DE DOMINIC RONALD W DODGE
CHARLES R DOWNEY JR CHARLES A EAKINS
GEORGE R EDWARDS LARRY A FAULKNER JOSEPH O FRIGAULT WILSON T GERALD JOHN J GUIST
STEVEN M HANIOTES LYNN C HAYES CLAUDE A HODGE GARY W HOGLUND GERALD D HUFFMAN
CHARLES W JOHNSTON JR JAMES R MICHAEL RICHARD L MOORE JASPER N NEWBERRY JR EDWARD A PAINE
JOSEPH D PRINCE JR DON A REDFEARN ARTHUR REYNOLDS JR JOHN E SCHEETZ ANDREW J SHORT III
TERENCE E SIMON WENDELL L SLAVENS GREGORY M THOMPSON ROGER D THOMPSON JOHN R TIGHE
WILLIAM C TURNER CHARLES E ARONHALT JR JACQUE J AYD FLORENTINO C BARRON JOE L DELONG
CHRISTOPHER W BEAVERS WILLIAM A BLACKWELL ALBERT C BROSE JAMES E BURCH JAMES T BURNS
JOSEPH CALHOUN KENNETH R CAMERON RONALD R CASSEL KENNETH N CHEEK ROY D CHITWOOD
EDWARD J CHRISTENSEN LOUIS W COLEMAN JR ESTEBAN COLON-MOTAS LEWIS C COOK PATRICK J FLAVIN
CHARLES L ANDERSON MARK A DALGLIESH ALLEN K DEARDEN LOUIS D DOBBIN II PAUL F DOYON
COIL EDMOND JR MICHAEL C FARRELL WILLIAM G FELLINGER JR WILLIAM A FISH DUAINE K FISHER
STEVE J CHURCHILL JAMES P FITZSIMMONS JAMES L FOREMAN EDWARD R FRANK SR WILLIAM C FREUND
JOHNNIE C FULLER JOHN C GAINOUS STANLEY M GODWIN HORACE R GORE WESLEY I GOSWICK
OTTO C GRABOW BRUCE A GRANDSTAFF WILLIE R GRIFFITH CARL R HALLBERG FRANKLIN G HAZZARD
JOHN W HUDGENS EDWARD C HULTQUIST HUGH L HURSTON COLIN F JACKSON STANLEY M JAMROZY
CLIFFORD A JOHNSON RUSSELL F KECK DANNY E KING STANLEY S KLECZ ALBERT KORONA III
DENNIS D KRAMER RICHARD L LAND JOE P LARSEN LEONARDO LEOS JOHN W MCCORMICK JR
JAMES S LEONARD ORRIE E MACOMB JR BOBBY G MCELHANEY JOSEPH T MCKEON JR CLYDE U MITCHELL
THEODORE R NELSON JAMES C OFFLEY PHILIP J OLOFSON RONNY L PALMER JEARL E RIMMER
JOHN J NEMCHIK JR KENNETH D PHARES CHARLES E RANALLO JR MICHAEL P RANDALL CHARLES O REED
JAMES W ROBBINS JOHN J ROBERTS ALFRED W ROBINSON ROBERT B SANZONE OTTO A SEAMANS JR
MICHAEL SESSA JR MELVIN L SHIELDS MARK SMITH JR MICHAEL F SMITH ALVIN R SPIDER
CALVIN L TAYLOR JIMMIE L THOMAS ROBERT J THOMAS LELAND H THOMPSON LEON THORNTON
ROBERT A TURNER OLIVER A WARE WILLIAM WELLS JOHN T WILSON JAMES A WORKMAN
PETER ALBERT KENYON E BEAN JERRY L BECKHAM MICHAEL A BODAMER HERBERT L ELLINGTON RICHARD K GILLINGHAM
ANTON T BORNSTEIN ROBERT J BRADY ROBERT K BRICE WILLIE L BROWN ROBERT D CAMPBELL
WILLIAM J CORBIN GEDIMINAS J EIDUKAITIS JAMES W ELDRIDGE DENNIS H FAIRFIELD
JAMES F AKINS REYNALDO S FERNANDEZ JOHN T FULFORD WALTER T GEIGER JUAN A GONZALEZ
RAMON GONZALEZ-RODRIGU JAMES L GRIFFIN WAYNE C HARMON BOBBY V HAYSLIP RICHARD RICH
HAROLD J HELLBACH VERNON L HENKE RICHARD P HILGART PHILLIP M HINES JOHN A HOLLINGSWORTH
WILLIAM D JINKS EVERETT E JOHNSON JR LEO J KELLY III MICHAEL A KIGHT ROY A KNIGHT JR
CHARLES W LARMAN RICHARD O LOZENSKI JOSEPH A MANCUSO WILLIE J MITCHELL JR GREGORY P MOSER
GUY E MCNAY JR JAMES M MOSGROVE JR EUGENE O OWENBY WALTER A PAIRAN ALBERT J PATRILLO
JOSEPH M GRANTHAM III JAMES K PATTERSON PAUL W RATLIFF ALAN T READ CHARLES R RHUE
THOMAS A RONALD HENRY M SARMENTO DONALD F SCHAFER LAWRENCE F SCHERRER BURTON I SHARP
ALTON SHEDD HAROLD D SHELTON JOHN C STECKER RAYMOND H TIGHE DALE W TOLBERT
MARTIN N TULL EDWARD J WAGNER JR RONALD T WALDROP JACK WALTERS JR CARNELL E WATSON
CHARLES B WATSON JR DALE E WAYRYNEN WALTER A WILKS JOE P WOODEN JR ROBERT D ALEXANDER
JOHN ATKINS STANLEY M BAKER GARY C BANNON RICHARD J BELICOSE ERNEST L CHAMBERS JR
LESLIE A BELLRICHARD DAVID G BENDORF FRANK H BERAN III RAYMOND J BOROWSKI ROBERT T BOYKIN
DALE E BROUGHT THOMAS BROWN WILLIAM J BROWN LEE B BUAN JAMES M BURROUGHS
GERALD L AYLOR FREDERICK A BUZA RONALD M COOLEY MARIO O DE LEON DAVID L FENNESSEY
VERNON E DE PEW JAMES T DOBISH WALTER E DUNCAN JR DONALD R ELLIS KARL F ERB
RUDOLPH R CORONA III HAROLD E FETNER REGINALD FLACK ORVILLE B FRITS EDWARDO J GONZALES
KEVIN T GORMAN WILLIAM M GRAMMAR JOHN A GRAVIL MACK E GREGORY GERALD C HAGUE
RICHARD A HARDIN RICHARD E HARRISON DAVID E HARTSOE NORMAN P HOWIE JR JEFFREY R HUGHES
LOUIS J INFERRERA DAVID J JOHNSON DOUGLAS O KEEFE GARY M KILLIAN ALAN R MAY
MARK R LANDER DANIEL H LAWLER JOSEPH LEDESMA JR VERNON L LEINO THOMAS L LESTER
RICHARD LEYVA JONATHAN F LOWMAN NOTLEY G MADDOX BRUCE A MANTON FREDERICK L MARCH
AUSTIN R JOSEPH ROBERT W MEISS JR FRANKIE Z MOLNAR RONALD J MOORE RONALD B MOS
IVY M MCCARROLL JR DOUGLAS W MURPHEY NICHOLAS A PAVLAKOVICH BARRY C PRICE ROY SMITH
ROBERT E PAYNE JOSH PETERS CLARENCE W PILKENTON EUGENE F POELING THOMAS W POORE
WESLEY R MCKEE GARY W RITCHEY ALLEN T ROGERS JR ROLAND E RUSH ALLEN B RUSSELL
CARL D NAGENGAST LUIS E SEGARRA JR RONALD L SHARAR HOMER L SMITH LONNIE L SMITH
RONALD D STARR TERRENCE C SULLIVAN ELISEO E TARIN GEORGE M TAYLOR LEON A WANGERIN
EUGENE A WARD GALEN E WARREN WALTER J WASHUT LARRY L WILLIAMS SANDY ZIMMERMAN JR
ROBERT G ANDERSON HAAKON W ANDRESEN CLEVELAND BATISTE JR EDWARD J BOHANNON WILLIAM P CENTERS JR
THOMAS B DAILY THOMAS E DAVIE JR HARRY K DAVIS STEVE C DAVIS EUGENE H DICKINSON
TERRY M ELSHIRE RICHARD J FEEHERY FRANCISCO J FLORES JOEL C FOWLER MICHAEL P GALLAGHER
DAVID A HARALDSON RONALD M HAYES GEORGE H HEPPEN JR DAVID H HOLLAND JOHNNY M JOHNSON
JERRY L HOUSER ROGER M HURD TOLER L HUTCHINS JR PHILLIP E IRELAND JAMES A JACKSON
THOMAS E HENDERSHOTT JAMES JOHNSON JR ROBERT KATAVOLOS ALFRED LEE JAMES D MCWHORTER
PATRICK M LOISEL WILLIAM W LUMSDEN CLIFFORD L MENZIES JR PETER E MILLAR THOMAS G MODISETTE
DAVID C LINDBERG HILDRA MCCOY JR HENRY D MCINNIS ANTHONY W ROYBAL RODOLFO A SAENZ
HARLEY E SPIVEY WILLIAM C STANLEY JAMES T STEIGHNER DWIGHT E TIMBERLAKE JOSE M VASQUEZ
CLYDE A WARD LARRY A WILLIAMSON RONALD E WISSMAN GEORGE N WRIGHT WALTER F WROBLESKI
RANDAL R AYLWORTH KENNETH F BACKUS WILLIAM K BATCHELDER GERALD D BEHLKE LESTER E HOLMES
THOMAS J BURKE MERLIN F CALDWELL GARY L CARLE FREDERICK J CARRATURO PEDRO A CRUZ
GEORGE P CUSTER HAROLD A FORD VINCENT J GABRIEL JR ANTONIO G GARZA JR
JAMES N BAUER WALLACE S DWORACZYK ALFRED R GREGORY DENNIS L HOLM JULIUS E JENKINS JOHN A MIETUS
WALTER Z MOORE JR LEONARD A MORGAN CLARENCE L MORRIS EDWARD T MURPHY ROBERT L MURPHY
HARRY J MCGUIRE III RUSSELL D NEEDHAM ELTON L PERRINE MOSES L POINDEXTER SAMUEL PROCTOR JR
MICHAEL W RAMSEY CARL W SCALLIONS MACK D SIMMONS III LARRY G STONE TERRY G STRAUB
PETER L VALENCICH DONALD E WALTERS JR RONALD W WARD KENNETH G WORMAN BOBBIE M AUTON
RALPH W BLACKERBY ROBERT J BOHMER JAMES W CARTWRIGHT ROBERT M DWYER WILLIAM D FARLEY
THOMAS L COLDREN CHARLIE M GILMER RICHARD F HENRICH RICHARD W HOMUTH BOBBY R JERMYN
CLIFFORD E KELSEY JOSEPH D KING CURTIS O MATIER TERRANCE W NELSON THOMAS E PETTIS
EUREKA L SCHMITTOU DONALD A SKINNER RONALD P SOUCY CARL R STOVALL ROBERT D THOMPSON
JOHN T TRIVETTE LAWRENCE N WELK MARK A ANDERSON JOHN C BETTIS CLAYTON H BYERS JR
MICHAEL J CAHALANE ROY L CASTLEBERRY BERNARD L FRANKE TIMOTHY P GUGLIELMONI MORRIS D NEW
FRANK J GUICHAUD STEPHAN C HIMES MELVIN E HOFFMAN STEPHEN K JENNINGS RONALD R JOSEPH
GEORGE DIKER JR JAMES L KACHLINE TERRY F LEAZER MICHAEL S LYLE GARY MURRAY
BRIAN R NORFLEET STEPHEN J O'SHEA JAMES B PATTERSON RODNEY D PICKETT JOHNNY C PRESTON FRED S ROTH
JOSEPH K PURELIS GERALD J PYSHER MICHAEL C QUINN SANDY M RIVERS LLOYD V ROBERTS
WILLIAM J SCHERLE JR COLERIDGE WILLIAMS JR CHARLES D WITT KENNETH R ABMEYER DANIEL A PATTERSON
EDDIE C BEGAYE WILLIAM H BETHEA III ALAN W BONNEY ROBERT K CADEAU PAUL J CAMIRE
MARTIN CARRANZA VAN CHAFFEE JAMES G CLARK ALFRED COBOS PETER M COONS
WENDLE C DAVIS HAROLD J DILLARD LEONARD A ENOS JOE A FUNK II PETER J GERSPACH III
GREGORY R GINGERICH TERRY A HARDING WILLIAM H HAWORTH MARVIN C HILL EDWARD M MCMULLAN
THOMAS R IKE ALFRED G KIRCHER REYNALD G LEPAGE LARRY J LILES JOSEPH A MAGGIO JR

253

THE VIETNAM VETERANS MEMORIAL COLLECTION

RICHARD C GRAVES HARRY MCCLAIN JAMES B MCGILL LEONARD K NUTE
DON M PERDUE WALTER L QUEEN GARY A RATHBUN JOSEPH A SICILIANO JR JIMMIE SIDDALL
RAYMOND M SIEGER EDWARD A STAHL ROBERT G STATON JOHN A SUTHERLAND CHARLES E THOMAS
GARY L STYMUS FREDDIE E THEIS EDWARD L TIEMAN BENJAMIN G WELLS KURNEY J WHITE JR
ROBERT J WHITE CHARLES R WISHAM ANDREW S WRIGHT CHARLES D ALLEN JR WILLIAM A BELAND
JAMES W AYERS GEORGE D BENNETT WILLIAM J BRESNAHAN JR THOMAS R BURNS DOMENICO CACCIOLA
MICHAEL W CAREY HARRY K CARTRETTE ANTHONY M CASS ROBERT H CHANDLER JAMES E COLEMAN
MICHAEL H COLLINS THOMAS A CONKLIN PATRICK CONNER ROBERT W COOK CHARLES A CRUMP
WILLIAM R DALRYMPLE LAWRENCE R DODD JACK L DODSON WILLIAM L DORNBERGH JR JOHN F DUGAN
DAVID R CUSHING EDWARD D DROHOSKY BROCK D ELLIOTT EDWARD S FISHER TERENCE P FITZGERALD
RODGER L FORTUNE DENNIS W FRASIER PHILLIP R GAINES JAMES L GALES JERONIMO GARCIA-SOTO
ROBERT G GODDARD THOMAS W GOODRICH MICHAEL J GREELEY GEORGE W HARRIS CLAUDE HOWARD
ROBERT HUGHES ROGER V INSCORE FRANK JAMISON EMMETT JERMANY JR CLAYTON W JOHNSON
XAVIER JOHNSON THOMAS G JONES SIGFRID R KARLSTROM ALLAN H KELLERMANN NORMAN R KIDD JR
THOMAS A LANE JOSEPH D LE GRAND LOWELL R LLOYD LARRY F MARKUS ROBERT D MILLAN JR
MELVIN L MARTZ GENE F MATTHEWS JOSEPH MATTHEWS JAMES J MENART DONALD E MESAROSH
WILLIAM G LANDON BENJAMIN G MOLLICA RAMON J MORALES SHELTON MORGAN JIMMY K MORRISON
GERALD F MCDONALD WAYNE R MCKENZIE ROBERT L MOSHER OXLEY C MOULTRIE DAVID L NIEMANN
RICHARD E POTTER JAMES C POWERS BENJAMIN RICHARDSON MICHAEL C ROELL JOHN D ROGERS
ALAN J RUDDELL ANTHONY J SALERNO JOHN E SCHON PAUL D SKELTON II WILLIE B SKRINE JR
JACK SMASO GARY M SMITH JOSEPH P SMITH LADDIE C STIERWALT RICHARD E WILKINS
LOREN C SURLES TEDDY G TALLEY DONALD R TROXELL ALEXANDER G WAINIO JERRY G WALLER
ALLEN W STATH ARNOLD G WILKENING III PAUL M WOOLDRIDGE JR NABIL M YOUSSEF ROBERT M BENNETT
GORDON B BLACKWOOD ROY R BOOTH THOMAS A BURKHARDT ROBERT B DANIELS PETER E DAY

PANEL 21E

HENRY A JOHNSON DENNIS J KEENAN GARRY D KLEIN THOMAS D NIEDERMEIER
HERBERT A RIPKA JAMES E SMITH ARTHUR V VIGIL DONALD L WHITE LLOYD M ADKINS JR
JOHN W AVELLEYRA WALTER L BABBITT JR RICHARD BROWN DONALD L CRANE CANDIDO SERRANO-GIRAL
TED L EDWARDS JOHN J FINNEGAN RALPH P FLINT JR BILLY L HAMMONTREE MICHAEL N HARLEY
NOBLE JACKSON FLOYD W KAASE EDWARD G LACEY DOUGLAS LLOYD GEORGE M WALKINSHAW
JAY D MCLAIN STANLEY T MELVIN ROBERT E MONAHON JOHN A PETERSON DONALD R RYBOLT
RICHARD A CASPER MICHAEL SOROVETZ FREDERIC C STYER GORDON M TRIPLETT RICHARD E VEACH
CHARLES E JOHNSON MICHAEL D WITHROW ENOCH A BALLANGER ROBERT H BEESON JR JOHN M BIONDI ARNOLD G KRAVITZ
MARGIE BROGDON GEORGE J CARR EDWIN J CASALETTO DAVID O CEDERSTROM CHARLES E CHERRY
ALAN B CIPRIANI FRANCIS C CLEAVER RANDALL V COOK CHARLES H CRAWFORD RONALD C DAILEY
WILLIAM A DIXON JR MICHAEL L DOTSON THOMAS F DREW RUSS E ECKHART GREGORY A ERVIN
WILLIAM H FARMER JR WILL L FOWLER JOHN H GARNER IVAN W GATLIN DENNIS R GLENN
HAROLD D GRIFFIN RAUL C GUTIERREZ GARY L JAMES WILLIAM C JOHNSON MATHEW L JOLIVETTE
FRANK E HARDY RICHMOND R LUCE BRUCE K MANNING BILLY C MCFALLS MICHAEL L OTTO
RONALD W PENN WILLARD S PRESCOTT ROBERT W PRYS GILBERT REYES MICHAEL G RUSHING
FRANK M SCARPULLA JR MICHAEL O SHELLEY WILLIAM G SILVA ARMAND R THOUVENELL RALPH B WALKER II
LEONARD A WYNN OSCAR BIEHL JR JOHN R CABRINI THOMAS J DEAN III JOSEPH L RHINEHART
HARRY G CARTER ALFRED ELLIS NOEL J FELICIANO JIMMIE L JONES DANIEL I NELSON
CLARK E SAPP KENNETH L STAGER GEORGE S SUTT MICHAEL W THOENNES GERALD A VIZER
DAVID L ADAMS HERVEY H ALLEN PETER M APODACA RANDALL ARBOGAST HAROLD A BEAVERSON JR
GERALD A CHAMPION NATHANIEL COLLINS WILLIAM E COSSA JR GEORGE A DOANE JOSEPH E FITZGERALD
MICHAEL F CONLEY TEDDY R DUNN CARL D FLOWER JAMES A GLOVER JERRY L HOLMES
JOHN A JAKOVAC DENNIS C JOHNSON CHARLES W KRUEGER BRIAN K MCGAR WILLIAM W MONEY
DENNIE NEACE THOMAS L NIGRELLI JAMES E RICKERSON CHARLES R ROGERSON EDWARD S ROUBA
GARY P STEFFUS JERALD A VOKISH PAUL D WILLIAMSON FRANCIS L ARB JAMES W ASHBY
CHARLES C BURNS WILLIAM G COATS GARY C CUPPLES ISAAC A DIEZ JR LAWRENCE D DUNLAP JR
LONNEY L EHLERS WILLIAM B ESSLINGER FRANK J GALLANT DONNELL HENDERSON FRANK J KILKENNY
LARRY W KNIGHT FRED V LEE CLAYTON B LOWE JR ROBERT S MATERN PAUL J PETERSEN
RODERICK D MCMURRY MICHAEL L PARISH WILLIAM T PARKER III EDWARD H RIXMANN DANIEL T SCHMIDT
JAMES R SIMPSON JOSEPH A TOMKO SAMMIE J VOLLMAR ROGER L WHINERY JOSEPH WAXFORD
RONALD G BABICH IGNACIO BARELA NORMAND L BEAULIEU BRUCE E BOYER DANIEL L CARRIER
JOHN L CATTON LARRY V CHMIEL DONALD R CHRISTY THOMAS E CRAIG DAVID L DIXON
KENNETH R ENDSLEY RUBEN ENGLISH JOSEPH S ESCOBAR ALEJANDRO F FIERRO LEONARD E GILES
ALBERT GRAHAM JR DANIEL L HARMON JOSHUA HICKMAN DAVID M JORDAN JOE MONTEZ
JOHN J KATONA JR DANNY J KEITH RICHARD M LOMBARDO PAUL J MACIUSZEK STEVE G MARCOMBE
DENNIS E HOFFMAN ALAN R MARSH JAMES F MCGOEY JAMES E MILLIRONS JOE MOYA
FRED G O'MALLEY PHILIP O PARRISH DANNY L PAUL GARRY O PRICE FIDEL RAMOS JR
WILLIAM A RAWSON RAYMOND A RENZ ALTON C ROCKETT JR JOSEPH J SELLER WILLIAM A SINCHAK
RALPH E SMITH RALPH W SMITH NEAL R THALIN JAMES E THEISEN SAM R TRIZZA JR
RAY L VAN ZANDT DAVID H WELLER HAROLD F WERLE JAMES E WOOD REX S WOOD
GERALD L ACKLEY STEPHEN A BALTERS JR RICHARD L BLASEN LARRY N BOATMAN MARION L DIRICKSON
TIMOTHY R BODDEN BILLY R BOYD ARTHUR M BYRD AVERY L COOPER JIMMY R CROOK
GARY B BAKER WILLIAM S DAUGHERTY ROBERT B DE MELLO JAMES J DEASEL JR RONALD J DEXTER
THOMAS S DONOVAN VICTOR M DRISCOLL WILLIE G DYER EDMUND G EXUM JR DUNCAN H FLEMING
JOHN P FRANCIS JOHN G GARDNER HARRY E GEARY LAWSON D GERARD AUBREY L HEWITT
KENNETH A GORE JACK E GOSS II JAMES A GRAHAM STEPHEN P HANSON ROBERT R HERNANDEZ
GERALD L FOELL DARREL L HOVENDEN GEORGE H JOHNSON JOSEPH T KEARNS JR STRAUGHAN D KELSEY JR
JOSEPH M KIERNAN JR BILLY R LANEY WILLIAM E MARTIN DENNIS E MONFILS KEITH M MOSER II
GARY W KLINE MICHAEL D MCCANDLESS TAYLOR H MCLEMORE CHARLES C MONROE LOWELL E MORGAN
CITY T NEW JR ALLEN T NEWMAN GARY M O'BRIEN JOHN R PAINTER JR BENJAMIN F PELZER II
JAMES W PRICE JR ROBERT RICHARDSON TERRY M RIMES KARL B RISCHE JR LUTHER ROBINSON
ROBERT R ROGERS LARRY V SAYERS STEVEN E SCHARLACH CHARLES J SCHULTZ CLIFFORD SHEPHERD
RODNEY H SMITH JORGE SOSA THEODORE SPRINGSTON JR MILLARD L TREADWELL JR CURTIS L TREMAINE
PRESTON H TURNER JR GEORGE D WALLACE JAMES A WEED JERELD E WESTPHAL DANIEL W WHITE
PABLO ALMANZA ROJELIO BOCANEGRA FRANKLIN T COLLINS GERALD W INGLETT
MICHAEL D GEORGE JAMES H OVERPECK CELSO A PEREZ LARRY L PRICE LEWIS M ROBINSON
CLYDE D SHELTON JR JOHN M ASTLEY JAMES P BURNS DOUGLAS H BUTTERFIELD EDWARD A CABRERA
DONALD L PATTERSON FRANCIS L COLLINS LARRY D GOOD MICHAEL D HALFORD DIR IBANEZ CHARLES W KANE
TERRY R MCCOMB JAMES W RAMAGE STEPHEN W SOKALSKY JR GRANT C TAYLOR THOMAS M WILLIS
NEIL W ALDRIDGE DUANE S BAKER DONALD J BARNES JOHN R BURKE NILES BURNEY
CHARLES F BUFF DAVID W CLOUTIER FREDERICK H ELIZONDO WILLIAM C GUNTER DARRELL W HEATHERLY
JOHNIE M HENNINGER MELVIN S HOOVER CHARLES A HUBBARD JIMMY KEMP LARRY E LAWRENCE
JAMES A MCMURDO ROBERT M MILLER WILLIE L PAGE DAVID F SHERRELL DALE L SPEIR
MITCHELL N STUPAR BILLY L TOBIAS EDGAR H VALLECILLO HOWARD H WHITEY JACKIE R BAIRD
EVERDENE BAKER JR JAMES L BLAZ JAMES D CARTER JR JOHN J CHASE HARRIS V DAVIS
LAWRENCE A BROOKS RONALD L CROOKS BUCKNER CRUMP JR ROBERT F ENDERBY WILLIAM L EVANS
EDWARD F FURLONG JR ALVIE W GAPP GALE E GOTTI JIMMY W HALL DOYLE L HARRIS
THOMAS M HEALY JESSE L JOHNSON KENNETH M JOHNSON KENNETH R KEEFER PHILLIP A VAN DEUSEN
REX A LA DUKE DAVID A LAND LUIS E MILAN-ANAVITARTE STEVEN L MILLETT LARRY L MORRIS
KENNETH P NEWTON JOY L OWENS WAYNE M PITTS HAROLD R SALE JR FRANK J SHOVLIN
RICHARD KNAPP EDWARD A VERCOUTEREN GREGORY P VERCRUYSSE WALTER L WARD FLETCHER D WHIPS
RONALD A WILLIAMS LARRY E WORTHEN EDWARD S YAMASHIRO JEFFREY L BARKER WILLIE J MOORE
JON T BUSCH LEONARD J CARTER TIMOTHY R CLARK JERRY L DAW HOWARD A DONALD
JACK ELENBAAS JOHN E FERGUSON WILLIAM G HENDERSON THOMAS L HOENIGES HANS D LANGE
VICTOR J APODACA JR DE J LEON JOHN T MCMAHON DONALD A MOURITZEN DAVID G MYERS
ROBERT M NAIL DANIEL M O'DONNELL THOMAS PRETTER HOWARD J RICE WALTER A WAGNER
GLENN A WATKINS HOWARD L WEBB ELWIN H BUSCH HERMAN R CULL GEORGE R DARRELL
LAWRENCE H DONNELL SAMUEL R DURHAM HAROLD L GIBSON FREDDY L GRAY RICHARD A GRAY
RICKY L HERNDON CONRAD T LANGE JAMES C MARTIN JR PETER W MORRISON GUADALUPE RENDON
JAMES L JOHNSON RICHARD W PODELL FRANK R RAGUSA RUFUS RAY RAFAEL L RIVERA-BALAGUER
CRAIG R SCHOENBAUM IRA E SCOTT ANDREW H SHIMP JEROME F STARKWEATHER HOWARD E SWANN
WILLIAM E TYREE WALTER L ADAMS LARRY W BLOODSWORTH GREGORY C COIN RICHARD P GLAUDE
JAMES L HAMLET GREGORY P KELLY JAMES M LOSO JIMMIE H MANTOOTH ROBERT W MAZZA
WILLIE A PARKS ROBERT L PLATT JR AUGUSTUS J PONTO III PETER W SHERMAN RONALD L STAPELMAN
ROBERT F STEVENS MILTON H THOMAS JR LAWRENCE C THOMPSON HENRY J WILHELMI JR JAMES R PAGE
WILLIAM L BONNELL EMMETT L BOOTH DAVID A BRILEYA KERMIT E BURKEY ERASMO C CASTILLO
CHARLES D CHOMEL DENNIS R CHRISTIE DEAN E CLINTON EDWARD J COLSTON FERGUS F CONNORS JR
JOHN J FOLEY III JOHN M FRAMBES FRANK R FROST III DARRELL F GASKINS JOSE J GONZALEZ
THOMAS M HANRATTY MICHAEL W HAVRANEK JAMES R HICKS DONALD M KLEMM JAMES K KOEHLER
JAMES W KOOI JOHN C LOWE EDWARD R LUEKERT ROBIN P MILOVICH MANUEL G MONTALVO
CURTIS R BOHLSCHEID JIM E MOSHIER JAMES R NELSON JOHN S OLDHAM JOSEPH L PARKS
ROBERT H PEARSON ROBERT G REYNOLDS THOMAS F RIGGS FRANKLIN J SUMICH RALPH E UHLMANSIEK
QUENTIN R BEECHER JOSE H VELASQUEZ JAMES E WIDENER JOEL T WILLIS SERGIO E ALBERT RONALD L ELZA
KENNETH C HURSE WILLIAM H JOHNSON JR MATTHEW D KENNEDY DANNY O KENNELL DENNIS R MANSKE
HARRY L HENDRICKS JAMES L KISTLER ALAN J LEE JAMES L MCCLAIN DARYL E ROLFE
GARY L TAYLOR ROGER L BARBER WENDELL L CARTER FRANKLIN D CHOPPER MICHAEL J CLIFFORD
JAMES L CUMISKEY SIDNEY E DENTON AMBROSIO S GRANDEA DON L GRISBY GEORGE B HAYS
CHARLES L HEMMINGWAY CLYDE R HOUSER JR EDWARD A LAPIERRE FRANKLIN D MCNARY PAUL R MYERS
LAWRENCE J SILVER TOMMY L SMITH BYRON M SPEER GERALD C STELLE MANUEL V TORRES
GLENDON R BARNETT JOSEPH R BLAIR RONALD J BONERT BERRY J BRIDGES RICHARD G BROWN
RICHARD A CABLE FRANK A GIACOBELLO JR ROBERT L HOLLAND FREDERICK J LECHAK JOSEPH H URMANN
JOSE A MONTOYA ROBERT R ROUSH HARLAN R SLUSSER ROBERT F STEIMER ROBERT E THOMPSON
JOHN R VAN NORMAN III HERBERT A WARNER JR BARRY L ADAM PAUL BOWMAN JR PHILIP G CHIPCHASE
MICHAEL O CROSSEN WILLIE DAVIS JR JOE R DE BAULT DAVID J ENMON JAMES C FEKETE
JERRY FOREHAND TOMMY R GARTON RANDY J GLENN JUAN J GONZALEZ STEPHEN M HENRY
LONNIE M HOLMES LAWRENCE A HURD WILHELM L KEGLEWITSCH PETER B LEHMANN DONALD A LEHUTA
HENRY L LITTLE WALTER J LYONS JERRY E METCALF CHARLES D MYERS JR MICHAEL R OJILE

JOHN A PENNA FLOYD H RUSSELL JR FRANCISCO L SAMSON JR ERNESTO SANCHEZ JR BEN D SNOWDEN
LOUIS J PURDY JOHN C SHAMEL JOHN W SWANSON JR VALENTINO TAUAESE FRANKLIN R THORPE
BRUCE TOWNSEND HUBERT C VAN POLL HERBERT WIGFALL JR FREDERICK J WILLIAMS WILLIAM W YOUNG JR
DAVID L ARENS DENNIS A COMBS TERRY L CONLEY PORFIRIO E ELIAS WARREN HARDY JR
JOHN E CAMINO GEORGE A GARCIA CHARLES E GRADOVILLE JOSEPH E HAMMAC JERRY M JENKINS
CHARLES R MEARS RANDY M MINOR LAWRENCE H MITCHELL EDWARD MORRIS ALVA N MYRICK II
JOHN E MCCULLOUGH NEIL C MCENTEE GEORGE M O'DONNELL DAVID P OPLINGER DEAN N RASCHKE
HARMON T RESPASS THOMAS A RIVERA CLARANCE W ROGERS JR LYLE E ROHLFSEN EUGENE SESTER
JOHN A SICKLES WILLIS M SULLIVAN JR MICHAEL T URSERY CHARLES E VICICH RICHARD A ANDERSON
JOHN E BERNARD WILLIAM D BLESSMAN JOHN A BRANTLEY EMANUEL K BRICKHOUSE ROBERT E BRIDGES
GUY W CLINGER JR WILLIAM N COLE JERRY R COOK WILLIAM H CROSSMAN ALAN W DENNEY
ROBERT L CLUKEY JR DON L DEATHRAGE JR HERMAN G EBBINGA RONALD D EDENFIELD JAMES M ELCHERT
GARY J ERNST ALAN J FARHAT JAMES R GARCIA RAYMOND G HAHN JR MICHAEL J HARE
CURTIS J HARMAN ROBERT T HARRIS EDWARD E HEYER SAMMY L HOLMES CHARLES W HOOK
HOWARD E HURST RICHARD L JENNER CARL T JOHNSON JAMES R JONES CHARLES P KELLY
PAUL E KELLY JR DOUGLAS A LOGAN ROBERT S MAGUIRE BRENT E MATHIS BOBBY MINTON
PAUL F KIECKER SAMUEL L MODESITT MICHAEL J MORROW HOWARD A MUCHA GEORGE T MURRAY
MORRIS A NOBLE STEPHEN M NOGGLE WALLACE G NYE DENNIS S PAZDAN WAYNE A PETTERSEN

PANEL 22E

THOMAS R RASCHEL LEROY REED CHARLES M ROACH BENJAMIN F ROBERTSON JR
ALAN J ROESE FRANK G ROMO DENNIS RUTH JAMES P SCHUELLER MICHAEL B SCOTELLARO
MAURICE A SHAFF JR VICTORIANO P SOSA JR JAMES E STARKS JOHN H STOUT WILLIE L THIGPEN
EDWARD A SMITH EDWARD E STROMBECK JOHN W VAUGHAN WILLIAM B WEIKAL JR CHARLES E WEST
LARRY E WILSON LLOYD C WOHLFORD JR VERNON H BAKER II JAMES E BERRY JAMES F BERRY CHRISTOPHER BONNET
LARRY W BURDETTE DENNIS L CASEY DALE D DWYER HENRY L FISHER EDWARD J GUILLORY
JAMES E KING WALTER J KRAUSS JR CHARLES R LAUER WILLIAM E LEMMONS HAROLD W RADABAUGH II
RICHARD L HIX ROBERT K MCCORVEY JAMES C MCKITTRICK MICHAEL D PINKERTON PHILLIP R VENEKAMP
JAMES E WERDERMAN DENNIS J ADAMSKI ROBERT C AGUADO FRED G BERTOLINO DENNIS W BROWN
ROBERT J CARA BOBBY L CORNS JACK E COSSINS ROBERT E CRAYTHORNE RAYMOND D CROWDER JR
WILLIAM J DILLON ALLEN N ENGEL EDWARD L FAILS JR WAYNE S FIELDEN RUSSELL L FILIBERTI
HUBERT J FINK KENNETH D FRAKES WILLIAM M GEIER RAYMOND W GODWIN PAUL E GOOD
THOMAS L GORDON MONTE R HARPER CHARLES J HILDENBRAND JOHN R HILL FREDERICK W SCHAEFFER
JAMES G HINCH ROBERT J HINDRA TIMOTHY A JOHNSON BLAINE W LANDERS LAWRENCE R LASITER
JOHN P LEE RICHARD C LUNDY JOSEPH T MARTIN GEORGE D MILLER STEVEN R MILLER
HOBART W MCCOMAS JR DONALD D MORRIS EDDIE L MOTON JR BOBBY L MURPHY DANIEL T NUTLY
IGNACIO PORTUGAL JR BOBBY W PRICE DAVID S RAINE GEORGE RANDOLPH BOBBIE J RATLIFF
WILLIE J RHODES CAMERON A RICE JOHN J RIECK JR DAVID A ROBIN RONALD J SAIZ
DAVID F HENRY DANIEL J SANDSTEDT SHELDON B SCHULMAN WAYNE T SCHUMACHER WILLIAM N SCOTT
LLOYD A SELLERS III WILLIAM P SHAFFER WILLIAM J SIPPEL KAZIMIERZ H SLOMIANY JAMES B SMITH
CLYDE W STEPHENS EDWARD H STEVENS JOHN D STPETERS MERILL L SUEDMEYER LEONARD V TEDESCO
RONALD G TROGDON JACKIE D WEATHERLY NOEL T WEST JOHN L WINTERS DAVID M WOOD
ROBERT F WRIGHT MALLEN P ZUM TERRY H BROUMLEY LESLIE A CHAMBERLAIN CARL H PRESNALL
BEN COY CHARLES L CRONKRITE LESLIE E ENGELHART JAMES E FIELDS WAYNE E HALSTEAD
LEHRON JACKSON JR FRANK P JENKINS JR WAYNE D KARN JOSEPH R KLUG GEORGE B LEE
BENJAMIN M BROTHERS III ROBERT E MASON RONALD A MICHAUD CHESTER D PAULL GARY T PORTER
FORREST L RAMOS JOHN W SCHWEYHER JR ROBERT E STAUFFER RICHARD K WELLS DAVID A YOUNK
HARLAN F ADAMS HOWARD L BRITT THOMAS E CAMPBELL RONNIE S CATANZARITI DENNIS M HIGGINS
JERRY F CLARK FRANK J CONSTANTINI JR JIMMY L COOK FRANK J COSTANTINI JR DEAN D CRANE ROBERT J DOUGHERTY
WILLIAM ESPOSITO MORRIS D GAGNON CARLTON E GOULD CARMEL B HARVEY JR STEPHEN C HASS
GERALD D BOYD JAMES W JOHNSON JR THOMAS A JOHNSON WELLINGTON M JOHNSON GARY L KENAGA
CLIFFORD W LEATHERS JR EDGAR L MCWETHY JR JOHN L OLSEN RICHARD G OSBORNE DARRELL J SPINLER
RUSSELL E PAGE WILLIAM C PETTY LARRY M PORTER RUSSELL R ROULIER ERNEST P SANTOS
DESIDERIO C LAUREL JR FLETCHER SEEBER JR HOWARD A SESSOMS ALAN A STEIN WILLIAM P WAGNER III
BILLY J WATKINS GERALD E WATKINS TERRY L ALLEN ERLING A ANDERSON JAMES ARNOLD
GARY E BEESLEY WILLIAM J BOEHM ERVIN L BURNS ALBERT BUTLER JR DARRELL W BUTTS
GENE E CALPH CARLIN M CAMPBELL JR THORNE M CLARK III VERNON T COCHRAN THOMAS A DESCHENES
JACK L CRIPE ROBERT A DAVIS LLOYD D DE LOACH LESTER M DE RISO CHARLES O DEEDRICK JR
RONALD C CLARK THOMAS B DUFFY JR TIMOTHY J EGAN JAMES R EMMERT RUSSEL W ENGLE
BOBBY L FINNEY HURRELL GIBSON KENNETH L GREENE RICHARD E GREENE JR RANDY A HARRILL
DAVID J HELLER ALVIN G HILL DOYLE HOLCOMB RICHARD E HOOD JR VINS R HOOPER
DAVID E JOHNSON HARRY J JOHNSON RICHARD J JOHNSTON DONALD R JUDD DONALD M MUNDEN
STEPHEN A KELLY ELI J KING KENNETH K LIMA FREDERICK H LIMINGA ROBERT R LITWIN
JIMMY C LOWRY GARY A LUTTRELL FRANCISCO S MARIN WALTER C MAYER STEPHEN A MIKA
RICHARD B JOHNSTON ROBIN D MACLEOD WILLIAM S MCBROOM WILLIAM A MUNN TIMOTHY J MURPHY
FRANK MCCRAY JR JOHN MCEACHIN JR DANIEL L NEGRO JERRY L NOE MICHAEL D O'CONNOR
CLYDE OWENBY GEORGE PATTON JOHN P PATTON LEONARD B POORE DANIEL V VALDEZ
ROBERT L PREDDY FLOYD E QUARLES RALPH J RIZZI TRINE ROMERO JR HECTOR M SAENZ
JAMES W SANFORD WARREN H SCHROBILGEN JR JEFFREY R SEXTON JOHN SHARBER JR LLOYD E SMITH
CHARLES H SNOW JOHNSON A STEIDLER DAVID A STEPHENS DAVID R STEPHENSON ROBERT L STEVENS JR
GEORGE A POOR JR EDMOND C SUTTON FA'ASAVILIGA V TAFAO LARRY B TURNER CHARLIE L WALKER
WILLIE C WARREN MICHAEL J WATERMAN EDWIN J WILLIAMS ALEXANDER C ZSIGO JR LARRY S BYFORD
EDWARD L CENTENO RONALD J CRANDALL CURTIS L DUCKETT ODDIE C HAILEY RONALD L HAMILTON
WILLIAM L HAMLIN MICHAEL G HARVEY ERNEST L HURD CHARLES L JOHNSON HARRY JONES
SAM R JONES EDWIN W MARTIN JR ELLIS A MCBRIDE JR CLIFFORD N MIZE JACK W PETERSON
LEONARD PHILLIPS WILLIAM C ALLEN JR ELWOOD BAKER JOHN J BIALKOWSKI ANDREW J DAVIS JR
EUGENE D HARVEY THOMAS M DICKINSON CRAIG B GARIEPY LARRY R GUENTZEL NAMON HINES JR ROY E SHANKLIN
GERRITH L KIBBE JEFFREY D MCGUIRE HAROLD C NYE MICHAEL C ODELL THOMAS H OHNESORGE
DAVID N PARKS MICHAEL D PERKINS GERRIT J SCHOUWBURG ROBERT C SHERMAN HAROLD E SOUTHARD
JERRY L STEED THOMAS C BENGE KENNETH H BROWN CHARLIE L BURNEY ALLEN J CAGLE
LUIS F CORREA WILLIAM K GARDELLA HUBERT E GORDON WAYNE V GORDON RONALD H GROFF
THOMAS C GUDEN CARL E HOLBROOK ANDREW JOHNSON ROBERT W KURTZ OREN K MILLER
ALFRED W MURPHY JOHNNY C QUENGA OTTIS REED RAYMOND D RHAMY KIERAN J STARR
JAMES S MCARTHUR JERRY T THOMAS RUFUS T WILLIAMS NICHOLAS M BERAN JR THOMAS C CARTWRIGHT
ANGEL M CORREA EARL DANIELS JR JAMES E DELRIE JOEL A ELLINGSON REYNALDO B FLOREZ
DANNY R GODSEY TEDDY M HART MICHAEL L MANGAN RONALD L SCHURCH JAMES G SCOTT
KYLE SMIDDY AARON B SPALDING DALE C ALLEN LAWRENCE E BACH JAMES A BLAKLEY
LAWRENCE J BOLGER VICTOR L BURNS FRANKLIN D BYUM JIMMY E CARTER FRANCISCO A MAZARIEGOS
JAMES E CRAWFORD ALLAN J DAMIAN JEFFREY J DAVID ANTHONY DICESARE JR CARL D DUDLEY JR
LEWIS B GAISER JOHN P GANNON ALEJANDRO R GODINEZ DONALD P HAMILTON ALLAN R HOFFMAN
CURTIS D JACKSON FREDDIE L JOHNSON PAUL E KINCAID CLYDE E LONG JR CHARLES A LYNCH
FREDRICK J BRENKE KENNETH A MILLARD DENNIS A O'CONNOR MICHAEL PARKER PAUL M RODRIGUEZ JR
JACKIE L SANDERS JAMES M SHEPARD JR JAMES R SNYDER RICK J STEWART EDMUND R TRAVIS
JAMES S STASSI RICHARD L WALKER ROBERT W WALLER STEPHEN G WASSENICH JONATHAN C WHITTICOM
IRA W WILLIAMS WILLIAM J WILLIAMS KENNETH R WRIGHT ROGER L BLAKE THOMAS E BROOME
MICHAEL G BROWN RICHARD W BRYANT FRED W CARPENTER DUANE E CAVARZAN ARNEL J DAVIS JR
DAVID R EDWARDSON RONALD E FIKE HARRY B FRANK JR ROY E GRANTHAM RODGER T GROSS
FRANKLIN D BYNUM PAUL E HALE DENNIS L HALL GEOFFREY L HAM WESLEY R KELBY GREGORY A KOSCHAL
BOB R LAYNE ROLF F LENZSCH WALTER N LOCHER GRAHAM N LOWDON JR DAVID A MOORE
CHARLES R MULLAN JR JOSEPH D NICHOLS JR JOSE H ORTIZ WALTER PRZYBYLOWICZ JR EDWIN L SHUBERT JR
WILLIAM D SIZEMORE ROBERT D SNYDER DONALD F SPICER JACKIE G STANLEY KENNETH M WRIGHT
FREDDIE L ALLEN WILLIAM J BACON DAVID E BOYER JERRY R CARTER CLINTON E CROFFORD
GAYLON D DAVOULT GARY L DUVALL JOHN J GULLIVER FELIX B HAWKINS ELWIN J LAMB
JAMES R LESTER GEORGE T MANGRUM KEVIN G O'CONNELL JUNIOR B PACK ROBERT PENDARVIS
GLENN E SANDERS HERBERT SHERRILL BING F STEPHENS GORDON W STOFLET CHARLES E SULLIVAN JR
WILLIAM A TAYLOR FRANCIS H TOENYAN MERLIN R ALLEN RICHARD A CARTER LEGRANDE O COLE JR
RICHARD H FREUDENTHAL RONALD A GILLY THOMAS A GODDEAU JOHN A HOUSE II LUTHER H HOWARD
JAMES T HUFSTETLER CHRISTOPHER P JOHNSON HOWARD W JONES MICHAEL B JUDD JOHN D KILLEN III
DALE R KOCH LARRY D MCKINNON NOEL S NELSON BRUCE G OCKEY THOMAS J POOL
GLYN L RUNNELS JR JAMES H SPARKS WALTER W VINSON MICHAEL O BARRETT STANLEY E BOWEN
PETER AVILES HARLAN T BILDEN GENE F COLVIN STEVE C CUNEO MICHAEL W DOWNEY
ANDRE E MARCOTTE LEON G NELSON DAVID M PREDMORE WAYNE M ROCKENBAUGH ROBERT A SAUCIER
WILLIAM SCOTT DANIEL R SMEESTER CLAYS TURNHAM ARSELL WHITLEY MELVIN R WRIGHT
JOHN M AINSWORTH III WILLIAM E ALLISON JOHN P ANDERSON DENNIS D ASCHENBRENNER LEON E BELL
THOMAS E BAILEY GARY M BARNARD WALLACE W BARNETTE GILBERTO BARRERA ROBERT C BARTA
ROGER D ADAMS MICHAEL L BEASLEY RONALD BOSTON CHARLES W BOWERSOX JR DAVID M BRADLEY
DANIEL W BRADY WALTER H BROOKS JR EDWARD L BROWN CESAR E CARVALLO RUSSELL L CASTLE
RONALD CHARLES MEDFORD A CHRYSLER FEDELE A CICERO KENNETH R CLOPTON MARK R EVERETT
KENNETH E COE PHILIP H CONVERSE GEORGE COUTRAKIS CHARLES E CRAIN FRANK DAVILA
DAVID J DE RUE ARTHUR E DEMERS JR VAUGHN L DEXTER ALAN L DIEDRICKSEN JOHN W DOHERTY
STERLING K COATES MICHAEL R DOTSON PAUL G FORBES JR JAY E FORSBERG ROGER H FRIESNER
HECTOR FUENTES MARGARITO GARZA PAUL J GOLEMBSKI WARREN H GRANT JR MICHAEL L GRAVES
RICHARD W GRIFFITH ROBERT L HAINES STEPHEN W HARSHMAN JEFFREY S HATISON STEPHEN J HONNOLD
ALAN M HANSON WILLIAM E HILLIARD TERRI L HIXES GARY A HOLSCLAW CHARLES E HUMPHREY
JAMES D IMERESE GENERAL F JAMES JR ROBERT J JAMRO DEE R JARVIS CHARLES E JOHNSON
LUTHER M JONES DARRYL R JUEL FREDERICK M KASCH WARREN O KENEIPP JR JOHN M KESSINGER
THOMAS G KING DAVID B KLINE JOE C LEUTENEGGER JIMMIE LEWIS GARY D LYONS
WILLIAM D LEWIS HARRY J LOCKHART FRANK T LOPINTO EDWARD R LOZANO CHRISTOPHER J MAGUIRE III
ANTHONY MARACZI STEVEN F MATHIAS STEPHEN A MENSHEK EDWARD C MILLER JERRY L MILLER
JAMES L MCBRIDE JIMMY MCBROON JAMES G MCCOY MAURICE K MOCK STEPHEN P MULLER
EDWARD J MCCUNE JOHN T MCGARRY THOMAS W MCMAHON JR RICHARD A NICHOLS BENNY F NIMOX
TEX D PATRICK RAY D PENDERGRAFT FRANKLIN H PENN DENNIS M PERRY STEVEN J POWERS
TERRY L QUIGLEY ALEX L QUIROGA DELMA L REED ALFREDO V REYES PHILLIP W ROE

PANEL 22E (*Continued*)

JACK R RUSH JOHN D SALMIERI STANLEY SANDERS FRANK W SAWYER JR JONATHAN A SAWYER
DENTON R SLACK MICHAEL D SMITH DAVID G SPEARMAN MARSHALL G STEFFANS WILLIAM L STEVENSON
RAYMOND E STERRY ALAN M STURDY WILLIAM J SUTTON PETER G TALMON III MALCOLM F TASSEY
THOMAS M THOMPSON WILLIAM H TOOMBS EARNEST L TURNAGE ROBERT VARGO STEVEN R WAGSTAFF
SHERMAN R WAITES TOMMIE V WHITE MARK A WHITT WAYNE V WILSON HERBERT C WRIGHT JR
BRUCE A YODER ROBERT E ZIMBERLIN JR WILMA J BARR BRUCE H EATON WILLIAM A JUNE
FRANK R ALLENDER JR TIMOTHY M FLAMMER JAMES H HINSON MARVIN R JOHNSON DAVID B NELSON
NICK PANELLA JR LLOYD F PHILLIPS HAROLD D PHILPOTT PETER C REYES JOHN S ROEDERER
BENNY E SEABOURNE TONY AHINZOW CLINTON H ANDERSON JR JAMES E BALL III WALTER D BUSCHLEITER
LEO E SEYMOUR CALVIN BELTON KENNETH P BIRELEY STEVEN A BROWN JAMES H COONEY

PANEL 23E

ANDREW CURRIE JOHN W DAVIS CECIL F DIXON EDWARD F FEE JR
DANIEL R COX WILLIAM O EDMONDS DWIGHT D EISENHOUR GILBERT FELICIANO EDWARD K FERGUSON
MARLIN J GOODHUE DAVID A HEDBLUM JOSEPH L HICKS RAYMOND L HYSON FREDDIE JOHNSON
THOMAS J JONES ARTHUR LANTEIGNE JAMES R LUNSFORD JOSEPH MARVIN ANDREAS MCCURRY
CHARLES H MCFARLAND RICHARD L MCKINNELL ROBERT C NELSON MELVIN E NEWLIN ROGER K NORTON
ROBERT J OVERMYER GEORGE A PACE ARNOLD R PALMER FRANK M PIETRAS WAYLEN L POWELL
RONALD D REYES RICHARD N ROBEY ANTHONY M SCHMUTZ MONTY R SEWELL STANLEY H SULLIVAN
ROBERT W SWIGART THOMAS L TERRY JAMES E TURNER SAMUEL E WITCHER ROBERT A WOODROW
KAY W WRIGHT DAVID A ACTON ANTHONY J BORREGO PATRICK G BRIDENBAKER ERNEST M CARTER
EDWARD M CORNELL PEDRO FERRA-FLORES BERNARD F FORD WILLIAM V FREDERICK ROBERT T MCDANIEL
CHARLES M GATTIS JR RALPH B GERKEN JOHN W GRANAHAN DONALD E HEINZ JAMES E HOEWELER
JERRY D HUDSON JAMES R ISBELL PAUL G KNIGHTON LARRY G LUDWIG JAMES E MATTHEWS
WARD K DODGE FRANCIS G MONIN ROBERT L MORNINGSTAR ROBERT S MUMMERT EARNEST G NELSON
DAVID S PALMER ERNEST F PETTY GEORGE R PFLASTERER CARLOS M QUIROS DANNY P RIESBERG
TIMOTHY J SAUNDERS RONALD D SHEPHERD ANDREW P STEIN JR MARVIN O STEVENS KENNETH J STUTES
LEONARD J TAGLIEBER NORMAN E TREEST FRANK B WESTERFIELD JOSEPH W BABILLO JERRY R BEEBE
EDWARD M BRADY VINSON BYRD GILBERTO CABALLERO JR JERRY M CASH DONALD E DILLON
ROLAND D DU MOND FREDDIE ESTERS VERNE M GREELEY WAYNE M HAYES JOHN K HELTON
MELVIN D HOLCOMB JOHN R HOULIHAN TERRY W JUDKINS JERRY L KASTER LEONARD MIRAMONTEZ
TERENCE J KILBANE MELVIN E KUHLMAN RONALD L LAKE JOHN J MALLOY CHARLES E MANNS
THOMAS L MCCARTER ROGER P MCDANIEL STEVEN W MCGEE THOMAS E MCKEE SYLVESTER MCNEIL
RICHARD F HAWKS DONALD C PIKE WILLIAM J PRICE JETTIE RIVERS JR FRANK I RIVIERE RANDALL K RUSSELL
RICHARD J SASEK DARRYL E SAUNDERS ROBERT J SLATTERY DANIEL J SULLIVAN JOHN J VAN VLECK
LEON L VIVETTE MILES E WHITE ERIK B WICKENBERG BRUCE J ALLEN KENNETH R ANDERSON
PAUL A AVOLESE CHARLES A BALLAUF DAVID F BITTENBENDER CHARLES H BLANKENSHIP JOHN H FERRIL II
WILLIAM J CRUMM ROBERT C DAMBECK GLEN V DAVEY RICHARD R DAVIS WILLIAM W DAVIS JR
WILBUR L COSSON THOMAS A DEROSIER DAVID M DURANCEAU BOBBY L FOREMAN DAVID W QUALLS
CHARLES J GLENN III GERALD R HENRY WILLIAM E HERRING FLOYD HOLIFIELD JR GATLIN J HOWELL
GEORGE E JONES KENNETH B KOOSER ROBERT J KUBINCIAK RICHARD H LOPEZ PETER MOSKOS
JACK A FUSON OLEN B MCLAUGHLIN THOMAS M MCLAUGHLIN GLENN R OGBURN STANLEY F PATTERSON
ANDREW C RABAIOTTI JOSEPH R RIEBLI CHARLES E SAUER PAUL J SIMON MICHAEL B SMITH
DONALD J SOBY WLADYSLAW STANISZEWSKI IVRA A TATUM HAROLD TAYLOR LEE R TAYLOR
JAMES F TRITT HILARIO P VILLANUEVA THOMAS R WALSH GLENDON L WATERS JOEL WILLIAMS JR
LAWRENCE W WILSON JIMMY O BARNES EDWARD L BROMLEY GENE W BROWN PATRICK R CALLAHAN
JAMES L COTTEN JR MERRITT T COUSINS JAMES T DAVIS WILLIAM G DELLVON GERALD DUNN
JAMES A GAZDAGH THOMAS GREGORY JR ANTHONY K JOHNSON RONALD E JOHNSON SZOLTON S KLEIN
HARVEY J KINSEY DONALD H KITO GARY D LITTLE THOMAS V MALLOY WILLIAM H PRITCHARD
PERRY K JONES DONALD J REYNOLDS JAMES J SUSSMEIER FRANK J BOWLES CLIFFORD G BURCH
CHARLES R LEE T C O'BRIEN WESLEY R SEXTON CURLEY J SIMON WILLIAM E STROBEL
MYRON S BEACH JR JOHN C BOROWSKI KENNETH L BROWN ROGER W CLARK DAVID P CROZIER
JIMMY E DARBY WILLIAM J DEUERLING LARRY A DORING ARTHUR A ERWIN JAMES FABRIZIO
ARLAN D GABLE FRAZIER D HUGGINS DAVID H JOHNSON MICHAEL C JONES DANIEL W JORDAN
PETER G LECHNIR EDWARD K KEA FRED A KELLEY REVELRY L KERWIN SIEGFRIED KOFLER DONALD R LAST
BUDDY R MARTIN SIGURD M MESSER CLAUDE P MILLER MICHAEL S MITCHELL STEVE V MYLANT
REX K OFFIELD ANTHONY S PAPALAS ORIS L POOLE ARTHUR C RETZLAFF JOEL M SABEL
WALTER A SAMANS JR WILLIAM A SCOTT FRANKLIN S SHEPHERD MALTON G SHORES JAMES A SMITH
HARRY D SPIER JESUS M TORRES JAMES C WEARS BEN WHITE LAWRENCE A WHITFIELD
WALTER D WILLIAMS ROBERT P WYATT ANTHONY ALLEN HOWARD W BANNISTER KEVIN M CLARKE
ASHER A ANTHONY LOUIE D BRISCOE JR CHARLES N BROWN ROBERT L CENTER THOMAS L CLELAND
MARTIN J CORONIS OLIVER P DAMROW DANIEL F DE BUTTS JEWELL F DODGE MARION T EAKINS
CHRIS S EVANS PHILIP A FERRO CLIFFORD K FRYE ELOY S GRIEGO JR FRANCIS A HUGHES
WILLIAM J IGOE LEWIS F JENKINS ELMER F KENNEY HAROLD W KING DAVE R KINGSBURY
CLARENCE E LOSSING JORGE J MALDONADO DAVID H MITCHELL ROBERT J NICKLOW GEORGE E SMITH
CLEVELAND PATTERSON DOUGLASS F PEAY EDWARD R REED BRUCE R SCOTT DENNIS D SKUTT
EMILE J LEGERE LUTHER T STOWE SAMUEL ALMENDARIZ CHARLES V AYLOR FRED G BRAGG JR
BOBBY M BRASWELL LEROY H CHARBONEAU PERNELL R CLAUD GARY T COLEMAN TYRONE COMBS
JACK J COOPERWOOD III RONALD E CRAIN JACK P DOVE SR ROBERT E ECHOLS CLAUDE E ELMORE
GERALD L FOX WILLIE K FULLILOVE DALE F GAGNE EDDIE C GIBSON STEPHEN J GROTH
JAMES M HAIDER WANDLE L HICKMAN DAVID M HORN JERRY L HUGHES OWEN R MONTGOMERY
ROCKWELL G JAMISON JOHN H JOHNSON CHARLES M JUDGE JR RONALD R KING JERRY D LANIER
JOHN A HARLAN CHRISTOPHER M MCGINNIS JEROME G MCGOVERN JOSEPH L MILLER CHARLES L MOORE
MILFORD G MCKEE FLOYD R NOE GAYLORD E NOOTZ SALVATORE F POLIZZI CHARLES D RAILING
JAMES A RAINWATER JR FRANK J ROSE JR BRIAN W RUSHTON LAURENCE G SERSHON ROBERT J SULLIVAN
TROY L SEXTON JERRY R SPITLER LOUIS D SPRINGER BOYD E SQUIRE ROBERT A STRANGE
JAMES F SCHIELE BERNIE L TATE BRADLEY O TILLINGHAST JAMES L VANBENDEGOM GARY L WAGUESPACK
EDDIE E WILLIAMS FLOYD C WILLIAMS MOSES WILLIAMS HARRY L ALWAY CIRO J ANDREASSI
MICHAEL P CASSIDY LARRY F FAULKNER FREDDY R GORE ARNOLD MATHIS EDWARD MCGRUDER
MICHAEL J SHEHL ROGER L ACREE TERRY L ADAMS MICHAEL S BEREK JUAN J BOTELLO
RICARD T BUNNIS ROGER D CECIL KENNETH L CULVEY WILLIE L DAVIS STEVE B FENKO
LARRY E FIELDS DANIEL R FLANSAAS LARRY R FOSTER JUAN F GUTIERREZ FRANCIS D HORLBACK
WILLIAM B MONAHAN JEROME MOORE GUILLERMO MUNOZ KENNETH M SCHRAMEL ROGER D SEGERS
JAMES H SPENCER PETER C SVINTSAKOS ELBERT T WILLIAMS JOHN W ALLEN TERRY D ALSUP
DAN W ARCHER JR JOHN S BERG RUSSELL L BLANTON CHARLES F BOSS WILLIAM L CANTER
ROBIN B CASSELL JOHN P COLLOPY DONALD J CROCKER GERALD E DAVIS ROBERT K DWYER
DAVID A FASNACHT KENNETH B FROMANT JAMES J GRAY PAUL M GREGOVICH FLOYD W HARTWICK JR
EVERETT A HERRITZ GEORGE A HOLLADAY CHARLES R HUMBLE RONALD R JONES HARRY A KELLY
PATRICK D LUCAS RONALD E MECKLEY JAMES E MESSENGER JOHN P OLMSTEAD DONALD PASKOWICZ
RONALD F POOLE JAMES H PRICE DAVID A RITZSCHKE RAYMOND RUIZ EDWARD S SACCO
JERALD K SUMIDA ARMANDO VILLA CHARLES D WARD CHARLES I CARTER EDWARD L FOLKS
ANDREW M HOVANCIK JR FRANCIS E HOWE ROBERT W JOOSTEN GARY T MARBUTT CHARLES E MERRIMAN
WAYNE F REED CHARLES H RICHARDS JR REYNALDO S TORRES WESLEY E BELLAMY JESSE L HARRIS
GERALD R BRINES JUAN V BUENDIA AUSTIN B COOK MICHAEL L HOGGE BILLIE MIMBS
SAMUEL PAOLETTI EARNEST D RITCHIE CLIFFORD W SILVIA DAVID A SMITH DALE F TEGELMAN
THEODORE E WESTBROOK DONALD B ADAMS JR GILBERT F BALLARD JAMES E BROWN WALTER BROWN
DAVID R CHATTERTON TYRONE DARRETT DON E DAVIS ROBERT L GENTRY RICHARD A GIOVANACCI
PABLO R GONZALEZ ROGER W GREETAN RICHARD D HARTMAN WILLIAM E HELLYER JEROME JOHNSON
LEONARD KUBIAK WILLIAM H LAMB PAUL A MACKAY JAY B MARTINE JR STANLEY TOMASZEWSKI JR
JOHN L MODGLIN GLEN E OAK ROBERT E PASCOE WILLIAM V POTTER ANTONIO RIBERA JEROME SIMS
RICHARD J TORTORICE WASH J LINDSAY DAN C STARNS JR PATRICK J SWEENEY JUAN M ZAMORA
WILLIAM D BIEVER MICHAEL K BOARDMAN GARY W BURNETTE DONALD P FRYE LAMOINE L SANDVIG
WALTER E GIBLIN JR WILLIAM A GUILLORY HERBERT P HUNTER WILLIAM B JACKSON JAMES E JARANSON
DONALD P MCGRANE NORMAN A MEAD RONALD A MOORE DENNIS W PETERSON KENNETH G STOKER
JOHN ALFONSO GERALD A LUPAS JOHNNY T BRANHAM MIGUEL Z CONTRERAS GARY R DANSER
RONALD R BARCALOW EVERETT E FOSTER THOMAS GURLEY RONALD B HAMBLIN MICHAEL J MENCHISE JR
RONALD K SCHUMACHER LOUGHTON SMITH BOBBY H SORRELLS RALPH M STACEY JR ALLAN J STEARNS
DONALD T STEINBRUNNER CLYDE J STEPHENS GARY F WALLACE IRVIN G WEYANDT WILLIAM F ABERNETHY
JOHN L ANDERSON DENNIS L ANTOINE JOHN J CAMPA JOSE CASTILLO THOMAS O CLARK
JAMES F BEAN RICHARD F COLEMAN OCIE D COOLEY ROOSEVELT C CURLEY JR LAWRENCE M DAWSON
PAUL L DOMKE ARTHUR M DRIGGERS JR WILLIAM M DUNCAN DONALD F FEE STANLEY FERBOS
GEORGE FOSTER WILLIAM F GAINES THOMAS F GANION DOUGLAS W HILL JAMES E HUCKABEE
ROBERT E JOHNSON FRANK D LEAL JOE LEWIS MARK T LINDERMAN HAROLD E MORROW
GARY A MCLENNAN DONALD W MCNAMARA HENRY MUCHA JR STEVEN J MULLET ALBERT A OUTWATER JR
WILLIAM E MURFF HAROLD R NIELSEN WILLIAM A POLLARD LE R RADTKE JR JOHN W RIVERS
BILLY G RODGERS CARL E RYDER RICHARD J SCHUTZ PONDER R SIMS GARY W STERN
RICHARD F SUTTER WAYNE J SYLVIA PATRICK J VASQUEZ MERLIN H VROMAN DENNIS J WAHL
GENE A WHITE JAMES L WHITFIELD REGINALD E WILSON ROBERT W WOOD PAULINO G LOPEZ
THOMAS P BRADY WILLIAM B BROWN WILLIAM B GRAVES CHARLES R LEONARD ROBERT MATRANGA
CURTIS R MCLAWHORN HEINZ A TAPIO WILLIAM S WHITE CHARLES A BARRETT II RICHARD J BEHRNS
DEAN M BERANEK RONALD P BLAESE MICHAEL P CARR GEORGE W CHILDRESS STANLEY W DIX
WILLARD D DURHAM JR CHARLES J EVANS JAMES R FISCHER ROGER D GOLDSMITH THOMAS M HUNTLEY
JOSE A IRIZARRY LEMOYNDUE JARRETT SAMUEL A JOHNSON STEPHEN LEBITZ JR GARY O MOOER
HUGH R MCCABE JAMES J MCCARTHY HARRY C MCMICKEN ROBERT A NELSON NELSON T NICELY
CHARLES E OLIVER EUGENIO RODRIGUES WILLIAM S ROSS JR JAMES J SALTMARSH JOEL P STAUNTON
STERLING D STEADMAN RICHARD D STINNETT LARRY I SUTTON DANIEL TRAMELL DANTE VOLPONE
BOBBY G WELLS LEO BELL JR NICHOLAS C BIANCONI DAVID N GREEN JR ANTONIO M SALINAS
WILLIAM G GROTH WARREN D JOHNSON RICHARD LOPEZ FRANCIS J LUDWIG ROBERT L MCINTYRE
ARTHUR E FISHENDEN CLIFFORD L RANDOLPH LAWRENCE J VIRGILIO ROBERT L WALKER RODERICK L WEISS
EDWARD BARDEN JERRY W CAMPBELL ROBERT M CRAIG JEFFREY C CROUSE DONALD V DAVIS
JERRY D GOOCH JEREMY M JARVIS JOHN L JEFFERS BRUCE E LARGE HERBERT L LUNSFORD
CHARLES D MATTERN WALTER L MCINTOSH JR DEAN R NELSEN CLIFFORD D NELSON WESLEY PARKER

PANEL 24E

CHARLES W WARNER LEONARD T WILLIAMS LEWIS D WILMOTH RICHARD BRAZIK
GEORGE S CAMPBELL RICHARD A CLAFLIN JAMMIE V FRANKLIN EDWARD C GOELZ CHARLES D HARMAN
MICHAEL R HARRIS JR JERRY R HOLBROOK HENRY LANGHAM JR LARRY J MELOY ROBERT P O'NAIL
ANTHONY RUTIGLIANO JOSEPH WHITE WILLIAM L AMOS WILLIAM O BARE JAMES W BEAMS
JOHN C BIONDILLO STEVEN W BOWERS EDWARD R BROWNE GILLAND W CORBITT FRANK B CRUZ
MERL W FERGUSON JACK W FINCHUM DAVID E FLANINGAM MARTIN A FLEISCHMANN CHARLES D HARDIE
LAWRENCE A DIETZ II GUILLERMO GAZAR KENNETH L HENDRIX MILES E JANSEN THEODORE P LINSKI
MYRON D LUCAS RAYMOND J LUDWIG DAVID L MEYERS HAROLD D MONEYSMITH HAROLD W MORALES
PHILLIP M MYLES LEROY A NELSON ROBERT W NELSON BRUCE M PATTERSON BOBBY G PETERSON
RONALD H PFEUFFER ERNEST PHILLIPS JAMES R POPE RICHARD SMITH JR RICHARD J WEHRHEIN
THOMAS A WELKER MICHAEL D WESSEL EDWARD J WISE HAROLD E YOUNG JOHN CAREY JR
JOHN R EVANS ROBERT O GAGNE MANUEL M GARCIA JR GERALD B KEENE KERMIT H LA BELLE JR
DOMINGO MUNOZ KARL W RICHTER MARVIN J ADKINS EVERETT A ALLEN GARY J ARDENEAUX
ROBERT D ARNDT JAMES P ARRAIZ TONEY A BARNETT DENNIS M BARTON DEWEY L BEATTY
STEVEN H BENNEFELD ROBERT L BENNETT HENRY W BERNARD JR MARK R BISHOP JAMES L BLASKIS
CECIL B BRIDGES WILLIAM V BRINDLE BOBBY J BROWN DENNIS E BROWN
ERVIL T BRAY JERRY D BYARS FRANCIS CAMPEAU JACK M CARLAN DANIEL G CAVAZOS RICHARD D CLENDENEN
WILLIAM D COLLINS ROBERT B COTTEN JAMES L CRENSHAW HUGH W CROSS MARIO C CRUGNOLA JR
ROBERT J DAVIES BLAKELY I DAVIS JR THOMAS J DAWSON JR JEROLD V DESPARD EDWARD R DORSEY
JERRY V DAVIS ERIC M DEWEY JOHN M DUDLEY JOSEPH G DUGAS PAUL A DUPERE
JOHN S DUPLAGA KENNETH DYKE WALTER T EADS JAMES A EARICK JOHN T EDWARDS
ROBERT L ELLISON ALAN C ERICKSON CURTIS D ESKEW GERALD W FARRIER KENNETH L FASTH
JOHN J FIEDLER RUSSELL L FIKE HAROLD FONTENOT JOHNNIE L FRAZIER GERALD G FREDRICKSON
HERBERT A FRYE MICHAEL F GAFFNEY RAMON GARZA ALFRED J GASPAR ROBERT E GELLER
RICHARD H GIBSON WALTER C GIBSON LAWRENCE J GILBERT WILLIAM T GILROY LARRY E GRACE
RUSSELL A GRAZIER CHARLES C GREGORY ROBERT L HASZ RICHARD A HATCHER LARRY D HOLLEY
WILLIAM C HARTGEN JOHN O HAYNES WILLIAM K HINCKLEY JR STEPHEN L HOCK CHARLES W HOLLWEDEL
CALVIN D HOWISON JULIUS B HUGHES DONALD N HUGO MARTIN M HUNT PHILLIP JACOB
RALPH W JACOBS DONALD W JEDLICKA RICHARD H JOHNSON WILLIAM B JUSTIN THOMAS M KANE
THOMAS L KEIRNS CHARLES D KIESER LARRY V KINARD ROBERT A KISCH JOSEPH KOSIK III
EDWARD L LA BARR RICHARD L LA FLAIR WADE A LANNOM JR ANTHONY M LEACH WILLIAM LEE
ROBERT C LEONBERG JOHN T LILLA ARNOLD E LOHSE WILLIAM E LOWE GEORGE C MCDONALD
KENNETH W LOZIER JAMES M LYNCH RALPH E MANNING ALAN R METZ GEORGE D MILLER
JAMES S MACVICKAR JR EARLE E MCAULIFFE JR EDWARD A MINDYAS HUBERT H MORGAN JR LEROY MOSER
CHARLES E LONG BRIAN D MCCONAHAY JAMES G MCGOVERN RONALD D MCILRAVY RONALD L MCJUNKIN
FRANK C MCNELIS JR WILLIAM V MCQUADE JOSEPH R NATOLI JAMES E NEUMEYER GEORGE NEW JR
GARY E NEWBY JAMES E NEWKIRK HUGH NORWOOD RONALD R OGRINC ROBIN L OLMSTEAD
CARL J OLSON THOMAS D OTT II WAYNE H OTT RICHARD L OWENS DANNY W PACE
STANLEY K PATRICK RICHARD T PINTA RAYMOND N PLESH JOHN C PODY II ERNEST E POLSTON
DOUGLAS A POST DAVID S PRENTICE ROBERT M PRIVIECH ROBERT A RHUDA RICKY W RICHARDSON
JOHN M PRUNER CHARLES R RICH EDDIE L ROBERTS JERRY P RODGERS CHARLES E ROLAND
DALE R ROSS JAMES M RUNNELS HARVEY D SCOFIELD WILLIAM F SEVENEY JOSEPH C SHARTZER
WILLIAM J SHIELDS RICHARD M SIETZ DAVID W SMITH RICHARD T SMITH JOHN F SNOW
JOHN C SPIESS NELSON E SPITLER JOHNNY W SPIVEY GERRY L STARK WALTER E STEELE
ROBERT A STICKLER KENNETH D STRAIN ROBERT H SWAIN BOBBY R TABRON LEE R TAYLOR
RICHARD H TAYLOR DELTON E TERRY NORMAN A THOMAS JAMES L TOWNSEND HAROLD D WATKINS
WILLIAM F THOMPSON RICHARD J VALLONE ROBERT J VELASQUEZ JUAN A VELEZ GEORGE E WALL
GREGORY L WEBB GERALD A WEHDE JUDSON A WELLS JR RICHARD L WESCOTT EDWARD J WESSELS
ALLEN J WHITE FRED D WHITE ROBERT W WILFONG WILLIAM A WILK KERRY D WISDOM
JERRY G WRIGHT ROBERT L BISCAILUZ EARNEST R BYARS GEORGE F CATALANO RAY A CHATELAIN
DAVID A FREDERICK LARRY A GARNER JOHN C GEMBORYS WILLIAM V HEARNS EARNEST L HENDRIX
JOEL R KOHLER DENNIS KUZER VICTOR A SPADARO RICHARD W TOSCHI FLOYD G TREAT
CRAIG H WATERMAN TERRY L WINTERS THOMAS R ALLEN JOSEPH W ALLWOOD DWIGHT L BENNETT
HUGO A BOCANEGRA BILLY E BROWN HENRY C CAUTHEN SR RODNEY O DAVIE EVERETT A EASTMAN
RICHARD L ERTL DONALD W HART JOSEPH E LAVIGNE JOSEPH H MIDGYETTE DOUGLAS R NOEL
ARNOLD O NAKKERUD LEROY O'NEAL RONALD L PACKARD RAYMOND A PETERSEN JAMES R POGGEMEYER
DAVID L SCRUGGS GLEN E SHROPSHIRE BOBBY D SMITH WAYNE G VAN LANT ROBERT M WALLACE
PAUL E WILLIAMS JESSE W ALLEN JAMES E BATTEN JAMES F BURKE JR ROBERT J D'AMICO
HERMAN C BROEGELER III CHARLES G BUTLER JR DAVID J CARLTON LEVAN A CHURCH PAUL S COLVIN
JOHN A DONNAL DONALD R ELMORE DOUGLAS M FRANKLIN ALVIN M GOODWIN GUSTAVE F GUDLESKE
ROBERT H HARDENBROOK ROBERT L JOHNSON ROBERT J KLAGES JOHN L LAVISH WILLIAM L MATHIS
CALVIN A MCGINTY JR BRUCE E MIELKE JOE N MONTOYA ELZIA R PITCOCK WILLIAM R PREWITT
JAMES P PROCTOR RICHARD J REMEDIES ERNST RILEY STANLEY J SEAVERS WILLIAM S SIMMONS JR
HAROLD SNYDER JR STEVEN M STOFKO MONTY N WILSON ROBERT L WILSON CHARLES C WINSTON III
WILLIAM O WINSTON RICHARD E WOODSON ROBERT L ZWERLEIN RAYMOND L ABBOTT
GLEN A BJERKE THOMAS M BLYSTONE CAREY A CUNNINGHAM ROBERT D DRAPER THEODORE H DREYER
PETER L DUBE THEODORE F FUSS RICKY G HALL PATRICK B HOPPE PHILIP L HUDSON
PAUL C BERTOLOZZI WALLACE G HYNDS JR JOHN K JOHNSON JAMES R MAJORS LEONARD G MARCUM DANIEL H MILLER
GLENN R MCCUAIG KEITH C PERKINS ROGER M POIRIER LARRY G SALISBERRY DAVID SANCHEZ
DONALD M SOWER RAY W STOTLER MICHAEL L TROMBLEY ALBERT F WRIGHT JR BORIS R BENTLEY
RUFUS W BILLS JOHN W BISCHOFF CLARENCE H BROOKS RONALD L BUMPUS FREDDIE D LAWSON
ZANE A CARTER JOHN A DE BOCK FRED M GARDNER THOMAS A GOPP ARTHUR H GREEN
DANNY L BOLIN ALAN E HENDRICKSON JOHN W MACGLASHAN JAMES P MCGRATH JOHN B NAHAN III
WILLIAM G PHILLIPS TROY M PUCKETT HOWARD J SCHNABOLK WENDELL W STEWART JOHN N WICKLIFFE
IGNACIO E SABLAN EDWIN F UPRIGHT DAVID L WIGHTMAN III JOHN D WILEY JACK WOLPE
JOHN YEAST GERALD D BAKER PATRICK R DONER DAVID A ECHOLS EVERETT STRATTON JR
RICHARD C FERDIG FRANK GARCIA JR MATHEW GIBBS LAWRENCE R KIMBLER DWIGHT D WOOLF
RALPH C BISZ THOMAS L MEIDAM WILLIAM A NOSEK JAIME PARRILLA-CALDERO LAWRENCE G STAPLETON
HUGH M JACKSON JAMES WILLIAMS DONALD M WILSON CHARLES F BRANDENBURG KENNETH R BROWN
FORREST E CAIN JAMES H CALLIS LARRY T CHANDLER ROBERT V DURBIN MICHAEL L ENDICOTT
ARLEIGH F FELCH KENNETH D HAAS GORDON G KROPP HARRY B MCFADDEN PHILIP G ONKALO
EUGENE D RAMON KENNETH L SPITZER LANCE D BRUNSON EARLE A DRAKE ROBERT W TUBBY
LOWELL C HANSEN DONALD R KEMMERER BOBBY R MEFFORD FRANCIS M MICHINOK DARYL L MILLER
DENNIS J MCCAULEY FREDERICK A NEWBY JR ALBERT L PAGE JR HERSHEL H ROHN JR JOHN C SOPER
MICHAEL A COFFREDO JERRY L SPENCER DONALD L THOMAS FREDERICK D WOOD JOHN R ANELI
DONALD C COULTER ROBERT J DAVIS JR WILLIAM C FITZGERALD FRANK D GEORGE GEORGE W SCHOOK
MICHAEL J HILLER WILLIAM J HINES JERRY K JORDAN BOBBY D LIVELY JOHN P MARLOW
THOMAS T BROWN RICHARD T MCANDREW JR MICHAEL A MOORMAN JOSEPH S PORTER JR DAVID L SCOTT
VERNON G STICH VAN V TRANTHAM III HAROLD S TURSKEY ALLEN R VILKAS NARVIN O WITTMAN JR
JAMES D DAVENPORT EARL K EICHBAUER ANTHONY L FRANKS BOBBY R GARDNER JOHN L MORELAND
JOHN R FREILING JR CHARLES A JONES ROBERT I KLOOTWYK ROBERT T LOHMAN SOTORIOS M MARGARITIS
WILLIE M RHODES LEONARD W ROBERSON HERBERT C SAMPLES ROBERT J SCOTT CLARENCE E TACKETT
JOHN B WALTERS JAMES J WEEST JAMES B WILTSE JR ENRIQUE BERMUDEZ-PACHECO JOHN M BEYRAND
ANDREW C CONRAD JR JOEL D FENDLEY HONORIO M FIDEL JR JOSEPH HARRISON GERALD L HOPPER
ALLEN S CHERRY MICHAEL J HOTCHKISS HAZEL H HUMPHRIES III GARY R KOOMAN CHARLES R LATTA
PRENTICE D LE CLAIR ROBERT J MAXWELL WILLIAM J MCRAE RAY E MORAN JR CECIL B NICKENS
CAESAR A PINTO FRANCIS A ROCHKES ALFRED F SIMPSON GEORGE F SODAITIS ROBERT A THOMPSON
JOHN K WILLIAMS HARVEY E WYNN RICHARD C BENNETT THOMAS G DINEEN JR PAUL E TIGUE JR
KENNETH A BERUBE EDWARD A COFFEY CLYDE G GENTLE HENRY B GRAMMER DONNIE W YOUNG
KENNETH R HUGHES JOHN K HUTTON JR RANDALL L MCINTOSH ALBERT MOORE JR RICHARD L MORSE
GARY F GATTI JOHN F RODENBERG ALAN R SCHULTZ RONNIE M SNIDER ROY M WHEAT JOSEPH S YANCY
GEORGE C ALVAREZ LARRY G ASBRIDGE EDWIN L ATTERBERRY EUGENE CASTANEDA
FAY K COOPER GARY P FONTENOT RICHARD J GILBERT LARRY B GORDIAN DANIEL J HEIBEL
JOSEPH A LISTORTI LEONARD R LUDWIG DAVID L MCMATH TERRANCE L MEIER VERNON J THORSTEINSON
RAY A LEACH ROBERTO M RAMIREZ EDWARD D RANDAZZO LEONARD S SCOTT JR JESUS YANEZ JR
CYRIL E STIRNKORB ALVIN R BOZARTH DOUGLAS D COFFMAN JOSEPH W CRUZ RODNEY L HOFFMAN
JOHN A CAMPBELL LONNIE J DUCOTE JR WILLIAM G FERGUSON DANNY L INGLES JOHNNIE H PATTERSON
WESLEY R PHENEGAR JR KENNETH W SWAFFORD MARK R BLACK FRANK M BOZZELLO GARY B STEPHENS
GARY S CURTIS LEONARD E EASLEY EUGENE FIPPS ALEXANDER JACKSON ERSKIN D LIVINGSTON
THOMAS J CARSTENS HARRY J MOSER IV GEORGE E PARTIN ANGELO C RAPTIS JR GEORGE D TAYLOR
RONNIE D BEETS GEORGE A ZOMBERG GLENN C BAER WILLIAM E BAKER LARRY E BOWMAN JERRY E BUTTS
CLARENCE R ANGUS JAMES F BROOKS DAVID A BUJALSKI JAMES L COACHMAN JR CLIFFORD K COONS
DOUGLAS R DICKERSON JR GORDON P EADIE PATRICK J FLEMING JAMES W HUNLEY ROBERT V KEMP
ROBERT A KOLAS RONALD H LOFTON EARL W LONG JAMES J MCCORMACK JAMES E MILLIGAN
PAUL MCEACHRON HARVEY J MCSWAIN DAVID A NOLAN VALENTINE D UNCAPHER HENRY O VIGIL
BRIAN F WALLACE GERALD B WEAVER MICHAEL J YARBER CHARLES E BORDEN JOHN C FRIEL JON J HAYDEN
ANTHONY H BENNETT GENE H ELLIS JR JOSEPH M HALLAS RAYMOND HARVEY MARVIN D HAWTHORNE

PANEL 25E

LAWRENCE E HOWARD LELAND W HYSLOP JOHN H JONES GEORGE P KLAUS
NATHANIEL KNOWLES THURLO M MCCLURE TIMOTHY V RHODES EDWARD J ROSSER RICHARD R SMITH
LARRY J PETERS HUGH E SMITH KENNETH R SPOHN LAMAR H TEMPLE DAVID VAUTOUR
ROBERT R WATROUS RONALD P WINTERS ROBERT W BATES JOSEPH BENSON JOHN C BURDEN
DAVID M CALABRIA STEVE D CAMPBELL GILL L CARTER LOUIS A COBARRUBIO RONALD F CORNS
RICHARD L CURD WENDELL L DAY LAURENT N DION DON R HARGER THOMAS A HARP
CHARLES D HOM JON R HONRATH RONALD J JOHNSON WAYNE E JONES KEITH W LIVERMORE
JOSEPH MAIURO JOHN T MCLAIN WILLIAM P REESE RICHARD E SHILT JOSEPH E SHUBIAK
ARTHUR T STACHOWSKI RANDY L TAYLOR JOHN W TELFORD ALBERT A WASHINGTON ROBERT F WHITE
JOHN W BADON JESSE R BAKER HAROLD B BARTON WILLIAM J BRYANT MARVIN D BUCKRIDGE
KERRY E CLARK BILLY CUNNINGHAM STEPHEN W DAVIS ADAN FIGUEROA BARRON A FRAZIER
RONALD E GERWIG JOHN C IMRIE THOMAS R KELLEY ANDRE R LATESSA KENNETH J MANDERFELD

CHARLES J HOLLAND DANIEL MAKAREWICZ FRED W MITCHELL JR LARRY J OROSCO CHARLES E PATTERSON
LEO PORTER ROBERT A SNAVELY DAVID P WERNET LARRY G CAMPBELL WILLIAM E COMPTON III
MARTIN W ANDERSEN JAMES W CLEMENTS ROBERT E CLOWE TONY W COLLIER MAURICE C DESCOTEAUX
BAXTER H ELLIS THOMAS E IRWIN WALLACE M JACKSON RANDALL G JACOB MICHAEL B KOONS
DARREL U MAHAN CHARLES W NEISZ JR JAMES W RAGLE RICHARD M SECANTI JERRY J TUCKER
ROBERT E VIGGIANO GARFIELD WEST JR HAROLD BAUCHIERO KENDAL L BENNEY JR BERNARD B BRITTON
ALFRED J CORNEJO DANNY J CORRIGAN JAY D HERR RICHARD A LASHER RUDOLPH MELENDEZ
ANTHONY M GALENO GEORGE D MOTTE JOSEPH B ODUM WAYMON M PARKER SIGFREDO PINTO-PINTO
DARRELL L REID GARRY G TALLENT RICHARD G THIBAULT JERRY L ALLEN RAYMOND E ALLEN
FRED H GATES II ISIDRO BACA EDWARD L BOBO JAMES L BOEHLER JIMMY L BUCKLEY CLARENCE L CHASE
PATRICK S COCHRAN BAXTER F ERVIN DAVID A FRANCIS LEROY L GERBER LUCION GILLISPIE JR
ROGER C LEWIS RICHARD A MCCORMICK WILLIAM L MILLER MERWIN L MORRILL DAIN V SCOTT
ARCHIE W MORRIS THOMAS PETRAMALO LYNN K POWELL BENJAMIN ROMERO-DE-JESUS ROGER D ROOT
WILLIAM D SOULE FREDERICK H TIMS J F TREMBLEY JUAN VALENZUELA BILLY F WATSON
LARRY R WIEGERT DAVID K AASEN EDDIE J ALLEN RICHARD J BALTHAZOR
ALBERT L BROWN EDWARD E DAVIES JOEL E FALLER RANDALL R FREEBERG THOMAS E GILLIAM
LINDSAY D BALDONI HENRY GRANILLO HAROLD W HADDICK ROBERT A HEISER CHARLES J HOBAN III LEONARD R JOHNSON
CLIFFORD F KANGAS JOHN C KERR CHRISTOPHER A LESKY ROBERT L MADLAND JAMES A MESSER
DONALD A MIDDLETON BURKE H MORGAN GEROLD L MOUNCE MAURICE J NILE BILLY W PLATT
ROCKE D RAMSEY JAMES E SCHLOTTMAN CICERO WHITFIELD JR HENRY T ARAGON GERALD F CARROLL
PAUL E HAHN WILLIAM D HANEY CHARLES LANE JR DAVID L MARTIN JR WILFREDO PUMAREJO-COLON
FRANCIS B MIDNIGHT MICHAEL P MOSBACH PATRICK L NESS DANIEL T O'LAUGHLIN CARLTON M OTTEY
COLEMAN J KANE JR RAYMOND M OTTMERS JR THOMAS W SITEK RONALD N SITTNER RODNEY L STINSON
JOHNNY C WHEELER DEREX WILLIAMS JR NAOTO YAMASHIRO RICHARD M ALLARD DUANE R BENTLEY
JOSEPH B COMEAUX PAUL M DALEY JIMIE D DUTCHER JAMES F GODSEY WILLIAM H GOEDEKER
KENNETH B GOFF JR DANNY E GOODWIN EDWARD R GUEST RONALD L HOLTZMAN ROLAND I JEFFERSON
MICHAEL E JONES JOE L LEE RENE L MALARZ OTHA L MONGER NORBERT A OVERKAMP JR
FRANK E PETRICK WILLIAM E RODKEY RICHARD J SCHELL STERLING A WALL MANUEL G YBARRA
DAVID F ABLE PERCY BEASLEY JR CLAIRE R BOIS PAUL D CARAMELLA DENZIL M CARDER JR
DAVID L CLARK CHARLES R FERRELL CHARLES C HENDERSON ALLEN L JACKSON EDWARD J JACOBS JR
EDWARD L JORY JR TERRENCE M LAVELLE RONNIE L LOGAN WILLIAM J MCCUE GEORGE L MILAN
LARRY J MCDONALD MARK W NEUMANN WILLIE C ROBINSON JR ROBERT L SCOTT GASPER A VOILES
CARSON L WHALEY JR ELDON W WILLINGHAM JAMES J ZAVOCKY FILBERTO AGUIRRE JR JOHN J ALMANZA
LARRY F ARNOLD JOHN B BOOTH JOHN P CAREY RIM M DUNGEY ILLINOIS EMORY JR
WILLIAM O FULLER CHARLES GREEN JR RONALD E KEGLOVITS THOMAS M KILCULLEN JOSEPH C LUPO
DENIS D MATTHEIS CARY P QUEEN ROBERT C SMITH DOUGLAS D WALLIN VLADIMIR H BACIK
JAMES C BANKS PASCHAL G BOGGS EUGENE C CAMPBELL DENNIS W COLE RENE R COUTU
GENNARO J DE CARLO DAVID R FAEHNRICH FRANK C FISHER RAYMOND FORT JR MEDFORD S HENSLEY JR
OWEN WEBSTER LARRY J GRICE ROBERT F HAINES RICHARD A JACOBS CLAUDE R JAMES BRUCE A JENSEN
JOHN A JENSEN EDWARD L JOHNSON WILLIAM O JONES MICHAEL C KAMPH ALBERT G LEGGETT
FRANK M LEYVA WILLIAM D MIGNINI JESSE L MOORE TOMMY R PETERS CLIFTON B ROBERTSON JR
GEORGE H RUSH JR WILLIAM J SANDERS FRANCIS E SMILEY TIMOTHY P VOGEL JERRY P WYNNE
JAMES E YOUNG, FRANK L BELLANT MARCUS BROWN JR THEODORE BROWN ORLANDO FLONORY
WILLIE C BAKER MICHAEL J CALLER PHILIP R CURRAN TERRY L ECKER DAVID H ESMAN
ANTHONY J GRASSO JERRY E GUERRA WILLIAM J HART JR MARCUS C JONES WALTER M LANKFORD JR
RAYMOND P LINK GARY L LOVE BERNARD M LUSK JULIAN MENDEZ LARRY L SEXTON
PHILLIP W LESLIE JERRY L NEWMAN JEROME D PATTERSON ALAN A SANTIAGO BLAIR W STARKEY
ROBERT H STEELE DALLAS E THOMPSON RICHARD J WAGER CHARLES F WALLACE OSCAR ANZALDUA
SHAREL E BALES RUSSELL R BANNISTER RUTILIO P CORDOVA FRED B CRADDOCK JR JAY R NORMAN
FRANK J DE MARCO GEORGE F GALLAGHER DONALD L GASSER RUDOLPH GORHAM DAVID C HALL
LONNIE O HILL ALBERT C HORACE JR THOMAS W JONES J D KERSEY TIMOTHY F LIESE
PETER S MARTINEZ REED M MAY JR JOHN J MCMONEGAL JR LOUIS C MUSER II LARRY S NEWBURN
GEORGE E CAHILL NICKOLAS R PALUMBO JR RICHARD L SCADUTO STANTON J SETKA ROMAN SISNEROS
LEROY SPILLER III JESSE A TAYLOR ROBERT E THORNTON JOSEPH L WHITAKER JR JOHN D WHORFF
MICHAEL J ALLARD TOM J BAGENSTOSE JOHN S BURFORD FARRELL R CAREW DOUGLAS COATS
DOUGLAS C COKER BENJAMIN D COY JR RICHARD E FERGUSON JULIAN R HOOPER DONALD R OKAMOTO
BENJAMIN E KELLY JR RALPH M KNIGHT TERRENCE J KUDRO ROY H LEACH HOWARD S LINDECAMP JR
CHARLES L MAGLIARO JACK I MAGUIRE ROBERT W MORGAN VAUGHAN S MORGAN REGINALD A MUNDY
HOWARD W JOHNSON JR EUGENE C PACHECO JOHN J PINDER EDWARD L RANKIN ALAN J SMITH
ALFRED J SMITH HARVIE G SMITH CHARLES D TURNBOUGH CHARLES R WILKERSON JACK W WILKINSON
REUBEN C WILLIAMS ROSS W WOOD JR PETER J CANELAKES MICHAEL F ELFLEIN DANNY W ENGESSER
MARVIN L FRANKLIN JR LAWRENCE G GRASS CLEMENT F LAJEUNESSE JOHN D MERRIMAN JAMES M MOORE
MICHAEL D LAYMON LAWRENCE R MOYER DANIEL L MULLINS FRANK M PACHECO RICHARD C PERRY
GERALD J ROBERTS JR RICHARD ROCKENSTYRE CLIFFORD L WENCKER JACK L BUCHANAN BENNIE L WEST
JAMES H COOLS DENNIS E GABBERT MATTHEW R GOOSSENS GEORGE L HAHNER JR JOHN M HALEY JR
MILO P JOHNSON ROBERT D JOHNSON DONALD W KEENAN SCOTTY L KEYES WILLARD R KNIPPERS
DENNIS W LUGAR EDWARD L OTT III GARY K RATH CLINTON M RHOADES JR MELVIN J RILEY JR
TIMOTHY B CALDWELL ROBERT R SWAN ERNEST TATNEY JR EDWARD J ANDRADE JAMES M BAGSHAW
JERRY BELEY BILLY J BENNETT WILLIAM G BENNETT CHARLES F BIGHAM JAMES G BOSLEY
CLAUDE L COLLINS JAMES L DANIEL JAMES R DUNCAN JERRALD L EDWARDS WILLIAM H ELMORE JR
JOHNNIE L GARNER JON J GIORGIANNI ROY L GREENSAGE WILLIAM A GUNTER JR CLARENCE M GUNTHER JR
JOHN D HEFLIN MICHAEL J HOLSTIUS JOHN T HOLTMAN LLOYD R HUGHEY DAVID R HUNT
JAY D JOHNSON ALLAN G KALFAS JAMES L KEENER WAYNE R KLOESE ARTHUR W REINHARDT
TERRY V LEACH WILLIE J LIGHTFORD BRUCE B LIVINGSTON JAMES E MANESS WAYNE J MARQUARDT
WILLIAM D MARTIN ALAN L MATTHEWS LARRY A MERRILL KYNARD MILLS RICHARD D MORSE
CRAIG E MCCORKLE WAYNE I MCDANIEL WILLIAM J MCGEE IV HOLLIS R MCKINNEY JR GEORGE E NORBUT
PERCY JULIAN GORDON M REEVES SANFORD SHROUT JR RONALD W SIMMONS ROBERT L STEBNER JR
JOSEPH W THOMPSON NICHOLAS O WAGMAN JOHN W WRIGHT JACK W ANDERSON JR BOB J GOODWIN
JAMES L ANTE VALLANCE G ARKIE ROBERT E BROWNING DAVID CARROLL DONALD E CUTLER
FRANCIS B AMOROSO GEORGE A DIDASKALOU LEWIS C GILDER KAORU HONDA WILLIAM L LOCKHART
RICKY P MATTERN JIMMY G MAYFIELD HERBERT W MOORE JR WILLIAM C ROUSE JOSEPH M SALVO
RAY A SCHOLD JAMES THOMPSON GAIL F WILSON ALFRED F ALVARADO THEODORE E ANDREYKA JR
JOHN R BARBOUR JACK A BERRY JACKLIN M BOATWRIGHT WILLIAM C BURNS JR VINCENT R CAPODANNO
FLOYD E CLOSE EARL R COBB HAROLD C COOK STEVEN T CORNELL ROBERT W COTTENIER
FLOYD C CRAVEN MICHAEL D DE CAMP JOHN DI DOMIZIO CLARENCE E DRAKES FRANKLIN D ENDICOTT
SAMUEL L DASH JR GALVIN L DUNCAN CLIVE L EVANS CHARLES FINKEL DENNIS F FISHER
THOMAS W FISHER FERNANDO V FOOTE TONY E GABALDON JAMES J GARRITY GERARD L GAUTHIER
KENNETH S GIBBS SAMUEL D GIBBS ANDREW M GIORDANO EDWARD L GOUCHER ED N GRANT
RICHARD GUERRERO JR CAREY HAMMOND JR TIMOTHY J HARTMAN RAYMOND G HENGELS KEITH F SHARP
CHARLES B HORTON LESLIE V HURLEBAUS JULIO A IGLESIAS III WILLIAM E JERKINS JOHNNIE W KELLEY
PATRICK G KELLEY VIRGIL K KELLEY JR ROBERT L KEMPKES BOBBY G KINKLE ARMANDO G LEAL JR
GARLAND P LITTLE DOVER L LOCKHART WILLIAM B MAHONE CHARLES F MARTIN BENJAMIN H MASON JR
JAMES R MAYO FOSTER B MILLER MICHAEL R MINER OSWALDO L MIRANDA CURTIS MITCHELL
DONALD L MCALISTER JAMES C MCKENZIE ROBERT R MOONEY ROBERT F MORGAN GENE A MORTENSEN
RICHARD J NASHAWATY JAMES C O'REILLY JR DENNIS A OMILIAN JAMES E OWENS CHARLES A PARADISE
JAMES S PEREZ LAWRENCE D PETERS HERMAN R PHELPS CHARLES W PIATT JAMES F POLLARD
TERRENCE L PRIEST JACKIE K REED EDWARD C ROZANSKI GILBERT S SALAZAR ALBERT W SANTOS
DOUGLAS J HOOTS GREGORY J SCOTT MICHAEL F SHEA LEON SIMMS VARDE W SMITH III
MANFORD D STEWART MERVYN D TEDDS JACK E TELLING FREDRICK L THROWER LAWRENCE D TORREZ
MERLE D TURNER ERIC M WARDWELL RICHARD A WORTH STEVEN J WRIGHT EARL W FERNANDEZ
WILLIAM R BRENNAN DIETER H BURGER ELMER D BYRD DAVID CALVITTI DONALD W DOWNING
ARNOLD BENSON JR CHARLES H GOBBLE THOMAS P HANSON WILLIAM E HARGROVE GEORGE W HENRY JR

PANEL 26E

WILLIE L JONES JR MICHAEL L LA PORTE RICHARD B LOZANO DAVID G WOODRUFF
WILLIAM T MCDANIEL CARL D MILLER DAVID R MILLER COSMO F PACETTA DAVID C PHELPS
MARTIN W PRATHER EDWIN P PRENTICE PAUL D RAYMOND GEORGE R ROLAND THOMAS E RUSS
DAVID A SCHULTZ BRAVIE SOTO DAVID S STEWART BENJAMIN A THOMAS GARLAND D WHITMORE II
KENNETH J KRAUSE TERRY C WILLIAMS REID C ARNOLD DONALD L BAKER JESSIE L BARLOW
HAROLD S BERN JOSEPH K BRADLEY CHARLES E BRENNAN JOHN G CALL JOHN T CAROTA
MANUEL G CASTILLO RICHARD W CRAWFORD JOHN D CRISP III SAM T CURIEL ROBERT B GRIFFITHS
EDGAR S DAVIS RODNEY M DAVIS WILLIAM N ERLING JR ROBERT D EVANS ANTHONY T FIELDS
PAUL L CLARK WILLIAM R FRANCE LYDES J GARNER JR DENNIS A GETTY STEPHEN L GRANT
DALE A GUNNELL JERRY H HEIZER JAMES V HEMBREE DONALD R HENRY PATRICK HERRON
COLIN K HIPKINS JOSEPH S HUME JR RICHARD B JACKSON REGINALD A JORDAN LEWIS H PROUDFOOT III
FRED K KAMA JOHN P KLABUNDE MICHAEL L LANGERIO DAVID B LE FEVER ROBERT MASON
CHARLES E MILLER JAMES B MILLER MACK P MOHAMED CECIL R MOORMAN JAMES T PEPPER
ROBERT S MCBETH SAMUEL R MCGEE III LOREN L MORFORD GEORGE A NASH JR SAMUEL A OATES JR
ALBERTO H MORAN RONALD A PATTISON DENNIE D PETERSON WALTER M PHILLIPS HUMPHREY J PRICE
GARY E HIBBARD RONALD R REINKE WINSTON T ROBINSON JERRY C ROYAL JAMES H RUST
ROBERT L SADLER RICHARD E SERWINOWSKI ROBERT E SHIELDS J D SINGLETON NORRIS R SMITH
THOMAS SOLIZ GEORGE S SPAK JR JOHN M SPIRES BARTLEY T STOKES III ROBERT W SWAFFORD
FRANK L SWINFORD III ALLISON L THOMAS JR MICHAEL J TOMASEK FOSTER J TOUART JR DONALD R WARD
JERRY L THOMAS WENDELL G VAUGHN RALPH P VILLEGAS ROBERT C WALLACE PRYOR L WHEAT
ROBERT G WILLOW GREGORY L YEAGER RAY A ARCHULETTA ROBERT S BARNES ROBERT D BLOUGH
DAVID A BRADSHAW ORRIN J CASSATA RONALD P CHERRSTROM DONNIE COLEMAN ARCHIE L COOPER
ALVIN CULLINS JAMES M DANIELS JOSEPH A DURLING III LARRY V FLORA GREGORY GAGLIARDI
ALLEN D GAILEY JR MICHAEL GIDVILAS WILLIAM A GILMORE HUGH C GOINS TERRY R LITZ
ALEXANDER GONZALES DONALD L GRAVES CHARLES G HAMILTON MICHAEL B HIMES DANNY J HUDDY
EDDIE D HAMM LEE B JARVIS NOEL A JOHN JAMES A JONES BRUCE H KRAGE
RANDOLPH M GAMET ALBERT C LAWSON JAMES E LEWIS GARY W LINDSAY JOHN P MANZI MARL W MCCUTCHEN JR
DENNIS H MARSHALL KEITH A MILLER WILLIAM F MILLER JERRY R MOON GARY L MOORE
BENITO MORALES DUANE L MORNINGSTAR ERIC P MULLER JEFFERY P MYERS STEPHAN J NELSON

ROY D O'NEAL DON T O'SHELL RICHARD L OTTE SAMUEL L PARKER THOMAS J PESEK
LEROY J PHILLIPS ROBERT R ROGERS CHARLES E RYBERG JOHN R SIBILLY JAMES H STUART
TERRY L SUMERLIN LEONARD J TAUSCHEK LYNDOL E TOLLESON RONALD C TOTH JOHN H WALKER JR
ROBERT M WARREN RUSSELL D WHELCHEL TONY L WHITE JAMES M WILSON JAMES S CAZARES
CURTIS E COTHRAN WILLIAM J DORAN LEROY J DRABY WILLIAM K ELLIOTT RUSSELL G GARRISON
GARY L GILLEAN FRANCIS E GLAZEBROOK JR DALTON T GOFF DURWOOD M HALLAM KURT L KUHNS
LARRY G LANCE DAVID A LE BEAU JAMES E LIGHTFOOT DONALD R MARSHALL OSCAR H PALACIOS JR
JUAN RAMIREZ JOHN D REYNOLDS ROBERT L RIGHTER JR FRANK E ROBINSON ROGER C ROSE
ALBERT F SAYER JR WILLIAM D SEASE WILLIAM L SLANE GAYLORD L WESTBAY FRANK L ZIGALO
LARRY L BARKER JAMES R LAUDICINA WILLIAM E LAWSON DENNIS D LOFTHEIM
GUADALUPE M ALVAREZ JOSEPH B SUMPTER KENNETH W TATE JAMES L TWEED JOHN R VANDERZICHT
THEODORE H VOIGT ARLON D WALL JR GERALD F WENDEROTH JUAN ALMANZA LEO C AUKLAND
CHARLES L BERNARD JR DENNIS L BOLMAN JAMES P BRASWELL JR DILLARD BROCK DAVID H BROWN
ALBERT M BUTSKO ALEXANDER CHISHOLM KARL H COUK WOODROW C CRONKRITE EDWARD R GAYTAN
DAVID T BRYANT DEIGHTON A DANIELLES LEWIS DAVIS JR RICHARD O FISHER ROBERT J GALL
ALLAN J HERMAN LEE C HITCHCOCK RICHARD L HOLYCROSS CHARLES W HORVATH LESTER HOUX JR
BRUCE HUNTINGTON STEPHEN L IRVIN LEE IRVING KENNETH C JOHNSON PHILLIP D JOHNSON
RONALD B KERNER EDWARD W KINES RAYMOND R LA POINTE JAMES G LAWSON EDGAR W THOMPSON
BRIT P LEMMONS HERBERT LINDER III JOHNIE B MACHAU PATRICK E MCBRIDE GEORGE F MEISTER
JOHN T MCDANIEL THOMAS J MCMAHON SIMIN A NAQUIN LARRY R PALMER WILLIAM F PELTON
DONALD R PETERSEN JR RAYMOND G POTTER DONALD R PRITCHARD ERIC R RADTKE DAVID L REASONER
HULAN D ROLAND MARTIN A ROSALES ANTHONY P SAWICKI JAMES R SMITH TIMOTHY N SMITH JR
THOMAS A KRISPIN RICHARD L SPAULDING FRED D STGEORGE WILLIAM B STUTES STEPHEN L TRAUGHBER
CHARLES WALJESKI RICHARD A WARDROBE WAYNE A WATTS HENRY M WHARTON JR DONALD M WHITE JR
JIMMY D WILLIAMS JAMES C WILSON LUCIUS WINFIELD MICHAEL F WOLF RONALD L BLACK
THOMAS D CULP MICHAEL T FINCH STEPHEN R FORD JOE GILLESPIE WILLIE J PAYNE
CHARLES A JOHNSON DAVIES L JONES BRICEY E LAMB RICHARD R MULLIN NELSON D NEAL
GAYLORD D PETERSEN DALLAS RATLIFF GLENN REVELLE DAVID A SCRITCHFIELD TALMADGE W CARNELL
DOW E STEPP EMERY C SULLIVAN III MICHAEL J TOMLINSON JAMES D TRAVIS JR ROBERT F BIGELOW
HOWARD A CHAMBERLIN GERALD A CULHANE THOMAS L FORBES THOMAS E FRANCIS CALVIN L MCDAVIS
DAVID J GULASH RICHARD W HAWTHORNE ELWOOD R HENDRIX CHESTER K HUTCHISON ROY J JUERS
RICHARD R KANE FRANK E LYON ROBERT K MATTSON JERRY B MENANE JAMES A MORRISON
BRADFORD T GRIFFIN JAMES L MCCADEN EUGENE PETTY ALAN E PILON MARLIN L PRICE
EFRAIN J ROBLEDO JERRY L ROGERS EVARISTO SANDOVAL THOMAS F SHANKS ROBERT J SULLIVAN
RUSSELL J SWANHART HARRY W WALLACE CLARENCE E WATERS MACK A ALSTON WILLIAM A ASPINALL
JESSIE C COFIELD WILLIAM P COLL GARY F FLYNN DENNIS R HODGE BRUCE A KERN
JOHN O KERNEY RICHARD M KROSSEN WILLIAM N LOOMIS MICHAEL L MULCAHY KENNETH C RAKENTINE
MICHAEL D MINER SIDNEY M RASNICK HAROLD E REID BILLY R SALYER WALTER F STEFFENS
DAVID L STRAIT PAUL R STRANGE LAWRENCE M SVOBODNY RONALD S SWEET KENNETH D WEIS
JOHNNY WILLIAMS JR MICHAEL S WILSFORD WILLIS L WOOD WILLIAM G YOUNG GARDNER BREWER
HAROLD J CANAN CLARK E CLEVELAND DONALD B DRAY JOHN M GALLAGHER EDWARD T HARRISON JR
ROBERT GARCIA KEITH E GERHARDT GREG L GESSEL RONALD B GOBER DAVID L HOWARD
WILLIAM D HUYLER JR PERLEY M LONG JR THOMAS E MURRAY TONEY NELSON JR JOSEPH S ROSE JR
DAVID C STANLEY HAYWOOD W TIPSY JR KENNETH E TREIBLEY GARY R WILSON RONALD L WILSON
RICHARD A CHEEK WILLIAM T CHERRY JR WILLIAM T DIAMOND JR RICHARD E GLAESMAN WILLIAM H LITTLE
NORMAN D GROVE GAREY L HENSLEY JOHN L HINES LOWELL D HOLDEN JOHN M KEPPLER
GLEN A MAKI CHARLIE M MCKEE ALFONSO A MONTERROSO JERRY W MUSTAIN RONALD E SHOWMAKER
MAURICE G WIDICK FRANKLIN D WILLETT WILLIAM G ANDRUS WILLIAM BELL JERRY C BENNETT
COBBIE J BENTLEY JAMES M COLITO JR ROBERT L GABLE LAIFELT GRIER FREDERICK HIRSCHMANN III
JERRY V HORN WILLIAM G JERRO ERNEST N KROLL DARRYL D LAWSON DONNIE R LUSK
JAMES R MERTELL JR HARLAN C RILK JAMES R SMITH WILLIAM M VAN ANTWERP JR JAMES D WISE
LAWRENCE J WOOD WILLIAM R YOUNG JR NICHOLAS E BRUZNACK BENNY G CARR JAMES W CHAMBERS
RAYMOND E CHAMBERS MERRELL J CLAYBURN ERVIN L CONDREAY THOMAS J DANIELS NEVITT D DAVIS GUADALUPE PEREZ
ROBERT N DECHENE MERLE L DUEMAN DAVID E DUMOND WALTER E ELLIS WILLIE ELLISON JR
MARVIN E GOEBEL MARVIN E GORDON PETER A GRUBB WILLIAM M HARPER THOMAS D LANMAN
STEPHEN J MELNICK WILLIAM L NELLANS CLYDE E PAUL JR JOHN C PEEL
WILFRED M PEREZ NOEL W ROBERTS CONRAD A STYBEL GENE L TWEHOUS OMAR D WITMER JR
RONALD G YACKS HENRY D BABERS HARRISON B BALL JOHN W BOYER MICHAEL J HALL
ROBERT P BREEDEN BRADLEY J CARSON EDWARD S DUFFETT RICHARD A GIULIANI KEITH R HENRICKSON
PAUL A HOLCK BURRNON E MILLER AMOS R OSBORNE THOMAS F REGAN LONNIE J ROBBINS
DALE G SIEVERS JR PAUL C SIRCHER EDWARD C STATELMAN JACKIE A TUOHY JOHN P VIS
EDUARD A AUER MICHAEL L BAUM GABRIEL BETANCOURT ROBERT L BLOUNT CLYDE W CARTER
RAY COLLINS GAILEN C CROSSLIN ELMER N DAVIS MARSHALL C FARLEY ROBERT E FOLSOM GAILEN C GROSSLIN
JOHN M HASKINS HERBERT A LOUCKS STANLEY W MCPHERSON CHARLES MILTON VICTOR M NEGRON
DAVID E RALPH DAVID L SCHOUWEILER RUFUS A THOMAS JR PIERRE A THREET WILBERT A TYNES JR
BARRY H WILLIAMS JAMES L WOODSON JR MAURICE P CHAPMAN JR ROGER L CORNETT KENNETH I FINKEL
DAVID E GOSSARD ROY G HARRIS JR STANLEY HORTON RICHARD D NORWOOD TERRY L OAKDEN
RONALD E PENE BILLIE T PRESSON JAMES W SAVAGE WARREN T SCOTT MALCOLM R WISEMAN
WILLIAM A WRIGHT GARY E YOUNG VICTOR P ANDREOZZI ROBERT S BAIRD WILLIAM H UPCHURCH JR
JEDH C BARKER WILLIAM A BERRY CONAL J BYRNE JR CHARLES M CASTILLO RAYMOND CLAY
TROY W COKLEY JOSEPH A COOMES JERRY K COVEY JIMMY D CURRY CHARLES E DENNY
THOMAS F DURBIN ARTHUR D ESQUEDA GLENN W FOSTER JR DAVID F GARRETT CHARLES M GOFF
EDGAR J GUIN RICHARD A HAMBLIN BRENT A HOLTE CHARLES E LOFTON MERLIN C STELPFLUG
RICHARD A JANIGIAN TIMOTHY P JENNINGS THEODORE JOHNSON MARK W JUDGE JOHN H KAVULAK
ALBERT A KEDROSKI JR WILLIAM J KILDARE RONALD R KING JOHN E KLETT GEORGE E LA LAND
JOHN L HARRIS JR KENNETH M MONTONE ROBERT S MUELLER LUIS ORTIZ-CORREDOR WILLIAM G PILCHER
KENNETH L PLUMADORE MORELL J POPE TIAGO REIS DONALD J RICHARDS NESTOR J RIVERA-TRINIDAD
CHARLES W ROBERTS MICHAEL A ROBERTS JUAN A RODRIGUEZ ROBERT C ROPER WALTER SAUER JR
WILLIE GREENE GARY R SCHAFER CLARENCE D SHEIBLEY REGINALD E SMITH RICHARD E SUTHERLAND
WILLIAM J BALFOUR WILLIAM E SWENSGARD HAROLD D TATUM JAMES E TRUSHAW MILTON J VESCELIUS JR
WILLIAM C WENTZEL DAVID G WILLIAMS WILLARD P WOODS HERMAN J BAER THOMAS H BENTON
JAMES R BOYER BLACKSHEAR M BRYAN JR EUGENE F CORMIER JOEL CROCKETT JAMES T DONAHUE JR
PAUL G GIROIR CARL M GREENE RAMIRO HERRERA JR RONALD ILLER DAVID A KRISAN

PANEL 27E

LEON L LOCHTHOWE NICHOLAS L NATZKE DAVID E PERSON JOEL B WARSHAWSKY
JAMES A LUBAS BRUCE E SAGERIAN FRANK M STREEKS JR PATRICK E BRODERICK OTIS L BUSH
LARRY J HIGH LASZLO HOLOVITS CECIL A MEARES PAUL L PRICE ROBERT E SIPE
CLAUDE A SMITH JAMES A SWANCY ELISEO A ANDRADE JR GORDON J BRULE JR WALTER BURNS
WILLIAM D CASS LAWRENCE B CRAWFORD GEORGE W DEKKER ONEAL DUNMORE RONALD O MCCLUNG
CARL W HEIDEN HARRY D HUSTON JR JAN KRAWCZYK RAFAEL LISBOA JOHN F PENDER
GARY L ROBERTS ERRAL D SMALLWOOD BOBBY L SMITH THOMAS M THATCHER JOE M THOMAS
KENNETH L TURNER ABRAHAM WOODS RICHARD C ARCHER JOSEPH ARCHULETA CHARLES D BOLDT
JAMES W CHEEK DAVID L COWART STEPHEN C CRABTREE WILLIAM E CRAFT DOUGLAS L FRIED
CLIFFORD W GIBBS GEORGE E GLENN JR KENNETH L GREEN RICHARD D HENREY JAMES P MCLAUGHLIN
WILLIAM C JOHNSON JR GREGORY J KASPER JOHN L KITZMILLER DENNIS W MARCOTTE PATRICK J MCGUIRE
RICHARD L O'LEARY KEITH F PERRELLI RONALD C ROGOWSKI JOHNNY S ROTTON GARY R SCHMIDT
ALLEN D SMITH DOUGLAS C STARRY PAUL R STATON HAROLD J STURGILL JR LEROY WILLIAMS
RICHARD M YELLAND SCOTT M BURGESS ARCHIE M CARLYLE JAMES D CLARDY BILLY K DE VASIER
STEPHEN J GEIST DEAN L GRETENCORD JEROME C HADLEY JIMMY D HATFIELD JOHNNY V HAYES
PAUL W HILL LYNN R HUDDLESTON RANDY L JOHNSTON KENNETH W MARTIN MICHAEL P SANTOROSKI
HENRY P JACKOWIAK HAROLD J MOE HAROLD REYES JAMES L SCOTT JAMES R WATANABE
WILLIE WHITE WILLIAM R YONGUE LOUIS W BELLACH JR ELDRIDGE M BRUNET WISELEE SMITH
CHARLES W DANIELS JR ARTHUR R EWING JOSE A FLORES PATRICK J GALLAGHER JAMES V HAMILTON
THOMAS L HOOVER JOHN W HOSE JR JERRY G INGRAM MARC S JAMES DAVID D KNOWLES
ALLEN R LOANE LOUIS N MALIN TOMMY E OSBON LOUIS E PORRAZZO ROBERT C PURGIEL
EDWARD A CARRUTHERS STEVEN B RICCIONE JOHNNIE D SANDERSON HUELYN B STOKER ROBERT TAYLOR
ROBIN L VARNEY MACK L WOOLLEY JR WILLIE F ASHLEY JOHN R BAMVAKAIS JR JOHN P BURGESS
GILBERT J GRAHAM CHARLES A JAMACK MICHAEL A JONES MARCUS T KENNEDY DONALD R WOOD
CLARK L MARSH CHARLES A MONDYKE JOSEPH T MUSETTI JR TRACY H RIFFEY JERALD A SLATER
JOHN M ZEHNDER DAVID M AGAZZI JOHNNY B ALBRITTON ROBERT D ANDERSON CHARLES W BALCOE
CULLEN BARKSDALE JR EDWARD C BECK DALE R BERG JIMMY L CRAIG WILLIE FARMER JR
JAMES B FIELDS DAVID A GENTRY KENNETH L GREEN WILLIAM E HAMILTON RICHARD K HARVELL
RONALD J HUMM JOSEPH J KELLER JR ROGER V KELLEY MICHAEL J KOLLER LESTER L MEADOWS JR
CRAIG A MCDANIEL WILLIAM L MCDANIELS FREDDIE MCWILLIAMS CLYDE V MOORE GEORGE E OVERSHINE
LYNELL NEBLETT NIEL B RIGGS CLARENCE RIVERS BOBBY J SHELTON WILLIAM M SKOVRAN
ROBERT J SMITH CULLEN G STARNES JR JAMES M SUNDAY GEORGE H ULRICH BENNETT G WILDER
WILLIAM E WILSON WILLIAM M BRADLEY MICHEAL E CONROY DAVID P COVENY MICHAEL J FRANCIS
JAMES L HAMMAR ERNEST B HANKS III MICHAEL J KRUG DALE M LAUSE JACKIE E TROSPER
WALTER VIEREGGE III WILLIAM H WALTERS WILLIAM E WILLINGHAM JOSE F ACOSTA CARROLL M JOHNSON
ROBERT R BROWN QUINNEN T CHANDLER JR LESSELL DUNN JR RAYMOND P FINLEY LAWRENCE B FLOWERS
PATRICK J BROPHY ROBERT G MONTOYA AUBREY G PARK ROBERT V SIPE BILLY L SNIPES
DAVID B TUCKER JESSIE S BREWER RICHARD E DUCHARME RODGER D ECKSTEIN IVAN C KING
ANDREW J GARRITY HENRY GOMEZ THOMAS E JOSEPH CHARLES H KILGORE GENE W LAY
EDWARD A BIRMINGHAM SANFORD S JOHNSON JOHN J LANDOR JAMES T LIKELY JAMES A NEISESS
PATRICK L OTT SAMUEL C PHILLIPS III RICHARD P RUIZ ELZIE E SAMUELS ROGER T SAWYERS
WILLIAM F SMITH JR ROY C WAGNER ALAN E WILLIAMS CHRISTIAN L WILLIAMS JOHN W YEAGER
MARK A BATEMAN ARTHUR R COUGHLIN MICHAEL D D'AIELLO WILLIAM W DUCK WALLACE W HOPKINS JR
ROLAND BALENTINE JR DONALD V FREEMAN THEODORE HOWARD RONALD R KING JAMES C KROUSE
STEVEN E LEGLER TERRY L MARTIN WILLIAM W MCCARRICK DANIEL R MEADOR MICHAEL L MILLER
VAN H NEWVILLE FRED C NUNEZ CHARLES J ROGIERS WILLIAM W SCOVILLE WALTER C WRIGHT
LAURENCE C ZIETLOW MAX W BATCHELOR JOHN F DE WALD HERMAN ELLIS JR RAYMOND W FRITZ JR
HOWARD M GERSTEL WILLIE F GREEN MARION M HOPKINS JAMES T LANE RONALD A MARTIN

PANEL 27E *(Continued)*

LAWRENCE GALLEGO WILLIAM A LILLUND MORRIS L MCDANIEL JR WALTER W MORGAN ROLAND A NIELSEN
JOHN A NORRIS III DUANE A NOVOBIELSKI DAVID B OWEN CHARLIE F SAULER TERRANCE H SCHNEIDER
DONALD G SCHRENK PETER A SPARKS CRAIG A VER LINDEN DAVID B WAINWRIGHT DAVID H ZOOK JR
RONALD L ALVEY RALPH E BOWEN HOLBERT E DAVIS HAROLD C DOSS JR JAMES E DOSSETT
NEVADA L ELLISON CHARLES E FARMER MARTIN D HESTER FREDRICK J HOFFMAN MARSHALL W HUNT
CARL F HYNEK III LYLE A JOHNSON WILLIAM B KISER DAVID R MALINS FRANCIS C MIDUSKI
DONALD R PHIPPS WILLIAM E REES DANNY E REID NATHAN RIVERS JAMES L ROBINSON
ROBERT R SANDSTROM STANLEY R UDING JOHN T WERTMAN JOSEPH A ALBERTINI GALE A ALLDRIDGE
DAVID B ALTMAN GABRIEL BACA DANNY D BURKHEAD ROBERT G BURLINGHAM JOHNNY R CRAWFORD
FRANK A ARMSTRONG III PETER B COOK JR CHARLES W DAVIS EARL DINGLE ROBERT L DUNCAN
ERNIE J ELFENBEIN LESLIE H FUNK JR JOSEPH L HOGGATT JIMMIE L JOHNSON JOHN L KEATON
MICHAEL S GOZDAN CHARLES E LEWIS DON W LINTHICUM EDWARD C MCGRATH PAUL A OESTREICHER
GERALD P PARKEL ROBERT G POREA CHRISTOPHER R SALEH TJEERD SCHOELIER PAUL R SIMON
THOMAS E SPRINGFIELD THEODORE N TAKACS JR LEWIS A TRASK CARL H WALL JR VAUN ANDREWS
IVAN D APPLEBY EARL D AUWARTER JAMES O BEASLEY RONALD J CARTWRIGHT CHARLES D EDWARDS
ALDWIN A ELLIS JR HUGH R FLEMISTER WAYNE E FULLAM MICHAEL GRIMES VICTOR M GROSS
RODNEY D HILL WILLIAM A JATEFF JOHN J JENSEN FRANK R KERBL JOHN E MADIGAN JR
DAVID L HODGES JAMES L LAWRENCE JOHNNIE R MCMURRAY ROBERT J PADGETT BENJAMIN F PHILLIPS JR
MARK A RIGGLE JAMES A STOEBERL JAKE H VAN METER JR SAMUEL D AMANTEA ROBERT W ANDERSON
RONALD L ANDREWS JAMES W ARMS WILLIAM H ARNOLD CARL R ARVIN JOSEPH W BAKER
CLOYCE O BURKETT JR SCOTT M BURKETT THEODORE J CHASON HENRY JOHNSON RONALD A VILARDO
JACK DEAVER DAVID G DUNKENBERGER STEPHEN E FEISTNER RICHARD G FERRUGGIA JEFFERY D FLOURNOY
LARRY L GASKINS RAY GEVARA JR JOHN H GILLILAND III FRANCISCO H GONZALEZ RAUL A GUERRA
GEORGE A GUY JOHN H HARDING ROBERT W HEBERT DEMETRIO L HERNANDEZ DENNIS H HEWLETT
CHRISTOPHER BRAYBROOKE GARY L HOLZ RICHARD V HUGGINS MELVIN E JOHNSON MITCHELL L KEMP
BERNIE C KRIDLER III TERRANCE H LARSON JOHN S MARTIN JOHN W MCMASTER ROBERT D NELSON
DANNIEL NETTER JR ROLAND R PINEAU TERRY M REHM NORMAN L ROGGOW DONALD A WILKINSON
RONALD P RUYFF JOSE C SANTIAGO-LUGO JR JOHN D SAVILLE JR JOHN E SHOWERS JR BOBBY D STEVENSON
SCOTT A CHRISTOFFERSON WILLIAM L STEWART JR JERRY F WALLS DAN E WARNER RICHARD A WEST
JOSEPH P ROWLEY DAVID E WIELAND THOMAS WITHERSPOON JR DONALD F WOLFE ANDREW G ZISSU
DOUGLAS E ATWOOD MAURICE J BIEHN EDWARD J BLOTZER WILLIAM R BRAY THOMAS U WAY
FLOYD E COLLINS JR WILLIS W EMERTON RICHARD C ENGROFF JAMES G FARMER RICHARD R IRWIN JR
DAVID L FARLEY GREEN L HART JIMMY R HOHSTADT BARRY A HUNTER ROBERT E KNADLE
ROBERT J LAZARO WILLIS L MCBRIDE BERNARD J MEIRNDORF CHARLES E MOLANO ODES H MOUTARDIER
WILLIAM E ANDERSON JR JOEL C ROPER RONALD S SANDEL STEPHEN J SMITH THOMAS C AUBERT
JOHN R COTTER JOHN E DAVIS LOREN L ERTEL RORY A MADDEN GERALD F MAYO
FREDERICK J MILEY JR JAMES B MOORE CHARLES O NEAL DENIS O'CONNOR EDWARD M SELKREGG III
WAYNE T MOLL HENRY E OATES CRAIG D PINCHOT THOMAS P RAY DONALD J RYAN
GEORGE H WINKEMPLECK ROBERT J WISCH ELLIS M BAILEY DENNIS A BEUKE JOHN T CARROLL
ALFONZIE CULVER HARRY E DRESHER JR RANDOLPH DUVALL JR JAMES E FLICKINGER VERNON L HARTMAN JR
SAMUEL M DAVIS JAMES C FREIDT JOSEPH A GELINAS DARRELL L GIBBONS JEFFREY C HAHN
ISAAC P HUFFMAN REESE A JONES JERRY C LIGHT GLEN LOCKLEAR ELMER W MAHURIN
WILLIAM H NEUSS WILLIAM V PENNY THOMAS D PIPKIN JR MILTON SNOW JR MICHAEL F WEISSERT
DAVID J UCKER JERRY D VARNER ABRAM J WELKER SALVADOR BAZULTO WILLIAM S BLESSING DALE A LASH
GERALD J BROTHERS RAYMOND V BROWNING WILLIAM J BURKHARDT KEVIN A CAHILL JAMES E CANIDATE
JOHN J CASTILLO TED H CHRISTIAN SAM CRUZ HECTOR CUBERO JAMES M DE ABRE
WILLIAM T EDGERTÖN JR JOHN K HARDY JR FRANK N HOLSOMBACK EDWARD C JARVIS JOSE SALAZAR
JOHN R LEE MALCOLM P LIBBEY WILLIAM J MCCARTY FRANK MELECA RONALD S PENMAN
THOMAS G DERRICKSON II WILLIAM T PERKINS JR JOSEPH L POKERJIM RICHARD V SMITH ROBERT M WADE
ROGER E WALTON GUY L BELLEW GARY L BINDER ROBERT W BOYD DENNIS R BROWN
GARY D BYRD LEONARD W CAMPBELL JOEL H CHAPIN JOSEPH D DAIGLE JOHN L EDWARDS
WALTER C EVANS KEITH E FRAZIER HERMAN B GAILLIARD JIMMIE W GREEN ABRAHAM HARRIS
ROGER C HEARNS CHARLES M HOUSER ANGEL IRIZARRY-HERNAND STANLEY J KERR MELVIN F SINK
GEORGE W LOCKE JR WILLIAM J MILLER BOYD E MORROW BRUCE A PAQUETTE WAYNE R POLLARD
RICHARD J JONES JAMES P PURKEY EDWARD J RAFFERTY GEORGE E SHADE ROLLEEN C SORIM
ROBERT L WHITE ROBERT C WING DOUGLAS G WINGERT ROBERT E ALLEN GEORGE M BROWN
ROGER D ATKINSON JOHN P AVERY ROBERT E BARDACH OLIVER BELL JR ERIC C EGGE
ROBERT J ARAUJO RICHARD BERUBE QUINTON M BICE CHARLES W BIRD MICHAEL A BIRD
ROBERT D BUCHANAN ROBERT J BURROUGHS ROGER G CAREY DENNIS A CARLSON LOUIS COLSTON JR
CLIFTON B BERGMAN MELVIN D EAST DUANE J FOSS FRANK FOSTER PAUL H FOSTER
PHILLIP S FRANCE WILLIE FRANKLIN WOODY J FROST HENRY J FUGETT GERALD L GASSMAN

PANEL 28E

GARY C GRISWOLD DAVID A HAMILTON DONALD C HANSEN JR WILLIAM R HENRY
JOHN I HIGGINS JR DOYLE G KING CORNELIUS C LACKS GLENN E LUHNOW WILLIAM F MULLINS JR
JAMES W MCCARTER JR KURT B PEARSON JACK W PHILLIPS JOHNNY M PLATA ROBERT A VAN BALLEGOOYEN
JOSEPH W PRANGE RONALD L RADIL JOHN W ROBERTS ROBERT C RUDD MORRIS J SENSAT
RICHARD MCGREGOR JAMES R SIMMONS EDWARD J SIMONS ROBERT R VAUGHAN RICHARD D WHALEN
WILLIAM I WHITE JOHN D WILLIAMS LAWRENCE A WOJCIK STEPHEN R WORLEY CHARLES YAGHOOBIAN JR
KEITH W ALLEN ERLE L BJORKE JAIME CAMBRELEN FRANKLIN L CAREY WAYNE A PODLESNIK
RALPH P COSTANZO NATHANIEL DABON PATRICK L DOYLE ROBERT J EDWARDS GAYLON G GIPSON
DAVID J GRONAU JAMES R HOTTENROTH FREDERICK L JACKSON ARCHIE J MAPLE JR QUENTIN D ZAMBANO
RONALD D MARCRUM LARRY T MCBURNETT JAMES F MORROW EDWARD MOSLEY EUGENE A PARISH
CHARLES L BANEY FRANK A PRICE III PHILLIP E REED WILLIAM A SCHULZ BURNELL SIMMONS
ORVAL L SKIRVIN JOHN H SNYDER DAVID J SPINALI HUBERT STACKHOUSE ARNOLD D SYROVATKA
KENNETH J LANDERS CHARLES E BEAVERS AUGUSTINE BELTRAM JR LAWRENCE A BERNESKI ROGER E JARVIS
JOHN W BURKE JUNIOR R BURNS GEORGE W CLARKE JR RICHARD A DEMERS KEVIN L FERGUSON
RICHARD D APPELHANS MICHAEL F FIELD LEE R HODGES HARVEY R HOWARD BERNARD F JONES
JOSE LOPEZ CLAYTON A MARTIN JAMES E MIDDLETON DENZELL R MILLS JAMES W PRATHER
GEORGE S SALEMA LARRY P STOTLER DON C THOMPSON JR WAYLAND K THOMPSON THOMAS J TORI
EVANS S WALKER DONALD W ADKINS LEMUEL L ALEWINE TERRY D ALLEN JR LARRY M ANDERSON
GARY L BARKER JAMES L BLACKWELL JR JACKIE E BOLEN JR CLIFFORD L BREEDEN JR ANTHONY B CADWELL
RALPH CARRASCO ELWOOD D CHANEY JR LAWRENCE H COLLIER MELVIN B COOK HAROLD B DURHAM JR
RICHARD L CRITES JOE A CRUTCHER JERRY F DE GRAY WESLEY E DODSON FRANCIS E DOWLING
SANTOS CAMERO EDWARD P DYE LEON N EAST MAURICE S ELLIS ANTHONY J FAMILIARE
MICHAEL J FARRELL PAUL L FITZGERALD JR FREDERICK J FORTNER ROBERT L FUQUA JR MICHAEL J GALLAGHER
ARTURO GARCIA MELESSO GARCIA STANLEY D GILBERT VERLAND A GILBERTSON WILLIE V GOREE
RAY N GRIBBLE OLIN HARGROVE JR CHRISTOPHER E HERDERICK DONALD W HOLLEDER ALLEN D JAGIELO
ALAN T JENSEN RICHARD W JONES CHARLES F KENNEDY JOHN D KRISCHE JERRY D LANCASTER
JAMES E LARSON GARY G LINCOLN JOE LOVATO JR ANDREW P LUBERDA EMIL G MEGIVERON
MICHAEL M MILLER RAYMOND B MINUS ANTONIO MORALES JR ROBERT J NAGY RICHARD D WEEDER
STEVEN L OSTROFF PETER A PENFOLD WALTER PLATOSZ EUGENE J PLIER GARLAND J RANDALL
EDWARD H RAUCH RONNEY D REECE ALLAN V REILLY HARRY C SARSFIELD JACK W SCHRODER
JACKIE E SHUBERT DANIEL SIKORSKI CHARLES E SILLAWAY LUTHER A SMITH THEODORE D THOMAS JR
JOE D MOULTRIE PASQUALE J TIZZIO GEORGE H TOWNSEND ANTHONY J VAICKUS JR KENNETH P WILSON
ROBERT YATES SR JOHN F BARR CLAUDE C BETTY JOSEPH O BOOKER JIMMY M BRASHER
LAWRENCE J CHURCHILL WILBERT R COCKRELL ROBERT H DECKER ALLEN E FIRTH NATHAN JOHNSON JR
CHARLES L GASS DONNIELL GOODMAN DELBERT W HAASE JERRY R HALL JACK M HAMMOND
TERRY H FENENGA NATHANIEL HARRIS CHARLES W INGELS JAMES S KELL OWEN C KELLEY
MICHAEL F MATTHEWS MATTHEW O MCKNIGHT LOUIE OCHOA HOWARD OGDEN JR DONALD T SLUDER
ANTHONY PEREZ ROBERT B PETERSEN ROBERT E PITTMAN ALLEN J ROY MICHAEL J SIGSBEE
DAVID A OBERLE TIMOTHY L VICALVI RICHARD M WOYNARSKI DENNIS G BLACKMON GREGORY L BROWN
ROBERT L FLECK BURDETTE D GRAHAM GLENN G JACKS DUDLEY N JORDAN KENNETH D KREHBIEL
RAYMOND E LONG FRED E MACGEARY GERALD W MCMILLAN JOHN F MCNAMARA GARY P POLLEY
HERBERT L THOMPSON GORDON W WILL CARL A BALLENGER GEORGE E CLARK JR WAYNE A COLANTUONO
JOSEPH DAUNIS BOBBY R GRIFFIN STANLEY D GUBBELS WILLIAM H JETT PAUL E LATOURETTE
DALE R LINDBERG JAMES E MORGAN GERALD S RYAN JOHN A RYAN JR STANLEY W THOMPSON
ALVIN R CHAVOUS RODNEY B CLINE WILLIAM L CUMMINGS JOHN L JONES DONALD P YARRINGTON JR
DAVID P KUSY FREDERICK M LOWE JR GERALD C MILLER JEFFREY L MORRIS PETER J PAELE
ARCHIE A PORTER LEE A TOYER KENNETH E TREADWAY DAVID E WARD MICHAEL A WYRICK
CLARENCE J HEMMEL CLAUDE YOUNG WAYNE M CARDINAL JAMES E DOOLEY FRANK B DUNFORD III
MERLE K CARTER ROBERT L EICKHOLT THOMAS L GRIFFEE BARTON E HAYNES JAMES R JONES
JIMMIE W JONES ROBERT M KAIL JAMES M MCCORMICK LARRY R MCDUFFIE LAWRENCE J STARK
EUGENE NAYLOR RONALD R PEARSON JOHN J RHODES ROGER D ROMINE DANIEL J RYAN
DAVID M LEWIS PATRICK J SUGHRUE JOHN F TERRY JR WAYNE F WHITEMAN RUSSELL L ADAMS
EDWARD L BIEBER ROBERT D CAIN WARREN D CAMPBELL KENNEY D CHAPPELL GEORGE H COLBERT
GORDON J DIBBLE ANTHONY J ESTELLA MICHAEL C ETTZ DAVID W FISHER WILLIAM FORD
DANIEL B HERRELL LEROY HOPKINS JR MICHAEL E LAVALLEE RAYMOND T MASHBURN JEREMIAH J SULLIVAN
RODNEY W MCLEAN DEAN H MESSERSMITH JON R MORVAY CHARLES E MULLIS JOSEPH P PINK
JOSEPH J RHODES CHARLES A RIEGER III ROBERT F SHAW ROBERT J SIME JOSEPH SOSINSKI
EARL GAUTNEY OSCAR L THOMAS JR ROBERT G TSCHUMPER EDDIE D TURNER GEORGE M VINEYARD
HARRY O WHITLOCK JR MICHAEL L BROWNING RICHARD C CLARK GARY L CONAWAY VAUGHN P FLIZANES
ROBERT D CRAWFORD GARY W HAWKINS ROBERT D JESSEN THOMAS S JONES FREDDIE J KEELEY
WILLIAM E LESNIK JAMES J MALLON JR GILBERT G MARCUM KEITH A MCENANY RICHARD L MCNEISH
RAYNALDO POLENDO MANUEL J RODRIGUEZ BASIL L SAUNDERS JOEL L SCHUBERT HAROLD J SOTZEN
FRANCIS J THIBEAULT MICHAEL C TOSH SIMEON A TUAZON JR GAROLD T WILSON ROY E CONRAD
GILBERT T BEAUPRE BOBBY J BONIN AQUILLA F BRITT GREGORY J CANDLER PATRICK J CARNELL
DONALD G STAYROOK JERRY D CHARLTON CHARLES R CHRISCOE CHARLES A DAVIS DONALD R FOSTER
LAWRENCE L GARDNER JOHN B GAY JAMES E GISH GORDON J GRAHAM MORRIS GRAHAM
RONNIE L GROS ROBERT C HARKINS DON C HARRELL JAMES E HENSLEE CHARLES E HOOD
GARY L GRISSOM ALEX R HOUSTON WAYNE JOHANSON RICHARD A JOHNSON JEFFREY M KROMMENHOEK
WAYNE O MARTIN ELEC MCCOY HOWARD E MORSE DONALD S MOSES ROBERT E MUSSELMAN
WALTER J NOWAKOWSKI CARL W OLIVER LAVERN L SALZMAN CARL S THORNE-THOMSEN CHRIS A TOTORA
ARTHUR C ROESLER DAVID M TOTH ELMER R ABLES JR RICHARD J ACEVEDO DAVID A BARTLETT
JOSEPH R BECK JR RONALD D BENNETT RUSSEL D BENTSON LARRY D BLEEKER RICHARD K BOYD JR
RICHARD J BROWN EDWARD CLEM JOHN O COOPER III ROBERT B CRANE ALEXANDER N DI GUARDIA
DENNIS J FRIES WAYNE A GRANT DAVID S GRIFFIN SAMUEL L HUNT GERALD H SLINGERLAND
GEORGE D LACUS JR MELVIN C LAPP JOHN J LAWENDOWSKI CONVERSE R LEWIS III JOHNNY MEANS
DANIEL P KEE III JOHN G ORSINO DONALD G OSBORNE STEPHEN F PETERS STEVEN A SMITH
RICHARD W STEIN STEVE M SUMMERLIN STANLEY W TUNALL BILLY R WOHLGAMUTH DUANE C AKKERMAN
HENRY ANDERSON JR MICHAEL E ANGERSTEIN ALLEN L ARTHUR RODGER G BARNES GEORGE P BARRETT
DAVID P BETTS HORACE CANN ROBERT M CARLOZZI ROBERT J CARMODY EDWARD CHARITY JR
JESSE N CLAYTON DOUGLAS F CLEMMONS LORENZA CONNER ROBERT P COOK JAMES A CORE
JOHN R DAWSON GARY F DISSINGER LINDEN B DIXON MICHAEL J FONSECA EVARISTO MARTINEZ III
WILLIAM R HACKETT JR ANGUS L HARE JAMES E HUFF EDDIE L JAMES JR VERNE D JOHNSON III
STEPHEN P JONES JOHN H LANCE JAMES LEATHERWOOD TERRY L MALOY WALTER A MARABLE JR
DENNIS H GRANT ALFRED L MASON EDWARD A MELTZER ARTHUR F MIRAMONTES EDWARD A MOLDAVAN
HARRY M MCNALLY JOHN T NELSON CURTIS W PAINTER MICHAEL PETERS MERRICK R PIERCE
ROBERT C RICE JOHN A ROBERTS GARY A RUCKTAESCHEL HARRY L SCHLEE ERICK L WASHINGTON
FRANCIS P SCHMAUTZ DAVID L STOLL KENNETH C STOMMES JON P TURK THOMAS F UHL
LAWRENCE B PRATER JUAN J VILLALOBOS JOHNNIE WALKER JAMES R WARREN JR BRONSON L WESTFALL
ROGER D WILFONG ROBERT A WILLIAMS MICHAEL ZARBO PAUL D ABBOTT DAVID BAKER
LARRY D CARRELL THOMAS S CLEM RANDY R COGDILL ANGEL L DIAZ DAVID J DONAHOE
ELMER E ELLSWORTH NELSON P HENRY TEDDY L HISAW JR DANIEL E HOPPER ANTONIO M MAVROUDIS
DONALD D MAKI JESSIE F GREENE JR NICK KOKALIS JOHNNY H LEBOFF WILLIAM D MIZE CHARLES A MOYER
THOMAS G NAILE JOSEPH R NORRIS ROBERT J REGINALD ALVIN P RIVERE HECTOR M ROMERO
WILLIS J SCHUBERT JOHN G TINKER ALVIN P TRONNES WILLIAM J WAGNER JR ROBERT L AGAR
LOUIS B ARNOLD MANVILLE L BARB THOMAS J CHIMINELLO WALTER L CLARK HERBERT C DONALDSON JR
WILLIAM F DYKES GEORGE W GABURO CHARLES E GENTRY LARRY R HAVERS EDWIN M KAHKONEN JR
WALTER T KAY JR LAWRENCE LANO MICHAEL D LAUER JAMES R PLAKE RALPH W PLUMMER III
CARLYLE B POMEROY JR JAMES L PREZIOSI FORREST D RAINS JR BRISTOL ROBERTSON JR JOHN C YAGER
JOE AMOS JOE H BASS LARRY F COGGINS RODNEY L EGGLESTON VICTOR R WOODEN
JAMES H BENNETT JR KENNETH G HANSON RONALD A HESSMAN MICHAEL W KENTER ROBERT L MULDROW
RAY E COLN ROBERT F RENSHAW LAWRENCE F REYMAN JAMES H TOMLINSON SR JAMES H WILSON JR
KEITH L BENSON DOUGLAS BROWN JOHN W CAVER CHARLES D CHAPMAN WALTER W CUNNINGHAM
RALPH J DIPACE JERRY D EVERETT HUGH M FANNING EARNEST R HINSLEY GREGORY G HUBBARD
ROGER L HUBBARD STEPHEN J KOTT WILLIAM E MILLER JAMES V MULLER RALPH J PARKER JR
STEPHEN E PARKS MICHAEL G PHILLIPS RILEY L PITTS FLOYD I ROBINSON MICHAEL J SEADORF
LAWRENCE A STALNAKER JOHN C STEER KENNETH W TAPPE JR SCOTT L THIRY ALBERT C WATSON JR
CURTIS F WILLIAMS JR LOUIS E ARMSTEAD HOWARD L BARTLEY EDWARD A BEILFUSS JR MICHAEL E BENNETT

PANEL 29E

JOHN B BURGESS RONALD J COSTANTINO MORRELL J CRARY NICHOLAS B ENRIQUEZ
ALBERT BRILLO JR RICHARD G DAVIS DENNIS R DIEBALL GARY L GASCON EDWARD E HARSON JR
DON A HAWKINS MICHAEL M HORNER KEITH V HUFFSTUTLER GERALD A IVERSON MICHAEL D JAQUA
CHARLES E KAHLER ROBERT W LARSON JOHN D MICHAELIS MOSES MICKLE BERTMANN E MILLER
LEWIS M OGLE FERDINAND J QUATRONE THOMAS S RICHARDS KARL F RYNEARSON GEORGE B SULLENS JR
FRANK R NOE LEO R SCHOFF STEVEN D SEARS RONALD D SHEFFEY KENNETH E SLATER
ARTHUR I THOMAS DAVID TUCKER MICHAEL VIEHWEG JOHN G WEATHERBY JOHN H WELCH
DAVID A WOODS WILLET R AMENDOLA KENNETH J ARENT BOBBY L BARBER STEPHANO J FIDUCIOSO
KEITH J ANDRES GLEN D BATES PATRICK J DEARBORN JAMES G EDINGER MELVIN E FOAD
ROBERT M FOLEY JOHN B HEADLEY JAMES E HOWARD JR PAUL J HUGHES MIKE G IBARRA
DAVIS A JONES FREDRIC W KNAPP GERALD KROPIDLOWSKI JOHN A MAY HEBER J MILLER
ROBERT P MILLS JR ROBERT E MOORE RICHARD D MORROW DANA A PITTS DAVID H SHOEMAKER
RICHARD E SMITH TRACY L WHOOLERY JAMES J WRIGHT JAMES E ANDERSON RANDALL W ERNSBERGER
PHILLIP W BROOM DUANE E CARTER JOHN H DAVIS JOHN C EGGER JR RONALD J ENSLEY JR
ERNEST D FUNICELLI JR HANS H GRAUERT CLEOPHIS HARRISON GARY L HENSLEY JERRY L JACKSON
MATTHEW JOHNSON JR PETER H KRUSI JAMES T MORRIS JR EDMUND L PALCZEWSKI FRANK J PAPA
JAMES E PAVLICEK JR DON POTTER MICHAEL ROMANO JR RICHARD W SANDIFER DAVID E THOMAS
GREGORY A WATSON ROBERT A ALBERTSON JIMMY R BAGGARLY JAMES W BROCK III ALBERT R MOLNAR
ALEXANDER COOPER RICHARD E CREASON KEVIN G FLAHERTY LEROY A HAYES DAVID M HERENDON
RONALD J BRITT ROBERT C HOWARD NICKLOS B JANES CLYDEWALTER KLINGENSMITH ROBERT A LOVELACE
HARVEY M MOSHIER JR C G NUCKLES BARNES W ROSE JR WILLIAM F SCHMEES JR LOUIS J SEBASTIAN
CURTIS E STIEFERMAN SANDERS K STROUD II FLORENTINO TAFOYA JR JOHN V TAYLOR JR RICHARD E WADE
JERRY L WIGGINS GLEN R WILLIAMS THOMAS E BALL JR EARL G COBEIL BOBBY G PATRICK
RALPH L FORD EMMITT R GEORGE ROY P GILLESPIE GEORGE R GREENWOOD WILLIE J HOLLAND
ALFRED L BERTULLI CHARLES K JOHNSTON RICHARD C LANGSJOEN CARL P MCCORMICK JAMES J MURPHY
LUTHER E PRESTON CLIFFORD W SCHNEEMAN JR MARTIN H ZUNIGA JOHN F ATKINSON JR JAMES D SHAFER
RALPH L AVERY ROBERT J BICKEL CHARLES G BOWERSMITH PAUL F BRUGMAN DAVID F BURNEY
JOAQUIN P CABRERA ROBERT L CARTER ROBERT H DARLING HAYWARD DENNIS JR JAMES L JENKINS
RUFUS J DOWDY DEWAIN V DUBB JAMES L ELLIS JR JIMMY E FLOREN ARDENIA FREEMAN
IRA L GARNER ROY A GIBSON ROBERT W HAGERMAN THOMAS G HAWKINS JERRY L HILL
LINWOOD C CORBETT CLARENCE JACKSON SHERMAN L JONES EMORY L JORGENSEN STEPHEN F JUMPER
BRADFORD S KING RICHARD F LAIRD BRUCE C LEISING WALTER W LEWIS WILLIAM A MICHAEL
CLARENCE A MILLER JR LOUIS C MILLER ROBERT W MILLER JR JOHN R NOVOTNY DONALD R OUELLETTE
ELBERT F PRICE JR ROBERT B REED PAUL F REID DONALD F SANSONE JOSE M SANTANA
ALFRED E ANDERSON RALF I SAUNDERS CLARENCE W SCOTT BERNARD M SHATTUCK DALE E SHUMBARGER
MARTIN F STERUD EDRICK K STEVENS RICHARD A STONE JOHN K TOOKE RICHARD Q WEEMS
GLENN E WHITE TERRY D WILLIAMS WILLIE A WRIGHT LARRY C BANKS LAWRENCE W BARKLEY
BILLIE J BARNETT JR EDWARD E BLUMER TIMOTHY F BRENNAN JAMES R BROWN WALTER C BUNYEA JR
DAVID E CALKINS GEORGE D CLAYTON MICHAEL D COCHRAN CLARENCE E DALTON JR JOSEPH MCLEMORE
WILLIAM C DIEHL JR LEE A DIXON JOHN R ENSELL KENNETH J HELSTROM TERRY A HENDRICKS
JACK P LANGLINAIS WILLIAM W LITTLE III CHARLES E LONG DALE R LOUDIN RONALD J MAYBERRY
DONALD R CAMPBELL GREGORY W MCFADDEN HENRY H MCGEE DENNIS E MOORE EUGENE MORRIS JR
RONALD H PAYNE JESSE J PEARSON PASCAL C POOLAW SR KRAG B ROYDES WILLIAM R RUSS
FREDERICK T SEBERS CLARENCE L SHAW SECUNDINO G SOSA JR ARTHUR D STIGALL LARRY E TURNER
RONALD G STOLTENOW ROBERT F STRYKER ESTEBAN W TADENA JAMES O THOMAS GAIL W THOMSEN
ROBERT S WALSH MELVIN O WELBORN JOHN E YOUNG JOHN R ADAMS JAMES W ALLEN JR
ROBERT R BAXTER JOHN W BROOKS ALPHA L BUFORD MICHAEL J CALLAHAN ROGER R CAUTHERN
ROBERT L DE VOE CHARLES DOTY RICHARD W DUNCAN LAWRENCE G EVERT DENNIS E HILL
THOMAS J CULLEN ROBERT C FERGUSSON CLINTON E HARRIS JR DAVID A HAYES MARION F HENDERSON
VAUGHN M HINES HENRY R HOCKNELL JR DAVID L JONES JOHN M JOYCE WILLIAM L JUETT
JOHN M KAPELUCK DONALD M KRETSINGER JOSEPH G KUSICK EARL D LAWRENCE GABRIEL LONA
ROBERT MATTHEWS JR RICHARD A MEHNE SIMON R MOLINA JAMES L NAVARRO MAURICE F NORTHRUP
RONALD P PRINCE WILLIAM D REEVES JR PAUL W RISINGER HOWARD L ROGERS JR DOUGLAS E SOLOMON
DARRELL E PRUETT GARY W SCHMITT THOMAS L SCOTT ALFRED C SPRINGFIELD JR LAURENCE C SUTTLEHAN
KENNETH W TINGLE WILLIAM A WHITNEY JOHN W WILSON JR JOHN W ARMSTRONG LARRY R ARWOOD
BARRY J BAKER STEPHEN D BARTELS ROBERT M BATES RALPH W BROWER ANTHONY E BUCKNER
STEPHEN H BYLER TERRY L CLARK EUGENE L CLAY JERRY W GENTRY RICHARD J GIEBE
ROBERT R GONNEVILLE EDWIN M GRAY KENNETH W HARRIS DONALD S HOLKE WILLIE C JOHNSON JR
RICHARD M HOOTS JAMES R HOWARD KENNETH R HUNTER MAX R IDOM RAYMOND L JARVI
ROBERT L HALE ROBERT L JOHNSON JR LARRY V LYLE LARRY W MAYSEY RAYMOND E MILADIN
ROBERT F NITZ DENNIS R PODGORNY TOMAS G REYES ROBERT E SCHARON III ROBERT C SEDGWICK
GARY L REHN PETER A SCHRADER DONALD M SEWELL LARRY D SHARP LANCE P SIJAN
BILLY TEMPLETON FREDDIE L THOMAS JR QUINN W TICHENOR PHILIP R WAHL DAVID H WAINSCOTT
CHARLES E WEAVER JAMES C WHITMORE ROBERT J WINTERS TYRONE WRIGHT VINCENT B BAKER
RAYMOND H CHASE JR KELLY F COOK JAMES T COON MICHAEL A HOGLUND WILLIAM H RICHARDSON JR
JAMES A CREW CHARLES W GRIZZLE THOMAS F HARDING ARTHUR L HAWKINS JR DAVID E HELM
LUIS BARRETO JR CHARLES J HUNEYCUTT JR JERRY D JONES BRENDAN J KEARNS RICHARD G KOHLAND
NORMAN J LIVINGSTON CLIFFORD J LYTLE JOHNNY W MCCAIN BERNHARDT W MILLER JAMES S MORGAN
WILLIAM T BROCK ALFRED TIMMS VICTOR R VELAZQUEZ-LOPEZ JIMMIE C WALLACE RALPH H BARLETT JR
FRANCIS D BATTISTA JAMES L BEYERLING ELZA M BREWER JR BILLIE W BRIGHT THOMAS J CARTER
JAMES A COLLIER JOHN J COLLINS WILLIAM G DAVIDSON HAROLD DICKERSON RAYMOND R HOLLOPETER
JOHN P FALCONE JR ROBERT R GROOM GEORGE B GUNN EDWARD B HARPER ROBERT E HAYNES
GREGORY J DELLAMANDOLA JOHN W HILL III CALVIN C HUDSON JESSE JOHNSON VERNON J JOHNSON
GLENN D KERNS LARRY MARTIN EDWIN J MARTINEZ-MERCADO WELDON J MILES WILLIAM G MUIR
JAMES H MCCRAE CARL J MCHANEY DENNIS C MCPHERSON DENNIS L ODELL CHARLES F RILEY
JIMMIE D ROGERS CHARLES D SAWYERS GARY F SHAW MICKEL M SMITH ROBERT M STATON JR
GEORGE E STIVERS JOHN S STUCKEY JR GERALD K TAYLOR JEROME THOMPSON NATHANIEL A THOMPSON
JOHN J TISCORNIA ANDERSON TURNER EDWARD URBANIAK LARRY WADE BRUCE A WAGNER
JEROME W WALSH CHARLES J WILLIAMS CHESTER A WINCHELL JR MICHAEL H YARTYMYK DAN S ALLEN III
JOHN H BARNES JOSEPH P CANDIANO JOHN D CAYCE HAROLD E COUCH JACOB ORTIZ
HUBERT CROOM ALDON J DEDEAUX ARMANDO L ESCARENO GARY L FARLEY CHARLES FAVROTH
DANIEL W FOSTER GREGG M GOSLIN WILEY GUERRERO ABRAHAM L HARDY GETER A HENSLEY
JAMES G HOOD JAMES E JENKINS JERRY C KELLEY DANIEL E KLOS JR ROBERT C MELENDREZ
JOHN A BARNES III FORREST A MCKINNEY CHARLES H MORRIS JR CHARLES R MOULTINE WILLIAM L NULPH JR
ANTONIO R PONCE JAMES D ROARK SYLVESTER S SAGAN ELZIE SANDERS JR BILLY G SMITH
JACK M SMITH CHARLES A SPRINGER LEONARD A THOMAS RICHARD J WARREN GOLER J WILLIAMS
DANIEL J YEUTTER JOHN L BARNHART JAMES C BERRY DAVID E BUNKER NATHANIEL CHATMAN
HORACE W COWDRICK JR GREGORY L DUNN GLENN R EISENHOUR LAMONT G EPPS ROBERT S FERRULLA
RAYMOND GARTH LA F HARDIMAN ALPHONSO L HARMON ZAN HESS VANESTER L HESTER
JOSEPH L HYATT MILFORD JONES RAY M JONES LAWRENCE A LETTERMAN FRANCIS L MAPLES
WILLIAM O MCKOY VERNON MEANS WAYNE P MURRAY RICHARD V MYERS JAMES E RAFFENSPERGER JR
ROBERT L ROSS LEROY A ROST RICHARD A SCHEIBER EDWARD A SCULLY WILLIE J SIMMONS
VERNON P SPRINKLE DENNIS E WARNE LARRY K WILLIAMS FRANCIS L BRYANT RICHARD KOVALCSIK
MICHAEL A CASP ROBERT A CRABTREE JAMES P CRYSTER III ROBERT E DOUGLAS JR JOSEF HEMER

257

THE VIETNAM VETERANS MEMORIAL COLLECTION

RALEIGH L HEWITT II   BRUNO A HOCHMUTH   PAUL E JOHNSON   MILTON G KELSEY   ROBERT G KIMMEL
THOMAS A CARTER   RICHARD D KLUG   JONATHAN P KMETYK   RICHARD KROLIKOWSKI   FRANK A MURRIETTA
RUSSELL F MCLAUGHLIN   RICHARD A NELSON   RONALD J PHELPS   LARUS W ROLAND   JOHN C RUBINS
RANDALL D SHAFFER   MANUEL SILVA   STEPHEN H THORNTON   GERARD M WYNN   ROBERT P CASPERSEN II
ORVILLE CAUDILL   LORINZER P CLARK JR   HENRY G CRIGGER   DONALD C DAVES   BRYANT D FANNIN
JIMMY L FISHER   JIMMY E FLYNN   JOHN S GORDON   DAVID I HARNER   HENRY B HAWKINS JR
WILLIAM F HUBER JR   DONALD E KREUSCHER   JOSEPH P MAREK   JIMMIE L MCMORRIS   WILLIAM G NUEBEL JR
WILLIAM D PETERSEN   DONALD L RICHARDS   JOHNNY A SIGURDSON   OTIS T SMITH   WALTER A TASHNER
ROBERT A WELLER II   FRANK A WILLIAMS   WAYNE R ADAMS   ROBERT AUSTIN   RALPH E BYRD
BOBBY R ALEXANDER   JOHN F BETTENCOURT   DONALD W BOYER   ROBERT W BREDE   LEWIS C CHILDRESS

PANEL 30E

RAYMOND P COX   PAUL M CRONK JR   DAVID K DEMOREST   MICHAEL J HOOVER
GERALD CRAGG   KEITH A FELTZ   LEONARD E FRITZ   RICHARD J HAMMER   MARK T HOWARD
EARL D JENKINS JR   ARNOLD E JOHNSON   W C JOHNSON   DAVID R KEATON   JERALD W KEMP
GEORGE K KOON   JOHN L LINDABERRY   PATRICK J LONG   JOHN S MCCONNELL   MARION L MEGGS
RICHARD W MIDDLETON   GREGORY C QUINN   O D SCOTT   LEWIS L SLOAN   JAMES E STONE   WILLIAM VELILLA
KENNETH L WITT   GLENN R WYLIE   WILLIAM C BULMAN   CHARLES E CAPPELLI   EDWARD J MURPHY JR
JOHN T COLL JR   JACKIE R COMBS   FRANCIS J CORMIER   ROGER E DALRYMPLE   ROBERT W DEYO JR
REY L DUFFIN   ROGER G EMRICH   TERRY M ENRIQUEZ   ROBERT J FARLEY SR   JOHN D FLANIGAN
MICHAEL E FLANNERY   KARL D HEZEL   WALTER D HOGAN   THEODORE W JOHNSON   LEROY J KLING
MAURICE BROOKS   JOHN T KOZIOL   GUADALUPE MARTINEZ   WILLIAM E MCDONALD   WILLIAM D MCGRATH
MAX E NICHOLS   JOHN W PAGE   HUBERT J PAYNE   RONALD J PERKINS   RICHARD P TEEVENS
JOHN W TERRELL   LARRY P THURMAN   DARRELL D VENENGA   JAMES D YEAKLEY   JIMMY D YOUNGBLOOD
DOUGLAS B BAUM   ERWIN BEEK   DAVID T BROOKS   LAWRENCE D BROWNOTTER   EDWARD B BURDETT
SAMUEL L CARMICHAEL   WILLIAM A COLLINS   MICHAEL A CRABTREE   JAMES A DAILEY   OSCAR M DARDEAU JR
JOHN W DRINKHOUSE   JOSEPH F DYER JR   RAYMOND GARCIA JR   ROBERT A HARTWELL   LESLIE J HAUER
DONALD H HOLM   MOMI N KANE   EDWARD W LEHNHOFF JR   FLOYD L LONG   JAMES E LYONS
JERRY E MAURER   EVERETT L MAXWELL   WILLIAM B MCGARVEY   RICHARD D MCGHEE   HARTWIG R POOLE
DOUGLAS G MAGRUDER   FRANK V RAZ   WILLIE REED   GARRY L REICHARD   THOMAS J RILEY
CHARLES H ROBINSON   IVAN D ROTH   HUGH D SCOTT   COTIES R SOWELL   RICKIE D SPARKS
HARMON S STONE JR   JAMES D SUGGS   IGNACIO TORRES JR   PAUL W WAHLER JR   LEONARD B WASHINGTON JR
RICHARD C ALLEN   NOAH WILLIAMS   HARRY C WILSON II   MICHAEL E ADAMS   FRANK ANDRISANO JR
ERVIN G ASCHENBRENER JR   DAVID W BARKFELT   JAMES A BELVEAL   FREDDIE J BENJAMIN   ROY J BLACKWELL JR
RICHARD K CARTER   MARIO A CISNEROS   TERRY R CLARK   GARY R COOPER   JACK L CROXDALE II
BENJAMIN D DE HERRERA   DAVID J DECKER   GERALD T DOBBS   MICHAEL L ELLIS   WALTER O ESTES
JAMES W FLYNT III   WILLIAM H FOWLER III   JAMES C FREDERICK   GERALD L GEORGE JR   WILLIAM H MURPHY III
DONALD M GRALLA   JOSEPH G GREGG   PRELOW GRISSETTE   CLARENCE L HARLOW   JEFFREY A HAWK
MARK R HERING   THOMAS P HUDDLESTON   CURTIS W HUTTO   DONALD IANDOLI   CLEVELAND KEAL JR
RONALD D KING   HARRISON H KLINCK   GEORGE F KNOWLTON   JEFFREY W KOONCE   ROGER A KROS
ROBERT C LAVALLEE JR   WITOLD J LESZCZYNSKI   JOE L LYONS   TYRONE C MARSDEN   ROGER R MARSHALL
DAVID L FARR   ROBERT E MILLER   PEDRO R MONTANEZ   DONALD T MORGAN   CHARLES C NELSON
THOMAS OLEARNICK   ANDREW J OROSZ   MARK C PETERSEN   LESLEY W REED   WALTER R RIDDLE
JIMMY D ROBERSON   CHARLES E ROBERTSON   RONALD N RODREICK   WILLIAM A ROSS   DONALD E SMITH
ARTHUR J SANDERS   ROBERT J SANDERS   JACK H SHOOP JR   LEWIS B SMITH   MARVIN R SMITH
DUNCAN P SMYLY   JAMES R SPELLER   HARRY E STEPHENS   JAMES E TEAGUE   RICHARD W THOMPSON
EDWIN W VAN ORDEN JR   DANIEL VARELA   ANTHONY VIGIL   RICHARD WALKER JR   RUDOLPH N WARD
CHARLES J WATTERS   REMER G WILLIAMS   JOEL S WILLIAMSON   ROBERT B WILSON IV   JOSEPH V ZELINSKI
LOUIS G ARNOLD   GREGORY C BAUER   BRUCE M BENZING   NEAL I BEST   MANFRED F CAMAROTE
DAVID B BETCHEL   ROBERT T BLY   HARVEY L BROWN III   RICHARD T BUSENLEHNER   ERNESTO S CANTU
AMBROSE J CERENE   THOMAS L CORBETT   CLAUDE L CRAWFORD   BRUCE W CUNNINGHAM   TROY A GALYAN
JOHN D'AGOSTINO   LARRY A D'ENTREMONT   ROBERT P DEGEN   CASIMIRO DIANDA   JERRY R DONATIELLO
JOHN M DUNBAR   JAMES C FARLEY   GREGORY S FENNIMORE   MICHAEL W FERENCE   ANGEL R FLORES-JIMENEZ
CHARLES R CREWS   JUAN M GARCIA   MICHAEL J GLADDEN   HERBERT H GRAY   EDWARD L GREENE
WILLIAM T HAGERTY   CLARENCE HALL   BOBBY G HASTINGS   WILLIAM A HAWTHORNE   STEVEN R POWELL
WILLIAM D HERST JR   AARON K HERVAS   KENNETH J JACOBSON   HAROLD J KAUFMAN   MICHAEL J KILEY
WESTON J LANGLEY   CARLOS J LOZADA   ROGER D MABE   JOHN M MARTIN   GEORGE M MATTINGLY
TRACY H MURREY   JOSH C NOAH   JAMES W NOTHERN JR   WALLACE L OGEA   JOHN M ORTIZ
EARL M FREEMAN JR   ROBERT E PACIOREK   THELBERT G PAGE   JOSEPH PANNELL   JAMES R PATTERSON   ROY C PAYNE JR
DENNIS GREENWALD   KENNETH A PETERSON   ARNOLD PINN   WALTER D RAY   LEONARD J RICHARDS
JESSE SANCHEZ   JOHN W SMITH   ERVIN SPAIN   HARRY H SPENCER   ERNEST R TAYLOR JR
JEROME C SHOMAKER   FRANK E STOKES   ROBERT T SZYMANSKI   NATHANIEL THOMPSON   ARTHUR TURNER JR
LESTER TYLER   ERNESTO VILLARREAL   THOMAS J WADE   EARL K WEBB   MERREL P WHITTINGTON
LEMUEL T WILLIAMS   JOHN R WOLF   JOHN W WOOTEN   RONALD W YOUNG   CHARLES R ACHESON
KENT E BAHNSEN   WILLARD T BATEMAN   WILLIAM A BEAUBIEN   DAVID R BLACKMAN III   THOMAS G BRADY
GARY M BRIXEN   HAROLD BURTON   RODGER K CAIN   MONROE W CROSS   DAVID L EATON
WILLIE L BROADNAX   HAROLD E CUMBIE   FRED R DODE   KINNETH G EDWARDS   NORMAN R GOBLE
WILLIAM C HINKLE   DAVID E HOMMEL   FLOYD A HYDER   GERALD KLOSSEK   ROBERT L MCCARTER
RALPH E JOHNSON   ROY R LEE   ROBERT W LINDGREN   ROLAND W MANUEL   RAYMOND W MICHALOPOULOS
JERRY D MCDONALD   ROBERT L MCLEOD   VAUGHN T O'NEIL   ROBERT OCHOA   RAYMOND PLUMEY
KEVIN A PORTER   OLIS R RIGBY   JESUS D RIVERA-MELENDEZ   JOSE E RODRIGUEZ   JESSE E SMITH
DAVID R REYNOLDS   RONALD G SMITH   MICHAEL J SULLIVAN   CHARLES M TAYLOR III   MICHAEL J UTTER
JAMES A WATSON   JEROME P WEBER   THOMAS B ALLEN   SHELDON D BOWLER   DEAN MOORE
BILLY R CUBIT   MARSHALL F FRENG   KENNETH E GREENFIELD   LEVESTER GRIFFIN   EDWARD D HANCOCK
JEFFREY J BROWN   DONALD W HOLLENBACH   JERRY D JOHNSON   ERHARDT W MATHIESEN   MCELREE MAYS JR
JOHN A MACDONALD   PAUL B MCKINLEY   GERALD L MCKINNEY   STEVEN P MORSE   GEORGE OSBORNE JR
DAVID B OTSEN   KENNETH G OWENS   JOHN L PONTING   TUNIS E RAPPLEYEA JR   VALDEZ SHARP
LARRY G POWELL   CHARLES G ROBERTS   ALLYSON Y SASAKI   JAMES P SAURINI   JOSEPH V SHERLOCK III
STEPHEN S SMITH   FRANK L TAFOYA   STEPHEN N THOMAS   JAMES L TRAVIS JR   ROBERT W WATTS
CHARLES E WILLBANKS   JAMES S YODER   KENNETH S ADAMS   PHILIP F ADAMS   DAVID W VEST
WILLIAM L CATES   JOSEPH CLOUD JR   WILLIAM W COLE   CALVIN L COOK   RONALD H ESSLER
LE R FLADRY   ROBERT L GUNTHER   ALAN J IMPELITHERE   RICHARD N KIMBALL JR   RONNY D ROBERTS
PETER J LANTZ   ROBERT L LEE JR   RODNEY E LOATMAN   ADRIAN L LYNN JR   RONALD V MAIORANA
JOHN J MARTINEZ   RICHARD F MASON   RICHARD L MORENO   FRANCIS J MURACO   RONALD W PATTON
JOHN C HUGHES   GARY D ROERINK   DOUGLAS E ROGERS   LLOYD C RUNNELS JR   GERRY G SIMPSON
LEONARD L BEVELS   JERRY W STANDRIDGE   CALVIN M STRONG   ROBERT D WADDELL   WILLARD B WALLACE
LARRY L WILLIAMS   JAMES R WORRELL   JERRY E BLACKBURN   ROBERT S CHAMBERS   RONALD A CROSE   SYLVESTER W WILSON
CLARENCE DARDAR JR   JOHN G DAVIS   THEODORE A DOUGHERTY   DALE E EGBERT   LONNIE B EVANS
MILLARD W FARBRO   BRENDAN P FOLEY   RICHARD GALAN   ROLAND J GRUNDER   MARTIN L HANNO
JAMES E HAYNES   DAVID L HILTON   WILLIAM C LANGHAM   JOHN W LUCAS   VERTIS L MACKEY
ALLEN H MARINSIC   RONALD M MAYERCIK   DAVID P MCCARTHY   CHARLES E METCALF   ANDREW J MILLER
GORDON S MCCLARY   MICHAEL S NYMAN   JAMES E O'NEAL   RICHARD H PARKER   RAYMOND PEREZ
HECTOR L RUIZ   RICHARD L SANDERS   ROBERT L SAS   MATTHEW F SHARPNACK   JOSEPH L SIMON
WILLIAM C SMITH   RAMON H TORRES   WILLIAM J TSCHUMI   CHARLES L WILK   DAVID R BLACKBURN
GEORGE R YCOCO   LEWIS H ABRAMS   CARL R BARNHART   BORIS F BORENSTEIN   JAMES F BROWN
JOHN M EKSTADT   DENNIS R ESTES   JOHN A GIBSON   ROBERT E HACKETT   ARTHUR J HENSINGER
ROBERT E HOLDEMAN   WALTER KOEPPE JR   DONALD M KROTZER   JAMES R LEMON   JOHN C LERCH JR
DEWEY A MIDGETT   ROBERT L MLYNARSKI   EVART E ROBESON   WILLIAM H SEARFUS   NORMAN J VANDERSKI
THOMAS C MAYS   ROBERT A VAN PATTEN   WOODROW D ADLER   JOHN B ALLEN   FRANK L ALLRED JR
DONALD A BASALLA   DALE P BERTHOUX   JONATHAN BLUE JR   HERBERT O BRENNAN   MICHAEL P BROWN
DOUGLAS C CONDIT   WESLEY D DAY   HANK J DE HOMMEL   GERALD A DE MUNDA   MICHAEL D DEESON
HAROLD A DOMAN   PAUL M DUMIN   DANNY L FRYE   RICHARD E HAYES   GERALD R HENDRICKSON
MANUEL HERNANDEZ   JAMES W HICKEY   EDWARD C HIGGINS III   ALBERT H HORTON   RICHARD P HOUSTON
GARRY L IHRIG   CECIL D LAMM   CHARLES P LIROT   JIMMY C MATHIS   JAMES L MELVIN
JOHN A MERCURIO   DONALD H MIKULECKY   CHARLES R PITTS   WILLIAM H PROTHERO   DIEGO RAMIREZ JR
ARTHUR W RIEGEL JR   RAYFORD N SEWELL   LONNIE L SILVER   CHARLES B STIGALL   DAVID L TASKER
ROBERT D TAYLOR   MICHAEL J THIRKETTLE   OSCAR L THOMAS   JEFFREY D ANNABLE   ALFONSO P BARTALOTTI
JOHN R BERRIOS   DAVID F BOWMAN   RUDOLFO CHAVEZ   JOE H FURCH   RONALD GILMORE
ROBERT L GRAY   EDWARD C HUGHES III   WILLIAM R HUNT   JAMES I KING   DAVID A LAPE
SAMUEL LEGLEU   JOEL A MATUSEK   WILLIAM W MCGREW III   MERLE B MORROW   GREIG R PARKHURST
JOSE RAMOS JR   JAMES SAMUELS   HECTOR L SANCHEZ   BILLIE E SANDEFUR   WILLIAM S SLOCUM
SAMUEL S THERIAULT   DAVID W WOODEN   THOMAS G CARAWAY   BILL E GAULT
WILLIAM G HALL   GARY B JONES   DONALD W KEMBLE IV   PAUL A LEONARD   DON N MAYHUE
JAMES B MEEK   DENNIS L MERRILL   DARRELL H MOREY   EDWARD R NAYLOR JR   WILLIAM T POSTON

PANEL 31E

DENNIS R SCHMIDT   ARTHUR SLOAN JR   BENNIE A SMITH   MINORU TANAKA
SAM TENORIO   HILLARD E WILLIAMS   EDWARD F ZACKOWSKI   DWIGHT F BENNETT JR   RODERICK W BREAULT
DALE C BREWER   VICTOR L CRUMP   LAWRENCE R DUFFY   WILSON N FLOWERS   STEVEN F FREEMAN
PETER M HANSEN   DONALD L HETTICH   LOUIS F JONES   JOHN M KOVANDA   JOHN P KURZ
GERALD L LATINI   HOMER R MIDDLETON   MICHAEL MILLNER   JOSE L MORENO   THEODORE MORGAN JR
HERMAN A MCBRIDE   KENNETH H NORE   WILLIE L SHEGOG   LARRY E SHEPHERD   RICHARD G STAMPER JR
KENNETH A ROE   JAMES A SNOOK   DANIEL S STEELE   CLARENCE J TIFFANY   GARY L TRUJILLO
WARD G WALTER   ROBERT T ABINA   ELEANOR G ALEXANDER   PETER N ANDERSON   THOMAS L BALL
GRIFFITH B BEDWORTH   EDWARD O BILSIE   GEORGE A BIRD III   ROBERT A BLISSETT   BOBBY G BROWN
LARRY G BUFORD   WILLIAM J CLARK III   ROBERT L CULBERTH JR   DONNIE L DARROW   DARYL L DAVIS
ARTURO DELGADO-MARIN   THOMAS J EKWELL   DONALD W GEBHART   WILLIAM R GODWIN   WHYLEY E JOSH
WILLIAM E GROVES   GARY L GROW   JOHN W HARTMAN   WILLIAM B HAYS   STERLING M JONES JR
ROGER G JUSTUS   ANTHONY E KISUCKY   BOBBY D LIKENS   NORMAN F LOEFFLER JR   LEON P MILLER
THOMAS J MCELYNN   KENNETH D MCKEE   JOSE L MIRANDA-ORTIZ   THOMAS D MOORE JR   PHILLIP A OGAS
NELSON W MCKENNA   JOHN J MCNABB   JEROME E OLMSTED   HEDWIG D ORLOWSKI   JAMES K OXLEY
CLARENCE L PALMER   LARRY T PARKER   DALE C PEHRSON   STEPHEN R PORCELLA   JACK ROGERS
KENNETH R SHOEMAKER JR   CLIFTON B SMITH   LAWRENCE D SNYDER   JAMES A STEGER   JAMES D STOKES

LAFFEY F STRAIT   HARRY C VANDERKLOOT   JIMMY L WARD   SAM D WARLICK   WILMER WATSON
TEDDY WAXMAN   LIBERT J WELDON JR   VERNON E WHETHAM   EDWARD L WILLIAMSON   WILLIAM D WILSON
STANLEY J YUREWICZ   JERRY L CARVER   JAMES K FRYE   JAMES J HAGEN   EARL D MILLER
PEDRO R AGUILAR   ROGER J HOOVER   HUMBERTO LARA   SALVADOR L MONTE JR   GEORGE E NAYLOR
CARLOS A PEREZ   HOMERO PEREZ   PHILLIP P SUMMERS   MARVIN D BANAR   JACK P BROADHEAD
GERRY G CHESNUT   RICHARD A CROSBY   GEORGE L DUPLESSIS   WILLIAM L DWIGHT   VICTOR A ENDERIZ
THOMAS L HERRING   RICHARD A HOLLOWAY   SAMUEL H HOWARD   DAVID A KREITZER   WALLACE W LEEPER
JOHN H MANN   RODNEY D MARTINEZ   THOMAS W MITCHELL   RUSSELL MOLDENHAUER   FLOYD W STRANGE
MANUEL J MOREIDA   ROBERT L MORRIS   TOMMIE PHILLIPS   WAYNE J STOKES   DONALD W THOMPSON
TOMMY R THOMPSON   THOMAS J WALKER   ROBERT A WENNES   LARRY G WILLIAMS   COLEMAN G HILLMAN
GEORGE F ANTONITIS   RICHARD C BALUKONIS   WILLIAM S CUTTER   WILLIAM M DALEY   LAURIER D DEROSIER
CHRISTOPHER ANDREWS   ROSS A DYKEMA   WESLEY GREEN   WINSTON C HAMILTON   JOSEPH HEALY
LAWRENCE E LEIBA   WALTER A OWENS   DWAYNE M PATTERSON   DANIEL QUINN   JOHN R RUOHO
LOUIS Z SILVERII   ROBERT T STEINSIECK JR   WILLIAM W STEPHENSON   OTIS F THOMPSON   WALTER L TILLER
PHILIP A VOLENTINE   WILLIAM T ALLEN   SIDNEY E BARBER   ROBERT H BRUNS   THOMAS P CIECURA
ARNOLD COLLINS   RAYMOND L CORK JR   DONALD R COTE   HAROLD W CUMMINGS JR   OMER P DICKERSON
WILLIAM E EMBRY   MERLE K FAGERLIND JR   RICKIE D FISHER   ALBERT W FRAZIER   JOHN L GARRIGAN
WILLIAM Y HADLEY   ADRIAN E HOWELL   JOHN JUAREZ   LOUIS F KEEVEN   DOUGLAS J KELLY
ROBERT D KING   JOHN F LAZAROVICH JR   CLYDE M LEE   WALTER L MATEJECK   DONALD W MILLER
WOLFGANG T MOHL   ROBERT J MORAS   WILLIAM F MOSELEY   EDWARD S O'BRIEN   CHARLES G SCHNEGG
ELGAN L MOORE   WILLIAM I POLLARD   JAMES L REAVES   DONALD S RIGGS   RICHARD A RUSS
TODD TATE III   GREGORY A TUHOLSKI   EDDIE L WEEKFALL   RONALD WILLIAMS   ALVESTER L WINSTON
BYRANT H YOUNG JR   WILLIAM J ZALEWSKI   DAMON E BILLINGSLEA   GARY L ENGLAND   DANIEL H LINDSEY
CHARLES D MAXSON   AUGUST H MONHOF   FRANK E MOREY JR   PETER W ROY   THELMER A RUDLONG
DONALD M RUSSELL   ROBERT I TERRY III   JAMES D VAN HOOSIER   RICHARD R WEISE   CARL E ADKINS
ROBERT J BAWAL   WALTER R BOETTCHER JR   FRANK BRACKETT   CHARLES E BROWN   ROBERT O BUCKNER JR
DANIEL P CAPPELLO   BOBBY D CARVER   GARY R CLARK   EUGENE COLLINS   JOHN C FILIPPI
SOLOMON W DE HART   DAVID T DICKINSON   MICHAEL J DINGUS   ALFRED DUGGER   RAYMOND E DYRDAHL
MICHAEL D BYLINOWSKI   GUY M FINLEY   KENNETH J FORET   GARY G HAHN   DONALD E HARP
THOMAS O HARPER JR   VINCENT V HAUSER   RONALD E HOLMES   AUSTIN A HORNE   WAYNE A HUTCHINSON
LANCE N JENKINS   ERIC W JOHNSON   JOHN W JONES   JEROLD L KASTRINOS   PAUL S KRZYNOWEK
DURWARD A LIMBACHER   RICHARD J LIS   MONTAGUE LYONS   GARLAND R MANN   DAVID M MIDCAP
LEWIS E MCDERMOTT   JAMES R MILLER   PAUL A MIRANDA JR   LARRY A MOORE   MARIO MOREU-LEON
KEVIN M MCGOVERN   DOUGLAS L MCLOUD   MANUEL C NEVES   MICHAEL J PASTVA   JACKIE R PERRY
JAMES D PLECITY   ROBERT A PRETTY   WILLIAM H PRUITT JR   DANIEL K PUHI   ROBERT L PULTZ
JAMES D RADER   JOSEPH L REYNOLDS   JOHN C ROMANSHEK   FREDERICK W SANDERS   PATRICK T SASSE
LEROY F SCHYSKA   JOHN W SOGNIER JR   CLAYTON M SPAINHOWER   TERRENCE L SUND   TYRONE TAYLOR
RICHARD W VAUGHN   BERT VELEZ   JAMES L WADE JR   NATHAN M WHITE   TEDDY G WHITTON
NORMAN P WILLIAMS   JACK M YOUNGS   EUGENE ZEIGLER   LEON ZUNIGA JR   RONALD R HAMMERSTROM
JAMES E BURNS   DONALD L CUMMINGS JR   JIMMY C ELROD   GEORGE F EUBANKS   WILLIAM G GILGER III
DUDNEY N ARLENTINO   TOM GONZALES JR   WILLIAM H GOODSPEED   JESSE A GORDY   THOMAS C HUBARD
RICHARD R KUCERA   THOMAS A MCDERMOTT   JAMES A MCKENZIE   LARRY D METCALF   RICHARD D OSBORN
JERRY PAIZ   RICHARD PLOTTS   CARL RATCLIFFE JR   JERI C SEEMAN   RICHARD G SHERWOOD
CLIFTON TANKSLEY   ROBERT W TEWKSBURY   FREDRICK W TODD   CHARLES C WILCOX   LARRY A WINSLOW
DAVID J WOZNICKI   DAVID L ZYWICKE   DOMINGO I AGUILAR   WILLIAM E AILES   GARY D AMES
KENNETH R BENJAMIN   LARRY H BOWERS   HUBERT C CARTER   MARK J CULLEN   RICHARD L DENNIS
LEON CANFIELD   PAUL E DUFFORD   GEORGE N FANIS JR   THOMAS M FLATLEY   THOMAS GRANT
CHARLES L HAUSCHILDT   MICHAEL KARPIAK JR   LARRY J MARTIN   VICTOR A MAZITIS JR   LLOYD D MICHAEL
DALE E MILLS   FRANK H MOORE   BILLY J MORRISON   RICHARD E PRATT   JOHN M RAY
CLAUDE J STEIN   DAVID A TANNER   JOHN E THIEL   CHARLES D WILKIE   JOHN P FLOOD JR
JERONIMO ALVARADO-RIVERA   CLYDE R COBURN   PATRICK E DUFFY   LLOYD A DUNCAN   LIVINGSTON GLENN
RALPH D HALE II   HERMAN L HILL   CHARLES JASMINE   JAMES LAMPLEY JR   GEORGE W NELSON
LESTER L PELHAM   GARY W PETERSON   LESLIE R SLOAN   FELIX D BEGAYE   LARRY W BIRCH   JOHN NISHIMURA
RHINE H BOGER   LARRY L BOICE   PAUL F BRANYAN JR   BOHDAN P BRYDUN   GENE DI RITA
SAMUEL V BULLOCH JR   ROBERT C CAMPBELL   JOHN C CAVANAUGH   RANDY E DILLINDER   ALBERT E DUSSEAU
WILLIAM P FARRELL   BARRY E FELDMANN   JOSE J FIGUEROA   DONALD L FLEETWOOD   JOHN J FULLAM JR
HENRY R GARCIA   DANIEL E GARDNER   MANUEL M GONZALES   JERRY GRANT   ROBERT H GROSS
DONALD H GUITTAR   JIM L HARNDEN   BRUCE L HOWARD   BILLY A KELSALL   ROBERT J LARSON
WASHINGTON C MABLE   WILLIAM A MACHACEK   IRA J MURPHREE   STEVEN H NELSON   JOHNNY VILLARREAL
RONALD L SANDMANN   MICHAEL J SAUNDERS   DREW D SHIPLEY   MELVIN SMITH   WALKER SMITH JR
MICHAEL R SHAPARD   SAMUEL J SMITH   MELVIN D SODOWSKY   RONALD C STALLINGS   RALPH M VALENCIA
IVAN D MILLER JR   HARRY R WHITE JR   JAMES E WRIGHT   ROBERT A ANSPACH   ALLAN E FOLLETT
JERRY W BRANNOCK   WILLIAM D DAVIS   HOWARD J DE WAAL   TIMOTHY M DICK   JOHN C FREPPON
SAMUEL GRAY   ANDRES LIMON   DANIEL J MAGUIRE   PETER T MELAHN   DOUGLAS I MOYER
LARRY E MCCLUNG   JOHN P PAULSON JR   FREDDIE J PHIFER   KENNETH L PUGH   JAMES G RILEY
JERRY M ROBERTS   DENNIS M STEVENS   DAVID E AILI   DENNY A BATTY   WALTER E MURPHY JR
RICHARD CURTIS   ROBERT C KUGELMANN   STEPHEN C MOSELEY   GEORGE L MYERS   GERALD R NEWBROUGH
GEORGE P O'TOOLE JR   JAMES W POWELL JR   ROBERT E BENNETT III   ROBERT D BERTA   BRUCE H BUMGARNER
DONALD R BURGESS   GRADY I CARRIKER JR   CLIFFORD R CARTER   THOMAS W COTTON   MELVIN E CROSSMAN
JOHN E DAVIS   CALVIN D DAWKINS   JOHN W FITZGERALD JR   PAUL G HAMILTON JR   LLOYD L HITCHINS
DOUGLAS R JOHNSON   VERNE L JOHNSON JR   GENE F LEE   LUIS M MARQUEZ-LOPEZ   MICHAEL R MCCORD
RICHARD D JENKS   SIM S STEVERSON   KENNETH R STUBBLEFIELD   JAMES G WHALEY   IAN W ADAMITZ
MATTHEW P AMARAL III   HARON L BROWN II   JUAN R BURGOS   WILLIAM K CLAWSON   GREGORY P CURTIS
JERALD F DE LOOZE   PHIL J DICKENS   HOWARD L DOYLE   BILLY L GODFREY   RICHARD D HARRISON
PHILIP S HOLLAWAY   ROGER E HUESTIS   GARY R JOHNSON   PATRICK M JORDAN   ARTHUR R KEELING
RONNY K KINDRED   JAMES L MILLER   MICHAEL A NEDERLK   DONALD C NELSON   MICHAEL D NISSENBAUM
STEPHEN W PICKETT   HERBERT PLUMMER JR   GARY E SCHUBERT   LLOYD SLACK   RAYMOND E STONE JR
ALLEN L VAN KEUREN   LOUIS W WADLINGTON   ELIJAH WATERS   DONALD C WILLIS   JAY L WRIGHT
ELLSWORTH SWANN   OSCAR AGUAYO JR   WALTER L ARMSTRONG   RICHARD J BOESHART   RICHARD A CHOPPA
RAMON CORTES-ROSA   KENNETH CUSHEN   KENNETH R DAU   MARVIN R DAVIS   RICHARD L DOOLEY
ROBERT L FLORES   WILLIE FRENCH JR   THOMAS E GRIX   CHARLES W HICKS   JOHN C HOUSE
FRANK A INDYK   EDDIE L JACKSON   DAVID P JEWELL   RONALD L KLAUSING   JAMES J KOPRIVNIKAR

PANEL 32E

OMAR LEBRON-DOMENECH   ROBERT LEVINE   EDWARD M LOONEY   WAYNE D RYZA
JAMES E LYNN   STEVEN MATARAZZO   JOHN E MOGAN   ALDEN G MOSHER JR   WESLEY A MOYLE
RICHARD L NORTON   RILEY C O'NEIL JR   ROBERT C OLSON JR   JUAN S OZUNA   MICHAEL B PAQUIN
JOE PENA JR   ERNESTO PEREZ   WILLIAM E PIERSON   RICHARD M PROSCIA   JAMES L REICHELT
JOHN H LATTIN JR   JOHN D ROCHE   MICHAEL D SANDER   ROBERT M SAWAYA   PATRICK J SMITH
SHERMAN A SORRELL   ROY E SOUTHERLAND   LAWRENCE STEWART   WILLIAM D THOMPSON JR   JAMES TIERNO
RODOLFO TREVINO   DAN WAGNER JR   STEPHEN J WHIPPLE   MICHAEL BERRIOS   LARRY K BILONTA
TERRI M BOETTGER   THOMAS R BOYDEN   STEVEN L BRUDERER   THOMAS B CHAMBERS   MICHAEL J MEDEIROS
MICHAEL T COLLINS   LOUIS N COOLEY JR   OMMIE T COX JR   EDWARD A FINLAY   DAVID R GIFFORD
JAMES C GROOVER   JAMES Y HIDALGO   VIRGIL L HITER   JAMES C HOUGHTON   FATHIES KELLY JR
KENNETH H CARPENTER   CHARLES D KERR   THOMAS R KING   WILLIE KNOWLES JR   KENNETH D KRALICK
WILLIAM F MCCARTHY   PATRICK R ROY   STEVEN T RUNYON   MARCOS SOSA JR   RONALD T STOKES
THOMAS E PRIESTHOFF   HARLEY R STANDRIDGE   JAMES T TAYLOR   JAMES M THOMAS   JOHN W VASILOPULOS
AUSTIN R VON KLEIST   JAMES W WEST   WILLIAM G WILKINSON   DEAN J CRAIG   RICHARD A HOUSE
MARTIN G MCDONNELL   PAUL J MONCILLO   HENRY L OLSON   BARRY L RUNYON   MARVIN SMITH
MYRON F SMITH   MARION B WEARING   GUADALUPE N ZUNIGA   DOYLE L BELL   JAMES D BLANDEN
PATRICK C CASSIDY   EDWARD L CLEMMON   ROBERT J GRANDE   THOMAS HUBBARD   KENNETH R JACONETTI
JAMES H BUSH JR   ERNEST MAY   JOSEPH MORGAN JR   MARSHALL L RITZ   GEORGE X ROCHA
MICHAEL P RUANE   DENNIS L SENZ   LARRY D TRAASETH   BENNIE ALSTON   DAVE E ASHFORD
JOHN D BARNETT JR   RALPH D BOBIAN   JAMES L BROWN   WALTER O BROWN JR   ANTHONY V CAMPANIELLO
EDGAR A CAMPBELL   CHARLES CARPENTER   GEORGE P COLANGELO   ROGER D EVANS   LEROY EVERETT
WILLIAM R FURLONG JR   CALVIN A GREENE   THOMAS E GRINER   DONALD P HAMILTON   LARRY A HARKE
PATRICK L HENSHAW   THOMAS S HENSHAW   CHARLES R HOLLAND   JOHN F HOLZ   RODNEY L HUDDLESON
ROBERT D KLINE   JAMES M KLOPMEYER   JEROME F LE VASSEUR JR   JUNIOR E LOTT   RAY TAYLOR
ANTHONY R MANTOUVALES   GREGORY MCCRAY   WILLIE C MCNAIR   RICHARD E MEHL   EUGENE MILEY
JERRY L NATIONS   GARY L NORMAN   LOUIE P PINA   RANDALL B PURDY   STEVEN N RADU
LESTER L RIDINGS   JOHN F RIEGEL   JUNIOR L SCHRINER   WINFIELD A SPOEHR JR   BRUCE W STLOUIS
EDDIE L LANCASTER   WINSTON A TAGGART   MURRAY D VIDLER   THOMAS M WEBSTER   JIMMY L WOOLFOLK
RAYMOND L ZIMMERMAN   DAVID ANTOL   TERRENCE D BECK   GLEN D BELNAP   WILLIAM A CARTER
DANNY J FISHER   GREGORY CORE   JOHN H HOLMES   CHARLES L HOUSLEY   CARL E MURRAY
WILLIAM C JANES   LEROY JEFFERSON   HORATIO L JONES   WILLIAM C JONES   BERNARD P MEINEN JR
RICHARD F GITTINGER   JEREMIAH D MCGARRY   MORRIS G MCPHAIL   FRANK G MICHULKA   RICHARD J PAYNE
GARY M RIST   HERBERT ROBERTS JR   TERRY ROBERTS   BARRY A THOMPSON   RAFAEL A VALPAIS-MORALES
RONALD S ALLEN III   RUDOLPH J BILLIOT   JAMES H BROWN   FRANK H BUCK   DANIEL S BUKALA
JAMES L BURNS   ARTHUR P COPELAND   MITCHELL J DUNCAN   MICHAEL J FEAGAN   LARRY E GONZALEZ
RICHARD J JANSKI   RICHARD A KASKE   CARROL G KEEHNER   WILLIAM H KENNEDY   JOSE A TINAJERO
THOMAS R KISNER   FRED D LAMBERT   EUGENE MANIGO   ROBERT D MASON   THOMAS R MATTY
RICHARD H MCHAM   JOSE M MENDOZA   DAVID W MILDE   WILLIAM C MOORE JR   DAVID R MYERS
JAMES M MCLEAN   GLENN L MCMASTER   LES H PASCHALL   DONNIE D PRESLEY   LEE D SCURLOCK JR
GLENN H SIMMONS   LARRY E SMEDLEY   DONALD L SMITH   MURRAY L SMITH   CHARLES F SORROW JR
MICHAEL T HOKE   LANE A TILSON   DANIEL A VERDUGO   ROBERT L WALLS   FREDERIC P WEBB
WILLIAM H BORCHART   WILLIAM E BRIDGES JR   TED W BURROUGHS JR   PETER B BUSHEY   EDWARD L POLSON
PHILLIP G CANTRELL   WILMER P COOK   ROBERT W COOPER   MARIAN J DOMINIAK JR   STANLEY W DRIZA
GARY H FORS   JOHN F FULLER   ROBERT A HANSELMAN   RODGER D HASTE   MERLIN C HOLLENBACH
HARRY W HORTON JR   STANLEY R HUTCHISON   ROBERT L LONG   STEVEN W MUELLER   PETER E NARVARTE JR
LARRY P BLACK   CLARENCE W OBIE III   CHARLES C PETERSON   TIMOTHY H RINEHART   THOMAS D ROBINSON
MARTIN P SCHWARTZ   JOSEPH L SEEKFORD   MICHAEL M SENGER   GEORGE C SIGALAS   EARL E TYREE
EDWARD RODRIGUEZ   LEWIS W SIGEL   GARY S STICKEL   MICHAEL E SUNIGA   ANGEL VEGA
GARY L WEAVER   KENYON G WELLMAN   DENNIS P WOOD   FRANK G ANTONE   RICHARD E BOURNE

PANEL 32E (*Continued*)

JOE E CARTER JAMES N CLEMONS MICHAEL J DI NAPOLI CARL R GOODFELLOW HUGH G WILLARD
HOUSTON GRANT JR EUGENE H HARRIMAN DUDLEY C HUGHES JR ROBERT R JACKEMEYER LEE B ZOELLER
THOMAS E LAYNE JR PAUL R MADDOX THOMAS L NELSON ANIBAL OYOLA-RABAGO JOHN R PHILLIPS
RAYMOND C EUBANKS JR KENNETH E THRESHER NICHOLAS G WALZ LESTER L WILLIAMS JOHN L WULFFERT
BOBBY J LAWRENCE WALERIJA CHULCHATSCHINOW WILLIAM D DICKSON DAVID MIDDLEKAUFF
JOHN M NEALON RONALD A PARSONS LARRY W PIERCE VERNIE H POWERS TRAVIS R SUTTON
GRADY M JORDAN MICHAEL B SWEENEY MATTHEW J AGUGLIARO RICHARD W BUDKA FREDERICK J BURNS
ANDREW M HUDAK DANNY W JETER BERNARD D JOHNSON TERRY T KOONCE BILLY E LANKFORD
THOMAS A GRUD DELBERT O LEWIS CHARLES D MCCLURG JOHN D MORRIS LARRY H OERTEL
KENNETH F OLENZUK HUGHIE OXENDINE DONALD W RICHARD FRANCIS E SANDERS PETER W SCOTT
PHILLIP E NEFF JERRY A SELLERS JOE T SHUMPERT RONALD J SIENGO EDGAR J UDELL HAROLD D WILLIAMS
RAYMOND S ADAMS LANCE B BARTON MICHAEL E BERDY WILLIE T BRICKHOUSE JR SAMMY BUFFINGTON
WILLIAM H CAMPBELL III JOSEPH T CLARK TOMMY L DANIELS ROGER A ELLIS DANIEL C FAULKS JR
ALLEN D FORD JAMES H GAMBLE DARRELL D GEHRKE DAVID R HAEFNER TIMOTHY J KENNEDY
BARRY S KYLE DARYL L LIGONS MATTHEW P MALCZYNSKI DONALD F MCDOWELL LARRY L ORCUTT
MICHAEL R RICE GERALD L ROWEN II JAMES L RUSS JR RENNY D SCHOEL STEPHEN M VUGA
BERNARD F POBLOCK ROBERT A SIKON THOMAS M VAN ZANDT ROBERT E WOODS CARL E ABNER
JOHN E ADDISON BRUCE C ALFRED RONALD P ALLEN HOWARD D ANDERSON JOHNNIE ANTONIO JR
DONALD L APPLEGATE JOHN R ARRINGTON RICHARD W BANNISTER LAWRENCE M BARNES GEORGE BINKO
JOHN P BARSCH CALVIN W BILES DAVID L BOGGS WILLIAM J BROWN GEORGE M BROZ
WILLIAM H CARPENTER JR WILLIAM A CASON THOMAS E CAST KENNETH L CHAPPELL BOYD E JONES
WILLIAM R CRITCHFIELD DONALD J CRUDEN GORDON T DALTON RICHARD N EDDY JUDSON W EMMONS
MICHAEL D FULLER GARRY L GABRIEL FRANCIS D GREENWOOD BRUCE HALL MOSE HEGLER JR
ROGER L HENSON ROBERT E HENTSCHEL TED D HOLLIMAN JR DONALD C HOPEWELL ALBERT L HORNER
THOMAS S HUBBELL MITCHELL HUGHES JR ROGER B INNES THORNTON I JACKSON JAMES L JAKO
NORMAN W CLEARWATER MICHAEL L JONES RONALD L KESLING DONALD R KIRBY III GUY D KISTNER
RONALD F KITZKE DAN T KLINDT IRVILLE J KNOX DAVID N LAFFERTY LEONARD M LEE
EARL L LEWIS RICHARD E LEWIS VERNON R LIPINSKI GEORGE E LONSDALE JAMES E LOUDERMILK
CARLOS F LOZANO GARY W MARTELL SAMMY A MARTIN ROBERT T MILLER ARPHALIA L RICHARDSON JR
JOHNSON MINNITEE JR MICHAEL J MINOR BEN OWENS RAYMOND B PALMA MICHAEL L PARKER
CHARLES D POPE VERNON B RAINS SHELLIE J REED HARVEY L REMBERT OSSIE REYNOLDS
THOMAS W MALLOY ROBERT T RIDDLE MARK V SCHMIDT WILLIAM D SCHMITZ GARY R SCHWELLENBACH
DENNIS L SCOTT STEVEN E SHEKELL DARNAY SHUBERT RICHARD J SOLCZYK THOMAS N STILES
ROBERT M THOMPSON THOMAS A VARNER JR ROBERT L VAUGHAN FRANKLIN WEBSTER JAMES E WILLIAMS JR
STEPHEN WILLIAMS KENNETH ALLEN PATRICK E ANGLIM MICHAEL E ANTILL ROBERT L BOYER
RONALD C BRESHEARS RICHARD W BROOKS III RICHARD L CARLSON CARL E CHAMBERLAIN JOHN G CORR
DANIEL D DENIPAH FRANK FLORIO WILLIAM G FRASER BYRON A GAINES JR DANIEL L HAVENS
JAMES B COX PHILIP N GANDOLFO ROLLIN E GOLIGHTLY SALOME HERNANDEZ THOMAS B HOLDBROOKS
ARTURO M LARA JERRY J MCDANIEL B L MURPHY JR RAYMOND A NIEDECKEN JUAN ORTIZ-RIVERA
JAMES K PALMER GENE R PHIPPS JOHNNY L ROBINSON RONALD J STRECKERT ERNESTO TARANGO
CHARLES D TOWNSEND HERBERT O ZINNEL JR RONALD M ADAMS RONNIE H BEALS DAVID A BLOUGH
JON M CAPPAERT GEAN P CLAPPER CHARLES P CLAXTON HOPSON COVINGTON CARLOS R CRUZ
EDWARD J DARCY JOHN A DELOZIER CHRISTY T DIMOULAS LARRY R DOYLE WAYNE A ECKLEY
DAVID F FISHER DONALD E FISHER PAUL L FOSTER ROBERT O GRAHAM KEVIN B HARDIMAN JOSE L LUJAN
FRANK H HENDERSON CLIFTON HENSON GLENN C HOPES JOE L JOHNSON ROBERT H MCWILLIAMS JR
LUPE P LOPEZ JACK MCCRARY LEO MENENDEZ JR HENRY L MORGAN STEVEN D MUNDEN
JOE E KINSEY EDWIN N OSBORNE JR FRANK C PARKER III WILLIAM PETROSSI JR WILLIAM J POTTER JR
BRUCE J ROTH JONATHAN P SHAFFER DENNIS C SMITH MILTON W SMITH GERALD G VAN BUREN

PANEL 33E

JAMES R WILLIAMS GERALD W ZIY DAVE M BARTHOLOMEW MICHAEL A STROSHANE
JOSEPH BUSUTTIL SCOTT H COOK RAY DELGADO HENRY L GEDDIS JR RICHARD G GODBOUT
TERRY W HOLMES DANNIE L JOHNSON TERRY A JONES WILLIAM N LOCKETT WILLIAM C MARKLE JR
JEROME J MACDONALD ROGELIO M MARTINEZ JAMES L MCILVOY JOHN F MORRISON JR WYLIE O PHILLIPS
CLARENCE M ADAMS JOHN W STILLEY LOUIS SUTERA JR SMITH SWORDS III THOMAS J TINGLEY
GEORGE J WILLIAMS MURRAY L WORTHAM THOMAS E ADAMS GLENN A BELCHER JAMES A BLANKENSHIP
DICKEY CHAMBLEE WILLIAM C CHENEY EDWARD A COMBS WILLIE F DAIL JR DAVID L DROUGHT
GUILLERMO ESTRADA JOSEPH L FARMER HENRY M HALE ROBERT J HALLETT WILLIAM D HOLLAND
IRA H HULLIHEN CECIL B JONES JR MOSES J LEWIS EARL F MACEY JR ERNEST D MARCUM
JOHN D PEACE III GORDON S PERISHO JOSE SANTANA JR JAMES E THOMPSON WESLEY G TUCKER
NORMAN R ANDERSON RAYMOND D BRETCHES ALVIA G BRYANT TERENCE H HANLEY GREGORY E WERNER
DAVID L CHANEY THOMAS B CORBIN JAMES R DENNISON DAVID DONNELLY DAVID L FRENCH
ROBERT L CAMPBELL CLARENCE H GENAU JR THOMAS B GRIFFIN JR HENRY H HERRIN JR PETER S KLEINBERG
PETER KRETZCHMAR RONALD E LLOYD RONALD L MARTIN ROBERT E MURPHY JR FELIX A SISARIO
PHILIP A TINGLEY JR FRANK VELAZQUEZ RONNIE E BALLARD JOHN W BECKETT THOMAS G BERNARDY
TERRY W BIRMINGHAM ALAN L BLAIR ROBERT E BOWMAN HOUSTON C BOX JR BILLY W BRITT
KENNETH B CARPENTER GARY E CLAYTON ENNIS E CROW JOHN H CURTIN FRED C DUBOSE III
ELDON GARAMILLO GERALD P GAUTHIER BRUCE R HARRIS FRANCIS G HOUDASHELT FURMAN L JOHNSON
WILLIAM S ILLMAN WILLIAM T JACOBUS DAVID L JARVIS HANS KLETINGER JEFFRY A LARSON
FREDERICK L MANLY RONALD O MARQUEZ GARY L MERIDITH JACK W MILLER JAMES W MILLER
JAMES W MCCAFFREY ERNEST J NICHOLS JR WILLIE PETTY JR FREDERICK A PINE TERRY D PITTS
JAMES A PRICE GERALD F RIEDLBERGER SAMUEL RIVERA-FERNANDEZ RALPH L ROTTER JOSE A SILVEIRA
FLOYD P SKAGGS DAVID R SMITH WILLIAM E STAINER ODELL STOKES JR ALTON L WATKINS JR
TOMMY G STOVER ABLE C STROUD III VICTOR D TOMCZYK HENRY VALENZUELA JR ROBERT L WILLIAMS
BOBBY J WINKLER FORTINO J APOLINAR HARRY R BARTHOLOMEW CHARLES M BELL JOHN M BRIMM
CHARLES BRISCOE DAVID R BURSON ANDY A CABRERA JAMES T CLAIR JAMES H CLAY
CHARLES T COOKE ARNOLD L COONROD CLAUDE DARDEN JR DENNIS D DAUTREMONT BILLY J ELLIS
FERDINAND W GLESSING JR ALLEN B GLINES RONALD D GOULET JUAN A GUZMAN RODNEY A PRICE
RICHARD L HATCH MORRIS B JONES KENNETH R LANCASTER ROBERT R LINDBERGH THOMAS P MOORE
WESLEY J MCKINNEY JACK W MCKINNON JR THOMAS D O'CONNOR IVAN A ORT JR JOHN H PATTON
RICHARD W FOX JR DARWIN E RAY CLARENCE ROBINSON EDWARD K ROBISON JESSE E RODRIGUEZ
HENRY E SCHANCK JAMES L SCHERER JERRY D SCHROEDER JERRY L SMITH MORGAN E STEWART
PAUL R STRIEPE JOHN W THOMPSON DONALD F WEBB MELFORD W WEST MILAN C WYDRA
FRED E ANDREWS THOMAS D BABIN JR REGINALD W CHUN DAVID M CLAVIER COY G STAYTON
ROBERT L CLINE HENRY C COUSINEAU GREGORY E COX KENNETH J FARRELL GEORGE F FLANAGAN
RICHARD H FROST JAMES F FUHRMAN MEREDITH A GABRIEL BILLY W GOBER ROGER D GRIFFITH
JAMES B HALL OSCAR HARDISON ROBERT C HENDERSON BILLY G JENT LARRY H MCLAUGHLIN
LOWELL JOHNSON WAYNE H KELMAN CURTIS L KENNEDY ROGER W LARCHER RICHARD L LONG
BOBBY F HOLMAN THOMAS MCCRAY MICHAEL F MEYHOFF RICHARD W MINNICH JR DENNIS E MONTAGUE
JAMES D OSENBAUGH WALTER J PETERS CLIFTON P PIERCE GENE A POLITO GARRY G PRINCE
DWIGHT F RAND NATHANIEL R ROSE JAMES W ROY III DAVID L SIMON DAVID R SIMONS
RUBEN BELL JR ROBERT W SORENSEN EUGENE F SWEET JR FRANK O TABOADA KENNETH J TAKEMOTO
THEODORE TAYLOR JR JOHN G TURK PAUL H VILLAROSA ROBERT V VINSCOTSKI RONALD R WATSON
GEORGE M WISHAM JR MICHAEL R BAKER DONALD W BORNMAN ERNEST F BRIGGS JR LARRY I BRIGGS
JOSE CAIQUEP JOHN R CARLOCK ALBERT M CARWITHEN SIDNEY H COOLER ARTHUR J EARLES
FREDIE R COX GUILLERMO DE LEON JR WILLIAM J DESILETS RICHARD E DEVORE LARRY A DIEFENBACH
NORMAN E COLOSANTI WILLIAM D DOWD ROBERT W DOYLE SAMUEL FANTLE III RALPH E FOULKS JR
JOHN T GALLAGHER GEORGE G GONSALVES JAMES C HARTNEY CARL E HIXSON DANIEL J JOHNSON
DENNIS C HAMILTON EDDIE H HOLLAND ALVIN S JOHNSON JOHN P JOHNSON WILLIAM E JONES
GENE R KUNTZ FLORIAN H KUSS LAFON W LADSON JAMES J LIND JOHN M LINDNER
JOSEPH LUCAS JR MIKE A MAKSIN RAYMOND D MCGLOTHIN BRUCE J MORAN BOBBIE J MOUNTS
ROBERT W RENAUD BOBBY R RODGERS GARY W RUNK FRANCIS P RYBAK JOSEPH SMALLS
DANIEL E RODRIGUES SHELDON D SCHULTZ KENNETH C SCRUTON RICHARD E SHAW THOMAS J SKAVARIL
ROBERT G SMOOT FRANK B SMYK RICHARD O WILLIAMS JAMES D WILLIAMSON FRED M WRENN
WILLIAM J ADAMS JAMES A BAILEY WAYNE S BATES TROY C BATTLES ROBERT L HILLEY
KENNETH B BERRY JAMES A CROSBY STEVEN C DRAKE EDWARD J DREW II ERIC R FASSITT
JOHN M GALATA BROMLEY H GERMAN ROBERT C GILLEN JERRY W GILLIAND HAROLD E HAGER
WILLIAM E BERNARD GEORGE L HORSMAN II RICHARD T JACKSON ROBERT L JONES JR JOHN MARTIN JR
JUAN H MARTINEZ SOCORRO PEREIRA ROBERT D PULLEN JORDAN E RAMEY HAROLD SMITH
GERALD W NORTON JAMES P ROBINSON STEVEN S SCHNACK LELAND STEWART ALONZO R TOAL
JAMES P TURNER MICHAEL F WALKER JAMES A WALL TERRY C WALLEY WAYNE A WHITELEY
JERRY W WICKAM ROY V WIEGAND DANIEL L WISELY RICHARD E WOLFE PETER A ZANCA
BRIAN P AHERN WILLIAM M ANDERSON THOMAS R AVILA ROBERT F BAHL JR JOHN L BAROVETTO
LOUIS W BRANCH THOMAS N BREWER ROBERT G BRIGHAM DONALD R BRUCKNER JOHNNY R BRYSON
KENNETH D BUTLER MANUEL CASILLA-VAZQUEZ JR LARRY L CLEEM ROBERT L HELLER DELMER R JONES
STEPHEN E COALSON CLAUDE H DORRIS DAVID W DYER ENRIQUE FERNANDEZ-LESTON DAN T WARDS
FREDDIE D FORD MARSHALL H FORD CONRAD N GONZALEZ BOB L GREGORY RENE GUERRA-HERNANDEZ
JOHN C CALHOUN RAUL G GUTIERREZ DARREL W HEEREN JAMES E HESKETT LOUIS HILLYER
ARNOLDO L CARRILLO SAMUEL F HOLLIFIELD JR RUFUS HOOD JAMES M INMAN DAVID L JOHNSON
TERENCE P JORDAN JAMES JOSEPH ROBERT C KEARNEY RICHARD C KEEFE ROGER D LEDBETTER
LLOYD E KNAKE ARTHUR L LAUDERDALE BLAZE MAGYAR III LAWRENCE M MALONE RICHARD G MANGRUM
WILLIAM A MARKARIAN ALLAN MENDELL ARTHUR MILLER JR DONALD E MONKMAN ELLIOTT W MOORE
BOBBY R MCKINNON MICHAEL J MENDENHALL JAMES J MORA ROBERT NIELSEN JAMES E PEAY
LOUIS G PETRONE JR EDWARD J REEDER HUBERT ROYSTER JR PHILIP E RUMINSKI JR ROBERT C RUSHER
WILLIAM G SCHRAMM LAWRENCE K SEPULVEDA KENNETH S SMITH JR JAMES M STONE FRANK SUTTON
ANDREW J TELLIS ROBERT S TRUJILLO ROBERT W VADEN DANNY R VANCE LAWRENCE R WALTON
GARY D FERNANDEZ THOMAS L WARD PAUL H WEBB JOSEPH C WIAR JR MICHAEL L WILSON
ROBERT C WOLF WOJCIECH WYSOCKI TIMOTHY H ARTMAN MELVIN BAKER ALAN J BARDACH
KENNETH D BARRY CHARLES L BIFOLCHI HOWARD M BISSEN RUSSELL K BLATZ LAWRENCE C COVINGTON
SAMUEL BLUNT DANIEL R BOWMAN JAMES L BURNEY FRANCIS E CANNON JOHN T CHAPMAN
FREDDIE A BLACKBURN DELL R CLAIBORNE DENVER D COLBURN JR PHELON H COLE ROBERT M CRAMER
ROBERT L CRAWLEY HOVEY R CURRY LAWRENCE J CYR MICHAEL R DAY LARRY G DEARING
DANIEL DIAZ GARY P DIETZ LEONARD E DORNAK ISHMELL EADDY PHILLIP J EBERHARDT
GEORGE W ELLIS ALTON J FENNELL RICHARD W FISCHER RONALD L FOX ROGER C FOXWORTH
GLENN W FREEMAN DANIEL R FULWIDER ENRIQUE L GARCIA JR VICENTE GARZA DONALD W KEEP
MICHAEL J HALL ROBERT E HAMILTON HOWARD E HANSON JR RONALD L HETLAND JOHN R HULBERT
JAROLD E HUMPHREY DONNEY L JACKSON BOBBY W JOBE BOBBY R JONES HALCOTT P JONES JR
THOMAS A GRIMES STEPHEN B KIRSCHNER RICHARD G LIGHTBOURNE PAUL J LIVELY MICHAEL D MARKS
CRAIG N MAY JAMES I MILLER JONATHAN MISKIMMON JR RAINER K MORGAN GLEN M MORRISON
DAVID D NICHOLSON JOHN G NIEDERMEYER MARTIN E O'GRADY NELSON M O'NEAL MICHAEL P OLIVER
BENNETT W OLSON JERRY PATRICK RONNIE D PENDERGRAFT JUAN J PEREZ CLYDE R PHILLIPS
JAMES A PINTAR MILLARD E PRICE JR GUY J PROTANO JR JERRY E PRY DANIEL REESE JR
RALPH O RODRIGUEZ RICHARD A RUMLEY LOUIS L SCHAUTTEET JR FREDERICK L SCHRAM J C STORY
WALLACE C SHAFFER JR HAROLD W SIGMON CHARLES H SMITH HALLIE W SMITH STEPHEN J STEWART

PANEL 34E

GARY A TEETER WILLIAM E TIEMAN JOHN J UGINO FLORENCIO G VILLANUEVA
ARNOLD H SULLIVAN MICHAEL E VAUGHT VERNON B VENEGAS ANTHONY R WATKINS JOSEPH M WATSON
CRAIG P WHITE RAYMOND WHITE ROBERT C WILSON DONALD WOOLEY ROBERT L WRIGHT
ROBERT E YOUNG EWALD ZIRFAS ROLAND BELCHER JAMES O BLANKENSHIP BRADLEY W BOEHM
SISTO B BOJORQUEZ MICHAEL J BRUNNER RANDOLPH T BUTLER LEE M CAPERS GEORGE S SEHI
TYLER W COBB JR THOMAS J DEAN VICTORIANO ESPINOZA JR BURLEY D EZELL JACKY L GARRETT
NORMAN M GREEN LOUIS T HAZZARD WAYNE C IRSCH BRUCE M THOMAS HARRY L WATKINS JR
LARRY R JACKSON RICHARD D LAKIN TIMOTHY LAMBERT GLENNON MARCUSSEN GENIE L MCDONALD
JOHN C MCDOWELL DOUGLAS S MCILROY WARREN E NEWTON PAUL H OLIVER JAMES L PHIPPS
MORRIS C PICKETT WILTON R PICKETT DENNIS L PRESCOTT TONY J QUITMEYER RAINER S RAMOS
THOMAS A BOOKER VINCENTE R GONZALEZ RICHARD R REHE FRED J SECRIST DERRI SYKES
EDWARD J HARRIS JR MARTIN W WELESKI III HAROLD J WESOLICK JR CHARLES K WILCOX JOHNNY WILLIAMS
ARNOLD G ABEL FRANCIS H ANDRYSIAK EDWARD W ARGY LOYDE D ARMOR NORMAN W BATES
PAUL L BERRY LEE R BIRDEN KENNETH L BLACKMON ROBERT D BLEA MURRIE L BLOCKER
EDWIN F BROWN WILLIAM B CAMERON GORDON A CAMPBELL THOMAS CARPENTER JR RICHARD J SEIBERT
WILLIE J COTTRELL BOBBY D CRAWFORD JOHN P CULLINAN DAVE CUMMINGS JR DAVID C DAILY
RICHARD D DEVINE JR HENRY J DONESKI SISIFO FALEAFINE HERMAN R FLETCHER DAVID H HERSHBERGER
PAUL M FONES THOMAS A GHELLI GORDON L GOINS ANDRES A GOMEZ PHILIP L GREGORY
GARLAND A GRIFFIN JR ROBERT P HAIN CHARLES L HANSELMAN WILLIAM R HARTWELL GARY O HEDIN
JEROME W ELLENSON SAMUEL J HELFENSTINE ALEX J HERNANDEZ EARL P HOPPER JR ROBERT L HUTCHISON
NORRIS F JOHNSON ARTHUR JORDAN JERRY W KIZZIAH MARTIN D KLANN ROBERT R LEWIS
JOEL R KOESTER LAMAR A LAWSON ANTHONY J LEDERER DOUGLAS J LEMAIRE JOSE A MANZANARES
JIM D MARTINEZ BENTON MICHAUD ROBERT I MOORE JAMES M MORGAN ROBERT W MUNCY
HARRY P MCFALLS DAVID E MCGLOCHLIN JEFFREY PEREZ ROBERT PFEISTER HENRY L PRATHER III
WILLIAM M BRIDGEFORD FRANKLIN H RAUB BILLY G RIGGINS PAUL W RUMRILL STEVEN W SCHMIDT
RICHARD W SHIVER JOHN C TINGLEY GREY H WAGNER JOHN T WEBSTER GLEN A ZEIGLER
DENIS L ANDERSON JOHN N BREWER ERNEST O BROOM ARTHUR C BUCK PHILIP E BURRELL
MONTE R BUSBY EMORY S CANNON MICHAEL D CRIBELAR DOUGLAS B GREEN III DONALD N THORESEN
PATRICK L HALL MARVIN HEAD JR WALTER M KEENE ROY B KEITH LARRY F KUJAWA
JAMES R LOY RICHARD M MANCINI ROBERT L MCCALLISTER TERRY L MEYER JOHN F OLESNANIK
DELBERT A OLSON GERALD M PINA PAUL W QUICK III MICHAEL L ROBERTS GALE R SIOW
HUGH J FERRELL WILLIAM P SMITH LEONARD H SNEAD JR PHILIP P STEVENS SWANTE A SWENSON
KENNETH H WIDON EUGENE M WILLIAMS WILLIAM P BACKER JOHN E BARRON KENNETH W BARSLOW
LOUIS E BERRY MICHAEL G BERRY ARLYN J BLAUWKAMP CLIFFORD A BOGGS DONALD C BROWN
JAMES D COHRON JACKY R COUCH LEE R DANIELSON ROY W EDWARDS WILLIAM O POFFENBARGER
MICHAEL K FRIESE JAMES R GILLESPIE WESLEY L GOOCH HENRY J GORDON CARL A HARRIS
WILLIAM B HUBBLE LLOYD H KENT ROBERT D KING DAVID W LEATHERBURY EARL LONDON
JAMES CASTALDI BERNARD C MATTSON BENJAMIN F MCCLARY PHILIP D MITCHELL JOHNNIE K PERKINS
WILLIAM D PORT PAUL F QUILL MAX R SPANGLER DARRY R STRAUSSER JULIUS THOMAS
DEWITT J WOLF DELMER ANDERSON ROBERT S BAGNALL RUDOLPH J BIELEK JR CULLIE W BRYANT
ARTHUR BUSTAMANTE CLARENCE J CLAYCOMB EVERARD A DAVIS WILLIE R DENNIS DONALD P FERGUSON
MICHAEL T GEORGE JACKIE W HALL GERALD A HIUKKA ERNEST HOWARD ROBERT A JACKSON
MARK A LAMPRECHT JACKIE R MCELWEE ROBERT J MOLOSSI BRUCE A MORRISON JAMES D SACCO
MICHAEL W ORR LEWIS J PARKER DENNIS K RICE ROBERT L ROGERS ANDERSON L RUDERSON
EUGENE LAW ALFRED B RUSS EDWARD SANCHEZ JR WILLIAM O SAUNDERS JR HAROLD L SCHRECKENGOST
JOHN M SCULLY CHARLES S SICKLER DAVID G STEWART JEFFREY D STRAFACE LARRY D WELLS
ROBERT A WOZNIAK ROGER L BATT HUBBARD D COBB ANDREW COCA EMILE COLE
BILLY G COLLINS DOUGLAS E GOOGINS JR NOLAN D HABERMAN CHARLES E HARRIS RICHARD J HEALY RANDALL D YEARY
FREDRICK H HEMPHILL HARRY G HODGES STANLEY H HORNE ALFONSO IBANEZ PATRICK C MORTUS
HARLAN T PACHE ANTHONY SMITH PAUL D STRAHM CLIFFORD O WARE ROY E WOLF
BOBBY K ALLEN STEPHEN P BARKER HARRY J BOSTON BRIAN T CADY
JOHN J DE NAVA KENNETH B DEAN JOSEPH W DUDEK HENRY W GORMAN TERRY A GRAY
GARY H GRUBB LARRY E HERBERT LARRY E HILL BERT H HINSON KENNETH R HOWELL
CHARLES W IRBY TIMOTHY R KESSLER JOSEPH L LONG ERNEST T MARTIN ROBERT MATHIAS
DALE A MILES RICHARD L MILLER JAMES B RUTLEDGE MICHAEL J RYAN THOMAS R WATTS
RONALD L MCDUFFIE ORVAL H SKARMAN RICHARD H WALKER RAYMOND N WEBER CHARLES T WHITE
PETER R WILLEY HERBERT R ANDERSON EARL R BIGGS JIMMIE R BLISSETT LARRY T BRENT
ORVILLE D COOLEY PAUL S GEE MICHAEL O GLENN EUGENE S HICKS DOUGLAS D HOLLAND
DARRELL C LINT FRED W MAGNUSSON KEVIN J MAGUIRE WILLIAM D MORELAND FRANK C PARRISH
DAVID L PERKETT HOMER E PIERCE JR WILLIAM H REEDY JR HAROLD E STANTON WILLIAM J THOMPSON
JOHN C WHITE JOHN H WRISBERG III JOHN F YOUNG HERLEY AYER JR SAM F BEACH JR
ROBERT L BURRELL DONALD L CHANEY WILLIE DURANT PAUL J GREENWOOD RONALD L STROOMER
CRAIG W HANDLEY DOUGLAS G JENSEN JIMMIE J JETT DANIEL M MEDINA JOHN ORTIZ
JAMES H POST JR VIRGIL R RICE JOHN G SCHMIDT LARRY S SEMENIUK WINFRIED A SHEETS
KENNETH R BELSAR ARTHUR D SINGLETON MIKE R VELASCO ROBERT F WILKE CHARLES E WUERTENBERGER
NORMAN E ADAMS JEFFREY S AKER CECIL D BELT JR WARREN W BOLES MARVIN W BOWEN
TYRONE BROWN SAMUEL BRUCE JR ROBERT E CONDON CARL R DAVIS RONALD H DERENBURGER
JOE R DOMINGUEZ RONALD FAIR NORMAN E FINE JR KERRY R GEDDES THOMAS J HOARE JR
JAMES A JOHANSEN THEODORE F JOHNSON THEODORE K KALEIKINI JR JOHN S KMIEC THEODORE O'BRIEN
MICHAEL KANE JAMES A MORRISON WILLIAM D ORDWAY RONALD L ROEHRICH STEVEN SOLARI
HAROLD D SPRAGG HOMER D SPRING WILLIAM R STALL ROBERT L STOLZ JAMES A TILLEY
ROBERT L TRACY CASIMIRO VILLON THOMAS L WHITEHEAD DONALD D WIELKOPOLAN RUSSELL L WILCOX
GORDON D YNTEMA RANDALL B ANDERSON VAUGHN M ANGELL RONALD BAKER JOHN L BARNES
JOSEPH W BENEDICT DONALD BOWEN WILLIAM E BRUNN KERRY M BUGAJSKY WILLIAM P BURGOON
ROBERT J BLACK JR JUAN C CASTELLANOS DONALD A COFFIN CHARLES E DAVIS JOSEPH F DE CROSTA
MICHAEL J DUNN DENNIS E FULLER JOSEPH GERWATOWSKI RAYMOND A GIGNAC DONALD L GLOVER
MICHAEL P HALPIN GENE D HICKS LAWRENCE M JENNINGS BYRON S JOHNSON WILLIAM D JOHNSON
RANDOLPH R JONES ROOSEVELT JONES JACK J KUPFERER FLOYD C LACHNEY BERT D LEFLER
JOHNNY W LINDSEY JOHN P MARKEN JR LESLIE D MATCHETT JAMES R MOORE MICHAEL E MORRIS
ROBERT M MCCONNELL PATRICK P MURRAY CHARLES E MUZZEY TIMOTHY M NAFE LEONARD L NEWTON
GEORGE H NUNEZ RONALD G PAHL FRED J PINSONAULT RONALD L RICKARD PAUL W ROBINSON
JOHN A ROGERS FRANKLIN E SOLLARS EDWARD O SPENCER CHARLES WALLACE JR HOBART M WALLACE JR
PATRICK R WOLFE JR MICHAEL YAWORSKY JAMES H BASS JR THOMAS D BRINDLEY CHARLES W BRYAN
WILLIAM S CALHOUN RONALD G CAMPBELL PHILIP M CIRILLO JAMES A COLLINS DANIEL P MCLAUGHLIN JR
MICHAEL E DE BUSK DAVID A DE COSTE RICK D DEEDS GARY L ELIA JOHN E ESTEN
PETER FLETCHER ANDY GARNICA STEPHEN A GUARDINO ELIOT F GUILD WILLIAM T HARTMAN
ANTHONY J HENDERSON JOSE B HERRERA TILDEN S HOLLEY GERALD N HUNTER DAVID A JAMESON
SOLOMON KALUA JR JAMES A KETTERER GENE M KOSEL EDWARD KUBISKY GERALD F LENZ
GEORGE A LINK JOSE D LOPEZ POLLARD H MERCER JR LEO E MICHAUD CLARENCE E MITCHELL JR
ROBERT E BUTLER JOHN J MOORE GERALD A O'TOOLE GUILLERMO B PAGADUAN JAMES W PARHAM
DONALD F PARKER WARREN H RALYA JR RICHARD P REYNOLDS JR PAUL M ROBERTS MICHELE M ROSEBERRY
RONALD L SANDLIN STEVE S SAROSSY ROBERT E SWALLEY MICHAEL H THOMAS MURRAY W VAN LONE SR

PANEL 35E

ALLISON A WESTBROOKS JR EULIS N WILKES JR ROGER L WILSON PETER L WOOD
JAMES F WRIGHT JOHN M ACOSTA GLEN R BARNHILL PAUL M BEDDOE JR PAUL R BELLAMY
JOE L BIFFLE JR LAWRENCE E BISONETT THEODORE BROWN JR CURTIS B BUGGER ECHOL W COALSTON JR
PAUL R COMBS JOHN J CONTRERAS REECE A CRITCHFIELD JR MICHAEL D CRUITT MICHAEL G DONOVAN III
MERLE C EICHER JR JERRY W ELLIOTT ALBERT EVANS EUGENE T FRALEY LARRY J FRITZGERALD
STEVEN L HELLWIG BILLY D HILL TERRY M JOHNSON CLIFTON R JONES SEABORN D JONES
WILLIAM A KIMSEY JR THOMAS L KINGSTON JOHN W KNIGHT GORDON L LAWRENCE MALCOLM G MOLE
HAROLD F MCGAHA GERALD L MCKINSEY JR CHARLES J RAMSAY THOMAS H RETSCHULTE JOSEPH P SEYMOE
THOMAS J MOODY MELVIN L RIMEL DAVID T ROZELLE JAMES L SIRON TERRENCE G SMITH
JERRY O STENBERG BOBBY WEST LARRY F WHITE DAVID A BINGHAM RICHARD S BYARS
THOMAS L COTTRELL HOWARD L JOHNSON DALE S PUISHIS JAMES T RANSTEAD GARY L SAXTON
TOM W SIMMONS JR RICHARD E STECKER NATHANIEL WEATHERS JERRY D WELLS JOHN O WHITE
ROBERT L WICKLIFFE RONALD W ADAMS JAMES M BERGE WILLIAM E BLACKMER JULIO A CALDERON
HILAIRE A ANDRY JR NERY J BRENES JAMES I BUCHNER ALBERT L CAMPFIELD TOMMY L CARPENTER
BRUCE W DUDLEY JR BOYCE L DUNCAN JR GARY B DUNCAN RONNIE J ESKEW MICHAEL F FANNING
EMILIO G GARCIA HERSHEL HIGGINS DAVID J KLIPPEL JOHN F LOBSINGER LEE A LUALLIN
DONALD G MACINTOSH JOHN T MCCHESNEY III JOSEPH S MCKINNEY THOMAS R PEARSON JR JOSEPH VIEIRA
WILLIAM A POLCHOW GERALD L RAMSDEN ANGEL O RUIZ RUDOLF A SCHRADER JAMES C STRANO
GEORGE M MOORE CLIFFORD J VOLKE II LEROY J YOUNG DAVID C AUGE GILBERT AYALA JR
GEORGE R CASTILLO THOMAS G CURTIS JR BOBBIE L DITZFELD THEODORE A FAULK RONALD A GALANTE
WAYNE C CHITWOOD JOHN R FAVOR KENNETH R GAY KENNETH V GOODMAN JON L GRIMMETT
DAMAS HERNANDEZ-FELICI THOMAS W HODGE GEORGE J HOLLY III ERNEST E HOOD JAMES MILLER
ARTHUR R JANSEN DANIEL W KENT FERDINAND J KORNICK JR PETER L LOVETT HAROLD I LOYD
CLAYTON M HOLLAND JR WILLIAM L MARLIN JR ROBERT J MCCARL CHARLES W MILLER ROBERT J MILLER
WILLIAM W MCCLENDON JR JAMES C MCHENRY ROBERT D NAWROCKI JOHN H NEAL JR GARY L NORDQUIST
ERNEST P PALCIC FRANCIS PENNETTI GREGORY F POPOWITZ RAMIRO R RAMIREZ JOHN O ROESLER

259

THE VIETNAM VETERANS MEMORIAL COLLECTION

JUAN A ROSA DAVE R SCOTT GARY D SCRIBNER EDMUND SKUNDA JAMES A STARK
MICHAEL E STEPHENS BILLY L STRICKLAND JAMES R WEST CHARLES M WHITE SR GEORGE D ANDERSON
JAMES B ANDERSON JESUS V AVILA STEPHEN C BARRETT CLIFFORD E BRYAN THOMAS E DENHOFF
JOSEPH L BEDOLLA JOHN A BURZAWA JR RAYMOND M CASWELL JACK P COTTERELL ROLAND K DAVIS
DAVID P DODSON KENNETH H DRESSEL CHRISTIAN F FEIT III BRUCE J FLETCHER JOHN J FODEN
PHILLIP E GARVER FRANCIS G GERCZ JR ARTHUR C GRANGE EDWARD W HEIFNER JOSEPH A KELNHOFER
ROBERT H KING ARTHUR J KLABUNDE JR HARVEY E KLINE II ROBERT C LANGFORD ROGER M LAY
EARL A MAILLOUX JOHNSON M MILLIGAN JOHNNY R MILLS JULIUS W MORRIS JR MICHAEL S ROMANO
PETER G NASH MITCHELL F SILVERS JACK B SUTPHEN NORMAN L TINKER KENNETH R TRIER
GEORGE R WASHINGTON LAWRENCE D WILLIAMS ROGER L BEAM LAWRENCE C BLOOM JOHN A BRISCOE
EDWARD J CRAIG JAMES C CURTIN JERRY W DEARING JAMES W FOLEY JOHN L REID
DWIGHT T DENNING MICHAEL E DUNN PAUL D EKART ROBERT D FAIRES GARY N FOSTER
HOWARD F COLES JR NORMAN E EIDSMOE FREDERICK J FALK JR TERRY D FINCH HARRY S FITEZ JR
ROBERT R FRYER ROBERT A GATES ALLEN GEIB JIMMY L JOHNSON JR BYRON C LOLLAR
WILLIE R CAULTON LYLE W MORRIS MAXIE L PRICE ROBERT L SCOTT PETER L SILLER
RAY O SIMONS JR FRED H SPEAR REGINALD A STANCIL ROBERT W TANKSLEY MICHAEL R ZUREK
LUIGI F ALBANESE KEITH R BACORN JOSEPH L BEGOTKA GERALD R BRENT JAMES M BUCK
SILVINO F BARREIROS JOHN R BURNS JR PAUL CHRISTMAS MICHAEL J COLEMAN THOMAS K COLEMAN
ROBERT J CORDOVA RUBE A COX JR WILLIAM E DONOHUE DANIEL ESCOBEDO JOHN A FELSHAW
DAVID D FLANAGAN EMMITT GALLOWAY JAMES R GOLZ HARVEY HARRIS JR WILLIAM D HART
JOSEPH T HUNT DONALD L HUNTER LORENZO J IOANNI WILLIAM N JOHNSON CHRISTIAN A LANGENFELD
HERLIHY T LONG MICHEAL A MIKITIS STEPHEN M MUELLER LESTER M NESS MICHAEL V PETERSON
WAYNE C MYERS GEORGE P NICHOLSON THOMAS J PENNINGTON JOHN L PRICHARD FRANK RAYMOND JR
WALLACE L REATHER JR WILLIAM J ROBERTS MARSHALL L ROBINSON WILLIAM H SCHEIBER JR LARRY WRIGHT
JOE C SMITH CHRISTOPHER J TOPPI FRANK N UZZELL RANDY N WARD DONALD E WEED
RONALD S RUSSO RALPH D WHEELER III ISAIAH WHITE KURT F ZIMMERMAN RICHARD A BALLHEIM
JOHNIE R BARBER JOE D BROWN THEODORE CHRYSTYNYCZ WILLIAM J DAVIDSON JR EDWARD K PETERS
GILBERT DIAZ JAVIER P FIGUEROA ANGEL A GARCIA EDWARD HADDOCK THOMAS W HOLLIS
ROBERT L KELLAS DAVID A MARKS ROBERT J MEREIDER WALTER J MIKOSZ JR WILLIAM H MOORE III
DONALD R BUCKLES TIMOTHY J MCKIERNAN KEILA PAOPAO ROBERT S PLUNKETT ROGER D QUILLEN
KENNETH E RASCO JAMES C RILES GREGORY J SINTIC KENNETH W SMITH DOUGLAS M SOROKA
DENNIS R STANLEY JAMES E WAGNER GEORGE W ZENKEWICH FRANK W ASP GARY L CRONE
ROBERT N BARBERY HERBERT H BUTT JR CHARLES A DELLINGER RICHARD E DENNY JR ROBERT B ENGLAND II
KENNETH J GRASSL THELBERT A JAMES VICTOR JOHNSON JR LESTER S KINARD ROY D MCGEE
GENE L KUVIK NARCISO LEOS JR MICHAEL T MAHONEY JIMMIE C MARRION JAMES D MILLS
ESTEBAN P ESTRADA RICKY A MYERS ROBERT W NEHER ROBERT L PITTMAN JOHN A RICKELS
JOHN F RUIZ RICHARD S RUSSELL STUART H THOMSON CHARLES N TREDINNICK JOSEPH G VOGRINEC
DANNY A WEBER HAROLD H WELCH CHARLES E WHITE WILLIAM E WHITE III JOHN P ZIELINSKI
THOMAS A BADGER NORMAN C BALLARD TIMOTHY M BARMMER CLIFFORD R BENNETT HOWARD R BISJAK
JOHN S AMBROSINI JAMES C BODISON BILLY C BOLTON GLENN R BRUST HARMON W BURKS
GARY R CARPENTER EDWARD E CERVANTEZ RALPH E CLARK RICHARD J CLEMENTZ FRANCIS P COX
WILLIAM L DAZEY JR DAVID W DE PRIEST RICHARD K DRAKE JR ALFRED T DWYER PAUL J EDGE
ANTHONY E ELLIOTT ARTHUR F ELLIOTT DONALD A EVANS BLAKE W FARRIS JR DONALD W RICHARDSON
ROBERT W FORKL NORBERT L FROEHLICH CURTIS T GAY PAUL E GERLACH PAUL S GOGGIN
JEHOVAH GRAVES RICHARD P GRAY JAMES L GREENE JR LAWRENCE D GREENE WILLIAM E GRENNAY
HOWARD W GULLIKSEN RICHARD T HEIMES CLEVELAND HOLMES WILLIAM J HURST PRINCE A JOHNSON JR
LOUIS C GROVE ROBERT N HUTTER JR ROY L JACKSON TODD R JACKSON CLIFFORD JONES JR
JOHN H JONES JR DENNIS B KOUHNS JAMES M LA ROUCHE ROBERT E LOCHRIDGE MARCELLO J LOFARO
RALPH E MABRY JR DENNIS L MAGRIE JOHN E MANNING ROBERT J MARIZ JERRY MARKUS
MILOSLAV J MARTINOVSKY MELVIN L MARTZ JACK R MCKEE PETE MELNICK LARRY D MILLARD
PATRICK J MCKINLEY GEORGE W MCREYNOLDS WILLARD E NELSON TIMOTHY C OCHS ROBERT V PETERSON
DELL C ODEGARD STEVEN C ODOM RICHARD W PERDUE ROBERT C PETERS DENNIS L PICKARD
MORRISON L PICKETT MONTE G PITNER STEVEN C POWERS WILLIAM J POWERS RONALD E RAY
PETER W FOOTE RICHARD F RIAL TONY RIJOS GENE A ROSS WILLIAM R ROSS JR
STEVEN R SMITH WALTER J SOUTAR KENNETH A SPILKER ROBERT L STALEY JR GEORGE D STIEHLER
COLBEN B STOKES JR THOMAS H SWINNEA BRAD J SZUTZ CHARLES T TATE JR JIMMIE P WALL
TUIOALELE T SUIAUNOA RONALD E THOMPSON JOHN H TIGNER JESUS R VASQUEZ ROBERT A WARNER
ALVIN J WESOLOWSKI JR ROBERT E WHITBECK RALPH E WHITE JOSEPH C ZAMIARA GHALIB A ABDULLAH
RUSSELL M AMOSS GLENN E ANKRUM CAREY C ANTHONY JAMES A BALLINGER GARY A BANGLOS
JERRY D BARKSDALE RICHARD L BARTLEY WILLIAM C BEHRENS RALPH T BERRY WILLIAM A BERRY
ROBERT C BIEGEL EDGAR L BOLDING RANDOLPH E BOONE LASZLO BOROSS JR ROLAND M BOWEN
STEPHEN L BRADDOCK JOHN P BRAGA JR CLYDE B BRAUGHTON JR JAMES A BRENNAN DAVID C BROWN
LESTER E BROWN ARCHIE BURNETTE JR WILLIAM L BUSBY PETER M BUTLER HOWARD E BUTTON

PANEL 36E

ROGER S CAMERON DAVID R CARSON PAUL C CARTER JR PATRICK C CARTNEY
HAROLD E CASHMAN JR ROBERT G CHENAULT JOHN L CHURCH LARRY R CLEMONS ALFRED J LEWIS
ALFRED P COFFROTH PETER M COLEMAN EUGENE J CONNER RICHARD CONNOLLY MODESTO COTTO JR
CHARLES E CRANDALL ROGER B CROWELL DENNIS T CUNNANE GORDON L CURRIER JR WYATT C GORDON
GREGORY V GRAY FLETCHER L LEWIS
WILLIAM J CYR CHARLES L DANIEL DWIGHT A DEDRICK HOUSSAYE A DELA
ROCHERS J DES FRANK DOEZEMA JR DOUGLAS W DOODY CARL W DORRIES BYRON R DUHE
WILLIAM B DUNCAN HARRY L ECTON CLARENCE L EVANS FRANK E FAUGHT ROBERT M FINNEGAN
LOUIS H FISCHER GERALD L FITTS MICHAEL T FITZGERALD WILLIAM J FLAHIVE JR MANUEL S FLORES
ERNEST E FREUND JR JOHN J FULLERTON JR SAM H GALLOWAY JOSEPH A GARCIA OWEN N GARNET
CALLEN J COURTEMANCHE SERGIO J GHERARDINI RICHARD A GILLEY AUBREY GOFF JR WILLIAM S GORDON
GUY E GREENFIELD CHARLES L GREGORY HERBERT L GREGORY III MICHAEL A GRIEVE
STEVEN A GUTHRIE CHARLES E HALL CHARLES V HAMPTON JR GARY W HANNA RICHARD W HARPER
JESSIE E HARRIS HENRY W HARTMAN FRED K HATADA JAMES M HAUCK CHARLES E HEBRON
RICKY D HENDERSON ROBERT M HENDERSON COMBLY H HENRICKSON DANIEL B HENRY THOMAS C HILEY
LLOYD A HIMES TROY E HIRNI II MICHAEL L HOLIDAY LUEY V HOLLAND IVAN D HOMSLEY
GORDON W HOOVER KENNETH E HOTCHKISS RICHARD D HOVLAND HENRY G HOWCOTT ROY HUDSON
ROBERT A HUIE ABRAHAM JACKSON DENNY M JACKSON RICHARD A JACKSON ROBERT W JENKINS
CHARLES F JOHNSON JR EVERETT W JOHNSON JR GIDEON P JOHNSON DUBOIS R JONES MARVIN H JONES JR
ROBERT KEMELMACHER WARREN E KENERLY RICHARD A KERR GERALD C KINNY FREDRICK M KITTLE
THOMAS L KLINZING CHARLES A KRONBERG RICHARD J LACEY HELMUT G LAKASZUS JAMES P LANIER
VERNON H CHRISTOFFER JR RICHARD F DELGADO DANNY L LASURE BILLIE L LEE WILLIAM R LEE
STANLEY LEWIS TROY A LITTLEJOHN JACK R LOCKRIDGE NORMAN L LONG JR ERNEST MADRID
REGINALD V MAISEY JR ANTHONY G MALDONADO MARTIN MARQUEZ JR DON PRIEN FLOYD B SPENCER JR
JOSEPH V MARRONE JAMES C MARSHALL JOHN F MARTIN FRANCIS J MAYER JR OWEN E MEBUST
JOHNNY MEDINA RUSSELL E MILBERRY ROGER B MILLS ROBERT W MOINESTER THOMAS W MOORE
EDWARD MCNALLY JUAN B MORALES-MERCADO JAMES R MORRIS WALTER M MURPHY MICHAEL V MURRAY
JAMES R MCCLINTOCK JAMES E MCCUE JOHN J MCHUGH EDWARD A MCKIM EDWARD G MUSE
JEFFERY C MCTEER CHRISTIAN H MORRISON LARRY F NEWCOMB VERNON L NEWTON JOHN L NIELSON
RICHARD E O'CONNOR NESTOR OJEDA DAVID L PARKER RODNEY G PASCASCIO JIMMIE PATTEN
LEE R PEEKS EDWARD M PIKE RAYMOND H PIKE JR BENJAMIN F PITTS MARVIN J PLATA
MICHAEL A MANGIOLARDO MICHAEL A POGUE JAMES F PORTER JOHN P PREZIOSI DONALD M RADICS
RICHARD J RHODES HARRY F RICHARDSON JR TERRY L RIEGEL CLARENCE T RISHER III DAMON L RITCHIE
ARTHUR J ROBERTS JR DAVID O ROBERTS RONNIE R ROUSH CLIFTON D ROY PILAR R RUIZ-DEL WILLIAM M SEBAST
TERENCE F SAGE DONALD B SCHAICH ROBERT W SCHULTZ RANDALL K SCHUTT
JAMES SEIDENSTICKER MARK M SERREM BRUCE D SHARP JAMES J SHERRILL LEON J SHRUM
MAXIMILIAN H SIMMETH BENNY J SMITH DANIEL J SMITH DONALD L SMITH JOHN T SMITH
GERALD M MARKOSKI ROBERT C SMITH WILLIAM E SMITH DENNIS W SONSTENG HAROLD R STAFFORD
ROBERT B STAFFORD JAMES STANCELL JR THOMAS H STAPLES STEPHEN W STARK JAMES L WAGES
WILLIAM J STEFFES PATRICK J STRAYER GERALD D SULLIVAN JOHNIE B THOMAS BERNARD D THOMPSON JR
THOMAS J TORRINGTON DAVID L TURNER ANTHONY F VANHULLE II MURRAY L VERON JAMES M VIELBAUM
LAWRENCE N STANGEL JOSE G VIRUET JAMES M VRBA JR JAMES E WALSH JOHN D WARD JR
LUCION P WELLS ROBERT L WHITLEY VERNON C WILDERSPIN MELVIN J WILLIAMS TERRY J WILLIAMS
ROBERT J WILLIAMSON DAVID R WILSON ALLEN L WINTERS JOSEPH R WISE JERRY R WOODALL
TIMOTHY L WORTH O'NEAL WRIGHT LESTER G YARBROUGH CHARLES A YEOMANS STEVEN W ZIEGLER
KENNETH H ALBRITTON WILLIE J BARNES JAMES T BERGEN III RICHARD L BLEVINS THOMAS G D'EUSTACHIO
REX A BOWYER ELVVIN L BROWN JOHN T BROWN GEORGE A CAMPBELL WILLIAM A THORNTON JR
CLYDE E CARTER JR CLYDE T CODY DAVID L COLLINS WILLIAM M COMER JR ROBERT L CONLEY
DAVIS J BOARDMAN RAYMOND L CONWAY CHARLES H COOK TERRENCE R FEIGENBUTZ JOHN E GAGNON
PHILIP M GERMAIN BENJAMIN D GRANT CLARENCE GRIEGO FRANCIS L GRIFFIN JAMES L GRIFFIS
CHARLES C GRISHAM GEORGE M HALL JAMES E HAMILTON MICHAEL W HASKINS JOHN R SHELL
FRANCIS G HENRY PEDRO A HERNANDEZ JOSEPH P HOLLAND ALPHONZO HOLMON JR ISTVAN MOLNAR
EDDIE G HUFFMAN WEDEN G HUMPHREY JOHN P HYLAND LEROY JOHNSON ROBERT E JOHNSTON JR
GENE L KEAHI MICHAEL Y KEETER NORTON Z KING DONALD A KIRKHAM KENNETH E KUSPIEL
ISAIAH LAWS JR WILLIAM E LEAMON MICHAEL C LINDSAY GILBERT R LISH EDWARD E LONG
GEORGE A LUBESKY JR GLENN A LUCAS WILLIAM K MARCIN THOMAS M MARTICH ALPHONSO S MARTIN
ELBERT H MAXWELL ALFREDO MEDINA JR JACKIE L MELTON JAMES A MELTON JR JAMES J PETREY
HORACE HOWARD STEPHEN P MITCHELL WESLEY R MOORE JR HARRY V MOSHER MICHAEL G MURDOCK
CHARLES R MENSCH STANLEY MURDOCK DWIGHT M NOVEMBER FRANK A PAPE HENRY H PERSONS
ROGER D PUCKETT JAMES E REED MAXIE R RICE KENNETH L ROGERS TOMMY G SANDEFUR
LAWRENCE E HECKMAN DORTY H SCOTT JR JEREMIAH SCOTT JOHN F SEVICK DARREL A SHELLIE
DIEROTHER BROWN LYNN H SMITH CURTIS D SNITKER GLENN D TAYLOR RALPH L THOMPSON JR
ARTHUR R TIMBOE EUGENE V WILLIAMS LARRY E WILLIAMS ROYCE H WILSON JR JOHN W WINTER
WILLIAM F WITEK LARRY E WITTLER MATHEW WOLFE ARTHUR G WOLTER BILLY L WRIGHT
CHARLES L ADKINS KENNETH J AINSWORTH RODNEY A ALFANO DONALD W ALLEN JR WILLIE J ANGUS
JOSEPH C APPLEGATE MOSES A ARNOLD RAY C BANKS CHARLES J BAUER JR ALBERT L BETTS
ROBERT B ANNAS KENNETH BOROWICZ GUY F BROOKS IRVIN BROWN JAMES A BUNN JOHN D EVANS
DONALD D BURNHAM JOHN H CANNON ROBERT L CHAPMAN PETER F CHERNEY HOLLIS R HALE

LARRY M CLARK PAUL R COLLETT JR DAVID W CRARY RICHARD L CULLEN JOHN P CULP
ANDREW J DANIEL JOHN M DASHNAW DENNIS P DAY DELFERD B DUNIFER TED W EDWARDS
QUENTIN W BINDER RICHARD E ENGLE CRISTOBAL FIGUEROA-PEREZ GARY R FITCH RUSSELL R FLESHER
ROBERT P FOLEY GARY L GABEL LEANDRO GARCIA SILAS E GIBSON HORACE G GIDDENS JR
RICHARD E GIDEON JAN R GILLHAM KENNETH E GOLDEN JOEL H GONZALEZ-VELEZ JAMES E GOSSELIN
PHILIP R CHASSION GEORGE J GOTTWALD JR PHILLIP O GUILLEN GILBERT L HAMILTON ALLEN C HARDISON
PETER H HEISSENBUTTEL RENE Z HERNANDEZ GUY R HIVELY LEON F HUBER FRED W JANSONIUS
DOUGLAS E HOBACK SAMUEL G HURRY WILLARD V JOHNSON JOHN L JONES RALPH A KEATING
ROBERT G KEATS KENDRICK K KELLEY III ROGER E KELLY RAYMOND E KRAMER JOHN F KUIPER
GARY J LANDON PATRICK J LAVELLE ELOY F LE BLANC NICHOLAS A LIA ROBERT A REYES
WILLIAM E LOZIER FRANCISCO MACHADO JR JOHN E MALONEY JR DONALD E MARTIN LARRY L MAXAM
HUGH R MCKIBBIN JR ALLEN T MERRITT IV DENNIS J MILLER LARRY L MITCHELL CHARLES W PERMALOFF
ALFRED L MCNABB WAYNE P NEWCOMB ROBERT J OATES HILBERTO ORTEGA WAYNE L SAPP
RAYMOND J MICHALOWSKI CHARLES T PARKER KENNETH J PATTON JAMES C PAYNE DONALD D PERKINS JR
ROY L PHILLIPS GARY S POSCOVER WILMER POTTS HUBERT PRICE JR JOE H PRINGLE
VINCENT P LANDON JOSEPH D PUGGI GLENN W RAMEY STEVEN L RANEY DELBERT L REESE
ROBERT I RICE JOSEPH M RODRIGUES THOMAS M ROSS FELIX A RUIZ HOMER A RUPLE JR
DANNY R NORTHCUTT BERNARD S RYAN SELMER E SALVESON ROGER L SCHNEIDER GAYLORD J SEBENS
RONALD J SELIG ROBERT L SHAFFER DONALD B SMALL HURLEY A SMITH JACK C TAYLOR
JOHNNIE N SHEARES JR STEVEN L SMITH PAUL A STENDER MICHAEL D STOTLER RICHARD A SWEDEEN

PANEL 37E

LEROY E VALDEZ JAMES D VAN HOOK RICHARD L WENDEL LEON ANDERSON JR LARRY W NORGAÁRD
TIMOTHY L WHITE KENNETH J WILLIAMS BILLY W WILSON JACK P WILSON JR EMMETT L YORK JR
CARL L WEST ROBERT C ANDERSON FRANK A AZZARITO JR ROBERT I BALLARD HOWARD D BENNETT
JAMES B BRANDON RUSSELL D BRYANT JR LANGDON G BURWELL LARRY G CANNON MICHAEL B CERVERA
CHRISTOPHER M DANIELS LESLIE A DICKINSON JR ROBERT L DICKSON JERRY R HALEY VERNON Z JOHNS
CARL DINGUS ORRIN L DYER JR BRUCE E ENGSTROM GLEN O ERVIN NOLBERTO FRAUSTO JR
ROBERT A GIFFORD DON R GILBERT JAMES R GODWIN HAROLD L GRAY GERALD B GREENDYKE
LESLIE L COWDEN LEON HAMNER HAROLD S HIGGINBOTHAM EDWARD W HUGHEY CHARLES S JACKSON
RUDOLPH V CISTARO JR ROBERT F JOHNSON JR LARRY H JONES JOSEPH F KARDOS EUGENE M KORECKI
HOLT LAU JAMES E MALONE EDWARD MANOWSKI JAMES K MCCANN STEPHEN B MURDEN
EDWARD MCCORVEY JR JOHN W MCGUIRE THOMAS W OTTE ROBERT G PAINTER JACK A PEACOCK
PAUL A PRZELOMSKI WILLIAM C QUEBODEAUX JR DAVID QUINONES TIMOTHY C REITHMANN SAUL ZAYAS
DAVID L RICKELS JIMMY K ROBERTSON ZACK O ROWLAND HOWARD SADLER JR JOSEPH SANTOS
DALE H SCHMIDT MANUEL T SEGURA RICHARD E STANTON BOBBY A TAYLOR BARRY L WOLK
EUGENE D TREADWELL ROBERT R VAN GILDER HOWARD G VAUGHN JOHN K WEBER WALLACE L WIGGINS
DANIEL PENA JR CHARLIE A STEWART JR MARION E WILSON THOMAS F YOUNG CHARLES E ZUNIGA
HENRY ADLER VAL G ALLARD MARK J ALLSTOTT GERALD R ANDERSON JOHNNY L BACA JR
LOUIS R BALOG DINGUS BANKS JR WILLIAM C BARNES JR FREDRICK H BECKMEYER BILLY J BLACKSTEN
LEONARD BREAUX WILLIAM L BRIDGES HENRY E CASIAS RUSSELL D CHASE LARRY G CLARK
EARL T CLASSEN THOMAS J CRAGHEAD JR ANDREW L DAWSON GARY M DIAZ JOHNNIE L DOUGLAS
JAMES DZIENCILOWSKI RONALD C FIELDS AUGUST H GENZLER ALFREDO GONZALEZ JOHN P GORDON JR
CHARLES H GRAHAM ROBERT E HALL PAUL T HALLMAN RICHARD E HARNER JR JAMES R HEDGER
ROBERT E HOPKINS ROBERT W HUBBARD ERNEST L JACOBS JR GEORGE P KENDALL JR HUSKIE Y TEN
RUSSELL E KEPHART LARRY D KING BRUCE N KNOX GARRY F LAWRENCE STEVEN P LINNA
THOMAS W LOOS CLYDE R MENZ WAYNE A MICHALAK GARY B MIDKIFF BENJAMIN A MONDRAGON
JOHN D MACLEAN LONNIE E MCNEILL JOHN P ONDERKO CURTIS R PATTON OTIS L PHILLIPS
HAROLD R REEVES LEON REID CHARLES E RICHARDS RONALD RODERICK JAMES D SERENA
MICHAEL D HOLLINGSWORTH ROBERT L STANEK MICHAEL L TOSTENSON KESTER ULREY JUAN F VAZQUEZ
WAYNE A WASHBURN PATRICK A WHITLOCK DONALD M WILLEY JOHN D WILLINGHAM ROY L WINER
RONALD W WOOD JOHN W WYATT JR CHARLES H YOUNG ROGER D ALBERTS JOHN J BURKE
JACK A BEARD MICHAEL W BERKERY JOHN F BIBBY LARRY J BLANKENSHIP JACK C BOGARD
WILLIAM J ANDERSON NORRIS L BRENDEN LARRY W BROWN JOSEPH S BURGETT ROBERT W CAMPBELL
GARY L CAMPEN RAUL CANDELARIA LARRY V CLASPILL KENNETH W COATES JERRY D MALLORY
REMBERT CRAWFORD JR RAYMOND N CURLEY M L CURRY ANTHONY DEGEROLAMO JR LEONARD R DEMKO
TIMOTHY J DINEEN ROBERT J EDGAR SOLOMON H GODWIN WAYNE L GOLON LAWRENCE G GRASSI
WAYNE D HAMEL TIMOTHY R HAMMOND JOSEPH E HEIMAN SHULER A HOFFMAN JAMES R HOLT
JOHN H JACKSON WILLIAM T JARVIS JOSEPH B JONES LEE R KING HAROLD A KRAM JR
RICHARD L KUNTZ TYRONE F LAMITIE MICHAEL S LANE MARK M LANGSTON THOMAS W LAUGHLIN
NORMAN O COPELAND JAMES A LOWERY CHRISTOPHER E LYON DAVID M MABERY THOMAS A MARCHUT
DOC H MARSHALL RONALD L MEANS JOSEPH A MOLETTIERE BRUCE W MONSKA JEFFREY P MORLEY
JOHN A MCINTOSH CLENZELL MORRIS PAUL J MYERS CARL J ORNELAS
GREGORY A MUSZALSKI THEODORE A PAPKE GERALD F PELZMANN WILLIAM T POTTER JAMES E PRIDEAUX
MARTIN L RIMSON ALTON B SEBASTIAN WILLIAM D SELDERS CHARLES J SHEEHAN III JAMES E STOVER
JAMES D SHELTON ALAN R SMITH ROBERT E SMITH VERNON P SMITH ANTHONY J SPIRITO JR
ANTHONY J SCHNELLER JR LOUIS F STAPLES CHARLES R STEVENSON STEVEN J STROUB ERNEST V TAYLOR
WESLEY G THURSTON ROBERT TORRES ENRIQUE VASQUEZ WILLIAM E WEST EDWIN R WIERZBA
STANLEY K WOODWARD HOWARD D AKEHURST PAUL J BACHMAN CURTIS F BAGGETT ROBERT E BALDWIN
LARRY G BARHAM IVYL R BENDER RICHARD BENJAMIN WILLIAM H BLAKE JR FORREST L BOLIN
EDWARD J BOVA SAMUEL M BOYCE WAYNE D BOYER KENNETH R BRADLEY MELVIN J BYERS
EDWARD J BREWER RONALD L BROWN RONALD W BRYANT WILLIAM T BUCKLES DENNIS E BURKE
DAVID L BOWMAN JR DONALD F BURNETT BERNARD J BURNS JR JOSEPH CAMPBELL JOSEPH F CONVERY JR
WILLIS G CARDIN ARMANDO CHAPA JR DONALD E CLARK PAUL H CLINE THOMAS E CORLEY
JAMES E CRAVEN III EDWARD W CRUM GEORGE W CRUTHIRD JACK DECESARO JR JOHN W DOBY
RAYMOND E DUNLAP JOHN H EDWARDS JR WILLIAM EISTER WILLIAM D ELTRINGHAM MICHAEL A HODGE
JOHN P ESPARZA JR ROBERT E EWOLDT WILLIAM F FARRIS ALBERT R FOGG III ROBERT E FORSHEY
JAMES L FUCHS DONALD L GALLAGHER WILLIE GARCIA JR REGINALD J GAUTREAU WAYNE A GOETSCH
JOE W GREENE WAYNE S GREER DOUGLAS H GRIFFIN PETER R HANSEN JR ALLEN H HARANO
CHARLES J EISENACHER EUGENE E HENRY STEPHEN M HERMANSON LARRY B HULSEY ROY A HUSS
MICHAEL W JOHNS JAMES JOHNSON JR GREGORY JONES THOMAS P JONES BEN JOWERS JR
RONALD L KOCH RONALD E KONWINSKI EDWARD J KOWSKI JR ANDREW M LARSON DUANE E LITZINGER
CHARLES W LOLLIS GREGORY H LUNDE GLEN T LUNSFORD ROBERT S LUTZ ALVIN P MASON
GORDON B MATTHEWS ALONZO E MAYHALL THOMAS A MEADE ROBERT F MEGLIO MICHAEL D MILBURN
CHARLES C MITCHEM RONALD E MORRIS MICHAEL MULLERVY JOHN L MURPHY FRED L SALYER
BILLY W MCGHEE HOMER E MCKAY DENNIS D NEHRING JAMES C NEWMAN JR WILLIAM W NORMAN
RICHARD C O'BRIEN ROY T O'KEEFE LOUIS J ORISON PAUL R PADUCHOWSKI JIMMIE C PALMO
LOREN L PAMPEL WALTER T PANNELL JOHN J PETRILLO CHARLES E PHILLIPS KARL W POST
AURELIO R RAMON JR WILLIAM E RANC ROBERT K RAYMOND WILLIAM R ROBSON CONRAD E ROSS
CHARLES L MORRISON DONALD J RUSSIN JR PHILLIP L SALINAS WILLIAM A SAWYER RANDALL J SCHWENDY
CURTIS D SCOWDEN JAMES SEFRHANS PAUL D SHAMP JR HAROLD G SHIRLEY NOLAN L SIMMONS
JERRY G SIMS TERRENCE E STAUDOHAR JAN M STODDARD LARRY W STULL LOUIS V SUPINO
JONATHAN E SYKES NABOR R TAFOLLA GARY L TALLENTIRE ROBERT H TAYLOR TENNYSON A THOMAS
MELVIN C THOMPSON EDWARD S THURMOND JERRY T TILLERY PAUL D TINSON JOSE A TRAVIESO
LYNN M TRAVIS BRADFORD L TROUT JAMES E VIOLETT RICHARD A VOORHEES JAMES R WALDEN
DENNIS R WALLIN EARL W WATKINS JR CARL J WIENEKE TOMMY A WIGGINS JAMES L WISE JR
MICHAEL W WEBSTER DONALD L WILLIAMS RAYFIELD WILLIAMS ROBERT L WILSON JR DARREL Z WRIGHT
HENRY A WRIGHT RODERICK M WRIGHT WILLIAM L YOUNG JR JOSE G ABARA EARL F BURKE
DAVID M ANDERSON SANFORD K ARCHER EUGENE ASHLEY JR STANLEY L BAKER THO-AS L BEIERLE
GREG B BELEW CHARLES E BENNETT JOHN A BRADLEY RANDY H BROCK MICHAEL A DEETER
WILLIE H ADGER RAYMOND BROWN RONALD H BROWN RICHARD BURBACH LIONEL BUTLER SR
LAWRENCE CHAPLIN PAUL F CHARNETZKI ROBERT E COATES ERNEST W COLE JERRY L COLLIER
JOHN H BRANCATO JR RUSSELL B CORBIN JR MICHAEL A COUCH ANDY P CRAWFORD RICHARD S DORSCH
JAMES W DURHAM JR RANDOLPH A EDWARDS MANZELLE A FORD VERN J FRIED JOHN GIBSON
WALLACE L GIESEN JOE W GRIGSBY CHARLES C HALE JR KENNETH HANNA BILLY C HAYES
JERRY W GLEGHORN RODNEY G HINTON GARY W HOLBROOK ISMAEL HOLGUIN JAMES W HOLT

PANEL 38E

KENNETH W HUDSON JOHN J HUGHES TROY H HUNTER ROBERT A JENSEN
HAROLD O HOSKINS CALVIN O JACKSON JOHN P JACOBS DAVID R JOHNSON EVERETTE R JOHNSON
RONALD G JOHNSON RONALD J JOHNSON EVARISTO P JOHNSTON GEORGE E JONES JR LOWEN L JONES
EVERETT E JUSTICE JR LARRY W KANE DANIEL J KAPLAN STEVE N LAMBERT ROBERT R LORD
MYRON KOT CHARLES W LINDEWALD JR MICHAEL D LONG MICHAEL J LONGABARDI RONALD R LOVELAND
ROBERT F LUCERO JOSEPH MANDARINO SAMUEL T MARSHALL JR ANGEL MARTINEZ TOMMY R MEDLEY
JAMES L MCCOY TIMOTHY D MCHUGH JAMES H MILICH DONALD E MOORE JAMES L MORELAND
DAVID L MCPHERSON ROGER D MCQUAY BOYD J NELSON DONALD L NELSON LEWIS J NEWBERRY
VICTOR C NORDSTROM CLAUDE E NORTH THOMAS T OLIVER ARTURO M ORTIZ LARRY K POWELL
JOSEPH OSBORNE JR LARRINGTON OWENS DANIEL R PHILLIPS ROBERT C PIERCY BOBBY L PORTER
RONALD R PRATHER JR ADRIAN A QUICK JR ROBERT L QUICK VERNON C RANDOLPH GUIDO S REALI JR
HARMON L REMMEL III JAMES J RICE LARRY D RIPLEY WAYNE D ROBBINS JAMES E ROBINSON
NORMAN E ROSE III PRESTON I RUSSAW CECIL L RUSSELL DAVID A SANFORD THEODORE SHINGLETON JR
JACKIE G SMITH LARRY C SMITH MAYNARD L SMITH STEVEN E SMITH WILLIAM H SMITH JR
ROBERT H SODEN SAMUEL L SQUARRELL ROBERT J STATEN ARTHUR A STEPHENS JOHN A SURGALSKI
BRUCE E STRATE LAWRENCE H SWANSON RONNIE L TERRY DONALD R THOMPSON DARRELL C TROJAHN
ROBERT C TURNBULL DONALD G TUYES ALFRED URDIALES JR RICHARD M VASKO JAMES L WALLER
ROBERT J WEBB DAVID E WEDHORN GORDON J WETJEN VORIN E WHAN JR ALBERT D WHITE
ALGER L WHITE JR ROY E WORTH EVERETT A WYATT JR ROBERT L YORK RICHARD F CAVANAUGH
TOMMY E ANTRIM LESLEY S AYERS JOHN BARBURY MICHAEL B BARRETT MICHELE BASSO
THOMAS J BLAHA AMOS H BOUTWELL DONALD R BOWMAN JOSEPH B BOWMAN THOMAS H BRIGGS
KENNETH J ALLEN DAN E BRYAN DAVID E BRYANT JR JERRY C BURKHEAD ALBERTO CARRASQUILLO-DEN
JAMES S CERIONE III JAMES T CHAMBERS GERALD R CLEMSON FRANKLIN CLOVIS WILLIAM K COLEGATE
THOMAS R CRAIG JR PETE F CRUZ BRUCE E CUNNINGHAM RALPH A DAHM BILL N DALTON
DOUGLASS J DENNIS GEORGE R DENSLOW GUY D DICKIE WAYNE T DILLMAN RICHARD W FRANCE

PANEL 38E (*Continued*)

DARRELL E DUNLAP BRIAN F DURR ROBERT L DYKES JR MICHAEL R ELWELL DAVID D EUKEL
DANNY E DANIELS RICHARD A FEATHERSTONE JAMES P FERGUSON ROBERT D FLEER KENNETH C FORDHAM
JAMES E GEORGE JR GREGORY A GIFFORD WILLIAM L GLASPER RICHARD J GLENN LEON G GRESHAMER
LANNY E HALE DENNIS W HAMMOND ANTHONY W HANDLEY JOHN I HASELBAUER NED LEE
JOHNNIE B JACKSON LEONARD JACKSON JR JOHN L JERVIS III CHARLES E JOHNSON LESTER W JOHNSON JR
HOWARD L JOSELANE LEE C KINNEY MARK A KOLVEK ROBERT A LA BUDA ARTHUR W LA MORTE
WILLIAM F HARRINGTON ROBERT G LAPHAM HOWARD W LEE THOMAS C LEWER JAMES L LOPP
INNES L MARLAND DANIEL MEADE JIMMY A METCALF GLENN D MOORE ROBERT N MORDEN
DONNIE R MCCORMICK LARRY J MCCUBBINS ALLEN L MUMMERT JOHN R MURPHY PATRICK M MURPHY
ROY D MCDANIEL ALLEN MCKINLEY BERNARD B MCKINNEY JR DAVID L MCKINNEY JAMES R NEAL
JAMES E PARKER RONALD L PEMBLETON LE R PETER AQUILLA A PHILLIPS JOHN C PONDOFF
JOHN R POSO SPENCER B POWERS JR WALTER R PRATT JESUS P RAMIREZ FRANK RAMOS JR
JAMES P RIZZO TERENCE R ROACH JR RONALD C ROUNTREE JAMES F SCOTT WILFRED L SOLOMON SR
JOSEPH B ROBINSON DANIEL E SIRIANNI ARVID B SKUZA JOHN A SMITH LEONARD A STALNAKER
TOMMY L STEWART KLAUS J STRAUSS MICHAEL X SULLIVAN FREDDIE L THOMAS ONNIE THOMPSON JR
RODNEY P TROYER LAWRENCE K TUTTLE JEFFREY M WALSH GREGORY C WEISNER JOHN A WILCOX JR
MANUEL P TORRES HENRY YORK JOSEPH S ZAWTOCKI JR ROBERT J ALLEN DONALD D ALVIS
RAY E ALWINE JAMES R ANDERSON ROY L ANDERSON WILLIAM E ANDERSON PAUL R ANZELONE
THOMAS A BACKY JOHN R BARFIELD ALFRED H BLEIGH JR DARREL A BONDROWSKI CHARLES J CRAWFORD JR
DAVID L BOYD FRANKLIN S BRADLEY JR JAMES J BRENNAN BYRON L BROWN RONALD L BROWN
DAVID BUURSMA ROBERT S BYRNES KENNETH CAMPBELL BERNARD J CARON ROBERT N CARTER
SALVADOR M BANAGA JR STEVEN E CLARK BONNIE L COLEMAN JOSEPH P CONKLIN JOSE G CORTEZ
DONALD E DAWSON JR CLYDE L DE MELLO LOYAL B DOTY ARNOLD M DURYEA STANTON R DYKE
CECIL W EPPS LEONARD E EULITT WILLIAM N FLINT JOHN C GLESENKAMP WILLIAM J GOLDBERG
CHARLES O GOODMAN DAVID H GREEN JR DONALD J HAILE PETER B HEDLUND NORMAN C KISSINGER
BISMARK W HENRY LAUREN J HEYDINGER FRANK E HILTE CHARLES E HOFFMAN GARY D HOLLAND
NORMAN W HOLMES NORBERT P HOLZAPFEL RICKY L HULL GREGORY T IDING JOHN A ILSTRUP JR
DAVID R JONES GARY C JONES MARK S KAYE RONALD N KELLER MICHAEL G KINDRED
LAMBERT A GOMEZ KENNETH L KIRKES RUSSELL W KRILL RAYMOND C LAWSON LONNIE G LE BOMBARB
DAVID E LITTLETON MICHAEL L LOVATO MICHAEL J LYNCH ROGER G LYONS CHARLES R MARTIN
CHARLES P MCCAFFREY WALTER R MCDONALD RAMON A MEEKER JAMES G MILLER MARVIN E MONROE
SAMUEL T MCDOWELL JR ROBERT J NARDELLI THOMAS NORTON JERRY A NOVAKOVICH CHARLES E NOVEL
JOHN A PAGE RAYMOND J PALACIO JOHN J PALMIERI RICHARD PEREZ LARRY L PHELPS
JACK C PLAHN MICHAEL PUMILLO DAVID D REID WILLIS C RHEAULT RONALD E ROHRKASTE
JOSEPH W ROUNSEVILLE GARY E SALISBURY ROBERT L SHARPLESS DARRELL W SIBERT HAROLD L SMITH
THOMAS J SPARKS FREDERICK M STEMEN HAROLD D STOKES JAMES P STRAIN BENJAMIN J TEREJKO JR
JESS THOMAS CHARLES P TORLIATT JR WILLIAM H UNDERWOOD DOUGLAS B WADE DONALD S WAITE
WALTER R WASCHICK GERALD P. WILLIAMS ED WORTHEY ROBERT E WRIGHT WILLIAM D WYANT
IGNACIO ALVAREZ JR RICHARD M ANDERSON JACKIE W BERRY EDWARD J BREFCZYNSKI SIDNEY L LEONARD
BERNARD P BREITENBACH WILLIAM L BROWN RAYMOND A BURGESS GLENN H CALVIN CLARENCE R HOLT
EARNEST W CARAWAY GARY S CHRISTENBURY JOHN D'ADAMO JR GAIL DENHAM JR DAVID R DEVIK
KENNETH L DEVOR THOMAS E DOBRINSKA JOSEPH H DOWNING JR GERALD T GALLAGHER ROBERT R GRAY
RONALD D BUNTING EARL W HAUG LARRY L HOYT HUGH R JOHNSON JR EUGENE V SONNER
MICHAEL P ANDERSON FRANCIS KAIRAITIS GENE D KILLGORE ROGER G LEADBETTER WALTER B MAKSYMIW
BOBBY D MATHENY STEPHEN D MAZZA JOHN J MCELROY WILLIE B MCNEILL HOWARD L PAINTER
CARL E PETERSON THOMAS M PINATELLI MICHAEL J RAMBERG JOHN W ROWDEN DILLARD G RYE
ARTHUR HINES VICTOR P SHERMAN JR DONALD B SIEKIERKA EDWARD H STUART THEODORE J STURTEVANT
GEORGE S SUTTON TROY T THREET WILLIE C TORRENCE LUIS F VELEZ GEORGE W WALBRIDGE
ALBERTIS WILLIAMSON CHESTER W WILSON JAMES D WILSON CHARLES WOOD MARLYN R ANDERSON
RONALD S BAGEN STEPHAN L BECHTEL JOSEPH P BOWLING GIVEN W BRADLEY DOYLE L BUTLER JR
ADALBERTO CACERES DONALD R COLSON JAMES P CROOK MONZIE D EDMONDS THOMAS G GAINES
DONALD A HAUSRATH JR PETER A HILL GEORGE J HOUSE DANNY R HOWELL GERALD A HUCZEK
DENNIS M KEEFE RONALD J KELLEY CRAIG G KNOBLOCH RAUL R LAMAS ANDREW E LE BEAU
CHARLES E MCDOWELL MICHAEL J MUETING MICHAEL NEMETH IRVING C PIERCE JR JEFFREY A PINHEIRO
RALPH H REID CLYDE A RHINEHART RONALD E SATCHELL KENNETH E SCHNEIDER WALTER M SCOTT
RICHARD L SORENSEN FRANK L STEC SAMUEL R STEWART III JOHN A SULLIVAN MICHAEL M SWEENEY
GEORGE E TAFOYA JAMES E TINSLEY ROBERT L TURNER GARRY F VICKERY DANIEL J VILLEGAS

PANEL 39E

STANLEY E WATSON JOHN K WOODS MICHAEL M ALLEY CHARLES E YOUNGBLOOD
WILLIAM J BLOCK JOHN N BROCKMAN HARRY W BROWN CRAIG H BUELL BERTRAM A BUNTING
GARY R CATES ALVIN R CHURCH JAMES L COKER GREGORY C CONANT TERRY M CURTIS
LEROY E DAMIANO LEO P DUNSMORE MICHAEL W ENBODY LESLIE J FROLICH GERALD GOINS
RONALD A GREENWALD WADE L GROTH LARRY L HACKLEMAN WILLIAM A HARTER RONNIE J HOFFMAN
ALAN W GUNN ELVESTER HESTER JR BRUCE G HOWERTER ROBERT L HUGHES JEFFREY A HULTS
MARTIN JASSO WILLIAM F JOINER DERYL R KIRKWOOD LARRY W LA POINT STEVE W LEWICKI
FREDERICK G LOPEZ GEOVEL LOPEZ-GARCIA DONNIE J MARLAR ROBERT W MAY LESTER E MAYNARD
CALVIN R MACKAY JESSE MECHEM ARNOLD E MELISH JOHN D MENDOZA DENNIS D NAGELKIRK
ROBERT M NIX DONALD B OLSEN JOSEPH L OSTIFIN RALPH E PETERS JOHN C PRICE
EDMUND A O'CONNOR THOMAS D POOLE ROBERT E PRESTON ROBERT W PRINE RONALD D ROACH
JERRY L ROE ROBERT J RUHL JR JOHN M RUPERT ROBERT C SCHULTZ WILLIE C SCOTT
KALEY A SONNER LARRY K SPANGLER ULYSSES STEWART VICTOR M STRIBLING BOBBY C SUTHERLAND
WILLIAM A SIMS JOHN H SUYDAM III KENNETH E TICHNELL GERALD A TUCKER JAMES P VOJIR
RICHARD E WAGNER WILLIAM J WEBER DAVID C WILLIAMS RANDALL A WOOLCOTT WILLARD G WRIGHT
MAX R BEAVER RONNIE L ADAMS JAMES C ALBERTINI LARRY ANDERSON FRANCIS I ARNETT
LARRY W BARNARD WINFIELD W BECK RONALD L BLACKSTEN JAMES L BROWN JR ROBERT G BURR
EUGENE M CAMPION RODNEY S CANTOHOS JOHN L CAREY ROBERT J CHAMBERS DONALD H COLEMAN
JIMMIE M COUTO WAYNE F CRAPSE JIMMY A DARNELL JOSEPH D DAUGHTON JR JOHN L STOW
ERNEST F DAVIDOVE MIGUEL A DIAZ-COLLAZO ARTHUR L EDMONDS JR ROBERT A ELIA EDWARD S ESTES
JAMES F FUQUA JACK W GRANDAHL EDDIE C HARRIS FRANKLIN D HATTON RONALD W SHIELDS
DANIEL A HILDEBRANDT PETER W JOHNSON DONALD LETA PERFECTO N LOPEZ CHARLES R MORGAN
DENNIS R LANGROCK JOHN M MARTIN ROBERT C MAURICE JERRY D MOUNTS ROBERT J NELSON WILBURN F VAUGHT
HARRY F PEEPLES GARY C PORT VERNON POST JR STEVEN E REICHERT AARON H REIGLE
RAMON H GONZALEZ HOBERT T ROLLINS JEROME A SCHUETT JAMES D SHAW RODGER W SIPP
LESTER E SMART JR JESSE L SMITH KELLYNN V SNOW FELIX SOSA-CAMEJO WAYNE J SPARE
NORMAN T D'AGOSTINO TIM THOMAS ALEX R TOLPAROFF ROBERT J WIGGIN ROBERT E WILLIAMS
TERRY W WILLIAMS RAFTKEITH E BAKER FRANK A BEAVERS HAROLD L BEGODY HOWARD C BELL
JOHN G BELLANGER WILLIAM BLAKELY LEONEL BUENTELLO FREDERICK W BUNGARTZ CHARLES M BURKE
FRANK P CAPUANO BEN E CAUSEY JR LOWELL T COMBS JEHU J COX JR RODOLFO DE LEON
GEORGE H DIZE DON M DOORNBOS JOSEPH P DUNN ROBERT M ELLIOT LARRY W ELLIOTT
DENNIS K FLEMING EDWARD L FRAZIER LAWRENCE E GIBSON JOHN GODFREY JR LARRY J GOSS
RANDALL J GUSTAFSON CARLTON B HALCOMB EDMOND HAMPTON JERRY A HURD THOMAS A JOHNSON
DAVID G ISBELL JERRY W JENKINS WILLIAM C JENKINS DOHN W JOHNSON MELVIN L JONES
LOUIS W KALB RONALD F KLOS MICHAEL J KURELLA DONALD L LLOYD ALLEN T SMITH
BENNIE L MARTIN ROBERT C MCMAHAN DAVID J MONCAVAGE THOMAS Y OSBORNE LUTHER PAGE JR
WAYMAN E PASKINS ROBERT J PASTORE ALBERT E PATRICK CHARLES O PENNEY LIONEL N PHILLIPS JR
DAVID W PIPPIN JOHN W PYLE WILLIAM R REESE BARRY L RIGSBY GERALD W ROBERTSON
JOSE J SANTIAGO FRANK J SCHAP DAVID F SCHNEIDER ORVILLE A SHEETS STEVEN G SLACK
LEMMIE D LUNSFORD CHARLES A STOVALL WILLIAM D THOMAS ALBERT A TIPPETT VERNON S TSCHERTER
JOHN F TYRRELL VITALIO VELA JR ERNEST M WEATHERSBEE JOSEPH R WEAVER JR JEFFREY R WENTZELL
JAMES W WILSON SPENCER ADAMS CHARLES L BAUGH JAMES H BENNETT JAMES G BLAINE
HARRY G BLOOMFIELD ROBERT F BRULTE JR EMANUEL F BURROUGHS DAVID M CASH DALE L DAVIS
PETER COLICCHIO KENNETH L CRYSEL DONALD M DALE LUNAS J DANIELS WILLIAM M DANIELS
MICHAEL M CADY HERBERT C DAVIS JAMES T DAVIS WARREN M DIXON DENNIS DORSEY
DONALD L DYRESON RUSSELL J FAUSER JR MARION F FERGUSON DOUGLAS M FRACKER VERNON H LACKEY
LESTER FREEMAN SPENCER S FREESTONE KENNETH L FULTON JAMES T GAYNOR FREDERICK W HAAS
JAMES M HILL JOHN B HOGAN EARNEST P HOLMES JR MARK E JAMES STANLEY M JAMROCK
CHARLES W EGLIN III ROBERT K KAWAMURA DAVID E KEISTER MICHAEL J KELLY ROGER G LEE
CLAYTON LIGGINS THOMAS J MARGLE CHARLES F MCGRATH DOMENICO MORGERA JR PATRICK W MURPHY
EARL MACK CLYDE R MCAFEE MURAL MCDANIEL RUSSELL W NAUGLE BRUCE A NELSON
JOHN R PERRETTA ANTHONY J PODEBRADSKY GARRY R POWELL EDWARD B QUILL JR ALVIN L RAPER
RAMON S RODRIGUEZ MELVIN H SANDERS STEVAN R SARGENT JIMMY L SILER EURAL STANLEY JR
KARL W SCHWANBECK JAMES J STEWART ROY F SWED HENRY M TABET WADE E THACKREY JR BRENT J TOSH
REX F TUTOR BENJAMIN S UNDERHILL DONALD W VAUGHN RICHARD P VELLANCE KARL M WALDRON JR
RALPH L WILLIAMS ROGER G WILSON JAMES L WOOD ROBERT E ALEXANDER CHARLES A ALVAREZ
CHARLES E ANDERSON WILLIAM BONEY ANTHONY L CAPOZZI GERALD E GORDON PAUL A JENSEN
KENNY L COLTER KEITH D COON DONALD W DIXON STEVEN E EMRICK JAMES O FEEMAN
TAYLOR W FOREMAN JR ARTHUR T FRILEY BOBBY F GALBREATH DERYL R GARVICK ALEXANDER GIEJC
RICHARD L BOSWORTH HAROLD P GRAY WILLIAM L GREENWELL BARRY N GRIGSBY STANLEY C GROVE
PAUL M ASH HERBERT D HAMMONS DONALD A HIERLMEIER ROBERT S HUTCHINSON II GARY D JOHNSON
KENNETH R JOHNSON JEROME R KELLY ERNEST F LAWRENCE WILLIAM A LEE GEORGE G LESCARBEAU
SUN T LITTLE ADOLFO LUNA HARRY E MATTHEW GERALD L MILBRODT ANTHONY MONTANO
BENNIE E MCCORKLE HAROLD G MCDOWELL JACKIE M MORGAN THOMAS H MORRIS DONALD J WIELINSKI
ROGER D PYNE CULLEN W QUIN JOHN H REYNOLDS JOHN K RIPEL RANDALL L SAUNDERS
HARRY W SCHNEIDER WAYNE T SEVERINO SANDY L SHULL EUGENE A SORENSON JAMES F SOSNOWSKI
JOSEPH V SPELLMAN DANIEL M STONE PEARLY J THOMAS ROBERT B THOMSON JIMMY E TOLLIVER
JAMES D MCALISTER VALENTINE B VOLLMER ALEXANDER K WARD CORDELL E WOODS HAROLD W ABBOTT
CHESTER L COONS CLAYBORN W ASHBY JR FRANCIS S BECHTOLD DAVID A BERNHEISEL ROGER L COUICK
FRANK A DAWSON CHRISTOPHER G DELGADO PAUL N DONATO WILLIAM L DRAPER DAVID W FRAVEL
JAMES T GORDON TERRENCE C GRAVES HENRY GREGORY BLAKE H HALFMAN GLENN M HAYDEN
HENRY F HENDERSON III FRANK L HOGE ROBERT A JACKSON SYLVESTER W MCFARLAND AMON F MOORE JR
GEORGE M KIHNLEY THOMAS W KLORAN JAMES S KRAVITZ JOHN F LEWIS CARL C LOWERY
DENNIS J LULOFS WILLIAM T MANGUM JR JAMES E MARTIN THOMAS V MAYBURY THOMAS O MEEK
CHARLES P HEADLEY JAMES E HONEYCUTT RONALD L MCELROY ALOYSIUS P MCGONIGAL JAMES F MEYER JR
LARRY R MCKINNEY DALE S MCWRIGHT LEWIS R NOBLE RICHARD W PERSHING KENNETH W RADONSKI
SAMUEL J SANTANGELO ANDRES SORCHINI KENNETH E STETSON WILTON H THOMAS JAMES C WONN
GARY R SMITH CURTIS F THURMAN DAVID H WARNER WILBURN E WESTER MAURICE T WILLIAMS
JERRY D ADAMS JOSEPH C ANDREW MICHAEL F AUSTIN BRIAN W BATES ROY V BERRY JR

PANEL 40E

TERRY L BOYCE TOMMIE BRANDON CHARLIE A BRATCHER JOEL K BROWN
JEFFREY R BYRNE DARRELL L CABELL BRUCE L CAREY HOWARD R CARPENTER JR JOAQUIN CASTRO
RHONDAL G CLAYPOOL DALLAS D CUMMINGS LOUIS W CUSSINS WILLIAM M DE VOS GREGORY J EVANS
J B CATHEY EDWARD E DEW JAMES D DOUGLAS DONALD T EWALT LAWRENCE J FARELLI
RICHARD H FOX DENNIS W FRISBEE CARROLL B FULLER NORMAN D GREEN JOE M GUTIERREZ
DENNIS F HAHN LAWRENCE E HAMES RICHARD M HAMMOND JAMES P HARKANSON DAVID W HECK
ORVILLE W HEIGHTLAND JR JOE L JONES REUBEN JONES JR DANIEL L KICK MICHAEL C KINSEY
MICHAEL L KOSKOVICH LLOYD G LAMMEY BOBBY E LEE RAYMOND R LEWIS WAYNE E LEWIS JR
PATRICK E LINDSTROM ADRIAN S LOPEZ CLARENCE F MAAS III BENJAMIN F MATTISON CHARLES J PATRIZIO
ANDREW MATYAS RONALD L MCCOLLUM CHARLIE R MILLER JR JAMES H MILLER ROBERT L MOSLEY
CARL L LJUNG JOHN A NEVELS ROBERT V NOWAK ROBERT L PETERSON LEONARD M PHIPPS
DAVID K POMEROY CHARLES B POOLE JOHNNIE W POTTS RICHARD C RAMSEY DAVID M SCHASRE
DANIEL R SCOTT THOMAS L SENN KENNETH M SHANNON KENNETH W SHAPLAND GARRY D SHEPPARD
JAMES G STANDEFER TERRY J SUTTON HOMER TAYLOR JR MARVIN H TERRY MICHAEL B TURNER
VINCENT M SORANNO WILLIAM J THORNHILL JOSEPH P TURNBULL LUKAS J VENTLINE RICHARD J VONASEK
CLIFFORD W WALKER ALAN W WILLARD DANIEL WILLIAMS III NOEL D WILLIAMS DOUGLAS A YOUNG
TIMOTHY C AGARD JOSEPH T BAILEY RONALD D BAPP WILLIAM E BOONE JAMES C FOSTER
ROBERT J BRIDGES JR ASHLAND F BURCHWELL ALEX L BURGESS STEPHEN COHAN TIMOTHY L COLLIER
ALBERT DANDRIDGE LARRY W DARLING BILL W DEETZ MELVIN C DYE KENNETH P EHNIS
STEVEN R ANDERSON MICHAEL W ELBEN TERRENCE E FEDOR JAMES L FELTY JOSEPH K FISH
EARNEST W FOWLKE GEORGE R FULLER JOHN H GFELLER DOUGLAS J GLOVER ROBERT D GRIFFIS
RONNIE HARRELL BOBBY R HATFIELD WILLIAM W HOOK KENNETH E HORNBAKER JOSEPH S SOBCZAK II
JOHN R HUSCHER WILLIAM JENKINS BENJAMIN F JOHNSON III TIMOTHY J KAPOUN MARTIN R KNIGHT
RONALD B LANNING DAVID H LEWIS THOMAS E LILLEY THOMAS J LOBACK JOHN B MADISON
ERNEST MAHONEY DONALD F MARSHALL II CHARLES J MARTIN JOHN E MILANOWSKI LARRY R MOORE
SYLVESTER MCCULLOUGH HERMAN MCKINNIE THOMAS J MOORE JAMES E MULLINS RICHARD D ODAFFER
WILLIAM L MCMAHON DANIEL A NELSON MICHAEL W NORMAN BILLY R NORRIS CHARLES E OLSON
JOHN PASS III WALTER M PATTERSON JAMES D PENTLAND DAVID A PITTS SEVENTY J POLLOCK
CARL A RATTEE MICHAEL J REINHOLD JOHN T ROBERSON RICHARD S ROBERTS RAYMOND RODRIGUEZ
DONALD P ROEMER GRADY SCOTT ROBERT W SEATON WILLIAM R SEIBERT
RICHARD A SHARPE WILLIAM C SHUMATE ADRIAN E SIGLER BOBBIE E SIKES JERRY D SISCO JR
ROBERT S GRIFFITH BERNARD E SMITH ENRIQUE L SOLIZ WILTON J SULLINGER JR LUCIEN C TESSIER
TERRY L SCHAUB FRANCIS S TORRE ROBERT E TYNER BARTON J UPLINGER ALFRED VALDEZ THOMAS C VAUGHAN
MELVIN U WANGESHIK MICHAEL W WARREN JAMES R WEBSTER JR DOUGLAS C WILLIAMS ARCHIE V WILLIS
KEVIN E VER PAULT JIMMY D WINCHESTER ARKIE J WRIGHT JAMES A ANDERSON MICHAEL A ANDREWS
JOHN A BAFILE JOHN F BARANOSKI RONNIE O BIGELOW DANIEL R BODIN DAVID R BOSWORTH
ROBERT R BOYLE DONALD G BRANT RAYMOND E CARPENTER ALBERTO COLON HURSHELL H GOUGH
JOE M COPELAND RAY D CROPPER THOMAS A ECKL ALEXANDER FEDOROFF KENNETH L FETTER
GERALD W CONNER JOSEPH T GALLAGHER ARMONDO A GOMEZ GEORGE W GRAVES III JEFFREY W GREEN
JAMES W GUEST STEPHEN M HANSEN JIMMIE L HARVIN STEVEN HERNANDEZ DONALD L HERNDON
JOSE B HERRERA JEFFREY L HOLBROOK DANIEL HOLCOMB ALEKI JEREMIA JAMES A JOHNSON
JIMMIE D JONES RICHARD J KELLEY DENNIS D KING LAUNEY E KING MICHAEL T LA COSTE
GUY E LEE NICHOLAS P LIGAMMARI DONALD J LOZANO ALBERT MARTIN DENNIS S MICHAEL
RONALD J MCCOY MARVIN L MILLER MICHAEL G MOHAREMOFF JAMES E MURRAY MICHAEL P PELLEGRINO
MICHAEL J MCGINNIS LARRY D NEASBITT TERRY Y OGAMI GALEN E OHLSON ALFRED R OLSON
DAVID L MOREHOUSE JOHN M OLSZEWSKI VINCENT B PARKHURST ROY B PARSONS DONALD D PHILBECK
MICHAEL W PICARD DARRYL W POINTER ARNOLD W PRICE GARRY E ROGERSON GEORGE W RUSHING
TERRY L SMITH SAM W STEWART BOBBY R TALTON STEPHEN P THUET PAUL R URBAN JR
RONALD M URBANSKI DAVID N VALERIO WALTER E VONDERCHEK JAMES L WEST ALBERT C WOODS JR
RICHARD D VICK HOWARD WILLIAMS JOSEPH P ZALE DALE E ANDERSON WALTER G ANDERSON
ROBERT N BAKER BARTOLOME A BALDERA JACK W BRASINGTON JAMES D BROWN RAYMOND D BURBAGE
FLORENTINO CANTU JR PAUL M DOUGLAS RICHARD P FRASCA PAUL D HERSCHBACH JOE L PEAKE
CHARLES R HORTON JOSEPH HUDSON JR ZYGMUNT P JABLONSKI JR THOMAS L JORDAN RAMON JURADO
WILLIAM T CONLEY JOHN W KINNEY JOHN J KOPFER FRANK R MANELLO WILBERT PETERS
LUCIEN ROBINSON ROY R ROBINSON WALTER ROBINSON ROBERT J ROSENWALD WILLIAM A ROZZI
LENNIE H SCHARFF CLIFFORD C SIMS WILLIAM G SMITH PAUL P SONSTEIN PAUL STASKO JR
TERRY M ABBOTT JOHN R ALLISON SAMUEL L ANDERTON WILLIAM E BOBBITT MAURICE BOGGUESS
TERANCE M BOZARTH ROBERT R BRETT WARREN R BROWN DAVID J CAVIS ALEXANDER S CHIN
KENDALL H CLARK WAYNE D CLEMENTS CHARLES W CLINE MICHAEL S COLLINS DAVID A CRAMER
THEODORE COAXUM JAMES S COMBS RICHARD A CONTRERAS HOWARD M COX LARRY C COX
TERRENCE M DALE DOUGLAS O DAVIS ROBERT E DOOLEY JAN D DOXEY THOMAS E FALK
GREGORY W FISCHER JULIUS C FOSTER ARTHUR D FREDERICK EDWARD W GERO DANNY L GILSTRAP
WILLIAM A GLEIXNER HENRY H GRAHAM RANDALL A HENZE RONALD L HILL JAMES L HOLLAND
JOHN E ISHMAN WILLIE JACKSON JON A JULIA JAMES A KOCH KENNETH W ROCHE
ROBERT C KRUMM JOHN R LAWRENCE ROLAND P LEVESQUE WILLIAM C LING FRANK J MADRID
BILLIE R MCCALL HERMAN MCGEE GREGORY MCINTYRE ROBERT J NEAL JOE M NEILL
ELVAIN E NIOUS BERNARD J NOVAK LARRY D POWELL CORNELIUS PRESSLEY FRED REAVES JR
ALBERT KAPLAN JAMES T RILEY GEORGE J SCHULTZ KENNETH D SCOTT ROBERT B SELBY
HECTOR L SEMIDEY CARY C SMITH JERRY W SMITH BRUCE A SWAIM LEE G TOLLEY
REGGIE L VANCE JOHN D VAUGHAN JAN B WAHL GENE J WHEAT THOMAS E WHITAKER
LOYD M WILLSON WESLEY L WOODFORD EDWARD L WORTHINGTON EMIL J WURTZ EDWARD ZAMORA
LARRY ADAMS GUY R BEAN GOLA C BETLEYOUN THOMAS H BIRCH JAMES R BRYANT
RUBEN A BURGESS JAMES CHISHOLM LONNIE W CLARK JAMES R ETHERIDGE JERRY D EVANS
ROBERT E GREEN DONALD G HICKS WILLIAM R HIGHT THOMAS W HILL LOUIS A MARTINEZ
WESLEY E HODGES GEORGE L HUBLER RICHARD A HUEFFNER DAVID ISOM MICHAEL E MCKEEVER
VICTOR GONZALEZ JR RODNEY W JOHNSON JACK G KRIDER DELBERT L LEASURE DAVID R LEHR
KIM W JOHNSON DOUGLAS M MCNABB RANDY C MOORE VINCENT A MOTTOLA DENNIS E MUSSMAN

PANEL 41E

WAYNE E PINGEL ALFRED E PLAEP JR JAMES S STRICKLAND JR JAMES C THOMASON
CHARLES E PURSER FRANKLIN D RAY HORRIS G ROBINSON PAUL E ROBITAILLE LEE M ROWELL
JOSE A SALDIVAR JOHN L SAUNDERS WILLIE F SHIPMAN DENNIS L SIEGEL RAYMOND R SPROUL
JAMES R OAKLEY DANNY R PIERCE JOHN SPURLOCK CHARLES F STROCK ALLAN F SULLIVAN
GARY W THORPE RODOLFO A VASQUEZ RONALD L WEAVER ALFONZIA WILLIAMS TINEY W WINTERS
EUGENE C WIRE CARLOS C AGUIRRE GERALD W ALLEN JOHN T BECK ANTON D BLOEMHARD
CLIFFORD G BORRELL NED R BROWN FELIPE CANTU JR LUIS A COLON ARTHUR CRESPIN
FERDINANDO DISTEFANO PATRICK H DOWNEY WALTER D FAITH JONATHAN R GADDIS BROADUS D HILYER
BRUCE J DENT JAMES GORMLEY WALTER H HUCKS ROBERT B HUDSON FRANK J WOLFE
KENNETH K HUTTON GERRIE G JEFFRIES HOWARD L JONES JR PAUL D KNOWLTON PATRICK C LUCA
DAVID G LUPIEN JOHN C MARTIN JOSEPH MCCLOYN MAX A NELSON RICHARD A ROTHERY
ALFRED S NAJAR JR ROBERT E OSUSKI CARL J REID JOHNNY ROSE JR LOWELL V SMITH
TERRY W SUTTON JULIUS N SZAHLENDER NORMAN E THOMAS WILLIAM R TRUSTY JR M B WALKER JR
LAURENCE J HERFEL LEON E WATERS JR WILLIAM L WATSON MORRIS A WHITEHEAD JIMMIE D WHITLOCK
JAMES L ZYPH MAXIE E ACKERMAN RONALD P AKINS MICHAEL B BAPTISTE JOSEPH C BATTLE
LAWRENCE F BEALS DONNELL BELL JAMES E BENTLEY JR FREDERICK A BILLINGHAM JR JAMES C BLOUNT
MICHAEL J BRELLENTHIN BARTON W BROOKS JOE H BROWN JAMES R BRUDER DANIEL D CALLAHAN
LESTER E CHAMBERS KENNETH F CHASTINE KENNETH W CLAIRE RONNIE L CLARK DOYLE G CLAY
NOBLE COLLINS JR JERRY L COLLISTER ROSA L DE LA JR JERRY L DODSON PETER J FILIPIAK
THOMAS J COONEY GERALD T DOUGLASS JR RICHARD J FAULKNER CHARLES G GELLER WILLIAM A GIBSON
DENNIS F GULICH PHILLIPS HAYES III ROBERT L HEARD MANUELITO L HERRERA VERLIN D HOLDERBY
WILLIAM E HUFF GORDON K HUGHES DONALD JACQUES STANLEY JOHNSON BRUCE E JONES
EDWARD KASNOW LARRY W KRAFT RONALD L KUSTABORDER MICHAEL J LADEROUTE DENNIS E LANE
LEWIS N LANGFORD JOHN A LASSITER LESLIE R LEWIS JOHN J MAGEE WILLIAM C MARSH
CHARLES T MARTIN GEORGE MCCLELLAND RICHARD B MCDANIEL KIM E MEADS LLOYD W MOORE
HENRY MCDONALD III RICHARD W MCKENZIE WILLIAM L NEWSOME FRANK D ORTEGA EARL E PARKER
GEORGE PAROUNAGIAN JR WILLIAM T PITTMAN ARNOLD J RIVERA CHARLES E ROBENA GEARWIN P TOUSEY
GUSTAVO ROTGER JR WILLIE J RUFF RICHARD M SCALA DAVID C SCARBROUGH DANIEL R SCHUEREN
MICHAEL D SHEAHAN STEPHEN A SHELLEY ROBERT L SIMMONS EDWARD SINGLETON JR PATRICK SKEET
WALTER F SKINNER DOUGLAS W SMITH FORREST F SPITLER JOHN R STEVENSON SIDNEY T STRATTON
NATHAN L ROBINSON FRANK A SZYMANSKI IV CLAYTON J THEYERL JAMES V THORNTON GERALD F TRACY
LARRY J TYLER ALBERT WARD FREDERICK C WEBBER DONALD E WHITAKER GEORGE D WHITELAW
ROBERT A WIEDEMAN FREDERICK T WILLIAMS BOBBY WILSON JERRY L WININGHAM JAMES A WOOD
BARRY M WOPINSKI MICHAEL C ZELLER WILLIAM E ADAMS ANDREW A ALLEN III ROY ALLEN
ROGER C ATKINSON WILLIAM M BAGSHAW CALVIN H BIGGER RAYMOND J BRERETON EUGENE M MOPPERT
ROBERT W BROWN JR ERNEST CHAFFINS JR WILLIAM D CHOI MICHAEL COTTON ROBERT S CRAGIN JR
JAMES E DEESE JR JAY C DYER GARFIELD EVANS MICHAEL S GARRETT RODGER R HERTEL
DENNETTE A EDWARDS III WILLIAM H GOINS STEVEN V GOLDSTEIN ROBERT B HEDGE STEPHEN L HUBER
WILLIE L JAMES ROBERT A JANS DENNIS J KROMREY ANTHONY LA ROCCO GARY K LANNOM
LAWRENCE G LEIGH JR DAVID J LINK BILLY D LIVINGSTON PHILLIP W LUCAS FRANK J MATHEWS
GERALD W MCCAFFREY ALLAN L MCCALL ISMAEL MENENDEZ-OCASIO
GERARD M MCDONALD SAMUEL D MCINTURF JAMES W NICHOLS JR WAYNE B PLATT MARK E POLICASTRO
ROBERT L REEVES SHERWOOD REYNOLDS JOSEPH M SINKEWICZ DAVID L SMITH JOHN M SPIELMAN
ROY S SPURGEON PAUL F STEDMAN JOHN L STEWART MILES B STUART RANSOM L STUCK
ALVIN R BROWN ROBERT D MURPHY JR THOMAS J SWEENEY EDWARD J TARIN MONTE E VANSKIKE TERRY L VINGE
ROBERT L WALKER ROBERT L WATTS RICHARD D WILLIAMS RICHARD J WILT MICHAEL V WRIGHT JOSEPH A ZUNIGA

261

THE VIETNAM VETERANS MEMORIAL COLLECTION

KENNETH E ALESHIRE RAMIRO ALVARADO KENNETH S ANDRADE RICHARD R BALLANTINE ERNEST E BEAM
JOHN E BERGER ROSCOE E BRYANT DOUGLAS J BURDICK ROY N BURRIS RAMIRO CARDENAS
JOHN E DILLARD STANLEY E GRAVES JR ROBERT L HAIR JOHN F HARTZHEIM ROBERT H MCCOLLUM
ARTHUR W HEROD DENNIS W JACOBS RAYMOND O KENNEDY MICHAEL S KRAVCHAK CHARLES H STANLEY
JAMES L LIEN LAWRENCE F LUBONSKI ABELARDO MALAVE-RIOS PAUL L MILIUS PAUL J MILLER
RICHARD E GRIER LOUIS H MCFARLAND ROBERT E MINO EDWARD L NIEBUR FREDERICK J O'CONNOR JR
GILBERT S PALMER LARRY W PETETT ROBERT L POWERS FERNANDO M QUINTERO RODNEY A ROAT
HAROLD M RENWICK JR WILLIAM W ROUSH RUFFIN J SATTERWHITE JR MITCHELL F SEK LARRY E SINKS
JOSE A HINOJOSA DUANE H SNYDER GEORGE E SPECK THEODORE A STAMPFLI CORNELIUS W STRASSNER
JOSE R TAVAREZ JIMMY M TROLLINGER ANTHONY N VALENTE VERNON L WALKER JEIDER J WARREN
RICHARD D WELCH CHARLES E WILLIAMS THOMAS C WRIGHT THOMAS T WRIGHT JAMES D YOUNGHAM
RICHARD C ADAMO FRANK T ALDAY ARCHIE ANDERSON DAVID Z BALADES JAMES F BAUCOM
ALFREDO BENIGNI MARTIN L BENNETT JAMES BOYD KENNETH R BRADLEY EDGAR J BROSSMAN
ROBERT E CALDWELL JAMES D CHAMBERS MELVIN E CHLOUPEK RONALD S CHRISTMAN KLAUS D EGOLF
RONALD T KRANSI DENNIS P CLANCY KYLE J COLES JOHN S COLLIER KENNETH L COOK HENRY A COONS
DONALD N COOPER HARRY J CORNWELL BENJAMIN CRAIG JR GARY L CRAMPTON THEUS E DE LAIGLE
RONALD L DEMPSEY JOHN L DENGLER JOSEPH C DOYLE ROY W DUNCAN MATTHEW M DWYER JR
CLARENCE H BURDETT GENE C EID JOHN P ELLIS ALAN G FLOYD JAMES N GALEY
DANNY D GARD TERRY A GILBERTSON JOHN D HALL WARREN G HARDING JR EARL W HARRIS
RONALD C GOODIRON WILLIAM L HARRIS WILLARD F HAYES THOMAS G HAZELWOOD THOMAS L HERD
ROBERT W HOWDEN ROBERT W HUNT WILLIAM J JACOBS RAY G JENKINS HERBERT A KEHRLI
CHARLES F KERR DONALD A LABONTE ROBERT W LAUZON JERRY D LEAK ROY R MADDUX JR
PATRICIO MALDONADO JR EDWIN G MEIXNER JAMES H MIKELS JR JERRY E MILLER JAY W STULL
MARC W MCCABE GARY W PAINTER CHARLES E PARSONS JUANITO PEREA DALLIS PERRYMAN
JOSEPH B PHILIPSON JR ROBERT L PLATT STEVEN J POPKIN WILLIAM P RAUBACH STACEY D REECE
WINFIELD W REID JOHN R RUGGLES III FRANK SARDINA JAMES SCUTTIER ROBERT L SEVELL
WALTER C SHELLITO ROBERT L SHORTER PERRY V SHROYER CHARLES A SMITH JOHN R SMITH JR
ALLAN D MASTELLER CHARLES O SPILLMAN EMMETT C STANTON THOMAS STEGMAN JAMES E THOMAS

PANEL 42E

JOHN A THOTLAND JIMMIE L TODD WILLIAM O TURNER WALTER W VAIL ROBERT E WESLEY
JOHN P TOTH RICHARD E BECKWITH DONALD C BENNETT JR GERALD CERVANTES JAMES F COLEMAN
JOHN W COOK JOHN W COOK JR RORY A COVINGTON GEORGE W DE JARNETT VICTOR DI CAVALLUCCI
CARL L DOWNS FRANCIS M DRISCOLL JOHN D DUFFIELD ROBERT W ELLIS EARL ERWIN JR
CROSLEY J FITTON JR HARRY I FUQUA JR PHILIP F GREENE RICHARD J GROAT JAMES C MCPHEARSON
CLEVELAND S HARRIS EARL T JONES EDWARD J KAMINSKI CARL R LEED KENNETH C LOCKWOOD
PHILLIP D LAFRAMBOISE DOUGLAS A LENTZ FREDERICK L MARTIN MICHAEL E MARTIN VERNON J MILLER JR
JEFFERY GURVITZ EDWARD E MCCLELLAN GEORGE A MUSSENDEN OTIS L NICK CEIZHAR V PAGCALIUAGAN
RICHARD A RANDOLPH LUIA RODGERS JOE S RODRIGUEZ RONNIE D SCHULTZ MAURICE L SIROIS
JERROLD P SMITH EDGAR C SPENCE KENNETH R STEPHENSON SAMUEL K STEWART GILBERT THIBEAULT
JOHN W TRACY ARTHUR J TURKSTRA LARRY P TYSON DARRELL R UMHOLTZ LARRY J WALTERMAN
WAYNE L WARD WILLIAM R WATT HAROLD C WHITTAKER RICKY F ADAMS EARL I ALTHOUSE
JAMES V BACKLUND BUDROW BASS JR STEPHEN J BOBKOVICH LINDEN W BRITTINGHAM CHARLES F DEUEL
ARTHUR L BRUNT RICHARD J BURNETT ROBERT I CRANE WILLIAM L CUNNINGHAM BERTRAM A DESO
LARRY W BENGE LAWRENCE A DODD JOE D DUNN ADOLPHUS ELLIS JERRY W FERREN
FRANK FETTUCCIA NICHOLAS H FRITZ RICHARD L GARLICK WILLIE GILES JR CARLOS L GONZALES
THOMAS C GOSCH PAUL W HEINZ JOHN C HILL NATHAN HOLMES MICHAEL W HOLZMAN
MICHAEL K HASTINGS RICHARD W KAPP JR LAWRENCE J KLAAHSEN WILLIAM R KLAWITTER BENNIE KSIAZEK
STEPHEN T KUCAS RICHARD C LANNOM DANNY LEDFORD STANLEY R LEWTER FREDERICK B LINK
RODNEY D LLOYD GERALD W MARKWITH GARY A MARTIN JOSEPH MAYES RICHARD D MILLER
EDWARD M MISIUTA BENNIE R MONCUS JOHN H MORENO ALDEN F MOREY JR ROBERT E MOSS
JEFFERY MCCLATCHY JR WILLIAM R MCJIMSEY LESLIE E MURRAY DAN L NEELY GARY L OLIVER
FRANK D PINA ROGER L REED WILLIE L RICHARDSON GERALD G ROSENBAUM VERE L WILLIAMS JR
THOMAS D ROSTAMO THOMAS E SCHEURICH JOHN S SIMMONS THOMAS SPADARO MICHAEL B SPICER
ANTHONY O STRINGER STEVEN P SWATEK ROGER A THOMPSON WALTER L THOMPSON JOHN TILLMAN III
RICHARD J PETRIE RODOLFO VALENZUELA JOE W VANDERPOOL JOHN H WHITE JR JOSE L ALVAREZ-TAPIA
CARL V ANDRE GERALD L AVERY GUY N BERNARD CHARLES E BONDS JOHN M BOYCE
HARLAN R BRANDTS ANTHONY J BREUER ROBERT G BURNS JERRY W BYERS MARK D COOL
RICHARD C BROWN HORACIO CARRANZA WILLIAM B CAWLEY JR ALVIN L CAYSON JUNIUS C COLLIER
JAMES A COREY NICHOLAS J CUTINHA DAVID K DEMATTEIS BRUCE ELIOT JR NORMAN J ERBLAND
MICHAEL A EVENSON EARL F FITCH GARY V FRAZIER REX B FREEMAN MICHAEL D FROST
RAYMOND L GALLAGHER ROY C GERDON WILBUR L GRAY JR RUSSELL C HAAS JOSE RODRIGUEZ-ACEVED
FLOYD HEGLER JR DAVID N HILL FRANK J HUTCHINS FRANCIS L JEANTET ROBERT J JENKS
CLARENCE S HILLS CAL D JOHNSON LAWRENCE JOHNSON JACK J JORDAN JR EDWARD L KOLKA
KENNETH M KREBS FRANK KREC LEE R LANIER CHARLIE F LEE KENNETH E LLOYD
ROBERT W LUECKE JAMES R MATHIS ROY A MEIER CHARLES E MELOTT DAVID L MELTON
WILLIE L MCGAUGHEY DAVID C MOORE LEONARD D MOORE BARRY L MOYER CHARLES G REHBERGER
ROBERT J MCGEE JAMES F O'LAUGHLIN TONY S OLIVER ROY D PAGE WILLIAM RASSANO
THOMAS L MORK PETER S REINHART JOSE A REYES DOUGLAS R RITCHIE MICHAEL R RIVERS
TODD A HANDY GEORGE F ROBILOTTO DANA H ROESNER RICHARD ROMERO RONALD L SALVANI RONALD L SALVANIA
THOMAS J SCULLEN ERWIN B SIMS WILLARD SKAGGS JR RONALD A SLANE MARK E SMITH
RONALD J STILLEY CLIFFORD G STOCKTON DANNY M STONEKING DANNY G SWAZICK NEIL S THOMPSON
ARISTIDES SOSA WARREN L TALL JOHN M THOMPSON CARREL J TITSWORTH MICHAEL R TRAVIS
WALTER C VELVET JR LARRY H WALDEN GARY W WATKINS TERRY L WEAVER PAUL E WEST
DAVID L WETHINGTON JR DARRELL E WHEELER LARRY A WIDENER JOSEPH J WILLIAMS LEONARD J ZELASKI JR
VIRGIL L WILLIAMS KENNETH W WINGET DANNY S YOUNG WILLARD F YOUNG HOMER L AKE JR
WILLIAM F ALSMAN HOWARD H ASHFORD RICHARD L BORGMAN FRANK L BROWN KENNETH A BUYS
DAVID A CARLI MELVIN CARRILLO RONALD J CASPER DAN E CHARLES JAMES M DARBY
MICHAEL L CHARLES ABRAHAM L COLON-PEREZ PHILIP M CREWS VINCENT A DATENA FRANK R DIMMITT
ALBERT R DISMUKE RONALD D DUCKER EDWIN R EDWARDS MICHAEL J FARRIS ERNEST E FAWKS
NORMAN A FOSSETT FRANCISCO FRANCO JACKIE W GARNER LAWRENCE L GASKA RICHARD S GINDER
LARRY R GOURDINE HAROLD HOLMES LAWRENCE E JONES WILLIAM A JORDAN VICTOR A JUSTINIANO JR
GARY A LARSEN DONALD W LATTMAN JIMMY F LEHMAN PETER MITCHELL GEORGE H NESTLERODE
DAVID W KNOUSE DIMITRIOUS C MCCALL WILLIAM L MOORE DONALD A NAHODIL JR HENRY NORFLEET JR
DAVID R OGLE DOMINGO ORTIZ JIMMIE E PARKER DANIEL L PENSON RODRIGO VELAZQUEZ-FELICI JR
HARMON W PERRY EDDIE L PLEASANT M R REEVES HAROLD E REKAU SAMUEL D RIDER JR
CHARLES G ROSS THOMAS P RUSSO THOMAS F SMITH JR RICHARD C SPENCER ALFRED W SPEYER
KENNETH L OLDHAM GEORGE T SWYMER DENNIS H THOMPSON JOHN W VAN SANT EARNEST S WARD
JOHN T WELSHAN JAMES E WILLIAMS RAY H WOODS RANDALL L YOUNG ROBERT W ABERNATHY
TERRENCE W ACHOR THOMAS B ADAMS TERRY E ALLEN CURTIS E BAKER GEORGE L BARBER III
GARY J BELL PRENTIS B BOYKIN JR DAVID K BRUNING ALAN D CARSON LEONARD O CHANDLER
CONRADO F BILDUCIA RICHARD L CLAVERIE JAMES CROCKRAN DOUGLAS D CROWE JAMES R DAVIDSON
THOMAS G DE FOSSE CAMP A DEL CHARLES C DUNN BERNARD J FLEMING WILLIE F FOSTER
DARRYL A GALLAUGHER EZRA GAVIN DAVID P GOLDSMITH GARY D HALL
MICHAEL D GEISE CARL C HARLESS EDWARD E HENRY RAMON S HERNANDEZ ROBERT J HODAL GARY O HOLSINGER
RICHARD G HUDSON WILLIE H HUNTER GEORGE R HUTCHINSON ISRAEL L INGRAM ROBERT E JACKSON
CHARLES T JOHNSON RICHARD JOHNSON RONALD B JONSSON DONNY R KIDD ROBERT W KOIVUPALO JR
EDWARD M LENTZ VERNON L LEUNING DARREL G LEWIS WILLIAM P MASON JAMES C SWANN
DENNIS H MUTZ PATRICK F O'KEEFE FRANK A OSTER GARY C PARKINSON PHILLIP K ROSS
VERNON F PENDERGRASS ROBERT E POE TERRELL L RANDALL ANTHONY E REED RONALD J RHODES
EDWARD W MILAN ROBERTO P RIOS JEREMIAS ROMAN CAMILO J SANCHEZ DONALD B SAUNDERS
LORENCE M LUNDBY TIMOTHY R SCHROEDER EDWARD A SCHULTZ JOHN W STEVENS JR VOYD E TIDWELL

PANEL 43E

JAMES R TOMLINSON JOSE E TORRES EVERETT J VALANDINGHAM ANGEL R VASQUEZ
ROBERT H WALKER CURTIS L WILLIAMS RICHARD E WINDBIGLER ROGER K YAMANAKA RONNIE E ALVORD
STEVE A BANNER JAMES H BANNING JR ELDRIDGE J BATH DAVID L BIDART DON A BOOZER
JAMES M BROWN GARY R BURNETT ALBERT E COLLINS ROBERT R CRISWELL SALVADOR B GARCIA
DEAN L DALBERG JUAN J DEMARA DAVID M DLUZAK PABLO DURAN JUAN FLORES JR
NELSON J BOURDAGE RODNEY G FRANK RICHARD GRANADOS JAZREAL L HAYWOOD BILLY M HOLLIMON
BARRY W HOOPER JULIUS J HOWARD JR LUCIOUS HUTCHINS JAMES R INBODEN THOMAS E JENNINGS
RALPH H JOHNSON MILES W KIMLING MICHAEL W LANGER FREDRICK E LARSEN GARY W LITTON
RICHARD S LOWES CHARLES LUDWIG ROBERT D MCMILLIAN BRIAN T MURRAY GEORGE D NOVAKOVIC
JAMES L PIPES JR THOMAS W PRYOR CHARLES SANDERS REED J SCHWEIGHOFER PAUL SCOTT
ARCHIE D SMITH JOSEPH B SMITH JR JOSIAH SMITH JR GARY L TALLEY VERNON R TWEEDY
EDWARD L VAN HORN AUGUSTINE VERGARA-ARBIL HERBERT R ALDRIDGE RICHARD J HALL DENNIS W KLEIN
CHARLES H BATOZYNSKI GEORGE E BEALE CHARLES R BEALL JERRY A BEATTY WILLIS BEAUFORD JR
DAVID H BOSWELL CHARLES G BOYER JOSEPH P BRIGNAC HENRY R BROMMANN FREDDIE BROOKINS
WARREN G BROWN DONALD R BUMSTEAD FRANCIS J CAPEZIO ALVIN CARR JOHN H CLARK JR
CLINTON R CARPENTER JR GARY L COLOMBO JEFFREY F CONLIN RONALD S DOBBS STEPHEN W DOWNEY
FRANK F DYKES WILLIAM W DZIARCAK GEORGE L ELLIOTT III RONALD L ELLIS GARY L ENGEBRETSON
JERE D FARNOW MELVIN B FENN MICHAEL J FERRARA JOHN A FISCHIO KENDALL T FORTNEY
MICHAEL D GRAY JAMES A GRZEGOREK JAMES D GUFFEY JOHN L HAINES BLUCHER R HALL
LAURENCE R ASHMORE FREDERICK J HAMPTON JOSEPH E HARTZ JOHN G HEISELMAN ELLIS E HELGESON JR
BILLY H HENDERSON PAUL E HICKS RALPH E HIGGS EARL H HILLS JAMES N HINCKLE
GLEN T HOBBS HOWARD E HOLLAR ROBERT J HORVATH SANDRA HOSEY GEORGE H HUDSON
HOOD H HUNT ANDREW JACKSON GARY L JATICH LARRY S KENNEDY DONALD E KENTON
DAVID G ANDERSON GREGORY P KERNAHAN JR EDDIE KITCHEN JR JOHN A KOZACH DAVID J LATRAILLE
HARRY K LATSHAW CHARLES T LEE ROBERT A LEEMAN ROBERT LOPEZ JOSEPH A MARTURANO JR
DENNIS M MEAD DENNIS J MEDEIROS ROGER C MINCH JOE A MIRANDA GILBERT L MITCHELL
JAMES E MILES ALBERT J MITCHELL DALLAS H MOORE JAMES E MOORE THOMAS J MOSS JR
THOMAS MACMILLAN WINFORD MCCOSAR FLOYD MCFADDEN FRED C MCHUGH JR LARRY MUNOZ
RICHARD C NELSON RICHARD J O'HARE RONALD M OBENOUR STEPHEN F PALAZZOLA ANTHONY PATRIZI

PHILLIP W PIGFORD RICHARD L PITZER VIC M PIZARRO RONNIE C PRESLEY JEAN A RAILLA
HOWARD E RANDOLPH DAVID L RAY SAMUEL P ROBINSON DOMINGO RODRIGUEZ JR WILLIAM H ROGERS
WILLIAM T ROGERS IV JAMES E ROSE CLARENCE A ROUSSELL JR JOHN M RUSSELL JR RONALD R RYAN
RICHARD E SALDANA ROBERT B SCHAMPIER DAVID M SCHUH MICHAEL SEARS JOSEPH D SEIBERT
WILLIAM H SEWARD GREGORY R SHAMBAUGH JOHN B SHANK ARTHUR D SHELTON GEORGE W SKAKEL
JAMES H SMITH JR KENNETH A STANCIU CHARLIE R STRICKLAND JR STANLEY G STRONG STANLEY A STYS
GLENN SULLIVAN JAMES O TAYLOR LOUIS G TAYLOR DARYL B TERHUNE JR WILLIAM L TERRELL
ARLIE TERRY LOUIS J TONER ROBERT L VICKERS GARRITY VOGEL HOWARD B WALDRON
RALPH J WEESE STEPHEN A WEST LEAMUEL A WHITE GREGORY K WHITEHOUSE MARK C WHITTIER
DAVID R WIENCKOSKI HOLLIS WILLIAMS JR THOMAS H WILLIAMS STEPHEN F WOODS DARRYL W WRIGHT
FREDERICK L ALLUMS JOSEPH W BAKER HAROLD G BEANE JR RALPH R BERG
RICHARD D BAHR ENRIQUE M BERNAL STEPHEN F BOOTH WILLIAM N BRITTON GERALD K BROWN STEPHEN G CARLOS
CARMINE CASILLO CALDWELL M CAUTHEN JR RALPH E CONSAVAGE LESLIE COOK EDWARD R CORDEAU
MATHIS DANIEL ABRAHAM R DERRYBERRY III RALPH D DI FATE THOMAS W FERGUSON RICHARD GINAL
RICHARD D HALL RALPH L HAMMEL STEPHEN W HATHAWAY DAN S HICKS KRAIG S HOGAN
EDWARD L HOOVER WILLIAM C HOPPER BILLY D JACKSON LITTLE J JACKSON STERLING P JOHNSON
CHARLES W JONES ARNOLD D KIRK GEORGE M LAMBERTON II THEODORE T LEO HOYLE MARTIN
BEN MCCOULLOUGH JR JOSEPH J MELNYK JR WILLIAM J MULDOVAN CHARLES H RAMPLEY DANIEL D WEBB
JAMES G RANDALL EDWIN M RIDENOUR JEFFREY E SMITH MARTIN J SOTO GEORGE E SWEATT
LOWELL T PETERSON WARREN G TEDRICK JR DONALD W TISDALE HARRY K VAUGHAN ESAU WHITEHEAD JR
NATHANIEL WILLIAMS JR HOWARD D WILLIS JAN F WILSON LEWIS B WILSON EUGENE YOUNG
ELVIN L ALLEN CRAIG A ARNDT JOHN D BEAVER BERNARD BONEY JOHN W BORDERS JR
WILLIAM J BOWERS FREDDIE J BRYANT DAVID L CAREY DONALD R CHAMBLIN JR DAVID W CUTSHALL
WILLIAM C DE LAPP III GUY L EISENHART TIMOTHY FULLER RICHARD GALLAGHER JACK E GORBEY
CLEMENT B GRUBER BRUCE W GRUNEWALD JOHN P HARTLAGE III BOYD L HERRING HAROLD F HEYMACH
CHARLES E HODGE JOHN W HOGAN SAMUEL B HUDSON CHARLES B JILCOTT JR EDUARDO JIMENEZ
DONALD E JONES GUY T JONES STEPHEN C JONES JOHNNY J JUNKINS WAYNE M KIDWELL
RICHARD A KOSKI JIMMY M LOGAN WILLIAM T MANNING MARGARITO MARTINEZ ELDON E NEVINS
FRANK W MARKS DOUGLAS N MCKENZIE II KENNETH C MOORE HOWARD S PONTUCK DELMAR W PROBST
WILLIAM T PUFFENBARGER MELVIN R RANSON DAVID M REYNOLDS MARVIN N RICHARDSON GARY N SHY
JAMES P ROGAN MICHAEL D ROLFE SAMUEL J RUMSON JR GEORGE H SAULS JR JOHN E SEVERSON
LARRY R REDMON PHILLIP E SEXTON MICHAEL A SHRAMKO JAMES P SINGLETON DANNY L SMOTHERS
SONNIE STEPHENS GEORGE W STORZ JOHN J SULLIVAN ROBERT L TAYLOR JR DONALD R TITUS
DONALD W VAN FLEET RODOLFO VILLAFRANCO HAROLD E WALKER JR RUSSELL L WALLACE DALE K WILSON
JOHN M TOMKINS BEN H WILLIAMS TERRY A WILLIAMS RICKEY E APPLEBY RICHARD T ARTHUR
JERRY S BAKER JAMES R BATEMAN WILLIAM H BECKWITH WILLIE B BRADFORD JOHNNY R BURTON
ROBERT L CLEWLOW ROBERT J COMSTOCK MAURICE A COOPER LONNIE J CRISMON RICHARD D FEIRO
FRANCIS R HITTINGER JR JOHN E HOOD DONALD R IRBY DALE R KARPENSKE DANIEL L KINNARD
MELVIN R LEAVELL PATRICK D MORIARTY JOSEPH E PEREZ LEON M PHILLIPS MELTON H PRESLEY
RICHARD N PROCIDA STEPHEN J RAGO JAMES RIVERA LEROY B ROBBINS DAVID A RUSSELL

PANEL 44E

WILBERT STOVALL HOWARD A STRAUSBAUGH JOHN R TWOREK KENNETH R WILLIAMS JR
EUGENE E SWIFT ALTON THOMAS JR HENRY E THOMAS SANTIAGO TORRES JR MCCREA B TUTTLE
LAWRENCE W SCANLAN EDWARD M STERNIN WILLIAM VAZQUEZ RICHARD E VINCENT JERRY O WOODS
JAMES E WYATT BENJAMIN F ALMAGUER WALTER E ANDERSON JR RICHARD C BROWN RUDY Y CHALAKEE
ARTHUR L CHISOLM SYLVESTER E CONLEY JR JOSEPH J DAFFER RAYMOND A DUBBS MIKE ESPINOSA
ROBERT E COCHRAN FORBIS P DURANT JR ROBERT W EAGLESON GEORGE F EDWARDS CHARLES D FLOOD
FRANK G GOELZ JACK L GOODWIN HUBERT H GORDON JR MICHAEL F GREEN CHARLES M HAIRSTON
DAN L HERDEBU JOHN A HOOKER JOHN F JOHNSON HOMER H LEE BOSCH D VANDEN
JAMES A LESSEG GRASSO R LO DURWOOD B LOMBARD RICHARD A MARSH BRIAN A MARSHALL
LEWIS W MOORE JOHN W MURPHY III MARSHALL D NELSON RONALD C OGLESBY CHARLES OLIVER
ROBERT RERA SCOTT C ROGERS JESSE E SCAVELLA JR STANLEY B SMITH FRANCIS X TURBERT
WARREN C LANE RICHARD C WESTBERG VINCENT D WESTBERRY WILLIAM W WIEBURG JAMES W WILLIAMS
JAMES W WOOD STEPHEN M WORLEY WILLIAM A ANDREWS DONALD W BEAN CLARENCE F BLANTON
JESS B BOICOURT JR RONALD D BOND BENNY C BURNS JAMES H CALFEE JAMES W DAVIS JAMES E FRANCIS
PORTER E CALLOWAY JOSEPH C CARVAJAL ROBERT D DAVIS RICHARD ETCHBERGER JOE F EVANS
THOMAS A FERGUSON JIMMY FLORES KEITH M FLUMERE DONALD S GILLMAN HENRY G GISH
OSCAR G GUTIERREZ WILLIS R HALL RALPH D HIRSCHLER JR WILLIAM S HUNT BENNY K SANCHEZ
HERBERT A KIRK ELDON J KIRKPATRICK JR DAVID W KMETZ ELMER D LAUCK DANIEL L MEYSEMBOURG
JAMES L NUFER GEORGE H OEHLER ERNEST A OLDS JEFFREY L PECK DAVID S PRICE JAMES W REESE
DENNIS D REED EDWARD RITSICK RAYMOND G ROCHA ALBERT E RODRIGUEZ JAMES L RUSSELL
MELVIN A HOLLAND PATRICK L SHANNON DALE E SHIRLEY FLOYD T SPENCER DONALD K SPRINGSTEADAH
TONY L TATE TERENCE P THOMAS DENNIS A TOADVINE JEFFREY A TURNER JAMES M WARR
GERALD F WERNSDORFER HENRY B WILLIAMS JR WILLIE A WILLIAMS DON F WORLEY WILLIAM E LILIENTHAL
BERND BACHLEDA JAMES W BETTIS LAWRENCE A BRANIGAN RICHARD P BRUCE THOMAS R FLEMING
LENARD COLEMAN STEPHEN R CUNNINGHAM LEWIS R DORSEY RICHARD L DUNLAP LEON G EDWARDS
JERRY W FRAZE CHARLES W GRAHAM JERRY L GREEN GEORGE F HAYES RANDALL L MCELREATH
WILLIAM L HOLLAND JR LOUIS H HUFF II WILLIAM A JONES JOSEPH M KNOBLOCK JR GLENN E KOLLMANN
PAUL T ARAMBULA RODNEY J LAWSON JAMES R LEDBETTER WILLIE B LEE JOHN L MATTOCK
JOHN G GRIFFITH JEFFERY E MEAD HAROLD METCALF DANIEL V MICHEL JOSE S MONTEMAYOR
ROBERT W O'DONNELL GARY W PERKINS ROBERT C PLEMMONS DONALD R ROBISON EDWARD F ROGERS
ESTEL D SPAKES RICHARD J STEWART JOHN R STROHMAIER CARLOS V TREVINO FRANCISCO L VALLE
RALPH L WASHINGTON KENNETH M WATKINS EDGAR W BLANKENSHIP JAMES L BUCHY LYTELL B CHRISTIAN
LEON J ATTERIDGE JR JOSEPH H BYRNE GEORGE M CHACALOS GUY F COLLINS WILLIAM D CRAWFORD
EVERETT DAVIS WILLIAM E DEAN JIMMY L DELANO DOUGLAS E DISHMAN FRANCIS J DOWD JR
DAVID K DITCH RAYMOND P DOBRZYNSKI DAVID L EDNEY CLEVELAND EVANS JR LAWRENCE A FULTS JR
RONALD F GOLEBIEWSKI EUGENE GUBBINS DAVID L HAMPTON WALTER E HANDY GUY E RAY JR
LEWIS M HAYWARD WILLIAM J HONDEL RUSSELL E HUPE KOSMAS P KAPETANOPOULOS GLEN H MOSLEY JR
DREK A LANDES RAMON LOPEZ EDILBERTO D MACAGBA LARRY J MOORE MICHAEL K MOORE
STEVEN W HEITMAN CARL M MORRIS HAROLD B MULLER ALVIN J MUNSON JOHN M NOONAN
KENNETH W HAAKENSON ANTONIO OROZCO RAUL PENA-CLASS ARNOLD P SARNA MICHAEL J SCOTT
LARRY D SHERMAN VERNON R STEAD TODD E SWANSON RUBEN N TACKETT J A THEODORE
TERRY L TRAINOR BOBBY D TUCKER JIMMY L WATSON TERRY E WEBB JOSEPH R WENZLER
DONALD E WESTBROOK MICHAEL L WHITE ELSWORTH WILLIFORD WILLIAM P WORLEY JUAN D AGUIAR JOHN J GUNTHER
LUCIUS ANDERSON JR JAMES R BIERNACKI ROBERT W CAWLEY HENRY J CHESTER JR
ANDREW D CHOWKA DAVID F COSBY GEORGE J COX WILLIAM G DOWNS JR HARRY J ELLIS III
ADOLFO AGUILAR MICHAUEL D FERGUSON ROBERT G FINDLEY DALE A GRIFFIN
EDWARD J HAGL JAMES E HAMM JIMMIE R HARRISON FRANKIE R JOHNSON DONALD E KIDD
WILLIAM S KLEINT THOMAS G KOLINSKI DOM E LEE ROGER W LETTO PATRICK A LUCERO
GERRY D MAJOR ERNESTO MARTINEZ KENNETH R MCALLISTER JOHN R MEDLEY TERRY L MILLER ERNEST W WIGLESWORTH JR
WILLIAM R MARYFIELD WILLIAM W MCCONNELL EARL C MINARD WILBUR L MINTER JR CHARLES F MORSE JR
RONALD G MCCRAW CHET E MCPHETERS EUGENE NELSON NICHOLAS PARASILITI DUANE R PASSIG
EDWARD L PATTERSON JOSEPH S PERYSIAN WILLIAM F PIASKOWSKI ROBERT G PINKSTON THOMAS R POPE
WILLIAM E PRICE GEORGE W RIORDAN RAUL ROBLEDO THOMAS J SALTMARSH SAMMIE R SNEED JR
CHARLES H SOWERS II JONATHAN N SPICER MICHAEL L SUCCI TOMMIE L SYMANK WALTER F TYRCZ JR
KENNETH J GREENE JOHN A VIRGONA DONALD E WEITZ LARRY E WELCH JAMES C WHISNAN
GARY L WILLMAN ERNEST H YOUNG III GILLES D ADAMS GREGORY F AMBROSE FRANKLIN C ARMENTO
WILBERT R BARBEE PAUL L BIGELOW DANNY E BLEVINS CHARLES L BONNER SAMUEL J FRIESON
THEODORE D BERNARD RICARDO CAMPOS DAVID A CHISHOLM WILLIAM W DAVIS JR MICHAEL R FINERTY
AUSTIN M GAUGHAN RAYMOND C GUEST WILLIAM HERSHAN JAMES M JENSEN RONALD E JOHNS
LEROY W KATTERHENRY JR EDWARD A LIONETTA STEVEN A MIDDLETON RONALD L WRIGHT PAUL A YOUNG
WALTER L MCCAHAN ROGER T NELSON WALTER J PANAMAROFF HOWARD P PETTY JAMES B RICKELS
PATRICK A SHUTTERS ROBERT SMEAL LARRY J TAGGART RICHARD R TESORO CHARLES S WALSH
CLARENCE H LEWIS WILLIAM S WILLIAMS JR EARNEST WILSON GERALD J WINCH PAUL L WOODARD
DOUGLAS R MOHRMANN DAVID R YOUNG JR CARL T ADAMS STEPHEN H ADAMS JOHN B AHERN
EDWARD J ARIAZ ELBERT A BALLANCE JAMES H BEAVER CHRISTOPHER H BELL CARL H BERNHART
ROBERT L BODINE DENNIS R CARR GARY A CLIFFORD ROY B COCHRAN DOUGLAS R COOKE
EDWARD J CROSS MARK L DICKSON MARK R DZIEDZIC ROBERT W ELSWICK ALBERT A ENGELHARDT

PANEL 45E

JAMES B FARMER II BOGARD L FLOYD DAVID L GILLIAM GARY P HADLEY
ROBERT W HARDESTY DAVID A JOHNSON HENRY L JOHNSON MICHAEL D KALB YOUNG D OGLETREE
BILLIE O KEAN EDWARD L KRAUSMAN BRUCE W LOISELLE JAMES B MAKIN WELDON B MERRILL
FRANK A UHLIK JR GARY D HICKS JAY D MCMURPHY RONALD S MOORE DEWEY R OWENS DAVID A PURSER
KENNETH T RABEY RICHARD A RATHBURN FREDDIE J ROBERTS THOMAS W SCOTT HENRY J SERVENT JR
DAVID L SIMMONS HOWARD B SMITH KENNETH R WELLS MICHEL T WHEELER BENJI YAMANE
TERRY ZIMMERMAN DENNIS J ZWIRCHITZ THOMAS D BARBER EDGAR D BELL LAWRENCE A GRENHAM
JOHN L BINGLEY JR JAMES G BLACKSHEAR RALPH A BRANSON JR JAMES R BURCH JR DANIEL L BURR
ROBERT B CANNON VIRGIL E CHILDERS GEORGE W COLEMAN DENNIS L CUNNINGHAM ALLEN P SHEEHAN
LEE D BENSON HERMANN DOELGER-LANDIVAR ROGER E DUNCAN JOHN FOLDVARY JR CARL E GARZA
RICHARD J GROOMS DAVID L GROVES JOHN J HARRIS LEON HENDERSON THOMAS T HENSLEY
DONALD R HUBBS ROBERT A ITZOE EDWIN O IVES DAVID E JACKSON FELIX LEON JR
DAVID L LIPSCOMB DONALD C MCNAC DAVID H MEALY RICHARD J MEIGHAN GEORGE F MYRICK
RANDALL J NIGHTINGALE JOE R PECK JIMMY R PIERCE LARRY J RODGERS JLYNN ROSS JR
MARIO F DE MATTIO DAVID H SEVIER TOMMY L STEPHENS JOSEPH P STRIPPOLI JR EDWARD A SWONKE JR
WENDELL G TAYLOR PATRICK J TREMBLAY BOBBY L WEATHERS JAMES WITT DAVID L BROWN
GEORGE F ADAMS GREGORY K ARTHUR CHARLES C ASSELTA JAMES D BARR ROBERT L BERRY
JAMES P ACHTERHOFF BILLY R BOWEN CHARLES L BOZEMAN MICHAEL D CARROLL MICHAEL J CASEY
WILLIAM E COFRAN PAUL A CONNER MONTE R COOLEY DARYL W CRUM CECIL L DAVIS
EDWARD A DE VORE JR FRANK C DEUSEBIO THOMAS W DUKE ROY L ESTRADA JOHN A FERA
ROBERT T FERRELLI ROBERT G FISHER LARRY L FITZSIMMONS EDDIE D GANT GRADY GANTT JR
EDUARDO GARCIA JR LOUIS C GOI ELVIN W GOSE WILLIAM R GOUDELOCK LARRY V GREEN

PANEL 45E (*Continued*)

MCARTHUR HAMBURG ARTHUR L HAWKINS JR EUGENE C JOHNSON LORNE C KRUEGER WALTER A WILLIAMS
JOHN P LARKIN GREGG E LAVERY RICHARD R LYNN TOMMY D MABE ROBERT P PAYNE
ROBERT A MARTIN THEODORE MAZON JR CARL L MERCHANT STEVEN L MESSERLI VIANE S MISA
DENNIS F MOORE WILLIAM MURPHY JUAN J NAZARIO ROBERT O'BANNON III SYDNEY PARKS
LAWRENCE J LE DONNE DOUGLAS B PARSONS ELLIOTT L PETERS WILLIAM D PRICE THOMAS R RAMEY
JAMES M RAY WAYNE P REEVES WILLIAM C ROBERTS EULALIO A ROMAN FRANK M ROSS JR
LARRY D SAIN ALFRED R SAPINOSA MARSHALL G SCHAFFNER JOHN C SEAMAN JR JIMMY L SHERRILL
CHARLES D SMITH ELLIOTT R SMITH THOMAS L SMITH ANDREW SPRINGS JAMES E SPROWL
GEORGE L STARKS CHARLES E SUTHERLAND JERROLD A SWITZER GARY D UTZ FRANK E WEISS
GARRY E KING KENNETH E WILLARD JR HOWARD K WILLIAMS CLINTON C WUSTERBARTH DAVID H WYRICK
THEODORE L ZAWISZA MARTIN BIONDO CHARLES E BLAIR JODY A CRON WILLIAM E DARNELL
SAM Z HUGHES CLARENCE JEFFERSON JR JEFFREY R JORDAN BILLY D KENNINGTON NIKOLAI KIATKIN
FREDERICK L KRUGER BILLY D MCDOUGAL EDWARD L MILUS VICTOR ROMERO WOODROW WILSON
HAROLD S WOOD JR JEFFREY J YARGER JIMMY R YOUNG DOUGLAS L ZELLER JAMES R ADAMS
ROY M ALEXANDER ALAN G BARETTI GEORGE D BARRETT JOSEPH C BAZA ISAAC BLAND
THEODORE BELTON DENNIS R CANTLER JOSEPH J CASSIDY JR MICHAEL J CORDIA BRUCE A COUILLARD
DICK E CUFF ALLEN E FELLOWS JAMES E FISHER WILLIAM GOODHEART WILLIE GRANT JR
DAVID E GREGOIRE ELGIE G HANNA RUFUS Q HENDERSON GEORGE A JUAREZ JOHN M KARES
MICHAEL H KETCH DAVID A MADDUX KENNETH D MOORE GREGORY F MOSSFORD WINCE I OVERTON JR
JAMES A PATTON GARY D REED ALAN R ROBERTS MARION N SALTZ FRANKLIN A SAPPINGFIELD
LESLIE B SAYRE EUGENE SMALL FRANKLIN E SPEIGHT ORIS C TAYLOR WILLIE S TILLMON
ABELARDO VERA TOMMY A WALDON WILLIAM J WEIDINGER JOHN E WHITE LOUIS C ZUCKER
ROBERT W ATWELL EDGAR BAKER JR CHARLES R BARTHOLOMEW DANIEL F BETTENCOURT JR LARRY W JONES
MICHAEL R CALLAWAY MICHAEL L EBERT EDDIE L EPHRAIM RONALD C FRANSEN ODIS L GOSNELL
JAMES L HENK GILBERT HERNANDEZ-CARRIO PETER D HESFORD LEONARD D HOLDER CHARLES E MCGEE
TERRENCE J BELLOMO EDWARD E HOLT JAMES E KESSELHON GEORGE L LAKEY CHARLES R LOVEDAHL
GARY L HANLIN RAFAEL A MADRIGAL-CORDERO JR RAYMOND L MASON JOHN P NAGY ANDREW R SMITH JR
SAMUEL R NIXON RONALD E RAKUNAS FARRIS L RICHARDSON WAYNE L ROBERTS JOSEPH E ROBINSON
WACLAW J MACZULSKI RONALD J ROMERO RUDOLPHO SANCHEZ CARL M STITELY CHESLEY A STORY
AUBREY E STOWERS JR DANIEL THOMAS JUSTIN G TURNBULL STEPHEN J WELSH RICHARD H WOODWARD
JAMES C ACKERMAN JR WALTER H ANSLOW KENNETH E BAKER JR GARY L BARNUM ROBERT L BELLAMY
JAMES E BLAAUW PAUL W BUSH PHILLIP J CAYFORD JR CHARLES E DANIELS CARLOS R DAVIS
DAVID W DERRY WALTER J EGGER FRED C FRAPPIEA JR WORDELL GAINES LARRIE J GOTCHER
BILL W GRANT DONALD E GREEN JOHN J GROHMAN JEFFREY G HAMILTON ROGER P KELLER
FREDERICK Y HOLJES BENJAMIN A JONES KENNETH R JOYNER MANFRED W KRAUSE MICHAEL E LINDERMAN
ROBERT LUNA DONAVAN L LYON JULIUS MADDOX RALPH W MANEY BRIAN S PERLEWITZ
CARL LYONS LINWOOD D MARTIN THEODORE V MCINNIS THOMAS J MURRAY THOMAS J PTAK
CHARLES R PYLE LARRY M ROBERSON STEPHEN C SHANNON BENNIE J SISSON THOMAS J STURGAL
ESTEVAN TORRES JOHN C WELLS C W WILLIAMS ROLAND R BELLAMY LARRY J CLANTON
RANDALL E COLE RONNIE C CURETON THOMAS E DONOVAN VERNON L DOWNS JR JAMES E LAIRD
IAN J FRANKS EULAS F GREGORY MICHAEL P HARRIS MASAKI HATTORI RAYMOND R JORDAN
CLARENCE DAWKINS JR ROBERT A KANESKI DONALD F LANDERS MICHAEL D LAWRENCE FRANK R MELL JR

PANEL 46E

JOSEPH M ROMERO WILLIAM M SAUNDERS EDWARD A SHARROCK DANNY E TUCKER
THOMAS Y REYNOLDS JOSEPH G ARTAVIA DOUGLAS M BACOT DAVID J BARDUSON KENNETH M BARKER
VAL E BARTON DANNY P BOUCHEZ GEORGE CAMPBELL GERALD G CHINO WALTER L GAWEL
CHARLES E DAVENPORT II JOHN J ENZINNA FRANKIE L FARROW SAMUEL E FOSTER RICHARD A FRIEND
WILLIAM R BREEDEN DARRYL B FULLUM BERNARD L GAINES FRANCIS L GAULOCHER DONALD L GEARHART
DARWIN D GORDON JACK W HALEY WILLIAM G HALL STEPHEN L HALSTEAD TROY R HAYDEN
ALBERT F HEUSEL JR PAUL L HUTCHINSON WILLIAM A IVES ROBERT L JACKSON WILLIAM C JENKINS
RONALD R LAKE GERALD R LEGER ROBERT J LORENZO LOUIS J MAHER JR GEORGE R MARTIN
EUGENE P MCKINNEY MICHAL A MERKEL KENNETH L NEAL GEORGE J NICHOLSON ERIC B NILSEN
FRANK A O'BRIEN III ERWIN A POLT CHARLES W PORTERFIELD ARTHUR O PRENDERGAST GEORGE F PROFFER
ALBERT J PETERS CARL R RASORI LAWRENCE R RAYMOND JOHN B REALE III ROBERT D REICHERT
RUDOLFO L ROCHA JR RONALD F SADLER DENNIS C SHIVELY TERRANCE E SMITH DANNY S THOMPSON
JEFFERY H VAN VLEET JOHN B WEILL TERRY R WHITE DAVID L WILKERSON FRANCIS A BARNES
PATRICK M BERWERT LEONARD E BORCHARD JR RICHARD E BOYD MCARTHUR CALLAWAY JOHN M CASEY
GLENN F CASHDOLLAR RONNIE J CHARLES BRUCE A COBB LLOYD A COLFACK EUGENE J CURLESS JR
TOM DAVIS JR DAVID R DE PRIEST DAVID E DEWITT LOUIS M GARCIA LARRY M GRONEWOLD
TRACY W HARGRAVE JOHN D HARPER JR JOHN E HEFTY RICHARD E HEIL BENNETT J HERRICK
JOHN L HIGGINS CHARLES A HINCKLEY ROY L JOHNSON WALLACE B JOHNSON III WILLIAM J SHORTSLEEVES
DOWARD L JONES JR EDWARD J JUREK II MICHAEL J KELLEY MONTE C KINASZ DONALD R KINTON
ALFRED F LANCE BALFOUR O LYTTON JR FRANK J MALSEED JR JOHN M MIHALOVICH FRANKLIN E MOORE
JOHN H MCCARTHY DONALD L MCHUGO PATRICK C MCILROY JAMES E MOORE JAMES M MULLINS
DAVID T ORWIG III MICHAEL L PFEUFFER WILLIAM L RAY WADE R REAUME ROBERT D ROBINSON
DANIEL C RUNKLE HOWARD L SAVARE DONALD H SCHMIDT GILBERT SERRANO EDWARD C SHELDON
RICHARD W HOPPER JOHN O SHERRILL DENNIS K SHOWERS RONALD SOCKEY JOSEPH T TANGARIE
JIMMY J TESSADRI FLOYD N THOMAN HERBERT F WELTZ JR BROADUS A WHITT ROBERT J WIEDEMANN
GARY R WIGINTON LARRY E WORKMAN JIM L AILSTOCK JR LONNIE D ALLEY FRANKIE E ALLGOOD
JOEL G ANDERS ROSS APPLEGATE EDWIN L ARMSTRONG CRAIG P AVERILL GENE T BAILEY
JERALD L BAKER MICHAEL J BANDY LARRY E BARGER JIMMY D BARNETT BENJAMIN J BELARDE
RICHARD L BELINGE STEVEN M BEZENSKI JOSEPH M BROWN RONALD W BURKHART ROBERT J PIATKOWSKI
ROBERT L BUTLER JAMES H CAMPBELL JR MICHAEL W CAMPOS BARTON W CAREY WILLIAM H COOK
ROBERT E CUNDIFF ROBERT E DAVIS JACK E DERRICO LARRY E ELMORE RICHARD EVANCHO
MICHAEL A FAY WAYNE J FIELDING DONALD C FOUST EARL W FRYE JOHNNY E GANTT
STEVEN H GERLACH ALVIN R GIBBLE JOHN P GIDDINGS DENNIS S GLEASON JAMES T GORSICH
BARRY L GRAHAM PAUL D GRASSO GERALD J GUNDERSON JOHNNIE D HARRIS LAWRENCE SKLODOSKI
CHARLES L HATCHER JOHN R HORTON CHARLES L HOWE GLEN D HUBBARD WILLIE JACKSON
KENNETH KAMINSKI ERNEST C KERR JR ALAN S KOHN PHILIP J KREK JR WAYNE D KRUEGER
ROGER M LINK RICHARD E LOMAX LEONARD LONG LEO J MATYLEWICZ MARVIN L MAYO
CHARLES R MOOMEY MAURICE MOORE ROBERT W MORRIS JAMES M MOSER ROGER L OLSON
CARL MCFADDEN JR CECIL R MILLSPAUGH ROBERT B MOSSO GLENN W MOWREY JAMES A OSTERLOTH
PHILIP C BENN LAWRENCE P PENNEL ERNESTO S PEREA ROBERT D POPE GARY M REEDY
WAYNE E RISNER ROBERT J RYLANDER RAYMOND F SCHOPMANN RALPH SIBLEY HAROLD J SIMMONS
LARRY E GREEN JOE W SMITH JAMES F STOLINSKI HOYLE TERRY JR HARVEY J TOMPKINS
JOHNNY W WANAMAKER HERBERT F WHITE SYLVESTER WRIGHT JR HARVEY G ADAIR JAMES L BADLEY
JOHN H BARNES THOMAS E BIXBY WILLIAM E CARROLL DENNIS E CHESTER ROBERT J FRISK
JOHNNY C CALHOUN MICHAEL L DOANE DONALD C EMERY STEVEN J GAFTUNIK MARVIN E GALBRAITH
FRANKLIN N GILES JR LOUIS W HAMIL RONALD J HASKO JAMES C HAUGH CHARLES K HENSON
RALPH HORNADAY JR WILLIAM C JUDGE JR LAWRENCE R LOPES RICHARD LOPEZ ROBERT E LUCAS
PAUL J MOODY CARTER L MOORE BERNIE J MOSLEY RICHARD W ORSUND ROGER W OVERSTREET
WAYNE W PEARCE WILLIE B RICHMOND MICHAEL C RUSSO RICHARD L SCHMIDT FRANK SCHUSTER
FREDRIC B DAVIS CARL A SHUTT JR JOSEPH E SINTONI IRWIN R SOBEL EXTRUMBERTO SOLIS MAC W SPEAKS
JACK D SUNDQUIST THOMAS L TAFFE LARRY D WEBB JAMES D WHITE RICHARD L WHITTEKER
CLIFFORD L WILLIAMS PEDER W ARMSTRONG PETER N BALDWIN JAMES L BOWMAN ALAN L BOYER
GEORGE R BROWN GEORGE P DESMARAIS WILLIAM C DIMAGARD RAYMOND C DOWNIN LEE M LAMBERT
ROY D ELSTON JR GERALD F GILBERT RAYMOND R GILLOCK DENNIS L GRAHAM CHRISTOPHER A GROSSE JR
RAY I HAAS JAMES A HARRINGTON JR RICHARD A HEWETT CHARLES G HUSTON GREGORY P KENT
EMERSON P COLE PAUL D KUEHL LARRY C KYAR ROBERT A LA FOUNTAIN FRANKLIN D LACEY
DOUGLAS F LOUDENBACK HENRY E MACCANN PAUL E MAYER FREDERICK D MCCARTY JIMMIE L MCRAE
LAWRENCE W O'MEARA JOSEPH C PARK JR BERNARD M RICHARDSON DAVID L ROSS VERNON D SANDVIG
VINCENT B SANTANIELLO JOSEPH F SCHLICK ROBERT S SHELTON ELMORE R SIMPSON JACK M WOLF
JOHN T SUMMERS III ARTHUR L TUCKER MICHAEL W WALLACE FRANK T WATTS HOWARD D WEEKS WALTER G WILSON
FRANCIS A ANDERSON MICHAEL M BARR HANS W BRUNNER THOMAS G CARLISLE II
CARL L CARSON MICHAEL L GANDY CORNELL H GIBSON HOWARD M GIFFORD THOMAS C HENRY

PANEL 47E

LARRY A IANNETTA KENDAL R KRUSE ANIELLO C NUNZIATO NATHANIEL WILLINGHAM
NORMAN E LANE JR JOSEPH LASZLO JOHN LEVINTHOL JR RAFAEL MARTINEZ JOSE MEDRANO JR
DONALD B MCCOIG PAUL R MCFADDEN JAMES W MULTHAUPT JON M MURPHY MELVIN D NEWTON
DAVID L HINZ MAURICE T NOEL GEORGE A OWENS MARVIN E PENRY HAROLD E PENSON
WILLIAM S PRICE THOMAS RENDON MICHAEL A ROSE MANUEL RUIZ GARY A SCOTT
FRANK L RODRIGUEZ MICHAEL L SLOAN TERRY C SMITH JOHN H VIVIAN CONNIE V WELLS
JACK M JONES PHILIP B WENRICK PAUL E WILLIAMS DAVID A ALDRICH DAVID B ANDERSON
JERRY D ATKINSON LUZON BEASLEY NORMAN L BLASINGAME WALTER L BRANNON MCKENLEY O MATLOCK
ROGER T BROWN PATRICK K BURKE WALTER A CICHON ROBERT E COLE DAVID CULP JR
JAMES T CUMMINGS JR CHARLES H DYCHES THOMAS B FERGUSON PETER J GALLO EDWARD L GLOVER
CHARLES D GOFORTH ROY L GRIFFIN JR GEORGE E GRUBBS PAUL R GULA MICHAEL K HARE
BARRY M HILLSGROVE NORMAN L HOWLETT JR ROBERT S JERNBERG JIMMIE L JONES BERT A KEELER
ROBERT F KLINE JR LAWRENCE R KOMAN JOHN F LINK LARRY G MANUEL JOHN G MARSHALL
TED D BRITT WAYNE P MOORE JAMES E MORSE JESSE A MURPHY WILLIAM P MURPHY
JAMES E MCPHERSON MARION H NORMAN RAYMOND L PLUNKETT DONALD R RASH FRANCIS L SHAFER JR
RONALD REYES MICHAEL M REYNOLDS JOSE RUIZ JR KENNETH E SANDS ALBERT R SANFORD
DENNIS M POTEAT GERALD A SCHIRO CHARLES E SHAW AUTHOR C SMITH KENNETH R TOTTEN JR
DONALD A WARREN STEPHAN M WIGGINS WILBUR L WILLIAMS JR DAVID R WILSON ROBERT E WILSON
ABRA J WOLFE JR EDUARDO ARANDA-SANTOS LESLIE A BALL FREEMAN BOLEN JAMES B BROCK
DEAN H BURNS STEVEN D BURTON GERALD L DE ROSE GEORGE R DE SHURLEY PATRICK M DERIG
ARNOLD J FERRARI WARREN J FLANAGAN JAMES K FLOURNOY JAMES F GALATI RICHARD GARCIA
MICHAEL R GREENIDGE MARK E HODEL WAYNE A HOKENSON ROBERT K HORSPOOL GERALD L JOHNSON
GRAT A KEENE THOMAS J KOVACEVICH RICHARD F LINKS ALLAN L MAIR JOHN P MATLOCK
ARTHUR C MCLELLAN CHARLES D MILLER KEVIN W MOORE WILLIAM R NEAL WALTER W ROSOLIE
ERASMO PALOS JERRY L PATRICK DANIEL PESIMER THOMAS P PRUETT JR DON J YELVERTON
EZEKIEL PAIGE JESUS A QUIDACHAY JAMES R RETZLOFF JR RICKEY L RICHARDS WALTER R RIGGS
TIMOTHY J SHORTEN ARTHUR B SMITH DANNY L STEPHENS EDWARD T STONE JR THOMAS P SWEENEY
WILLIAM VANCE JR SHERMAN T WASHINGTON JAMES O WEST JOSEPH K WHEELER STEVEN R WOLTER
JOHN F PEEK KENNETH R YANTIS FRANKLIN D AUDILET JOHN H BLALOCK EDWARD A BOARDMAN
DAVID A BRENNER JAMES M BRINKMAN III DONALD W BURNSIDE DAVID C CARDINAL LESLIE A DEVERS JR
KENNETH L CRIST WILLIAM S CUTTING LARRY E DARDEN MUNOZ A DE JESUS GEORGE A FISCHER
RICHARD L GIAMBRONE FRANK E HAND III GARY B HARRIS FRANK E HEADLEY IV CECIL L JONES
RAYMOND O KINCANNON DONALD E KULACZ GERARD A LAVIGNE DELMAR L LAWRENCE ROBERT A LULLA
BRIAN J MATHISON ROBERT E MENTZER JR RONNIE MILLS GEORGE L MYERS RODOLFO C SERRANO
STUART M MCLELLAN RICHARD D NICOLINI MORTIMER L O'CONNOR MICHAEL J PURCELL ROGER W RAIH
JAMES H MORGAN CURTIS A RHODES DARWIN B RIDENHOUR PETER W SHAGOVAC JR ANTHONY SIMOES
HARRY S STAYER JAMES J TEDESCO DONALD E VAN DER SCHANS RONALD E WILSON EDWARD O WYNDER
ROBERT C STRICKLAND DONALD F WOOD ALVIN G YOXSIMER HERBERT H CATO III GEORGE J KOHLMEIR III
DAVID T CONNORS WILLIAM E EDWARDS DOUGLAS L HARRISON ARCHIE A HAYMAN GENE J HOWARD
BRUCE L BADGER FRED C JENKINS JOE T KEMMERLING CARL M MABE LARRY J MILOT
ROBERT A MOWERY BARRY M PATTON KARL F PERRY LAWRENCE E PHILYAW DONALD L STILES
DONALD W QUEEN ROBERT G QUICK JEWEL L RAINWATER ROBERT H RASSEL DOUGLAS C RUSTINE
JOHN J PALL PABLO D SANCHEZ BENNY M SANTISTEVAN JR KENNETH F SCHORNDORF ALBERT SHILLER
JAMES STRECHA JR WATSON UNDERWOOD JR WESLEY W WHITE WILLIAM G WILKINS DOYLE WILLIAMS
INGO J WISKOW THOMAS S WOODLAND JR CHARLES L YATES LARRY W BARRETT JOHN E BLACK
HARRY L BLALOCK JOHN C BONNEY WAYNE BOYD JOHN J BRADY CANDIDO CABRERA-RODRIGUE
FELIPE D CAMARILLO GARY M CARTER ROBERT L CASWELL DAVID W CHAMBERS LEVERN COSOM
LESLIE L CRANEY ALBERT W CUDWORTH STANLEY J CYGON EDWARD DAY PENA G DE LA
RAYMOND L DILLON MICHAEL W DOWNING RICHARD L FAHRENBRUCH JOHN W FOX ROBERT GONZALEZ
GREGG R FOURMENTIN WILLIAM J FREY GEORGE H GILLIAM FRED R GLOVER JOHN C HARDY
KENNETH J HONEK JAMES G JOHNSON JOSEPH L JORDAN PHILIP L KONIGSFELD JOSEPH B KUBE
JAMES M LANGFORD LESLIE J LANTOS CLIFTON MALONE JAMES MIRACLE JR QUINTEN E MULLEAVEY
RALPH C MCCOWAN ROGER A QUINN JOSEPH G QUIRION JR DANNY J RICHARDSON PAUL T WRIGHT
DOUGLAS C RISTINE ERVIN L RUSH GARY A RYDEN CHARLES P SCARANO RONALD L ZACH
WILLIE SHELTON EDGAR L SIMMONS HAROLD R SMITH ROBERT SMITH DON C SYKES
DAVID L SKUMURSKI WILLIE J SMITH ROBERT J SOVIZAL LENARD STREET JR ROOSEVELT THARRINGTON JR
DAVID C THOMAS JAMES C THOMAS THOMAS P VISKER ELBERT B WALKER GARY E WATSON
RONALD R REXROAD THEODORE W SANDIDGE JOHN T WILKINSON TERRY L BAXTER JERALD A BORMAN
ERNEST L BRIDGES LEON C BUEHLER MATTHEW J BUONO JESSE C BURROUGH RICHARD J CALL

PANEL 48E

RONALD T CAVAZOS JOHN L CHAMBERS SAMUEL C CHAVOUS JR BRADLEY E CLARK
ROBERT G ELGIN MICHAEL L FARMER CLIFFORD L FAULL DOUGLAS E FULCHER JOSE S GARZA
LORN D COMPTON HEINRICH GERSTHEIMER TAHER F GHAIS ROBERT O GIRDNER WILLIAM E GRACE
DANIEL GUARDADO LEO B GUNNING FRANK V HERRERA CARL L HILL JR CECIL R HOBBS JR
JAMES O HOLLOWAY JR ROBERT M JACOB RAYMOND J JOHNSON WALTER C JONES III DONALD B KEARNEY
JOHN R KEMPER CHARLES L KING TOMMY D KNAPP LAWRENCE H KOCHER FRANKLIN O LEGGETT
BRIAN V LINDBERG CHARLES C MILLER ROBERT J MOORE JOE M MORAN DOUGLAS G MORTON
LAWRENCE E OSBORNE DONALD B PAYSOUR GEORGE R PECKHAM DONALD L PERILLO ROBERT R PERRINS
DAVID A PETERS RONALD G PHEARS JIMMY D PICKLE MIKE R RASBERRY GENE K ROSS
ROBERT H RANGES JR JAMES R REDFORD DAVID A ROSENBERGER ROBERT L RUNKLE DAVID J SCHULTZ
JERRY W SHAIN MORRIS R SHEPARD JR JAMES G SIGNETT DENNIS SMITH MARK G STICKELS
LARS P SUNDELL CHARLIE B THOMAS EDWARD L TOWSLEE FAUSTINO TREVINO STEVE M TRIVELPIECE
ROBERT L TAYLOR WILLIAM C VANCE LUTHER T WILDER DAVID L WILLIAMS JOHN D WOODARD
JON M YOUNG DOUGLAS G BAILEY WALTER J BERNREUTHER VANCE A BERRY CHESTER BOB
ANDREW Z BUCIOR JOHN F CANDELAS JAMES A CARDINALE PATRICK J CONROY DONALD J MATOCHA
LARRY R CREECY GEORGE E EDDEN ROBERT E GIRSCH CEPHUS GRIFFIN JR ALAN R GUYMON
DOUGLAS R HARP DONALD A HARRELL JOHN C HAVLICK JOHN R HENDRIX CARL E HOSNANDER
PETER Y CLAW ERNEST A LANG RAFAEL MARTINEZ-SANTIAG DOUGLAS D MCMAHON CHARLES H NEEL JR
WALTER M OSTAPCHUK JAMES A PEMBERTON BURTON W PETERSON JR JOHN R PIERINI GARY A RHODES
KENNETH R ROBERTS NORMAN E SMALL WESLEY W SPERLING KENDALL A STAKE PAUL H STEIN JR
JOHN P SUPPLE ROBERT R THOMPSON DAVID W TIMM BRUCE TORTORICI ROGER E WARD
RICHARD E WILLIAMS JOE A WITTKOP FRED YOUNG RICHARD M BARGAR IVAN R FEBO-BETANCOURT
ROBERT L BARKER JR RONALD M BEECK ROBERT J BENSON JAMES T BLALOCK LEE A BOWDEN
JOSE BRENES-ESCOBAR ELMER W BROWN WILLIAM F BROWN MARVIN E BURROWS WILLIAM D CANUP
MARK O CHARETTE ROBERT E COOK PAUL P DAVIS SAMUEL L DAVIS JACK D DOWNS PAUL F NEWMAN JR
LEE S ADAMS DALTON M ESTEIN GARY D FORTNER ORONZO GEMMATI BOBBY J GRAVEL
JOSEPH F GULLUNG III DANNY E GUTHRIE WILLIAM T HANCOCK ALAN R HAUGEN WILLIAM D HOFFMAN
JOHN B HURTADO ALLAN H JORDAN WALTER E JOYCE JR GREGORY R KELLY ROBERT B KERCHNER
DANIEL R KETTMANN HARRY J KORDASIEWICZ HERMAN A LOHMAN JR FREDERICK E LOVE LARRY J LYONS
ALLEN G MACK EDWARD U MASTERS MARTIN H MILEK VICTOR R MILLER CHARLES W MOODY
EDWARD A MCGRATH MICHAEL P MCLAUGHLIN TIMOTHY J NIGHTENGALE JOSEPH S NITKA DEAN G OWEN
DALE W PARKER DAVID A PARKER ANTHONY J PEPPER DANIEL F REID BENITO B RODRIGUEZ
ROBERT G PIAZZA JAMES E RICHARDSON DANIEL A ROCHA MANUEL V ROMERO RUDY J SALAZAR
JAMES R SANFORD JR LUIS G SCAMARONI RUSSELL W SCARBOROUGH JAMES E SILFEE ALFRED D SMITH JR
MICHAEL A SNYDER JIMMY R SPACH RONALD D SPARKS STEVEN L SPARKS JAMES M TRIMBLE
LAWRENCE A SWANGUARIM WILLIAM M THOMPSON DANIEL R TWITTY CLIFTON WALKER DONALD L WALL
LEE A WATSON RALPH C WIGHT JR GEORGE L WILSON LARRY M WOLPERT GERALD F YOUNG
GILBERT J ADAME JOHN ADKINS THOMAS J BAYES SILVESTER BEAUREGARD JOSE R BERNAL
CLIFFORD BIAS JAN E BOBOWSKI JR RICHARD S BROWN MICHAEL J CAIN EFREN CARMONA
RICHARD M CORRALES LIONEL R CRASE MELVIN L DOLBY LEONARD D ERICKSON LEO F MALONE
PAUL D FLOURNOY LORRENCE T FRIDAY ALLAN J GAINES DOUGLAS W GUEST JR JOHN L INGRAM
EUGENE M JOHNSON JR VICTOR E KIDD DENNIS L KNOTT JERRY F LENTZ ARMAND P LESAGE
JOHN H LIBBY ELMER R LINDSEY JR GREGORY L LITTLEJOHN RICKEY J MARSON ROBERT L SAMUELSON
ROBERT W MCCASKEY ARTIS W MEADOWS JR GRAHAM L MILLS CLIFTON MOSES JOHN E MOUNT
WILLIAM R MCGEE FRED H MCMURRAY JR THOMAS S NASH ROGER M NELSON TILO R OESTERREICH
JEARL R PATTEN ROBERT C PEDA JOHN F QUATTLEBAUM MICHAEL L RANSBOTTOM JOSEPH M REES
DANIEL J CLEVENGER JAMES D RICHARDSON WILLARD M ROBINSON DONALD R SCHROEDER OTTO W SEE
JAMES P SMITH JOHN M SNYDER JR ROBERT L TATE JEFFRY R THARALDSON GEORGE M WEITZEL
JAMES R WELLS RALPH N WELLS GLENN A WESTPHAL WILLIAM J WHITEHEAD GILBERT WILEY
WILLIAM L YOHN GILBERT L ZERBST GLENN U ANDREOTTA RICHARD G BAMBRICK HAROLD E BARRICK
MELVIN B BROWN ROBERT H COLEGROVE GENE F COLLIER CLAYTON A CRAFT JERRY W DILLOW
EDWIN D CONNELL HERBERT T CROSS CHARLES M DUTTON STANFORD M GOUGH ALLEN E GROSHONG
ARTHUR W HUNT III ALAN P JONES JOHNNY R KING STEVE D LEDFORD PAUL L SAWYER JR
FRANK J MASTROMATTEO RANDALL C PHELPS JOHN F PLUNKARD GEORGE A PRUITT JUAN N SEDILLO
HARRY E SMITH RICHARD J SMITH JON F VAN DUYN BILLY J VICKERS WILLIAM O WAGNER
ALBERT W WARTHAN ARTHUR J WEINPER SALVATORE AGRI JR ANDREW J BABYAK JR THOMAS F CAMPBELL
JAMES R CHINN JAMES W COOPER PATRICK C COUGHLIN THOMAS F DAZEY JR JAMES D DILLON

PANEL 49E

RONALD L FRAZIER CHARLES W GARBER JR CLAUDE H GREEN GREGORY H WATKINS
GERALD S HANSEN KENNETH A HARDIN RICKY G INLOW BILLY L JACKSON LARRY B JENKINS
PHILLIP M KIDD BENJAMIN K KISSLING LOUIS M LANE KARL W LAWSON WAYNE R LE FEBER
PHILIP T LINDSAY GEORGE E MCDONALD JR ROLAND E MOORE KEVIN S MULGREW MICHAEL D NEWLAND
JOSEPH R PAULETTE EMERY N POITROW CHARLIE RAINEY DENNIS W REED JACK R REINKE
DOUGLAS G THOMPSON PEDRO VALENZUELA ROBERT L VANDERMUELEN DAVID F WAGNER
GREGORY J WILLIAMS WILLIE G WILSON ROBERT H WOOD EDWARD A ZAGER DANIEL L ACKERMAN
RONNIE F BRANAM SHERRICK C BRITTON AUBREY A BRYAN GARY L BURKE FRANK H BUSHEY
DONALD E CALHOON CRECENCIO CARDOSA CLYDE C COLLINS RONALD DAVIS ROBERT J MARCANTONI
GEORGE N DEVERALL LAWRENCE W ELLER ALAN R GAULT WILLIE E GLOVER ALLEN D HANLAN
CHIP R HARRISON KIMMEY D HOBBS DENNIS F HUGHES WAYNE C JESTER RAYMOND E KELLER JR
ROBERT J KLINE DONALD C LEE GARY D LOKKEN THEODORE D VAN STAVEREN GORDON D WALENSKY
HARRY F CARVER CHARLES A MAJER ROBERT D MARCO WILLY R MICHALIK BRYAN T MUKAI
RICHARD L MURRAY JONATHAN NEAL SAMUEL J PADGETT JAMES A PALENIK JR WILLIAM POWELL
JOSEPH A PURYEAR MARTIN J REIDY LIONEL L ROBINSON RONALD P SCHWORER WAYNE A SLANKARD
STEVE KLARIK YLDEFONSO SOLA-MALDONADO ROBERT J SOWINSKI HAROLD TOMPKINS MICHAEL P UMEL
ROBERT W MADSON TOMMY D WALKER CHARLES E WILCOX JR MAXIE R WILLIAMS JR JESSE L WILLOUGHBY
RONALD J WOJTKIEWICZ ROBERT N WRIGHT STANLEY ZALEWSKI JR FRANK P ADDICE PAUL J ALLEN
GARY W ARNOLD KEITH N ATCHLEY RICHARD ATWOOD ROBERT W BELCHER LEONARD G CHESLEY JR
JERRY D CLARK DENNIS R DAVIDSON MICHAEL G DEMARCO PERRY DICKEN JR FREDERICK H WHITTEMORE
EDWARD J DOWNEY JR RICHARD E ERWIN CHARLES R FINLEY DELLWYN A FITCH LAWRENCE L FULLAWAY
EUGENE R GANNON FREDERICK D GRATEN LARRY D HATCHER TIMOTHY HENDERSON JOHN A HOGGATT
JOHN P HOLDEN II WILLIAM L KINNARD DOUGLAS W MCCARTY JOHN M MILLER GEORGE W MOORE
JAMES R MCCLELLAND JOHN W MCFARLANE BRUCE F MCMILLAN JERRY R NICHOLS JOHN A NIXON
FREDERICK R OHLER JACK W OSBORN PETER E POWELL RONALD E RIEDE GUILLERMO A RUIZ-BERNARD
JOHN A OSCELUS CLAUDE ROBERTS JACK A SANDERS JR CHARLES C THOMPSON KENNETH D THOMPSON
JAMES A DILL DAVID M TOMLINSON PATRICK F VAN DUYNHOVEN ARTHUR C WILLIAMS JR JAMES C WOOD
CHARLIE K WOODEN DAVID P ANDERSON WARREN M BEAUMONT PATRICK M BIERLEIN ALAN P BUTKUS
EDWARD C BECKWITH DONALD J BOAZ BILLY J BROWN CARL L CARLSON ROBERT S CLARK JR
RUSSELL H CORNISH JOHN E CUNNINGHAM JR WILLIAM J DE LISA WALLACE J DIETZ STEPHEN J ECKLE
ROBERT W ELLSWORTH ROCKFORD G EVERETT PHILIP F GAINES EDWARD L GOODMAN EDWARD L HARRIS
JOHN F FITZGERALD ROBERT G HARRIS DARREL B HELMKE JACK W HESS ALAN J HETTICH
GARY R HOLLAND BENNIE F HUMPHRIES RICHARD W JOLES BYRON N JONES DWAYNE C MCCLURE
WILLIAM E MAXWELL ROBERT L MELTON JR PETER A MENDOZA MICHAEL W MILLER ARTHUR L MILLS
MORRIS K JAMES CLEATUS W MCCLANAHAN PATRICK G MCGARVEY THOMAS M MCVAY GLENN L MOLLER JR
REYNALDO N OROZCO NOLAN R RAY JOSEPH J STEIMBACH LOYD E STROISCH HUBERT E WAFORD
DAVID A STRUPP HAROLD A THARP JR DONNY G TIDWELL JONES E TOMLINSON GEORGE F VISE
FLOYD W PETTIE III DOUGLAS R WEIHER RAYMOND ARMSTRONG FRANK W ATHERTON ROLAND L BALLEW

263

THE VIETNAM VETERANS MEMORIAL COLLECTION

AUGUST T BATTAGLIA JOHN M BELL ROGER A BOOMSMA LUIS B CAMPOS RICHARD E CAWLEY
RAY T COMFORT PATRICK H COOK JR CHARLES C CROW RICHARD L EMBREY JAMES E HODGE
ATANACIO GOMEZ JR AGAPITO GONZALES JR JOE E GRIFFITH RANDOLPH M HARRISON JOHN OKEMAH
FRED J HAYES ROBERT C HEALEY JR DOUGLAS R HEATH STEPHEN J HINDS KENNETH L HINNANT
ROBERT L DODSWORTH LARRY C HOPPER GLENNIS R KELLAMS ALAN A KETTNER RODNEY H KOEHNE
WILLIAM J KRALIK ERNEST E LESURE DOUGLAS L LONG JR BARRY D LORD QUILLARD F LYONS
RICHARD A ESTRADA DONALD L MANSFIELD GERALD C MULL JOHN E NELSON JAMES L PARKER JR
RICHARD PEGUERO PAUL E POIRIER ALFRED L POWELL WILLIAM E PROPST JOSEPH C REID
WILLIAM G PARKER RICHARD A RENFRO WAYNE A RHODES WARREN J ROBINSON JOSEPH W SHORT
JERRY A SNIPES STANLEY SPIKES JUAN P VALDEZ LAWRENCE J VARGAS ALFRED V WHITMER
GRADY THACKER KENNETH M WATSON STEPHEN J WESTPHAL PAUL L WHITTHORNE JR WILLIAM W WILSON
GEORGE E WINFIELD DENNIS J YETMAR ANTHONY A ALENCASTRE RICHARD A ANDERS ARTHUR BOBBITT
WILLIAM H BOSWELL DANIEL A BRANSON ROGER L CARPENTER JORGE A CASTRO JAMES C COCHRAN
GEORGE A DILLON JOSEPH EDMONDS TERRY L FUHRMAN JAMES J GREB CHARLES J NIELSEN
DE W KING GARY H LEARY BENJAMIN E LENNARD JR HECTOR R MARIN-RAMOS TIMOTHY G MATTSON
JOSEPH A JANOWICZ REUBEN C MCMACKINS JR STANLEY J MICHALOWICZ JAMES R NASH JAMES A PETTITT
RAY L FERRY III

PANEL 50E

GEORGE QUAMO RICHARD F RENNOLET PHILIP F SHERIDAN RONALD C SMITH STANLEY R STELLMACH JR
GEORGE D STONE STEVEN E TAYLOR MARVIN L VOTAW EUGENE WALTON ROBERT F WILLIAMS
RICHARD G ANDERSON WALTER J CHRUPCALA CHARLES M CORRY BENJAMIN S FORDHAM BILLIE JAMES
ROBERT FRITSCHE JR HOMER H HAWS JERRY W HEUER RONALD L HOLTZHOUSER ROBERT E MALONE
GEORGE J ECONOMOUS JR ROBERT W GRANT LAUREN D HUERD DENNIS L KLIMPKE ALBERT G MAROSCHER
WILLIAM L MATTHEWS JR JAMES T MCMASTERS JAMES H METZ JAMES E NICOLAISEN JOHN J O'BRIEN
KIM R PARLIAMENT PATRICK C PATTERSON MICHAEL P PAVLOCAK JR EDWARD A RHODE RICHARD N RIVARD
PATRICK F SCHAROSCH KENNETH D SCHWARTZ DENNIS R SIETSEMA LARRY E SLOAN LOUIS WILLIAMS
STEVEN D SMITH DENNIS R THORPE JAMES A TREMBLAY ROBERT L TREVATHAN JOHN E WALTERS
DANIEL F SANDOVAL ARNOLD S WHITE EDWARD C ADAMS JOSEPH H ALLEN WILLIAM R AMMON
WILLIAM C AVERITTE CHRISTOPHER P BATTAGLIA REGINALD C BELL CHARLES B BOYNTON JR BRUCE K CRAIG
DAVID D BROWN JR DANIEL K CHRISTIAN ROBERT D CICIO BILLY J COLE WILLIAM F COLEMAN
WILLIAM ANDERSON JR GALE E CRAUN HAROLD D DANIELS JOHNSTON DUNLOP WENDELL GUILLORY
DAVID HABERMAN LESLIE P HAGARA MICHAEL P HAYDEN LAWRENCE HIMMER JACK L HINKLE
RONALD D HINSON WILLIAM G HULWI JR ROY D HURLBERT NATHANIEL E JACKSON DANIEL J JASKIEWICZ
RICHARD W JOHNSTON JOSEPH M JONES DANNY R KILGORE ALFRED L LE BLANC JAY A PRICE
CHRISFINO D LEAL DENNIS W LINVILLE ROBERT H LITTLEFIELD JOHN E MALONE JACK W MARLOWE
MAURO MARTINEZ WILLIAM C MEDEIROS JOE R MELCZEK GARY P MERINGA HERVE J MOISE
DENNIS N JOHNSTON AUBREY D MCCLELLAND LARRY G MOORE ROBERT F OWENS TIMOTHY E OWENS
TERRY J RAMPULLA DAVID G REDENIUS ROBERT RICE JOSEPH RODRIGUEZ JOSE RUIZ
MARVIN G RUSH JOHN R SCHAAF HUGH E SCHAVELIN LOUIS C SCHLOTE STEPHEN E SEIFERTH
DONALD C SMITH ERNEST W SMITH SAMMY R SMITH ESMOND E SNELL JR NATHANIEL M WILLIAMS
NORMAN W TARPLEY LEROY TOWNES LARRY D WARREN NATHAN WASH JR ROBERT J WELLS JR
JERRY A SWEET SETH L WEST JR WILMER D WILSON ROBERT WRIGHT WILLIAM W WYMER
JAMES E YOUNG WARD L ANTHONY GARY M ARCHIBALD HOWARD W BANDELIER VERNON W BURGESON
CHARLES E ALLEN JAMES P BOYLE JAMES C BRYANT TOMMIE A CHAMBERS LARRY L CHAPMAN
JAMES C DELAPLANE JAMES E DICKERSON GEORGE S ELBERT CHARLES R FRANKLIN WILLIAM D WINSLOW
EUGENE L FREEMAN JR JERRY F GARCIA JAMES A GEROU MANUEL J GOMEZ ROBERT C HAMPSHIRE
THOMAS J HAYES IV JOHN W HELD JOHN D HOUSTON JR THEODORE HUBBARD JR GEORGE A HUDSON JR
JAMES L KELLER JEFFREY E LAMBERT FRANCIS W LAMON JR CHARLES T LANGENFELD ROGER L NEGER
CARLOS J MEDINA VICTOR G MIKA JERRY MOSBY WILLIAM W MOUTON LOUIS S MUCHA
WILLIAM A LAWRENCE KENNETH A MCCLAIN JIM C MCNAMAR JOSEPH W MULLEN JR WILLIAM P O'FARRELL
MICHAEL L PHEIFFER ALVIN L POUNDS LARRY G RUSSELL ROBERT F SERIO FREDDIE L SONAGGERA
JAMES T SUTTON RUDY M THOMPSON ROBERT G TOTH JOHN J VENNARD EDWARD J VICKS JR
WILLIAM J DOLAN DENNIS F WESTBROOK HOWARD C WILLIAMS JR TOMMIE D WILLIAMS DAVID K WYRICK
GEORGE G ADAMS PAUL E ADAMS MEL R BALLARD JERRY L BOYLES ROBERT J HESS
THOMAS E CARNEGIE DEMPSEY CHALMERS JR JAMES P CLARKE SAMUEL P COWAN JR DAVID W DORRIS
BARRY H DULYEA WILLIAM F ELDRIDGE ROBERT L ELMORE BERNARD L FOX WILBUR C GASKINS
GILBERT E BUCHANAN UDO HANNIGAN EARLIE H HICKS JR MICHAEL P HOUGH TAYLOR B HOWARD JR
THOMAS J LAWSON JOSE A LOPEZ JR STEFAN MAZAK ARNOLD PAIRIS CECIL L RENDER
STERLING G RIDDICK ROGER D SAUX WILLIAM C SHEARIN ROBERT J SMITH JAMES V SOLOMON
GARY E RUSHA DONALD E SMRTNIK PAUL M SPENCER JAN A ULMER ROBERT K VARICK
ERNEST VETTER JR JOHNNY R WEBB FREDERICK D WESCOTT REGINALD WILLIAMS JR GROVER C WRIGHT JR
LEE C ADAMS WILLIAM ADAMS JR DONALD R ALLEN CHARLES C BEARD DOUGLAS R BLODGETT
JOHN R BROOKS MICHAEL J CAPORALE JAMES D CRAFT CLIFTON H DAVIS DAVID K DEETER
WILLIAM R DENNIS KEVEN T DIREEN WILLFORD L DYER FRANK L FREEDLE ROBERT E GARDNER
JUAN GOMEZ-RIVERA TOMAS GONZALES JESUS A GONZALEZ FORREST GOUDELOCK OREN B MCCARROLL
DENNIS R HARTPENCE HERBERT R HAYASHIDA ANTHONY F HOUSH ALFRED JACKSON MELVIN L KIRK
JOHN L KOEBKE PAUL N LARSON MICHAEL G LIPSIUS ARTHUR J LORD CARLOS A MARCANO
WALTER F MATIS JR EDWARD T MELLO JR GILBERT MENDOZA JANIS MICULS CHARLES W MILLARD
CHARLES J HARRINGTON JERRY V MCDONALD JENIES I MOBLEY GEORGE W MONTGOMERY DAVID J NESSET
MARCELO ORTIZ JR DENNIS E PAINTER JAMES L PARSONS ANDREW J PAYNE JR RICHARD S PENNAMON

PANEL 51E

CURTIS R RILEY ARTURO R RIOS TIMOTHY G ROBINSON CASIMIRO RODRIGUEZ JR
DAVID G SALINAS CLIFFORD L SELL PHILIP R SHAFER CARY J SMITH MICHAEL J WALLACE
WILLIS W SMITH JR LAWRENCE J SNYDER TOMMY L TAYLOR RUSSELL L THOMPSON PERVIS B VALENTINE JR
MICHAEL R WERDEHOFF FREDDIE WHITAKER JOHN E WILBURN JEROME I WILSON WILLIAM P YORK
LEWIS J YOUNG KENT R BOLTER LARRY J BRANAUGH EDWARD E CARTER JOSEPH A CESTARE
JERRY J CHAPMAN MICHAEL M CLAYTON FRANK M DARLING ROME E DIMMERLING ROBERT W GLIDDEN
JOHN M GOODRICH LARRY E GOSWICK FRANCIS G GRAY JERRY R GRUBBS ROBERT C HAWES
JOHN B HUDSON LARRY J JENNINGS CHARLIE M JERNIGAN JOHN V JOHNSON JR WILLIAM G LAMBERT
LARRY W MACK JESUS MARTINEZ PAUL E MATTSON DAVID J MORENO JOSEPH A ZUTTERMAN JR
JAMES F MACMANUS CLAUDE MCCAN JR TERRY W MOTT PATRICK H NATALE LARRY L NEFF
ROBERT J NOTO RICKY L NULL TIMOTHY J O'KEEFE MICHAEL D PADILLA JAMES E PANTIER
WARREN C PARSONS JR RUSSELL G PETERSON JOHN E QUILLEN JR JOHN A RODGERS ROBERT B THOMPSON
SAMUEL REYNA ANTHONY R SMITH JERALD D SWAN LEO E SWAN JR JOHN B THOMPSON
RICHARD J TURBITT JR EDWARD D ULMAN RICARDO VILLARREAL WILLIAM J WALKER ORTEN L WARE
DARRYL C LINTNER BURNELL WILLIAMS JR SCOTT A WRIGHT ARNOLD AGUILAR MICHAEL B ALVAREZ
BILLY C ARMSTRONG IRVING D BARROWS MCDONALD E BOYCE WILLIE G BRIDGES ALFRED B CAFRELLI
GARY A CHABERT GERALD COHEN JOHN L COLEMAN PETER E CONLIN ROBERT L JOHNSON JR
JAMES E CREAMER JR JOHN L CZECHOWSKI JR ALBERT DAVIS DON E DAVIS JOSE A MARRERO-RIOS
RONALD P DEAN ROYCE E EDDLEMAN NEIL H EXUM ROBERT D FULKERSIN DOMINGO R GONZALES
JACK D GOODE RONALD D GRIFFIN LANE K HARGROVE EUGENE HARRIS HIAWATHA HICKS
KEVIN R CASSELL THOMAS M HOLCOMBE SAMUEL R HUGHES LARRY C JAMERSON FRANKIE B JOHNSON JR
FRANCIS X KANE RONALD C KEARSLEY RICHARD C KLINKENBERG ROBERT C LINK LYLE E MACKEDANZ
GENE T COVEY RALPH M MAHONEY CECIL J MOSER CHARLES MRDJENOVICH JOHN M VAUGHN
WILLIAM M NEELEY BERNARD J NEWHOUSE ROBERT L OLLOM FLOYD W OLSEN CHARLES W REBERG
JAMES W RUDD RICHARD J RUDD JR JOHN G SPINDLER ROBERT J STAVINOHA GRIDLEY B STRONG
CHARLES J MEERHOLZ JR MICHAEL G TURNER DAVID S URIAS RONALD F VAN AVERY FELIX VAZQUEZ JR
TIMOTHY R WILLIAMS THOMAS J WORLEY JR DAVID P ZIMMERMAN CLARK E BARLOW JAMES E BELL
RAY W BERG JR HARVEY W BOOKER JERRY L BOOKER JACKIE A CARRANO WILLIAM L CHIFOS
ALEXANDER CHISOLM WILLIAM CHOMYK DAVID L COOLEY ROGER A DAINS JOHN A GREENFIELD
JAMES E GUSTAFSON HERBERT L HAMMOND HENRY A HEAL JR RICHARD A HILL REYNALDO A SANCHEZ
GEORGE P KLEIN DANIEL MASON BOYD C MINK LESTER L MOORE SAMUEL MORALES
THOMAS F NORTON EDWIN D PALMGREN JOHN W PARCEL HENRY PASILLAS MICHAEL G PRICE
NORMAN L HINKLE CHARLES J RACHON SIMON RANDALL ROBERT P RIGGINS RONALD E SPROUSE
JOHNNY S TAITAGUE THURMAN T WALLS EDWARD E WHALEN ROBERT R WHITE JR WALTER R WINDER JR
DANIEL E WOLFE THOMAS S ALFRED JAMES W ALLEN ARTHUR W BALL WILLIAM G BANEY JR
THOMAS K BEAMON DAVID M BRANCIO STANLEY A BULLIS MICHAEL CACCIUTTOLO MORRIS E CASH
RONALD H CHILCOTT JESSE J COON CLAUDE H COVINGTON CHARLES S COX JAMES B CROCKETT
THOMAS J DAVIDSON THOMAS J DAVIS DON F DIAN AMOS O FOX WILLIAM M PANGLE
HARLEY F GRIGGS LEWIS A HARMON DONALD G JACKSON LOUR LE DESMA TORO S LOPEZ-DEL
GARY LODUHA RUSSELL L MATHENY ANDREW L MCDANIEL ROBERT E MEEHAN DAVID MURPHY
HENRY T CURTIS II ANDRES L NARVAEZ-MARRERO RONALD OGLESBY LYNN A PIERSON ASHTON H PRINDLE
JAMES E RAINBOLT ARTHUR W ROMERO JOSEPH SANTORI HARRY L SOWELL JR DAVID P SPEATH
JOHN L VINCENT JACKIE D WALKER JAMES L WALLACE JOHN S WISEMAN HERMAN A HESSELSCHWARDT
GEORGE B AYERS JOSEPH R BENNETT JOSEPH J BRADY DAVID J CABALLERO MICHAEL J COX
PAUL B CREIGHTON STEVE DAVIS RUSSELL F DEITCHLER RALPH FREDENBERG CRECENCIO C GARCIA
LARRY E ANDERSON DONALD M GUTRICK GEORGE B HERTLEIN III FERNANDO J HUGHES WILLIAM G KEYES
BUFORD G JOHNSON LARRY A JONES PAUL KASSATKIN KENNETH E KOTYLUK DALE L LAMBERT
CHARLES L MCLAURIN JOHN E MULCAHY LUIS A ORTIZ-PEREZ WOODROW W PARKER II TERRY W SHOOT
BRIAN H PHILIBERT ARDEN K RENVILLE JAY D RICHTER FRANK R SIMMONS JOHN H SOUTH

PANEL 52E

BOBBY G VINSON RALPH VOSS LESTER T WALKER JOHN M WEATHERFORD
STUART A WERNER CURTIS R WRIGHT CARMELLO ANGE JR DONALD BALKIT JACK BITTING
ALBERT BURCIAGA JOSEPH BURKES RONALD J CAMPBELL JAMES P CAWLEY ARTURO OLIVARES-MARTINE
ANDREW P CORBIN GREGORY J CROSSMAN PAUL L DENNIS LINDEN D EILER JR ERVIN J HOYT
ERIC FICKLIN BILLY R GIVENS PATRICK J GRAHAM PHILLIP W GRINDOL HUBIA J GUILLORY
RONALD J COLONE DONALD R HANNA DENNIS W HOFF JAMES O JAYNES DANIEL M KELLEY
JAMES D KENDALL ROBERT C KIMMEL EDGAR C LAYE JR KARL LUCAS MICHAEL P MAKUCK
WILBUR F MATTOX HENRY T MCCRIMMON BOLEN P MCGEE ALBERT C MITCHELL VICTOR A MOHR
RICHARD A BROOKS JERRY D MCMANUS BRUCE P NETTESHEIM WILLIAM D NODDIN CARMINE NOVEMBRE
ANIBAL R ORTIZ-RIVERA ROBERT D PATTERSON WILLIAM RAUBER EDWARD C ROOT JESSE L SAMFORD
BROCK R SCHRAMM DAVID L SCOTT FRED SENA JR KENNETH G SPENCER GARY A STADING
RONALD T STETTER THOMAS E TONGRET RONALD J WALBER RONALD N WANBAUGH MICHAEL J WARREN
DALLAS T ADAIR JR ANJELO J APRILLIANO ELDON A BAKER MICHAEL J BALITCHIK GEORGE R BENNETT
BERYL S BLAYLOCK PAUL D BOYETT DAVID A BROWN ROBERT L BROWN GENE M BURKELL
RUSSELL D BURGESS MICHAEL F CAMPBELL THOMAS J CARROLL NATHANIEL B CLARK HARRIS L COLLINS
HARLEY R COWAN JESS W CREASON JR DALE A CRULL THOMAS F CUMMINGS WILLIAM C DE WEESE
PETER F DONNELL WILFRED DRAPER DONALD K DUDLEY MICHAEL T EVANS WILLIAM L FIX
BILLY R FOSTER JOHN A FRANKLIN RUSSELL R FYAN STEVE A HARDING DAVID L HARTY
CAREY D HARMON STEVEN C HEFFNER DANNY E HEREAU WAYNE H HOFFNER ROY D HUMPHREY
WILLIAM R JENNETT KENNETH L JOHNSON TERRY J KENNEY MARC J KUZMA ROY A LAMON
ROBERT E LEA MILTON A LEE EDDIE L MILLER FRED A MILLER KURT MUELLER JR
JOHN L MCDANIEL JAMES J MCKINSTRY JR CALVIN I NESBITT DANIEL J O'CONNOR RICHARD J OLSON
ALBERT A PETERSON DONALD W PRATT DENNIS E PURCELL THOMAS E RAUBOLT GEOFFREY D SAUNDERS
JAMES C SMITH RAYMOND J SMITH MICHAEL P STILES LILBURN R STOW EARL P SUMMERSILL
TERRY L TEBBETTS ROBERT E TERRELL JAMES W TERRY LARRY R TODD JAMES L TURNER
WILLIAM F VANDERVORT JR LARRY A WINCHESTER ROBERT L WORRELL EDWARD J ZEWERT JR ROBERT E FUSS
DONALD E ANGERMAN ROBERT BADCOCK CHARLES J BONGARTZ ROBERT J BOWDERN JR JOHN P KELLEY
HOLLIS W BUCK JAMES R CAMPBELL RICKEY L CHRAN THOMAS S COLE ROBERT S CROKE
GEORGE B ALLISON MELVIN J DECKER JONATHON L GENS MARTIN W GUARD FERNANDO GUTIERREZ
KEVIN P BEAUCHAMP GARY N HALL HOWARD H HOMINICK GEORGE E JACOBS WILLIAM JURSZA JR
LOYD E KINSWORTHY TIMOTHY L O'DELL FRED OLIVER JR MICHAEL W ORASH DANIEL PERRY
WAYNE E SEXTON WILLIAM J SEYKORA LAWRENCE WILLIAMS ROGER D ZEIGLER RICHARD S BANKS
DAVID L BARBER DAVID T BARNES FREDRICK E BAUERLE III JORDAN BELCHER DAVID J BERRY
LARRY C BOLYARD JOSEPH C BORS JERRY W BRYAN JAMES D CAIN COYTE D CAMPBELL
LEONARD CARABEO RICHARD W CARDINALI RICHARD A CASSANO WILLIAM R COOK JIMMY L CURRY
ARTHUR L DAVIS CHARLES E DAVIS FRANKLIN R DU LONG JOHN DUFFY JACKIE L ELSTON
BILLY K FORD JOHN B GINGERY ROBERT L GLENN JR WILLIAM H HARFF JR DALE E HILL
ELMER D HILL ROBERT E HOLEYFIELD WILLIAM H HOLLMEN SIDNEY A HOWE ROBERT L MENDIOLA
DANIEL W KEO THOMAS P KLAUSING JAMES F LANG JOHN W LANKFORD MICHAEL R LUCAS
JOHN T INTIHAR JOHN S MANCHESTER PEDRO A MAYMI-MARTINEZ STEVEN M MCARTHUR LUIS R MUNOZ
ROBERT L MCDUFFY DICKIE O NELSON LEWIS C NELSON ROGER NESTER VALENTINE A OCHS
EDGAR D PAGE MILLARD L PALMER RICHARD W POWELL JR MELVIN PRYOR SR ROBERT W ROMERO
AMEL D ROYALTY ROBERT SAAVEDRA JAMES E SAND MICHAEL J SAUNDERS ROBERT P SHELLEM
RONNIE G SLAY MICHAEL F SMITH HOWARD W SNITCHLER THOMAS C STRICKLIN HENRY WUNDERLICH
IVOL M YORK WILLIAM E ZIMMERMAN JR GERALD D AITON LYLE E ALLEN JR ROBERT E ANDERSON
DIXIE C BERGER BEN S BITEL GERALD R BROWN ELMO L BUTLER WALTER K CLARKE
RONALD D COBB THOMAS S COOK LARRY O COPELAND RONAL E CRITZER GARY L DANIELS

PANEL 53E

EDWARD A GAFFNEY HAROLD HENASEY JAMES A HERING GEORGE L MAUGHAN SR
HARLEY J JENKS ANDREW J JOBEY LEROY JOHNSON ROBERT W JOHNSON JR ARTHUR L JORDON
JOSEPH T KOVALOFF DAVID G LEDGERWOOD JAY L LIEBERMAN JOSEPH A MAAG JR VERNON W NIX III
JOHN T DUNLAP III GARY L MACK ELMER MARTIN DAVID L MASSA ANTHONY L MOORE
GEORGE LATHAN ARTHUR F MCQUADE JR HURIEL L MOORE DONALD L MUSSELMAN THOMAS A NYSTROM
LLOYD W PEELE JR WILLARD A PERRY JR WALTER G POPE JAMES W POWERS JR STEPHEN R WHITE
WILLIAM A ROAR LORENZO STEGALL DAVID F STRICKLER ALEXANDER TATE JR THOMAS L TWYFORD
ADOLFO M PEREZ CLIFFORD E TYSON JAMES E WALKER JR DAVID V WHINNERY LUCKY G WHITE
GARY WISNIER GARY L YOUNG WALTER F BARNES CHARLES J BEHM JR JAMES S BENNETT
LARRY F BRASHEARS PATRICK L BRUCKNER MICHEAL A BURNS ERNEST BURTON BENNY D CASH
WALTER A CICCHIANI JOHN R D'AGOSTINO JR LOREN K DAVEY ROBERT J DIEDRICH RICHARD L ENDICOTT
MICHAEL R DIGGS ROBERT J ENEDY DAVID K FELLER PHILIP G FRANKLIN CHARLES L FRISBY
EDDIE A GARDNER MARCELLO C GARZA JR CARL R GIBSON ROY L GIBSON JOHN A GLORIOSO
GEORGE GREGORIUS LOUIS F GUILLERMIN CECIL M HAIGLER WILLIAM H HANCOCK II EDWARD L MANN JR
DALE J HESS JOHN P HOLCOMB NICHOLAS L HOLLINGSWORTH JOHN F HUTZELL RAY D JAMES
DONALD R JOHNSON PAUL C JOHNSON SEEBER J KELLY DALE L KRUSE LARRY J LEINDECKER
GERALD A GRANSBURY GIANCARLO LUCCHESI SAMMY R LUSK LARRY E LUTZ EDUARDO MARQUEZ JR
JOHN C MATTHEISEN PAUL L MILLER ROGER D MILLS MANUEL MOORE ROGER W MORGAN
ROBERT A MCPHERSON LAWRENCE J MCRAE GEORGE C NORRIS ROLLIE M NORTHOUSE RUSSELL W NOYES
ADAM S NAJAR JOHN M ODELL RONALD E PARR JOHN E PASQUANTONIO EDWARD L PERRY
ELMER J PERRY JR DONALD L PETERSON NORMAN I PHIPPS ROBERT E PIETSCH SOREN PRIP
JEROME RAWLINGS JOHNNIE G REID DAVID R ROGERS MICHAEL E SANTOS ARTHUR G SCHAUERMANN
EDWARD M SHELTON JR SAMUEL A SINGER BRUCE W STAEHLI RAYMOND E STANLEY CHARLES E TATE
ALLEN L TERRY ARIE TERRY PAUL THORIK JR ALEXANDER TSIROS HAROLD J VIERHELLER JR
ROBERT A VINTON JR ALLAN C WARD JACK A WHETSEL JR EDDIE J WHITE JAMES E WHITE
ROBERT E FLOYD GERALD S WILLIAMS ROBERT L WILLIAMS ALFRED M WOLFE JAMES R WORLEY
MICHAEL L ALFORD KENNETH C BAXTER THOMAS E BONDERER JAMES L BOSHEERS PATRICK J HARRINGTON
WILLIAM G BUTLER JR GEORGE G CAPPARELLI DONALD L CARNES GARY S CAYWOOD JAMES M CHRISTIE
PAUL J COCHRAN ELBERT E COX JR RUSSELL D CRIDER HOWARD R CROTHERS DANIEL W DALEY
HERMAN B DE LEON HERALD L DELANEY ROBERT A ENGELSEN DONALD R EVANS JIMMIE L GROOMS
JAMES R FEDRO SR BARRY L FRAZIER ANTONIO GARCIA LESLIE N GENERAL DONALD P GERVAIS
AMIE J DURAN GELASIO N GOMEZ JR JAMES R HAMMONDS DENNIS I HARDIN WAYNE L HARLAND
THOMAS E BUMP REYES C HERNANDEZ JR GARY P HILL WILLIAM L HILL ROBERT S HOSKINS
JOHN K HOUSE DONALD E HUNTER SHERMAN J HUSSEY KENNETH E ISER CHARLES E JOHNSON
DAVID A JONES RICHARD W KANONCZYK LARRY D KELLEY DENNIS D LAWVER LAWRENCE J MERSCHEL
STEVEN J LAYTON JOSEPH F LODISE JR RONALD D LOVELADY THOMAS K LYONS ROBERT T MADEL
RAYMOND P MARKHAM RICHARD D MARTIN DENNIS R MASON EARNEST L MASON JR MICHAEL J MASSEY
DONNIE S KEGG RAYMOND G MENDIBLES JACKIE G MONTGOMERY TERRY E MOORE PAUL M NANCE JR
JOHN R NEARY II MICHAEL B O'CONNOR GEORGE C OLSEN GASPER ORLANDO DANNY R WEST
GERALD L PARSONS RAPHAEL A PERALTA GEORGE E PETERS JR DWIGHT G REICHLE DONALD R SCHAFER
JOSEPH L SHREVE JR RICKEY D SMITH EUSEBIO SOLIS DAVID A STREMLER THOMAS F STROTHERS JR
ANTHONY TAYLOR JOHN H TEETOR WILLIAM A THOMAS JR WILLIAM P TOWNSEND JR BARRY W VAN HORN
MICHAEL M O'BRIEN THOMAS M WHITE WARREN T WHITMIRE JR CLIFFORD D WILLIAMS DAN R YOUMANS
PAUL L ABRAHAM RICHARD F ABSHIRE JAMES S ALLPORT RALPH T ANDERSON JOHN A ANSELL JR

PANEL 54E

REGINALD BAKER ERROL M BARRIMOND RICHARD L BARTLOW O D BRUNNER
DAVID R BINGHAM KENNETH BLACKWELL GROVER W BOSTON THOMAS J BRADFORD EARNEST W BROWN
RONALD BUKOWSKI JAMES R BURKE STEVE BUTOROVIC WILLIE C CLARK WALTER K CLEVELAND
LOUIS G COHEN MICHAEL D CRAIG ROY R CRAM EVANS B CROCKER JR GEORGE L CRUSE
FRANCIS S DEVINE JR ALAN J DICK THOMAS E DIEFFENDERFER RONALD G DOBBS LAWRENCE J ENGLANDER
RONALD L FAVOURITE JERRY FIELDS ROBERT B FINDLAY WALLACE B FOARD JR NELSON E FOURNIER
EUGENE FRANKLIN RICHARD M GALLERY JESSE E GARCIA JAMES S HADLEY JR THOMAS G IDLE
LEON G HAMILTON JR MICHAEL L HANSON PAUL A HARRISON JOHN E HAWTHORN FOSTER E HILL
EDWARD F GUTHRIE BENJAMIN A HONEYCUTT WILLIAM J HUGHES NATHANIEL H JACKSON RONALD JONES
RONNIE J JONES ROLAND R LAFOND RICHARD R LANDERS CHRIS J LARSEN III MICHAEL D LEE
THOMAS I LONG JOSEPH M LOUGHRAN JR JOHN M MALNAR ROBERT W MARTIN ADOLPH A MARTINEZ
HERBERT L MEADS EDWARD C MILLER JOHNNY MILLER JAMES D MOLPUS WILLIAM J MORSE
JAMES MCDONALD LARRY S MCKIBBEN LLOYD F MOSSEAU LLOYD F MOUSSEAU EDWARD L MUNSON BERNARD M PELLEGRINO
CLAUDE E MCQUEEN RICHARD H NALEY JAMES P NICHOLSON FELIX OCASIO MICHAEL D OLIVER
JOSEPH C PICKETT JR JEROME PRYOR DONALD D RANDALL JR CHARLES B REMER JR HUMBERTO REYES
THOMAS O REYNA MARK J ROMAN ROBERT A ROMO ALLEN D ROWLES ROBERTO SANCHEZ
THOMAS H SCHOFIELD LARRY C SCHWEBKE EDWARD S SMITH GEORGE A SMITH JERRY W SMITH
JACK L SNODGRASS GREGORY J STAPLES RALPH C STEWART PIERRE L SULLIVAN MATTHEW E SUTTON JR
MICHAEL A TEAGUE HOWARD M THOMPSON DENNIS S TOTCOFF CHARLES H TURNER JR CLYDE J VALSTAD
GEOFFREY R TAYLOR ISMAEL J VALDEZ JR DEAN VASQUEZ JULIUS L WALKER JR THOMAS M WALKER
JERYL L WATKINS BRIAN F WEDLAKE ROBERT L WEEDEN STEVE C WILDER PAUL M WILLIS
LEROY N WRIGHT PAUL L YOST PAUL A YOUNGMAN OLIVER ANDERSON BILLY W BRIDGEMAN
ROBERT D AVERY PAUL L BARKER ARNOLD L BOLINDER LONNIE A BROOKS JACK C CARCLAY
JESSE CARMONA JR ARTHUR F CHANEY STEPHEN W CLARK THOMAS D CLEM WALTER J DANCER
DANIEL F FENNEWALD RONALD R GAMBLE BRIAN G HUGHES WILLIAM I INMAN EDMOND A JABLONSKY JR
HERMAN JACKSON ROBERT P JOHNSTON DERVIN J KEISLING MICHAEL L KIDD CHARLES W KINNEY
JAMES A LANIER JOHN E MANSON RICHARD M MARTIN DENNIS R MCCOY BOBBY L MCKAIN
HOLLAND I LANGHAM WARREN F NICKEL JR ALAN P PAGLIARONI WILLIE L PONDER GREGORY G PRITCHETT
SCOTT D REED GEORGE J SINGLETON JULIAN SOLIZ JAMES R SOUTHEY ROGER H SPARKS
FRED P STAFFORD ORAL R TERRY RONALD C ANDERSON STERLING C BANKS SAMUEL H BONIFANT
JAMES R BOWDEN WILLIAM R BROOKS FRANKIE N CARTER JIMMY R CLARK ROLLIN D DAVIS
DARRELL W COTTRELL KENNETH M CRYAN ROBERT W DAMERON LARRY D DANIELS JOHN M DURHAM JOHN E SWANSON JR
JERRY T EVANS ANTHONY P EVERSULL ALLEN L FALER DOUGLAS B FOURNET ROBERT A FOWLER
EDWIN G GALINDO ROBERT D GARIEPY KELLUM W GRANT PAUL V GRASSO BILLY R GREENE
DWIGHT D JOHNSON WILLIAM W JOHNSON GERALD D KLEIN DOUGLAS B SMITH
JAMES E KRALOWSKI ARTHUR T KRAMER JR JOHN T LANE ROY B LEAGUE JERRY LENNON
GEORGE C LETMATE BRUCE S LINDSAY JOE J MASK BERNARD R MAZURSKY RICHARD T MILLS
THOMAS A MCCORMICK JR LAWRENCE MOBLEY SUTTON MOBLEY JR JOHN W MORAN SAMUEL T NEIL JR
DONALD E NIPPER DEMPSEY W PARROTT CHARLES L PERRY ROBERT G PRICE JACK E REYNOLDS
RONALD L HURST SANTIAGO RODRIGUEZ-LEBRON DAVID C SCHULTZ DONALD E SLATER ROBERT R SMALL
PAUL C KING JR DONALD J SWEAT ANTHONY W TORRES EGBERT R VAUGHAN JEFFERY A YERION
DARRIUS W ADAMS ROBERT S ALLEN BRUCE R BACKES CHRISTOPHER J BARBER FREDERICK A BARCLAY

PANEL 55E

JAMES W BARTON WESLEY G BAUGHMAN RENE G BAUMANN JESUS E BAUTISTA
JOHNNIE H BEASLEY ELROY E BEIER DAVID L BLATTEL DANIEL J BLOMFELT WILLIAM D BREIGHTMYER
ANTHONY R BELLAMY THEODORE R BONHAM JR GARY L BOUNDS JAMES E BOWMAN THOMAS G BROCKER
MARTIN E BROPHY BARRY L BROWN RICHARD A BROWN PETER BRUM FREDERICK BURGE
BERNES E BURRIS DONALD A CAMPBELL JAMES N CARROLL III GARRY R CHAPMAN MICHAEL J CHARLEY
PAUL E CHAVEZ EDDIE E CHERVONY RONALD W CHILD LOUIS CHIMERI FREDDIE J CIGAR
NICHOLAS S CONAXIS EDWARD W CONNELLY JR DANIEL J CONTESTABILE DAVID E DEVINE RICKY L DOYE
JOHN R CROUSE WILHELM K DAMMER GLENN E DAVIS THOMAS N DEAN CHARLES K DEERE
RAYMOND L COOK DOUGLAS J CRADEUR CORTLAND E DENNISON JIMMIE A DOLEN JOHN L DOWNING
MALCOLM C DULAC JERRY R DUNDAS JOHN W ECKELL RUSSELL W EGGERT PAUL R EVANS
JAMES D FERGUSON GERALD W FIEGLE MORRIS L FLEMING JAMES P FREEMAN THOMAS GARTLAND
GLENN T FEY BOBBY S FRYE SAMUEL R GARDNER RAYMOND L GEE JR ISADORE S GEIGER JR
JOSEPH G GILL LARRY F GLEASON RICHARD C GONZALES HARVEY D GRAY WILLIAM E GREKELA
HERMAN G GOODALL RICHARD A GREEN MATTHEW E GREER GARY A GUASP CARLYLE GUENTHER
RICHARD W HAGEL GARLAND G HALEY FOSTER HAMILTON SHERRON E HARBISON LENWOOD T HARRELL
DAVID A HAEFNER LESLIE E HARRIS JR WILLIAM E HEILMAN DUANE A HELMICK HAROLD T HENESY
ARTHUR R HENNING DENNIS E HINTON RALPH J HITCHCOCK PAUL R HOLLEY JOSEPH H KAZEKEVICIOUS
GREGORY T INDRECC JEROME E JACOBS JERRY L JANEWAY GERALD L JOHNSON MICHAEL L JOHNSON
RONALD A HILLMAN SANTFORD B KEMPKE ALVIN C KNIGHT JOHN R KNORR CARL KOLLMEYER
EDWARD C KRAWCZYK GENE A KUNST WAYNE C KURLIN STEPHEN M LASHINSKY JR ROY L LEDE
ROBERT J LESKA RICHARD G LEWIS STEVEN LEWIS DONALD E LOWE RONALD MIDDLETON
RICHARD C MADISON JUAN P MARTINEZ CHAD D MEADOWS GARY M MEIER RODNEY W MELTON
LLOYD LOCKETT DONALD L MERRY KENNETH E MESSENGER DONALD R MOCK MICHAEL MOMCILOVICH JR
JIMMY R MOORE KENNETH P MORROW LOUIS H NELSON GLENN E NICHOLSON ISRAEL PEREZ
MAX E NIMPHIE JR DUANE M NORMANDIN LYN D OBERDIER MICHAEL S OSTEEN THOMAS R OUILLETTE
WILLIAM J PAPA GARY L PARSONS JOHN H PATE JR ERNEST PAYNE DONALD M PERDUE
MICHAEL M MONTGOMERY JOSEPH R PIERCE ELBERT D POFF MILTON P POTIER ROBERT E QUICK
NELSON R RAMIREZ LYNLEY L RASH WILLIAM A REES BARRY T REINHARDT DAVID J ROBERTS
FRANCIS J ROBINSON CRAIG A ROOD ERNEST ROSADO SR MIGUEL A RUVALCABA-LOPEZ WILLIAM J SAFRIT
RONALD SAPORITO GARY O SCHLAMP WILLIAM E SHAFFER WALLACE W SHANE KENNETH P SHASTEEN
TOMMY L SHEHORN WILLIAM C SHELDON WILLIAM T SMILEY PAUL W SMITH HOWARD J SPEAR
LOUIS L SPEER ROBERT L SPRINGER DONALD R STEPHENSON ARNOLD L STEWART BRUCE W TABOR
TOMMY L TAYLOR JOHN M TIFFANY TEDDY J TOMCHESSON PETER R TURCOTTE RICHARD W WACKERFUSS
GORDON L TERRELL JOHN L VORIES CRAIG C WALTERS SAMUEL E WATKINS AFTON M WATTS
MARION E WAUGH FRANK W WEBB ROBERT G WEDDENDORF RICHARD F WELLS BOBBY R WILLIAMS
LARRY D WILLIAMS JOSEPH G WOLFE BILLARA WOLFORD JAMES W WRIGHT II RICHARD C WYATT
JERRY A WYMAN RONALD J ZIEMANN EDWARD D ABBOTT TERRY H ALDERSON LAWRENCE L ALDRICH
TERRANCE W ALLEN STEPHEN A ALLSOPP DAVID AZORE THOMAS H BAILEY RONALD E BAIRD
CURTIS E BANDY ALLAN G BARNES DENNIS E BASDEN ROBERT L BAUMGART JIMMY BEDGOOD

PANEL 56E

DAVID L BETEBENNER EDWARD L BROCK DONALD R BROGDON BOBBY R CHILDS
LARRY BRISCOE KARL L BULLARD ANGEL L BURGOS-CRUZADO BRIAN J CANNADA ROBERT L CLAMPFFER
JAMES L CLARK JOSEPH A CLINGERMAN EDWARD W COLLINS III DENNIS L COOK JAY A COOK
HARVEY L COOLEY GARY R CRAIG RODNEY A CRANDALL THOMAS F CREWS FREDDIE I CROCKETT
GEORGE L DALE CURTIS E DANDY THOMAS J DE NISCO JAMES W DIAL DENNIS P DUNSING
THOMAS A FOX SANFORD R GABORIAULT JAMES B GARD ROBERT J GARRIDO SYDNEY W KLEMMER
CHARLES E GIBBS LA V GIDDENS JERRY E GRADY JAMES L HAMMONS RALPH P HAYDEN
PATRICK B HESSION STEPHEN HINKLEY BENJAMIN L HINNANT CLETUH HOLLOMAN JR JOHN A JOHNSON
DONALD R HAYES JOHN T HOSKINS BRUCE N HUFF VICTOR J HUMPHREY HAYWOOD JOHNSON JR
MICHAEL R KALE WILLIAM A KEKAHUNA LARRY L KELLY WILLIAM B KIMBALL JR EUGENE H KIRKLAND
JIMMIE A FANCHER TERRENCE E KOHLBECK MICHAEL J KUSTIGIAN THEODORE E LEYDE JOHN A MARTINEZ
MICHAEL W MELVIN EARNEST L MILLER HARRY E MITCHELL BENNIE F MONFORT TERRY L MOORE
PATRICK J MCCABE LAWRENCE M MCGINTY CHARLES F MCGOWEN ORVAL W MCLEARY ROBERT H MUNDY
TILGHMAN R MCLEMORE KENNETH R NEWSOME PHILIP E PENNINGTON DENNIS PREMOCK DANNY K RICH
ROBERT L PERRY WILLIAM J PRITCHARD KENNETH R QUAN RONALD L ROGERS ROGER L ROWLAND
WILLIAM L RUSHING JOHNNIE C SMITH JR MILTON E SPEARS LONNY L STEWART ALLEN A STRAUS
WILBUR E SMITH JR HOWARD A THREET RICHARD F TURPIN III JOHN R VELASQUEZ STANLEY J VOSSEN
BRENT F WARD JERRY R WHITMAN CHARLES R WILLIAMS ROBERT A WILSON RAYMOND G WITZIG
ROBERT L WORLEY LEE R WRIGHT ALONSO ARAGON JR TERRY W BETTS ROGER D CAULEY
ROGER C ACKERMAN GARY L BRADEE ALLEN R BRADFORD RANDELL H BURNSED RICHARD M CAMPBELL
JERRY W CLARK AMBROSE W CLAY JR CHARLES J COOK JERRY W CORLEY PHILIP L CULVER
WAYNE C CYR STEVEN F DAVIS ROBERT J DEIKE ROGER A FESSENDEN JAMES D FEUCHT
FRED K FISH KENNETH W FLOYD GREGORY R GAINES MICHAEL A GEROME JAMES R MCDONOUGH
PATRICK M GOBLE THOMAS GORE JAMES W GRANT BEN J GREENE AARON HARTNESS
RUSSELL J HELIKER ROBERT F HOLDEN GARY E HOWARD GARY L HUDSON MACK S JEFFRIES
ISIDRO B JIMENEZ ADAM D KNECHT HARRY G KOYL GLEE R LIGHT DONALD J MATTARO JR
WARREN M KIRSCH ARTHUR MANOS CARL J MARINO SIGIFREDO MONTALVO JR BILLY E MYERS
RICK H FOSBURG DALTON H MCWATERS THOMAS W MYERS DANIEL L NAVARRO ANTHONY J NEMETH
ROBERT F NOLAN KENNETH B ORSZULAK PEDRO M ORTIZ DAVID R OWENS PAUL W PAINE
WAYNE P PUMA PHILIP H RADECKI WILLIAM RANDOLPH JR DUANE F REDTKE EDDIE B SANDS
GEORGE RANDLE JR ROBERT RICHARDS SAMUEL E ROUSH WILLIAM E SANZOVERINO BERLIN R SHUMATE
ARTHUR W SMITH MICHAEL A SMITH DANIEL E STROBBE DONALD A TESTA JOHN R THORNHILL III
JERON F VALENTINE GEORGE M VICTOR DONALD G WAIDE GEORGE T WALKER DONALD W WILLIAMS
ROBERT E ABBOTT JR MIGUEL A ABREU-BATISTA JR DALE C ANDREWS RONALD N BANKSTON GARY E CANAPP
SAMUEL P BEAUFORD JOHN W BEZECNY ECKHARD G BRENKER ANDRE M BROOKS JOE CARRILLO JR
JAMES L CHAMBERS JERRY L CHERRY BRADLEY R CLARK CLINT COLLINS GLENN M CONNOR
GEORGE T CONDREY III LLOYD A CONE MICHAEL D CONNOLLY JAMES E COOPER JOHN A COUNTAWAY JR

PANEL 57E

PAUL L DARDEN JR RAYMOND M DASILVA JR JAMES L DAYTON GREG A DU BOIS
DAVID S EASTON ELLIS L FAIRCLOTH JOHN C FIFFE DAVID F FLETCHER NORMAND E FONTAINE
MICHAEL J FORDI FRED S FULLERTON JR EDDIE D GADSON RICHARD GONZALEZ CARL O PEARSON JR
DEN J HAWKINS ROBERT S HUBBARD FREDERICK JARRETT ROBERT E JENNE ARMSTEAD JOHNSON
DANIEL E JURECKO FREDERICK D KEMP DAVID B KNAPP ROBERT A LANDRY THOMAS J LANSDEN
VICTOR L LAYNE JAMES E LOTT GERALD W MAYBERRY DAVID W MEISTER JOHN F MORAN
GERALD W MCCONNEL JR ROBERT MCKELLIP JR STEVEN MURRAY WILLIAM D NIXON KENNETH B NORTON
RICHARD W FRINK ALBERT F O'BANNON JR RONNIE L OBNEY DONALD W PICKERING STEVEN J PRESCOTT
ALVIN L PRESTON JEFFERY M QUIRK RONALD D RICHARDSON DAVID B RODMAN JAMES D ROY
RICHARD M SENG JAMES S SINGLETARY CARL W SPARROW MICHAEL H STEWART WOODROE W WARTH
DONALD W SPERL WILLIAM D TRENT LLOYD E TRIBBETT ROBERT E TUTTLE JOHN W VIKTORYN JR
ROOSEVELT WHITE ROBERT E WHITTEN LARRY E ADOLF GEORGE V AIREY JR ALBERT K AKAMU
ROBERT ALEXANDER SANFORD T ALLEN ANDREW C ANDERSEN JAMES B ANDERSON JAMES A DAUGHERTY
KENNETH W ARNOLD JAMES C BANG GEORGE J BEDROSSIAN HARRY T BOWMAN II CHARLES T BOYER
DWIGHT E BOZEMAN MICHAEL L BREWER IVAN C BROEFFLE JIMMY R BROWN LARRY G CALDWELL
ROBERT J CAPANDA FREDERICK R CASPER JOSEPH F CATT JR KURTIS N CHAPMAN ROBERT L COLE
SAM COLE JR CARLOS W CORNETT FREDDIE J COX JR LESTER W COX EUGENIO E FERNANDEZ JR
JAMES V ANTOLINI WINFORD R CRABB THOMAS W CRANFORD JOSEPH N D'AMBRA GEORGE W DARNELL JR
JOHNNIE W DAVIS CASTILLO M DEL BOYCE R DICK JOHN C DOUGHERTY RENDLE DULEN
ROY A COX FRANK W ELLIOTT RUSSELL L ENGS III LEROY FERGUSON TIMOTHY G FITZMAURICE
CHARLE C FLORES VIRGIL J FOWLER CHRIS W FRANKHAUSER PAUL L FREDERICKSON JOY T FRENCH
ALLEN R GIBNEY EDWARD A GILLASPY DANIEL G GLADDING JOSEPH GREENE JOHN W GRUTSCH JR
ROBERT E HARRIS QUENTIN HAYES LA M HORSLEY PRESTON L HOWELL EVERETT S JONES
GEORGE E GUYETT RICHARD A HUFFMAN EDWARD J HUGHES JR RUSSELL W JARICK CHARLES W JOHNSON
ROBERT N JONES TERRENCE A KANDLER TIMOTHY W KELLER BILLY R KIELY RAMIRO F OLIVO
RONALD N KOITZSCH PHILLIP L LACKEY DAYTON W LANIER BARRY W LEWIS SAMUEL S LINVILLE
CHARLES A LOTT CHARLES E MARISKANISH RONALD J MARKEL MARVIN H MARTIN MICHAEL M MICUNEK
SIDNEY B MACLEOD JR ROBERT N MINETTO HOMER MITCHELL JR MICHAEL L MITCHELL MERRILL A MOSER
MICHAEL C MCCAIN STEPHEN D MCGEE JOE L MCGILL MITCHELL MCGUIRE DONALD K MCNEIL
JOHN H KIRCHNER JR RICHARD E NOBLE DAVID G NUNEZ JR JORDAN J OZANNE ROBERT P SICKLES
WINSTON G PARKER JACK E PORTER CHARLES R ROSENBUSCH RAMON R RUIZ BILLY G STEWART
GARRETT T O'CONNOR LEO F RUPERT RALPH SANCHEZ JR JOHN M SCHNEIDER RONALD W SHEPARD
THOMAS A SINGLETON ALBERT E SMITH STEVEN A SOMMERS ROBERT E STALEY PAUL R STANDRIDGE
CLAUDE D PROTZ RANDOLPH J STERNS NELSON C SWANKER LARRY L TOLLIVER FRANKLIN A TOWNSEND

PANEL 58E

EDWARD TYLER CLIFFORD D VAN ARTSDALEN DURWOOD W VERRETT JIMMY R WHELESS
HERBERT L TUTTLE JR CLARENCE H WASHINGTON JR WILLIAM J WAYSACK FRED L WHILES JR PHILIP G WIGTON
WALTER J WILLIAMS JR MELVIN G WINDHAM PAUL D WOLF MARK D YOUNG ROBERT L BAKER
WILLIAM G BEHAN HENRY C BIGGERSTAFF THOMAS J BLACKMAN GARY A BOCHE JAMES S BROWN
JOHN M CALLAHAM JR FRANK V CALZIA KENNETH A CARROLL LEROY CONE JOSEPH F COOK
SHELBY E COOLEY PAUL S CZERWONKA LELAND P FINLEY HORACE H FLEMING III THOMAS C SCHRIVER
RICHARD J FLORES ADAM A FONTANA THOMAS W FRITSCH GARY L GADZIALA WARREN GRAY
CARL F GREEN PERRY E HANEY DONALD L HARDEN LAWRENCE HARVILLE BARRY L HEMPEL
RAYMOND T HEYNE PATRICK A HIGGINS PAUL E JACKSON ROBERT M JACOBS RAUL SERRANO-ECHEVARR
GERALD E KING DAVID L KIRKEBY OLIVER K KORANDO RICHARD D KOSAR CALVIN R LEE
ROBERT C LOPEZ JAMES L MATHEWS WILLIAM D MCGONIGLE GLENN E MILLER DONALD W MITCHELL
RUDY LOPEZ WILLIAM J MOLTZAN JAMES R OVESON ROBERT L OWENS WAYNE T PROVENCHER
ROBERT C ONSLOW LARRY G PATTERSON THOMAS H PERRY DAVID M POWELL HOWARD E QUERRY
JOSEPH A REICHLIN JR THOMAS J RICHARDS JR JOE E RILEY JR PEDRO ROMERO JR JAMES R SARGENT
ROGER L DUCE FRANK P JENCZYK JR EDMUND B SCARBOROUGH VERLE J SKIDMORE WILLIAM C SPROULE JR
THOMAS F SWANN JR HERSHALL TALLENT HERMAN L TAYLOR DAVID G THOMAS ARTHUR C TIJERINA
JOSE L VIERAS JERRY WHITAKER WILLIAM E WILCOX JR RANDOLPH R WILKINS LONNIE R YOUNG
ROGER ZIMMERMAN JAMES K ALLES JERRY L ANDREWS SAMUEL K CULBERTSON PATRICK V FITZGERALD
LEONARD J BELL ROBERT V BENNETT THOMAS H BERGREN PEARL BUSH JAMES G COLLINS
FLOYD C BAILEY GARRY R ELLERMAN OLLIE C FREEMAN OSCAR C GALLEGOS RONALD D GALPIN
WILLIE F GARNER CALVIN L GOOCH DAVID D GRAHAM MARVIN J HANNA LARRY R JOHNSON
JAMES S HAY JAMES W HILL JR DONALD E HONEYCUTT RICHARD C JACKSON JUAN M JIMENEZ
TOMMY W JOHNSTON GEORGE G KOKOSH REECE L MARPLE BOBBY J MARTINEZ WILLIAM L MENCONI
JOHN M MICHALSKI CRAIG W MITCHELL JOHN T MOORE JR MICHAEL D MUELLER WILLIAM E PASCH
CHESTER J RADGOWSKI JR ROBERT C RANSOM JR ARCHIE J ROBERTS JR GREGORY A RUSSELL LEROY F VALDEZ
JAMES S RYLEE JOHN E SCHERTZ EDWARD M SIMPSON SAMUEL D SMITH STANLEY R SMITH
EDWARD W PIGG MICHAEL B TURNER KEITH D VINCENT THOMAS L WADE EDWARD WALKER
DAVID C WELLS PERRY L WHITTINGTON EARL WOODS KENJI J YAMASHITA EDWARD A ZIMMERMAN
STEVEN G ABBOTT PAUL G ALANIZ JR GARY L ALLEN MICHAEL A BAILEY DONALD K BAKKIE
ROBERT R BEANNER ARTHUR L BEATY RICK W BEZEAU IVY L BLAIR RICHARD A BOWERS
DAVID A BRENT LAWRENCE J BRONCZYK BERNARD L BUCHER ROBERT H CARROLL JOHNNIE CARTER JR
DAVID R CARUSO JOHN H CASH JR WAYNE W CHAMPION FILIBERTO CHAVEZ HARRY B COEN

PANEL 59E

GERALD W COX JR ANDREW J CRAVEN LEONARD J DALMAN ROBERT M FLETCHER
EMMIT C DANSBY CHARLES D DORMAN JAMES R LEE PATRICK L MANSFIELD
BENNIE DALE CHARLES A GERONIMO ROBERT W GOTTHARDT ANTONIO GUZMAN-RIOS LYLE W HANSEN
CHARLES W HARBERT JONATHAN HENDERSON FRANK M HEPLER PAUL J HILL TYRONE HILL
JOSEPH H INGRUM JOE J JANAK STEVEN A JARRETT DENNIS K JONES MICHAEL B JONES
WILLIAM J EISENHOWER JERRY FLETCHER OMAR D JONES JACK H KAMRATH JOHN E LAIPPLE JAMES L LAKE
JACKIE G LEISURE RANDALL L LLOYD RICHARD L LOHSE GEORGE W LONG FRED G LOSEL JR
JULIUS R ELLIOTT JOHN E MAGEE JACKIE E MARSHALL RONALD J MILLER MAURICE H MOORE
JOHN L MCELROY STEPHEN C MORELAND JACK A MORRISON RICHARD A NUBER JAIME A RIVERA-LOPEZ
ARTHUR E NULL JR WILLIAM J O'CONNOR JR WARREN R ORR JR ANTHONY P PALUMBO WILLIAM PATE
ALLEN W MCNEIL ANTHONY R PRIETO FREDERICK J RANSBOTTOM FREDERICK D RICKELS GREGORY A RINDY
ALBERT M RIZO WILLIAM F ROGERS EDWARD J RUVOLIS RICHARD E SANDS DANNY L WIDNER
JACKIE R SELTZER JOSEPH L SIMPSON HARRY D SISK WILLIAM E SKIVINGTON JR JOHN C STULLER
DANIEL J TABABOO JR LAWRENCE F TURNER RICHARD W VAN BLARCOM DARRELL V VANCE JOE L WARE
GRIFFIN E SCARBOROUGH IMLAY S WIDDISON BRUCE J WILDER ROY C WILLIAMS ALVY E WOOD
PHILIP M WOOTEN DONALD H ZILLGITT JOHN A ANDERSON ALLEN R BARNES THOMAS M BOYD III
JOSEPH ADAMS RALPH R BLACK SHERMAN C BRADY SAMMY L BREWER OLLIS BREWSTER
FRANCIS P BRICMONT JR RICHARD B CALDWELL JR STEPHAN CODRINGTON ALBERT E DAHL JAMES A DAVIS
JOHN E CASHLEY GEORGE COLEMAN RALPH R COLLINS JR SAMUEL G CONNELLY MOSES J COUSIN
FERNANDO CALLE-ZULUAGA ROGER J DANA ARTHUR L DAVIS GLENN P DAVIS JAMES A DAVIS
LELAND S DEEDS CARLOS DOMINGUEZ DOUGLAS G FACTORA PAUL E FITZGIBBONS WILLIAM D HANSSEN
AMOS L FRANKLIN DAVID A GARCIA GARY J GILIN JEFFREY W HAERLE TOMMY L HANKISON
ANDREW L HEIDER JAMES D HESS BURL D HEWITT PAUL R HOAG JR ROBERT G HOOP
ABRAHAM JACKSON BOBBY JAMES VINCENT E JENKINS FREDDIE L JONES PAUL R LOZANO
GARLAND D JACKSON WILLIS G JONES MICHAEL J JUNEAU PAUL J KINGERY EDWARD G LEE
RALPH J LYDON JR FRANK J MAKUH GEORGE D MATTHEWS JAMES E MAYS JOSEPH A MENA
JOHN P MCGONIGAL JR OCTAVIO MOLINA-ROSARIO GENE C MORACK GARY F MYERS RAY W OWEN
RICHARD D MCGOVERN PATRICK V MCNEARNEY EARL J NETZOW TIMOTHY J NODEN KENNETH L OLSON
CHARLES I MILLER WILLIAM A POHL RICHARD F PRECOUR ALEXANDER E PRUNKA JR THOMAS F PRZYBELSKI

PANEL 60E

JOHN RECK DANIEL P REISTROFFER JAMES A RIDER JR CHRISTOPHER J SCHRAMM
WAYNE RICHARDS KEVIN H ROSS ROBERT E SALMELA CHARLES H SANDBERG NELSON SANTIAGO-APONTE
LOUIS P SPENSKO ARMOND J STEIN JR HAROLD A STONE STANLEY J SUKOWATEY DAN P VANNOY
EDWARD E STROUD THOMAS N TEAGUE MARVIN G TOZOUR CHARLES A URDIALES JR DIXIE D WALLACE
FREDERICK F WALTERS JAMES R WALTZ SYLVESTER WASHINGTON ROBERT E WELCH ALVIN E WILES
RONALD E WILTSE MICHAEL C WITTEVRONGEL JOHN L WOJCICKY BOBBY C WOOD
RICHARD D WOOD DAVID A WORTHEY STEVEN D ZUCROFF VESA J ALAKULPPI EDWARD ANDERSON
JON A BAKER THOMAS A BARRETT SEYMOUR R BASS RICHARD J BECK JR DALE L BLUME
RONALD E CLARK ERNEST K COTA JIMMY R COX EDWARD D CROW JAMES S DAHL
MICHAEL F DALTON EDWIN P DAVIS JOHN DI NAPOLI JR JOSE R DIANA-DIAZ RICHARD L GILBERT
RONALD T DOGGETT JAMES W FOUS ROBERT J GROTHAUS II RICHARD J GUERRERO ROBERT R HAMMER
JOHNNY J HON DANIEL G JOHNSON LEE F JONES FRANCIS E JORDAN JEFFERY C SETTLEMYRE
JAMES D AMES BARRY E KARGER DANIEL D KEYES JAMES J KLINE LANCE J KOHANKE RICHARD M KUCHEK
DONNIE G LEWIS LOUIS C LOWE MICHAEL H LYNCH JAMES R MAURER JESUS MEJIA
DENNIS E MCDONALD JOSE MUNATONES JR GEORGE L MUNDY JR ROBERT D MURPHY ROGER D STEPHENS
LARRY J HARDY STEPHEN R POWELL RICHARD V RIGGS JAMES R RINGEL KENNETH D RYNNING
MARTIN R NIEMI WILLIAM R SMITH JAMES F TURNEY WILLIAM H ZEIGLER WILLIE E ALSTON
STEVEN E AMESCUA DENNIS K ANDERSON LESLIE G APUTEN STANLEY W BEHM HOMER B BELL JR
DAVID R BINNS WARDELL BORDERS ANDREW J BRINZO III NORMAN C BRUBAKER DONALD D CROWTHER
ROBERT H BYRNES DAVID L CAMPBELL WILLIAM CHAPMAN JR DORIS W CLARK CHARLES A COPE
THOMAS W BISHOP GEORGE H COPPAGE III FRANCISCO DIAZ ROBERT M DONOVAN MICHAEL T DRYDEN
RANDOLPH P ESTRADA JAMES R FISHER THOMAS W FOY JOHN D FRAZIER EDWARD FURTADO JR
BENJAMIN N GOLDBERG RICHARD L HARROTT PHILIP HAWKINS III FRANCIS J HAYES JR THAD B JESSIMAN
DENNIS E ISGRIG ALFRED L JASNOCHA JR HERBERT KOLIBA WILLIAM L LAMB EDMOND J LANDERS
DAVID J LATORIA JAMES H LEDFORD LELAND E LOFSTROM CHARLES R MARSHALL ROGER W MIDTHUN
BOBBY MOORER FRED W MORRILL MARCO F MUELLER CARL T MURDOCK PATRICK J MURPHY
RANDALL G MILLIGAN FRANK G NAVARRO DAN L NEUENSCHWANDER JOHN R OGLESBY ROBERT G OLSON

PANEL 61E

MIGUEL PAGAN DONNIE L PATRICK DENNIS I PEDERSEN JOSEPH H PICARELLI
RILEY D RAULSTON JOHNNIE B RICHARDSON THOMAS L SEIFERT GARY J SHEA JOHN J SLIFKA
STEVEN D RUGAR WILLIAM D STIRRUP VALENTINE J SYNKOWSKI DUNCAN TAYLOR JR FREDERICK W TAYLOR
WILLIE R VARNEY DONALD F VOGEL MICHAEL W WEBB FRANCIS M WEBSTER ROBERT W WEST
JOE R WHITTED RONALD L WIGFIELD MELVIN A WILDMAN LAWRENCE G ZIEGLER MILTON G CLAYBORNE
EDWARD J ALLEN FORREST L BARTRAM LOUIS L BRADLEY JR MARVIN A BULLOCK EARL R BURNLEY JR
ZACK T ADDINGTON ROBERT M CASEY DANIEL H CHATFIELD ROBERT E CHURCH PAUL F COBB
VINCENT S COLES STEPHEN E CRAWFORD GERALD J CROSSON JR CLIFTON CUBBAGE DARRELL J DE PRIEST
JOHN H DIXON EXCELL FICKLIN DOUGLAS E FOSTER ROBERT G FREEMAN EDWARD T GORMAN III
EUGENE GREEN JAMES D GROSS LEON H HAHN JR MICHAEL E HAMILTON JACK HENDERSON JR
DAVID W HENDLE CHARLES R HENDRIX JAMES L HILL JERRY G HOLLINGSWORTH JR HENRY J KIRCHNER JR
CARL R HUTTULA OTIS E ISBELL MICHAEL E JOHNSON ROGER K JONES HUBERT C KNIGHT
WILLIAM E KOEHLER GARY L LANTZ ALVIN A MACK JR HOMER L MEDLEY CHARLES R MENTON
ORMOND M MILLER MICHAEL J MORRIS RICHARD K MORRISON RICHARD L MOSS RICHARD J MYSKYWEIZ
WILLIAM D MCCLAIN ERNEST C MCCRIMMON JR ELMER M NANCE EDWARD L NIX CLIFTON OLIVER
JOHN M PAMPLIN WILLIAM L PATE JAMES T PAYNE JEROME J PEDICONE EARNEST PERRY
LARRY D PHELPS JOHN D PONDER LEROY W POPPEMA HARRY L RILEY JR FREDERICK L ROHAN
DAVID J RICKEL ANUND C ROARK SAMUEL F ROLEN ALBERT W ROMINE JOHN ROTONNELLI
LOUIE J SANDOVAL GEORGE H SCHROEDER JR ERIC L STAUFF ROBERT L STEWART WILLIAM J TARPLEY
BRUCE E TEAGUE REN F U DANIEL L UNDERWOOD CHARLES C VAN ALLEN PAUL E WATSON
ROBERT A WAGNER GEORGE H WALLINGTON TERRY M WARD STEPHEN L WOODARD ABRAHAM K AHUNA
RICHARD J ALLEN FRANKLIN V ANDERSON WILLIAM N AREY JAMES A ASHFORD ROBERT L BAUER
BRENT J BERTSCH JOHN A BIFARETI JR LYLE P BILLS DENNIS B BLACK SHERMAN J BOULWARE
KENNETH C BERRIER GHERALD E BLALOCK REGINALD A BOWMAN CHRISTOPHER BRYANT ROBERT C BURKE

PANEL 62E

ALLEN W COURTNEY JR DAVID A COX THOMAS H CROOK DENNIS O CULLUM
LANNY D CUMMINS CARL R DAGGER JAMES N DAVIS STANLEY R DAVIS LUIS DELGADO-CLASS
HARRY H DESORMEAUX PAUL J DI CAPRIO REX W DOYLE DENNIS E DYER DENNIS L EVERTS
SHERMAN R FIELDS JR CHESTER J FONTENOT JOHN A GIBSON IV JACK B GORTON LARRY J WEST
ALLEN R GREEN TIMOTHY M HAMILTON JERRY W HAMMOCK ALBERT W HAWKINS RAYMOND A HENSLEY
BERNARD M HIMES THOMAS S HUGHES REID A ISLER STERLING H JOHNSON BENNIE R JONES
WILLIAM F JULIUS III EDDIE KELLY JR MICHAEL D KUHSE GERALD T LE BLANC NATE F LEE
LOUIS R LORDI RONNIE D LUMAN ROLAND T MARSHALL SAMUEL C MARTIN FRANKLIN H METZKER
CHARLES E MCMULLIN MARIO F MUSE JR JEROME PARRIS JR CHARLES H PERKINS RAFAEL SANCHEZ-SALIVA
DALE L POSEY STEPHEN W QUINN THOMAS H RALPH JR CHARLES D RAVER CHARLES E REINER
PHILIP D MILLER ROBERT J ROSAR DAVID L SCHETTL FRANÇIS B SCHMITT VICTOR J SCHWEIG
WILBUR A SKAAR QUENTON E SLOCUM JR JOHN C SMITH VINCENT J STAMATO JR GEORGE THOMAS JR
MARCUS G FIEBELKORN RICHARD TURNER SYLVESTER G TYLER GARY L WALKER JACK L WHITE
AARON L WOOD CHARLES L YOUNG STEPHEN R YOUNG HAROLD B BAYLOR LARRY G CALHOUN
RICHARD C ABBATE DAVID M BLANCHARD JOHN T BURTON MELVIN CAMPFIELD MARK J CARTER
DAVID W CASEY DANIEL B CHRISTENSON STEPHEN F CHUTE HARRY L CRAIG GARY R DAVIS
WALTER L ENSIGN JR JULIAN T FIELDS KEVIN L FORBES BYRL W GAERTNER ALAN S GELB
DAVID GIBSON PETER M GUENETTE ROBERT W HAMMER JOE D HELVEY JOSEPH A PADILLA
FRANK G HERRERA THOMAS L HUBBARD LEWIS P IORIO DONALD B JONES BRUCE LEVY
BENNY J LEWIS WALLACE S LITTLE EUGENE K LUPE CHARLES B MASON DONALD R MATE
LEROY MCKEEVER VINCENT D MONROE GILBERT H MUNCY RAYMOND V NORA ROLAND R OBENLAND
TOMMY E GIST DAVID E PADILLA HAROLD D PEPPERS JERRY L PETTY TIMOTHY J RIZZARDINI

PANEL 63E

CARL F SCHMALZ JR THOMAS E SHARPE CARL E SHIRLEY HOWARD R SPITZER
CHRISTOPHER J SCHERER JOHNNY W SITTEN NEIL B SULLIVAN DENNIS W THOMPSON JAMES N YOUMANS
GARY J THOMAS DOUGLAS A WALKER THOMAS J WEISS NATHAN WHITE JR JAMES R YOUNG

265

THE VIETNAM VETERANS MEMORIAL COLLECTION

RICHARD L AKEL MELVIN A ALLEN THOMAS M BAKER WILLIAM C BALDWIN DANNY L BOONE
EDWARD A BIES JOSEPH A BODNAR JOSEPH BONNER GEORGE BOTES HARRY W BRAUN JR
GORDON C BROWN MICHAEL F BURLESON JOSEPH F BURNHAM PEDRO J CAUDILLO LYNN B COLEMAN
RICHARD C COLEMAN JAMES W COOPER JESSIE F CROW PAUL F DANIELS JR JOHN W DAVIDSON
JOSEPH E DAVIES RICHARD H DILLON JR JOHN D DONOVAN BENJAMIN T FOLCK DANNY R SWOFFORD
JAMES L FOSTER CARLTON A FROST GARY N FRYE FRANCISCO FUENTES GERALD JAMES
ALLAN M FREDRICKSEN ALBERT A GILLESPIE SIGARD R GRIMSTAD OVERTIS HINTON JR ARTIE INGRAM
THEODORE JANKE JR ROBERT E JENKINS GUY L JEWETT LARRY V JOHNSEN DONALD V JOHNSON
JIMMY J JONES CARSON M KING DAVID G KIRK WALTER B KRUPSKI ROGER E MONTZ
JAMES L KRISELL RICHARD P MARTINEZ GREGORY V MAYNARD ISAIAH MITCHELL JR GORDON T MOLAISON
GLENN D MCCUBBIN HAROLD MOORE WILLIAM H MORTON JAMES MUIR DENNIS R MUVICH
HASKER L NESBITT JR GARY P NOBLE TROY R OLIVER JR PATRICK J THIROWAY JR RAYMOND F TRANTHAM
ALBERTO L PEREZ JOSEPH J PETERLICH GEORGE R POPE THOMAS R PURSEL DONALD K RAHN
WALTER J REECE PATRICK C RIORDAN SAMUEL H RODRIQUEZ WILLIAM K ROSS WILLIAM G SACHEN JR
LON B EWING STANLEY A SCHROEDER JAYE A SHARPE GEORGE O SPANGLER EUGENE M SUTTON JR
EDWIN G NEWELL ROBERT J PALENSCAR WILLIAM B THOMPSON WALLACE R THORSON JR DWIGHT T VALRIE

PANEL 64E
JERRY M WALDRON THEODORE G WEYMOUTH GERALD P WILLIBER RICHARD L WOZNIAK
GARY L WILKINS KENNETH R WILSON WILLIAM L WILSON GARY L WITHERELL WILLIAM C BAER
MARTIN G BLAKELY JERRY A BOCKBRADER ROBERT CROUTER JOSEPH R DAIGNEAULT CLARENCE R WARRICK
GARY W DUNN JOE EVANS RICHARD T FLATTERY JR CLAUDE J GASPARD JR MICHAEL GILLARD
NEWTON M GRAY JR RONALD E HARRISON ROGER F JORDAN RICHARD H JUNK PAUL A PARAMATTO
GREGORY S KOWALESKI GENE A LA BOUNTY JOHN D LARRY JR LARRY L MITCHELL GARY K MORRIS
ROBERT J HARTLEY WILLIE J MCCLAIN JR THOMAS E MCKNIGHT ROBERT D PLATO CORNEALUS PUMPHREY JR
MICHAEL D REEVES JOHN H ROBERTSON TOMMIE A ROLF DARYL L STITH RONALD G SWAIM
LARRY K BRYANT MICHAEL J SWIECZKOWSKI JOHN H TURNER RICHARD M WEAVER FREDERICK W WEIDNER
RICHARD A WESTERN JOSEPH M WILLIAMS DONALD C WOOD MELVIN WOOD BILLIE R ACREE
ERNEST A BAKER JR JIMBOB BICKLE RICHARD E BIESIADA JAMES A BILLINGS JR JOHN P BROWN
ROBERT L ANDREWS JR ALLEN J BOUDREAUX CHARLES P BROWN VINCENT J CARAVELLO MARK P COLLINS
ROBERT DAVID MICHAEL F DEENY III ROGER L DILLMAN MARCUS R ECKENRODE LARRY M GROSS
JIMMY W HAMBY GREGORY A HARPER VICTOR R HEESACKER AURELIO G HERRERA JAMES JOHNSON JR
ROBERT L HARRISON JAMES J HEWLETT DALE A HILL THEODORE R HOLLIS BRENT R JONES
WILLIAM T JONES KENNETH J KNOWLES DENNIS W LANE DAVID E LEMCKE JAMES W LIEBESPECK
DARRELL G MARTIN LEONARD D MCGINNIS WAYNE H MCKINLEY DONALD MILLER ALBERT E PETERSON

PANEL 65E
JEFFREY B SEGAL EDWARD C SIMS ALTON L SINGLETARY JOSEPH A SOMMERHAUSER
LEROY SHANNON JR JERRY E SPICER JAMES W STARKEY GREGORY W THOMAS BRIAN E TIERNEY
ZBIGNIEW J TOMASZEWSKI GEORGE E TONGEN ALLEN W VANDERHOOF CHARLES E WALTHALL RICHARD A WESKE FLORIAN J ZAHN
STEVEN L ZOBEL LEE M BARGER JUNIOR W BARR JERRY L CHAMBERS
DENVER J BERKHEIMER WILLIAM R BISSELL DARRELL D BRATTON BILLY M BRISTER DAVIS F BROWN
JOHN Q ADAM DAVID B CAMACHO WILLIAM M CLARKE JR LIONEL T CLOVER JOE R COURTNEY JR
JOHN H CREWS III ROBERT L CREWS JOSEPH V CZAJKOWSKI HOZ C DE LA ALEJANDRO DIAZ
ALONZO L DIXON GERALD L ELLIOTT PAUL A FROEHL CALVIN C GLOVER WILLIAM H MASON
ANDRES A GONZALEZ GEORGE GUERRA JR JOHN H HALMAN JR CLYDE R HAMBY WILLIAM B HUGHES
ROBERT E HARRIS CHARLES W HASKELL ANTHONY D HATCHER ROLANDO HERNANDEZ ROBERT L HICKS
WILLIAM B HAMACHER STEVEN G HICKS JOE R HINES DUANE F HORGAN JAMES E JOSHUA JR
DANIEL J KEATING JR EDMUND J KELLY CHARLES S KIRKLAND JR THOMAS E KNEBEL CHRISTOPHER L KURTZ
GALE W DIXON FRANK MARCH JR THOMAS B MITCHELL WILLIAM D MORROW DAVID W MOSELEY
RICHARD A MCCLAIN WILLIAM T MCPHAIL JAMES R MUCKLEROY HAROLD J NICHOLES TERRENCE P O'BRIEN

PANEL 66E
PAUL A PROEHL RAYMOND B RALLS MELVIN D RASH JOHN H TOMENY
CLAIR F RITCHEY JR LARRY J SAMPLES ANGEL L SANCHEZ SAMMY L SCOTT KENNETH C SHEMORY
GARY PATE WALTER S SIMPSON PHILIP SMITH JR PIERRE D ST ARTHUR L WALDORF
VICTOR D WESTPHALL III MICHAEL W WILLIAMS RAY WILLIAMS WILLARD L WILLIAMS CALVIN K WOOD JR
JERRY D WRIGHT JAMES L ZIMMER TOM P ACTON JOHN E ALBANESE JR THOMAS F BUHR
GRANVILLE J ALLEN JR EDWARD N BEERS LAURIER G BOSSE ROGER W BOYD FLORIAN A BUGNI JR
BILLY CHAPMAN ISOM C COCHRAN JR JOHN L COON JAMES R CORDER RICHARD I CULLEN
CHARLES L DANBERRY FRANKLIN V DE LARA BRUCE H DYER THOMAS J EISCHEID RALPH B FECTEAU JR
ROBERT A FINK HENRY C FLIPPEN LARRY W GILLISPIE ROBERT E GONZALEZ DAVID E GORE
EARL J GUILLORY TOMMY HARDWICK HAROLD R HAYDEN GLEN O LANE JAMES M LEVINGS
RODNEY E MARRUFO JR PAUL R MARTIN JOHN U MCALISTER CHARLES R MILLER CLIFTON P MOAK
JAMES P MCCOLLUM TIMOTHY A MCGURTY DONALD E NELSON TERRENCE E O'NEIL STEVEN W OLSEN

PANEL 67E
MARTIN L OWENS BILLY J PARRISH LEONARDO RAMOS JR JOHN C ROBERTSON
IVAN K PASCAL MARTIN J RAPCZAK BENJAMIN H REID JOSEPH D RUTTER JR JAMES A SMITH
CLIFTON T TAYLOR WILLIAM H TAYLOR DANIEL F THOMPSON RUSSELL U WEST JOE E ALLEN
MICHAEL F ANDERSON FREDERICK V ARENS JR STEPHEN L BEAN JAMES P BIRKS
CLARENCE J BALDWIN JAMES D BOWERS MICHAEL J BURKHART DONALD B BUTTON FRANCHOT T CALHOUN RICHARD A CARLSON
RICHARD CARRILLO DWIGHT W CARROLL WILLIAM E CASSIDY CLINTON CHAPMAN CHARLES M CHESSHER
JERRY M CHITWOOD JOHN C COLLINS THOMAS C CONNOLLY RONALD J COOK JOSE DAVILA
GEORGE W CLARK KEVIN CORCORAN DAVID W CRAWFORD RONNIE J DAUGHERTY MICHAEL L DEANE

PANEL 68E
MELVIN DIVENS FRANK G EAVES ROBERT A FEDEROWSKI RICHARD C FINA
WALLACE A FORD GARY D FOX RONALD L FRAZER ROBERT A HAYDEN PAUL LEWIS
LYNN G HIEBERT JERRY L HILBERT JERRY J HILL DAVID A JACKSON JOSEPH M KAMINSKI JR
JEFFERY A GOSS DALE D KENYON WILLIAM E KNOX JOHN G KOMERS AL R LEWIS
JOSEPH D MACK GEORGE E MASSIE LARRY R MCFADDIN RUSSELL A MICHALKE LARRY D NOVAK
GERALD T PARMETER JOSEPH J PASSAVANTI III GARY L PATTERSON ROBERT M PAULK GARY W PURCELL

PANEL 69E
HU B RHODES GLOUSTER RHYNES LARRY L RILEY EMMETT RUCKER JR
GERMAN A SANTIAGO HERBERT E SCHMIDT JAMES L SHANKS RONALD J SHEWMAN MICHAEL A SMOGER
FREDERICK G STEFFEN BRENT L SWABBY PAUL R THERIAULT TOUSSAINT L TITUS PHILIP G TURNER

PANEL 70E
DAVID H WHITEHILL FLOYD L WILLIAMS JR ROGER D WILLIAMS JESSIE C ALBA

PANEL 70 WEST
EARL E BARNHART JR JAMES E BATES GERRIT L BLANKSMA

PANEL 69W
JAMES C BUTLER JR CHARLES BYRD BRIAN E CAMPBELL THOMAS J DAVIS III
GAZZETT B BRUNSON JR FRED D CARTER JR NICHOLES W CHARLES ALONZO C COLLIER MELVIN D DECOW
THOMAS W DULIK KELLY FIELDS JOHN E FLASKAMP DANIEL J FLYNN MICHAEL E FORD

PANEL 68W
HENRY L GOFF STEVE GOMEZ LINWOOD GOUGH WILLIAM A GRIFFIS
LONNIE J GAY DALE E GRANT JOHN J HANLEY JAMES L HARRIS JAMES D HODGES
DANIEL J HOMMEL MICHAEL E HOPPERS DANNY HOSKINS JAMES H JACKSON BARTON W JOHNSON
LARRY W JONES ANTHONY KNOLL LEWIS D LAMKIN JOSEPH T LASLIE JR DON K LEDFORD
WILLIAM M LEVENDIS WILLIAM R LINDSEY JERRY A LONGTINE ANTONIO LOPEZ JR THOMAS R MALONEY
DENNIS L MACK JOHN B MARCELLO GUY W MARTIN JOHN P MASTERSON MERL R MEADOWS

PANEL 67W
JERRY L MILLER HERBERT W MOODY ROGER D MOORE LEROY PALMER JR
RONALD C MCEUEN JOHN J MONAGHAN JR WILLIAM J MOORE JR MASON NIXON JR EUGENE G O'CONNELL
SAMUEL W PARNELLE III JOHN L RAMSEY JOE A REED LEONARD A ROY JOHN C SEEBODE
KENNETH R SEMON BRUCE SHERFIELD JR JAMES H SHOTWELL BERNARD A SMALLS JAIME VILLALOBOS
LARRY STERN DENNIS L STIGLITZ DENNIS R SWANTAK JOHN A THIELE JR ELMER W THOMAS
ROBERT L SMITH JAMES THURMOND HERBERT L VAUGHN DAVID E WATKINS DENNIS D WEHRS
RICHARD J WEIDNER ROBERT A WHITNEY LLOYD L WILLARD ERNEST C WILLIAMS JR DON C WILLIAMSON
WILLIAM D WILSON BERNARD F YARBINITZ ROBERT E ZESKE OTIS L ALLEN EVERAL F AVEY

PANEL 66W
EDWARD E BEACHAM GARY E BECKER KEVEN W BOWDISH ALTON BOYCE
KENNETH E BRADLEY MICHAEL W BRAUN TERRY L BROADY BILLY R BROWN JAMES P CRAWFORD
HOWARD E BURDICK GEORGE W BURR RUDY CARDENAS HAROLD J CLIFFORD GEORGE L COBB
ROY L BRAGER JAMES W COCKRELL JR RICHARD W CRICKENBERGER ARTHUR A CROWELL WILBERT W CUCH
JESSIE J DANNER JACK D DEESE RONALD W DURBIN LESTER ERBY NATHANIEL HALIBURTON JR
RAYMOND I GARCIA MICHAEL J GARDNER RALPH A GEARHEART DANIEL E GOLDSMITH MARTIN J GRACE JR
RICHARD FERRALEZ RONALD E GRIER HARRISON L HALEY STERLING H HILL CLYDE S HIMES
CRAIG B HOLT GENE E HONCHAROFF RICHARD L INCROCCI HARRY W JOHNSON JAMES E JOHNSON
LARRY JONES RANDALL W KELPINE WALTER R LANG ROBERT G MARVIN DAVID H MILLER
MITCHELL L MCGUIRE HERCULES L MOORE JIMMY L MOORE MICHAEL MURPHY THOMAS W PETERSON
THOMAS MURRIN JR WILLIAM B O'HALLORAN LEROY PEGROSS RAY L PENLAND JR LARRY J PIERSON
DANIEL L POWELL ALBERT J RAPPOLD JR DE W SELBY HENRY E SHELTON LARRY J SINEGAL

PANEL 65W
LUKE A SMITH JR RONALD L SMITH DENNIS M SOLLENBERGER REID T STYERS
DOUGLAS R SUTTON MORRIS E THOMAS ROSALIO VALENCIA ALVIN C VAN RIESEN FREDRICK H WILLIAMS JR
JERRY L WILLIAMS WILLIAM O ADAMS JR EDDIE H ALLEN JESSE J ARMWOOD ROLLIN R AUSTIN
NIKOLA BABICH THOMAS E BAGLINI WILLIAM J BALLINGER DONALD E BEATTY CHARLES T COATS
FIDELE J BASTARACHE BRADLEY BOWLING WILLIAM F BRICE JR LARRY J BURKHARDT LARRY A CARAVETTA
JAMES L CUMMINGS ALFREDO DAVILA JOHN P EDWARDS JAMES F ELLIS GUY B EPHLAND JR
MICHAEL J FALLON FRANCIS I FOILES WILLIE L FREEMAN TOM GALVEZ FRANK W GARAPOLO
THOMAS H GOODMAN JR RALPH S GORTON III PHILO D GRANT III JOHN W GRASER SHERRY J HADLEY
FRANCIS J HEFNER KENNETH R HELLMAN RONALD W HERREN LEE E HIMEBAUGH RUBEN L HORTON
THOMAS HILL CARLTON H HOOD ROBERT D JENKINS GARLAND JONES PATRICK A LAYTON
JOHN R LINDEL MICHAEL E LUDWIG ROBERT G MARX ALAN L MATTE VERNELL H MILLER JR
BILLY J MCCARTY TIMOTHY P MCGUIRE JAMES D MCKELVEY WILLIAM J MCNAMARA THOMAS H NERINI
FRANK T NEVIDOMSKY BERNARD J OSTERBERG JR WAYNE A PAINTER FRANKLIN D PETE JR ANTHONY G PRIOR
EARL D REED MERRILL D REICH JR HECTOR RIVERA-COLON KENNETH R RUCKER SCOTT B SALTER

PANEL 64W
CHARLES D SCHOEPFLIN GARY J SCOTT CARL H SEXTON JR GARY C SHAFER
MELVIN R SIMPSON GEORGE R SMILEY PATRICK M STEELE CHARLES J TREWEEK THOMAS J WALTERS
GEORGE R SOSA JERRY W VANDEVENDER RONALD R WALLACE CARL G WARD CHARLES G WARSING
SYLVAIN L WHITE RICARDO YBARRA JOHN C YOUNG LAWRENCE K ARTHUR MOSES J BACOTE
STEVEN D BAKER RAYMOND F BARDET BARRY G BARTLE PERCY BETTELYOUN JR SAM H BOYD
WILLIAM E BRICKER JOHN C CARNEY ALAN G CARTER GERALD D CONLEY EZRA D CRAFT
RICHARD E CUTBIRTH MICHAEL J CUTRI RANSOM C CYR RAYMOND A D'ANGELO PONTE A DA
FRANCIS A DANIELS JOHN J DONAHUE MICHAEL L DRAKE WALTER L DROSD SAMUEL H EASLEY II
WETZEL L ELDRIDGE WILLIAM P FLYNN PAUL A GONZALES ROBERT P GREEN WILLIAM A GRIST
RONALD G HEMBREE JOSEPH A HILL JAMES W HOLBROOK BEN W HOWELL PHILLIP D MILLER
RANDY S HUBER RICHARD J JONES JR GARY L KESTLER PAUL J KOHLER RALPH J LUEBBERS JR
JOHN E HAZELWOOD WOODROW MAKIN JR DENNIS R MASON CARROLL R MEIER WALTER M POWELL
JOHN W MCVEY ROY J MOHR MICHAEL J MOON ROY W NEAL LEONARD M NOWAK
THOMAS W MILLS RAUL A OBREGON STEPHEN E PETERSON ROBERT J PLOURDE STANLEY F PONIKTERA JR
JULIUS D PRITCHETT WILLIAM RUSSO DONALD P SCHUCK JOHN C SMITH JR MICHAEL S SMITH
RONNIE W SMITH ROBERT M SOPKO THOMAS A STEVENS JR STEPHEN T SULLIVAN PELESASA S TAUANUU
BERNELL TAYLOR FRED L THRIFT ROGER W VOLZ GEORGE N WALKER CHARLES E WARD

PANEL 63W
CHARLES J WHYTE SHIRLEY WILDY JR JOHN H WILKENS EARNEST L WITT
PHILLIP E WYATT LEONARD L YAZZIE ROBERT J ANDERSON DANIEL M ARIZMENDEZ KENNETH N BLAIR
ANANIAS BOYD ERNEST BOYD JR GARY A BRECK CHARLES W BROWN JR LAURENCE C CAPLAN
ROBERT M BROWN PHILIP S BRYANT FERNANDO CAMARILLO JR ANDREW J CHICANTEK HENRY R CLAUSSEN
MARVIN E COLE STEPHEN S DONOHUE JUAN A ELIAS JOHNNY P FIECHTER MILTON E FLOWERS
RICHARD E GITHENS GENE T GRANT BRUCE R HAYES BRADFORD J HIPPIE MICHAEL L HORN
ROBERT R HUFF GARY A HUSTED KENNETH M ILER REGINALD R JENKINS JAMES C JEWELL JR
JOHN M JOHNSON OBBIE JOHNSON MICHAEL T LATHAM JOSEPH P LOGAN JR RONALD L MABE
TRISTAL MACIAS CLIFFORD B MARTIN JR HAROLD MASON JR WILLIAM J MOSES JOAQUIN NERIS-APONTE
CARL T MCCOY JR JAMES R MULLINS ROBERT L MYERS NICHOLAS A NATALE VAN A NORRIS
DONALD S PALMORE ARTHUR M PARKER III FREDERICK J PERKINS ROBERT K PERRY JOHN D PETERS
JAMES L PRIDEMORE FREDERICK F RAY RODDNEY A RODDAM MARK C ROKASKI JAMES A RUSSELL III
RONALD E SEGINE VICTOR SIMON JAMES A SMITH WILLIAM E SMITH DANIEL J WEIXEL ALBERT D MENTON
JIMMY S WILLOUGHBY GERALD L ADLAND ROBERT C BARNES JR JAMES L BATES BRADLEY M BOYD
PAUL J COATES GERALD A COLLIS JAMES DAVIS CHARLES E DRAEMER IGNACIO DURAN BILLIE H FULK JR
JOSEPH H GRAHAM ROBERT R HAYNIE CHARLES E JACKSON RANDALL C JEREMIAH CLEM S LOWERY JR
MARSHALL D JOHNSON CLARENCE JONES MICHAEL A JOSEPH THOMAS W KEMP JAMES G LA FLEUR
GREGORY R JOHNSON APIMENIO LARA GEORGE F LONG ALPHONSE J MACCHIONI MARK E MELLOR
EDWARD M MCNAMARA ERNEST A MOLZON WILLIE F OXENDINE III JOHN D PAPE JOHNNIE E POWELL

PANEL 62W
WILLIE J ROSS JOHN W ROUSE RICHARD L RUCKER PAUL E SCHIEVE
PEDRO A RODRIGUEZ ROBERT H SANDERS JOHN R SINNOCK LEWIS P SMITH II HERBERT D SNELL
JERRY M STONE DAVID E SWIHART JAMES L THOMAS WILLIAM WILBUR JR ANDREW K YOUNG
HOWARD J ALAIMO SEVERIANO AMADOR BRUCE F ANELLO JOHN J APPOLONIA GARY M MARTORELLA
LARRY W BENDER EUGENE P BERESIK JOHN W BOWDEN HENRY J BOYE JR HAYDN EVANS
PHILLIP L BROCKMAN CALVIN F BUTTERFIELD JAMES R BYERS JR LAWRENCE H CARSON GEORGE G CASON JR
JAMES A CASTLEBERRY CHARLES L COLEMAN JAMES E COWELL JOHNNIE L DANIEL LEROY DAVIS JR
ANTHONY L BENNETT JOHN A DENNIS ERIC V DICKSON JOHN B DURST RALPH FERGUSON
CHARLES H GATEWOOD WILLIAM G GIFFORD THOMAS H GOODSON HAROLD D GORE JOHN P GRAY
RUZELL GRAY LEROY C HALLER FRED L HAMPTON PAUL O HARMON JR DENNIS HERRON
NORMAN E HICKS JR CECIL H HUMPHREY JR HARRELL W JOHNSON PETER J KAULBACK DOUGLAS M ROGERS
ROBERT C ALLEN JOSEPH E LAUER FRANCIS A LAUTNER THOMAS L LOSCHIAVO MICHAEL A MACHIE
SQUIRE N MAYBERRY JR O L MIDKIFF DONALD R MILLER JOSEPH P MISIASZEK HARRY T MOORE
WINSTON MCELRATH JR TIMOTHY P MCGUIRE CHARLES L MORGAN WAYMAN D MORRIS JEFF MULKEY
JOSEPH D MCNEIL GLENN N NISHIZAWA CRAIG S PETTIT LARRY D PLILER CHARLES T POWELL
SAMUEL T HILL ANASTACIO D QUILALANG JR GEORGE M RAMOS HOWARD T ROBERTS CARLISLE A RODNEY
PAUL F SANCHEZ JOHNNIE A SHEPPARD JOSEPH SMARSH II ROBERT L SMITH WILLIE TUCKER JR
LOREN F STUDER DARWIN C STURTZ JIMMY R THOMAS JOSEPH M THORN DONALD R TRANTHAM
ROBERT J SCHATZMAN JAMES E WEST JR SAMUEL WILLIAMS DONALD E ARNOLD GLEN R BECK
PAUL BELCHAK JR JOHN N BOURNE STEPHEN G BOYER THOMAS L BUTLER JACK W CALFEE
FRANK W CAMPBELL JR JERRY A CAMPBELL WILLIAM J CARPENTER JACKIE D CHAMBERS GLENN T CIARFEO
BILLY E CLARK JERRY J COLE MITCHELL P CONELLY MICHAEL J CONRADY GARY K DARRAH

PANEL 61W
WALTER B GROVE JR ROBERT HANSON NORMAN W HASSELL ALGERNON P KAAKIMAKA JR
ROBERT L GRAHAM JAMES E HOPKINS TOMMY B HOSEY MICHAEL P HOURIGAN THOMAS G HUGHES
VAN ETSITTY HARRY L HUMMEL BRUCE E JOHNSTON III JOSEPH C KING JR HAROLD J KNITTLE
MARCEL A LA ROCHELLE MARTIN R MANESS DONALD D MEIS MICHAEL J MUSZYNSKI JOHN T WOLFE
DONALD R NORTH JR RUDY M OLIVERAS OSCAR C PHILLIPS JR FRANK M PROCTOR GEORGE R PROCTOR
STEVEN G RAMSEY ARTHUR M ROWE MICHAEL G SAKELLARIS NILE D SHUMATE MARTINIS G TIPTON
EARNEST R SAUNDERS GREGORY H STALEVICZ ERNEST R TAYLOR RICHARD K TAYLOR STEVEN D TOWNSLEY
OTIS TURNER DANNY E WARD WILLIAM F WASHINGTON JR LOREN D WHITE CAL W WILLIAMS
DAVID L LA JEUNESSE FRANK E WILLIAMS LARRY L YORK JOSE Q AGUON CHARLES C BAILEY
HARRY J BEADLE JR STEPHEN W BOWMAN CONLEY A BRADSHAW GERALD F BROWN JAY Q BUCKWALTER III
PETER A CLAVIO JR RONALD A COLEMAN ALBERT E COOK JOHN D CREWS JR DENNIS E DILLON
WILLIAM J DUNCAN COLIE ETHERIDGE JR CHARLES D FARRELL CLEM C GILES HERVE J GUAY RICKIE LUKER
LEONARD E DUTCHER THOMAS J HARBOUR WILLIAM W HENCE JAMES L HILL
ROBERT G GALLOWAY JAMES M HOFFMAN ROBERT L JONES BILLY J LACKEY RAYMOND VILLALPANDO JR
WILLIE L MORGAN JR JACK E MUISENER PHILIP F NESTICO STEVEN I OLNEY JESSIE G POE
JAMES H PRESLEY DENNIS M RAMON THOMAS E RILEY ARTHUR D SINKSEN EDWARD L SIZELOVE
AUDRON L SMITH JAMES G SMITH LLOYD M STARKEY TIMOTHY L STROHM RICHARD F TRISKE
MICHAEL P MINEHAN JOHN R VAN HORN JOSEPH T VANDEVENDER ANDREW J WANG DAVID A WASHBURN
ROBERT L WEST AVERY WILDER RANDALL L WILLIAMS DALE E BADGLEY CHRISTOPHER R HARTLEY
MICHAEL J BECK JAMES E BELL THOMAS N BLADES STEVEN C BUSH TERRY L FYOCK
HARRY W BUTLER JAMES E BYRD JR JOHNNY D CABE DARRELL E CAMPANELLO EARNEST E CAMPBELL
HAMP CARTER JR MICHAEL F CHUBBUCK BRIAN J CLARK DANNY J DART JESSE W DOWLING
DELBERT R BROCKMEYER TERRECE E EDGAR DANNY G FLANDERS RONALD S GILLIAM STEVEN M GILLMER
CARL K ALL JOHN A GOLDSBERY II MILTON D GRUBER CHAUNCEY I HALL HERMAN E HANTZ

PANEL 60W
JULIO A HERNANDEZ EUGENE HILTON JR ROBERT D JANSSEN GUSTAV A JOHANNSEN
CHARLES F HUFF WILLIAM L JARBOE KENNETH W KING BILLIE C LOOMIS LUIS A LOPEZ-RAMOS
GEROLD J MCADAMS GENE F MORRISON MARVIN W MURRAY FRANK J NESTICH ANTHONY P O'REILLY
ALAN R OTT JEFFERY S PATTERSON BILL D POFF DAVID A PROVOST CLARK D STICKLER
EDWARD QUINONES GARY L RUSSELL JOHN SALAZAR DAVID R SQUIRES CLIFFORD STAPLETON
LARRY T OWENS NICKOLAS SZAWALUK ANDREW J THOMAS KENDALL W THOMPSON JOSEPH R VALENTINE
PETER J WEIDEMIER ALLEN WILLIAMS DAVID C WILLIAMS MICHAEL L WILSON IKE O BONNER
RAYMOND A BORDUAS TADEUSZ J BOROWSKI ERIC P BRICE EARL W COBBLEY JR DANIEL J DABREU
MARCIAL B GARCIA JOSEPH J GRILLO JR JEROME E GRUNEWALD DARL K MCDORMAN AMELIO NINO
JOHN C HARRINGTON ROBERT V HOLLAND RONNIE L JONES NORMAN L KELLER EARL R LERCH
RANDALL M DAVIS WILLIAM S HARALSON JAMES F LEWIS JAMES D MOFFETT RICHARD A POLLEY
WAYNE S PROCTOR RICHARD A ROESLER ALDO E RYDER LOUIS A SNAKOVSKY JR MICHAEL D SODERSTROM
RAYMOND T STEELE MATAU TOIA JR LONNIE M WEDRICK THOMAS D WILCOX BENJAMIN J WILLIAMSON
DENNIS O AKERS JAMES J ALLEN RODNEY R BERNARD FELIX R BOCANEGRA DANA R CALL
JAMES W BARBOUR BRUCE W BURKES LUTHER BURNS VICTOR J CANALES WOODROW F CARBAUGH
JOHN H CARSON LONNIE L CLEAVE JAMES W COX CLIFFORD L EATON JAMES O ELLSWORTH
JEFFERY E FESER JUAN F GARCIA-FIGUEROA MACARTHUR G GEE CLAUDE M GEORGE AUGUST GONSALVES JR
KURT E HACKER KENNETH P HUTCHINSON JR EDGAR D JOY DAVID R KELLER WILLIAM G POOLE III
KENNETH E KIDD GEORGE L KING JR JOSEPH KLEIN JOSEPH W LYONS LARRY D MAGGARD
TRUMAN J MCMANUS THOMAS J MORRISSEY JR TERRY L MULKEY TONY V NASTOR DENNIS R VOLK
GAYLORD B HENDRICKSON JOSEPH P NOEL ELIEZER ORTIZ DOUGLAS R OTT BLANE M RUBY
MICHAEL W SIMON DAVID A STOKES DENNIS L SUTTON RICARDO R TEJANO RICHARD L VINES
JOHNNY M SCOTT JR HARRY L THEURKAUF NORMAN M TURONE DERRIS L UUTELA RICHARD L VINGE
THOMAS L MCBRIDE THOMAS E WALKER CHARLES D WENDT DAVID A ACKERMAN DENNIS ARCHIBALD

PANEL 60W (*Continued*)
ALLEN J BAKER MICHAEL H BIA SAMUEL BOYD JR JOHN K BRAZIER ANTHONY B BROWN
JOSEPH L BROWN JR PAUL E BURGARD LEE R BUSH WILLIAM R CAMPBELL MANUEL CASARES
FRANK A CONDON LEONARD E CRUCE ROBERT W CUPP RICHARD S DAVIS JR STEVEN F DOLIM JR

PANEL 59W
THOMAS L DUNITHAN WILLIAM R EBRIGHT JACK G ENIX FELIX F FLORES
FORREST J FLYTE HARRIS A FOLMAR JACKIE FRANKENSTEIN TIMOTHY J FRAZIER JR ELIGIO R GONZALES JR
FRANK E GREGORY DAVID J GUNSTER MICHAEL S HAINES WILLIAM E HALE WILLIAM E HANNINGS
RALPH L HARPER WILLIAM A HAYES ALVA D HENTHORN EDWARD H HIGGINS JASON A HOLES
JAMES HOLT RICHARD A HOLT FRANKLIN W HOOPS JR CLARENCE E HORNBUCKLE JR JAMES B HOWARD
ROGER L INBODEN ALBERT ISHMAN JR KURT E LA PLANT MELVIN D LANGSTON DENNIS L LOBBEZOO
LEWIS R LOVELL JR GERALD MATTERA JAMES MAY JR THOMAS J MEENAN DENNIS C MELTON
CHARLES E MICKLES LOREN R MILLARD STEVEN J MINER ROBERT N MOORE CATARINO MORELOS JR
ALFRED MCCULLOUGH NORMAN L MCKENNEY LARRY H MORGAN WILLIAM T MORRIS III ANDREW PERRY JR
MARVIN E MCLELLAND ZACK W NAPIER RODOLPH L NUNN JR CECIL T OSCAR GEORGE R PACKARD
DENNIS W MOURGELAS LUIS F PALACIOS WILLIAM H PARKER PAUL J PELLETIER TERRANCE A PICCIANO
LAWRENCE E PORTER DANIEL L PROCK LARRY B REED JAMES A REID LOUIS G RHOADES
GARY K ROBERTS RICHARD J RUDOLPH JOSE R SANCHEZ ANGELO C SANTIAGO DONALD S SATTER
KENNETH W SCHAUBLE WALTER L SEAWRIGHT PETER M SHEPHERD LONNIE SHEPPARD JR ROGER W SHIPLEY
WILLIAM SIMMONS CHARLES W SMITH DONALD L SMITH ROBERT L SMITH ERNEST G WINSTON
JONATHAN L STOOPS MIKAL J SULLIVAN HARRY THOMAS JR JOHN P THOMPSON FRANCIS V TODARELLO
F R TOMON DOUGLAS M WASHINGTON ROGER D WEBER JACOB R WELDIN JAMES K WHEELER
GERALD D SORRENTINO EUGENE WILSON JAMES S WOOD DAVID O AUEN DAVID E BARBER
ROBERT E BARNES MICHAEL P BECKER FRANK E BELCHER EDWARD L BRADFORD DAVID W BRANTLEY
WYNNE L BURLINGAME JERRY N CHRISTMAN JOHN A COMBS RICHARD F CORCORAN THOMAS R CORES II
KEVIN M COYNE DONALD M CUFF NORMAND C DESCHAINE DAVID E DIXON MICHAEL J DONOVAN
CONEY ELLIS JOHNNIE B ESPY GEORGE A ESSARY PETER C FERGUSON SAMUEL J HANNAH
DAYTON J HOOKS RALPH E HUNT JR BENNY L HUSKON JOHN A KEEPNEWS CARL M MIDDLEBROOKS
JAMES A KING RODNEY E KINYON RICHARD C KNACK ANDY KNEVELBAARD JAMES F KONECNY
ROBERT J KUCWAY JEROME D KUPPERSCHMIDT ROBERT V KURILICH ROBERT M LEAHY RAMON LEYBA
DONALD H HARTNESS PHILL G MCDONALD PAUL M MCGRATH DAVID A PADDOCK JOHNNY L PROCTOR
MICHAEL E RAINS RONALD E ROCKEFELLER WILLIAM E SAPP JOHN A SCARPINATO GREGORY A SHELLEY
DEAN C SPENCER III ALTON L STAPLES III EDDIE T TERRY REYNALDO L TORRES JR MICHAEL W TRAVIS
LELAND D WELCH MITCHELL A WENTZ ERNEST L WESLEY ROBERT J WESTRATE LOY N WHALEY

PANEL 58W
WILLIAM C AHOUSE ERIC A ANDERSON JAMES O ASHTON STEPHEN E AUSTIN
RENATO M BEVILACQUA ANTHONY CARRA SCOTT D CORRELLO ROBERT L COUSIN GERALD J FROST
PHILIP G COLONNA JIMMY O CROFT THOMAS A EDMOND RONALD E FORGET KIRBY L HAMBY
CLARENCE O HENDRICKS III CHARLES JONES JR DAVID KNOX ARTURO S RODRIGUEZ JOHN H ULBRICH
DOUGLAS M MALLETT DANIEL L STOCKER ARTHUR T TURNER TERRY L ALLEN JUAN ANTU
DONALD BAKER ARDREY W BARRINGER JR RONALD E BELL LAWRENCE F BOND WILLIAM F BURDICK JR
EDWIN L CAHALL JOSEPH M CHEARNLEY PATRICK B COPPO NATHANIEL CUMMINGS WILLIAM M DRAPER
CLIFFRED M EVANS CLIFFORD E FORD JR MICHAEL B FULLER LARRY H GIFFORD MERVIN D GOLDEN
ANGEL L GONZALEZ-MARTINE BERNARD T HANSEN ELMER L HOLDEN MARVIN L HOUSTON PHILIP P REED
RICHARD J IANIERI MELTON L KIDD DONNIE H LITTLE JAMES D LOCKER BARRY LOWE
HARRY P MARTIN MANUEL F MARTINEZ GERALD L MILLER DARRELL C MIZNER JERRY W MOTSINGER
DAVID E NASH RICHARD L NOWRY JOSEPH OLESON JR RAMON OQUENDO-GUTIERRE DAVID A WENGER
CHARLES W HAMMOND JOHN C PENNINGTON PETER PEREZ ROBERT L POLK JAMES E PRINGLE
JACK C RITTICHIER AUGUST ROMANO WALTER R SCHMIDT JR RICKY L SHACKELFORD DONATO J SIMIELE
LARRY E SMITH GARY G STEVENSON DAVID L STOEHR EDWARD M SULLIVAN ARTHUR C TOWNSON
WILLIAM A PATTERSON EMORY D VOORHIES HAROLD A WILLIAMS WILLIAM H WILSON JR JACK L WOOLSEY
RICHARD C YEEND JR ROBERT BALL EDWARD D BENNETT WILLIAM W BOETJE ROGER T BURROWS
EDWARD R CLAY TERRY W CRUTCHFIELD LEROY DIGSBY ARTHUR J ENQUIST KIM W FLETCHER
LOUIS M GIROLIMON WAYNE D HEINTZ KENNETH D HINKLE ALEX L JOHNSON JULIO SERRANO-RIVERA
TODD D KELSO LARRY T MILLER DAVID Z NARAMORE JR LAWRENCE O ROSE JIMMY H SMITH
LARRY D SWANEY WILLIAM E WILSON MILTON R ALLERBY JR DANIEL F ANDRUS CHARLES G CLITTY
WAYNE W BERNHARDT JAMES A BURTON GLADSTON CALLWOOD LARRY D CARLISLE ROBERT S CASTELOT
MICHAEL BARD DE L CHAP CHARLES J CHASE TOBY E COLLINS DAVID M CRONIN
ROBERT H DAVIS MICHAEL L DEWLEN BERNARD W DICKERSON JR MICHAEL L EWING JAMES D FAZZINO
OLLIE FORTE ROBERT S GROSSHART PAUL R HARRISON GORDON A HAWKINS KENNETH J HAWKINS
TERRY L IVENER DONALD W JACOBS SAM JONES THOMAS H JONES WILBER D MONROE
DAVID H LALICH GEORGE W LARGE CONRAD LERMAN WILLARD D MARSHALL HERBERT N STEHLE
ROBERT J IRWIN RAYMOND C MORA WILLIE OVERSTREET JR JAMES A PHIPPS DWIGHT A PRICE
CHARLES E LEE DAVID M PRUITT THEODORE P RAYMOND BERNARD J SNEAD JR RAYMOND W TEMPLETON
RUSSELL J WEEKLEY CHARLES C WHITE ROY A WINTER GERARD T WOLTERMAN EDWARD T WRIGHT
BILLY J WYATT GLENN J ZAMORSKI ALTO ANDERSON JR OSCAR GENTRY JR RAYMOND L GOODMAN
DENTON J HASDORFF ROBERT C HAWKINS JOHN L HOLMES LARRY D HUMPHREYS CLIFFORD JENKINS JR
RAY E MCCUNE

PANEL 57W
MICHAEL J KAPLAFKA CARLOS L KNIGHT JAMES L LAWRENCE JR STANLEY E SPANGLER JR
KENNETH R MENGEL LEONARD M MILLS JIMMY C NEWFIELD JOHN T O'DONNELL RALPH H PADILLA
JAMES D RAAB DONALD L RANKINS WILLIAM M ROWLAND ROBERT E SANDERS HENRY C SANFORD JR
ALAN D LYLE EDWARD D SCOTT HERBERT W SCOTT III DONALD G SMITH TERRY H SMITH
COY F STARK RAYMOND R VARNER JR DALLAS A WEST JOHN C WHEELER MICHAEL M WHITE
DAVID WILSON DONALD E YEAROUT FRANK A BARKER JR PAUL J BONETTI DAVID G BRENNER
SEFERINO ALBAREZ JR JAMES D CARTER DUANE R COTTINGHAM DONALD C CROTTS FRANK O CUEVAS
JOHN C CUPP JEFFREY L DARGAN WAYNE A DECKER GARY G EVANS NORMAN E LODHOLM
JERRY R FERGUSON CHARLES A GAUDREAU DONNIE A GEERDES EDMOND J GREER WILLIAM A GRITTS
BERNARD W EDWARDS JR RICHARD T HUGGETT JAMES L JENNINGS WILLIAM A JOHNSEN JERRY H JOHNSON
PAUL N LOYA DONALD T LUTZ EARL R MICHLES GARY A MILTON RAUL RAMOS-JIMENEZ
ALAN R LYMAN KENNETH O PALMER MICHAEL L PHILLIPS RONALD D POOLE GARY L RICHARDSON
JAMES R RICHMOND CRAIG L SEIDEL EMORY M SMITH JOE A SNITKO PORFIRIO S SOLANO
ROBERT L SPROUL MILO H STRATTON COY E STROBLE GARY L VAN TOL FORREST E WARD
ALLEN R WEAMER ROBERT W WERLEY LEONARD R WHITE RONALD A WILSON HENRY E WOOLEY
DANNY W ALDAY CHARLES S BERANEK RONALD W BLEVINS RICHARD T CHRISTY CHRISTOPHER E CLAY
DONALD G DENNEY JOHNNIE L DOUGLAS JOSEPH D DUELK JR RICHARD H FERGUSON JOHN J KEDENBURG
LARVON FLOYD DOUGLAS D GONZALEZ JESSE V HAWK III JAMES L HAWTHORNE RICKIE J JACOBS
JASPER ELLISON JR STUART O KIEFER GERALD E KORSON GARY W LINK HAROLD S LOCKWOOD
ROYAL C MANK DARRELL W MAYNARD CRAIG S MUHICH ROBERT L RODRICK ROBERT R WHITE
DOYLE W OVERTON KENNETH D SMITH HAROLD R VOGEL RONALD V WEARMOUTH ROBERT D WOOD
JOHN W WRIGHT JOHN V AKIN ERVIN L AUMAN CHARLES O BAKER II DAVID M BERTRAM
R B BRIDGES JR ROBERT D BROCKMAN JOSEPH T CAMPBELL DENIS M CHMEL RAYMOND N MCINTYRE
LARRY G CLARK RICHARD D CONKLIN DENNIS CRANE JAMES D CRUSE MICHAEL D DAVID
WOODROW DAVIS JR RICHARD L FITTS JR RALPH H FRANCK JR STEPHEN M GRANT CLEMENT J GRASSI
THOMAS E GREGORY THEDORE S GRIFFIN WILLIAM F GUNSET GEORGE S HADZEGA HENRY KOLAKOWSKI JR
DONALD R HAWYER RODGER D HEBERT ARTHUR J HOYT KENNETH R HUGGANS STEPHEN D JOYNER
ALBERT L GUNN GERALD H LAVOIE GUADALUPE LERMA JAMES W LITZLER DOUGLAS E LONG
ROBERT F LOPEZ FRANCIS E MANUEL GERALD MCCLINTOCK WILLIAM I MERCER RICHARD B MURPHY
JAMES L CHIVERS ROBERT A MCCLOSKEY JOHNNY A MCDANIELS PAUL V MCHENRY RANDALL T PLANCHON II
WILLIAM G ROSS WILLIE P SEAMSTER GARY C SEYMOUR CHARLES D SMITH ROBERT J WILLS
JAMES E SULLINGER NAPOLEON E TALIAFERRO JOSEPH E TAMAGNINI JEFFERY A THIBAULT NATHAN THOMAS
MARK D TYLER REGINALD B TYNES OSCAR VALENZUELA JR JACKIE E WALLACE CARL R WARD
ALOYSIUS F SPICZKA JR LEEVERNE R ACHOE BILLY S ARMSTRONG JESSE S AYRES THOMAS D BERNARD

PANEL 56W
THEODORE C BOND FRANK BOWMAN JAN A CARMODY ANTHONY G CHANDLER
EDWARD C CRUZ ALAN R DUKE NED T DYBVIG WAYNE A FERGUSON MANUEL A GALINDEZ
DAVID W GASKIN WILLIAM D GROOMS CHARLES M HANNAH PATRICK K HANNON CLARK L HENSON JR
CARL W HOLLER JOHN M HOVER GARY C HUTCHERSON JAMES W INMAN PAUL L JOYNER
JOHN F KENNEDY CHARLES F LANDERS RICHARD A LANE JAMES K LEACH ARNOLD L LEONARD JR
JAMES L MARTIN FREDDIE L MCNEIL THOMAS L MILLER ROY L MOORE MICHIEL D MURRAY
DAVID K OMSTEAD STEPHEN B OWEN GEORGE P POWER JOSEPH PRESTON JR GERALD A SZYSZPUTOWSKI
BERNARD F RUPINSKI CHARLES A RYGG JOSEPH F SCHILLER KENNETH W SKINNER III JOHN G SOUTHALL
REGINALD F POWELL FRANK SPOTWOOD JR DONALD H STEPHENS JOHN R TAGUE DENNIS W TAYLOR
RIGOBERTO TORRES-LOPEZ ROBERT E TULLY CHARLES V VASQUEZ JR WALTER D WEEKS WHITNEY L WHITE
ALFRED E WHITEHEAD RILEY C AUSTIN CHARLES A BEDSOLE CHARLIE E BERRY CHARLES E GOODMAN
TYRONE E CARNEY DONALD S FUJIMOTO DAVID M HOLLINGWORTH ROBERT W HUGHES JACK W OAKES
JOHN E KELLETT MICHAEL J KENNEDY STEPHEN W KURTTI JOHN A LA BUNDY ALLEN W LEWIS
LUIS G GONZALES JR RONALD J LOCKHART RICHARD R MACHUT VERNELL OWENS JOSEPH W RICH
STEPHEN W SHAW NYLES B SKYLES HOWARD W STEWART ALLEN S STROUD CLARENCE TOLENTINO
ROOSEVELT TOWNSEND WILLIAM T WEDGEWORTH MARVIN L WYATT RONALD L ALESHIRE LEROY C GEYER
ROBERT L BALL CLARENCE BOWMAN JR THOMAS J BRENNAN VERNON BROWN JR ROBERT B BUCHANAN
RAMON P CANCEL FERGUS J CARROLL ALVIN P CHRISTENSEN SIDNEY M CONOLLY JR PETER F FONDA
AUDREY J COOK RONNIE D DAVIS GERALD G DEDMORE JR JAMES E DEGNIS ROBERT C EWALD
JOHN J CIMORELLI JR ELMER L FAULKNER JR JERRY FLEMING RONALD D FOGARD JIMMIE F GENTRY
RICHARD R ANTONOVICH JAMES T GIBSON WILLIAM T GIBSON CALVIN GOLDEN JR BASILIO GOMEZ
RONALD K GROOMS CARLETON P HASTINGS JAMES C HEARD MARCOS HINOJOSA DONALD R HOFFMAN
CAREY L JOHNS CLAYTON H JOHNSON NORMAN JONES JR LITAEL JORDAN JR STEVEN B LA VIGNE
BOBBY R LANE AMOS D LAWSON LEROY LELAND JR DENNIS M LONGO ANTHONY R LOVE
DAVID J MARSH JAMES M MATHEWS RANDY L MATHIAS EDDIE L MAULDIN EDWARD H MEEKER JR
CLARENCE V MOBLEY JOSE R MONCAYO ELWOOD OWENS CARL A PAULINO DAN L PFISTER
ANDREW J PACHECO ARTHUR QUEZADA JAMES A RAVENCRAFT JAMES R SALISBURY RANDY S SCHELL
JON R SCHURRER RICHARD A SKAGGS ALBERT R TAYLOR II KEITH D TAYLOR NATHANIEL WADE
CALVIN L TERRELL CHARLES B THOMAS EARL THOMAS CHARLIE V THOMPSON BOBBY R TRAPP
CHARLES L COLLEPS RITO SILVA STEPHEN F TURNER MARK A WENZEL DONALD E WHITERS DANIEL A WITKO
ROBERT M WOODS HERBERT M ALLEN DAVID R BARTHOLOMEW RONALD L BEST MICHAEL D HELMSTETLER
WILLIAM A BLEWITT JR PAUL A BOGUSKI JOHN S BROWN PATRICK A CONNELLY CHARLES M COTTON
JOHN R DOWLING GLENN H DUSBABEK RICHARD T DUTRO TIM L FRITZE LEONARDO LOPEZ-VAZQUEZ
JERRY L ADDIS JEFFERY H HALL WILBUR L HALLOCK JR KENNETH W HICKS B C IZARD
MICHAEL J JOHNSON DAVID W JORGENSEN ARLAN J KENNEDY JR CARL S KIZER NEFTALE J LABOY
JAMES R FRY JR JOHN J LINK EUGENE L MANSELLE III FREDRIC C MCCASKILL RUBEN D MERCADO-GUTIERRE
CHARLES A MCKINNEY ROBERT A MCLOUGHLIN JR PAUL L OAKES JR LARRY R OLSON GERALD A PHILLIPS

PANEL 55W
ANDREW G RICHARD GEOFFREY T ROWSON ERNEST S SAKAI MICHAEL V SORTER
JOHN V QUINTAL MARVIN SCOTT LUFKIN S SHARP WILLIAM D SISLER BOBBY D STANLEY
ROBERT E VEACH RICHARD E WHITE FRED WILSON JON R WINGER GARY D WOODS
ROBERT G ZINK ROSS O BARLOW TOMMY J BREHM THOMAS R EDWARDS STEPHEN W HADLEY
ERNEST L ELLIOTT RANDOLPH W FORD HAROLD F GENTILE MICHAEL GIGLIOTTI JEREMIAH GREEN
DAVID T BELL THOMAS E HARRISON WILLIAM D HEADRICK HOWARD P HOWLAND JR GERALD L JOHNSON
LARRY R KENNANN MICHAEL B KOPETSKI THOMAS D LATANOWICH LARRY G MASSIE THOMAS M WERNER
MARVIN R MCCAIN JR ROBERT L MCGEE JR HAROLD N MINNIEAR TERRY L PARSONS EARL T PELHAM JR
ROSS M PRESTON MICHAEL G RINDONE GREGORY M ROSS CHARLES SEGAR JR LAWRENCE A SHAFFER
WILLIAM R LA PLANTE III SIDNEY C SQUIRES JAMES L STILES DAVID L STOCKMAN DONALD D WILLIAMS JR
CHARLES P BARNES CHARLES D BOYER JOHNNY D CASEY RICHARD M CHAMBERLAIN UDELL CHAMBERS
ROOSEVELT CLARK SCOTT C DELPH WILLIAM E DENNIS KENNETH R ESCOTT TERRY L FETZER
KENNETH C FLEMING JR PATRICK O FORD WILLIAM H GLASPIE JOHNNIE JACKSON RUDOLPH JENNINGS
BRADLEY J JOHNSON BARRY E KINCAID WILLIAM L LAW JAMES L LUTTRELL DAVID L MCDONALD
DONALD D KORB FRANCOIS A PETERSON GEORGE R POWELL JR EUGENE RICHARDSON III ASTOR SCALES JR
DAVID B TAYLOR RICHARD L TIRICO WILLIAM J VAN GORDER BOYD J YOUNGBLOOD JAMES R ZBOYOVSKI
STEPHEN A WALKER JERRY D ABEYTA LE R ARELLANO JOHN D BABINSACK JOSE E BENITEZ-RIVERA
CHARLES K BURKART JR GEORGE C CURRIE FREDDY GREENE TATE T HACKNEY III WARNER C JACOBSON
CARL I JOHNSON RONALD SAUNDERS FRANK J STRNAD NEIL W WEINTRAUB DARYEL J YOUNG
RONALD L SHAVER TERRY ALLEN JR JAMES E BOOTH GARY R BURNETTE DONALD F CASEY
DAVID A DENTON HAROLD E GRAHAM LOUIS G HEIL DWIGHT E HINMAN DENNIS R KINNARD
RUPERTO MEDINA-GONZALEZ TERRY J NEILL KENNETH E NOLAND DAVID L POWELL RICHARD L RUSSELL
MONTY D PRUSH JAMES RICHARDSON EDDIE RIGGINS ERNEST SANAZARO JR GEORGE D SCHILLING
ERNEST V SHOMPANY JOHN J SHORTER DAVID SMITH II CLETUS D TUTTLE JAMES B WASHINGTON
GARY WILKINSON THOMAS L WINES WILLIAM E BADER TERRY N BARTLING DANIEL R BROPHY
LEROY J BROWNING JAMES D BUDAHAZY II NICHOLAS M CARPENTER WARREN N CHAPMAN CARL B HELM
TERRY W CRESSEL JESSE J CUNNINGHAM JR CARL L DOBY ERNEST W GARRETT GARY B GRISBY
MARCUS E CLINE KENNETH W HALL RAYMOND R HITCHCOCK JR ERNEST M HODGES JERALD L JONES
RICHARD A JONES JOHN A LAFFERTY ANDREW A LANG JAMES F MEGA KENT F MILLER
CHARLES C PEDRICK II JESUS R PEREZ RICHARD S POHL BOBBY R PORCHIA MICHAEL G THOMPSON
DONALD J ROE PRESTON R SCOTT WALTER A SOUTHER III RICHARD P STASIO ARTHUR W THOMAS
JOSE H RAMIREZ MICHAEL P VAUGHAN DONALD L WASHINGTON HARVEY C ADDISON ANDREW BATTIEST
TERRY H BROOKS JOSEPH G CATOIR JR IVY G CHILDRESS GEORGE D DELL JAMES B TASKER
JESUS G ESCOBAR OTHA D GIBSON JOHN M GOLDEN JIMMY R HARRIES DAVID R HOFFMAN
JEROME GARCIA RALPH M HAVNAER ROBERT G HENRY FRANKLIN J HINER CHARLES J HUZICKO
ANTHONY J MANCUSO EDWARD MARZENELL JR ANTHONY J MELLO THOMAS R MORRIS HENRY L PAGE III
JOE F PEREZ JR ROBERT POWELL MARVIN K ROBERTSON PHILLIP ROGERS ARVI ROHTVALI
CHARLES C SALES ALBERTO V SANCHEZ ROBERT M SCOTT RICHARD SIMMONS THOMAS J SMITH
ROBERTO BRACHINI JR WAYNE M SMITH LEE R SPROUSE DENNIS E THOMPSON DOMINIC UNGARO JR

PANEL 54W
MACK W WILLIAMS JORGE L BATISTA-RODRIGUE RICHARD T BRONSON
JOHNNIE C CORNELIUS ROBERT L COULTER PHILIP M CRANE II JOHN FONSECA JUAN R GARCIA
WILLIAM A CLIFTON LAWRENCE JACKSON TIMOTHY L MCLEAN JAMES E NIEHAUS MARK PATTERSON
GERALD N REMPER ROBERT C STEELE WILLIE R THOMPSON WAYNE C WILLIAMS ROBERT F WOODS
BILLY W CHILDRESS RAYMOND P DE LUCA LUPERTO GARCIA VINCENT J ROSSOTTO ELTON S STALLS
CHARLES A GORDON BENNIE E HODGES JON W LAYTON III MANUEL T LOPEZ DAVID W ROBERTSON
VINCENT F GIAMMARINO JAMES H ROULETT MICHAEL E WALKER MELVIN R WHITE JAMES B WHITTIER
JOHN H BAKER DAVID R BURKES JR JAMES T COGGINS JOHN R COOPER JR MARK E VANDERHEID
WILLIE G COOPER ERNEST P DAVIS ROBERT C DAVIS WILLIAM N DODSON JR OSCAR R JUAREZ
CHARLES E DUNCAN RONALD A EWING STEPHEN M GARDNER RICHARD D GORDON WILLIAM L HARRIS
CHARLES D CROCKETT JR EDWARD M HEISER HAROLD J HERRING PAUL F JOHNS LARRY T JOHNSON
BLAIR L KEOWN STANLEY R KILTON JR LOUIS C KIMBRELL WILLIAM E MCGUIGON GEORGE L MYERS JR
WADE L BROOME LORENZO RAMIREZ JR HECTOR SANTIAGO-COLON KENNETH W SEIDEL YANCEY SMITH JR
LARRY E ADAMS DOYLE T ANDERSON WILLIAM J BOLAND JR DENNIS L BROWN WILSON B BROWN
ROY G DORSETT KENNETH L DREW ROBERT L DUTRA RONALD E EBERLE PETER FEDASCH
RONALD G GATTERSON JOHN A GERO RONALD L GRIFFIN ALFREDO GUZZO RONALD V HARBERT
GARY R HINTHER ROBERT W JARONIK GUERRERO K LEON MICHAEL L LEWIS JR EDWARD B LINDSEY
JOHN T O'CONNOR ROMMIE OLIVER RAYMOND ORDONEZ TIMOTHY S OWEN RICKY V RILEY
EDWARD G RAINFORD JOHN P ROGONE JAMES G ROWE JR PETER G RUIZ ROBERT L TYES
CLARENCE R ROOT DAVID T SHIELDS LARRY H SMITH RICHARD E SWAB LARRY L THORNTON
DAVID L VOYTKO DAVID E WAFER JAMES W WINKLES DAVID W YARBER ROBERT W YOUNG
LARRY D AUSTIN ARTHUR C BALLEW GORDON F BROWNE RICHARD C BUSBY JR WILLIAM C WHITEHEAD JR
JAMES V DENHAM TERRY E DIFFENDERFER GEORGE B DUKES JOHN C FIELDS JOHN D GOLLAHON
DONALD HICKS FRANK W JONES WILLIAM G KANE JR WAYNE W KNUPP JOHN D POWELL JR
FRED BUFFINGTON LAWRENCE B RYAN GEORGE A SCORSONE GERALD L WALTERS WILLIAM T ANDERSEN JR
PETER J ANGLE JAMES G BELINSKI AUGUST F BOLT GEDDES C BOYTER JR NICHOLAS J BUFFIN
RICHARD F BURNHAM JR JOHN M BUTTS LESLIE L CARTER TERRY L COGGINS JAMES L CROCKETT
ROBERT C DICKINSON WILLIAM B EOFF JR GERALD A FOSTER LUDIN GARCIA EDGAR GODBEY
JIM R GONZALES WILLIAM W HESTER ROBERT E HICKMAN BERNARD HOLLIDAY NICHOLAS A ROMANO
STEPHEN C HOUCK CHARLES E HOWARD CHARLES C ISLER JR FRED V JURADO CHARLES C KALKA
ROGER L LANE JOHN A LE COMPTE ALBERT F LUPOLI JR HOLLIS R NORRID HENRY J O'KUSKY JR
MILES R GREGOIRE MORRIS E OSTRANDER ROBERT L PULS ROBERT J ROSS THOMAS RUIZ
SAMUEL RUSSELL LYLE E SLANE DON S STANLEY TONY TROMBETTA THOMAS M WASHINGTON
ROY L WHITTLESEY JAMES A WILLIAMS THOMAS H WILLIAMS GEORGE J ANDERSON ROBERT L DAIGREPONT
DARELD N BORDERS JAMES A BRADY SR ALBERT L BROMLEY DOUGLAS A CANN WILLIE B CATLING
ALVIN K BENCHER DICK DE GRAF RICHARD A DEXTER FREDERICK L DYER WILLIAM J HAUPERT
EDWARD E HENDERSON JR ALFRED J HOLTZ JR BARRY D JENKINS LANCE LA GRANGE CARL B MELLINGER JR
JOHN E MILES MANUEL G OROPEZA GLENN A PRANGER RONALD W SEBRING JAMES C TULLIS
CLARENCE C RATLIFF HENRY A TIPPING RONALD G WHITE SR JAMES J WILLIAMS ARNOLD A ADES
JAMES E ANDREWS RONALD L BELLINGER JOHN C BILENSKI GREGORIO C BUSTOS JIMMIE HANKERSON
LAWRENCE N CONEY JOHN D COX JR RAYMOND C DALEY JOHN D DALHOUSE THOMAS A DAVINO
JOHN L CARTER KENNETH E FISCHER RAYMOND C GARCIA BASIL L HAREFORD JOSEPH HODGES

PANEL 53W
GARY D HOLTON JOSEPH M HOUTZ WILLIAM D JOHNSON JR FREDERICK F VAN DEUSEN
JOSEPH J JONES COLIN E LAMB JAMES S LANGWORTHY DILLARD R LAYNE RANDELL B LITTLE
JAMES L LITTLER III RAYMOND S LOFTUS III CHARLES A MARIA WILLIAM G MONCRIEF WILLIAM C MOON
ROY H MCCLAIN WARREN MOYER JR FRANKLIN D RATLIFF PAUL SCHECKLER CRAIG L SMITH
DONALD W OLSEN JR MELVIN J SCHEUBLE DANIEL C SCHUSTER HAROLD R SILVEY FAY C SIMMONS III
ALTON HOUSE THOMAS A STRANDE GARY D TISDALL SHERMAN D VANCE CLARENCE WALKER
RONALD K WEISTER PHILIP L WHITNEY RAYMOND P BOSWORTH JR BRADLEY D BOWERS BRUCE A MURRAY
ERNIE L BURGAMY RONALD M CLOUD LARRY E COLLIER JESSIE E COY JAMES W DAVIS
BERNARD F DUTTON JR JERRY N ELLIS EARL E FAULKNER DENNIS FERNANDEZ MARSHALL W FISHER
DANIEL N GLOWACKI JOHN W GREENE STEVEN F HARPER MILO S HOMSTAD PAUL L KAPP
WILLIAM A BECKWITH EUGENE L MARKWELL DAVID R NELSON WALTER J O'NEIL LAWRENCE PINALES
MICHAEL A POWELL MORRIS POWELL JOHN B REED ROBERT A RESNICK LEVI R REYNOLDS
ALEXANDER A ROCZEN CHARLES P SEARLES RAYMOND B SHAWN DON T SHEARER WILLIAM L SNODGRASS
LOUIS J SKANSON WARDELL SMITH STEPHEN R STEFANIAK FREDERICK G TERRY JR DAVID J WARD
DIRK J WESTRA WILFREDO P ZAMORA OLIVER ZINIMON JR ROBERT A AUSMUS TONY A BAKER
JERRY P BARBEE HARRY W BASS JR ISIDRO S BAZAN RICHARD S BROWN MAC C BUCKLEY
RAYMOND L BUNCH JR RICHARD J CEGIELSKI MICHAEL E DAVIS JERRY D DEWBERRY DAVID F LANGLEY
ARTHUR W DILWORTH GERALD T DUFFEY JERRY ECTOR DAVID B EMOND JOSE G GARCIA
WILLIAM H GIBBS JR TIMOTHY W GILKEY STEVEN L GRAHAM LOUIS G HEALY JOHN H HERRING
CARL P HETRICK GARY W HOPKINS ROOSEVELT HURST JR ERIC J JEDNAT HERBERT B JOHNSON
CARROLL S DIEUDONNE LAWRENCE E JOHNSON JACK P JONES JOSEPH R JONES BRUCE E LAWRENCE
HENRY A LEDFORD RUFUS M MARTIN GLENN R MILLER WILLIE R MOBLEY JOHN B MURRAY
THOMAS L MCELROY WILLIAM REYES GERARD J SANDERS EDWARD D SILVER HERMAN SMITS JR
GARY D TEMPLETON MICHAEL J THIELEN LOUIS K THOMPSON THOMAS G TURNER JAMES W VAN TASSELL
JAMES TAYLOR RANDALL M WAUGH ROBERT E WILLIAMS JON R WOODARD JAMES A WOODS
WILLIAM R CURRY JOHN W DUNLAP DOUGLAS P FRASER WILLIAM J HANSEN ARTHUR HARMON
JOHN L HASFORD JR ROBERT L HOLLIE JR RONALD E INGRAM MICHAEL J KILDERRY THOMAS P MAHONEY III
ELWOOD L HOUSTON GERONIMO LERMA RONALD B LOWE FRED E MITCHELL III CHARLES R MORRIS
DONALD W MORRIS ARTHUR B MULLINS MICHAEL R NAWROSKY BRANDT S NEUBACHER ALLEN PASCO
EUGENE L RILEY JOHN L ROBERTS CRES P SALAZAR FREDRICK J SMITH JERE L WHITAKER
PATRICK J SCOGNAMILIO JEROME S STARCKS RICHARD L TRISLER CHARLES E WIGHT JOHN ANTONACE JR
GERALD L BALDWIN RAYMOND BATEMAN WILLIAM A BATTLE CHARLES D BENNETT WARREN L BIBBS
MARLIN J CALLIES RONALD D COLEMAN HUGH COYLE CHARLES J DICKEY DONALD M FURR
DONALD R BLANKENSHIP ROBERT G DODSON CARROLL W EAVES LAVAUGHN ELLIOTT DAVID A FIELDING
JAMES A GOODMAN ANTHONY W GRUNDY IVORY HILL JR JOHN T HOLTON JR ROBERT B HORTON

267

THE VIETNAM VETERANS MEMORIAL COLLECTION

DONALD C JOHNS PAUL K JOHNSTON THOMAS R KEPPEN PATRICK D KOPP JERALD L LAW
STEPHEN H LEWIS JAMES T LOVE LUIS R MERCADO-COLLADO JOHN B MORENO WILLIAM C PENDLEY
RICHARD N PINSONNAULT GREGORY K REEVES WILLIAM K REGAN HARLEY R ROBERTS SHARBER M ROWE
LESLIE W ROYALL III DAVID J SHARP LEONARD C SHARPLEY WILMER F SIMPKINS MICHAEL E SINGER
THOMAS T SPRINKLE ROGER L STROUD JOSEPH E THOMAS ALAIN J TREMBLAY RUSSELL D WAKE
HAROLD L WALTON KENNETH G WATSON WILLIAM P WEBER WALLACE B WERNER DONALD C WILSON
DONALD E BEAR VAUGHN L BROWN ROBERT N BURROUGHS CRAIG J DEVORE WILLIAM R HOPKINS
LOUIS L CLANTON PAMELA D DONOVAN JOHN R GALABIZ TIMOTHY L HREN EDWARD D JACOBS JR
JAMES E JORDAN JR DONALD C KYLE LOUIE J MCFARLAND CHARLES E MOORE JR JAMES D NANSEL

PANEL 52W
LOUIS F PERALEZ HERBERT W ROLEY ROLAND M SHEREDOS DOUGLAS SOWARD
WILLIAM I TURNER JR HOWARD C WILLIAMS THOMAS L WILSON JIMMY R YOUNG HUGO C CASTANEDA
MANUEL V ARENAS JR ROBERT E ASH JOHN J AVELLA JAMES W CARR EDWARD W WASHINGTON JR
SAM S ALLISON R G CAUTHRON CHARLES COOK JR ANGEL M CRUZ-VAZQUEZ DANIEL L DAWES SR
JOHN P DELGADO CHARLES B FOX JR LE R GEE ROBERT W GIBBINS GEORGE A GRAY STEPHEN L WRIGHT
CHARLES F HARGER JR HUGH L HARRINGTON MILTON J JOHNSON ANTHONY I LEE EDWARD LESTER
KENNETH E MATTSON ELLAS L MIHALAKIS FREDERICK R MILLEDGE ROBERT L MILLER DALE E NORTH
HARRY A BARBER LINWOOD P RICKARDS JAMES J STRANGEWAY JR MICHAEL E THOMAS FREDERICK R WILL
LONNIE M BURCHETT ARTHUR D ELMANDORF WILLIAM F MOCKER DUSSEN G VANDER
MONTE E HENDERSON ROBERT HERNANDEZ STEVEN P IRONSIDE DOY R KENDRICKS RUDY P KRISSMAN
DENNIS W ALLEN JAMES T MCCONNELL III DOUGLAS SCALES PHILIP G SPENCER JOHN R STOCKDALE
KENNETH W ECKMAN GARY L STROUSE ROBERT V TILLOTSON LARRY G TREVARTON WILLIAM O TRUJILLO
EDWARD C VANOVER LEMON WALLACE JR JOHN L ADAMS ADOLPH W ALBRECHT HERMAN D ROBERTS
DAVID L BINGAMON WILLIAM E BLAIR DAVID S COOK GENE E FECTEAU EDWIN Z FLOYD
JIMMY L GOLDEN GEORGE W HAMILTON JR ERIC R KOEPPEN RICHARD P LONG JOHN J MICHELS
KENNETH D ARMSTRONG JOHN E MINCEY ERNEST W RUTHERFORD RONALD W SHALLER BILLY J SISCO
RONALD J TEBBE RANDALL N ARNEY ROLAND N BARNABY JAMES L BROWN FRANK R CAUTHEN
CHARLES R CLARK OTIS COOPER JR ROY K CORLEW MARIO COSTA JIMMY D FULFORD
GERALD E HETRICK KEVIN B MCGOVERN CECIL S MURRAY GEORGE W PATTERSON WILLIAM E WATTS
WILLIAM J MATHEWS CLIFFORD H SCHECK MARION N TAPP WILLIAM A THOMPSON DAVID C TOMLINSON
NORVELL J WEBB JOHN L ABRAMS LEONARD A BIRD CHRISTOPHER L BURTON STEVEN L BYINGTON
RONALD R COE ROBERT CREECH JR AUGUST E CZERWONKA ISAAC R DRAUGHON RICHARD J GAFFANEY JR
PAUL C HEWITSON RANDALL S HILL JOHN C HURST WILLIAM M JOHNSON THOMAS B LUKES
RONALD E PILLOW RAYMOND D ROBINSON JAMES H ROMANSKI CHARLES K RONZANI DENNIS M WOBBE
BOBBY E REDD RUSSELL D SPIEROWSKI BRUCE L TRUHLER JERRY L WEAVER LEROY WOOD
DENNIS D ANDREWS FRANK L AUTEN HENRY D BANKS WARREN K BROWN DONALD R BUSHONG
DOUGLAS M CAIN JOHNNIE R CAMDEN FRANK W COX JR HAROLD L DAVID JR DAVID T DURHAM
JOHN H FEEZER ERNEST J HILL CHARLES B KEATHLEY RICHARD G LIEWER HAROLD L LLANES
GERALD A MCCALL JAMES E MCCLAFFERTY RANCE A MCEACHERN JR GILBERT MORALES DONALD L MURPHY
RICHARD A MCGEATH JAMES G MCWHIRTER JESUS F ORTEGA JR JOSEPH S OTT DONALD R PHILLIS JR
MELVIN POOLE GREGORY R RAYFIELD ALAN J ROBINSON STEVEN C SANTY JAMES W SCHULZ
STEVEN J SCOTT SAMUEL T SMITH JR RICHARD B TAYLOR WAYNE J VESSELL CLAYTON D WRIGHT
DONALD R WILLIAMSON JAMES A ACOSTA JR DAVID M ARNOLD CURTIS C BROWN JOHN W HANSARD III
ANTHONY N CONTI LARRY E CURRY TERRY L DAVIS NORMAN K DOUD ROBERT B RAY
MICHAEL A BEALS STEVEN GIACOPPO JR CHARLES R HENLEY ROBERT D HICKOX ROLAND H JENKINS
GERALD J LA FLEUR LARRY E MARTIN HARLENE E MILLETTE HENRY A MITCHELL DAVID M PRICE
CHRISTOPHER COWEN JEREMIAH J SAULNIER ARMAND A SYLVESTRE LARRY M WELSH ROBERT J ZENICK
GARY W BALL RICHARD A BANKS WILLIAM J BARR HAROLD E BOWMAN KENNETH J CANTWELL
PAUL R FUSCO JESUS GRIEGO THOMAS N MANSOR ROBERT T MCJUNKIN JOHN W SIMPSON JR
CHARLES W SRADER JR RAYMOND E WRIGHT JACOB BENNETT PRENTICE J BENNETT EDGAR L BOWERS
JACK E BURTON ISAAC N CLARK ARIEL L CROSS ROBERT A CUCCINELLI WILLIAM F REILLY III
LARRY L CULLNAN CHARLIE J DOMINICK ARTHUR R DUKES JR EDWARD W FELL JR AUGUSTO J GARCIA
LARRY A GARRISON ISAAC D HAMPTON ROBERT D HAZLETT DOUGLAS A HENNING RICHARD L PROSTELL
ANTONIO HERNANDEZ MARVIN L HUNTER WILSON JACK JR RANDOLPH T JEFFERSON MICHAEL R KLINSKI
GARY L LABONTE ROBERT D LETSCH JR MICHAEL P MADRID DEAN E NICHOLAS LIONEL PARRA JR
STEVEN A BUTLER PEDRO C GONZALES WILLIAM POWELL GARY P ROWLETT GEORGE A SALCIDO
PATRICK R SCULLY JR DONALD J SMITH GARY D TICE DALLAS R TRAVIS WILLIAM B WEATHERS III

PANEL 51W
JAMES R WILLIAMS JOE B WILLIAMS LARRY D WINTERTON THOMAS A WOOLRIDGE
DAVID J ALEXANDER JR LEWIS D BLACK MANUEL A CASTILLO GEORGE A CAVALARATOS TERRY K HUFF
BILLY L COOK LAWRENCE A DAVIS VICTOR L DODDY HERMAN D DUNCAN MICHAEL ELKINTON
JAMES R FALLSTICH EDDIE T FRIERSON FRANKLYN W GERMANY STEVEN A GERSHNOW JOHN E HALSELL
WILLIAM E BEALL JR RAYMOND C HANIK JAMES W HARRIS JR ROBERT C HARTLEY JAMES G HILDEBRANDT
GARY S JOHNSON ALVIN M LASTER JR THOMAS G LE DUC DENNIS S MALEC JEROLD W MEISINGER
ANTHONY F MCNELLIS RONNIE G MOORE RONALD J PUSKARCIK WILLARD T REDMOND RONALD C ROSS
THOMAS M ROYBAL JR GARY B SANFORD JOHN C SCOFIELD EARL F SEABLOM ALLEN C SHELINE
JOHN E SWEENEY JOHN A TEMPLETON KURT E WARD HARRISON E WOEHNKER JR DONALD E BROSIUS
WILLIAM L CARR JR ROBERT W DAVIS CHARLES D EBERT DONALD L GIBSON STANLEY L GRUNSTAD
JOSEPH J GUCWA THOMAS L GUTHRIE DENNIS W KEEFE GUY R KING MELVIN S LAMAR
MICHAEL C LARSEN CECIL L MATTHEW JR ROBERT D MORRIS CHARLES L O'NEILL JR GERALD P OGLESBY
RENE T PRUDEN JOSE A RIVERA-BERMUDEZ CHARLES F RUBADO AMOS C SHERRILL II DAVID P THIBODEAU
VINCENT PISCAR JR JACOB F SIRATT III GEORGE SOLIZ RONALD F SOSNOSKI RANDALL F SWANCEY
SANTIAGO TORRES JR CLARENCE E WATSON EARL R WELSH JR RICHARD A WHIPKEY ROBERT L WILLIAMS
RAYMOND A YOUNG ALAN F ANGELL ANTHONY W ARELLANO WILLIS J BILLEAUD JR HUGH B BROWN III
RENE CARBAJAL-AZMITIA JAMES A CLEVELAND ARTHUR COLEMAN JR ERNEST EVANS JOHN C GAETH
MARCELLUS GARLAND JR AUSTIN D GIBSON GEORGE W GIPSON ROBERT L GRAHAM MICHAEL J GWINN
DONALD E HEGGAN GARY C JONES BRIAN F LE FEVRE BRUCE A MARRON ARTHUR P MURPHY JR
TERRY L MCNEAR JAMES E O'TOOLE JR DAVID J OHM RICHARD G PIXLEY ROBERT D RYAN
ROBERT C SHANNON ROOSEVELT SHERMAN JR DONALD J SLICHTER ALLEN L SMITH ISAAC SPARKMAN
JAMES A STELL GEORGE A TODD LESTER A WATSON MICHAEL R WILEY DENNIS H WIRT
STUART J WOOD STEVEN A ZIMMERMAN EDWARD G ASH JR EDWARD R BRAUN RUSSEL E BUTLER
JESUS E CHAVEZ JR JIMMY CONCEPCION-CHAPM LARRY D COOK TIMOTHY P DORAN ROBERT M LURIE
DAVID J ECKENRODE SAM J FAVATA SHERMAN E FLANAGAN JR ARTHUR M FLORES WILLIAM H FOSTER
CHARLES L CALLAHAN III DAVID L GLOER DAVID K HAMILTON CHARLIE E JENKINS BRIAN S KRILL
JOHN T LYNN SOLOMON L MCMILLIAN WILLIAM C MOORE CHARLES L MYERS JR JIMMY L NORSWORTHY
ROBERT W PARENT ROBERT D STONE ROBERT W THOMAS RALPH J WILLARD ALTON K WOOLF JR
LEONARD K STEWART EDWARD A WILLING RONALD D ALBERTSON JIMMY A AWALT LESTER E BOWMAN JR
GILBERT CARLO EUGENE F DAVIS GEORGE N DAVIS HUGH M DAVIS JOSEPH HILLMAN III
DAVID M DROB EVERETT W EVERETT CHRISTOPHER GARCIA SIEGFRIED L GRAEBNER JAMES R KEIM
JOE M DAVIS JOHN E GREESON ALLAN F HAMSMITH ISAAC L HENDERSON LYNN A HOFFMAN
TED S FERGUSON MACKLIN O HUGHES WILHELM S HURKMANS JR SALVATORE C INSANA DAVID B KELLEY
GERALD D KIESLING GERALD KIRBY DONALD J KRUSSOW HERMAN P MAGEE DAVID M MAYMON
GARY A MEYER JOHN P MURPHY STEVEN R OLSON JACKIE R POLING MYRON J POOCK
LUTHER J ROSS JR EUGENE D SCHINDLER ROGER D SHAFER JERRY L SHULTZ VALENTINE TUCKER
WILLIAM L SHRUM RONALD A SKELTON FREDERICK D STEPHENSON MARC G VAN DALSEM GARY R WILLEKE
JOHN F BOBB HARRY L BOYLE KENNETH A BUTLER JR DOUGLAS D CHANEY DANNY E DEESE
ALBERT GONZALEZ LAWRENCE D GOSEN BILLY M GROSS ARTHUR HADDOCK GREGORY P HELSLEY
THOMAS W DULER CHARLES T HESSE CHARLES G HEYDORN SID HILL HARKLES L HODGES
JOHN M HOGUE RAY HOWARD JR DENNIS E IAMS FRANCIS D JOHNSON GARY E LEE
JAMES H MARTIN HARRY M MATHER DAVID G MITCHELL JAMES S MITCHELL RICHARD A MULLINS
THOMAS R OWENS EDGAR E PARKER DAVID A PEARSON RICHARD L ROUSSEAU JACK W SCARBOROUGH JR
JOSE A ORTIZ-BURGOS CHARLES S ROY DONALD W SEIDEL FRANK J SHAREK JR JAMES D SMITH
DENNIS J SPECK GLENN E SPENCER JOHNNY R THAXTON JR BENJAMIN TILGHMAN WAYNE E TIMOTHY
THOMAS J TOMCZAK ROY N UEBLER JR BRUCE R WENBAN RANDY R WERNIG WILLIAM H WHITE
ROBERT C WITZEL ROBERT F WORLEY MICHAEL V AURADY THEODORE L BIGHAM JOHN R BUSH
JOSEPH T CAMBRON IDUS J CONNER MICHAEL S ELLEDGE JOHN C FOY THOMAS C FYFFE
RUSSELL M ERICKSON DAVID S GREILING HARLEY B HACKETT III JIMMY L HAIRSTON RICHARD S HAYMES

PANEL 50W
MARVIN P HUBBARD JIMMIE L JEFFERSON HOWARD L KLENSKE CHESTER J MOSHIER JR
RICHARD L JUSTICE JOHN C LUEBKE JR JOSEPH J MILLER JR LARRY MONTGOMERY JOHN V SARTOR
ANTHONY J SIVO DOUGLAS D SLOAN RANDOLPH M TARJANY PERRY E THOMPSON ROBERT R THOMPSON
JOHN R WILSON WILLIAM S BAKER BRENDON J BERRIGAN PAUL BLACK JR RONALD H GABLE
NORMAN K BRISTOW LUCIEN G CARPENTIER LON G CARR CARSON G CULLETON LARRY H GALLAGHER
HECTOR GONZALEZ MICHAEL F HENDRICKSON KENNETH J HOFFMAN VAN A IRWIN WAYNE A KELLER
JOSEPH A L'HUILLIER DAVID R LANG WILLIAM M LIVINGSTON SALVATORE J MANCINO RICHARD R TOLETTE
JAMES E MANSON JR GARY R MCKENDRICK PAUL H NABORS CHARLES C PARISH JOE PIERCE JR
IRVIN W MOSLEY CHARLES D PEKNY CHARLES H PETERSDORF JR GREGORY M ROUSE JACK R SANBORN
THOMAS A LUTGE JOHNNIE B SEWELL RICHARD S SIMMONS DONN L SWEET ALFRED L TRIPP
LEE D TSOSIE MERVIN E WALLACE ROBERT L WENZEL THURMAN W WINSTON CHESTER L WITANEK JR
HILLMAN G CHAMBERS ROBERT M CHILDRESS THOMAS R COOK JR MERLIN G CORNELIUS JR PERRY R CRISE
GENE A FRAZIER STEVEN A FRINK ALLEN J GROVNER RICHARD W HANLEY VERNAR SLOAN
ROCCO R ISAAC DONALD A JONES JAMES R LONG RICHARD C MANNERY RALPH W MCLENDON
TERRY A FRECHETTE CHARLES T MCNUTT RICHARD M O'NEAL ERIC PARKER MANUEL M SIQUEIROS
JACK S SMITH PAUL D SPILLANE WILLIAM J TELLIS FERNANDO M VALDEZ JOHN W ACOSTA
WILLIAM A ATWELL ROBERT J AUCOIN THEODORE N BOLAK DURWOOD CAULDER FRANK E FULLERTON
TERRY L DILLARD DAVID P DUNYON JAMES EDSALL WILLIAM L FOLEY JOSEPH R FRANCKOWIAK
RICHARD V DALY RUSSELL G HOFER MICHAEL T MAJESKI RICHARD R OBERT DONALD G PACHECO
WARD K PATTON ROY E PHILLIPS CHESTER M RENCEVICZ THOMAS M ROLAND ROBERT A ROMERO
LARRY TAYLOR JAMES H YOUNG ROSCOE D ADAMS DAVID L BROOKS JOHN C GIBSON
WAYNE M CARON GEORGE L CARR WILLIAM S CLARK GUY W DOHERTY TERRY L DOUGLAS

DONALD B CAMPBELL EDWARD J DOWNS RALPH M DRYDEN JR GARY G GORDON PHILIP L GOSSELIN
JERRY L GRAVES RAY G HAWK GEORGE S JOHNSON DOUGLAS M KELLY FREDERICK J KRUPINSKI
JOHN M LANCASTER ROBERT C LEE DANIEL E LLOYD ERASTE J MARCEAUX JAMES C MARKEL JR
CARL R MILLER DANNY OVERTON JR ANTHONY C PINO RAPHAEL J RENDON JOHN E RICE
JORGE MARTINEZ STEPHEN R RICHARDS RONALD L RUSEK JOHN R SERRANO ELWIN R SHAIN
ALBERT P SMITH WILLIAM S SMOYER JOHN J TILL RICHARD E URBAN JOHN W ZUEHLSDORF
PAUL D ATON JERRY E AUNIER GARRY W BAKER ALFRED J DAVIES JR MICHAEL R GLASFORD
DONALD J GREENE JOHN V GRESSEL BILLY G INSALL SOLOMON LEARY PHILIP MARASCO JEFFREY L MARTIN
DONALD S MCGINLEY CARLOS G MUNOZ DOUGLAS G ORVIS WILLARD O PACK TERRY A ROBINSON
GARY V ORSLAND WILLIAM L PEMBERTON LUTHER M SEXTON JR PAUL SHIREMAN JR ROBERT C SMITH
JACK M STRONG JAMES L TANGEMAN JOSEPH R WHITE JR JAMES M WITHERSPOON WILLIAM R ALMON
WILLIAM E BERZINEC THOMAS J BEYER ROY E COOPER JOHN P DELANEY III CLIFFORD L ERVIN
ROBERT L GARDNER PAUL J GORMAN JOHN W JACOBSON SR THOMAS O JIMENEZ JR ROBERT QUINN
JAMES E KANDEL DAVID S KOSSOWSKI KENNETH D LINSE DENNIS D MANNING RICHARD H MCKINNEY
GUIDO FARINARO JERRY L PATTERSON GERALD D SACK FLOYD E SELLERS LOWHMAN S SUTTON
VERNON E BELCHER LLOYD W EVANS JR GEORGE A GARRISON CHARLES HAMNER MICHEAL E RICHARDS
THOMAS J HARKNESS JR GARY D KELLER ARMANDO D MARTINEZ JOSEPH E NEAL THOMAS R PULLEN
GEORGE A ALFORD JR RICHARD D SULLIVAN JR JAMES M WILKINS EDWARD M BABIARZ LARRY G BANDY
HARRY M BECKER EDWARD J BROMS JR DONALD L CARLSON CHARLES W EPPERSON WILLIAM FERNAN
DONALD R FOWLER DONALD N GLENN ROBERT GRIFFIN GLEN R HICKS EARL A OKUMURA
DAVID L HOPKINS LARRY W HOWE JAMES H JONES GUADALUPE M LEAL JAMES R WILLIS
STEVEN M HASTINGS HAROLD L MARCUM LEONARD T MARLIN HUBERT A MEREDITH JIMMY L NATION
WILLIAM D PEARSON GERALD L POPPA JOSEPH S ROSS PETER J RUSSELL SCOTT G SMITH
WILLIAM F HOOK JR ALLAN G SWAIM WILLIAM J THOMPSON THEODORE J WHITLOCK MATTHEW WOODS
JOSEPH A ALBRECHT WALTER J ALYEA JAMES W ARVIDSON RAFIEL AVILA JOHN J MCGLEW
RONALD C BAKEWELL RONALD N BLOOM RICHARD I BORNHEIMER BRUCE E CLOUGH DAVID C CRANE
WILLIAM C CUE MARTIN J DAVIS JOHN C DE MARR CHARLES H DELLINGER RONALD H DYE
CARL L GENERAL RICHARD D GOEN RONALD L GRENIER MICHAEL A GRIGGS ROY W HOWARD
LARRY A JAMERSON KENNETH R JONES DENNIS L KELLY PETER J LOVAN PAUL F LUCE
WILLIAM P ARMSTRONG EDWARD M MAHER JR AL D MEMORY CHARLES H MILLNER DAVID E MORTON

PANEL 49W
CRAIG F SWAIN BILLY J TAYLOR WILLIAM R TAYLOR CHESTER A WRIGHT
RICKY E SMITH PAUL W TRAINOR CARL D WAKEFIELD ROBERT S WILHOIT ALFRED L WYANT
NATHANIEL BUGGS JR LARRY B BUZZARD RANDALL B CHOATE JAMES B COOK SERVESTON D POPE
LARRY L ELZINGA GEORGE W FISCHER JR WILLIE E GRANGER FRANK A HARAH STEPHEN L HAVAS
GARY E HOADLEY CLARENCE J JACKSON WILLIAM S JONES RONALD K LEWIS LOUIS U MENARD JR
CHARLES R CRIM RICHARD E PALOWSKI RONALD P SANTORO MILAN E TURNER MICHAEL L UMDENSTOCK
DON R BACHELOR EUGENE M BARNETT RICHARD J BECK HENRY M BRUCE ANTHONY J EDWARDS
JAMES I FOWLER JR JOHNNY E FRISK RICHARD W HELLARD JR MORRIS E HOLCMAN ALLEN P HOUCK
OSCAR L HOUSE LEDELL JOHNSON JR RONALD J MURPHY DARNELL P MURRAY RAMIRO L SALINAS
JAMES A HUFF MIGUEL A NEGRON-RODRIGUEZ JOHN R SCHMUDE RONALD B TAYLOR GEORGE C VASSEY
THOMAS A WARREN GREGORY B WHITMORE TIMOTHY M WILBANKS JONES L YAZZIE EUGENE BAKER JR
GERALD D BERGER STEVEN C BLOSSOM WILLIAM G BREWER BRUCE N COLSON RONALD L DAVIDSON
THOMAS K FAHRENHORST ANIBAL FALCON CHARLES V FIRTH DAVID A GULBRANTSON MICHAEL N HOBAN
WILLIAM B DECKER MARK K HAGE DWIGHT S HOWELL THOMAS G HUDSON DENNIS M HYLAND
HARRY KIM ROBERT D LONG GARY M MABREY ROBERT W MATTHEWS
LUPE MONSEBAIS JAMES L MOORE TONY S OROZCO JR RODOLFO PEREZ BLAINE C SCHAFFER
DANNY W JOHNSON HERMAN W SCHERMANN IRVING B TCHAKIRIDES JACOB R TRUJILLO EDUARDO VELOZ JAMES P YOUNG
MARCUS P ANDERSON BERNARD G BAKER EDWARD G BAKER JOHN W BARBEE LAWRENCE G BARGAHEISER
ERNESTO F CASTRO JR THOMAS B CHRISTIAN ROBERT G FANTE STEVEN W HUTCHINGS CHARLES T NANCE
PATRICK M LORDITCH JOHN C MARTIN ANDREW C RACKOW JAMES L RATLIFF JAMES E RUDD
RICHARD L TATUM RONALD D WHITLOW TERRY L BALDWIN THOMAS C BAMFORD MALCOLM M ESPARZA
RICHARD R CERRA ROBERTO COBARRUBIAS DARYL C CULVER COLON J DE JESUS DAVID R HOWARD
THOMAS J BLANCHARD WILLIE FIELDS JR TIMOTHY C HANNIGAN DANA A HARRISON ANTHONY HEIN
STANLEY R BUSTAMANTE JR BRYAN T KAY DAVID C KEEFER DONALD H MABRY MORRIS A MALLARD JR
WILLIAM E MCDAVID EMMETT D MCLELLAN THOMAS L PIPER SONEY RAMEY JOHN E REYNOLDS
JAMES M ROBINS NICHOLAS L SCHROEDER JOHN R SHEROKE JR BEN W STEPHENS LARRY W SWIGGUM
WILLIAM J THIESFELDT-COLLA JAMES E TURNER JAMES E VERNOR WALTER L WALLS ALDERMAN C WEST
MARSHALL D WOLFORD FRANK D ADAMS CHARLES D BARTLETT RONALD D BUSBY LEE T CLARKE
EDDIE DISMAYA JR JAMES M EDWARDS REESE C ELIA JR GERALD P GATEWOOD GARY L HIGBEE
MARTIN S GRUBER JR GRADY H HARRIS HERBERT E ILGENFRITZ JR WILLIAM S IRBY PHILLIPS H IZARD JR
JOHN A JABLONSKI ELIAS C JURADO JR DICKIE L LEACH JAMES A LEAHY JAMES F LUCAS
DWIGHT E MOONEY LEONARD L MOORE ZACHARY P NEW RONALD L NOLDNER EUGENE M WOODSON
RICHARD A OVAITT ALLEN J PRETNAR PAUL R SAVACOOL JR LESLIE J TEGTMEIER MYRON THOMPSON
JOSEPH P TOOMEY ALAN D TRUCANO LARRY J TYLER ROBERT A VON BISCHOFFSHAU JAMES M WALSH
MELVIN L MCARTHUR WILLIAM C WIESKUS STEVEN E WILDMAN ROBERT O BUMILLER FRANKLIN I BURRIS JR
TERRELL W HALE ROY L JENKINS VICTOR B MEYERS STATUE MOSBY JR MICHAEL P BOYLE
LEROY NEWSON JR JOHN P RILEY MICHAEL E SMITH PAUL J SULLIVAN WAYNE B WOLFKEIL
JOHN A HOLDERBAUM DANIEL L AULT MICHAEL C BRUNNER ROBERT L CARMAN WILLIAM V CLARKE
KAROL CLAY JOSEPH O CLINE III RICHARD K CRISWELL III LUIS CRUZ JOHN F DIGGS
ANTONIO V GARCIA DAVID A GULEY FRANK C HARRIS ROBERT G HARVEY WENDELL H MCKENZIE
ALBERT R HAYNES BEN L HERRERA DOUGLAS W HILLIN ROGER HULSEY MARK D JACKS
SAMUEL R JAMES II RAYMOND G KRISKOVICH JAMES E MARSHALL JOHN J MATARAZZI JR PAUL H MELOY
DANIEL L EDWARDS PAUL G OLENZUK CHRISTOPHER L RAINS JAMES T RANDOLPH DONALD M REDMOND
FRANKLIN RENFRO JR CARLOS M RIVERA JOHN C ROBINSON II STEVEN M SCHLOSSER MICHAEL B SNYDER
KURT P STEPHENSON EDWARD STEWART DAVID R THOMAS GEORGE E VALKER III STANLEY R WOHLMAN
TONY J AYALA FRANK J BELTRAN ROBERT L BOUCHET HOWARD F BURNS KINSEY A DAVIS
WILLIAM L DEBO JOHN J FLOOD JR CARL R FOSTER ROBERT J GILLESPIE JR JAMES H HILYARD
WILLIAM A JOY JOHN C MILES HERMAN A MILLER II THOMAS D NADEAU GARY G POOL
JOHN K SCHMITT JR DONALD L STONESIFER CHARLES E TEAGUE ROBERT WILLIAMS JR MICHAEL R WILSON
JOHN A TESAURO DONALD E AUSBORN MERLIN H BERGAN KENNETH R BLAIR HENRY L BRADSHAW
STEPHEN M CARNINE LEONARD W CHRISTESON BOBBY J CLARK GEORGE R CLAYPOOL
DAVID C DAISHER RALPH P DAYHOFF THADDEUS DURRETT EARNEST EATMAN JR FRANKLIN M ELLINGER
DOUGLAS L FREDERICK BOBBY FREEMAN LEONARD Z GURWITZ HARRY J HAAS ROGER D HEDDEN
MILTON COOK JAN V HENRICKSON STANLEY G HOLTON TERRY R JENS JR WILLIAM W KENT RONALD P LEE

PANEL 48W
ROBERT F MCMANUS ARTURO D MONTION RONALD L MUEHLBERG KENNETH L WORLEY
JOHN A MCCLUNG THOMAS E MORTICE III JAIME ORTIZ-RODRIGUEZ RONALD L PANZER DENNIS A PRICE
DONALD L PUMPHREY LARRY J PURCELL RICHARD A SCOTT PETER W SLABINGER THOMAS C TREADWAY
JOSE A MATOS-CORREA HARLIN P TREEN LONNIE J TULLIER WILLIE WHITFIELD JR GERALD A WILSON
MARCUS R ASPLUND LUTHER BETHEA JR DANNY C CASEY ROBERT M CATES JR LONNIE ELLERBE JR
PHILIP R FINK TERRY R HINKLE DUANE A JOHNSON JIMMIE L KRATZBERG FREDDIE LEWIS
FRANCISCO X LICEA JAMES A LISENBY CHARLES L LYMAN JAMES A LYONS THOMAS W MATTESON
TERRY R MEYER EARNEST R MULLINS VICENTE D PEREZ THOMAS R POLISKY DONALD E PRAGMAN
EDMOND R TOLER DARRELL L TRUMBLE ALLEN L WARD LEON D WILLARD JAMES A WILLIAMS
ROBERT W WOODS WILLIAM J ZEMANICK MICHAEL P AARON ROBERT I BROWN RAYMOND L DANIELS
ROBERT A BULMER RODRIGUEZ P CAMACHO GORDON E COLE GARY L MALOY HAROLD L WHITE
ROY L EDELSTEIN THOMAS L EICHENAUER ANNIE R GRAHAM LEO L HADLEY SCOTT D HENRY
ROBERT G COOPER DALLAS L JOHNSON STEVE D LEE BARRY A MANTHEY BEN O MASADAS
JOHN B MULARZ DANIEL L NEUBURGER RICHARD D NOVAK LEONARD M PARRISH KERMIT C PETERSON JR
BOBBY L RILEY RICHARD M SAMORAY ROBERT J SANTORO FRANCIS A SCHWARZ MICHAEL W SINIBALDI
BRUCE W COLLINS HENRYK T SULATYCKI LARRY E VAN GESSEL GEORGE J BODNAR BAY B BOOTHE
ROGER D BOWMAN CHARLES F CRICHTON ROBERT E CROWLEY PHILLIP J ESSIG ROLAND L FLORIO
TERRIN D HICKS OSCAR K HIGGINBOTHAM JR JAMES K KNUTSON MICHAEL E MEANS DERRYL L MOORE
ARCHIE L NELSON JR JAMES R PARKER ANTHONY J PORTIS ROBERT V SIMONS WILLIAM F SOULE
BYRON C TUCKER WILLIAM N URSIN ROBERT K WAGNER LEROY A WHITLOW AUGUSTUS L WILLIAMS
JOSEPH B ADAMS GEORGE R ANDERSON ROBERT M ARNOLD JR WILLIAM T BANNA JR DARREL E BARNHOUSE
JOHN L BEGAN JEROME BELL LURAL L BLEVINS III DAVID R BOEVER THOMAS W MUSICK
GARY D BOWLING CLAYTON C BRANNON ROBERT J BROWN DAVID CHISUM JOHN P COOK
ROBERT M CRAVENS JR JOHN E CUMBRY ELLIOTT L DE CORA JAMES C DICKERSON ALEXANDER M SLUSSEAR
ARTHUR R DUPREY ROBERT C GARDNER JOHN A GERDESMEIER LEWIS C GILLS JOSE A GRANIELA JR
RICHARD L HALL CHARLES M HARDY OTIS L HARTRY DAN D HAYES DENNIS W HEFFNER
PAUL L HUFF CRAWFORD JACKSON JR PATRICK L KORTESMAKI GARY D LAWSON STEPHEN W LEONARDIS
JAMES E BLUE THOMAS L MERICANTANTE ROBERT MILLINER RAMIRO M MORA ROJELIO O MUNOZ II
DONALD C MCALLISTER JR MICHAEL O MCELHANON JOHN F OVERLOCK JEPPIE J PAYNE GARY R RALPH
KEVIN R REMER ROBERT M REYNOLDS JOSEPH F RIBEIRO JOHN E ROE GORDON A SKINNER II
DENNIS O CROCKER CHARLES D SONNKALB JR JOHN D STRATE JERRY L WILSON TERRY R ZIMMERMAN
HENRY E BENTON JR CARLOS GONZALEZ ROBERT A HANNAMAN PAUL J MEAUX HOMER L MULLINAX
MICKY R HIGHLANDER JOHN W IGERT NOBE R KOONTZ JR DAVID S LASSITER LOREN V LEE
WILLIAM R CORCORAN ARTHUR D EDGERTON JR EDWARD K MILLER WILBERT H NEAL JR RAYFORD NELSON
LEON A PALMER WILLIAM E POWELL WALTER SEALS JOSEPH R STEINER III JOHN C THOMAS
STEPHEN M TULLY THEARTIS WATTS JR BILLY L WILSON RICHARD E ADDISON JR ROBERT ARNOLD
RUSTON L BAKER KENNETH M BALDWIN GERALD R BALLARD MARTIN J BEGOSH CHARLES T BELASCO
WILLARD G BELLOMY JOHN C BIENEMAN GEORGE A BRANCH STEPHEN C BRUNTON DANIEL CARDENAS JR
JOE D CARROLL JAMES CAUDILL JOSEPH C CERRONE JR ROGER D CHEEK EDWARD R DARVILLE III
GARY R CRUSE PHILIP A D'AMICO JR GILBERT T DELGADO ARTHUR L DOILEY JR JAMES D EISENHOUR
NORMAN L EVERSGERD ALVIS R FAVERTY JR GERALD M GISCHER PATRICK J GRIFFIN WILLIAM A HADSOCK
MICHAEL C POLISKI MICHAEL D HAHN MICHAEL D HALE HARRY D HAMM LLOYD HARMS JAMES R HEETER
RONALD M HEINECKE WILLIE L HENRY RICHARD M JARVIS ROBERT A KEHOE ROBERT F KELLY
RANDOLPH C KETT JAMES C KRAYNAK KENNETH L KROM LARRY J LA POINT FRED E LAND
THOMAS A LEIGH JR ROY D LOWE JR HECTOR LUGO-MOJICA JAMES R MONCRIEF DOUGLAS S SCROGGINS

PANEL 48W (*Continued*)

ROBERT A MCALLISTER KEVIN J MCARDLE LARRY D NELSON MICHAEL J O'NEILL LEWIS W PAGE
DAVID CHISUM BRUCE W POULSON CHARLES R REFF BILLY D ROY JOHN SANEDA KENNETH F SCHWAGEL
JOHN R MILLIKAN ARTHUR SEABROOKS LORENZO SEWELL DONALD F SLACK JR JAMES O SPAW
DAVID M STJOHN JOHN F SULLIVAN LEE W SWAIN JR KENNETH L THOMAS WALLACE O TRAVERS JR
MARTINIANO VALENTIN JR PAUL VELEZ FREDERICK M VICKERY III LARRY W WALKER SHERMAN L WALTERS
FREDDY R WILLIAMS MICHAEL R WITT ARTURO S ZAMORA DAVID L ADAMS GARY C BAIZE
GARY A BARNES STEVEN K BRANDENBURG BRUCE C BROGOITTI TERRENCE E BUTLER THEOTHIS COLLINS
ALAN C DABBS GALE E DEERING WILLIAM J DEORIO JR LEWIS A DITTMER CURTIS JOHNSON
ROGER T FAST WILLIE S FIELDS ANGELO GIACOBBE WAYNE W GROSS ROY A HARBAUGH JR
DONALD D HAWKINS JAMES J HEFNER AUBREY R HENLEY ROBERT H HERING TERRY A HODGES
ERROL W ESQUILIN-ORTIZ TERRY A HOFFMAN JOHN W HUTCHISON HORACE JOHNSON JR ALDON C JONES
JAMES M KARRAS JAMES K KELLY DWAYNE E KEVER ALVIN H LANGFORD JOE E LOFTON

PANEL 47W

SALVADOR J MENDEZ PATRICK C MILES GENE A MOONEY JR ROY T WESTBROOK
DENNIS L MCCORMICK EDWARD A MCKENZIE DEAN O NEWSOME JAMES A PACE JACK P PASHANO
HERMAN G PAYNE CHARLIE PERKINS JR THOMAS L POLLARD ROBERT B PURTELL RICHARD RAMIREZ JR
WILLIAM L SANDERSEN ROGER L SCHWARZ FREDERICK V SEABORNE RENE SERRANO LEONARD E SEXTON
RALPH W MILBOURNE VICTOR D TRUJILLO JOHN V VEARA ARTHUR WATSON JONAS BENFORD
VICTOR BOOCHKO DAVID M BOTTS BOBBY J BYRD GREGORY V CARR VERNON W CHRISTIAN JR
JOHN A CONNELL FREDDIE L COUCH MARTIN ESPINOZA CLARENCE FULTON RONALD D GOLDEN
SAMUEL A FEW JAMES W GATES LOUIS E GAU ISREAL GIBBS MICHAEL R GOINS
JOAQUIN C GONZALEZ MICHEAL R HARLAMERT RICHARD HUNT JEROME E JANSEN ROY M JOHNSON
RONALD W KEMPFF ROBERT W LAIS DONNIE J LAWHORNE CHARLES D LINDBLOOM DONALD E LISENBY
FREDDIE K MARTIN RAYMOND E MUSICK JR BRINSON I PAUL RAYMOND L PEREZ BILL A WEBB
DONALD E RUMMEL JERRY R SANSING DONALD R SIZEMORE ALBERT D SMITH JOSEPH E SMITH
ROBERT S STRAUSS FREDERICK H TAPPAN EUGENE S TINNIN PEDRO A VERA CLIFFORD C WALKER
STEVEN C MARTINEZ J C WHITING JR ROBERT L ZORNOW ALFRED L BAILEY JR EDWARD V COFFEY
DANNY L BLAKE JOHN A BOSCH JAMES L BOWDEN HERSHEL J BULLOCK SR GEORGE A CARNEY
BRUCE E BARTLETT FRED A CHITWOOD JR DOUGLAS W COLLINS JOSE R COLON-RIVERA JERRY W COMBEST
FRANCIS J CONNOR RICHARD A DAMSCHEN JR GARY L DOBBINS EDWARD J DULL CHARLES H ELLIOTT JR
WILLIAM E FENNELL DICK D HAMILTON JAMES R HAMILTON LOWELL R HANSON JAMES L HARBOTTLE
JOHN IMBACH III GEORGE K KAPALU LEWIS M KING JR MAINOR D LANG JR DAVID W LEDBETTER
MICHAEL R MANGAN HUBERT W MARTIN ARTHUR W MEYER STEVEN P MURPHY JOSEPH T PIGEON JR
DONALD K POWELL WILLIAM G RASH DONALD P REAMER ROY J RECTOR JESUS RIVERA
ERVIN B ROBERTS JESUS ROBLEDO JR JAMES E RUSH JR JOHN E RUSSELL ELIAS SALAZAR JR
RICHARD E SMITH EDWIN C SONNICHSEN WALTER C STEELE DELBERT R STOGSDILL R D SULLIVAN
HEYDEN C VANDER DANIEL E WARK EDWARD T WEST JOHNNY L WHITEAKER MARVIN R YOUNG
CHARLES R BALES DAVID A BALLOU KENNETH N BRANDES CHARLES W BROWN PAUL E PARKER
JAMES B CARLSON LARRY D COOK DONNIE L DAMEWOOD PHILIP T DE LORENZO JR FREDFOR EDWARDS
DAVID N EMBREY DAVID L FERRY ROBERTO L GABANA WAYDELL GETTER ALBERT H GIDDINGS
RONALD A GOLWITZER PHILIP W HUNT PAUL A JEROME JR JOHN C KENNEBREW ARGESTLAR KING JR
GILBERT KING NEWELL F LEIGH JR PETER J MEARS JR VERLYN G MEYER JAMES M MORIARTY
HUMBERTO ACOSTA-ROSARIO DAVID A MCAFEE JAMES K MCALEER III ROBERT D MOYE PAUL F O'LEARY
JAMES H PIGOTT ANTHONY N REVAK JAMES M RICHARDS PEDRO J RODRIGUEZ ROBERT L ROSS
DWAYNE L SALTER ROBERT B SANDERS STEVEN M SCHLUEB JAMES E SELF LAWRENCE E STEVENSON
PETER L RUSSELL KENYU SHIMABUKURO THOMAS K SMITH WILLIAM E SPENS III JOHN D STRINGFELLOW JR
WAYNE E THOMAS REGINALD G TOLBERT ARCADIO TORRES JR RICHARD L TREAS PATRICK E WARD
ALLEN P WEAVER WILLIAM E WEBER BLAINE A WELCH THOMAS R WELLS BENJAMIN G WILLIS
ROBERT M WORSHINSKI DAVID L WRIGHT BILLY E YARBROUGH ARTHUR L ADAMS JR TALMADGE H ALPHIN JR
HENRY H BALLEW BARRY J BECANNEN CHARLES L BERGEVIN DANIEL J BERMINGHAM DAVID T JUDD
WILLIAM H BRIC III DONALD W BROWN THAL A BROWN CHRISTOPHER L CHAMBERS HYLAN L CROWDER
RONALD L CALENTINE ROGER O CHARLAND HAROLD L CHEADLE JR CHARLES A COATS PHILIP G DAVIS
JOHN L DIEDERICH RONALD F DONOHUE CLIFFORD A DRAPER STEPHEN A ELLENWOOD JR JOHN A ELLER
MIKE P ESPINOZA MIKE P ESPONOZA JOSEPH E FALARDEAU WALTER FERGUSON JR MICHAEL D FIX DAVID A FLESKES
RAMON GARCIA WILBURN C GIDEON CHARLES R GOLLING FRANK GOMEZ RICHARD D HARNED
THOMAS S GARRETT JOHNNIE GOODEN NORMAN W GRANT JR WILLIAM R GRANT DANNY L GRIMSHAW
BILLY D HARRIS RICKY G HARRISON PATRICK S HEDERMAN WALTER M HENRY EUGENE J HILL JR
ANTHONY J BLEVINS HENRY HILL JR ROBERT G HOLLEY DONALD E HORINEK LEO M JENNETTE
CHARLIE E KEMP DONALD R KERNS JAMES T KICKLITER HAROLD J KLUSENDORF CHESTER R MCCLELLAND
GEORGE A KYRICOS RAYMOND L LA GROU JR JOEL M LA ROCHE WILLIE J LAMAR LORIN E LONG
EDWARD LOPEZ HAYWOOD MAHONE JR HARRELD P MARTIN CHESTER H MAY ROBERT G MILLER
ROBERT J MILLER JR GILBERTO M MOLINA ROGER R MOLL DENNIS E MORGAN ROBERT D MURPHY
TADEUSZ M KEPCZYK ALBERT MCBRIDE JERALD T MCKENZIE SHERMAN D MCLESTER EDDIE L MCMILLAN JR
JAMES E NEELY CHARLES R NORRIS RICHARD E PEGRAM JR GEORGE E PERDUE PAUL D POTTER
ROBERT D PURDIE KENNETH W REID LON D RICHARDS ROLF E RICKMERS LEONDIS E RODRIQUEZ
RICHARD L ROWLAND JR ANTHONY J SANTANA ROBERT W SAWYER WILLIAM O SCHMALE JAMES W SMITH
ROBERT W SALTER DANIEL G SCHWAN GILBERT A SECOR FRANCIS L SETTERQUIST HENRY F SMITH
LARRY M SMITH RICHARD O SOPER JOHN L STABLER EDWARD S STEWART JOHN P SUPERCZYNSKI JR
LUTHER J THEDFORD ROBERT S UNDERWOOD ROBERT J UYESAKA HOWARD S VARNI STEVEN C VINTER
HAROLD R VOORHEIS ALBERT M WALTER JERRY A WEIMER DONALD W WELCH FREDDIE L WHITLEY
EARL C WILSON GREGORY WOODS CHARLES F WRIGHT WILLIAM R YOUNGBLOOD DANIEL O ABERNATHY
MICHAEL ALBERICI ROGER C ANDERSON EDWARD R ARNWINE CARL L BORGEN DONALD P CALDWELL

PANEL 46W

RICHARD P CAZIN MICHAEL L COOPER RANDALL S FLETCHER HERMAN D ROBINSON
STEVEN J FOSTER JAMES T GRIFFIN JR DENNIS A GUNDER ALBERT R GUTIERREZ JR WILLIAM A HEEP
THOMAS F HERKINS ROBERT J HIMLER LESLIE E HINES III ROBERT D HUGHES JOSEF P INTIHAR
NELSON JEFFERSON JR KURT K JOBST JR GARY B KILGORE LEWIS KING HAROLD F KLINE
PETER F KOVACH FRANK J LACEY MELVIN E LADEWIG DONALD G LAMMERS DEAN L LANG
ROBERT W MCGILL WILLIAM N MCMURTREY JOHN E MILLER LEWIS NANCE LUPE P OCHOA
BENNETT E EVANS RICHARD A PARKER DONALD R PYRANT DAVID N RASMUSSEN CHARLES H READ JR
WILLIAM P RYLAND JAMES E SANDERS JR RONALD D SHOCKLEY ISIAH SIMMONS BILLY SMITH
GEORGE W SMITH JR CARMELO SOSA-HIRALDO RAYMOND P SPINLER JAMES L TARTE ROBERT R TOLPA
IVAN L VINCENT JR JAMES WALLER RICHARD A WARE THOMAS H WILLIAMS CHARLES R WYATT
DANIEL L ANDERSON WILLIAM T ANDERSON ROGER E BISHOP CARL L BROWN LESLIE L BRUCKER JR
RONALD F BUSS CARLOS G CARBAJAL TIMOTHY L CARMODY ROBERT O CATO MICHAEL R CLASEN
CHARLES R CORNETT JEFFREY T CRAMER WILLIAM T DAVIS GUY A DAVISON DONALD L MCCLANAHAN
ALLAN G DECKER BRUCE E DOLBOW MICHAEL B DOOLEY ROBERT J DORSHAK GERARD J DUNNE
JOSEPH E FUNSTON ELVING P GUTIERREZ-OLIVER JAMES E HALL STEPHEN R HILTON STEPHEN M KRINKE
EDWARD J GRAY RAY L JACKSON GEORGE JOHNSON STEPHEN A JORDAN ROBERT M KEENE
RAYMOND G KROBETZKY LEO N KRYSKE WILLIAM C LAWSON BYRON J MITCHELL DANNY J MITCHELL
JERRY L DAVIS PATRICK J MCCORMICK GARRY M MCCULLOUGH FRANCIS T MULVEY ARDEN G SONNENBERG
BRUCE J NELSON JOHNNY B NESBITT STEVE O NUSSBAUMER MARVIN R PEARCE JOSE M PENA
FRED D PENLAND ROBERT PETRACCO CALVIN B PIERCE PAUL H PIRKOLA JEFFREY W POHJOLA
JUAN M QUINONES LELAND E RADLEY DANIEL D REZENDE JAMES B RICHEE THOMAS E RICHEY
ANDRES RIVERA-RUIZ KEITH W ROWELL WILLIAM W SEAY PAUL R SEVERSON JERRY L SIMMONDS
CORNELIUS F MURPHY JR EUGENE R SKOCH FRANKIE L SMILEY FORESTAL A STEVENS THOMAS J STOPYRA
GLENN C STROMBACK JOHN C STROME WILLIAM A SWOVELAND EUGENE TURNER CARMELO VASQUEZ
CLAUDE F VAUGHN THOMAS J WALKER JAMES F WATSON JAMES B WESTBROOK EDWARD J WOODS
WENDELL W ANDERSON EARL S BAZEMORE LEWIS L BIGGERS WILLIAM J BILBO JR RICHARD L DAUGHERTY
ROBERT G BULL II DUANE L BUSSELMAN GARY L CLAPP ROBERT W CLARKE THOMAS R LIND
NORMAN E BALDWIN DWIGHT C COY JR JOHN CURTIN III RICHARD L DAVIS EDWARD DAY
JAMES A FERGUSON LEE O GLANCY III ALLEN E GUY GARY L HARMS DALE M HUSTON
LAWRENCE R BULLEN KENNETH M KARDASH BRUCE T KENNEDY RICHARD O KROGH FRANCIS J LE BLANC
RALPH W MANNERS BRUCE M MCCLELLAN MICHAEL O MELLON ROBERT J MORRIS PETER P MURNER JR
RONALD G NOBLE FRED O PRATT WILLIAM F REITER CRAIG A RICH DALE R RICHTER
TEODORITO RIOS-ROSARIO FERNANDO A RIVERA JR DENNIS T ROBBINS JAMES L SCHIBI VERNON L YARBER
DAVID F SLEEPER CHARLES F SMITH ROBERT J SMITH RICHARD M SPROUT JAMES A TAYLOR
MICHAEL P TROLIA ROBERT J TWIST BILLY R VENABLE VERNON M WALLACE PHILIP W WEAVER
MICHAEL B SHUMAN CHARLES A WHALEN JOHN E WICKHAM RONNIE G AVERY JAMES C BARBOUR JR
JACK A BARNHART JOHN S BAXTER JOHN B BECKER GERARD F BERGIN BENNY D BESS
EARL J BLUNKALL RICHARD A BROWN JERRY CELLETTI VINCENT A CLARK PETER F COMACHO JR
KENNETH D COMBS TIMOTHY J COTTRELL WILLIAM F CROOK JR GLENN F DEAN JOHN K HILL
DANIEL P DROSZCZ LESLIE M DYSON JR GLENN C FISH WILLIAM F FLAHERTY III ROGER L FRAKER
DENNIS P FRIEDHOFF DAVID U FRITZ ALLEN A GRIFFIN PAUL R GRINE JAMES R HARRIS
MICHAEL J DERRIG CHRISTOPHER L HAYES WASHINGTON L JAMES FRANK H JOHNS JOSEPH K KIRKENDALL
ROBERT P MCCORMICK ADOLFO V MORENO JAMES C NAU BRUCE C PALMER HAROLD L ZUG JR
RONALD W PHARIS DONALD W PICK ERNEST POSTORINO ROY C REGISTER RUDOLPH S RENTERIA
JIMMIE J RICHARDSON CHARLES J SNYDER ARTHUR O SOTO ARTHUR L STOCKBURGER JAMES D WAGSTAFF
SAMUEL F MORGAN HENRY L WARNER III ROBERT G WASHBURN JEDD E ASHBY BOB BARBER
BOYD CANFIELD CHARLES D CHAMPION ARLIN D COLLINS BOBBY C COVER BRADLEY R DEGENAARS
ROBERT L COONROD JAMES J CRISWELL JAMES CURRIE JR WILLIAM T DAVIS PEDRO DIAZ
JIMMY L HARRIS JOHN T HARTLEY CLAY HOLT JR MARK L HOOK ARMANDO S NAVARRO
MICHAEL G HUTSON MICHAEL J INGRASSIA JOHNNY F JACKSON THOMAS R LAMB CHARLIE M LEONARD
ANTHONY MANGANELLO JR DAVID P MCCORD JOHNNY L MEEKS ROBERT C MILLER MICHAEL J MITCHELL
JAMES L GLOVER JR WILLIAM MCKNIGHT JR MARCELINO NIEVES-COLON JR ELBERT A PHILLIPS WILLIAM L PITT
JAMES R PIZZANO VICTOR M PLOURDE CHARLES SOTO PAUL M STOCKWELL JOSEPH E TAFOYA
ISIAH THOMAS TOM M THOMAS MICHAEL H TUTEN LAWRENCE WAITERS WILLIAM W WATERS JR
ROBERT J WASHINGTON THOMAS V WILLIAMS JR RONALD E ADKINS KERRY ALEXANDER DAVID ALICEA
DAVID L ANDREWS ALAN F ASHALL DANIEL J BOTTAN LARRY L FINCHER
MELVIN COPELAND JOHN L DAVIS ALLEN S DUNBAR ROBERT R DUNCAN ROBERT C PERRY
MARSHALL E CALLAHAN LYNDAL R CALLIHAN RICHARD A EVANS JR RICHARD D FAIRCLOTH WILLIE J FAULKS ROBERT J FOLEY
LARRY E FRANTZ GARCLEE M FREDWELL ERNESTO R GALLARDO DANIEL GUEST GARY A HALL
HOWARD J HARTMAN LOUIS A HERRERA JACK S IMLAH BENTON A JETER LILE L JOHNSON JR
DAVID V MCCOLLUM ROBERT J MCDONOUGH LOUIS C MOORE RICHARD S MOXLEY MICHAEL L NATHE
HAROLD C DAILEY II MARSHALL W PHILLIPS JR RICHARD L POWELL RONALD L POWERS ROBERT B RANDALL

PANEL 45W

JAMES D RAYNOR RAYMOND P REILLY GERALD R ROY EDWARD L SANDERS
THOMAS R SCALISE DONALD W SIMONSON CLAIBORNE J SKINNER JOHN B SMITH ELK C YELLOW
GERALD W SPRINGER JEFFREY S TIGNER KENNETH K TOWER JR JAMES E WELLS ROY R WEST
TERRY D SMOCK JAMES C BAXTER JOHN R BECK DANNY L BITNER THOMAS B BUSH
DONNY R CAMPBELL SAMUEL R CASTELLANO JAMES A DALTON JOHN E DAVIS WILLIAM L VICK
MAURICE J HAAS EDWARD O HASKETT RAMON S HERNANDEZ JR JAMES H JESSMAN RICHARD E TRASTER
JAMES W JONES GARY L KLINGLER JAMES A MANGER PAUL S MAREK TOBIAS E MARKUSEN
ROBERT J MERCER GARY W MORGAN PEDRO J MOTA DANIEL J MURPHY MARVIN R PARKER
WILLIAM F PEPPER FRANK S PORTER WILLARD W RIGGS ROBERT S ROBERSON JR GARY G RODGERS
ORIL W HAWLEY JORGE A SILVAS WILLIAM H SMOCK TADEUSZ SOSNIAK JOHN L TRACY
HAROLD P GRASSER GERALD W VAN DONKELAAR JIMMY WILLIAMS DAVID L WILSON WILLIAM E WOLFE JR
RICHARD F YATTEAU JOHN E BARTOCCI WILFORD L BLUMER EDDIE S BROWN ERNEST R CARR
REX G CHRISMAN LESLIE D CROUSE JOHN C DAVIS JR WALTER S DAVIS PETER M DONOVAN
MORRIS G DUNN RONALD C HIGH RAYMOND K HONAKER JR JAMES J JENKS JR JULIAN S KEE JR
JOHN R MCINTOSH WALTER R MCKEE CHARLES C MEYERS ANTHONY MILLER JOHN L MOLYNEAUX JR
DAVID L MCRAE MAGNUS C NIELSEN JOHN PANAK JR LARRY H PATTERSON ERNEST E SANVILLE
STANLEY L SIETING HENRY B SMITH JR STEPHEN R TUBRE ROBERT L WILKES KEITH L WILSON
FRANKLIN E ANDERSON DANIEL D BUSSE BENITO CONTRERAS JR KIRBY J DOUGHERTY WILLIAM J FLINT
LUIS G GOMEZ-MESA GWYN T HENSON WILLIAM R HINSON LARRY F HOADLEY MELVIN J OWCZARCZAK
JAN D JAMISON WILLIAM L KINKADE JAMES W LAHTI LONNIE C LAWS JAMES M MOORE
EDWARD M JACKSON JOHN P NOWICKI STEVE M OHARA JOHN T PEEK RONNIE C PIMENTEL
ANGEL L REYES JR ROBERT F RIGGLE ROBERT L ROSS JAMES J SHAUGHNESSY JR ROGER L SHREWSBERRY
WILLIAM D TAYLOR EDDIE WILLIAMS PAUL E YONKIE DENNIS C BOONE RICHARD A BRUNNOW
JAMES P BURNS WILLIAM R BUSBY LARRY D BUTLER NORMAN J CHANEY HAROLD D COLLINS
MICHAEL E CONSTANTINE RONALD E DAVIS CURTIS N EVANS JOHNNY FOGLEMAN JEROME FORT
HECTOR M GONZALEZ STEVEN L HILMES HOWARD W JONES GREGORY J KELLOGG MICHAEL E LOUGHREN
HERBERT G LUCAS WINSTON E MARCANO THOMAS H MOON CHARLES E OSBORN JAMES D PEOPLES
JACK C PLUMB RODNEY L RANSOM JERRY L ROBINSON LAWRENCE C ROSE ROBERT L SMITH
MICHAEL J STANLEY TOM D SUGIURA GEORGE V SZCZEPANCZYK KENNETH L THOMAS ROBERTO TORRES
MANLEY G WALKER RICHARD A AKIN JR RICKY J ALMANZA GEORGE J BELANCIN TERRY L BLOOMER
DAVID C BURCH RONALD M CEDERLUND LARRY D COATS CHARLES E DAVID JR RICHARD A GROSS
JAMES W DACY PAUL R FRAZIER FREDRICK M HECKLER ANTONIO B HERNANDEZ PAUL E HYLAND
THOMAS D KESTER GARY R KORSMYER STEWART A MELNICK RONALD W NEAL ROBERT L PINKARD
THOMAS F POST STEVEN J RIGGS TIMOTHY E SHANOWER MARC E SNELL RUSSELL L WRIGHT III
MICHAEL D WILSON THOMAS A ACKERMAN FERDINAND O BARGER JR ROGER D BELL RONALD H BINGMAN
JAMES E BOWDEN RICHARD W BROOKS ROBERT J COBB WOLF-DIETER DIETZ ROBERTO ESCOBEDO
GERONIMO L GRIJALVA DAROL E LAWRENZ HORACE J LEJEUNE JR ROBERT D LITTERIO JAMES G ZEIMET JAMES G ZEIMET
JIMMY LOCKLEAR RANDELL H LOY WILLIAM H LUCAS GERALD D POCHEL EMIL H SMEVOLD
BRUCE J GREENWOOD DAVID P SULLIVAN BARRY S WELLS DAVID E WOODS JAMES M BARBARE
TOMAS A BARRERA ROBERT E BOTTS ROBERT L FAIRBOTHAM FREDERICK GOCZAL CARLTON T GOREE
CHARLES H HARDISON JAMES S HATH GLENN O HELKA GLEN M HUFFMAN LAWRENCE F JAWOROWICZ
ALEXANDER JOHNSON JR ROBERT L JORDAN JR CLEE A KIRKENDOLL JAMES E MURCHISON GEORGE R POSEY
THOMAS LANE ALLEN W OREM BOBBY J PAPPAN HERMAN PARKER JR JERALD P PERETIATKO
DAVID A REED DENNIS K RENO JOHNNY F RICHARDS ALBERT L RICKERSON FRED P RUGH
LIONEL A RYAN JOSEPH E SMITH EUGENE H STEPP RAYMOND V STOLPA LLOYD E VALENTINE
DAVID D SIEGEL JOSEPH M TURK TERRY C WELTY MICHAEL D WHITE EUGENE W WICKER
ROBERT J WRIGHT DENNIS L AHRENDSEN JAMES H ANDERSON JAMES E BARNHILL DEAN A BELL
GREGORY L BOMBERRY ROBERT E BOONE MARSHALL J BROWN WILLIAM CANNION ROBERT O CHAMBERS
ROBERT D CRYDER LLOYD T DARLING JEFFREY A DAVIS BENJAMIN T DAWKINS SAMUEL M DEICHELMANN
GERALD M DUARTE JEFFREY A EVANS ROBERT A GAMBER MERRILL T GERAGHTY GEORGE A GERALD
MICHAEL L GRIFFITH WILLIAM R GUENTHER TERRANCE R HANSON MICHAEL O HARDESTY DAVID H RISHER
EUGENE W HARTMAN NED A HEATH JAMES C HOLMES DOUGLAS A HOUSE RONALD D HUTCHERSON
KENNETH B JENKINS GUS W JOHNSON JR LARRY A JONES JOHN F KELLY MICHAEL C KOLAROV
JOSEPH J KULL JR JIMMY D LEMLEY STEVE A LIVENGOOD ANTHONY J MONTES RAYNER E WILLIAMS
BARRY R MOREE HERSHEL E MORROW JEFFREY W NORVELL JESUS OCHOA EDWIN A PENN
THOMAS W HARRIS MARLEN L PHILLIPS JERRY G RICHARD RANDOLPH SAMPSON EDWARD W SECREST
LEONARD SELANIKIO PATRICK E SINCLAIR ROY B SQUIRES BRADLEY A STCLAIR FLOYD L STILL
WILLIE L TONEY BENJAMIN R TOONKEL RUBY K WALSTON RAYMOND L WHELPLEY DONNIE R WHITE
RALPH J LUND DONALD M WILBANKS CAROL E WILLIAMS JOHN W WOOLBRIGHT MICHAEL J ABRUZZESA JR
DAVID C BROWN WILLIAM T CLONEY III WILLIAM M COOPER PETER DE HAAS LLOYD D DOERING
GEORGE R DORCHAK CECIL V EVANS JAMES E FARO ALAN R GERRISH JOSEPH SCHMIDT
ROBERT B GILRAY JR HERBERT J GLAZER EDGAR J GRISMER CARL N HORNER JOHN W JOHNSON
DAVID R KARR ROBERT E MACKEY JOHN P MCDERMOTT JAMES J NEIDLINGER ERWIN G POWELL JR
MICHAEL A FAULKNER CHARLES G RUSSELL GEORGE D TAYLOR CARLOS D VIBBERT STEVEN A WINTERS

PANEL 44W

BRUCE C CHRISTIAN RONALD B CLARK GERALD J CLARKSON DALLAS R PRIDEMORE
JOHN T CORLEY JR TERRY C CORSON PATRICK L DE WATER RUSSELL N FERDIG ISAAC R GARCIA JR
JAMES E GLEGG WILLIAM P HARWOOD LARRY F HORSLEY REDLICK S KOPPEL ELLIS E LAIR
WILLIAM O LANG DAN V LINDHOLM FREDERICK W MCHUGH KENNETH R OLIVER HARRY S ONETO JR
DAVID J BULKLEY JESSE J PALMER EDWARD E PEA ROBERT S PRIESER FRANKLIN RAMBERT
DONALD R ROBINSON TERRY A RUTH REX R SAGE BOBBY R SUMPTER MICKEY L SWATSLEY
GROVER L SUIT THEODORE A THOMPSON JR JOHN W THORP MICHAEL P WHELAN RAYMOND C WILLIAMS
SANTIAGO D ADAMES JR HOWARD D BURKE DONALD A CAMPBELL PAUL E CHRISTJOHN CURRY B DAVIS
ALDO A DORIA ROBERT T ELLIOTT III WILLIAM E FISHBACK KENNETH C FRAZER EUGENE O FULLER
MICHAEL S GODETTE RICHARD P GRAVELINE HOMER L HODGES JR EDWARD W KNAPPER DAVID R LILLY
CLIFFORD D LOGSDON NAPOLEON MARTIN GURNEY L MILLER JERRY L MILLER PERRY S WHISENANT
DAVID J POPP RAYMOND POWELL JR BILLY M REA ROBERT J RUSNAK TIMOTHY J SMITH
ALVIN MONDAY DOMINGO M TERRONEZ JERRY A TREZEK DENNIS L TYSON PAUL M VARA
JESSE L BARKLEY THOMAS M BINA RONALD R BLOHM JIMMIE W BOGGS ARTHUR B BOWMAN JR
RALPH W BYRNES JAMES B CALDWELL SCOTT M CARPENTER DANIEL L CARR GLENN CARTER
MICHAEL J ROWCROFT REX A DAVIS RICHARD J DRIVERE CARREL C EALUM PATRICK D FAY WILLIAM R GAST
RONALD G HACK RICHARD L JERNIGAN LOYD E JONES THOMAS E LANGH ALFREDO LOPEZ JR
HOWARD H LUSCIER NICHOLAS MARINO III ALAN J MEISHEID HAROLD E MOSELEY MERLE E ROBERTSON
SAMUEL J NUNN MICHAEL J PELCH MICHAEL L POLETTI JUAN PORRAS BERNIE ROSALES JR
PETE W SOBACKI PAUL J STEWART TERRY L STOUT PETER S TYRKA DENNIS W WEAR
WILLIAM M WILKERSON LAURENCE O WOODSON CREED L BRYANT CECIL W CAROTHERS BRUCE L CARTER
WAYNE E CHRISTOPHER ROY CISNEROS ELDON D COLDREN JR JERRY D COPELAND JOHN G COULON JR
BRUCE W CRABB GARY F CYSEWSKI RICHARD G DANIELS PHILLIP F DE FAZIO JERRY B EVANS
STEVEN R FRESE WILLIAM J GAGNIER JESUS M GARCIA ROLAND A GORSCHBOTH DAVID K HUFFMAN
WILLIAM A GIBBS LEONARD O GRAVES GARY J HALVERSON W C HERNDON JAMES K HOYEZ
PHILLIP L INMAN MICHAEL T IVORY LARRY W JOHNSON RICHARD N KLOOS ALBERT L LAZZAROTTO
LARRY L LISKOW ARMANDO LOPEZ LONNIE E LUNDY HAROLD J MATHEWS JR CYRIL MITCHELL JR
GEORGE W MCGEE DAVID O PAINTER RUSSELL A PEDERSEN KESTUTIS A PETRAUSKAS THOMAS W ROBERTS
HEINZ RUCHTI VINICIO F SANTUCCI BILLY J SCOTT ROBERT L SCOTT WILLIAM SLADE
PHILLIP E SLAUGHTER CURTIS O SMITH JR DOUGLAS M SMITH THOMAS D SMITH STEPHEN D SPARKS SR
FRED C SPINA THOMAS W STEELE AKOS D SZEKELY EUGENE C TIBBS JIMMIE W YOUNGS
FRANK VALLONE HARRY L VAN ALST JR RICHARD H VAN DYKE GARY A WALDORF WILLIAM E WARK III
FRANZ TINES TOBY J WATKINS THOMAS E WELKER OWEN WHITE JR ROBERT J ZERILLI
DONALD P ABBIE JAMES L ADAMS RICHARD H ARRUDA PHILIP K BAKER BRIAN P COLLINS
MICHAEL R BALDWIN EUGENE R BOYCE BRUCE W BROWN DONALD R BUTLER DONALD R CRAVEN
CARL R CRONE DAVID C DAHLIN JOHN A DICKINSON WESLEY G DOTY ROBERT W DUNN
WILLIAM E FOSTER JR DENNIS W GLYNN WILLIAM H HANSON ISAAC HARRIS MICHAEL L HEITGER
WAYNE D JENKINS HENRY L JOHNSON JR RICHARD D LE MAY LEONARD J LIPAROTO SAMUEL C MAXWELL
LARRY W JANSEN JOSEPH MACON KENNETH L MARTIN RONALD S MARTIN WALTER W MCGINN
GUSTAV OSTRAKOVIC MARION L OXNER DALE A PALM JOHN E PERRY WILLIAM J PINTER
KURT F PONATH WILLIAM H PRATHER CLIFFORD L SCHOLL EARL E SHARK LARRY R SIMS
DAVID M SOWARDS PHILIP L TANK EDGAR L TOMLINSON SAMUEL G UMSTOT JR WILLIAM WITTMAN
JAMES A SMITH KENNETH A WEDMAN ROBERT R WEISS JAMES H WHITE J C WILLIAMS JR
LESTER L WOOD ARLEY G ABRAHAM SAMUEL L AKINS CURTIS L ANDERSEN JAMES O ARROWOOD
RAYMOND BEAM STEVEN L BECK FRED A BELCHER ROBERT J BENZ STEVEN R BROOKS
REX L BROWN RICHARD T CLARK KENNETH G CUSHMAN JOHN W DAVIS JOSE D GUTIERREZ-VELAZQ
JAMES L DILLARD III JOE A ELBERT EUGENE J FEELEY JR LARRY L GAMBOTTO JOHN A GERMEK JR
RAYMOND COBB MCVINCENT GODFREY JR HOWARD B HANDLEY DWAYNE HELTON GILMER E HUMPHREYS
TERENCE M HUSTEAD THOMAS C JACOBS JERRY E JARRARD JON C JONES VERNON D JONES
RAYMOND E LANTER GARY L LEWIS MELVIN R LONG CHARLES L LUMM DAVID A MAHAN
WILLIAM MANZANARES JR ARIEL MARINO GARY R MCFALL LONZO J MORAN JR ARTHUR D MOSCRIP JR
CHARLES A NOLAN JR MANUEL G ORTIZ ANTHONY P PATRICCA ERNEST D PEINA DONALD E POWLES
HENRY M OLIVER THOMAS M PHILLIPS EVERETT A PLANCK GERALD W PLUNKETT ERVIN PROCTOR
EDWARD K RYAN GARY L SMITH STERREN C VANDER JOSEPH A VENABLE JAMES D WARDLOW
KEITH L WARE RICHARD W WELCH JOHNNY L WILKS BOOKER T WRIGHT DANNY R AYERS
JAMES M BAKER CLIFTON L BOWEN RONALD M FRASER ALAN R GIANNELLI JOHN W HEAPS
RONALD L COLWELL SIDNEY HAYNES JR LAMAR HUBBARD GEORGE V MARTINEZ BOBBY G MESSER
CHARLES K FINK CARY F MCAFEE JOHN T MCINNIS CHARLES J MOORE ALVIN G MUTTER JOSEPH P NAIMO JR
DONALD A OBEY ROBERT PARKER CLAUDE PERRY JOHN T PETERS RICHARD E PLUMMER
CHARLES W SETH PHILLIP W TOMPKINS HARRY W UNDERWOOD ROBERT P WALSH LILO E ALDOUS
JAMES D ARNETT TOMMY L BERRY JAMES P BORDEAUX JR LEON D BULLOCK GILBERT CARVALHO

269

THE VIETNAM VETERANS MEMORIAL COLLECTION

RICHARD L COOPER FRANK W CROSS JUAN R FELIX-TORRES THOMAS F FLANIGAN II
DAVID A FORSYTHE DOUGLAS G FOSTER ROBERT L FOSTER WILLIAM A FREY RICHARD GREEN JR
HARRY B HAMBLETON III VERN A HARRIS ROBERT HERALD LARRY C HIGGINSON DOUGLAS G IMPSON
GEORGE F KEIPER DUANE J KUEHN TIMOTHY K MAHONEY TIMOTHY J MELVILLE WILLIAM M MILLER
HAROLD O'NEAL JR STANLEY R PETTIT JERRY L POE PETER B RICH EDDIE L RILEY JOAQUIN ROBLES
LOUIS J COFRANCESCO JR ROBERT H STAHL ETHER A TINKUM VINCENT J WARGO JR BRADLEY K WATTS

PANEL 43W

DWIGHT L ADAMS RAYMOND D BAKER WILBUR R BRANNING JR RICHARD J MARTIN
ANDREW T BROWN JOSEPH R BROWN LAWRENCE G BRYAN THOMAS E BUCKLEY PAUL BUSTAMANTE
EDWARD CUNNINGHAM ROBERT P D'EMANUELE GARY R DAFFIN BILLY R DENT MICHAEL H DESCHENES
PERRY DI BERARDINO JOHN M DONOHUE JAMES C DURHAM JR JAMES R ENGLERT KENNETH R FARDEN
DOUGLAS GAINES JR RUSSELL J HEATH BRADY W HERRING DELON HUNTER CHARLES M THOMPSON
RODNEY BRADFORD FREDDIE R KELLEY RALPH W KUCHCINSKI LOWELL E LUNZMANN JOHN M LYONS
GEORGE F MCDAVITT JAMES R MILLER WILLIAM J MOORE CLYDE E MORGAN RANDALL A THOMPSON
D L MCDONALD WILLIAM J OSKILANEC NORMAN W PARTRIDGE TONY G POWELL JOSE M QUESNEY
HARRY E RIVERS JOSEPH E ROBLE JOSE M RUIZ ALFRED V SCHOFIELD ANTHONY R SIGNA
DONALD E GLIME DALE A MORROW EDGAR D STANTON JR SAMUEL R SUMMERFIELD MARTHELL TRAYLOR JR
WILLIAM H WHITE JOHNNY B WILLIAMS ARNOLD B WIMBERLY MICHAEL E ADAMS ERNEST J BAYNES
NEAL G BOLLINGER SAMUEL E BRYANT ROBERT A BURKE RICHARD A CHAMBERS JAMES R COATES
BERNARD J COOK DEWAYNE CORBITT EDGAR F DAVIS STEVEN J DAWSON TERZO C DEL
KEVIN H DUGAN DAVID L EISENBRAUN RANDALL L FARLOW BRUCE J FEDLER JOHN W GEORGE
KEVIN C HANLEY WILLIE C HARDY RAY A HAYES TRISTAN W HAYES RAYMOND J MAZYCK JR
REX M HOOVER MICHAEL W ISSENMANN G B JACKSON JR GARY F JOHNSTON HAROLD J KISSINGER
LEON E KIZZIE GEORGE LEE JR LIONEL MALDONADO-TORRES JERRY L MARCUM JAMES E MARLOW
GARY HILL FRANK J MCMANUS WAYNE E MONISMITH GREGORY S MUNDELL FREDRICK E NIGH
CHARLES E OWENS WILLIAM T PARKER RONALD J POINTER DOMINICK POLLASTRO MICHAEL W POUSSON
WILLIAM T PRATT PAUL M PRESSER THOMAS R RANGE JR JAMES P RAWLINS STEVEN J REICHARDT
LARRY E RICHARDSON WILLIAM A RIDENOUR RONALD L RONDO ALBERT E ROSE JUAN O SANCHEZ
GEORGE SANDOVAL GEORGE D SHANNON ALBERT W SIRMANS JR LARRY D SMITH GEORGE A YARBROUGH
FRANK A SKOCICH LLOYD H SMITH WARREN A SMITH DARNELL J SONGNE BILLIE G STICKLAND
PHILIP E ZELESKI RONALD W ZYDEL LARRY H ALLEN MICHAEL R BARTELL ROBERT J BECK
JOSEPH S BRAVIN RONALD L BROWN GARY L BROWNING WILLIAM E BRUSTER DEWAYNE T WILLIAMS
ALBERT J DAIR GILFORD F DASHNER STEVEN W DECKER JOHN F DOWNEY JR RAYMOND J ENNERS
WALTER H FENNELL CHARLES L FREEMAN JAMES O FRYMAN JOE A GALVEZ PEDRO G GARCIA
ROBERT E GRAY RALPH L GREEN WAYNE A HAYS ROBERT L JANOWITZ AARON G JOHNSON
FREDDIE L LOWERY CHRISTOPHER D LUCCI GILBERT M MAESTAS JAMES R MCCOY CHESTER MCDANIEL
STEVEN M ORT WILLIAM D ROBINSON JR JOSEPH SAROCAM ALFRED M SCHROEDER JR EUGENE SMITH
J B SPEARMON GARY E STRAKER ISAAC TAGGART DONALD E TURNER KREG A VIESTENZ
CALVIN K COON KERMIT L WILLIAMS RICHARD F WILLIAMS DENNIS E WITKOWSKI MICHAEL E ZIBURA JR
ALBERT A BANUELOS JR JOSEPH F BIBER JOSEPH A BISHOP FRANK O BONNARENS ELWYN R CAPLING
THOMAS J CAVANAUGH THOMAS H CLARKEN III ROGER O CLEMENS RAYMOND T CONWAY JOHN J VISSER
STEVE J DOCKERY JAMES A DONALDSON KURT W DUNCAN MICHAEL A FIGUEROA DAVID B FREED
LLOYD E GREENE JR ROBERT A GREGORY MICHAEL K HAMNER BENJAMIN C HARTMAN JR JAMES D RINEHART
RICHARD A HOFFMANN ROBERT A HOLT ROSS T HULSLANDER JOSEPH L JACKSON LLOYD W JACKSON JR
TED R JAMISON DAVID C JOHNSON JAMES D KELLEY MARK A KNOLLMEYER JOHN L KROL
JOHN A LA VOO CALVIN D LARGO BRUCE S LARSON JOSEPH P LOPEZ LARRY D MASSENGILL
PETER D MATARAZZO ROBERT M MCVEA TERRENCE MORAN PETER J O'TOOLE PEDRO S RODRIQUEZ JR
VERNON L HEADRICK GARY E NOLES ELIAS J PAULK FRANCIS S RHOADES ROY W RICH
LESTER E ROPETER JAMES C SCHULTZ JAMES C SIMMONS JOHNNY C SIMPSON EDGAR A SMITH
RICHARD L SPARKS DANIEL R SPURLIN JAMES J STITES ROBERT G TATE MARK L TRIPLETT
WILLIAM E DICK JR WILLIAM R TURNER JR PHILIP J WAJDA MICHAEL K WONDERLICH RAYMOND H ALBERT JR
JOHN M BATH DONNIE W BROWN ROBERT A BROWN II DERRELL W CLEMMER LARRY D DOSS
WILLIAM D EALY GARRY G GREEN ROGER W GRUBBS JOHN C HARPER FELIPE HERRERA
LARRY A JOHNSON EDWARD C JONES RONALD W LEWIS MARK W LONGTIN DANIEL B PERSONS
MICHAEL R MANNO WILLIAM R MORLEDGE PRINIS W ORSO HAROLD E OWENS JOSE A PABEY
WILLIAM R KAUSE RAYMOND A POWELL MIGUEL ROSARIO-CRUZ JR ROGER H SCHOENER JAMES R SCHULTZ
RONALD E SHEPPARD MICHAEL P SIMPSON JOHN P VAN DUSEN JAMES E WALKER JOSEPH K WOLFE
DOUGLAS K BARON VINCENT BERNARD WILLIAM M BERRY ADRIAN C BRITTLE JR THOMAS F SUDLESKY
BLAINE E CALLIHAN DOUGLAS J CAVIN FRANCIS CHARLES DAVID L CLARK TED D COLQUHOUN
JAMES P CONCANNON JR EDWARD L DAUBERT CLIFTON A DAVIS RONALD W EIGHMIE STANLEY G LAWSON
HAROLD E FEEZEL LAWRENCE E GARRON JR MICHAEL I HANNEMAN GEORGE B HESSE THOMAS S JESTER
ROBERT F CONLEY ANTHONY K KERCOUDE DAVID R LATSCH STANLEY R LEWANDOWSKY ROBERT A LHOTA
STEVEN R MAJOR JOHN A MCGEHEE THOMAS A MITCHELL DANIEL E NELSON JR MICHAEL D NYSTUL
HOWARD OWENS MICHAEL R PAGE LEVERET R PROSKY RONALD L REIL LEONARD F SKONIECKI JR
MARVIN V BELL RONALD R STROSCHEIN DONALD L TEMPLETON THERMALL THOMPSON WILLIS A TOOMES
DONNY R STEWART JAMES L WARNER DAVID L WHITE MICHAEL N ANDERSEN MICHAEL D ARMSTRONG
BENJAMIN F BARNETT DEXTER BELL SARGENT J BROSHEAR HAROLD R BRUBAKER ROBERT H BUEHLER
ROBERT J BYRNES RICHARD P CAPUTO JAMES J DEW RICHARD W FALK ROSCOE GLOVER JR
STEVEN C GASSEN FRANK C GONZALES HERSHEL L GOSSETT ADOLPH B HAMM JR ROY L HENLEY
JAMES R HOCKETT WILLIAM J HOUSTON LARRY D JOHNSON ROBERT P KEMER CHARLES F KUHLMANN
WILLIE R LAY RANDALL P LESS DAVID L LICATE JOSEPH M MAZZONE WILLIAM L MCFARLAND
CHARLIE L PARTIDA WILLIAM G PEELER HENRY R PHILLIPS JOHN H PRIESTHOFF II GREGORY W RODGERS
SAMUEL ROSAS-SANZ NATHAN R SALES MERREL G SARVELA JAMES B SCOTT STEVEN G SHIRK
THURMAN H SMITH MODESTO VALDEZ WILLIAM W VAN MATER KARL R BIESER THOMAS D BROCK
GERALD A CAHELA DAVID F CALLAHAN JR GREGORY CARTER WILLIAM N FARMER AARON Z GLAZAR
ROBERT W HARRIS ALLAN F KOEBERNICK DENNIS W KOSEBA RICHARD G MADDOX JOSEPH A MAISANO

PANEL 42W

MICHAEL D PERSONETTE MICHAEL J ROMANKO TEODORO SANTELLAN JACK SIZEMORE SR
BOBBY L SPENCER KENNETH C SPENCER JOHN M TANNEY DONNIE E WATSON JOHN M WHITE
ROBERT E WILLIAMS WILLIAM C WRAY JOE C BERRY KARL R HARING THOMAS J SMOCZYNSKI
LAWRENCE W BREITNITZ GEORGE M CUNNINGHAM NORMAN N CUNNINGHAM MARIO P ESTRADA
STEPHEN E BREINER DENNIS L GILES ALLEN W INGRAM KENNETH H MASHLYKIN CHRISTOPHER A MINTON
WILLIAM T DAVIS JERRY MCCONNELL WILLARD F MORELOCK LOUIS A NIEMEYER JR MICHAEL A NIEZGODA
JAMES E PENNINGTON JR ARLON G SCHAEFFER JOSEPH K SEARLE DARWIN H SHELTON PAUL J SILBERBERGER
SAMUEL F ANKNEY JOSEPH H THOMAS THOMAS N TRAINHAM MICHAEL R TROUT STANLEY E WEST
MICHAEL D MCNAUGHTON RICHARD G WOLFF DENNIS K BLAIN SAMMY BURROLA JR WILLIAM A CAMPBELL
JAMES B COLLINS RONALD L DELVERDE LARRY G DROWN JOHN W EASTON ERNEST L ROWE
MARK A ELLSWORTH ROGER A FULKERSON JERRY F GRAJEWSKI RANDOLPH C GRIMES DANIEL J HILTON
DONNELL HOWARD JOHN A JENKINS III TERRY J JOHNSON ROBERT J LOEHLEIN JR HARRY L MAYES
HERBERT P CHO JAMES H MORGAN WILLIAM H PALMER NORMAN M PAULSEN DAVID T SEATON
CURTIS L BATTON JOSEPH W SEBASTIAN EVERETT H SMITH JR MICHEL K SUBLETT HINEY WILLIS
ROBERT V BOLLMAN FREDERICK E BORCZYNSKI JOHN L BOYD ANDREW T BUKOVINSKY CECIL O BUNDAGE
FREDERICK J CARLSON BENJAMIN F CASTANEDA GEORGE M COX II PETER J DANILUCK WILLIAM F LEMOINE
MICHAEL D ECKERFELD ALFRED A FILIPPELLI BARRY K FISK DOUGLAS E GOSSAGE RONALD F GREEN
JAMES D HACEK DANNY C HAYES JAMES R HEARD JR MAURICE H KINKEAD RICHARD A LARRICK
GREGORIO M CAMACHO NICHOLAS P LESANDO JR LARRY L LOWER DALE A LUSTER DARRELL L LUTRICK
LEE R MCELHANEY BARRY A OLSON RANDALL A OLSON JEROME OVERTON DOUGLAS A PAIGE
LARRY E WRIGHT CLARK E PEDEN JACK A PLUCINSKI OSCAR K PORTER JR JAMES R PRUETT STEVEN P RANCE
DAWSON J ATWOOD TERRY D RATLIFF JON A RIPPEE ARTURO B RIVAS CARLTON ROSS JOHN A RUSCITO
CHARLES R SLUSSER GEORGE J SMITH JR JOHN C SMITH III JOHN W STAHL JOHN W STATES
JOHNNY W THOMPSON MICHAEL J TOBEY STEPHEN L TOWNSEND FREDERICK E TRANI JR RONALD R WALLS
RICHARD B TROTTER JOHN C WALLACE JAMES W WEBB JR WILLIAM A WESTLAKE JOSEPH G AMBROSIO
LAWRENCE B BANEK MARK A BARNES TOMMY R BOWMAN DERRIS BROWN JEFFERY C NILES
GEORGE A CARTER DAVID K CHAHOC DELFIN H COOK JAMES W CRAMER RICHARD DAVIS JR
CHARLES E DE LASSUS JERRY E DENSON DONALD L ELDRIDGE MITCHELL L FIRMIN RONALD L GRANVILLE
PAUL D GROSICK KEVIN L GREENE PAUL HOLSTON QUENTIN F HURST TYRONE JACKSON RICHARD L JONES
LEROY A KING ROBERT E KNOLL EDWARD L LAWTON CHARLES J MASON LAWRENCE R MERSCHROD
LUTHER C BERRYMAN BLAINE S MILES JR ANTHONY J MONTOYA JR JAMES A MORRIS JR GORDON W OGILVIE
JOHN L JOHNSON DAVID H PITTARD ISHAM I QUICK PHILIP D REEDER ROGER A RICKERT LARRY J SMITH
WILLIAM A SMITH JR EFRAIN SOTO SR HERBERT G TAYLOR DENNIS W VAUGHN VIRGIL J WEBB
JOHN A WOOD BRADFORD D WRIGHT WALTER C BLANTON GARY D COLLINS WILLIAM T DECKER JR
DAVID L DIXON RAYMOND E EVANS DAVID P HALPIN ROBERT L HAMILTON JR AUSTIN W HAVERKAMP
CARL V HANSEN ROGER L JOHNSON JR JOHN R KLOTZ JOSEPH D LILLY DAN B NORTON RONNIE L POUNDS
FREDERICK E ROUSE CLIFTON SPILLER GERALD S STOZEK CARL R USSERY WILLIAM M VALENTINE
ALEJANDRO B BAGASOL STEVEN R BINKLEY RONALD T BLEACHER TERRY P BRADY LYLE G BROOKS
ARTHUR B CREWS WERNER C BROWN II GORDON BUTLER FRANK E DAVIS TERRY B DAY VAN L DURHAM
WILLIE G GADDY JOHN E GIBSON RICHARD O GULLIXSON ROBERT R HAMILTON SHERWOOD D KREIS
LEE M HALSTEAD JERRY L HARRIS HAL K HOWELL RONALD J HUELSKAMP DAVID L MACE
JOHN J MATUSKA MERLIN E MILLER WALTER L MOORE JR WAYNE E NEWBERRY ROBERT D NOELLSCH
WILLIAM C PERDUE STEPHEN B PUGH WILLIAM P ROLLINS BLAINE J SHEPHERD EDWARD P TURNER JR
JOHNNIE L VAUGHT JR WILLIAM A VOSS CECIL B WAGNER JR CARROLL W WHITE GEORGE L ANGLIN
GENE A LAUER PHILIP S BANCROFT ROBERT J BARRY PHILIP A BEASLEY BOBBY J BROWN SAMUEL M CAVINS
LOUIS V DAIGLE JOHN DALTON JOHNNY T FULLER EDWARD GOLDA WALTER J HOWARD JR
CLIFFORD W FIESZEL ULYS F HAMILTON ALBERTO HERNANDEZ-VELEZ CHARLES A HOLBROOK JERRY JONES
GLENN R LAWFIELD RONALD W LAZICKI THOMAS C MARTIN JAMES G MESA KENNETH W MILLER
DAVID L JUDY MICHAEL D MCCLAIN RICHARD L MCCLAIN FRANKLIN L MCPHAIL LARRY G NEWBERRY
JOHN J QUICK FREDERICK P RHOADES HARRISON B SHAUGER GARY R SHEPPERDSON TIMOTHY D SINES
HOWARD H SMITH DOMENICK A SPINELLI RONALD STUCKY GERALD F SUBLER GARY R TOWNSEND
LARRY J VAN RENSELAAR HAMP E ZORNES ROBERT ALICEA TIMOTHY G ARENS ROBERT F ASHER
FRANK A BAGGETT CHARLES A BRANCH ALLEN P BROEKHUIZEN RONALD D BROWN FREDERICK H FLYNN
LANCASTER BROWN-BEY RICHARD B CLEMENTS ROBERT J DAVIS JOHN W DINGUS JR ROGER W ELLING
GARY W BROWN PATRICK M FARLEY WILLIAM G FERGUSON JR ALLEN G FUSSNER MONTIE H HENDERSON JR
ALFRED I BROOKS JAMES A HUNT LEMUEL JOHNSON HENRY JONES JR ROBERT L KNISELY JR CURTIS J KRAUHS
JOHN E JACOBS JOSEPH LANNON JR JOE R LAURENCE ROCCO R LUCISANO JOHN D WILLIAMS
RICHARD L HALGREN WILLIE J MCKENZIE FREDDIE MCQUEEN REUBEN MILEY JR VICTOR PEREZ JR WARD E SEE
KENNETH M PLAVCAN RONALD E POCHRON JOHN A RAUSCH JAMES R RONE RICHARD W SANDERS
ALLAN S MAJOR EDDIE L SIMMONS JOHN STIRPE EUGENE R SUAREZ BERNARD J UHREN FRANK WELLS JR
JOSE D MELENDEZ-GONZALE RUDY E EAY DONALD E ERWIN EARL B ESTEP JAMES A HOLLIS
JOSEPH L HOPKINS JR LARRY E KING LARRY D KITTRELL ARTHUR G MARTIN CURTIS O MILLER
CARL W MYLLYMAKI III STEVEN L PALMQUIST ROBERT C PROFILET EDWARD L SAENZ JIMMY A SMALLWOOD
JOHN M QUIGLEY LARRY M SABO JOHN C SHERIN III CHARLES R SMIDSTRA FRANK J SMITH ALLAN R WALSH
FRED Z WASHBURN RICHARD M WELCH DONALD L WESTER THOMAS E ALDERSON MARTIN E BIXLER
WAYNE P BUNDY MICHAEL J BYRON GEORGE A CABANO JR DAWSON CLEMENTS DANIEL L LEE
JAMES K CONNOR RONALD L CONROY LARRY L COSTLEY DONALD J CRAMER JR DAVID J DELL'ANGELO DAVID J DELLANGELO
DAVID A DISRUD ALLEN E GOMES DALE G GRANGER JOHN B HARLOW JR WILLIAM L MCLAUGHLIN
DONALD G CLEAVER RALPH T HIGDON RONALD D HORN THOMAS E JOHNSON GREGORY T JONES
JOHN W LUCIER JAMES E MANN JAMES L MERRICK JR ROBERT W MILES DONALD L MONTGOMERY
MICHAEL L MCCAFFERTY CALVIN E MCGILTON WAYNE T MCGUIRE DENVER MOORE JR CHRIS D MUNSON
JOE HIBBLER JR VICTOR M ORNELAS-ARELLANO CALVIN M PERKINS DAVID B PERREAULT JERRY L PIERCE JR

PANEL 41W

CLAUDE T ROPER MYRON R ROSS II RALPH SCHIAVONE ROBERT D TOMLINSON
KENNETH W SHOOK MICHAEL D SEE ROGER L SMITH CHARLES J WALLACE BILLY WELLS DENNIS A WIRT
WILLIAM R YOUNG BILLY A ADCOCK JOHN C BECHARD ROBERT J BERGERON DOUGLAS M CLARK
GEORGE M CLAYTON JR MICHAEL J CORRIGAN DANIEL J CZAJAK JR TIMOTHY J DUNCAN DONALD R GISE
MELVIN D HEBERT JR SHERRILL N HERALD WAYNE D JOHNSON GARY L KUNSHIER GARY G LA CHAPELLE
LOVETT L HARRELL JAMES M LAWING JAMES E LOTHMAN HUBERT W MILLER ANTONIO MILSTEAD
ARNOLD R PARKER HARRY A PETERSEN RONALD E POWERS WILLIAM L ROGERS JOHN P STEPP
GEORGE D OSBORNE WARREN L RUTLAND CHARLES N SCHALL JR TERRY A TOWNE CHARLES L TOYIAS
LUIS A VELEZ-RIVERA DANNY WILLIAMS JOSEPH R AJSTER JOSEPH C ARONCE JEFFREY L BEARD
LAWRENCE L BONACCI CURTIS E BOOTS GREGORY P BROOKS HENRY E CARMICHAEL JR KENNETH J NERVIE
JOHNNIE R COMPTON LONEY EVANS JR GEORGE FLOHR JR WILFREDO L GONZALEZ JOHN P O'HARA
ROBERT J GOODMAN RAYMOND L HOPKINS JOHNNY W HUMPHREY AUBREY E JACOBS JR ALEX L MITCHELL
ANTONIO B JAIME DAVID A JOHNSON HENRY L KERTIS JR GREGORY P LAWRENCE RICHARD E LETENDRE
DICK H CHRISTENSEN GERALD E HAMMON JR GERALD E HAMMOND JR CECIL C MCKINNEY LEO R MEYER JAMES C MOORE
DOUGLAS W DEVOE RONALD J REDENIUS MICHAEL C SAPORITO WALTER SHERROD JR LOYDE H SIMPSON
PAUL L SMITH EDWARD B SPEAR JAMES D STRIDE JR EDWARD O WEIMAN ALBERT D WESTER
CHARLES W WILLINGHAM DAVID W WILSON JAMES A BRINKOETTER JAMES T HENDRICKS EDGAR L SMITH
THOMAS J HOWE DENNIS E KOEPP JOHN R MARSH RICHARD L MARTIN ROOSEVELT WILLIAMS
DANIEL A MILLER LAWRENCE T MYERS ROBERT G OWEN DONALD J PARKS STEVEN D PERRY
GEORGE R ANDERSON RICHARD SAENZ ELDON W SMITH GILES W STALLARD RICHARD D STEVENS
RAYMOND R HERNANDEZ FRANKLIN D TINSLEY LARRY L WARBIS JOHN K ALLAIRE DEAN L BEACH
GEORGE H BREWER BRUCE G BROWN CHARLES CLARK II DANIEL P COLGAN RICHARD A DUDEK
MICHAEL R DUNKEL AARON F FERGUSON RAMON A FLORES REINIS FOX CHARLES D GARVEN
JOSEPH E GUENTHER DAVIS E HARDY HILTON HAYES JR SHELDON D HOSKINS BILLY R JEFFERSON
JAMES R JONES NATHANIEL KELLEY ROY R KOENIG JOSE L MONTES JOHN E POLING
DANIEL L QUIMBY WALTER G RICE JR STEVEN O SCHNELLER CHESTER J SCHULTZ CARREY E SCROGGINS
JAMES R SHERWOOD WILLIAM C SHUMAN KENNETH H SILLS LARRY E VAN METER WILLIAM D VAN TASSEL JR
GREGORY J WEBER STEPHEN D WOOD HARRY W ANDERSON JR GEORGE A BOND WILLIAM A BRABANT
WILLIAM M BREES JR WYMAN B COLEMAN SHERMAN A FURROW JR EUGENE HINGLETON JR STEVE J PERRY
JOSEPH W JONES III JAMES T LONG PIERCE MALMQUIST KENNETH F MOORES FLOYD E PARTON
DANIEL J COONON R T PERRY WILLIE C PRICE CHARLES H RICHARDSON LUCAS H RODRIGUEZ
GERALD SAMOLEJ MANUEL A SOARES LYN D SPARRE JOHN B STEVENS RONALD L SUMMERS
ROBERT L URBAN LARRY W WATSON DANIEL E WINTERS WILLIAM E WYROSDIC WARDELL L ARMSTRONG
JAMES E ARNOLD JOE E ARNOLD SAMUEL L BOYD JR ELIEZER DOMINGUEZ-CORTES ROY S FISCHER
JOHN A GIACONE JR LLOYD D GILLESPIE RICHARD O GRIFFITH DONALD C HAMM RONALD E HIBBARD
GEORGE M JOHNSON ULDIS J MALMANIS FRANCISCO H OLEA VENUS D PAYTON JR MORRIS J ROSS
PAUL M KOLENDA JERRY D PIERCE JOE T RUSSELL GARY H SMITH RAYMOND J STEVENS
GREGORY W STEWART PHILIP J TAFT RONNIE BLAIR MILARD L BLEDSOE DONALD R BROOKS
STANLEY G DENISOWSKI MICHAEL E EVANS GENE D GROVER ERISTEO GUTIERREZ JR JOHN W ROBINSON JR
EUGENE A HANDRAHAN JONATHON J HAWKINS ROBERT D HERREID HENRY JAMES VON M LIEBERNECHT
ANGEL LUNA BAYNES B MCSWAIN JR WILLIAM W MEISEL JR ROBERT L MIGLIERINA JOHN R NOBLE
EMMETT S ORR RAY W PHELPS JR LOUIS J RAMIREZ ANGEL L RAMOS MICHAEL E RANDALL SR
EVERETT L DAUGHERTY JR GARY C SMITH JAMES W SZCZUPAJ WAYMON L TRIGGS ROBERT W TUSKEY SR
FRANK C VAN LOON JR TIMOTHY P WEAVER CARROLL E WHITE HENRY A BLANDING JOHN E CANDY
DOUGLAS COMPTON VARISE H CRABTREE JR WILLIE S DAVIS WILLIE C FERGUSON JR WILLIAM T HALE
THOMAS F HANKINS LANTIE L HARRIS JR BRIAN T HEAVER IVAN L HELLER WAYNE G HENSLEY
STEPHEN J HOOGTERP ALVIN R HOOVER III CHRISTOPHER H INAY DENNIS C JERDET URBAN H JOHANNES JR
BENNY J HICKS GARY D KEMSKI LAWRENCE C KLEINHANS PATRICK S LAIRD STEVEN W MARTIN
PAUL NARCISSE EARL D OSBORN JEFFREY W RAINAUD PETER E SCHRYVER JAMES J SHOWS
J D WALTERS MARVIN WESLEY JR VIRGIL H WILSON JR JAMES J ABRAHAM RONALD E ALINCIC
ADOLFO M BEJARANO JOE C CARDENAS JAMES R CARROLL GARY M CULBERTSON DANIEL R DYE
WAYNE M BELL STEWART C EMERSON ROBERT D FACCIO DREW FIEDLER WALTER E GOLEMBIEWSKI
HENRY J KUYKENDALL JUAN J MARTINEZ MELVIN C MAULDIN JR JOHN E METZLER DAVID A PIETRASZAK
WILEY L MARTIN LUIS F SAAVEDRA ROBERT H SANCHEZ JAMES A SOWA DAVID W TARANTO
JAMES L THOMAS JR JOHN W VALENTINE MICHAEL L WASSERMAN DONALD R WEBB JOHN R WIEST
HERBERT J WISHER WILLIAM O AUSTIN ALEXANDER BEARD JOHN D BELLES SYLVESTER L BROWN
BRYAN M CHILCOTE AL D CORBO PAUL J CUMMINGS JR WILLIAM L DRUSCHEL JUAN C DURAN JR
GERALD L EGYED WAYNE C ELLEDGE JACK D GOLDEN JERRY L HALPENNY JOHN M HANSEN JOSEPH L POWELL JR
FREDERICK R HORRIDGE JAMES D HUNT PERRY O JACOBS PIERCE M KIMBALL DAVID L LOCKARD
WILLIAM G MARTIN ROBERT A MICHEL ROBERT D NEASHAM QUINLAN R ORELL SAMUEL R PLUMMER
MICHAEL J MASTERSON JOHN P PELLEGRINO RICHARD J PRICE RICHARD C STAMAND ROBERT J BONNICI
DAVE W BRANT JOHN P COUGHLIN SYLVESTER J HOWARD CLIFFORD A KUEBLER JR JOHN R PARSONS
DANNY V SCURFIELD TERRY L TIMMS MICHAEL J WILSON SCOTT T WIMMER OTTO W AUE
HAROLD W BUTTZ JULIUS C FAIRCLOTH EARNEST L LOWE NEIL J MORRIS STEPHEN G MONTAGUE
GARY J PALMER HARRY L PUCKETT JOSEPH H RIFFLE CHARLES E SMITH OLLIE R STAPLETON
JAMES A CROWLEY II RICHARD N DE ANGELIS JERRY A DILLARD GEORGE B HAMILTON DAVID J LE VIER
DALE L DAVIS GLENN S MILLER WILLIAM J PASSANANTE MICHAEL L RUSSO III ROBERT J TREASURE
GEORGE A VANDERHOFF JR ROBERT M CHEEK MARK C CHENIS FREDDIE D DICKENS
JOHN R FERRAZZANO WILLIAM D FRANTZ JAMES P MASON DAN R MOORE TIMOTHY J MURPHY
RALPH O DAUGHERTY JR THOMAS L MCKINZIE SIDNEY G POLLARD DAYNE Y SCOTT JAMES N SWEET
JOHN C YATES BENITO V ALANIZ CYRIL A ALVERAZ WILLARD L ARNTZ GARY W DOOLITTLE
LARRY D BENNETT RICHARD O BICKFORD TIMOTHY COLE JR RONALD M DELP ROBERT W DIEFFENBACH JR
WAYNE J BENES DANIEL E FIKE JIMMY C GREEN VICTOR R HERNANDEZ HARRY H HERNDON
HERBERT C LANGENHORST ANTHONY R LUX RICARDO R MARTINEZ LESTER C MCGINNIS II JOHN P MILLS

PANEL 40W

OTIS L NORRIS JR DANNY L ROSE RANDALL E WELCH ROBERTO GONZALEZ-MORALES
ROBERT L COTTMAN GEORGE E DEHNER RONALD L DOOLITTLE KENNETH W DUSART DOUGLAS EALEY
PERRY W GRIFFITH DENNIS A GROTH JOHN M HORTON JR JOHNNY L JOHNSON DERRELL W JOYCE
DANIEL MATTEI-SANTIAGO PAUL E MCGINNESS SAMUEL MENA MICHAEL D PAONESSA JAMES J RAIOLO
STEPHEN J SALUGA III CHARLES F STRAFELLO HENRY L TEJADA PETER G THOMPSON RAYMOND C WALDROP
EDWARD J THIBODEAUX JERRY G BRIDGES CHARLES E DEITSCH PAUL E FOUGHT JR JIMMY L HOWARD
MICHAEL K KLEIN HENRY C KNIGHT CHARLES H MELDAHL MATTHEW MINOR JR ALONZA W PHOENIX
ROBERT E REHDER IGNACIO E RIOS JERRY W SNYDER TIMOTHY L SPRING RONALD STANTON
JAMES E WILLIAMS FRANCIS V BARON WILLIAM P BOWMAN ARTHUR L BREWER DONALD W BRUCK
GERALD E BURGENER EDWIN E CARSON BASIL L CIRIELLO RAY E CODDING WILLIAM P COHN JR
PAUL L COSGRIFF GERARD COYLE LESTER A DOAN EDWARD K DUEL DICKIE W FINLEY
LUTHER A GHAHATE JAMES P GULIE EUGENE W HENDRICKS KARL E KELLEY JR BERNARD F KISSELL JR
KENNETH K KNABB JR GLENN E MILES BRUCE M MILEY BILLY R MORRIS RUSSELL E NIHILL
ALDEN W O'BRIEN ANTHONY J PEARSON MICHAEL A RANDALL SR RUBEN E REYES ROBERT B RICHARDSON
MICHAEL E ROBERTS COUNCIL L ROYAL KLAUS D RUHLAND GAYLAND O SCOTT STEVEN P SORICK
RICHARD W STRONG JR JOHN D THOMAS HOWARD E VAN VLIET RALPH R WENSINGER ROBERT R WRIGHT JR
GERALD D ZIEHE CHARLES J ANGRISANI COLIN J BACH ANTHONY J BELLETTI JOHN A BURLESON
DENNIS R CAIN ARTHUR J CARL RODNEY R CHASTANT JACK A CORN FREDERICK E HARRINGTON JR
DAVID H FISHER JAMES E FOSTER ROBERT L GARRETT RICHARD A GURULE THOMAS D HARDY
JEFFERY W EVANS JAMES M HOLMES FREDERICK G JACKSON JR EUGENE W KIMMEL IRWIN L KNICKERBOCKER
BILLY KNIGHT JOHN C KORINEK WILLIAM W LESTER JAMES E MCCORKEL DAVID W MURPHY
ROBERT C PAHCHEKA KENNETH A PAHL BENIGNO RIVERA-GALARZA ROY H WILSON TERRY H BEARDSLEE
JAMES R BECK HARVEY BLACK DONALD L BROWN RAYMOND G CLARK ROBERT M CROSBY
ROGER K DRAKE RICHARD L EDWARDS ERNEST U GAMELIN JR ROBERT A HAGAN JR JAMES B HANSARD
ROBERT L JONES HAROLD D MARTIN CHARLES J PARKER MARION E REED JOHN T REILLY
DAVID RIELLY JOHN R SHINER DENIS L SIMONE EVERETTE R BAILEY JAMES T BLANKENSHIP
DONALD R BURNSIDE CLARENCE B CUNNINGHAM PAUL R DARTT FRANK M DE NARDO JR WILLIE R TUCKER
CLYDE D DOWNARD JR ROBERT T DUNN DAVID L EVANS ARNOLD M MARCHLEWICZ LARRY E MARTIN
JUAN MASILLO EVERETT J MEESTER JOHN J MORLEY JR CHARLES L MOSS JR JAMES P MRAZIK
LONNIE T PARKER TIMOTHY M PORTER RICHARD S RILEY JR DAVID L SPARKS ROOSEVELT SPEIGHTS
ROBERT V DIMITT GEORGE E TYLER JOHN R WILSON RICHARD M BANASZYNSKI NORMAN W BARTELS
TOM G CASEY JOHN W DORIO JAMES M ESPOSITO EDWARD E GOLDER III LEONARD A GUY
JIMMY W HARDWICK NOEL HURLEY ROGELIO LEBRON-MALDONADO BILLIE M LONG DAVID R MERRELL
PAUL M MOORE THOMAS F RAY JR JAMES G SANDERS ALLAN E SCHWARTZ BILLY E SCOTT
JAMES G SORIANO BENJAMIN A THOMPSON JR DENNIS R TRIPP MICHAEL E WITKOP JAMES A WRIGHT
CARROLL J BAILEY TERRY H BATES THOMAS H CARSTENS PILAR J CUELLAR JAN A ELKINS
FRED W CARPENTER CLYDE GARTH JR WAYNE B HOLLAND CHARLES R HUTCHISON SAMUEL JOHNSON JR

PANEL 40W (*Continued*)

MARLOWE E KEELS ANTHONY J LASKOWSKI ABEL LUNA STEVEN A MATHERS DONALD L PERRY
CHARLES L POOL STEPHEN H SAMPLES THOMAS A SENNE WILLIAM G SMITH STEVEN A STROUD
KEITH L SWANSON LOUIS W WASHINGTON MILES G WILDMAN DAVID K WILHELM JAMES A WORLDS
DENNIS C ACKERMAN THOMAS A BIDDULPH RICHARD L BRAY III ROBERT E CANNON STEVEN C CANRIGHT
STEVEN E COLLIER DONALD M COOK JOHN L CRANE ROBERT L DELLINGER WILLIAM L MICHEL
DAVID D DUMAS ROBERT C EDMUNDS JR LOUIS A FRYE ALFRED D GARRETT JAMES L HAMILTON
NOBLE T HEAD LARRY D HOSFORD ARLEN J HUNTER DOUGLAS C KLOSE JIMMY R LIPE
RICHARD R COOMER JOHN M MANSFIELD EDWARD J MASLYN ROBERTO MENDEZ EDWARD P MULLINS
JAMES J MCCAFFREY JR MICHAEL J NOVAK JERRY S RATLIFF RICHARD A SABLOTNY WAYMOND A SAYLOR
ROBERT C SIEBENALLER RAYMOND M TANNER GARY W WEIR HILTON E WOOLSEY EARL H ZAEHLER
ROCKY L BLAIR CHARLES R CONNOR JOHNNY L EVANS KENNETH W FAUL RONNIE L RUSSELL
CLINTON M GAULT JR WILLIAM LUEDKE GERALD MARTIN LUTHER O MCCORMICK CHARLES S PETTERSON
REGINALD W MERRIMAN JAY W PAROLA DONALD T PENNEY WILLIAM E RICKER FRANCIS L ROSSELL JR
BARRY A COPP DAVID C SCHULTZ KENNETH A STONEBRAKER WILLIAM H STROVEN DONALD F STURGEON
DAVID S TAYLOR JR GEORGE R TUNISON HARRY L WELLS DANNY G WEST STEVEN N BEZOLD
CLYDE R CARTER JR CLARENCE R CHAFFIN RICHARD C EWALD DONALD L HARRISON RAYMOND J HARSTER
CHARLES E HAZLIP JOSEPH E HEATH JAMES D HUNTER HERBERT N JOHNSON GEORGE M PRICE
ROBERTO RAMOS CHARLES T ROEDER JAMES G SCOTT WILLIAM E STONE TERRY L WILLIAMS
DALE H AMUNDSON GREGORY J BARTKOWSKI JOHN V BERG MERRITT L MURRAY HERBERT J PARZYNSKI
LARRY B DURST JOSEPH FERRO GERALD H FORGUE HARLAN L GRAHAM DANNY M GRAY
RICHARD W HORSLEY JAMES V HOWARD RAYMOND L JANSENIUS GEORGE J KENDRA GARY L MATSON
JOHN M AVERY JIM G BELL JR KEVIN E MOLINE KENNETH R PAYNE RUSSELL J ROTKO JR
LARRY E SCHWARZ MARLIN L SIEGWALT RICHARD E TURNER DAVID F WORKMAN JAMES S ALLISON
ALEXANDER A AMES DONALD H BARTLETT RONALD A BEARDSLEY THOMAS M BEHRENS EUGENE CROSSLEY
JIMMY D BLALACK LAWRENCE G BOURNE JOSEPH M BOWMAN KENNETH W CASSEL GARRY W CATRON
PHILIP J BATTAGLIA JR STEVEN I CAVIN JAMES R COOPER JAMES A COX ANTONIO H DELACERDA JR
PAUL R DRISCOLL RAYMOND M ENCZI PATRICK B EPPS DONALD F FLETCHER JAMES M GHEER
LARRY K HENDEE FARIS E HOLLAND DARREL E LA FEVRE CHARLES R LEMUS JR ALFRED R MAHONEY JR
TOMAS R MESA MAURICE G NEWMAN JR THOMAS E NEWSTEAD GREGORY L NUTTER MILTON D PATE
ROBERT M PRESS JR WARREN H RAINES BILL E RAMSEY JR ANGEL A RIVERA-VELAZQUEZ RONALD L SCHUYLER
THOMAS E SIRBAUGH ALBERT P SMERIGLIO EUGENE SPENCER ANTHONY L SPINO ROBERT G STANKO
JOHN T STIMSON JR WILLIAM D STOVALL ROGER W SWANSON JOHN E URBELIS NORBERT O WERNER
RONALD A WOLTER WILLIAM K ALAMEDA MICHAEL P ALONGI JR THOMAS W BAYONET EDWIN E BLAGDON
LESLIE V BOWMAN JACKIE C CARTER THURL G CARTER III RICHARD C CARTWRIGHT TIMOTHY C DUNNING
EDWIN H CASE NORMAN G CATES JAMES M CIUPINSKI ERNEST F COOKE JR THOMAS G FUNKE
CHARLES G COSTIN DUANE L COTTET MICHAEL B COUNIHAN RONNIE COURTNEY KENT A CUNNINGHAM
THEODORE H DALTON GARY L DAUCH WOODIE J DEAN KEITH W DUFFY EDWARD L GUSTAFSON
WOODROW W BRADLEY JR WILFREDO CINTRON-MENDEZ DAVID G FELL ALBERT L GAY JR JAMES E GRAVES
CHESTER D DALE GERALD E HAMM STANLEY M HARRELL GREGORY L HEGGEN MICHAEL G HOFF
FLOYD W HOUGHTALING III ARISTOTOLES D IBANEZ WILLIE L JAMES PAULL D JOSE SAMUEL K KAHANA

PANEL 39W

ELMER M KIVEL GEORGE E KOTTYAN WAYNE K LAINE JERRY S LEONARD JAMES E MARTIN
WENDELL MCBURROWS JOSEPH A MILLER JR WILLIAM J MORRISON DONALD H OUILLETTE
EASON J MAXEY DENNIS K O'CONNOR DANIEL C PATTERSON RODNEY W PETERS MARVIN N PROPSON
CARY F RUNDLE REINHARD J SCHNURRER JR WALTER J SEIDEL ROGER E SHEPHERD THOMAS H SMITH
EDDIE E SPRADLIN MICHAEL J SYNOD ROBERT J TODD ANTHONY R TORCIVIA DIETER R VATER
LARRY T WALTZ JOHN C WHITE III LESTER WILLIAMS JR JOSE R ALVAREZ DAVID A ANDERSON
TERRY L ARMSTRONG REFUGIO CANALES RALPH R CARPENTER JR EUGENE T DALY JR JAMES E DUNKIN JR
MURIEL S GROOMES ROBERT G HUFSCHMID DARRELL S LOVE WILLIAM D MEARA JR JAMES I SCHLINGER
JACOB MCKIE ROY W MILLER JR MARVIN B MULLIS JR PHILIP L NICHOLS RAYMOND F ORR JR
TERRY A JOHNSON WILLIAM L SFERRUZZI JAMES A SINGLETON WILLIAM D STURDEVANT NOE TAMEYOZA
FRANK J YOKES ROBERT W BENJAMIN JOSEPH E DAVIS JR LARRY D DU BOSE MICHAEL J FOY
JAMES L FULLER JOE L MASCARENAS JAMES R NORRIS BILLY J PITTS FRANKLIN W POOLE
VAN V RIBUCAN MICHAEL E RITCH BRUCE A ROBINSON MATTHEW A RUDEN JOHN F SCHROM
SHERRELL V SHELTON JOHN B THORNTON THOMAS E WELCH DAVID A WENCL BRYAN L WILSON
RICHARD C SIMON ELTON G ANDERSON THOMAS H BAKER DOUGLAS H BERGERON STEVEN W BURNAM
BENNY D CLAYTON JOHN M FILIPPELLI EDSALL A FRICK JIMMY L GRIER DAVID B HENDERSON JR
DERRICK HENDERSON EDDIE L JACKSON JR MARVIN C JONES BURT E MILLER RONALD K MOORE
PATRICK I NELMS GREGORY L PHILLIPS ARTHUR J ROSS JR RICHARD A SETTER OTIS R SIMPSON
ALLAN R TYLER TIMOTHY H WEAKS BARNEY J WHITE BILLIE W WILKINSON HERBERT WILLIAMS
JOHN J ZIMULIS EDWARD E DANIELS CHARLES I DE GRAW MICHAEL M FARMER PETER J JIRSA
KENNETH J DELL LLOYD R GREENE ARDON HALT FREDDIE J HANNAH DAVID A JOHNSON
DENNIS O JOHNSON KEITH G JOHNSON CHARLES C MANN JR HERMAN L MCINTIRE CLIFFORD J ROBERTS
ROGER D JUSTICE DEAN W OLTMAN JEAN P PELLICANO MICHAEL R RICH JOSE G SANCHEZ JR
TIMOTEO M SANTIAGO JR JOHN G SCUCCHI WILLIE D SPIVEY JOHN F SUGGS JR DAVID J ULMER
GEORGE F WALLACE JR WAYNE A ALLEN THOMAS L BECKER LARRY R BELLAMY LANNY J BURDETTE
WILLIAM G CAMP WILLIAM R EMBRY JR LATNEY D FERGUSON JAMES A FROST VERNON R FYALL
LAURENCE B GREEN EDWARD D HENRY DENNIS G INIGUEZ ROBERT G JOLLY RODNEY S KIAHA
GEORGE A MARKS JR GERALD C MULLIN WILLIAM D NELSON GERALD R PETERSON LAWSON J SCHROYER III
DAVID L MERRILL JOSEPH M PIGNATO RUSSELL J POWELL ALLAN L SCHMIDT MARVIN I SIDERS
RAYMOND G SKAGGS DUNCAN B SLEIGH RAFAEL SOLER JAMES M TIMMONS FREDRICK R TURNER
JOEL VRUGGINK JOHN C WELLS CHARLES L ADKINS CHARLES D BALLOU JOSE D BERMUDEZ JR
DAVID W BROOKS RANDELL L DOCKSTADER PHILIP D ENGLISH THOMAS J EVANS PHILLIP F KAPLON JR
LARRY P BROWN EDWARD A FRYER JR CHARLES W HALL THOMAS M KUBICA ROBERT M KUMMELL
PAUL E MALESZEWSKI WILLIAM F MEINECKE KAZUTO MORIWAKI JOHN F SCHAFFER JAMES R SPRINGER
JERRY L PHILLIPS JAMES T STOVALL DAVID L THORNTON CRAIG L WALTON KENNETH F YBARRA
PETER P BLASKO JR GARY R COOPER JAMES A COPELAND JOSEPH F DESMOND JAMES A HARDMAN
JOHN H HAYS DONALD J HERTRICK MITCHELL L JOLY JOHN E LUTZE ERNEST M PLATTNER
MARVIN E LIVELY RODNEY S PEARSON MARK H PIETRZYK THEODORE SMITH FLOYD A STINSON
ALLEN W THOMAS STEPHEN T VOLZ RICHARD C WALLACE GARY J ALLEN LARRY W BOWEN
GARRYL D CARDINAL FRANKLIN N CURL LAWRENCE DE WITT RICHARD EDWARDS JR JIMMIE L HARVIN
STEVEN D KRECH FAGALII L LEATUTUFU ALLEN L LUCAS HOWARD G PEOPLES ROGER E WICHMAN
LARRY J WOLOSONOWICH JOSEPH E AMEJKA JOHNNY M ANDERSON THOMAS L CARTER JOHN H COLE
SAMMY J CROSS ROBERT D DREW JOSE GARCIA RICHARD GREENSPAN EUGENE D HILL
GEORGE W HOLL RONALD J JENSEN LARRY R LALAN MICHAEL C MANNINA WILLIAM MILLER JR
JOHN P MURPHY HAWK J RED JOHN G RITCH BILLIE G RUSS HARRY W WICKERSHAM JR
EDDIE M ADAMS DONALD N ALBERTSON PHILLIP D BARGER ROBERT B BARRON JAMES E BRASWELL
MICHAEL W CHANEY RONALD E COLVINS GEORGE W COONE JR HOWARD K COOPER JAMES HAMBRICK JR
JOHN L BRATTON ALBERTO DUNES JR ROBERT R FOLEY JR STEPHEN L GLORE GARY E GRAVES
JERRY R HARDY THEODORE HARRISON JR JAMES G HUMPHREY LARRY A JACKSON LANE C JOHNSON
DAVID A KNOX CHARLIE L LOGAN WILLIAM E MORMAN JR RICHARD L MOYERS THOMAS B RAINEY
ROBERT J MCCARTHY ERNEST L MORA CLIFFORD A NEWMAN LANNY J NORMAN WILLIAM B REAMS JR
FRANK J ROBERTS GARY A RUST BENJAMIN SADBERRY JOHN D SHERMOS WILLIAM C WINSTON
DOYLE W CLARK JAMES E CUMMINGS JR DAVID A DENNIS JOHN Z FICKUS MARVIN E GAY
RALPH GUARIENTI ROBERT E JACKSON FRANCIS J JURANIC JR FREDDIE L LAMKIN DALE K LARSON
JAMES C MAIATO JR CHARLES R MCCURTAIN JR WILBUR L MONG EUSEBIO MONTOYA JAMES A MYERS JR
HENRY L NIX RUSSELL K OGDEN RONALD L REED DOYLE E SALLEE WILLIAM H SCHAEFER
LARRY E SOMMERS DANIEL E SPENCER JR WYATT S THOMAS TERRY M WESTERGARD CHARLES R BOGART
MICHAEL F BRANIN JR JOSEPH W BUCHANAN PATRICK J CARROLL ANTHONY T CULOTTA JAMES W HARNESS
JAMES A BOOTS LOREN E ENGSTROM JAMES L EPLIN FREDERICK M GILSINGER JR DENNIS G HANSON
CHARLES T HERSHEY ROBERT W JASURA ARTHUR E KEESEE DONALD L KEETER JACK W RICE
THOMAS H KLOSTER STEPHEN M MACCALLUM LARRY E MAYBERRY THOMAS W MORRIS THOMAS A NORRIS
JAMES C HATHORNE JR LASZIO RABEL ROBERT R RADES DALE F ROLLINS JOSE C SANTOS ELMER O WRAY
GREG P STIGER JERRY A TRUELOVE CHARLES E YOUNG FRANCIS BALDINO DAVID A BRADSHAW
JEFFREY L BUCHANAN WILLIAM E CARLSON LESTER R DAVIS FRANK L DOMINGUEZ DONALD H GREINER
ALAN C DONNELLY WILLIAM H FABIAN DAVID A FIALKO JR JOHN E FLETCHER MASON O FOLMAR
RICKY L CORNELL MONROE GREER RANDOLPH E HATTON GABRIEL HERRADA JERRY D HILL
KENNETH A HODGES WAYNE M HORNE ROBERT T JONES JR BRUCE J KENNEDY DAVID M MORRIS
LARRY L JOHNSON LESLIE C PASCHAL JR CHARLES D PLUMMER DELMAR SHELLEY DONALD A THOMPSON
JACKIE S UNDERWOOD KARL E WEBER FRANCIS C AKI JR JAMES D BIRCHIM WILLIAM E BROWN
JAMES M CURTIS PETER H GARMS FRANK HOGENMILLER STEVEN E JOHNSON ROBERT J KOWALSKI
WILLIAM R KUCZEWSKI ALLEN R MELDAHL BRENT A REEDER LEONARD L THOMPSON ROBERT TRIVISONNO
LARRY R WOOLRIDGE STANLEY W ARMENTROUT ROBERT F BALSLEY JR WILLIAM M COPLEY EDDIE C KIMBLE
JAMES CRAFT MANUEL DE LUNA JR JAMES G DESCHENES ROBERT R HILLIARD RUSSELL A HODGE
EDDIE W BROWN ERNEST C HOMER MARIAN JAMILSKI MICHAEL D JARRETT CARL F KARST
JORGE L NIEVES WILLIAM H NOLTE GORDON L PATTERSON LEONDA SARTOR GEORGE A SCHWALBACH
LARRY C LARA RICHARD A SITO SR MICHAEL VILLARREAL ROBERT C WIECHERT STANLEY F WILTON
RONALD A YANCHAR JAMES M YOUNG PHILLIP R ANDERSON JACK A BOWMAN PAUL D DERBY
JOHN W CIALLELLA RHONNIE L CLARK RICHARD G CLEVELAND CHESTER COSGROVE GARY D COX
THOMAS F CALLAHAN TIMOTHY A CRANDALL FRANCIS M FINNERTY JR RONALD E FISHER RYAN J GALLOW

PANEL 38W

ROBERT E GREENE RICHARD T HAVEL ALVAH W HENSON JR WILLIAM C WYMER JR
JACOB JOHNSON THOMAS J KILLION JR JAMES L LANG HAL R LONG JOHN K MARSHALL
WAYNE E KOHN ROBERT B MARKUM ROY E MAY MARTIN E MENDOZA DAVID H MERRIAM
LARRY D NICHOLS ERNEST D PERINOTTO THOMAS A REICH GARRY E REMILLARD DANIEL A RIDDICK
ALLEN J RANKE GERALD F ROCK GEORGE C ROWLAND JR MARTIN D SHIELDS AARON TAWIL
DAVID E HOFFERT LLOYD K TURNER DAVID S VOLLMER JEFFREY R BEARDSLEY MICHAEL J CROMIE
WILLIAM B EZELL DAVID R HOLT DALE W JOHNSON FRANK MARTINEZ WILLIAM J MURRAY JR
WILLIAM G REICH JOAQUIN RODRIQUEZ WAYNE SANGILLO MIKE A SOLANO WILLIE J WASHINGTON JR
IGNACIO SANCHEZ ELIE E SWARTZLANDER DWIGHT J TAYLOR HERMAN W WRIGHT JR CHARLES F ABENE
LEWIS R CAIN YALE R DAVIS JR ROBERT A DESROCHERS JERRY E DOROUGH CALVIN FIELDER
ALBERT M FIGUEROA RICHARD H GREENE JOSEPH J HERNANDEZ JR PHILLIP A HILL DAVID C JASPER
PETER B LIVINGSTON WILMER T LUTZ BILLY C MCDANIELS WILLIE D MCVEA RAYMOND S REEVES JR
JOHN N REILLY JR TED L SHARP LEROY SPENCER JR WAYNE A TICE JAMES D ARMSTEAD JR
RAYMOND L BROWN ROGER C BROWN ROBERT L BROWNLEE KEVIN G BURKE ROBERT L DETRICK
THOMAS J BURTON MICHAEL W CLIFFORD TERRY W CLIFTON CLAUDE COLE JR WILBERT E COLEMAN
LEONARD BEATTY JR ALBERT D CONTREROS JR MICHAEL J CRESCENZ RICHARD W DIERS WILLIAM EMERSON
DONALD P EVANS RONALD R FITCH WALTER A FRY CHARLES W HAN JOHN R HARRELL
ARTHUR J HERINGHAUSEN JR JEFFREY L HICKS DANNY C HUDSON WASHINGTON HUNTER JAMES L JONES
JAMES M MARTIN DONALD W MCBRIDE DAVID W MYERS GARY D PAGAN HARRY C PANNELL
JOHN F PRISET MICHAEL D REIFF MELVIN D RUMSEY BENNY J SAPP WILLIAM P SMITH JR
HORACE V ROBINSON JR THOMAS P SCHWAB JIMMY L SHIELDS PAUL W SMITHSON JAMES E STONE
GERALD D WILLIAMS JESSE L ADAMS DANIEL J ALBERT DOUGLAS W ARMSTRONG JERRY BAKER
RICHARD A BARBOLLA CHARLES R BEARD GERARD J BLUME JR CURTISS E BRAATZ THOMAS W DESSELLE
JAMES L BROOKS HARRY L BROWN THOMAS E BUSH HERBERT R CURTIS JOHN P DEIHL
LARRY DUNN SAMUEL J EVANS GLENN E FORD JEAN C FOSTER JOSEPH R FRANKS
MARTIN G GIVEN STANLEY N GREEN WARREN G HAUGEN JR JOHN W HINKLE RICHARD L MATTHEWS
THOMAS HOPKINS GARY W HULSE CURTIS J KAUPP DOUGLAS H KIKER CLIFFORD M KUHN
JOHN E HEYEN JOHN R MILLER ARNOLD L MULHOLLAND MARVIN J NASCHEK CARMELO NAVARRO
RICHARD A NICHOLS BILLIE J ONTIS GERALD M ORTEGO PAUL J PAMANET CHARLES F REIN
WILLIAM J RUSSELL JR WAYNE E SKOLITS CHARLES L SMITH JOE H STANLEY EDDY G SUMPTER
THOMAS L STANLEY ROBERT L STOREY MELVIN E THOMPSON ANTHONY F WASHINGTON WILLIAM S WATTS
CLIFFORD K WELDING DONALD R WENTZ KENNETH A BAKER GEORGE L BARNES BEN C BURGE
WALTER L BURKE IVAN J CAMPBELL DAVID A CASSIDY GREGORY B CHIAGO BRIAN D CLAYTON
JAMES L CRANDELL FRANKLIN D EFIRD GEORGE W FISH JR CLARENCE E GOSS LEROY D HOFFMAN
DONALD L FORD GARY R GOUDY WILLIE C HAMILTON PATRICK R HENDRICKSON TONY G HUBBARD
ALLEN V JACKSON RAYMOND B KYZER DAVID G LENGYEL HAROLD D MILLER LEO J MILLER
DAVID M MISZEWSKI THEODORE MOSTOWSKI CHARLES A OLSON RONALD J PANICCIA ANDREW A RUIZ
JAMES K SANDER RAYMOND P SANTORA THOMAS E SHEPPARD JAMES W SINCERE PAUL A STEIN
DOUGLAS R SEAVEY GALON G SPAFFORD BRUCE R SWEENEY RICHARD C SWIFT ADOLPH W TAJCHMAN
RANDALL K NAUERTZ LOUIS A TAYLOR DAVID J WILCOX JACK BERKEBILE DAVID I BRIGGS JAMES C CARLSON
LONNIE V BYRD MICHAEL B CLARK JOHN W COLBERT DONALD F CORNELL BRADLEY G CUTHBERT
THOMAS G DICKERSON ARNOLD R DIEKEMA ELMER E FREESE HAROLD L GLOVER DONALD L GOLDSMITH
JAMES R GOLDING DARIO D GUERRA JAMES R HARRELL DAVID W HEMPHILL LESLIE A LEWIS
FORTI P LO MICHAEL N LOITZ JUAN A MARTINEZ-QUILES JR RICHARD A MILKS RONALD Y MILLER
HILARIO MORENO DANIEL L NEISWENDER GRADY R NELSON ROBERT J NIXON SAMMY C ROMERO
LARRY W RYCROFT FRANK SANFILIPPO ROBERT L SANGSTER EDDIE L SHAFFER NOAH L SMITH
RICHARD C STEVENS JOSEPH D SZIDOR TERREL J VIDRINE THOMAS W WARREN HOWARD R WILHOIT JR
MITCHEL R TYLER CARL J WINTER LARRY L BATES LARRY M CARROLL THERON W COBB
DAVID F GARRINGER ALFRED HIGHTOWER JR TERRY L HINKLE LARRY JENKINS HARRY T KITE JR
JOHN R LARIMORE JOSEPH M LIGHTCAP LONNY L LOYD JOHN J MAILLOUX LARRY J MASON SR
TIMMY L MILLER CHARLES T NALLEY JOSE J ORTIZ-NEGRON THOMAS L PETERSON ISREAL D REED
MICHAEL J RAMBUR JACK J SANDERSON THOMAS H SCHNEIDER STEPHEN F SELGRADE LAWRENCE E SIROIS
JERRY N SCOTT ALFRED J SMALL MARK S STEINER JOHN S WASILOW DANIEL F WEST DANIEL L MCKECHNIE
FRANCISCO ALVAREZ MICHAEL D BELL JOHNNY W BENTON MELVIN E BEVIER WILBERT A ELLISON
MICHAEL D BIRDWELL PAUL E BONNETTE KENNETH J BRITT JOHN E BRIX THOMAS E BROWN
DAVID M BARRETT MATTHEW M CANFIELD JR GARY M CHAPMAN RICHARD K CHILTON MICHAEL P CUSICK
LAWRENCE ELLSWORTH JOHN F FITZGIBBONS SAN D FRANCISCO LARRY G HETZLER ROBERT G HODGES
ROBERT E HOSKINS KURT C HUSSMANN FREDRICK B KING JAMES E KING DONALD G LEWIS
ROBERT K HOULE LAWRENCE D KUTCHEY BRUCE A LYNCH ROBERT E MARSHALL FLORENTINO MARTINEZ JR
JOSEPH ALLESSIE RAYMOND B MCKINNEY JOSEPH C MORRISON CHARLEY L MOUNT RALPH B MULKEY JR
DENNIS E NAYLOR JOSE T NETO LAWRENCE J PUTZ JR MICHAEL L SIMMONS JOSEPH V STACK
ERNEST A STAMM GARY G THROCKMORTON RICHARD C THUM THOMAS M WHITFIELD GEORGE L YOUNG
CHARLES G STANLEY JACK M ZAITZ KENNEY M ADAMS JR RAYMOND J AHERN JR ROGER D ALGIRE
JOHN S ALLING JR STEPHEN C BEALS WILLIAM D BEESON JAMES J BUONAIUTO LLOYD A CHESS
DARWIN J DELANO CHARLES DENNIS JAMES D DORAN WILLIAM M EBEL MONICO FLORES JR
MARVIN J GAINES JOHNNY G GREGG GREGG HARTNESS HAROLD D HOUSKER MICHAEL J PASSAFUME
LAWRENCE G KOCH MICHAEL G LANDKAMER DUANE A LIKKEL RONALD R LOWRY RONALD J MOE
ROBERT E JONES MIGUEL F MONTANEZ BOBBY J PERKINS PIETRO PICONI CURTIS H RAINER
GEORGE A SHAVIES MARSHALL R SMITH PATRICK E SMITH JR DAVID J STANSBURY RODGER A BLATNICK
JAMES C ADAMS NICHOLAS R ALEXANDER HENRY F ASUNCION ERNEST L BARBER ROGER J BARTHOLOMEW
JAMES G BRADY JOHN W BRINKMEYER JOHN C BROWN DAVID A BRYANT RICHARD W CASEY
DAVID D CREEL RONALD C CUNNINGHAM JERRY M DAUBER GORDON E DE GARMO FREDRICK H FRAZER
JEROME D CHANDLER ALLEN E DUNEMAN OLIVER E DURHAM DENNIS J FETT DANIEL P FLORES
WILLIAM GIBBS JR JIMMIE R GREEN WILSON F HALLEY RICHARD L HAMMETT BILLY C HUNTER
ERIC D JENKINS ANTHONY E JOHNSON JOE A JOHNSON LESLIE H LAROCQUE BOOKER T LOFTON JR
MALCOLM E LOMAX VINCENT L MAGER MYRON W MAGNON LOREN D MARTINSEN JACKIE M MEDLIN
EDWARD E MCBRIDE RAYMOND MCCUMBER DONALD S MIHORDIN MICHAEL G PARR WILLIAM J SIMPSON
WILLIAM D RAY AUGUST K RITZAU WAYNE J ROGERS JOHN R RYAN JR DWIGHT C SARJEANT
SALVATORE J PISCITELLO DAVID W SMITH GENE P STUIFBERGEN THEODORE A SWEATT DANIEL C TEDROW
WILLIAM R THIEM JOHN B ULFERS CARLOS VEGA-LOPEZ EDWARD B VOGEL RANDALL W WAGNER
CHARLES D MILLER LONNIE WILLIAMS JOEL D WOLFE JOE I WOOD RODNEY B YARDLEY JIMMY J LA COSSE
CHARLES E BESTMANN THOMAS L BRATTAIN RICHARD C DEVINS DONALD J DRAKE KENNETH JOHNSON

PANEL 37W

JOHN MOULDEN JAMES K PARKS LONNIE M REEVES LAURENCE E WILLIAMS
JOHN H ROACH RUSSELL L SMITH FERDINAND STROYE WALTER STUCKEY ANDREW J TOPORCER JR
PAUL P POTTER MICHAEL D TURNER SAMMIE L WATSON JR DWAYNE J WHORTON HAROLD L BASHAM
HERIBERTO BLANCO EVANGELOS K CARANASIOS GARY L CARLSON JOHN L CHASE THOMAS R STEINBACH
VESTIE T DRIGGERS GEORGE A FOSTER III JOHN R GASTON JR JOHNIE R GODWIN JR JESUS E GOMEZ JR
MELVIN R GREEN ERVIN E HARRIS BILLY E HUGHES II ALFRED F MCCANTS JESUS Q MENO
TERRYL G PARTSAFAS JOHN S POOLER GARY D PRINCE TED J RULE HURSTON E WORRELL
THEODORE R CONLEY JR ROBERT J TARANTO WILLIAM M VITALE DOUGLAS L WARNER RICHARD A WEAVER
HENRY L ROGERS JOHN R WILLIAMS GEORGE B ALGER RICHARD D AMBRUSO ARTHUR E BADER JR
JAMES E CHERRY WILLIAM T DAMRON RICHARD A FITTS ROBERT L FOX JR GENE FREEMAN
LAWRENCE C GARRETT JAMES E GLISSON JAMES H HALL SHERLIN A HEIMAN JEFFREY D HOUNSHELL
RONALD E JAMES JERRY W JEFFERSON JAMES KENNEDY ROGER R KERNS JOSEPH KRESIC JR
GARY R LA BOHN DONALD C LEPAK LONNIE G MARTIN MICHAEL H MEIN BRUCE J MORI
DONALD D PANNO LEE V PORDEN JR KLAUS D SCHOLZ RAYMOND C STACKS GEORGE S STRASZEWSKI
SAMUEL K TOOMEY III KING D WASHINGTON ALLEN E WHITE CALVIN E YOUNG RAYMOND ALANIZ
THOMAS E ALFORD III ERVIN P CANOY JR CURTIS R CRUM FREDERICK L GRUBER ROGER A HOLTE
ALFREDO D GRANADO-AVILES LARRY S HEATER DAVID P HELLENBRAND JERRY A KISER MICHAEL E LAWTON
JOSEPH A MERRILL NORMAN A MILLER WILLIAM A PERKINS JR NEWTON R PLUMMER LARRY E RICKS
MICHAEL D ROGERS TULLIE R SMITH JR JAMES M STANDEFORD THOMAS R STUTTS RICHARD D WALLACE
DOUGLAS M ALLEN JIMMIE M ALVAREZ VINCENT J ANASTASIO GEORGE H BELANGER BENNY R GUY
THOMAS W BLAKESLEE EARL T BROOKE JONATHAN BROWN ROBERT T BURTON JESUS ESCAGEDA
ROBERT K ANDERSON WALTER D FREEMAN WILLIAM G KEELER JAMES R KNIGHT RAYMOND W TYMESON JR
DONALD P KREMER RICHARD E LATIMER JR CLARANCE L LOVE JOHN E MARASON DUNCAN B MCINTYRE
JAMES R REESE JOSEPH L RINEHART JAMES D ROBINSON THOMAS W ROWLAND PATRICK SALAZAR
TERRY L SAVOTH CHARLES E SEATON GEORGE H STAMPS LARRY A STEINER DAVID O TIMSON
JOSEPH A HADLEY FRANCIS P TRUANCE RONALD E VAN BARRIGER WILLIAM M WEBB VICTOR B WEISSMAN
DENHAM A WHITESELL JR ARTHUR WILLIAMS JR JOHN R AUSBERN WALTER T BAHL MICHEAL R BAKER
JAN D MILLER EDWARD A BELL LESLEY BOLING JR JAMES J BOLSON DON W BONNER DANIEL J BURDICK
JOSEPH T BURSIS JR NOLAN D BYRD CLAUD W CAPRARO ROBERT A CARNEY HARVEY W CARTER
BILLY J CLAYBORN RONALD R CONKLIN ALEX B CONLEY LARRY L CUNNINGHAM JOHN C DAVIDSON
WILLIAM J DAVIS JR JAMES B DILLARD MARK L FUSILE RICHARD L GOODMAN WILLIAM J MCATEE
FLOYD GRAHAM JR KENNETH G GREEN JOHN N HOLCOMB HARLEY M HOWARD THOMAS A HOWER
MARION B HUGHES JR WEBSTER B JOHNSON JOHN A LANGSTON BOBBY D LEWIS DANNY J MAWDSLEY
ADOLFO M ESTRADA HOWARD H MAYER BENJAMIN MELVIN STEVEN V MERSHON DAVID L URBAN
ROBERT L NORTON FRED J PAUL RICHARD D RANDALL HAROLD J ROBINSON JR LESLIE D ROSEKRANS
STEVEN M CONNELL DENNIS J RUSSO JAMES T SHEFFIELD IRWIN N SOKAL DONNIE M STOKES HENRY SZOR
TERRANCE L MERCKE ARTHUR L WARNER STEPHEN BABULJAK RICHARD L BALES WALTER F BYRD JR
GABRIEL CARDONA JR ROBERT CLOKES THOMAS E CONKEL FREEMON EVANS ROBERT P FISCHER
JAMES R GAGE JERRY W GLAZE WILLIAM J HODGES JAMES C HOLT FRANK JOHNSON JR
JAMES E JONES WILLIE G JONES JEROME A LONG WILLIAM F MARASCO RICHARD E NITSCHE JR
ZENEIDO ORTIZ JR GARY L OWENS ALBERT L PEGGS JOSEPH W PITTS JR REID R ROSS JR
MARLIN SMITH DONALD R STOLTZ RICHARD D TAMM JAMES C TARRANCE JOHN R THOMAS
JOHN A TOWNSEND JR CROW@ B TWO BROADUS W VERNON STEVE E WERTZ GARY N WHIPPLE
WILLIAM C WILLIAMS CHARLES J AKINS MICHAEL W ANDREWS JOHN A BERRY MELVIN L BOLAND
WILLIAM W BREECE JR NYROON CHADEE RICHARD E DRYER BILLY K EVANS JR JOHN D FLOYD
ROBERT C FOX HENRY M HAMES JR HARRY J HARRIS HERIBERTO S HERNANDEZ GUY HOLDAWAY
JOHN F KANACZET JR GARY M O'KEEFE ALLEN N PALM DAVID L ROBISON RAYMOND SINGLETON
GUENTER R THONUES JOSEPH R THORNTON DONALD D WEYKER GARY R BERG JOE P KLIPFEL
JUNIOR B EARNEST WILLIAM B FERGUSON JOE J GONZALES WARREN J GOSS AMEDEE G GRANELLE JR
DAVID GROENE THOMAS J HADLEY LARRY E HAMILTON ROBERT H HARMAN JAMES W HEAGY
GUY B CREEP JR GLENN E HEFLIN WILBURT N HINES JAMES C KERR CHARLES A LAUER EVERETT D RIEPE
STEVE R LUKE RAY MCKIBBEN MICHAEL M MEGINN RONALD L MILLION LONNIE R MITCHELL
DAVID E SCHWARTZ SERGE W SPOTANSKI HAROLD C STILLS CARLOS A VELAZQUEZ-ORTIZ
WILLIAM W WAGNER RODOLFO J ARCHULETA JIMMY D BIGGS JAMES W BOWLING LAWRENCE J BROWN
DENNIS W BURIAN JAMES H BURT MICHAEL J CADORETTE RICHARD CRAWFORD KARL P DENCY
RICHARD F HARRIS HERMAN C HARRISON JR BENJAMIN L HOOPENGARNER JR ROBERT T KEAG WALTER C LEE
JAMES R LEWIS JR KENNETH MILLER KENNETH W MOLTON LARRY J OWEN BERNARD R WOEHLCKE
ROBERT L PACHECO DAVID H PHELPS LANNY W PHIPPS BABE PINOLE FRANK PUGLIESE
FRED A RATLIFF LARRY G RATLIFF KENNETH W RUBBO JAY J SCHMID HERBERT K SKINNER

FEDERICO MATIAS-SANTANA DON E TURNER JOHN A VIALPANDO JOHN L WAUGH MICHAEL R BACH
WAYNE A BARNUM HARRY E BATES MARTEE BRADLEY JR JAMES E BREWER CHARLES W CALDWELL
DONALD K CHEEK ALFRED P CLAYTON PAUL L DAINS CARROLL E DERRILL DOUGLAS DUPREE
ROBERT P ENGLISH DOUGLAS D ESTES PAUL Q ETTER FIAPAI FANUA JR EDDIE D FOSTER
FRED GERTZEN MICHAEL E GIBIS RICKY D GIPSON NICHOLAS V GONZALES DANIEL L GREGG
VICTOR HALE CHARLES W HALL JR WAYNE D HAMILTON JOHN D HANCOCK JOHN C HARDING JR
MARVIN L HARTMAN JOHN F HIGGINS RICHARD D JAMES JOHN K KOSTER LARRY L MARSH
DAVID M JALBERT CONNARD D MALLORY CARL J MILLER DAVID N MOORE JOSEPH S PIRRUCCELLO JR
LEROY C MARTINSON FRANK F MUSICK STEPHEN E NEAS JERRY L OWENS ROBERT A REX
EARNEST L REYNOLDS FELIX D RIDGE LARRY G SANDNES JACK D SCHAFFNER CHARLES L SMITH
PETER S STRATEGOS KARL G TAYLOR PHILIP A TERRY JIMMIE M THOMPSON DAVID R TURNER
MICHAEL C WALKER DENNY L WASHAM BRIAN L WEBBER ARMOUR D WILCOX III JIMMIE K WILLIAMS
HARVIE P WINKLES III WILLIAM C WIRICK ARTHUR W WOOD THOMAS D BERKFIELD MICHAEL J CIESIELKA JR
CHARLES A ATWOOD JR GARY W CHAPMAN IRA D COOPER DENNIS C ERFORD EDWARD FORD
ERNEST L GOMEZ LEO S GORALSKI ERNEST J GRASSI WILLIAM F HARRELL GARRY D HAYNES
ROBERT F HINKSTON RICHARD M KEEGAN JOEL M LEIGH PETE LOPEZ TALTON L MACKEY
LEONARD R MARTIN LYNN M MATTESON CARROL W MINOR KENNETH L NEWBY JR JOHN V O'CONNOR JR
VAN L RANDOLPH JR MICHAEL G RAY DAVID F RHODES CHARLES E ROBINETTE EARL T SHAFFER SR
CURTIS H SHARP JR SAMUEL D SHIMEK ERVIN D SMITH JOHNNY C TURNER WILLIE G ALDRIDGE
THOMAS T CHAPMAN MELVIN E CLARK ROLLAND E DARLING JR DANA E DIEHL CHARLES D SPRINGFIELD
CHARLES A DIXON FREDDIE J DOBBINS WILLIAM J EDER JAMES E FARROW DEXTER N GAMBLE JR
BOYCE L HALL JOHN K HOBSON GARY S HODGES LATHAN HOUSTON LAMONT JACKSON
WILLIAM A LOWRY JOHN P MELOY ROBERT K MERYS JOSEPH T MONAGHAN DENNIS R WEGNER
DONALD F MCKENZIE MELVIN D NELSON JOSE A RUDON PEDRO SANCHEZ JR BOBBY C SNYDER
DAVID M DICKMAN JOE M JUAREZ ATWELL A ARMSTRONG STEVEN P BRODRICK CHARLES E COFFMAN

P A N E L 3 6 W

ALFRED J CRITELLI ROBERT W CROMWELL LAWRENCE G EANS DENNIS E EDGE
MARTIN C FRITZ RUSSELL D GALBRAITH DAVID E GARDNER BILLY L GOINS WILLIE L HALL JR
GERALD C HOAGE JAKE E HURST ROBERT E LACKEY STEPHEN D LANGLER PAUL E SCHMIDT
MELVIN D LEMBKE JOHN C LIVERMAN WENCESLAO R MATIAS JR ELIJAH MILES JR RONALD A OSINSKI
ROBERT G PENDLEY JOHN PIZZUTI ALEXANDER POZMANN JR RALPH E ROACH RONALD M ROMERO
LEROY H ROMIG AGUSTIN ROSARIO HERMAN F RUBIN CHARLES E RUSSELL III THOMAS C RUTTER
RAYMOND H HIGHLEY VINCENT R SALEMI BOBBY G SIMPSON TIMOTHY D STICKLE WILLIAM J SUGDEN
ROBERT TEASLEY DANIEL TELLEZ GREGORIO TREVINO JR DONALD K VADAKIN EUGENE WALTERS
ROY J WEATHERFORD JR JAMES O WEAVER DENNIS M WOOD JAMES WOODWARD DAVEY M ADAMS
ROBERT L BELTRAN DAN M BENNETT JAMES K BRIERLY GALE W CROON FREDERICK G DEROCHER
HARRY C DORSETT STANLEY C FULLER DOUGLAS B KEHOE JOHNNY KING JOE E LADELL
JAMES A MERRETT MICHAEL T MURPHY ANDREW R SINCHAK JR WALTER L STARLING RONALD S STEPSIE
WILLIE C WALKER JOHN S ALBRIGHT II DONALD R ALLEY CHRISTOPHER O BOLSTER RONALD L NIEWAHNER
FRED L CLARKE DOUGLAS V DAILEY RANDY W DERRICK MORGAN J DONAHUE THOMAS W DUGAN
THOMAS C ELDRIDGE JOSEPH P FANNING LEON R FIELD EARL R FRAY ROBERT R FREGIA
BRUCE B GREENE CHARLES F GRIFFIN JAMES C LEWIS ALAN C LOCKARD DURWARD G MORSE
GILBERT S BELL JR WILLIE J MCCLENDON FRANCIS J MCGOULDRICK JR EDDIE J NEELEY THOMAS F SMITH
DONALD A PETTITT DAVID W PIERCE SALVATORE A ROWE JOHN J RUSSEK ORLANDO A SALAS
SAMMY R PALMER ROY STOWE WILLIAM E VANWEY MARION F WALDEN JR SAMUEL F WALKER JR
RAYMOND J WEST JERRY M WHITE RAYMOND D BANDY BILLY F CLARK RICHARD J CONLIN
BRUCE T GOODMAN MITCHEL C HANSEY RONALD R HOBBS WILLIAM K HOPKINS FRANKLIN P WILLEFORD
RICHARD G JESTER GEORGE F JOHNSON LARRY G LAMPHIER DAVID J LEHMAN III DANNY A MCGEE
MARK J O'BRIEN JOHN C ROBERTS RICHARD L ROGERS AINSLEY C SIMONS RICHARD SINCAVAGE
JOSEPH H HANKS III OSCAR E SANABIA ABRAHAM TRUJILLO-TRUJILL GARY A WARNER RAYMOND D WEISS
KENNETH B BIXEL EUGENE M CHRISTER CHARLES E GAY WILLIAM C GRIFFITH STEVEN A HAMPTON
DAVID A LENCHNER MARK E MADSEN KENNETH C MAJOR JR DAVID PIOTROWICZ EDWARD D POWERS
THOMAS E RAMSEY EARNEST E SHEFFIELD TEDDY R SININGER JOHN E SLATER JOHN M VITELLO JR
DEAN F SPAULDING JR DAVID H ALEXANDER ANDRES BALAI MICHAEL R BISHOP RENE A BOIS
TOMMIE J CLARK RICHARD O FISK DAVID A FLEISCHER RAMIRO INFANZON-COLON TERRY PENSONEAU
GARY W GROSS CHARLES L KNEECE ZYGMUNT KOWALEWSKI JAMES M LUDWIG WARDELL PERKINS
RICHARD W RANDOLPH JAMES M RUSHING RONALD C SAFFELL ROBERT N SANDERS CEDRICK L SMART
JOHN D STUART JR JOHN A BLANCO JR BRADLEY J BOURQUE JESSE J BRADSHAW LEON R BROOKS
RICHARD A BROWN NEIL R BURNHAM RAMON CASTRO-MORALES JAMES F CHASE BROOKS M SCRIVNER
KENNETH R CRIST RICHARD G DRAKE RICHARD C DREWES TOMMY R EATON PHILLIP H ENGLE
JAMES R HAMMERSLA JOHN R HARTKEMEYER JOHN K HAYWARD JOHN P KOOB JOHN D KROUSLIS
GRAYSON CRAFT THOMAS M KUPIEC ROBERT R MASCARENAS HERMAN L MCCLAMB GEORGE W MORTON
WALLACE F SIMPKIN MORTON H SINGER FRANK N SMITH ROBERT F STOCKARD DONALD L STONEMAN
ROGER H STROUT GERALD J SZOSZOREK GEORGE A WEAVER JOHN R BABCOCK GARY J MEYER
ROGER A BROWN NORMAN H CLARK MANCOL R CLIFTON RICKY F COSSEY CHARLES M DUMDEI
JOHN J GOTT JR RONALD L HOVIS DONALD A KASKI BENJAMIN C LARABEE CARL J METCALF JR
GREGORY I BARRAS ROGER C MCCORD KENNETH B MILLHOUSE RICHARD OLSON ANGELO A PETRAGLIA
HAROLD R REEVES ROY H SHEFFIELD JAMES E SPARKS DANNY W TIFFT RUSSEL J WHITTINGTON
DAVID L AERTS GERALD A BENSON ROBERT L BONE SHERL K BONNETT CURTIS L BROWN
BRIAN H BURDICK THOMAS G DANOWSKI JAMES P DELANEY JOSEPH W EDWARDS STEVEN J FOY
BEN H IDE ALTON D KELLOGG JOHN A KOCAK DENNIS R MAXWELL LAWRENCE ORTIZ JR
WILLIAM J PAHR JR NORMAN PAYNE DONALD A PLEDGER RENE J SALAZAR WADE T SHAW
MICHAEL P WALSH LANNY L WESSON DONNIE L WORTHEY ROBERT W BENSON JACK P BLAKE
MICHAEL L BOUCHARD GEORGE H BURRELL THOMAS CLARK JR KEVIN T CONNOLLY JOSEPH R DANIELS JR
ROBERT A CLARK WAYNE S CRANDALL VINCENT T DAIELLO DOUGLAS O DUKE LARRY R FOX
RAPHEAL J FROST ALBERT B GERDES JR STANLEY R GILMORE DOUGLAS J HAAN JR DARRELL L HAGGARD
WILBUR O HAKE RAY W HESTERLEE JOSEPH R HUDSON JR RONALD A JARVIS CARL F KASHIEMER
ROBERT D KENT JAMES R KING FLOYD N MARTIN JOHN J MICHAELS MICHAEL MILLER JR
DENNIS F MCGUIRE RICHARD G MORIN WILLIAM J NEUBIA DALE H RANTHUM THOMAS G SIKES
MICHAEL J O'TOOLE LOUIS RODRIGUEZ ROBERT F SCHNEBEL ROBERT E SMITH JR HOWARD J VAUGHAN
RICHARD K ALLEE RICHARD C BACHERT WILLIAM W BLAIR JR ROBERT G BLANK CHARLES J BUCKLEY
JOSEPH P CASTAGNA ROBERT C DREWICZ LARRY A GOFF ROBERT C GREEN JR ROCKNE L HARDWICK
ROBERT H INGRAM SYLVESTER JOHNSON MICHAEL J MCDONALD EDWARD C MCHENRY JOHN B MOORE
ADELBERT E MCRAE THOMAS E NOVAK WILLIAM E O'CONNOR RODNEY T PRATT RUBEN PRIETO
JAMES F RUMMAGE EDWARD SALONIES JR EDWARD J SCALISE ELMER G SIKORSKI EARL W THOMAS JR
LEONARD WEBB JR LAWRENCE J WISSELL ROBERT L WORTHINGTON JUSTIN K ANDERSON DENNIS M AYERS
RICHARD G BARNARD RICHARD T CHAMBERS TERRY L COOPER EDWIN H CORWIN DON HINSON
DONALD I CULSHAW DENNIS L DULEBOHN GARY W EVERETT JAMES F FLETCHER GARRY M FORKUM
DONALD G BOUSLEY CHARLES P GLENN THOMAS L GOODALE TERRY L GREENHALGH ARNOLD JANSSEN
JOSEPH JOHNSON JR ALLEN I LIMBRICK MANUEL D MADRUGA HENRY E MAUL MICHAEL A MINKO
ROGER W MCCLATCHEY EDWARD A MORRISON DONALD A RITTLINGER DIONISIO SANCHEZ-ORTIZ
ERNEST J STIDHAM WILLIE J TATE MALCOLM R TRUE JR ALFRED VIEL TERRY J WARD ALBERT G WINGFIELD JR
LEWIS C WUESTENBERG DENNIS G BENSON GEORGE J BURD ROBERT K CHASE TRAVIS R CROCKETT JACK H CURRY DARRELL L ENGLE
GARY L FAIN RICHARD J FORTE THOMAS J HOECKELBERG
WALLACE GOING GERARDO H GONZALES DWIGHT HODGES GARY L HOGAN HERBERT E ING III
DAVID M MCCORD RICHARD R MEIGGS WILLIAM T OVERCASH DONALD W SENTMAN FRANCIS C SOLLERS
JAMES A TUELLER JAMES U WILLIAMS III DENNIS A BORLAND LEE M BROOKS CHARLES R BROWNLEE
EVERETT F COX KENNETH R DEVORE BOBBY B EDWARDS JIMMY C HESTER CHARLES H HODSON JR
BRUCE M JOHNSON CHARLES D MAURIN JAMES D OZBUN FREDERICK G PARKER JR JOHNNY L RICHARDS
ROGER A ROSS AMBROSE P TANASSO JR GEORGE L TATARYN EDWARD L VANDERPOOL ALBERT G VINSON
PATRICK L WOODS LOUIS A WUEST JR ROBERT A AMSPACHER PAUL W BAKER KENNETH M BRYANT
SANDY L HOOKER CHARLES D KING BOBBY S MALICHI THOMAS F O'DEA JR JIMMIE L ROBINSON RUSSELL L WELLS JR DAVID A JOHNSON
MARK S LUTES JAMES P MCCONNELL JON M RUMBLE
ALBERT W MCKINNEY JR SYLVESTER ROACH LOUIS W ROBERTS KENNETH D SHOOPMAN IRVIN WALKER
THOMAS D WALKER JOHN W BAKER JR LOUIS A BARASH BARRY M BARBER LARRY M BARTELL
CHARLES R COOK EDMUND V CUDNIK JOE L EMERY DARYL L ENGLISH LARRY E FOSTER
THOMAS HAYES THOMAS L LEWIS FAGATOELE LOKENI WILLIAM E MAXWELL STEVEN D WILKERSON
ORLANDO MEDINA KENT D PIERCE JEAN W PUCKETT EDWARD J STANKEVICH DAVID A UECKER
R W GIPSON GERALD WOODS JOSEPH ANTOGNINI III RONALD W BRUTSCHER GERALD D MARKLAND
VERNON T BULLIN FRANCIS D DONOHUE WILLIAM E FERGUSON REID E GRAYSON JR A W HOWARD JR
JAMES B ARTMAN ROBERT G KIMBLEY WILLIAM E MCDONALD JR ISMAEL MENDEZ JR DENNIS E MICKELSON
GERALD G MCGINLEY WILLIAM E MCGUIRE STEVEN J PERRY THOMAS P PETERSON STEPHEN C PONTY JR
RICHARD C PUGH CLYDE A REITER ALVIN W ROBERTSON DONALD J SHANG JOSEPH G TAYLOR

P A N E L 3 5 W

JOSEPH R TWIGG JR CLARENCE L WELSCH JR JAMES G WRIGHT SR VICTOR L AUSTIN
AARON A BARNES JR EDWARD J BOGGESS LEONARD E BRADFORD WILLIAM L BROWN JAMES A BUCKLEY
BILLIE BYRD JAMES I CUTLER SAMUEL V DAVIS ARTHUR J ELLIOT II JOSEPH E STRAWBRIDGE
EUGENE FELTS JR DENNIS W FISHER WILLIAM H HAUPT III CARL R HINKLE DAN N JAMES
CLIFFORD R JONES JR WILLIAM D KINDLE BARRY D KINGMAN JON P LA FRANCE JAMES J MORRISSEY
DAVID P NASH EUGENE L RATHMANN RONALD E ROBERTS ROBERT F SCHERDIN ROBERT F SCHERIDIN MICHAEL C SPOTSWOOD
WILLIAM S DE BOER HENRY J TEWS EARL D WAGNER GEORGE L BAILEY WALTER C BLACK JR
GARY W BOUGHNER JAMES R BOYLE ELTON B COLLINS ROBERT E COUCH ALLEN S FARNHAM
JERRY D GIBBS MARC C GORHAM JAMES R JERSON LELAND S MCCANTS III ANTANAS A PRIZGINTAS
RONALD L SHATTUCK MARK A SMENYAK ROGER D SPRINKLE STEPHEN O WHITE REYNALDO ARENAS
FREDERICK N BONNER ANTHONY P BUSCEMI STEVEN C CZARNECKI DOUGLAS A DUGGER JOHN J MCLAY JR
ROBERT E ENRIGHT RICARDO GALVAN ERNEST E GARRAHAN STEVEN E HESLER CHARLES A JACKSON
JOHN O NACY JAMES J BRITT JOHNNIE D KNIGHT BYRON L NOTT JR MARTIN G SAUBLE JR HARLAN SECRESS
ROGER L BROWN ROBERT H SINCLAIR JR FRANCIS C SULLIVAN JR ROBERT M SULLIVAN KENNETH A TUTTLE
CECIL J CLACK LONNIE A DILBECK CHARLES S DUDDY STEVEN GALLEGOS JAMES M HALL
WAYNE L HAWES KEVIN M HURLEY ISABELO JIMENEZ-GONZALEZ CARL A JONES THOMAS F JOURDANAIS JR
DONALD G KING MICHAEL J MCKIBBAN JOSEPH NEMETH JR VICTOR W OSNESS EDMUND J SCHMIDT

BRIGGS K SICILIA CLAIR L WESTLAKE JR RODNEY J YANO LAWRENCE J ZELLER ARTHUR F BARTLETT
MICHAEL F BASTIAN DEAN F BOLHOUSE RICHARD J BOROVICK RONALD W FREEMAN CHARLES D GROH
ROBERT W JANTZ ROSS A JOHNSON JR LEE E MOORE JR MELVIN D MORGAN JR JAMES C NICHOLSON
WILLIAM J HAYES ROBERT J MORRIS MICHAEL PAGALING MURPHY PLEASANT JR JAMES A SCARBOROUGH
RICHARD C SEELY CHARLES E SELLNER BOBBY G STEVENSON RICHARD H SWEGER WILLEY E WILLIAMS JR
RAYMOND D THURMAN HAROLD WILBERTON JR PAUL W BARNETT CARL W BEERS JR ARTHUR L BELT
PETER BINSTOCK JR RONALD K BLOOM DONALD W BROWN GLENN E CASE ERNEST D DODSON
PHILLIP E BENJAMIN WILLIAM S CHILDERS JOSEPH P COLASURDO JOHN V COUTURE ELDRIDGE M DANIELS
JERRY DUNLAP WAYMON C ELROD HERMAN E GANT PATRICK C GOLLIHER CHARLES E HEINE
CARL L HOLDER CHARLES A JOHNSON JOHN H JONES THEODORE R KLINGENSMITH JOHN R KUNKEL
WILLIAM R LIDDYCOAT JAMES S MATCHETT GLENN P MCADOO RONALD S MCCRARY CLIFFORD T MULLEN
LARRY R MCPHERSON MOISES A REYES JR KENNETH L SHERMAN DENNIS J STANLEY STANLEY D WHITE
ROBERT M STEC WALDON J SWART MICHAEL J UNSINN GERHARD W VANDERFORD PHILLIP D WATTERS
WILLIAM E PARKER III TED A WHITE EDGAR W WILLIAMS JR FREDDY T WILLIAMS RONALD P ZENGA
JANIS ABOLINS ROY A AUBAIN DARRYL V BARNES LAWRENCE V BEATTYS FRANK E BRAWNER
TERRANCE L BROCK CHARLES J CATELLI RICHARD W DAVIS PAUL M EVANS GARY D FALK
KENNETH L FOUNTAIN DAVID O HERSHISER ALFRED D HILDEBRAND GARY L JAMIESON WILLIS L MIDGETTE
RALPH E ICKE II MITCHELL S LANE ROSS W LIVERMORE JAMES R MACY ALVIN E MILLER
BOBBY G NEELD WILLIAM H PLESS JOSEPH M RANKINS THOMAS A SHERMAN ROGER L TROXELL
STEVEN A WESSEL RAYMOND W BLANDIN ROBERT J CHALLENER MICHAEL CROWDER WILLIAM J ELSTEN
LLOYD A FEDER DAVID D FOSTER MICHAEL GALEA LEO A GEORGE ERIC S GOLD GERALD R ABBENHAUS JR
RONNIE P GRAYSON GERALD R HORRELL HORACE JONES RAYMOND P JONES KENNETH A MASON
LA V OENS CARL R PETERSEN HUBERT SINEGAL JR RAYMOND L SIP GREGORY H STANCIL
DAMIAN T TOMASKO DAN A VANEREM JOE J BRACKENS ROBERT R CHACON JOHN E FRANCEWAR
GARY W ARNAUD ROBERT L CHANDLER DANIEL B CHENEY ARTURO P GONZALES JAMES J GROMPONE
WILLIAM A HERNANDEZ DAVID L JOHNSON WALTER N KOSLOSKY CALVIN LEWIS JOSE L LOPEZ
JAMES F MALLOY DALLAS L PADGETT MARVIN C PEDERSON CHARLES F THOMAS TERRY L THOMPSON
RICHARD G THUNMAN RALPH L VOGELI JOSEPH WALTON CARL WASHINGTON PATRICK D BALLEW
ROBERT J BOWLIN KENNETH R CLOUGH CHARLIE A DAVIS TOMMY C DONOVAN II JOHNNY R VERASTIQUE
PAUL J FLAHERTY PAUL D FLEMING ALVIN W FORD GLENN J FORD III DAVID E GAARDER
RUSSELL J HEVERN GLENN E HOBART III VINCENT L JACOBS RONALD J LEAKE JR JAMES A LONG
ROBERT D MARTIN JAMES K MERRELL RONALD L MORRIS SHIRL B NANCE RICHARD D WINNINGHAM
CRAIG S OLSON ROBERT V PACK DAVID F PEAK RICHARD J QUINN DANA L RAGER
WAYNE H FISCHER CHARLES J ROBINSON GLENN W ROMERO DANNY R SCOTT STEPHEN L TRONERUD
LEO R MULLEN LARRY D WELSH JAMES L WOLTER JAMES A ASCHER STEPHEN H DEMERJIAN
GERALD F APPERSON CHADWICK M BARBER STEVEN D BARTMAN WILLIAM I BOUTON JR ROBERT D CASE
GERALD J DOWNEY KENNETH F DUPONT ALAN C GILLES ALLAN B HILL NORMAN F RIDLEY JON P ROCHE
DANA J KAEBERLE THOMAS B ORR JR WILLIAM R POLGLASE JOHN A RIVES JR
ANGEL L GONZALES-MADERA HARRY SIMS STEVEN SLUSHER BILLY E SMITH LARRY E STEPHENS
GERALD D STONEMETZ BILL F WILLIAMS JR JUAN BAUZA-PEREZ JAMES F BERRY ANTHONY J DE BONO
REX W BLISARD HUGH M BYRD JR JOHN R CAMPBELL STEPHEN B CARLIN DALE E COLLYER
ANTHONY C ARMBRUSTER RONALD L DAVIDSON BOBBY J DUNHAM JOE H ELLIS STANLEY S GASTON
FLOYD I GRANGER JR LARRY GREEN BRUCE B HARTMAN JESSE B HAYES LYNNFORD H HIGLEY
KEVIN O'BRIEN BENNY R PRESTWOOD WILLIAM M RIDDLE RICHARD C SEE MICHAEL J TESSARO
CRAIG J LOFTUS THOMAS J SHAFER WILBUR J SIEGRIST RALPH P TERRY TODD L WOOD
CARL T ALEXANDER RONALD K ASADA MELFORD K BLAKELY DONALD S CARTER JOHN C FITZWATER
WILLIAM W FORD TERRANCE D FRANCIS WILLIAM FRANCISCO JR PETER F GERSTENLAUER DANIEL L WESTLIE
RICHARD C GILLHAM JOE E GRAYSON ROBERT G HAYES JOHN L HENDERSON BERNARD G HITRO JR
MARTIN R JOHNSON DAVID K MANNING STEPHEN R MULLINS WILLIAM B OFFERDAHL GERALD R OLMSTED
DOUGLAS L RANSHAW ARTHUR R SPROTT JR CURTIS R STOCKLIN WILLIAM H SWISHER RUDY R TAYLOR
MICHAEL A FONTAINE DANNY G SCHWARTZ VINCENT VENUTI JR NORMAN L VON AHRENS
FRANCIS J BIRCHAK LEE R BRUCE JR THOMAS C BULLARD DANNY T CLARK ABRON E DAVIS JOHN P DAVIS
CHARLES K DAY CLYDE L DICKASON IRINEO GUEVARA ROCKY W HANNA DENNIS H HAYNES
JOHN T HINES CONRAD J KUFFEL ANTHONY L LEMA ROBERT LOVE HAROLD J SLINGERLAND JR
JOE MACIAS THOMAS C MANN DARRELL E MILLER DAVID T MOORE WILLIAM R PORTER JR
VAL L LAFON JOHN M ROUSCHER LEAVY C SOLOMON MICHAEL D THOMAS MATTHEW W THORNTON
EDWARD M TYSZKA DAVID M WILLIAMS LAURENCE D WORTHINGTON JAMES P BARRIOS DENNIS B FARRIS
DAVID T BREEN JIMMY CARTER DOUGLAS K CHUNG JAMES S CLOSSON CHARLES H DAVIS
LARRY G BRADLEY FRANCIS X DE VILLE GEORGE A EVANS BRIAN R FREDRICK RONNIE J FULLERTON
ALAN D HAVENS LAWTON A KEENER JAMES M KELLY DONALD R LUCAS ANTHONY P NASH
WILBERT OWENS MELVIN L REED JR RICHARD A RENNING CALVIN ROBINSON ARCHIE D ROGERS
JOHN B ROLLE JAMES T RUSH LESTER A STEPHENS EDWIN F TUBBS GABRIEL ZOLDI
GROVER W THOMPSON JOSEPH H WACKER TAKESHI YABIKU RICHARD E ZIMMERMAN JOHN F BALDWIN
JIMMY C BOWER GEORGE W BROWN JAMES D CRESSEY JR PATRICK T DE MARCO HARRY J DORSEY
VAUGHN O DOTY NORMAN D EATON PHILIP C ERICKSON PAUL E GETCHELL CHARLES E HIGBEE JR
DARRELL E HOLDING STEPHEN G KELLY WILLIE J MARSHALL JOSEPH C MARTIN DENNIS J MINKUS
WILLIAM MACFARLANE WILLIAM A MORRELL RUDOLPH PEARSON GLEN E ROUNTREE MICHAEL R SPANGLER
JAMES R ROBERTS ROGER D SHULER DEWITT STUDWAY JR TERRY L TIPPERY GARY P TRYON
EDDIE WALLACE GARY R WEATHERHEAD DAVID V ADAMS DWANE L ADAMS RICHARD ADIUTORI
GERALD O BAKER CLUSTER L BEARFIELD PAUL E BELANGER DANNIE L BIRD MICHAEL A BLAKEY
EMIL E BOADO JOSE B CAMPOS DONALD E COLLIER CHARLES N CORNMAN GARY W DUDLEY
WAYNE O FEINAUER DAVID A GAUCH NORMAN E GOODMAN IRVIN H HILL KENNETH L JONES

P A N E L 3 4 W

LYLE T MOORE MICHAEL T MORAN DANIEL L NAPOLI GILBERT G TORRES
DAVID A LAND JOHN M O'FARRELL GREGORY L RICE JACK D SHOCK PAUL A STONE
JOHN E WARREN JR TIMOTHY L WILLIAMS DAVID A WILSON JOSEPH G WILSON III RICHARD P YANCHUK JR
SCOTT J BAILEY RICHARD A BAKER BRUCE G BOWLES GERALD G BRADLEY JOSE R CANO
JAMES D CAREY JR PETER R CARROLL AUSTIN R CHENOWETH JAN P CHRISTENSEN JUAN E CORTEZ
FRANCIS H CORWIN JR STERLING E COX WILLIAM A CURRENCE NICKEY W CUTRELL HAROLD T DABNEY
DENNIS M FAIRCHILD EDWARD F GRANDPRE FREDERICK W GRESCH GARY L HEEMAN JOSEPH E HURNEY
STEVEN L JENKINS HAROLD L JONES FREDERICK D KANSIK JOHN F KAPP JERRY W LANEY
GARFIELD M LANGHORN TED E MCCLINTOCK WILLIAM C OLSON JERRY D PEARCE JAMES B PETTEYS
ROBERTO RAMOS STEVE R REISER RONALD D SLAYTON MICHAEL M SPARK NICHOLAS J SWIDONOVICH
DEANE A TAYLOR JR TIMOTHY M TELLEFSEN LARRY B THOMAS JOHN M TREJO CHARLES F WADE
MARVIN F WEHR ERMIL L WHISMAN WILLIAM L WILBURN JR MARION WITHERSPOON JAMES H DIECKMAN
DOYLE ATKINS ALFRED BAUER FRANCIS D CAMPBELL DAVID A CARLIN PHILIP B CURRIER
ROBERT D ARMSTRONG JOHN C DEATON PAUL R DEW RICHARD L DIXON JUAN V ESTRADA
FREDRICK L HOLDER DAVID L HOLDREDGE ALEC H HORN GEORGE F LAPAN GIUSEPPE MAGRI
HOLLEY D MATTHEWS HARRY A MATTINGLY JR RAYMOND C MINKS JOHN MIRICH WENDELL A MORRISON
CHRISTABOL T MCCLURE JERRY A MCFALLS JON O OSHEIM DAVID J RIDEOUT STEPHEN F ROBAR
STEVEN R ROWLES KENNETH M RUSSELL ALLAN N SCAVELLA EDWARD E STOCKWELL JR RAYMOND E TIFFANY
ERIK N RUDZIAK RANDALL J WICKLACE MILTON J WORRELL CURTIS S ANDERSON JOHNNIE M AYERS
JAMES D BAILEY WALTER E BARNES WAYNE F BOLTON CHARLES L BRIDDELL JAMES W BRIGHAM JR
PATRICK E BROWER FRANK H BROWNE II DANIEL CASSANO NORMAN L CATES RONALD I CRODY
RICHARD T CULP ALBERT J DAVIS JAMES G DAVIS ROGER A DIXON CLARENCE E ELLIS
GREG B ELLISON JOSEPH ESCAMILLA EDWIN J FICKLER RICHARD A FLEMING BARRY R FRANKS
JAMES M GAHAGAN DONALD A GUERTIN LEE R HARRIS DENNIS W HIPPO RUFUS W HODGES
ARELINN L JACKSON ROBERT J KUHLMAN JR ROGER L LANGFORD JAMES D LASER KENNETH W MEASELL
EARL L LEIGHTON VICTOR LOPEZ JUAN A MALDONADO WALTER W MARTIN STEPHEN W MAYNE
GEORGE A KURTYKA BRUCE S MCFADYEN RICHARD R MELADY MARK D MITCHELL JAMES M MONTEMAYOR
RONALD F NEAL MICHAEL F NOLAN JR ROBERT W O'NEIL GARY N OLSOWSKI BRUCE M REITER
JEFFREY D RUPP STANLEY K RYKACZEWSKI TERRY C SIMISON VICTOR A SMITH CURTIS F THORNTON
JIMMIE E TRENT JOHN H WEAVER PAUL J WILSON JEREMY R WOJTKIEWICZ JOHN R BARTLETT
RAYMOND G BEAM BENJAMIN P BENTON FREDDIE A BONETTI JOSE A CASTRO ROBERT F COADY
JACK R DANCE HAROLD M DAVIS JR EUGENE L DOTSON HARVEY J DOUGLAS JAMES F EISMAN
ALAN D ELA JAMES E ELLINGSON DANIEL J HOLT WAYNE H KNOWLTON FERRELL E MESSER
KENNETH W PETERS WILLIAM B ROLLINS JR ORMAN STONE TOBY W STREET DAVID H TOMIKEL
JERRY L WARBRITTON DAVID WILLIAMS JR RICHARD B APLAND DAVID R BALZARINI STEPHEN W MCKINLEY
DAVID L BELLERIVE RICHARD A CARLSON JOHN N COTTRELL MICHAEL L DORN DAVID C HALL
WILLIAM R CHRISTENSEN DENNIS B GREEN RONALD L HARRIS FRANK E HICKS CLARENCE M HILL
PAUL A HOLTZ BARRY C KELLENBENZ LEO L KOTKE JOHN T KUNF JR ROBERT T MILLER
WILLIAM R ADAMS CLARENCE MCCRANEY RONALD E MITCHELL JR LARRY W MORELAND CHARLES A PRICE
JUAN C QUINTANA GENE L SCHUKAR DONALD J SMITH JAMES L SMITH PAUL A BALLARD
JAMES F BOYCE THOMAS A FOREMAN JOSEPH J FUNK JIMMY L GREEN ENCARNACION A SUAREZ
MIGUEL HEREDIA OTIS KENNEY FRED D KESTER ALEXANDER KING RAYMOND J KOZIK
EDWARD H MANN LARRY A MARTIN TERRY L MARTIN DAVID E MORGAN ALFRED M QUIROZ
DAVID P OKER JOHN M PAGE ROY F PHILLIPS NORMAN W PIERRE WESLEY R POTTER
LARRY BROWN ROBERT W SMITH WARREN L SPINK RONALD E STOKER DAVID E TAYLOR
QUINCY H TRUETT ARTHUR WATSON RICHARD K ZIMMERMAN LOUIS V ALBI JR DONALD E ALLAN JR
DIEGO AMADOR VICTOR W BULLARD JR JOHN K CHILDERS BRUCE A CLARK THOMAS E DRAUGHN
DANIEL P GALLAGHER EDDIE G GAY GARY B GEHRKE ALTON G GIBSON MARVIN A GIES
GERALD L HABECKER TERRY N HARDIG RUSSEL H HEWIT JR HENRY E HOLDER JR RAYMOND J KREKELBERG
FRANK M GREER DALE L KAGEBEIN JAMES R KNOX JIMMY W LESAINE JOHNIE LOMAS
MILO G MAAHS KEN E MICLOSKEY JAMES L MILLER JOSEPH J MOLLOY JOSEPH L MOORE
TERRENCE W MCFARLAND VERNON L NELSON NORMAN J NOBLES JAMES H PORTER MICHAEL A RADZIECKI
ANTONIO REYES THOMAS V RHOADS MARIANO RIBILLIA JR ERNEST E RITCH RAY L SHARP
JAMES W SPIVEY ALVA R TERRELL WILLIAM J THOMPSON DONALD J TURNER ELLIOTT VELEZ-RODRIGUEZ
JOHN W VOWLES MICHAEL J WHITE JAMES J WILEY CHARLES H AYRES ROGER C BANGERT
GEORGE H BARGER ROY G BARNETTE KENNETH D BROWNLEE HARRY D BRUESKE JACK E CAMPBELL
GEORGE G CARLOUGH JOHN F DENEEN JR CORNELIOUS P DUKELOW II WILLIAM D FARRELL EARL K ZIEGLER
DENNIS E GEST DAVID F HEAD RAMON N HERNANDEZ DAVID C HOGAN JOHNNY S HOLT
WILLIAM C INGRAM ARDEN L KRUKOW JERRY P LAIRD THOMAS W LOUGHRAN RICKY L WIKLE

PANEL 34W *(Continued)*

FREDDY A MCGEE DANIEL J MINAHAN KENNETH W MOKUAU JR WILLIAM M MOOERS AUBRA E MORGAN JR
GARY L PAYNE VIRGIL J ROBERTS DOUGLAS A ROSS WILLIAM L STJOHN JAMES D STUESSEL
GILTON W JOHNSON MARK A TAYLOR MICHAEL L WARNER JOHN F WEAVER MICHAEL D WEEKS
MARVIN L ERICKSON JOSEPH A WILK JR TYRONE M WRIGHT PETER L ALAGNA LARRY M BECK
GERALD J BUDBILL KEITH N CANTRELL BENNY E DAVIS SYLVESTER DAVIS HARLON J GILMORE
DENNIS H GUTHRIE WILLIAM R HENDERSON ROBERT L LUSTER FRANK J MARCONI TOMMIE L MITCHELL
FRANK D MOORMAN JAMES R MULVANEY JR ARNOLD G OAKES EDWARD P OGDEN MICHAEL L OVIEDO
JERRY A PALMER HENRY E PEARCE II HERBERT L PIERCE JR BRUCE H RAWLING LEONARD D ROSE
ROBERTO RUIZ-PEREZ ARVID O SILVERBERG JR ROBERT R SLOPPYE EDWARD SMITH JR BENEDICT J TRIPODO
ANTHONY J WIECKOWICZ CHARLES R YATES JAMES A BURTON DOUGLAS M CADY DONALD R CARLYLE
OSCAR CORDOVA JAMES T GRAVLEY SCOTT C GRISWOLD PAUL R JORDAN MICHAEL A LEDERLE
JAY B LEVINSON IRVIN E MARTIN WILLIAM H MCDONNELL ROBERT C RIGGS BRUCE W WESTMORELAND
GLENN H ROLLINS RICHARD J SADICK RAYMOND W SULLIVAN JOHN O TAFOYA PAUL F TERSTEEGE
LLOYD I LUTTRELL GREGORY C TUCKER RICHARD R BELLWOOD LAWRENCE G BORQUEZ ALVIN R NARCISSE
JOE R BOSWELL ANIBAL S CABRAL JR SANFORD CLOSE JR JAMES R COPELAND BRUCE E DEERINWATER
WILLIAM C DEFER JERALD G DEWVEALL ROBERTO DOMINGUEZ JOHN J FOGARTY III RALPH L GLOVER
DENNIS A HOLZHEIMER AMIL JACKSON JR RALPH E JOHNSON STEVE E JORDAN STEVEN T KIEL
ROBERT M LANGSLOW FERNANDO L LOZANO JAMES A LUCKEY JOSEPH L MEADE RONALD D MELTON
ANDERSON D BOLTON JACKIE L MORRISON GORDON E MYERS CLIFFORD L NEWBERRY BRUCE D OAKES
RAMON F ORTEGA JR ULYSSES G QUEENER JR DAVID W RIEMER JAMES P RIGGINS JAY D RUMSEY
JOSEPH M SCHMOLKE FRANK D SMITHERMAN JERRY W TALLEY ROGER L VICKERS JON F WARMBRODT
CHARLES M WOODALL JR JOSEPH A AGUIRRE LORAN L BERGER SHERMAN D BRADFORD MARTIN J GIMBERT
CHARLES A BREZINSKI HENRY R BROADTMAN JR MARVIN COOK JR DONALD B DEAN DAVID P DOLAN
JOHN A BOYLE CHARLES D DRYSDALE RUSSELL L EQUI WILLARD J EVANS JORGE L GUZMAN-PAGAN
JAMES E HANNIBAL JACKIE V HENSLEY GARY D HUMPHRIES DOUGLAS D JANSSEN KENNETH P JOHNSON
ROBERT L JOHNSON IVAN W JONES LAWRENCE L KEISTER MARIO M LAGUNA ALAN K LANGER
RICHARD M LUBIN GARY W MAY JOHN F MEYER MICHAEL R MICHELS WILLIAM R MOHRHAUSER
WILLIAM D MURRAY JR WILLIAM R NEVILLE STANLEY H NEWMAN RODNEY W PAVAO CHARLES H WATKINS JR
CHARLES L PEDDY DAVID C RUSH MICHAEL J SCHICKEL LYLE W SCHROEDER DANIEL E SINGLETON
LAWRENCE W SOLTAN DAVID W STERLING BRADLEY E SUCHKA DENNIS E ULSTAD STANLEY F URBAS
JERRY L O'NEAL RUSSEL K UTLEY BRUCE R WELGE ROGER C BEALL RAYMOND F BEAUCHAMP
JAMES S BURNETT JR ROBERT M CAMPBELL RICHARD CLARK JOHN E CONGER JR WALLACE T CORBITT
NATHAN E CROUCH AUBREY G DAVIS CAMERON J DEVINE WALTER L FERRELL ROBERT J GNIADEK

PANEL 33W

PARKER K GODFREY THOMAS GRAHAM JR ANTHONY G HARBORD KENNETH D HAYS
HAROLD H HUNTER MARK N JACOBSON ELTON L JENNINGS JR WILLIAM J JONES JOHN D KEEL
ROMAN G MASON PARIS W MONTANEZ LEON D MOORE JAMES A NICHOLSON WILLIAM D NUHFER
JEWEL E MCCLATCHEY BERNARD G PURVIS EUCLIDES RIVERA STEVEN J ROUM DIOSDADO SANTOS-IZAGAS
RICHARD ARIAS ANDRE R BELLEMARE MICHAEL P BIEDRON DENNIS L BOLTON THOMAS G BURGE
ROBERT J CAMERON JERRY R COLE GARY E COLLINS JOHN W COWART ALVIN R GALE
LEWIS A CALLAWAY III THOMAS P DUGGAN WARREN R ESKRIDGE WILLIAM R GRAY JR PHILIP B JONES
DON R KLEIN DENNIS V LEE MERLE J MARTIN THOMAS L MORELAND ALTON D PERCIVAL
ROBERT E POORE JESUS QUESADA JOHN L REAGLE DANIEL P ROSE DARRON F ZICCHINO
JEROLD J SHELTON GARVIS K SIMONS CHARLES E SMITH GARY L SQUIERS STEVEN M STEINBACHER
CARL D PIPHER WILLIAM M THOMAS PHILIP A TRITSCH LAVALLE WALKER MICHAEL W BAILEY
GEORGE A BAKER LANNY W BANTA CHARLES D BULLARD WILLIAM E CAMPBELL WILLIAM R DOUILLETTE JR
HUGH E BEST III DAVID F CLEEREMAN JIMMY L CULWELL WILLIAM DALEY JESSE L ELLIS
DENNIS C ESHLEMAN JOSEPH E GREENWELL CAL T HAMMACK LARRY R HARRIS ROBERT E HOLTON
LARRY F HUNT JOHN R KAAWA DENNIS E KOCH FRANK M KOERNER SAMUEL D REEVES JR
DENNIS L KURZ FRANK LEPTRONE CHARLES M MCGOVERN WILLIAM L MOTT MIGUEL A PUENTES
DAN L JENKINS SAMUEL RODRIQUEZ ROBERTO A ROMERO BILLY J SIMMONS REYNALDO SOZA
LARRY A STEPHENS JAMES W THOMAS CARL J ANDRUS LUDWIG G BAUMANN LEON BEARD
EDWIN BLAKLEY JR JERRALD J BULIN ROBERT A FIREBAUGH STEVEN E FREDERICK MICHAEL B FRYE
LEE H HARRA GARY N ISAACS WILBERT D KANOSH HARPER B KEELER RONALD N SAMPLE
RICHARD A MOORE WILLIAM J MURPHY JOSEPH Y RAMIREZ JR JAMES E REEDER JAMES R RUSSELL
REMI H GREEFF JEROME J SCHLICHT RAUL L SEGOVIA L C SMITH JR CHARLES J STOHLMEYER
RONALD A VAN WAMBEKE HOMER WEST JAMES W AMBROSE III BOBBY D ANTHONY WILLIAM T ROBERSON
ROBERT L BLAIS RALPH L BLAUVELT DAVID E BROOKINS BOYCE D BURGETT HILDEFONSO M RAMIREZ
HARRY J CLOUD ROBERT D CODY THOMAS R DAVIS JOHN W EUTSLER DONALD M MICHELS JR
NORMAN A FREDA DONALD G HEIDER ROBERT E HENDRIX WAYNE R HOYLE EDWARD A LAMB
JOHN F DARBY III WILLIAM G LE CLAIR ROBERT E MILLER III WILLIAM P NOGIEWICH KENNETH E NORRIS
NORMAN R BETTIS RONALD CHAPMAN IRVIN W PROSSER JR CHARLES W RICHARDSON DAVID RODRIGUEZ
BOBBY D ROGERS JOSEPH B RUSH PAUL G TELLES LAWRENCE M WEICHE GARLAND G WHALEN
WILLIAM D WINKEL JACKSON D BARNES MELVIN E CLAY LARRY G CURTIS ANTHONY M CUSUMANO
CALVIN S DAY EDWARD L EBY RUSSELL H ELLIS JOHN H GORDON HENRY L GUTIERREZ JR
REGINALD M HERBERT STEPHEN R KUTSCHBACH JOHN M LAMANNA DAVID A LANNING STEVEN L LEACH
DONALD A LUNA NEIL H MACKILLOP TOM R MUELLER THOMAS E NICHOLS MICHAEL P RICE
LEE F LINCH RONALD L OSTENSON MELVILLE B ROSE III GEORGE S SANCHEZ FREDERICK SCHMITT
HENRY G SCHULTE JAMES E TAYLOR JAMES H WARD JAMES L WOODWORTH JIMMY E ABERNATHY
ROBERT L ANDERS LARRY E BOYER RICKY C BRADLEY ALLEN D CHESHIRE ALAN R RAMSEY
RELL CRIGGER JR LEROY B DANIELS ALBERT A DAVENPORT WILLIAM H DENNEY JR EDMOND Q WILSON JR
JAMES T FEENEY RAYMOND G FELD WILLIAM E FINLEY JOHN D FREPPON RENALD L GAGNE
JAMES GAINES JR CLIFFORD M GARDELL CHARLES J GIBILTERRA JR LAWRENCE F GREER WAYNE D GROAT
THOMAS R GROVER LINCOLN HARDY DAVID F HEISER DOUGLAS E HOFFMAN HOMER W HOLLISTER
CHARLES E INLOW GEORGE E JACKSON RANDALL L JENKINS CARL R KECK ASA MARTIN JR
ARTHUR A CALLISTER CLARENCE L MCKINNON JAMES J MORRISON LARRY W NEILL RAYMOND N RIVERA
JAMES M ROBINSON JOSEPH ROMERO PAUL C RUDY THEODORE M RUSH RONALD SABIN
DENNIS W SCHONBERG DALE W SCHWEFEL JOHN J SENOR KENNETH H SHELLEMAN LEONARD D SMITH JR
JERRY R DAVIS THOMAS T STAPLES II DANIEL A TRESSLER JR JAMES B WHITE RAY M WILLIAMS
RICHARD ANDRADE GLEN L ATKINSON ISIAH BARNES JR RONALD G BAUGHMAN DONALD C BERRY
BRIAN L THORNTON ROBERT A BYE MICHAEL O CASSIDY THOMAS CLARK OTIS J DARDEN ALVIN J DERRICK
RUSSELL T FANT GORDON D GARDNER GARY L GLEAR DENNIS J GULLA LEONARD H HOLMES
DALE A ECKOFF RONALD C JENSEN LESLIE A JERSTAD LESTER JOHNSON JR WILLIAM R LARKIN
WILLIAM F LESTAGE LARRY R MADDY MICHAEL S MASSONE RICKEY C MCCOY WILLIAM H MILLER
JOHN R POFF JON S RASMUSSEN JOHN R REBITS ROBERT E SHERLOCK JAMES E SKIPPER
ERNEST A SPONG MALONE B TEMPLE JOHN T WALLS DENNIS R WHICKER DAVID R AUGUSTUS
ROBERT L BALLARD MICHAEL A BARNES ROBERT E BEAUMONT BENJAMIN H BINEGAR JR JAMES M DONSTAD
STEVEN M BRITTON JOSEPH H BRUBAKER JR LEE E BURNOR JIMMY O CALL JAMES D CAMP
ANTHONY A BARBARINO KENNETH C CLIFTON KENNETH J DAVIS JOHN A DURHAM ROBERT L EATON
DONALD W EDNEY THOMAS J GILDOW OTIS GREEN ANDREW M HAGLAGE ROBERT K HALL
JOHN D HARRINGTON LAWRENCE E HOUCK II DAVID HOWZE JR ANTHONY A KOSTER GREGORY J NICCOLI
ROGER D KNUDTSON JAMES D OPSAHL ANTHONY L QUINN HAROLD R RICHARDSON JUAN RIVERA
JOSEPH J SMITH WILLIAM A TENNANT GERALD L THOMAS HOUSTON F THOMAS JAMES W TUCK JR
EDWARD P VANDERVORT STEPHEN C WALKER FRANKIE R WILLIAMS WILLIAM E BOEHM RAY L GOOD
WALTER F BURKE WILLARD H BURKHART JAMES L CLARK LOUIS J CLEVER JAMES V DORSEY JR
BRUCE B BERNSTEIN JAMES T EDMONDS JAMES L FRANCISCO ALVIN GORDON JR GERALD J JOHNSON
ALLEN J GREENE TONY L GRIFFITH GARY R HALEY ROBERT W HAMLIN TIMOTHY M HARRINGTON
WILTON N HATTON GEORGE E HAYWARD WILLIAM C HIX JR KENNETH E JACKSON GARY M JOHNSON
RODNEY H GOTT GEORGE L KELLAM CHESTER J KMIT HOMER M LYNN JR BENJAMIN MALDONADO-AGUILA
SALVATORE MANCUSO ROBERT W MCCLUSKEY CLARENCE L MCNEILL JAMES R MCNISH FRED A NEUBAUER
HARRY T NIGGLE THOMAS P NOONAN JR JOHN E NORDELL JR CHARLES R O'STEEN ROBERT E OLSON
OTHA L POOLE WILLIAM J PRYOR RUSSELL E REINEL JULIAN C RIVERA DEWEY D RUIS JR
DARYL G SCALF HUGH L SHERBURN JOHN W SPAFFORD WILLIE SUMMERVILLE JR PAUL E SWIGART JR
CARL J TANZOLA JR GLENN R URQUHART JR DANA L ZALESKI RONALD D BRIGGS EUGENE F CHRISTIANSEN
JAMES T DOUGLAS ROLAND L HARRIS LEWIS C JONES JR DENNIS M KEITH MICHAEL J SINCAVAGE
TERRENCE P KILBANE JOHN V KUCHTA RAFAEL MELENDEZ ROBERT C O'HARA WILLIAM S OGDEN
DAVID E PADGETT DAVID W PARKER DONALD E PARSONS MISTER REDDIX JR WILLIAM B REEDY
WILLIAM M HARRISON MARK SIEDENTOPF TROY N SITTON CHARLES I STANLEY CHARLES L SUTHARD JR
CHARLES J SWINT RODNEY D WISE RICHARD L ALLEN ERNEST E BARTOLINA JR CHARLES BEDFORD
WALLACE C BERGSTROM JR DWAIN L BIBEY GERALD R CARR EDWARD CLEMONS LARRY H COLEMAN
GARY J COYLE ROBERT M DAVENPORT RICHARD L DAVIS RICHARD A DELEIDI PATRICK E MCCULLOUGH
STANLEY D FARRO RICHARD B GARRETT ALFRED A GATES RAYMOND E GLOVER ORVILLE E HILL
PETER C HURLOCK PAUL R JARVIS GAYLAND E KEROHER EDGAR LEE CHARLES W MILLER JR
LINWOOD R CUMBO DONALD K MCLEAN CHRISTOPHER MITCHELL MICHAEL L MITCHELL RUSSELL E MOKE
CHARLES H OXENDINE STANLEY PATTERSON JAMES E PIERCE JOHN A PROMBO KENNETH E ROBERTS
RODNEY G SHANK JAMES R SMITH LARRY STEVENSON DARREL T SWANSON WALTER R TYRRELL
JAMES L WARD GARY N YOUNG LONNIE BRIDGES JAMES G BROWN GEORGE J CANAMARE
THOMAS E CLARK ROBERT D DE BOARD WARD C EVANS FRED R FRAZIER JR ANDREW P GARCIA
DAVID B GRAHAM DAVID P HAEGELE LAWRENCE C HAWLEY RODGER D HOWARD CHRISTOPHER S SMITH
LLOYD J HUCKS NATHANIEL IRVING PERRY D JOHNSON DONALD L KIPP ARTHUR L KLAUS
VICTOR R LANDES ROBERT O MAYHEW JAMES B MCKNIGHT STEVEN H NIPP HENRY L PALMER
ROBERT H PARCHER JR ALEXANDER A PEOPLES THEUS J POUND BRADFORD P SAWYER JACK E SCHULTZ
KENNETH C HESS ALVIN L SHADWICK JAMES M SKOMSKI RICHARD L SKOUBY MICHAEL J SPEAR
JOSEPH O STRICKLAND MANUEL G ULLOA CALVIN W WILKINS KERRY F WILSON RUSSELL B ADAMS
JOHNNIE W ATOR STEVEN R BAUER DOUGLAS J BEVERIDGE RONALD E BOYER CLAUDE E BRAGG
BENITO CONCHOLA WILLIAM T CUMBIE BILLY J CURBOW MICHAEL M DAVIDSON MICHAEL T DECKER
LYMAN R DITSON RONALD J FLOYD BOBBY G GAMBLE JOHN L HAWKINS JR JOE E HESTER
ROBERT L HETTINGER JERRY D JONES ROBERT S KNADLER GREGORY M LEINEN ROGER A MEYERS

PANEL 32W

LEONARD A MORSE CARROLL P O'NEILL RICHARD A PATON WILLIAM P WEIMER
WILLIAM R PROM MILTON A ROSS DEWEY I STRUEBING JOSE M TREJO JOHN L WEHR
THOMAS M NEAL MICHAEL J WILSON FRANKIE YOUNG JR JEFFREY R BRUCE JOSEPH K BUSH JR
ALBERT G CHRISTY JR RICHARD L COTTER LONZO S CUMMINGS BARRY V DETREMPE CARL E GOLDSMITH JR
JOHN T COLEMAN THOMAS R DICKEY HENRY R DUELLMAN DANIEL A FOSS ROBERT G GARRETT
THEODORE L GYULVESZI ANDREW HARBIENKO CHESTER E HILL ROBERT L HOWELL DALE R JACKSON
RICK V JENSEN DENNIS A JEZIORSKI JAMES R LOVELL EDDIE A MARTINEZ JR HUGER L PHELPS
FREDERICK J MCLAUGHLIN WILBUR L MILAM III MICHAEL L NESS SAMUEL J PARRISH WILLIAM A PHALP JR
JAMES R PHILLIPS FRED E PITTS MCKINLEY RICE JR CESAR R RODRIGUEZ JAMES W SMITH JR
CLARENCE C ADAMS DONALD M ASHTON JR MACARIO S BANDA THOMAS W BENNETT DUANE A DE VEGA
JOHN A BELFORD RALPH CANNON LARRY A COCHRAN DALE E CRICK RAFAEL CRUZ-CRUZ
DANNY J DODD JOEL L GABRIEL WILLIAM D GOUGER JR RONALD L GROVES ROBERT T HAMILTON
EDWARD M HOLTZMAN LONNIE E HOOPAUGH JAMES E KIRBY HAROLD W KROSKE JR ROBERT B MADDOX
RUSSELL L HARRIS BILLY G LANGLEY CHARLES K LARKINS HARVEY E LOTT LARRY J LUCKETT
MICHAEL J MCGLOTHLIN JAMES E MCKEE ALLEN D MULLER VICTOR C NAVONE JR FRED L PETTIGREW III
ROBERT L RAMSEY JR GARY R REED GARY E REYNOLDS LINUS R ROE MICHAEL W SCHUMACHER
JAMES STEPHENS MICHAEL P TAYLOR JACK D WADLEY LARRY K WHEELER RUSSELL D WOOLLARD
KIRK A WOOLLEY ROBERT J ZUKOWSKI ROBERTO ACEVEDO THOMAS L ARMITAGE WILLIAM D BAKKEN
RANDOLPH BROWN JR WILLIAM E BROWN VINCENT COLASUONNO WALTER N CRAWFORD JOE J MILES
GEORGE K HAMILTON BILLY F HARPER WESLEY P HENDRICKSON LELDON E HOCK JR ANTONINO RUGGERI
RICHARD D BARTHOLOMEW JR ROBERT W HOOK FRANK A JENSEN VERNE C KELLEY JOHN MATULONIS
ROBERT E GILMORE BILLY D MOORE DARIS W NICKELS RICHARD W RIALE SALVADOR D RIOS
WILLIAM G SCOTT JR MICHAEL A SHEPHERD ROBERT D SHOEMAKER STEPHEN A SHORTALL DAVID W SMITH
KENNETH R SAWYER RUBEN ANGUIANO DANA R BARKER JOHN D BENIEN JAMES BRANCH
THOMAS E CREEK DANNY K CROTHERS DENNIS E DAWSON THOMAS G FISHER DANIEL L HENRY
KEVIN L DAY PHILIP R FRANKIEWICZ RICHARD P GATES DAVID A HILL RICHARD M HILT
TERRY K JACKSON NORMAN A JENSEN DONALD N KENNON JOHN W MENDEZ ROGER C NESBIT
MARK L KLINE JAMES P MCKEON BEDFORD M MORRIS JR LYNN P NAYLOR JAMES T PENCE
GERRY A POLEGA DONALD B SCHROEDER WILLIAM R STOCKS ROBERT J TURNER LARRY G WHITEHEAD
DONALD E SCHWARZ JOHN E WEST JR GARSON F WHITE STEVEN L WISSINK RAYMOND J BALDAUF
DAVID L BELL CHARLES N BONDI STANLEY S CLARK GARY L DUBACH JEFFREY H FOULKE
ALVIN R FRITZ JOHN M HOLLOWAY CHARLES S JONES REGINALD D KING THOMAS W KUSTABORDER
LAWRENCE C LOOBY LAWRENCE H MOORE JAMES PALMER JUAN R PEQUENO LARRY J STEVENS
MARK F POWERS SALVADOR O RICARDO BILLY D ROBERTS THOMAS L ROSSI STEPHEN L SCHUMACHER
ROGER D LEWIS DAVID O SULLIVAN JUAN J WILSON JAMES P WITT MARC A WOODWORTH
EDWARD F BARRY JOHN E BOHNSACK BENJAMIN F BOLDING CHARLES BOYD EDWARD E COX JR
ERSKINE L CRUMP CLARENCE W DUNBAR JAMES T FIELDS BILL W GENTRY FRANKLIN B GILBERT
THOMAS S HAMILTON ALVIN J HO RICHARD R HURLIHE FRANCIS K KULBATSKI RONALD A MONISH
WILLIAM C NIEDECKEN DENNIS C NORTH HUBERT PALMER WILLIAM RIVERA-GARCIA RICHARD A WALSH III
WILLIAM S RIGGS KURT L STARKEY HAROLD R TYSON LEWIS R VALENTINE LEWIS W WARNER JR
BRIAN L WELLS FRED D WHITAKER WAYNE A WILCOX MICHAEL J WYMAN LARRY M ALCOS
STEPHEN BLANN THOMAS J CASEY JR THOMAS M CASEY JR MICHAEL R COON ROBERT DUNBAR
RALPH G DUNN WILLIAM H FARVOUR GERALD Q HANCOCK EDWIN H HARDESTY JR EARL F HOUCK JR
ERIC A FISHER CRAIG M HEMPHILL VERNON G KNUTSON KENNETH J LEWIS LONNIE D LOYD JR
HUGH R MCKINNEY GARY L MILLER JERRY L MOORE RICK A OLIVER ARTHUR L PAPALE
JOHN S PINNEY NELSON RAMIREZ JACK L RIGHTMYER DENNIS L RILEY ROBERT D ROGERS
NORMAND P PERRON HAROLD J VAN WINKLE JR ROBERT W WHITNEY WILLIAM M WOGAN JAMES W BELL
CHRIS F BRUNN MICHAEL A CLUTE PATRICK J DUGAN ROGER L ELKINS ROSCOE C GRAY JR
HAROLD H HLADIK DENNIS J KANE DICKIE G KEELER DONALD L KUJAWA RICHARD M KULAVIK
ROBERT J HALL KENNETH G LIEBHABER WELDON G LYNN CORNELIUS A MCCAFFERTY JR ROY E PITTS
THOMAS W SANDER CHARLES E SCHOOLCRAFT LEE V SILVER JAMES D SNYDER RUSSELL W WENDLER
REGINALD J RODRIGUEZ ULYSSES BATTLE ARTHUR L BROWN SR JOHN M BRUCHER JAMES V CAVANAUGH
RODNEY M CHAPMAN VIRGIL C COMBS JOHN P COOK CLEVELAND E DYKES RALPH E EBBS
IRWIN L EDELMAN CLIO C FEATHERSTON JR RODNEY R GREEN NATHANIEL L JOHNSON RONALD M NOWAK
MARLIN M JONES JR CARL E KELLY JR MARWICK L KEMP ROBERT I MEEKER PHILLIP E MINTON
STANLEY M JEROME DAVID Q PATTERSON RONALD L RAKER PATRICK J RONAN EDDIE R SCHIMMELS
THOMAS M SKALLY EDWIN A ACKERMAN JR WARNELL E ATEN THOMAS M BLACKWELL LARRY A BODELL
DAN R BYHAM JAMES W DALTON HOWARD L EARLY DANIEL J FOSTER GARY R GENTH
CHARLES M DOWNS CHARLES FOULKS JR RICKIE N GUNDERSON RONALD J HILLMAN CHARLES R JAMES
CHARLES D JONES JOHN A KUCICH CHARLES R MAIN ABRAEL MALDONADO E G MAYS JR
WILLIAM O'SHEA II JOHN W POE DAVID A SCHNEIDER JONN J SEERY RICHARD L WAYCASTER
RONALD D SHAFF BARRY W SMITH ROY D STOFFREGEN STEVEN D TANNER ELTON R VENABLE
MICHAEL T ROWE MACK H WILHELM ROBERT G WIMP HOWARD E WRIGHT MICHAEL D ADAMS
ALAN C BURTNESS QUENTON L CHRISTENSEN THOMAS R DANIELS MARVIN A DE VAULT WILLIAM T FRANKE
DENNIS W CRIPE MANFRED W FITZGERALD EDWARD L HANDY FRANK R HOWE EARNEST L KAUFFMAN
DAVID G KING BILLIE J MCCLURE ANDREW L MILLS DAVID P NEISLAR EDDIE V OLIVER JR
ALLEN E OLSON RICHARD E PARKER ROGER L PIFER JUNIOR F RONIGER MICHAEL WILSON
LARRY T ROSS HERBERT H STAUFFER HAROLD SULLIVAN ALFREDO J VILLANUEVA WAYNE A WHARTON
ALLEN C YEOMANS III FLOYD S ATOLE GROVER C BOWEN ALLAN B CALLAWAY RANDALL M CARLTON
HAROLD E CARTER ROBERT D CHRISTIANSEN HOWARD L CLACK RONALD J CORBIN MICHAEL G DINKINS
RONALD L GARNER PHILIP A JOHNSON CHRISTOPHER W MEAGHER DONALD W MILLER RICHARD J RIKER
ISMAEL LAUREANO-LOPEZ JAMES W PENDERGRASS PETER P POLAK EDWARD D POWERS DALE E RAUBER
CLARENCE ROBINSON JR RICHARD J ROCHACZ HARRY Q ROSE VICTOR S SCHLICHTING WILLIAM B SCOTT
HERBERT H SWEAT JR PETER S TIMMERMAN GEORGE D TINKO JUAN M VELEZ-VILLAMIL EVERETT N WILSHER
WOODROW W ADAMS WILLIAM J ALLEN HOY E AU JOHN R BAIRD JR LARRY J BOEHM
EDWARD W BOLAN MORRIS BRANNOM II FRED BUTLER III DAVID A CHACON NORMAN P CHITTESTER
WILLIAM J CHRISTMAN III MICHAEL L CRUSE JOHN F DEDEK GEORGE E DUSCH ROBERT D LAW
MIGUEL A GONZALEZ-RIVERA ALAN R GRAHAM EDWARD S GUM RONALD L HARKEY LEE R HERRON
RICHARD P HODGES ANTHONY L JOHNSON VICTOR M JOUVERT WALTER A JOYCE CARL N KOZMA
DALE C FISHER FREDERICK W KULICKE III NATHAN C LUNAPIENA CHARLES MACKO DANIEL W MARGRAVE II
ALBERT MCCULLOUGH GEORGE MEERDINK JR LAWRENCE P O'TOOLE II WINGFIELD PAGE JR ROBERT SELLERS
DONALD E PAXTON WAYNE E PEARSON DAVID J PELLOSMA JOSEPH H PIERCE JR RICHARD POLLARD
VICTOR G MCCALL ALFRED A PURVIS BRUCE E ROBINSON RANDAL L ROGERS DONALD V SALLER
LESLIE H SHAFER ALLEN THOMAS JOHN W THOMAS BOBBY D TIMMONS GERALD WRAZEN
ROBERT W TOPHAM JR KEVIN E TWEEDLE MICHAEL A VOSS RHENA C WEBSTER RONALD C WEEMS
WILLIAM B TARRANCE ALONZO W WIGHT DOUGLAS J WINCHELL JR TOMMY L WYATT ROBERT M YSGUERRA
GUY F ABBOTT KYLE A ADDAIR WILFORD H ALDERMAN ARTHUR J ANDERSON HENRY L ASHFORD
HOWARD ATKINSON OSCAR P AUSTIN JAMES A AZBELL LARRY D BARKER CARL F BELDING JR
ANDREW L BELFIELD DAVID E BELVER ROBERT L BENNETT HOWARD S BIESANTZ RANDALL L BROCKWAY
JAMES BERENDS ROBERT BLAUT JR MICHAEL J BRADY HAROLD G BRETON MARVIN H BROWN
THOMAS M BROWN JOHN C BROWNING JOHN L BRUMBAUGH JR ROBERT R BUCK JOHN A BUSCHKE
BILL D CALLAHAN CLYDE CALLAHAN RAYMOND W CALLAHAN JR JESSE D CARPENTER CHARLES O CRAIG JR
CHRISTOPHER CASIAS EDWIN D CASWELL PAUL F CLARK RAYMOND A COLE BENNYE W COWLEY
MARVIN D CANTERBURY KEVIN F CREGON THOMAS H CROOK JAMES E CUMMINGS RICHARD J CURRY
CURTIS DARRISAW GEORGE L DAVIS JR JOHN H DAVIS PAZ A DE LA DONALD M EDWARDS
WILLIAM W DICKEY DUANE A DOWNING MICHAEL J DROBENA DAVID W DUNFORD EDWARD J DUPERE
HENRY D CUSTEN ROBERT D EICKLEBERRY RANDOLPH EUBANKS WESLEY E FLANIGAN EUGENE J GARRITY JR

PANEL 31W

DANIEL W GLEASON EARNEST W GRAHAM HERBERT R GRANT GARY D JUDD
EDWARD L GRIGGS III GERALD W GWALTNEY DONALD W HALLOW WALTER S HAMNER LEE A KEITH
GREGORY E HANKINS ROOSEVELT HARDY JR LARRY A HARTIGAN ROBERT W HARTSOCK KENNETH R HEIFNER
NORMAN M HARMON PETE G HECKWINE THOMAS M HIDAY DOUGLAS L HINKLE WILLIAM R HODGE
ROBERT A HORCAJO CALVIN L HOWELL JR JERRY R HOWERTON NATHAN E HULLETT GARY E JOHNSON
PHILIP GIGLIO KENNETH R JOHNSON ROBERT L JONES MARTIN R KEEFE EDWIN T KEEN
FREDDIE R GUINN JOHN J KENNEY ANDREW J KIEFHABER GREGORY L KOUPE WOLFRAM J KRETSCHMANN
KEITH T LANDERS WILLIAM R LAWSON JAMES W LEAF ROBERT M LEE GREGORY T LINDSAY
HAROLD S LONERGAN DENNIS J LORENZINI ROBERT M LOUGH JR LOUIS V MARCIANO RICHARD S MARK
JOHN E MARPO ANDREW M MATTIE EDWARD D MERKLE PHILIP C MILLER JR GARY R MIRACLE
PAUL J MITCHELL ROBERT C MORA RONALD G MOSS PAUL W MOTLEY WILLIAM E NULL
MICHAEL R MCCABE RONALD MCINTOSH CHARLES L MCMAHAN REID M NANEY WINFORD A NASS
JESSE B MONTEZ FRANK W NELSON JR ORLAN M NELSON DALE A NICHOLL CHARLES K NOWELL JR
JESSE M NUNEZ JOSE A OLLIVIER RICHARD E OLSON CHARLES R ORNSBEY STEPHEN J PASTULA
GERARD F PAULSEN RICHARD A PENKE JOHN A PETERSON LAWRENCE POET JAMES B RICE JR
DANIEL L POFF CHRISTOPHER D PRATHER THOMAS R PRESTON THOMAS G PRICE WILLARD F PROCHASKA
NICHOLAS I PYLE VICTOR A RABEL STANLEY M REED JAMES S REYNOLDS JR MYRON E RHUE
THEODORE J PAWLOWSKI JR CARL J RIEDERER HAROLD K RING RICHARD P RITZLER FRED L ROACH JR
JAY L ROBBINS JR JON P ROBBINS HENRY M ROBINSON JR DUANE C ROMEO CLARENCE D RUSSELL
GENE L SALZER RONALD L SANDERS BOBBY SANDERSON WILLIAM H SATTERFIELD JOHN S SHOEMAKER
RANDALL F SCHWARTZ LARRY R SHORT DARRYL W SHUSTER SCOTT M SIBSON MICHAEL E SIDOR
GEORGE L SILVA DONALD H SISSON ADRIAN J SMITH JIMMY V SMITH RICHARD C STEVENSON
JERRY D SPRADLIN LARRY D STAGGS JOHN J STAHL JERRY W STANBERRY EDWARD B STEELE
RONALD L SMITH KENNETH E STEINHEBEL THOMAS G STEVENSON JR HENRY R STROBO WALTER STURGEON
MICHAEL J STONGE RAYMOND SUAREZ JR DAVID H SUNDQUIST RICHARD J SWEENEY ERNEST W SWONER
JOSEPH G TARASZKIEWICZ DE W TAYLOR JERRY L TAYLOR DAVID E THAXTON FRED L THOMAS JR
FREDDIE L TIPTON PAUL H TOBER ROGER M TYNER JAMES D TYUS JR BILLY L UNDERWOOD
JAMES F UTTERMARK JOSEPH M VAN DANIKER KENNETH E WADE WOOTS E WADKINS JOHN F WALKER
JIMMIE S WARREN JOHN W WASHINGTON LESTER W WEBER KELLY W WEITZEL JAMES L WHITE
CHARLIE L WILDER RONALD J WILKINSON WILLIE L WILLIAMS CHARLES E WILSON JOHN S WILSON
RAY G WILSON WILLIAM R YASKANICH JOHN P ZIEGLER JAMES C ALDERIDGE XAVIER A ARVIZU
JON BAILEY MORRIE C BARBER LARRY L BROOKS THOMAS J BURGESON MERLE F BUTLER II
DANIEL F CAHILL CHARLES E CARPENTER GILBERT M CHAVEZ WILLIAM C CLINGER III DANIEL COLEMAN
DUANE M DAVIS ROY H DAVIS VASILIOS DEMETRIS MICHAEL B DUFFY JESSE R ELLISON
STEPHEN D FACCHINI LEWIS M FORMAN THOMAS A GARMAN HARLAN L HAHN EDWARD M RUDITYS
JAMES K HALL TIMOTHY J HALL EUGENE S HANCOCK FREDDY P HEUGEL JOHN R HILL MICHAEL N HUBERT
VICTOR C JAUER TOMMY JOHNSON WILLIAM J LEVETT HAROLD S LEWIS ADALBERTO R VERDUGO
ANGUS W MCALLISTER JR BYRON D MCQUINN JIMMY L MYERS JAMES NICKENS JOHN C ODLE

RICHARD W FORD JOSE R OVERMAN-RODRIGUE MARVIN L POSPISIL WILLIAM E PRICE ALAN M ROYSTON
LEROY E SHELDON ROBERT L SHIRODA JR RICHARD L SHUCK GAROLD R SIMMERS GARY W SMITH
JOHN G JOYCE TERRY D TAYLOR WAYNE L THOMAS RONALD T VARNEY JOSEPH A WEBER
EDWARD J WOLFENDALE CLARENCE J BABIN JR JEFFREY M BARRON ARTHUR W BARTLETT SR LOUIS F GRIFFIN
DOUGLAS B BASTYR MARTIN T BATCHELOR JR HAROLD D BILLER ROBERT H BROGAN RICHARD C BRUNN
KEITH C BUCKINGHAM MICHAEL C BURNS MICHAEL T CALANDRINO FRANCIS W CODY THOMAS N GROSE
ROBERT A COFFEY CLIFFORD D COMBS BRUCE W CURTIS WALTON G DALEY KENNETH DAVIS
ODELL DICKENS LAWRENCE G DONALDSON SAMUEL A EKLOFE RAYMOND L FLINT DOUGLAS B FORSBERG
HOWARD T FOX JUAN GASTON KENNETH R GILLIAM JOSE L GONZALEZ PHIL D JOHNSON
ARTHUR L ANDREWS FRANKLIN D BRYAN JOHN T HARE RICHARD W HEIM ARNOLD HILB-SCHELEIN
CARL W HILL RUSSELL J HOLLAND RODGER D HOLMES ERNEST C HOWLE WILLIAM H HUNT
STEVEN V GARCIA LEMUEL ISABELLE MICHAEL L JENKINS ROOSEVELT JOHNSON JR WILLIAM B JONES
HARRY D KELLAR NORMAN W KELLUM ROGER M KITTLESON CHESTER J KOZDRON JAMES F LAIRD
WALTER L LAMARR RICHARD L LANCTOT DONALD R LEWIS JAMES D LOGAN JOHN LOPEZ
MARION W LYONS SAMUEL C MACON DAVID A MALLORY CLARENCE S MILLER TOMMY N MILLER
ROBERT A MCCARTHY THOMAS H MCGRATH WILLIAM D MORGAN JOSEPH B OLIPHANT JR FRED L RICARD JR
THOMAS E PARKER JAMES D PESCHEL VICTOR L POOR CALVIN R PRATER JAMES E SCOTT
PATRICK J MURACA GERALD PRZYBYLINSKI RANDOLPH R RAMSEY FREDERICK R RATLIFF JR ROYCE E ROE
JAMES M ROOT DAVID L RUTGERS ROBINSON SANTIAGO BRUCE A SAUNDERS JOSEPH R SCHNELL
PORFIRIO M OVALLE JR WALTER P SEEL JR ALLEN M SHARP LARRY J SIKORSKI CAREY W SMITH
JAMES E SMITH WILLIE F SMITH JOHN M SULLIVAN JAMES K SUTTON JAMES E TITUS
NORMAN R SURPRENANT DAVID E THOMAS ROBERT H TRAIL III JAMES E TUCKER DONALD K WALSH
SAMUEL R WALL TRUMAN J WALSH THOMAS C WARNER RONNEL L WAUGH GEORGE W WELDY JR
JAMES E WELLS LARRY A WESSINGER JOHNNY G WILLIAMS JAMES E WISE LARRY L WOOLUM
MICHAEL L ZAPPIA GERALD D ZAWADZKI VINCENT N BANKS IRIA D BARNETT STEPHEN S NIEDERHAUSE
JOSEPH F BAUER JR TIMOTHY P BAUER CHRISTOPHER BROW JOSEPH K CARROLL EUGENE COPELAND
CHARLES E CLAY GEORGE P COLLINS HOBART E COVINGTON DAVID G CUMMINGS LAWRENCE J DEFELICE
DAVID W DENLINGER RICHARD L DESPER JIM L DICKSON ALBERT ERSKINE DENNIS K MILLISON
JERRY R FRAZIER MICHAEL J FRENCL GORDON P GIPNER MANUEL GONZALES LEON R GOODALE JR
DUANE A HIPPLE DAVID C JACKSON RONALD D JEWELL RICHARD M JOHNSON SAMMY E KINNAMON
LARRY C KOSKI CHARLES J KURTZ KENNETH A LAVINE JR DONALD C LE BLOND WARREN G LIZOTTE JR
JERRY L ALFERINK DANIEL G ELY WILLIAM C MATTHEWS SALVADOR L NORZAGARAY RAYMOND YAZZIE
JAMES E PALMERI VAN H PEARSON THOMAS V PILSON HENRY L QUIGLEY RONALD L QUIGLEY JOHN R TENNANT
GLENN B RAO ALFREDO RIVERA ROBERT L ROEBUCK JAMES W SIMMS TERRANCE L SNYDER
EDWARD C SOUTHERN BARRY G SOWDERS BENJAMIN F STOFFER II ISAAC STRINGER JR
JIMMIE R TICE FREDDIE USHER RICHARD A WALLICK JOEL K WATKINS RICKEY J WHITEHEAD
RAYMOND C MROCZYNSKI DANIEL A WIDOMSKI WILLIAM B WILSON THOMAS E ADAMS MARVIN D AVERY
MACK C BOBLETT ROBERT A BROTHEN EARNEST J BUCKELEW JOSEPH F BURINDA JR BERT E BURTON
SAM W BUSBY CECIL F BUSH MARSHALL L CALENDER JAMES P CARNEY JR WILLARD G COEN
TERRY L CRAWFORD ENRIQUE S CRUZ PAUL A CUMBERLAND CRAIG N DE MICHELLE ELROY MORRIS
CHARLIE M ELLISON JOHN H ERBES DONALD J FISHER RONALD J GEBBIE MIKE M GODINES
GARY V HALL THEODORE S HAMNER III JAMES P HANLON DAVID W HAWRYSHKO DONALD M HORTON
DONALD M JENNINGS JEROME M JONES GLENN K LEINO ROBERT P LEVIN JAMES T LIEBNITZ
HENRY MADISON JR ADOLFO MARTINEZ MANUEL MARTINEZ DANIEL J MINOR EARL T MOORE JR
BRUNO W DE MATA WILLIAM H MOORE RALPH E NATHAN DANIEL L OVERRIGHT ROBERT E PETSCHKE JR
WILLIAM S POTTER MARTIN R POWERS PERCY I PUGH LARRY S RAINEY DONALD R RHODES
MICHAEL R ROMMEL MELVIN L SELLERS MILTON SHAPIRO CRAIG E SWAGLER WILLIE L WALLACE
RUDOLPH SWOOPE CHARLES A TAVARES LOUIE J TROUTT JR GARY L VANDERBROOK DAVID S WHITMAN
RONALD P YUHAS LYLE D ZACHER DENNIS M ADAMS RONALD J ALLEN MARVIN D BARNES
IRWIN BEYDA DONALD L BLANKENSHIP WILLIAM J BRENCICH CHARLES BROWN ROBERT D CALHOUN
ELVIE BELL JR CLIFTON L BROYER WILLIAM J BRUCE JOHN A BURICH JR RICHARD A BURNS
ROBERT M COOKSON EUGENE COUTURIAUX JR JOSE CRESPO LARRY B CURTTRIGHT RICHARD M DONLAN
VERNON W EAST GEORGE F EVANS JAMES T FERNANDEZ RUSSELL D FLANAGAN ROBERT J FRANKOWIAK
CARTER J FREUND WARREN R FURSE JERRY W GOBBO DENNIS A GROFF WILLIAM A HANNA
JERRY D HARSSON HOWARD T HAUGHT JR WILBUR L HICKS DAVID K JACOBSGAARD GARY L JOHNSON
JAMES J JOHNSON EDWIN A KEEBLE JR RICHARD W KEITHLINE DONALD J KRAJEWSKI VITO VITRO
GERALDO MARQUEZ THOMAS A MCADAMS JERRY S MCDONALD BURT J MEYER JR STEVE MIRICK JR
DAVID A PARKER BRUCE E REED PHILLIP E ROSSON EDWARD C SANCHEZ JOE B STUART JR
RONALD L KIELPIKOWSKI BYRON L TENNANT STANLEY E UR GLEN O VENET DONALD C VOLTNER
JAMES L VROOM MICHAEL C WHALEN JAMES W WRIGHT DAVID YBARRA ROBERT J COSTA
CALVIN E ALEXANDER DANIEL D BRUCE THOMAS L BURTON CLYDE W CAMPBELL RICHARD A CARAPEZZA

PANEL 30W

RAY R DAVIS LEONARD P DEINLEIN RAYMOND R DELGADO ERIC T DUFFER
JAMES A CRAFT DAVID A FLOYD LOUIS A GEORGE JOHN B GIBSON JR LARRY G HIGGINBOTHAM
RODNEY M GOODE JOHN P GRIMENSTEIN JR JIMMY R GROSS RUDOLPH GUARDADO EDWARD L HARRIS
THOMAS L GAINES JR MICHAEL A HARVEY DALE G HELGESON CHARLES M HOBBS GEORGE V JMAEFF
WENDELL R KELLER JOSEPH R KING JR DAVID E LOVEGREN GREGORY A MARVIN FRANK WILDER
JOHN W MASSEY JR DONALD R MAYBERRY GEORGE M MAYS JR ROBERT P MENNINGER VIRGIL K MERONEY III
LAWRENCE W PORTER HENRY PULLUM JR WILLIAM D RYAN JOHN C SCHIFFHAUER DAVID E SCHULZE
STEVEN R SEGURA JOHN E TIPTON ALVIN C TOOMBS JR WILBERT M WEBSTER MOUNCE E WEST
DOUGLAS J MARKOVICH BEN H WILKINS JR DENNIS E WISNIEWSKI DONN P ZARINA WARREN L BEACHAM
JOSEPH L BIDDLE CHRISTOS C BOGIAGES JR ROGER C BURNHAM HENRY CALDWELL JR DENNIS S COKER
ANTHONY B CURCI CARL S DOUGLAS PETER A DUPERRY BRIAN R ESTES EDWARD L GILLIARD
ROBERT E DIEHL WILLIAM A EVANS CLYDE W GANZY ANTONIO M GARCIA MICHAEL D HYATT
FRANK P EVANGELISTA DAVID GOMEZ-BADILLO DAVID L GUILLEN ROBERT L HARTER ROBERT L HEINMILLER
RICHARD W KULPA GEORGE R LOVELLETTE MICHAEL F MAY DOUGLAS F MENARD MARIO J MENDIAS
JOHN J MEYER JOHN A PETRIC CARL L RADTKE GEORGE H RIPLIE THOMAS D THOMPSON JR
FRANK MESZAR III GORDON L SARGENT JR HAROLD J SMITH KENNETH L STRITTMATER JAMES R TAYLOR
RAYMOND E TOLSMA WALTER B TULLY JR DAVID F VAN DEN HEUVEL JOHN E WALTERS JASPER M ALEXANDER
RAUL ALVARADO JR LYNN D ANDERSON MICHAEL E ANGEL MELVIN L APPLEBURY PHILIP L BAKER
BILLY H BEST GEORGE M BINNS PAUL J BUCZOLICH FRED D BURTON JOSEPH L FREEMAN JR
ROBERT J CAMPBELL RONALD F CHRISTIANSON DENNIS J COLL GEORGE COLUNGA PAUL D COOKE
HAROLD E CROWDER JOSEPH N DECKER AUSTIN I EDWARDS MICHAEL ENGLAND HAROLD E MUSSELMAN
JAMES C BURKS CHARLIE FIELDS RODGER D FORCE EDWARD L GARCIA ROBERT E GODING
RUPERT W GOEBEL JR GLENN R GORDON ROBERT E GRIFFITH HARRY T HARRISON MANUEL HIGUERA
JEFFREY K GOSS SAMUEL N HART JOHN L HEISER STEVEN M HICKMAN BARRY D HORTON DAVID J PUGLIESI
WILLIE J HUDSON DENNIS R ISOM DAVID A JOHNSTON JAMES M KALTER KENNETH R KENT
ARLIN W KOEHN JACOB C LAAN VERNON E LAIL JR AUSTIN C LANE HARRY B SEEDES III
WILLIE E MADDEN LEO J MANGOLD GENE O MERRIWEATHER DEAN W MOEHRING RANDY R MUELLER
CALVIN EDMUNDS DARRYL E MCCARTNEY JOSEPH B MCCARTNEY WILLIAM C NINOW DUANE C PAEPKE JR
JOHN L PRATT WILLIAM T RECTOR JR GEORGE R ROBINSON JOE G RODRIGUES JR DONALD L RUDD
WALTER W RUDOLPH MICHAEL D SAMS LAYNE M SANTOS WILLIAM J SCHAAF THOMAS K SCHAEFER
ROY E LYNN JOSEPH SCHMICH JR GERALD W SCHULTZ VERNON E SCOTT DAVID A SEIBER
RONALD J SHIER DELBERT L SINGLER JR WILLIAM M SMITH WILLIAM C STINSON JR BRUCE W THOMPSON
RAY T SHAUM JR LESTER R STONE JR PHILIP J TAYLOR WAYNE W TEEPLE RONALD C THIEX
GLENN A TOMPKINS RONALD J VANDENBERG WILLIAM O WALTERS OLIVER K WEBB GEORGE P WHITE
ALFRED M WILSON WILLARD A WIMMER VENCEN ACKERSON JEFFREY C BARTHOL HENRY BETHEA
FRANK W BOSSONG ARTURO A CAUBLE RICHARD L DIEMLER MICHAEL S GARRETT JOSEPH A GOODSON
ARTHUR S HILL JR PHILIP M HUNT ROBERT C JORDAN LAURI KANGRO WILBUR J MILLER JR
ROBERT A MCGILL LARRY MURDOCK CHARLES R OUTLAW JR CLYDE E RAINS BENJAMIN J RAWLINGS
WILLIAM C NORTHINGTON RONALD P RUSSELL VICTOR R SCHEELER FRANK SHARTZ JR DOUGLAS R SLEDGE
ROBERT L SLOAN CHARLES L SMITH RYUZO SOMMA JOHN A SORRENTI DAVID J WARCZAK
FREDERIC N ASH JUAN AYALA-MERCADO NELSON BEY BOYD L BRAKE EFRAIN FIGUEROA-MELENDE
GEORGE L BROWN GEORGE A CALLAN MICHAEL A CLAUSE JIMMIE D COOK JACK P DE LANGE
PETER F DE WILDE JR STEVEN W DUNDAS MICHAEL A DUNNEBACK RICHARD F DUSSEAU WILLIAM T HARRIS
WAYNE G BERNOSKA ANTONIO GARCIA HAROLD S GLADNEY JIMMIE L GORDON ALLAN R GYORE
DAVID C FERGUSON EDWARD R HICKEY EARL W HIMES DAVID P JACOBS GARY F ROLFE
ROBERT H JENKINS JR CARLTON J JOHNSON SANDERFIERD A JONES LARRY G LACAEYSE ALFRED LALLAVE
LAVERN M LAMEY GERALD B LANE DANIEL W LAWSON JOHNNY R LYNN KENNETH MARTIN RAYMOND L TACKE
ROBERT V JAY DENNIS G MERRYMAN RANDY W MOLKENTINE JOHN A NOWAKOWSKI JOHNNY L PALMER
MARTIN T SCOTT II ALVIN M SLATON CLAYTON A SONGLE JOSEPH J STRUCEL JOHN K SUBLETT JR
PHILLIP E TAYLOR CHARLES W THOMAS LESLIE D THOMPSON RONALD L WARNETT STANLEY B ZIEGLER
EDGAR ACUNIA RAL J ANDERSON JR GEORGE R AVGERINOS THOMAS A BECKER JIMMY BOOKER
CARL D CAIN WEYMAN T COOK RICHARD D COYLE BILLY G CREECH EUGENE ELDER
JIMMY L COLEMAN RONALD D DUNTZ CLAYTON E FRALEY IRA M FRANKLIN JR RICHARD L FRY
WILLIAM L GOUGH JOHN A GRABBE LOWELL R GROVES BRUCE J GUEX GLENN B HAINES JR
THEODORE C HALL WILLIAM E HART CLARENCE M HOLLAND ROBERT JACKSON JR DANIEL M NOELDNER
JERRY JOHNSON FRANK D JOYNES JR JOHN W KOBELIN II STEPHEN F KOSTANSKI RICHARD J LEAHY
ROBERT E LEAMEN DOUGLAS O LOONEY DAVID G LOVITT STEVE E LOWERY PHILIP N MALONE
GERALD L JAMES MICHAEL P MALUEG WILLIAM D MCALLISTER JOHN T MCDONNELL RICARDO J ORTEGON
WILFRED PEREZ KEITH J PUHI LARRY M RODGERS CALIXTRO S RODRIGUEZ MICHAEL L WOODSIDE
TERRY L SAYER HAROLD L SEAMAN PAUL E STROUSE LYLE J THOMPSON PAUL P VAVROSKY
JAMES E RAMSBY CLINTON L WHEELER CRAIG E WILLIAMS GLENN S WINGENBACH JR WILLIAM W ABSHEAR
JOHN I ALECK WILLIAM F ANSELMO ALLEN R ARNOLD RAMON J ARROYO JAMES L AVERY
RICHARD J BOIS MICHAEL G BROWN MARION M BURKE EDWARD DUTY KENTON E HENNINGER
MICHAEL R FORCK GARY R GEORGE JAY B GILPIN ORANGE GOODING WILLIAM F GOODWIN
LINNELL BUTLER DALE E GREENWOOD CLARENCE A HECKMAN STEVEN H JOHNSON VICTOR JOHNSON JR
JAMES E KINNARD WILLIAM J KOLENC ADOLF J KROISENBACHER DAVID D LAYNE LARRY W LISS
CARLOS O MALDONADO ROGER J MAZAL WILLIAM L MCCORMICK RICHARD L MUSSER JOHN H WEST
LEWIS L MCDONALD WILLIAM J MCNAMARA JOSEPH E NESKE JOHN S OTAKE TED Q REED JR
NOEL L RIOS JOHN A RIVERA JERRY C ROBBINS JOSEPH C RUSSO RANDALL J SANDOVAL
NELSON L SMITH ROGER J SPENCE BILLY D THOMAS LEE D THOMAS TERRANCE L WEANT

DAVID R MORGAN RICHARD L ADCOCK WILLIAM A BEARD ROBERT J BENEDICT JEWELL C BLANKENSHIP
ALFRED E ALVEY JR WILLIAM R BLACK THOMAS J BOWE LARRY D BROWN WILLIE L BROWN JR
WALTER A CARPENTER LEONARD R CATON WILLIAM T CRAIG JR DAVID H DE FORGE EDGAR A DEES JR
MICHAEL W DOYLE JOHN P EMRATH LARRY E EVANS PETER L GORVAD JOHN W ISRAEL MICHAEL S MASSEY
ROBERT E GRANT THOMAS R GREGSON VINCENT F GUERRERO DANNY L HANSON RANDALL L HARVEY
RALPH A CONE PAUL D HAYDON GRANT H HENJYOJI EARL T HOAG JOHN R HORNSBY ROGER H HOWES
WALTER B HOXWORTH DANIEL IRIZARRY-ACEVEDO SAMUEL J IZZARD JAMES E JANKA DEAN H JOHNSON
JERRY G ERVIN KENNETH M LEE CHARLES D MACKEN MICHAEL A MARSHALL SIXTO R MARTINEZ JR
KENNETH E MILLER MATTHEW E MORTON JR JOHN L MOTLEY JR JAMES M NORMAN DOUGLAS R POLLOCK
GORDON C MURRAY KENNETH A PEDERSON DAVID J PHILLIPS THOMAS J ROACH JR PETER L TRIPP
DONALD L RUPE ROGER W SMELSER CHARLES D SNYDER GLENN R STAIR NYMAN W STELTER JR
FREDDIE C POTE JR EARL E TAYLOR DAVID E THEOBALD LEON TISDALE RALPH D VEALE GORDON L WHEELER
HECTOR M VEGA-DIAZ CLIFTON F WAGNER JACK E WILLIAMS ROY D WIMMER ROY G ZUFELT
DREW J BARRETT III DONALD F BAYSINGER LEON BEARD RAYMOND J BECHARD RAYMOND L BETHEA
RANDY R BOYKINS CLARENCE P BURLESON LARRY D CARROLL TIMOTHY M CARROLL BUDDY E CHANNON
BOBBY D CLARK KENNETH G CLARKE JR MILO D CLEMENTS RODNEY L CRANE LESTER DANCHETZ
RONALD E DEDMAN DARRELL W DONALDSON ALTON L ELLIS STEVEN C ERBENTRAUT CALVIN NORMAN JR
LINDELL FRANCIS CHARLES P GIRARD JAMES M GONANO JOSEPH GRASSIA JR ROBERT S GREGG
JUAN E GARCIA-DIAZ JOHNNY P GRISSOM JAMES R HARRISON ELIJAH HERRING JR BLAINE L HONEYCUTT
DAVID J HORDERN TIMOTHY L HURLEY RICHARD A LAMEIRAS WALTER J LEMIEUX ARTHUR D LINDSEY
WILLIAM R LUCAS LARRY D MATHENY RALPH E MAYERS III JOSEPH H MEARS ROBIN B MILLER
JERRY C MCDONALD FULTON B MOORE III JACKIE R MORGAN CLARENCE NOFFORD RUDOLPH WILSON
RICHARD T FORESTER JOSEPH E NOHE JR MICHAEL P O'CONNOR DANIEL J O'NEILL FRANCIS S OBERSON
DENNIS A ORMOND GREGORIO L PANGELINAN JOHN J PETRIE DAVID A POLEY WILLIAM T PROSE
ROBERT B PROTTO JR ROBERT F REX BOBBY J ROLLINS DOUGLAS N ROWE RICHARD D SHIELDS
DONALD L SHIRLEY AARON C SMITH LARRY M SMITH WILLIAM T SPEARMAN III JESSE B STEVENSON
CHARLES F STURMA THOMAS G TURNER JAMES H WALL TIM L WALTERS HUEY WILLIAMS
EDWARD J MILLISON III JOSEPH W WYSONG FIDEL J AGUIRRE JESSE H ARCHER JACK BERNSTEIN
JAMES L CAMERON JEFFREY T CASSIDY FREDDIE P CHAVEZ CALVIN J CHILDRESS DAVID B CHRISTIANSON
ARTHUR W COFER LEON COIT WILLIAM R CRUICKSHANK LAWRENCE DESMORE RICHARD A DOSECK
WARREN L LONG KENNETH E GAYER ARTHUR GEORGE-PIZARRO DONALD C GILLETT JOHN P GUTTMANN JR
CLARENCE E FETTY BUFORD HARDY JOHN W HILL JR CALVIN JOHNSON JOHN E LORTZ III CARTER P LUNA

PANEL 29W

RICHARD E MATYAS EDWARD R MEIEROTTO LEONARD C MILLER JULIUS A MITCHELL
CLARENCE E NUNNERY JR JOHN B PETERSON JR LARRY L RAUSCHER AARON L SMITH JAMES L YARBROUGH
ALLAN D MORTENSEN WILLIAM J STEDL CECIL W TILLMAN MICHAEL G ALLENDORF DAVID B ARNOLD
PHILLIP R BAILY WILLIAM H BARKSDALE DARYL C BAUER JOHN L BENDOR PERRY L BOZEMAN
WAYNE A BRATZ HERMAN F BROWN WILLIAM H BROWN JOHN V CALLANAN JEAN R CLEMENCIA JR
GEORGE A DEMBY ROGER E DENNY MICHAEL DI GENNO MILFRED H DINGMAN KENNETH M FRAIN
HENRY A DYE JR VANDERBILT ELLIOTT JR WHITNEY T FERGUSON III DONALD L FOWLER JAMES E FOWLER
EDWARD T COOPER BENNIE J GRAHAM MICHAEL J GRUENWALD MELVIN GUYTON RICHARD H HAAG JR
PAUL E GARRETT TERRELL T HAM STEPHEN HARDER LEWIS C HARRIS LARRY L HODGES LARRY A JACKSON
JOSEPH R HERMOSILLO SAMUEL L HOLDER JAMES H HORTON ARCHIE H IYUA JR JOHN R JACKSON
WILLIAM B TERRY WALTER A KOEHLER VINCENT G LEW JOSEPH A LEWIS JEAN D MARTIN DOYCE G MILLER
NEAL E MONETTE WALTER L MOORE JOHN F MORRIS DENNIS L MOYER STEVEN B OAKS
DEAN R ORN THOMAS POLDINO ROBIN W RICHARDSON KENNETH J ROBINSON TOMMY L ROBINSON
CHARLES D ROGERS CLARENCE L ROUSE ROBERT N SAULS RICHARD M SCHMIDT JOHN E SHIRAKA
ALAN C MARTIN PAUL W SHREWSBURY LARRY L STONER LARRY STRAHAN CARLOS L TARTT JOHN R WEIR
GEORGE J SMITH JR DAVID C TEUTSCH HOWARD R THOMAS JR DANIEL W TINDLE HOWARD G WEBSTER
JULIO C WELD HARRISON WINE JR JACK B YOUNG FRED J BRIDGES JR THOMAS BRIGHT JR
CLIFFORD M CORK HARLAN M CRAFT JACKIE L CROSBY LAWRENCE R ESSER RONALD L FRANCE
JAMES A FRANKLIN LOUIS W FRERICKS JAMES A GAZZE JAMES C GILBERT THOMAS E HACKER
EDWARD J HAUGEN ALAN R HOSNEDLE PAUL H JACKSON JR FRANKLIN A JOHNSON NORMAN S SALIMAN
FRANKLIN M LANIER PATRICK M MCINERNEY FELTON L MIMS FRED A MOODY GARY L MOORE
DALMACIO P PASCUA JR PAUL J PEOPLES THOMAS C PRANGE JOHN A RAMIREZ DAVID G RANKIN
CHARLES J REVIS FRED E RICHARDS LEMOND RICHARDSON FLOYD H ROBINSON FRANKLIN J RUNGE
PAUL E IRVIN HENRY C SANDERS ROBERT E SHAFFER SIGMOND M SIKORSKI EARL S SNYDER
ROBERT E SPIRES GERALD L THARP TYRONE G THOMAN RICHARD L THOMPSON JR TOMMY L TRIMBLE
CHARLES J TURRI KYLE WALDROP WILLIAM T WHEELER GORDON G WHITE JERRY O YOUNG
THOMAS A ZIMMERMAN JAMES T ANDERSON DOUGLAS W BICE DON R BREWER JOSEPH M BUCHANAN
DONNIE W CAUDILL HENRY CHAMBERLAIN CORNELL R CLARKE ROBERT A CONLEY CHARLES V DUPRE
RICHARD L DURAN CLARENCE A EARLEY JAMES P FULLERTON ALBERT T GLANTON DANIEL W LLOYD
CHARLES R GRANT WILLIS F HOUSE RONALD C KATZ THOMAS J KOOB GEORGE R LEVESQUE
ALVIN L LOWERY CRAIG S METTLING THOMAS C MOFFITT ROBERT T ORR TIMOTHY C PROUDFOOT
PAUL V QUAGLIERI ISIEAH RELEFORD JR RANDALL L SHACKELFORD DONALD E SIZEMORE JAMES L SMITH
DONALD J SPATAFORE JOSEPH M URBANCZYK THOMAS L VENDELIN KENNETH L WATSON CYRIL T YECKLEY
JOHNNY G STAMPS RICK YAMASHITA MICHAEL H YEATES RONALD J ALFONSO HOBART AXSOM JR
LEON E BARNARD RAYMOND E BAUMGARNER EDWARD R BEASLEY THEOPHILUS BOWLES SAMUEL HOPE JR
FREDDIE N CHASE RICHARD C CHUBB BERTON DECKER EARL F FALCONBURY HADLEY FOSTER
JAMES A CARPENTER ERNEST R FRANKS FURNACE FREEMAN JR MICHAEL J HAYES JR HERMAN B HOSE JR
SYDNEY C HOWARD WILLIAM J HUTTON WAYMON L JONES JR ANDREW J KUKURUDA STEPHEN W LUCIA
WILLIAM L MCFARLAND JOEL L MILLER PHILLIP R PANNELL JAMES R POLLARD JR DAVID F POPP
JAMES L RIPANTI VERN E ROOT ANTONIO E RUIZ ELBERT J SAULS RICHARD W SMITH
ALVIN T STAHL WILLIAM R STOLLEY JR ALAN W THORNTON GEORGE R WARD JR SYLVESTER WILSON
ARTURO F ALARCON BRUNO BARAN HARVEY L BASCO SIMEON J BERGERON MICHAEL E BRADY
WESLEY BEAVER DONALD R BLEDSOE PAUL BONAPART ROBERT W BOWMAN FRED E BROWN
JOHN W CAMP FRANK A CANCELLIERE STEVEN D CHURCHWARD TOMMY J DIXON JAMES DOLLARD
GEORGE R GARRIS JULIO HERNANDEZ JR WILLIAM J HILLARD II CARL W HUGHES DENNIS R HUNSLEY
HENRY R LONGSTON MICHAEL LYNCH DONNIE J MARTIN ANTHONY J MORINA JEFFREY L WHYNAUGHT
EDGAR G MCADAMS BRIAN F MCCARTHY JOHN MCMANUS MICHAEL L PADDOCK RONALD L PEARL
JOHN W PRICE DAVID J PUGH WILLIAM REYNOLDS JOHN E ROBERTS JR BENJAMIN A SMALLS
WILLIAM J GRIFFIN ROBERT E SPIEGEL MICHAEL L STACY LARRY A STARK WILLIAM L TANNER TERRY E THARP
WILLIAM JACKSON MORGAN THOMPSON MANUEL B ALONZO CHARLES R BARNES MICHAEL L BATT
DAVID W BAZZLE ALBERT A BEAUCHAMP RAYMOND E BOBE WAYNE E BRANTNER JOSEPH T CHATBURN
EDWARD C COFIELD JR DALE W COLDIRON ROBERT G DANIEL F M EUDALY MARVIN L FOSTER
JOHN L GAWEL DOUGLAS D GAYLORD DENNIS M GROVES RONALD H HOWARD RUDOLPH JONES
WILLIE J KIRKSEY DICKIE D KOELL JR JAMES M LEE MILFORD LOONEY JR WILLIE E MALONE JR
PHILLIP H MARKS FRANK J MATTERA RICHARD M PEARSALL LOUIS V ROMANELLI ROLANDO G VILLARREAL
FRANCIS E SIEVERS JR DAVID R SMITH LARRY R SWISHER SELVWYN R TAYLOR TERRY L TAYLOR
RICHARD M ROCCO MARLON W TROXEL CHARLES W WARRINGTON JR LOUIS G WHEELER JEFF WHITEHEAD
STEVEN R ARMITSTEAD TERENCE E BARNEY HERBERT M BEAUMONT LOUIS M BECKMANN EARL L WILSON
HAROLD P BERG RICHARD A BROWN EDWARD L CHAPPELL BENEDICT M DAVAN JOHN C DAVENPORT
CHARLES E DAVIS JR HAROLD P DEGNER CHARLES E FINNEY RODGER L GARLICK DAVID A MITCHELL
ROBERT E GREEN LARRY D GREENHALGH LYLE C HANSBROUGH JOSEPH W HUDSON VERNON D JACOBS
DAVID T DINAN III JOHN A LESTELLE II RAIMUNDO MARQUEZ-QUINONES EARL T QUILLEN JOHN L RUETH
JAY H MANCHESTER JOSEPH A PETRARCA DEWEY J RAY ROBERT J REGENHARDT JR THOMAS L ROBINSON
DENNIS R LAWRENCE DAVID A RUSSELL DON SMITH JOSEPH C THORNE JR FIRMAN A TITUS
DELMER V ASHBROOK BERNARD A ZAMBRANO ROBERT L BALDWIN ROBERT L BARRETT JR DAN M BRITT
PAUL A CABRAL HARDY E CALLOWAY MICHAEL J CAPUTO MARK F DANIELS ISAAC E HEATH
LARRY K DAVIS EDWARD C DE BOW THOMAS M DEITZ LEONARD DODSON JOE B EASTERN
RICHARD B BRUCE DALE L EISAMAN GEORGE T FARAWELL MARGARITO FERNANDEZ JR WILLIAM E HOPKINS
DARCY A HOUCHIN BARRY JACKSON RAY R JOWERS KENNETH J KNOEFERL BARRY D MURPHY
JIMMY L LARSEN WILLARD S LUND DANNY R MACK DANNY J MAGGARD RICHARD H MEHEGAN
WILLIAM L JOHNSON ROBERT A MCINTOSH ROBERT L MITCHELL JOHN W PARHAM ROBERT W PATTERSON
DAVID S PELLEW JAMES L PHILLIPS WILLIAM M PHINN JAMES M PINTOLA EMMETT T PRINGLE HERBERT J STOBER
ROBERT L WILSON KENZEL M RACEY EARL C RIDER JR JERRY E SAMSON CLYDE E SAXON RICHARD W STITT
HERBERT A TATUM JOHN R THIELEN JOSE TORREROS THOMAS J YOLKIEWICZ JACKIE L DAVISON
DAVID B ARNOTT JAMES M ASTON HARVEY C AVERY HENRY P BALDWIN DONALD R BARTLEY
BARRY W MURTAUGH JOHN F ALLEN BRAD D CHRISS MILAM E CLOUD DENNIS F ELLIS TERRY R MONIA
RONNIE L ECKENROAD KENNETH R EYRING RICHARD GILLIAM ANTHONY A GIRETTI JOHN M GOODWIN
CHARLES E GROOMS JR LEE T HAMMAN JOHNNIE R HANSON ROBERT R HIGHFILL WARD E HOMER
GARY L HOSKO JOE S HUSTON CHARLES W JENKINS ANTHONY JOHNSON JAMES G JOHNSON
JESUS ENCARNACION-BETE LOREN C JONES FLOYD M KEEFE EDDIE R KELLEY BARRY L KOPP
THOMAS J MCMAHON DEAN L MOON JAMES H MOORE WALTER L MOSES JR GEORGE N MYERS
JESUS C OLETA JR DONALD L OLIVE WILLIAM D OVERSTREET DAVID R RAY ROBERT C ROGERS
JACK L REXRODE MERVIN R RICHTER ELLIS A ROBERTSON CHARLES ROECKL HECTOR M SANCHEZ-ROHENA
RICHARD D SATTERTHWAITE GENE W SOMERS JR GLENN L SPARKS HERBERT C SPENCER JOHN A SWORDS
WILLIAM W UTTS JOSEPH R VAN DE HEI RICHARD A VOLK LORING W WATSON JACKIE J WEBB
RONALD E FORSTER DANIEL G WESSLER CHARLES E WHEELER PAUL WILSON MAX I BAER RONALD K BATTLE
JOHN M BURKE VAUGHN D CONNELL DAVID L DAVIS RICARDO G DAVIS RICHARD R MAYNARD
DOUGLAS G EDWARDS BARRY L EICHELBERGER ERNEST F ELDERS RICHARD L FIFFE JEFFREY S FORRY
GEORGE M GORRERA JR JAMES H JEFFRIES HAROLD B JOHNSON MAX A JOHNSON VICTOR D KAHLA JR
TERRY T KAWAMURA LARRY W KNOX BILL G LEE RICHARD L MALONE WILLIAM H MAUTHE
JIMMY F BURCHFIELD MICHAEL P MCCORMICK JOHN G OSTERHOUS RAUL V PEREZ JOHN D PETAL
ROGER L PHILLIPS NIGEL F POESE JAMES C REED DAVID J SANDVIG FRANK D SARACINO JR
FILEMON SERRANO CLARENCE E SMITH DENNIS A SMITH LARRY D SMITH KARL J TASCHEK JR
ROBERT A TATE JR ROBERT E THOMPSON LARRY M WHITIS BILL ASHFORD JR FRANKLIN D ASHLEY II
ROBERT A BAETZEL ALAN M BERNSTEIN PATRICK L BLAIR WILLIE E BOLTON WILLIAM M CHURCH
RICHARD C BENICEWICZ JOSEPH G BOWMAN JR WALTER T BRYANT RONALD B CASSELL JUAN P CASTRO
RONALD S COLSON ROBERT A DALTON ROBERT S DAVIS JOE E DEMERSON WILLIAM L DENT
JOHN ENGEDAL JOSEPH M EUSTAQUIO JERRY L EWING HARRY H GIBSON MICKEY W HILL
JOHNNY L EDWARDS BARRY W GRAF THOMAS J GRINDSTAFF DAVID E HERSCHBACH ERROL A HUGHES

PANEL 29W *(Continued)*

MOSE C HUNDLEY LOUIS H JONES THOMAS E JONES JR WESLEY S KERR LARRY T MOULDER
JAMES M KING ALBERT O KRAUSSER FRANK A KRIEGER LYNN R KROTZER HERMAN E LASSITER
EUGENE PIZZINO II EARL L LEWIS DALE D LINGLE JAMES J LISTER RICARDO LOPEZ ALAN F MARSCHALL
EARL M MATTHEWS GEORGE E MENNINGER FREDERICK C MILLER III TED D MILLS ADGER E MOODY
DONALD R JOHNSTON MITCHEL T MORTON BILLY D MURPHY THOMAS M NEWMAN ROBERT E O'BRIEN

PANEL 28W

DAVID B PETERSON ROBERT E PIERSON LEONARD L PRESTON JR RENE A SANTOS
BILLY W RAPP JAMES R REGNOLDS ROBERT L RIGGINS JR MIGUEL A RIVERA WILLIAM E ROWE
RICHARD B PHILLIPS GILBERT RUIZ GEORGE T SARGENT JR LARRY SCOTT WILLIAM W SHERMAN
ALBERT E SMITH JR JAMES E SMITH CHRIS A SOUZA DALE L STOCK CLIFFORD M TAYLOR
GERALD R THOMPSON MICHAEL K THOMPSON PHILIP B THOMPSON JOHN J VALERO KELLY P VAUGHN
JAMES A WALKER JR STEPHEN L WEIGT CHARLES F WHITE RONNIE R WHITE THOMAS W WHITTEN
CARL R WILSON JR DONALD R ALEXANDER RICHARD W ANDERSON KENNETH D BAILEY LARRY D BALDWIN
ROSCOE W BALL JR JOHN BARCA JR MORRIS S BEESON RALPH N BICKFORD ARMIN J BLAKE
CLARENCE H BOOLIN JOHN R BRANDBORG TONY L BUHOLTZ ALBERT C BUTLER WILLIS CORMIER
CARL L DI NUNZIO HARVEY G ENZ THOMAS FOLDEN RICHARD W GODEN WALTER GREEN JR
CHARLES L GUTHRIE MICHAEL E HERMSEN STEVEN D HOOPER CHARLES D HOWELL ALBERT M MENDOZA
DANNY E HUBBS ROBERT P ILSLEY EUGENE J KOCK ROBERT E MCAFERTY GILBERT E MCDANIEL
JAMES A MCKECHNIE DAVID D OUELLETTE DAVID E OVIST LAUVI P PETERS ANGEL REYES
LEONARDO RIOS-VELAZQUEZ JR RICHARD F SALAZAR LAWRENCE L SMITH FRANK SPIERS TERRY L STAMAN
CLYDE S SWEATT CLIFFORD L SWISHER MOISES TAPIA ROBERT C TEDFORD DAVID C VALLANCE
LYNN C WHITFORD JAMES D WRIGHT JR WILLIAM J AHLUM KENNETH R BARKLEY TOMMY L BARNES
NORMAN E BECK MICHAEL L BERRY STEVE E BYARS REX F CHURCH EDDIE L EVENSON
STEVEN A BELL LARRY J CONKLIN ROBERT C DAVIS HOWARD K FITZGERALD MICHAEL A GEHL
CHARLES D HENRICKS ROY L HOWARD HOWARD M MEUTE JOHN L MORRIS BILL A MOSCHETTI
GREGORY E NEWMAN DAVID D OVERSTREET EDWARD W PAWLOWSKI CARL H PETERS JR LOUIS B WANER II
JERRY L PETERSON ANDREW L PRESLEY JR LEON SEARS JOHNNY L SMITH LEO B SMITH
ROBERT A OSBORNE ALLEY O STEPHENS THOMAS M STRUCHEN ROBERT F WHITTEN JAMES W WIDDIS JR
JOHN R YARGER DARRELL E ANDERSON LARRY E BAILEY RICHARD L BOWERS JOHN M FOSTER
WILLIAM M BRYANT DANNY V CASEY RONALD L COKER JUAN A COVARRUBIAS CARL J CREW
GERASIMO ARROYO-BAEZ RAYMOND F EADE TOM EMERSON PHILLIP H FLEMING JIMMY G FREEMAN
JOHN M GREENE DAVID S HARRIS ROBERT A HOLAN JR JAMES K JOHNSON ALLEN R MILLER
JOHN D HAMILTON JR WILLIAM H KEELER MONTY G LACKAS THOMAS L LOAN ROBERT T MANNING
ARTHUR J MCINTYRE GARY R MOSS BOBBY J NEWMAN CURTIS ONCHI JOHNNY R PARKER
MINOR W PATTILLO RONALD E PLAYFORD DONALD S REPACI WILLIE J SANDFER JR DENNIS M SILVERI
RICHARD W PELLETIER GERALD R SCHIESL JOSEPH F SCHIMPF MICHAEL A TORRES BENJAMIN R TURIANO
MICHAEL VALUNAS ROBERT M WALKLEY GARY L WEEKLEY DENNIS A WILLIAMS JOHNNY YOUNG
LUCIANO ARIAS JAMES H ARMSTRONG JIMMY D BEAN GERNOT BENDER DAVID F BLACK
GARY M BRANNON JAMES E BRANNON WALTER E BROWN JR EDDIE D CARPER
JACK D CARTER STEPHEN H DOANE WILLIE C DOZIER MICHAEL R DUNN FRANK J ELLIS JR
STEVE FLAHERTY HOMER L GLEATON CARTER L GRAVES EDWARD GREEN JR ROBERT F MCDONALD II
JEWELL R GREEN JOSEPH C HAGA EARL M HAYES MILES B HEDGLIN FREDERICK D HERRERA
PRENTICE W HICKS BOBBY D JENNINGS LEONARD W LABOWSKI EDWARD D LAMOREUX PHILLIP E LYNCH
EDWARDO FLORES MICHAEL L MALIN GREG W MILLS RENE C MISCHEAUX CHARLES N MOSS
GENE O BLOSKY DARREL G NAPIER DENNIS M ORBINO AVEY PRESLEY DENNIS R RICHARDS
RICHARD D ROBERTS LEWIS E SAMPLER DOMINIC M SEMENTELLI JR DAVID G SMITH NORMAN C SMOOTS
CARL E TODD WILLIAM J TORPIE JAMES G UPCHURCH DAVID A WEBER WILLIAM R WILSON
ANTONIO L ALHO ROBERT L ATKINSON JR MICHAEL R BALL DONALD E BARNETT PATRICK H BENZE
WALTER C BOOTH JESSE C BOWMAN OWEN D BROWN JR JOHN R BUSCHMANN EDDY R CASEY
RICHARD E BRENNEMAN NICHOLAS CANCILLA TIMOTHY L CARLEY STANLEY M CLINGLER FRANK A DI FIGLIA
JERRY DISHMAN WILLIAM C FENTON JR ROBERT W FIELDS DONALD S FOREST JAMES R GENTILE
LARRY A GILLASPIE WILLIE F GREEN DENNIS D GREER GREGORY L HABETS GEVIN P PASTORES
EDDIE L HATLEY DANIEL K HINKEL JOE E HOLLEMAN DAVID J HUFFMAN FREDERICK R KUTZER
THEODORE E HEINSELMAN GUY F JOHNSON FRANCIS J KING DONALD G LE PARD J B LEVESQUE
WILLIAM C STREVEL JR JOSE LEZAMA JR ROBERT D LIESER BOBBY P LINDLEY JAMES L LOCKE CLYDE A LUCAS
FRANKIE B MCDANIEL RAND R MERKER CARLTON L MONROE TERRY D MOORE ANTONIO R MORALES
LEONARD J HALL CLAUDE J OWENS J C REEL DONALD J RICHTER DONALD R ROBERTSON
WILLIAM J ROGERS IV CARLOS W RUCKER WILLIAM W SCHOTH II MICHAEL J SELLITTO ROBERT E SHERIDAN
ROBERT V SHRACK JR JAMES L STEWART DAVID STONE DOUGLAS E STOVER JAMES H WATSON
ALFRED H SUHR RONALD W THOMPKINS JOHN M TURNER CHARLES C VICKREY MAURICE J WASHINGTON
ROBERT O WELLS STEVE R WHITAKER LAWRENCE M WILHELM JR DONNIS G WILLIS JOSEPH F WILLIS
ROGER D YOUNG ROBERT L ANGLIN DIMITRIOS G ARNIOTIS DONALD R ARNOLD EVERETTE W BRIGGS
WAYNE MONEYMAKER JERRY BAXTER WILLIAM B BELL RENE A BULLER LARRY E CHRISTIE WILLIAM D CODY
LEE R COMBS EVERETT T CULP BARD E DAVENPORT LOUIS K DIXON HENRY F FAIRCLOTH
RAYMOND G CZERWIEC JOSEPH J DOBYNES THOMAS W DURHAM VICENTE T ESPINOSA ROBERT D EVANS
DAVID E FLANNERY ROBERT S HARDISON ALLAN G HARPER GARY P HEIZER LEONARD C IVY JR
WILLIAM M JODREY OSCAR G JOHNSON JR ZANE E JOHNSON RICHARD S JONES ALLISON W LOCKLAIR
RONALD JONES JAMES R LONG HAROLD W MAHER WILLIE D MARTINEZ ALFRED MORENO JR
ROGER W PATTON WILLIAM D POTTER SAMUEL A ROBERSON FERROL S SMITH WILLIAM P THOMPSON JR
CLYDE SEILER ANTHONY J URRUTIA RODNEY A VORE JOHN B WALLER BOBBY J WALTERS
DAVID O WILSON KENNETH L WITHAM LESLIE W WORL ROBERT A BELCHER PETER J BOUCHARD
STANLEY T BRADLEY LEROY BRANTLEY GERALD J BRATRSOVSKY GEORGE E BROWNING WALTER V CROCCO
EARL F BROWNE VICTOR A BURRIS WILLIAM J CAREY CHARLES F COOK ALBERT L D'ADAMO JR
ROBERT D DAVENPORT SEAN T DORAN BILLY W DUKE ROGER J DUMONT JOSEPH D GOODALE JR
EARL FERGUSON FRED L GABBIN THOMAS M GIBSON DONALD R GLASS GEORGE K GOLDEN
TERRY D GRAHAM ALVIN F GUNTER ROGER L HAWLEY KENNETH R HUGHES THEODORE E MOON JR
DENNIS G JOHNSON WILLIAM P JUSTICE JOHN P LANDRY WILLIAM J MASKE DUSTAN W MEEKS
GARY W GROW THOMAS MICHAEL LARRY A MILES MICHAEL A MILLER VINCENT MORAN
CARL D NALL DANA E NELSON PAUL A NELSON RICHARD L NOTTINGHAM MICHAEL L POGGI
WILOFARD A MCCLAIN II LAWRENCE D PERUSO JULIUS P PIGNATARO GARY J POLLOCK ROBERT E PUGH
ERIC V PULLIAM RONALD F RICCIARDO MARVIN J ROBERTS ROY G RUBIN ALVIN C SCHULTE
BRUCE W SHAFFER CHARLES O SNYDER LON A SPURLOCK II JAMES M SULLIVAN JOHN W SUMMERLIN
CHARLES WALKER ROBERT L WEIHER JAMES C WEST JR LORNE J WILSON ROLAND S ZIERDEN
PAUL J BAKER TERRY J BARNHOLDT ROBERT D BENGTSON STEPHEN D BOARD MARTIN J CANAVAN JR
ROY B BOYD KENNETH J BRENNER JOHN J CLARK JAMES B CLAYBAUGH ROBERT O COLE
ROSS W COLLINS JR THOMAS L COTTRELL BRUCE W DANIELS JOHN J ELSENRATH RICHARD J SCHWICHOW
WILLIAM C GOULD JR GEORGE C GRAY RICHARD E GRIEGO FREDERICK W HESS DAVID I STYLES
LARRY K HOCUTT FRANK L KECK ROBERT D LAUBER ROMAN H LEICHT MARIO R LEON
MARK D MARSHALL CHARLES E MARTIN JAMES M MCKINLEY JOSEPH M MERMEJO RONALD R MEYER
JULIO MALABE ROBERT A MULHOLLAND LEA E NIBBELINK JOHN L PARTEE DANNY F PERKINS
CHARLES R PRCHAL VICTOR H PRITCHARD SAMUEL V RAMSEY JR MARTIN J REGAN GEORGE F REYNOLDS JR
DONALD F ERVIN RICHARD W ROSSIGNOL MACK D SHARPE GLENN T SHIBATA RICHARD E SLAVEN
ANTHONY G HARNESS WAYNE R SWAN KENNETH H VISINTIN CHARLES C WALKER RICHARD A WHITE
THOMAS A WIESE MICHAEL L WILKINS LYLE G ASTON ELMER E BARR RAYMOND BROWN
ROBERT P AHERN ARTHUR M BRADBERRY BRET F CRANDALL DANIEL J CURRAN CHRISTOPHER L DELLAPINA
BENITO DIAZ JR JERRY T DRIGGERS GLENN L FETTERMAN JAMES C FOX JERRY A GARRICK
JOHNNY A GIBSON WILLIAM A GOULD CHARLES L HODGE NELSON L HORCHEM JR CLARENCE A LATIMER
LAMARR L JOHNS RUSSELL L JOHNSON CHARLES M LAMBY JACK N LOUALLEN PETER J MCCALLUM JR
LAWSON D NELSON DONALD L NIXON RONALD G PACE JOSEPH J POLASEK JR EUGENE R SHERIDAN
WILLIE J SIEGLER FRED D SMITH MELTON E SMITH WALTER D SMITH CHESTER H TERRY JR
THOMAS J TYRELL PAUL B WEST WILLIAM C WILLIAMSON ROY A WOMACK HOWARD E YOST JR
RICHARD C BEHNKE HERBERT E BELCHER JAMES C BRANNAN DONALD L BRUCKART WILLIAM G BURKE
RAMEY L CARPENTER CHARLES R CUNNINGHAM JEROME A DE GALLEY TERRY L DELCAMBRE CHARLIE HILL III
DAREN L DRINSKI CLEMENT A DUPUIS EDGAR A FLOWERS RAMIRO M GONZALEZ WAYNE H RUSSELL
MELVIN H CONNER JR ARTHUR P KONEVAL EDWARD B LAMA PETER M NEE JAMES C O'SHEA
EDWARD J FRENDLING GARY L PACE JAMES A SALAMONE ROBERT E SHAW KENNETH E VERRETT
DANFORTH E WHITE JAMES H WILSON LEROY I BLANKENSHIP JAMES E BOUYER ALVIN L GAY
FRANK J CARROLL LELAND S CROWLEY JR JAMES J CURRY WILLIAM A DEBATES CARMELO DIAZ-ROMAN
LAWRENCE T ANDREWS TERRY W DICKERHOFF GARY L DUGGAN BARRY L GOLDEN JAMES L HALL
RONALD J LONG EDWARD L LOO JR JESSE D MORRIS JR WILEY B MOSS JON D PETERSON
REX E RADER RICHARD C SIMMONS PHILIP C STAFFORD JOHN F TAYLOR MICHAEL G TAYLOR
RICHARD A THURSBY ROBERT E VAN DUSEN DALE A YATEMAN PAUL H ABRAHAM CHRISTOPHER D BANGS
HURLEY M BOYD WILLIAM H BROWN JR LOWELL L CRAWFORD THOMAS R GORRILL PERCY L GULLEY JR

PANEL 27W

VERNE E LOCHNER CHARLES D MOSSER WILLIE J PERKINS CARL J PETERSON
RICHARD C JOHNSTON LOWELL S POWERS JAMES H RODGERS LARRY D RUGGLES STEPHEN A SHERLOCK
ROBERT J STORK JR JIMMIE M TILGHMAN JULIAN V VELASQUEZ DAVID A WALDERA LENWOOD WHITE JR
JAMES W AGNEW RICHARD B BRUSH PETER B CHRISTIANSON LONDON CONAWAY RONALD D DESKINS
RONALD V HACKER LONNIE H HENDRICKSON JAMES H HUFF PERRY H JEFFERSON JOHN T MONTGOMERY
ARTHUR G ECKLUND ROBERT T JOHNSON D J KELSEY JAMES E KLCO EDWARD F MORRILL
FRANCIS L PEARSON ROBERT N PRETE THOMAS A ROSS THEODORE V THOMAN JOSEPH B TOLER
GENE L WHITE ROBIN R ANNIS THOMAS M BOULE LAWRENCE J BUTLER MICHAEL H FLOOD
ROBERT M BECK GERALD W CANTRELL WALTER W CHASE FELIX M CONDE-FALCON JAMES O DAUGHERTY JR
MICHAEL D GILMORE IVEY J HAYES EDWARD A HOPKINS KENNETH B JAMES J C JENKINS
RONALD D LAYTON TERRILL M LISLE DANN J LOBKER TEDDY C LOFTIN KENNETH G MISNER
DAVID H MCDONALD ROGERS PULLINS JR THOMAS W QUINN DOUGLAS W RICHARDS THOMAS H WEIGLE
RALPH T SAND JOSEPH D SLAWEK JR CLINTON D SMITH PHILIP C STEIN HAYS C STEPHENS
CHARLIE R MCDONALD WILLIAM D TYRON DAVID B ANDERSON STEPHEN E BELCHER THOMAS E BEST
WILLIAM E BOONE IV JAMES A BROCK LOUIS BROWN DAVID L BURNETT DONALD L CLINE
JONATHAN COLLINS III STEVEN E DONALDSON LAWRENCE W DUDLEY JR JOHN N EDWARDS ISLAM OZGER
KENNETH ESTES JIMMIE L FORREST DAVID H GAMBOA JR WILLIAM S GEARY ROBERT J HARRIS
HUGH G HILL JR STEVEN J HUBERT LARS P HUSTAD GEORGE J HYATT WAYNE L ISAACS
BURLEY D KIRACOFE PAUL R LE HOULLIER RICHARD T LEAVELL WILLIAM M LIGHT ROBERT C LIRA
WILLIE L LOWE JERRY W MARTIN MIKOLAW MELNYK STEVEN MICHALSKI LEE R NOLLEY
STEPHEN A DANIEL BOOKER T PATTERSON JR RICHARD W PERDUE BOYCE D PHILLIPS LARRY A REYNOLDS
LARRY R RIEKEN PAUL A SMITH CHUCK M STADEL VEGTE D VANDE MICHAEL L WERTMAN
EDWARD F AYERS JERRY D BECK JAMES A BROWN TERRANCE L BROWN STEVEN J SMITH
OLLIE J DANIEL THOMAS S DE LUCA JR ANGELO FIGUEROA TERRY L GLASSCOCK RANDY L HANSEN
LAWRENCE A HILKIN MICHAEL J KELLY DAREN L KOENIG MELVIN LEE ROBERT P LYONS
PAUL E MAPLES GEORGE W MCDONOUGH LARRY D MILLING JOSEPH NESBITT CHARLES O OLIVER
JOHN W BLACKWELL LEO J SCHROLLER JR GLENN W THOMAS RICHARD T WARNER DAVID R WIGGINS
ROBERT A WOJTYNA WILLIAM ALLEN JR JAMES L BARTON JOHN E BATCHELOR JR JACK B BEERS
KENNETH R BIRD JAMES A BISHOP ROBERT M COCHRAN JR FLOYD A DEAL JAMES M DERDA
TIMOTHY E DYE ANTHONY J FANFA GARY W GILLIS PETER GODOY JR JOHN T GRAY
MICHAEL D GRIFFIS CHARLES L HATHORN JR THOMAS E HOOVER DONALD M KINNEY EDWARD T PETERS JR
JAMES J LYNCH III RICHARD G MAY STANLEY E MCCREARY THOMAS V MITCHELL HARRY L MORRIS JR
LARRY M KELLEY RICHARD L PORTER LARRY G PYLE DAVID W RANSON WILFRED G SAM
RONALD A SEHESTED ROBERT W SNYDER DOUGLAS S SOUTHER JR JAMES A STAPLES WAYNE Y STEWART
THOMAS J VASIL DARRELL E WALDEN WILLIAM J WOOLSEY JOHN C ALAIMO FRANCIS D ALIVENTO
EDWIN P ANDERSON KENNETH G BLACKWELL ROGER D BRAGG GLENNIE W CAIN VICTOR J CARTIER
DONALD R COOPER KENNETH J ELLINGTON ROBERT A FULKERSON CHRISTIAN G GIRARD DENNIS L ROADS
MICHAEL A GIUNTA RAYMOND A GRAY IVAN I GREEN ISMAEL F HORNELAS EDWARD M KACHMAN
LE L KAHLER ORVILLE L KNIGHT KEITH N MILLER JAMES R O'BANION JOSEPH M ORLOWSKI
CHARLES C DICKERSON JR TONY PALACIOS GERARD P PORTA ROBERT M RASMUSSEN ROLAND A RICHARD
FRANCIS M SAMZ LARRY D SIMPSON GERRAL A SMITH WILLIAM O STEED TOWNSER STEELE JR
JACKIE L TATE VINCENT A TAYLOR JAMES M TRUELOVE CARL R VANN JOHN E WALLACE
JIMMY R WESTMORELAND STEPHEN D WILKINSON LEON WILSON JAMES H ADAMS JAMES G BUNCH JR
ROGER BROWN THOMAS L BROWN RONALD C CONLEY GARY L CROSS DAVID R CROW IV
DELMAR C DENNIS RODNEY T FUKUNAGA NATHANIEL HUDSON BRUCE T KING THOMAS E LEAP JR
DAN S LONG WILLIAM L OVERSTREET DANNY L PATRICK ROBERT A PORTE MICHAEL J VERHAEGHE
RAYMOND M WINFREY JESSIE ARREDONDO WILLIAM F BAGGS JR JOHN T BOONE STEPHEN J BORYSZEWSKI
JOSEPH CLERKIN GEORGE A DASHO JR WILLIAM J DAUBERT GERALD A DECKER DWIGHT M DURHAM
LONNIE D EVANS RANDALL L HAWK WILLIAM A HERING THOMAS E HOFER THOMAS J HUCKABA
ROBERT A JINES DANIEL S KEITH MICHAEL W LIZARRAGA THOMAS G MANDERFELD RONALD S ROSSINI
RICKY D MAUNEY STEVEN L MCFARLAND JOHN L MORGAN JR JOHN G NURSE STANLEY J OTTMAR
LOEL F LARGENT EDWIN H PUMPHREY JACKIE L RATCLIFF OLIVER E REYNOLDS JR JOSEPH F SPINNICCHIA
WALTER S STRAHAN RONALD J TOWARD EUGENE C ZAMORA JOHNNIE L ANDERSON EMMONS E FUNK JR
WILLIAM J BANNON JR LAURIE E BARNES BEVERLY L BARNHART DONALD C BOSBERY KENNETH E BROWN
RICHARD D AUSBROOKS ROBERT M CHRISTIAN JR EDWARD V EIDEN JR NEIL P FARMER GUY T FLETCHER JR
DALE H HAVER BRUCE D HENDERSON RICHARD E HUFF ROBERT L KNIGHT JR ANDREW M KUEBEL
MARTIN LECHUGA STEPHEN M LEWIS MICHAEL E MATTA DALE L MILBRADT GONZALO H VILLASENOR
LAWRENCE S MILLS WILLIAM L OWEN JR JOSEPH F PAEZ CLIFTON D POTTS PETER E REECE
JEFFERY T SAPP ROBERT L SCHEIDEL JR ROBERT H SMART MATTHEW E SMITH LAWRENCE E ZAPOLSKI
CHARLES H MEEKS JR BRUCE M SOURS PETER L STITH LARRY T TURNER ALFRED WEBB JR
DONALD S SAWYER DANIEL E WILLIAMS STAMATIOS G ALEXANDER JR SA ATUATASI JR PATRICK E BLAGG
LARRY D CHANDLER BERNHARD M CHRISTIANSEN DUANE R DAVIS ERNEST L DE SOTO JOSE R DIAZ
FELIX A CALDERON DONALD G DROZ JEFFERY S DYER JEFFREY S DYER STEPHEN M FRY FREDRICK M HALL
THOMAS E HOLLOWAY DANNY W HOULE CLAUDE T JENKINS MARYUS N JONES CORBIN C TINDALL
RONALD J KILLING ROBERT C KING ARNOLD W LAMP JR RICHARD K LEMMON JOHN C LEONARD
CHARLES L LIPTAK WALTER L PRITCHARD JR DONALD G RESPECKI THOMAS H ROBERTSON MICHAEL L SMITH
MANUEL A RIVERA-DELVALLE SCOTT D SCHOEBEN SYLVESTER V SEKNE ROBERT T SMITH JOHN THIERY
LLOYD E JONES FRANK E TIMIAN MILES D TOUCHBERRY JR JERRY G WEATHERFORD STEVEN E WETTERGREN
MICHAEL B WIER ELROY WILSON LOREN E WOOD JR CURTIS S WOODS ROBERT L WORTHINGTON
KEITH D ALLEN JR LUTHER E BALL JR LARRY B BARFIELD RICHARD I BRENNER ROBERT J BRINKMAN
HARRY P BURTON LOUIS CASTRO IRVING S CHENOWETH III ARLIE R COLLINS ANDERSON N RENSHAW III
GARY J DASHER DAVID F DECKER BOBBY L DENTON GARY G DETRICK GLENN W DOMER
RONALD B FERGUSON HAROLD L GREEVER TERRY L GUMP ROGER W HOOD RICARDO I ROMERO
MICHAEL D HOWARD HAROLD N JENSEN KENNETH V JENSEN BRUCE E JOHNSON TERRY E JONES
ALVIE J LEDFORD JR JAMES O LYNCH JOSEPH D MACY LARRY C MARTIN WILLIAM H MARTZ JR
RALPH D MCMURTRY FRANCIS J MELLAR JR JOSEPH D MELONSON JR DAVID T NELSON JOSEPH A ORETO
RICHARD A BROWNE WILLIAM C PIERSON III JOSEPH J REMEIKAS JR LARRY O ROBBINS THOMAS G ROMAINE
JOHN HALE JR JOHN J SCHMELZLE WILFRED F SCHMIDT JR CHRISTOPHER L SENESE NELSON O VAN HOUTEN
LOUIS J WEHRHEIM RONALD H YOUNG ROYCE H ADAMS JAMES N BLAVAT MICHAEL R BURNETTE
NORMAN C BYRD JAMES W DEAN FRANCIS E DUNLAP JR ROBERT M GENDRON MICHAEL K NICKERSON
DAVID W HILDRETH VICTOR M HODSON MICHAEL D HOLMES GARY O JACOBS ANDREW E JENKINS
CHARLES D CROSBY WALTER B JOHNSON FRANCISCO LICON JAMES W MOORE JR ALEXANDER D NEIBAUER
MICHAEL G PORTER LLOYD D QUILLEN THEODORE F SIEGEL THOMAS M SMITH WILLIAM L SPERB
RICHARD B TUTEN MICHAEL N VITALE JAMES W WILSON ROBERT B WOODARD BILLY C ALSTON
BOBBY R BAKER STANLEY A CARTER ALBERT E CREAMER STEPHEN W CUMMINGS TERRENCE J MORTENSEN
RAFAEL DE LEON JR JAMES W DERBYSHIRE LYLE E DROWN DOYLE D DUNBAR BRUCE G FRIEL
JOHN G GLASSEY ROBERT J GORDON MICHAEL E HARR HERBERT S HILDEBRAND WILLIAM F HITCHCOCK
WILLIE B JACOBS JOHN F JONES WALTER J JUNGER JR LAWRENCE O KELLER JR JOHN A LA POLLA
CLIFFORD G LABOMBARD NEAL W LOVSNES JR RALPH MAYNARD RONALD M MONTAPERT LARRY P TREGRE
VERBIN E DAVIDSON JOHN E MCDONALD MARTIN J NICKELSON ANTHONY A PROIETTI WAYNE R QUARLES
PETER T RASMUSSEN LAWRENCE D RICKEY JOHN L SMITH FREDERICK V SUCHOMEL JAMES W TAYLOR
JIMMY D LESTER JERONE J WARNICK ROBERT A YOUNG JR JOHN E BANISTER HARRY D BEECH JR
CARLYLE M BOWDEN III WILLIAM O BURKETT WAYNE E BYRNE KARL H CULP ROBERT E FINAN
WALTER E GIERMAN II ROBERT E GILL ROBERT E GULBRANDSEN RALPH W ISRAEL JR CHESTER JARMOLINSKI JR
JOHNNIE W JOHNSEN ANTHONY E KUPKA JOHN E LEWIS MICHAEL E LEX LARRY A SMITH
PETER C LITTLE THOMAS K LONG ANTHONY G MARKEVITCH JR RALPH C MUNSEY LEON J PIERCE
WILLIAM M KONYU ROBERT L RODGERS ROBERT P ROEHMER ROBERT W SATTERFIELD FREDRICK S SHAVEL
THOMAS W SNYDER ROBERT L BITTINGER JR ROY E BRIGHT KENNETH R BULL JOHN J CORWIN II
DOUGLAS E DAHILL JOHN C DRIVER MIKE D GEARHEART LARRY E GRAHAM WILLIAM W GRIFFITH
TOMMY C HEATON DANA B JENSEN JAMES C JOHNSON JOHN M JOYCE FRED KARAMAN
MICHAEL P RIBICH KEITH KESKI ALBERT A LADD LAWRENCE J LAUZON ANTHONY LAVITE III TRAVIS B LEE JR
ARLIE B MILAM CHARLES V NEWTON WILLIAM ORTEGA JAMES W PATTERSON JR LESLIE A POWELL
CHARLES F PREVEDEL WAYNE M RANDALL CHARLES D ROBINSON WILLIAM H SMITH ROBERT V WILLETT JR
JAMES C SWANSON SR WALTER M TAYLOR ROBERT W TORESON JAMES M TRIPLETT ROBERT J WHALEN
WILLIAM RACCA JAMES A BAKA LARRY D BLEYTHING KENNETH R BRINKER JOHN BURGESS
CHARLES CHANDLER JOHN B COMBS CURTIS K COOK JR ROBERT M CUNNINGHAM GEORGE C DAHLMAN
THOMAS A DAVIS JOHN T DE PRIEST DAVID A DITTMER RANDALL S ELLIS FRED G HAUG
HAROLD L ECKERT JR THOMAS M FITZPATRICK MICHAEL E GORDY DAVID D HANBURY ROBERT C HERMAN
JERRY D HUGHES ROBERT L HUMPHREY LLOYD W JONES GARRY L KUBLER DANIEL M LEAHY

PANEL 26W

JOHN P LYON ROY F MAAS DON J MCATEE VICTOR L MILLS
ROBERT L MORGAN JR JOSEPH E MORROW JR ROBERT J NEVEL HOWARD R PAQUIN PAUL D SAVANUCK
ROBERT L PARK RONALD E PONGRATZ AUBREY A REID JR RONALD H RILEY PERRY J SCOTT
JOHN C SHELLUM LOUIE J SHIANNA CHARLES D SHORT CHARLES C SMITH JR TIMOTHY T TIPTON
GLEN D TOMEK WILLIAM B WATSON FRANK C WILLIAMS REX W ACKERMAN JOSEPH J AGRI JR
REESE M ANDERSEN GERALD D ANGELLEY JOHN O BAUGHMAN ANDREW A BIEDRON JR ROBERT R BRADLEY
PAUL E ALLARD HAROLD G BOTTOMS DENNIS R CAMA LARRY H COOKE JAMES C CROSE
GAYLEN R GALLION RICHARD L HANNON LARRY N HARPER JOSEPH K HOLLINGSWORTH GERARD V PALMA
ROBERT D HUIE JR JAMES P JENSEN WALTER E JUSTICE SR ROBERT C KIJOWSKI ROLAND C LABONTE
JOE G LONGORIA DARYL L LOWERY TERRY B MILLER PERCY MOORE CARL P MORRISON
ARTHUR F HENDERSON DAVID L MCGILL ROY T MOSS ROLAND J PANARESE THEODORE S ROLSTAD
GEORGE H SMITH CHARLES L TANK BERNARD R TERHORST CHARLES E THOMAS JOHN J BACH III
RONALD BOHANNON ROBERT C BOUCHER CHARLIE P BRYANT JR ROGER W CUMMINGS CHARLES H VESEY
NICHOLAS ESPARZA JR GEORGE A HUBBARD RUSSELL H KITCHEN JR ANGEL M MEDINA-RIVERA TIBOR SOTAK
GLENARD J GREGORY GEORGE J PARKER JR SILAS W PAROBEK TYRONE J STATEN WILLIAM C STATES
CARL M CREAL GARY W THORNLOW ELISEO M VILLALOBOS SULLIVAN W WATSON BOYED T ADAMS
JONATHAN W ALLMAN BUEL E ANDERSEN JULIAN R ANDERSON JAMES H AUTREY DAVID L BANKS
PAUL T BAZAR RALPH BURKHALTER JR THOMAS A CHIALASTRI SANTANA S FERNANDEZ JR JOSEPH FICARA
JIMMY M GARDENHIRE THOMAS W GAUDET ROBERT K GILLIES DWANE G HOWARD MAXIE JACKSON JR
KENNETH C JENKINS CURRAN M JONES STEFAN MALKUT JERRY MORGAN JR RALPH R OCHOA
FRANCIS S KOVACS WILLIAM A MCCALL JR BERNARD G OLIVER JR BERNARD F RITCHIE ROBERT T ROHWELLER
CHARLES G RUSH JR TOMMY Q SEGARS JR RICHARD H SIMONSEN JAMES A SPENCER JR ALFRED STARK
GERALD W STEPHENS TIMOTHY R VAN TONGEREN EARL S WEMPLE CHARLES J WILSON JACK L BAKER
WILLIAM H BAZEMORE CHESTER E BINGHAM ROY A CARROLL ROBERT W CLIREHUGH JR WILLIAM J COUSAR
NICKOLAS G GARCIA JAMES HUDSON JR FELIX JACQUES DAVID LEE OFALEE PERKINS
GUADALUPE FLORES THOMAS W LENZ DALLAS E MCKINNEY JR RICHARD MCNEAL MEADDOW J OLSON
THOMAS D PERRY VINCENT C SCOTT JR MICHAEL R SKIPPER ARTHUR W SMITH HARLEY A SMITH JR
JOHNNIE P STEPHENS JR THOMAS J TISCHLER WALTER S VAN CLEAVE JERRY L WALL JOHN M WALSH
DAVID E WILLIAMS WARREN WILLIAMS MICHAEL J WINTERS ROGER M AULD JR OTTO P BARNHART
ALLAN V BARR JULIAN W BERG STEWART S BURR JACK D CAMPBELL HENRY W CARDWELL
JULIAN D DEDMAN RICHARD P DEXTRAZE JAMES H DUNN III ALLAN D EYLER DONALD O MCGRAW
TROY D FAULKNER MELVIN J FREISE OLLIE J GROSS JAMES P HEIM JOHN F KOEHLER
ROGER D CURTIS JOHN H MCSWINE JOHN R MIFFLIN CHESTER A MOLLEY ROBERT W MOON
GARY P NEIMAN DENNIS J OLIVER DARNELL M PAYNE KENNETH R PEDERSEN STEPHEN R PETERSON
STEPHEN L PLOTKIN MARTIN D REYNOLDS WILLIAM F ROCCO TOBY S RODRIQUEZ JR DANIEL F ROSANOVA
DONALD E ROSS ARNOLD SANFORD JOHN R SPEAR CHARLES D TANNEHILL JOHN W TIDERENCEL
WILLARD H TILL JR THOMAS J WATTS JOHN J WITTS JR WILLIAM P WOFFORD JAMES A WORTHINGTON
DONALD D BLAIR JAMES E BOUSQUET JAMES A BROWN II WILLIE BROWN LAWRENCE J BUDZINSKI
BILLY C DAVIS FRANK W FLONNOY JR JOSEPH J GAVIA CARL J GREEN JR GREGORY M HARRIGAN

ERNEST C JAMISON CHARLES R JOHNSON DAVID G KELLISON JAMES A LEACH EDWARD D MARTIN
DARWIN D MCGEE ERNEST M PERRY JR RANDALL RUGGS JERRY M SHRIVER JAMES J WAGNER
JAMES M ABBOTT RICHARD L ANDERSON GILBERT D ARROYO-BRENES JAMES H BELFLOWER JOHN J HICKEY
JOHN E BLADEK ALBERT N BOOKER THOMAS M BRANDOM JR VIRGIL BURKS JR ADRIAN D CARBAJAL
MICHAEL COTTERILL RALPH L CUTLER JERALD C DAVIS RONALD C DEFORREST WARREN C DELANEY
JOHN E DOBASH MICHAEL R DORMAN PAUL FAULK FRED A HARTMAN JR PAUL R LUNSFORD
SAMUEL A BESSENT CLAYBURN M HATCHER EMERSON E HELLER LARRY D JOHNSON MICHAEL J KELLY JR
GEORGE R KIDD ROBERT L KING DAVID L KITCHEN DAVID M LACEY RODGER P LANTER
KENNETH W FOWLER LARRY G LEOPOLDINO JOHN M MADDEN JR JOHN A MARSH MITCHELL MESSING
WILLIAM C MCCORMICK JR JAMES D MOORE JACK M ORNELAS JOHN T PATRONE CARL E PILKINGTON SR
GEORGE ROBINSON JOHN W SADLER ELTON L SEARCY MARK M STEELEY WILLIAM D STEPP
THOMAS G STONGE RONALD B VANN DAVID W WATSON DELVIN K WILSON GARY ALLEN
LEO M BRELAND JAMES D BURNS THEODORE H BURTON ROBERT J CARTER FRANCISCO GREGORY
JOSEPH M CORNELISON JAMES R DORSEY JR JAMES B EAST JR GEORGE E EATON FRANCISCO M GARCIA JR
CHARLES W CHANDLER ROBERT J GOEDDE JOHNNIE L GRAHAM JR MARK J HANSEN JAMES E JOHNSON JR
MARK S LENNON DWIGHT A MCNEES WILLIE J MURRY DONALD W NOEL LARRY D PARR
RICKEY A PROCTOR JOHN F QUINN SETH E RANDOLPH DON M ROBERTSON FREDERIC L SCHRECONGOST
DAVID SCOLNICK CHARLES R SINK LARRY E SMITH MARCUS W STODDARD ROBERT L TRISDALE
RICHARD L TURLEY VINCENT VOSYLIUS RICHARD H WALKER BEVERLY C WARE ALTON D WOODRUFF
JAMES D VALOV ALFONSO A WEBB ALBERT D AUSTIN JR DARYLE W BATT ARNOLD R BRAY
LARRY D BROCK BENJAMIN BUGARIN WALTER C CARTER BILLY C CHAMBERS RICHARD J CORDOVA
MICHAEL E COURTRIGHT JAMES D CROW RICHARD I CUNNINGHAM BERTRAND J DACEY EARL M DENEEN
ALAN B DENHOFF BILL J DUPREE CLYDE A GIDDINGS WILLIAM W HENDERSON ROBERT E HOY
JEFFERY A HARVEY GERALD HUFFMAN CHARLES W JENNINGS DEAN R JOHNSON JIMMY D JOHNSON
DANIEL A KEENE WILLIAM H KINDLE RODGER M KOEFOD JOHN D LEARY WENDELL W LESLIE
LARRY D LOWERY LAWRENCE W MAHURTER WILLIAM J MCFARLAND PHILLIP S MOHNIKE ARVIN L OQUINN
JAMES C MOORE JR PAUL J NEELY RICHARD A OMAN RICHARD D ORLANDO FRANK J PROKOP
CHARLES E REDD PHILIP T REGAN JR LESLEY S REITER LORNE J SIPPERLEY GARY R SMITH
ALFRED W SPINNER DENNY L ASHER SHELDON O BARNES HUGH B BLEVINS JR GALE L BROWN
HAL C CASTLE JR ALBERTO G CORTEZ GERALD F COULTHART JOHN S DAVENPORT JOHN C DAVIS
JOHN R EARLEY MELVIN G EHRHART KENNETH K EPLEY FREDERIC R HARBOT JOSEPH F HART
MANUEL HERNANDEZ JR RICHARD D HERTZLER EDWIN E HOFFMAN CARL R HOUSER LARRY L HOWELL
MURRAY J JACKSON BERT M JENKINS HERBERT L MALONE WALTER L NUTT III ROY E PARKER
KENNETH E POLK RICHARD J REARDON JAMES H REHBERG LARRY W RHODES PHILLIP E ROTHAR JR
MICHAEL E SCHAFERNOCKER RUFUS SIRMANS COURTNEY A SKINNER WILLIAM H STOUT III ROGER L WARD
PETER M STENGEM AUSTIN TEETH DANIEL WELSH PHILLIP W WILLIAMS RONALD K WILSON
NICHOLAS L FRANZER BERT M ADAMS III PAUL A BROUSE JAMES W CLEARY SIMON DEAN JR MARK H DIXON
LESTER E DOWNING DANIEL E FECK RICHARD J FISHER ROBERT M FLANIGAN FREDERICK E FURR
ERWIN J HARDER JAMES A JENSEN RICHARD L KELLER ROY L LIPSCOMB WALLACE J MOSLEY ELMER L SPIVEY
STEPHEN M GABRYS ANDREW B RANKIN DENNIS M RAY FRANCISCO RODRIGUEZ JR CLINTON W SHAVER JR
ARTHUR R STRAHIN JERRY E THOMPSON TERRY N THOMPSON ROBERT P TIDWELL JAMES W TUTTLE
ROBERT H WESCOTT JR FRANK C AMBROSIO LAWRENCE E BAUER WALTER P BEM RICHARD P BLANTON
DAN A BOLTON JR JOHN P BYRNE LOVELL F COEN DENNIS CONRY LARRY A CUNNINGHAM
ALBERT J DAVIS MICHAEL D ERHART HOWARD W ERICKSON JR PHILLIP W FLANNIGAN FRANCIS E STEWART
GERALD E GORAL GLENN A GORDON STEPHEN T HALL DANNY W JARVIS GARY A JOHNSON
CARL E KLEINAU RAYMOND J KRUPINSKI JOHN F LAWRENCE SAMUEL D LOVETTE DARYL G MEIDINGER
MICHAEL E METOYER MICHAEL MIRANDA JOHN W OSBORNE ESPIRIDION PEREZ DAVID P ROY
ANTONIO FALCO FERNANDO S SALDANA GEORGE SIDELKO HARRY N STONESIFER HAROLD P TATEM
ERNEST W TEWS GUYLER N TULP DENNIS G WARFIELD FRED T WILLIAMS LLOYD J WOOD SR
ARTHUR W BAILEY JR WILLIAM H BAUER STEVEN D BELSLY JAMES D BLASKO KERNELL P BRADSBY
LARRY R COLLINS ROSARIO J DEL IGNACIO E DURO MARTIN F FOLEY JOHN F HATFIELD
GARRY L HAYES CHARLES B HIGHT RONALD A HILL EDWARD A HORN JR PAUL S LAVEROCK
MICHELE L JACKSON JOHNNY LISBON GABRIEL H MADRID DANIEL C NELSON RANDY D OLIVER
RANDY C PARO LAWRENCE W PARRANTO JR KENNETH A PREJEAN KENNETH E ROSS FELIX J SALAS
DAVID R SCHAEFER JOHN D SEXTON RICHARD S SLY AMMONS E SMITH JR WAYNE A STEVENS
LESLIE J STEWART WAYNE O TAYLOR JOHN R TINE JOSE R TORRES-RODRIGUEZ JAMES C VANDEVENTER
KENNETH L WHITE GERALD D ANTHONY FRANKLIN G ATKINSON JR RICHARD B BENNETT RODNEY J BLACK
JOSE C ALVAREZ FLETCHER W BOLES II NEIL S BROWN DANIEL CARRASCO JAMES G CASE
LUIS P CRUZ MELVIN W EAKINS JAMES D FLURRY FREDERICK J FOLLETTE MICHAEL J FRATTO
ROLLAND K FRY BRUCE E FUNK EUGENE GASTELUM GARY E HOLTZCLAW LARRY E KIGAR
JERRY R LANGLEY WILLIAM A MANSERGH JR PHILLIP L MASCARI JERRY R MEADOWS EDWARD C POWERS
RENE MEDEGUARI EARNEST D MENLEY WALTER J MORRIS DAVID F OSBORNE CHARLES W POOL JR
GLENN R MEARNS TROY E POWELL WAVEL W POWELL TIMOTHY H PYLE SAMUEL F RYAN
CHARLES H SHELTON JOHN F STEWART LARRY D STOLLAR THOMAS N STRICKLAND JAMES H SUMNER
WILLIAM P THOMAS ROBERT E TRIGALET STEPHEN A VIX JR DENNIS R WAGIE ROBERT L WALTERS
EDDIE J WILLIAMS JR THOMAS E WILLIAMS JR ROY L ARNOLD EDWARD N BARR LARRY C BEEBE
ROBERT W BOWE LLEWELLYN P DICKENSON RICHARD C GARCIA DAVID L GIRARDO SILAS L HICKS JR
GERALD W FORTE NORVILLE M HENN JR PAUL JONES MICHAEL R KITCHEN DAVID A LA COURSE
ARMAND D MASTEN RICHARD D MILLER RAMON MORENO RONALD R SOMES MICHAEL D STEVENS
EARL P SNOW LEMUEL E TERRELL GARY W WRIGHT MICHAEL T ADAMS CHARLES H BEST
GORDON D BIRDSELL RAYMOND H BRODIE JR RUSSELL W EADS JAMES P FLAGELLA MICHAEL E LE MASTER
DENNIS R GUSTAFSON WALTER S HATHAWAY GREGORY A HEINRICH BOBBY R JOHNSON PEDRO M MAES
WILLIAM D BRITTON RICHARD W HOUSEHOLDER JOSEPH R KARPY JOHN R KLAPAK JR JOSEPH T MURPHY JR

PANEL 25W

JEFFERY M PARENT NORMAN L PLEMMONS WILLIAM D QUINN III ROBERT L THOMAS
DON L ROSS ALAN E SINGER BILLY R STUBBS RICHARD D SWEET CLIFFORD TABOR JR
MILTON W REMMLER JR JAMES L URNES FRANCISCO VILLANUEVA JR RAYMOND C WILLIS ARTHUR L WOODS
RICHARD L BAUMBERGER JR WOODROW W BISHOP JR ODELL CRAIG CURTIS C DEES JAMES M ELLIS
WILLIE J FRAZIER LEROY J GENTRY HERMAN L GRAYSON GEORGE R GREEN JR KEITH T HAMMOND
RODNEY A HOHN LAFE INGRAM ANTHONY B JONES RICHARD L LASSITER SINCLAIR B LEWIS JR
ROBERT D HARKER MARTIN J MAHER ARTHUR T MALLINCKRODT JR BARRIE M NEWTON HENRY C RAMSEY
LOUIS SOLIVAN JOHN W STEWART DONALD T TAYLOR JAMES L WASHINGTON SR ALLEN W ALLUMS
TYSON V BEALL OLIVER A BEST JR NORMAN K BILLIPP JAMES A BLAIN JOHN O BOWMAN
MICHAEL L CHRISTMAS GEORGE L COODY STEEVE A CRAWSHAW RICHARD J DALEY IRENARDO F PADRON
BURTON W DALKE KENNETH L DULLEY CHARLES M FULLER JOHN R HAGAN MICHAEL J WOEHRL
LARRY D HOCH ROGER L JAMISON PAUL J KRONTHALER RICHARD M LUCKENBACH JR JACKIE R MCKENZIE
LARRY H BRINKEY ODIE C MCMURRAY WILLIAM L NEGRINI FRUTO J OQUENDO MARVIN R PAINTER
GILBERT G PALACIO KENNETH PARKER JOHN M PRATT VICENTE ROSA-URBINA FOSTER L SONNIER
WALTER A ELAM JOSE SOTO-CONCEPCION BRIAN E SWANE CHARLIE C WILLIAMSON JR JOSEPH WOODARD
ANTHONY P AGAR JAMES A BORDEN DALE A FAHRNI JOHN J GLYNN JR WALLIS G PATTERSON
JOHN A KEESLING CLYDE T MARTIN PAUL D MARTINEZ JR JOHN F MATTAROCCHIA JR HENRY E RUSSELL
ALTON S ELLIS ROY L MCDONALD NORBERT MONTOYO-RODRIGUE GARY B NICHOLS ROOSEVELT F PENN
DONALD R HAYWOOD LOUIS A PEREZ RONALD S PIERCE JOHN M SHINAULT DANIEL TIRADO
JIM A BARTON DARREL G BITTNER CHARLES G BOLING MELVIN BOLTON ARTURO PELAJIO
JOSEPH W BORGES WILLIAM J BRASHEAR MIGUEL E BRIALES CARL N CLUTTER RONALD B REYNOLDS
ALBERT COBB JR EDWIN R DANEHART ARTHUR M DAY FRANK E GARLEY WILBUR L GREEN
ROBERT J HAWKS LARRY K HENSON PETER L JAKOBSEN HAROLD L JONES ANDRE L KNOPPERT
MARK S ANDERSON JOHN S MERRIMAN HENRY G MUNDT II CHARLES E OUTMAN DWAYNE R PICKART
MICHAEL J BRULL JAMES E RICKETTS THOMAS J SIMS LYNN L STEPHENSON ROBERT E TURNER
ALLEN TYLER THEODORE D WARD SAMMIE L WARREN MAHLON H WATKINS ANTHONY R WERNER
ROBERT J ALERT JR ROBERT A BANKS HAROLD D BEACH GARY L BROOKHART GERALD L CALL
RICHARD D CHENEY SAMUEL CHRISTOPHER JR TERRANCE B CLANCY BRUCE D DICK DARRYL T DOMBROSKI
GREGORY L FLECK GEORGE T HALL JIMMY L HENRY JOHN M HENSON MELVIN JOHNSON
EDWARD M KLANIECKI MICHAEL LA BIANCA THOMAS W MARKUNAS ALVIN MERRICKS JAMES A REASONS JR
GERALD MCCORVEY VICTOR D MORALES MARVIN L NOE JOHN A OLSEN JUAN ORTIZ-RAMIREZ
FREDERICK J MAGSAMEN DAVID M PETERSON RICHARD J PICKARD GUY L PRATT JR JAMES A SANDERS
PAUL J SEYMORE ISMAEL SOLIS LAWRENCE E STRAYER JIM A THOMPSON ALBERT J VAN HORN
JAMES C WARD LARRY W WATKINS OSCAR L WHEELER ALBERT A WHITTLE JOE ALMEIDA JR HAROLD B DEEL
SAMUEL W BELL BENJAMIN C BLISS ROBERT E BOWMAN LAWRENCE S BOYCE RONALD D KELLER
GERALD G BROUSSARD STANLEY W BURGESS CANDELARIO P BUSTOS MARCUS R BYOUS PHILLIP E COMBS
JAMES C BYRD NICHOLAS F CERRATO JAMES C DEWAR RUSSELL M DOBYNS JR SAM EGGERT
KENNETH J EYER JR PETER F FEGATELLI ALBERT D FOSTER CHARLES J FREELAND HENRY GARCIA JR
PETER GIBSON DEMETRIUS J GRAYS ROBERT W HANSEN THOMAS H HEISE ROBERT J HYNES RUSSELL L PLATT
EDWARD ATKUCUNAS PAUL N KUPCHINSKAS VIRGIL L LARKINS PAUL D MANNEROW ROY J MROSEWSKE
HERBERT B MURPHY PATRICK E MURPHY REX F NELSON JR DENNIS D PALM DELBERT P WRIGHT
MAURICE E LUNDY JOHN F PAYNE DAVID A PROTAIN EDWARD A PUTNEY PETER E SIPP JAMES E TANKERSLEY
DONALD R SANDERS JR ARTURO S SISNEROS CHARLES P SMITH JR RONNY SMITH ALLAN E STAHLSTROM
JAMES R THOMAS ROY S THOMAS RICHARD A WADE BILLY G WAID WILLIAM WALTERS
ANTHONY J PASSERELLO KENNITH W WHEELER ROBERT L WILLEY ERVIN H WILLIAMSON TERRY L ADKINS
JAMES L SIPES EDWARD A BARLOW MILLS BEALE III MALCOLM F BELL RONALD J CARTER GARY G DAGLEY
ERVIN J EMRICK ROBERT M FUENTES JAMES M GILBERT BRUCE A GOURLAY THOMAS E GRAY
MARTIN L GREEN JR JAMES E GREENE JR EDWARD W GRIFFITH ARTURO B GUTIERREZ HEINRICH RUHLMANN
DARRELL E HARTMAN THOMAS W HASTINGS WILLIE R HORNBURGER JOSEPH E JACQUEZ GERALD D JERDE
GEORGE H JULES ROBERT C KERCSMAR ROBERT G KOVAL TERRY L LARSEN MICHAEL L LICKEY
JOHN H LINN STEPHEN R LOPEMAN JOHN R MCLAUGHLIN LONZIA R MOORE R C MYERS
TERRY K MAREADY JOHN E MCCARRELL TERRY A MCCARTHY PATRICK R MCCLURE MICHAEL S NAKASHIMA
CHARLIE T NEAL ROBERT N NEWMAN RICHARD M PACO CHARLES M PENLEY JR DENNIS R RANK
MICHAEL W GREEN AARON L ROSENSTREICH JOHN M RUCKER WILLIAM C RYAN MICHAEL A SCHROEDER
SAMUEL B SCHWARTZ DAVID H SHIFLETT RONALD L SHROPSHIRE HAROLD R SIMONDS HUBERT S TILLEY JR
WILLIAM S SLAUGHTER ROBERT B STARKES JR WILLIAM H SWANSON CLIFFORD K TAIRA DAVID A TRINKALA
NORMAN L TUNGATE MICHAEL A WALTERS CARLISLE O WARK JR CHESTER J WARTMAN LARRY L WEEDEN
RONNIE G WEESE JAMES C WILSON VICTOR M YANEZ RICHARD L ZODY GERALD R ACTON

JOSE J AGUILLON RICHARD M AMICK CHARLIE C ANTHONY ALAN ASHER DON L ATKINS
ROY L BALDWIN CHARLES L BARBIERE ALFRED BARNES THOMAS M BARR BARRY R BAUSCH
LARRY L BAXTER DAVID M BECK ARTHUR F BELL RICHARD J BENNETT ALLAN C BENSON
DAVID J BORON CURTIS BREEDLOVE KENNETH L BRINKS CHARLES L BROWN GEORGE A BROWN
WILLIAM J BURKE JR HUGH P CALDWELL JR CHARLES C CASE DAVID E CHERRY JR STEPHEN W DE ARO
JOSEPH C CHISHOLM ROBERT W COMPTON DONALD J COOK GARY A CORRIE ROBERT L COWAN III
ROBERT G CEVALLOS HOWARD E CRAMBLET JOHN H CRISP THOMAS W CUMMINS RONALD DE LORENZO
DAVID E DEMINGS PHILLIP R DOEBERT TIMOTHY C DONAVAN EDWIN A DOWNS JOHN W DRANE
PETER P DUBIEL JOHN F ELAND JAMES T ELSWICK JR PAUL D ELWART MICHAEL D FIELDS
WILLIAM M FIELDS RICHARD J FLAGIELLO CHARLES W FORD EARNEST T FREEMAN DONALD W GARRETT
THOMAS H GENTINNE RONALD L GRAY CLYDE R GREEN MELVIN GREEN JR ROBERT E GRETH
DENNIS M GUILMETTE MARLOYE K HALGRIMSON CURTIS L HARDIN JAMES R HARRISON JAMES W HARTER
LAWRENCE D HARVEY RICHARD W HAYNES TERRY R HEISER GERALD E HENRY ALVIN C HINSON
RICHARD L HOPKINS ERNEST J HUGHES JAMES IDLETT JAMES E ISAAC JR WILLIAM E JERSE
FRANK E JOHNSON JAMES S JORDAN ORVAL C JORDON III ROBERT L KLEINSMITH MICHAEL A MATHISON
WILLIAM C KNAUS ROBERT G KRELL THOMAS E LATHAM ALFRED L LAWYER DAVID A LEFLER
ROBERT D LEWIS MORTEN A LIND JR JOSEPH L LOGAN JR JOHN LOVE JR AARON H LOWE
RANDY T KENDLE WILLIAM L LUTZ ADANO H MADRID CHARLES E MANNING JOHN A MARTIN III
RODNEY H MAUNAKEA JOSEPH E MELVIN JORGE L MENDEZ-MATOS JEROME MENTER RICHARD T MILLER
RICHARD H MCCORMICK JR DENNIS A MCELROY LESLIE W MCKILLOP MICHAEL J MITCHELL WAVERY MOORE
JOSEPH P MCKNIGHT ROY L NATIONS DAVID R NEFF JOSEPH A NURZYNSKI LYLE C PALMER
MICHAEL S O'BRIEN TIMOTHY B O'REILLY CARL E PACKARD JR LARRY G PADBERG FIDEL PADILLA
RAYMOND F NORVELL MARVIN E PARK WASHINGTON PAULEY BRUCE E PETEROY ERNEST A PINAMONTI
MARION D POWELL ALAN N PRENTICE CECIL W QUEEN FELICE N RATTA CLARENCE I RISHER
ROBERT A ROOSSIEN CARLOS J ROSE JOHN ROZOW ANDREW R SABO WILLIAM E SCHAEFER
ARTHUR E SCOTT RONALD M SETTIMI RICHARD D SHANNON JR LAWRENCE R SHEPARD RICHARD L SICKLES
NATHAN B SIMMONS OLEN W SMITH RONALD G SMITHEE JAMES R SOWERS LARRY E SPAULDING
JAMES V SPURLEY JR EDSEL W STEAGALL JAMES R STEVENSON THOMAS A STRATTON RICHARD A WHYTE
ISAIAH T STUKES CHARLES G STULTZ MICHAEL J STURGILL ROBERT T TAYLOR HARRY E THERIAULT
CHARLES THOMAS JR CARL THOMPSON JOHN F THOMPSON LARRY L THOMURE EDWARD R TOLLEY
BERTALAN J TOTH ESTEBAN A TREVINO JR PRESTON TRIBBLE JR MICHAEL R TUCKER RODGER A VANDERGRIFF
ALBERTO R VASQUEZ JR SAMUEL L WABLE GARY T WALZ DAVID E WEIDNER DARRELL C WEST
WAYNE D STIGEN WENDELL A WESTON THOMAS A WHITBY CHARLES E WILSON JR JOSEPH W WOODARD JR
ROGER E WOOSTER DENNIS H WRIGHT JOHN M YEATTS BOBBY J YEWELL REX C ALLRED
SCOTT F ANDRESEN CARL F ARBOGAST JR DANIEL R ARNOLD EVANS BENBOW JR DANNY W FANN
BRUCE C BESSOR PATRICK W BEST JIMMIE R BICE JAMES L BLANTON JR MICHAEL D BLEA
JERRY C BOCK KILBERN D BOUDRA OSCAR D BOYDSTON JOHN H BROOKS JERRY T LEE
GALEN C BROWN DAVID F BUKOWSKI EDWARD A CLARKE THOMAS M CONNELL DONALD J CORBETT
KENNETH T CRUISE JR MARTIN L DAMITIO WILLIAM C DICKERSON MICHAEL J DOMINKOWITZ JOEL R KELLY
ODELL D BEASLEY JAMES R DUNKLE JAMES H DYE WILLIAM G EGGENBERGER JOHN V FOLGER
THOMAS E FOSTER MOULTON L FREEMAN MARION L GARDNER JAMES R GOHAGIN FELIX G GONZALES JR
PAUL V GOODWIN PAUL E GOONAN JR ERNEST L GORDON ASA P GRAY JR GARY J GREINER
ALVIN GRIMES ROBERT A GRUHN JAMES C HARPER JR WILLIAM L HAYDEN CLEABERN W HILL JR
RAYMOND A JINKS ERIC B JOHNSON LARRY P JONES JAMES J JULIAN JR RICHARD R KELLEY
THOMAS W DAVIS HOMER P KENDRICK HARRY W KERKSTRA DONALD R KRAFT BOBBY G LAWRENCE
RANDY K BRONSON JOHN A LOVE JEROME K LUKAS PAUL R LUKINS ROBERT R MALECKI
JESSE A MALLOBOX JAMES A MARGRO RONALD W MARRS BRENT T MASCHER STEPHEN M THOMPSON
ROBERT S MASUDA BRUCE J MATTA ARLEN J MILLER DANA L MILLER TEDDY R MOORE
LARRY I BROADHEAD DOMINGO F MORADO MICHAEL R MUNCH DAVID L MUNOZ JOHN C NELSON DANIEL C NICHOLS
PHILIP G NICHOLS WARREN P NIX STEPHEN V PARKER SAMUEL L PATTERSON FRANCIS G PATTON
JOHN A PEREZ GEORGE W PICKEL WILLIAM D POOLE JR JOHN E RAY MICHAEL R ROSS
ROGER D ROSS THOMAS W SADLER RALPH M SANTINELLO MIKE J SCOTT WILLIAM F SILVER JR
FRANCIS L SOUZA WILLIAM V SPRINGFIELD WESLEY W STEVENS JEFFREY C STOWE IRA J STURGEON
SALVATORE P MANINO LYNN C SWANSON SAMUEL C THARPE ALBERT C THOMPSON JAMES M THOMPSON
THEODORE R VIVILACQUA JAMES R WALTERS ALAN C WARD JOHN WEISBROD TERRY A WENDER
MYLES D WESTMAN LYNN J WIESER RAYMOND L WILLIAMS KENNETH E WITMER DANIEL T ABNEY JR

PANEL 24W

CHARLES E BOUTTRY JOE E BRAGG TOMMY L BROWN TYREE CARDWELL
ROBERT E BELT DAVID BRUNER THOMAS E BUMGARNER DAVIS C BUTCHER LEONARD B CASTILLO
WILLIE J CHAPMAN HENRY A CHEVALIER FREDDIE L COFFMAN RAYMOND CRITES DANIEL E ROSEN
WILLIAM DANIELS JR RAYMOND W DE MEOLA WILLARD J DUFRESNE JR JOSEPH W FREEMAN JR ERIC J GRECO
RONALD W FEROUGE MICHAEL K FULTZ GILES W GILMER MARK J GIRON FRED G GUSMAN JR
WILLIAM R HALE CURTIS R HARRIS GEORGE G HEATHERLY PHILLIP HERNANDEZ ROBERT M HIGGINBOTHAM
MICHAEL A HUNTLEY GERALD R HWANG RONNIE W JOHNSON GERALD J KELLY JR JAMES C KOPSENG
MERLIN J LABER ROBERT F LAUBACHER JAMES A LEE MICHAEL D MELTON MICHAEL W MILNER
LESLIE L MCCORKLE WILLIAM L MCGOWAN JIMMY L MCLELLAN LUTHER MORGAN JR HENRY L OWENS
FLOYD J PARKS REESE M PATRICK STEPHEN T PERRY STEVEN G PETTIS CHARLES H PILKINGTON JR
GARY R CLODFELTER DONALD W PRIEST JR CLAUDE D PULLEN MICHAEL W RECTOR DAVID B SCHACHNER
WAYNE K SCHALTENBRAND DANIEL J SHEA JAMES B SMITH R J SMITH WINSTON O SMITH
RUFUS N STEVENSON JR DAVID A STIYER LARRY E THOMAS DONALD W VALLEN JR SAMMIE W WADDLE
LARRY S WEIL WILLIAM J WINTERS LARRY V WOLFRUM LUIS C BORREGO JR DAVID J BREDESEN
EMMETT R BROWN JAMES T COBLE JUAN L CONTRERAS WALTER E DAVIS DEWEY R DECKER
WILLIAM C DONICS JAMES EPPS DANIEL GAUNA JR GARY L GILLARD KENNEDY JACQUES
JEROME D JORGENSON DAVID M KIRK ALBERT L KOON GEORGE A LAMOTHE TERRY L LESH
MICHAEL P LYDEN JOHN G MASINSKI ARTHUR R MCFARLAND ANTHONY J MINOTTI ARTHUR J MURRAY JR
FLOYD C NEVINS DUANE W NYBLOM JOSE L OSUNA GEORGE P PERKINS NORRIS A PHILLIPS
RONALD C PHILLIPS JOSEPH M PRICE RALPH A RAMIREZ JR PAUL I RODERIGUES PHILLIP D SANDERS
HARRY D SARAKOV BRUCE SAUNDERS JOHN L SCHULTZ WILLIAM H SHULTZ LARRY W SMITH
EDDIE W SNIPES WALTER R STACY RICHARD W STINDL JERRY D THOMAS AMADO A VALENCIA
ARTHUR G VILLALOBOS LINDBERG WADE CARL W WALLS LARRY WARREN GEORGE D WILLIAMS JR
AUTHRAN W WINFREY ROBERT L WORDEN DAN YAZZIE JAMES A BATEMAN LEONARD A COLES
MELVIN T COWDELL ROY W DUNBAR JR JOE L FOWLER PATRICK R MCNELIS ALEXANDER A MONGELLI
ROGER W PEDUE GARY W PLANTE DENIS G SCHMIDT JOSEPH V SCHMIDT GEORGE D THOMAS
JAMES G WITHAM RONNIE G ALCOCK DAVID ALICEA-SERRANO FELIX ARROYO-SIERRA JR EDWARD DEITMAN
ARTHUR J ARTKOP DALE F BROWN THOMAS L CHRISTIANSEN PAUL A COWAN LEON D COX
ROBERT W ANDREWS JR DAVID R CROCKER JR LAWRENCE DE MILIO JERRY L EWING JAMES R FIELDS
JOHN R FRONGILLO HERBERT L GAY LARRY GRACE BERNARD HAMLET JR LLOYD E HANDSHUMAKER JR
HARVEY N HEDSTROM LAWRENCE E HITCHENS RICHARD J HORNBACK JAMES A HULL JR JOHN A NICHOLAS
JAMES D KLUGE RICHARD E MAY JOSEPH MCCANTS JR LOWELL W MEYER CHARLES M MOE JR
JAMES B JOHNSON SR DOUGLAS E LOHMEYER PHILLIP L MACLEOD RONALD E PACE GILBERT W PAGE
WALTER PALMER DENNIS H RHEN WILLIAM R SESSIONS RICHARD E STAAB VIRGIL G STEWART
EARL R TURNER JR KENNETH E VAN HOY DAVID W WILSON RAYMOND C WOOD WILLIAM J ADAMS
PETER A ARKOETTE GREGORY G BECK PAUL G BELLINO LARRY J BUDDE MILTON J BUSH
ROBERT A BONEBRIGHT LINCOLN E BUNDY STEVEN B CALHOUN JAMES P CASEY DAVID P CHENEY JR
JAMES T COFER GREGORY D CORNETT ROGER M COURVILLE JAMES A COX RALPH J CRUTTS
CHARLES J CUDLIKE ALLEN R CULPEPPER THOMAS J DE MARINIS JAMES A DIMOCK JR DOUGLAS M EVANS
HENRY F EVANS DAVID G FINNEGAN JAMES R FIUME JAMES O FOGLEMAN ROBERT L FREEMAN
NUN P GA JOSE GARZA JR KITCHELL S GIBBS DANIEL J GIORDANO III PHILIP L GRIESER
DUANE L HARTENHOFF NEIL W HAYDEN HAROLD C HEDDEN JR CARROLL F HERSEY LEONARD M HICKSON
LARRY L HOLMES LEO J HUBER III STEVEN R HUFFSTUTLER RUSSELL L JETT KENNETH J JOANIS
WILLIE L KIRKLAND JOHN J LASKOWSKI BIRDEN J LAWSON THOMAS D LIPSCOMB KENNETH E LOCKHART
JERRY M LOVELL DONALD J MALICEK CALVIN MEADOWS JR HANS L MILLS MIGUEL O MORENO
GARY D MCCRAY BRIAN R MCNEW DAVID E MOVCHAN JOHN L NALLS BOBBY G NEWBY
ANTHONY J O'NEILL FRED H PADDLEFORD RONNIE E PARKER WILLIAM J PETERSON NORMAN P SINGER
CHARLES W PIGOTT JORDY J PITRE JORY J PITRE EDMOND C POLENSKI PATRICK L RICE KERMIT B ROBERTS
JOHN C PAPE RUDOLPH ROSSI GARY J SCHEULEN JIMMY D SELLS THOMAS C SOTO
OTHA T SPRIGGS JR DANA M SYKES GEORGE E TACKETT GARY R TROWER GARRY L UPLINGER
GARY S VANN JOHN M VOLLMERHAUSEN JR CARL J WANNER JOSEPH J WILLIAMS JOHN C WILLIAMSON
CHARLES D BUCHANAN RICHARD CARBONE JAMES C COCKERL W K CREASON WILLIE C DAVIS
HAROLD C DAWSON JR CHRISTOPHER C DONAHUE WILEY B EARLEY JOEL W FORRESTER DAVID P GAUCHE
WILLIAM C GEARING JR BILLY R HEAD THOMAS M HOFFMANN JEREMIAH JUNE DONALD G KELLY
DONALD L KELLY TIMOTHY K LE CLAIR EDDIE MONTGOMERY JR KENNETH A PAVAN THOMAS C TREIBLE
RANDALL A MEE HOWARD M PETERSON DONALD F SCORSONE ROBERT A THOMPSON DONALD A TURSO
FREDERICK C THOMPSON JR WILLIAM E WHALEY III THOMAS F BARTH DANIEL S BEHAR SAMUEL C HALL
EDWARD A BROOKS ROBERT W BUCKLEY JOE T CONKLE LARRY F DODDS DONOVAN R FLUHARTY
ANTHONY BONGO ARTHUR K FORBES RAEFORD J GERALD JR ROY W GRAHAM BENJAMIN W HAIRE
JAMES A JENKINS BRUCE I LUTTRELL WILLIAM L MARCY ROBERT J MCDOWELL JR TOMMY D WRIGHT
JOHN M RANDALL TIMOTHY F ROBSON JAMES B SHELBY RAYMOND M SHINELDECKER DALE G SMITH
JOSEPH C STONE JON R SUMMERS JOHN S TAYLOR PASQUALE TORRE DOUGLAS D VAUGHAN
GUADALUPE E MONTOYA DAVID H WILKERSON HARRY D ASHCRAFT JIMMIE V BOCK L C CARTER
ERNEST L CLARK ROBERT L COOPER PATRICK R DIEHL MICHAEL K DIXON CAREY L DOBSON
DONNIE BIARUM PATRICK W DWYER CLYDE S EVANS LOUIS E FENCEROY GENE T GIETZEN PETER J GLYNN
ROBERT E GOODNER JAMES R HASH MARK J HAVERLAND JR CHARLES E HAWKINS JR KENNETH D PETTIGREW
EDWARD J HOGAN THOMAS P JACKSON JR ALBERT JOHNSON JR JERRY J KOCANDA III JOHN E LOGUE JR
CARL R MARTIN ENRIQUE MARTINEZ ROY G MATTHEWS PHILIP J MODDERMAN LEE A NAPIER
MICHAEL M HATZELL ALBERT O NELSON JR CHARLES H PEARCE JR EDISON R PHILLIPS THOMAS A POTTHOFF
TIMOTHY R PTACEK JAMES T RALPH JOHN W RICHARD PEDRO A RIOS KEITH N STARNES JR
JAMES I SANFORD JAMES S SCARMEAS JR LYNN D SHUGART CLARENCE SIZEMORE WILLIAM W SMITH
SAMUEL RAMOS KENNETH D SPENCER LAWRENCE M STUCK DOUGLAS G SWANSTROM RICHARD E TAMER
ROBERT L VAUGHN JR JOHNNIE B WESTERVELT GERALD L WILSON ROBERT W ARNOLD EARL P BEECHING
JOHNNY L BRYANT RALPH W CONNERS JR CALVIN E COOKE CLARENCE CREAGHEAD JOHN L CROY
JOHNNY M CRUZ DAVID J EWING ULYSSES C HASSELL JERRY W HESKETT CHARLES A JONES

PANEL 24W (*Continued*)

THOMAS C DE PALMA CHARLES A HILBERT JOHN E HUESTIS JOHN R JACKSON RALFORD J JACKSON
DONALD L JUSTICE FRANK J KIEWLEN JR ROBERT E LAYMAN JR CLOVIS L MAY GEORGE O MAYO
JOHN J MCANDREWS DOUGLAS F MOORE STEVEN D PAXSON ERROL W PERREIRA CLYDE R PERRY JR
RICHARD D PICKETT JEFFERY A RICHARDSON KENNETH L SMITH PAUL E SPEAKS RANDY A STRICKLAND
HARRY M TRAMMELL FREDRICK S WALTERS WILLIAM WARD JAMES L WILKS BUCK E ALBRIGHT
ROBERT L ANDERSON GREGORY R BENTON JR GERALD A BLAIR ROBERT L BOESE MARTIN BROWN
RONALD A BROWN CLEVELAND BROWNING HOWE K CLARK JR MILFORD E COBB DOUGLAS R MATHESON
RAYMOND L COLLIER JACK V CRUMP ROBERT A DOBBS JOSEPH D FISCHER JOSE M GALARZA-QUINONES
YVON E GIROUARD GARY O GRIFFIN KENNETH W GRUBB VAUGHN O HALL JAMES L HARRIS
HOWARD S HILL GARY L HISLE GRAHAM HUGHES HENRY D JOHNSON EDWARD H KENNEDY
KENNETH W KRUKEMYER DAVID J KUHN DONNY R LAWSON THOMAS C LONG JR JAMES S LUCKETT II
LOUIS BRUNSON RUDOLPH G MACHATA HERIBERTO MARRERO-ESTRADA AUBREY R MAYS GENE L WARE
EDWARD MENDEZ-QUINTANA ROY C NEWSOME JOHN D OLENICK WILLIAM W OLSEN RONALD R WARD
SANTIAGO V QUINTANA ARMANDO RAMIREZ ROBERT J RANDALL JR ANDREW W RICE JR DAVID S ROSS
PETER F RUSSELL ROBERT P SCIBILIA KENNETH D SHOAPS DOUGLAS J SOMMER JAMES W SPEER
FREDES V MENDEZ-ORTIZ JOHN M O'DONNELL PHILIP W STROUT JAMES E WORKMAN JAMES BOSTON JR
MILLARD R ANDERSON TIMOTHY J BALLINGER WILLIAM H BESKE JR DAVID T CHAPMAN HENRY L CHAPMAN
ROY E CLARK TERRY D CLARK WILLIAM H DARDEN JAMES M DAVENPORT EMMETT L DAVIS
CARL DEYNEKA HARLEY D DIMICK MARK W FENNER ELMER E FIELDS JOHN A GILLEN
ALLEN M GRAFF ORVILLE HAMPTON DAVID A HARGENS GEORGE HOSKINS JR CHARLES R JONES
RONNIE G KLOMSTAD RONNIE G KOLMSTAD JOHN H LAKIN CARL F LYBRAND CHARLES J MANSKE ANASTACIO MONTEZ
JOHN N MCCARTHY GARY A NEAVOR THOMAS P O'DEA ROGER L OLIVER JOHN H PLATT
STEPHEN L MCCARVEL GRAFTON L PERRY DERRILL L PRICE JR CORTEZ A RANDOLPH JOHN L ROSEMOND
RICHARD M SCHNAKE CECIL F TAYLOR GARY C TOWLE JACKIE W TROGLEN STANLEY TURNER
FARRELL J VICE GARY A WALLACE RONALD A YASHACK KENNETH W YOUNG JOHN W ABBOTT
BYRLE B BAILEY LARRY E BOYER GARY R BUTTS GARY D CARTER JIMMY K CHURCH
EDWARD F CLENNON DUANE L CLOUSE DONALD J DEEVERS JAMES P DUFFY JR WAYNE E GARVEN
DAVID B HERRING RONNIE E HOGBIN WESLEY G ICE DONALD W IDE GARY MCCOLLOUGH
OPHREY A IRVIN JACK L JOHNSON KEITH A KAHLSTORF JOHN P KARR MARIO LAMELZA
PAUL A GRAFF LIN A MAHNER JOSEPH F MCCARTHY JR GEORGE C MELTON ARTHUR R NEWKIRK
EDWARD T O'DONOVAN TIMOTHY M O'NEILL GREGORY J OLSEN CALVIN R PATRICK THOMAS B PAYNTER
MICHAEL A POWELL JAN RAUSCHKOLB LAWRENCE N SAVINO WILLIAM F SKAGGS TERRY A SUNDEEN
BILLY L THOMAS RALPH A VITCH ALBERT C WALLS JR JIM J WALTERS MONEK WEITZ
RICHARD N WHITE LEROY C WILLIAMS JOHN WINTERS MERRILL BARNES TIMOTHY K FOSTER
PHILIP L GAMBLE JR CLIFFORD E HAYNES JR JAMES F HILLIARD JAMES D JOHNSON ERNEST C MUNOZ
LOUIS H GODLEY MAX LISENBY CHRIS R MARTINEZ LARRY D MULLEN STEVEN E MURRAY
HENRY L MCARTHUR ERIC D NADEAU GEORGE H NOE EUAN J PARKER EDWIN ROMAN-RODRIGUEZ
SCOTT E SAYLOR ROBERT H SIGHOLTZ JR JOHN M STENBERG JAMES TITMAS III RALPH H CROWLEY
ROBERT C VAN VLEET WILLIAM L ANDERSON CHRISTOPHER J BELL ROBERT T BENSBERG SCOTT E COCHRAN
THOMAS R BLISS ROBERT H CARTER JR ALBERT J CARTLEDGE III ALPHONZO L CHAVIS JAMES W CLARK
GARY K SMITH RICHARD L COX CHARLES D ERVIN GARY C FASSEL CHARLES C FLEEK GARY R GUEST
JAMES P FRANCIS MICHAEL E GERBER KEITH E GIBSON GAREY L GRUBBS RAYMOND R GUTIERREZ
THOMAS R MCCORMICK

PANEL 23W

HENRY R HAUSMAN JR JAMES HEBERT III JOHN W KIRCHNER CORDELL B ROGERS
JAMES P HICKEY MATTHEW T LOZANO JR THOMAS W MYERS JIMMY W PHIPPS ROBERT A PITTS
GAIL G SANDERSON ISAAC SAPP WILLIAM A SEIGLE KENNITH M SEWARD CONRAD A SOVA
DONALD Y SCARBERRY KENNETH W SMITH DAVID L TESSMER CLAUDE R VAN ANDEL HAROLD J WARMSLEY
ROBERT C YATES DENNIS L BABCOCK FLOYD E BARBER DUDLEY J BENEFIEL JR RONALD C BOOTHE
DUANE C BOWEN MARVIN C BRISS RICHARD L BRUMFIELD JAMES S COLOMBERO CALVIN E COOPER
GAYLORD M COUCH GARY W COX FREDERICK N CURTIS JOHN T DAVIS PATRICK M DIXON
JAMES L DREW VALENTINE M DWORNIK VALARIAN L FINLEY EARL A GODMAN LAWRENCE H GRILLO
STEVE F GRUBB ALBERT HILERIO JR KEITH B JANKE EDWARD T KIEZKOWSKI FRANKLIN L KOCH
DAVID R MANN DENNIS R MEETZE THOMAS A NEBEL THOMAS J ORR CHRIS M PYLE
ROBERT B READ JOSEPH L RHODES ROBERT G SCHMIDT FORREST L SMITH CLARENCE TAYLOR
WILLIAM J THORNHILL DAVID L TIFFANY STEPHEN L UPTON RAMON L VAZQUEZ-NIEVES DICK E WHITNEY
WILLIAM K WORD MATTHEW J BAURLE JOHN W BLANDING JOHNNIE L BRIGMAN IRAN C BROWN
RUDY A CARNLEY JAMES W CLAY DONALD E DALTON CURTIS R DANIELS JOHN A DIXON
ROGERS L HAYWOOD CRIS HOLLIDAY HERMAN L JUDY JR JESSE P KENT GARY W LEIGHTON
LOUIE Z LEIJA EMERSON MARTIN CHARLES E MCMILLION TERRY V MILLER RONALD E MORGAN
RICHARD L PATTERSON GARY M PAUL CHARLES C PFORDT JR GERALD W POSTEN WILTON S PYLE
JOE RODRIGUEZ ROBERT J ROSENOW LEE E SINCLAIR MICHAEL C VOLHEIM CHRISTOPHER WILLIAMS
JAMES B WILLIAMS JR CRAIG E YATES JAMES F BECKER GERALD D BELL STEVEN E BROWN
JEROME L COLLINS NATHANIEL COOK EDWIN E DOTTER RICHARD F DU BOIS EDWARD FROWNER
VIRGIL V HAMILTON DANNY W HARGIS THOMAS E HAYS FREDERICK P JOHNSON JR LOUIS JOHNSON
HARRY MASSEY EDWARD C MCGINN RALPH J MEARS JR DAVID C NELSON ERSKINE J OLIVER
GORDON D PERRY THOMAS C PIGG DONALD P SEBURG JR CRAIG M SIMEONE ROBERT L WATT
WAYNE M WILSON PETER R ADAMS WILLIAM L ALEXANDER JACKIE D BASS THOMAS L BLEVINS JR
JOEY L BOLES PETER S BORSAY BYRON B BOWDEN BYRON T CALKINS LARRY E DIKEMAN
JEROME N DOLL RUSSELL EVANS ROBERT J FULLER RICHARD F GLINIEWICZ JOAQUIN R TELLO
PATRICK M HAGERTY PRENTISS HARRIS JR MICHAEL F HEATH JOHN M HOHMAN CLARENCE JONES JR
DAVID W KINNEY JOHN N LA CHICA JAMES M LEONARD JAMES R LEWIS BILLY J MARTIN
STEVEN L MARTIN LESLIE T MCMACKEN JR RAYMOND L MORRIS PAUL V NELSON STEVEN C OWEN
BILLY W PETTIS DENNIS M PHILLIPS JOHNNY M PILSNER PHILIP A PRATT ROBERT F ROSE
SALVADORE I RUIZ KENNETH W SCURR WILLIAM J SEWELL STEVEN K SPRINKLE LANDUS S TAYLOR JR
JAMES G FLYNN DANIEL P THOMAS JR SCOTT W THORNBURG SALVADOR P TRIANA RALPH H ZERINGUE
STEPHEN E TURZILLI GARY L WALLEN THOMAS A WATSON PHILIP G WEIR JOSEPH C WILTSIE
RUDOLPH R TREVINO JAMES J WISE JAMES A WRIGHT ERNEST ABEYTA FREDERIC G AGATHER
EARLE J BEMIS DAVID A BRACK CARL T CAHILL BILLY W CAMPBELL BERTRAM A CARR
ROBERT W GETZ MICHAEL D GOELLER JERRY L GOODLIN LOUIS A GORDILS WENDELL J GRAHAM JR
ROBERT L GRANT IRIS H HARRINGTON DANNY L HOPKINS MILTON JOHNSON JAMES L KIESTLER
RAY E KNOLL LEONARD L LEWIS RUBEN LOPEZ-MERCED JESSE S MANUEL JR DAVID L MILLS
JAIME PADILLA-JORGE DARRELL V PECK STEPHEN J PEONIO JAMES W POE JOSE L SANCHEZ
RICHARD J SIGWORTH JAMES M STOTTS THOMAS M TROTTER ALBERT B WASHINGTON JR BLAIR C WILKEY
JAMES A WOODRUFF LYMAN C BACH MICHAEL O BAKER SCOTT D BALDWIN JACKIE L DICKENS
WILLIAM D BLOOMFIELD RICHARD L BRECH MURRY L BRITTON WARREN F BROWN MICHAEL H CAVANAGH
DUANE R BAUMGARDNER EMMETT L DAVIS MARK S DREIER RICKEY D DYCUS DAVID R ELLIOTT
JOHN H FARLEY JEFFREY L GELDIN JAMES R GILMORE JR MARVIN J GUDE JOHN HENSLEY
PAUL C JANTO BRIAN R KELLY JOSEPH G LA POINTE JR ROBERT H MARTIN JR MICHAEL MONTIJO
FRANCIS R MCGOWAN KENNETH R MCNEILL GEORGE R PALERMO DONALD J PORTER ROBERT L POXON
DENNIS G PRINCE DANIEL L PUCCI JIMMIE L REED MANUEL RODRIGUEZ JR EMANUEL L SAUNDERS
JOSEPH R SCOTT WILBUR A SMITH KENNARD E SVANOE PRESTON TAYLOR JR SAVAS E TREVINO
DENNIS TUINSTRA RAY L ULRICH BARRY L UNFRIED PAUL F WEBER GERALD W ALBRITTON
ROBERT J BEAMAN SAMUEL E BENGE DENNIS F BIBERDORF THOMAS M BONINE BRUCE E BROWN
DAVID F BURCH LEON T CULVERHOUSE JIMMY D CUMBEE ROBERT D DIXON WILLIAM A DUNAJ
LAWRENCE A FANELLA ANDREW S FARLEY JR DONALD F GINART TOMAS GOMEZ-ROBLES LOUIS RODRIGUEZ
ROBERT J HOFFMANN HARRY R ITALIANO CLAYTON D JENKINS STEPHEN D JOHNSON GAYLORD G KERR
GEORGE A KIGER DARWIN L LABAHN SAMMY L MEAD JR THOMAS J MEAD PAUL W MILLER
HENRY MCCLENTON GERARD MCGRADE TULELE MISA CHARLES E MOORE LONNIE D MOORE
LARRY D MCKENZIE MICHAEL J MCPARLANE FLETCHER J NOWLIN JR GUILLERMO PARISI RODDIE L PERRY
JOSE GARCIA JR BILLIE W REED DONALD H RICHARDSON ALLEN H ROBERTSON ANDREW C ROSE
DOUGLAS D RUEHLE BROOKS E SABLE MITCHELL H SANDMAN MICHAEL G SCHERF STEVEN G SCHIMMEL
WALTER S SEDDIG JACK L SILLIMAN JAMES H SMITH JOHN R TAYLOR HARRY N THOMPSON
CHARLES VALE CLEMENT VALENCIA JR GREGORY R VOGLER RICHARD W WATSON RANDALL R WHITE
RICHARD L BARNES DOUGLAS W BARNITZ MILTON BLACKWELL STEPHAN R BROSE WILLIAM A BUCK JR
JOSE A CALDERON-PACHECO ANTHONY L' CAMP LEROY R CARDENAS MAX F DE SULLY JR DAVID J KOEHLER
DONNEY DELANEY FRANCO A DI TULLIO PATRICK D FINCH GREGORY G FUCHS JOE R GARCIA
ROY P GARGUS THOMAS A GREISEN BENJAMIN HARRIS GERALD R HILL JAMES H HOPKINS
WILLIAM C BURGESS JR ROBERT L JENNINGS CHARLES L KING JAMES A KUMMINGS OSCAR C MAYER III
DENNIE MCMEANS JAMES MICHALSKI JAMES G MILLER DANIEL S MULLER MICHAEL M O'CONNOR
ROBERT L PEARCY DAVID B PLATT DAVID R PORTER ANDREW S RAHILLY STEPHEN L ROBERTS
EDWIN F SHOLAR GARY W SILMAN HAROLD A SKAGGS MICHAEL D TURNER DONALD F VAN COOK JR
FREDERICK A VERRY WILLIAM M WELLMAN JR JOSEPH V ZAPPINI JR WILLIAM H AYERS RONALD R BAKER
JOHN B BALITSARIS JOHN M BELLAMY RONALD L BRASHEARS ROBERT B BROUGHTON ROBERT P RUTTLE JR
GERALD B BROWN DAVID P CALLAHAN GARY A COX JIMMY W CRISP KEVIN R CROWE
JERRY M DAILEY ROBERT S DANKERT DONALD G DISSELKOEN JOSE A ECHEVARRIA JR RORY T HARAN
LOUIE F DALIE MCARTHUR GAFFNEY SHERMAN W GREGORY JACK HATFIELD FREDERICK J HENRY
STEVEN W HERRING KERRY E HESS MERLE R HIGGINS RICHARD J HOLMAN THOMAS G HORAL
JOHN W HORAN DAVID T HOWARD EDWARD E KING CLYDE D LAHR ROBERT E LANGSTON
DAVID L MANN JAMES A MARDIS JR JOHN R MAXSON CLAUDIE METCALF TORRANCE MITCHELL JR
LAWRENCE P MULVEY JAMES H MYERS HAROLD L PARKIN LAWRENCE E PAULSEN PATRICK E POPPENGA
CHARLES H BRITTIAN JR GERALD S POWLISTHA MACK L PRESTON JR CHARLES M RAMSEY ROBERT L ROMERO
HANK SALLY ALEXANDER P SANTIAGO JR ANTHONY J SESTITO DENNIS L TAYLOR PAUL R TILLEMAN
FRANK TORTORICI BRENDAN X TURNER HUGO H ULLOA JOSEPH VALESKO JR JAMES D WALKER
NORMAN G WELCH MILFORD H WENSEL THOMAS J WILLIAMS FREDERICK A ALLMEYER LUKE J AZLIN
HOWARD R BAKER LARRY H BARBEE JOHN P BECKERS WILLIAM P BENN THOMAS A BERG
SAMUEL G BOSENBARK JOHN R BRAGG JOSEPH BRESKI JR WILLIAM L BROOKS NORMAN D BROWN
ROBERT M BRUPBACHER WILLIAM H CLEVENGER JOHN P CRAIG WILLIAM M CRUSIE JR RICHARD E CYRAN
ROBERT DRAK ROBERT C ESSMANN MICHAEL J EVANS ROBERT M FULLMER FELTON R FUSSELL
PHILLIP D GARDNER DANIEL A GATTO STEPHEN B GEURIN LARRY G GOSCH MICHAEL F GRISAFE JR
STEPHEN R GROSS TEDDY M HODGES JR RALPH HONAKER JOHN D INGUILLO TERRY L JENKINS
WILLIE L JOE GARY A JONES NOEL F JOSEPHS MICHAEL S LAFROMBOISE DUANE H LANDWEHR JR
DON H LASCELLES RONALD D LAYTON PETER A LEHMAN CARL D LYNCH DENNIS J MANSON
LEO R MARCOULIER BRUCE C MAYNARD TERRANCE R MESENBURG TERRY D MILLER LARRY J NICHOLSON
DANNY L PARKER STEVEN J PHILBRICK JAMES F PUARIEA ROY L RAMEY JOHN D RHODES III
ERNESTO ROSARIO-SOTO JR JOHN D SHARP RONNIE D SHAW RONALD L STORBO VICTOR B SUTTON
FRED T TEAL PHILLIP F THERIOT FRANCIS L THOMPSON JAMES L TODTENBIER RICHARD P VALADEZ
JOHN K VOGELSANG MELVIN E WHITE ALEX J ALVAREZ ALLEN R AMBROGI JOHN C ARCHBOLD
DONALD ARRIBI LARRY N BAKKE FREDERICK D BARGE FREDERICK L BENISHEK JOHN M BLACKFORD
LARRY H BOWEN DAVID J BREDENKAMP DAN BULLOCK DONALD W BUNN PHILLIP D BURFOOT
WAYNE R BURRAGE MICHAEL P CALLAHAN RONNIE L CLAYBURN SAMUEL C COPELAND ALF E ERIKSEN
WILLIAM C COSTA DAVID A CRILLY WALTER J DART JR FREDERIC H DAVIS LARRY C DAVISON
ROBERT R CATHERMAN RICHARD L DELANEY ANTHONY DUTY LARRY J EGLINSDOERFER HENRY C ETTEL JR
KENNETH L FORD TERRELL GIBSON DALE E GRIFFITH DAVID A GRILLY CURTIS L HENDRICKSON
SHELDON W HICKS JASON D HUNNICUTT DENNIS A IASELLO SALVATORE IOZZIA JOHN A KALIVAS
GEORGE D KINNETT JOHN E KRZMARCIK THOMAS P LANDMAN STEPHEN E LARSEN CLIFFORD J LEFLER
JOHN S LEWIS RALPH T LOMEN WILLIAM T LYNN LARRY W MARTIN MICHAEL W O'LEARY
JOEL C LOFTIS BENJAMIN L MCCULLOUGH STEVEN H MONTGOMERY JOSEPH A MOTT BRUCE A PANKUCH
DAVID A PATTON JOHN T PAULIN KENNETH J PITRE JOHN R PONTIERE RONALD H PORTER
CHARLES G RAWLS EDWARD R RAYMOND III JAMES RUNDLE JR KENNETH L SMALL JOHN S STAFF
RAYMOND T TALBURT ISAAC THOMAS JR DALE E THOMPSON JOSEPH TREJO JR STUART H TYSON
GREGORY J WELCH LEON WHITE WILLIAM F ZAHN JR JAMES D ADKINS GALE L BARNES
DON L BARTLEY DAVID L BELL PAUL M BOWLIN DAVID A BROWN KENNETH E ENFINGER
JERRY L ERVIN GLENN R FLEITMAN WILLIAM H GREEN MICHAEL W HAGIE CARL W HUDGINS JR
DALE L JOHNSON JAY A KAUFMAN CARL J KEAHEY III KEO J KESHNER GEORGE F LANDI
SHARON A LANE ROBERT N LATIMER MALCOLM F LEGER JOHN E LORENCE THOMAS W STRATHMANN
GEORGE F MARTINEZ DAVID L MCKEE RONALD W MCLEAN HERMAN R MORRIS ALBERT D OWENS
MELVILLE A LURTH JR JAMES A PERSON JOHNNY B ROBERTSON JR ROBERT R SHERIDAN DEANE F SMITH JR
ROBERT G STRICKLIN TERRY E TOOLE IGNACIO L VILLALOBOS ROY L WALKER WILLIAM R WILSON
ROBERT A WIMER ROGER L YOUNG LEON H ADAMS DONALD W AKINS GARY L BARNES
CHRISTOPHER J BEAN MARK W BELL WILLIAM M BELLILE RICHARD A BURINGRUD WILLIAM D BUSHARD
JOHNNIE J CARAWAY ARTHURO CARRASCO JAMES N CLARK LEROY CONWAY DARELL L COVINGTON
CLINTON L DAY STONEY L DEEL BRUCE J DUNHAM PAUL R EDMOND JUAN J FIGUEROA
WALDEMAR J GEIGER GORDON M GEORGE JR LARRY R GILBERTSON WILLIAM R GREGORY JAMES F HAIDER

PANEL 22W

DONALD O HARTMAN THOMAS A HILL JOHN H HUGHES JOHN D INCE
JIMMY A INGRAM FRANK W JEALOUS-OF-HIM@ LARRY R JENKINS LARRY D KEELING DENNIS A KELLUMS
KENNETH J KREUTZ TOMMY R LAWSON ALLEN L LEWIS HARRY L LONG ROBERT W LONG
WILLIAM H MILLER BRUNO J MLODZINSKI JR JOHN M MOORE JR JEROME D MORNEAU NORMAN W TEETER
STEVEN W MCCLOUD RICHARD D MCKENZIE JAMES H MCMAHON GENE A MYERS CHARLES NELSON
BRUCE F PEARSON MANUEL J PENA LUTHER R PERKINS GUADALUPE PRADO JR LIONEL T RACHAL
TERRY G RADA CHRISTOPHER R REED JESSE L RIDGE KARL A SCHOFER LARRY E SCOTT
LLOYD M SCOTT JR DONALD R SHOULDERS JESSE W SINGLETON JR DONALD R SMITH EDDIE L SMITH
RONALD J MATEL WILLIAM D SPARKS DANIEL T THURSTON JASPER H TRUSLEY JR HECTOR M VALENTIN-PEREZ
MICHAEL A WHITE MICHAEL R WICK GARY J WINKLER DENNIS S WOSICK SAMUEL L YOUNG
RONALD W ASHBURN GEAROLD L BRANDT LAWRENCE J BUYNOSKI III GLYNN T CAHOON JOHN A NORTH
MICHAEL P CURRAN LE R GARIS RICARDO J GOMEZ JAMES R GOOLSBY ROGER L GRAHAM
LONNIE H HARRISON HOWARD C HEARD JAMES HOPPER JR ROBERT L HOWARD MYRON D KJELLERSON
JAMES A KRUSE ANDREW A KUHN JAMES D KURTOWICZ EVERETT R MATARAZZO CRAIG A NEWELL
LAWRENCE COPPEDGE ROGER A PARRISH ANDREW PARTIDA EMIDIO PASQUALUCCI GERALD W SHAKLEY
EUGENE W SMITH GARY D STOCKLIN RAYMOND W SWANSON DAVID W WALSH LAWRENCE L WHITE
LEE A WILLIAMS JAMES L ASHER EDWIN E AXTON DAVID O BIGGS HAROLD M BROWN
CHARLES M BEAR DANIEL H BOLDEN ALEXANDER B BRANTLEY RUSSELL D BUCKNER CARLOS M COLLAZO
PAUL CORR JR HAROLD J CRAWFORD RONALD G CROWE THOMAS P DAWSON FRANK F DE MARIA JR
ROLAND F DIPOLO TERRY F DROWN PAUL G GONZALES CHARLES D GREEN DAVID E KENNEY
JACK L HAGER PHILLIP D HARDY MICHAEL E HICKS FREDDY L HOLLOWAY MYLON R HOPKINS
CHARLIE W FARMER JR STUART G HOSTETTER EDWARD JOHNSON HARRY G KUNKLER III JACK C LEE
ROBERT L LOCKHART JOHN B LYLE PETER LYNCH CHARLES R MANAREL ARTHUR J MARTIN
HUMBERTO C MELENDEZ DAVID G MICHEL RICHARD L MILLER IVAN H MUNRO ROBERT G SEKVA
BOBBY G OLIVER DUANE E OLSON EDWARD V PALMENTA JOHN B PARKER FLOYD L PITRE
RICHARD M RANDOLPH DANIEL G REID RICHARD R REVOIR THOMAS J RILEY CHARLIE ROBINSON JR
KARL W MILLS RANDALL C ROBINSON MOSES RODGERS RAYMOND R SCHIFRIN EDWARD J SHAUGHNESSY
GARY R STAHLECKER DOUGLAS L STRICKLAND JAMES C STRUBE TERRY L THORNTON BRUCE H TIBBETTS
JAMES M WANDRO CLARK L WILLIAMS MICHAEL G WORLEY DONALD J ZASTOWSKY FRED J ZYCK
BENJAMIN R ALDERSON LEO R ASSELIN STEVEN P BARNETT KENNETH L BARTLEY ALAN R BRESNAHAN
GIOVANNI H CAMPBELL ROBERT D CLATFELTER FRED J DANIEL MICHAEL F DAVIS THOMAS W DOLAN III
THOMAS M BRYANT JAMES F ENGELMEIER KURT W FRANZINGER JR MICHAEL A FULLER WILLIAM E GOODEN
GREY L HAGINS TERRY R JOHNSTON EMANUEL JONES JR BENJAMIN F LEWIS JR TERRY W LOVETT
THOMAS M MARCHAND WILLIAM T MATLOCK THOMAS H MCSTOOTS CARL G MOTES DENNIS B MURRAY
ALFREDO OCHOA JR JAKE OSBORNE GEORGE M PAGE JR DAVID H PALMIERI LORENZO R PETTIS
LEO PIERCE RICHARD B PROVEAUX PAUL R ROSS CARL M SNEED MICHAEL A SYLVIA
JOSEPH B WALKER DONALD M WAYMAN GREGORY I WERTS THOMAS M AARON JR FEDERICO ALANIZ JR
RALPH A BARCELONA JAMES B BURTON JUAN H CAMARGO WALTER J CARNEY TEDDY E HARGROVE
DONALD CHRISTIE RICHARD R CLAXTON STEVEN P ETHERTON DARRYL G FRANCISCO NEAL C WARD
CHARLES M ANDUJAR JEFF L FRANKLIN JR KENNETH R HARRIS THEODORE S HERIOT JR ADRIAN J JOHNSON JR
CHARLES H JOHNSON STEPHEN J KINGHORN JOSEPH S LABAY MICHAEL K LEWIS DANIEL J LIPETZKY
JAMES C LUCERO JAMES MCCONNYHEAD JR MICHAEL H MOBILIA THOMAS E OWENS RUDOLPH PARKER
CHRISTY A PEEBLER ROY M PING ROBERT V REKER ARTURO SALAZAR DAVID F SCHLUTERMAN
WAYNE G SCRIMSHAW CLARENCE M STONER JR JAMES C STORY GARY L TAYLOR THOMAS H UTEGAARD
KENNETH L CONNER HENSON F WALKER THOMAS J WILK CARLOS A YOUNG BOBBY R BROWN
JOHNNY F DAVIS MICHAEL J DODGE STANLEY O EVERETT PAUL S GOC JR JAMES W GRACE
CUTBURT HURTAULT HAROLD KAHLER ROBERT J KAZMIERCZAK LOUIS J KELLEY JEROME D LUBENO
ARMANDO A MINOR MALCOLM E MITCHELL JAMES E PULLEY LYNN M RANDALL DAVID A WORRELL
KIM RAUPACH JAMES E SAWYER JR DAVID T SITTON HARVEY N SLAUGHTER ROBERT M SNELL
ROBERT B TUFTS RUBEN URDIALEZ RICHARD D WALKER JOHNNY WILES BOBBIE G WOOTEN
REX D MORELOCK JR JEFF H UPP DONALD L BRIGHTMAN VALERIANO D CONTRERAS EDWARD C FANNING
JAMES L GALKOWSKI RONALD R GARNER CARLOS M GONZALES KISH L GREEN JAMES G GRIENER
JAMES G GRINER ADAM HOLMAN JR DAVID M KAUFMAN JERRY C KLUTE LARRY D LEMASTER
JOHN E LYNCH FRANCIS B MADDEN JR JERRY MCCARTER WAYNE O MCCLUNG HAROLD L SHATTUCK JR
CALVIN M MINOR ALTON R PHILLIPS FRANK J PICELLE JR PETER P RUBIO WILSON D THOMAS
EDWARD VOYT DONALD L WICKLINE JR MITCHELL B WYSEL GARY D BENDER RONDAL L BURNS
MARK D CLOTFELTER DAVID L COLLINS DAVID A CURTIS RAYMOND L DOCK JR HALLIA L GRIFFIN JR
JOSEPH GUILMETTE JR JOSEPH J HELTSLEY RAYMOND C HOLMAN MICHAEL A MAHOWALD LARRY A RUSH
TONY L MARTIN DANIEL D MCNEILL ANTHONY M NOTICH PHILLIP A PAGE GEORGE J REED JR
THOMAS E HUGHES LEROY H SCOTT ALBERT J SMITH HARREL E STEARNS RUDOLPH M STEFANIC
SASA ULI DAVID E WEISS MARVIN C WHITE WILLIAM G WHITE SAMMY H WHITWORTH
EDWIN A ZUMWALT JERRY A ASHBURN ROBERT E ASKAM WILFREDO AYALA-REYES DANNY R BAKER
BILL L BERSTLER HIRIS W BLEVINS RONALD S CAMPBELL BILLY R CHADWICK DERRICK CORE
MICHAEL D DAWSON LEON T DUNCAN EDWARD J EDMUND JOHN A FELSHER JOSEPH D FOURNIER
FRANCIS G FRECHETTE LARRY A GRAHAM ROBERT L HANSELMAN CHARLES E HUNSINGER LARRY R MARTIN
RICHARD A KELLER BRUCE KOLTER LUTHER J LACKLAND DANIEL B LEDIN DAVID W LOEW
JOHNIE F GRANBERRY DANIEL A MAY DOUGLAS W MCPHEE GREGORIO M MORA GERALD K NEER
ROBERT G NICHOLAS WAYNE L NOTH DAVID PEREZ WILLIAM E PREWITT WILLIAM J REVELL III
MICHAEL S ROBERTS ROGER D ROSENBERGER WILLIAM H SCOTT DONALD L SPARKS DAVID M STEELE
WILLIAM M STONE JR NOE TAMEZ WAYNE R THOMAS EVANS J THORNTON JOHN B THURNHAM
FRED E TRAYLOR MARVIN L WATSON SAMUEL M WHITE JR ROBERT W WITTY WALTER W BECKER
PETER V BLAZONIS MICHAEL D BOYER JAMES P BRADY GEORGE R BROWNING WILLIAM D BURKE JR
JAMES CABARUBIO TIMOTHY J CAROLAN GEORGE D CARR ROBERT G CARR EDWARD W CHARLES
CRAIG M CLANCY JAMES A COWAN JR FRANK CRUZ ROY J CURRY TORRE J DE LA
HARRY G DIEHL JAMES R DOLVIN CHARLES W DORNON MICHAEL L EARP CHARLES W EMMERT
ENRIQUE T ENRICO ROBERT M FEGAN EDWARD F GOSHORN HARRY D GOWIN ROBERT L GRAHAM
ALAN H GREENLAW WALTER J GRIFFIN BARRY R GRULKE HAROLD F HAWKINS JAMES D HENNESSEY
MICHAEL L HODGE CHARLES L HUNTER PAUL T HURT III CLAUDE C KASIAH JAMES J LANE JR
GARY W LETSON HOWARD J MANER LIONEL L MARCAURELE HOLLIS G MILLER DENNIS G MURPHY
DAVID W MCCONNELL ROBERT L MINGLE ENRIQUE MIRAMONTEZ MELVIN L MIZE RUDOLPH P MUNOZ
MARTIN A MCZEAL PAUL R NARVAEZ THOMAS D NAUGHTON JR ROYAL P ODEN STEPHEN OROSCO
PAUL A REZENDES MICHAEL W RICHARDSON DARYL J SCHMIDT JOSEPH F SMITH JR EDWIN F TURK JR
GARY C SALANITRO SOLOMON E THOMPSON EUGENE K WALLACE THOMAS A WILLARD DIETER E WILLERT
JAMES J AHRENS RICHARD D BACA GILBERT R BARGMANN JOHN P BATTERSON JR TROY BETHEA
CARL J BIEKER THOMAS J BRADLEY LLOYD L BUZZARD GARY W CARLSON LARRY R CLARK
FREDERIC D BLACKWELL LUTHER M CHAPPEL HAROLD R CHRISTENSEN RALPH J CLIME RICHARD W COLE
DAVID B COLLINS HARVEY C CRABTREE JR DONALD L CURTIN JAMES R DANIEL DAVID DEITCH
GEORGE R DOVER LLOYD J DOWNS HARVEY A DUHY JR ANTHONY H FIGUEROA JR CRAIG HABERLEIN
EDWARD M HARDWICK GLENN S HAUKENESS JR ROBERT L HIVELY JAMES D HOAG CALVIN G HUNT
ELIJAH INGRAM GARLAND B KING JR KEITH W LARIMER PAUL F LITTLE ROBERT W O'KEEFE
DAVID A MADDEN ROBERT T MARTIN JR HENRY D MATHEWS KENNETH L MCFALL JOSEPH R MCILVOY
WILLIAM J KUHNS JAMES M NESSELROTTE DANIEL G O'CONNELL JERROLD S PEARLSTEIN BERNARD L PIERCE
JOHN H PRIEST JR ISRAEL RODRIGUEZ ALAN M ROUCHON PAUL H SCHAEFFER VICTOR T SHAFFER
RONALD E SIMPSON STEPHEN D VAN DYKE RAYMOND A VOSS ALBERT C WALL JR ROBERT A WILLIAMS
LUIS J SIMANCAS JAMES T WOODS JOHN H ALDRICH JOSE F ARROYO THEODORE E BALTEZORE
DONALD L BLACKSTON JOHN DE MEY DENNIS R FORNEY JOSEPH J GOETZER JR ROBERT R GUERRA
DANIEL H HACKETT CRAIG H HANSEN BUFFARD C HARRISON HARVEY J HASSLER BRIAN C HEATH
GLENN R JENNINGS JIM F JENNINGS RICHARD D JOY LEON L LANINGER LOREN H LARSON
WILLIAM L LONG ROBERT C MAHAN LUIS A MONTOYA TONEY F MYCKA JR KEITH OLSEN

JAMES M PANKIEWICZ JAMES E PARKER DALE R PAVEY JOSE L SALAZAR JOSEPH W SELL JR
DALLAS C SHELTON JR TIMOTHY A SHOBER FLOYD L STEWARD JOE A WADLEY THOMAS R WILLIAMS
JAMES J BARTON DOUGLAS R BITTLE FRANK J BOSCO ANTONIO G CASTILLO HAROLD J FINNEY JR
LORANZEY P CHAMBERS HARRY J COLON BRUCE COPLEY ARTHUR C COUNCILL III JAMES H COVEY
JERRY M BORKHOLDER ROBERT L CRITES JR WILLIAM A DANIELS JR DANNY G ENDICOTT ROBERT E FREITAS
CHARLES G GRAY JAMES O HALL JR REGINALD W JONES ROGER L JOYCE JOHN L MURDOCK
HERBERT C FROST RICHARD L KERKHOFF ANDREW F KOKESH GORDON A MACMILLAN WILLIAM F MALONE
PHILIP E NICKERSON ROBERT NOZEWSKI EDWIN P PAGAN WILLIAM L PETERS JR JOHN K PETERSON
PAUL E PETROLINE JOHNNY W PHILLIPS JERRY E ROGERS FRANCIS G RUPPERT ALLYN T STEVENS
DENNIS M RESINGER HARLIS C SALES WILLIAM G SCHANCK JR KENNETH J SUSMARSKI JOSE M TORO
CHARLES F TYSON III JORGE VARGAS MICHAEL P WARNER RICHARD A WEIL JR WALTER WILLIAMS
JOHN M BORG CHARLES E CLUBBS RICHARD L DAVIS ERICH C ENGELHARD WILLIAM D HEGWOOD
TERENCE A HUEBNER ROBERT H JOY JOHN G KOPRIVA EDDIE L LOCKLEAR GEORGE M LYONS
JAMES E MCMAHON JAMES H MCNEILLY WALTER R MILLER JR MICHAEL J PARMERTER RICHARD RAMOS
JAMES A ROBERG JOHN W ROBERSON MICHAEL A SEAGROVES GARY J WEBB KENNETH P WEST
JEROME P ZINDLE DAVID P ACHORD EDDIE D ACUFF EARL E ANDERSON KENNETH T ANDERSON
FRED M BAILEY MICHAEL E BARROW KRIS BILMER JAMES L BISHOP JACKIE L BLANKENSHIP
JOHN E BRAID MARVIN M BURNS GERALD W CAMERON WILLIAM H CONDIT JR JAMES J HOCHSTETTER
RICHARD C DANIELS GEORGE D DEITRICK DEWEY M EUBANKS MICHAEL FORBES GARY FREEMAN
EDWARD B FULGHAM JR ANSON T GERONZIN JR DAVID R GILL WILLIAM G GRAY STEVE HATHAWAY
GARY E BRUNNER THEODORE M HATLE TERRY A HOUSEHOLTER ANTON J JECMEN JR LORENZO R JOHNSON
MONTE R JONES PAUL D JONES JEAN A KEARBY CHARLES H KELLER II LARRY W KINDER
CHARLES E KUHN JR DONALD T LASKAY MARZEL R LEE ADRON L LEWIS WILLIAM F LINDQUIST
GEORGE D MCCLELLAND BILLY W MCDONALD DANIEL R NELSON DAVID L NORD MARTIN J PAMONICUTT

PANEL 21W

GEORGE C PETERS EDGAR S PITTMAN TERRY M REED JOSEPH B RIGGS
ROBERT J ROBINSON WAYNE RUSSELL LELAND C SAGE DOUGLAS P SAVAGE RONALD L VAN DUZER
STEVEN J SKEEN JOHN C SMITH CHARLES S TAYLOR HOMER D THICK FRANKLIN W UNDERWOOD JR
TIMOTHY H SIMPKINS PERRY L UNDERWOOD CHARLES G VICKERS RICHARD E WEISS DENNIS M WILLIAMS
ROBERT C WILLIAMS BOBBY R ADKINS JAMES K AMEIGH RICHARD M ARANN JOHN A BERRIO
DONALD L BRICKLE GARY L CLARK TERRY L CRUTCHER FERNANDO DE RUBEIS ALFRED DE SIMONE
RICHARD A ELLSWORTH JOHN V GILKER ROGERS S GORDON LAWRENCE K HINSCHBERGER ALBERT J JONES
MICHAEL D HAMPTON HUGH B HOLMES RODNEY A JANNETTA BOBBY C JOHNSON JOSEPH H KENNEY
RICHARD N MAMIE JAMES T MOORE JESUS A PEREZ LAVON N PRATHER RICHARD D ROBERTS
ALAN E SANDERS RONALD SCOTT JAMES A SLATER WOODROW N TRISSELL JR MICHAEL J WATERLOO
DELBERT E WEBER DEAN C WILSON DAVID C ASBURY JAMES R BRIGGS DAVID J CORCORAN
KRIS BLUMER DONALD H BUTTERWORTH JAMES H DANKOWSKI MARK J DE FRANGE WILLIAM M ELBRACHT
DARNELL HARVEY WILLIAM E HIBPSHMAN CARL E JANOWSKY JR ROBERT L KING JERRY L SOUTHARD
TERRY A LOFFER STEPHEN G MAUSEN HERBERT L MEGAR JR MITCHELL E NORTON CALVIN C RICE JR
THOMAS W FABER PATRICK D ROBIRDS HOWARD ROSEDIETCHER TIMOTHY J SHELTON ROBERT C SNETHEN
WILLIAM F STRINGER BARRY N THOMPSON ROY K WILLIAMS JR CHARLES D AYERS ANTON W BOROSKI
JOHN L BOWEN ROBERT C CAMERON CHARLES E CARPENTER JACKIE COOTS GUILLERMO DAVILA JR
JESSIE J GARRARD ROBERT C GONTERO MICHAEL D HAVEL LUTHER A HINTON ANTHONY J MARINELLI
JERRY A NICHOLS JAMES L PLUMLEE JR ROBERT E RATH WILLIAM H RODDICK OTIS J RUCKS
JOHN T RYAN JAMES E SHORT ROGER L SIMPSON RICHARD P SPEAKMAN JR RAFAEL G TENORIO
LARRY W WILLIS ROBERT K WITTMAN RONALD R BEAMAN HAMMETT L BOWEN JR WILLIAM C HACKETT
KEVIN G ALDAM FREDDIE L DANIEL ARTHUR R DAVIS CLAUDE C DE NARDIS FOSTER E HARRISON
HAROLD S HUGGS JERRY A HURIANEK MICHAEL J JABLONSKI ZDZISLAW B KADLEWICZ ALFRED H KUNKEL JR
RONNIE LAWSON LEON S MADDEN PHILIP MASTRAMICO MICHAEL G MENNONE MARVIN R MILLER
DANIEL L ONEY LARRY D PLATT CHARLES H ROBINSON HUMBERTO R SANTIAGO JR WILLIAM M WILSON
MICHAEL L MCMASTER WILLIAM J SEILER STEVE O STRASSHOFER MICHAEL J THEMMEN MICHAEL A WELLS
CLIFFORD D WRIGHT JAMES D ZEBERT JAMES P BROWN JAMES R CASH THOMAS A CINCOTTA
WILLIAM C DABBERT ROGER D JENSEN PATRICK B KEMPKER EMERY L KOREL VICTOR M ROMAN
HERBERT LOGSDON JR KEVIN D LOW STEVEN L MCGINNIS CHARLES L MOSS JR MICHAEL J PADDOCK
RUDOLPH HINOJOSA JR BARRY I RABINOVITZ RICHARD T SELLERS JR CHARLES E BATTLES JAMES E BOWMAN
TIMOTHY G BURCHETT CHARLES F CLENDENIN COURTNEY J COSGROVE RONALD R DEWYEA LEVIL HICKS
DONALD P DAVIES RICHARD E DOPP WAYNE H EMERSON JOHN C GUENTHER JR GREGG C HINDERKS
ALAN M HORN ELGIN J JURI CHARLES M KINIYALOCTS FREDRICK A LISIEWSKI HERBERT J LOTTES
HARRELL S MEFFORD PATRICK J O'SHAUGHNESSY ROBERT D PAULUS ERNEST M STAINES BENNY D STUCKEY
DANIEL L TERRY DANIEL K WAPINSKI BOBBY R WILKINS STEVEN J WOODCOCK DELBERT E BRIMMER
ANTHONY J CABOT JR ROBERT J COLEMAN EUGENE T COX GERALD C DALEY JOSEPHUS DANIELS
GERARD J FLIEGER MICHAEL E FOWLER EDDIE L GARCIA EDWARD H GERNERT GEORGE T GIBNER
REX D HARLOW WAYNE S HORVATH JOHN W HULME JAMES W JONES JAMES A KLYNE
GLEN C LUDBAN JOHN D MORRISSEY STEWART W OBERLE GLEN E POTEET LAWRENCE RASPBERRY
RONALD E ROBERTSON JEROME E TUCKER LARRY C VALLELONGA CLOVIS B WALKER JAMES H WORKMAN
LARRY J WHITE DAVID J COLLINS RICHARD GARZA JR CORDELL GROVE CHARLES O HAMILTON
JOHN W HOLLE ELMER G IRELAND STANLEY N IRVING JAMES A JOHNSON JOSEPH H KELLEY
RICHARD A LAVENDER JACK E LUNTSFORD JAMES T PROUE HENRY L STAFFORD LARRY M BRYAN
RICHARD F CRUDO ELDON G CRUMLEY ALBERT L DELANEY BENNY H FERGUSON CALVIN J FEWLASS
JOHN L FLINN ALBERT M FRANSEN JR MELVIN S FUJITA HOUSTON GULLEY ROBERT W HOLDITCH
DAVID P INGERSOLL GLEN C KEENE JR MICHAEL P KLOTZ KENNETH A MAHL JOHN C MOSLEY
CARL E LAMBERSON JR BOBBY L MCCOY ROBERT R MCGINNIS STEPHEN T MOODY TIMOTHY C NUNNALLY
RALPH B ORTMANN JULIUS L PETERSON JAMES R RAINWATER ROBERT C RIZZO THOMAS J SCHNEIDER
DANIEL B SINNOTT DONALD L TOVEY DAVID R VORENKAMP EDWARD L WILLIAMSON JIM A WRAY
ROBERT ALBANESE MICHAEL R BLANCHFIELD HENRY J CABALLERO DANNIE A CARR CHARLES B DEDON
RICHARD W FELT MICHAEL F FOLLAND JOHN L FORDHAM THOMAS V HAGEMEIER PHILLIP T IVES
GARLAND D FLOYD STEPHEN C HARRELL ROBERT S HOLLEY III DUANE R KEIL JAMES E KELLY
RICHARD J KEY DONNIE L KING ROBERT E KING RONALD E KNIGHT FRANK L KOBOR JERRY W POFF
ROBERT A LAYTON JR ABBIE E LEAZER ROBERT A LEWIS JOHN S MANFERDINI THOMAS N MOTTO
DARRELL E NICHOLS SANTOS S NUNEZ BARRY L OSBORN ANTHONY E PETERSON
GERARD M REGGIO CHRISTOPHER J RICETTI WILLIS ROGERS JR PATRICK A RUSSELL FELIPE O SANTIAGO
TAKESHI SATO RICHARD G SONNEBERGER BILL H TERRY JR RICHARD J WHITEHOUSE AMOS L WILLIAMS
RODNEY D WILSON GLENN R WORKMAN THOMAS S BONVENTRE JOHN R DRISCOLL III BEN G DUGAN
PATRICK M FALLON AMBROSE GASSAWAY JOHN W GLADNEY DREW M GREENMAN
ROBERT P GARDINER ROBERT A GRIFFIN ALFRED W HUBBARD CHARLES F HUGHES JOHN C JAVORCHIK THOMAS W JOHNSON
EPHRIAM R LILES II STANLEY W MARTENS FLOYD J MATTHEWS JOSEPH J MEYER JR TIMOTHY S MICHAEL
DARRELL E MCGEE JOHNNY E MCIE WILLIAM R MCNELLY MICHAEL D NOONAN RAYMOND L PIRRMAN
MICHAEL T SHUEMAKER STEVEN M STICKS LANCE W STLAURENT DENNIS W SYDOR FLOYD WATTS
JIMMY D WEST JAMES M WITHEE JOHN C WOOD THOMAS J CAMPBELL APOLINAR CASTILLO JR
GEORGE D CRISWELL DAVID E FOGG RALPH J GREER HERMAN H HUEBNER HENRY E IMES JR
ARLAND J JONES PATRICK E MCGOVERN CECIL V MILLER LEON V PARKER GERALD R PUGH
JOAQUIN RAMOS-RAMIREZ JOHN J SESLER LORENZO TUGGLE JOHN A WELSFORD JR SAMUEL L WILLIAMS JR
DAVID F ACKERMAN DENNIS BAGLEY ALBERT D BENSON KURTIS A BERRY ROBERT A BROWN
DAVID E BUTTRY RONALD W CARDONA THOMAS R COLLINS JR JAMES L DAVIS RODNEY J DELISLE
THOMAS R DWYER KAYLE D HENDERSON LARRY H JOHNSON ERVIN JONES GOLSBY KIMBROUGH JR
JOHN D LINDBERG RICKIE A LOOMIS WILLIAM F RIGDON PATRICK R SCOTT JERRY W SPEARS
RUSSELL C NICOLAI WILLIAM M SHORT WARD G SNEED DARRELL L TUCKER LEONARD D WARD
LEROY WARD MICHAEL D WEBB THOMAS J ZELENKA JAMES W BEDELL DAVID L BONESTEEL
STEVEN K BROOKS BRUCE E COLEY HAROLD A COX RONNIE L DAVIS LEONARD G GREVILLE
TIMOTHY W HANSLEY RONALD J HAUPT DEWEY W HEROY DONALD F HOVANEC PAUL E JOHNSON
JAMES D KNOWLES RAYMOND P KURTIK FRANK LEVATO THOMAS J LYONS DANA L MACE
JOHN W MANNING RONALD E NEWELL JAMES L O'HARA BILLY E PERRY DAVID W SHAFFNER
PAUL H SHEEHAN THOMAS J SIZEMORE CHARLES E SMITH CURTIS A STEPHENS SHELBY M TROTTER
CARL L WALKER DAVID D WRIGHT DANNY K YELLEY COLON D YOUNG WILLIAM O ANDERSON
HOWARD V ANDRE JR VERNON D ARTIS BISHOP S BARANOWSKI GEORGE H BEASLEY THOMAS BROOKS JR
VIRGIL A CALKINS JR RUSSELL B CARSON CHARLES P CHANDLER GERALD S COLVIN DONALD L COVINGTON
JAMES N CROCKER JR STANLEY S FENNER ROBERT V GAPINSKI WILLIAM R GARNER SALVATORE A GELUSO
BOBBY L GENTRY WESLEY O GRANT DONALD L GRUBB FRANK W HUMES HENRY D HUNTER
THOMAS W HURLBUT JAMES H MANNING JOHN D MARTIN GEORGE L MUMMERT ANTHONY A NEVILLE
JIM C PAGE ROBERT W PETERSON HERBERT L PHELPS JOHN S REAVES JR RUSSELL A SCHWARTZ
ROY L SINGLETARY WILLIAM E SISLEY JAMES E SIZEMORE JOHN C TODD JESSE UPTIGROVE
ANTHONY VULTAGGIO JERRY BARFIELD THOMAS J BARNES JR WILLIAM C BOBO DANIEL SULLIVAN
JOHN B CORNWELL JAMES R DAVIS ROBERT DIAKOW JAMES C DOLOUGHTY BENNY T GISH
THOMAS H GREEN WILLIE C HAUGABOOK ANASTACIO JIMENEZ ROBERT E KING LARRY LUSTER
STEVEN L PORTER SANTOS RIVERA JR WALTER E ROBERTS JIMMIE C SCROGUM MICHAEL D SPRINKLE
EARL L COOK JUAN L TERRAZAS PETER E ULRICKSON STEVE ANDERSON ELIJAH W BURKETT
THOMAS A CERES WILLIAM B CHRISTENSON KENNETH J CYMBALSKI JOHN M ELLIS BOBBY G FARMER
JOHN R FRYE DAVID N HARROW THOMAS W HERBST LON M HOLUPKO WILLIAM A HYMAN
MICHAEL L KROM JACK V LACKEY JR ERNIE R MARTINEZ PETER F MCLAUGHLIN DAVID D PEPPIN JR
RICHARD F RUNZO HENRY E SPARKS CHARLES T STOCKBAUER WILLIAM L TOLIVER RAYMOND TORRES
ALEXANDER J URBAN JR ROBIN K WETZLER OSCAR L WHITE MALCOLM D WHITING III RICHARD H WILLIAMS
TIMOTHY T WILLIAMS JACKIE L WOODARD ALLEN C ARGENTA ELBERT J BAKER JR RENNIE J BAKER JR
PATRICK L BASILE ROBERT BATES JR NORMAN H BLOOMFIELD MARK L BRUNER WILLIAM R BURT JR
LARRY I CORNISH RICHARD T CORRIVEAU ROBERT W DEAN RONALD L EIDSON THOMAS P FENUSH
CURTISS FERNHOFF CLAUDIE FOWLER GEORGE H FRY ALAN G GEISSINGER JAMES R GEUY
JOE R GLASSBURN ARNOLD C HAYWARD HERMAN HAZELTON WILLIAM C HELM DANIEL J JONES JR
JOEL R KITCHENS BRADLEY W KLUKAS LARRY K MOTLEY MARVIN K RICHARDSON MICHAEL F ROGERS
CANOY L SISTRUNK BYRON D STEWART JOSEPH A TAISLER GEORGE B TEAR ALLAN C THIBOU
JAMES P WARD ROBERT W WHITE DAN B YARBROUGH RALPHAEL S YOKOI RUSSELL C YOST
ROBERT J BAKER PAUL W BANNON BARRY W BICKEL RALPH O BRAY JR ARTHUR D BROWN
RICHARD L BUCKLES DELOS R BUXTON CODY R CALKINS LUIS G CERVANTEZ JOSE B CISNEROS
RONALD M CREMER STEVEN T CUMMINS DANIEL M DENNIS RICHARD A ENGLAND DAVID C GORMICAN

CALVIN HARRIS PHILIP N HUTH II TOBY L JACKSON GEORGE S KIMMELL JOHNNY L KING
CALVIN G MAGUIRE LARRY D MCKOY PETER X PIKE ROBERT J SIRES OTTIS E STRINGER
JAMES W THIBAULT JOHN C USILTON DANIEL L WAGENAAR ROGER G BOVE STEVEN W BRADBURY
ROBERT H BURGESS RONALD D CHALOU JAMES W COLE THOMAS L DUKES THOMAS F FANNING JR
BYRON R HALL RONALD S HOLEMAN GRAHAM H HOWISON DAVID R MAIER JERRY MANNING
JOHN D MARTIN WILLIAM T MARTIN REYNALDO MARTINEZ JOSEPH MORRIGGI JERRY G ROSE
RICHARD D SCHWIDERSKI STEVEN C WEBB CLIFFORD W WEEKLEY GEORGE A WORK ROBERT E WORRELL
DAVID E YATES WILLIAM D ALBERT EDWIN C ALLEN CHARLES D BRASIER ERNEST D BURNS
DEWEY R BUTLER GEORGE L BUTTS WARREN C DEYERMOND THOMAS M FELTON
RAY G DAVIS WILLIE J DAVIS PETER A DROUHARD ARNOLD F GARCIA LEONARD M GOMOLICKE JAMES H SMITH
TERRY L HAWKINS CHARLES W HUGHES MICHAEL D HUGHES BRUCE E INGMAN EDWARD L KINGREY
DENNIS F LORDEN THEODORE MENDEZ SR JOHN V MORASCINI GEORGE J PASCALE GREGORY J PEARSON
PHILLIP C PETSOS JUAN M RAMOS ELDON L REYNOLDS JOE I RODRIGUEZ RICHARD J SCHOONVELD
WILLIAM D GILLINGHAM EDWARD L SHELTON HAROLD M SLOAN LARRY L TECHMEIR RONALD G THOMAS
DAVID C TOBIE MICHAEL J TROYAN JR RALPH A WELLINGHOFF ROY S WILLS TIMOTHY G CARTER
JOHN E BLINER PAUL J BRAGG ARNIM N BRAITHWAITE STEPHEN J BRENNAN ADOLPHUS CHRISTOPHER
DAVID H DUNN LUCAS R ENRIQUEZ WILLIAM F ERICSON II HAMPTON A ETHERIDGE III JOHNNY N EUTSLER
ROGER L GLEI SAMUEL E GODBEY JOHN C HANSEN THOMAS E HEMPEL MICHAEL A LACKNER

PANEL 20W

RICHARD H MCGUIRE KENNETH J MEULEBROECK TEDDY E MIDDLETON DENNIS E NEWMAN
CHARLES D ORSUA HARMON POLSTER HENRY R REYES HARVEY F ROUNTREE JR WILLIAM D SMALL
JACKIE L SMITH WILLIAM E SUTTLE LUIS TORRES-SERRANO NICHOLAS L VENDITTI GEORGE J VIEHMANN JR
MICHAEL S WALKER JAMES N WALL ROBERT H WOOD ARTHUR R ALLISON BRUCE C ANDERSON
ROGER C BRATHWAITE JERRY A BUNN DUANE J CABALA STEPHEN R COSTELLO CARL E CUNNINGHAM
JAMES V DAWSON ROBERT G EASTON JAMES M FLEMING RONALD A HOFF KENNETH M WILLIS
DARRELL V HURT JOHNNY L KIDD RONALD I KIRKPATRICK JESSIE R LEWIS RODGER D MCELHANEY
JOHN T NALL WILLIAM F OLSEN JACK L PRICE PEDRO RODRIGUEZ-RODRIG WILLIAM J SIMS
DENNIS K HOPPOUGH ELWIN E SINGLETON BENJAMIN J SULLIVAN ROBERT D ANDRADE ROBERT F BACON
DENNIS W BINGHAM PAUL W EDWARDS MICHAEL G EMEIGH ARLIN D FRANKEN NOEL K GARRISON
JAMES E LEACH RICHARD G PHILLIPS LEWIS D PROBART JULIO QUINONES JR GARY W REED
LESLIE REYNOLDS JR DANIEL M SHEEHAN ROBERT J SLANAKER WILBUR J VACHON III JONATHAN R VARS
KEM L WALLACE DEAN B ALLEN HERBERT F AMRHEIN MARVIN L DIPERT DOUGLAS S DRESSEN
LAWRENCE A ESTERLY RODNEY J EVANS ROGER E FOREMAN DAVID L HASTINGS RICHARD L HUPP JR
JOHN S KRAABEL DONALD A LAPES ROGER D LAWSON JOHN P MADDEN THOMAS J MARTINO
ROBERT V MOORE WILLIAM C PROCTOR JR ROBERT S SHEGOGUE HECTOR VALLE HENRY O WILHOITE
THOMAS L WISNIOWICZ BRENT L ARVESETH WILLIAM T BASS JR DENNIS M BELONGER MICHAEL R MCCANN
JOHN D COSSEY RONALD E DASCOMBE WARREN K DAVIS BERNARD F DEUTSCH JAMES R DEVNEY
JERYL F DRISKILL RALPH S FLADGER JOHN G GERTSCH TERRY L GILLIAM RAYMON D HALES
RICHARD A HAVLIK MICHAEL A HAWK WALTER KARAS BERNARD M LUEBKERT AUBREY G MARTIN
RONALD I BUCHANAN CARROL F MEADOWS DONALD K MINK MACK L MITCHELL MICHAEL T MITCHELL
JAMES E MCPIKE JAMES E NULTON II ALFONSO OLMOS THOMAS E ROSE MICHAEL SCOTT
ROBERT L SEEKAMP ROY D SIKKINK WILLIAM D STEELE WAYLAND D STEMBRIDGE WALLATE F THIBODEAU
DUREL S WOODS HARRY P YINGLING BENJAMIN F BROWN JR JAMES R COUCH DENNIS EITEL
RONNIE G GREENE RONALD G JETT ALEX E MARTINEZ DANIEL E MCGRATH DANIEL W MCGRATH
JOHNNY K PARKER LARRY R REATHERFORD DAVID P RUSSELL ROBERT R SANFORD DAVID A SEMERARO
STANLEY K SMILEY GEOFFREY S SMITH LEE TRYON JR JOHN E ANDERSON NORMAN J CHAVARIE
RICHARD S CLARE ARCHIE G CULVER RICHARD A CUTLER EDWARD M DENNULL EDWARD S HAMILTON
MARTIN W DROICK YOUEAL D ERWIN MICHAEL B FINN JOHN T FUDGE LUIS A SOTELO
JAMES M COX GEORGE A GRINNELL MACDONALD B HALSEY WILLIAM D LOUNSBURY RICHARD D MCNABB
BOYD K NEWBOLD RAYMOND J PALANDRO ROGER R PANGAN RICHARD J PARNELL EUGENE R RIPPEL
JAMES N GAY ANSELMO SANTIAGO-ARROYO JOHN M SROKA JR ROBERT D STAGGS DUNCAN A WARWICK
RONALD F WILDER JOHN S BAILEY JR DENNIS S CABE DAVID L ELROD BERNARDINO F GENCHI
ROLAND C HAMILTON CHARLES W JOHNSON JOSEPH A MARASCO LARRY G POOL CARL D SHIRLEY
ALLEN E STARR GAIL L WHITLATCH SAMUEL V BURRUANO CHARLES E FORD PHILIP HAMMONS
JOHN F KITSON THOMAS H MCCARTY GLENN E PELTON FRANKLIN W PICKING FRANK C WALLENBECK
CARL O HENLY MYRON K RENNE MICHAEL A RUHTER JAIME A SALINAS DAVID A STRONG
MARTIN R BECK FRANCIS M BEVERLY EVERETT W BRAUBURGER DANIEL L CAREY JAMES D EARNEST
GREGORY C ENGEL LOUIS J GENESEO ROBERT L GLASGOW STEVEN J GRECO THEODORE E GRENSBACK JR
ELI W KNIGHTON JR STANLEY J LENTO JAMES W LOONEY PETER J MORKA LEON L MORRIS
ARCHIE H MCDANIEL JR CALVIN L MCDURMON JOHN P ROE PAUL J SALMINEN DOUGLAS L STIGGINS
GARY D TATE ROBERT J WHITES LARRY D AIKEN MICHAEL M BARTHOLOMEW JAMES L CLARK
JIMMY D COURTNEY JOSE A DELGADO GERALD E DU BEAU JAY L EVERETT JOHN B GAINGER
WILLIAM L HAAK RONNIE L HERRIMAN MICHAEL JENNINGS CURTIS JONES JOHN E KELLY JR
WESLEY E MUELLER ARTHUR T PFEFER VINCENT F SABATINELLI ALAN P SANDOVAL MICHAEL L STPIERRE
ALBERT VICK JR SILAS C WRIGHT LARRY G BELDEN RICHARD D BRENNING ALPHONSO D COWAN
JULIUS L BROWN ROBERT D BUSWELL MICHAEL J CAPRIO LESLIE D CARTER JR JOSEPH S CHIACCHIO JR
JOHN A BRAXTON GEORGE H CLIFFORD THOMAS J DION ALFONSO M DURAN RONALD K DYCKS
EVERARDO GALINDO JR STEWART B GOLDBERG GLENN A HAMILTON CLYDE L HOLLIDAY HENRY J ROY JR
TOMMY HUERTA RAY G HUFF ARNOLD B JACKSON JACK C JOHNSTON JR RICHARD K LARSON
FRED J MCCLAIN KELLY S MORRIS MICHAEL C NIELSEN ELVERNON PEELE REYNALDO S RODRIGUEZ
DONALD E FLETCHER ROBERT J RUNSER MICHAEL O THOMAS GARY L TINKER HARVEY R WATSON
JAMES F WOHRER JAMES A AMOS ROBERT W ARMENIO HENRY BALLEW JR JOHN A ALBASIO
LEON R BARICKMAN WILLIAM G BARKER ROBERT H BARR ERIC E BERGQUIST LAWRENCE J BERTAGNA
FRED W SHATTUCK JAMES A CARR JAMES L COLEMAN JAMES R DANIELS JERRY R DEES PAUL M DU CHARM
WILBERT C FLECK RAYMOND GIBEL JAMES D GIBSON DAVID M GLASCO MICHAEL F GRAMLICK
CHARLES L HACKWORTH JOHN H HARRIS JR THOMAS A HINSON CHARLES E JOHNSON DONALD J MACCIO
JAMES C JACKSON DELMER L KINNEY GARY P LEACH THEODORE E MANGUM JR EDWARD A MISKOWSKI
JOHN T MCDANIEL MARK L MCMANUS GARY R MORTON JAMES J MOTES STEVEN NAGY
JOHN H PEARSON RICHARD PISKULA FELICIANO ROCHA THOMAS R ROOT DAUNT B SANDERS
RONALD J SCHARF WILLIAM E SHEEN RALPH D STORM CLAUDE E TABOR CLINTON E TIBBETTS
EDWARD W WYATT RORY M BAUM LANNY R BAUMANN THOMAS A BLAIR FRANCIS J COULOMBE
TIMOTHY W BEVERFORD DANIEL M BROWN THOMAS L CALLAGHAN DANIEL G CASEY MICHAEL N COLTON
JERRY D DE MARCUS GREGORY J DENTON STEPHEN DOWDELL ROBERT L ELLIS PAUL E FABRISI
ROBERT W FLETCHER JOHN R GAINER PETER J GERRY JACKIE D HAMBY ANDREW J KINIRY
HOWARD W LAKEY BERNARD J MATTHEWS BRIAN G PARROTT JOHN M RENNER DUANE M ROUSSEAU
FRANKLIN D SIBAYAN CHARLES M SIKES CURTIS D SMITH ERVIN R SRB JR LESLIE E WALKER
MICHAEL WALTERS DAVID E WESTOVER HERMAN WHITE JR MICHAEL C WUNSCH JAMES J AMENDOLA
RICHARD T BLAKE DANIEL A BOLDUC PERRY N BROWNING JAMES P CHITTWOOD RANDALL M DENTON
HARRY E BLACK ROY N GIVENS STEPHEN D GLECKLER EDWARD J HALBERT ROGER P HARRELL
JOHN E HISEY ROBERT J KEIN FRED M KERNS JAMES C KOTRC JAMES A LANDRUM
BRUCE M LANGAUNET DANIEL LEWIS MELVIN LOYD CURTIS MARION ROBERT E MITCHELL JR
JOHN F MURPHY LARRY MURRAY DAVID P QUINLAN HUGH E REVIS SOLTERO R CARRASQUILLO
LARRY L RIDDLE JOSEPH P RUEBEL KRIS E SHAW HENRY E VILLALOBOS JOHN W WHISENANT
WILLIAM T POCHER DAVID E BRAMSEN JERRY D CANTRELL TERRY L DALLAPE JAMES E GASSER
FRANK R GILCHRIST JR AUGUST F HAMILTON TONY HARPER CORNELIUS F HUBBARD EUGENE M ROBINSON
WILBERT E JONES JOHN D MCARTHUR PERLUM M PARKER JR ANGEL L RODRIGUEZ-COTTO FRANK G SMITH
ERNEST L STANFORD JOHN R STASHONSKY HAROLD O STUMP SAMUEL W WALTHOUR JR
RICHARD L WINDSHEIMER JOHN K WINSLOW RONALD J BATES MICHAEL P BURNS CONN K CLARK MICHAEL A DWYER
THOMAS L FULLER RAYMOND H HARDIN ROBERT A HOFFMAN WILLIAM J KARAS PAUL D MCKNIGHT
DENNIS P NEAL RONALD R NILES RANDY L OWENS HENRY C POLZIN JOSEPH RENDON
JAMES E SHELTON WILLIAM R WILSON JR JOHN L BRADFORD DOUGLAS G BURD TOMMY L CALLIES
THOMAS CASTILLO GAYLORD K DE FRIES JAMES L HICKS RICHARD E HOLZER JR JOHN D MUIR
JAMES THACKER FRANK D WALTHERS HAROLD D WILLIAMS ROBERT G ARDOIN DAVID M BALL
WALTER D BROWNE WILLIAM E CAMPBELL GEORGE D CONRAD JR DAVID L DE LOACH
THOMAS L DIVES JR JAMES S DRAVIS JR DAVID E FITZGERALD WILLIAM T GRESHAM JR HAL K HENDERSON
DANIEL A IRELAN THOMAS L JUSTICE RICHARD K LEWIS RONNIE D LINDLEY GERALD S LOTRIDGE
GARRY D BARBEE DWIGHT P MCKEATHON ROLAND H NADEAU DAVID C O'CONNOR ALEXANDER P POMEROY JAMES F POTTER
THOMAS K RYAN ROBERT L SHOOK JAMES S STACEY GEORGE F TALKEN RICHARD C WATSON
DAVID TORRES ALBERT A VAQUERA VENANCIO VERA CARL R WARD JR ALLAN T YOUNGKRANS JR
BOBBY W ARMES JAMES W BLAKE DENNIS M HARTER LAWRENCE A HAYES FRANK A HILL III
CHRISTOPHER KELLY DAVID R KINK GLEN A MILLINGER JAMES E MORTON JR DAVID H SHERLOCK
TERRENCE M MCDERMOTT CARL E MORGAN DENNIS R ROBERTS GEORGE C SCHOETTNER PHILLIP C SMITH
STEPHEN E SROKA JAMES D WHITE CHARLES W BEESLER ROY D BRATTON WYMAN G BRITT
GEORGE S DORMAN RICKEY E HARRIS GEORGE F LOSTUTTER DANIEL L MERSHON EUGENE C OATES III
JAMES H OWENS JR FRED M RAGLAND RODNEY F STEVENS DANNY L BARRON MICHAEL L COX JR
JAMES W DONNELLY JR WALTER J GUTOWSKI JOHN E HUGHES JR RICHARD L IRVIN ROBERT E JONES
PHILIP V MACKINNEY MARTIN J KERBY ROBERT L KRAFT VERLE N LARSON LYLE G LEPPKE FRANK E LITCHFIELD
RONALD H STGERMAINE DAVID M SWAN JOHN H SWEET DAVID H WILSON II JOHN L ALLEN
SAMUEL BETZ JAMES C BINK JR GARY M CLEMENTS NORMAND A CORBIN ALEXANDER A KAOPUIKI JR
JOHN F CRIKELAIR ROY L FELTY DAVID H FINGER ARTHUR GRASSER JOSEPH M HASHIN JR
GEORGE E CANNON SR STANLEY B HOJNOWSKI ROBERT B HOWARD BOBBY J JONES MICHAEL D KELLY
GREGORY L MEYER ANDREW MONTANIO PAUL A NELSON SCOTT T NELSON DAVID M VALDEZ
MICHAEL W NORTH VIESTURS REIKMANIS FRED G RINEHART DAVID F SMITH JAMES F TALBOTT
SYLVESTER NELSON JR AKKE J TIMMER JR LAWRENCE O WOOLDRIDGE ROOSEVELT ABRAHAM JR LEO J ADAKAI
NORMAN L BARTON GEORGE L BOURNE TERRENCE C BRASILE EDWARD BRUNO CHARLES M COLLIER
CARLOS A BALDIZON-IZQUIER JOSE A CARRION BRUCE W CARTER PEDRO A DE LORA JERALD M HYATT
THOMAS L CLARK JR EARNEST HEARD JR LAWRENCE H JACKSON RONALD R KIRKPATRICK JOHN J MASLAK
ROBERT F OLSON STEPHEN B PEEL BOBBY R QUESENBERRY CHARLES L REEFER STEPHEN P SHANER
LEWIS L SHORT FREDERICK WELSH RICHARD L WILSON EDMOND D WIMMERGREN LIONEL WORKMAN
MILFORD M TOGNAZZINI JAMES A WINFREY CHARLES W ADAMS ROY O BUCHANAN DONALD P CANDLER
ROBERT W COOPER GARY W COX ROBERT L DANCE PEDRO DE HERRERA BRUCE A EAMICK
DWIGHT D FOSTER HARRY GARRIGUS DENNIS J GREEN LOUIE E HAWKEY JIMMIE E KEITH

278

OFFERINGS AT THE WALL

PANEL 20W *(Continued)*

LUIS A MASSA SAMUEL J MATHIS LONZO O MCDONALD RICHARD J NOLDIN RICHARD R OLSON
MICHAEL H PAINTER MANUEL F PARRA GEORGE W PIERCE HENRY L PIPPIN STANLEY R RAJALA
DUANE N SCOWDEN FREDDIE M SHERLIN ARVEL R SMART JESSIE J TYLER HUMBERTO LLAMAZALES
JOHN D BRING VIRGIL L CASTLE PAUL A DE VEGTER LAURIERS P DES JAMES C DINE
JEFFERSON S DOTSON FRED A FEDDER LAURENT L GOURLEY RONALD J JANOUSEK RAYMOND P JOHNSON
EDWARD E BECK JR BRUCE E KANE MICHAEL W KIRKPATRICK DONALD H MCMAINS JR MICHAEL R SEIBERT
MICHAEL S SPRATLIN FRANK M STREAMER GWYMAN STRIBBLING STEPHEN A YOUNG JOHN K ANDERSON
ALBERTO T ANZALDUA LEVI L ARMSTRONG RONALD L BERRY DAVID E CARTER SAM CATALANO JR
WILLIAM R DICKEY BILLY W EARP DONALD L ELLIOTT STEPHEN G LOWE JEFFREY A SCHONFIELD
JAMES C HARMON JOSEPH L HESSON III JAMES G HILLIARD ROGER D HOLLIFIELD RICHARD A JOHNSON JR
PETER F KRISTOF JAMES J KROLIKOWSKI ROBERT T MARMIE WILLIAM E MICKELSEN JR MICHAEL J MOONEY
LARRY D MCGHEE RONALD R OZIMEK CARL A PETERSON PAUL G PLACZEK CHARLES A POE
JERRY GORE ABELARDO RODRIGUEZ-GUZMAN THOMAS A ROSENOW REGINALD M SATER BRIAN E WOLFE
CHARLES B SEMINARA JOHN S SERATTE MICHAEL F SHERIDAN THOMAS D SNYDER LARRY J TALLEY
DONALD F ROBINSON LINDSAY C TURNER LUTHER WALKER JR DALE S WILKINSON KENNETH E BURCH

PANEL 19W

CHARLES R COPE JOHNNY J CURETON JR LAWRENCE K DOWD DAVID M FREEMAN
ALAN D HARVEY ROBERT W HOCK TERRANCE F KANE EDWARD L KANTER KENNETH MARCUM
BERNARD L HOLZKNECHT RANDALL F KASER JAMES J KESTER RANDOLPH L LARSON MICHAEL H LAWHON
STEPHEN R PRINCE ROY V RAWLIN RONALD ROBBINS LARRY L SHAW STANLEY J SHUMINSKI
JOHN C SIMS JR BRADLEY L SINN SAM J SMALL JR JAMES C STONER LAURENCIO VIGIL
TOMMIE WATSON FRANKLIN D WILLIAMS JOHN C WILLIAMS JAMES R WOODS DANIEL M ZUNIGA
SAMUEL ABRAMS JR CARL E ADKISON LEONARD L ALVARADO MARK T AMANN GREG A BARKER
BRUCE M BARNES THEODORE F BENVENUTO JR BOBBY L BEVARD ALAN W MEDIATE CHARLES D ROBERTS
HENRY BRABO JAMES J BRANHAM ALAN W BRESHEARS GRADY L BREWER CLARENCE F BRISTOL
DEWEY F BUTCHER JAMES A CABRAL JR CORNELIUS J CASHMAN MARTIN D CHILDRESS LARRY D GARNER
EUGENE P CLARK ALBERT V COLLETTO JR JOSEPH COLORIO JOHN R CONSTIEN FRED J DE LORENZO JR
DAVID S DETERS DONALD G DILLARD JAMES P ECKLES JOSE L FLORES DALE E FRUHLING
THOMAS W CARRINGTON CHARLES J GARITY JR JAMES F GASE FREDRICK P GILLEN LAWRENCE D GREEF
LEO F GREEN JR MELVIN GREEN MICHAEL J GREGORIUS PHILLIP GUZMAN JR DAVID O HAAKE
RICHARD L HARDESTY JONATHAN P HASH JEREMIAH M HAYES JR RAY E HOMBEL CHARLES A HOOD
GARY L HOSKINS JAMES L JOHNSON STEPHEN J KELLY GENE R KOSKI CECIL W LAMBERT
DENNY R LAPPIN KENNEY E LASSITER JAMES LINDER JR JOHN M MAHONEY JAMES H MARSHALL
TILMEN V BARTHOLOMEW FRANCIS MCDOWALL JR STANLEY A MENSING HAROLD G MILES PETER R MILLS
WALLACE T MCMAKIN ROBERT A O'CONNOR RODNEY G OXENDINE SAMUEL A PAPIN JR CARL PARTON
HARVEY A PEAY STEPHEN J PENTA GEORGE R PLATTER HOWARD M PYLE JR RONALD G QUINN
MARCELLO N BARRIOS RONALD J RAY JAMES R RICE PHILIP O RICHARDSON GERADO P RIOS
JOSEPH G SANDS LARRY R SCHMIDT WILLIAM J SCHMIDT WILLIAM B SCOTT LEE R SHAW
RONALD L SHORT BRADLEY J SIMMONS THOMAS J SIMON JOHN J SINCLAIR AARON B SMITH
GARRY G SMITH WILLIAM T SMITH STEPHEN A SNIDOW GEORGE E SNYDER LEONARD P SPARKMAN
THEODUS M STANLEY JAMES STANTON GARY L STEPHENSON BEN W STONE DON R SYKES
JON TASCH WILLIAM M TREADWAY CLINTON J WEAVER CHRISTOPHER C WEBSTER LARRY J WHEELER
MILLARD P WHEELER DONALD H WHITE ADVERT WOODS JR MARION L ZIPP RICHARD J ZISKO
NELSON ANDINO ALFRED BARNES JR PAUL V BARRINGTON JR RICHARD L BROWN DOUGLAS J BRUSTMAN
JAMES R BYRNE MOISES CARTAGENA-ACOSTA JAMES W CASTOR STEVEN V CRUM JAMES W DAVIS
GUIDICE G DEL JOHN A DOWD WILLIAM J DURHAM JOHN L FIELDER JERRY L FORDHAM
RUSSELL P FORRISTAL MICHAEL J HOLLOWAY WAYDE M HUSO CARL F KROH DANA E MEANS
LESTER A HANSEN GARY E MARXMILLER CHARLES C MATTHEWS THOMAS J MENDENHALL RICHARD MILLAN
ROBERT F MCCLAFLIN KENNETH R MCDANIEL KENNETH R MCLEESE JAMES A NORRIS JERRY W OFSTEDAHL
MARK J PHILLIPS JERRY D REED LARRY M ROBINSON NORMAN D SCHULTE PHILIP T SMITH
RUSSELL M STAUDT ROBERT E SWINDLE MICHAEL J THOMAS JOHN B VALDEZ CHARLES VELASQUEZ
ROBERT A WASHINGTON RICHARD D WELLMAN JOHN C WHITESIDE JACK M APODACA DAVID E BEAN
DONALD A CONTARINO MICHAEL H DERAGON DONALD L DUNN JEFFREY C ELSON LESLEY H HENSON
HERMAN T FIELDS THOMAS L FOWLER KENNETH G GOODNESS MELVIN L GRANT JOHN S HALL
MICHAEL L BRUNDAGE KENNETH J HAMRICK JAMES B HIEMENZ HORATIO W HURSTON RICHARD J KILWINE
JOHN A KUEFNER SIDNEY G LAZARUS JR ROBERT W MAJOR ROBERT S MITCHELL DARYL M MOGCK
EARL W MCDOWELL EDWARD L PENNINGTON CARL J PICHAUFFE DANIEL T ROY JAY C SACKS
RICKEY E SWANEY STEPHEN J TORBETT GIL S WILFONG RICHARD M WISE HUMBERTO R HERNANDEZ
JAMES D ANDERSON FRANK C ARMIJO JOHN M BOZINSKI ROGER D BROWN DANIEL E CAREY
TYRONE CHATMAN RICKY W CHURCH VALLE S DEL CHESTER L GOINS JOHNNIE GRAHAM JR
VINCENT L SHEPERSKY JACKY E LANDERS RICHARD D LAXSON DAVID B LENTZ MICHAEL L LEWIS
RAYMOND LIGONS RAYMOND G MASSE TERRY K MCDONELL JOSEPH W MITCHELL EARL J OVERACKER
PAUL PONCE PAUL M ROBERTS RONNIE L ROBERTSON ROBERT H SHIELDS II JOHN G SMITH
WILLIAM H SOMERVILLE JAMES L SPRINKLE BOYD L WHITTED TOMMY J BERRIER WILLIAM K BLACKBURN
GEORGE F BONNETT JOHN M DAVIS ISRAEL ESPARZA MARK W EVELAND JERRY A FRAKES
CLIFFORD M GIBSON WILLIAM S HEIDER LAWRENCE J HUMPHREY THOMAS D JONES WILLIAM N LA GRONE
RODNEY D LITTLE CLIFFORD P MCCRARY MICHAEL D MUSE ARTURO A NAZABAL JR SAMUEL H PIERCE JR
RONALD E SHIPLEY CHARLES L TROXEL EUGENE TUCKER JOHN E WIBBENS TERRY L BARR
CARL C BATES JR CURTIS BOWMAN GERALD L CATON KIM M DILIBERTO DAVID A GAY
FRANK A FRANGELLA GREGORY J GEE WILLIAM P GOODING PAUL R HOPKINS CHALMERS C HUMPHREYS
JAMES R HURST DONALD JAMES JR FREDERICK MEZZATESTA GEORGE L MINER STEVEN M MIOTKE
RONALD W PANNO MATTHEW PETERSON CLIFFORD SEALS VERNON D SOUTHERLAND RONALD D TILLERY
DANIEL R TURNER JAYSON F ULRICH JAY D WEBSTER JR DOUGLAS W WILKIE SCOTT E WISE
HOWARD C ARD NORMAN D AUTEN DONALD R BARRETT WILLIAM J BASSIGNANI NEWTON T BELL JR
HOWARD R BRUCKNER DANIEL R DAVIS MARIO P DE LEON STANLEY H DICKERSON ROBERT H DONAWAY
RODNEY L ENGEL ROBERT A FOX RIGOBERTO GOMEZ-DIAZ MARK W GRIGSBY GEORGE A GUY
GARY W HARVEY GEARLD A HENRY EDWIN C HOCKENBERRY JAMES G HODGSKIN JR JAMES W KIRKSEY
DAVID LEWIS VINCENT T MASCIALE FRANCIS MCLAUGHLIN DOUGLAS C MERRILL VINCENT J MUSCO
BENNY B PARKER BOBBY RIDDLE JOHN C RODGERS EDWIN J SMOLAREK JR ROBERT K SPILLNER
RICHARD W NELSON THOMAS L STRADTMAN DAVID R TIBBETTS PAUL W VANDERBOOM JR GARY E YOUNG
RODOLFO P ALLAGONEZ RAYMOND J ASHNAULT ROBERT C BECKMAN JAMES R BOHLIG JOSE LLAMAS
REGINALD W BURRIS JERRY N CREASY GASPAR CRUZ-LEBRON JERRY J CURTIS WILLIAM J DAWSON
RICHARD A DORIA ROBERTO C DUENAS JOHN D DUNCAN ODELL EASLEY JOHN N FLANIGAN
JARED A FRISBIE FRANCISCO GONZALEZ JR DONNIE L HACKNEY ELI P HOWARD JR MARTIN E KIRIK
FRANCIS E BRANCHEAU II JOHN A KOLWYCK DONALD G LANHAM STEWART J LAVIGNE BOBBY J LIKENS
EUGENE A LUNN WILLIAM M MACKAY WILLIAM L MAGERR III ROSS E MANDEVILLE STEPHEN L MARTINO
JIMMIE MILLER JOSEPH P MOBUS TIMOTHY A MOHLER RICHARD T MORRISSEY JOHN L MUTSCHLER
HARVEY R MCCUISTON ROBERT M NELSON JOHN S ORLEMANN GEORGE W PEARSON JR JOHN D PLUMMER
MICHAEL E POLIQUIN FRANKLIN D ROWELL RUSSELL M RUFFNER JR DENNIS F SHINE GUS SIAMBONES
GERALD L SILVERSTEIN ROBERT N SMITH ROBERT G SOLOMON PAUL A SPARKS JOHN W VOYLES
ROBERT J WAGNER JAMES R WALLACE MARK H WARD JOHN R WATTS PHILIP M WERBISKI
DONALD F WOOD LEONARD J ZIGALLA RICHARD P ALBERT THOMAS W BAZEMORE LESTER J BRANTLEY
JOSEPH E BUGAR JR DAVID L CAUSEY CRUZ F DELA MICHAEL G DEMORE STANISLAW J DROZDZ
BOBBY J EVERETT DAVID T FORD FRANCIS B GARGUS MICHAEL GARLO GARY D GRABER
WILLIAM H HAND CARL C HARRIS JERRY W HILL CHRISTOPHER A JACKSON MILTON J MENDOZA
JIMMY L JONES EDGARDO R LA TORRE RICHARD R MCINTOSH JOSEPH H MUSSELMAN FRANK R NESTOR
RANDALL I ORTIZ JOSEPH J PAPARELLO CLYDE E PHIFER JR STEVEN M POE MAXIE D REGISTER
JAMES E RUTTAN FRED A SLEMSEK JAMES D SPILKER ARTHUR STROYMAN MARTIN L TABER
JOSEPH D THOMPSON DONALD D TRIPP GORDON J TURPIN JR JAMES R WALDOWSKI RAYMOND L WILCOX
JOHN W WILSON ROGER D WRIGHT DAVID R BAKER JAMES H BROWN JR THOMAS L BUSCH III
JACK L CONNORS DENNIS A CUNNINGHAM JAMES M EARLY DENNIS L ENGLISH RUPERT A FUNDERBURK JR
JAMES L GORDON MICHAEL L HARP MICHAEL J HAVARD CHARLES T HEINEMEIER DANIEL P HOLTREY
JEFFREY L HULBERT ROBERT A JONES DANIEL J KIRCHGESLER CHARLES R LE BOSQUET RANDY J LUNDY
WILLIAM D MARTIN MICHAEL N MASUEN EUGENE L MILLER WILLIAM MIRANDA MAJOR B MORGAN JR
CHARLES H PARKS JR RUDOLPH S PARRISH LUIS E QUINTANA-SOTO ROBERT T RAZZANO JAMES C TOSH III
WILLARD D RICHARDSON JR JOE C SHAW AOULIULITAU F TAUFI ADOLPHUS N TYLER RAY M BARKER
JACKIE D BIRD JR MICHAEL T BOAT BARRETT C BROWN ALBERT J CARRIER III CURTIS P CHALLBERG
ANTHONY B BLAIR HAROLD E CUSHMAN LAWRENCE R DETWILER JR MICHAEL J DUGAS EDMUND FURMAN
BERTRAND R GAGNE DENNIS A GATTI LAWRENCE R GOODMAN JR MICHAEL J GRECU JOHN M HILL
LUIS M GONSALEZ RICHARD R GRINNELL STUART F HEMP JOHN L HURD ARTHUR H JOHNSON
ROBERT L KETELAAR PETER A KIDD MOSES I KUAHIWINUI JR ADREN A LEE ROBERT D LINGLE
DANIEL H LOVE DOMINICK J MADONNA ANTHONY V MIONE STEPHEN D MOORE RAYMOND L WHITMAN
PHILLIP G MCCALL JAMES E MCWHORTER JEFFREY C PETERSON ROY K PETERSON DERWIN B PITTS
THOMAS M RALSTON ERIC D SALTZ THOMAS R SAYERS WILLIAM R SPEIGHT DARRELL D TAYLOR
PETER LOPEZ HOWARD F TAYLOR BENJAMIN T WALANGITANG WILLIAM J ZELTNER III WILLIAM C ADAMS
STEPHEN E CUNNINGHAM TOMMY G ELLIOTT WILLIAM W ELLIS III DENNIS M GILLERAN JAMES A WINGERT
BORIS W GURDCILANI RICKEY W HALL DENNIS C HUCKABY RONALD A HUNT HAYWARD K PELEIHOLANI
KENITH L JARRELL KENNETH D JOHNSON GEORGE M LABANISH JAMES MACK JOE W NORWOOD
FREDERICK C KINSLER JR DENNIS M MATTOX ALEXANDER M MORALES NORMAN L RICHARD JON E DAVIS
JUAN L DUENAS JOHN R ROMO KENNETH E SINGER JIMMY J TENORIO PHILIP J VEVERA
EDWARD AMBROSE WILLIAM J ANDERSON JR BERNARD P BAILEY JAMES R BEATTY JAMES N STEEN
STANLEY R HONEA JIMMY M DOLAN DANIEL E FARAN ROY A FRYMAN GUADALUPE GALINDO JR
WILLIAM F GOLLIDAY DENNIS L HENRY WILLIAM D KAYGA JOSEPH J MILANO LENARD F MOEGGENBORG
ROY D MCLENNAN JESUS D NIETO JR GARY A OHMAN JOSE A ORTIZ WILLIAM F RIDGE
BOBBY L ROBERTS JOSE F ROSADO-BORGES CHARLES H SCHAEFER ROBERT C SCHELL JR LARRY SHEA
RICHARD A ANDERSON DENNIS M SKOGERBOE BOBBY L TARTER RICHARD J WHITE JOHN R ZIMMERMAN
LA B BAKER BARRY B COERS THOMAS J DOSTAL JAMES A FRANCIS ROBERT E GAFTUNIK
JEFFERY L GEIB TERRANCE N GENTRY EDWARD R GRUSCZYNSKI HERBERT C HEINTZ FELIPE HERNANDEZ
STEPHEN E BEBOUT ALLEN L HITES DIXON T KINARD PAUL F KOSTICK MICHAEL J LAWRENCE MELVIN W LAY
MICHAEL G MCGILL DAVID M MILLER DAVID E NELSON DONALD W PARMLEY RAYMOND J PORTER
GERALD J ROSSOW ROBERT A RYAN STEVEN R SANDERS JOHN J SCHMIDT DENNIS C SHARPE
RICHARD P SHELTON JAMES STINGLEY ALAN P STRAZZANTI EARNEST ALLEN JR GAETAN J BEAUDOIN
GUY A BLANCHETTE DON C BROWN GARDNER J BROWN DENNIS J CANNITO WAYNE L CARLSON
JOHN W COCKERHAM JR MERLIN J CRAIG WILHIMON GARDNER RICHARD E GENEST WILLIAM A GORVET
GARY G GRAY ROGER T GUEST GEORGE E HENRY NORMAN R HETZEL WILLIAM G HOWELL
GUY M INKEL VERLON D KING JR JAMES C MCGLASSON JIMMY T MORRIS WAYNE MUSKETT
DONALD E NELSON JUAN R PEREZ-PADIN JOSEPH J PINTO JAMES D RAYCHEL RICHARD P RAYMOND
HERMAN RICHARDSON JR RUBEN RIVERA MARSHALL E ROBERTSON ROGER E ROBICHAUD ALFRED D RUTH
JAMES R SHIPMAN FRANKIE STANLEY RUSSELL A TAYLOR GLENN E TRUEX KENNETH W WORTHLEY
CHARLES L BALDWIN LEROY L BELL LESLIE R BELL JAMES M BOGACZ DAVID E FREESTONE
RODGER L JAMESON DUANE G LANDIS SANFORD J LEDBETTER DALE J LENIO PETER H MCMURRAY
BRIAN A HUBIS RICHARD W RILEY JOHNNY E SHOUFF EFRAIN VAZQUEZ-SANTIAGO WILLIAM J WICKWARD
LARRY G BELL JOHNNY S BOSSER CHARLES C BUCHANAN BILLY J CAUDILL SALUM E CHARD JR
DOUGLAS A COOK DENNIS D DAVIS WILLIAM F DAVIS JR JAMES A DOUGHTY KENNETH R FORD

PANEL 18W

ROBERT GONZALES WELBY H GRAYSON III CHARLES E JACKSON EDWARD H SHERROD
JOSE F JIMENEZ RICHARD K JOECKEN RICHARD E MARTINEZ MICHAEL A MCANINCH JOHNNY MUNOZ
ROBERT W MCCABE JR THOMAS P MCKERNS WILLIAM F RABURN JAN I RASENYUCK JOHN C REEVS
EDWARD C HAMMERBECK GERALD H SAMPSON PATRICK A SANTO DAVID T SCHAFFER THOMAS E SEMANS
CHARLIE SIMMONS JR ALVIN W STALLCUP CLARENCE H STCLAIR JR CARL B AYERS JR WILLIAM T CHAFFIN III
KEITH A DE VRIES JACKIE C DEHART MONTE D DYKES RALPH D GODFROY ALBERT S GRAF
JOHN H GUTHRIDGE LOUIS V HERMANN JR RICHARD D KRUPA ROBERT F MAURER DOYLE A MORRIS
CHARLES J MACDONALD JAMES T MOSES WILLIAM G NELMS JR EDWIN J OLMEDA MICHAEL P QUINN
JACK E SCHOBER GERALD A SMITH THOMAS D STONE GARY W WITHERS JERRY A ZIMMER
RICHARD M ARNOVITZ MARVIN J BUTTERFIELD RONALD B CHURAN DUANE A CLEFISCH ROBERT V GRAY
ROBERT A HANEY RALPH E JOHNSON WILLIAM F KELLEY ISRAEL MARTINEZ JR JAMES F MOTT
NICHOLAS J RYMOND CHARLES E SMITH JR JAMES E SQUAIRE GREGORY N TRIMNAL SCOTT M VERNER
ERNIE L WALLEN RICHARD T WILHELM ISMAEL B ARANDA DOUGLAS A BENNETT JEROME E BOWERS
CHARLIE L COCHRAN ROBERT I COX PAUL D DUKES DAVID J GIVENS LAWRENCE W GLOVER
TERRY G GRAFT RICHARD W HOFFLER RALPH M HOOKS EUGENE HUNT RONALD JOHANSEN
DONALD W KIMSEY DANIEL W MAJORS HOLLIS G MAPLE LAURENCE A MILLETT LAURANCE R MOHN JR
JOHN A POLEFKA ROY L PORTER MICHAEL PRESLIPSKI JR RONALD D ROGERS EDWIN B RYDER
WILLIAM C WEAVER MARK S WITT ROBERT P ACHER JR WILLIE W ALLEY KENT S ANDERSON
GEORGE D BROOKSHIRE LESTER M CAVALLIN JAMES T CLARK MICHAEL D DUNAGAN BOBBY EDMONSON
JULIAN ESCOBEDO JR LIBERO C HANDEL GEORGE D HUTCHESON ROBERT A MARSH ALBERT C MCBRIDE
RAYMOND G PARKS CORNEL PETTEYS JAMES S PITCHES FRED W SMITH LARRY A STEPHENS
HARRY H WECKER ROY C WILLIAMS JR JAMES K WOZNIAK DONALD W WRIGHT DAVID B ATKINS
SAMUEL D BARBRE WILLIAM G BATTS JOHN A FUTO DALE R HEIDEBRECHT THOMAS A HIGGINS
DONALD F HORN DENNY L JOHNSON DONALD R KILPATRICK ERNEST KISH CARL S MIKULA
WILLIAM E MCCORMACK BRENT B NAUSS RONNIE J PETRE EDWARD R SARGENT RAYMOND W VAUGHAN JR
DELMIS C WATSON MARK C ALFORD RONALD J BRITZ ANDRE G BROUMAS MICHAEL L COLLINS
MICHAEL M COX TONY CRUZ NEAL D EPIFANIO GARY L EVANS MCKENZIE W GENWRIGHT
LEN M HANAWALD DAVID R HANNA CARL P HUGHES DEAN R LANGE ALAN C MANESS JOHN G WILLEMS
RICHARD C MILLER LOUIS T MILLS NORMAN L NESTERAK MARVIN E SCREEN WILLIAM E TITTLE
LEROY RUTHERFORD BEN F SUTTON ALLEN J VAN FREDENBERG CHARLES B WALKER JR TROY L WALKER
REGINALD P BEGNOCHE LAYNE H CONNEVEY CLIFFORD J CONSTANTINO KENNETH T CUMMINGS
GEORGE H DANIELS II EARMON R DERRINGTON RUSSELL C FORDHAM LARRY D FRALICKS ROBERT L HARRIS
WALTER E HUTCHINSON JAMES M KARDOS GEORGE L KLEIBER JR JOHN E KLINGEN FELIX D KNUTSON
CHARLES E LONG MARVIN J LOUVIERE WILLIAM M LYONS III STEVEN L PESSIER MICHAEL R REITZ
TERRY S SMALL RICHARD A STANLEY CHARLES T THIELGES BILLY D WEITZEL DAVID ALBERT
ELTON H ALEXANDER DWIGHT F BABEL ASBERRY BEARD JR CARL G BECK JONATHAN R BORTLE
LEE R SCHAAF JERRY BRYANT DONALD N CARTLAND BARRY R CLARK LOUIS S DI BARI CHARLES R GEIGER
RONALD P CUASITO JAMES R FIELD KENNETH E FOUST JACKIE L GOODNIGHT CHARLES L HARRIS
GARY C HARWELL RON J HAYNES RICHARD R HUGHES CHESTER L JACKSON FRED O JACKSON JR
GEORGE W JINKINS III JOHN K KAUHAIHAO DOUGLAS S KEMPF GARY W LAHNA TERRANCE E LEDDEN
MICHAEL L LITSEY TERRY D MASON LEE E MONTAG JAMES L MOORE ARTHUR E MORGAN
DENNIS J MURPHY HARRY W PIERCE JR RICHARD P POWERS BERNARD A PROPSON RAY W PURIFOY
BRETT G REAVIS JOEQUIN ROBINSON CHARLES A ROMERO PETE S SEGUNDO DELBERT R SMITH
JOHN C STERLING JOHNNY D SWANN CHARLES F TAYLOR RAYMOND B THOMAS RONALD C VLIEK
DENNIS R WARTCHOW ARTHUR E WOJAHN ROBERT E AHLSTROM DALE R ALCORN JR FREDERICK H BARRETT
LARRY D BOOBAR MICHAEL T BURNS WENDELL M BURNS BOBBY G HAYNES JERRY W HICKERSON
JULIUS C HOULDITCH JR ARNOLD N JACO JOYFUL J JENKINS ROBERT W LA FLEUR CHARLES R LEMING
LESTER H LEOPOLD JOHN E LOGES DANIEL M LYNCH DONALD B MANCILL MICHAEL M MAYE
BERNARD A MCDERMOTT III CHARLES R MOORE GAYMAN C OGBOURN RONNIE PAGE RICHARD E PEREZ
GUNTHER H REHLING DAVID RIVERA THOMAS C RUSH JR THOMAS A SALVATORE WAYNE J SANDERS
NEAL A SMITH DENNIS A SPENELLI JERRY SYLVIA MICHAEL J TRUSTY GILBERT C TURNER JR
WILLIE J WASHINGTON STEVEN W WILSON STEPHEN W YOUNG TOLLIE BAILEY MICHAEL F BANKS
ROBERT C BENOIT JR RICHARD J BEST JR ROGER W BISHOP GARY L BOWDLER JOHN L ERFORD JR
PAUL F FOULK DAVID M HARTOGH LEO F HARTSUFF DOUGLAS J LAMBERT MICHAEL G LOYD
CAMERON T MCALLISTER JAMES W MEGEHEE ALBERTO MILAR JR RONALD E PEETZKE ALLAN W PERSICKE
LARRY K ROBILLARD JAMES W SAMPERS LARRY T SANDERS CHARLES W SHARMAN III RICHARD J SWIGER
PETER J TROY JESS H VAN WINKLE JR FRANK WRIGHT JR JESSE J ARTHUR III GARY T BENJAMIN
AMBROSE H BROOKS JR ANTHONY J BROULLON EDWARD L DAVIS THOMAS E GUY ENOCH HAMPTON
THOMAS M HUX GARY R JACKSON CLARENCE E LOWDER CARL L MEIER EUGENE F SMALLWOOD
SCOTT N STANTON MARVIN J TAYLOR JEFFREY BORR JOHN R BOX VICTOR P CASSMEYER JR
DONNIE J CLOUGH TERRY L DENNEY DELBERT DOUGLAS DAVID D ELSBERND MICHEL J GRECO
ANTHONY L JENKINS LONNIE V MERCHANT GEORGE L METZGER DONALD E MOORE JAMES R MORROW
LEWIS D ROSS GREGORY E SCOTT ROBERT P TITCOMB ODELL B ACKER RALPH M BOGGESS III
LONNIE BROWN JR DAVID T FELLOWS GEORGE S GOODE CHARLES E HANCOCK EDWARD C KALINA
PETER T LUNDBERG MICHAEL J MCGOVERN JR GEORGE W PEPE DAVID S SELDON JAMES W SMITH
DONALD E STEPP JERRY D WHITE LEWIS E WOOD ALFREDO E AVILES ALDEN J BULLWINKEL
JOSEPH S BURRIS III GILBERTO BUSTAMANTE REGINALD T BYRD JOHN H CAMP JR THOMAS R MCDONALD JR
WOODROW J EWALD JR KENNETH W FIELDS DALE S FULK JOHN P GOGGIN TILLMAN D RODGERS JR
JOSEPH L GOLC JR NEIL N GREINKE ROGER D HELWIG LARRY D LEDBETTER DANNY R METZ
RANDY G CAGLE GEORGE F MCGEE SHERMAN D MONK MICHAEL A MONTELLANO CALVIN MOULTRIE
MICHAEL T MCGLONE MICHAEL R ODUM ALFREDO PACOLBA JAMES R POTTER MARION C ROBB
BRUCE S GIBSON MARVIN R ROBINSON CHARLES B ROSS JERRY V RYAN DENNIS W SHEW
THOMAS L SMITH ROGER H STEARNS JOHNNY L WARD PATRICK M WARD PATRICK A WHITTEN
ROBERT P WIESNETH FREDERICK WILHELM LEO J BROUSSARD JR JOSEPH W COX STEPHEN A DE SANTIS
JAMES S BRISTER STEPHAN L HARGRAVE RONALD C HUDSON LAWRENCE D JACKSON BEDFORD F WHITE
HERBERT R RAGANS GERHARD M ROLFS RICHARD A SAWRAN RAYMOND SERNA JOHNNIE M SPEIGHT JR
TERRENCE E KIERZNOWSKI BOBBY G BAKER ALBERT L BELANGER ROBERT BRUCE DEWEY R BURNS JR
JAMES A BURNS JAMES F CAMERON GEORGE D CHUNKO THOMAS G CORNWELL THOMAS W NORMAN JR
JOSEPH W DANISON JAMES D DARWIN EDWARD M HANSON ROBERT T HOLMES STEVEN D LUND
RICHARD W SHERRILL WILLIAM R SQUIER JR ANTHONY M STEEN JAMES B STOCKDALE MANNIFRED YATES
ROBERT R BAADE II THOMAS E CHAMPAGNE DONALD W CHURCHWELL RICHARD K GRAY JEFFREY J JOHNS
JOHN A HALLADAY PETE B HAMMOND HAL HARRIS STEPHEN C HENDERSON WALTER E HEYER JR
CHARLES W BECKER JOSEPH A HOEKER MICHAEL E KOONCE ROGER D LOWERY LARRY G MARSH
GARY R MASON JOSEPH V MATHIAS CHARLES W MCLEOD PAUL W MURPHY JR ROBERT L PERSON
LESLIE M POCS LEONARD L POTTS GALE S PRITCHARD CHARLES W PROSE JR DANIEL P RATLEDGE JR
RICHARD J ROUGHGARDEN TONY E SCOGGINS JAMES E SCOTT JOHN P SHANNON JR DONALD S SKIDGEL
DEWEY V RAY THOMAS L SNYDER GARY K STANFIELD MARK J STEPHANAC LARRY E SWEET
MICHAEL H THOMAS LOYD D ACOSTA ROBERT J ARNOLD WILLIAM T BUSHEY WILLIAM F DIGGS
JERRY G GATLIN STEPHEN A JOHNSON DONALD R KREGELOH KENNETH E LEONARD DONALD A LIEBL
DAVEY A LIEURANCE PATRICK O MORIARTY JOHN F PETTIGREW JOHN F PITTIGREW JOSE Y POLANCO JR JOHN J WALKER
STEVEN A RICKERSON JAMES S ROGERS WILLIE ROGERS JR EDMOND R SACCOMEN JAMES A SICKLES
KENNETH A MEYER THEODORE L WYKOFF ALAN ATTARIAN JOHN A BENNETT ALLEN CAIN
JOHN E CARLSON FREEMAN A CARR WILLIAM E CARTER WILLIAM E CLANCY TROY O COKER
ROBERT F DALEY JAMES M FLOYD JOHN F GOODLETT MICHAEL E HAIDER THOMAS R POUNDSTONE
JACK HARRIS JR JOHN J KALEN HARRY F LA LONDE JR WALTER B LOWE JR CHARLIE H MITCHELL
JOHNNY R MCKENZIE LARRY G MOOTHART JERRY L OGREN WALTER S OLINSKY JR M C PAGE
ARTHUR C FAIRCLOTH KENNETH W PEASE LARRY PYPNIOWSKI FLORENCIO RAMIREZ JR WILLIAM J ROBERTS
ALFRED G SAPP SR ROBERT E SCHMITZ JAMES L SELDON DONALD J TRAMPSKI ELISEO VERGARA
THEODORE W WEBB JAMES M WILLARD ROBSON W WILLS WILLARD E WILSON LESLIE M ALY
JERRY E BARKER RONALD B BISHOP KENNETH C BURLOCK JR JOHN L CHESEBROUGH MELVIN R CHILDERS
EDDIE N CORSINO DALE J CRITTENBERGER GARY J DAVIS DENNIS A DENTON JOSEPH A SERVANTEZ
DENNIS W FERGUSON WILLIAM A FITCH RONALD J HAGEN GARY L HAUGHT STOKELY J JONES
WILLIAM C JOY DONALD L KENNEDY PAUL J LAFRENIERE JR DAVID R MACKEY ROBERT P MAYER
JAMES E MCGARRITY JR JAMES B MCGARRY MICHAEL B MCGINNIS RICKY L MEEKS DANA W MITCHELL
DONALD W DIETZ WILLIAM T MCNAIR RICHARD E PEARSON ENCARNASION RODRIGUEZ LEO P SIKORSKI
THEODORE V SKILES SCOTT P SMITH RICHARD A SNOWDON RICHARD W STARKEY ERICH L TIDWELL
RICHARD M TURNER WILLIAM H WAIDMAN JR JOHN W WALKER MICHAEL D WEEKS HARVEY L WILLIAMS
THOMAS E YOUNG SCOTTY G AUSTIN WALLACE S CARTER CURTIS R CLINE PAUL J KNEELAND
JAMES BETANCOURT DANNY C CRAVENS BRYAN J DE MELLO MACK DENNARD JR DAVID L HOLLMAN
RANDALL L KRUEGER ROBERT W LABRECQUE ARTHUR LEWIS PAUL D LUCAS JOSEPH E MAZZANTI
JOHNNIE R MILLER JERRY D RICE JAMES D SLATTERY ANTHONY STANDIFER LARRY D STROUSE
JOHN W TRACY CORDIS R WHITE RICHARD G BOUCHARD TERRY L CHARLES STEPHEN E CRIST
MARTIN B DYER JR MONTY J EICHHORN ROBERT L FISHER RONALD L GUTKE WILLIAM HALL JR
BERNARD J HENRY JOHN P LAMBOOY KENNETH L PERRY LARRY G PINSON JOHN A REED
CLYDE W SAUNDERS J L STENHOUSE JR THEODORE A TROCK ROBERT L TUELL III CHARLES H WRIGHT
LELAND A BAILEY WILLIAM C BIFFLE ROBERT M BUCHECK TIMOTHY A COOK CECIL DAUGHERTY
WILLIAM V FLYNN ROBERT E LAVENDER WALTER V LEMMOND III FRANK J MONTEZ DANIEL NAPIERSKIE
GEORGE W SIMMERS JR WILFREDO B ANDRADA DENNIS L BARTLEBAUGH CHARLES H BEARE CARL A DEAN
CHARLES L ATKISON GROVER BOWEN GREGORIO P CASTILLO ALAN B CECIL LARRY W DENNIS

STEVEN V ELTING JOE A FOSTER JR DAVITT J FRANKS MERLE W HABEN LARRY C HATHCOCK
GREGG W HEIDRICH JAMES W JACKSON JR NATHANIEL JACKSON JR TOBY E JAECKELS NELS V ROSENLUND II
THOMAS A LEICHLEITER RAYMOND P MILLER II JOHN O MOORE MICHAEL J PACHECO GARY D PRICE
THOMAS L LARSON LEONEL M SILVEIRA LARRY R SKINNER DAVID W SMITH HENRY M STEWART JR
BARRY K ALEXANDER GLENN M BRADLEY EUGENE L BURBEY DANNY L DUPREY LARRY W ELLIS
JOSHUA B STEWART FRED E GOLD ROBERT L HAGER JR JAMES H HALL JAMES C HENSLEY GARY G LAMB
ERIC A LORD JOSE C RENTAS JR MARK W SURBER JAMES T TUCKER JOHNNIE L WILLIAMS JR
CLINTON E MILLER JAMES I YATES ROWLAND N AGARD SHELTON F BARRS DENNIS J BROWNING
THOMAS E CARUSO JOHN M CHAVEZ ROBERT A COOKE JOHN E COTTINGHAM JUAN A DIAZ-DOMENECH
STEPHEN J CHANEY SHERBERT L COX GALEN E HAYNIE MICHAEL A KNECHTGES ELWOOD J ROEHL

PANEL 17W

HUGH H SARAH ALBERT J SCRUGGS RICHARD R SEABRIDGE THOMAS J SIMETH SR
MARVIN G STEPHENS SHELBY D STOVER MICHAEL L WHITE JOHN E WRIGHT SOLOMON H BRYANT
JOHN L BURTON FREDERICK R CLARK GREGG L COCHRANE MICHAEL COLLINS KENNETH E PENNINGTON
JAMES E CROSBY CHARLES W ELLIS JR FRED A GRIFFIN JR KENNETH N HATCH ARCHIE E HICKS
KENNETH D COSTANZA THOMAS F LAWLER JOHN W SAUNDERS JR BOBBY D SCHEUER DONALD E SCOTT
WALTER L SMILES LESLIE W WILLIAMS JAMES B WOODS JR LOWRY T CUTHBERT JOHNNY R ESQUIERDO
CHARLES H GOLDMEYER DAVID P HENRY DAVID R JACKSON JAMES I JAQUISH JOHN W LUPU
T Z MERRIWEATHER LONNIE R PARKER WILLIE J SMITH JAMES E TOMPKINS RANDY V TURNER
ROBERT L CROSBY NORMAN K FORK RONALD M GOULET MICHAEL D GUNNELS GREGORY J HUGHES
DENNIS FRENCH RICHARD A GWINN BRUCE E HAZLE WILLIAM M JOHNSON JOHN F MACHUL
KENNETH J MCCLUSKEY ERIC A REAM LARRY C VASTINE HARLAND L WILKINSON LARRY C WRENN
ALLAN T ASLETT ROBERT E BITTNER JR MARK L BROWN RICHARD A CARABBA WILLARD DE LONG JR
ROBERT L HENNEGHAN JOHN N HUNTLEY JOHNNY NEWSOME TOMMY R THOMAS JAMES A TONON
FRANK F AUGUSTINE LEONARD O CAAMANO JAMES C CAMPBELL LESTER C COOK DUANE C SCOTT
CLARENCE A CORLEY JR CHARLES T DEATON STANLEY W DOAK CHARLES H EMERY JR THOMAS J GABBARD
DONALD J GARVEY JR LONNIE L GIBSON JOHNNY W GLISSON STEVEN T HOWE EMMETT D JAMES
WILLIAM A MAGUIRE JR DENNIS O MCGHEE STEVEN P MULLINEAUX KENNETH A SCHIMANSKI PAUL H REESE
TIMMY VALADEZ PATRICK R CURRAN ELTON DAVIS JR JAMES JENNINGS JR JIMMY KUHLENHOELTER
MICHAEL A PIACENTINO LUTHER A LONO LAURENCE T MCDOWELL THOMAS J PRICE JOE RODRIGUEZ
PHILLIP B COONEY JOHN M ANANIAN TIMOTHY A DAHL LOUIS T ORTIZ PHILIP H REITHER JR
FRANKLIN D SCHOPPE PHILIP P TOMASZEWSKI HERBERT WALTER TERRY L BERNEY MURIL S COLE
DAVID L COPELAND MONROE FRANKS HENRY W GARRETT ROBERT G HARTMAN MICHAEL J KEBERLINE
RAYMOND M KILBY CRAIG G KLOTZ MARK D MANGIN EARL T SOMMERHOF FREDDY K STALEY
EDWARD A ULIBARRI CHARLES W BACHMAN JR CLIFTON A BALDWIN TERRY L BECK RICHARD W BELL
MICHAEL L BOWMAN NATHANIEL BUSH ROLANDO C DAYAO DONALD C DEAN HERBERT H DILGER
CARL J ELLERD JAMES J FOWLER ROY G FOWLER LEONARDO M GAN JAMES O GODWIN
JOHN F DUARTE JR ROBERTO GONZALEZ-SANCHEZ PAUL E GORE WILLIAM D GORSUCH ALLEN B GOYNE JR
RONALD E HAGSTROM RAYFORD J HILL EDISON D HULL DELVIN L KOHLER RONALD W MONTGOMERY
PAUL H KRUSE JOHN R LAKE JR DENNIS M LAMBERT WASHINGTON M LANGLEY ROBERT B LEONARD
HOWARD M KOSLOSKY RICHARD A LIVINGSTON DONALD R MOORE JR WILLIAM R MOORE PAUL K MOSER
RONALD L MUNSON KENNETH M PRENTICE JOHN A QUINN BILLY J RENFROW FIDEL G SALAZAR
KEAVIN L TERRELL MICHAEL J TYE REYNALDO R VIADO CLYDE A WENRICK RICHARD L WISSLER JR
LARRY O ADAMSON HARRY L BOLES KENNETH L CUNNINGHAM FRANCIS W DEAL JR ALTON L ELLISON
JAMES R WEISLER ANTONIO GARZA FRANCISCO GIRON PAUL L GRAFFE DAVID A KUHNS RONALD J MILLER
ALEX L MCLEAN RALPH D RABER WILLIAM C AVERY RICHARD B CANNING PAUL W LARREMORE
STEVE D CARTER THOMAS H CHURCHILL GEORGE C DAVENPORT JR WAYNE R ELKINS RONALD P HUFFMAN
JAMES A BIEHL SAMUEL R JESSEE GREGORY L LA FLEUR RALPH E LOUNDERMON JOSEPH E MUENCH
WILLIAM F MCLAUGHLIN GEORGE MULROONEY THOMAS M SHROBA GARY D TAYLOR ORVAL A BALDWIN
ROCKY D ARMSTEAD STEVEN E ARNOLD JAMES ATKINS WALTER BARTASCH DARRELL G BATTIN
RAFAEL BERRIOS-GARCIA MICHAEL L D'AGRELLA WILFORD L DONOHO GARY S POSS HUBERT D SUTTON
SHELBY G FOSTER MICHAEL GALLEGO ROBERT M HAYNES JR WALTER J HOGANS HOWARD T LENHARD
CHARLES W MALONE MICHAEL E MCDANIEL BILLY L MILLER ELVIS E MULLEN GORDON L NAGEL
WILLIAM L ERICKSON JR JAMES H NOBLE RALPH E PIANO JR DENNIS J RODRIGUEZ BILLY D SHORT
LARRY G BURKHOLDER JOHN R VINNEDGE IRVIN L BOWER JR JAMES L BUSEN BRUCE L CARDY
ISAAC J CORBETT WENDELL P CURRY GENE P FUSSEY ROBERT W HAYES MICHAEL E LUCAS
GEOFFREY J LUKEY GARY D MILLER NORMAN R SWEAT JOHN F WARD TROY D WILHITE
TERRY L ALBRIGHT LARRY R GLOVER CLARENCE J HALL VICTOR W JONES JOHN F KAZANOWSKI
MICHAEL K KNIGHT KENNETH D NORTON ROBERT L SHEPPARD JR ROOSEVELT WALLACE LOUIS B ALBERT JR
ALBERT H ALTIZER JOSEPH H BENSON WILLIAM F DAVIS CLAUDE E ELLARD JR JAMES L GASSELING
DENNIS GONZALEZ ELMORE L HALL WILLIAMS O JACKSON RONALD A KLINGMAN RONALD H KNIGHT
JAMES T LUSCINSKI FARRIS E MAY LESTER MCCABE ALEX R MOSHER LARRY R OWENS
BRADLEY R RANSOM SYLVESTER W REDMAN CHRISS L ROEDIGER MAX E ROSEN JOSEPH SLAVENSKY JR
MICHAEL L STIGLICH JEROME M TAYLOR ROBERT J WATKINS JR LAWRENCE D ACRE GEORGE L AIKIN
ADRIAN L ALLEN ELDIN G BERGER JR TERRY W BOOKER JOHN P BRENNAN EARL E CHARLES
JIMMIE D COX BENNY R DUPREE GEORGE A ELKINS ROBERT FIELDS JR JAMES H GRAHAM
OWEN T HIRANO MICHAEL L HOLTZ GEORGE D HOWARD DARRELL D IMBORNONE CHARLES D JAGELER
EDUARDO J JIMENEZ-LORENZO ROBERT S KING JR JOHN E LOPEZ JR ROBERT S MASON JR ROBERT R MILLER
WILLIAM H MORRIS JR TONY L O'NEAL GREG B SCOTT JAMES C SHIELDS RICHARD A SMITH SR
DANNY R SPENCER STEVIE TAYLOR FRED R THORPE LEON TRECINSKI MARK A VAN BEUKERING
TONY M VASQUEZ WILLIAM R ADAMS DAVID H BENALLIE THOMAS F BROWN JR CHARLES F BURRELL
RICHARD L CUMMINS WILLIAM E FINCHAM WILLIAM R GODFREY DANNY R HESSON FRANKLIN L WEISNER
LELAND C JOHNSON LAVOYN A JONES GILBERT KETZLER JR MAURICE P KRAEMER JR STANLEY G KREBS
NICHOLAS P LANNOYE ROBERT L LAZARUS CALVIN W MAXWELL EUGENE J MORSE TED PIERCE
LARRY G PREWITT JAMES L RHODES JOSE C SALINAS HARRY C SHEPARD JR MANLEY E SILER JR
ROBERT FLORES JR MARSHALL F THOMAS WILLIAM F UNCKRICH MOSES L ALVES ELLSWORTH S BRADFORD
RONALD L CANNON LARRY E CROW DOMINGO Y GARCIA ALAN D GROOM JOHN H HATHAWAY
LEO F JOHNSON VICTOR L JONES FRANK W KINKAID JR BERNARD R KNAPIC MARVIN D LARSON
WILLIE G LEWIS JR ROBERT LOONEY DAVID L MCCOMBS TIMOTHY R MIEDZIELEC ABRAHAM L MOORE
DAVID L NICHOLAS HERMAN J O'BYRN WILLIAM ORTEGA JR JEROME J RICE JOHN J RODEN
ROY R WHITESIDE GREGORY CARTER JAMES R DUFAULT ROBERT C GREATHOUSE ROBERT E JENRY
FOREST D JOHNSON JR JAY L KECK WAYNE M LENDERMAN RICHARD J RINCK RICHARD R STOLARUN
MICHAEL D TERRY JOHN D ARQUILLO JOHN T BAKER JOHN W BROOKS CHARLES B CAREY
WILLIE F CATO MICHAEL P DZIENGEL RONALD C EDWARDS THOMAS A FRITZER JR JOHN K KRUEGER
JOHN A LEE RONALD L MARTIN GARY L MCCLOUD DONALD R OSBORNE KEITH A PATTERSON
JOHN P PICKETT RONALD C RUDOLPH WILLIAM S SHADE JOHN M WHEELER ERNEST B WHITE
FRANK N WILLIAMS JOHN W BENNETT DENNIS A BROWN JIMMIE L CASTLEBERRY WALTER G WICKER JR
HENRY M GNANN EDWIN R GROTTKE JR LANNY M HAMBY JERRELL R JONES DAVID E KUCZYNSKI
DOUGLAS A LE MOND JERE R LOWE GEORGE P MCCLINTIC JAMES T SAVAGE BURTON E SMALL
MARK A BABSON JR JACKIE L SWINK DONALD H TROTT DONALD R WASHINGTON GLENN WASHINGTON
GEORGE R ANDREWS BOBBY BAXLEY TERRY L BOOTH EDWARD L BORREGO FRANCIS P CREAMER
LAWRENCE D LARSON MARSHALL T MARKHAM RAYMOND O NOVOSOD EDWARD E PIERCE
DANIEL G RULISON TONY E SEAY RONDALL P SPEARS DAVID J TRBOVICH CLYDE W VAN VALKENBURG JR
DAVID L JOLIET BEN C WARD LAWRENCE R BOOTH JIMMIE D BROWN LAWRENCE L DWYER JR PAUL E WALL
RAYMOND A GIBSON DAVID R GOODINE EDWARD L GOODMAN ROBERT F HEILIG JR JOSEPH HOLMES
ROBERT N DEMGEN HAROLD F HYSMITH MICHAEL K PRICE DENNIS M RATTIN MICHAEL K SAWYER
RICHARD T WILKINSON DAVID J BAITINGER MICHAEL E COTES MARCAS J GARCIA ALAN T GEE
WILLIAM T HANEY DAVID L NICHOLAS CHRISTOPHER S STUEWE LEONARD D COOPER RALPH CUSTODE
PETER E GUTLOFF WILLIE M JONES ROBERT L LA COMBE PAUL L MARCHANT WILLIAM A RUDDAN
STEPHEN L SHARP VALENTINE B SUAREZ JOHN H TAYLOR WAYNE L ADKINS DAVID P BABEY
FRANK H BRIGGS FRANK DAVIS JR WILLIAM L DAWES GERALD J GUILLORY EARL E HOWERTER JR
ALLEN F KEATING EDWARD S KOCH PETER J MOLDENHAUER JAMES E PETTIJOHN JOHN P SOUTHWICK
PETER V MESTAS ALVIN R STOVALL JR ROBERT L THANE EDDIE L WALKER JAMES C WOODS
ALBERT N WRIGHT JR JAMES V ALDRED STEPHEN H ALLISON DENNIS R BAKER PHILIP W BAUGHN
LARRY D BUNCH JACK CALAMIA JOSEPH V CAMERLENGO JAMES I COLEMAN JAMES E CONKRIGHT
RICHARD J COSTON HAROLD G CURTIS THOMAS F DANIELL ALBERT L DAVIS DENNIS G HALL
MICHAEL E DAGNON ALLEN W DUMKE CHARLES K EDWARDS MARTIN W ESSARY JR PATRICK M GRELLA
BENNY C JACKSON WILLIE L KEITH DENNIS W KIPP RICHARD D LEAR CRAIG T MARRINGTON
JOSE E ORTIZ LARRY S POLING STANLEY D ROSS MICHAEL R SAMPLE ARNOLD R SCHUH
WILLIAM W STUBBS ALEXANDER VIGIL JOE N WATSON MICKEY R ALEXANDER DANNY E APPLETON
JESSIE R BATEMAN BENNIE C CLAYTON GLENN R COOK JOHN E COOK FRANCIS E CORTOR JR
JOHN L ESPENSHIED THOMAS V FELDHAUS FLOYD E GOLEMON JR KENNETH G HAVENS STEPHEN M WELCH
BUDDY E HENDERLIGHT ROBERT KENNEDY JR TIMOTHY E LARMON KEITH D MEHAFFEY MARK J PREIS
MARTIN Y NAMER DALE F OLMSTEAD MONTE L PAYNE JOHN D REVIER GLENN M SCHROEDER
NEVIN O FARNSWORTH JR DALE E THOMPSON JAMES D TRAYLOR CRAIG H WEBER WILLIAM B BISHOP II
DONALD R DESMARAIS RICHARD H GREENE PAUL A HUGHES KENNETH A KUBIK SHELBY M LONG
BILLY L PETERS ROBERT L REIPLINGER HARVEY C REYNOLDS JOSE T RIOS TIMOTHY C ROBINSON
VINCENT SALDANO RUSSELL F SMITH RICHARD W YATES ANDREW J ABRAMSON LARRY M CLEVELAND
HENRY E BARBER JR JOSE L BORRERO-SANCHEZ DENNIS M CLARK VANCE M EVANS GERALD L YOUNG
KENNETH E HEATH KERRY B LOVE EUGENE O MARTINEZ MANUEL G MARTINEZ GALEN M SMITH
RAYMOND R BLOSSEY DENNIS N HUDSON SETH H MATTHEWS III ROBERT P SHEELY STANLEY R TOKARSKI
CHARLES V REDDING III ROBERT L ADAY STEVEN BOAL BENTON BROWN GARY W BRUHN
RODNEY R COLLINS JOHN T DE MARCHES JOSEPH R HAGY JR RALPH W JOHNSON HENRY R LAMBERT
WILLIAM F LARSON JAMES C MCPHILLIPS HERBERT L MOORE JR HELMUT W PAIER MAX W PUGMIRE
CLIFFORD J RUSH DAVID L SACKETT WILLIAM J SCHUSSLER VERNON J SEGER RONALD SOWELL
THOMAS D TOMASZEWSKI JERRY L WAGES ALBERT O WAYMAN JR MELVIN M YAMASHITA JOSEPH V WHELAN
BENJAMIN F BENNETT JR RONALD H BOZIKIS LEE F CLICKNER MARTIN J CRIBBS THOMAS T FLETCHER
MILBERT W HAMILTON DAVID N HEBERT FLORENCIO Q MARQUEZ CARL E OLDFIELD ROBERT J OLLIKAINEN
ADRIAN A AKINS MICHAEL J RODOWICZ CHARLES E SHULTZ JAMES D STEVENSON DWIGHT J THORNTON
HERBERT ARVISO JOHN W BEITLICH CALVIN BLANTON JR JIMMY D BOUDREAUX NEIL S BYNUM
LORENZO CHAPA JR JAMES A DOANE DONALD M DYCE ROBERT N FUNK JOHN K GOETT EDDIE B STORY
FRED D HIGHBERGER JR JAMES JONES RAYMOND J KIESLER CLAUDE B LANDIS II BILLY J LEMLEY

RICHARD M LOGAN MICHAEL L LYTLE KEITH M PARR GRAY D WARREN RONALD D WESTPHAL
DAVID D WINKLER DENNIS AKERLEY GARY R BOUSHELE THOMAS A ENGELMAN THOMAS R FOSTER
JAMES W HERRICK JR EDWARD A JAMES JOHN M MCKENNA MICHAEL G O'CONNELL JOE L PETERSON
RALPH M SMITH CLARKE K VICKREY JAMES A WILKS GEORGE H AYALA CHARLES E BARNICK
GARY A BEST CHARLES E BOXLER THOMAS E CAMPBELL TERRENCE C CONNOLLY CHUBBY D LOWREY
ERLE F DAVIS BILLY W DENLEY ARTHUR FOXWORTH CHARLES F GAMBLE JR WALTER M GIBSON
RALPH S CINOTTI PETER G HEINZMAN ANGEL L HERNANDEZ-RIVERA FERMAN B HODGES MARK JACKSON
CHARLES E MILLER DONALD L NEELEY JAMES A ROBERTS RALPH D TADEVIC BARRENT O TORGERSON

PANEL 16W

BRUCE A UGELSTAD JOHN P WRIGHT CARMEN DE CUBELLIS JR GERALD T GREENO JR
JUAN B BERUMEN JEROME G HATTER GEORGE R HUNTZINGER STEPHEN S MACVEAN DAVID C BRANNON
RUSSELL M LE COMPTE CLYDE J BENNETT NOLAN E BLACK CLYDE L CANADA WILLIE J KELLY
ROGER E CARROLL CHARLES C CHILD THOMAS E CLARK GERALD W DURTKA ROBERT M GROSCOST
CONRAD J WHEELER MAURY W HEARNE JAMES E HERIN PERRY B HOPKINS ROGER J KOPKE
WILLIAM C LEGAT DOUGLAS H LOTT JR EMILIO RIVERA LARRY S SLAYMAKER WESLEY W VERMEESCH
JOHN A WARREN JAMES N WOOLLEY ROBERT L ALEXANDER LARRY M BAUGH MICHAEL D BRIGHTMAN
ADAMO E DE ANGELIS STEVE L ESCALLIER DENNIS L GAUTHIER PAUL R GETZ FLOYD S GIEBELL
MICHAEL L HOSEA ROBERT L LYNCH LARRY J MCGRAW PAUL E REAUME RONALD A ROSS
BRIAN J MORROW MICHAEL D ROSENTHAL JR EDWARD E SEE THOMAS J SMALLWOOD JR DANIEL L STARKEY
MURRAY J WYMAN ARTHUR B BENGEN STANLEY A BROWN JIMMIE J BUTLER OLIVER COLEMAN JR
CHARLES F DANIELSON JR MICHAEL A DE MAGNIN OLIVER E DEAL JR LARRY D DUPRE ALLEN T ELDER JR
PHILIP J ENLOW JOHN R HAGOOD JIMMY K HARRISON ERIC T HARSHBARGER JOEL T LAU
RICHARD W LYTLE SAM H MANGUM FRED A NELSON LONNIE P NEWLAND GERALD W NICHOLSON JR
ROGER D PARTINGTON JAMES A ROSS WILLIAM D SIROCCO JR HERSHEL C SMITH CHARLES R TIPTON
BERG J VANDEN JOHNNY D VOLLRATH GILBERT E WALLACE DONALD G WEHR DAVID F ABBOTT
MICHAEL D CAMERLENGO THOMAS M CURTIS LEWIS B GILL GEORGE A GILLESPIE RICHARD R MANEMANN
GEORGE W GREGA GARY E GRUBBS MICHAEL L HARRIS WESLEY H HARRIS JR DONALD G VOLLMER
PATRICK H CARROLL MOISES R HERRERA JR LEO C HESTER JR HULUS E KEY JR DAVID M LIVINGSTONE
DAVID L MASON KEITH F SAUNDERS ROBERT E SCHROEDER JR JAMES F SPENCER JON W STOKKERMAN
ERIC E GITTENS LAWRENCE W WHITFORD JR JOHNNY WILLIAMS LABON R WILLIAMS NICKOLAUS C ZOZULA
JOEL A BALCOM WILLIAM T BROWN JAMES E BUCHANAN FLOYD J CRAIGMYLE FRANKLIN T JAMES
DENNIS J KEMPF STANLEY C KENTON KENNETH R LEACH DAVID L NAPIER MICHAEL R NORTON
WILLIAM J ROEGLIN DONALD M SHUE SERGE B SIMMONS MICHAEL W STEFFE LOUIS R SUSTERSIC
GUNTHER H WALD GAYLE E WILLIAMS JOHN H WILSON JAMES H WOOLARD STANLEY L ADAMS
TERRY L ALFORD JOHN S ANDERSON DERWIN M BAILEY RICHARD G BAUER JAMES C BEAVER
JOHN P BRADY JR DAVID R BRANSON ALFONSO R CASTRO JIM R CAVENDER HARRY J COATES JR EDUARDO RIVERA-PAGAN
PETER M CONNOR CARL L CROWLEY CHARLES P GEISERT KENNETH A GROVE ROBERT J GROVER
LARRY J HANLEY ROBERT D HARRIS CLARENCE L HOLMAN ROGER L JONES CHARLES L KARR
ALLAN G KENNEDY JAMES R KLIMO ERNESTO L LARACUENTE FRANCIS M LOGAN III ROBERTO J MACIAS
RICK E MEDARIS JOHN A PAYNE MARION L ROACH LAWRENCE E SCHMIDT
ELMER M SHIELDS WILLIAM D SMITH BENNIE V STEPHENS JR JOHN D THRASHER JOHN A WARE
FRED J CARTER PATRICK J DONOVAN JOSEPH Y ECHANIS ROBERT B ELDRIDGE KEN A MCCARTNEY
HOWARD L FLAMENT DRANNON R GORDON WADE A GREER EUGENE R JENKINS DOUGLAS P LEFEVER
GARY K BARNETT RICHARD L MOOREHEAD CHARLES A POSEY WILLIAM T QUILLIN GEROULD M RUMBLE III
MICHAEL T RUTHERFORD ROYAL R SHAFER CURTIS M WEEKS JR WILLIAM A ANDERSON JIMMY R CAIN
DONALD A CLARBOUR RONALD L DE LONG ROBERT A DONDERO JAMES W ROBERTSON ROBERT J SCHEELY
JAMES L DOWNING DAVID J GAMBLE HERMAN D GIBSON DONALD G HEDGECOCK RICHARD L HONEY
RAYMOND C FOERSTER THOMAS E HOLMES LENNIS G JONES JR BRADLEY J LOGAN CHARLES W LOWERY
JOSE C CARRILLO THOMAS A PUTMAN WILLIAM C RAY LARRY W ROBISON CHARLES B ROLLER JR
MICHAEL A CAPUTO SR RAYMOND A SHOEMAKER II LA V TEGTMEIER HENRY J VAD DAVID R COOK
LAWRENCE M DART ANTHONY M FIRAK JAMES A GAISER DAVID C GREESON HARRY E UNDERWOOD
GERALD D JOHNSON JAMES E JOHNSON ROBERT A MCMILLIN CHARLES C NAPPER JOHN W RASMUSSEN
DAVID R JACKSON NATHANIEL J RILEY JR GREGORY P RUGENSTEIN RICHARD SHIRMANG RICHARD L ADAMS
FRANCISCO H DELGADO RONALD W GIBSON KENNETH L HENKE MICHAEL S HRUTKAY JAMES L NELSON
CLINTON D PIERCE DARREL G PIERCE STEPHEN J PRASZYNSKI NICHOLAS R PROCINO WILLIAM L REGER
EDWARD T REYES GERALD SAUERS ANDREW B SEXTON THOMAS F SHIPLEY ROGER P WALLING
ARIEL J SMITH TOMAS C TUCKER RODNEY C TURNER MICHAEL G BUCKMASTER MICHAEL A BUSTAMANTE
DONALD H DWIGGINS JR MICHAEL R ETHERIDGE JOHN E GUROVICH WAYNE G HUBBARD MOSES B LUCAS
ALLAN J EASTMAN RICHARD S MCFARLAND IRA E MCGOWAN RONALD RODRIGUES FRANK D STEIBEL
JAMES J STROBLE JIMMY W WILLEFORD RUDY L BALDON RICHARD L BARIGLIO STEPHEN E BAYLES
ARTHUR J CASTILLO DANIEL J DAVIDENKO JAMES L FERRELL ROBERT J FULLER JAMES M HASENFLUG
VERNON G HOLBROOK SCOTT W IGGULDEN FRANK J LILLEY JAMES J MCMORROW ROBERT E OWENS
EARL T PEARSON JR ROBERT P QUERY ROBERT J SALISBURY LESLIE F SHENK DANIEL J SMITH
RAUL J VARGAS PAUL B WOOLFORD FRANKLIN E WRIGHT ROBERT C BARR ROBERT C BECKMAN
WILLIAM A BLACKBURN WALTER G BURKHART RUBEN J CARBAJAL CLARK R DOUGLAS HARRY J JACKSON JR
MERLIN G BEER JOHN K FOWLER CARL F GOACHER JOHN D HARRINGTON JAMES A JACKSON
CHARLES J KEITT CLEATUS P KIMBLE RICHARD S LEACH DENNIS P LINDSEY WILLIAM F LITTLE III
EDWARD W MCCARTY WILLIE E MCINTOSH MICHAEL P MCQUEER JOHN W MEADOWS ROBERT L OAKS
DANIEL L SEEKFORD ERNEST SERNA ROGER A STEELE ROGER L TALLMAN JIMMY L VAULTZ
MICHAEL E YOUNG KENNETH P BARKLEY JR JOHN M BELLAIRE JON K BODAHL JEFFREY L BOGUE
D C CARTER DANIEL CARTER JR KENNETH L CASWELL ROSA G DE LA JEROME HIGGINS
JAMES E DENNANY RALPH E DIAS ROBERT P GALLAGHER DONALD W GILL JR PETER O HAJMAN
ROBERT B HAMBLETT FREDDIE N HAYNES GERALD R HELMICH CARL HENDERSON HOWARD B HENRY
THOMAS W LANDRUM RONALD G LAUDERDALE JOSEPH A LOFTON GORDON W LOGAN JR
DANIEL F LYNCH JR LARRY C MOSHER LIONEL E PARSONS WILLIAM M PIERPONT RANDOLPH V RHEA
DONALD O FONZI MARK R ROSE DENNIS W ROSS WILLIAM SCOTT HARRY W SMITH R C SWEETEN
DENNIS E TIMMONS ROBERT L TUCCI BRUCE E WALTERS NORMAN F BENEDIK GORDON W BENT
JEFFREY L BOBULA EDDIE D CARPENTER RALPH R EVILSIZOR RICHARD A FORBES LUIS A HILERIO-PADILLA
EUGENE LENOIR JOHN M MCLELLAN DENNIS E MILLIARD JAMES M MOORE PAUL W PLAMBECK JR
RONALD E RAY STEVEN T SCHOOLER STEVEN G SKELLY RANDOLPH B SUBER WILLIE G TURNER
MICHAEL J ROBINSON CYRIL H TOWNLEY TERRY L ANDRESEN DAVID P BEDROSIAN HOWARD M BURNS
MICHAEL J DALTON GERALD R DASEN III RONALD G DE WEESE KENNETH G ELMORE EVERSON B FAISON
JOHN W FRITTER VICTOR M HAGLUND JR JOHN A HOWE DANIEL L JURGENSEN ERNEST J LA GRAY
JOHN E LEASURE JAMES R LINDSAY JOEL A MAY JR RICKEY J MEDLIN MILLER E MORGAN
JAMES C RUMMERFIELD JR DENNIS L STEVENS EDWARD E STUMP THOMAS H SULLIVAN DAVID L TEICH
CARL A THOMPSON OLIVER N THOMPSON CARL A THOMSON RUSSELL E UPRIGHT JAMES R VAN HATTEM JOHN D WALKER
ARTHUR N WELCH CHARLES R ALEX DEE O CANADY JAMES R CULWELL RONALD L DUCOMMUN
RALPH E FLOWERS JR ANTONIO M FUENTES JOHN G GRAF ALLEN F GROTZKE VICTOR M GUERRERO
JAMES J GUNDERSON FOREST C HODGKIN EVERETT R JORENS JR RICHARD T KASTNER JOHN M ROSA
WILLIAM D MCGIVERN CORDELL J PONAK JOHN E POOLE JOHN R RANKIN RICARDO W REGALADO
BENEDICT J LINNEN III JOHN J ROBINSON WALTER D ROMERO DONALD L WILLIAMSON ADAM WILSON
FRANCIS ZAVACKI TERRY L ZUMALT MARVIN R BERHOWE MICHAEL L BILES PHILIPPE B FALES
GEORGE R FAZZAH ERNEST D FORD LARRY D HOLLOWAY RONALD W IRELAND ROBERT E KUSHMAUL JR
HENRY L LIMBACH LARRY B PERRY JOHN P RACKHAUS KENNETH D RANKIN DARYL J RUPKE
ROBERT C SKINNER JERRY D SMITH JOSEPH G AUTORINO JR WILLIAM J BROWN MARK W BURCHARD
ALLEN H CALDWELL DAVID R CASTILLO CHARLES M COHEN JOHN M CONE GEORGE J FUERST
THOMAS L GRAVES RICHARD H GREEN DANIEL L HART HAROLD J JUNGA THOMAS K KAMP
BRIAN L LONG WILLIE D MCNEIL MICHAEL A PASTORINO DUANE K PETERSON CHARLES R PITTINGER
KENNETH G KLINE JAMES F POLUSNEY ARTURO C RODRIQUEZ THOMAS F ROGERS JR JAMES F ROST JR
MARK F TEARL NORMAN E THOMAS DAVID TORRES JULIUS ZAPOROZEC KENNETH D HARJO
ROGER D ALEXANDER JOHNNY L BURRISS DAVID L DOYLE THOMAS M GOULDIN OSCAR L GRIFFIN
ALAN B TURNER THOMAS J HARTMAN ANDREW G KIRCHMAYER JOSEPH M RAGSDALE ROBERT J SCHARES
DONALD E SPENCE MATTHEW A THOMAS JR KANJI YOSHINO ROGER J BACHMAN PAUL H DUNNE JR
DOUGLAS E PETERSON WALIS W GARST DAVID GARZA CRAIG S GREEN RORY W HUNTER HUEY L ISHMAN
WILLIAM C JAMES GEORGE E MILLER MICHAEL A PFEUFER DON L ROCK REX M SHERMAN
RICHARD E WALTERS ARDEN D ZHE JAMES A BAILEY JOHN R BALDRIDGE JR ERIC G BLANTIN
ANTHONY J CARLUCCI RAYMOND A CHARTIER JAMES M DALE LESLIE A DALRYMPLE PABLO B GARZA
ALAN E DICKEY WILLIAM A DUNCAN FRED A EXNER III LESLIE T HAMMACK LEROY L HOWLAND
WITHERS T JACKSON FRANCISCO JIMENEZ-O'NEILL HARVEY P KELLEY DAVID S KLINE DAVID A LERNER
BILLY R MARSHALL PETER K MATTHEI BRENT H MCARTHUR HAROLD W MCDONALD CHARLES E MOAKE JR
GUY E MCKEAN JR ROBERT M NEWBERG JOSEPH C PETERS ROGER S POWERS ROBERT J PRUDEN
RODNEY K RANSON WALTER A RENELT BARRY J SMITH ELDON W TOZER JON A TURNER
JACKIE C WALKER LARRY L BETTS DONALD R BOYLES JAMES H BRASWELL ERNEST J DAVIS JR
HARVEY DUDLEY JR DWIGHT G FOREMAN CURTIS R FRANTZ JOHN J HAYDEN JR MICHAEL J MCCLELLAN
PHILIP L JEWELL PETER J LACEY III WILLIAM F LEASE GRADY L LEWIS JAMES M MINCEY
ADOLPHUS HALL JR CHARLES I MITCHELL JAMES T SMOAK JR JOHNNY W TRAINHAM ANTHONY A VIRBICKAS
ROBERT K WORTHEN CHARLES D YLLAN RICHARD F COLLINS KEITH COLWELL JOHN J CROCE
MICHAEL L DE BOLT RICHARD C DEUTER KENNETH G EWING PETER A GRUCA JOHNNY V JOHNSON
GERALD E KEESLING FRANCIS M MONROE PATRICK L PURDIN MICHAEL E QUINN WESLEY M SIDENER
LAREST C SUTTON DAVID WILLIAMS III ALEXANDER C BROWN STANLEY J EGAN LESZEK A KULACZKOWSKI
ROBERT A CLEMENTS GRAYLAND JONES VINCENT B LEE ROBERT MOORE JR ALBERT E PARKER
MICHAEL J POLL ROY M STILWELL ALFRED L TURNER JOHN J ADDUCI HENRY G ALLEN
CHARLES J ARMSTRONG MICHAEL D BALAMOTI RAUL R BARRERA JR BARRY J BEDARD EARL C BROWN
ROGER L BYUS BILLY L COKER LARRY E COLLINS HOWARD B COMER JR ROBERT F CONTI
ROGER A DE DIE REXFORD J DE WISPELAERE PHILLIP A DUNCAN CHARLES R FELLENZ LAURENCE A YOUNG
RICHARD O GANLEY MICHAEL F GONZALES LARRY I GREWELL JOSEPH E HARDY JOSEPH R HARRIS
JAMES R JONES JR PETER R MATTHES RONALD L OLSON ALLEN D PERKINS BURTON K PHILIPS JR
CHARLES M RUSSELL III JOHN J SEXTON THOMAS M TAYLOR JAMES B WHITE JOHN H WHITTINGTON
JACK E DEETER EVERETT E WOOLUMS JR DONALD L WRIGHT EDWARD J CORMIER RAYMOND K DISMUKES
EVERETT GORE JR TEDDY L HAMEL GARY P HERSHBERGER PAUL R LAVEZZOLI ROBERT J NADEAU
JOHN R NAUGHTON JR WILTON PADIER JR JOHN PATTISON JR JACK W POMEROY JERRY D RAWLS
ROGER B SCHAEFER EARL M STANFORD HECTOR VILLEGAS-VILA MARVIN A VOELKER JR JON A ALLEN

PANEL 16W *(Continued)*

TIMOTHY E BADOSTAIN GARY W BUCHANAN EDWARD T DAVIS JR CLIVE GARCIA JR WILLIAM A KUHNKE
THOMAS L DAUGHERTY JERRY L GREENE WILLIAM F MERRILL LEROY NESMITH JAMES R PLATE
ARTHUR J RAMBO TERRY L REXROAT DAVID G RITZ BARRY F SCOTT WILLIAM F VAN CLEAVE
WILLIAM O BRANTLEY JR CHARLES R DE WINDT LARRY L FOWLER LINWOOD E HYMAN ROBERT J SILVA
LARRY A BROWN JOHNNY C JONES WYLIE C KING JOHN M SMITH KENNETH J SMOLAREK
JOHNNIE M WAHL ULYSSES WALLACE BLAINE H WALSH ANGEL L ACEVEDO-MILLAN THOMAS E ASKEW
CARL E DEAN JR ROBERT W DONAHUE JR MICHAEL L FERGUSON ROY E FICKLING MICHAEL T GIBSON

PANEL 15W

DANIEL T HUNT MARSHALL P IVEY KENNETH R KIENER ROBERT B KOSTICH JR
DELVIN C MARTINSON NATHANIEL SCOTT RONALD L SPENCE JOHNNY L YOUNG LAWRENCE J BABYAK
PAUL B BENOIT DENNIS D BOGLE RICHARD H BOISE ROBERT S CLEMENTS ROBERT O EDER
ROY A EPPERSON JAMES M GARRETT HENRY N HEIDE II DENNIS W HOLTORF JERRY E KEKEL
JACK D KNEPP KENNETH B KOZAI MELVIN LEDERMAN RICHARD J LEFFLER CLARENCE LOGWOOD
RAY F LONG JAMES W LUNSFORD JR KENNETH A LUSE CALVIN B MATTHEWS JOHN E MATTINGLY
JAMES I MCCARTHY JR MICHAEL A O'KEEFE JR HENRY B PARSONS III CHARLES V PENN JOHN M PIASECKI
DENNIS J REARDON JOHN W ROLES JAMES R SMITH CLYDE E THOMAS LARRY E WATSON
JOHN A BOSSOM JIMMY R BURK DONALD A DEMOND TOM HABADA RUSSELL JONES JR
THOMAS H JONES DONALD L KINGERY DAJVID L NICHOLSON ROBERT K PARKER CLAUDE B ROGERS
JAMES ,N ROYAL DEAN R SHILLING DENNIS SMITH JR ROBERT E VANDERGRIFF RICHARD O WOLFE
TIMOTHY E ACHISON ROBERT R BROWN JACK CAMP JAMES L CLARKSON GEORGE B COLGAN III
DOLROY FRANCIES PATRICK J HAYES WILLIAM C KEELER FREDDIE L LONG DANNY G MARTIN
WILLIAM V MOORE STEPHEN L RAGSDALE BILLY L ROGERS DONALD F SCHNABLY FREDERICK W SIEBERT JR
DENNIS A WATSON JOHN S ASH TRINO B BENAVIDEZ KENNETH W BROWN THOMAS E BROWN
JAMES F CARLONI ROBERT G CURL COSTA J DA ROBERT L DALTON JONATHAN W GARRETT
JOLLY J DAY WILLIAM C DUNLAP DONALD L GREIGER JOHN C GUIRE CHARLES C HOWZE
STACY KRESHO ROBERT R LEISY ROBERT J MCINTOSH DARNELL MISTER WILLIAM D SANDERLIN
LYLE F KELL EDWARD L NEAL ALFRED PICKARD RUSSELL T PICKERING FRANCISCO M TRUJILLO
ROBERT S RAINES MARVIN H SANDERS MICHAEL H SHANLEY JR JONATHAN TOWNSEND DENNIS L VANCE
EYKEL M VANDEN II FRAZIER T DIXON JOHN H FREY CLARENCE M GATEWOOD CARL B RAY
JOHNNY R GILLINGS ROGER L HUNDT STEPHEN D LYNN GORDON J NORMAN MICHAEL W PRENGEL
WAYNE M ANDERSON ROBERT E ROMERO CALVIN E THOMPSON JR LESLIE R TRENT MARTIN S DOHERTY
DAVID A HICKMAN CHARLES R JONES JAKE MARTINEZ CLEVELAND PITTS DAVID C SCHOENEWALD
LOUIS D PALLAYE EMORY L REA EDWARD R SMILEY JR DON E STEVENSON JOSE A VELEZ-HERNANDEZ
HIRAM M WOLFE IV ROGER C BARTZ WILLIAM J BEKSI JOHN C CLARK II BENJAMIN F DANIELSON
DAVID M DAVISON TONY C FOSTER PATRICK K HARROLD JERRY L HAUSCHULTZ JOHN J HEALEY JR
STEVEN D LE VESQUE JOHN E MARTIN EUGENIO MOLINA-RODRIGUEZ MARK R MUEHE DAVID NIEVES
THOMAS M MCMAHON JR ROGER L MCRIGHT STEPHEN S OVIATT DANIEL A PETERS RUBEN D REESE
RALPH L TAYLOR ROGER L VENTERS RICHARD F WATERFIELD RICHARD A WATTS JEFF L WENGER
JOE WITHERSPOON FLOYD J BANKS FOSTER CRANMER ALAN D CURTIS ROLLAND L DURFLINGER
ROBERT A FALKENAU CHARLES E FERRELL GARY L HEIN LARRY L HOHMAN ROBIN MANGUM
GEORGE L MILLER PETER K MIRANDA PHILIP J SCHROCK CHARLES G SCHWARTZ TONY R TURNER
RICHARD M THOMPSON DANIEL R ZUTTER PEPITO R ACERET ALBERT L BELL ROY J BUTTS
ROBERT E DE VINNEY DANIEL R FANKBONER ISSAC D FAUGHN CHARLES E FULKS RUSSELL E GEDEON
THOMAS P GILL III VINCENT J HALL CHARLES E JOHNSON LEE D KENNEDY DANNY R LATHAM
WEBB H LAYTON JR MICHAEL W LEIF JERRY D PATTON KENNETH A RICHEY HOWARD E WILLIAMS JR
JIMMY L FOMBY JOHN A HANCOCK JOSEPH E HARDEE ROBERT L HATCHER RANDALL B MILLER
CARL R DICE DALE A MACARTHUR WILLIAM P MCCARRON JR MICHAEL L MCGOVERN GARY H MITCHELL
GERALD R ROSS KENNETH B SESSUMS TERRIL W SNELSON FLOYD G TALLEY ROYCE W TRUSSELL JR
WILLIAM J ZABOROWSKI WILLIAM A BARNES ANTHONY W DEAN EDWARD F FRATUS DOUGLAS T GRAY III
ROGER W HEINZ RICHARD G HILL WARD L HOOPER JR WILLIAM R KIMBALL KARL F LANGE
MICHAEL J MCCLANE JOSEPH H OBMAN JOE B OJEDA REGGINALD W PLUMMER DALE A SCHEPP
EUGENE P SHUMBRIS JEFFERY N SMITH THOMAS E SUMLIN ROBERT J SWEDENBURG CHARLES S TARBERT
ROBERT R ALLMERS CHAD L CARSON JAMES F GHEE RONALD F KEENER KENNETH W SMARR
REGINALD J SUTHERLAND RONALD J TAYLOR DAVID A WEIR CHARLES P AUVE HERMAN D BUCHANAN
JOSEPH F BENAK ARTHUR B CLARK STEPHEN G CONNER LARRY R DAMERON DAVID D DICKERSON
ROBERT D FARRINGTON GARY L FOLZ THOMAS-R MARSHALL THOMAS A MAY JIMMY R PATRICK
RAYMOND R PISENO JR GERALD L BALDWIN ALBERT F BAST JR JAMES W BISHOP KENNETH E DE MORE JR
JOHN A FEDELE BRUCE R FRANZ ARTHUR T GALLAGHER CHARLES P HOOD JR ROBERT A HUGHES
CASIMIR KULIK ARLYN L LAMPERT THOMAS V MARCHESE JOSEPH L MENDOZA WILLIAM C WHITLATCH JR
DONALD A MARTIN CHARLES B MOORE LAWRENCE G REMUTH OTTAWAY L WILLIAMS REED E CAMPBELL
JAMES M CHEATHAM GARY M GRYZEN BRUCE G GUSTAFSON DEARING M JACKSON JAMES E MELVIN JR
TIMOTHY J MCCREIGHT DAVID A MCINTYRE WALTER A PETERSON JR GARY T PHILLIPS RICHARD H BRIGHT
EUGENE CAULEY JR ROBERT E HEWITT GRANT H HIGHSMITH CARL L HUGHES JR CHESTER L HUGHEY
LARRY R JOHNSON KENNETH L MARSHAND PAUL C MEDLIN GREGG A NEWELL DENNIS P POELSTRA
ROBERT T RUSSELL II WESLEY R THOMPSON CARL E WHEELER WILLIAM S BARRITT DONNIE J BRAGG
RONALD C COLLINS FARRISH COMBS DANIEL M DAWSON JAMES M GRANT DEE A HYDEN
LARRY D KEELER BILLY B LEYERLE EDWARD LOPEZ JAMES P NUGENT DARYL W PATRICK
DAVID A PENDELL JOHN ROCHE DONALD R ROSE MONTE L STAMM DON E STOCKTON JR
DAVID B THOMPSON JOE D WRIGHT OSCAR L BRITTENUM JR VICTOR P BUCKLEY ALLEN A BULLARD JR
DANIEL C CAPITANI JOHN W CREWS JR THOMAS E DEVINE MICHAEL J DRAKE JOSEPH N EVELAND
ROBERT F FAVOR NICK A FINLEY KENNETH A FORD JR JOHN T GAGE FRANCIS M GIRARDOT
JAMES E HAYES GLEN E HOWARD DAVID W JERO SVEN S MASON RONALD D MCMILLEN
TERRY L PERZ ROY L ROYSTON RALEIGH J SNELL JR LEONARD J SUGIMOTO AARON WALKER
CHARLES L WASHINGTON JUAN CARRILLO JAMES D CASTEEL GARY V CLARK JOHN J GALLAGHER
NEIL E HARVEY GLENN R MANNING BILLY J NEELY CHARLES Q POLK MICHAEL T SOLTYS
WILLIAM R SPILLERS WILLARD E SPIVEY THOMAS T TOMSIC DE W VANCE RICHARD E WESTFALL
SAMUEL H WILLIAMS RONALD J BINKOWSKI RICHARD W BOSWELL JR WILLIAM R CRANE PATRICK M DILLON
ROGER J FLYNN JERRY D GIESECKE WILLIAM R HASSELL ROBERT C HOUSMAN CHARLES D NEWMAN
ROY D BASSETT JR CLYDE R CARRICO JAMES A COOPER CLIFFORD E DRAHER CHARLES B DRAUT JR
RICHARD W FRANK II ROBERT N NORRIS MACEY L RUCKER RICHARD G BUCCILLE GERALD E BUTLER
PATRICK A CADWALLADER ANTHONY W FELDEN LLOYD M HAMMOND JR DAVID W JONES CARL E LONG
J C MILLER JOEL A SANDBERG GLENN C SHUEY DAVID L SMITH CRAIG D SMITHSON
WOODROW W SNYDER JR WILLIAM M STEVENSON LARRY L WOOD DOUGLAS W YOUNG ROY J BURKE
RUDOLPH E ARAUJO STEVEN E BACKHAUS DAVID L BARBER DONN W BELANDER DAVID R BRUCE
THOMAS L ANDERSON JAMES H DEAN THOMAS J DOWD DAVID L EGGLESTON BOB J FORD JR
THOMAS L FORSYTHE CHRISTOPHER J GRAY ARTHUR R HERNDON BARRY P KALETTA JAMES E LOWRY
THOMAS M MAYS KENNETH B MEADOR WAYNE D MORGAN DAVID L RECK GARY P SINCLAIR
GARY M SMITH THOMAS S STAFFORD MELVIN SULLIVAN STANLEY E TAYLOR FRANCIS A TRINCHITELLA
ROBERT A YATES THADDEUS M YONIKA JR DONALD D BURRIS JR FRANK HALL JR JAMES E KENNEDY
JAMES P HALEN WILLIAM T HATTING CHRISTOPHER A MILLER STANLEY D MONTGOMERY JAMES C MOORE
BRUCE A MCCORMICK GERALD E NIEWENHOUS JR PETER P PARNELL JR CHARLES R RAINES JOHN N RANSON
DONALD A SELKEY JR JAMES L SWAIM HARRY F ZALESNY JR REYNALDO L BARRAGAN JR JAMES E FORE
DAVID E BERGFELDT RUSSELL L BROWN EASLEY P BYERS JR JOEL L COOK DANIEL W EDWARDS JR
SANDERS R BALDWIN ERROLD R FARRAR TRUMAN J GILBERT WILLIS W JOHNSON OSCAR B LYLES JR
RICHARD A MARFURT JR CLIFFORD MONTGOMERY FRANKLIN W NEEL ROBERT J OSBORN DAVID N REED
EDWARD L ROGERS GERALD R WADE ROBERT L WEHUNT TIMOTHY C WHITE ALFRED L WILLIAMS
FLOYD I BEACH RONALD A CHRISTEN WILLIAM J DAHL RONALD G DENNIS LAUREN D FRITZ
THOMAS V HAAS GLENNON HAYWOOD THOMAS M HIRES ELKER G KATZ TERRENCE M KUZAK
PATRICK R MARTIN GLENN E MITCHELL EDWARD MORRISON JR TERRY C NEWKIRK DAVID RAMP
WILLIAM A THEISEN WAYNE H WALKER WILBERT L GILLESPIE HARRY R SINE JR DENNIS M BOLAND
GENE T WRIGHT DAVID B BOWLING ROGER R BROWN TERRY B DYER RICKY M GLASPEY GLYNN B HOLLEY
TERRY L JOSLIN DAVID L KNOTT WALTER H KOSKY JR MITCHELL MAGEE JR GARY O MANCHESTER
EARL G LEACH VINCENT O MCCANN JR HARVEY R MCCONAUGHEAD JR RICHARD J ROMESSER E J WELCH JR
RAYMOND L MCCASLIN WILLIAM H RUFF DUSTIN C TROWBRIDGE GERARD J WALKER CURTIS M ASHTON
DONALD W ATWELL JR WILLIAM E BONNER ERIC A BOSCH GLENN A CAIL MARK C CORBETT
MICHAEL R EARL ISOM J GOODWINE PERRY W HALL JACK E HOLMES DONALD R LAMBERT
ALLEN J LAMS CHARLES W LOVE JR TOMMY L MARKS DAMIEN J MESSINO THOMAS V PAKULA
DONALD I PRINGLE THOMAS A SCIBELLI ROBERT D SHERADIN REGERNAILD WEBSTER LOUIS ZABROWSKI
ROBERT A ABRUZESE JAMES M ALDERMAN WILLIAM L BEADNELL DONALD J BERGER WILLIAM L BUNCH
CHARLES K BUTLER OTIS CARTHAGE JR ROGER D COX WILLIAM N CUNNINGHAM ROBERT L EMERY
JOHN W FOREMAN ROBERT S GATES STEPHEN F GEORGE DEAN E HALL RONNIE L HAWKS
DANIAL G HEIDERICH WILLIAM P HIGGINS RONALD F LISCUM CHARLES E MERRITT JAMES H PENCE
JON M OLSSON ALAN R RADER LESLIE L SHELTON DOUGLAS L SNEAD EDWARD R STORM ROBERT R SWAIN
RANDALL K TETER TERRY A THORNTON RICHARD D WALSH MICHAEL H BEAVER MICHAEL J DINDA
FRED M ELLIS CURTIS GOOD GLENN R GRADECKI CLARENCE E HARPER JR GARY V LOVELLETTE
LAWRENCE A LUCIANI GEORGE P REED EDDIE SAILOR WILLIAM E SPENCER WILLIAM E ALLEN
FREDERICK A CAINES JAMES R DEAN JR WILLIE J DELACROIX FIELDING W FEATHERSTON III DOYLE H PARSON
DOUGLAS D FERGUSON JAMES H FRY FREDRICK A HASSLER ELLIS S MARLIN THOMAS A MOORE
MICHAEL P DIMMER THOMAS W MYNES WILLIAM H RAPP JR ROBERT L ROSE ROBERT L SMITH
THOMAS E SOMA RICHARD P STOTSBERY GERALD C SWAYZE JAMES E TOWNLEY SR WILLIAM O VAUGHN
RICHARD C BABB JR GOLGUIS COLON-RODRIGUEZ THOMAS J CROSS CHARLES F GODFREY TERRY B LUND
BENJAMIN J BUCHANAN GARY L DEMPSEY ROY W GODOWNS ROGER K GREENWAY HENRY C KLINGER
SCOTTIE S MASSEY CHARLES E MOORE JR WILLIAM C REDDICK JOHN M REILLY JIMMIE D STILL
DONALD A SUDBRINK KENNETH W TODD ROBERT G WARREN JAMES O WATSON DUANE G WILLIAMS
NICHOLAS G BROOKS TANNER M BROWN JR ROBERT E CARMICHAEL JOSEPH M D'ANGELICO JOHN T WEST
GARDNER DORSEY FRANK M DUNSMORE JR HARRY E FARMER ROGER W FELLERS BRUCE C FRYAR
RAUL GARCIA JR STEVEN L GREEN WILLIE J HAYES ROGER W KVERNES RONNIE G LINDSTROM
KENNETH H MCLENDON BARNEY M SMITH DALLAS R SNODGRASS EDDIE L SPIVEY WILLIE B WALKER JR
DENNIS E DEBNER ROBERT C WRIGHT GARY L DAVIS RICHARD T DEROSIER GARY E EICHELER
ROBERT J FATICA CYE GARY RONALD A JENNIGES CLAUDE A KNIGHT STEWART R MOODY WILBERT WALTON
CHARLES R OLSON GENE J OLSON KENNETH E PERRY MATTHEW P ROCHE JR JIMMY D SANDERS
LAWRENCE R WARF HERMAN H BAN THOMAS L BLANKS PAUL B BLUNT JR ROY L HAMMONDS
JOHNNY L HAWKINS DAVID S JONES REGINALD W LINDSEY RICHARD M MAHON DANNY W OVERTON
PETER PULASKI JR FRANCIS J SNEE JR BERNARD A SOWDER JAMES S VANCE WILLIAM S WADDLE
JAMES R WHITMORE JIMMY A WHITSON RICHARD C WILLIAMS WALDO A WILLIAMS BILLIE M BEDSWORTH
JAMES F BRENNAN JR HUBERT F BRINSON ROBERT W BURNES GARY W ERICSON WILLIAM F GILMORE JR
PATRICK H HU MAX D KERSEY LARRY N LAMB DONALD E LEWTER MICHAEL O LUND
JOEL M MAGRASS TOM A METCALF CHARLES T MOORE EUGENIO ORTIZ RANDALL E RAMSDEN

PANEL 14W

HERMAN P SANCHEZ RICHARD C SCHMIDT ROBERT S SOMBATI LARRY VILLANUEVA
ROY L BASS CLIFFORD C BLEND JR NORRIS R BORGMAN KENNETH W BOWARD DANNY K RAYBORN
RICHARD F BRANT JR CLAIR B BUTZ CHARLES C CHAPIN JOHN A DE ROO GARY H GARNER
CARL E GILBERT RUSSELL E GILBRECH JOHN J HARGREAVES CHARLES L HARTUNG MICKEY L HAWKINS
RUSSELL W KAYSER JOSEPH A LOZANO CHRISTOPHER H MARKEY EARL W MARLIN JR BERYL G PETERS
WILLIAM M ADAIR JULIAN R RODRIGUEZ CLINTON G RUCKLE FRANK M WALKER JAMES F WESTPHAL
DEAN A WILDERSPIN LARRY A BRADLEY RICHARD L DICUS ROBERT E DORSE JR WILLIAM J ERKES JR
REID C HENNINGSEN MICHAEL G HOFF JOHN A HURST MICHAEL W LYNE LENUS E MEAD
ROBERT OCHAB JOHN D RETSECK JR MICHAEL B ROBINSON CRAIG R ROGERS LA R ROTH
OLIVER C STAMPS GENE G WELLS RAYMOND A WHITE III CHARLES R WILLARD JR FRANK ZYDZIK JR
WILLIAM E BARNES STEVEN M BROWN GALE W BUTCHER JR WILLIAM L CAMPBELL JR DAVID W COPPERNOLL
LEO C CASEY JR WAYNE M COLE WILLARD W CROY WARREN L DONAHE XAVIER GOMEZ
TERRY E GORSLENE GEORGE M HINES RONALD F HOPKINS EDWARD J JUSTICE KENNETH T KLEPPIN
JOSEPH M LAUINGER JAMES L MCCABE JR JAMES C MITCHELL JR JOHN E NIERER RONALD E PICKART
HAROLD K RAPPAPORT JOHN M RICE JAMES R RUTLEDGE JR JOHN SMITH JR FELIX SOLIS
MICHAEL C VICKERY WILLIAM J AHART LARRY P BARTLETT WILLIAM J BECKER EDGAR L BISHOP
HOWARD E BROWN JR HAROLD B EISERT JR RONALD E EMBREE HARLAN K GAMMONS JR WILLIAM C STEFKO
LARRY D GRIFFITH ALFRED F HALL RICHARD W HIBBLER GEORGE A HOLTSCHNEIDER BOYD L WADE
GERALD A JACKSON JERRY A KAYS CHARLES W KLANCKE ROGER R LEASER TEDD M LEWIS
RAYMOND A MAY DENNIS L PEEK DANNY J PETERSEN RODNEY R ROGERS RICARDO SERENIL
WALTER J GARSTKIEWICZ JR JOHN W SPARKS MANUEL A TAVARES RICHARD A THOMAS MARK D VINCENT
JOSE F GUERRERO JR WAYNE C ALLEN HERBERT C CROSBY MONTE R DE VERE FRANCIS G GRAZIOSI
GEORGE A HOWES DENNIS F KABARA JAMES G LEGA JOHN A LEHECKA NEILE C MACKAY
JOHN A ORDNER THOMAS D TIGHE JAMES H ZUMBRUN KENNETH B BECKMAN GROVER C BOWERS JR
VERLYN C BRUNS RICHARD D CHORLINS JERRY M CUNNINGHAM MICHAEL E DARNELL JAMES W SALTER
DAVID W FELKNER EDDIE D GLINNEN EDWARD J HAMRICK ROBERT A HARRISON MICHAEL R JAMES
RONALD W JONES ROY R LEWIS WILLIAM B LIBERSKY EDGAR R PULLIAM JR TERRENCE P RYAN
JOHN C BREWTON RICHARD B SPENCE EDWARD A BISCHOFF JIMMY L CHAMBLISS JAMES G DALTON
DANIEL E ECKENRODE GORDON E EVANS EUGENE HOOD JOHN J JANOSKA JR JAMES D PLANK
RICHARD L SCOTT DAVID D TETTLETON ANDRUS J BLANCHARD RALPH L HAMPTON CLYDE P MEREDITH
HARVEY T PINKNEY ROBERT G POTTER MARK P RUDOLF STEPHEN G SAMPLE GLENN E TUBBS
JOSEPH P ANTONELLI HERMINIO A BONILLA LEE A CONNERS ROBERT D FARNHAM WILLIAM G LITTLE
GILBERT A BENAIM ROGER G KIDWELL WILLIAM LEONARD REINALDO SANTIAGO-CASTILL JR
GARY W MORRIS ANDREW M PHILLIPS JOHN M RIZZO JR MARTIN S SCHILLER JR HENRY L TAYLOR
JOSE M MANGUAL GERALD L SCHWUCHOW CLARENCE S TURNER III DANIEL L WOOD RICHARD H BAHL JR
DAVID C CHAVEZ LARRY D FLORANG MICHAEL H HIPPACH ROBERT D KRAMER SAMMUEL E SURBER
WILLIAM BUGOSH GREGORY J THOMAS TOMMY R WARREN DAVID K AESCHLIMAN RICHARD L BLOWERS
RONALD J FUITE PAUL L BINDER JAMES D CONN NEDWARD C ESTES JR KEITH B LACKEY ROBERT M MILDNER
JESSE D CANFIELD CARLTON F MCCAGG JR KENNETH C MCTIER BRIAN J O'CALLAGHAN EARL A PEAK
CHARLES J GIRARD WARREN S HALL JOHN M JENNINGS JAMES E LAKINS ROBERT H MILLER DAVID A SWEET
OTTO J OSTENFELD DONALD P SLOAT PHILIP E SMITH JR JAMES L THONEN LYNWOOD K THORNTON
FRANK BLAS STEVEN F EDWARDS RICHARD E FORD DAVID A FOWLER KENT D MATTHEWS
DONALD R COLGLAZIER CHARLES R GAMBILL BILLY G HARRISON GEORGE A HECTOR JR DONALD L MARTIN
STEVEN A MUELLER CHARLES J NOLDER KENNETH L STOKES DAVID H STOPPELWERTH MARK E TONTI
DENNIS M TOPOLINSKI ROBERT L WILLETT EDWARD J WITEK RAYMOND J AQUINO MARION CROOM JR
GARY L ERVIN ROBERT P FITZHUGH DALE R FORSYTHE JUAN A FRET-CAMACHO AUBREY A WIGGINS
JOHN M MCDAID WARD NORTON III OSCAR F RODRIGUEZ MEL E SALAZAR JR FRANKLIN D SCHRADER
ROBERT G MITCHELTREE JR VAN S TURNER JR JAMES E COOLEY HAROLD D DARNELL JAMES D FOX
ROBERT J GASKO JR GERALD A GAUTHIER ROBERT J HOLLAND CHESTER T HOWARD JR EVERETT D KEATON
FRANK A PECORARO WILLIAM L PHILLIPS ROGER L SCOTT WILLIAM W SURETTE JR RONALD S ATHANASIOU
TERRY L BANNING JAMES C BAUMER LARRY D BEEBE LARRY D BOYER CLAUD A DAVIS TERRANCE L DREA
MICHAEL G FOUTZ THOMAS M GAITHER PEDRO A GONZALEZ WILLIAM E HAGGARD ROGER E KEY
JOHN C KROEGER KENNETH R KROEHLER RICHARD L METCALF MORRIS C MILES JR BILLY E MOORE
FLOYD S MCCREERY LARRY D MURRAY WILLIAM W O'NEIL JOHN D PIES JOHN C REITWIESNER
SCOTT J RODERICK ROBERT H RUGGLES CHARLES T RUSSELL JEROME R SAIN JOHN B STIZZA
VICTOR B STRIBLING KERRY L TAYLOR NEELY C WALKER WILLIAM N WILLIAMSON ROBERT F BULLA JR
PEDRO C GARCIA LENNIS C GENTRY, JAMES C GRAFTON JACK D HANSON JR WALTER W NUNLEY JR
DONALD H MAJKOWSKI LOWRENZO NEELEY GEORGE D QUICK JR DEAN A BORNEMAN ROBERT J MULLENS JR
RICHARD T CARTER MICHAEL D CASEY WILLIAM H CLARK JR RONALD C DAVIS TERENCE J FOLSOM
WILLIAM H BARTHOLOMEW JR MALCOLM J GRIM FRANK D HAMMOND DONALD J RICE WILLIAM E SEMPLE
CAREY A FOSNAUGH FRANK SPENCER III ALLEN R TOWNER DENNIS C WARD DANIEL L BEHM
MARK S BUNDY WILLIAM A GRIFFIS III OLIVER Y HARRELSON MILFORD D ISAACSON PAUL N JACKSON
THOMAS E LITTLEPAGE RANDALL E PERRY ROBERT W SHELTON NATHANIEL THOMAS DONALD R YARBORO
ROY C BEASLEY ALAN L BRACKEN NORMAN R EVERETT KENNETH FRIERSON BENJAMIN GARCIA
OSCAR C GONZALES RONALD D HECK BARRY V HOPPER ROBERT L JOHNSON THOMAS J KORDOSKY
HAROLD V MANN JR DUANE J MARHEFKA JEFF MILLER ROBERT G ROGERS DENNIS W SMITH
CARL J PREUSS NICOLAS V SAN GEORGE T SPILLERS JAMES V VINCIGUERRA VERNON M WIGGINS
MICHAEL E STYER FRANCIS M AUD DAVID E FARR HARVIE R FRADY PATRICK H HALBERT RICHARD J HAWCO
JOHN J KOS THOMAS A MADDEN II DENNIS W MOORE RAYMOND PLATERO ROBERT W READY
LARRY S RUTHERFORD THOMAS R TENNIS RICHARD WILLIAMS JR WILLIAM L WOOD ERICK W BEATTIE
WAIN P CRAIG RICHARD A DORNELLAS PRESTON L HALL EVERETT D HERREN STEPHEN A KRAMER
WESLEY W CARROLL III GARY L HOBBS JACKEY V KNIGHTEN THEODORE R LEIGHTON JOSEPH V OLSZEWSKI
FLOYD D WIMER ROBERT L YOUNG GREGORY L ANDERSON ANTHONY B BATTEL HOLLY G BELL
KENNETH S BERCIER TERRY A CARTER STEVEN O DILE PETER D GUZMAN JAMES F HACKETT JR
MICHAEL W HUNTER CLEVELAND O JOHNSON JOHN M JONES JR KENNETH E KOCH LEONARD C LEESER
FRANK D MADRID RICHARD J MALLON ROBERT J PANEK SR JOHN J POLLACK WILLIAM D PRUETT
JOHN A SHAFFER WILLIAM C SHINN WILLIAM C SUTTON HOWARD BLANDINO CLARENCE F BROWN JR
ROBERT W FLOYD RONNIE D FULMER CHARLES C HINTON JR MERLE G HUBBARD LARRY E KREBS
LYLE M JOHANNES RICHARD C KNAPP BILL B LONG JOHN A MOREAU LEON C POLASKI
WILBERT REED JOE H RUFTY ROY L STRINGER LAWRENCE O WASHINGTON WILLIAM A DIXON
KENNETH A STEWART JOHN A SMITH GARY A CHESHIRE CALVIN L JOHNSON BOBBY E JONES LUIS A LE BRON
DANIEL I MAMBRETTI VERNON W WOODY MICHAEL L ARRANTS JOHN L BEEK HENRY D BELL JR
PAUL B BOWMAN JERRY D DENNY PAUL F DORONZO BLAINE W ENOS JR JOSE M LLANTIN-ORTIZ
RONALD J FULTON ROGER L GIVENS KENNETH R GODWIN RAYMOND D HARRELL DAVID L HEMKE
PAUL H CARDENAS JR DAVID A JOHNSON RICHARD M MADER ROBERT L MCARTHUR RICARDO MENDIOLA
GLEN A JACKSON III GUY T MCAULEY ALAN B PARTRIDGE O'NEIL J PELLEGRIN JR NORWOOD R RICHARDSON
JOHN T RODGERS EDWARD A ROZELL WILLIAM H SMITH JR DONALD L SWANSON JERALD D WEST
JAMES B BROWN JAMES C CARMAN CHESTER C CARRICO JR EDWARD L CRAIG RUSSELL A STEINDAM
LEON A FENTRESS ROBERT FORD MARK A FOSTER WILLIAM K GARRITY CHARLES V GREEN
GEORGE D HARPER JOHN M KOENIG RAYMOND N PELKEY THOMAS J PROTACK CHARLES L RIDDLE
FRANCIS M ALLEN JR RONALD E ROBINSON BERNARD RUSSELL CRUZ J SANTA LARRY H TRUSSELL
RICHARD W WILLIAMS VON S ANDERSON BARRY L ARMSTRONG DONALD E BARTEK ALAN W BERRY
TERRY A BRYSON CHARLES E DIAMOND WILLIAM E FOLLON GERALD L GARDNER JOHN D GUILLEN
VICTOR OCASIO JR DAVID L JUDY JAMES K KIRKBY DOUGLAS L KONING FRED J LE BLANC ERIC O LEWIS
ANTHONY J METZGER JR RICHARD H MILLER GIRAUD D MUNTZ CARL A OLSON PAUL R PELUSO JR
JAMES W STEWART DONNIE J SWATSELL HENRY B WRIGHT ARTHUR CLARK EDMOND E SMITH III
JESSE C CREEKMORE DWIGHT S DOUGLAS DENNIS A HAINES ANTHONY J HAINS JR ADOCK V JOHNSON
J M CHILDRESS DANNY L JONES LARRY E NEWMAN ERNEST A RIVERA JR WALLACE A STOCKSTILL JR
VINCENT R THORNBURG ROBERT M WARNOCK CHARLES H WRIGHT JOHN M BURNLEY DUANE C LARSON
PATRICK L COLE ROBERT O COLLINS ROOSEVELT G DOCKERY LAWRENCE N DUBIA LARRY E DYER
GARY A BULLERDICK LARRY GREEN JOHNNIE L ISHMAEL DANNY R MAGAHA MICHAEL L NEUDAHL
DANNY R ROBERTS JOHN M SMITH GERALD D TOMLINSON ROBERT L UFFORD LUIS A ALANIZ
ADAM CANTU MICHAEL DI PASQUANTONIO PHILIP B GOODWIN LESTER W KIMBLE CARLOS VALENZUELA
PAUL E LEES JAMES M LYON RALPH MARTIN RONALD D PATE WILLIAM SMITH JAMES J O'SHAUGHNESSY
OWEN T MCCANDLIS KENNETH M PERRY RAYMOND D REGIER DANIEL SAVAGE RICHARD C STEPHENSON
ALLEN M HUTCHINSON WALTER H BUCKA JR RONALD J CHAPMAN WILLIAM R CULVER JACKY L DRURY
ROBERT J DUPELL JR DAVID B FOGG JOSEPH R HARDEE DWIGHT HAYES ALAN H JOHNSON
FRANK M KAISER PETER M KOMAROWSKI PATRICK A MCLEOD ERICK O OLSON RUSSELL A SHIELDS
DARRELL J SMITH KIRK I TEMPLE GARY D THATCHER JAMES L WALDEN RICHARD F WALTON
LAWRENCE H WILLIAMS JR MORRIS E WILLIAMS JESSE A WISDOM JAMES H ALEXANDER MICHAEL H BAIRD
TED J BISHOP ROY E COUCH RAYMOND J DI LORENZO JAMES M FUHRMAN ARTHUR M GARCIA JR
ROBERT E HUNT KENNETH R LASSETER TERRY S LOPRINO CARLTON B MILLNER ROBERT A WHITTED
THOMAS W MUIR JAMES A NIEMI WILLIAM D SCHIERMEYER JR ROBERT C SMITH JOHN L TAYLOR
STEVEN M KUSTER WILLIAM V YOUNG MAHLON R ARNETT GILBERT BLANDON ARLIS R BRANSCUM RODRIGO F IBARRA
BOOKER T DAVIE JR HARMON O DONALD JR BRADLEY A KINDER
JAMES L BRITT WILSON C KOEHLER JOSEPH W MCDONALD THOMAS L MORANO GREGORY P WAKULICH WAYNE K WOODLAND
CHARLES R BERRY OSCAR J GOMEZ ROBERT E GRIFFIN JOHN A GRINER THOMAS F HAGEN
GEORGE A JOHNSON JR JOHN J KOS DENNIS W PFEIFER BURTON K WALKER BILLIE J WILSON
RONALD B BAKER TOMMY L BARNES RICKY L BOWDEN ROBERT G BROWNE STEVEN L CATINO
DANNY C DAVIS BILLY F DODD JOHN V FRANCIS BOBBY G FROST TIMOTHY J GREEN
ALVIN L HALVERSON THOMAS M HILL JR RALPH A HOWARD EDWARD J KULIKOWSKI EDWARD D LOCKETT
GEORGE R MATTHEWS JOHN MAYNARD RONNIE L MCCORMICK MICHAEL MERENO RAYMOND G MILES
TARRY T O'REILLY ANTHONY P ODDO DUANE L RICHARD KENNETH ROSS DAVID F SCHUETTE
JOEL R STEPP DOUGLAS H TANNER LANNIE R ANDERSON JOHN J BURNS JR MORGAN L CAHOON
JIMMY L CAMPBELL FRED E CARRINGTON RICHARD B DAVIS JR TIMOTHY C FARRELL HAROLD W SHULER

MICHAEL R GLENN KENNETH L KELLER WILLIAM L KIEFFER JR PAUL H KNECHT VINCENT M LA ROCCA
JONATHAN L LAMM ENRIQUE LUJAN CHARLES T MALEY TIMOTHY L MCCURLEY RAYMOND R MOON
ROBERT R DAVIS THOMAS L NORWOOD JR MARLIN T PETERSON MICHAEL D PUETZ CHARLES M SHUMPERT
LAWRENCE P WALKER DARRELL G ALLISON PERCILL BATTS KENNETH D BOSTON ROBERT S BRADSHAW III
MICHAEL H BREEDING EDWARD F BROWN JR THOMAS C BURKE SAMUEL N BURTON RICHARD W COONS
WALTER K DENNIS CHARLES P DUESSENT DANIEL A FREY CHARLES T GENITTI JOHN M GIBBONS

PANEL 13W

JOHN B HIGGINBOTHAM PAUL E JONES WILLARD D KELLY LEE M LESHEN
JERRY E LINEBERRY WILLIAM J MONTAGUE LARRY H MORFORD DENNIS W NELSON CLIFTON T SMITH
JESSE J PENA LARRY R PRYOR HAROLD R SCHULER BOBBITT SCHWINTZ MICHAEL A SIROUSA
DONALD R MCINTOSH BILLY J SMITH MARK A STRAUB ARCHIE N WADE ROBERT L WALKER JR
ROY W COBB THOMAS E COPP ROSS E HARDT RONALD L HAUG LAWRENCE W YOCHUM
RICHARD J GORGES JESUS J MEZA JAMES O OLZER JR TRINIDAD G PRIETO CHARLES E SMELTZER III CHARLES G THORNE
BOBBIE H BREWER JAMES E BURKE WILLIAM L CLINE ERNESTO CUEVAS-RIVERA
JERROLD B DAY KENNETH L DELANEY JOSEPH W DUNCAN HAROLD P FESPERMAN GARY L GIOVANNELLI
JAMES D HAGELSTEIN DELMAR J HERRIN JR MICHAEL A HUGHEY SAMUEL J JORGENSEN ELDON R PAYNE
WAYNE E KAUFMAN ARTHUR W KINSER HERMES P LAS BERNARD E MEISTER ROBERT C MILLENDER
THOMAS A GUENTHER LOUIS W MCLIN III WAYNE D MCRAY VICTOR A MORENO RONALD G NEUBAUER
GREGORY C SCHOPER GARY SMITH FERDINAND J SOCHUREK III CHARLES E THOMAS JR EARL C TIDWELL JR
JOE N WATSON JAMES H WILBANKS CLARENCE C YOUNG JAMES S BAIRD MICHAEL A BOSOWSKI
JOHN E CARTER JR GREGORY M COONS FERNANDO B ESTEVES MARK R HORNER GERALD E HULL
RAYMOND D BRAGG DAVID H JOHNSON JOHN W KELLY JOHN MARKS CHARLES E MELTON
CONNIE W PARRISH ROMAN D RODRIGUEZ THEODORE F SAS RICHARD J SEXTON II SPENCER SMITH
ROBERT G O'CONNELL WINSTON J SMITH NORMAN A TAYLOR JOSE E VILLANUEVA FRED C ZIMPFER
JAMES A BARNES GEORGE O BOATWRIGHT MICHAEL S CARTER BILLY D CRELIA JOSEPH W DAVIS
ALAN C DE CRAENE JAN D GARRINGER CLAUDE V GILES J D MILLER ROBERT E NEAL
EDEWIN C HARMON DON R MCINTIRE DONALD W MORIN WILLIAM J MURPHY EDWARD YEE
CHESTER A MOLLETT PASTOR F RUIZ JOEL W SAMPSELL ROBERT J WIESE JAMES T BATEMAN
ROBERT L BLACKFOX KARL E BROWN CHARLES L CORDLE JACK L DRYE SAMUEL JAMES JR
THOMAS H FREASIER JAMES B GORDON JR BRUCE G GREENE CRAIG W HAINES JOSEPH P HONAN
HERBERT L MARSH RAYMOND MAYS RONALD L MEANS GEORGE G MITCHELL JOHN L MITCHELL
DON L PAPPAS ARLEN D RICHARDSON THEODORE A WILLIAMS JACK A ZOODSMA PAUL E ASH JR
DANNY E BLEVINS JOHN F BRADMAN RICHARD A BURGESS JAMES R CLARK ARTHUR E CLOUGH
THOMAS C DAFFRON JAMES N DIEDRICH GARY J EARLYWINE ROBERT E ELLIS ROGER W FIKE
BRIAN M FLANNERY THOMAS E GILLEN MICHAEL S GRYDER DAVID L HARDING EARL F HOFMANN
ARTIE E JOHNSON ABBOTT R JONES MAXIE D LINAM CHARLES F MORLEY MICHAEL E MULLEN
PATRICK O POMPELLA DAVID F SKALA ERIC W TAYLOR RONAL L WILLIAMS THOMAS A WILLIAMS
NIXON D PIKE HENRY T RAVA MICHAEL V BLUDWORTH DEAN W BORROUSCH WILLIAM R COGGINS
DICKEY L COOLEY THOMAS H FURNISH LARRY T HARRISON PHILLIP F HULTS MANUEL T MONTOYA
JAMES R HARDIN JIMMIE R MARSHALL TIMOTHY J NORMAN GREGORY A PARSONS ROBERT T SUDDUTH
RICHARD A WHITMORE DARRELL G WOOD JR LOSSIE F BONE WARREN J FERGUSON JR DENNIS E JOY
WILLIAM C HAGERICH LARRY E HAND DEXTER D HARBOUR MICHAEL L HELLER STEVEN L HESTER
EDWARD C CALDWELL III KENNETH L HIGGINS REGGIE W HINSON DAVID A HOCKETT FLOYD R JOHNSON
LESLIE E LIVINGSTON III CHARLES M MEDLEY LEON A MILLER SCOTT F MOORE JR LARRY D PALMER
THOMAS A PORTER DAVID A ROGERS CLYDE D ROOT CLYDE B TATNALL JAMES H WAULK JR
LARRY D WOOD WILLIAM W WOOD THOMAS E WYNNE VICTOR ZARAGOZA GORDON F ZIMMERMAN
ROBERT L WILSON VICTOR W BADWAY JR JEFFREY T BEARDSLEY THOMAS E BEWLEY RODERICK W CALHOUN
STANLEY D CALVIN JAMES C DE FRANCO LON DOUGHERTY JR STEVEN G EPPERSON JOHN E JORDAN
FREDDIE L EDWARDS JR ROBERT L HAWKINS ROBERT L SCHRAND RAYMOND R TAYLOR JR JOHN G WILKES
CRAIG A BAUER ROGER J BERNIER JERRY K BRIGHTER ANDREW J DUSZYNSKI WILLIAM C MCCONNELL IV
FRANK N FIGUEROA FREDERICK C FORTE JR ROBERT D FROST RONALD J HAMILTON DAVID W JANISH
MARK A JENEWEIN ROBERT W KUHN LISTON R LEONARD FREDERICK E LEOPOLD JACKIE L LEWALLEN
HAROLD L CHITWOOD BRUCE E MARTIN DENNIS P MARTIN GEORGE E MATTOCKS THOMAS R MOORE JR
THOMAS A PALLADINO JOHN W ROBERTS III MICHAEL J WAGNER MALCOLM G WILLIAMS DANNY K WITT
PAUL E DOLIK JOSEPH F ERICKSON NORMAN G GAGE ALBERT MALDONADO-LLUBER CALVIN E SERAIN
EDWARD B MELODY BARRY A MOLETTIERE DAVID J NACHTIGALL CLARK R PEDERSEN JUAN A RUBIO
THOMAS L CHANDLER DENNIS P SCHNEIDER RUSSELL M STODDARD WAYNE S ZACH WILLIAM A ALDAG
ERNEST L BROWN JR MICHAEL W HOPKINS LAWRENCE E LUNDGREN FRANK C NEWMAN STEVEN D STRUBE
JAMES H SACHASCHIK PATRICK L SMITH HENRY L VALO JR WALTER L WILSON JR RONALD E YOUNG
CHAD A CHARLESWORTH THOMAS G DICKSON JESSE C FREY ALAN P JOHNSON JERRY L STOUT
ROBERT B MOSSGROVE GEORGE A ODIORNE ROBERT L PEARSON JEFFRY R RIEK JOE L RIVERA
BOBBIE R BAXTER ROY J ROGERS THOMAS J VEZEAU DONALD J WADE MARTIN WALKER JR
RONALD S BAY NORMAN K BYASSEE ROBERT B CROSBY MARK S DIORIO MANUEL GALVEZ-PASTRANA
MARTIN J BENSON THERMON H EMORY JR ROBERT L FALLOWS MICHAEL J FLEMING FRANK B GLENDENNING
DAVID P HOFFMAN HENRY HUDSON JR WILLIAM D KRISTJANSON BERNARD L LEFEVRE
DONALD F HARTZELL JR GENE B NICKERSON DAVID S REID JAMES P RICHARDS TIMOTHY R ROE GERALD M STAATS
ARCHIE C WABSCHALL III PETER R WIESNEIFSKI JOHN M WIKE GEORGE A YOUNG DARRELL W ASPEY
FRANK M BACA DANNY C BERRIER RICHARD S BOVIO ROCKY A BURNS RICHARD J CONNELLY
FREDDIE C DE FOOR CHARLES W DOKES DONALD HALL JAMES B HEARD RONALD L MCCORMICK
JOHNNY J GALLARDO RAYMOND C HETZLER DAVID A LARSON JOE LONG HOWARD L LUCAS JR
JESUS M ENCARNACION-COLO MARK S MILES JAMES T PACE JAMES E PIVA DANIEL V PROCTOR
FRANCIS J PRUITT RONALD W STAFFORD FRANK L STATON GARY L SWARTZ ROBERT T TAYLOR
CORNELIUS TERRY JAMES D AALUND DANIEL A ALEGRE CHARLES R BAGGETT SHERMAN BOCHNEWETCH II
WILLIAM BOYLE GLENN E BUNDY DONNIE R CHASTAIN LARRY E DAILEY DOUGLAS M WOODWARD
JAMES P DEVANEY GEORGE A FINTER KENNETH M FLASHNER ROBERT E GUTHRIE WILLIAM J HODGE
BILLY J ROBERTS WALTER T SMITH GREGORY SQUARE EDWARD J VAILLANCOURT JACK A VAN WIEREN
EUGENE CARTER MARK E WILLIAMS MICHAEL J BLOTTENBERGER TERRANCE L BOWELL DANIEL L BROCK
SAMMY W GOLDMAN JIMMIE L JOHNSON MICHAEL E KELLY HERBERT W KLUG LARRY D LEITCH
EVERETT C PUGH JAMES J PUMPHREY ROGER J ROWELL DONALD R SAMUELS RUSSELL R BEELER
JOHN J BENNETT GUY R BRISTOL JAMES J BURGOYNE SYLVESTER COLLINS PHILLIP G CREECH
GRECO V DEL JR MILTON GOLDSMITH RICHARD A HOSTIKKA MARTIN J KEOGH JOSEPH C LAZICKI
THOMAS G LOVLEY LA V MCVEY WILLIAM J PARTINGTON DANNY J QUAITE DAVID W SKIBBE
ERVIN L TUTTLE DANIEL L WALLACE HARLEY D WHITNEY JOSEPH W WIRTH DANIEL AGUILERA
LARRY D ARONHALT PAUL D BRUMMET JAMES E BURTON JR KENNETH S DEE ANTHONY GOLSON
DANNY D HANKS JAMES D JOHNSON KENNETH H KANAMAN GEORGE G KARR RICKY N LOWDER
BRADLEY T MACE STEPHEN B MURRAY GEORGE T OLSEN RICHARD V PAWLAK WILLIAM H SCOTT
JARED B WALDING RUDOLFO R ALURA REGALADO M APEROCHO HARMON J BOVE JR MICHAEL W BOW
DENNIS M DAUGHERTY THOMAS DRUM BARRY C HIATT JOHN P JAROSCAK JAMES M STANLEY
JAMES A PARKER JOHN J PARKER EDMUND A PETRECHKO JR TIMOTHY E QUIGLEY ROBERTO RAMOS-LOPEZ
JOHN M CHAVARRIA JUSTIN R SPISTO JOE N TUCKER BRIAN L WILSON JAMES D ANELLA
RICHARD D ATOR HECTOR L CARABALLO RONALD D CAREY JOHN J CRAVEY MIGUEL R GARCIA
MARIO GONSALEZ JAMES L HOWELL WILLIE JOHNSON BRUCE D KLINGAMAN THOMAS M PEAVY
ELMER R PERRY DENNIS H RILEY JOHNNY F ROACH ROBERT P ROSENBACH DONALD C TAYLOR
WALTER L BECKWITH JR THOMAS C CHANEY MICHAEL J CONNELL OREN L CROOK JAMES W FINZEL
WALTER B FOOTE BERT A HAMILTON JR IRVING G PARK JAMES D PRESSON GEORGE E RAILEY
OSSIE RICHARDSON JERRY W RUSSELL ROBERT D SHIPMAN WILLIE D STEPHENS FRANCIS L WARE III
ROBERT L WEBSTER CHARLES WHATLEY JEFFREY L WILSON KENT M ZERR PAUL V ADAMS
GLENN F AUSTIN JAMES R BOWERS JR THOMAS M BROCKMEIER CLIFFORD M DAVIS JR JAMES L DOWNS
ALBERT H GATES JR DENNIS R HEERMAN PAUL J JAMES JIMMIE J JONES JR KAY K KIMURA
JAY W LADNER STEPHEN L LANE MAX LIEBERMAN GLENN A LOVETT CHARLES D MCCARLEY JR
JAMES R MUTH MARVIN L RINGOEN THEODORE M ROPCHOCK ANDREW W SMITH CHARLES A VAN HORN
THOMAS J WHITLOW JR DONALD R WISHON CHARLES E BROOKS THOMAS L BUDDI MACK C BUSTLE JR
JOSEPH W DEVLIN JAMES E DODD DAVID K ERENSTOFT WIM GOEREE ROCKY Y HIROKAWA
JAMES E HYLMON DOUGLAS R JONES JACOB L KINSER JOHN E LOCKHORST JR JAMES W MCCLURG
JOHN R PENMAN JOSEPH J POSTIGLIONE WILLIAM R ROGNE PATRICK TRACY TERRANCE W ANDERSON
GEORGE A BAMFORD RICHARD A BRUECK PHILLIP L CLARK LARRY W COTTEN JOHN L FORTNER
WILLIAM J FRANCIS ENCARNACION LEDESMA MICHAEL J MCCARRON REX L PARCELS JR HAL E PERRY
KEITH H REITZ EDWARD ROBINSON LEONARD J SCHOEPPNER RICHARD L STILL LOTHAR G TERLA
DONALD R WEBB JOHN P WONER WILLIAM R ALAMED JR THEODORE L CADENHEAD RICHARD J COWELL
KENNETH W COWSERT THOMAS W DEAN DONALD R DONALDSON LARRY W DUKE PHILLIP A ELLIOTT
BILLY J GREAVU JOHN P HENRY CHARLES D HICKS JR DONALD W HOLMAN LEONARD KELLER
STUART B LAMKIN WILLIAM LORIMER IV ROBERT D MCFALL FLOYD MOYE STEVEN L PETERS
WILLIAM PISHNER JR BYRON M RICHARD PAUL A RICHARDS LESTER RILEY JR DOMINIC N SCATUORCHIO JR
DON R RILEY LAWRENCE H SANTINAC GEORGE T SCARBOROUGH THOMAS E SEVERSON DENNIS G SMITH
ROBERT M SMITH CARROLL W SPRAGINS LARRY A STRUSS ALEX V VARDY KENNETH E WEDLOW
STEPHEN A SPIERS MARCELINO VARGAS JR CLIFTON WRIGHT EDWARD F YAPSUGA JR DONNIE S BARTLETT
ARTHUR T BIEMERET HARRY L CEARNEL JOHN M CHAPPEY JAMES W CLEMENT PAUL F KLUG
ROGER L COFFMAN WILLIAM A COMLY MARTIN J DE HIMER SAMUEL A DUMAS DENNIS F GRACE RODNEY G HEISEL
RODNEY G HELSEL GARY R LARGE ROGER D LEGG JOHN W LUTTRELL
DAVID L MATHIS OLAF T OLSEN JOHN R PINER PETER L PROCOPIO
LESTER P SABA JOSE L SANTOS-LOPEZ RANDOLPH SCOTT TERRY M STEINER MICHAEL N SULLIVAN LARRY G WILLIAMSON
GERALD T ATKINSON KENNETH J AUSTON LESTER V CAFIERO JR CHARLES H CUMMINGS TERRY E GUENTHER
LEONARD D CUNNINGHAM JAY T DANDURAND AARON L DARR DUDLEY DAVIS RICHARD H DURANT
ANTHONY M BLAS ALBERT J FARRELL JR JOSE O GARCIA WALTER J HAMPTON DANIEL N HEATER
GARLIN J HENDERSON JR EDWARD W HOLMES WARNER P HUGHIE FRANK JACARUSO OLIN J LEONARD
WILLIAM T MCCORMICK GARY D MCNICOL JACK W MESSER WILLIAM C MOORHOUSE TERRY L MOSER
JOHN P PAPPIN BENITO A PONCE GARY B SCULL GERALD D SHANOR RONNY D SHATTUCK
MITCHELL W STOUT RAYMOND W TEAL VENEY E THOMPSON DAVID R WELCH DANNY R BISHOP
STEPHEN B BOEHNE ROBERT H GOOSEN BENJAMIN F JACKSON LARRY D KNIPPEL FLOYD B LOCKHART JR
DAVID W MARTIN DARWIN S PETERSON JOSEPH M PILOTTE KENNETH W PREVOST DOUGLAS R ROEST
JAMES C ROLAND PAUL W ROSE ALLAN RUTTIMANN EUGENE E SPOONER CHARLES K TRUESDALE
THOMAS URQUHART CHARLES A VARNER SAMUEL G YBARRA ROBERT A BANKS GLENN R BREWSTER

JERRY D COPELAND JESUS H DE LEON DANA A DILLEY CECIL L DOBSON CALVIN W KOLB
TIMOTHY D ECHOLS DONALD B FINCHER BOBBY G HANEY GERALD R HAUSWIRTH
MARTIN J DI MARZIO MICHAEL A MEEHAN THOMAS P O'NEILL LOUIS A PAVLACKY JR JIMMY D ROBERSON
JOHN J ILLINGWORTH PAUL E RUSS LANE W WISEMAN LORING M BAILEY JR RONALD L BIEGERT TIMOTHY Z BORDEN
JOHN J BOYD JR THOMAS R BREWER PAUL D CARSON TOMMY D COOPER ISIDRO GARCIA
WILLIAM R GRAVES JR ALBERT W HASLAM JAMES A HUGHES WILLMER A MATSON PAUL R MORAN

PANEL 12W

HAROLD O RICHARDSON MICHAEL A ROMERO ROBERT D WALDEN FLOYD D WEBBER
WILLIAM T VOHRINGER ROBERT A WOOD ROBERT F YOUNG HARVEY C AIAU DANNY R ALLEN
FLOYD E ANDRUS III GREGORY J ASBECK JOHN M BIRCH WILLIAM P BLETSCH GARY L BURKETT
THURLE E CASE JR GERALD E CORLETT MICHAEL D DAVIS CRUZ F DE LA GUY T DENTON
VINCENT E DUFFY LOUIS C EMERY JOHN C FERN BRADLEY K GAUS MICHAEL L GEISTER
FREDERICK E GILMAN BEN A HUGHES JR JOHN D INGRUM JORGE V MAESE LARRY O MARCHBANK
HENRY C MARTIN JAMES M MASTERS JR GEORGE L MORNINGSTAR WILLIAM A NORWOOD JOHN T NOWAK
AVERY M NYE III JOSEPH E ORLANDI JR WAYNE D PEAGLER ROBIN A PEARCE CHARLES E PRESSLER
RICHARD H PROPST RALPH S PURDUM ROBERT RODRIGUEZ JOSEPH S SAUKAITIS STUART J SCRUGGS JR
WILLIAM J RISSE JOHN S SCHAEFER BARRY M SEARBY ARTHUR D SIMMONS JEAN P SOUZON
JAMES S STANLEY GORDON C STAUFFER FORREST D SUMTER DAVID WALDEN DONALD W WILSON
WILLIAM F BROOKS HUGH CLOWER JR ROBERT W CULVER ROBERT F DICE CARL L GILBERTSON
JAMES M GRIBBIN DOUGLAS G HOWES MICHAEL C JACKSON RAYMOND S KIPP DAVID R KRUEGER
RICHARD A MOHR RAY MURPHY TRUMAN D NORRIS ALEXANDER F POTAS THOMAS L RYAN
ERWIN R SCHMELING LESTER K TAYLOR JR ROBERT J THOMAS RODNEY R UBERMAN CHARLES A WALTERS
MARK A WHIKEHART RICHARD H WILSON LAWRENCE R BARNS GARLAND D BENOIT MCARTHUR JOHNSON
OSCAR A CONNELL NATHANIEL COX JR RALPH R CUMMINGS CAROL D DALE LAWRENCE S MILLER
JOSEPH MONSON JESSE J ONISHEA DONALD J PIERCE JR HUGH J RONNEBERG DOUGLAS L SHORTLEY
WILLIAM J SWARTZ DORRIS W TRAINER RICHARD L WISEMAN DARRELL E AYERS LARRY A BRANAM
JAMES E BROOKS ROBERT A BROWN LARRY E CALDWELL FRANK J CWIOK CLYDE W ENDERLE
CARLOS A ESTRADA JR JAMES W GREENWOOD WILLIE HENDERSON ROBERT A JARDINE JR FOSTER LOCKLEAR
GALEN G LUDWIG PHILLIP W MEADOR DENNIS G PUGH ROBERT E RICHARDSON PRESTON D SHARP
BOBBY T SIEGLER BENNY D SLOAT ATILANO U TOVAR GEORGE W WARD JESSE L WEST
LEONARD M ACKERMAN DALE A BLAKE JAMES E BUTLER CHARLES A CONNELL ROBERT G COZART JR
JAMES L DAVIS HAROLD R HARRIS ARVELL B HOLSTON PHILIP G KNIEPER JR JAMES P KURTH
RONALD F LEONARD RUDOLPH D LOVATO DENNIS L MORRILL JAMES E SCHUNEMANN WILLIE T WALKER JR
MICHAEL J MCGUIRE GARY R STACEY ROBERT N THOMPSON TINSLEY J WELLS JR RICHARD J WIDMER
LOUIS J BARBARIA GARY J BARNETT JOHN C BLAKE ROBERT E CASTLE JOHN R CHAPMAN
RONALD L CREAGER RICHARD L EHNES STEPHEN A GOLSH DAVID GONZALES CLIFFORD N GREEN
JOHN T GUTEKUNST EDWARD M HUDGENS ROBERT M KELLY JOHN P MALLOY THOMAS W UNDERWOOD
JOSEPH B MUELLER LARRY PARKER CHARLES A RAULSTON DONALD B REES ROBERT S RICHMOND
FREDDIE D MIZE ANDRES SANTIAGO-MARTINE BUFORD E SUMNER JOHN P WANTO RONALD W WILLIAM
RICHARD P COX THOMAS A DELANEY DONALD T GRAHAM NOEL A HARRIS JR MICHAEL J HATFIELD
KERMIT W HOLLAND JR EHRHARD H POHL JOHN W SAMS JR FRANK H ADAMS RONNIE E ASH
PERCY C GAGNON RICHARD D HULSE JAMES M KLEIN ROBERT D MORRIS GORDON L ZIMMERLE
RAYMOND E OTT SCOTT K PARDEE WILLIAM I PIRKLE JOHN S RICK TOMMY H SWAIN HOWARD G BENFORD
RONALD W HURT WILLIAM E TAYLOR RUDY M BECERRA JOHN A BORONSKI LARRY M COMIS
JAMES E CRAWFORD FRANK W DAWSON CARRIS M FRANCIS BERMAN GANOE JR GUADALUPE GONZALEZ
WILLIAM F HANNIGAN GARY A HARNED JOHN C HOSKEN LARRY L JORDAN DONALD W MCKEE
MICHAEL D ODONNELL JERRY L POOL KENNETH R SMITH ARCHIE L WHALER RONALD L WHITE
KENNETH E WHITMER WALTER E ANDREWS JR ERNEST J BROWN ROBERT L CHAVEZ FLOYD B COATES
TOBY R GRITZ HAROLD J HARTWELL DENNIS L HAYES KENNETH H HEITMANN JOSEPH B HORSMAN
HARVEY L JAY MICHAEL E JUSTUS ROGER A LAKIN SANFORD G PACK THOMAS PADILLA
MALCOLM J PICKETT FRANK E SACHARANSKI WILLIAM H THOMAS JR JOSEPH WAKEFIELD JR HENRY L ALLEN
WILLIAM L ANDREWS RAYMOND H CRULL JOHN P DIDIER JR RICHARD G ELZINGA JOE A ESCANDON
ROBERT FOREMAN JR JAMES A GRIFASI ANGELO R MORALES DON M O'SHELL MARVIN SHELL
DAVID T SOLIS JOHN A STEEL NORMAN H STRENGTH JOHN R WYNNE RAYMOND AGUIRRE
JOSEPH BENOSKI JR GARY L EDWARDS ARNOLD G GARZA BILLY J HARTSFIELD JOHN L HOUSE
MATEO SABOG NORMAN E LITTLE CECIL E MCCLAIN JAMES R MITCHELL GARY D POLK RALPH R QUICK JR
LESLIE E REMBERT RICHARD M ROVINSKY ROBERT T SCISLO BAXTER WARREN WOODROW ALEXANDER
RICHARD A BROYLES DARRELL A CAMERON DONALD W COOK PAUL J FRANCIS KENNETH J GARSKI
CHARLES G HEWITT FRED G KOVARIK THOMAS E LA COSTE EARL L POOLE SIDNEY E ROHLER
DENNIS M SCHULTZ DARRELL SMITH JOSEPH P SOULE BOBBY G SWANSON JR DANIEL R TROYE
JAMES T WATSON THOMAS J WILLIAMS BILL R ACKERMAN DWIGHT I ADE BARTOLO A BARELA JR
MICHAEL A BLONDIN GEORGE R CUTHBERT JAMES M FURGERSON GORDON M GUNHUS MURL A MOYERS
WILLIAM R HAINLEY JOSEPH L HART PAUL E HARVEY JIMMY I HICKS JAMES R HOLMES
WILLIAM A BROWN STARET J INGLESTON RAYMOND S INSLEE DAVID M KING DONN M LORBER
GILBERT C PEIXOTO MICHAEL J PYNNONEN MICHAEL J RANDOLPH WARNER STARKS PAUL R STEPP JR
MICHAEL J WAINWRIGHT GEORGE M ANAYA DAVID W BARRUS BRUCE W BRACE FLOYD S FRANKLIN
CLIFFORD E HALEY JAMES R HAWK GLEASON C HELTON RUSSELL C HIBLER NICHOLAS M MOLNAR
JAMES JACOBS JOHN A KIMZEY JACKIE L LUNDELL EZEKIAL MARTINEZ HARRY E BAKER JR
PAUL T BURRIER WILLARD C DEBOLT ROBERT H FENNELL DAVID H HARLOW HARRY E HAYES
DANIEL K KOHL RAYMOND C MEEKINS KIMBALL H SHELDON THOMAS J SHRINER JACK R SMITH
JOHN S SPOHN NEWTON L TAPP ROBERT E WILLS BOBBY L BARKER BENJAMIN V CHILDRESS JR
DONALD H BLOOMER WILLIAM R BOND THOMAS R BOWEN CLEAVELAND F BRIDGMAN JAMES C CARLIN
CARL E BARNETT BILLY P CARLISLE RICHARD M DELL'ARENA CARTER W DOWD DAVID G DRAGOSAVAC
OTTO J DRAKEN LEROY J FASCHING CRAIG P FIELDING ROBERT G FLOYD DANIEL L FLYNN JAMES J BYSZEK
LARRY GILBERT JOE W GREEN SYRIAC HEBERT JR DON R HEIMARK ROBERT A HILL ROCCO J DE MECURIO
KENNETH R HODGE DENNIS V JOHNSON WILLIAM P KASTENDIECK JAY W KING MICHAEL R PATTERSON
RUSSELL T LA FAVE ROBERT H LANE JR DAVID H LASSEN ROBERT M LIDDELL CLARENCE LOGAN
NATHAN J MANN EZRA B MARTER JAMES C MILLER ELDON W MOORE LARRY E MULLINS
ROGER J MCINERNY JR JAMES M MCMILLAN JR THOMAS J MURPHY LEN E NIXON GEORGE F PATTERSON
FLOYD D KETELS SIDNEY E PLATTENBURGER GERALD R POLLARD JR GERALD W PURDON MELVIN D QUINN
JOSE L QUINONES DONALD R RAGSDALE TERRY W RATCLIFF BILLY J SCHAFFER TERRY L SCHELL
KLAUS D SCHLIEBEN DAVID J SCHMIDT VINTURE SCIARRETTI JOHN L SMITH PHILIP J STEMPER
WILLIAM F STEPHENS JR BRENT A STREET LAWRENCE E SUTTON MILTON T SWAIN GEORGE M UNDERDOWN
BLYTHE N VAN DE VENTER WILLIAM P WALL III CASEY O WALLER DAVID WELCH CLIFTON P WHEELHOUSE JR
STEVEN J WILLIAMS THOMAS E WILSON JOHN E YOUNG DONALD G ARMSTRONG MICHAEL E BORGES
JAMES E BYRD DONALD E CHAMBERS DALE E CHRISTENSEN JOHN H DILMORE RICHARD ELLIOTT
WILLIAM M FINK ALVIN W FLOYD CARL L FRUECHTENICHT SPENCER A GOETHE LARRY GRAVES
MICKEY E GRIFFITH DALE A GRONSKY KENNETH R HAWLEY MELVYN H KALILI STEPHEN M KENOFFEL
DAVID M KESTERSON ROBERT P KETTERING ORVILLE E KITCHEN JR RONALD V KOLB HAROLD J MCDONALD
JOHN J LYONS FREDERICK MAREZ DANIEL L MYERS DENNIS N PIPKIN JOHN E RARRICK
WILLIE J RIDGEWAY EVERETT E RINES SEVERIANO RIOS HENRY N ROCKOWER WILLIAM T SMITH
CHARLES E SUPRENANT JR JAMES A SWARTZ JR MICHAEL F THOMAS STEVE W TRAIN WILLIAM L VASPORY
ROBERT J WROBEL DENNIS L YOUNG ROBERT S ALEXANDER EDWARD J BAKER DWIGHT H BALL
CARL S BERGER JR MANCE BROWN WILLARD L CLEMONS EVERETTE E COFER RAINER L COLE
GEORGE R CRABTREE JAMES A DE CARLO SAMUEL FIELDS JR NICHOLAS L GARDELIS GERALD L GRIFFIN JR
CARL J HELRING JOSEPH D JOHNS JAMES F LEE WILLIAM A MILLER RONALD N PARSONS
ARNOLD T RIDER THOMAS J SILVA WILLIAM T SMITH RICHARD L WILKERSON JOHN W WILSON
EVERETT L ANKROM MANNIE A BARBER STEPHEN L BUSBY CLYDE L COFFMAN FREDERICK W DAUTEN JR
CLARE A BARRETT JACK W CONNER MARCUS R DAVIS JOHN E DUFFY THOMAS E FRASER
JAMES A GRAY RUSSELL L KLEIN LEONARD E NYBERG SAMUEL L ROBERSON DAVID P ROY
CECIL R SMITH JR WILLIAM M WALMSLEY GARY W WEEKLEY DANIEL K WELIN JEFFREY J YOUNG
KENNETH N BAILEY JR LAWRENCE C BIGELOW DAVID R BORZYCH PAUL M CAHILL CLARENCE J CARSON JR
BRIAN L BUKER CHARLES M COBB CURTIS H CROPPER ELIGAH L DAVIS LANCE A DE ROO
EUGENE P GEE RAYMOND C GRAVER JR RAYMOND M GREENE OLAN J HOWE CALVIN J LAYTON
ROBERT LOCKET JR WILLIAM L LOWERY CLARENCE J NOVAK JOHN W ROHR ANDREW M SIMKO
PAUL E THOMAS STEVEN M TORREY WINSTON C WALKER STEPHEN J ALSUP FRANCISCO J BORREGO-RUIZ
ANDREW T BRASSFIELD LAWRENCE P CHRISTMAN KENNETH J COTTER GORDON M GAYLORD ISMAEL SOTO
THERON C FEHRENBACH II CARL B GOODSON JULIUS P JAEGER MICHAEL L KLINGNER STEVE L STEWARD
GREGORY W STODDART HENRY K WEITZ DONALD P WOODFIN PAUL C BOVAN LARRY P DANIELS
ROBERT M ROBERTSON DALE A ERDMAN PAUL J FRINK JOHN E HILL HARRY D JOJOLA WILLIAM W KLEFFMAN
JOE B GIBSON ORLAND T LLOYD DOUGLAS G MACNEIL GLENN W MILLER MICHAEL PAULSEN
WILLIAM B TURNER CLAYTON D WHITCHER BRIAN J WILLIAMS DENIS J ZIMPRICH PAUL W ANTHONY
TROY H BATTERTON MYRON W BERG LARRY L BROWN RICHARD T CALDERON PETER K CHRISTIAN
LARRY W DOUGLAS CHARLES A FRALEY JEFFREY A FREEMAN JAMES M MCDONALD ROB G MCSORLEY
ARTANZIE NETHERLY LEONARD A NITZSCHE LYNN A OSBORN RANDALL L PELL THOMAS A SCARBORO
WILLIAM A SHARPE JR DONALD B SMITH THOMAS C SMITH JR LAWRENCE G THODE ROBERT J THOMPSON
CRAIG A VAN AKIN MICHAEL J YEAGER JAMES E ABBOTT NICK A AGUILAR JR CHARLES D ANNIS
ROBERT D BESCH EDWARD H BEYER GARY L BROWN BRIAN L BUSHNELL ANDREW A HORCHAR JR
HERMAN A CLAY JR JAMES COONEY DAVID R EASLEY DAVID P EVANS PHILIP A HARRIS THOMAS L GATES
JOHN A AVERA CHRISTOPHER JACOBS RALPH M JENERSON RICHARD J KAUFFMAN JOHN A KITRILAKIS
LARRY C KNIGHT PAUL A LECRONE JAMES D MACE JOHN B MULLIS LEROY NELSON
JAMES J PASTORE JR CHARLES B PFAFFMANN WILLIE R RASCOE JR CHARLES G SELMAN WILLIAM H SMITH
DONALD C TANNENBAUM RAYMOND L WILLIAMS JACK L WRIGHT JIMMY CARRILLO DANNY L DAWSON
MICHAEL L FARLEY FRANCIS X GAWORSKI JACK A HAWLEY JAMES T HOWARD DAVID C KAYS
PHILLIP M LONG THOMAS M LOWE DOUGLAS C MABEE DWIGHT A MASLINSKI JOSEPH S NEMETH
FRANCIS J O'REILLY DONALD R PERKINS JR ALFRED N POTTER CHARLES A PURSELL RICHARD L WHITEMAN
FRANK D RYAN JR DONALD W SISTRUNK GALE STOPHER JR KEVIN A STOUT EDWARD W STRAIN
JOHN C ROSE ROY WALKER THOMAS L WATERMAN HOWELL F BLAKEY EMILIO A DE LAGARZA JR
WAYNE A BLOMSTROM JOHN C CHAVES MICHAEL D CLICKNER HARLAN E DANIELS JIMMY R HIGDON
CRAIG N BARRY DANIEL C CASE ALONZO GARRETT VALENTINE B GOMEZ JR GERALD M HELLMANN JR
RICHARD L HIGGINBOTHAM EDWARD E HOWARD GARY D JEFFERSON RONNIE L JOHNSON JAN H NELSON
LEO MCEACHERN PATRICK M NEVILLE BRADFORD G RACEY DANNY G RUYBAL ROSENDO F SILBAS

PANEL 12W (*Continued*)

CLIFFORD L TARBELL ROBERT L WADE GARRY W WARD GEORGE H ADAMS BRUCE E ARMSTRONG
JAMES M ATCHISON TIMOTHY R FAUST DONALD R HOFFEDITZ SHERMAN D LANNES JR ROBERT F MERRILL
THOMAS J PRICE HENRY P RATHMELL DANIEL P RICHARDS GUS B ROBINSON CHARLES N RUFFIN
RAFAEL S SANTOS JAMES C SHUKAS FRANKLIN D SUMMERS CHARLES R TOWNSEND JAMES F AUSTIN
WILLIAM M CALDWELL TROY V CANADY JAMES J COOK STANLEY W CRAWFORD CLIFFORD J EARNHARDT
RALPH C EMBREY II LARRY E FRANCIS CARLOS H GARCIA JUAN GARCIA-GARAY BENNY D GREENE
RICHARD F HEATH JOSE HERNANDEZ JR JAMES A HULSEY WLADISLAW KAUS THOMAS J LAUGHLIN

PANEL 11W

LEWIS C OUELLETTE ROBERT L PENDERGAST ROY L PHIPPS JAMES M REINHARDT
GEORGE B ROBINSON ROBERT J SHURR LESLIE J WATSON CARL L BRUTON HENRY L BURTON
HAROLD V CUMMINGS JR ALAN D HELMICK JERRY W LOFTN RONALD I MCDONALD PAUL F SAYERS
RONALD D SCHULZ WALTER L TAYLOR JR JOHN L THOMPSON DONALD W TINNEY JR WALTER C BARTLEY JR
WILLIAM R ALFREDSON SANDRO N BARONE ALBERT L BARTHELME JR HERNDON A BIVENS JAY O CLARKSON
ANTHONY E CURRIE DEAN B DAFLER JOSEPH DI GREGORIO WILLIAM R DI SANTIS ALLEN M GARRETT
MICHAEL C GOMES MICHAEL W HAYNES JAMES D HOUSLEY DENNIS E JACKOWSKI MICHAEL V KUROPAS
JOHN T LANKASTER JR JAMES W LINDEMANN CHARLES L MERRILL JR ROSENDO MONTANA ROBERT J MUSSIN
JIMMY H MCCLUNG DENNIS W NEAL JOHN H POHLMAN JOSE L RIVAS TRAVIS H SCOTT JR
LARRY R SLAGLE BRUCE A SMOKE CHARLES E STEFFLER GENE S SWAGER JAMES A TYNER
RANDALL R SIMMONS CLARENCE W TEMPLETON RICK A WILCOX LOUIS H WILSON THURMAN W WOLFE
PERRY L WOOSLEY BOBBY A YOUNG RICHARD L AYERS ROY L BERGERON JOSHUA COLEMAN
JEFFREY L DAVIS JOHN F DOWNING JAMES K FLANNERY DENNIS R HEINZ EARL HENDERSON
EDWARD L HUBLER JR GARY C JOHNSTON PAUL S MANDRACCHIA CLEVE D MILLER ROBERT E RAUSCH
RALPH E REED FRANK L RIDEN EDWARD D SOSSAMON JOHN D THOMAS JOHNNY B WHITE
HOWARD R ANDREWS JR RAFAEL COLON-SANTOS AVIN E CROSS DEAN A HARIG WILLIAM K HUNTER
FRANK M KITCHENS JR HOWARD D LANDRY MARK A LILIENTHAL FREDERICK C MARSH DANIEL P OUELLETTE
NORMAN D PEERY JERRY L PRENTNER LOEL F REXROAD LAWRENCE D RICHMOND HARVEY D ROGERS JR
FREDERICK M SIMEONOFF ROBERT W SMITH JACK D TUGGLE JR BARCLAY L VOLK MICHAEL J WEIK
LEONARD W BAUER JEROME E BOWERS JR KENNETH L CROW ROBERT L DANGBERG TIMOTHY E SULLIVAN
JAMES F DEEBLE WILLIAM A EATON ROY W GARDINER WILLIAM H HAAKINSON III WILLIAM S MONAHAN III
MARTIN C CARR RONALD E HODGE DANIEL F KASZUBOWSKI ANTHONY S LUGO LEROY MITCHELL
MICHAEL J VAGNONE WILLIAM R WALBRIDGE ROBERT A WALL JOSEPH A BOBANICH JR CHARLES A BUSINDA
WILLIAM H PEASE DEAN L FREY BILLY W GLASS LAWRENCE L HENSEY JR JAMES D JARRETT JEFFREY J JOSEPH
RICHARD L MCMINN GLENN T RIDLEY JERRY L RISINGER JON C SAPP JEFFREY P SEARLES
LEE A STEDMAN FREDDIE THOMPSON JR ROBERT C TRIGG CLARENCE E UMSTOT STANLEY WILENSKI JR
GERALD T BUTLER DAVID J FALK GERALD D GRAY GERALD L HARTZEL MARLIN J JOHNSON
JAMES E LOCKETT KENT W LONGMIRE DOUGLAS F MAHAN DAREK N RICHARDSON STEVEN P STEELE
RICHARD H WARD ROBERT J ZONNE JR BILLY W ADDIS CARL T BAUER DENNIS M BOYER
RALPH N BRIGHT ROBERT A BURNS SCOTT R COPLIN JERRY M CORP WILLIAM R EMMANS
MARK FARREN DANNY W JOHNSON ANTHONY W MANSTIS VAL G MEYER RANDE L NICHOLS
ERIC G OHM GEORGE E POWELL WILLIAM F RICHARDSON GARY A SCHOBORG RONALD B STILLIONS
KERRY L VANCE EUGENE L WHEELER BRUCE L WOLD DOUGLAS F WORTMAN HERMAN D YOUNG
THOMAS Y ADACHI KENNETH E AZNOE WILLIAM L BROOKS MICHAEL R CONNER CHARLIE B DAVIS JR
DONALD G FISHER JOHN B GOLZ ELY GRANTHAM JR SEVIER GRAY JR STEPHEN W HARRIS
RONNIE L HENSLEY ROBERT N IRELAND WYMAN T JOHNSON JOHN S KEENAN ALAN J KULTGEN ROBERT J QUINN
DONALD C LAMB JR DONALD M LINT KEITH A LOCHNER DENNIS L LONGDAIL RAY T MARTIN
JAMES M MCDONOUGH THOMAS A MCKINNEY THOMAS MILLSAP III CHARLES S ROWLEY DON R SCOTT
RICHARD M SPEER JOHN C TOWLE JAMES N VARANSKY GEORGE M WALL HAROLD E BASEHORE JR
CHARLES COOK MICHAEL S CORREA DENNIS K EADS ROBERT A GOMEZ HARRY C GREER
KENNETH R JONES GEORGE T KELLY III DANNY L LITTLE ALBIN E LUCKI LARRON D MURPHY
BENJAMIN A NICKS III JOSEPH D POGUE JOHN W SNELSON LORAN E SWEAT JR THOMAS D WORREL
ERIC L TULLER ALLEN T WHITE GARRY L WORLEY JAMES R CASE TIMOTHY G FRANK DOUGLAS W MURPHEY
STEVEN M CRONRATH JAMES E CROSS MYRON DIDURYK ERNEST E ENGLISH JAMES R FOWLER
DONALD E CARPENTER OSCAR T FRANCIS WILLIAM D GALLAWAY RICHARD G GARDNER MICHAEL P GINN
PAUL J GUELIG GERALD W HAY JEFFREY K HOAGLAND FRED D LARSON RICHARD A MOIREN
WILLIAM P MCCONNAGHY JOHN L PENA ALBERT C POWELL GOMER D REESE III JOSEPH R SMOYER
NORMAN D ADKINS RODNEY K ARNOLD MICHAEL G BAZEL JAMES H BROOKS JR RONALD G CLINE
JAMES T CONWAY WILLIAM F DACUS JEFFREY B DODGE DAVID J ELLEFSON DOUGLAS P MCCORKLE JR
PAUL W HANDERHAN RALPH O HILL ROBERT R LEWIS JOHN C LUNDIN BOYD MAGEE
CHARLES K HACKETT JR JOHN R MATTOX MICHAEL J MAYBERRY WILLIAM R MCKIBBEN WILLIAM W NOETZEL
JOSEPH L NUNN ROBERT L PIERCE JOHN R POWERS MASON E RAGLAND SCOTTY H RHEA
ARMAND E RISTINEN BILLY J SEBASTIAN GUS SMITH JR RONALD H ALLBRIGHT SAMUEL E ASHER
DONNIE R BOGGS PETER K BOYEV TONY CLOUGH RANDALL L CRABTREE ERNEST L THORSON
DARRELD E FISHER DAVID J GEISER CHARLES R KING EUDELL L KOTROUS RONALD E NEWMAN
BRUCE H BARDON GERARD F O'CONNOR ROBERT L ROGERS MANUEL R TORRES JOSE G VAZQUEZ
MICHAEL D BROWN GERALD W BYRNS JR ZETTIE J DULIN CARL N FISHER JR RICHARD M FORTE
ROBERT W GARDNER ROY V GRAY HAROLD G GRISSOM DELBERT E HALL JOHN R HILL
ROBERT T KOEHLER LARRY J LONCON RANDALL W LOVE GERALD E MCKAY STANLEY J MILLER JR
JAMES H PALMER MICHAEL R PICKLES JOSEPH T ROBERSON JAIME RODRIGUEZ-RIVERA CARL D RUENGER
JAMES A RUSS GARY A SANCEVERINO BLAINE P SMILIE JAMES T SWIFT JR GEORGE W TOM
ROBERT D WALSH JOHN L WARD ROBERT E WILLIAMS MEREDITH G ANDERSON STEVEN R SANDLIN
KEITH W AU ROBERT E BACKMAN DAVID C BUGMAN CLINTON A COOK ROBERT F FAGE JR
JOSEPH C JESZECK CHARLES M KNOWLES THOMAS L LUBBERS GILBERTO PADILLA VERNON R RILEY
PAUL E ANGERT FERNANDO RIOS-MALDONADO HUGHIE F SNIDER RAYMOND P SUSI JOHN D VANDIVIER
MICHAEL J VANGELISTI WILLIE AUSTIN JR EDGAR D BERNER EDWARD J BISHOP JR ROBERT S BOGGS
PAUL D BRANNON WENDELL L BROWN DAVID M BURKE JR WILLARD S CANNON III LOUIS A FAVUZZA
RONALD L HAZEN DENNIS W HUNTER CHARLES E JOHNSON JEFFREY J KLAVES PAUL J KOSANKE
JAMES W MCGUIRE TED R MILLER JOSE H ORTIZ CARL E PATTEN WILLIAM J SATTLER III
JOHN C SEEL CLINT J SIMS LORA W SNYDER ROY H SNYDER WILLIAM J STIEVE JOSEPH S HENRIQUEZ
ANCEL J TERRY LINWOOD A WALKER WILSON L WEBB JR FREDERICK E WORTMANN BILLY R BAKER
VERNEL COLLINS RICHARD H DAVIS LUTHER J DOSS JR ROBERT F ELSTON JACK C EVERTS
DONALD BARRETT DANIEL FLORES JAMES R GILREATH JOHN A HERNANDEZ DONNIE E HORTON
JOHN R HUNTER LARRY N JONES LARRY K KAISER KEVIN R KELEHER GLEN L KNOBLOCK
DONALD R LEDLIE DONALD R MARLOW ROBERT E MASSETH WILLIAM A MEISTER LUIS A SANTELLANO
JON L PADGETT ROBERT D PALMORE LARRY W RABREN LONNIE B ROBERTS JOHN L SENSING
ROBERT J SHANNON CHARLES L SMALLING JOHN R SMITH DAVID W STATON LEON A TETKOSKI
FRANK M VALENTINE JAMES C ADAMS KEITH S ARNESON JOHN H BARRETT JAMES BUSH
ROBERT L COLLETT JR PAUL M DAILEY ROBERT DOERING LARRY R HENSHAW JIMMY A HILL
MARTIN S HUSKA EDWARD JACKSON JR LOWELL T JARBOE THOMAS J KAUFMAN CHARLES H KEFER JR
SAMUEL S LANCE CHARLES D LOWNES CALVIN E NOLT JACK A NOON PAUL F ROGALSKE
WILLIAM S SIGMON JR JOSEPH S TATUM CARL D WOOTTEN ROBERT ALMASY DAVID W BARNETT
JOHN P BECKER RICHARD D BREWER FRANK R CORONA HAROLD G CRAFT DAVID W DASH
WILLIAM W DAVIS EDDIE R EATMON CURTIS GAITHER STEVEN J GREENLEE VASSAR W HURT III
KENNETH L DEFENBAUGH RODNEY L GRIFFIN EDWARD C HAGGERTY LARRY HERRERA DANIEL C JOHNSON
GRADY R LESTER JR LANE F LEVI LEO J LUDVIGSEN JR ROBERT R NEEL DONALD L PARKER
MILTON PEREZ-RIVERA JERRY N PHILLIPS BUNYAN D PRICE JR FRANK L RICE JR DALE W RICHARDSON
JOHN C SHERMAN GEORGE D SLYE DAVID W SMITH RODNEY H STONE ANDREW J TAYLOR
RAYMOND N TAYLOR MICHAEL B VARNADO DONALD L VOORHEES ROBERT M YOUNG WILLIE BEDFORD
CARL R CHURCHILL LAWRENCE Y CONAWAY ROGER G CRAIG OSCAR A DAY FRED DENKINS JR
GLENN C DUNCAN RAY F EVANS ROBERT B HANEY JR JOSEPH J HARPER THOMAS G HESS
JOHN L KOTORA ARTHUR E LA CHANCE ERNEST R LASHER JR PERRY A LE CLERC RANDALL S PHILLIPS
THOMAS T SMITH EDWARD W STONE KENNETH B THOMAS JAMES M TREESH GLEN R WITYCYAK
THOMAS O AHLBERG JAMES G ANDERSON DEAN L BONNEAU RONALD CHISOLM JAMES E RIMMER
STEPHEN B EMERY LEON GARNETT JR JAMES F HOPKINS GEORGE E HUSSEY TOMMY L KEARSLEY
DEAN L AITKEN FLOYD W LAMB JR ARMANDO C LUNA LARRY F MATTINGLY RICHARD W PAQUETTE
THEODORE I ROBERTS ALBERT C SMITH RODNEY A TAYLOR EDDIE G TERRELL ROBERT V THOMPSON
WAYNE L TORSIELLO MICHAEL A VANCOSKY LARRY L WATKINS DOUGLAS N WINFREY CHARLES E AARON
PHILLIP C ADAMS HORACE ANDREWS LARRY M BEAUDETTE NICHOLAS J BRAICO EVERETT L BROCKS
GARY W BROWN LARRY D BUFFINGTON FRANCISCO T CARVAJAL ROBERT R DOWDS
CHARLES G DOUGAN JOHN R FEESER STEPHEN P FINKE CRAIG J FOX RAMON L GRAYSON DAVID C GUNDERSON
ROBERT E HERNDON ROGER E HOLLER JAMES M KELLER GERALD A KULM JACK D LEOPARD
ANDREW Z LISOWSKI WILLIAM E MALCOLM JR PETER J MARTINEZ JR GEORGE A MASON RICHARD S MODEN
TSCHANN S MASHBURN THOMAS M MCDONALD GREEN E MILLER JR RODNEY K MILLS CHRIS A MITCHELL JR
IVORY L MCKINNEY VERNON L OKLAND DUANE A PETERSON JAMES L PULLAM ROBERT I RABB
WILLIAM H SHALLER BOYD W SMITH JAMES D SMITH DENNIS A SPRENKLE DERRICK SUDLER
ROSCOE SYBERT JIMMY L THOMPSON RICHARD L VAN DE WARKER STEVEN E WASSON JOHN A WHITE
ROBERT W WORTHINGTON WILLIAM G YOUNG MICHAEL L ANTLE ROGER B BAXTER GEORGE W BENNETT JR
MELVIN BOWMAN MICHAEL F BROWN JAY M BYERLY DENNIS P CALLAGHAN DIONISIO G CARRIZALES
GREGORY A CHAVEZ THOMAS L CRAVENS DOUGLAS W DAY ROBERT A DENTON JAY T DILLER
JON H DOOLITTLE SYLVESTER ELLIS KENNETH L FOUTZ LAWRENCE L GORDON JOHN E GRANATH JR
BRUCE E HAHN PHILLIP R HARDIN RICHARD A HAWLEY JR FRANK S HERNANDEZ LARRY G KIER
TOMMY I HINDMAN JAMES D HOWE LEROY HUNTER JAMES D JENNINGS MICHAEL A JOHNSON
ALBERT L HARRISON JESSE G JUAREZ ALLEN G KINNE ROBERT L KIRK AUGUSTO C PADUA-LEDESMA
FRANK F LEWIS RAYMOND L LONG JR GARY L MCKIDDY WILLIAM J MITTON DAVID E OGDEN
GARY R KIESELBURG MICKEY D PEARSON CHARLES W PHILLIPS JR ROBERT L PHILLIPS CLIFFORD E POE JR
ROY C RANSOM DICKIE W REAGAN MITCHELL ROBINSON GARY F SNYDER REFUGIO T TERAN
RONALD D VAN BEUKERING EDWARD VESER PHILLIP R WARFIELD WILLIAM C WEISS JR TOMMY L WHIDDON
JOHN G WIDEN JOHN J WILLEY BILLY J WILLIAMS DAVID YELDELL FREDERICK P ZIEGENFELDER
WILLIE D ARMS PAUL A BAPTISTA RICHARD J BARBER EUGENIO BARBOSA-OYOLA TERRY D BAXTER
WAYNE R BEBO ROBERT F BERGER JOHN A CAPASSO ROBERT L COLEMAN JAMES M COMBS
PETER A COOK JOHN E DAYTON RAYMOND W DEGE III FRANCISCO P DELGADO RONALD E DILLS
RONALD E FITZGERALD LAWRENCE E FLETCHER JOSE A GONZALEZ TIMOTHY L GREEN JACK S GROUF
THOMAS E HASLET LAWRENCE J HERMAN III WILLIAM E HOWELL LLOYD W JACKSON ARTHUR N KANGAS
KENNETH B KENDALL RICHARD S KENDRICK DENNIS D KIGER JOHN R KNAUS ROBERT R LOHENRY
NEAL A LORD JR GERALD V LUNDY JOHN J MCCARTHY DAVID C MCCRANIE MICHAEL J ORWIG
RAYMOND D MARECK WILLIAM A PEYTON ROBERT C PHLEGER JOSEPH PIPPENBACH CHARLES D PLUMB JR
GARY P RADER JOSEPH V REDMOND ROBERT P SHEPPARD LENNY M TIPPETS WILLIAM T WADDELL
JOHN L WILSON BERNARD H BAX CHARLES D BETHEA DAVID A BUTCHER HAROLD CARSTARPHEN JR
SHELBY M CARTER CHARLES A DAVIDSON JAMES M DAVIS CARL D DIXON HARRY G FLIEGER
LARRY A FOSTER GARY D FRASHER CHARLES J HEIN JR PATRICK E HENNEN DAVID J HUBERTY
CLIFFORD E JESSE MIGUEL KEITH MONROE D KING MICHAEL J LALLY JOHN D LONSDALE

PANEL 10W

RICHARD A MATHEIS ROBERT E MINCEY ALLAN J MOORE LARRY G MORGAN
MICHAEL L MCPHERSON PETER F NOLAN ROCKY P O'HAM MERLIN G ORR ELIAS B PEALER JR
JOHNNIE PICKENS JR PHILLIP J SMITH WAYNE K SMITH THOMAS G STANDLEY MICHAEL S TUFF
FRANKIE C VASSAUR HARRY L BUCHER BILL D CARPENTER CHRISTOPHER J CHILDS III DAVID J CORPUS
RHONALD L DURHAM THOMAS J FOX JR JOHNNY L FULTON STEPHEN H HAIGHT CHESTER G HALL
TERRY L HENRY WILEY D HOOKS COLIN P HURD DOUGLAS J ITRI MICHAEL G JENSON
WILLIAM O LASSITER III RONALD S LOWE NELSON C LUTHER JERRY R MARCO JOHN A MARR
JOHN D MCCLUSKEY EDDIE L NAILS JR RAYMOND L PARADIS KRIS M PERDOMO MICHAEL M USSERY
RAYMOND M MORRIS ROY L RICHARDSON CHARLES D SLAYTON OSCAR A SOLIS DAN R STEWART
RICHARD A WELLS CHARLES R WEST LARRY C YOUNG JAMES A BLACKMON LELAND M CHESTNUT
CHARLES A COVEY LAWRENCE N DE BOER JAMES E DEBREW TIMOTHY C DRAKE ALFRED J GAIDIS
WILLIAM J GOLDEN FREDERICK W HARMS JR RONALD W HOLT TERRY L KETTER JOHN A LARGENT
ROBERT B LUTHER CLIFFORD F MACOMBER JR JOHN S MELIUS THOMAS B MERRIMAN RALPH O MURPHY III
GERALD J LYNCH BRIAN E MCCARTHY JOHN W MERSCHMAN EDDIE MOLINO JR ERNEST L MOORE
ANDREW C MCCARTNEY ESTILL R MCINTOSH LESLIE H SABO JR PHILLIP N SCHMITZ RONALD O SMILEY
ALLAN L SMITH DONALD W SMITH GARY A TURNBULL LESLIE J WILBANKS GARY P BAKER
STEVEN W BOEGLI JAMES W CHARLESWORTH JR RAYMOND D ELLIS ROBERT C GEIGER WILLARD D O'BRIEN
GEORGE E FOGLEMAN BRYAN T KNIGHT DAVID M KOZAK ALBERT MILBURN DAVID MUNOZ
JOSEPH W CUNNINGHAM JR ROBERT L O'CONNOR JAMES R OLSON JERRY W PYLE SCOTT E SUTHERLAND
DANNY J TAULBEE DANIEL J VAUGHAN JOHN A VERNO MORGAN W WEED ROY L WILSON
DANIEL J YADOCK CARROLL E ADAMS JR GLENN A ADAMS JAMES V BALLAY KENNETH D BENNETT
PHILIP M BENNETT WILLIAM D BOOTH EDWARD F BRADY III RONALD E CAMPBELL ROBERT CHILDRESS JR
FRED V COLE ARDIE R COPAS JOHN A DILLARD JR THEODORE G DREW RAYMOND R DULAK JR
TROY L FLINT HORACIO A FONSECA-VARGAS KEITH K FRANKLIN DAVID A GALLION ROBERT E GREEN
TERRANCE L HOOD ROBERT J HUDDLESTON ROBERT H JOHNSON GRIFFITH A JONES STEPHEN J KEESLER
CHARLES M KOON ROBERT L LEMONS LEOPOLDO A LOPEZ STAN MENDY RONALD J MILNE
CHARLES D MCMAHAN RAMON MOYA JR BARRY T MULLINEAUX BRIAN S ORR GREG E WEIGHTMAN
ROBERT F PREISS JR JAMES H RAWSON MICHAEL W RAY STEVEN R RENNER KENNETH F ROGERS
STEVEN C SEEMAN MICHAEL P SEGICH THOMAS SHERRY JAMES G SHRADER THOMAS A STEPHENS
DAVID L PALMER ROBERT C THOMPSON STEPHEN L YONTZ JOHN B ABBATEMARCO RONALD M ANTWINE
CHARLES A BAZZINOTTI GARY L COX WILLIAM M COZAD RANDY M DAVIS EDWARD J DELIKAT JR
RICHARD G DESILLIER RAYMOND J DI SANTI DANNIE FITCH ROBERT C HARDWICK WAYNE H HEDEMANN
JOHN L HENDON RICHARD A HENKE ERIC J HUBERTH DAVID E HUBNER RICHARD D HUMPHREY
SIDNEY W JARRELL ERNEST L JOHNS RHEA M KIDD RANDY G KITTLESON PAUL H KRIEGEL
THOMAS W MATTHEWS JR ALLEN A MUNSON DAVID R NASH WALTER M NOVAK WILLIAM J OLSON
RICHARD A PATTERSON PAUL L RAMOS JR CURTIS E RINGHOFER FREDRICK W SHEFFIELD VAN T WRAY
RAYMOND J SOUZA ALAN R TRENT DONALD R WHITE DAVID F WINDER ROBERT T WOOD
GORDON A SHAW BARNARD BACON JAMES R BARTON MARC B BELON CHARLES D BLAIR
WILLIAM J BREWER JR FRANK K BUSH STEPHEN C CHASIN RICHARD S CUNNINGHAM ROBERT K EVEREST III
ALLEN L BONEY JAMES C DAIGLE GARY M DOMINIQUE STEEN B FOSTER LAWRENCE R GEIGER
DAVID R GOLL EDWARD G HUNTLEY RAYMOND H KRUG JR DONALD G KUZILLA THOMAS J LARKIN II
JAMES L LOISEL ROBERT E LOWE JAMES E MIREMONT DEREK W PATRICK THOMAS J PETELA
JAMES PORTWOOD JR SILVESTRE M RIVERA RONALD E SCHMIDT HERMAN SERNA JACK R SMITH
KENT C TAYLOR LEROY WALLACE KENNETH M WALLS JR DOYLE W WEAVER CLEVELAND G WYNDER
DOUGLAS CARROLL THEODORE W HIGH IV LLOYD G HOWIE PETER P KELLOGG STEVEN LE BARS
DAVID E MEADE STEVEN D MERRELL THOMAS M MOREAU EDWARD E NISEWONGER DOYLE G PULSE
ARNOLD L ROBBINS JESSIE F SANDERS KENNETH E SMITH ARLIE SPENCER JR JOHN R STINN
MELVIN R THOMAS GEORGE W BEAL JR LESTER E BUNNER DAVID L CHRISTOPHERSON EDWIN R CONNER
RAYMOND F CONTINO HARRY A COTTERMAN JERRY L COZAD JAMES E CUMMINGS GERALD C MAUNEY
WILLIAM B DOUCET WILLIAM H FILLION NEAL R FRANK CHARLES H HAMILTON NED R HEINTZ
DAVID W HENSEL DOUGLAS E HOBBS WALTER L HUFFMAN DAVID L JONES SIDNEY K KOGER
MICHAEL D DAWSON CLYDE W LAWRENCE JR DAVID B MAGRUDER JOHN R MARIANI WILLIAM D MENSCER
BILLY R MCCULLOUGH EUGENE F MCNALLY CHARLES R MCNULTY JOE E RABER DONALD E RILES
MATEO RUELAS RICHARD R SKEEN SIDNEY M SOLOMON GUY L STOKES JR EMILIO C SUPNET JR
GARY R WHITE AUBREY WILLIAMS SAMMIE E ALEXANDER PHILLIP F ARNOLD WAYNE BENNETT
MICHAEL L BLOOMFIELD PAUL R BROWDER WILLIAM W COLYER MICHAEL H CORWIN JERRY A EATON
RICHARD A HAITHCOX ROGER A HICKOK DAVID F JOHNSON HENRY J KETHE DAVID W SMITH
PAUL J MARCIN ALAN D MARTIN DANIEL H MUNIZ ROY A PETTY JR GEORGE C SCHULTZ JR
NASH FRY FREDERICK D SNYDER MICHAEL A WAINWRIGHT NORMAN P WESTWOOD JR WAYNE G WUTZKE
MARK W BACHER CARL T BARNETT GARY W BRITTON ROBERT K COLE ALBERT B CROUCH
JOHN E DARLING JR LARRY R GARCIA HARVEY G GRAHAM CARLTON C GRAY EDWARD F HABBLETT JR
MICHAEL HEINRICH CARWAIN L HERRINGTON NICHOLAS G SAUNDERS HARRY J STONE ROBERT D UNRUE
JAMES J WILKINSON JR WILLIAM C AIRLIE GARY J ANDERSON CHESTER L BALLEW EUGENE BROWN
ROBERT W COONS LEWIS E COX FLOYD E FULLER JR KENNETH W GONDER RICHARD L HERRINGTON JR
THOMAS W JOHNSON LANNY G LADOUCEUR ROGER T LAGODZINSKI BOBBY J LEMONS JACK T NEGUS
BILLY R LUCAS BILLY R PARKER JOSEPH S PRINCE LARRY J RIGNEY FRANK D SALTER ALLEN D UDINK
WILLIAM R SPEIGHT JOHN S SPREWELL LARRY E STONE THOMAS P TALBOT ROBERT J URBASSIK
CRAIG M YANCEY CURTIS BOARDMAN ROBERT E CAIN JOSEPH A CARDENAS JACKIE L FORD
RICHARD C BRULE ROY L CARTER JOHN A CLAGGETT DAVID L DAILEY SALVADOR G DURAN
ROBERT L FOZZARD GARY W GEAR KENNETH M GRAY JAMES J HAZARD THOMAS J KELSO JR
MICHAEL J MANIERE DONALD J MORRIS RALPH T MUELLER PETER J PENNUCCI RANDALL C VAN HAITSMA
PAUL B LAMBERTSON ARTHUR G QUALLS CRAIG RATHBUN JOHNNY J SMITH DAVID L VIGIL
KENNETH S VORE JOHN H WAALEN TONY R WARD JAMES C WHEELER WARREN L WOZENCRAFT
LEON N BOBO DONALD G BUSSE PATRICK F CAWLEY ROBERT P COTE JUANITO M ESCANO
CHARLES H EUBANK ROBERT E GORSKE THOMAS A GOWERS STANLEY R HANSEN LEONARD T HIGDON
LAWRENCE W HOYT CHRIS A KEFFALOS RICHARD H KEITH LARRY J KIRKLAND MICHAEL S MESICH
BRUCE J NICHOLS JOE D RAMEY JON W RICH WARREN L SCANLAN JR JAMES L ABLER
ARTHUR P ADAME CHARLES F ARMENTROUT ROBERT L BEAVER RALPH W BIGELOW JOSEPH A CERIO
ANTHONY L CLARK JOHN T DONAHUE WILLIAM F DUFFNER NORMAN A EMINETH JOSEPH M HARTL
MAXIMILIANO DAVILA-TORRES NEIL B HAYES JR PEDRO HERRING JONNY HINES JIM H HOLMES
WILLIAM N JENSEN JR RICHARD A LARSON ROBERT F MARTHALER RICHARD W MEACHAM JR JOHN C REILLY
RICHARD W MEHLHAFF THOMAS H MOLES GARY R MOWER DANIEL E NELMS RICHARD D NELSON
VALENTINO J LA SCOLA JR DAVID J ORTALS RONALD R SAGERS LAWRENCE W THEIS GEORGE F BARRY JR
JAMES H CRAIG GEORGE F FELL JR CHARLES D FOLEY MICHAEL J FRANTA ELLIS D GREENE
ALAN H GROSS JAMES W HESSING CHRISTOPHER M HOBSON JOHN R HUGHES III MICHAEL S JETT
LARRIE J LANDERSHEIM WILLIAM E LEACH LARRY A MAY PETER J MCCOY EUGENE S MILLER
STEPHEN J PERKINS RICHARD T PRIDDY CECILIO ROBLES JR GEORGE RODRIGUEZ JAMES E RUSS
CECIL C SCHOFIELD SHANE N SOLDATO WILLIAM H VAUGHT III FRANK T VER LIHAY JR FRANK T VERLIHAY JR JOHN D ALLEN
STEPHEN R BARKLEY RONALD M BLUE ROBERT L BROCK DENNIE L CARNETT DONALD A DAVIS
THOMAS L FARMER TERRY W FOREMAN PETER W GILMORE REUBEN A LESS DWIGHT A MCKINNEY JR
JOHN KAUGARS ANTONIO L MORETTI SAMMY R MORRISON MICHAEL P MURPHY ROBERT B PRITCHARD
ROBERT E RAGLAND ALAN ROSS DENNIS R SILVESAN NICHOLAS E THOELE RUSSELL D WATTS
GARY L TAYLOR NICHOLAS W VROOMAN TOMMIE R ANGEL ERNEST C BALLAND CHARLES E BATCHELOR
JEFFERY J BENJAMIN GEORGE A BIRDWELL GREGORY A BLAKENEY BERNARD BRAY PETER N BRUYERE
HAROLD R BURTON CLAUDE H CARGILE MICHAEL J CHAMBERLAIN ROBERT L COLEMAN DAVID L MITCHELL
LAWRENCE J CRAWFORD LUTHER E DAVIS PABLO G DE LOS RIOS JR GARVIN W DILL JAMES E DOLAN
RAMON FLORES JR DANNY L GOSS DALE E HUTCHINS KENNETH L KELLER MICHAEL R KERNAN
TOMMY M CLAYTON BILLY E LAWRENCE DONALD G LUKENS LE R MARTINEZ GREGORY J MAYNARD
LESTER N MOULTON RAFAEL OLIVO FRANCIS E PARKHILL JR SIDNEY PIPER JR RICHARD RODRIGUES
CHARLES D SHARPE CURTIS SMITH JERRY L SMITH RICHARD D SMITH ROY J SNYDER
CHARLES R STEVENSON RODNEY W WILSON WILLIAM J BUNTING CARL W CROWE ARTHUR A DEHN
DAVID J GARCIA MONTE L GATES JAMES L GIEGEL ROBERT J GOSSELIN BRUCE E GRAHAM
SAMMY M GULLART WILLIAM E HAWKINS ALAN HILL JR HANCIL E HOWELL JR WILL ISAAC JR
STEVEN M JANEDA DAVID K JOHNSON CLARENCE R LAVOIE THOMAS A LOLLAR EDWARD M MILLER
HAROLD R MCCORD JR ROBERT L MCCURDY EDWARD T O'BRIEN VERNON E SCHROCK KENNETH W SCULLY
RICHARD L RISH ROBERT E SCOTT WILLIAM E SMITH GEORGE E WALKER JR ROBERT WASHINGTON
JOHN A WHEATLEY CURTIS WHITTED FRANKLIN J WILLISON DONALD A BAKER DANNY W BOWERS
DAVID J COMBS JOSEPH W CRARY GARY C EATON WILLIE E ELSENBURG CHARLES G FLOYD
JOHN L HARLEY GEORGE R KELLER GLENN H LEE MICHAEL R MAIDENS EDWARD A MATHES
FRANK M MEBS DONALD W MYERS ALAN H PARKS ROBERT D RHODES LARRY A RIPPE
ANDREW P SUSI WILLIAM J WHITE JR WAYNE L YINGER JR JOHN R ANDERS ALAN BEDROCK
ANANIAS BENTFORD ROBERT R BERNING JUSTIN P BRDA CLYDE A BROWN EATTERSON BYRD JR
MICHAEL G DOMINGUEZ JAMES R DUNAWAY JAMES T FISHER MICHAEL A FRESE DENNIS J GATTI
JOHN R GMACK FRANCIS J KELLER RONALD A KREBSBACH ARTURO LOPEZ JR EDMUND M LOUGHLIN
DAVID L MAZE ARMANDO MONTERRUBIO ANTON C MYLES JOHN H PARHAM III THOMAS E PRITT
WILLIAM L REYNOLDS TIMOTEO F ROMERO ROBERT B ROSHON GREGORY W SHEELER CLAYTON E SAVOY
GREEN THOMAS LAWRENCE A BIERBAUM BILLY FERRELL KENNETH L GILL DANNIE L HAWKINS
JERRY R JOHNSON JOHN MARQUEZ DALE REISING GLENN D RICKERT RAYMOND L ROBERTSON JR
ANDREW D SMITH III GARY L SPIEKER CHATWIN A STROTHER JOHN L THOMPSON JR FREDDY L BRATTON
TIMOTHY J BROWN JOSEPH R CLINCH DOMINICK L CUCCIA BRIAN J DEVANEY MICHAEL E DUVAL
WILLIAM E GAY JR RICHARD G HAILE JR STANLEY R KIMMEL PATRICK E LAWLOR KEN S MAXWELL
PATRICK E MCDANIEL HARRY D PICKARD DAVID F SANTA-CRUZ WILLIAM H STEPP RICHARD G WEID JR
BENTON F ASBURY JOHN S BONNER JR JOHN C BURRIS ROBERT K COOLEY JOSEPH P DASTOLI

283

THE VIETNAM VETERANS MEMORIAL COLLECTION

THOMAS S LIPP ROBERT S DUNBAR HAROLD J FORD LARRY M GASSNER JAMES D GRIFFIN JOHN L GRIMES
GARY D HULTS WILLIAM H KILBURN HOMER V LEE STEVEN R LOWE LEONARD MORGAN
THOMAS W MORIARTY ROBERT P O'BRIEN HILARIO O PEREZ FRANK M PERRY JR MARK D PONTIUS
BRUCE RICHARDSON RODNEY R SANDERS HAROLD J SHEA DOUGLAS E SIMPSON RONALD R TANNER
JERRY L THOMPSON JAMES H UNRUH KURTESS H WALKER BEN WILLIAMS CALVIN WILLIAMS
DURWYN L WOLF STUART A WOODMAN LLOYD L BOWLES JAMES H BRADY DOUGLAS J DAANE
ROBERT M FITZGERALD WILBER D FRAHM KEITH A HELD ROE HOPSON JR JAMES G HOWARD JR
RICKEY L JERGENSON ROGER J KOSTKA ROBERT D LOPEZ DAVID C MOSSNER JOHN M MULCAHY
RICKY E PERSELY JOSEPH J SMITH EDWARD VAN EVERY JR AULDON K WHITE GLENN L WILLIS
MELVIN R WINK THOMAS J BERNING MICHAEL D BOHRMAN DAVID G CAMPBELL JOHN J CLARK

PANEL 9W

GARY L GILES JOSEPH M GIUSTA DARRELL W HANSON DANIEL W HARRISON
THOMAS E JOHNSON ARNOLD J KULHANEK KENNETH B LUTTEL DAVID E MITCHELL WILLIAM R PORTER
MICHAEL A RASMUSSON JAMES M STOKES DOUGLAS R ULM DALE A ANDERSON MICHAEL P BOUCHARD
EDWARD M DUGAN FRANK R GUERRERO KENNETH F HAYES JOHN S HUGHES JR EDGAR D MATTHEWS
RICHARD L KESTER WIELAND C NORRIS DANIEL R PARTIN THOMAS E PEACOCK RONALD E ROGERS
BUSTER L SCOTT RODERICK K TOLBERT EARL R WEBB JR BILL G WILLIAMS HOWARD L WILLIAMSON
SYRES M BROWN ALAN G DEMOROW STEPHEN C FOHT JERRY C GILLETT ROBERT G GUINN
BOBBY G HUGGINS DAVID H MARINE ALVIN E MATHER FRANK E MCCLELLAN DAVID G MCKAY
RAYMOND P MCMAHON ROBERT E PHIPPS MARK H RIVEST RICHARD E RUTHERFORD LARRY A SALMON
EUGENE SELDERS RUSSELL D SHUE ANTONIO SILVA JOHN F TILLOU JR ARCADIO TORRES
ROBERT E UTHEMANN ARNO J VOIGT WILLIAM T WALLACE JR JOHN E WELLS HARRY T WILSON
ROOSEVELT J BRAGGS SCOTTY R BROADSTON PATRICK BRYAN MICHAEL L CHASE ROBERT E COOK
DANNY L DEWEY DENNIS W DOTSON JOHNNY L DOVER JR ROBERT M GOSELIN PATRICK A HARTWELL
ROBERT H HILL JR HERBERT D HORNER VERNON F HOVEY III DONALD J LUNDEQUAM STEPHEN A MCCAULEY
RANDY L MAST GRADY E MCBRIDE III DAVID A MEIROSE WILLIAM A MORTON VINCENT P MURPHY JR
JAMES P HASSETT ROBERT J PODNAR EVERETT D RATLIFF CHARLES A RICHARDSON RALPH S ROUSSELL JR
RONALD A STALEY STEVEN R STEFANSKI ARCHIE E TRIMM ALFRED F WIGGINS JR GEORGE E BECKLEY
MICHAEL J BLANSCET ROBERT R BOESKOOL WILLIAM A BRANCH RALPH J BUFORD LAWRENCE D BURGESS
WILLIAM L BYRD EVERETTE B CALDWELL MELVIN E DAVIS BILLY J DEMARCO RICHARD D PLINER
DALE F FLEISCHMANN JR DENNIS N HOGENBOOM ADAM JACKSON GERALD L KALIS MARK E KLEVER
ALBERT R CORTEZ JERRY L MARTIN ANDRES ORTIZ-LEBRON RONALD E PACE JOSEPH S SANCHEZ
GARY L STEWART JAMES R STUTES TERRY S WOODROFFE CLYDE D ALLOWAY CHARLES L ATHEWS
JERE A BARTON CHARLES R CRANFORD WALTER GOLASZEWSKI DONALD D HALL ORLA D HAMMACK
MICHAEL C HOPE ROBERT C MURRAY MARVIN E NEELEY BRUCE R NEESON CRISTOBAL RIVERA-CRUZ
MICHAEL C ROCKEY VICTOR A TAFOYA FRANCIS P VALDEZ LEONARD C WARNICK KURT M WILBRECHT
DAVID L WOMBLE ALBERT C BACHMAN JR BRUCE W BLAKELY STEVE BLASKOVICH JR CARL EALY
THOMAS E HEALY DAVID F HELM MICHAEL J HIGGINBOTHAM MAHLON L KELLEY ALBERT A STLAWRENCE
JOHN T KREBS JR MARVIN D LAMBDIN GARY L MERCER JOSE C MONTANO ANSEL W MORSE
DONALD W OLLILA WILLIAM V REED JOHN ROBINSON CLARK F ROGERS CREIGHTON W SISTRUNK
JAMES GILES WINFRED L SMITH WILLIE L STEELE JOHN T THORNTON GEORGE L TUCKER JR
DENNIS W VALUSEK GEORGE W BAKER RICHARD A BOWMAN RICHARD T CARLSON JOSEPH J CHISKO
WILSON DAVIS SARKIS DERVISHIAN STEVEN L DOBRY ANDREW J ELLIOTT TIMOTHY F FEWELL
ROBERT J GARRETT JOHN A GIOIA ROBBY D HANVEY BARRY W HILBRICH MICHAEL G JONES
ELMER L KEASLING KENNETH H LAMBORN JERRY W MCGLOTHLEN JEFFREY H MILLER LOWELL E MOON
DANIEL J MCMAHAN MICHAEL L OEN FRANK J QUINLAN JR JOHN L RYDER MICHAEL P TOMSIC
RANDOLPH M VAN HOOK JOHN C VAUGHN DAVID G WEBER GEORGE O WILKERSON MARION B ANDLER
GARY M BOOE DAVID CONCEPCION-NIEVE JAMES M DAVIS JAMES L DELMONT LONNIE A DYKES
EDWARD L EVANS STEFANO GIARDINA JIMMY L GOODELL DALE E GREIFE LOWELL G HARDMEYER
JERRY L HURLEY VYRL E LEICHLITER JR JOHN W LONG JR WILLIE E MACK JOHN F MALONEY JR
DONALD P MARKLAND III JOHN R MUNGER PHILIP M OVERBECK WALTER M PIERCE RONALD W RASH
CLYDE D SANDERS RONALD W SIPKA BIRCH U STEMMONS JOHN J VARDNER BILLY D WEHUNT
EDWIN T WINTER JOHN R WURTENBERG SHOJIRO YAMASHITA VERNON G BERGQUIST JAMES G BULLOCH
JOHN L DAVIS DAVID W DE LAAT JOHN A DOSSETT JR STEPHEN J GEER WILLIAM J GULLEY
GORDON T KIMBRELL JR ROBERT C MCANDREW FRANKLIN D MEYER CLAYTON W NEAVES RAYMOND R UHL
ERNEST L RAMSEY HARVEY T ROSS JR DENNIS A STEPHENS ALONZO H TAYLOR THOMAS E TAYLOR
KENNETH R MCKENNA JR REX E THORNLEY GARY A UTRIAINEN JOHNNY L WEBB STANLEY M CIESIELSKI
JAMES D CRAWFORD DAVID L EX JAMES T GLADDEN JR EDWARD L JAMES II STEPHEN E KRAJESKI
RICHARD D MASSARI TERRY L MORELAND CARL M REYNOLDS DANNY R SCHMIDT DAVID D SNOVER
RICHARD W KUYKENDALL LESLIE M TATARSKI WILLIAM F WALTERS JOHN S WILSON HENRY E COPLEY JR
PHILLIP W GREEN JR MICHAEL A GROSS DENNIS E HEITNER LEWIS E HUGHES II JAMES D RUMMEL
ARDEN E KERSEY JR FRANKLIN J KRANTZ JR DENNIS C MILLER JAMES R MOORE JR RONALD C MORGAN
GARY L GRIMES ASCENSION R PEREZ DONNIE R SIZEMORE JAMES P YOUNG CHARLES A BROOKS
CECIL R CLAYTON JOHN W EMMONS JR JEFFREY L GAYNE MICHAEL J LE LEAUX MAURILIO MENDEZ
JIMMY C MONTANA MICHAEL E MOORHEAD DAVID G PRENTICE GARY W RAGSDALE JOHN C TOBIAS
DALE E WILLIAMS JAMES L WOOD MICHAEL L WRIGHT DOUGLAS R CURRY KURTIS L GAYNOR
ROBERT L HENDERSON ROBERT M KUNER JR RONALD MANNING KENNETH W MARTIN MARK S BEHRENT
GERARD R BONIFAZI WILLIAM D BRIDGE WARREN G FRANKS JR ROBERT L GRAY FREDERICK R LEVINS
MARCUS W MADDOX JAMES R MCCRONE ROBERT W MCDONALD BOBBY W POWELL ROBERT L SEARGENT
JOHN D BELL DEVERTON C COCHRANE PRESTON H ELLIS HAROLD A GREEN THOMAS G HAGER
NELS I HEMMINGSON FRED C HENRICKS WILSON B KEE CARL J LAKER CHARLES D MALONEY
WAYNE C MOUSEL MARION D OVERBEY JAMES R POWELL MICHAEL S SPEAR JAMES R SWANGO
RODNEY G WOOD LARRY M ALLEN FRANK BOWENS JOHNNY C BRISENO PHILLIP CASTILLO
RAFAEL A CHAVEZ HENRY P CLARK ROBERT C DAWSON DONALD D DOUGLAS SCOTT E KILLINGSWORTH
PAUL DUFAULT JAMES A GREEN EUGENE R GUDISWITZ EARNEST HARDIMON JR ROY J HOLMGREN
CARL W DRAKE HARRY L MCLAMB WESLEY E MELTON JAMES A SCRUGGS RODRICK A SKEINS
STEVEN R STOLTZ RALPH M TRIPLETT BARRY G TUCKER THOMAS M WHARTON FRANK C ZONAR JR
FRANCIS R ADDIS JERRY J ALLEN GORDON G ANDERSON WILLIAM P ARTHUR JOHN R BLOSCHICHAK
FRANCIS A BOND JOHN W BROWN LEROY C CECH ROBERT K HENDERSON JR HERBERT L JOHNSON
PATRICK D KADOW PHILIP A KALHAGEN DONALD E LAYFIELD MICHAEL W NOTERMANN BARRY K WEAVER
ROBERT H PILK FRED S SMART ROBERT F STEELE RONALD R STEWART CHARLES E THORNTON
LARRY R LADD JOHNNY M WATSON WILLIAM R BONNER MARK C BRANTLEY ROBERT F COLATRUGLIO
THOMAS L CUSSON DANIEL J DESOCIO DAVID G DOBOSZ JERRY G GIBERSON RICHARD J GRIEME
THOMAS D GRIFFIN MERRIL HOLT FREDERICK W HOPSON LARRY J LOWTHER JOSEPH P LUTZ
GLENN A PARKS ROBERT L PORTER ROGER L PORTER MELVIN N RUTHERFORD RONALD E UNDERWOOD
DONALD J MURPHY BILLY R SARGENT ALEX C SPENCE JR DENNIS M STOPPLEWORTH BURDER S ATHEY III
JAMES D GARDNER ERNEST L GARNER DENNIS A LA DAGE JOHN N MCCLENDON JR STEPHEN J SMITH
BUFORD R SPENCER LONNIE H WEISHEIT MICHAEL S BEZEGA MARK J BUSH GEORGE CHAMBERS-QUIROZ
CHARLES C CISNEROS RAUL DE JESUS-ROSA WILLIAM M DUNNING JOHN S EARLE ALLEN E OATNEY
RALPH A GADDIS ROBERT W GUMBERT JR CHARLES E HANN TRACY R HYATT HERMAN MOORE JR
JIMMIE L CHAMBLEE WILLIAM J MCTAGGART WILLIAM W MORROW GARY L PEAT THOMAS M SCHALK SR
JOSEPH M TUROWSKI JR RUSSELL L WILLIAMS DANIEL K WILSON LARRY W ANDERSON MICHAEL L BALDINI
THOMAS R BROWN DARRELL E BURNS NEWTON S CLEMENT HAROLD E COWAN DENNIS J DILLON
JOHN J DONNELLY III JOHN S DURLIN JAMES R GORE DANIEL J HALLOWS MYLLIN G HENRICH
EUGENE HUGGINS REGNOLD J LA COST JAMES W LENZ HAROLD L LINVILLE PATRICK D LOVELL
JOHN J MCCULLOUGH CHARLES W MCLAUREN LAWRENCE M MOORE JOE P PEDERSON ROBERT P PHILLIPS
THOMAS L POOLE DANNY L ROBINETTE DONALD A ROWLEY JAMES M ROZO RICHARD J SOLANO
TOBY A THOMAS GEORGE R WALL WAYNE R ANDERSON GEORGE A CAPUANO THOMAS D CATLIN
MICHAEL L CONKLIN JAMES W CRIDER MICHAEL R DADISMAN ALBARO Q GARCIA JAMES B HICKS
TIMOTHY C MCCARTHY JOHN A RINGHOLM RUSSELL E SLOUGH RUSSEL E VORIS THOMAS E WATSON
RICHARD L BARNES BERNARD G BRANTMEIER CARLOS CHAVEZ JR THOMAS J DAVIS GARRY L FRANKLIN
WILLIAM A JURICH JOHN A MARTINEZ OSBORNE MATTINGLY JR DALE P MEEHAN CLARENCE M OVERBAY JR
OSCAR B PATTERSON DENNIS L RITTER MARVIN D SNIDER DAVID M WALTERS DAVID J WIKANDER
DENNIS J BRAULT VICTOR B CAMBAS WILLIAM J CARIVEAU JERRY D CARVER DENNIS D CHAMBERLIN
HALQUA D CLIBURN WILLIAM J ENDRESS GARY L FLECK JOHN A GARZA CLARENCE GOBER JR
MICHAEL T GUZZETTI JR EDGAR HARRIS FOREST G HIGHLAND JR FREDERICK E HUGHENS MELVIN L PULLEN
OTIS R JONES RODNEY L KOERNER DAVID J MOYLAN STEPHEN O'BRIEN LAWRENCE L PETERSEN
WESLEY C HOWLEY JR JAMES A PETRIE WALLACE ROBERTS EARL W THARP JR DOUGLAS S VERGAMINI
JERRY M CAREY ALAN D GARDNER STEVEN L HIENSMAN JOHN F HOLLISTER LANCE M LOFMAN
GERALD L MCDOWELL PAUL E PAQUIN JR CHARLES D PEDIGO GARY M PRIDGEN ROBERT J WALTERS
JAMES A WIMMER JACK L WOLFE TERRELL R GALBREATH JOHN A MCGINN JOHN P SHARPLESS
JAMES T WEBBER DONALD D ALDERN CALVIN W BINDER II ROBERT P HAMPTON JR BRUCE W HESKETT
WILLIAM L HUDNALL LEROY B MUDD JAMES A SCHACHTNER CURTIS E STELZER MARVIN E BELL
HOWARD E CAFFERY JUAN COLON-DIAZ MICHAEL F DEAN MERLE A DENTINO DONNITH H FLETCHER
JOHN L BURGESS LESLIE F DOUGLAS JR RICHARD DYER JAMES F ELKIN JOHN W GOEGLEIN
CHARLES R HESTER GORDON C HILL PHILLIP M HORST STEVE L INBODEN PAUL L JENKINS
STEPHEN L KLEIN JIMMIE F NABOURS LESTER E PARKER STEPHEN K RAMOS ANDREW J ROGUS JR
MITCHELL O SADLER JR WILLIAM S SANDERS LEROY C SCHANEBERG GARRY M SHANNON EDDY E WHITE
MICHAEL R WATERS PETER H GERTH ROBERT J GLADU MICHAEL E KISCADEN RANDY S MORRISON
TERRY A MOTE WALTER M PUCHALSKI PAUL A THARP JOHNNY ALLEN JR LARRY R BRENNER
RANDALL A CARVER RICHARD J CONRARDY WILLIAM F EMANUEL CALVIN R GISH ROBERT W ZOLLER II
DARYL R GROTHAUS STEPHEN J HARBER THOMAS H HERNDON THOMAS T HEWITT LEE N LENZ
JAMES R MERZ JR DAVID B MILLER JOHN E MITCHELL JR JOHNNY L MOORE ARTHUR D NEAL
ROBERT P RADCLIFF JR WILLIAM D SECOR ROGER D SUMRALL FRANK A WEBSTER REXFORD E WILSON
SHERMAN P DAVIS DOUGLAS R ANDERSON DAVID L BROOKS RICHARD A BROWN DONALD D CAMPBELL
JOHN W CARPER JR LOUIS J CROSBY WILLIAM T DORSEY WILLIAM D FRAKES NELSON M HYLER
WILLIAM A JUSTICE JAMES E OLINGER JR JOHN W OWEN DONNIE H RUSSELL TERRY L SANDERS
BOYD A STEPHENS JR ROBERT S UTECHT ROBERT L WELCH CHARLES F BOOKOUT JIMMIE L ROBINSON
JERRY O EMERINE WILLIAM T HANEY MARK T JERNIGAN GEORGE JOHNSON WILLIAM P LYONS
CHARLES L MATHEWS KELLY R DAVIS CARL L MICKENS WILLIAM C RAY BRUCE W SHURTLEFF JIMMIE F SLIM
RANDOLPH SPIERS NADE M STANICH FRANK E STEARNS WILLIAM L SULLIVAN GARY D THADEN
RICHARD J WARDEN ROBERT J WINGENFELD E G AKERS JR DANNY L ARCHER WILLIAM F BROWNING

ROBERT L KING GEORGE LISHCHYNSKY MICHAEL R PEDDLE DONALD H PRATER FRANKLIN G SCOGGINS
RICHARD L SMITH FOREST M STONE MICHAEL K WAYMIRE CHARLIE C BENTON HOWARD T BLEDSOE
LANNY H BUROFF ROBERT G CHOQUETTE JR WENDALL J JARRELL PHILIP J ORGERON SANDY H PORTER
FIDENCIO G RIOS JR JOHN R SIEVERS ALBERT F TRISTAN STEVE A VESTAL RICHARD C WORTHINGTON JR
GEORGE W CASEY WILLIAM L CHRISTENSON KENNETH W COOPER THOMAS W DAMM RONALD F FULLER
THOMAS D GILLASPY BOBBY E GRAY MICHAEL J GRIMM NED H HARRIS DAVID M HAVEARD
JOHN A HOTTELL III LEWIS HOWARD JR DAVID L MEADOWS WILLIAM F MICHEL RONALD J NATALIE
KENNETH N REBER GERALD L RISINGER VERNON K SMOLIK JR ROBERT F WOODHOUSE JR STANLEY J CRUSE
HOWARD L ELDER TONY M FLOREZ HAROLD L FRANK RANDOLPH E GRAVES JAMES E HUPP
DANIEL J MALONEY JOSEPH F MCDERMOTT III HARRY MCEWING JOHN W MURSCH RANDAL G SOWERS
WILLIAM L NETTLE LARRY L NIEKEN THOMAS B OWENS MARK P RAIFORD RICHARD G REPOLE
LEE E MARSH JR RICKEY L SCOTT JOHN D SKIRVIN JOHN F SPANGLER ALLEN R STROUD

PANEL 8W

JOHN L WADSWORTH WALTER L WALKER HERBERT D BEMBOOM WILLIE BOZIER JR
CHARLES E BRAY JR GREGORY A DODGE JOHN W FISHER LARRY M HORNER JAMES L JONES
MILTON J JONES JAMES L KRULL JULIAN LUNA JAMES LUTTGENS BERNARD LYNCH
RUSSELL D MILBERGER JOHNNY W OGLE NATHANIEL J PHILLIPS ROGER L PHILLIPS WALTER ROSS JR
LEO M SANDERS CHARLIE SINGLETON JR LE R THELEN TERRY E WILLIAMS PRESTON T WILLINGHAM JR
PATRICK J BOHAN THOMAS A CAMPBELL JOHNNY R COBB ROBERT J CUNNINGHAM ROBERT L OLDHAM
VICTOR L DE FOOR JOE B DELAPHIANO PAUL J FOUCHE ROGER D HARTNESS DANIEL R HIVELY
DONNY J BRASWELL ROY A JOHNSON DENNIS K MARTIN JOHN S MYERS FREDRICK C RAYMOND JR
DAVID P SCHULTZ CARLOS F TODD ALBERT TSOSIE DAN R HUBBELL WARREN LIVELY II
GLENN E MAIER MICHAEL P VULLO LARRY G YEAGER ROBERT E BIRKHOLZ WILLIAM K BOYER
HILBURN M BURDETTE JR TERRY P BURK MICHAEL E BURNS MICHAEL A DE MASI WILBERT R DRANE
KENNETH W HINDS THOMAS D KLOSS EDDIE D MAPES PHILLIP A MILES JR JESUS C NUNEZ
CAREY J PRATT RICHARD F QUINN HANS A RAJCEVAC THOMAS WALL JR WILLIAM A WICKS
ROSS E BEDIENT ROBERT L BRYAN LARRY D ENGEBRETSON RICHARD W EVANS DAVID B HAYES
SANFORD L JOHNSON FRANCIS E KLAIBER RICHARD W LITTLETON JOHN E MOODY JR JOHN W BLOUNT
JAMES L CAMPBELL BRUCE C CANDRL PAUL G GUIMOND JAMES T HEMBREE JR HARRY E LAUCK
ROBERT BRADSHER JR DENNIS W HUFFINE WILLIAM E JONES JOHN L KEISTER HOWARD W LAYNE JR
MELVIN D MILLER TERRY A PALM JOHN READY III THOMAS S ROGERS GARY L SCHNEIDER
KEITH E UTTER BOBBY L BAILEY JOHN P BARTONE HARRISON BELL DENNIS E CLARK
EDWARD R DIAZ CLIFFORD GRAY JIMMY L HILL LENTON E MIZER STANLEY V NEWMAN
JERRELL D SCROGGS CHRISTOPHER L SHAEFFER NELSON P TUTTLE FRED G VANDIVER JOSEPH D VAUGHN
WILLIAM E WHEELER ERNEST R DAVIS MICHAEL J HEINDSELMAN DONALD A KRUMREI ALBERT L LANE JR
FRANK E MCNUTT RONALD H REILLY WILLIAM F SETTLE FRANK SMITH RICHARD R TIMMONS
JERRY M WEAVER PETER P AULETTI ROBERT G CRICHTON GREGORY K KRUEGER GREGORY D UNZICKER
DONALD G MARCH LLOYD A MCGREW CLIFFORD E PARSONS JR PAUL L SALERNO JAMES D SCHMIDT
STEPHEN W BARNES CLIFFORD P SCHOLL JR LARRY L SEADORE TERRY J VAN OCHTEN LOUIS L ZITTERGRUEN
RANDALL T BAER MICHAEL E BAUM DAVID R BEYL DENNIS L CLYMER MICHAEL J DICKUS
JAMES M DUNNAVANT JR JAMES L FORE JOHNNY L GODFREY WARREN G INGRAM GREG KELLER
BURKE H MILLER WILLIAM A NORRENBROCK THOMAS A PARDO WILLIAM D ROLLASON MICHAEL A WALKER
OTIS PARKER KENNETH J SIMMONS JOHN ULICNI PRESTON P WINLAND JR JOHN F BARNETT
LEWIS E CASNER JR RICHARD W DODD RICHARD E FAY DANIEL B FELL ARTHUR P GRAY IV
WILLIAM J MARTINEZ JUAN M REYNA JOHNNY M RODGERS JOSEPH A SEAMAN MICHAEL L THIBODEAUX
RUSSELL A ROWE ELROY SIMMONS DAVID M TESH THOMAS E VAIL ROBERT L ARGENTI ALLAN L DUNNING JR
DAVID W AYERS BILL G BROWNING DURL G CALHOUN EDGAR F CROUSE JR JOHN C KNOTT
SAMUEL T CARROLL JR PATRICK T DE WULF DENNIS F FISHER CHRISTOPHER GUTIERREZ HAROLD A HOLMES
DENNIS R LEVIS DAVID J MAGNUSON LARRY J PLETT ELOY R VALLE MARK J WEBB
LEON D WITHERSPOON FRANK L ASHER ROBERTO C FLORES FREDERICK D GREENE ROBERT B HAYS
PETER P HUK DAVID E JOHNSON WALTER J KACSOCK JR JAMES R KALSU BRENT R LAW
FRANCIS E MAUNE RICHARD M PEARL RONALD J SCHULTZ JOHNNY F SCOTT DONALD R WORKMAN
LOYD H SANDERS GARETH M SILVER MARVIN L WAGNER LANNY J WALLACE SCOTT F WEMETTE
PHILLIP G WRIGHT JOHN M BABICH VIRGIL M BIXBY ROBERT J BROWN JR STANLEY G DIEHL
MARK G DRAPER DANNY J FRIES LARRY E GLATFELTER LARRY D JOHNSON ROBERT M JOURNELL III
GEORGE R KELLEY LYLE A KLOEK JOHN W KRECKEL THOMAS A LONG RONALD A OLESEN
STEVEN A OLSON WILLIAM A PAHISSA THOMAS R SCHULTZ DONALD J SEVERSON GERALD B SINGLETON
KENNETH W SLAUGHTER LAUREN W STANDRING DANIEL J TURCOTTE GUS ALLEN DERREL K DICKEY
LARRY A GATLIFF PAUL L HAINING ANDRE C LUCAS BERTRAND C MEDINE JR TERRY L MERRITT
MITCHELL JONES JR KENNETH P TANNER WILFRED W WARNER JR JOHN J ZAGATA DONALD B BLOODWORTH
ROBERT L BOLAN HARRY J BORT BILLY B BULL JAMES M BUTLER STEVEN L FAWBUSH
EDWARD F GLENN JR KENNETH D HAMMEL BRUCE D KIEME EDWARD G KILUK JR JAMES W REED
WILLIAM L SAWYER JR GREG D STEVENSON JOHN A SUNIGA JR WILTSE L WEBER ROBERT J ADAMS
WILLIAM A FAUGHT JR TIMOTHY M GREELEY PAUL A GREGORY HAROLD M HARDIN EDWARD D JOHNSON
SALVADOR LEAL JR DONALD R SIMON JACK E TAYLOR WEG P VANDER RICHARD H VOKES
ROBERT W WARD J V WATSON MARTIN W WRIGHT DARWIN O BRANDON MURVYN E HARGRAVES
ROBERT L ASMUTH JR WILLIAM D CHAMBLEE WALTER W HAMILTON ROY E HARRIS CHARLES E HARRISON JR
JIMMY H MERCER STEVEN B MILLS DENNIS R NOBLE ROBERT D OSIER JR WILLIAM A PARKER
RICHARD W PENNINGTON LARRY W RASEY MARTIN L RODGERS RONALD J SCHAAF JIMMY D SMITH
ALTON L STEGALL JAMES E TAYLOR GREGORY C THOMPSON CLEMENT J TROIANELLO SAMUEL W WILLIAMS
DOUGLAS P ATKINS TERRENCE R BILLINGS MICHAEL R BLANCHETTE ALBERT CALMESE THOMAS F DELANO
GRADY L EILAND JAMES W HUDSON LEONARD W KIDD MICHAEL A LAUCHMAN LARRY J MCDOWELL
HARVEY R NEAL JOSEPH R NEHL GRADY L NORRIS CHARLES D RIFFE DAVID R WEIGNER
GEORGE F BEELER LAURENCE G BROWN ROBERT N CHINQUINA WILLIAM B CLEVERLEY STEVEN S CROSIER
KEVIN M FRYE ANDREW L HILL RALPH V LA CAGNINA TERRANCE D MARPLE FRANK M PASCARELLA
ALAN K BARTON DICKIE C CURRY OTIS C MORGAN JOSE M PEREZ BOYD L SHOOK ROBERT W TAYLOR
GERALD M VETRANO TIMOTHY A WHITE DAVID E ZIMMERMAN KARL T ANTEAU LEE T BAIZ
STEPHEN W BANCROFT ROGER J CARR JACK H DILLON JAMES K EMCH NICK U FLEENER
WALTER B GOLOMBESKI RICKY J HILLS DANNY L HILTERBRAN RONALD T JONES JOHN J LAVELLE
ROY W MARLATT PLEASANT MCCRAY JR RONALD F PERSYN GARY L ROSE ROBERT A SZPONDER
DAVID A ALLEN DONALD E AUTEN CLYDE J BALL DONALD A BROWN GARY A CHAVEZ
JEROLD FRANKLIN EDISON A HARKINS III HAROLD U HAYES FORREST H HOLLIFIELD ROBERT MASEDA
VINCENT P MOREHAM LEE R PETERS RICHARD A POMERINKE STEPHEN A RUSHING CLYDE L TENSLEY
WILLIAM J MCPHERSON DALE E SATHOFF WILLIAM R SCHROEDER TIMOTHY M SPRINGER EDWARD J WHITTON
WILLIAM E AUSTIN JAMES M DOTY ANDREW G HAWTHORNE PHILLIP J HILDERBRANT EDWARD P MOORE
JAMES K MUSSELMAN PHILLIP A PAULE GREGG A SMITH GREGG F STEIMEL LUIS A ALTAMIRA
JAMES W BLACKMON DALE R BUXTON DAVID L CAPLAN JOHN J HOOPER RALPH W HUNT
FRANK I KRANNER LARRY J MALATESTA RAYMOND M MANINGER DANIEL L MITCHELL JON H NORDQUIST
ANTON J SCHOEPKE PERRY G BLACK JAMES A BOYER GEORGE W CHARTERS JR JOE H FULGHAM
TERRY L GILPIN RUDOLPH W GRIFFIN LESTER KING JOHN J RUSSELL TERRY S SELLS
RAYMOND L WILLIAMS STEPHEN L BOYD EARL D BROACH MICHAEL W BROWN JAMES FINNEY JR
JACK R GILBERT BARRY F GRAHAM JOHN A GULDAN ANDREW L LEWIS LARRY J MEADOR
JOHN B PROFFIT KIRK L RAUCH PORFIRIO ROMERO-PEREZ ROBERT D SPENCER FRED D STORY
KENT C WOLF WAYNE V BLAKE JAMES L BLOW JR JOHN H BURGESS JR WILLIAM M CLARK
GLENN R GILBERT ARTHUR F GLEIM JR PAUL A JOHNSON DONALD D LAYTON RICHARD W MINDOCK
RONALD P MCNEILL JESSE L MOSES JOHN R POE HOLLIS C SANFORD JR OVELL SPRUILL
JAMES K ANDERSON STEVEN R CAUCCI DAVID R DENNA MANUEL L DICK GERALD L HAMILTON
WILLIAM A CRAIG MONTE W FORREST STEVEN T GRIGGS MARK S HAILEY RONALD W HERD TERRY J PAYNE
JEAN M KRAUS ANGELO G LARRAGA ROBERT J MUELLENBACH MARGARITO RODRIGUEZ JR DAVID R TOMAS
DARYL D SHONKA ROBERT VELASQUEZ GARY G WINTER ROGER H BOUCHARD ANDREW C GRANT
JAIME HERNANDEZ-CARRAS RODNEY G JOHNDRO RICHARD J LEONARD ROBERT C MOLLENHOUR
LLOYD A MURPHY WILLIAM C PRCHLIK RONALD E SAMUELSON WILLIAM F SHAW KENNITH W TAPSCOTT
ERIC P BUSCH JOHN N CRAWFORD JR GORDON A DADISMAN JOHN H EVANS JR JAMES F GILLIES
ROBERT G HANSEN RALPH B MITCHELL PAUL V MOORE WILLIAM MURPHY RICHARD M SEYMORE
THEODORE C KAPPMEYER ROBERT W MACNAUGHT THOMAS W SHEA STEVEN M WADE STEPHEN C BRIESE
JOSE J CASTILLO PETER CHARLIE DAVID L CLIMER THOMAS G EDGREN MICHAEL R HALIBURTON
JOHN W KISIELEWSKI LEWIS D MOLES CALVIN W RAMSEY CARROLL E RAYMER JR ROBERT T RICE JR
SAMMY P RODRIGUEZ WILLIAM M SCANLON GARY D SENGSTOCK JOL N SMITH WILLIAM W WALKER
DANIEL S WALKO WAYNE E WALSH JR PONDEXTUER E WILLIAMS DON W AVERY KIRK O BARKLEY
DENNIS W BAXLEY IVERY L BAXTER SHAWN G CANNON ROBERT W ELLIOTT WILBERT J JONES JR
JOHN H LIGHTSEY DAVID T MADDUX ANTHONY V MARTINEZ WILLIAM F MCNULTY JOE REYNA JR
HERMAN V STURM JR NEAL V BAINTER MICHAEL A CAFFEY JOHN E CROWLEY JOSEPH F MARCANTONIO
DANNY L EVANS ANDREW J FRITSCH III STEPHEN T HENNESSY ANTHONY G KUBELUS JR WILLIAM H KUSCH
DWAINE E MATTOX RICHARD W MCFARLAND BERNARD F MORRILL KENNETH J SORENSEN JAMES D BRADLE
ANTHONY L RAMSEY GRANT R WAUGH WILLIAM L WHITMORE GARY J WINTER DONNIE D ASBURY
LUCIEN J MIGLIORE ROBERT J PIERCE MARCOS PIZARRO-COLON THOMAS L PORTER WALTER L REDDING
DEAN F ROGERS MARK J TOSCHIK ALAN W ASHENFELTER JAMES A BROWN DAN G FEEZELL
GARY L JENKS KENNETH E OLIVER CHARLES K PUDERBAUGH JIMMIE D RYALS BLAIR H SIMPSON
EDWARD TARVER RUBIN W WESTFALL JR RUSSELL L BAHRKE JR ALAN B CHEESEMAN DONALD C COLLINS
HENRY T COX TROIT D FREELAND MICHAEL A GAGE NICKALAS P GURNIAS JAMES C JUNGE
GEORGE D HENRY JR NICHOLAS G JOHNSON SR EDWARD C JOHNSTON LESTER E OONK JOHN P POWELL
WILLIAM L RIPLEY STEVEN C SCOTT GREGORY C STITT LAWRENCE G SWARBRICK ROBERT H WESTON
GORDON S WISE SHERMAN F ARMSTRONG WILLIAM E BARRITT MICHAEL J BRENTON DENNIS H HERRICK
HAROLD D HOLLIFIELD LESZEK S KARSZNIA FRANKLIN K NELSON HECTOR D OYOLA ALVIN L PEMBERTON
JOHN A PREMENKO TERRY D REAMS DOUGLAS THOMPSON DANIEL C UPTON DUANE E WALDRON
ORLANDO TORRES-OYOLA BRUCE D WAGNER WARREN C ANDERSON WILSON P BAILEY JAMES C BECKER
BRIAN J BENNETT HARRY E CHESSER CURTIS COOPER DONALD R HILLIARD BEN JACKSON JR
HERBERT M HADDEN FREDERICK E HUTTIE III JAMES W MATTHEWS JOHN E MCGUIRE PETER A SCHMIDT
WILLIAM H VAN GELDER JR ELVIN JAMES JR BILLY N JOHNSTON JR STEVEN R OTT ROBERTIS PINKNEY
RAUL RIVERA ROBERT L SCHOFIELD STEPHEN A SHARP GARY L WASHENIK ROBERT A ATER
CURTIS C COLYEAR PAUL A DEMALINE ROBERT W HART RICHARD K JOHNSTON MOSES E JONES
JOHN L MCCLURG STEVEN B MELNICK PATRICK R O'BRIEN ROGER D PARMENTIER GUY W PATTON

PANEL 8W (*Continued*)

DAVID L RAMSAY SCOTT E SCHNEIDER RAYMOND L STANSBURY II CHARLIE W TAYLOR PHILLIP R WELLONS
MERLYN L WENTZEL JAMES W WOOD ROBERT N BOLLMAN RALPH N DUEMLING THOMAS L GUNDERSON
DON W LOVE GEORGE H MEYERS THOMAS H PAPPENHEIM JOSEPH H SHELTON III DAVID L SMITH
GARY W WALKER JIMMY R WALTON JOHN E ANTHONY DENNIS M BAILEY ROBERT L BROWN
FREDERICK W CROSS FRANK R FRATELLENICO EVELIO A GOMEZ TERENCE M KJOS DANIEL L AAMOLD
WILLIAM E BROUGHTON JOSEPH H DENIG FURMAN D HUGHES MARSHALL K JONES DON MANAC
PAUL MILLER WAYNE W MULLIN HORACE L WARDELL MICHAEL J DOUGAN ROBERT L FRASCH
JAMES E HOLDER BEN O JOHNSON KENNETH J KOSOWSKI ROBERT W LANCASTER RONALD W MUNGER
LARRY W MCCOY CHARLES E MCLEISH DEAN M WIEGAND DEAN M WIEGAND JR DAVID W YOUNGBLOOD LARRIE C ALLEN
KENNETH D BILLS DAVID J CAMPBELL GLEN A CHAVEZ WAYNE R DAVIS JAMES A DONAHUE
ROBERT L DUNAWAY JR ROBERT M DURALL GARY L FRAZIER JOSEPH D GAGNON LAWRENCE GEIGER
JEFFERY A MILLER ROBERT O NIMAN EDWARD J NOVAK THOMAS J ROBERTS DONNIE P SMITH
PAUL WARD RONALD L YOUNG RAYMOND S BRAMWELL CLARENCE BROWN CLARENCE B COLEMAN
JAMES R HUNT GARY W JONES ARTHUR MEDINA DAVID W OSBORNE JOHN D PHILLIPS
ROBERT D ROTHER JR ROBERT G SIMES JR SAM E STOUT EVERETT E WELLS JR JOHN F WERNER

PANEL 7W

RICHARD W DEVINE PATRICK G FITZSIMMONS JOHN C HINES ASA T JOHNSON
MILTON R KENNEDY LARRY K LEIMBACH JOHN P MORGAN JR SHELDON SILVERMAN RONALD G DICKSON
JOHN S NUTWELL BRUCE G TINDALL IVAN L BARGER JR RONALD D BELARSKI DONALD G CHMIEL
RALPH M JOHNSON CARL E DUNN BARRY W GODFREY JOHN P HEARSCH JR JOHN JASSO GARY E JENSEN
THOMAS E KESSING JR JOHN J KLIGAR III ROBERT E KOONCE JAMES M KOZLOWSKI JOHN D MALCOLM
CHARLES H MEAKINS DORSEY MINCEY III JACK MOSS JR TERRELL L RAWLINSON RICHARD H SAVIEO
JOSEPH A CARDINICI JERRY M STILL JERROLD L VESEY MICHAEL E WHITE REX T ALLEN WILLIAM ANDERSON JR
STUART L BARNETT DENNIS G BATESEL THEODORE F BEDRA KEVIN E BONJOUR PAUL E BRIDGETT
RONALD E CHANDLER WESLEY O CODY ONNIE D DUNCAN CURTISS ESTRIDGE BENNY R HALSTEAD
STEPHEN D CARR HENRY R EXPOSE FLORENTINO FLORES ISIAH C GARNETT JAMES M GINN
JOHN D HERINGTON THOMAS S HICKMAN LARRY B JACOBSON ALBERT L JOHNSON FRED C KRAEMER
WILLIAM H LAURENCE JR CURTIS J MANRING HIMA D MCDOUGALL JR MICHAEL L MORGAN DANIEL W YORK
ROBERT P MCMASTER DWIGHT P O'BRIEN JOHN L PIERSOL JR DAVID P REESE JOHN W REESE JR
DAVID E ROSE LEE E SALTERS HECTOR M SANDOVAL GEORGE E TEFFT WILLIAM D THORPE
RUBEN MARTINEZ-ZAYAS CHARLES G WEHRHEIM JOHN W WIDDOWS JOEL C YORK ERNEST M BARBER
ANDREW R BARRETT DANIEL M BENNETT JAMES C CAIN MARCUS J HAMILTON WILLIE H HAWKINS JR
MICHAEL R KEMPEL JOHN J LAFLER DAVID MONTOYA CHARLES W NURISSO RICHARD W PALCOWSKI
EDWARD J PARADA STEVEN L COFFEY ALFONZA FOSTER RAYMOND L HODGES JR JOE LUNA JR
THOMAS H MESSER ERIC P MISTRETTA JAY A MUNCEY SAMUAL K RANKINS NICK E SANCHEZ
DONALD R SMITH RALPH H VON DER HOFF THEODORE A WOLTERS DAVID J AMHEISER MELVIN C BATES JR
WILLIAM D BLENKINSOP DAVE S CARRUTH JR MICHAEL J COURTNEY JAMES W FENTON DONALD B GREENE
DANIEL L GROVER HARRY T HENTHORN CECIL JACKSON JR BRIAN E JAY MARK W MINEAR
HAMILTON PAUL JR HOWARD E SATTERFIELD LAWRENCE E SCHEIB JR JOHN F SHIEFER PAUL J AUSTIN JR
RODGER P CROW KEITH R DAVIES ROBERT E DEW ANTONIO A GRAU GARY K MORE
RUBERT G HUMPHREYS JIM M RHEAD OTTO STONE JR LEON P TRIDLE EUGENE E WOLTERS LARRY R CARTER
DAVID G CHANEY JAMES E DUCKWORTH JOHN L ERVIN CONRAD L FLYINGHORSE@ NICHOLAS C STEFANICH
CHARLES H GRAY JR JAMES H HEPPLER CHARLES P HUTTON HARRY C INMAN III FREDERICK R KILLMON
MICHAEL J MCGERTY GARY R METZ EDICTOR RIVERA-MONTES ROGER A SCARBROUGH CRAIG A SCHMITZ
LORENZO FOX LARRY G TAYLOR HENRY B THOMAS DOUGLAS P ZERBA RANDY C BRACKIN
JOSEPH L CHAMBERS CHARLES R CONOVER TYRONE CONVERSON GILBERTO GARCIA JIMMY R HOLKEM
BILLY R HUNTER WILLIAM R KERSEY JR JAMES R KING JOHN D LAWSON DAVID R NOLL
DALE A PENNINGTON LARRY SCHOONMAKER RUSSELL C SCULLY WILLIAM A SEELEY BRUCE W WRIGHT
WILLIAM F BENOIST III RONALD E HARWELL BOBBY L HOLZER WILLIE HOOPER JR JOSEPH PERITO
ROBERT L JAMES MARION D LA ROSA EDWARD C MORROW ROBERT W ORTIZ ROBERT P PAPE
EDWARD P DEIBEL III NICOLAS R SAN WILLIAM G WALKER II ROBERT J WEIDLE RONNIE CHAVIS
GARY A CRAVEN LOUIS C DI FINIZIO EDWARD G MATHERN CHRISTOPHER G MIRACLIA GARY L RUFF
CRAIG T WATERMAN RUSSELL R COSTELLO JOSE L GONZALES JR JOSEPH K GRENIER WILLIAM HARP
OTIS E PLANTS MICHAEL E QUICK RONALD D SWINFORD RODNEY E TAYLOR KENNETH S GNIEWEK
JACK M BAKER EMORY T COATES THOMAS M CRISP ROBERT D HAUER DANIEL F KLEIN
EMIL J NAASZ RONALD L POLAND LUIS RAMOS CHESTER R REESE JR PRESTON L SMITH
VERNON A WRIGHT LARRY E BROOKS GEORGE W COLLINA LAWRENCE S MARTIN JESUS MORENO JR
PAUL D MYERS ROBERT L PORTER JON E REED RICHARD M SCHWAB KIRK W SIMS
THOMAS P SMITH GUILLERMO VALLE WILLIAM L WILHELM EUGENE A AARON MONTY D BOYER
JOHN C DAVIS GLENN H ENGLISH JR DON M JUSTICE JULIUS D NELSON EDDIE J PADILLA
DAVID A PRATT WILLIAM E ROLLER BRENT W SVEEN MICHAEL ASEP ROBERT M BOLES
DAVID H BRADY DAVID L CONLEY GLEN A FIESTER THOMAS C LARSEN KENNETH J NOLEN
FRANKIE NORTHERN ROGER D OTTO JAMES B PERKINS CARL R RAYMOND WALTER L STANKO
WILLIE J THIGPEN FRANK N VAVRIN JOSEPH M BROWN PATRICK J CONNOR ROBERT R SIZEMORE JR
ELTON W LEWIS KEVIN F LYNCH GALEN S MILES RICKEY D MILLS TIM E NEWELL
CURTIS J PERRODIN NICHOLAS C PETANOVICH ERNEST D PETTY DARREL M PICKETT JAMES M SCRIVER
GARY R FRIEND WILFORD A YOUNG MERRITT ADAMS JOHN J ARTEAGA BRUCE A BAIN
WILSON CAMPBELL FORREST C CHILDS HERMAN EVANS DANIEL F GALLAGHER RALPH J GIORDANO
DONALD R HUEY JOSEPH E JACKSON GEORGE L LOPEZ WALTER L POINTER CHARLES M REED
CALVIN R JOHNSON ERNESTO V SALAZAR RICHARD C ALEXANDER ALAN S BOOR ERNEST R BROWNLOW III
DENNIS J BULLOCK GARY B GLASSFORD GORDON M JOHNSON LARRY JOHNSON JAMES W KNIGHT
JAMES L KNOBLES ALBERT MCDONALD JR BARNEY K NEAL JR DOUGLAS A NIEBOER MICHAEL D NOEL
BERNARD H PLASSMEYER LONNIE M SWINSON JOHN W CANNON DEVON M ENMAN DEAN W HARDMAN
JUAN AVILA JR LUTHER A GENES HAROLD O HARPER LEONARD J KOWALSKI JR CHARLES V LANG
CHARLES D MATHEWS WAYLAND F MCCAULEY JR FERRELL E MEALER JR STEPHEN C NAHER JOHN G PAGE
CURVIN CLAYTON THOMAS P COFFINO JON COLE FRANKLIN M CORL JR DENNIS C MARSHALL
DENNIS L DAVES DANIEL R FENN GARRISON D FIELDS DENNIS W GENTRY DANIEL M HEDGES
RICHARD L THOMAS WYATT MILLER JR EDMOND W RICHARDSON HAROLD R SPILLMAN JAMES T WALDRON
TYRONE C WATSON NICOLAS WHEELER PERCY E BLY JR ROBERT FREDA KENNARD K KANOSH
AARON VINSON ALBERT F AMMANN LARRY F DAVIS DAVID F FREEMAN HAROLD L MACDONALD LEE D MEADOWS
BRADLEY L BOSWELL WILLIAM R GOOLSBY JR CRAIG W HIRSCHI DONALD L KAHRE
WAYNE A MCCONKEY KEVIN C MCELHANNON JR WILLIAM A PEDERSEN JOSE P RAMOS PABLO I SEDA
DAVID B TOLER FRANCIS J TROTTA JAMES M BALL JAMES R BODISH JAMES BROWN JR
ALTON D BYRD WILLIAM J FRANKLIN JOSEPH F KEENEY DONALD L PERCY HARRY R SCHETTLER
JERRY E BEVAN JAMES O CARR DAVID L CONNER JAMES J DALY EZEKIEL FRALEY JR
MARK T HEAVRIN WALTER W HUTTON RONALD L HUXTABLE JAMES L STRONG JOHN R TAMBURRI JR
ROGER O WELLS DAVID W BAKER JOE M BROWN JAMES C DU PONT ROBERT W NAPIER
TODD W OTTMAN LUCO W PALMA EDWARD L REYNOLDS LAWRENCE C WILLIAMS JR MARK E HAMBLETON
MARK A HENSLEY TORY D LAWRENCE MILAN L LEE JESSE L LENLEY LELAND M MEHLS
JOHN G MELCHOR FRANK H MILLER JR ROY C OLGYAY MICHAEL SANCHEZ JOHN E TOUART
ROGER D OVERWEG THOMAS A SHIPE RAYBURN L SMITH III GARY L ABRAHAMSON RAYMOND H APELLIDO
LARRY G BALDWIN LARRY R BUSICK FRANCO DIANI WILLIAM T DOTSON III DAN O FELTS
ALBERT M FINN JOSEPH J GAGNE ANTHONY J GALLINA GORDON K GATHMAN DALE A GRAY
ALFRED J HERRING JR JOHN P JOHNSON MICHAEL T LINVILLE CARL R MCCARTHY JR JOE H MONTOYA
RICHARD D MCFARLANE MICHAEL L MCVEY JOE PENA JR GLENN G RITCHIE JR HAROLD E SIDES
RICHARD H STUBE JOHN BOWEN JR BENJAMIN V DOMAN GERALD F FILIPPI WILLIAM J HODGES SR
TERRY L DEAN EARL E FORD ROBERT W GREBBY DAVID L HICKS THIERRY T MAXIM
LAYNE J ROMAGOSA FRANK B SANDERS STEPHEN T SMITH KENNA C TAYLOR LEO A BEACH JR
JACKIE R BROOKS WOODROW M CANNADY WILLIAM S DAVIS BOBBY G FIELDS MICHAEL J GAMBINO
JOHNNY C JONES HAROLD B KIMBROUGH NATALIE NOWACZYNSKI TOMMY W ROBERTSON JOHN D BASS
STEVEN F JINDRICH CALVIN R SEGAR FREDERICK J SMITH JAMES R TEFFS HIRAM E EDENTON JR
ROBERT C RIVEIRA RAYMOND D WOODSON JAMES R FORTENBERRY FRED FRENCH WILLIAM J FROSSARD
LARRY D HICKS JOHN W HINES EDWARD J LAKWA MYRON R NABOZNIAK BILLY H RATLIFF
RICHARD N SEGLEM THOMAS H ZAREMBA WILLIAM D BOTHWELL ALFRED L BRADLEY BERTRAM WOOD JR
GERALD A COOPER ROBERT J FISHLEIGH LLOYD H GRIMES II CHARLES M HALLSTROM JACKIE P HEIL
HERMAN LANCASTER JR GUS PIPPINS CARROLL S PLUM BRUCE E THOMAS ROBERT B WIRKS
DALE S CHAMBERLAIN DAVID D WOOTEN THOMAS M BARNETT ROBERT E BAUER BENJAMIN R BOSTICK IV
FREDERICK P BROYLES JOHN F BUESCHER DONALD D CRAW JR DONALD A HALL JR JOHN R HELMS
MARK R HOLTOM PAUL P KEEFE ERNEST H LAIDLER WARREN S LAWSON THOMAS S MALMAY
JOHN A OGRIZEK ROBERT A PAINTER JR JOSEPH A SILVA FRANCIS J SULLIVAN RICHARD A TAYLOR
DOUGLAS M WOODLAND MICHAEL L BRADLEY STANLEY A GOFF ROBERT O HILL JR WILLIAM J LANGMAN
EUGENE BEAN JR PHILLIP H JACOBS STEVEN H KRUPKIN DAVID W MACLURG KENNETH C NOKES
JOHN W PARSELLS ROBERT F RONGA JR JEFFREY M WHITE BLAKE E ASTON WESLEY W DAVIS
ANDRUS F DUPLECHAIN WILLIAM B HERN DAVID M HOPKINS JOSEPH O MCGEE JOSE MUNOZ JR
WILLIAM M PREDOVIC DOUGLAS H YUKI ALAN G CARLBORG BRYCE L KINDRICK LEONARD W KNOX
JAMES M BENICEK EDWARD P MCCARTHY III IGNACIO MONTERO ROBERT W NELSON WILLIAM J ODSTRCIL
JAMES A ROBERTS JR FREDDIE L TAPPER HARRY E TAYLOR BOBBY R WILLIAMS OTIS CARTER
RONALD E FIELDS JEROME R FRILLING BERNARD J RAFFERTY LARRY W BERKHOLTZ MELVIN G BRYANT
DAVID A CASON HASKELL J DOLAN GARRETT E EDDY RANDY L FISHER MARK A MATTER
JAMES MCDUFFIE JR JERRY W STEWARD LEE C TAYLOR MICHAEL S VRABLICK LEVERETT E YARBROUGH
MARK A OLSON RONALD K ALLGOOD WILLIAM I ALLSBROOK JR ROBERT W ALVERSON JR MICHAEL D BANTA
BENNETT J DAIGLE KENNETH O DICKSON ROBERT I GARCIA GEORGE R JOHNSON ROBERT W KERR
GERALD L MASEDA JAMES T MORIN JOHN L NESOVANOVIC ALFREDO SANUT BRUCE J STICKEL
MARK A TAFOYA DAVID F TINSEY KARL W TITUS JOHN L WAGNER MICHAEL G WARNICK
JIMMY W WESTBROOK JOHN H WINBORNE STANLEY H BARRETT RALPH G BARTLEY JR KENNETH J KOCH
STEVEN E LUCAS MICHAEL J SAMPSON OLEN L UPSHAW WALTER R WINTERS GARY P FORMICA
DAVID GADDIE JR STEVEN E GROVE DAVID W LARSON DENNIS L MIKOLAJCZYK BRUCE POLESETSKY
MARK T SORCI JOHN D STARRETT BRIAN D UPRIGHT CLARK T BOOTZ DAVID A DAVIDSON
TERRY L DEER FRED A GASSMAN VAUN A GORBE RICHARD M HOPE WARREN E KINDSVATTER
JOSEPH MCGUCKIN ANDRES MORENO JR ELPIDIO J RAVELO-TORIBIO DENNIS E VACENOVSKY WILLIE J RAY
RICHARD J WATTS CHARLEY A WILBORN MICHAEL D GENTRY JAMES M KELSO JOHN B MARTIN II
JAMES V LLOYD DANNY J SHORES RUBEN B SUNIGA JOHN V WILLIAMS JR EDWARD W WITHEE
RICHARD R YOUNG MICHAEL A GRAHAM DAVID E HENDRY JON C JACOBSON STEVEN C JOHNSON
CRAIG MARATTA ALBERT E METTINGER JOE H MORRISON DOUGLAS H SILVERNAIL RICHARD W BEEBE
CLEMMIE BROWN JR DOUGLAS E BYRD WILLIS COBB GUY W HESTER JR WILLIAM A OTT
DONALD E SHAY JR ROBERT TRUGLIO DAVID A CONNEL GEORGE W DANIELS JR FREDERICK A HOLST
WILLIAM E JOHNSTON CHARLES E KOBERLEIN WILLIE J MCLAURIN JACK A PERRY EUGENE J TONI
DAVID M ALLEN JAMES A BAILEY DALLAS A DRIVER JIMMY R GARBETT EDWARD B IWASKO
DON JENKINS DANIEL S LAZAR HARRY J LUMPKIN RAYMOND G MOORE THOMAS C SCHIESS
JAMES L SUYDAM DONNY L TUCKER JAMES H TURNER FRANK L WILSON ROBERT W BRUNSON
TERRY R ALBRIGHT GREGORY W BEECY THOMAS M BOYER MARTIN G GILLIAM PETER R GOODNIGHT
LEONALD G GUILETTE PETER S HAWLEY LARRY D SHELTON MICHAEL SMITH MELVIN E TUCKER
CLYDE E WALTER JR DONALD N WHITE ROBERT B BAKER JR LARRY G BATCHER ROBERT J BELTRAN
WILLIAM E BOONE MICHAEL R BORG TERRY M CONWAY AMOS M CRAIGE JERALD S DE LONG
JOHN S HUNT DONNIE R MARTIN WILLIAM A NEU CASEY C PERRY FRANCIS E POWERS JR
THEODORE T ROWLEY JOHN A SPENCE III GARRY L WEAVER CLIFFORD I WRIGHT EUGENE O BROWN
STEPHEN M CADY LARRY R CONLEY LEWIS L FOWLER MARK I GROSS RICKS A HUTSON
JOSEPH L CHESTNUT ROBERT E HARPER LOUIS E JANCA GEORGE H KINGSTON JR ANIBAL P LOZADA-WICHY
LARRY A MACKEY PHILLIP A NICHOLS ALBERT M REED LAWRENCE M SULLIVAN LARRY A WALKER
ROBERT L BRUNCKHORST JR ROBERTS P BURROWS EDWIN H CURTISS TROY DURDEN LAMAR MCLEOD

PANEL 6W

WILLIAM H STROUD JOHN H THOMAS JR CARL J WANKA CECIL A WELLMAN
WILLIE J FLEMING KERRY R GOSSMAN JOE R ROBERTS JR JONATHAN C SHINE ALLEN J SMITH
JOHN S FAKO ERNEST D CARDWELL DOMINIC J DE ANGELIS WILFREDO GAVILAN-TORRES STEPHEN E JESKO
JOHN D LIVINGSTON BERNARD J LOVETT JR DAVID A MOORE ROBERT T WILSON JOHN R BREGLER
GARY W ENGELHARDT WILBERT E JONES WILLIAM M KOTNIK GUY L MEARS JR JAMES J QUINN III
JOHN M THAYER CHARLES E THOMAS BENTON C WILLIAMSON JOHN C ZAGER RAE A BAILEY
WILLIAM J CAHILL LEO A COLEMAN RANDALL C KNISELY RANDALL C KNISLEY SIDNEY A KURZ GREGORY M KUTKOWSKI
FREDERICK L NUTTER DONALD B SOWELL DOUGLAS F STRAIT DENCIL R BLANKENSHIP DAVID E BRYANT
CLEATIS L BURGESS DICKEY CRAIG DONALD E FISCHER DANIEL L FRIES MICHAEL P ZACHARZUK
HAROLD C MARSH RALPH P MILLER III DARRYL K SCOTT DAVID E WEST PETER J WILSON
DONALD C GAY GARY R CADY ALEXANDER CAMPBELL JR HAROLD C GAY BYRON M HANNAH
JOHN D DRAKE TERENCE A HANDLEY LARRY W KILGORE VINCENT R KOTARSKI JR RICHARD W MARSHALL
THOMAS S MCGARRY KENNETH M SCHLIE FLOYD A SCHLIEWE GARY L SCHROEDER JOSEPH J STOJINSKI JR
THOMAS R WEISS GARY R WILLIAMS LINWOOD C CARTER JR JAMES W DICKEY RONALD A FELKAMP
MICHAEL V SOLOMON GARY W BARTMESS VICTOR L BLACK ROGER L COEN TOUSSAINT O DALTON JR
GEORGE A HAIN MILO C ISAACS ANGEL J MORENO ROBERTO L PATINO STEPHEN P SCHRIVER
KENNETH C THORNTON DAVID T WILLIAMSON RAYMOND R BERGER NATHAN L INGLE MICHAEL J LE BOEUF
TIMOTHY J O'CONNOR RICHARD L TATE WILLIAM H CLIFFORD WILLIAM M DAULTON JERRY S FORD
THOMAS E HEIDEMAN RUSSELL W MULDER CARTER PARKER JR MICHAEL H PETERSON CRAIG B SCHIELE
JEFFREY M SHAW GREGARY A WILKS DENNIS C CANNAN ZANE CHRISTIE MANUEL D DOMINE
MAX E CARROLL ALBERT F GRAHAM JR PHILLIP H KILVER TIMOTHY R OWNBEY KIM W WIDMER
JOSEPH P JURGELLA ROBERT M SHUPTRINE PETER P BOHNWAGNER JOSEPH BORRUSO JR DONALD R COOK
ROBERT M GAFFIGAN THOMAS A GOEBEL DALE V HARGROVE KENNETH W HENDRIX GEORGE A MILIKA
DENNIS E REESE KARL L REINECCIUS CHARLES F SMITH JACK L BAGLEY JAMES E MILLER
BOBBY J PARRIS ALEX D PYSZ ROBERT E RINGENBERGER JOSEPH D CASLER MONROE J CONLEY
JOHN E STRAUB GERALD M WILLIAMS WILLIAM T FINDLAY JAMES T GERMAIN NATHANIEL LEWIS
ALFRED R MATTHEWS JAMES R MAYES GARY R MCHUGH MICHAEL A MICKO DERRELL L PONDER
JAMES A QUINN JUAN F ARANDA CLIFFORD G BURDETTE HAYLEN F GLENN PETER B STADDON
LARRY E HENDRICK OSCAR R LAYPORTE BRUCE A MCNEIL JOHN P MUSICH CARL E OWENS
FRANCISCO M ASANOMA MOSES PLACERES GARY W RICHARDSON LESTER S VESS JOHN E WINTERS
FRANCIS J BUNCH JERRY A DENNIS DOUGLAS G EHLERS RICHARD M FACER LEON E KISER
JAMES A LAIRD ROBERT E LINVILLE JIMMY E MARCHESI TIMOTHY F MURPHY JR PAUL E REED
PAUL SIRIANNI JR WALTER L MAURER JOSEPH E ROHLINGER ERHARD J ADAMS GREGORY W AULTMAN
THOMAS R BRADY KENNETH L BROWN DOUGLAS J CAMPBELL GARY W COKLEY CARL D COOPER
STEPHEN J KASTER JOHN C KING OSCAR MALONEY JOHN T ORRICO FREDERICK W PRUDEN
GEORGE H ROGALLA JEROME M ROUSE WENDELL TAYLOR EUGENE H CRUMPTON ROBERT A DERRICK
TERRY A HALE PERRY C KITCHENS ROBERT E MORRIS JR BILLY H PEEPLES RAYMOND TANNER
RAY ARNETT JR ROBERT H BENNETT JOSEPH B BRITTAIN LUIS A CRUZ JOHNELL WITHERSPOON
CHARLES D HOFFMAN BRUCE C HUNT LEONARD A LANZARIN JAIME RESTREPO JOSEPH M SOTO
KEVIN R HUMPHREY RONALD W ISENHOUR PETER J LANDRY ROBERT K MILBRATH SEWALL K LAWRENCE
WALTER J ROBERTS PATRICK D ROSEN LYNNE H RUTTER GORDON B SEARS NICHOLAS R TUNNY
J C DAVIS MEREDITH L BARNETT WILL D BILLINGS LONNIE D FIELDS RUBENEDID HERNANDEZ-RODRIG
GARY D MCMILLIN HERBERT H MOORE JOHN T PETTITT SR DONALD R SOLES CHARLES V DONOHOE
RAYMOND C HUOT JR ANDREW S PIERCE JR ARTHUR L SUTTON ROBERT E BARNHILL HERMINIO G CENTENO
RONALD L CLELAND DARRELL L COLFORD JOEL CORONA CARROLL D FISHER CHRISTOPHER W MORGENS
WILLARD FREEMAN TERRANCE J MCGOVERN DONALD W MCINTOSH HUGH J SHEVLIN WILLIAM K VADEN JR
TIMOTHY D AMICK JAMES P CODDINGTON RANDALL L ELLIS REX L FRAZIER RONALD E GERSTNER
FRANCIS W HARTER HARRY S MASON JR LUIS E MUNIZ-GARCIA HARRY T PETERSEN JAMES H SAXTON JR
JOHN W HERRING JOHNNY P COSTNER BENTLEY T DAVIS VICTOR M DE WALT WALDEMAR S GRZESKOWIAK
CHARLES V MCGOVERN GEORGE E ROYE FRANCIS X BUNK RONALD E GARLAND CURTIS RICHARD
CHARLES M GEORGE MCKINLEY H HARVELL JR JOHN E HOLLIS CHARLES G HUGHES DANIEL J JEDNEAK
RONALD J DI BARTOLOMEO DENNIS R LINNELL GREGORY L WHITE ROYCE L ADDINGTON JOSE G BARRERA
JOHN D BARRETT DONALD W CHIPP JR ROGER D COLE FREDDIE L DACUS TITUS L EPPS
GARLAND P FELTON DAVID L HATCHER DAVID B HOCKENSMITH JESSE L KESTLER JOE B MCNETT
DAVID A NUDENBERG EDUARDO C RAMIREZ WILLIAM C REED CRAIG T RESKA WILLIAM L AIKEN
SALVATORE J ARMATO WILLIAM W BANCROFT JR KEN D BURNS JOHN J FARNSWORTH JR ROBERT H GUMM JR
JAMES L HATCHER MONROE A POWERS CHARLES W ROBINSON ALVIN J SCOTT JOHN G STRACHOTA
DONALD L VALENTINE DAVID I WRIGHT CHARLES H ADAMS LEONARD P ALLEN PAUL T COE
JOHN W CONRAD BRUCE C ELKINS WILLIAM R ELLIS FRANK R HITESHUE ROBERT S ROCHA
FREDRICK J HUGHES MICHAEL C JENSEN JOSEPH R KLUGG JAMES M MEEHAN PERRY A MITCHELL
RONALD J HILL RAE K RIPPETOE STANLEY H TRYGG JR BENIGNO ZAMUDIO JR CLARENCE R PRITCHARD JR
WILLIS E EALEY BERT M GUENTHER JR THURSTON C HEAGGANS VINCENT L ROSSI SR RICHARD W SALMOND
JAMES W SCHELLIN COUNCIL D VAUGHAN DOUGLAS E WHITE ROBERT G DRAPP BRUCE L HANKINS
MICHAEL K JOHNSON RICHARD L KELTON DEXTER J LOMBAS JAMES F RILEY JOHN M ROE
DAVID A SAIDE CHARLES R SELLERS NORMAN R STODDARD JR KENNETH D ADKINS JOSEPH CARTER JR
LARRY A DAHMS DENNIS E STECKER ROGER S URBANI RICHARD R BUTTRY RUSSELL G DANIELS
ENVER BAJIN DONNIE L CUNNINGHAM DAVID V DELOZIER ROBERT A DONNELL II CLEVELAND R HARVEY
GARY D HUDSON THOMAS A KNOPIK WILLIAM G LEFTWICH JR RANDALL P MANELA BENTON L MILLER
CHARLES A POPE JR ORVILLE C ROGERS JR JOHN F STOCKMAN JAMES E STOLZ JR ROBERT E TUCKER
FERNANDO VILLASANA ROBERT H WILSON JR WILLIAM R ASQUITH THOMAS R BIERLINE JOHN R GRISARD
BRUCE C HALBACH FRANKLIN A HAMM WILLIAM A MONTANO THOMAS L OSTEEN JR WILLIAM J PERRYMAN
JUAN J PLAZA STANLEY D STRUBLE JAMES C WASHINGTON JR FRANKLIN R AKANA PHILLIP J BARBA
RALPH W BASNIGHT DENNIS H DALE ARTHUR FISHER WILLIAM E FLEMING JR THEODORE ISOM
JAMES JOHNSON JR MARION E MEE TERRENCE P O'BOYLE ROBERT L SHRINER RAY E TANNER
FRANCIS A ZERGGEN DENNIS L ZIEBARTH JAMES I BOWDREN JR THOMAS R BRADLEY CURTERS J BURNETT
JIMMY R CALLISON JOHN R MUCCI RICHARD C SCHOENBERG TOMMY BOWENS JEFFREY A COFFIN
BRENT A HAYTON ROBERT L HUDSON MATEO JUAREZ ROBERT D KAVICH MARK A LARSON
RONALD D LE FEBURE MICHAEL T MARTIN ROGER L RITSCHARD DOUGLASS T WHELESS DANIEL J CHAVEZ
DARRELL B RICKER ROBERT C RUNGE CLAIR E SAINT VERNON G ZORNES IAN MCINTOSH
MARTIN I ARBEIT DAVID A BRYAN VICTOR L ELLINGER JAMES E ESKRIDGE NORMAN F EVANS
BENJAMIN J ANTHONY MICHAEL D GEHRT ROBERT C GOTTIER PAUL G KELLEY WARREN H MOBLEY
NORMAN F PALEY ROBERT D PERRY SAMUEL R SAITO WILLARD G STORIE FRANK D TINSLEY
CHARLES R HAMILTON MICHAEL N HUGHES FREDDIE L LOCKHART LAWRENCE E SCOTT LYLE D HAYES
EDWARD D BURKETT SAMUEL L GANTT RALPH HOWELL DAVID E KILLIAN PHILIP E RICHARD
WILLIAM C ARIAS JR MARVIN S ARTHINGTON ROBERT L BAKER ALLEN J BODIN RAMON A HERNANDEZ
PAUL T GILLASPIE THOMAS W GOSZEWSKI JORGE L JOURDAN-FONT FREDERICK R NEEF WILLIAM B O'KIEFF
FREDERICK M RADER III MACARIO SANCHEZ JR CHARLES F CREAMER III GARY E FIELD DAVID C JAUREGUI
FRANKLIN U BRECKENRIDGE ALBERT HALL ROBERT J KOLY JAMES B POWELL JR EUGENE PRINCE JR
RONALD E SMITH CRAIG N WARD EARNEST WILLIAMS GARY ANDERSON JOHN R BEAN
GEORGE BEEDY JOSEPH C BLACKWELL ELMON C CAUDILL II FRANKLIN D DEFENBAUGH JACK R GIBBS
RAYMOND H GRAY SAMUEL A GRAYSON III PHELBON M GREEN RONALD R GREENHOUSE RALPH S GUCK
BILLY J HOGAN JR CHARLES A JOHNSON III ROBERT B JOHNSON WILLIAM D KENNEDY III JAMES F SAXBY
WILLIAM A KETCHUM JR JON M KING CHARLES L KOLLENBERG LEE R LINTON SAMMIE J LONG
ARTHUR J MENN CECIL G MOYER JR GRAYSON H NEWBERRY DOUGLAS H PARRIS NORBERT A PODHAJSKY
JOSEPH A JACQUES ROBERT J POLNIAK ROBERT D SCHNEIDER BOBBY D SEAY DONALD A SLATE
JAMES C STARNES JAMES E STUBBLEFIELD RONNIE C TESCHENDORF HARRY A WATSON JAMES B YOUNG
ROBERT E YOUNG CLARENCE E BAKER ROBERT A BOJANEK DOUGLAS S BRIDGERS CHARLES R COILEY
RAFAEL A DIAZ EUGENE EDWARDS FREDERICK L FIELDS ROBERT S GEER DONALD L GOLDEN
JAMES D JONES ROBERT G MOORE BENJAMIN R NELSON JR PATRICK J PAULICH JOHN C STRINGER II
FELIPE MORALES KENNETH L ROBERTSON DENNIS M SMITH ROGER W ANDERSON JR ROBERT L BLACKWELL
LAVERNE D COYLE KENNETH E CRAYNE THOMAS W FRECH ERIC L GRIFFITH JOHN H HOLMES
WALTER D LAMBERT ARTHUR W MACHEN III JOE M PALACIO RAYMOND B PENN JR STEPHEN C SELLETT
JOHN L STALLINGS JESUS M BERRIOS-RIVERA LEONARD P KUNSMAN JR JAMES H MARKLAND PAUL E WOLFE
FRANCISCO VEGA DAVID M BAUM JOHNNY P GARCIA LARRY E GILLIAM ROBERT L HOWELL
ROBERT L KING SCOTT L SCHMIDT JERRY D WALKER PETER C BEHRENS RICHARD L BLASKOWSKI
HENRY L CHAVIS GEORGE C GREEN JR JAMES R HEIMBOLD TERRY D KINMAN JOHN I LASSITTER
ANDREW MACHRISTIE KERMIT L MATTHEWS HOWARD J SCOVILLE JOE D TORRES ROBERT A WILLIAMS JR
DAVID J SCHMERBECK WAYNE L KENT SAI G LEW RANDY D RAY BOBBY L ROBERTSON BRUCE W SPRING
BILLIE R STROHL ROBERT W TOLER JR STEVEN C WILLIS MICHAEL H ALSEVER GEORGE E BAILEY
ALVIN L EVANOFF BERNARD HODGES WALTER V MARCUM ROBERT J SEUFERT ROY E SHAW JR
WALTER J TAYLOR JR ROY ANDERSON JR CLIFFORD K BAADE NICHOLAS A BERGER WILLIAM E BERRYMAN
OMER P CARSON PAUL COLWELL CHARLES W COX JOE E CRENSHAW HAROLD N FLIEGER
THOMAS L LAFFERTY CARMINE A MACEDONIO CHARLES T MORTON RICHARD L REED DENNIS L ROUSKA

285

THE VIETNAM VETERANS MEMORIAL COLLECTION

JOHN D BRYANT ARDEN R LYBERGER WILLIAM H MARTIN MARK C WITTBRACHT GEORGE T CONNOLLY
OTIS E ANDREWS MICHAEL J PETRASHUNE GUILLERMO RODRIGUEZ BERNARD L SWIGER ALVARO BARBOSA
ROGER A BARNHART THOMAS C CISAR BARRY E CLARK THOMAS A DUCKETT GARY L GAINER
LUTHER GREEN JR RONALD K KELSEY CARLOS RIVERA JR OWEN G SKINNER JOHNNY D VERSCHEURE
DAVID L NORRIS MICHAEL K WOODCOCK RICHARD L FERGUSON RODNEY C GREY DONALD R JENKINS
JOHN T KILE TOMMY G MORRIS EARL E SHANNON TIMOTHY J THOMPSON PAUL R BRASS
DUANE G CORDINER RANDALL G FREEMAN TERRENCE T JACKSON STEVE F JOHNSON JEFFERY D KUERSTEN
KENNETH H LOVE RICHARD L MAYNARD JR DENNIS R MORENO JOHN W MURPHY JOHN W RUCKER
ROGER W SWEET PAUL W BURNETT CARROLL J DEUSO RALPH T GLIM WILLIAM D GRIFFIN II
HERMAN F IVEY MERIL O MCCOY JR CLYDE C OWEN ANTHONY J PIERSANTI JR WILLIAM S STEWART
JOHN F SZLAPA III THOMAS D YOUNG ROBERT T CALLAN JOSEPH J DANNA JR GARY J FACULAK
STARR F FRYE DAVID L GILMOR VAL C ROBINSON RONALD C WALTERS JOHN O WARREN
FRED A WILLIAMS JOHN J WILSON PHILLIP A WILSON JOSEPH P CURTIS GREGORY A GYDESEN
RAYMOND J FLYNN JR ANDREW C GUERRERO THOMAS F HERRING WILLIAM T JOHN FERENC J RAMM
JAMES P ALLENBERG ELWOOD C BAKER GARY L BARTELS JAMES W CARTER DONALD C CORDLE
CLAYTON G CRAIG ROBERT D CRANSON HARVEY G JACOBSON PAUL D LACROIX BRUCE G SEMPSROTT
SAMUEL R LYNCH STEPHEN M LYNCH MICHAEL B MARCUS JOHN MARTINEZ BOBBY L PALK
DAROLD JETERS ROY L SIMMONS FLOYD D SOLOMON JOSEPH W BLICKENSTAFF JR RICHARD H BUZZELL
DAN L COOMBS III DERALD J HOOD GEORGE A KNETSAR AVON N MALLETTE ANTONIO O ORTIZ
KERRY W PHILLIPS JOHNNY RATLIFF ROBERT W RICHARDSON ROBERT E WORTH FRANK W BOMAR
BOBBY R DAILEY SAZIN D FABACHER KEITH D HOLMES WILLIAM H REMELTS II JAMES L RITER
HAAG A VANDER ROBERT P NOWICKI GEORGE H PACIO VERNON R ANDERSON JR TONY H MYERS

PANEL 5W

DAVID N STEGER DENNIS N VATISTAS GARY P BOOTH WILLIAM N BULTHUIS
RAYMOND D KAMINSKI JESSIE R LINDLER MICHAEL W MCANDREWS ERVIN J MURRELL THOMAS W SHAW
JAMES V DRAGONE RICHARD W SCOBY DALE E SHULTZ MICHAEL M SIKICH GARY W SMITH
BAIN W WISEMAN JR JOHN G BUCHANAN PAUL J DAMATO JR SAMUEL E DICK GREGORY W FELKER
TERRENCE L HARRIS LARRY M HEEN ALBRO L LUNDY JR CALVIN D MACK WILLIAM E MCLEAN
THOMAS G NOBLE MICHAEL R NUGENT VERN E ODOM JR WESLEY L PHILLIPS STEVE POHANCEK
HENRY E SANTEE JOSEPH C SPENCE JR MICHAEL J TECCO WILLIAM H YOUNT JR THOMAS G BRUBAKER
DONALD J KNEBEL RICHARD J KNICKERBOCKER ANTHONY A BRESE RICHARD W DOTSON BILLY R FARRIOR
JOSEPH W GUINN CLIFFORD T JOHNSON MICHAEL D MCADOO GARY E MCDANIEL MARSHALL MILLER
ARTHUR H PRICE PAUL R VILLALOBOS LAWRENCE G BANGS RAYMOND R COOREMAN ELROY F WELLS
MARTIN J HANLON RAYMOND C HOLT ROY D JORDAN JACK W MCCANN ESTEBAN V ROCHEZ
JERRY E HANCOCK BRADLEY E SANDFORD DAVID L TEMPLETON CARVER J VAUGHAN ROBERT D ARNALL
FREDRICK K BRANDT KENNETH W GRIFFIN JAMES L SMITH ROGER L TEETER ROBERT J CURTIS
LONNIE E DUMAS TIMOTHY H LACY JOHN E NORTON HOWARD W BRAMLETT JR PARK G BUNKER
STEVE S DE NIKE BRIAN A HORINEK LARRY J ANDERSON HAROLD E ASHER EDGAR P BECK JR
ROY L CHANEY RICHARD E DODD JERRY B EDMONDS JR RICHARD M ESCALERA PETE E WILLIAMSON
RONALD E GERTEN IRA E GIBBS LEROY E HALBERT JR STEVE L LAVERTY JOHN F NEUBAUER
JOHN J ORSINI JR THURSTON C ROBERTS WAYNE S RUSHTON ALFREDO SALAZAR HENRY J SIMS
THOMAS H HUDSON JACK E HYATT FREDERICK R FRACIONE WENDELL L WALLACE DENNIS W WEBSTER
MICHAEL A PIERCE EUGENE I SMITH DONALD D WINN STANLEY G CROCKETT GARY L DENT
ROBERT A HARRISON FRANK J LUKITSCH JR BAEZ R SERVERA HARVEY G SOKOLOF JAMES H AYRES
LUIS G HOLGUIN BRUCE M KELLER HARRY LEWIS JR PATRICK J MAGEE THOMAS R OKERLUND
ROBERT L OLIVER DENNIS W OMELIA CARL A PALEN MICHAEL D PARSONS KENNETH POWERS
FERRIS A RHODES JR LONNIE L STERN WILLIAM T STODARD CHARLES W STRATTON DAVID A TRESTER
JONATHAN T WILSON ROBERT A DOTEN GLEN C KLEIN BRIAN R KOEHN BOBBIE L WILLIAMS
DENNIS L BUTLER WINSTON BUTLER JR DONALD M CRAMER RAYMOND R ENYEART JR HOWARD W GIPSON
LARRY O HARDEN GLENN E KELLY DOUGLAS B KENT JOHN W LYNCH III RODNEY E MORGAN
EUGENE H MCKAY III RONNIE V ROGERS GLENN C VALENTE FREDERICK W BALDAUF GARY R BOECK
LARRY T DUCKETT BRUCE L GOODSELL STEVEN MIKE CARLETON P MILLER JR NELLO BALDWIN JR
STEPHEN E BOOTS RICK S BROWN GERARD CORRIVEAU JAMES L CRAIG GORDON A FISH
GERALD W HILL ROBERT B MICHALK RUSSEL C NELSON ROBERT L PAYNTER CHARLES M PRICE
KENNETH R RUSHING RICHARD E TABOR WILLIAM C VASEY DOUGLAS M BECKMAN JAMES H CARTWRIGHT
KEITH R CURRY ROBERT DEGEN ROBERT D DUFF BILLY W HARTWICK PATRICK J KIHL
JAIME LABOY CECIL C OLSEN JAMES R SHAW JOHN E STEWART ROBERT L WALKER JR RICHARD H SANSBURY
DENNIS R WATTERSON BENNIE F JONES DAVID W LILLEY LOUIS PAYNE SR CLINTON C ROBINSON
CRAIG A SYSAK GORDON L WIRTH JR WILLARD E WOODY BARRY H BERGER CECIL E CALLANDER
KENNETH A DAHL DOUGLAS O FORD LEWIS S HALL JERRY T HICKEY WILLIAM T JOHNSON
PHILIP J ADAMS STEPHEN P KRUG JOE H LILLIE CORNELIUS H RAM JACKIE L SAWNEY JAMES T ABBOTT
EDWARD W BETHARDS ROBERT D BLACK JR RICHARD V BLACKBURN LEE W CLORE ALLEN R GRAY
JAMES F HUGGINS THOMAS F IRVIN WILLIAM F JOHNSON DAVID L MEYER LEO J ROSE
RICHARD L RUSHLOW JOSE R SANDOVAL WILLIAM E STRACNER FRANCIS J THORPE REX A VOGELPOHL
DARREL J CLODFELTER STEPHEN E HENDRICKS EDWARD J KAPUSTA BILLY R PRICE JR ROBERT J LA FLAMME
HAROLD E CARR DENNY R EASTER ROBERT D HERTZ JERRY L MOFFETT ROBERT R ENOS JR
DONALD W SMITH RUDOLPH C THOMAS EDGAR L WEST JR BILLY R ANDERSON DAVID L BUTLER
DANIEL F COX JOSEPH W GAA JR JAMES A HARWOOD GERALD F KINSMAN LARRY D LOVE
WILLIAM A MALENFANT CURTIS W MOORE WILLIAM NAKI III DELBERT R PORTER BRIAN P RUSSELL
ROBERT E SHARPE WILLIAM R ZEYEN JEFF T BARNETT SR CHARLES R BESS DEWAINE L BRICKMAN
PAUL DARBY JOHN E DAVIS DONALD G DETRICK JOHN M GRAHAM NOEL B HERNANDEZ
HERBERT S HINSON ROGER G HOLLER MARTIN JIM JR PAUL E LEARY JR CARLTON J MENDALL
TERRY F MEZERA EARL NELSON REINALDO R RODRIGUEZ ROY R SALINAS BRUCE C SHOVER
CHARLES D STCLAIR LEE D STUART JR WILLIAM H THIGPEN JOHNNY N WARD JR JOHN S WEAVER
WILLIAM B BLACKMON JR ALBERT L BROWN DAVID W COON JOHN L DOBROSKI DANIEL K ERLANDSON
JOHN H GEDDINGS MALCOLM J LYONS ROBERT H MIRRER JESSE E NIXON JAMES M SCHERER
PERRY M SMITH CECIL W SOUTHERLAND JOSEPH S TIDWELL WILLIAM F AARONSON IV RONNIE BRICE
JOSHUA M DANIELS EUGENE T GILMORE BILLY J PLASTER JR LARRY J PRICE WILBUR D LATIMER
STEPHEN A ALTSCHAFFL GLENN R ETHINGTON JESUS A GONZALES RONALD D ROWSEY WILLIAM RUIZ JR
JAMES F THAMES HESSIE A BROOKS JAMES R GARTEN TOMMY H IVEY ROBERT P MARSDEN
ARTHUR S NABBEN RONALD D STEPHENSON RONALD M GARRISON ROBERT HRISOULIS LOUIS W TRAVERS
SAMUEL H BARNETT GREGORY S KARGER EUGENE J LEVICKIS STEVEN W MOLL BARTOW W POTTS JR
RONNIE G VAUGHAN LARRY D BEAN FRANK A CELANO ROG JOHNSON KENNETH LOVELACE
HUGH D OPPERMAN GREGORY L PEFFER MICHAEL H PETTY DENNIS R SCHOSSOW WILLIAM H SEABORN JR
DONALD L SENTI FREDERICK A VIGIL ALFONSO A BRITO JERRY W CUTTING GEORGE R MARR JR
RONALD J REVIS JAMES L COLWYE STEPHEN L LINDSAY CALVIN E MILAM WILLIAM L MORGAN
RICHARD C PORTER MERRELL E BRUMLEY JR WILLIAM O CREECH JR JUAN E GONZALES GERALD L CARTER
JAMES P MARKEY JR WILLIAM D NICODEMUS GEORGE L ROBERTSON ROBERTO L CANAS JOHN M NEILL
DEWIGHT E NORTON STEVEN J OLCOTT WILLIAM F REICHERT JAMES E WEATHERSBY GARNEY BURLESON JR
DEAN A HARRIS RONALD M RIGDON ARTHUR A SMITH MICHAEL E WILLIAMS HAROLD B LINEBERGER
DAVID I MIXTER ROBERT L PULLIAM JEFFREY L BARLOW HAROLD E BIRKY JAMES P DUNCAN
ALLEN C ELL RAFAEL GARCIAPAGAN RONALD W HACKNEY RONALD N JASINSKI PAUL E LEE
JOHN R MILLER ROBERT A SISK JOHNNY C SPEARS JOHNNY E TIVIS PATRICK G CARTWRIGHT LARRY J PEPPER
JOSEPH W CASINO CLYDE W COBLE GORDON L CRAWFORD JAMES C HARRIS LOREN D LEBEAU
KEITH M JACKSON WALTER X MENDEZ THOMAS C MILLER STEPHEN A MOORE STEPHEN E WARREN
RICHARD D RANDOLPH KEITH A STODDARD MICHAEL P AUSTIN DARRELL W COWAN ROBERT E TAYLOR
FRANK S MCCUTCHEON III FLOYD RICHARDSON JR JOHN C STRAUSER PHILIPP R VOLLHARDT
LUTHER N BAGNAL III MARTIN J BURNS MILFRED R GREEN LENNART G LANGHORNE THOMAS A MRAVAK
ROBERT L STANDERWICK SR JOSEPH L STONE WALLIS W WEBB TERRENCE W WELDON ROBERT J WILLIAMS
JACKIE L DENNY SAMUEL H EBERHART LARRY H MARSHALL DANIEL J MULLEN GREGORY S SOMERS
DAYLE R HALL ANDRES L RAMON NELSON G RICHARDSON STEPHEN M TRAYNOR PATRICK J TROTTER
CLIFTON E CALLAHAN DAVID C JOHNSON CLIFTON C NEWCOMB JAMES L PAUL DAVID A SEMMLER
CARL M WOOD LARRY A WOODBURN RICHARD A AARON DAVID L ALEXANDER KENNETH W BONESTROO
FRANK J GASPERICH JR AMBERS A HAMILTON ROBERT P JACQUES MICHAEL J KERL CARROLL R MILLS
WILLIAM B RHODES ROBERT J ROGERS JOSEPH A TERESINSKI CURTIS L WILLIAMS THEODORE R MASON
BRIAN R FOLEY THOMAS P KING RICHARD S KULWICKI WILLIAM A LARGENT GARY LEWIS
RUSSELL G BLOCHER DONALD L MEEHAN JR CHARLES L PEACE JOSE M ROCHA DOUGLAS R SCHMALTZ
ROLAND D TROYANO BRUCE A VAN DAM CHARLES E WITHERSPOON HARRY WOLFENDEN LEWIS R YATES
THOMAS A SONY RAFAEL R BENITEZ CHARLES G BOBO TYRONE C BRADLEY BARRY L BRINEGAR
LONALD R COLEMAN THOMAS P DOODY MICHAEL B FIRST DAVID N FOX ROBERT B GENTRY
RANDALL L HARRIS KEVIN P KNIGHT DALE W MEAD LEWIS D MEYER JR JOSEPH W MILEY
LENOX L RATCLIFF JOHN E ROBERTSON CHARLES H SOULE PAUL C STEWART JOHNNY M TINNEY
GERALD J TWOREK GREG R CARTER BRUCE A CHRISTENSEN DANIEL F FARRELL SHELBY G HENSLEY
MELVIN J FELTON EDGAR MCDANIEL STEVEN D MCDOWELL JAMES A MCINTYRE EDMOND S BLACKBURN JR
FRED D PAKELE NORMAN J PEARSON PHILLIP J SANDOVAL STEPHEN L WHISENANT BLAKE D WHITNEY
JAMES F COLLINS MICHAEL C LAWSON DONALD A MACKEY JOSEPH R PIETRZAK CHRISTOPHER L RAIMEY
MARK J ROBERTSON MONETTE V WHITE JOSEPH R ANTHONY KENNETH A BARGER RAYMOND F CARROLL
OLAN D COLEMAN JAMES F CONNOR JR CHARLES M DEAS DONALD L DUNN ROBERT A EISENBEISZ
CLYDE W HANSON ROY L HELBERT GEORGE G HUTSON MICHAEL D MCGOVERN CHARLES P MONTROSS
RICHARD W OKEEFE WAYNE O PATTERSON VERNON E RAINEY LUCIO J REIS DANIEL H TATE
WILLIS G UHLS WILLIAM L WILLIAMS JOSHUA E CARNEY AARON DAVIS JR STEVE C ENGLISH
WILLIE GARDNER JR WILLIAM J JOHNSON GARY W LARSON KENNETH A MEYER DAVID A MORAN
ARTHUR E MCLEOD JAMES V PICARAZZI JAMES G SIDDONS CLYDE D WILKINSON EDWARD S WISSIG
MICHAEL D ADKINS JOSEPH V MARTIN JAMES A MICHAEL WILLIAM E PIERCE KENNETH R PRICE
KARLHEINZ S SEIBERLING STEVEN L SEIGLER FREDERICK P SMITH DONALD G VOGET RICHARD D COVERT JR
DOUGLAS L HORN JAMES R JESKE PERRY METZLER ANDREW J NEWCOMBE RONALD C RUFF
STEPHEN H WARNER IVAN R ASPER JR JAMES R BROBST RICHARD N BRUSO BENJAMIN BURGOS-TORRES
JOSEPH S BURKE JAMES P COBB DAVID W COMBER RICHARD N CONCANNON WILLIS C CREAR
DONALD E CRONE STEVEN G ENGLAND BARRY F FIVELSON JOHN W HOWELL ZEBULON M JOHNSON JR
MARVIN M LEONARD JULIAN E MARQUEZ JOE L ORTEGA JR LARRY F OTT JOHN L POWERS
STANLEY E REDMON RICHARD B RINEHART WILLIAM D SAPP ROY D SHINGLER JAMES L SMITH
KENNETH M STEINKIRCHNER YOSHIO TAKEHARA TAGIPO V TAUALA JAMES H TAYLOR JAMES P THOMPSON

GABRIEL TRUJILLO KENNETH W TUCKER GERALD P WICK THOMAS W WIGGINS JAMES B CARTER
RICHARD W ELLISON CHARLES L HOSKINS MICHAEL R HUNTER LESLIE L KARNES EVELYN F LANKFORD
RALPH N PATTILLO JAMES M SIMON JAMES H STAFFORD GORDON A STOAKLEY RICHARD D BUCKLES
MICHAEL P DAMON TIMOTHY V HARPER JOHN D HODGE RICHARD E STUDIER HOWARD K WILLHITE JR
WILLIAM R HIGGINBOTHAM LESTER W ALIPIO JAMES E AUSTIN RICHARD T BAKER GEORGE P BERG
JOSEPH G BROWN GREGORY S CRANDALL WALTER E DEMSEY JR ROBERT J ENGEN DONALD G GIBLER
EARLEY C GRACE LARRY R HATTER WAYNE R HYATT GARY L JOHNSON COLEY L KENDALL
FRANK J KOHLMYER WALTER E LEWELLEN RICHARD A LILLIE ALLEN R LLOYD JAMES A LONG
JOSEPH H MARSHALL III ALLEN K MCELFRESH DANIEL O MURPHY WILLIAM C ODOM JR GREGORY A SLOAT
RONALD L WATSON STRATHER F WOOD GERALD E WOODS JACKIE W BARNWELL WILLIAM M FERNANDEZ
CURTIS E BURKETT ANTHONY J CARACCILO JR ROBERT L DALTON GERALD A GRAY JAMES L HULL
CLIFFORD W MARSHALL CHARLES T MATTHEWS LEONARD A MONNETT WADE H ROLLINS LYLE E SMITH
ROY M SMITH JAMES E TUCKER JR FRANCISCO N VALDEZ CLAYTON L WOODS ROBERT J ACALOTTO
CHRISTOPHER L CLEARWATERS CARLOS M DELGADO RICHARD B FRAZIER DENNIS E GILLILAND
DAVID N HEAD DANIEL J HOHMAN JOHN C HUNTER RANDOLPH L JOHNSON ROBERT W JOHNSON
BRIAN W KONG CHESTER G LYONS BENJAMIN K MALABEY WILLIAM W MALONE DAVID M MAY
GLENN W MCCARTY CARL NACCA JR JOHN V RAUEN JON E REID JAMES K SCHMOLL
CHARLES E BOVINETTE JR GEORGE T TAFF JR DAVID T TAYLOR PETER L BARILI CARL H CACCIA JAMES P CALIFF
ROBERT CORONADO ROBERT E DE CELLE II EDWARD F DOWNEY JR SABINO LARA JR JOHN J LEVULIS
ROGER L MAKI RICHARD L MARTIN TERRY L NIELSEN ROBERT J POTTS JOHN R SELAK
MITCHELL B SMITH ROBERT J THELEN FREDERICK A YOUNG CHARLES E ENGLE LARRY G MITCHELL
RONALD G CURTIS MONTY L HARBIN RICHARD L SARVIS EDWARD E SCOTT JR RAYMOND L ARMENTROUT
JAMES E BARTON JOHN W BRUIN DOUGLAS J CRAWFORD LARRY G DAHL RANDOLPH B MCKELLIPS
RONALD J FISHER RICHARD J FRAZIER GENARO GARZA JOSEPH B HART TERRANCE A OGATA
CHARLES R HAUSHERR STEPHEN M HISCOCK JAMES E JOHNSON III MARVIN A LUERKENS DANIEL J MAES
FREDERICK L BEATTY DENNIS C FARRIS VINCENT J MEDJESKY JAMES A MINER PEDRO C PANGELINAN

PANEL 4W

ROY Y SHINKAWA RICKEY A SLANDER TERRY M USHER WILLIAM T WALERZAK
THOMAS E BENNETT STEVEN W GOELZ VERNON A GREEN CLARENCE D HAKES STANLEY A JACKSON
CRAIG J JAKEL ARTHUR K KAWACHIKA MICHAEL H KEYS DENNIS A SMITH JOSEPH M WILSHER
TOMMIE BAINES DAVID A BARTON DENNIS A DAVISON ADOLFO GONZALEZ-LOPEZ MICHAEL K MALONEY
FLOYD H GOFF EDWARD A JOHNSON JR GERALD JOHNSON DAVID D PEOPLES JR WILLIAM S WOODS
PETER M LOPEZ JR LUISAR QUINONES-RODRIGU RICHARD K SOMERS RICHARD L HAMILTON ROY L PETTY
LARRY G HARRISON MICHAEL W LANGNEHS WALTER H NAYAR JOHN M SOUTHER JON E SWANSON
SHERMAN R TAYLOR DALE A WALKER RONALD L BABCOCK LARRY G LEWIS FRANCISCO QUINTANILLA JR
DENNIS L CRAVER JOHN A CUKALE JR ZBIGNIEW J DALENTA MASASHI NAKASHIMO JAMES L STEINKIRCHNER
RODNEY D COLLINS FRED MOONEY EMILIO N NEDEDOG CHRISTOPHER J SIX KEVIN G THORNE
CHARLES R TRICKER GERALD L EVANS RANDOLPH G HART JR JOHN W KUPKOWSKI LARRY E SMITH
ALBION J BERGANTZEL HOWARD S LAMB EARL E MCCARTY MORRIS A SIMPSON CHARLES G TAUBERMAN SR
ARNOLD R BENTON PAUL V BLACK RICHARD S BOWERS JAMES H COLBERT GARY C DAVID
KARL R GANTZ SHELDON L GULSETH ALFRED L KINCER III MILTON H RAMSEY THOMAS E ROSS
FRANK A SABLAN STEPHEN L SMITH ALBERT TIJERINA JR ROBERT D UHL JAMES T WILLIAMS JR
STEVEN V AST BYRON A BANGERT PAUL L BRADSHAW PAUL G BRIGHT JESSIE M BROOKS
KEITH D HEFFNER HERBERT E MULKEY JR RICHARD D SALDANA RICHARD L STOCKETT DELAND D ZUBKE
LESLIE C HICKS ANDREW J TOTH JR CHARLES R ANDERSON ORIE J DUBBELD JR ROY R DUKES
JAMES E DUNCAN MOSES HAYWOOD JR TOMMY R HENDERSON RICKY L JAMES NEIL S KENDALL
GARY T PADILLA RICHARD L PARK PAUL A SCAMBATI DALE M SNYDER HAROLD L ALGAARD
MICHAEL R COLLINS CHARLIE T GAZAWAY RICHARD J HENTZ MICHAEL W MARKER RODNEY D OSBORNE
JAMES J SHERECK JOSEPH A SILON JR GEORGE A SPENCE JOHN T STRAWN ARVID P THORMODSGARD
KENNETH J WAGNER CHARLES R BIGLIENI STEVEN R BURCH RICHARD S DENNISON GILBERT DOWELL
FRANKIE G BAKER WILLIAM L HASHAGEN JOEL C HATLEY LARRY P JOHNSON MICHAEL E KING
LARRY D LODEN RALPH A MOREIRA JR DAVID L NELSON GARY G PRENTICE EDWARD L RAYBURN
BARRY M STRAW JAMES C TUBB JR RALPH L WARD DANIEL W ALLEN JR GEORGE C BASS
STEPHEN W BURGDORFER HORACE L BURTON JERRY FLORES JAMES R HICKS JOHNNIE L PRYEAR
RONALD T HOFFMAN JOHN F HUMMEL KENNETH H JONES JOHN A LUKE FRANCIS D LUPO
WILLIAM L COFFEY TERRY L MCCLANAHAN WILLIAM P MILLINER MORRIS W PIERCE JR THOMAS A TOLEDO
HARVEY W WRIGHT MARK AFFLERBACH RANDOLPH J ARD TERRY L BLAIR PHILLIP M BRANDON
SHELDON J BURNETT PATRICK L FRICKE GEORGE R MORGAN DAVID J NARANJO HYRUM B PORT
THOMAS VALERIO JAMES L WIELER BRUCE A BOWMAN ROBERT E GRANTHAM JOHN D HALE
MARC J MEEKER DALE M HOLLOWELL MERLE E LOOBEY MICHAEL G MCKINNEY MATTHEW M RENNER
ROBERT J SCHOENHOFF BRUCE WOHLRAB WILLIAM E BAILEY BRUNSON A DERRICK SR DALE M MOZDZEN
BRUCE H HEIL ROBERT T KISER KEVIN C KRAMER RICHARD D MILLER ROGER M PISACRETA
JAMES L RANDALL GARY H ROBISON CURTIS R SMOOT GORDON K SPEARMAN JR EDMOND D BILBREY
KENNETH L BOYKIN DENNIS A CALTON FRANK L CASS GARY M COHEN JAMES D DEACON
DAVID E EASTON WILLIAM J FLOOD JR DONALD R HAMRICK PHILIP B HOLTZCLAW JOHN T LOCKHART
AERIO J LUCCHI JR MICHAEL J LUSE RONALD R NORTHROP DAVID H SMITH RAYMOND J BAKER
JERRY L DANAY JOSEPH J GOMEZ JOEL T HAGEMAN MELVIN HAZLEY MICHAEL W HILL
CLIVE G JEFFS VAN J JOYCE JERRY D KUNEY WILLIAM T LA FIELD JR NAZIR MOHAMMED
JIMMY ODENEAL SAMUEL T OWEN MICHAEL R REBER BENJAMIN E SLAGOWSKI ROBERT W THORNE
GERALD WELSCH EUGENE ALLEN MELVIN R CLEAVELAND BARTON S CREED NEAL S CROWDER
ROBERT S GOOD JR WILLIAM J HAMMER SAMMY F ISAACS EDDIE W VENCILL JAMES C WARD
STEVEN R WHITE ALVIN ADIKAI JR JOE L AVANT ROCCO DIPHILLIPO BOBBY J FIELDS
JAMES B FOSTER JR WILLIAM L HILL RONALD JACKSON JACK D MOORE JR RANDY M RIGSBY
CLIFFORD R OSTERHOUDT STEPHEN R PHELIX HARRY G PRINCE JR RONALD W STEWART MARCUS S STOEN
JAMES BINGENHEIMER FRANCIS M CURRY THOMAS A DELLWO JOHN ELAM JR PATRICK D ERB
JUAN ESPINOSA RAYMOND J GEORGE RICHARD E HARLAN SAMUEL M HARRELL PHILIP R JAMROCK
JERRY W KIRKENDOLL CHARLIE L LANIER WILLIAM D MINER PHILLIP D MONSON GREGORY S MORGAN
JAMES C MULLINAX JR STEVEN R PECK JERRY W PEOPLES MICHAEL H RICHARDS DAVID M SEXTON
CLYDE THOMAS CLIFFORD E BENCH GARY J FUQUA JAMES L GETTER LOYD V MCCARTHY JR
CHARLES D ALLEN JR DUANE G HOWELL ROBERT E RATAJCZAK EDMUND E ROBERGE RAYMOND J SAATHOFF
ENRIQUE R SANTOS RICHARD L BAUMAN LEWIS A DAVIS MICHAEL J DEPAUL CRAIG M DIX
ROBERT C GREEN HARRY C KING LAWRENCE E LILLY WILLIAM G NEWBOULD STEPHEN R SCRIVENER
BOBBY G HARRIS RONALD O SCHARNBERG WILLIAM D SCHLUTTER DOUGLAS M SEELEY BRYAN J SUTTON
THOMAS E TESTORFF RUSSELL G AHRENS ALAN B BOFFMAN KEITH A BRANDT JOHN R CHAMPLIN
DAVID ELIZONDO RICHARD W FORD FREDERICK L CRISTMAN RICARDO M GARCIA JON M SPARKS
GENE R KENNEDY THOMAS M KENNEDY CAESAR MURRAY THORNTON L WOOLRIDGE JACK L BARKER
WILLIAM B BEARDSLEY JOHN J CHUBB DENNIS T DARLING WILLIAM E DILLENDER JOHN F DUGAN
RONALD D KARAU THOMAS E KINGSLEY MICHAEL E KOSCHKE ROBERT P MARTIN JR VINCENT C MAURO JR
VERNON G LOVE RICK E MCFARLAND WILLIAM E ROYAL JAMES D SCHOOLEY JOHN L TRUESDELL
MICHAEL D WOODARD ALAN E DAVIS DONALD J FRAZELLE ERNEST L HIRTLER DAVID C LANCASTER
JAMES W MANTHEI BILLIE J MARLING LARRY M MASON CLAUDIUS A SMALL ANDRE B TIMS
REGINALD J ABERNETHY CHRISTOPHER Z CZARNOTA TERRY W DOAN KARL W DRUZINSKI WILLIAM H FELLS
REGINALD D CLEVE BENJAMIN W DUNCAN WILLIAM S GLENN STEPHEN D GUCOFSKI WALTER R HALL
MICHAEL L HARRIS DAVID R HAYWARD DONALD P KNUTSEN JEROME E LE ROY LARRY D LEAMON
ROBERT N LEBRUN CHARLIE M LOGAN JOHN W MCLEMORE JR PETER G MORIARTY ROGER W STAHL
CLARENCE M SUCHON JOHN G TRAVER III GARY S WHITE THOMAS L ZEIGLER SHERMAN AVANT
PAUL J FOTI JESSIE J GARTH JOHN D HEINZ DENNIS M HOTALING JEFFREY C KEETLE MICHAEL J BOSILJEVAC
DONALD K OSBORN JEFFERY I QUINTANILLA LANCE A ROBINSON WILLIAM L SCHELL WARREN P SEAWEL
MANASSEH B WARREN DOUGLAS E AYERS CURTIS D BAUER HARRY M BECKWITH III DAVID L COKER JR
JEROME D KLEIN STEVEN M LARRABEE JOHN C MERRITT WILLIAM E NEAL HERMAN E PICHON
THOMAS C SHEPHERD SR WILLIAM D SMITH GREGORY M STONE WILLIAM F THOMPSON JR RONALD F YALE
BERNARDO K RAMOS ROBERT D WALTERS ARTHUR WILSON JR MICHAEL D WRIGHT EDDIE L DODD
CHRIS BROWN JR EDWIN G CALHOUN MAXIMINO ESTRADA DOYLE FOSTER GARY G GEIGER
GARY D HALLIDAY OLIN D MARLAR III R D MCDONELL JEFFREY M PARMELEE
JEROME E JACKSON MANUEL R PUENTES RICHARD J ROSSANO LARRY A SIMONSON RANDALL A THOMPSON ROBERT L WUNDER
GEORGE THOMPSON JR DENNIS L WASZKIEWICZ JACOB B BABIN JR ROBERT D COFFEY JAY J FISHBECK
JOEL R HANKINS MARTIN R HUART JR WILLIAM A KINDER VINCE R KISELEWSKI DEAN W KRUEGER
DAVID R MENDOZA LAWRENCE PHILLIPS JAMES M RISCH GARY A SCHULTZ GORDON E TIBBETTS
ALBERT A VENCEL OTTO T WIEBEN GERALD ZLOTORZYNSKI ROBERT T BRADLEY ROBERT C CHAUDOIN
ARTHUR L GALLOWAY JR WILLIE JOHNSON JR THOMAS P OLSON PAUL E SERVEN GLEN H YELL
MICHAEL J BAYNE RONALD J BECKSTED DONALD C BENNETT VICTOR R BENNETT JR MICHAEL L CROSSLEY
LARRY D AUSTIN RICHARD J BOEHM DAVID A BOND RICHARD R CARSON CLIFFORD W CORR
WILBERT S DUPREE JR JAMES E EDGEMON KYLE S HAMILTON DRUEY L HATFIELD JOHN L HOGAN
MICHAEL S HOLLOWAY MYRON B JOHNSON WILLIAM W KIRKPATRICK RICHARD V KNIGHT JR LARRY P LAND
CARL B MCGEE LARRY W MCKEE WILLIAM J MILCO LAYMON PALMER STEVEN D PLATH
TERRY H PRICE CARL W PRITCHETT WARREN P RITSEMA DALLAS D ROBINSON PAUL A SHEER
JOSEPH R RYAN JR ROBERT J SCHUMACHER CLARK V SHAWNEE DONALD M STOTTS ROGER D WHIRLOW
RUSSELL L CLAY WILLIAM G COX CHARLES H EDWARDS JR KENT D ERICKSON MICHAEL A FRATTALI
ROBERT M GRIBBLE TERREL O KIMBER LESTER J MOE ROGER A PEDERSON BARRY A RHASH
RICHARD L STANSBARGER ANDREW R STEWARD JR CRAWFORD H TRAVER JAMES H ALLEN ALLEN E KINSMAN
AMADO ALANIZ JR TERRY L BOSWORTH DEWITT W BROWN III RONALD CLEVELAND DAVID F NIDEVER
GARY L PACE THOMAS H RATLIFF ROBERT J SKEWES MICHAEL A WADE MICHAEL A YOUNG
DONALD R BAILEY RAPHAEL L COLLAZO ROBERT LEE RANDOLPH L MARTHE HAROLD E MYERS
MICHAEL S MCLHERN BILLY R PARNELL ROGER G REID JAMES SALLEY JR GUY G SHANNON JR
CHARLES W STERLING PHILIP B TERRILL MICHAEL L THOMPKINS HARRIS L WILLIAMS JOHN W ANDERS
JERRY K BOBBITT JAMES D DAVIS DONALD J HAVEL ARTHUR HERNANDEZ JAMES A HIGHSMITH
COLLIE JOHNSON JR MICHAEL E MCPETERS PETER L WINTER STEVEN C WRAY GEORGE W YOUNGERMAN JR
DOUGLAS E CROOKS GLENN L HATA JAMES R MEADE JAMES E SUTHERLAND JOSEPH M YOUNGERMAN
GARY G ZELLER ARTHUR BEST RONALD R BLACKSMITH WAYNE R BOROWSKI HOWARD J BOWER JR
GARY BUTT ALAN D GILBERTSON RAYFORD H KING ROBERT J KISER KENNETH A THOMASON
JAMES B LOW EDWARD J ROG JR FRED B ROSENBERRY FELIX M TRUJILLO HOWARD O WARBINGTON
THOMAS L BLATZ KRAG C BULLIS SR MICHAEL E GIESE BENNY E HART ROBERT W HOMSCHEK

PANEL 4W (*Continued*)

TERRY V KNIGHT NOEL C LAPLANTE JOHNNY H LAWRENCE HARVEY M REYNOLDS JOSEPH S SMITH
LARRY E STEPPEE LARRY D SUEDMYER III MELVIN C WHEELER JR JAMES P ALEXANDER KARL R BERBERT
PAUL P CABE RAY G DESMOND GARY J FIEDLER DAVID B FITZGERALD ARTHUR GLASS
JAMES A LOUX WILLIAM C MCDOWELL MICHAEL M SCOTT FRANK T BURTON CLAUDE R GIBBONS
MARTIN D GOEN JOSEPH W JOHNSON RICHARD J LOCKWOOD DONNIE C TAYLOR LEONARD J TRUMBLAY
JOSEPH L ARMSTRONG DALE R HOOD EARL H KING RICHARD MORGAN GROVER C PIERSON JR
RONNIE A ROSS BILLIE J WILSON DENNIS R DEATHERAGE JOHN GLOVER THOMAS L SONDERMAN
CHARLES F THOMAS IV MOUSE J WHITE ALLAN F WILKINS LEVI J WILSON MATT J WODARCZYK
JAMES H ABRAM WILLIAM R FURR WILBUR GREENE CARROLL B LILLY NEWELL F APPLEGATE SR
BILLY G CHANNEL ROBERT N FIESLER JOHN H FRANKS ROBERT L GROF GREG N HENDERSON
DENNIS E JAHN RALPH W JONES JACK L KING STEVEN W MANESS MARTIN T MCDONALD
ERIC M KELLY HUGH M PETTIT JAMES L ARMSTRONG WAYNE C BAGGETT CLARENCE R FRANKLIN
JACK P BEGLEY JR MERLE D BROWN WILLIAM C BUERK THADDEUS DENNIS JEAN P HUMBERT
JON M MELIM PIUS L MILLER KENNETH E MIMS EDWARD P PILKINGTON JOSEPH A SCHOOLMEESTERS
JOE R SILVA DOUGLAS A VARNER RICHARD M WARREN DENNIS G DONOVAN ALFONZO L ESPINOZA JR
ROBERTO PEREA CHARLES L THOMPSON JOHN V WENTWORTH BENJAMIN J BENAVIDEZ JAMES A NICHOLS
ALTON R ROBERTS ELMER T ROSS LAMAR L WILLIAMS RENE A ZIMMERLE TERRY J BAILEY
CHISTOPHER L MAHER WILLIAM C ELROD JR ROY R HALL JAMES JILES JR RONNIE A KERR THOMAS E MACKEY
JAMES H MACDOUGAL RODGER H MITCHELL PAUL M NOLEN ABRAHAM POWELL RONALD L SANBOWER
JAMES D WADDELL RONALD E BALES LARRY L BROWN BRUCE E BUTCHER JEFFRY E COWLEY
ROBERT J DUTKIEWICZ THOMAS J GETTELFINGER TERRY W GREENE ROBERT C HEIN PAUL MCKENZIE
MANUEL C NAJERA JR GEORGE A PACHECO JERRY S STEARNS GREGORY A TYNES WILLIAM J WARD JR
JOHN L WILSON JR REX M DANIELS DAVID R DEKKER LEE E GRIMSLEY DAVID R KOWITZ
CHARLES D MCGINNES JAMES B MCLAUGHLIN PAUL C SAWTELLE ULMER J WATSON MICHAEL L WEMHOFF
MICHAEL J WHALEN BERNARD G ALBERTSON WILLIS N ANDREWS MICHAEL E BALL BARRY E BROWN
EDWIN F FISHER PETER KAPAS JR GEORGE J ORR GARY L REYNOLDS JAMES R THOMAS
RICHARD G TOLER ROGER N CARPENTER JOSEPH L COX RAYMOND E HAUSER RONALD J PETERS
ALLEN J DUROY MIGUEL A MONTES ANTONIO QUILES-HERNANDEZ JOHNNY SAXON GABRIEL L TWOEAGLE
PAUL O APPLEGATE LAWRENCE E CRAWLEY JOHN S GENTKOWSKI KENNETH M HATCHER BRUCE D OLSON
GEORGE J VANGUNDY JAMES A WALL JAMES M CARDWELL ALBERT F COAST DANNY G DRINKARD
KEVIN D GROGAN JOSEPH L HALL SCOTT W JONES JOHN T WALLACE CHARLES R LABOUNTY

PANEL 3W

STANTON G SARGENT KENNETH W SHAMBLIN GENERAL D SMITH CLAUDE A WILLIAMS
WILLIAM E WOOD JR LOUIS A YUGEL WILLIAM D HOLMES DENNIS A JENKINS ROBERT M PERSINGER
LEONARD REZA JOHN G SCHWARTZ TERRY E SCHWARTZ ROBERT B YOUNG MICHAEL L BRUMMER
WILLIAM E COLLUM EDWARD W CORCORAN JAMES R FIRKUS NORMAN C FISCHER FIDENCIO FLORES JR
ROBERT M FUHRMAN ROY L NELSON DALE E SORENSEN PATRICK W TERRY GEORGE H WILLIAMS JR
MELVIN J WILLIAMS BERNARDO R ALVAREZ BILL E BLANTON ALLEN T BOEHM JOHN W WILSON
THOMAS D CHENAULT RICHARD E COLBURN MARTIN V FANNING LOWELL V FERGUSON JR
JAMES A CHAMPION JAMES B HARRIS EDWIN HEISSE BENNIE R HIVELY GABRIEL A JEFFRIES JR LARRY C JORDAN
KEVIN A RINARD JOHNNIE R SLY TOMMY D SMITH JOSE A SOTO-FIGUEROA ROBERT F SPEER DIETER H DISCHHAUSER
STEPHEN A SPENCER BRUCE D STEPHENSON THOMAS H TAFT HILBERT W TEETER CHRISTOPHER L VOLLMAR
RICHARD M BEAUREGARD JOHNNY G WILLIAMSON EDWARD M BALL LENO R DILLETT KEITH E HANEY
JEFFREY C LEMON JOHN D NIX WALTER H SIGAFOOS III CHARLES W WARNER JR JOHNIE K WOODARD
DENNIS M CRAVER RICHARD H FANNING RICHARD J GOGGIN FRANCIS J MCCANN JR ROBERT J NICKLYN
DAVID B WOOD TONY R BINGHAM FREDERICK KRUPA RICHARD A LIKELY WILLIAM E LOCKE
HOWARD D PAYNE III LARRY L ROGERS WILLIAM D STONER JAMES E WESTON JUAN S BORJA
RICHARD L DE MUTH BENJAMIN G LANG LAWRENCE R PEEL GERALD C SEYBOLD DAVID W WINDSOR JR
DONALD E WEISMAN DONALD F WEST TERRILL E BRADFORD ANTHONY G BROZICH RONALD L EVANS
WILLIAM G HASSELMAN ROBERT L LONG ALBERT MCCOY JR DENNIS E MORGAN PATRICK O ORR
RICHARD STEWART HAROLD K ARMSTRONG CANTRELL M DANIEL III JOSEPH M EASON JERRY D HELMS
ERNEST R HOWELL CHARLES T KALLAHER DAVID P MEDINA ALIN E NORRIS JAMES E SHANKS
LARRY T YIELDING ALAN H HOLM RALPH B CORDON ROBERT B DICKERSON III GERALD T GINDLESBERGER
JEFFERY C GOODRICH RONALD J LARSON EDMUND L MACNEIL III CHRISTOPHER J NEALE JAMES R STOUT
WILLIAM H WALTON JR LAWRENCE L WIESENDANGER DERRILL L BURNSIDE JAMES R KIGER ROBERT H ROYER
MATTHEW A BOWEN CHARLES A LEWIS JR MICHAEL D BONDS JOHN W BREWER JR EUGENE M FRICKE
JOSEPH R SCHAFER FRANK W BENGTSON ARCHIE D CARNELL DAVID P MEYER JOHN E POESCHL
LARRY W ROTHEL GARY D COCHRAN STEPHEN F GRAY ALBERT R HANKINS GARY A KIRCHNER
MARTIN R LLOYD CHARLES T WILCOX THOMAS P CADIEUX JOHNELL L CHASTANG RONALD L DOOLITTLE
HERBERT D GOTT III HENRY R MARTIN JOHN J WOODRUM KLAUS Y BINGHAM DAVID D CAMPBELL
CLAYTON W JAMES JAMES M LUTTRELL HERBERT OHLER THOMAS J PATTON ALEXANDER QUIROZ
PAUL R RIVET JOHN W SIMMONS JOHN A STALEY DAVID W STARCHER LEWIS C WALTON
HENRY L WATTS SR MICKEY L WILSON NOEL B WITMER GARY D CHRISS CHRIS B CORDOVA
LONNIE D FOLEY JERRY A JOHNSON JERRY W LAMBERT STEVEN L MARTIN GEORGE W WINKLES JR
NATHAN L LEE JAMES L SHEFF JAMES R COOPER GUY V FEARN EDELMIRO L GARCIA SR
JEFFREY L COOPER ROBERT B DEWINE PHILLIP S GLASS EDWARD F HEASLEY SAM HOLMES JR
DONALD M POKE ALLEN D SCOGGIN HOWARD WILLIAMS STEVEN C BURNS LAWRENCE R DANCE
CLYDE DAVIS STEPHEN J HADLEY CHARLES T MEADOWS THOMAS E SNOWDEN CHRISTOPHER M WINTERS
PHILLIP C BLACKMOND DONALD O CARTER CHARLES L MARTIN LEONARD D MONTES DAVID R WINKLE
THOMAS KUKOWSKI JOB NAVARRETE JR ARTHUR C STEPHENS JR WAYNE R WILLIAMS GEORGE C YOSHONIS
DALE A PEARCE LARRY L ROBINSON DAVID P SOYLAND DALE W DEHNKE DANNY D ENTRICAN
LARRY J GAMMON WILLIAM M GEORGE GARY L HOLLINGSWORTH JAMES E TORRENCE RICHARD L BARBEE
HERBERT S BARNES PHILIP R DEARING MIKLE E DIXON MICKEY D LANG HAROLD D WALLER
JAMES D AGUILAR ROBERT G BRUCE LOWELL T GLOSSUP SCOTT H NEWPORT TERRANCE R SCHENE
GREGORY A SMITH MARCUS E ARNESON VINCENT M BENEDETTI JAMES E BODDIE RANDALL J GLASSPOOLE
CHRISTOPHER J BIGLEY CHARLES M CRAWFORD ALVIN C CURRY THOMAS F DELEHANT JOE F GAYOSSO
COLUMBUS V GROSS BILLY D HERRING WILLIAM H HJORTH WILLIAM C JENNINGS BILLY J JONES
WILLIAM M KENEDY CHARLES N KOWALK KARL J LAVALLEE ROBERT B LE CATES DAVID B MATYKIEWICZ
STEVEN M MITCHELL JOHN H NAJMOLA LEO C OATMAN JEROME A OLSON JAMES E TIGHE
OSIER L PRUITT ALBERTO A RAMIREZ WILLIAM SAYLOR JR WILLIAM T SMITH J C SUMMERLIN
BENNIE L NORTH GEORGE T TAYLOR JR KENNETH G WESTERBERG WILLIAM E WOLFE HAROLD M CROWE
GARY A DORE THOMAS R LUSHER EDWARD W METCALF JAMES W PETERSON RICHARD D PLUMM
RALPH E POSEY ROY G SHADDON PATRICK WEBER ARMANDO M ZEPEDA HENRY D ADKINS
TOM R ADLER JOHN H GRUBER PHILIP D SHARP ROBERT K BLOSSER RANDALL C SHORT
ROY L MEADOWS LARRY R DEWEY JIMMY D HUMPHRES GERALD M LUBBEHUSEN JACKIE D STOGSDILL
WILLIAM E ADAMS JOHN D CURRAN DENNIS C DURAND ROY IGNACIO JOHN W LITTLETON
MICHAEL D RIDDLE MELVIN ROBINSON LEROY J WESTRA ROBERT L GREENSTREET STEVEN W HENDRICKS
HARVEY E HUMPHREY PAUL D CARTER JERRY FOY THOMAS W KNUCKEY PHILIP C TAYLOR
ROBERT L BROWN STEPHEN CHAVIRA JOSEPH D ESPARZA DONALD R MATHIS PAUL D URQUHART
THOMAS G BLAIR JR STEPHEN G DAVIES JOSEPH E SWEENEY JOSE M ARREDONDO WAYNE S CRAIG
MITCHELL O BARNES ROBERT K CAIN II ERVIN B CHERRY ROY M SEABROOK JACK W BRUNSON
STEVEN J KEARNS CLINTON A MUSIL SR GARY J SHINN AUGUSTUS ADAMS GEORGE H GLAWSON JR
DEAN R ISAACS LEON J JACKSON PAUL G MAGERS DENNIS L MEDUNA THOMAS C MICHEHL
ROBERT D MCKINNEY DON M RAMSEY JAMES R SAXON ANDREW C STRONG III MARK R TAYLOR
DONALD L WANN SCOTT W WAYT EDWARD A WERMAN KEVIN P FORCUM DANNY R KING
ROBERT P SANCHEZ JR MICHAEL A LAMUSGA GEORGE H POTTS EDGAR D THOMAS MICHAEL J VERSTRAETE
TERRY K BEGGS RANDALL J BOYD JOSE A SANCHEZ DANIEL M BROWN KIMBER L HALL
JAMES W MYLES REY F TORRESRAMOS LEM CLARK JOHN R JONES WILLIAM J LAMMERS
LARRY L MILLER DAVIS J MORGAN WILLIAM K TAYLOR BILLY H WYATT EDMOND T BALLANCE
HAROLD E BARNARD CARL W BORCHERS MARTIN E LOVING MICHAEL R STREET BERNARD BARNES
THOMAS E BAUMGARDNER JR DAVID C BROWN ANTHONY M EILERS JERRY L THOMAS MAURICE H BRYANT
THOMAS H FARMER HIAWATHA H WILLIAMS THOMAS E EPPERSON STEPHEN K MASDEN JOHN R MICKLE
MICHAEL M DALTON HUGH A SEXTON JR ROBERT L SIMMONS JOHNNY ARTHUR CARL W BREWSTER
LOUIE G MONTOYA WILLIAM C BILY THOMAS J CONNIFF JOHNNY JACKSON LOYD E ROBINSON
THOMAS W BEATTY CARROLL J BENTON RALPH L CHURCH GARY L PFLASTER STEVEN J ELLIS
RICHARD J GRAY JOSEPH D HAYES JAMES D JACKSON CHARLES A SANCHEZ GARY L WESTPHAL
LEONARD L BROENNEKE FRANKLIN T CRITES DENNIS M DICKE EARL R LESTER JR JEFFREY D SCHUMACHER
WAYNE A GARBER MANUEL MIRANDA ANTHONY A PRICE WILLIAM T WALSH JR DEE BERGERA
FLOYD L BRADSHAW III SYLVESTER C MARTINEZ BILLY D PEDINGS JAMES A SOUTHER RICHARD WILSON JR
DONALD WOOD THOMAS P HARVEY DANNY G STUDDARD ERNEST K TYLER JAMES R VALTR
WAYNE J BILLEAUD DAVID L CURTIS ERNEST D HART JR HAROLD E IMLER JR TERRY L KELLY
PHILLIP L LEE VINCENT WRIGHT BARRY A BIDWELL RAYMOND V DEBLASIO JR JOHN T DOZIER II
LON P GREGORASH GARY L JOHNSON JOHN R PAINTER JR WILLIAM E REED ROGER E WITTE
DWIGHT T BLACKWATER REGINALD W FITCHETT JOHN W HAYNES RANDY V HINES HOWARD H NELSON
ARTHUR P ROBERSON FIATELE T TEO JEFFREY S WESOLOWSKI WHEELER D BROOKS JOHN E LEIS
ELBERT MARCANTEL MARLIN M MILLER JOHNNY SOTO FRANK R YBARRA BILLY J WATSON
EARL W ELLIS DONALD P LOCKWOOD DOUGLAS E LUSCOMBE CHARLES D METZLER FLOYD W WOODS
MELVIN V LE VAN FRANK R MAKI MARSHALL G MILLER MADISON A STROHLEIN DONNIE W ANDERSON
RICKY D GILCHRIST RONALD D CALLOWAY ROBERT EGGLESTON GILBERT L MATTHEWS JR TOIVO B NOMM
ROBERT L MORGANFLASH ALBERT P CARDEN CHARLES T JONES RICHARD N LEE RUBIN MATHIS II
WAYNE S MURPHY LOUIS J SPEIDEL MICHAEL J WHITAKER MICHAEL R WILSON SEBASTIAN E DE LUCA
JOHN L SONES JAMES M YOUNG HERBERT J ARTIS RICHARD W JONES DONALD F MCKIETHAN
CHARLIE T TANTON ROSS A TROVATO STUART M BINKLEY BERNARD F BRZEZINSKI CHARLES W COOK
DONALD L DELAPLAINE GERALD J DOWJOTAS WILLIE JAMES JR LARRY M LIVINGSTON DARRYL W TAYLOR
ANTONIO ESTEVES-NEGRON MASON A KEITH MICHAEL W NICOL WILLIAM P WALTERS HARRY T WALTON JR
CALVIN D GUNTER PHILLIP W BRIDGES PAUL A DODSON SR RONALD H HALL GERALD C HINSDALE
JOHN R HOUSTON MARK J HOUSTON GARY L LEWIS PATRICK B MORRIS STEVEN C ONEAL
ROBERT J SABATINI JOSEPH W YINGLING JR ANTHONY J LAMERE DUANE M MCBEAIN GLEN L FULLERTON
FREDERICK W MURPHY JIMMY R MURRELL FREDDIE TURNER PHILLIP R BERGFIELD DONALD L EVANS
ROGER W FAREWELL GERRY A HARR RUSSELL C MANN TERRY J MARTELL RICHARD SALLEE JR
ROBERT S SCHETTIG GARY P TOMLINSON STEVEN G WILLIAMS MANOLO B AGNES VICTOR W LEW
RICHARD M PURCELL NAPOLEON JOHNSON GILBERT LEDGER PAUL LOPEZ ISRAEL MEDINA

WINDOL W MCNUTT EDWARD L MORTIMER JR LAWRENCE WILKERSON DONALD G CARR ROBERT F DAVIS
ALAN S GOFF RICHARD S PATTERSON RUBEN RUBIO FREDERICK B SUMMERVILLE DANIEL W THOMAS
PAUL R WITHROW MICHAEL J KNOX RAYMOND R MAYS CHARLES P PANQUERNE CHARLES E BEALS
RONALD E BEUTLER MARION T GRIFFIN SAMUEL W MCDANIEL II WAYNE C PISCIOTTA JOHN H MORRIS JR
RONALD J KRIEG ROBERT J MANIAS BRYAN L WILKEN THOMAS W BICKFORD ROBERT L KING
THOMAS T COLLINS DANIEL G DORMAN MICHAEL E LUKOW LANCE D WORKMAN CURTIS G VAN WINKLE
MICHAEL WATKINS ROY D RUSSELL WILLIAM R ROBISON HOWARD J BECKER JR STEPHEN A BEDNAR
CHRISTOPHER C COOK JAMES M DICKEY ALEXANDER W DUPLESSIE ROBERT M LARSON TED J TAYLOR
ALLEN J DYER JOHN H LOPOCHONSKY JR ALLEN E NOBLE GREGORY I SAHLBERG JAY S ASTON
PHILIP D CHEEK JAMES A JOHNSON STEVEN J MINKLER CHARLES W ROBERTS JR RUDOLPH STEVENS
ALTON J HEBERT NORMAN MAXIE ALBERT E PETERSON JR JOHN L FETHEROLF GERRY D COULT
RICHARD L PAGE DAVID B BEGLAU LUIS J MONROIG MARGARITO R GOMEZ TONY ANGUIANO
RANDALL D DALTON RONALD N GOODWIN STEPHEN E SLOCUM MARVIN B STUART JR CHARLES R HARRIS
GREGORY A ANTUNANO WILLIAM J DONOVAN JOHN C HALSEY DANNY L LIGHTSEY LINWOOD L BAKER
HARRY K HARRIS JR RALPH E MCELRATH CLIFFORD F DOWLING RANDALL H GEIS JOHN A GROSS
GUNTER W SCHEU ROBERT E SCHULZE DOMENIC SMIGLIANI KEN H TAKETA CHARLES CLARK
WILLIAM E MURPHY DONALD E SCOTT ROBERT L WILLARD EDWARD J CAVANAUGH ALLEN H CLARK
ROBERT J DI PIETRO HOWARD L JONES SAMUEL L MCAPHEE NEIL ADAMS JR MANUEL GOMEZGUTIERREZ
RANDY L CAYLOR EVERETT E DE LONG JR RICHARD J DU PLESSIS RANDY A FLESHMAN ROBERT A PIPER
ANDREW M BORDES WILLIAM J BRADFORD CLINTON H EPPS WILLIAM C HINES TOMMY M MCCLEER
JOHN L ROBERTS WALTER R CAPPS JOHNNY W FREE ROBERT MIRANDA THOMAS E REIMILLER
GLEN J TALIAFERRO EDWIN N TROXEL ROBERT A PULASKI MARK L HAMILTON RAYMOND A ROSE
DONALD B WHITLOCK III DAVID E CINKOSKY ROBERT B CURRAN DAVID L GARCILLE ROBERT D SEVERSON
WILLIAM A THOMAS JR MARSHALL E NAFFZIGER JAMES C REAMER RODRICK TROUP MARK J EKLUND WILLIE MCCLOUD JR
WALTER J VICHOSKY JR BRUCE A BERG ORAN L BINGHAM LOREN D HAGEN ALFRED F POSPISIL
WILLIE R WILLIAMS JAMES R BROWN THOMAS M HANKINS HAROLD B FLYNN ARNOLD LOVINS
LOY W PIERCE DELBERT B RANDALL PAUL J BATES JR SANTOS CASTELLANOS JR THOMAS A DOLAN
WILLIAM L LOGAN NATHANIAL C MATTHEWS WILLARD F PAYNE PETER J GAUVIN VIRGIL J BATES JR
DUANE CRUM GARY L HOLIAN ERIC S KELLY LAWRENCE L KELLY LARRY MCCOY CHARLES D MCGONIGLE
ROBERT T NELSON JOHN M RYDLEWICZ GAIL L STRICKLAND JOHN C THOMPSON JR JAMES WRIGHT
LAWRENCE B COLEMAN JR MARK H EATON JOHN F PEPIN FLOYD W KOTEWA JR HAYWOOD RODGERS
WOODROW B CHASTAIN SCOTT T GRABER VERNON HART LEROY REID JR JOHN W KENNEDY
TIMOTHY J LYNCH ANTONIO T TOSA ARTHUR G DENTON WILLIE C KUYKENDALL JOHN L BRANNON
MELVIN L WEAKS JEROME A BROWDER JR DANIEL E GOODIN CHRISTOPHER G MORBITZER BRUCE MORGAN
JOHNNY H CHAPMAN JOHNNY E JONES MICHAEL J GUIDRY JAMES J WINSON TROY E BRANTLEY JR
BILLY W DISHEROON DAVID W FRADY DWIGHT B HOWELL WILLIAM E LAMAR

PANEL 2W

BILLIE D DUART CHARLES T GILLEY WARREN D HOLEMAN JOEL K KAMALOLO
BOBBY F LIMERICK DANIEL A BRANCHEAU GEORGE A CHAPMAN KENNETH R GULLETT RODNEY C HARSCH
JOHN P HOFFMAN CURTIS C KASTLER RODOLFO VALDEZ ROBERT N VENNIK ROBERT F GARTNER
ROBERT A BEAVERS WILLARD J BOUCHARD JR FRANK L BROWNING DENNIS BUCKLEW STEPHEN L GARI
EUGENE GRIFFIN CURTIS L NELSON RONALD S SHEPHERD ALLAN L HARRIS OSCAR B WILLIAMS
TERRY M HAMMOND HAROLD C HUNTER II DONALD N PENSYL SAMUEL O SMALL ROBERT L WEISSER
FREDERIC C SAUNDERS JR EDWARD M GARCIA LARRY J KLUEVER JOHN P QUINN JR ARTHUR TOMASCHEK
WILLIAM K AUSTIN GERALD A DAVIS GORDON L KIMMEL RICHARD RUSS JR MARION H STANLEY
HIGINIO R TORRES JOHN F WEBB JOSE E ZAYAS JAMES A MARESH
ROBERT E WOODS JOHN H BATTLE BERNARD G DILLENSEGER MARTIN W GRONBORG JR EDWARD L HARRIS JAMES P PETTIEGREW
THOMAS E SWEINSBERGER ALAN R HINZPETER RONNIE S MARSHALL BRUCE A CANNON JIMMIE D HINTON
CLIFFORD L BYRD CLAUDIE L COX ROBERT J ELLIOTT WAYNE C ROCHOWICZ JOHN A SERVICE
DONALD E SMITH RAYMOND W CULVER CHARLES C SNIDER JR LEROY J CORNWELL III ANDREW IVAN JR
JOE COOPER MICHAEL J KILDUFF ALEJANDRO MAKINTAYA ALFRED J TUTTLE ROBERT L GROOMS
WALTER C HARRISON JR ANTHONY L RYCKAERT CHARLES D CASERIO ROBERT G FORTIN GEORGE R MORRISON
ROYSE W REHWALD DON R GILBRETH STANLEY R RHODES HEINZ K ROESCH DIETER J FISER
GEORGE A FLOYD JOSEPH R YOUNG GEORGE W BOULWARE DONALD E LARUE JR JOHN W LAWRENCE JR
PAUL J LUECKING LYNN M MORGAN JOHN SENECHEK JAMES A WELLS ELBERT A WELSH GARY W BUTLER
MIGUEL A BYNOE LARRY D EHLERS HERSHEL D CUDE JR KENNETH L JONES GERALD V VAN WINKLE
LYNN JONES FREDRICK A THACKER GERALD F VILAS RUEBEN T ARAGON ARNOLD W BARDEN JR
IRA C BRANK LAWRENCE L COVER HAROLD E COWEN DUANE G FORGETTE LAWRENCE B FORRESTER
CHARLES H GOLDBIN JOSEPH B POE LEAGRANT BADGETT RANDALL B BERNARD DUDLEY F BRADBERRY
FELIX MALONE THOMAS W TRUELOVE CLIFFORD L CLARKE III ROBERT F HOJNACKI CHARLES E JAQUINS
RALPH L MCCOY JR DAVID L SHEAFFER MELVIN D BARNETT DUANE A COTTRELL RICHARD A SUPNET
STEVEN R HANSON JEROME D TODD JERRY O LAFAYETTE JOHN J MILLER JR EMIL M MILTNOVICH
STEVEN W NEVILLE KENNETH W ELLIS JOHN H GREGORY JR WILLIS E KERLIN JR ROGER L SVIR
CHARLES W TURBERVILLE HERBERT E ARMSTRONG JAMES F BISHOP LUIS H CAMPOS RANDALL K CLEMENTS
STEVEN D KARNEHM JOHN J KINTARO HERSHEL G ROGERS RONALD B RUEPPEL DONALD D BRUBAKER
ORVILLE CAUDILL BERNARD L CORO LEO F GRADY DWIGHT H JONES EDWIN A KUDLACEK
PHILIP R WAGNER ROBERT W WENDT DONALD E PIERPOINT ALBERT T BALL CHRIS R BEHM
RONALD L BOND MICHAEL L DONOVAN FREDERICK C HEBERT GEORGE W KAMENICKY RONALD G RICKS
THOMAS R STANSBURY HALTON R VINCENT JEFFERY L WRIGHT ROBERT E ELDRED ROBERT H MAGGS
JAMES V NEWENDORP CLAYTON PLOURDE ROBERT E THOMAS JR ROBERT O GOODMAN JR
FREDERICK O JONES DAVID L HANN LARRY W CHANEY SIDNEY A COTTRELL GARY L MIZNER JEFFREY R STOKES
CARL W THOMPSON PAUL R CARSON GERALD F MCGLONE ADDISON W PAGE JR RAFAEL PEREZ-VERDEJA
RUDOLPH G VALENTA DANIEL R HOFFMAN JOSEPH M FEENEY DAVID J FUNES DENNIS R HINTON
CHESTER A LUC ELDON L SHAPLEY FRANKLIN R SILOS THOMAS J STANUSH WILLIAM JIMENEZ-ACEVEDO
AUDLEY D MILLS JOHN S CHRIN MICHAEL L DARRAH HUGO A GAYTAN RICKY A PATE
RONALD K SCHULZ IRVING J BROWN JR CARL S MERLINO EDDIE B HUBRINS RALPH N LEE
JOHN C HAYES LARRY F MILLER HARRY O BOWLES BARRY A BOWMAN JACK E SEARING KENNETH W SCURLOCK
ALVIS T BARRINGTON JR BARRY L BROWN WALLACE J DEPREO LAUREN R EVERETT DAVID R HOUSER
PAUL A STOKES ROBERT M WEBB JR ROBERT J BARTON PATRICK J BRESLIN WILLIAM E WHITEMAN II
RICHARD H DEFER WESLEY S SHELTON RICKY M ARIENS ALAN R BOONE
JOHN H BROWN ROBERT N BROWN CALVIN B CHILDRESS FLOYD W FRAZIER JR MARSHALL W WILLIAMS BILLIE L COLEMAN
EDWARD J DOGGETT RICHARD J PRIVITAR WILLIAM A SHELTON HERMAN C CAHOON PAUL R FOLTZ
JAMES M HINKLE WILLIAM J MAKOWSKI LARRY J PORTER DANIEL S SALAS ROY D BARNES
HARRY H BRACK JR PAT G BRANNON DANNY A COWAN DANIEL G DYE MAURICE E GARRETT JR
RANDALL E MAGGIO ANTHONY J MENSEN BILLY V MORRIS NICK N RODRIGUEZ ANTON J SCHNOBRICH
WILLIAM R LEWIS JR ROBERT H CLIFTON WALTER C FRISBIE LONNIE W MITCHELL ANTHONY P QUINT
CLIFFORD A HOSTEN HARRY D MCWHINNEY JR ELLIOT M YOSHIDA BRUCE A ABDELLAH MICKEY E EVELAND
RUFUS P FALKNER JR SANFORD I FINGER THOMAS F GREEN EDWARD L HIMES MICHAEL LAUTZENHEISER
LEONARD G MAQUILING ROBERT A NICKOL JAMES C SKINNER STANLEY W TAYLOR ALBERT R TRUDEAU
SAMUEL A AMEY BRENT P CLEVELAND DAVID L JACKSON DONALD F VAUGHAN JAMES C WAYNE
JAMES L VAUGHNAN BOBBY B WHITE JOHN P CARR III JIMMY L HAYNES LINUS L OAKLEY GENE W STOCKMAN
JERRY E TEW VICTOR D WILLIAMS KENNETH M BERBLINGER HARDY E CLEVELAND MICHAEL M FARLEY
JACK A GARNES DARRELL HOGAN ERNIE R MARTINEZ ROBERT E RYAN JAMES M SELIX
DAVID G SMITHWICK DONALD C TALLMAN LUTHER B WARD JR STEPHEN J HUSKEY GUFFEY S JOHNSON
ANGEL A QUEVEDO CARL D TOMLIN JR THOMAS P FRANK MICHAEL L HINO JOSE MALDONADO
ROBERT F QUANDT JACK L DECAIRE ALBIN L KENDALL ERROL L KENT ERNEST J MONTELEONE JR
JERRY G THOMAS DENNIS I DAY RICHARD C DORITY DAVID L GINN HARVEY D JOHNSON
ARLIE R MANGUS JERRY D MARTIN CALVIN A NORRIS JAMES R PANTALL JERRY L WALKER
JOHN D SHEWMAKE SR PAUL TRUJILLO MARTIN M VASQUEZ DAVID W WOODS LEROY WHITE JR
ROLIN J CROSBY DENNIS R DEBICKERO CHARLES D DODD RICHARD R KAPSHA JAMES G CONLEY
EARL D BARKLEY JAMES P MALONEY JR DAVID J WATSON JOHN M CLARK JAMES P DELANEY
HENRY F DELLECKER DENNIS M HIGGINS RAYMON H JAMES JR FRANCIS J KLASSEN HOWARD M STEINFELD
DANNY T JETT PAULINO F JIMENEZ-ROIG WILLIAM E SUMMERS ROGER D DAVENPORT ERIC G HEROLD
HAROLD J RITCH DANIEL S BROOKER JOHN A CHARNOPLOSKY DAVID A GORTON ROBERT D PIERCE
VINCENT P MARTIN JR WILFRED N POEPPING THOMAS J PUFF BRADFORD M GRAHAM CHARLES H RICHIE
CHARLES A POPPLETON WARREN K WOLFF RICHARD R LANGE HAROLD D BOWLEN DANIEL L CHAMBLEE
ROBERT R CHESSER HENRY V CLOSSER DOUGLAS D EASON CARTER JEFFERSON JR JOE L LOVE JR
RONNIE SHARPE KEVIN J HAUGER ROBERT W ALTUS EUGENE R JOHNSON WILLIAM PHELPS
JOHN W GEORGE THOMAS D PROSE LOWELL R SAUNDERS ROBERT B SWENCK JAMES R THOMAS
ROBERT D BEUTEL JAMES H NEWCOMER DOUGLAS J PIERCE LAWRENCE C SMITH JAMES E STEADMAN
JAMES H SPANN JOSEPH A AUBAIN VINCENT BERNAL RONALD D CARLETON JERALD W CARTER
BILLY R COFFEY HOWARD L COLBAUGH MICHAEL A CRAWFORD RICHARD E GARRETSON JOHN H HARE
WILL R DANTZLER JOEL S IVEY JR TERRY G KUGLER ROBERT J LADENSACK EDWARD J LOPEZ
ARCHIE T LUCY GEORGE P MARTIN ALPHONZA MASON MICHAEL O MAYBEE ROBERT D MAYNARD
STEVEN J MCDONALD MARTIN K NISKANEN DANIEL E NYE WILLIE J OAKS JAMES E PALMER
OSCAR PAULLEY JR BRINSLEY B RAMOS JOSEPH J SAVICK JR ROY K STEWART RONALD K SWEETLAND
WILLIAM D THOMPSON CARL L THORNTON RAYMOND A TRUJILLO GARY D WILSON JOHN E WINDFELDER
ROBERT L WYNN STEPHEN C RUBY BERT O LAWRENCE HARRY M VANDIVER JR JOSEPH B ZIEL
JOE S BURCHFIELD THOMAS H FOLEY JOHN M HIEBERT THOMAS W KEENE MARVIN R KEETER
KENNETH R PERRY WILLIAM T WARREN JR SCHYLER WATTS RICHARD A GREEN CHARLES P RUSSELL
THOMAS E FIKE RONALD P REMBOLDT DENNIS R STEWART ROGER L CHRISTENSEN RICHARD C PAWELKE
GEORGE S MENO LEWIS A WALTON MARVIN C BRIESACHER SCOTT W MCINTIRE RANDY L CLIFTON
PHILIP S GALLAGHER III ISADORE JENKINS RONALD A SPUDIS HOWELL W BURNS JERRY N DUFFEY
BERNARD J MORAN JR LLOYD S RAINEY JOHN G BOYANOWSKI DWIGHT A BREMMER FLOYD D CALDWELL
GREGG N HOLLINGER CECIL C PERKINS JR OTHA L PERRY ROBERT WILLIAMS WILLIAM BELL JR
ANDREW H MESHIGAUD PETER C FORAME DANIEL R POYNOR THOMAS W SKILES HERBERT R STONEKING
LEO T THOMAS JR RONALD W NUTE LUTHER BARNEY DONALD H POWERS HENRY E EVANS
RONALD J COLEMAN WILLIAM R FINN TIMOTHY M TUCKER JAMES C WATSON ROBERT E FURSTENWERTH
VINCENT E GALKA DALE F KOONS LAWRENCE G STOLZ ALBERT S ROBALIN JR FREDERICK L HOLMES
ROBERT L DENMARK WILLIAM Y DUGGAN CHARLES R EGGERS NEIL W JONES FREDERICK J SUTTER
HARVEY W BAKER CHARLES M KALANI ROBERT O BAKER JR BEDFORD L DRINNON DOUGLAS E TROTTER
RAUL LOSOYA STANLEY C PERRIGO DAN A BOLSTER STEPHAN A DAVIS ROGER J KOJETIN MICHAEL SCHMIDT

287

THE VIETNAM VETERANS MEMORIAL COLLECTION

JAMES LOSPINUSO JOHN D EDDY LEONARD H MANTOOTH JR GARY W TAWNEY ROBERT W VEHLING
KENNETH C WILLIAMS CARLTON L DIXON STARLING G HAWKINS DAVID E VICKERS RICHARD L WILSON
RICHARD J HOCK PATRICK W RABACAL BENJAMIN E YARD JR DAVID D BERDAHL HARRY J EDWARDS
RONALD A LONGFELLOW HAROLD D KRASHES DWIGHT J MINNIEAR JIMMY L DUNAGAN JOSEPH J SLIFKA JR
WALTER C MORAN FERNANDO FIGUEROA BARRY L SMITH ROGER L PIERCE MICHAEL J WELCH
MARK E ALLEN WILLIAM J CRANE II EDWARD E TAYLOR LAWRENCE M OXX JR PANORMITIS STAVLAS
KURT INT-HOUT KARL D PORTER ROCKY L COOPER ERHARD J MELLO FRANK E WILLIAMS GREGORY C DAVIS
DONALD G BAILEY GARY W YORK PAUL G BAST DALE B MOILANEN CHARLES H STONE JAMES J CRAWFORD
CHARLES E GREENE DONALD W LOWE DANIEL D COOPER LEONARD J MATELSKI THOMAS W LIPSEY III
JAMES E MAXWELL GEORGE H TOUSLEY III ROBERT E LUTZ JR JAMES L ENNIS CARL D JOHNSON
JAMES W KIEHNE ROBERT M LAIRD LUTHER M LASATER III JESSE W MONTAGUE JR CHRISTOPHER R SEITZ
ROBERT E PRYOR CHRISTOPHER H TURK ALBERT E LEE RICHARD N CHRISTY II ROBERT H IRWIN
PAUL D KREGER BRUCE P ROWE JAMES M HAMRICK JR RUDOLF MICKA THOMAS E SMITH
DON H WARE BERNARD L JOHNSON II SCOTT B WESTPHAL WILLIAM M CLARK DAVID E CLARKE
MARK J FITZGERALD ROBERT G GALBREATH WILLIAM A GUNNELLS MARVIN L HALL DOUGLAS A HOWARD
DAVID N JOHNSTON ROMAN L JONES RONALD J MANCA WILLIAM J MORGAN ALBERT W SMARR JR
ROBERT L DAUGHERTY SCOTT N JACOBSON ARTHUR E LIKENS TERRY L BROWN ERICK R WELENOFSKY
ROBERT M DELGADO REGEN A MONETTE JAMES R BRYANT CARTER A HOWELL STEPHEN A RUSCH
RAYMOND F ANTHONY JR BRUCE D JONES JOHN E GREENE ARTHUR H HARDY GAVIN W PILTON
GEORGE W SEVIGNY RICHARD A CROCKER DONEL J DOBBS HOWARD E DRAIN TURNER C JOHNSON
JOHN M MINOR JOHN J MOYNAHAN JAMES J POCKEY CHARLES H SCHELLING ALBERTO VADIRODRIGUEZ
COLUMBUS WATSON JR JAMES C WILLIAMSON THURMAN WOODY JR SAMMY L WEAVER JOHN R WALKER
LARRY W HARVEY JAMES G TAYLOR MIGUEL A ALICEA RONALD S ANDERSON JAMES T JACKSON
BILLY J HAMMOND DENNIS S PIKE JAMES E WHITT RAYMOND J CROW JR RICHARD E DREHER
JAMES MANOR DAVID E PANNABECKER RAYMOND A WAGNER EDWARD P WONG JR LARRY J WOODS
LARRY BATTS HENRY P BRAUNER JAMES K CANIFORD RICHARD CASTILLO OLLIE E CRENSHAW JR
RICHARD C HALPIN CURTIS D MILLER MERLYN L PAULSON EDWIN J PEARCE DENNIS N PETERSON
DAVID P SHELTON ROBERT E SIMMONS EDWARD D SMITH JR HOWARD D STEPHENSON KENNETH R VOS
IRVING B RAMSOWER II WILLIAM A TODD CHARLES J WANZEL III BARCLAY B YOUNG CHARLES J BRITT
BRUCE A CROSBY JR MELVIN W FINCH MELVIN R GLEATON GARY P WESTCOTT CHARLES W BUNTION
DALE W FARRIS JAMES M MCCRACKEN DAVID C BRUGGEMAN JOHN A JELICH JAMES D OWENS
JAMES F WORTH WAYNE L BOLTE JOHN W FRINK ANTHONY R GIANNANGELI BYRON K KULLAND
ROBIN F GATWOOD JR CHARLES A LEVIS RONALD P PASCHALL HENRY M SEREX ALLEN D CHRISTENSEN
THOMAS R MUREN DOUGLAS L ONEILL EDWARD W WILLIAMS LARRY A ZICH HENRY M SPENGLER III
CHARLES C WINDELER JR JAMES H ALLEY ALLEN J AVERY JOHN H CALL III PETER H CHAPMAN II
THOMAS E DUNLOP ROY D PRATER ROBERT L HORST JOE D HUDSON
WILLIAM R PEARSON HOWARD B LULL JR RICHARD D MILTON LARRY F POTTS RICHARD S SCHOTT ROBERT A STERN
ROBERT H ALDRICH BRUCE C WALKER FRANK T BROCHETTI JOSEPH R HARRIS GARY S SCHWARTZ PATRICK A TALTY
JAMES M BARRY SCOTT D KETCHIE DANIEL K KUSHNER JERRY D LAWS CALVIN C NASH
JOSEPH C SZEKELY EDWARD C RIETSCHY STANLEY S TILLITSON MARVIN L BISCAMP JOHN M CHRISTENSEN
DAVID L LEET RONALD A MALL MITCHEL A DOWDY JOSEPH G GREENLEAF CLEMIE MCKINNEY
DAVID H STAMPER ROY E THOMPSON GEORGE W MAINARDY DALLAS L NIHSEN JON H SANDERS

PANEL 1W

ORVIN C JONES JR CHARLES D LANDIS ALAN P MATEJA ROBERT A STERLING
LEONARD R DAVIS TOMMY J BECKER GREGORY W HERMANN DAVID D STOVER RONALD H WIGGINS
GEORGE K BARSOM III ALBERTO ORTIZ JR PAUL J PESCE THOMAS S POWELL ARNOLD J RAHM
THOMAS H AMOS MASON I BURNHAM WILBUR H CHILDRESS JOHN J STEGELAND III CHARLES TURNER
STEVE POROVICH MICHAEL D BAKER GEORGE W CARTER MICHAEL D CLEAVES WADE L ELLEN
JAMES E HUNSICKER JOHNNY M JONES KENNETH J YONAN LEROY B AIKEN ROBERT W BROWNLEE JR
HARRY A AMESBURY JR CALVIN C COOKE JR RICHARD E DUNN DONALD R HOSKINS RICHARD L RUSSELL
KURT F WEISMAN THOMAS K DUFFY THOMAS F SHAW ROBERT L SOWERS CLAUD P STROTHER
FRANKLIN ZOLLICOFFER FRANKLIN EAST WILLIAM A HAINES JR PAUL V MARTINDALE PETER R MILLER
ROY J DAY JOHN J MOTT LARRY D EPSTINE MELVIN D SEAGRAVES JOSEPH M BERKSON GEORGE M COUCH
KENNETH R BROWN TERENCE F COURTNEY WILLIAM C JESSE CHARLES V MORGAN JOHN J PETRILLA JR
DALE K PORTERFIELD DAVID R SLAGLE JOSEPH C HOPPER JOSEPH W MCDONALD THOMAS C WIDERQUIST
LESTER BRACEY ALEXANDER MCIVER FREDDIE L SLATER DON L UNGER DAVID B WILLIAMS
LINCOLN R WRIGHT GLEN S IVEY MARVIN B WILES JOHN W CONSOLVO JR JOHN M LEAVER JR
REMBRANDT C ROBINSON EDMUND B TAYLOR JR JOHN T CONRY MIKE J AGUILAR OSCAR AGUILAR
HARRY L BLACKBURN JR WILLIAM A BOATRIGHT STEVEN E BOWERSOCK EDWARD D BURNETT CLINT E CARR
DENNIS G DUNNING ALVIN R ELENBURG DAVID C FLORES DIETER K FREITAG JAMES D GROVES
SAMUEL HARRELL JEFFREY L HARRIS DALE L HAYES WILLIAM F HENAGHAN FRANK T HENSON
DONALD E HOWELL FREDDIE JACKSON THOMAS A LAHNER ROBERT A LODGE KENNETH ROSENBERG LANNY A YORK
DAVID A LYDIC GARY R MONTELEONE LARRY S MUSTIN TERRY D NEISS DEAN A PHILLIPS JOHN C KOZUCH
JAMES C JENSEN JACKIE RAY RICHARD RIDGEWAY EFRAIN RIVERA-AGOSTO JOHN T SABLAN
CLARENCE L SAULSBERRY JR RAYMOND J SHIKO DAVID W SULSER DENNIS E WILKINSON THOMAS E WOOD
BARRY C TOMLIN BARRY K ALLMOND MICHAEL J BLASSIE HAROLD J FALDERMEYER JOHN H HASELTON
JOHNNY C MARTIN RODNEY L STROBRIDGE ROBERT J WILLIAMS SAMUEL Y ADAIR JR LONNIE P BOGARD
DENNIS C CRESSEY WILLIAM H OSTERMEYER THOMAS J WILEY RALPH P DU PONT JR JOHN W ADAMS
ELLIOTT CROOK RAYMOND M DAUBENDIEK CRAIG L FARLOW RICHARD H HAGMAN TIMOTHY J JACOBSEN
JAMES LATHON CYRIL H MADISON JOSEPH P NOLAN JR DAVID L WAGNER JONATHAN B BEDNAREK
CLYDE C LOVE WESLEY D RATZEL SANTIAGO H ESCOBAR DEAN K LEACH CLARENCE P LEWIS
GORDON E STONE THOMAS D WOOD JR CHARLES E BARNETT JAMES A BAREFIELD DAVID A BAUSCH
DAVID L BROOKS JR JOHN R HENN JR ISAAC Y HOSAKA DAN C KINGMAN JR BRUCE E KLINE
TIMOTHY J MONKELBAAN FRANK A NEWMAN HARRY L THAIN RICHARD S VOIGTS
FRANCIS C BROCKMAN III GARY B FARRIS DARYL R KUNZLER JAIME PACHECO ROBERT F WILCOXSON
HENRY H STRONG JR RICHARD R ARSENAULT CHARLES D GIPSON LARRY K MORROW GERALD D SPRADLIN
BARTLEY A WALLACE MONT S SMOOT JOE W EUBANKS FREDERICK N SUTTLE JR HAROLD D JONES
MICHAEL J KONOW BENJAMIN L TEBAULT PAUL D BACON KENNETH L BARNETT ANDEE CHAPMAN JR
CHARLES L FLOTT CALVIN T GORE JAMES F HOLLIS MICHAEL L HUTSON WALTER S MULLEN
DAVID S KRANER THOMAS M LEJEUNE RONNIE A MENDOZA KYLIS T PAYNE NICHOLAS QUINONES-BORRAS
ANDREW F UNDERWOOD MELVIN S DRY JAMES A FOWLER JOHN W SEUELL JOSEPH L MARSHALL
RONALD E DOUGHTIE JEFFREY A MAURER ELVIS W OSBORNE JR ROBERT A ROBERTSON STEPHEN W LYNCH
WAYNE BIBBS JAMES E HACKETT TERRY L HOCHSTETLER ARNOLD E HOLM JR JAMES R MCQUADE
ROGER E WILSON ROBIN R YEAKLEY MAURICE CLARK SAMUEL H POWELL RICHARD D WILEY
MARK F BIAGINI WILLIE HOOVER JR FRANCIS J DAVIS PAUL H LAWING JR JESUS G SEPULVEDA
THOMAS R HAMMAN RICHARD J MEECHAN JOHN J CABRAL ESEQUIEL M ENCINAS LEON A HUNT
GERALD F AYRES RICHARD M COLE JR MARK G DANIELSON PAUL F GILBERT ROBERT H HARRISON
LARRY R KILPATRICK DONALD H KLINKE STANLEY L LEHRKE JACOB E MERCER LARRY J NEWMAN

RICHARD E NYHOF FRANK L SETTLE ROBERT A WILSON BURR M WILLEY BURDETTE D TOWNSEND JR
RONALD A WENZL LOUIS K BREUER IV EARL W FREDERICKSON EDWIN G NORTHUP STEPHEN E SHIELDS
CHARLES L BUTLER THOMAS W JACKSON CORNER M DAVIS GEORGE R HENSON JOHN L DILALLO
JAMES L MCCARTY ROBERT D MCLAREN THOMAS J JOZEFOWSKI GEOFFREY R SHUMWAY DAVID L YOAKUM
MICHAEL J MARTIN ROBERT T MILLS FARRELL J SULLIVAN DONALD F YERYAR GORDON R UHLER
STEVEN L BENNETT PERCY G BROCK JR STEPHEN M WHITE JOHN M COLE ROGER M SMELSER
STEPHEN H CUTHBERT STEPHEN M BRUMFIELD ROBERT D HAMILTON JOHN E PARTON JOHN H BROCK
HARLAND M DAVIS JR PHILLIP R DUFF MANUEL A FERNANDEZ THOMAS P KEOGH FREDERICK M KOSS
LEONARD ROBERTSON LOUIS HAZEL ROBERT F TOWNES JR STANLEY J KUICK JOHN A TODD
PETER M BENTSON RICHARD J TALLMAN FRANK C GREEN JR KENNETH L CRODY JERRY W HENDRIX
JAMES L HUARD SAMUEL ODONNELL JR ROBERT R CECIL MICHAEL A HILL WAYNE G BROWN II
LEON F HAAS RAYMOND P DONNELLY EDWARD G HAYEN II LARRY J YOUNG STEVEN A TRANT
LEE W BILLINGSLY JAMES R LAYTON GLENN E NOWAKOWSKI JOHN A SPIRES STEPHEN H GRAVROCK
RONNIE L GIPSON GARY L SHANK LARRY F JAGARD HAROLD MCCASLIN JR OSCAR HERRGESELL
LESTER RUSHIN PHILIP D SELLERS RONALD A ASHE JAMES E HUDELSON DAVID J PRICE CHARLES F HAYNES
THOMAS W REASOR JOSEP L RUZICKA JR FREDDIE L SLAUGHTER JR LUIS ALONZO ROBERT M LANKFORD
DAVID N LARSON CLYDE K NELSON JAMES J SANSONE WILLIAM G CHANDLER PATRICK T MATHEWS
PATRICK A DECK JR HERBERT D STARK EDWARD J BRUE MARSHALL B COLLINS JAMES W FULK TERRY KOHLER
MERRILL H MASIN RAYMOND R REESE DANIEL M RICHARDS CHARLES P ROBERTS WILLIAM G SAARELA
BEN O SHEPPARD JR PHILIP H STEVENS RAY E TANNEHILL JERRY D VANCE TIMMIE J WARD
DAVID M THOMPSON FRANCIS W TOWNSEND JOSEPH E FRASHER RONNIE HOLLY ALLAN W HOLMES
LAWRENCE C DEAN ORLAND J PENDER JR JOHN R PITZEN GRADY T TRIPLETT CATALINO B ANTONIO JR
ROGER E BEHNFELDT RODERICK B LESTER HARRY S MOSSMAN WILLIAM J CROCKETT LEE M TIGNER
THOMAS W STALEY JR MICHAEL W DOYLE SAM G CORDOVA GEORGE B WARING RICHARD W HEROLD
CHARLES H PIPER JR ROBERT R GREENWOOD JR WILLIAM C WOOD FRANK G OLIVER II CHARLES H STEPP
DONALD J HANNING DONALD F LINDLAND RONALD F BOEING DONALD A GERSTEL ALAN P AHLFIELD
STEPHEN O MUSSELMAN ROBERT L HARLEY JOHN L SMITH MICHAEL P RICE GEORGE E GILLILAND
CARROLL T JACKSON MELVIN L STEVENSON KENNETH R BUELL VERNE G DONNELLY THOMAS A GOETSCH
CHARLES W GACHES MICHAEL S TUROSE THOMAS O ZORN JR ROGER W CARROLL JR DWIGHT W COOK TIMOTHY J SWEENEY
DANIEL V BORAH JR PETER CHAN VINCENT C ANDERSON RICHARD B LINEBERRY ROBERT A BRETT JR
WILLIAM C COLTMAN SCOTT L BIRKET HERMAN C ACKER JACK S BERGMAN JR WILLIAM CLARK JR
CHARLES W CLINARD RONALD P DALEY RAYMOND R DAVIS TERRY W DEAL WILLIAM H HARRISON III
TOMMY M HAWKER ROBERT M KIKKERT EDWARD R MCELENEY JR ROBERT T MOORE STANLEY G PILOT JR
RALPH L ROBINSON WESLEY H ROSE RICKY L RUCKER JEFFREY L SCHELLER DAVID L SCOTT
WILLIAM J TERRY RICHARD C TESSMAN JOSEPH GRISAFI ROBERT D ANDERSON BRUCE E BOLTZE
CARL O MCCORMICK PETER M CLEARY LEONARDO C LEONOR FRED G MICK JOHN R PEACOCK II
WILLIAM M PRICE JAMES L CRAIG JR JAMES D DUGGER JR ALLEN U GRAHAM JAMES A HOCKRIDGE
AUBREY E NOBLES MICHAEL S BIXEL CLAYTON M BLANKENSHIP DANIEL P CHERRY ROBERT A YANKOSKI
ROBERT W HAAKENSON JR KEVEN Z GOODNO CARLOS A PEDROSA MELVIN E WOLFE JAMES W HALL
DEXTER B FLORENCE FRED OBERDING JR JAMES E SULLIVAN JAMES D BROWN RAYMOND L GOODCHILD
LOUIS O CALDERON ROGER R CHAMBLISS DENNIS W FINNEGAN RICHARD B FREEMAN MILTON C HUNTER
STEVEN D HOWARD CHARLES A MCSWINEY JR KENNETH J SPENCER JAMES M STEVER CHARLES L STEWART JR
TIMOTHY A THOMAS RONALD L VANLANDINGHAM DAVID E WISCHEMANN HOWARD W JOHNSON JR
DELBERT R WOOD WILLIAM L MILLER III STEVEN L TAYLOR JOSEPH F DE NARDO CLARENCE O TOLBERT
ROBERT M BROWN JOHN L CARROLL ROBERT D MORRISSEY FREDERICK W WRIGHT III RONNIE N TOPPS
DOUGLAS T MANKA DONALD C BREUER CHARLES J CAFFARELLI WILLIAM S HARGROVE ROBERT A KOHN
JOHN W RYON RONALD D STAFFORD CALVIN B TIBBETT WALTER H TRISKO CHARLES M EARNEST
JACK R HARVEY BOBBY M JONES RICHARD E BRUNDRETTE JR ANTHONY C SHINE MICHAEL S MCNEILL
LOUIS R TAYLOR BILLIE J WILLIAMS BILLIE J WILLIAMS WALTER L FERGUSON JAMES R MCELVAIN
DONALD L RISSI ROBERT J THOMAS RONALD J WARD RICHARD W COOPER JR DONALD A DIX
ROBERT M DOW FRANCIS X EGAN CHARLIE S POOLE LARRY D SCHUMACHER ARTHUR V MCLAUGHLIN JR
IRWIN S LERNER CRAIG A PAUL RANDOLPH A PERRY JR WARREN R SPENCER JOHN F STUART JOEL R BIRCH
RANDALL J CRADDOCK CHARLES E DARR DELMA E DICKENS ROBERT T ELLIOTT
CHARLES J BEBUS CHARLES F FENTER JAMES R FULLER FRANK A GOULD ROBERT S GRAUSTEIN THOMAS T HART III
KEITH R HEGGEN EDWARD H JOHNSON BOBBY A KIRBY HARRY R LAGERWALL
ROBERT L LILES JR GEORGE B LOCKHART ROBERT R LYNN GEORGE D MACDONALD PAUL O MEDER JOHN Q WINNINGHAM
RONALD D PERRY ROLLIE K REAID BARTON S WADE FRANCIS A WALSH JR DONOVAN K WALTERS
GERALD W ALLEY THOMAS W BENNETT JR JOSEPH B COPACK JR WILLIAM R BALDWIN
STANLEY N KROBOTH JAMES L GRUNDY JR HAROLD L MISCHLER HENRY J REPETA GEORGE F SASSER PHILIP S CLARK JR
PAUL V JACKSON III STEPHEN L RAYBURN DWIGHT G RICKMAN ROBERT J MORRIS JR NUTTER J WIMBROW III
DALLAS C ALEXANDER JR RALPH J CHIPMAN RONALD W FORRESTER DONALD A JOYNER ROY T TABLER
LAWRENCE J MARSHALL JAMES M TURNER BENNIE L FRYER MICHAEL F HAIFLEY ALLEN L JOHNSON
GARY L BOYCE KENNETH D SCAIFE STEVEN B JOHNSTON JOHN S SATTERFIELD MICHAEL C SMARTT
JOHN C LINDAHL ELBERT W BUSH WILLIAM L DEANE JOSE J JAVINES RICHARD A KNUTSON
MANUEL A LAUTERIO WILLIAM S STINSON MICKEY A WILSON ROBERT A CLARK MICHAEL T MCCORMICK
PAUL A GUIDA JAMES D FARMER KEITH A CHRISTOPHERSEN CHARLES L PARKER JR RICHARD D WIEHR
ROBERT L FRAKES MARK J MILLER HARLEY H HALL GEORGE W MORRIS JR WILLIAM B NOLDE
MARK A PETERSON JOHN O RUCKER PAZZO A DAL JR ANTHONY DAL PAZZO JR ANTHONY DAL POZZO JR
JAMES A DUENSING ROY E HAVILAND
WILLIAM S STRINGHAM ARTHUR R BOLLINGER DALE BRANDENBURG PETER R CRESSMAN GEORGE R SPITZ
DALE L DE WOLF TED B HALLENBECK JOSEPH A MATEJOV TODD M MELTON SEVERO J PRIMM III
ROBERT E BERNHARDT FRANK W PAULOS DONNIE R CONNER JAMES L SCROGGINS JOSEPH GAMBINO JR
SAMUEL L JAMES DOUGLAS K MARTIN EDWARD R SITZ LARRY E LAWSON JEREMIAH F COSTELLO
EMME R GALBRETH II RICHARD T GRAY JAMES D BEAVERS DAVID V MCLEOD JR FRANCIS E MEADOR
GILBERT A ROVITO SAMUEL B CORNELIUS JOHN J SMALLWOOD JAMES T ONEILL SAMUEL W YATES
PAUL I VEGAS STEPHEN E BULLARD WILLIAM D HARRIS DAVID L WEEKS CHARLES F SCOTT RICHARD M REES
GARY C HALL GARRY W HERMANSON BRYAN A RYE DENNING C JOHNSON MICHAEL G PAGET
JAMES K HURLEY WILLIAM S WILLIS FELIZARDO C AGUILLON DONALD T DIONNE SR MARY T KLINKER
GARY B SIMKINS EDGAR R MELTON WENDLE L PAYNE JOE CASTRO KENNETH E NANCE WILLIAM M PARKER
DARWIN L JUDGE CHARLES MCMAHON JR WILLIAM C NYSTUL MICHAEL J SHEA JIMMY P BLACK
BOBBY G COLLUMS GERALD A COYLE THOMAS D DWYER BOB W FORD GERALD W FRITZ JOHN G STROBL
LAURENCE E FROEHLICH JACKIE D GLENN DARRELL L HAMLIN GREGORY L HANKAMER DAVID A HIGGS
FALEAGAFULA ILAOA JAMES G KAYS MICHAEL D LANE DENNIS W LONDON ROBERT P MATHIAS
WILLIAM R MCKELVEY GEORGE E MCMULLEN III EDGAR C MORAN II TOMMY R NEALIS PAUL J RABER
ROBERT W ROSS ROBERT P WELDON DANIEL A BENEDETT LYNN BLESSING ANTONIO R SANDOVALL
GREGORY S COPENHAVER BERNARD GAUSE JR GARY L HALL JOSEPH N HARGROVE KELTON R TURNER
JAMES J JACQUES ASHTON N LONEY RONALD J MANNING DANNY G MARSHALL JAMES R MAXWELL
WALTER BOYD ANDRES GARCIA RICHARD W RIVENBURGH ELWOOD E RUMBAUGH GEER R VANDE

Dear Charles L. Hosking,

As you lay lost somewhere
Somewhere in the cold night air.
When you lay down to sleep
You really want to weep.
We miss you don't you know
Are you in the snow?
When we find you, and we will,
we'll take away your sadness
and chill.

from
Anne
Grade 5

HAPPY
HOLIDAYS

Merry Christmas
!MARTIN!

JAMES N SPANGLER

BENNY L STOWERS

KENNITH ALSTON

VALENTIN G MATULA

MELVIN E TAYLOR

JAMES P O'DONNELL

ABRAHAM SCHWARTZ · RONALD W RINGWALL